PREFACE.

In presenting to the people of Iowa the debates in the convention, assembled at Iowa City, January 1857, for the purpose of revising her constitution, after the same had been in operation for nearly eleven years, it may not be inappropriate to give a brief history of the facts, connected with the formation of her first constitution, and the circumstances which led to the calling of a convention to frame a new one.

On the 19th day of December, 1836, a resolution passed the House of Representatives, directing the committee on territories to enquire into the expediency of erecting a new territory of the southern portion of the then territory of Wisconsin. The committee, after investigation, reported a resolution to that effect, which passed the House of Representatives on the 14th of December, 1837.

During that session of Congress various petitions and memorials were presented to both Houses of Congress, from the people of Wisconsin territory, for the formation of a new territorial government, and the settlement of the boundary line between that territory and the State of Missouri. The proceedings of the territorial legislature, relative to that boundary line, were presented to the Senate on the 2d of January, 1838. The committee on territories of the House of Representatives made a report, on the 6th of February, 1838, on the expediency of establishing a separate territorial government for Iowa. This report was accompanied by a bill, and on the 12th of June, 1838, the President approved an act to divide the territory of Wisconsin, and to establish the territorial government of Iowa.

On the 18th day of June, of the same year, an act was passed authorizing the President of the United States to cause the southern boundary line of the territory of Iowa to be ascertained, and properly marked. The Secretary of State reported to Congress the maps and surveys in compliance with the resolution of the two Houses of Congress. And on the third of March, 1839, were passed and approved, an act to define and establish the eastern boundary line of the territory of Iowa, and an act to alter and amend the organic law of Wisconsin and Iowa. The difficulty in regard to the boundary line between Missouri and Iowa continued, and during the session of Congress of 1839 and 1840, sundry communications were made to Congress from the territorial council of Iowa, and from individuals in relation to the subject. A bill was reported in the House of Representatives, on the 4th of February, 1840, to establish and define the northern boundary line of Missouri.

The President transmitted a message to Congress, on the 12th of February, 1840, with additional documents in relation to the disputed boundary line. And on the 5th of March, 1840, a bill was reported from the committee on territories of the House of Representatives "to enable the people of Iowa to form a constitution and State government, and for the admission of such State into the Union."

In the Senate, on the 11th of February, 1841, a bill was reported for ascertaining and settling the southern boundary of the territory of Iowa. The committee on territories of the House of Representatives made a report on the 26th of May, 1841, accompanied by a bill fixing the boundary line between Missouri and Iowa, which bill passed the House, but failed in the Senate.

In 1844, a convention met in the territory of Iowa, and proceeded to frame a constitution for a State government, a copy of which was presented to Congress in the session of 1844 and 1845. An act was passed, on the 3d of March, 1845, for the admission of the States of Iowa and Florida into the Union. In December, 1845, a bill to repeal so much of the act of March 3, 1845, as relates to the boundaries of Iowa, was introduced into the House of Representatives, and referred to the committee on territories, which committee reported to the House on the 27th of March, 1846, an amendatory act.

The people of the territory of Iowa held a second convention in 1846, and refused to agree to the change in the boundaries as previously fixed, and a copy of the constitution, affirming those boundaries, was presented to Congress in December, 1846. And on the 28th day of that month an act for the admission of Iowa into the Union was passed and approved.

The question of altering and amending this constitution was more or less agitated for several years. The people of Iowa were anxious to repeal the restrictions upon banking in this State, and other amendments were desired in relation to the election of judges of the supreme court, &c. Finally, on the 24th of January, 1855, the legislature of Iowa passed "an act for the revision or amendment of the constitution of this State," which provided for the submission to the people ot the question of calling a convention to revise the constitution. The call of the convention was adopted, and an election for delegates held in November, 1856. The convention assembled, in Iowa City, on Monday, January 19, 1857, and organized by electing Hon. Francis Springer, of Louisa County, President.

AN ACT

PROVIDING FOR THE REVISION OR AMENDMENT OF THE CONSTITUTION OF THIS STATE.

SECTION 1. Be it enacted by the General Assembly of the State of Iowa, That at the next general election in this State, to be holden on the first Monday of August, A. D. 1856, there shall be a poll opened in each township and election precinct, for the purpose of taking a vote of the people, for or against a convention to revise or amend the present constitunion of this State.

SEC. 2. Voters desiring such a convention shall have written or printed on their ballots, the words, "For a Convention," and those opposed shall have written or printed on their ballots, the words, "Against a Convention."

SEC. 3. The election shall be conducted in the same manner as the general elections of the Stafe, and the poll books shall be returned and canvassed as provided in the Twenty-fifth chapter of the Code, and abstracts shall be forwarded to the Secretary of State, which abstracts shall be canvassed in the manner provided for the canvass of State officers.

SEC. 4. On or before the first day of October, A. D. 1856, the Governor shall issue his proclamation, declaring the result of said election, and if a majority of the votes cast at said election, shall be in favor of a convention as aforesaid, then an election of delegates to sa id convention shall be held on the Tuesday after the first Monday in November, in said year, and the election shall be conducted in the returns according to the provisions of the Code, regulating general elections.

SEC. 5. The number of delegates shall correspond to the number of Senators in the General Assembly, according to the apportionment at the time of the election of said delegates, and each senatorial district shall constitute a district for the election o f delegate.

SEC. 6. Said delegates shall possess the qualification of Senators in the General Assembly, and shall meet in convention at the then Capital of the State, on the third Monday in January, A. D. 1857, for the purpose of revising or amending the constitution of the State.

SEC. 7. Should a vacancy or vacancies at any time occur by death, resignation, or otherwise, the Governor shall issue writs of election to fill the same, in the manner prescribed for filling vacancies of members oi the General Assembly.

Sec. 8. Each delegate shall receive three dollars per day from the State Treasury, for each day's attendance in said convention, and three dollars for every twenty miles travel in going to, and returning from said convention; the mileage to be computed by the usually traveled route.

Sec. 9. The convention shall have power to appoint its own officers, and to fix their compensation; and shall also have power to provide for the necessary printing for said convention; it shall also keep a journal of its proceedings, containing all amendments, revisions or alterations agreed upon, which journal shall be filed in the office of the Secretary of State, to be kept as other official papers of this State.

Sec. 10. Said revised or amended Constitution, when agreed upon by the Convention, shall be submitted to a vote of the people for their adoption or rejection, and if a majority of the legally qualified electors shall approve the same, it shall then become the Constitution and supreme law of the land.

Sec. 11. The convention shall fix the time and prescribe the manner of submitting the question to the people; it shall also provide for the publication of the proposed amendments, a journal of its proceedings, and for the manner of canvassing the votes given for and against said amended constitution; it shall also have full power to make all necessary regulations for the taking effect of said amended or revised constitution; Provided, That all elections contemplated in this Act, shall be conducted, as nearly as practicable, in the same manner as is provided by law, for the regulation of general elections in this State.

Sec. 12. The Secretary of State is hereby required to furnish a suitable room for the meeting of said delegates, and also to furnish stationery for the use of the Convention, which shall be paid for out of the State Treasury.

Approved January 24th, 1855.

I certify that the foregoing act was published by direction of the Governor in the Iowa Capital Reporter, on the 14th of February, and Iowa Republican on the 21st day of February, 1855.

GEO. W. McCLEARY, Secretary of State.

ERRATA.

Page 19, second column: Change the name "Patterson" to "Johnston," wherever it occurs.

Page 21, 1st column, line 13 from the bottom: change "Jeffrie's" to "Jefferson's."

Page 41, 2d column, line 6 from the bottom: strike out the word "each."

Page 47, 2d column, line 20 from the top: "Bills and Rights," should read "Bill of Rights."

Pagy 85, 2d column, line 13 from the bottom, for "Warren," read "Edwards."

Page 93, 1st column, line 29 from the bottom, for "reports" read "remarks."

Page 95, 1st column, lines 17, 21 and 22 from the top, for "Bill of Rights" read "right of suffrage."

Page 97, 1st column, line 23 from the top, insert between the words "shall" and "be" the word "never."

Page 151, 2d column, line 1 from the top, for "State," read "counties."

Page 156, 2d column, line 27 from the bottom, for "Hominy Nation" read "Hairy Nation."

Page 177, top of the page, in heading of names of speakers, for "Clarke" read "Hall."

Page 191, 1st column, near commencement of the remarks of Mr. Clark, of Alamakee, for "I became, however, in the days when Know Nothingism flourished, a member of that organization, and yet," &c., read, "I have lived in a county where Know Nothingism flourished, but was never a member of that organization, for," &c.

Page 238, 2d column, line 8 from the top, for "here," read "keen."

LIST OF MEMBERS AND OFFICERS OF THE CONSTITUTIONAL CONVENTION OF THE STATE OF IOWA;

ASSEMBLED IN IOWA CITY ON MONDAY, JANUARY 19TH, 1857.

NAMES.	DISTRICT.	POST OFFICE TOWN.	COUNTY.	NATIVITY.	OCCUPATION.	AGE.	YEARS IN STATE.
Edward Johnston,	I	Fort Madison,	Lee,	Pennsylvania,	Lawyer,	41	19
William Patterson,	I	Keokuk,	Lee,	Virginia	Pork Packer	54	19
Squire Ayers,	II	Bonaparte,	Van Buren,	Pennsylvania,	Farmer,	56	—
Timothy Day,	III	Winchester,	Van Buren,	Ohio,	Farmer,	53	12
M. W. Robinson,	IV	Burlington,	Des Moines,	Ohio,	Farmer,	42	18
J. C. Hall,	IV	Burlington,	Des Moines,	New York,	Lawyer,	47	18
D. P. Palmer,	V	Bloomfield,	Davis,	New York,	Lawyer,	40	10
James F. Wilson,	VI	Fairfield,	Jefferson,	Ohio,	Lawyer,	28	3
Rufus L. B. Clarke,	VII	Mt. Pleasant,	Henry,	Connecticut,	Lawyer,	37	6
George Gillaspy,	VIII	Ottumwa,	Wapello,	Kentucky,	Farmer,	42	16
John Edwards,	IX	Charitan,	Lucas,	Kentucky,	Lawyer,	42	3
Amos Harris,	X	Centerville,	Appanoose,	Ohio,	Lawyer,	34	8
Daniel H. Solomon,	XI	Glenwood,	Mills,	Virginia,	Lawyer,	27	3
Daniel W. Price,	XII	Council Bluffs,	Pottawatamie,	Kentucky,	Lawyer,	30	3
David Bunker,	XIV	Richmond,	Washington,	Indiana,	Farmer,	46	17
Jeremiah Hollingsworth,	XV	Richland,	Keokuk,	Indiana,	Farmer,	47	16
James A. Young,	XVI	Oskaloosa,	Mahaska,	Virginia,	Merchant,	41	8
H. D. Gibson,	XVII	Knoxville,	Marion,	Tennessee,	Merchant,	37	12
Lewis Todhunter,	XVIII	Indianola,	Warren,	Ohio,	Lawyer,	35	7
J. A. Parvin,	XIX	Muscatine,	Muscatine,	New Jersey,	Farmer and Engineer,	49	18
W. Penn Clarke,	XX	Iowa City,	Johnson,	Maryland,	Lawyer,	39	12
George W. Ells,	XXI	Davenport,	Scott,	Connecticut,	Bookseller,	48	2
Robert Gower,	XXII	Gower's Ferry,	Cedar,	Maine,	Farmer,	53	16
Aylett R. Cotton,	XXIII	Lyons,	Clinton,	Ohio,	Lawyer,	30	12
Hosea W. Gray,	XXIV	Marion,	Linn,	Pennsylvania,	Farmer,	40	19
J. C. Traer,	XXV	Vinton,	Benton,	Ohio,	Banker,	30	11
Harvey J. Skiff,	XXVI	Newton,	Jasper,	New York,	Banker,	36	7
Thomas Seely,	XXVII	Guthrie Centre,	Guthrie,	New York,	Farmer,	33	3
William A. Warren,	XXVIII	Bellevue,	Jackson,	Kentucky,	Mail Contractor,	45	23
A. H. Marvin,	XXIX	Monticello,	Jones,	New York	Farmer,	49	2
J. H. Emerson,	XXX	Dubuque,	Dubuque,	Virginia,	Real Estate Dealer,	49	16
John H. Peters,	XXXI	Delhi,	Delaware,	Connecticut,	Lawyer,	28	3
Alpheus Scott,	XXXII	Strawberry Point,	Clayton,	Massachusetts,	Real Estate Agent,	32	4
Sheldon G. Winchester,	XXXIII	Eldora,	Hardin,	New York,	Druggist and Bookseller,	26	5
John T. Clark,	XXXIV	Wauken,	Alamakee,	New York,	Lawyer,	40	3
Francis Springer, President,	XIII	Columbus City,	Louisa,	Maine,	Farmer,	44	18
W. Blair Lord, Reporter,	- - -	Baltimore, Md.,	——	Maine,	Reporter,	30	—
Thomas J. Saunders, Secretary,	- - -	Davenport,	Scott,	New Jersey,	Physician,	37	2
Ellsworth N. Bates, Assistant Secretary,	- - -	Cedar Rapids,	Linn,	Massachusetts,	Lawyer,	27	3
S. C. Trowbridge, Sergeant-at-Arms,	- - -	Iowa City,	Johnson,	Virginia,	——	45	20
Francis Thompson, Door Keeper,	- - -	Iowa City,	Johnson,	Connecticut,	Stone Cutter,	49	17
James O. Hawkins, Messenger,	- - -	Iowa City,	Johnson,	Iowa,	Student,	15	15

OFFICIAL REPORT

OF THE

DEBATES AND PROCEEDINGS

OF THE

CONVENTION OF 1857.

MONDAY, January 19th, 1857.

The Convention met in the Supreme Court room, at the Capitol.

Mr. GRAY, of Linn, called the Convention to order and said.

Gentlemen of the Constitutional Convention;

For the purpose of a preliminary organization of this body, I move that the Hon. J. A. Parvin, delegate from Muscatine, be chosen President, *pro tem.* Carried.

Mr. PARVIN took the chair, and said.

Gentlemen of the Convention:

Accept my thanks for the distinguished honor, you have conferred upon me, in calling me to preside over this temporary organization. In return for such an unexpected favor, I can only assure you, that nothing in my power, shall be omitted, to promote the happiness and harmony of the members of this Convention.

On motion of Mr. ELLS, Dr. T. J. Saunders was appointed Secretary; and on nomination of Mr. Traer, E. N. Bates was appointed Assistant Secretary, *pro tem.*

On motion of Mr. CLARKE, of Johnson, Samuel C. Trowbridge was appointed Sergeant at Arms; on motion of Mr. Wilson, Francis Thompson was appointed Door-keeper; on motion of Mr. Warren, J. H. Merrill was appointed Fireman; on motion of Mr. Todhunter, James Hawkins was appointed Messenger, and on motion of Mr. Clarke of Johnson, George Clearman, was appointed Assistant Messenger.

Mr SPRINGER moved, that Mr. Clarke, of Johnson, be appointed to invite a clergyman to open the Convention with prayer, who introduced Rev. Mr. Young.

Prayer by Rev. Mr. YOUNG.

On calling the roll all the members appeared, except Messrs Bunker, Cotton and Peters. Mr. R. L. B. Clarke, moved a committee on credentials —carried; and the chair appointed Messrs Clark of Henry, Hall, Todhunter, Palmer and Wilson.

Mr. CLARKE of Johnson moved to adjourn till 1 o'clock to morrow, which motion was withdrawn at the request of Mr. Johnson, to receive propositions for a future place of meeting.

The president then read propositions from the Common Council of Dubuque and Davenport, respectively inviting the Convention to meet at those places in case they should adjourn from Iowa City.

Mr. ELLS moved that the propositions be laid on the table, untill a permanent organization was effected.

Mr. HARRIS moved as a substitute, that the propositions be referred to a committee of three to report at a future meeting.

Mr. GOWER moved to amend by inserting five members, which motion was accepted. And the motion as amended, prevailed. The President appointed as that com. Messrs Ells, Emerson, Springer, Clark of Johnson, and Edwards.

Mr. Clarke renewed his motion to adjourn to 10 o'clock to-morrow, which prevailed.

TUESDAY, January 20, 1857.

The Convention met at ten o'clock, and was called to order by the Chairman.

The journal of yesterday was read and approved.

On motion of Mr. CLARKE, of Johnson, the Rev. Mr. Kynett was invited to open the Convention with prayer; which he did accordingly.

Credentials of Members.

The CHAIRMAN announced the first business in order to be the report of the Committee on Credentials.

Mr. CLARKE, of Henry, from the Committee on Credentials, made the following report:

The Committee on Credentials and Qualifications of Members report the following persons as duly qualified, and entitled to seats as members of the Constitutional Convention for the State of Iowa, assembled January 19, 1857:

First	*Senatorial*	*District,*	Edward Johnston.
"	"	"	William Patterson,
Second	"	"	Squire Ayres,
Third	"	"	Timothy Day,
Fourth	"	"	Jonathan C. Hall,
"	"	"	Moses W. Robinson,
Fifth	"	"	David P. Palmer,
Sixth	"	"	James F. Wilson,
Seventh	"	"	Rufus L. B. Clarke,
Eighth	"	"	George Gillaspy,
Ninth	"	"	John Edwards,
Tenth	"	"	Amos Harris,
Eleventh	"	"	Daniel H. Solomon,
Twelfth	"	"	Daniel W. Price,
Thirteenth	"	"	Francis Springer,
Fourteenth	"	"	David Bunker,
Fifteenth	"	"	Jer'h Hollingsworth,
Sixteenth	"	"	James A. Young,
Seventeenth	"	"	Hiram D. Gibson,
Eighteenth	"	"	Lewis Todhunter,
Nineteenth	"	"	John A. Parvin,
Twentieth	"	"	Wm. Penn Clarke,
Twenty-first	"	"	George W. Ells,
Twenty-second	"	"	Robert Gower,
Twenty-third	"	"	Azlett R. Cotton,
Twenty-fourth	"	"	Hosea W. Gray,
Twenty-fifth	"	"	James C. Traer,
Twenty-sixth	"	"	Harvey J. Skiff,
Twenty-sev'th	"	"	Thomas Seeley,
Twenty-eighth	"	"	Wm. A. Warren,
Twenty-ninth	"	"	Albert H. Marvin,
Thirtieth	"	"	John H. Emerson,
Thirty-first	"	"	(*not present*)
Thirty-second	"	"	Alpheus Scott,
Thirty-third	"	"	S. G. Winchester,
Thirty-fourth	"	"	John T. Clark.

On motion of Mr. CLARKE, of Johnson, the report was adopted.

PERMANENT ORGANIZATION OF THE CONVENTION.

Mr. WINCHESTER offered the following resolution:

Resolved, That until otherwise ordered, the officers of this Convention shall consist of a President, a Secretary, an Assistant Secretary, a Sergeant-at-Arms, a Door-keeper, a Fireman and First and Second Messengers.

The question being taken, the resolution was adopted.

Mr. CLARKE, of Johnson, offered the following resolution:

Resolved, That the Convention do now proceed to the election of a permanent President and other officers, *viva voce.*

The resolution was adopted.

The CHAIRMAN stated the first business to be the election of President, and requested members to make their nominations.

Mr. CLARKE, of Johnson nominated Francis Springer, Esq., from the Thirteenth Senatorial District.

Mr. JOHNSTON nominated Jonathan C. Hall, Esq., from the Fourth Senatorial District.

The Secretary then proceeded to call the roll, which resulted as follows, viz:

For Mr. Springer—Messrs. Bunker, Clarke of Henry, Clarke of Johnson, Clark of Alamakee, Edwards, Ells, Gower, Gray, Hollingsworth, Marvin, Parvin, Scott, Seeley, Skiff, Todhunter, Traer, Warren, Wilson, Winchester and Young—20.

For Mr. Hall—Messrs. Ayres, Cotton, Day, Emerson, Gibson, Gillaspy, Harris, Johnston, Palmer, Patterson, Price, Robinson and Solomon—13.

For Mr. Parvin—Mr. Springer—1.

For Mr. Gillaspy—Mr. Hall—1.

The CHAIRMAN thereupon announced Mr. Springer duly elected President of the Convention.

Messrs TODHUNTER and GIBSON were appointed by the chair a committee to conduct the President elect to his seat; which they did accordingly,

Upon assuming the chair,

The PRESIDENT addressed the Convention as follows:

Gentlemen of this Convention:—I return to you the homage of my hearty thanks for the honor of being chosen to preside over your deliberations. In signifying to you my appreciation of this distinguished testimonial of your confidence and regard, I must confess that I feel embarrased by a sense of my inability to bring to the Chair the experience and acquaintance with parliamentary practice, the possession of which would be considered necessary to justify your choice. Under these circumstances, I shall have to throw myself upon your kindness, and bespeak your forbearance and friendly co-operation in my endeavors to discharge acceptably the various, and sometimes difficult duties of a presiding officer—praying you to be assured of the disposition I cherish to serve you faithfully and impartially, and of my hearty readiness to contribute my mite toward a satisfactory performance of the important work we have been sent here to accomplish.

With us, the "Sovereignty of the People" is a conceded axiom. We are the representatives of that sovereignty, charged with the duty, and clothed with the power, of revising their organic law. I am sure I need not remind the intelligent members of this Convention of the high responsibility of this trust. The constitution of a State may be regarded, to a certain extent, as a fixed and permanent instrument, a higher law, for the guidance, not only of individual members of the body politic, but also a law to which the various departments of the government, in their action, must conform. It is the foundation upon which the superstructure of the legislation and jurisprudence of the State rests. Upon its character and principles the prosperity and happiness of the social compact may be said much to depend. It is looked upon as embodying the spirit and policy of a people. It is in a word "positive law."

That this great trust will be performed by the members of this Convention, wisely and well, I entertain no doubt, meeting the just expectations of an enlightened constituency, and imparting fresh vigor and vitality to the advancing steps of our noble young State in her career to the high destiny which lies before her.

The PRESIDENT announced the next business to be the election of the remaining officers of the Convention, and requested members to make their nominations for the office of Secretary.

Mr. ELLS nominated Thomas J. Saunders, of Scott county.

Mr. GILLASPY nominated Phillip B. Bradley, of Jackson county.

The roll being called, it resulted as follows:

For Mr. Saunders.—The President, Messrs. Bunker, Clarke, of Henry; Clarke, of Johnson; Clark, of Alamakee; Edwards, Ells, Gower, Gray, Hollingsworth, Marvin, Parvin, Scott, Seeley, Skiff, Todhunter, Traer, Warren, Wilson, Winchester and Young—21.

For Mr. Bradley—Messrs. Ayres, Cotton, Day, Emerson, Gibson, Gillaspy, Hall, Harris, Thurston, Palmer, Patterson, Price, Robinson, Solomon—14.

The PRESIDENT declared Mr. Saunders duly elected Secretary of the Convention.

The CONVENTION then proceeded to the election of Assistant Secretary.

Mr. GRAY nominated Ellsworth N. Bates, of Linn county.

Mr. PALMER nominated J. C. Burns, of Johnson county.

The SECRETARY proceeded to call the roll, which resulted as follows:

For Mr. Bates—The President, Messrs. Bunker, Clarke of Henry; Clarke, of Johnson; Clark, of Alamakee; Edwards, Ells, Gower, Gray, Hollingsworth, Marvin, Parvin, Scott, Seely, Skiff, Todhunter, Traer, Warren, Wilson and Winchester—21.

For Mr. Barns—Messrs. Ayres, Cotton, Day, Emerson, Gibson, Gillaspy, Hall, Harris, Johnston, Palmer, Patterson, Price, Robinson, and Solomon—14.

The PRESIDENT declared Mr. Bates duly elected Assistant Secretary.

The CONVENTION then proceeded to the election of Sergeant at Arms.

Mr. GOWER nominated Samuel C. Trowbridge, of Johnson county.

Mr. GILLASPY nominated D. F. Gaylord, of Wapello county.

The roll was then called, and resulted as follows:

For Mr. Trowbridge—The President, Messrs. Bunker, Clarke, of Henry; Clarke, of Johnson; Clark, of Alamakee; Edwards, Ells, Gower, Gray, Hollingsworth, Marvin, Parvin, Scott, Seeley, Skiff, Todhunter, Traer, Warren, and Winchester—21.

For Mr. Gaylord—Messrs. Ayres, Cotton, Day, Emerson, Gibson, Gillaspy, Hall, Harris, Johnston, Palmer, Patterson, Price, Robinson, and Solomon—14.

The PRESIDENT declared Mr. Trowbridge duly elected Sergeant at Arms.

The CONVENTION then proceeded to the election of Door-Keeper.

Mr. TODHUNTER nominated Francis Thompson, of Johnson county.

Mr. AYRES nominated J. Page, of Johnson county.

The roll was then called, and resulted as follows:

For Mr. Thompson—The President, Messrs. Bunker, Clarke, of Alamakee; Clarke, of Henry; Clarke, of Johnston; Edwards, Ells, Gower, Gray, Hollingsworth, Marvin, Parvin, Scott, Seeley, Skiff, Todhunter, Traer, Warren, Wilson, Winchester, and Young—21.

For Mr. Page—Messrs. Ayres, Cotton, Day, Emerson, Gibson, Gillaspy, Hall, Harris, Johnston, Palmer, Patterson, Price, Robinson and Solomon—14.

The PRESIDENT declared Mr. Thompson duly elected Door-Keeper.

The CONVENTION then proceeded to the election of Fireman.

Mr. WILSON nominated J. H. Merritt, of Johnson county.

No other nomination being made—

On motion of Mr. WARREN, the vote on his election was ordered to be taken by acclamation, which being done, Mr. Merritt was unanimously elected Fireman.

The CONVENTION then proceeded to the election of First Messenger.

Mr. WINCHESTER nominated James Hawkins, of Johnson county.

Mr. HALL nominated Willis Conard, of Johnson county, for the office of First Messenger. He is a worthy young man, poor and unfortunate, having broken his hips not long since. I do not know what his politics are. (Laughter.) I believe he has none.

Mr. CLARKE, of Johnson.—The young man nominated on our side is an orphan boy, who is endeavoring to educate himself, and I am anxious that he should be elected.

The roll being called, resulted as follows:

For Master Hawkins—The President, Messrs. Bunker, Clark, of Alamakee; Clarke, of Henry; Clarke, of Johnson; Edwards, Ells, Gower' Gray, Hollingsworth, Marvin, Parvin, Scott, Seeley, Skiff, Todhunter, Taer, Wilson, Winchester, and Young—20.

For Master Conard—Messrs. Ayres, Cotton,

Day, Emerson, Gibson, Gillaspy, Hall, Harris, Johnston, Palmer, Patterson, Price, Robinson, and Solomon—14.

The PRESIDENT declared James Hawkins duly elected First Messenger.

The Convention then proceeded to the election of second messenger.

Mr. SEELY nominated George Clearman, of Johnson county.

Mr. HALL nominated Willis Conard, of Johnson county.

Mr. CLARKE, of Johnson. I would ask the gentleman from Desmoines (Mr. Hall) if the young man he has nominated, is not now in the employment of the Legislature?

Mr. HALL. I do not know as to that. All I know is that he will fill the office creditably, if elected.

Mr. CLARKE. I do not question that; I asked the question merely that we might be informed as to his present employment.

The roll being called resulted as follows:

For Master Clearman—The President, Messrs. Bunker, Clark, of A., Clarke, of H., Clarke, of J., Edwards, Ells, Gower, Gray, Hollingsworth, Marvin, Parvin, Scott, Seeley, Skiff, Todhunter, Traer, Warren, Wilson, Winchester and Young. 21.

For Master Conard—Messrs. Ayres, Cotton, Day, Emerson, Gibson, Gillaspy, Hall, Harris, Johnston, Palmer, Patterson, Price, Robinson, and Solomon—14.

The PRESIDENT declared George Clearman duly elected Second Messenger, and announced that the list of officers was completed.

Oath of Members.

Mr. TODHUNTER offered the following resolution:

Resolved, That the members elect, of this Convention, be and they are hereby required, severally, to take an oath to support the Constitution of the United States, and to faithfully discharge their duties as delegates to this Convention.

Mr. SKIFF moved to insert after the words "United States" the words, "and the Constitution of the State of Iowa."

Mr. HALL. Mr. President; I differ from the gentleman from Jasper, (Mr. Skiff) I understand that we come here for the very purpose of altering and violating the Constitution of the State of Iowa, and I do not therefore, feel that I can take the oath to support that Constitution. I want to alter it, break it down, tear it to pieces, and build it up again. I am willing to take the oath to support the Constitution of the United States. That I think is a very important oath these times; but I want to be above the Constitution of Iowa in this Convention.

Mr. CLARK, of A. Mr. President; It very frequently happens that in the legislative enactment that authorizes the calling of a Constitutional Convention, there is a provision requiring its members to take a certain oath. There is no such provision, I believe, in the act providing for the assembling of this Convention, and if there is not, then I am apprehensive that a resolution passed by this body requiring its members to take that oath would not be obligatory upon any one. They would be at liberty to take it, or refuse to take it as they should see fit. Now, I believe every member of this Convention will act in good faith without any such oath. I am willing to take one to support the Constitution of the United States, and the laws of this State. But as the gentleman from Des Moines (Mr. Hall) has said, it certainly cannot be expected that we will take an oath to support the present Constitution of Iowa, as we have met here on purpose to overthrow that one and build up another.

Mr. PALMER. Mr. President; I believe if this resolution is to be passed, the amendment should be adopted. I think that if we are sworn to support the Constitution of the United States it is proper that we should be sworn to support the Constitution of the State of Iowa.

Mr. PARVIN. I hope the resolution will be adopted without the proposed amendment. I think it is but right and proper that we should be under the obligation of an oath to support the Constitution of the United States, but it would be improper to oblige us to take an oath to support the Constitution of this State. The act which authorized the meeting of this Convention, says nothing about an oath. It is with us whether we shall take one or not. In my opinion it is proper that a body of this kind should be under the sanctity of an oath, and one that should not include too much. As the gentleman from Des Moines (Mr. Hall) says, we have met here to amend, overthrow, disregard and change the present Constitution. Let us adopt the resolution without the amendment.

Mr. TODHUNTER Mr. President; I do not think we have any right to say that we will not take any oath at all. I believe we are under obligation to take an oath, and I am of the impression that the one indicated in the resolution I have offered is a proper one for us to take. As already suggested by the gentleman from Des Moines, (Mr. Hall) we have come here expressly to alter, violate, amend and change the whole of the present Constitution, and therefore we should not be required to take an oath to support the Constitution of the State of Iowa. But it is only right and proper that we should take an oath to support the Constitution of the United States, and to faithfully discharge our duties as delegates to this Convention.

Mr. CLARKE, of Henry. Mr. President, in regard to this matter, I think if we are to adopt the resolution we should adopt the amendment. We meet here, it is true, to alter and amend the Constitution of the State of Iowa, but we meet here under that Constitution, and we will be under it until the one we may get up, if we get up one, shall have been sanctioned by the people of Iowa. Until then this is still the constitution of Iowa. But I cannot see any necessity for our taking any oath at all. There is no provision of law for it; there is no necessity for anything of the kind. It would seem as if we were very anxious to show to the people that we are going to be very honest and very upright, and therefore we will swear upon the Holy Evangels that we will support the Constitution of the United States, &c. Now I do not believe any one of us will be more inclined to do this duty after taking an oath than before. I think that at all events, if we pass the resolution we should pass the amendment also.

Mr. MARVIN. I would enquire if the present constitution of Iowa does not require every person elected to any office in this State to take an oath to support the Constitution of the State of Iowa? If so, I think that we are obliged to take that oath as members of this Convention.

Mr. HALL. We stand here as the representatives of the people in their sovereign capacity; in a capacity above and stronger than the Constitution itself. Now I want to put a question to members here. If we take an oath to support the Constitution of this State, of course me mean that we will not violate that Constitution, and we intend the taking of this oath as a support to our moral principle and to our consciences. Well, if gentlemen will show me how we are inclined to violate the Constitution, and that this oath will be of any assistance in keeping us from violating it then I could see some necessity for it. But I am opposed to an oath as a matter of mere formality. We might perhaps frame a Constitution here in conflict with the Constitution of the United States; but I cannot see how we could frame one in conflict with the Constitution of this State. And an oath to support the State Constitution would be nugatory: it would be folly to take an oath that would have no effect on our action in any way. Hence, I shall oppose the amendment, and I have no objectious to the original resolution.

Mr. SKIFF. I will further modify my amendment so as to have the resolution read "the members of this Convention are hereby requested to take an oath to support the Constitution of the United States, the Constitution of the State of Iowa, &c." I change the word "required" to "requested."

Mr. JOHNSON. This same question arose in the Convention of Ohio in 1851, and about the same arguments appear to have been used there as have been used here. The conclusion to which that Convention came was that it was not necessary to insert the words "to support the Constitution of the State of Ohio." That proposition seems to have met with very little favor there. I find by reference to the reports of that Convention that Mr. Vance, of Butler, introduced the following resolution:

"*Resolved*, That the members of this Convention be and they are hereby required severally to take an oath to support the Constitution of the United States, and also an oath of office."—To this an amendment was proposed similar to the one offered here by the gentleman from Jasper [Mr. Skiff] but it was not favorably received. Mr. Harris, in order to bring the debate to a close offered the following as a substitute:

"That the members elect be, and are hereby required severally to support the Constitution of the United States, and to faithfully discharge their duties as delegates to this Convention."

The form of oath afterwards unanimously adopted, was this:

"You solemnly swear that you will support the Constitution of the United States, and that you will honestly and faithfully to the State of Ohio, discharge your duties as members of this Convention."

Now some such oath as that I think is sufficient here, and I see no necessity for anything more.

Mr. WILSON. I hope the substitute of the gentleman from Jasper [Mr. Skiff] will not be adopted. I consider it proper that the members of this Convention should take an oath of office, and I believe the form of oath embodied in the resolution of the gentleman from Warren [Mr. Todhunter] is a proper one. For one, I should not like to swear to support the Constitution of this State for reasons already suggested by the gentleman from Des Moines [Mr. Hall.] I think there should be an oath of office, and such an one as members will be obliged to take, and not merely request them to take it. Let it be put in such a shape that all will have to take it, or we may find a portion of our members under the obligation of an oath and a portion not under that obligation; and I suppose that any one who would take an oath to support the Constitution of the United States, the Constitution of the State of Iowa, &c., would not object to taking an oath even if the Constitution of the State of Iowa was left out. I hope the substitute will not prevail.

Mr. BUNKER. I do not see any serious difficulty either in the original resolution or the substitute. Yet as the original resolution seems to embrace all that is absolutely necessary, I prefer its adoption. But I do not conceive that this Convention will be violating the Constitution of the State of Iowa by any act we may perform here. The Constitution itself provides for this very Convention, for the altering and abolishing of this Constitution, and hence I do not see how we can be acting in violation of that instrument. But it seems to me that the original resolution is all that is necessary for us here.

The question was upon the substitute offered by Mr. Skiff.

On motion of Mr. Tracr the substitute was laid upon the table.

The question being then taken upon the original resolution, it was adopted.

On motion of Mr. Clarke, of Johnson, the Sergeant-at-arms was dispatched for a competent officer to administer the oath to the members of the Convention.

Rules of the Convention.

Mr. GRAY offered the following resolution:

Resolved, That the rules governing the present House of Representatives of this State be adopted temporarily as far as applicable for the Government of this Convention until otherwise ordered.

Mr. WILSON moved to amend the resolution by striking out the words "present House of Representatives" and inserting the words "Constitutional Convention of 1846."

Mr. GILLASPY. I think one of the rules of that Constitution ought to be excepted; the one relating to the appointment of the Standing Committees. If the gentlemen will except that rule I will support this amendment.

Mr. WILSON I will accept the amendment and move to insert the words "Constitutional Convention of 1846" in lieu of the words "present House of Representatives" and insert after the words "of this State" the words "except the 10th rule."

The resolution as proposed to be amended was then read as follows:

Resolved, That the rules governing the Constitutional Convention of 1846 of this State, except the tenth rule, be adopted temporarily, so far as applicable, for the Government of this Convention until otherwise ordered.

The question was taken upon the amendment and it was agreed to.

The resolution as amended was then adopted.

Miscellaneous.

Mr. EDWARDS offered the following resolution.

Resolved, That the Sergeant at Arms be instructed to procure from the Secretary of State for the use of each member of the Convention a copy of the code of Iowa and the Acts of the Legislature of 1855-6.

The resolution was agreed to.

Mr. TODHUNTER offered the following resolution.

Resolved, That a Committee of eight members be appointed, of equal number from each Congressional District, whose duty it shall be to report a method of conducting the businsss and deliberations of the convention and to designate the necessary standing committees.

On motion of Mr. HALL the resolution was laid upon the table subject to the order of the convention.

Standing Committees.

Mr. WILSON offered the following resolution:

Resolved, That fifteen committees be appointed by the President to which shall be referred so much of the Constitution and other matters as relate to the specific subjects hereinafter designated as appropriate to each committe, as follows:

1st. A committee on the Legislative Department to consist of five members.

2nd. A committee on the Executive Department to consist of three members.

3rd. A committee on the Judicial Department to consist of five members.

4th. A committe on the apportionment of representation to consist of seven members.

5th. A committee on the Elective Franchise to consist of three members.

6th. A committee on Corporations, other than Corporations for banking, to consist of three members.

7th. A committee on Banking and Currency to consist of five members.

8th. A committee on Public Debt to consist of three members.

9th. A committee on Education and School Lands to consist of three members.

10th. A committee on Militia to consist of three members.

11th. A committee on Finance and Taxation to consist of five members.

12th. A committee on the Public Institutions of the State to consist of three members.

13th. A committee on the Preamble and the Bill of Rights to consist of five members.

14th. A committee on Future amendments to the Constitution to consist of three members.

15th. A committee on such Miscellaneous subjects and proportions as are not referred to in the foregoing fourteen committees, to consist of five members.

Mr JOHNSTON the name of this resolution seems to be legion. It is one of the most important resolutions in relation to the labors of this convention, and I think time should be allowed members for an examination of it. With that view I move that it be laid on the table subject to the order of the convention.

The question being taken the motion was agreed to.

Mr. CLARKE of Johnson, offered the following resolution:

Resolved, That a committee of five be appointed to draft rules for the government of this convention.

The question being taken the resolutions was adopted.

The PRESIDENT announced the following gentlemen as constituting said committee:

Messrs. Clark of Johnson, Johnston, Edwards, Hall and Bunker.

Mr. PALMER offered the following resolution.

Resolved, That the Secretary of this convention be instructed to procure for each delegate 25 daily newspapers, or their equivalent in other newspapers at the option of the Delegate.

Mr. JOHNSTON. It appears to me we ought to settle some other matters before we proceed to act upon a resolution of this kind. There is one matter, more important than all others, in the preliminary stages of our proceedings, and that is whether we shall sit in this city or remove to some other place. We may otherwise go on here until we get ourselves so fast anchored that we cannot remove from here. I will therefore move to lay this resolution on the table subject to the order of the Convention, in order that we may have a report from the committee appointed yesterday upon the subject of removal of this Convention.

The question being taken the motion was agreed to.

Mr. CLARKE of Henry, offered the following resolution:

Resolved, That this Convention will employ a reporter to report the debates and proceedings of this Convention, and that a committee of three be appointed by the President to ascertain and report the name of a suitable and competent person to be thus employed.

The resolution was then adopted.

The PRESIDENT announced the following gentlemen as members of that committee, viz: Messrs, Clarke of Henry, Hall and Clarke of Johnson.

Mr. CLARKE of Johnson, offered the following resolution:

Resolved, That John Teesdale be employed to print 100 copies of the Constitution of this State for the use of members of this Convention.

Mr. HALL. We have just adopted a resolution the purpose of which is to furnish each member of this Convention with a copy of the code which contains the Constitution, and if we get that it seems to me that it would be a useless expense to print the Constitution separately. I know that it is necessary for every member of this Convention to have a copy of the Constitution, but we have it already in print, and if we desire it for circulation, when we print the one we may propose here, we can have the old one printed with it.

Mr. CLARKE of Johnson. The object I had in view in submitting this resolution was to place in the hands of our committees copies of the present Constitution to assist them in preparing their reports, and in preparing their reports it will be necessary for them to cut up many copies of the Constitution and use them up in various ways. And it would be better to have them printed than to employ clerks to copy them. That is the object I had in view. I think it will very much facilitate the business of this Convention to have 100 copies of the Constitution printed, and the cost of printing will certainly be much less than that of copying and enrolling the old Constitution.

Mr. HALL. The gentleman's suggestion would be very proper if the Convention shall decide that they will revise the whole Constitution. But I do not regard it as certain that the proposition upon our table to refer the various articles of the Constitution to their appropriate committees, will be adopted by this Convention. I shall not be in favor of any such course for one. There are many things in the present Constitution that require no revision whatever, and when we decide what we will do, there will be time enough to prepare the material to do it with. I therefore move to lay the resolution upon the table subject to the order of the Convention.

The question being taken the motion was agreed to.

Mr. JOHNSTON. Mr. President, I would now call for a report from our committee on locomotion—the committee upon the subject of the removal of this convention to some other place.

Mr. ELLS. I would say that the committee have not come to any definite conclusion as yet, and would ask for further time in which to prepare their report.

Mr. WARREN. I would move that the committee be instructed to report this evening at two o'clock. If we are going to move, let us do so; if we are going to remain let us decide to do so.

Mr. JOHNSTON. I understand from the Chairman of the committee that is is impossible for them to agree. If that is so I do not see why they should not report that fact and let the matter come up before this convention in some form for our decision.

Mr. CLARKE of Johnson. This committee consists of five members. They have never yet met. It is true the rival towns of Davenport, Dubuque and Iowa City are represented but I apprehend there will be no trouble in agreeing upon a report. Now if I am to leave home, I want to have a choice of places to which to go. And so I suppose it is with the gentleman from Davenport (Mr. Ells) and the gentlement from Dubuque (Mr. Emerson.) Let us have a meeting of the committee and come to some understanding and then we can report to the convention and they can decide whether they will go from this place or not.

Mr. ELLS. I understood that the proposition from Davenport is this, and from Dubuque it is the same; in case this committee determine to go to either of those cities, the city authorities will furnish them with a hall, light and fuel. That is all. The idea of furnishing the members with board free of expense, as I have understood is the impression among some, is entirely imaginary.

Mr. JOHNSTON. If there is any prospect of the committee agreeing and reporting this afternoon, I will withdraw my objection to allowing them further time.

The question being taken upon instructing the committee to report this afternoon at two o'clock it was agreed to.

The President laid before the convention, the following communication:

To the President of the Constitutional
Convention of Iowa.

HONORED SIR:

I herewith present to the members of the convention copies of a Journal of debates containing the terms upon which a similar publication of the doings and debates of the body over which you preside may be published so as to be subject only to newspaper postage, should it be the pleasure of the convention.

Yours Respectfully,

S. STORRS HOWE.

Iowa City, January 20th, 1857.

The communication was received and laid upon the table subject to the order of the convention.

Mr. CLARKE of Henry from the committee on the subject of reporting made the following report.

The committee appointed to ascertain and report the man as a suitable and competent person to be employed as reporter for this convention, report the name of W. Blair Lord of Baltimore, now present.

Mr. CLARK of Johnson. I would state for the information of the members of this convention that I hold in my hand certificates from various public men of all parties as to Mr. Lord's ability as a reporter. He was the reporter to the Kansas Investigating committee and brings with him a highly commendatory certificate from all the members of that committee.

The question being taken the report was adopted.

On motion of Mr. WARREN the Convention took a recess until 2 o'clock, P. M.

EVENING SESSION.

The Convention assembled at 2 o'clock, and was called to order by the President.

The PRESIDENT stated that Judge F. H. Lee, of Johnson county, was present, and prepared to administer the oath to the members of the Convention.

His Honor then came forward and administered the following oath to all the members present:

You and each of you do solemnly and sincerely swear that you will support the Constitution of the United States, and that you will honestly and faithfully to the State of Iowa discharge your duties as members of this Convention. So help you God.

Removal of Convention.

Mr. ELLS, from the Committee to which had been referred the invitations from the cities of Davenport and Dubuque, for the Convention to hold its session in one of these places, made the following report:

Your Committee have had the same under consideration, and a majority of the Committee have instructed me to offer for adoption the following resolution:

Resolved, That while we duly appreciate the patriotic motives of the city authorities of Davenport and Dubuque in thus tendering the hospitalities of their respective cities, we deem it inexpedient to accept of either of these invitations, at the present time.

(Signed) GEO. W. ELLS, Chairman.

Mr. CLARK, of Alamakee, moved that the report be accepted, and that the Committee be discharged; which was agreed to.

The question was upon the adoption of the report.

Mr. ELLS moved the following as a substitute:

That we duly appreciate the patriotic motives of the city authorities of Davenport and Dubuque in thus tendering the hospitalities of their respective cities, and that we deem it expedient to accept one of those invitations at this time.

Mr. CLARKE, of Johnson. I had not intended to say a word upon this matter, for I am well aware that whatever I may say, may be subject to the imputation of selfishness, as I am at home in this city. But I wish to remark this: that I am authorized by our city authorities to say, that if the Convention shall decide upon remaining here, a suitable hall will be provided for our sessions, free of expense to us, until we can have possession of one of the legislative chambers in this building.

The question being thus taken upon the substitute, it was adopted, as follows:

Yeas—Messrs. Ayres, Clarke of Alamakee, Clarke of Henry, Cotton, Day, Edwards, Ells, Emerson, Gibson, Gillaspy, Hall. Hollingsworth, Johnston, Patterson, Price, Robinson, Scott, Seeley, Skiff, Solomon, Todhunter and Warren—22.

Nays—The President, Messrs. Bunker, Clarke of Johnson, Gower, Gray, Harris, Marvin, Palmer, Parvin, Traer, Wilson, Winchester, and Young—12.

The question was upon the adoption of the report of the Committee as amended.

Mr. TRAER. I should like to know what is the state of the case now; as I understand the nature of the invitation is somewhat different from what we had reason at first to understand it.

The PRESIDENT. The invitation from the City of Davenport is, that we shall have suitable rooms, fuel and lights for our sessions.

Mr. TRAER. Then I should like to know what particular advantage there will be in our removing from this place to Davenport? I see none. I have no objection to going to Davenport or any other place, provided there was some good reason for it. But I want to see that before I vote for anything of the kind.

Mr. ELLS. The advantages of going to Davenport are, that it will cost us nothing to get there, and when we get there we will be able to obtain good accommodations at fair prices Here we have not. Half of the members of the Convention have to sleep three in a bed, and two on a bunk, in consequence of the want of good accommodations here. It is to avoid that that we should go to Davenport.

Mr. TRAER. I do not wish to discuss this question; but it occurs to me that before we adjourn to Davenport or any other place, we should ascertain what the accommodations there will be. If they get us down there, and charge us more for board than we are charged here, we shall not have gained much. However, I have no doubt they would do the fair thing by us; but I would suggest that before we determine to adjourn there, we should send a committee there to see what can be done. That, I believe, is the usual mode heretofore pursued by conventions.

And I must say that I have some scruples in regard to the legality of this thing of adjourning. I know there are gentlemen here who understand this question better than I do, but I have not heard them express any opinion upon this point. Until I have some further light upon the subject I shall be rather of the opinion that this convention has no legal right to adjourn away from this place. The act authorizing the assembling of this body prescribed that we should meet at the Capitol of the State. And I understand that in all cases where conventions of this character have adjourned to places other than the one where they were called together, it has been done under some provision of the law calling them together, which gave them the privilege of so doing. The Ohio Convention adjourned from Columbus to Cincinnati. But the law that called that convention together contained a provision giving them the power of adjourning from one point to another as they should see fit. Now I would like to hear some gentleman of legal ability and experience express his opinion upon this matter. I might probably be induced to view this matter in a different light, but at present I shall feel compelled to vote against this resolution.

Mr. ELLS. I ought to state that the LeClaire Hall—a large hall lighted by gas—has been secured for the use of this convention if they decide to go to Davenport. There will be no expense attending their going over there, and when they get there they will find everything free and liberal to their hearts' content.

Mr. HALL. I am in favor, Mr. President, of going to Davenport or Dubuque, I am not very particular which place. I do not think there is any provision of law prohibiting our adjourning to any other place we see fit. I think the power of the Legislature extended only to doing what the Constitution provides, and that is to provide for the calling of this Convention and designate a place at which it should assemble. After we have met, we are not subject to Legislative enactments at all. There can be no impropriety or illegality in our adjourning to some other place, for we are not confined or governed by the directory portion of the Act calling the Convention farther than to meet and organize.

Now we have got to take something for granted in this matter of removal. I am satisfied that so far as the accommodations and attentions we receive here are concerned, go where we will we cannot get in a worse place; we cannot go to a place where we would have less hospitality, courtesy or accommodation shown to us. I am for the experiment of a change at all events. Davenport and Dubuque have, through their City Councils extended to us an invitation to meet in their midst, and I am willing to believe that they will treat us properly and that we will be fully and fairly accommodated there. There will be no inconvenience in going there, and I think we shall be well accommodated after we get there I do not wish to be regarded as saying any thing against the people of this city more than against any other town of a similar character. This city was created for the purpose of holding meetings here, Legislatures and Conventions, and the people have got into the habit of treating all who come here like sheep who are to be shorn. It is so every where. It is proverbial that in State Capitols persons receive harder treatment and less accommodation than at any other place. Now we have the power to avoid all this and we should exercise it. Let us show that we have at least the instincts of the lower animals, to flee from danger and hard treatment By going to Davenport or Dubuque we will be conferring a compliment upon the people there. And a constitution made there will be as good as one made here, provided it is ratified by the people.

Mr. PARVIN. I have no desire to detain the Convention by any extended remarks upon this subject. I have no constitutional scruples with regard to our right to remove to some other place. I believe we have the undoubted right to do so; but I have doubts about the expediency of so doing. My friend from Des Moines (Mr. Hall) alludes to the dangers that are to be incurred here, and says we ought to flee from them. Now, we read of certain characters who flee when no man pursueth. (Laughter.) I do think that the citizens of this city have been held up in rather too severe a light. I have been here several times, and I have always had a good bed to lie upon and plenty to eat, and that which was good. In fact, I have always been treated as well as I deserved.

Now, I think we should inquire a little before we decide to remove to Davenport or Dubuque. Is it possible for them to accommodate us with as good committee rooms there as we can have here? It is well known that the Legislature will soon adjourn, and before they adjourn we can occupy some other hall and quite as good a one as any we can obtain in Davenport or Dubuque. When the Legislature shall have concluded their labors, then we can be accommodated better here than in any other city in Iowa. There is no city, without a house prepared for the purpose, that has as good a hall as our Senate chamber, and we have now, and can have, just as good a hall before the Legislature adjourns, as can be found in the State; and with regard to committee rooms, I do not think any tavern or hotel can accommodate the committees of this body as well as they can be accommodate in this building, which was prepared for that very purpose.

Now, with regard to the hospitality of Davenport and Dubuque, that is known all over the State. But I am under the impression that there is some little hospitality in this city, notwithstanding what my friend from Des Moines (Mr. Hall) may say of his bad luck here. I rather think he must have got into some bad place—where, I cannot imagine. (Laughter.) I am opposed to removing our sessions from this place, unless I can be convinced that we can better our condition as a convention.

Mr. TODHUNTER. With regard to this question of removing to Davenport, I desire to say this: Before we organized here, a proposition was made to us by the citizens of Davenport, which was generally understood to be something like this: that we should pass over the road to that place free of charge, and when we arrived there should be provided with a hall for our sessions well warmed and lighted, free of expense to the State, and that each member of the Convention should be boarded without cost to himself. In short, there was to be no expense to a single member, in any shape or form, nor expense to the State, should we remove to Davenport. When that proposition was presented here, I was favorably impressed with it. I thought it one of the most liberal offers I had ever heard—knowing what board costs in this place, and what I suppose it costs there. I came to the conclusion, as many other members did, that it was a very generous offer, and that we would be ungrateful if we did not accept it.

But we are assured this morning that a change has come over the minds of the people of Davenport about this matter. The gentleman from Davenport (Mr. Ells) says it is all imaginary about the board of members being paid. But he says there are other advantages, and among them is a free ride over the railroad. Now, that may be so, but it might prove the last free ride on the railroad some of us would take. We might run off the track, in consequence of the difficulty of traveling now. There are many weighty members of this Convention, and it has been suggested that they might be put in a very unpleasant condition in such an event.

I have about come to the conclusion that we ought to remain in Iowa City. And one word in regard to members being obliged to sleep three in a bed and two on a bunk. I have found a different state of things here. I can say with my friend from Muscatine (Mr. Parvin) that I have very comfortable quarters and am well attended to and well supplied in every respect, and I have no cause to complain at all; and the complaints made with regard to the people of this city, if intended to apply to all, are without good foundation, so far as the house where I am stopping is concerned.

Mr. BUNKER. It seems to me that the principal question for us to decide, is, whether the public business requires our removal from Iowa City to one of the places referred to in the resolution. I have no doubt but that so far as we are individually concerned, we shall be sufficiently well accommodated in this city. In my experience here, I have found it different from what appears to have been the case with my distinguished friend from Des Moines (Mr. Hall.) I have always experienced the greatest difficulty from the excess of attention that has been paid to me here, and the result has been that when I went home, I expected too much attention there, and not receiving it, I was dissatisfied. (Laughter.)

Now, in regard to the accommodation of this body. If we were obliged to occupy this hall until the Legislature adjourned, and they were to defer their adjournment for some time, I should be in favor of a removal to some other place, as we cannot all be well accommodated here. But the gentleman from Johnson (Mr. Clarke) has informed us that there is a hall in this city in waiting for us. I do not, therefore, see the necessity of adjourning to any other place to transact the business of this Convention, and consequently I shall vote against a removal at present. It is probable that the Legislature will adjourn in a few days, and then we can have the Senate Chamber for our use.

Mr. CLARKE, of Johnson. I feel some delicacy in speaking upon this question, from the fact that I am from the city most directly interested in its decision. But there is a view of it which I desire to present to this Convention. It is almost certain that the Legislature will adjourn on Monday or Tuesday of next week. I am so advised by many members of the Legislature. Now, so far as the business of this Convention is concerned, it is a matter of very little consequence whether we meet from to-day or to-morrow, until the adjournment of the Legislature. As soon as we have completed our permanent organization by the appointment of our standing committees, and have assigned to them the work they will have to perform, there will be ample business for them until the adjournment of the Legislature. This body is not like a legislature where members introduce bills and other matters of their own accord. All our business here must come from our committees, and they should have time to prepare it. We shall not suffer for the want of a room in which to hold our sessions until the Legislature shall adjourn. And, besides, we shall have committee rooms for the convenience of our committees more suitable and convenient than can be obtained elsewhere, and these rooms, I apprehend, are at our service at any time.

As for removing to some other place, because our members are not well accommodated here, I apprehend that is rather the fault of the members themselves. This question of removal has been sprung upon them, and they have all squatted down at the hotels, in the expectation of, perhaps, being obliged to leave this city, and are now liable to imposition there. But I trust the misconduct of a few in any community will not be imputed to all of that community. And I would say to the gentleman from Des Moines (Mr. Hall,) that so far from the people of Iowa City being niggardly in their treatment of strangers, there is no city in this State that has spent more, and done more for the accommodation of strangers than Iowa City has done. This is a public assembling place for all parties, and constant demands are being made upon the hospitality of the people of this city, such as is made upon the people of no other city or town in the State. I think the gentleman is a little unjust in saying that the people of this town are niggardly in their hospitality. It is true we are crowded at present, but as soon as the legislature shall adjourn there will be abundance of room. And those members who desire rooms in private families, where they will be more quiet than they can be in hotels, will find enough, who will be willing to receive them, and entertain them well, for a reasonable compensation. I know some families myself who would do so.

And I beg leave to add further, in behalf of the people of Iowa City, that some two months ago, the subject of accommodating the members of the Legislature and of the Convention was much talked about among the citizens. At one time we talked about appointing a committee to go around among our private families and find out all who could provide accommodations for that purpose. But many, myself among the number, took this view of the matter, that perhaps the members of the Legislature, and of the Convention, would not thank us for taking this matter in hand, but would prefer to look out boarding houses for themselves, and we were afraid that in place of accommodating them by doing this, we might give offence to them.

And so far as getting a hall in readiness for the Convention was concerned, it was anticipated that the Legislature would have been adjourned at the end of the fifty days from their first assembling, and be out of the way. I think all these circumstances afford an ample excuse for the conduct of the people of this city. I am aware that stories are rife of impositions upon the members of the Legislature, but these same impositions are practiced upon us also. We had occasion to send a messenger some distance from here, and the same exhorbitant charges were made upon the people of this town as are said to be made upon the members of the Legislature. Gentlemen can but see that it is the same with us as with every other community; there are persons who will always take advantage of circumstances; that needs no argument, for it is too evident.

I trust the convention will consult their own convenience and dignity in this matter. As was well remarked by the gentleman from Washington, (Mr. Bunker,) the first question for us to consider is, what is best for the public service. However fine a hall you may find in Davenport, you will find no such convenient committee rooms as we can have here. And if the hall we now occupy is not sufficiently convenient, there can be one furnished for our use. I am told that the Odd Fellows Hall, which is a fine one, and well furnished, can be at once obtained for our use.

Mr. HALL. I desire to set the gentleman from Johnson (Mr. Clarke) right. I am glad to hear, for the first time in my life, that the people of Iowa City are distinguished for their hospitality. I did not say they were niggardly. That word is one the gentleman himself used. I do not ordinarily use such expressions. But I say this—and I do not say it more about Iowa City than all other places that are seats of government—a man must be crazy, or nearly so, if he expects the same kind of civility, and civilization, too, if I may be allowed the expression, in a seat of government as in other places. It has happened to be my good or bad fortune to spend two or three months a year in this city since the organization of the State Government—perhaps for one or two years it was not quite so much—and I think I have some right to speak upon this matter. And I do know that I got less accommodation, and less of everything, for the amount of money paid, than in any other place in the State of Iowa. This is no slander upon the citizens of this city, but the necessary result of the fact that they have had these public gatherings here, the sittings of the Legislature, and meetings of Conventions, until they begin to look upon those bodies for their support and money making. Every man who has observed it, knows and feels the difference between this city and other places. I do not believe board is as high at Davenport as it is here. I do not believe the ordinary expenses of travelers and strangers is as high there as it is here. All that is a matter of no great concern, it is true. It is a matter of taste and choice and feeling; members feel that they would be more pleasantly situated there than here. I would prefer to go there, and will go there if the Convention will let me. But I can stay at either place. I have no doubt that many gentlemen have places here with which they are satisfied. I am glad to hear that such is the case. But I believe they can get as good places in Davenport as they can get here, and they would lose nothing by the journey.

Mr. CLARKE, of Henry. Having voted upon the affirmative side of this question, it may perhaps be well enough for me to explain that vote. My reasons for desiring to remove from this place are different from those given by the gentleman from Des Moines, (Mr. Hall.) As to the hospitality of the citizens of Iowa City, my experience has been such as to enable me fully to endorse the remarks of the gentleman from Johnson, (Mr. Clarke.) I do not think there is a very general feeling in this body adverse to the hospitality of the people of this city. I I think the reasons governing members of this Convention in desiring to remove from Iowa City are other than those caused by a want of hospitality. It is true there have been some difficulties in getting accommodations for boarding here. But besides that, we are assembled in a hall but inadequately adapted to the purpose. No other provision was made, as it was anticipated that the Legislature would adjourn. But such is not the case. We find ourselves hanging on from day to day, and we do not know when the Legislature will adjourn.

When the proposition was first intimated to me of an invitation, from Davenport, I understood it in the enlarged sense mentioned by the gentleman from Warren (Mr, Todhunter.) But my views have not been changed by learning that the proposition is a very different one. The mere matter of a board bill has nothing to do with my determination in this matter. I have no particular feelings to gratify upon this subject, and nothinb of that kind influences my vote upon this question. I think that perhaps if we should go down to Davenport we might relieve the citizens of Iowa City, who have had such an influx of strangers attending the Legislature, and the several Conventions here. Perhaps, also, we could not only get better accommodations for ourselves, individually, in Davenport, but also better accommodations for the discharge of our public duties, which would enable us to dispatch our business sooner than we will be able to do here. If we go to Davenport, in all probability, we will get through our business by the time the Legislature will adjourn. I shall therefore vote in favor of going to Davenport if we can go immediately. But if we have to send a Committee there to inquire what can be done, we had better decide at once to remain here, and go ahead with our business. It is only for the purpose of enabling us to do up our business promptly, that I am in favor of adjourning from this place to Davenport.

Mr. WARREN. Our Legislature is still in session, and there is yet a great deal of business before them. I am told by members from my county that the Legislature is hurrying through, and neglecting their business in order to leave and give their room to this Convention. Now I am not myself disposed to hurry them. I think if we were to leave here, the Legislature would then go on and complete the business before them in a proper manner, but if we remain here they may in their hurry leave much of their business undone. That is one reason why I am in favor of going away from here.

Mr. ELLS. I would say here, that if we conclude to go to Davenport we will not be delayed at all in our business, as I understand a hall is now being prepared for the meetings of this body.

Mr. TRAER. I desire to ask the gentleman from Davenport (Mr. Ells) what is the cost of living in his city? Much has been said here about exhorbitant prices we are obliged to pay here. Now if we go to Davenport without having some previous arrangement made, we may possibly find some little exhorbitance practiced there. I can live tolerably well for a dollar and a half a day. I have talked with some gentlemen and they say that the cost of living in Davenport is two dollars a day, so that we shall make nothing in that respect by going there. But that is a small matter.

There has been considerable said about the hospitality of Iowa City. I have not been here very much, but so far as my experience goes I have had no reason to complain at all. I was here last winter at a Railroad Convention, and I thought there was about as much hospitality shown here then as I have seen anywere.

Now I am willing to adjourn to Davenport or to Dubuque if I can be shown any good reason for doing so. But I insist upon the idea that if we conclude to go, we should send a Committee there to see what accommodations we can be assured of there.

The PRESIDENT. The Chair would say that the report is indefinite at present, and does not say where we shall go. It merely declares that it is expedient to accept one of the invitations extended to us.

Mr. TRAER. Then I would suggest that we might perhaps as well insert the name of Chicago. (laughter) If we are to go anywhere for the sake of good accommodations, I have no doubt we can get them at Chicago.

Mr. GOWER. I have been in the habit of visiting Iowa City for some fifteen years past, and fared very well, except the first night of the first Legislature here. I stopped at the American Hotel then, and had rather a hard time, I will confess. But since then, I have found good accommodations here. I have stopped in Burlington, in Davenport and in Dubuque, and I must say that I have got the worth of my money as fully in this city as in any other. So far from sleeping, three in a bed, or anything of that sort since I have been here, I have had a bed and a fire to myself, with a plenty to eat and cheap enough, too. The gentleman from Davenport, (Mr. Ells) says that he understands the people of Davenport are fixing up a hall for our accommodation, and the gentleman from Johnson (Mr. Clarke) tells us that one is being fitted up here. Now, we have good committee rooms here—better than can be obtained in Davenport—and I can see no good reason why we should go to Davenport. And, as the gentleman from Warren (Mr. Todhunter) remarks, we have several fat members here, and we may be thrown off the track, or something of the kind, and injure them very much. [Laughter.] I shall vote against the adoption of this report.

Mr. AYRES. I have been listening attentively to this discussion, as, before it arose, I did not myself feel properly prepared to give my vote upon this question; but after listening to all that has been presented, I can see but very little difference in the accommodations of either place in question. The friends of each presents the claims of his own city in the most favorable light, and the claims of the other in the most unfavorable light. Hence, I draw the conclusion that they are all unparallelled, either one way or the other. [Laughter.] As to the question of eating and drinking, that is but a small matter to me. I get a plenty to eat and drink here, and a comfortable bed to sleep on. But one difficulty suggests itself to my mind. Suppose that we determine to remove from this place, and the Convention or some of its committees should want some of the public documents for reference, or something else to be supplied by the State Department here? we will have to dispatch a messenger here merely to bring them from here, which can only be done after considerable delay. I do not know that such an exigency may arise, but it may. For that, and other considerations, I shall vote against the adoption of this report, as it is now amended.

Mr. ELLS. I wish to state that I will guarantee to every member of the Convention that he shall have a good room, fire, lights and every accommodation for a dollar a day.

Mr. CLARKE, of Johnson. At private houses or hotels?

Mr. ELLS. At the best hotels in the city.

Mr. CLARKE. At the Le Claire House?

Mr. ELLS. Certainly.

Mr. CLARKE.. Then, if the Convention decides to go to Davenport, I wish the gentleman would engage me a room at that hotel at that price.

Mr. PATTERSON. It does seem to me that this city is so crowded at this time, that however much the people here may be disposed to accommodate us, it is utterly out of their power to do so. Now, I have nothing to say against the people here. I have many friends among them. But it does seem to me that it would expedite business if we were to remove to some other place. That is what will induce me to vote for an adjournment to some other place. And, as my friend from Jackson (Mr. Warren) remarked, if we go away from this city, the Legislature may get along with their work a little more cautiously than they are now doing, in their efforts to hurry through in order to give us their rooms.

Mr. CLARKE, of Alamakee, moved to amend the report so as to read "it is expedient to accept the invitation from the city of Dubuque."

Mr. HARRIS. I hope the gentleman from Alamakee (Mr. Clark) will withdraw his amendment until we shall have decided whether we will adjourn from this place or not. If it is pressed now I shall be compelled to vote against it.

Mr. SKIFF moved to lay the amendment upon the table.

The question being taken, upon a division, the motion to lay on the table was agreed to—ayes 20; noes not counted.

The question recurred upon the adoption of the report as amended.

Mr. PARVIN moved that a committee of two be appointed to visit Dubuque and Davenport to ascertain and report the accommodations.

Mr. CLARKE, of Henry, moved to strike out the word "Dubuque."

Mr. HALL. I would ask whether gentlemen cannot take the word of members here as to the accommodations at those two places?

Mr. PATTERSON. It does seem to me that if we cannot believe gentlemen who are here, we cannot appoint a committee who will be entitled to more credit.

The PRESIDENT. The chair would suggest that it would be better first to decide whether the Convention will remove at all, before the gentleman submits his motion for a committee to visit the two places.

Mr. PARVIN. I will withdraw the motion.

Mr. CLARK, of Henry. I move, as a substitute, that it is expedient to accept the invitation from Davenport.

Mr. EMERSON. I move to amend the substitute by striking out "Davenport" and inserting "Dubuque." Occupying the position I do, in relation to this matter, being a citizen of Dubuque, I did not feel called upon to enter at any length into this controversy, while Iowa City was one of the points in question, But as the committee has indicated a disposition in its amendment to the report to adjourn from Iowa City, I feel that it is now my duty to say a few words in favor of Dubuque; and I certainly shall not undertake to disparage Davenport, or any other place that may be mentioned. I certainly do not feel like disparaging Iowa City, and as I said before, I did not feel that it was my place to say anything until it was decided that we should leave Iowa City.

You have received a communication from the Mayor and Council of the city of Dubuque, and you know from that about what we propose. Now I know if you determine to adjourn from Iowa City, the citizens of Dubuque would be much pleased to have you come there. I do not know as they are more hospitable than the people of any other city in the State. But I suppose that the facts are that so far as hotel accommodations are concerned they are better in Dubuque than in any other city in the State of Iowa. There are more rooms in the hotels and more hotels, and probably as well kept—I will not say better kept—than in other places in Iowa. There would, therefore, be no difficulty in obtaining hotel accommodations. So far as the price is concerned—which is no small item with us. I suppose gentlemen will acknowledge that we have advantages there that are not to be had in any other portion of the State. Therefore as regards these two items, proper hotel facilities, good eating and sleeping—and if you should want a little good drinking you can get that, too, (laughter)—they can be obtained in Dubuque as well, I will not say better, as in Davenport, I have been in Davenport a few times and must say I was very well entertained there.

Then so far as libraries are concerned, I suppose ours are not excelled by any in the State. I am told by members of the Bar, there, that there are probably some three libraries there that are equal to the public library here—so far as regards that class of books that this Convention would be likely to require. Now what the people of Dubuque will do for you, how many bills they will pay for you, or what they will say your bills shall amount to per week, or for any other time I do not know. I think the price of board at our first class hotels—and I would have you understand that we have no others there—is about two dollars a day for day boarders. I should imagine that as our session will be likely to last—I hope not more than two or three weeks, but I fear at least five or six weeks—the great probability is that they would be ready to put board down to about ten dollars a week, which is about as low as they can afford it. I think they could not put it lower than that and do justice to themselves, and it is a first law of nature that justice and charity begin at home. I am satisfied they would put it down to the lowest figure.

That much said, I wish to say a word about getting to Dubuque. I want that matter understood so that there may be no mistake about it. I have had no conference with the line of roads between here and Dubuque. I do not know positively what the fare will be between here and Dubuque, I believe somewhere between ten and twelve dollars. So far, however, as that is concerned I will say that I had a conversation this morning with several gentlemen from Dubuque, and they instructed me to say that as many of the members had their fare fixed to places beyond this city to Davenport, so far as the expense of traveling is concerned between Davenport and Dubuque, going and coming, the expense will be theirs, not yours. You can judge therefore how much they want to see you That is all I believe that I shall attempt to say now. These are as near the facts as I can get at them. At least for one I shall endeavor to make them the facts, if an opportunity is afforded.

Mr. WILSON. I think the better way to decide this matter is to call the roll of members and let each one as his name is called designate the place of his choice.

Mr. EMERSON. I will withdraw my motion if that is agreed upon.

Mr. WILSON. I will submit that motion then.

Mr. PARVIN. As the Convention has not yet fixed upon any place I will move to amend the motion by inserting the name of Iowa City as one of the places to be chosen from.

Mr. CLARKE, of Johnson If some of the members should vote for Dubuque, some for Davenport, and some for Iowa City, there might not be a majority for either of those places, and our vote would be useless.

The PRESIDENT. If the Convention decide upon taking the question as indicated by the gentleman from Jefferson (Mr. Wilson) it would be equivalent to going into an election with three candidates.

Mr. HALL. If we are serious in our action in this matter we have decided to leave Iowa City altogether, and now all we have to do is to decide to which place, Dubuque or Davenport we will go. And now to bring this matter all up again, I think would hardly be exactly right. It is gone on our record that we have determined to leave this city, and now let us proceed to decide which one of those invitations we have received we will accept. As we cannot accept both of the invitations let us accept one and proceed at once to designate which that shall be.

Mr. WILSON. I think with the gentleman from Des Moines (Mr. Hall) that so far as a removal of our sittings is concerned, we have already decided upon leaving Iowa City. I voted against that proposition but I am willing now to choose between the two places named, and shall vote for going to Davenport. That place occupies a more central position than Dubuque. So far as law libraries are concerned, I understand there are as good in Davenport as are found in the State. The library of Judge Grant is said to be as good as any other in all Iowa. And the advantages in other respects would be as good in Davenport as in Dubuque; and for other reasons I shall vote for Davenport. I think we have already determined to go away from this place and it would be but doing the work over again to vote upon the Iowa City proposition.

Mr. HARRIS. It is an old maxim that "it is never too late to do good." If we haved decided to go away we can decide to come back again. I was one of those who voted to remain in Iowa City. Now if we take the vote as proposed we will be voting for different candidates, and if Iowa City receives a majority of the votes then it will prove that some were a little hasty in voting for going away, and I am for giving them an opportunity to correct that vote.

From the remarks made here it would appear as if it was supposed we must accept one of the invitations tendered us if we would act like gentlemen. Now I do not think so. I do not think we have yet incurred any obligations, and I am told by those who are better fitted to judge than I am, that from the severity of the winds to day the railroad to Davenport is in such a condition that we cannot possibly get either to Davenport or Dubuque for a week to come. The road is filled full of snow, and we could not get away if we were to try.

Mr. EMERSON. As the gentleman from Muscatine (Mr. Parvin) by his amendment will defeat the object I had in view in withdrawing my motion, I must insist upon my motion.

The PRESIDENT. The gentleman from Henry (M. Henry) moved as a substitute, for the report of the committee, as amended by the Convention, that it is expedient to accept the invitation of the city of Davenport. The gentleman from Dubuque (Mr. Emerson) moved to strike out the word "Davenport," and insert the word "Dubuque." The question is upon the amendment of the amendment.

Mr. GILLASPY. I think it is necessary that I should define my position also. I have voted all the time for a removal from this place, and I wish to give my reasons for that vote. I am satisfied that while some gentlemen may have very comfortable quarters here, others have not. I come here on Sunday afternoon, and was told I could have a place at the hotel where I applied if I would sleep in the parlor upon a cot. I hunted around until about nine o'clock and made out to find a cold room with one wash bowl and one towel for two persons. That is the best I could do. I do not make complaints of the people of Iowa City, for I believe this is the best they could do with all the members of the legislature, the lobby members and the conventions here.

Now I am for going away and going to the nearest point. I repudiate all idea of being influenced by my board bill and everything of that kind. That consideration alone would not induce me to go a rod. I am willing to pay three, five, seven, ten, twelve or fifteen dollars a week if it is necessary. But I want to go somewhere where we can be comfortably accommodated. I repudiate the idea of gentlemen coming here and offering to board us for nothing. And board at seven dollars a week at Davenport would not induce me to go there. I think such a thing as that is all wrong—not wrong in the gentleman for it was drawn from him by questions—but wrong to let it influence us in any way.

Now if we could get the Hall of the Senate or of the House of Representatives I would not be willing to go away from here. But I heard them discussing the question of adjournment to-day and they could not agree even upon adjourning on the 26th of this month. There is no telling when we can get either of the halls, and I am in favor of going where we can be suitably accommodated.

Mr. EDWARDS. I do not care a fig whether we go away from this city or remain here. But it has been intimated here that if we decide to go away from here, we ought to go this evening or to-morrow morning, and if we decide upon that we will meet with difficulty upon the railroad. I hope, too, that the members of this Convention will take into consideration that the Republican Convention is to be held here on Thursday, and many members would be glad to remain here to attend that Convention. I am satisfied from the tone of the discussion that the minds of the gentlemen are not made up yet. I therefore move to lay the whole subject upon the table until to-morrow morning at ten o'clock.

The question being taken, the motion was agreed to.

Miscellaneous.

On motion of Mr. PATTERSON it was—

Resolved, That A. T. Walling be admitted to the hall of the Convention as reporter for the Keokuk Times, and J. B. Howell, reporter for the Gate City.

On motion of Mr. CLARKE, of Johnson, it was—

Resolved, That S. S. Howe be admitted to the floor of the Convention as reporter for the Iowa City Republican.

Mr. CLARKE, of Johnson. The Convention passed a resolution this morning instructing the Secretary of State to furnish each member of this Convention with a copy of the act of 1855, calling this body together. That gentleman desires me to inform the Convention that the Department has not a sufficient number of copies of that law to furnish the members of this Convention.

Mr. WILSON. I move that the resolution which I offered this morning, in relation to standing committees, be now taken up.

The motion was agreed to, and the Convention proceeded to consider the resolution which was read.

[For resolution see report of this morning's proceedings.]

Mr. TRAER moved to strike out all after the word "Resolved," and insert as a substitute the following:

"That the following shall be the number and character of the Standing Committees of this Convention:

1st. A Committee of five members upon the preamble and bill of rights.

2d. A committee of three upon the right of suffrage and distribution of powers.

3d. A committee of seven upon the legislative department.

4th. A committee of three upon the executive department.

5th. A committee of five upon the judicial department.

6th. A committee of three upon the militia and military affairs.

7th. A committee of five upon state debts.

8th. A committee of five upon incorporations and banking.

9th. A committee of five upon education and the school lands.

10th. A committee of three upon amendments to the Constitution.

11th. A committee of three upon miscellaneous subjects.

Mr. CLARKE, of Henry. I offer the following as a substitute for the resolution:

"*Resolved*, that a committee of five be appointed by the chair to report the number and character of the standing committees of this convention.

Mr. PATTERSON. I desire to say but few words in regard to the programme of our business. The act of the legislature under which this Convention is held, provided for the amendment and revision of the present Constitution of the State of Iowa. I do not think it necessary for this Convention to do more at present than to refer the different articles of the present Constitution to as many appropriate committees, commencing with the preamble and bill of rights, then the right of suffrage and distribution of powers, the executive department, &c.— I see no particular necessity for the motion of my friend from Henry. [Mr. Clarke.] My objection to the resolution of the gentleman from Jefferson [Mr. Wilson] is that it provides committees for a number of subjects that I do not find in the Constitution. I think all that is necessary is to refer the several articles there to their appropriate committees.

Mr. WILSON. The gentleman from Lee [Mr. Patterson] is right in saying that the number of committees provided for in my resolution is more than there are articles of the Constitution. But I provide for no committee to which there will not certainly go some business of the Convention. I provide for a committee on incorporations other than incorporations for banking; and another committee on banking and currency. I did that because I considered that the question of banking in this State was one of the controlling, if not the controlling reason for calling this Convention, and I tho't it would be highly proper to have a committee especially upon that subject. Besides that my division of the committees covers nothing but what may be found in the present Constitution. I deemed it advisable to divide the committees in such a way that each one might have something particular to attend to, and thus divide off the labor.

Mr. CLARKE, of Henry. My own views concur with those of the gentleman from Lee. [Mr. Patterson] I think his proposition for the division of the committees is the most natural and simple one; that is, to have our committees based upon the Constitution we are called upon to amend, and let each separate article be referred to its appropriate committee. But knowing that others entertained a different view I was willing to have the subject of standing committees referred to a committee to report to this body the number and character of our committees. We have two propositions submitted to us, and the gentleman from Lee [Mr. Patterson] has suggested still an other plan. Let them all be referred to a committee and something may be prepared that will meet the views of all.

Mr. PARVIN. I had prepared a resolution which I had intended to offer, precisely agreeing with the views of the gentleman from Lee.—[Mr. Patterson.] But when the gentleman from Jefferson [Mr. Wilson] introduced his resolution, I thought it would answer every purpose.

The question was then taken upon the motion to appoint a committee of five to report upon the number and character of the standing committees, and it was agreed to.

On motion of Mr. HARRIS the several propositions relating to that subject was referred to that committee.

The PRESIDENT announced as the members of that committee the following gentlemen:

Messrs. Clarke of Henry, Johnston, Barvin, Traer and Wilson.

On motion of Mr. CLARK, of Johnson, the convention proceeded to consider the following resolution, laid upon the table this morning.

Resolved, that John Teasdale be authorized to print 100 copies of the Constitution of this State for the use of members of this Convention.

Mr. CLARKE, of Johnson. I move to amend by inserting after the word "State," the words "and also 100 copies of the act authorizing the calling of this Convention."

The amendment was agreed to.

Mr. CLARKE, of Henry, moved to amend by striking out the words "one hundred," and inserting the words "two hundred," which was agreed to.

The resolution as amended was then adopted.

Mr. TODHUNTER then offered the following resolution:

"*Resolved*, that the reporter of this Convention be furnished with stationery and documents such as is furnished to the members of this body.

The resolution was adopted.

Mr. EDWARDS. Several members of this Convention have expressed a desire to have the question of the removal of the sitting of this body from this place, settled this afternoon if possible. I will therefore move to take from the table the report of the committee upon that subject, which was laid upon the table upon my motion.

The question being taken upon taking up the report of the committee, upon a division, ayes 11 noes 15, it was not agreed to.

Mr. CLARKE, of Johnson, offered the following resolution:

Resolved that the Secretary of State be authorized to purchase for the use of the members of this Convention thirty-seven copies of the "Constitution of the United States" published by Barnes.

Mr. PARVIN. I do not like to oppose the motions and resolutions offered by fellow members here. I think every member ought to have a copy of the work referred to in this resolution; but let them do as some of the rest of us have done, purchase them themselves. I do not think the State ought to be called upon to furnish these things to members.

Mr. CLARKE, of Johnson. I hold in my hand a copy of this work which members can examine. I think it will be of immense importance to us in our labors.

Mr. MARVIN. We have been furnished with other things here which we do not need so much as we do this work. I had a very good knife when I came here, but the State has furnished me with one that cost some two or three dollars. I have not any copy of this work and I think we should have one. If I can get it in no other way I would be willing to exchange my knife for a copy. (laughter.)

The question being taken the resolution was adopted.

On motion of Mr. EDWARDS,

The Convention then adjourned until to-morrow morning at ten o'clock.

THIRD DAY—WEDNESDAY, Jan. 21, 1857.

The Convention met at ten o'clock and was called to order by the President.

Prayer was offered by the Rev. Mr. Kynett.

The journal of yesterday was read and approved.

Mr. HALL presented the credentials of Mr. Peters from the 31st senatorial district which were read.

Mr. PETERS then came forward and after being qualifed took his seat in the Convention.

RULES OF THE CONVENTION.

Mr. CLARKE, of Johnson. The committee to draft rules for the government of this Convention have instructed me to make the following report, viz:

Your committee recommend the following rules for the government of the convention:

1. The President shall take the chair every day precisely at the hour to which the Convention shall have adjourned on the preceding day; shall immediately call the Convention to order, and on the appearance of a quorum shall cause the journal to be read.

2. He shall preserve order and decorum, and may speak to points of order in preference to other members, rising from his seat for that purpose; and shall decide questions of order, subject to an appeal to the Convention by any two members.

3. He shall rise to put a question, but may state it sitting.

4. Questions shall be distinctly put in this form: "As many as are of opinion that (as the case may be) say 'aye;' " and after the affirmative voice is expressed "as many as are of the contrary opinion say 'no.' " If the President doubt, or a division be called for, the Convention shall divide; those in the affirmative of the question shall first rise from their seats, afterwards those in the negative.

5. The President shall examine and correct the journal before it is read. He shall have the right to name any member to perform the duties of the chair, but such substitution shall not extend beyond an adjournment.

6. All committees shall be appointed by the President, unless otherwise especially ordered by the Convention, in which case they shall be elected *viva voce*.

7. The first named members of every committee shall be its chairman, and in his absence or being excused by the Convention, the next named member and so on, unless the committee by a majority of their number, elect a chairman.

8. All addresses and motions shall be made to the President, the member rising from his seat for that purpose, and shall confine himself to the question under debate, and avoid personality.

9. On any question, the yeas and nays shall be taken if requested by two members.

10. (See report of Committee.)

11. When a question is under debate no motion shall be received, but to adjourn, to lie on the table, for the previous question, to postpone to a day certain, to commit or amend and to postpone indefinitely, which several motions shall have precedence in the order in which they are here arranged.

12. A motion to adjourn, and a motion to fix a day on which the Convention shall adjourn, shall always be in order; the motion to adjourn and the motion to lie on the table shall be decided without debate:

13. The previons question shall be put in in this form: "Shall the main question now be put." It shall only be admitted when demanded by a majority of the members present, and its effect shall be to put an end to all debate, and bring the Convention to a direct vote upon amendments reported by a committee, if any, then upon pending amendments, and then upon the main question; on a motion for the previous question, and prior to the demanding the same a call of the Convention shall be in order, but after a majority shall have demanded such motion, no call shall be in order prior to the decision of the main question.

14. All incidental questions of order arising after a motion is made for the previous question and pending such motion, shall be decided by the President without debate, but subject to an appeal.

15. When a motion has been made and carried in the affirmative or negative, it shall be in order for any member voting with the majority to move for a reconsideration thereof, on the same or the succeeding day, of the sitting of the Convention, and such motion shall take precedence of all other motions, except the motion.

16. The rules of parlimentary practice comprised in Jeffrie's Manual shall govern the Convention in all cases to which they are applicable, and in which they are not inconsistent with the standing rules and orders of the Convention.

The question was upon the adoption of the report.

Mr. CLARKE, of Johnson. I would say to the Convention that the Committee reported no rules concerning the standing committees, inasmuch as that subject is now in the hands of another committee of this body.

Mr. CLARKE, of Henry. I would state that the committee upon the standing committees are now prepared to report.

Mr. JOHNSTON. I move to lay the report of the committee on rules upon the table, until the report of the committee on standing committees can be received and adopted, and we can then include their list of committees among the rules.

The motion to lay on the table was agreed to.

Mr. CLARKE, of Henry, made the following report.

The committee on standing committees for the Convention have had the same under consideration and report the following:

"That there be twelve committees of five each to be appointed by the President, viz:

1. A committee on the preamble and bill of rights.
2. A committee on the right of suffrage.
3. A committee on the distribution of powers and Legislative deportment.
4. A committee on the executive department
5. A committee on the judicial department.
6. A committee on militia.
7. A committee on State debts.
8. A committee on incorporations.
9. A committee on education and School Lands.
10. A committee on amendments to the Constitution.
11. A committee on miscellaneous sucjects.
12. A committee on the Schedule."

Your committee intend hereby to provide a standing committee for each seperate article of the Constitution to which appropriate committee the same shall be referred, together with such other matters as shall relate to the same.

R. L. B. CLARKE, Chairman.

The question being taken, the report of the committee was adopted.

The report of the committee on rules was then taken up and amended by inserting as "rule ten" the list of committees just adopted, and then as amended was agreed to.

The PRESIDENT announced the following gentlemen as composing the standing committees of this Convention;

Committee on the Preamble and Bill of Rights.

Geo. W. Ells, Timothy Day,
S. G. Winchester, A. R. Cotton,
J. T. Clark.

Committee on the Right of Suffrage.

John Edwards, Wm. Patterson,
Robert Gower, Amos Harris,
J. Hollingsworth.

Committee on the Distribution of Powers and Legislative Department.

John A. Parvin, Edward Johnston,
J. C. Traer, J. H. Emerson,
Thomas Seeley.

Committee on the Executive Department.

Lewis Todhunter, Squire Ayres,
A. H. Marvin, Daniel W. Price,
Hosea W. Gray.

Committee on the Judicial Department.

W. Penn Clarke, D. H. Solomon,
James F. Wilson, J. C. Hall.
R. L. B. Clark.

Committee on the Militia.

H. J. Skiff, George Gillaspy,
J. Hollingsworth, J. C. Hall,
Wm. Patterson.

Committee on State Debts.

James F. Wilson, Hiram D. Gibson,
Wm. A. Warren, Squire Ayres,
Alpheus Scott.

Committee on Incorporations.

R. L. B. Clarke, H. J. Skiff,
Edward Johnston, John A. Parvin,
J. H. Emerson.

Committee on Education and School Lands.

A. H. Marvin, J. C. Hall,
John Edwards, Geo. W. Ells,
Amos Harris.

Committee on Amendments to the Constitution.

Wm. A. Warren, J. T. Clark,
David Bunker, Timothy Day,
Hiram D. Gibson.

Committee on Miscellaneous Subjects.

David Bunker, David P. Palmer,
W. Penn Clarke, J. C. Traer,
M. W. Robinson.

Committee on the Schedule.

James A. Young, George Gillaspy,
Lewis Todhunter, Hosea W. Gray,
A. R. Cotton.

Miscellaneous.

Mr. TODHUNTER offered the following resolution:

Resolved, that the Secretary of this Convention make an arrangement with the Post Master for the payment of the postage of the members and officers of this Convention in the same manner as has been heretofore made with the General Assembly of this State.

The resolution was adopted.

REMOVAL FROM IOWA CITY.

The Convention then proceeded to consider the report of the committee to which had been referred the invitations of the cities of Davenport and Dubuque to the Convention to remove their sittings from Iowa City.

The Convention on yesterday adopted a resolution reported from the committee, which had been amended to read as follows:

"*Resolved*, that we duly appreciate the patriotic motives of the city authorities of Davenport and Dubuque in thus tendering the hospitalities of their respective cities, and that we deem it expedient to accept one of those invitations at this time."

Mr. SKIFF moved to reconsider the vote by which the Convention adopted that resolution.

Mr. CLARKE, of Johnson. Upon that subject I desire only to say that I am authorized by the city authorities of this city to tender to the Convention the use of either the Masonic Hall or Odd Fellows' Hall, both fine and commodious rooms, which will be fitted up by this city for the use of the Convention. There are three or four good rooms in the Masonic Hall which will make good committee rooms, and with those we have here will be amply sufficient.

Mr. WINCHESTER. I move that the whole subject of removal be indefinitely postponed.

Upon this motion the yeas and nays were demanded.

The question being taken by yeas and nays upon the motion to postpone indefinitely, it was agreed to, yeas 20 nays 16 as follows:

Yeas—The President, Messrs. Ayres, Bunker, Clark of A., Clarke of J., Edwards, Gibson, Gower, Gray, Harris, Hollingsworth, Marvin, Palmer, Parvin, Skiff, Todhunter, Traer, Wilson, Winchester and Young.

Nays—Messrs. Clarke of H., Cotton, Day, Ells, Emerson, Gillaspy, Hall, Johnston, Patterson, Peters, Price, Robinson, Scott, Seeley, Solomon and Warren.

Mr. CLARKE. of Johnson. In order that the Convention may have choice of the two rooms offered to them in this city, I move that a committee of two members of this Convention be appointed to visit these rooms and select the one to be occupied by this body until we can have one of the halls above. I think both of the halls are fine rooms, but one may suit the committee better than the other. After one shall have been selected, the City Council will proceed at once to provide the necessary desks and furniture which may be desired. I would say here, that I desire not to be upon this committee.

The motion was agreed to.

The PRESIDENT announced Messrs. Todhunter and Hall as the committee.

Mr. HALL asked to be excused from serving on the committee, and the President appointed Mr. Harris in his stead.

Miscellaneous.

Mr. PATTERSON offered the following resolution:

Resolved, That the President of this Convention be, and is hereby authorized and requested to invite a minister of the Gospel to open the sessions of this Convention each morning with prayer.

Mr. PATTERSON stated that he offered that resolution to obviate the necessity of a special motion every morning for that purpose.

The resolution was adopted.

Mr. WINCHESTER offered the following resolution:

Resolved, That a committee of five be appointed by the Chair to take into considerrtion and report the course to be adopted in publishing the proceeding of this Convention.

Mr. CLARKE, of Johnson. I move to lay that motion upon the table, and for this reason: the Committee upon Reporting have this subject under consideration, and will, perhaps, be able to report to-morrow morning upon it. They contemplate reporting a plan for publishing these debates and proceedings during the session of this Convention.

Mr. WINCHESTER. I withdraw my resolution. I did not understand that that committee had this matter in charge.

The resolution was accordingly withdrawn.

Mr. PALMER moved to take up the resolution providing a certain number of newspapers for the members and officers of the Convention.

Mr. PATTERSON called for the reading of the resolution, and it was read as follows:

Resolved, That the Secretary of this Convention be instructed to procure for each member and officer of this Convention twenty-five daily newspapers, or their equivalent in other newspapers, at their option.

Mr. WILSON. I hope that resolution will not be taken up at present. I understand that by to-morrow the Committee on Reporting and Printing will have completed a plan for publishing the debates and proceedings of this Convention, and that will, to some extent, take the place of the newspapers.

Mr. CLARKE, of Henry. I cannot conceive how any arrangement that may be made for printing the reports of this Convention can affect the objects of this resolution; we shall want the newspapers most certainly, whether any arrangement is made for publishing the debates or not.

Mr. CLARKE, of Johnson. I have no doubt the Convention will need a certain quantity of newspapers, but I apprehend if we adopt the plan suggested for the publication of these debates, members will find it to their advantage to take a large number of copies of the debates for circulation among their constituents.

The question being taken, the resolution was taken up, and the Convention proceeded to its consideration.

The question was, upon the adoption of the resolution—

Mr. EDWARDS moved to amend by striking out the words "twenty-five daily newspapers," and inserting the words "five copies each of the Iowa City Republican and Capitol Reporter."

Mr. HALL. I hope that amendment will not be adopted. I should, at least, desire the privilege of selecting my newspapers.

Mr. PALMER. I think twenty-five newspapers is a small number, if we wish to distribute any among our constituents. Five copies will be of but little service to us for that purpose.

The question being taken upon the amendment it was not agreed to.

Mr. CLARK, of Alamakee, moved to amend by striking out "twenty-five" and inserting "ten."

The question being taken upon the amendment, upon a division, it was agreed to, ayes, 21; noes not counted.

The resolution as amended was then adopted.

Mr. EMERSON offered the following resolution.

Resolved. That H. B. Lacosit be admitted to a seat upon this floor as the reporter for "The North West," published at Dubuque.

The resolution was agreed to.

Mr. CLARKE, of Johnson, offered the following resolution:

Resolved, That John Teesdale be employed to print 200 copies of the rules of this Convention, together with the list of Standing Committees.

The resolution was agreed to.

Mr. WILSON offered the following resolution:

Resolved, That there be appended to the printed rules of this Convention a list of the names of the members and officers of this Convention, together with the age, occupation, nativity, and Post Office address of the respective members and officers.

The question being taken, the resolution was agreed to.

Mr. WARREN offered the following resolution:

Resolved, That P. Moriarty be admitted to a seat upon this floor as reporter for the Maquoketa Excelsior.

The resolution was agreed to.

On motion of Mr. CLARKE, of Johnson, it was ordered that the various articles of the constitution be and are hereby referred to their appropriate and respective standing committees.

Mr. WILSON offered the following resolution:

Resolved, That it is expedient to amend the 16th section of article three of the present Constitution, relating to the legislative department, by inserting between the words "either" and "and" in the fourth line of said section, the words "and on the final passage of all bills the vote shall be by yeas and nays and entered upon the journal; and no bill shall become a law without the concurrence of a majority of all the members elect in each House."

Referred to the committee on the legislative department.

Mr. CLARK, of Alamakee, offered the following resolution:

Resolved, That the proprietor of any newspaper in this State shall be entitled to have a reporter in this hall without a special order to that effect.

The resolution was agreed to.

Mr. GILLASPY submitted the following resolution:

Resolved, That the Convention continue to meet in this Hall until the general assembly shall have adjourned.

Mr. GILLASPY. I offer this resolution because upon reflection I have become satisfied that it will be very inconvenient for the many fat gentlemen we have in this body to be climbing up and down the stairs of either of the halls offered for our use in this city.

Mr. WILSON. I move to lay the resolution upon the table until we can get the report from the committee we appointed to examine these rooms.

Mr. GILLASPY. I would suggest another reason for the adoption of this resolution. It will obviate the necessity of the city council fitting up a hall at considerable expense for this Convention.

The question being taken upon the motion to lay the resolution on the table, it was not agreed to.

The question was upon adopting the resolution.

Mr. PALMER. I would suggest that the resolution be modified by striking out the words "until the general assembly shall have adjourned," and inserting the words "until otherwise ordered." It is not certain when the legislature will adjourn, and it may be necessary to hold our sessions in some other place.

Mr. GILLASPY. I accept the amendment.

The resolution as modified was then adopted.

Mr. JOHNSTON. The only important preliminary matter we have now to settle is this question of printing, and I understand from the chairman of the committee on reporting and printing that they will be prepared to report to-morrow morning. I therefore move that this Convention do now adjourn until to-morrow morning at ten o'clock.

The question being taken, the motion was agreed to, and

The Convention accordingly adjourned.

THURSDAY, January 22, 1857.

The Convention met at ten o'clock, A. M., and was called to order.

Prayer by the Rev. Mr. KYNETT.

The journal of yesterday was read and approved.

The PRESIDENT laid before the Convention the correspondence between himself and the Rev. Alpheus Kynett, of this city, in reference to the daily opening of the Convention by prayer, which was read and laid upon the table.

The PRESIDENT also laid before the Convention the petition of sundry citizens of Delaware county in reference to a constitutional provision relating to banking, and one also in relation to township and county officers.

The petition was read, and on motion of

Mr. WILSON, it was referred to the Committee on incorporations.

Miscellaneous.

Mr. CLARKE, of Johnson, offered the following resolution:

Resolved, That John Teesdale be employed to do the incidental printing of the Convention at the prices now paid the State Printer for similar kinds of work.

The resolution was agreed to.

Mr. CLARKE also offered the following resolution:

Resolved, That John Quaintance be appointed Assistant Fireman to this Convention, whose duty it shall be to attend to the committee rooms.

The resolution was agreed to.

Mr. HARRIS made the following report:

The committee appointed to examine the halls tendered by the city authorities of Iowa City, for the use of this Convention, have discharged the duty assigned them, and beg leave to report, that in the opinion of your committee, it is inexpedient to remove to either of said halls.

The PRESIDENT. The Chair would state for the information of the gentlemen, that while they were absent yesterday, the Convention adopted a resolution to continue their sessions in this hall until otherwise ordered, and therefore no action upon this report is necessary.

The report was received and laid upon the table, and the committee discharged.

Standard of Parliamentary Law.

Mr. ELLS. I move to amend the standing rules of this Convention by striking out the words "Jefferson's Manual," and inserting the words "Cushing's Manual" as our standard of parliamentary law. I do this because Jefferson's Manual is out of print now, and cannot be obtained. Besides Cushing's Manual is now most commonly used.

The PRESIDENT. The Chair would say that he has a copy of Jefferson's Manual to guide him in his decisions of parliamentary questions.

Mr. PARVIN. I care but little which standard is adopted, still I rather prefer Jefferson. There is some difference between the two standards, and I hope the rules will not be changed.

Mr. ELLS. Jefferson's Manual is not used by any parliamentary body with which I am familiar. Cushing's Manual is used by our own Legislature, and almost universally in other parliamentary bodies. It is substantially the same as Jefferson's Manual, with the improvements and changes which time and experience have suggested. I do not know much about either of these works, but from all I can learn, I believe Cushing's to be the best work.

Mr. CLARKE, of Johnson. It seems to me that resolving that we will be governed by Jefferson's or Cushing's Manual will not be of much use to us, unless we can have the work here for reference. I would suggest as an amendment to the resolution that a sufficient number be ordered for the use of this Convention. Many of us here, I think I may say all of us, have acquired our knowledge of parliamentary law from observation rather than study. I am sure I have never studied either of these works. If we are going to become parliamentarians I trust we may have the books furnished us to study.

Mr. ELLS. It is my intention, if this amendment to the rules is adopted, to move for a sufficient number of Cushing's Manual for the use of this Convention.

The resolution of amendment, and the rules was then adopted.

Mr. ELLS offered the following resolution:

Resolved, That the Secretary of State be required to furnish each member and officer of this Convention with a copy of Cushing's Manual of Parliamentary Practice.

Mr. PATTERSON. I would enquire if that resolution would embrace all our officers, firemen, messengers, &c.?

Mr. ELLS. It was not intended to embrace those officers.

The PRESIDENT. The Chair understands

the resolution as it now reads—to embrace all the officers without limitation.

Mr. CLARK, of Alamakee, moved to amend by striking out the words "and officers," which was agreed to.

The resolution as amended was then adopted.

Newspapers for Members.

Mr. HARRIS. I was not present yesterday when the resolution in regard to newspapers for members was before this Convention, and I am hardly advised as to the definite action of the Convention in regard to this matter.

Mr. PALMER. It was to allow each member ten daily newspapers.

Mr. HARRIS. I would like to enquire if it would be in order at this time to offer a resolution to increase that number? I think that number is entirely too small, and I have conferred with several other members, and they concur with me in that opinion. My object is to get those papers that contain an account of the proceedings of this Convention, and send them to my constituents, that they may understand what we do here, and know how to vote upon the Constitution when it is presented to them. I want to keep them posted so far as I can in regard to the proposed action of this Convention. In my opinion ten papers would amount to but little for that purpose. Suppose that you have ten daily newspapers, you can send them to only ten men in your respective districts. And when, as is the case with myself, a number of counties are represented here by one delegate, that is not enough. I represent three counties here, and I should like to have the privilege of sending at least one paper to every Post Office in my district. There are others here who represent as many as ten or a dozen counties. This resolution would not give us that privilege.

The PRESIDENT. The Chair is of opinion that the object of the gentleman from Appanoose (Mr. Harris,) can only be attained by a reconsideration of the vote by which the resolution was adopted.

Mr. HARRIS. As I did not vote upon it at all I do not know as I have the right to move a reconsideration.

Mr. PALMER. I move a reconsideration of the vote by which the resolution was adopted.

The question was upon the reconsideration.

Mr. HALL. I think ten daily newspapers as many as we ought to take. I have resided in the State of Iowa for 18 years, and I have been a constituent nearly all my life here. I have seen the effects of this promiscuous sending of papers through the country by members to their constituents, and I do not think that it has produced any very beneficial consequences. I do not believe we can scatter enough of these papers through the country to make it any particular object to undertake the business. Besides I do not believe in increasing our expenses by any such measure as this. Ten daily newspapers are more than we can read and as many as we ought to send off.

Mr. TRAER. I think the gentleman from Appanoose [Mr. Harris] will be better accommodated by being supplied with a certain number of the reports of our daily debates. I understand it is the calculation to publish our debates daily and have them laid upon the table the next morning after their delivery. In my opinion a copy of these debates will be of more value to our constituents than the papers we get here now. So far as I am concerned I should prefer to allow each member a certain number of copies of these debates to send to our constituents instead of increasing the number of newspapers. The object of taking these papers is, I suppose, two fold. In the first place members here wished to be informed of the opinions of their constituents, as expressed in the public papers, from different portions of the State. Secondly, they wish to inform their constituents what they are doing here. Now it appears to me that by taking these daily reports of our debates and sending them to our constituents we will inform them of our doings here a great deal better than by sending them ordinary newspapers. It is not to be supposed that any of our papers will report and publish our debates in full.

I would suggest that we let this matter remain where it is, and when the committee on printing make their report we can then make some arrangement to allow each member 25 or 50 copies of our daily reports. That I think would be much better than increasing the number of our papers.

Mr. HARRIS. I had not been informed of any particular plan by which we were to obtain these full reports, but had supposed they would be obtained in some way from our daily papers. If the Convention will agree to allow us a certain number of copies of these reports by which to inform our constituents with regard to our doings here, I shall be satisfied with the number of papers allowed us at present. But I want a definite understanding about this matter.

In relation to the remarks of my friend from Des Moines (Mr. Hall) I would say this: I have not been in the State as long as he has and I may not be as well advised in regard to this matter as he is. But I know there is a very great anxiety on the part of my constituents as to what is being and to be done here, and they expect me to do all I can to inform them at as early a day as possible of what is done here, in order that they may form their opinion concerning our labors here.

Mr. SKIFF. As it is understood that the committee on reporting and printing will indicate some course to be pursued in printing and publishing our debates, I would move to lay the motion to reconsider upon the table until to-morrow.

Mr. PALMER. I would enquire of the chair what would be the effect if the motion to lay upon the table should prevail?

The PRESIDENT. The chair would consider it as equivalent to a rejection of the motion to reconsider.

Mr. PALMER. Then I trust it will not prevail.

Mr. CLARKE of Johnson. I am satisfied that ten papers each for the members here are not sufficient for circulation among the people if we adopt no other mode of communicating our doings. The committee on debates expect to make a report, which, if the Convention adopt, it will enable members to give their constituents sufficient information concerning our proceedings here. But as their report is not yet in shape the committee will probably ask for further time this morning, say till to-morrow morning.

The PRESIDENT. The chair would observe that the motion to reconsider can be agreed to, and then the pending question can be laid upon the table.

Mr. SKIFF. I will withdraw my motion to lay upon the table for that purpose.

The question was, upon the motion to reconsider.

The yeas and nays were demanded and being taken resulted as follows:

Yeas—Messrs Ayers, Bunker, Clarke of H., Clarke of J., Ells, Emerson, Gibson, Gillaspy, Harris, Marvin, Palmer, Peters, Scott, Todhunter and Wilson.—15.

Nays—The President; Messrs. Clark of A Cotton, Day, Edwards, Gower, Gray, Hall, Hollingsworth, Parvin, Patterson, Price, Robinson, Seeley, Skiff, Solomon, Traer, Warren, Winchester and Young.—20.

Accordingly the motion to reconsider was not agreed to.

Miscellaneous.

Mr. PALMER offered the following resolution:

Resolved, That the following be considered as one of the standing rules, viz:

Previous notice of one day shall be given of every proposed amendment to these rules.

The resolution was adopted.

M. HALL offered the following resolution:

Resolved, That the Secretary of State be requested to furnish this Convention with a list of the organized counties of this State; also a copy of Parker's sectional maps in pocket form, to each of the members of the Convention.

The resolution was adopted.

On motion of Mr. CLARKE of Henry, the committee on reporting were allowed until to-morrow morning to make their report.

On motion of Mr. PARVIN the Convention adjourned until to-morrow morning at 10 o'clock

FRIDAY, Jan. 23, 1857.

The Convention met at ten o'clock and was called to order.

Prayer by the Rev. Mr. Kynett.

The journal of yesterday was read and approved.

PUBLICATION OF THE DEBATES.

Mr. CLARKE, of Johnson, made the following report:

The committee to whom was referred the subject of employing a reporter to report the proceedings and debates of this Convention, beg leave to submit the following additional report:

Resolved, that twenty-five hundred copies of the proceedings and debates of this Convention be published in book form to correspond in size, appearance and workmanship with the Debates of the Massachusetts Constitutional Convention, on good paper, each page of which shall contain at least 3000 ems of solid matter.

Resolved, that it shall be the duty of the reporter to report at length and accurately the proceedings and debates of the Convention, to perform which, he shall employ at his own expense, and be responsible for, the necessary corps of reporters, and that the report of each day's proceedings of the Convention shall be ready for delivery to the printer as soon as the same can be written out, and as rapidly as he may require the same.

Resolved, that the reporter shall be allowed as a full compensation for his services, the sum of three dollars per page, and the President of the Convention is hereby authorized, from time to time to furnish to said reporter the necessary certificates on the Auditor of State for such sums of money as may be necessary to enable the said officer to meet his necessary expenditures, not at any time to exceed the amount of labor performed.

Resolved, that A. P. Luse & Co. be employed to print and bind the said proceedings and debates; and that they be allowed for said work the prices now paid the State printer for similar kinds of work.

Resolved, That it shall be the duty of the said A. P. Luse & Co., within thirty hours after the delivery of the copy of the proceedings and debates of each day to place upon the desk of each member of the Convention a proof sheet of said days proceedings, etc.

Resolved, That it shall be the duty of each member of the Convention at once to examine the said proof sheets and correct any errors that may be found therein; and the said proof sheets shall then be returned to the said printers to make the necessary corrections.

Resolved, that as soon thereafter as possible, and not to exceed forty-eight hours after the return of said proof sheet, the said A. P. Luse & Co. shall print on a good quality of newspaper copies of each form of said proceedings and debates for each member for distribution, which said sheets shall be placed upon the desks of the members without delay, after which the said printers shall proceed to print the volume above provided for without delay.

Resolved, that the President of the Convention be authorized to draw certificates of payment in favor of A. P. Luse & Co., on the Auditor of State, as the said parties may require means to prosecute the work; provided that the payments made to the said A. P. Luse & Co. during the progress of the work shall not exceed three-fourths of the value or amount of work performed; and provided further, that if the said parties fail to perform the said work or complete the same, after the same has been commenced, they shall forfeit the amount due for work already performed and unpaid for; and the said A. P. Luse & Co. shall execute to the State, a bond similar to that required of the State printer.

Resolved, That it shall be the duty of the Secretary of State to furnish the said A. P. Luse & Co. with the necessary paper for printing the said work herein specified, as the same may be required by the said printers.

Resolved, That the said volume shall be bound in sheep binding.

Resolved, That a committee of three be appointed whose duty it shall be to superintend the reporting and printing of the proceedings and debates.

Resolved, That the said work during its progress, and when completed shall be the property of the State of Iowa.

The question was upon agreeing to the report.

Mr. CLARKE, of Johnson. I would say that I desire this matter disposed of as soon as possible, but I am not anxious to press it now, in the absence of the gentleman from Henry, (Mr. Clarke), who is chairman of the committee, and the gentleman from Scott (Mr. Ells). I would therefore move that the report be laid upon the table, subject to the order of the Convention, until those gentlemen come in.

The motion was agreed to.

Subsequently, on motion of Mr. CLARKE, of Johnson,

The Convention resumed the consideration of the report of the Committee on the Debates and Proceedings.

Mr. CLARKE, of Johnson, moved to amend the first resolution by striking out the words "twenty-five hundred" and inserting the words "three thousand," as the number of bound copies of the debates, &c.

The question being taken, the amendment was agreed to.

Mr. ELLS. I move to amend the fifth resolution by inserting after the words "wlthin thirty hours" the words "unavoidable delays excepted." As these resolutions are to be the foundation for the contract to be made by these gentlemen, all saving clauses should now be put in, that they may be enabled to avail themselves of them.

The question being taken, the amendment was agreed to.

Mr. WARREN. I move that this report be referred to a special committee of three for further examination. I am told by gentlemen here who are practically acquainted with printing, that this work will cost an immense sum printed in the form indicated in this report. I hope, therefore, it will be referred to a special commistee.

Mr. CLARKE, of Johnson. I hope, for many reasons, that this motion will not prevail. In the first place, it is necessary to settle this question so that our reporter may be enabled to telegraph for his assistants. It is of the utmost imperthnce to him that it should be settled at once. Now, in regard to the expense of this work. Being a printer myself, I have made an estimate of the cost of a work such as is contemplated by these resolutions, and I have estimated that the cost of 2,500 copies—it has now been increased to 3,000 copies—of these debates, provided they make a volume of a thousand pages, wlll be between $5,500 and $6,000, reporting and everything else included. That, I think, is as cheap as could be expected for a work of this kind. Now, if this matter is referred to another committee, the work of examining this subject must all be gone over again, and the delay thus caused will very seriously affect the production of such a work as we may desire this to be. This subject has been thoroughly canvassed by the committee who have reported upon it, and they have aimed to get up a plan which will insure us a correct, accurate and creditable report. I cannot see what a new committee could do more.

Mr. HALL. If there are any gentlemen here better informed upon this subject than the committee who have had this matter under consideration, I am willing to have it referred to them. If any member can show any good reason why this report will be improved by being considered by a new committee, and will come back from that committee in a better form than it is now, I will go for the reference. I will confess that this was a new business to me, but I have acted according to all the light I could obtain on the subject The Convention has already decided to employ a reporter, and in that respect have acted in accordance with the course pursued by all State Constitutional Conventions in the Union, at least for many years past. If we intend to have our debates and proceedings reported we must pay for them. And if we have them printed we want the work done up in fair style, and not, because we happen to be a young State, make a poor job of it. It will cost but little more to make a good job of it, than to get it up in the style of a mere journal, like that of our House of Representatives.

These resolutions have been framed to meet all the points in the case, and intended to effect all we desire. It might be that you could get the reporting done somewhat cheaper, I do not know about that. I find that other States have paid about the same that we propose to pay. Now if we look to what others have done we will find the price proposed here to be about the same. I can say this, that assuming these debates shall be reported and published—which was the basis of the action of the committee—I do not believe any other committee can make a report which will be of any service to the convention, different from this. I do not believe they can better the plan, or cheapen it to any considerable extent. They may cheapen the manner in which the volume of debates shall be got up, but I do not think that ought to be done. This volume should be placed in the State libraries of every State in the Union, and in the li braries of every college and historical society in the United States, so far as we can obtain a list of them, It should go into every county and township library in this State. It is a book which I think will sell, too, to a considerable extent. At first I had thought the number of copies were too large, but I think now that the number should be increased rather than diminished.

Mr. CLARK, of Alamakee. I trust, for several reasons, the motion to refer will not prevail. As has been already remarked, it is of the highest importance to have this matter settled definitely, as soon as possible. It would be rather a novelty in legislative proceedings, it seems to me, to make the reference proposed. This whole matter has been referred to a committee; they have examined it and made their report and that report, as I understand, has been received, and the committee discharged, at least so far as that part of the business is concerned. Now, as the gentleman from Des Moines (Mr. Hall) has remarked, if we are satisfied that this committee have not had the proper and requisite information before them, or if we believe any other committee can be raised that would have any better foundation upon which to base a report, then there would be some reason in the proposed reference,. But unless we believe that, I cannot see any advantage to be gained by the proposed reference.

Mr. WARREN. I will withdraw my motion to refer. I did not make it because, I thought myself, the prices reported here were out of the way, but because I had been informed by printers who ought to know, that the committee were mistaken in their estimates, and that the work would cost an immense sum. But I am satisfied with the explanations given by the members of that committee, and will withdraw the motion to refer.

The motion to refer was accordingly withdrawn, and the question recurred upon the adoption of the report.

Mr. CLARKE, of Henry. I would suggest to the gentleman from Jackson (Mr. Warren) or to any other member who is not satisfied with the report of the committee of which I have the honor to be chairman, that a motion can be made to recommit the report with instructions upon any matter not embraced in the present report. But I consider it as full as could be expected.

The question being taken upon the report of the committee as amended, it was adopted.

The PRESIDENT stated that there was a blank to be filled in the seventh resolution, in relation to the number of copies of the daily reports to be furnished each member by the Convention.

Mr. TRAER moved to fill the blank with the number "twenty-five."

Mr. HARRIS moved to fill it with the number "one hundred."

The PRESIDENT stated that the question would be taken first upon the highest number, the motion to fill the blank by inserting the number "one hundred."

Mr. GOWER. I understand from the report of the committee which we have just adopted, that these reports will cost about $2 a volume, and for the 3,000 volumes the expense will be about $6,000. Now as I understand it we are called upon to vote a certain number of copies of the daily reports to each member for distribution, either twenty-five or one hundred copies.

Mr. YOUNG. As I understand it the question now is upon the motion of the gentleman from Appanoose (Mr. Harris) to fill the blank with the number "one hundred."

Mr. HARRIS. With the permission of the Convention I will modify my motion by substituting the number "fifty" for "one hundred."

The PRESIDENT stated the question to be upon the motion to fill the bank with the number "fifty."

Mr. YOUNG. I hope this proposition will not prevail. Whatever number of copies we order to each member, the cost to the State will be something. And besides, if we undertake to distribute among our constituents 50 copies of these reports daily in addition to the newspapers we have ordered, we shall have to employ persons to do our franking, for we shall not have time to do it ourselves. I think if each member distributes ten copies daily among his constituents he will find that number amply sufficient. I do not think very highly of sending papers to our constituents in this way. We send a paper to one man to-day, to another man to-morrow and to still another the next day, and neither of them obtains a mere outline of what we are doing here. I think it is an unnecessary expenditure to frank 50 or 100 copies of this report among our constituents when it will be to them of no especial benefit. I am willing to give our constituents all the information that can be reasonably expected of us, but I am not in favor of voting money for something that will be of no especial service whatever.

Mr. HARRIS. As to the labor of franking these reports and sending them off, that is a matter for ourselves. If the gentleman chooses to send his off separately he can do so. I shall bunch mine and send them to some one in my district who will distribute them over the district. I desire to have every side informed upon this matter. I am acquainted with persons of both parties in my district with whom I can make arrangements to receive these documents and distribute them through the district. I do not think the labor of doing that will be very great. And you must recollect that some of us who live a great ways from here, represent 2,500 and 3,000 votes, and they are all interested in what we are doing here and they want to know what the Convention does. It is to inform them that I desire these reports for distribution.

Mr. PALMER. The members of the Legislature for the county which I represent—the county of Davis—are supplied with twenty-five newspapers each, which they distribute among their constituents: and, notwithstanding they thus send seventy-five newspapers to Davis county, each day, I hear considerable complaint of their not receiving enough of this kind of intelligence concerning what is going on in the Legislature. Now, I think as much interest, if not more, is felt with regard to the proceedings of this Convention as with regard to the proceedings of the General Assembly. I have been requested by a number of persons to keep them posted as to what is being done here, and a great number have complained to me that they are not supplied at all with papers by the members of the Legislature. I think, therefore, that fifty copies of these reports will not be too many. As to the trouble and time in directing and franking them, I believe that number can be sent off in the way indicated by the gentleman from Appanoose (Mr. Harris) in ten or fifteen minutes by any member here. Let the member write upon each paper the name of each person to whom he wishes it to be given, and then have all put up in one package, and direct it to the post office from which it is to be distributed, and the whole matter will be disposed of with very little trouble, and ten to fifteen minutes each day will not be too much time for each member to devote to this matter. I am therefore in favor of the proposition to fill the blank with the number "fifty." There are also to be three thousand bound copies of these debates and proceedings, which will furnish each member of the Convention with about eighty copies, which will not be too many to supply to his district.

The PRESIDENT. The gentleman from Davis (Mr. Palmer) is under some misapprehension with regard to this matter. The bound copies of this work are to be the property of the State.

Mr. PALMER. That presents another reason for ordering a large number of copies of these daily reports.

Mr. HALL. For one, I would not have more than five copies of these daily reports, if they were given to me. I sincerely believe that if six hundred copies—some fifteen or twenty to each member—were brought here each day, one half of them would be thrown among the waste paper. If gentlemen desire a large number of these sheets I am willing they should have my share. But I think the result will be, if we order this number to be furnished us, that we will get but a few stray sheets to send off before this Convention will adjourn, and leave here. I am willing to gratify gentlemen, if they desire this large number, but I think three hundred copies for the use of the Convention will be amply sufficient for all purposes.

Mr. WINCHESTER. Perhaps the gentleman from Appanoose, [Mr. Harris,] has not accurately calculated the number of copies which will be brought here every morning for members to distribute, if his proposition is adopted. Fifty copies each for thirty-six members will make eighteen hundred copies which is a very large number to be sent off from here every day. The gentleman from Davis, [Mr. Palmer,] says his constituents complain of not being fully posted in regard to matters here. I would say to him that his constituents should take the papers more than they do. We cannot be expected here to furnish public documents for every man in the State. The gentleman from Appanoose, [Mr. Harris,] says that he represents three thousand voters. There are gentlemen here who represent twice that number. I represent five thousand myself, and ten organized counties. But I do not think it is necessary for me to send fifty copies of the debates to my constituents. Twenty-five copies I think will be an abundance.

Mr. BUNKER. So far as I am concerned I do not care about taking any of these daily reports of the debates. But I am willing to vote for twenty-five each to accommodate those who desire them. But I do not believe in the practice of taxing one portion of the community for the accommodation of another portion. Now whatever number of copies we take here, must be paid for by a tax upon the people of Iowa, while we will send these reports to our personal and political friends; we tax the whole community to gratify a few individuals. I shall therefore oppose the giving a larger number to each member than twenty-five.

Mr. CLARK, of A. My constituents have a great deal of anxiety to know the doings of this Convention, more than with regard to the ordinary legislation of the State. And permit me farther to say that my constituents are in the habit of reading the papers. But there is no means by which they can inform themselves of the doings of this convention, other than the journals of debates we propose to publish. It seems to me that fifty copies each, is the least that members can send to their constituents in order to keep them well posted in the matters upon which we are engaged. I shall therefore vote most cheerfully for the fifty copies, and I am satisfied my constituents will support me in that vote.

Mr. YOUNG. I move to fill the blank with the number "ten." I think that is amply sufficient.

Mr. GOWER. I have kept the post office in my county for some twelve years, during which time I think I have seen considerable of this printed matter coming from this place and the city of Washington, and when sent in bundles, as suggested by my friend from Appanoose (Mr. Harris) they have often laid in the office a long time before they were called for, without being distributed. That is very apt to be the case, where the population is scarce. Now my opinion is that this convention will not be long in session here—not more than a couple of weeks, I think. These reports are to be sent to Davenport, and be returned within thirty hours, "unavoidable delays excepted," which are very apt to occur this season of the year. We will therefore get our first sheets the first part of next week. Suppose we send them to our constituents in bunch, they will hardly get before the community during next week. Some of the rest will come here, and we will not be here to distribute them, as we will have adjourned and gone home, and those sheets which come here after we have gone, will be of no service at all but be wasted. I am willing to vote for ten copies of the reports to each member, and even for twenty-five copies, if a majority think that number advisable. But I think it would be money thrown away to order fifteen hundred or two thousand copies for the use of the Convention.

The question being then taken, by yeas and nays, upon filling up the blank with the number "fifty," it was not agreed to.—yeas 7—nays 28, as follows:

Yeas—Messrs. Clark of Alamakee, Clarke of Henry, Edwards, Harris, Marvin, Palmer and Scott.

Nays—The President, Messrs. Ayres, Bunker, Clarke of Johnston, Cotton, Day, Ells, Emerson, Gibson, Gillaspy, Gower, Hall, Hollingsworth, Johnson, Parvin, Patterson, Peters, Price, Robinson, Seeley, Skiff, Solomon, Todhunter, Traer, Warren, Wilson, Winchester and Young.

The question being then taken by yeas and nays upon filling the blank with the number "twenty-five," it was agreed to.—yeas 27, nays 8, as follows:

Yeas—Messrs. Ayres, Bunker, Clark of Alamakee, Clarke of Henry, Clarke of Johnston, Cotton, Day, Edwards, Ells, Emerson, Gibson, Gillaspy, Gower, Harris, Johnson, Marvin, Palmer, Price, Robinson, Scott, Seeley, Skiff, Solomon, Todhunter, Traer, Warren and Winchester.

Nays.—The President, Messrs. Hall, Hollingsworth, Parvin, Patterson, Peters, Wilson and Young.

Resolutions of Enquiry.

Mr. JOHNSTON. The preliminary business of the Convention having been disposed of, I suppose there is not a great deal that we can do in session now. The most of our work, for a while at least, is to be done by our committees. Now the idea suggested itself to me this morning, that as we have all probably come here with notions of our own about the different portions of the Constitution, it would be as well to have these views and ideas presented to the Convention in order that they may be referred to their appropriate committees. In this way the standing committees of this body, will have before them all the ideas of the different members of the Convention, and they would be enabled to digest and report to the Convention appropriate provisions for our adoption. I myself have some desire to see the Constitution amended in several of its articles, which have been referred to committees of which I am not a member. I would like to present my views to those committees in the shape of resolutions of inquiry. I think that would be a better way than to move to amend the reports of those committees after they have been made. I am on the committee upon the distribution of powers, and the Legislative department, and I desire to propose some amendments to other portions of the Constitution. That I may be the better understood I will offer a resolution of enquiry that I have drawn up embodying my views, as follows:

"*Resolved*, That the Committee on the Distribution of powers and Legislative Department be instructed to inquire into the expediency—

"*First.* Of amending the second section of article number three of the Constitution of Iowa by providing for annual sessions of the General Assembly, and fixing the day of their meeting on the first Monday in January.

"*Second.* Of amending the third section of article number three so as to provide for the election being held on the Tuesday after the first Monday in November."

That is the day of the Presidential election, and is the day fixed upon generally by the new constitutions of Western States.

"*Third.* Of amending section number five of article three by striking out "twenty-five" and inserting "twenty-one."

This is a bid to Young America. The old constitution provides that a man shall be twenty-five years of age before he shall be entitled to a seat in the Senate. I remember that I myself was in the Council of the Territory with yourself, before I was twenty-five years of age, and I think I had as much wisdom then, and was as well qualified to legislate upon the affairs of the Territory as I am now.

"*Fourth.* Of amending section twenty-five of art. No. three by striking out "two" and providing that the per diem of members shall be three dollars until the meeting of the next General Assembly, who shall be authorized to fix the per diem of the members of the succeeding General Assembly, and thereafter that the per diem of members shall be established every fifth year.

"*Fifth.* Of amending article three by striking out sections twenty-six and twenty-seven.

These sections require that laws shall be of uniform operation and contain but one subject each. They also provide for the publication of the laws. Now, I suppose the truth is, the laws of this State have never been technically in operation, for in some of the counties they have never been in published at all.

"*Sixth.* Of amending section thirty-one of art. three so that the census shall be taken by the authority of the State in 1865, and every tenth year thereafter, and then that the apportionment of members of the General Assembly be made according to population."

I name the year 1865 and every tenth year thereafter, because the census is taken by the General Government in 1860, and every tenth year thereafter. By this means we will secure a census of this State every five years.

"*Seventh.* Of amending article number three by striking out section thirty-four.

That is the section limiting the salaries of State officers for the first ten years of the organization of the State Government, which has now become inoperative by the lapse of time.

"*Eighth.* Of amending article 3 by adding the following section:

"No bill shall be passed unless by the assent of a majority of all the members elected to each branch of the General Assembly; and the question upon the final passage shall be taken immediately upon its last reading, and the yeas and nays entered upon the journal.

"*Ninth*. Of amending article number three by adding the following section:

"The assent of two-thirds of the members elected to each branch of the General Assembly shall be required to every bill appropriating the public money or property for local or private purposes."

I will not say that upon mature reflection, examination and deliberation, I shall support all these propositions; but they have suggested themselves to my mind and I thought I would bring them to the attention of the committee. I therefore move the adoption of this resolution, and its reference to the Committee on the Distribution of Powers and the Legislative Department.

Mr. PARVIN. The reference of resolutions of this kind will affect our business to a very great extent. My own views differ a little from the gentleman from Lee, (Mr. Johnston) in regard to this matter. As to the alterations in the Constitution, I agree with him precisely. But if every member of the Convention is to make out a list of the alterations he desires, and they are to be referred to the different committees, it will, I think, throw a great deal of unnecessary labor and business upon us. The different provisions of the Constitution are now referred to their respective committees And it is not very likely that some member of each committee will introduce amendments for every portion of the Constitution before them, which any member of this house would desire to see offered. As a member of the Committee on the Distribution of Powers and the Legislative Department, I have drawn up a statement of the points I wish to have examined, and I intended to present them to the Committee as soon as we can get together. And I venture to say that there is not one item to which the gentleman from Lee (Mr. Johnston) has referred, but what I propose myself to bring before the Committee. It does seem to me unnecessary to bring in all these various propositions, when each Committee will probably act upon every proposition which could be made concerning that portion of the Constitution referred to them. When they come to make their report, if they have failed in any respect, then any member can move to amend in any particular he may desire.

In regard to the various amendments indicated in this resolution, I would say a few words. In regard to the day of election, I shall go for fixing it in October, rather than in November. And the gentleman is mistaken in his supposition that the new States have generally fixed upon the month of November for the time of holding their elections. Ohio and Indiana have not done so, at all events. In regard to the taking of the census, I had thought it necessary to have the census taken oftener than the gentleman has indicated, until 1870, and then provide for its being taken in 1875, and every tenth year thereafter. By that time the population of the State will have become to some degree permanent and established. As to the per diem of members, that will, undoubtedly, be changed. I think all that is necessary is to cut off the perquisites.

I refer to these matters to show that a vast amount of views and opinions will be thrust upon the Committees if the idea of the gentleman is adopted by this Convention. I think his suggestion unnessary, as these various matters will come before the committees, and be digested by them without any such resolution. If any amendments to their reports should be necessary they can be offered in Convention.

Mr. JOHNSTON. I wish to say but few words in reply to the gentleman from Muscatine. (Mr. Parvin.) I did not suppose my resolution of enquiry would lead to any discussion. The truth is I am not possessed with the spirit of my friend from Muscatine. I desire every man in this house to come and tell me, as a member of a committee, of the Committee on the Legislative Department, and the Committee on Incorporations, what he thinks should be done to amend those two portions of the Constitution.

My object in offering this suggestion concerning resolutions of enquiry was to expedite business. I supposed that many of the plans, ideas and notions of members could be presented to the committees in this way, and disposed of by them without being brought forward here, and taking up the time of the Convention. I drafted my resolution of enquiry in reference to the Legislative Department, because I had had my attention called especially to that matter, and because I was one of the members of that committee. I have another resolution not quite completed upon the subject of Incorporations. By to-morrow morning I expect to have another prepared upon the subject of the Judiciary, &c. We all have our opinions upon these matters, and I think the committees will want to know what those opinions are. I hope every man who has opinions upon the subjects referred to the committees of which I am a member, will present them in the shape of resolutions of enquiry, that we may know what their opinions are.

It is only to expedite business that I make this suggestion. I have no particular desire to take a prominent part in this matter. My object in offering this resolution was to call the attention of the members of this Convention to this subject. If they think the committees are already so fully instructed upon all these matters that it is not necessary that they should receive any information and suggestions from any source, I have no objection. But I confess that I for one shall want information from every source, and will be thankful to any member of this Convention who will give me the benefit of his ideas and opinions upon any of the subjects I may be called upon to act in Committee.

Mr. EDWARDS. I hope the resolution of the gentleman from Lee, [Mr. Johnston,] will prevail. It appears to my mind that the views of members upon the various subjects which come before the respective standing committees should be laid before them in this way. Now I may have a proposition for the amendment of the constitution which should go before a committee of which I am not a member. Now it appears to me that in order to expedite matters as has been suggested by the gentleman from Lee, it is but right and proper and expedient that the views of each member should be brought before the committees of which he may not be a member. Numerous petitions and memorials will probably be presented to this Convention during its session, and they will be referred to the standing committees. They will thus have the views of the different members of this body, and the different portions of the State at large, and they can proceed to prepare their reports understandingly. I hope this Convention will adopt no course in this matter which will restrict members from getting their views fully before the committees. The course indicated by the gentleman from Lee, is the course generally pursued in bodies of this sort. Gentlemen are not thereby debarred afterwards from offering amendments to the reports of the committees when they come up for our consideration and action.

Mr. CLARKE of Johnson. I differ with the gentleman from Muscatine, [Mr. Parvin,] upon this question. I think the plan suggested by the gentleman from Lee, [Mr. Johnston,] is the usual and proper way of bringing these questions before the Convention. I think it will materially assist the committees in their labors, if members will express their views in this way, and have them referred to the committees. But I differ with the gentleman from Lee, [Mr. Johnston,] in one respect, and that is in having these resolutions referred without any discussion or action in the Convention. I think these resolutions should be fully debated here and either adopted or rejected. If a resolution of enquiry is adopted after full discussion here, it will operate virtually as instructions to the committee to which it may be referred. Therefore it is I think these resolutions should not be referred without discussion. I have myself a similar resolution of enquiry, addressed to the judiciary committee, which I propose to offer. I trust all these resolutions will be debated here. I think we can discuss them here much more fully, before these various committees shall have reported, than we can in committee. In this way the committees can obtain a general view of the opinions of this body.

Mr. PARVIN. I have no opposition to make to this resolution if it is the general opinion of the Convention that such would be the best way to expedite our business. My only objection was that I thought such a course would delay our labors here unnecessarily. The different portions of the constitution have been referred to their appropriate committees. I had supposed, and I suppose yet, that those committees will report all the necessary amendments to their respective portions of the constitution without further instructions from this body. But if the Convention think differently I have no objection to make.

Mr. AYRES. The great objection made by the gentleman from Muscatine to this resolution and others of a similar character, is that it would cause labor to the committee. Now I supposed we all came here to work. I know that I came here to labor in my humble capacity as far as was necessary. Now there is to my mind much reason in the suggestion made by the gentleman from Lucas. [Mr. Edwards.]—There may be subjects that will come up in committees of which he is not a member and still he would like have his views presented to those committees. I have been, as is the case with most of the gentlemen here, placed upon but two committees, out of twelve that are filled by members of this body. It is to be supposed that all of us are interested in the labors of the various committees, and the mere fact that we are not upon a committee is not sufficient to warrant us in saying that we have no interest in the labors of that committee. We are all as interested in the subjects before one committee as in those before another We were placed upon the different committees in such a way as to divide the labor, but it was not intended to deprive us of the expression of our individual opinions, and the opportunity of bringing those opinions before the various committees of which we may not be members.

I differ with the gentleman from Johnson (Mr. Clarke) a little, and upon this question. He says that he regards these resolutions as instructions, as the expression of the sense of this Convention, to the different committees to which they may be referred. I do not so regard them at all. I regard the resolution of the gentleman from Lee (Mr. Johnston) simply in the light of a petition in regard to the various subjects embraced in it, and it should be treated as a petition presented here, be read and referred to the Committee as a matter of courtesy. It is not supposed that the Convention endorse those views; they are merely the views of the petitioner. We ought to be anxious to get all the opinions we can before the committees, that they may be able to digest and codify those opinions, if I may use the expression, and be the better able to prepare a report. But I do not want to be understood, in voting for any of these resolutions of enquiry, to endorse the views expressed in them. I do not say that I am in favor of all the views expressed in the resolution of the gentleman from Lee, (Mr. Johnston.) But I want those views presented to and canvassed by the committee, and I may learn something from them, and perhaps have my own views changed by them. I think the view of this matter entertained by the gentleman from Johnson, to be entirely wrong. If we do not refer these resolutions, without regarding them as instructions, we shall be called upon to shape the whole course of the labors of this Convention before the committees report. I am for referring the opinions and views of any member of this Convention germain to the subject, but I do not want to be considered as endorsing his views, because I may vote for their reference to the appropriate committees.

Mr. MARVIN. While I am in favor of a reference of resolutions of this kind, I want to have it done without discussion. We cannot discuss them intelligibly at first, because we may not have examined the subject of which they treat Therefore, I would have them received and referred without discussion

Mr. CLARK, of Alamakee. I am in favor of this resolution. I have the honor to be a member of twc committees of this Convention, and I certainly would feel under great obligation to any member of this Convention, who should feel disposed to do so, if he would favor me with his opinion, and all the information in his power upon the subjects I shall be called upon to act. But I am in favor of having these resolutions referred without discussion, at the time they are introduced, for the simple reason that I would not have the committee regard them as instructions, but to be at liberty to adopt and reject what portions they should see fit. Should they reject any portion of these resolutions that fact would not preclude the members who introduced them, or any other member of the Convention, from offering those rejected portions as amendments to the report of the committee. When their report comes up for consideration, then is the proper time, it strikes me, to discuss the merits and demerits of these resolutions.

The question being taken, the resolution was adopted, and referred to the Committee on the Distribution of Powers and the Legislative Department.

Mr. CLARKE, of Johnson, offered the following resolution :

Resolved, That the Committee on the Judicial Department be instructed to inquire into the expediency of limiting for a term of years, the number of Judges of the District Court, fixing their salaries, apportioning the State into Judicial Districts and providing for a re-apportionment every five years.

Mr. CLARKE said: I am advised that in consequence of the legislation of the present winter, all, or nearly all, of the District Judges of our State, who have any reputation as judges, are indignant at what has been done, and will resign their places, thus leaving only the indifferent Judges upon the bench. A large number of new District Judges have been created, leaving to some of the present Judges only two or three counties, where there is but little, if any business. This has been the result of that legislation, while it has not provided for an increase of their salaries sufficient to warrant their remaining in office. I desire to have this resolution adopted and referred, as an intimation to those Judges that we have this matter before us, and will make all the provision for them that is necessary.

The question being taken, the resolution was adopted, and referred to the Committee on the Judicial Department.

Mr. WARREN offered the following resolution:

Resolved, That all resolutions offered referring matters to committees be referred without debate.

Mr. PALMER. I am opposed to this resolution. I understood the object of offering these resolutions of enquiry to be to ascertain the sense of the Convention before hand so as to avoid labor for the committees. If these resolutions are referred without debate, then they will amount to nothing in the way of instructions to the committees, and can be considered only as the sense of the individual members offering them, and not the sense of the Convention. Now I believe if we discuss these subjects as they are brought in here, we will obtain a correct knowledge of the sense of the Convention, and the committees can act with a view to that sense as expressed by the passage or rejection of these resolutions. For that reason I think we have seen resolutions of this kind passed too hastily here this morning. If the resolutions offered here are discussed and the committees to which they relate obtain in that way a certain knowledge of the sense of the Convention upon those subjects, they can shape their reports accordingly and may calculate with something like certainty upon the passage or rejection of provisions they may report.

I hope these resolutions will not be passed so hastily. I think such resolutions as those which have been offered here this morning should undergo a thorough discussion before they are acted upon in this Convention. If committees report upon resolutions referred to them without discussion and merely as a matter of course, they cannot know the sense of the Convention upon those subjects and their reports may be in part or wholly rejected and they compelled to do their work over again. I hope therefore the resolution of the gentleman from Jackson (Mr. Warren) will not be adopted. I believe we came here to discuss and act upon the subjects presented to us, and I think we ought to do so. These resolutions when adopted, are at least tacit instructions to committees to report according to the tenor and spirit of the resolutions of enquiry. I cannot regard them in any other light, and for that reason I think they should not be referred without discussion.

Mr. CLARKE of Henry. There seems to be different views entertained upon this subject.

The PRESIDENT. The chair begs leave to say that the resolution of the gentleman from Jackson (Mr. Warren) is not now in order. It being a change of the rules of this Convention one day's previous notice must be given before the resolution can be received and considered.

Mr. WARREN· I will then give notice that on to-morrow I will offer this resolution.

Mr. TRAER offered the following resolution:

Resolved, That the committee to whom was referred so much of the Constitution as refers to amending the same be instructed to enquire into the expediency of so amending the Constitution as to provide for a vote for or against holding a Convention to amend the Constitution at least once in ten years.

Mr. CLARKE of Henry. I can offer what few remarks I desire to make upon this resolution as well as upon the one of the gentleman from Jackson (Mr. Warren). I concur entirely with the gentleman from Lee (Mr. Johnston) in the views expressed by him here this morning. I think the object of these resolutions should be to give to each committee the views of those members of the Convention not on that committee. Of course it is to be supposed that the members of each committee would exchange views among themselves when they must together. But they must desire to know the opinions of the members of this Convention on other committees. I am opposed to the introduction of resolutions instructing committees. Let these resolutions be simply resolutions of enquiry and be referred without discussion to their appropriate committees. In that way those committees will have before them the views of those members of the Convention to assist them in their deliberations and labors before they make out their reports. This as I understand it, is the sole object of this system of introducing resolutions of enquiry. Otherwise I think with the gentleman from Muscatine (Mr. Parvin) that they would be labor thrown away. If these resolutions are to be considered instructions to the committees, we will find ourselves called upon to act here in Convention upon the resolutions as they are introduced without deliberation and opprtunity for examination. Now let each member have an opportunity to look over the Constitution carefully and prepare such amendments as he may think necessary and have them referred without debate. I am opposed to this system of the members of the different committees instructing themselves or getting the Convention by a vote upon these resolutions to instruct them.

The question being taken, the resolution was adopted and referred to the committee on amendments.

Miscellaneous.

Mr. PATTERSON offered the following resolution:

Resolved, That the use of this room be given to the State Colonization Society this evening.

The resolution was adopted.

Mr. TODHUNTER offered the following resolution:

Resolved, That the Secretary of State be, and he is hereby required to furnish each delegate with an abstract of each organized county in the State of Iowa.

The resolution was adopted.

RESOLUTIONS OF ENQUIRY.

Mr. GIBSON offered the following resolution:

Resolved, That the committee on state debts be instructed to enquire into the expediency of so amending the constitution that the entire indebtedness of this State shall not exceed $500,000 for the next ten years.

The resolution was adopted and referred to the committee on state debts.

Mr. WILSON offered the following resolution.

Resolved, That the committee to which was referred Art. 10 of the constitution be instructed to enquire into the expediency of so amending said article as to embody in it the following proposition, viz:

Any amendment or amendments to the constitution may be proposed in either house of the General Assembly; and if the same shall be agreed to by a majority of the members elected to each of the two houses, and such proposed amendment or amendments shall be entered on their journals with the yeas and nays taken thereon and referred to the legislature to be chosen at the next general election of members of the general assembly, and shall be published in at least one newspaper in every county where such papers may be published for two months previous to such election; and if the general assembly so chosen shall agree to the proposed amendment or amendments by a majority of all the members of each house, then it shall be the duty of the legislature to submit such proposed amendment or amendments to the people in such manner and at such time as the legislature may prescribe; provided such submission shall provide for a vote of the people before the next session of the legislature; and if the people shall approve and ratify such amendment or amendments by a majority of all the votes cast at such election voting thereon such amendment or amendments shall become a part of the constitution.

The resolution was adopted and referred to the commtitee on amendments.

Mr. CLARKE, of Henry, gave notice that he would on to-morrow or some future day, move to amend the rules by adding the following:

Resolutions of instructions to committees shall lie upon the table one day before reference, and be debatable.

Resolutions, petitions and memorials praying or suggesting amendments to the constitution shall be referred to their appropriate committees without debate.

Mr. PARVIN offered the following resolution:

Resolved, That the committee on State debts be requested to enquire into the expediency of preventing counties and cities from creating a debt for the purpose of aiding incorporated companies in works of internal improvement.

Mr. SKIFF moved that the resolution be amended so as to refer it to the committee on incorporations.

Mr. PARVIN. I should prefer to have this resolution go to the committee on state debts, though I am not very particular about it. I wish some committee to examine this matter and report upon it. I think if all our counties and cities become indebted it will be fully as bad as though the State had become indebted.

Mr. SKIFF. I am not particular about the reference. But I thought municipal corporations and their powers would properly come before the committee on incorporations. As the gentleman prefers the reference of this resolution to the committee on state debts, I withdraw my motion.

The resolution was adopted and referred to the committee on State debts.

Mr. TODHUNTER offered the following resolution:

Resolved, That the committee on Legislative Department be requested to enquire into the expediency of having the constitution so amended as to provide that every bill or resolution which shall have passed both branches of the Legislature shall, before it becomes a law, be presented to the Governor; if he approve he shall sign it; if not he shall return it to the house in which it shall have originated, who shall enter the objections at large upon their journal; and if it be not repassed by a majority of all the members elect of each branch the same shall not become a law.

The resolution was adopted and referred to the committee on Legislative Department.

SUPPRESSION OF DEBATE ON REMOVAL.

Mr. CLARKE, of Johnson, offered the following resolution:

Resolved, That the Reporter be instructed to omit from the report of debates, the debate on the subject of the removal of the Convention.

Mr. GILLASPY. I certainly shall oppose this resolution. I want everything we say and do here to go to the country.

Mr. CLARK, of Alamakee. I shall vote for this resolution. The idea suggested itself to me at the time this debate occurred that some measure of this kind should be adopted by the Convention. I apprehend that every member of this Convention has that interest in the proceedings of this body which will lead him to desire at least that the records and debates of this Convention shall be of a dignified character, and confined to subjects of a public nature, and those subjects germain to the objects we came here to accomplish. If we have all these minor debates published it will certainly take up some time and cause considerable expense, and be of no earthly benefit to any one.

Mr. YOUNG. I would like to know if the present debate is to be reported and published? If it is I shall vote against this resolution so that the people may understand to what the present debate refers.

Mr. CLARKE, of Johnson. I did not apprehend any debate upon this resolution. If it is adopted I suppose it will be understood that this debate is to be left out also.

Mr. TRAER. I am opposed to this resolution. If the gentlemen will examine the debates of Indiana and Massachusetts and most of the other constitutional conventions they will find these debates upon this same subject of removal. I am in favor of having the whole thing go upon record. I am not afraid to let my remarks and position be put upon record, and I believe I said about as much on the subject as any other member.

Mr. JOHNSTON. I am opposed to this resolution chiefly because it is setting a bad precedent. I have no doubt that during the discussions of this Convention there may be a great many little things said which members may not care to have placed on record. But that is to be expected. I am not interested that this debate shall be placed upon record, because I did not participate in it, at all. But there were some admirable speeches made here which I should not like to have lost. There was one made by my friend from Des Moines (Mr. Hall) and also one by my friend from Wapello (Mr. Gillaspy) who was so patriotic and unselfish that he said he would submit to pay ten or fifteen dollars a day for board here, if it was necessary for the public good. (laughter)

Mr. GILLASPY. I call the gentleman to order; he is indulging in personalities. (renewed laughter.)

Mr. JOHNSTON. I will say nothing more about that then. As the gentleman from Benton (Mr. Traer) remarked, there have been some very extended discussions on this subject of removal in other conventions. I well remember the discussions which took place in the Massachusetts Convention on the subject of removal, which took up several weeks, and was a much more pungent and spicy debate than that which took place here. An effort was made to remove the Convention from the State House to Lowell Institute, and I understand one objection to the removal was that there were some odors about Lowell Institute which were more noted for strength than agreeableness. Some of the greatest men in the Union were in that Convention and participants in a very interesting discussion upon the subject of odors.

Now I think it is bad policy at the very commencement of our debates to begin to expunge the record. There was nothing said the other day upon the subject of removal to which any one could take objections. Even those who spoke in favor of removal spoke very highly of the citizens of Iowa City. I am opposed to this resolution.

Mr. HALL. I rise merely to set myself right upon the record, and to have it understood that the reason we did not remove from here was that the roads were blocked up, and we could not get away from here. (Laughter.)

Mr. CLARKE, of Johnson. I offered this resolution merely to get an expression of the wish of the Convention upon the subject. So far as Iowa City was concerned in that discussion, I do not feel that she suffered at all. It was not to suppress anything said for or against her that I offered the resolution. But the Convention are aware that this matter is somewhat expensive, and it is now uncertain to what extent the debates of this body will reach. I desired to exclude from them merely that which had no tendency to enhance the value of the work either at home or abroad. So far as I am individually concerned, or so far as my constituents are concerned, have no particular interest in suppressing this debate.

Mr. WINCHESTER. I shall oppose this resolution. I was sent here by my constituents to act in a public capacity, and I do not intend to say anything that I shall be ashamed for them to read. If I do, then I shall ask the Convention, as a personal favor, to permit me to withdraw those remarks. The object of the gentleman from Johnson (Mr. Clarke) to save expense, is a very meritorious one. But I think the better plan to accomplish that object would be to make speeches shorter. If any very long winded gentlemen here would curtail their speeches, they would make the debates much shorter, and benefit the Convention.

The question being taken upon the resolution, it was not agreed to.

Mr. EMERSON moved the Convention adjourn to Monday at 2 o'clock P. M.

The question being taken, upon a division, it was agreed to; ayes 20; noes not counted.

The Convention accordingly adjourned until Monday afternoon at 2 o'clock.

MONDAY, JANUARY 26, 1857.

The Convention met at two o'clock, P. M., and was called to order by the President.

Prayer by Rev. Mr. Kynett.

The journal of Friday was read and approved.

Reports from Standing Committees.

Mr. EDWARDS, from the Committee on the Right of Suffrage, made the following report:

The committee to whom was referred that portion of the Constitution relating to the right of suffrage, have had that subject under consideration, and have unanimously instructed me to report the same back without amendment, and recommend its adoption by this Convention.

The provision is as follows:

"ARTICLE 2—RIGHT OF SUFFRAGE.

"1. Every white male citizen of the United States of the age of twenty-one years, who shall have been a resident of the State six months next preceding the election, and the county in which he claims his vote twenty days, shall be entitled to vote at all elections which are now or may hereafter be authorized by law.

"2. Electors shall, in all cases except treason, be privileged from arrest on the days of election, during their attendance at such election, going to and returning therefrom.

"3. No elector shall be obliged to perform militia duty on the day of election, except in time of war or public danger.

"4. No person in the military, naval or marine service of the United States shall be considered a resident of this State by being stationed in any garrison, barracks, or military or naval place or station within this State.

"5. No idiot or insane person, or person convicted of any infamous crime, shall be entitled to the privilege of an elector.

"6. All elections by the people shall be by ballot."

On motion of Mr. CLARKE, of Johnson, the report was laid on the table and one hundred copies ordered to be printed for the use of the Convention.

Mr. WARREN, from the Committee on Amendments to the Constitution, made the following report:

The committee to whom was referred so much of the constitution as relates to future amendments of the constitution have had the same under consideration, and a majority of the committee ask leave to recommend the following:

Sec. 1. Any amendment or amendments to this constitution may be proposed in both houses of the General Assembly, and if the same shall be agreed to by a majority of the members elected to each of the two houses, such proposed amendment shall be entered upon their journals, with the yeas and nays taken thereon, and referred to the Legislature to be chosen at the next general election, and shall be published as provided by law for three months previous to the time of making such choice; and if in the General Assembly so next chosen, as aforesaid, such proposed amendment or amendments shall be agreed to by a majority of all the members elected to each house, then it shall be the duty of the General Assembly to submit such proposed amendment or amendments to the people in such manner and at such time as the General Assembly shall provide; and if the people shall approve of and ratify such amendment or amendments, by a majority of the electors qualified to vote for members of the General Assembly voting thereon, such amendment or amendments shall become a part of the constitution of this State.

Sec. 2. At the general election to be held in the year one thousand eight hundred and sixty-seven, and in each tenth year thereafter, and also at such times as the General Assembly may by law provide, the question "Shall there be a convention to revise the constitution and amend the same?" shall be decided by the electors qualified to vote for members of the General Assembly; and in case a majority of the electors so qualified voting at such election, shall decide in favor of a convention for such purpose, the General Assembly at its next session shall provide by law for the election of delegates to such convention.

(Signed) W. A. WARREN, Chairman,
JOHN T. CLARK,
DAVID BUNKER.

Mr. EMERSON moved to lay the report on the table, and that fifty copies be printed for the use of the Convention.

Mr. SKIFF. I would suggest that there be printed two copies for each member, which will make near seventy-five copies.

Mr. EMERSON. I have no objection to that.

Mr. CLARKE, of Johnson. One hundred copies can be printed nearly as cheaply as fifty copies can.

Mr. SKIFF. I move that one hundred copies be printed.

Mr. EMERSON. I accept the amendment.

The question being taken, the motion was agreed to.

Mr. GIBSON. I hardly know how to get at the matter I wish to reach. The Committee on Amendments differ a little in regard to the last section of the report of the majority which has just been read. Two members of that committee thought there ought to be a different wording to that section in reference to submitting the question of amendment to the people once in ten years. I would ask if the minority can offer as a minority report a substitute for any portion of that report?

The PRESIDENT. It would be in order to submit a minority report.

Mr. GIBSON. The views of the minority are not at present drawn up in the shape of a report, but they will be prepared to submit a report at some future time.

The PRESIDENT. The chair would suggest that the object of the minority of the committee could be accomplished by moving an amendment to the majority report when the same shall come up for consideration.

Mr. PARVIN from the Committee on the Distribution of Powers and the Legislative Department made the following report:

The committee to whom was referred so much of the Constitution as relates to the distribution of powers and the Legislative Department, have had the former provision under consideration, and instructed me to report the same as existing in the present constitution, without amendment, as follows:

ARTICLE 3.—OF THE DISTRIBUTION OF POWERS.

1. The powers of the Government of Iowa shall be divided into three separate departments: The Legislative, the Executive and the Judicial; and no person charged with the exercise of powers properly belonging to one of these departments shall exercise any function appurtaining to either of the others, except in cases hereinafter expressly directed or permitted.

Mr. PARVIN. I see no necessity for having this report printed, nor did I see any necessity for printing the report made by the gentleman from Lucas (Mr. Edwards), as no amendment was proposed to the article which was reported back. I did not like, however, to oppose the motion to print, as other gentlemen seemed desirous to have it printed. But I do not see any necessity for printing this report, and shall make no motion to that effect.

The report was received and laid upon the table.

Mr. JOHNSTON. I was going to make the same suggestion as my friend from Muscatine, (Mr. Parvin). If I had voted on the resolutian ordering the printing of the first report, I should now move a reconsideration. There is certainly no necessity for printing that report, as we have the article to which it refers in the constitution which we have had printed for our use, and also in the Code which has been furnished us. It is a very short article, and I see no necessity for having it printed.

Mr. WARREN. I move to reconsider the vote by which that report was ordered to be printed.

The question being taken, the motion to reconsider was agreed to.

The question recurred upon the motion to print, it was not agreed to.

Mr. COTTON. I see no necessity for any delay in regard to the report from the committee on the distribution of powers, but think we can go on and adopt it and have so much of the Constitution disposed of.

The PRESIDENT. The chair would state that there being no motion the report as a matter of course, was laid on the table until called up for action.

Mr. COTTON. Then I would move that the report be taken up and adopted if there is no necessity for delay of any kind.

The motion to take up the report was agreed to.

Mr. CLARK of Alamakee. I do not know as I have any objection to having this report adopted as part of the Constitution of this State. But this is a matter in which I would prefer to have a little time for reflection, and presume other members of the Convention desire the same. Some of them may have amendments to propose to this clause. It strikes me that it would be better to have this report lie over until we all have had time to examine it, and think upon the matter a littte. I do not think we will gain anything by acting upon this report now.

Mr. BUNKER. I concur entirely with the gentleman from Alamakee (Mr Clark). We will probably have in this Constitution which we are now to make, a provision binding the Legislature so that they shall pass no bill without being read three several times and by a yea and nay vote. Now I think it would hardly be proper for this body to dispense with the ordinary Legislative practice in acting upon the organic law of the State.

Mr. HALL. As I understand this report the committee have reported back *verbatim* the article as it stands in the old Constitution. They have decided that it is best not to revise or amend that portion of the Constitution. Now I would like to know what we have to do with that provision? Would it give it any more efficiency for us to adopt it? It is now Constitutional law and if we leave it as it is will remain so.

The PRESIDENT. The committee propose to leave it as it now stands, and the question is upon adopting the report of the committee.

Mr. HALL. This perhaps is one of those provisions, one of those obvious propositions which every one can understand. No amendment to it in any form can be thought of or suggested. I think we are as well prepared now as we ever will be to discharge this committee, and have that portion of our labor completed.

Mr. TRAER. I would ask whether there is not some rules of this Convention under which this report should be read more than once? If it is to be understood that reports are to be received here, read but once and then adopted without any further time, I should like to know it.

The PRESIDENT. These reports can be read as often as members may desire. It has now been read as often as the rules require, once by the member offering it, and once by the clerk in reporting it to the Convention.

Mr. TRAER. I think it should be read as often as bills are in the Legislature. I now give notice that I will offer an amendment to the rules requiring that all reports of committees relating to and containing provisions of the constitution shall be read on three several days and the question upon their adoption be taken by yeas and nays.

Mr. CLARKE, of Henry. I think that as a matter of precedent here in our transactions of business this report had better be laid on the table. Do not let us be in too much of a hurry in these matters. I think we should be deliberative in our method of transacting business. Though the proposition contained in this report may be a self-evident one, but I think it will do no harm to defer action upon it for a while. If we get into the habit now of acting in a hurry upon these reports, we may do so in some matter not so self-evident, and thus be compelled to do our work over again.

Mr. EDWARDS. I think that this is one of those obvious propositions to which there can be no objection. But at the same time I believe the proper course would be to let this report lie upon the table for a time in order that the members may have an opportunity to examine it.

Mr. GIBSON. The question before the Convention, as I understand it, is, upon the adoption of this report. I would enquire of the Chair what would be the effect of adopting this report or rejecting it? Would not adopting it or rejecting it amount to virtually the same thing? The committee report in favor of letting that portion of the constitution remain as it now is. If we adopt the report, we will be virtually endorsing that portion of the constitution. If we reject it, we do not change that article of the constitution.

The PRESIDENT. The Chair conceives that by the adoption of this report the Convention would resolve not to amend that article; by rejecting the report it would leave the matter open for further determination.

Mr. GIBSON. It occurs to me that it would amount to about the same thing.

Mr. WILSON. So far as this report is concerned I am prepared to vote on it now. I presume there will be no change in that portion of Art. three of the present constitution. But inasmuch as some members of the Convention desire it should lie over for the present, I think it would be the better course; it certainly would be following out the usual rules recognized in bodies of this kind. Therefore, for the benefit of those who desire time to examine this matter further, I think it would be better that this report should lie over for the present. I would therefore make that motion.

Mr. PATTERSON. Instead of laying this report upon the table, I would suggest that it be made the special order of the day for to-morrow, which would give members time to prepare any amendments if they had any to offer, and to examine this subject to its fullest extent.

Mr. EDWARDS. I would enquire of the Chair should no motion be made with regard to these reports when they are offered, would they not lie upon the table subject to a motion from some member of the Convention.

The PRESIDENT. That would be the case. But a motion has been made in this case to take up this report and adopt it. The question now is upon the motion of the gentleman from Jefferson, [Mr. Wilson,] to lay this report upon the table, subject to the order of the Convention.

Mr. JOHNSTON. I hope this motion will be agreed to. The fact is that although there may be no opposition or amendment to be offered to this particular proposition, yet to adopt it thus hastily would be to establish a precedent which may become very inconvenient in some of the further transactions of this Convention. Suppose that some other report is made to this Convention and adopted without any consideration or time being allowed for its examination. We may find in some of our subsequent proceedings that some other matters would be adopted that would require a reconsideration of this whole subject. I trust this report will be laid upon the table, and if there is no rule in reference to this matter, I hope some gentleman will prepare one which will provide for such cases as this.

The question being taken upon laying the report upon the table, subject to the order of the Convention, it was agreed to.

RESOLUTIONS OF ENQUIRY.

Mr. WILSON offered the following resolution:

Resolved, That the Committee on Incorporations be instructed to enquire into the expediency of amending the 8th Article of the constitution by adding thereto the following section:

Section —. That property of corporations now existing or hereafter created shall forever be subject to taxation, the same as property of individuals.

Agreed to and referred to the Committee on Incorporations.

Mr. WILSON also offered the following resolution:

Resolved, That the Committee on Legislative Department be instructed to enquire into the expediency of amending that portion of Art. three of the constitution which relates to the legislative department by adding to said article the following section:

No extra compensation shall be made to any officer, public agent or contractor after the service shall have been rendered or the contract entered into; nor shall any money be paid on any claim the subject matter of which shall not have been provided for by the pre-existing law, unless such compensation or claim be allowed by two-thirds of the members elected to each branch of the General Assembly:

Agreed to and referred to the Committee on Legislative Department.

Mr. EDWARDS offered the following resolution:

Resolved, That the committee on the judiciary department be instructed to enquire into the expediency of providing for the election of district attorneys in lieu of county prosecuting attorneys, also to provide for the election of supreme judges by the people.

Agreed to and referred to the committee on the judiciary.

Mr. BUNKER offered the following resolution:

Resolved, That the committee on incorporations be requested to enquire into the expediency of amending the Constitution so as to authorize the legislature to provide for the organization of a State Bank and branches.

Agreed to, and referred to the committee on incorporations.

Mr. SOLOMON offered the following resolution:

Resolved, That the committee on incorporations be requested to enquire into the expediency of making the following, or its equivalent, a part of the Constitution, viz:

The power of issuing paper money shall not be granted by this State.

Agreed to, and referred to the committee on incorporations.

Mr. CLARK, of Alamakee offered the following resolution:

Resolved That the committee on incorporations be instructed to enquire into the propriety of so amending the portion of the Constitution referred to them, as to allow the general assembly to pass a general banking law.

The question was upon agreeing to the resolution.

Mr. SKIFF. It seems to me that two antagonistic resolutions have been handed in here. Now, suppose they are both passed and referred to the committee on incorporations, what instructions will the committee derive from them? It is to be understood that these resolutions express to some extent the sense of the Convention. If that is not to be the case, but one gentlemen is to introduce one resolution, and another is to introduce another on the same subject but diametrically opposed to each other, and both are to be referred to the committee, as a matter of course gentlemen may as well hand in their resolutions of every kind to the committee without troubling this Convention with them. No good can be accomplished in taking up the time of the Convention in this way, but every committee will be encumbered with these resolutions, and the result will be that none of them will be attended to at all. I have no objection to this resolution being referred to the committee, but I cannot see any good to result from it.

Mr. WILSON. There is some necessity for the resolution being handed in in this way. Members of the Convention may hand their resolutions in to the various committees who may put them in their pockets, and pay no attention to them; but if the Convention refer them to the committees we can require a report in relation to the propositions contained in them. It is necessary, therefore, to have these resolutions introduced here and referred by a vote of the Convention, in order to have some attention paid to them.

The resolution was agreed to and referred to the Committee on Incorporations.

Mr. CLARKE, of Henry introduced the following resolution:

Resolved, That the Convention consider the expediency of amending article four of the constitution by providing for the election of a Lieutenant Governor who, by virtue of his office shall preside over the Senate, having the right of debate in Committee of the Whole, and having the casting vote in case of a tie, and who shall exercise all the powers and have the title of Governor in case of the death, removal, or other disability of the Governor.

Mr. CLARKE, of Johnson. As I understand this resolution, it calls upon the Convention to consider this subject instead of its being considered by a committee.

Mr. CLARKE, of Henry. I think the resolution is in a proper form now. It is in the shape of a memorial to the Convention praying them to consider this matter. I move its reference to the Committee on the Executive.

Resolution agreed to, and referred accordingly.

Mr. PRICE introduced the following resolution:

Resolved, That the Committee on the Executive Department be instructed to take into consideration the propriety—

1. Of limiting the term of office of the Executive to two years.

2. Of the creation of the office of Lieutenant Governor.

3. Of the restriction and qualification of the pardoning power.

4. Of the election by the people of all State officers, and regulating the succession to office in cases of removal or other disability.

5. Of restricting legislative action whenever the Legislature may be specially called together to the passing of such acts alone as are referred to in the message of the Executive thus specially convening them.

Agreed to and referred accordingly.

Mr. SOLOMON introduced the following resolution:

Resolved, That the Committee on the Preamble and Bill of Rights be requested to consider the expediency of adopting the following, or its equivalent, as a section in the Bill of Rights, to wit:

No law shall be passed prohibiting the manufacture of or traffic in property which is a production of this State, or a legitimate article of traffic, with the other States and foreign nations, or destroying or in any manner impairing the right of property therein.

Agreed to, and referred accordingly.

Mr. CLARKE, of Johnston offered the following resolution:

Resolved, That the Committee on Suffrage be instructed to inquire into the expediency of amending the constitution by providing that all elections in this State shall be holden upon some other than the second day of the week.

Agreed to, and referred accordingly.

Mr. JOHNSTON offered the following resolution:

Resolved, That the Committee on Education and School Lands be instructed to inquire into the expediency of amending article nine of the constitution of Iowa—

1. By providing that there be selected, either by election or appointment, a board of edu-

cation consisting of ten or twelve persons residing in different parts of the State, who are interested in and familiar with the subject of education; that they shall be paid their necessary traveling expenses, and a per diem not exceeding three dollars for four meetings in each year, and of not more than three days each; that they shall be the trustees of the State University, and have the general charge of the common and other public schools of the State; that they shall have power to appoint a secretary of their board, who shall be their general executive agent, and required to perform such duties in connection with the public schools and education of the State as the board may assign to him, and that the office of Superintendent of Public Instruction be abolished.

2. By providing for the gradual withdrawal of the school funds from the hands of the school fund commissioners, and directing the General Assembly to provide for the investment of said funds in the bonds of the United States, or of solvent interest paying States.

3. By providing that the entire University fund of the State shall be diverted to the support of a State University, one and indivisible.

4. By providing that the State University shall be located at ———.

Mr. PALMER. It appears to me that we are getting into the difficulty I apprehended a day or two since, when these resolutions of instruction were first offered. We are getting on our hands resolutions almost innumerable, and they are adopted here without discussion; and in the manner they are passed they can hardly be considered as expressing the opinion of this Convention at all. I would rather that these resolutions should receive such consideration that the opinions of delegates here might be known to the committees to which they may be referred, so that they might be able to ascertain something in regard to the opinions of the Convention upon the subjects expressed in the resolutions. I hope, therefore that some time will be devoted to the discussion of this matter. Let us have an expression of opinion in regard to the proposed amendment, so that the committees may form some idea from the adoption or rejection of these resolutions, of the views of the Convention upon the different subjects to which they relate.

We have instructed the Committee on Incorporations to enquire into the expediency of measures in exact conflict with each other. That committee I do not think will be enlightened at all upon the subject of the views of this Convention upon these matters, and in relation to what is expected of them. This resolution of the gentleman from Lee, [Mr. Johnston,] embraces subjects which have not received much of my consideration, and I hardly know now how to vote upon it. If it is to be regarded merely as the opinion of the individual then I have no objection to vote for its reference. But if it is to be regarded otherwise, I cannot tell how I should vote.

Mr. JOHNSTON. The object of all these resolutions of enquiry appears to be misunderstood by some members of this Convention. I certainly did not intend when I offered the first resolution of this kind to call upon the Convention by their vote upon its reference to express their opinion upon its merits. My only object was to draw forth from all the members of the Convention some expression of opinion, some suggestions in regard to the various subjects before our different committees, and in that way endeavor to enlighten them upon the several not joint opinions of the different members of this Convention. Several resolutions have been introduced here and referred to the Committee on Incorporations, of which I am a member. I should be pleased if every member of the Convention were to offer resolutions upon the subject referred to that committee. It is a difficult subject, and I am anxious to receive all the information in regard to it that I can. The voting upon these resolutions does not commit any one. I do not consider that I commit myself upon them by voting for those I introduce myself. Some of the subjects to which I have referred have been suggested to me by other members, and I offer them here merely to bring them to the attention of the several committees so that they can examine them and bring them before the Convention in a matured form. I think the proper time to discuss these matters is when reports on them have been made and they come up for consideration.

The resolution was agreed to, and referred to the Committee on Education and School Lands.

Mr. CLARKE, of Johnson, offered the following resolution:

Resolved, That the Secretary of State be requested to furnish the Committee on the Judiciary Department a statement showing the number of Judicial Districts in this State under the laws now in force, and those created by the acts passed at the present session of the Legislature; when the terms of the present judges expire; the number of counties in each Judicial District, and the number of inhabitants in each of said counties in each of said districts.

Mr. PETERS. I would move to amend the resolution so that the information thus obtained, should not be confined to the Committee on the Judiciary, but that each member of the Convention be furnished with a copy of the same.

Mr. CLARKE, of Johnson. I have no objection to that, if it is considered necessary. But this subject will come before the Judiciary Committee in the first place, and any statement made for their use will of course be for the use of the Convention.

Mr. PETERS. I withdraw my amendment.

The resolution was then adopted.

PRINTING OF THE DEBATES.

Mr. TRAER. I desire to move a reconsideration of the vote adopting the report of the Committee on Printing, and I have one or two reasons to offer for making that motion. In the first place I think that the number of copies of the bound reports specified in these resolutions is unnecessarily large. I have been looking over the reports of Constitutional Convention in different States, and I find the number we have adopted to be much larger than the number adopted in any of the other States. Massachusetts ordered but 1,500 bound copies of the reports of the Convention. In Ohio the number of copies ordered was only 2,000. In the State of Indiana there were only 700 copies printed. Now it strikes me that it is unnecessary for this Convention to go to the expense of publishing at this particular time so large an edition of the reports and debates of this Convention. Now, while I am willing to vote for anything that is necessary, any expenditure of money that I can be convinced is necessary. I certainly think this Convention should be very careful how they appropriate the funds of this State where there is at least a doubt of the expediency of the appropriation.

Another reason why I wish for this reconsideration is that I think that if we publish the journal of the debates of this Convention in the form proposed by the report of the committee, that is, in the form of the Massachusetts reports, it will be entirely unnecessary to publish any journal separately from the debates. You will find by examining these reports that they contain a complete journal of the proceedings of the Convention, every motion that came before the body, every vote, and the yeas and nays upon the votes,—all these are embodied with the debates which is to be bound, and 3,000 copies of which is to be printed for distribution. Now if this is to be the case, I think it is an unnecessary expense to have the journal of this Convention published separate and apart from the debates. That is another reason why I am in favor of this reconsideration.

But again. I think the amount paid for this publishing is too high—in other words, the amount paid our State printer—which is the criterion for this printing—is too high. I am satisfied from what experience I have had in this matter, which is little, it is true, but sufficient to enable me to form some calculation what composition and press work will cost. I am satisfied that this work can be performed at a much lower figure, and yet prove a paying operation to the printer. I believe that the law now regulating the State printing provides that there shall be paid to the State printer seventy cents per thousand ems for composition, and about the same amount per token for press work. I am also informed by gentlemen who profess to be posted in this matter in this city, that the same amount of work for which we pay seventy cents, costs the printer but thirty-two cents without his turning his hand over, and the rest is clear profit to him.

Now, while I am in favor of voting all that is necessary, I am not in favor of voting money into any man's pocket merely because we have the power to do so. We are acting here as the agents of the people, and I believe the dictates of conscience and fair-dealing should be acted upon in this convention by gentlemen here, as much as out of the Convention in the regulation of our own private affairs, and that we are just as much called upon to look closely after the interests of the State in our action in this Convention, as after our own private interests if we were at home and looking out for the purchase of a horse, a piece of land, or anything else. For that reason, I now make the motion to reconsider, and I hope that it will be agreed to, and that members will look into this matter, for the people will undoubtedly hold us responsible for what we do here. If the reconsideration is agreed to, I hope the number of copies of the bound volumes of the debates will be cut down at least one-half, which I think will prove to be a sufficiently large amount. I also propose, if it is not too late, under our rules, to move that the motion to print the journal independent of the debates of this Convention, be reconsidered, and that matter struck out entirely.

Mr. HARRIS. I would ask the gentleman from Benton (Mr. Traer) how far he proposes to have his motion to reconsider reach, whether to the bound copies only, or to the printing of the daily sheets of debates?

Mr. TRAER. I understand that the motion to reconsider the vote adopting the report of the committee on printing will, if carried, bring up the whole report of the committee for the reconsideration of the Convention; and, as I understand it, I have the right upon a motion to reconsider to discuss the merits of the whole report. But what I was about to say when the gentleman from Appanoose, (Mr. Harris) interrupted me with his question, was, that if it was not now too late, I would move to reconsider the motion of the gentleman from Muscatine (Mr. Parvin)—if I am not mistaken—that the printing of the journal be given to Mr. Mahin, of Muscatine, in order to have that entirely done away with, and struck from the expenses of this Convention.

Mr. PARVIN. I wish to correct the gentleman from Benton (Mr. Traer) in one statement he has made. I have made no such motion as he has intimated, nor, so far as I know, has the Convention had any such motion before it. I think the records of this Convention will bear me out in that.

Mr. TRAER. I beg the gentleman's pardon if I have been mistaken in assigning the authorship of that measure to him. I think, however, he is mistaken in stating that the Convention has had no such motion before it. I think if he will examine the minutes of the last Thursday morning he will find such a motion there; but I will not say who made it.

Mr. ELLS. I hope the motion to reconsider the action of this Convention in relation to printing the report of our proceedings and debates will not prevail. I dislike to see such childs' play in a Convention like this, embodying, as it ought, the intelligence and dignity of the State. The gentleman from Benton (Mr. Traer) is entirely mistaken with regard to the Ohio reports. There were two volumes of those reports, embracing 1600 pages each, and the State printed 3,000 copies of them. In addition to that, them employed Mr. Samuel Medairy to print their entire proceedings in their journals, which were sent all over the State, besides having these 3,000 copies of the debates printed; and by reference to those debates gentlemen will find that they spent more time—as we may do here, if we continue in this way—in discussing the question of printing the report than would amount to the whole cost of printing the entire work. That, I think, would be poor economy.

Now with regard to this idea of printing 1,500 copies only of our debates—the debates of a Convention representing already a half a million of people, whose number by 1860 will have increased to over a million. Now if these debates are worth printing at all—and that is the only question with me,—they are worth enough to justify us in printing a large edition of them,—enough to give every intelligent, reading voter in the State a copy. I am for a larger edition rather than a smaller one than we have already decided upon. If we meant what we said when we said to our reporter, we will employ you and pay you for your work, go on and make your contract; and if we meant what we said to our printer then I think that good faith requires that we should not reconsider this matter, but we should go on with it, or else do nothing at all. That is my view of that matter.

As to the price paid the printer, I do not know anything about the justice of it. I understand it is the price paid to our State Printer, and if so, I think the same price ought to be paid to our printer. The Legislature have had this matter under their consideration, but they have taken no action cutting down the price. It may be that the price is high. But we must consider that we are living now in a progressive age, that the price of printing as well as of everything else is increasing, not only articles of sale and merchandise, but man's labor. I could live better twenty years ago on a yearly salary of $2,500 than I can now on twice or three times that sum. I think that where everything else has increased in price and value, the laborer should be well paid. And I am in favor of paying not only the professional man well, but also the laboring man and the mechanic. I have myself been through all the grades from that of farmer's boy up to that of a professional man. I shall vote for the largest number of copies of this work—it can be but a small one as we do not differ very materially—and at a fair price, and I trust the report will not be reconsidered.

Mr. CLARKE, of Henry. The committee who made this report are not tenacious at all in regard to this matter in having their report sustained. But this subject was thoroughly considered before the committee and—barring the question of the expense of printing—we, I think, looked well into what were the wants of the State, and we settled upon the number of 3,000 as what were necessary to supply those wants, and if the gentleman from Benton will reflect for a moment, he will perceive that at least that number will be demanded. In the first place we are receiving in this State in our State library and in all our public libraries throughout the State. the journals of the debates and proceedings of the Conventions of other States, and we must reciprocate the courtesies thus shown to us. A large number of copies will thus be required to be sent to the different States and Territories and the public libraries throughout the country. Then we must be prepared to supply the demand from the citizens of our own State. Let the gentleman ask himself how many will probably be required in his own county, and let other gentlemen make the same enquiry, and they will soon see that this number of three thousand will all be needed. And as to the economy of this matter, why the whole expense to the State about which so much has been said, is only about one penny to each inhabitant of the State.

Mr. PRICE. I shall vote for a reconsideration upon the ground that this report pre-supposes a quantity of labor and an amount of delay unprecedented. Now I am disposed to shorten those labors and to limit the debate. If we do that we shall not be under the necessity of having three thousand volumes published. It seems to me that with the lights we have already before us, with the constitutions of thirty other States shining upon our pathways, we shall not have need to remain here two or three months to revise and re-form our constitution. Such a course as that seems to be unnecessary, and for that reason, if for no other, I would support the motion for a reconsideration. It will be found by reference to the reports, proceedings and debates of all parliamentary bodies, that they serve the purpose of preserving a great many flies in amber, insects which buzz through whole periods of sound, gentlemen who talk a great deal and yet in fact say very little. Now my highest ambition will be to have it found, when the labors of this body shall have closed, that I have said less and made fewer motions, consistent with my duties to my constituents, than any other gentleman. And hence to limit debate, and that we may get away from here as soon as possible I shall vote for a reconsideration of this report.

Mr. TRAER. In reply to the gentleman from Henry, [Mr. Clarke,] as to the number of volumes I could distribute in my District, I will say that I suppose I might dispose of about 6,000 volumes, if I had the privilege of doing it, as there are about 6,000 voters there. I suppose each man there would consider himself as equally entitled to a copy of these reports with the gentleman from Henry, and every other gentleman here. Now if we are going to publish these debates to supply our constituents and give each one of them a copy, the number should be greatly enlarged. But I do not understand that to be the object in view. From the debate that took place upon the adoption of the report, I should suppose the object was to supply certain institutions of the State, and the others were to be the property of the State, to be sold for the benefit of the State. Now gentlemen tell us that 3,000 copies is not sufficient to supply the demands they have laid out to be supplied.

Mr. ELLS. I do not desire to be understood as saying any such thing. I merely said it would be necessary to supply those who would want to get them, and I should receive them.

Mr. TRAER. I did not refer at all to what the gentleman from Davenport (Mr. Ells) said. But I understood from the committee who made this report, that at least one-half of this amount would be sufficient to supply all the places it was then expected we should supply, and the balance was to be turned over to the State as the property of the State, to be sold for her benefit. Now, I imagine that the copies sold for the benefit of the State would be very few out of the three thousand we propose to print. I understand from the Secretary of State that there is nothing on record to show that this State ever received anything from the sale of the Code which was published for the benefit of the State. And I undertake to say, that in nine cases out of ten the State will receive nothing for works published in this way. Every gentleman who comes into the capitol who feels a desire to have one of these books, will take one under his arm and walk off with it, and that is all the benefit the State will receive from it. Not one will be sold for the benefit of the State.

I am willing to vote for all expenditures that I conceive to be necessary, but if I am not convinced they are necessary, I will vote against them. In regard to what the gentleman from Davenport (Mr. Ells) says about child's play, I do not understand that, if this Convention vote upon a question, and a member proposes to reconsider that vote, that thus they show anything like child's play. I would refer gentlemen to the Massrchusetts debates, and there was certainly as much talent in that body as in any other body of the kind that has ever assembled in the United States. They will find there the most extended debates on motions to reconsider. That is the case in all deliberative bodies. Motions to reconsider are made to enable members to have a better chance to debate the question to its fullest extent, far better than they could under other circumstances, and this charge of child's play upon those who are in favor of this motion to reconsider, has very little weight with me. If I vote in favor of any resolution, as I did in favor of those embodied in this report, and upon mature reflection I come to the conclusion that it would be better to have that vote reconsidered, I hold myself responsible for that change in my opinion, and I do not consider that it shows any sign of weakness or child's play, either; on the contrary, I hold that it shows an honesty of purpose for a man to acknowledge that he has changed his opinion, when he becomes convinced he was wrong.

Mr. CLARKE, of Johnson. As a member of the committee on the subject of reporting these debates, I desire to say a few words, and especially to answer the position of the gentleman from Benton (Mr. Traer). The committee investigated the question as to the number of copies to be printed and bound, and we first fixed upon the number 3,000; then we placed it at 2,500, and upon consultation with other gentlemen, we concluded that our first estimate—3,000—would be none too many, from the fact that the State printed three thousand copies of the Code, and it is now impossible to obtain a copy at any price. I have been endeavoring for the last week or ten days to purchase ten or a dozen copies to send to the city of New York, to a publishing house there, and I have been unable to do so. Now, if the State has received nothing from the sales of that book, it is the fault—not of the law, but—of the officers of the law. Now, I think we do not call for too many of these books. As remarked by the gentleman from Henry (Mr. Clarke) you need a great many copies of these books to circulate through the public libraries in this Union, in return for similar favors received from them. It is by works of this kind that public libraries are kept up, and the people of Iowa have as much interest to see this work in the Eastern States, as the citizens of those States themselves.

As I understand, then, the gentleman from Benton (Mr. Traer), and the gentleman from Pottawottamie (Mr. Price) are opposed to the publication of any number of these debates whatever. If that is the case, we should decide at once whether we will have printed this number or none at all, for that is all that is left to us to decide. Now as to the price of the printing: The Legislature, I understand, have had a committee upon the subject of the price paid the printer for the State, and after all the examination they have made, they have reported against reducing that price. The only change they propose in the present system, is to cut off some constructive charges which have sometimes been made. If that is true, should we not pay our printer as much as is paid the State printer? If it is said he is paid too much, we can refer to the action of the General Assembly and rely upon their judgment and decision.

I am aware that there are certain persons in this town who have been getting large prices heretofore for printing—a dollar a thousand ems for printing and a dollar a token for press work. Being deprived of that, they are now hanging around like birds of prey, striving to obtain the State printing again for themselves, at a lower price. I am aware, also, that this Convention has been beset by these men, who have in times past fleeced this State, by charging prices far greater than what we now propose. I think it will be safe to pay our printer the same as our State printer is paid, and the people of the State cannot then complain. Gentlemen should remember, also that we require from the printer of this work far more trouble and greater dispatch, than is required of the State printer, while we pay him only the same. We are told that he pays only thirty-two cents per thousand for his printing, while he receives seventy cents per thousand for it. That may, perhaps, be so, but after he pays his compositor thirty-two cents per thousand, what does the rest of the money go for? It goes for office rent, for lights and fuel, and for the wear and tear of his materials, and the other necessary expenses of such an establishment. Now, as I have before said, we may safely rely on the prices paid our State printer.

I trust, Mr. President, this subject will not be reconsidered. It has been quite fully and thoroughly investigated by your committee. We have endeavored to examine this subject fully, and ascertain all concerning it. We have made a report which meets this whole question, and disposes of it. If we reconsider it, now we must at least place the report in such a condition as to cause delay; and another question also presents itself. Suppose we print only twelve or fifteen hundred copies of these reports; in a short time they are exhausted. They are declared to be the property of the State, and in a year or two we will have an application to the legislature to print another edition of the work, which will greatly increase the cost of it. The great cost of publishing a work, is the setting up of the type, and when that is done, the press work and binding would cost but little more for a large than for a small number of copies. The same thing will occur here, I imagine, that has occurred in New York, and in Massachusetss, and in Ohio and in Indiana. You will not find this work in the book stores, or at least but few copies of it. Now I want to place this work in all the public libraries of our own State, and one in at least every county, and perhaps in every township. In addition to that, every gentleman of reading and intelligence will want a copy of this work in his library as a part of the history of the State. In your courts, upon every question of constitutional construction, it will be considered authority for the purpose of ascertaining the intention of the members of the Convention, in adopting any particular clause of the constitution. It then becomes an authority, a law book, and used as such. In view of the uses to which this work will be applied, and in view of its importance to the future history of this State, I trust that we will print a number sufficiently large to answer the demand, until another Constitutional Convention is called and assembled.

Mr. MARVIN. I move to lay the motion to reconsider upon the table.

The PRESIDENT. The Chair is of opinion that the question must be taken directly upon the motion to reconsider, and that the motion to lay upon the table is not strictly in order.

Mr. TRAER. In order that we may have a test vote and know how the matter stands, I call for the yeas and nays upon the motion to reconsider.

The yeas and nays were ordered accordingly.

Mr. JOHNSTON. Mr. President; I came to this Convention with the idea that we were going to take up but a very short time in our deliberations here. I came here as a party man, a member of a particular political party, but as I supposed and still suppose, above all partizan purposes. Now if I had desired to carry out any partizan purpose, I should oppose the reconsideration of this report, for I think the majority of this Convention is about to saddle the State with a debt of some ten or fifteen thousand dollars for which the people will require an account. But, although the party to which I belong cannot be held responsible as a party, for this expense, yet I feel that I am to some extent individually responsible, and I shall endeavor to get rid of that responsibility if I can.

Now I state frankly, that I do not see any necessity for publishing these debates at all. This assertion may surprise, gentlemen, but it is nevertheless my opinion. We have had two Conventions in this State, composed of gentlemen as intelligent, and as wise as we of this Convention are, and their debates were not reported and published. I do not know what new light gentlemen may have to shed upon the subject that may come before us. I would suppose that nearly every subject had been thoroughly exhausted in the Ohio, Massachusetts and Indiana Conventions, and I might say with the gentleman from Potawattamie (Mr. Price) that some of the longest and most able debates in the Massachusetts Convention were really but embalming flies in amber, as for instance the debate upon the meaning of the word loan, and also the debate upon the subject of removing the session of the Convention.

I did not think when we came here that we should be in session more than ten days. I am a member of two committees; both of them have had meetings and I think there is no doubt of their being able to agree upon a report. Therefore, it is, I see no necessity for having our debates reported and published. Now if this report is reconsidered, I would gladly do this: resolve that the gentleman employed as the reporter of this convention should prepare a synopsis of our debates and proceedings here, and have it published in a paper here, and we could scatter that among our constituents, and it would be more intelligible to them than these sheets which we have ordered to be placed upon our tables I therefore hope the motion to reconsider will be adopted.

Mr. PARVIN. I came here to this Convention thinking there was no necessity for publishing the debates of this Convention, but whenever I heard the subject mentioned by other members of this Convention and found them almost unanimously in favor of it. It was certainly not a political movement, for all were in favor of it, of both parties. I gave way to the better opinion of other members, as I did not wish to stand out against a large majority. The subject of reporting and printing the debates of the Convention was brought forward without any bearing as a political movement, it was voted for by members of both political parties and the contract has now been entered into. Now I have no right to break that contract though I will go as far as the farthest to restrain unnecessary expenses of the Convention even to the extent of one dime, yet this matter has gone so far as to have a contract entered into, the terms fixed, the reporter engaged and set at work, and I have now no right to rescind that contract.

Mr. CLARK, of Alamakee. The only question in my mind, Mr. President, is the simple one in relation to the price we have agreed to pay for the reporting and printing of the debates of this Convention. I am now of opinion, and was when the subject was before us on Friday last, that it would prove beneficial to the people of this State to have the debates of this body printed and scattered over the country that our constituents at home might have the means of knowing what we are doing and be enabled to vote understandingly when the Constitution we may make here, shall be submitted to them for action, and they certainly cannot be enabled to do that unless they have the action and debates of this Convention upon the Constitution placed before them in some shape. Nor do I think that the number of copies of this work to be printed are any too large. The simple question in my mind is as to the price we have concluded to give. I hear complaints from different sources as to the price being too large, being altogether exorbitant. I for one am not acquainted with this sort of work, and do not know myself whether the price is too large or not. But I see that there is dissatisfaction exhibited by different members of the Convention upon this point.

I disagree with the gentleman from Muscatine (Mr. Parvin). I believe that even if we have agreed to pay an exorbitant price and have entered into a contract to that effect, we are not yet entirely in the power of the men with whom we may have made the contract. So far as that is concerned, I think we may reconsider the whole vote, and although we may have entered into a contract with these men to do this work, still we have the right to say to them,—gentlemen we do not see fit to go on further with this work. They have no power to compel us to go on with it and their whole remedy is in an action for damages for losing time, &c. They have no right to say to us as a body that because we have entered into a contract we are therefore bound to carry that contract out. All they can do is to institute damages, if we now give them notice that we will not pursue this matter any farther. But I anticipate nothing of this kind.

As I voted for the adoption of the report I shall now vote for its reconsideration in order to satisfy all parties. The argument that we have agreed here to pay no higher than is paid the State Printer does not satisfy me. It is said the State Printer is paid more than he ought to receive for his work. I do not know how that is, but I think it is a matter which, perhaps, should be investigated. If the State Printer does receive more for his work than he ought, it is not necessary, because the Legislature has made a bad contract, that we should make another one like it.

Mr. HARRIS. I was in the first place and am yet in favor of having everything done in this Convention placed in such a shape and spread before the people that they could derive information from it. I was in favor of having our debates published in the papers and thought that with a very little expense we could secure all that was necessary in that shape. And hence I took the position I did in regard to the increase of the number of the papers to be allowed us. But in conversations I and others had upon the subject we were assured that we were to have the reports placed upon our tables daily and we could take them instead of papers. With that understanding I acquiesced. But in doing so I understood that we were to have the printing done in this city and not be dependant upon the contingency of the roads being blocked up with snow, as I now understand is the case. As I now understand the matter I shall vote for a reconsideration.

The question being then taken by yeas and nays upon the motion to reconsider the vote by which the report of the committee on reporting and printing was adopted, it was agreed to, yeas 24, nays 11, as follows:

Yeas—The President; Messrs. Ayres, Clark of Alamakee, Cotton, Day, Edwards, Emerson, Gibson, Gray, Hall, Harris, Hollingsworth, Johnston, Palmer, Patterson, Price, Robinson, Skiff, Solomon, Traer, Warren, Wilson, Winchester and Young.—24.

Nays—Messrs. Bunker, Clarke of Henry, Clarke of Johnson, Ells, Gower, Marvin, Parvin, Peters, Scott, Seeley and Todhunter.—11.

The question was upon agreeing to the report of the committee.

Mr. YOUNG moved that the report be laid upon the table until to-morrow morning at 10 o'clock.

The question being taken by yeas and nays, upon the motion to lay upon the table, it was agreed to, yeas 25, nays 10, as follows:

Yeas—The President; Messrs. Ayres, Bunker, Clark of Alamakee, Clarke of Henry, Clarke of Johnson, Cotton, Day, Edwards, Ells, Gibson, Gower, Gray, Harris, Hollingsworth, Marvin, Parvin, Scott, Seeley, Todhunter, Traer, Warren, Wilson, Winchester and Young.

Nays—Messrs. Emerson, Hall, Johnston, Palmer, Patterson, Peters, Price, Robinson, Skiff and Solomon.

The report was accordingly laid upon the table subject to the call of the Convention.

Resolutions of Enquiry.

Mr. CLARKE of Henry introduced the following resolution:

Resolved, That the committe on suffrage enquire into the expediency of referring the first section of the second Article of the Constitution to the people as a separate clause to be voted upon, so that if a majority of the voters shall vote in favor of retaining the word "white" in said election it shall be retained; but if a majority thereof shall vote in favor of striking it out it shall be stricken out, so that said section shall read "every male citizen of the United States, &c."

Resolved, That the committee on the Legislative Department enquire and report upon so amending Section four of Article three, so that it shall read,

Any person may be a member of the General Assembly who shall be entitled to the right of suffrage in the State at the time of his election, have had an actual residence of thirty days in the county or district he may be chosen to represent.

Mr. HARRIS. I hope the gentleman from Henry (Mr. Clarke) will not think me discourteous to him if I feel myself called upon, according to the pledges I made to my constituents not to permit a thing of this kind even to come in here without showing my opposition to it. I therefore move that it be indefinitely postponed.

Mr. TRAER. I would enquire if this is merely a resolution of enquiry?

The PRESIDENT. The chair understands it to be an ordinary resolution of enquiry.

Mr. TRAER. Then I can see no reason why this resolution should not be referred as an act of courtesy merely to the mover. I do not say that I am in favor of the proposition it contains.

Mr. HALL. Is it in order to move to amend a resolution of this character?

The PRESIDENT. It is not in order at present, as a motion to indefinitely postpone is pending.

Mr. HARRIS. I withdraw the motion to indefinitely postpone.

Mr. HALL. I now move to amend the resolution, so that "the committee on the right of suffrage be instructed to report against privilege," &c.

Mr. CLARKE, of Henry. I apprehend if this course is to be adopted in this Convention it ought to put an end to all resolutions or propositions offered in this body requesting committees to give their attention to certain subjects. We have all understood that these resolutions were to be received only as resolutions of enquiry, and not as resolutions of instructions at all. The proposition contained in this resolution is merely that of enquiring into the expediency of referring the section named to the people for their direct vote upon it. That is the whole proposition. Now for the gentleman to move to amend the resolution so as to instruct the committee to report against it, seems to me to be uncourteous, and I think he had better not commence that game here in this Convention.

Mr. EDWARDS. I do not see the necessity of sending this report to the Committee on Suffrage, as we have already reported that article back to the Convention, and recommended its adoption, without amendment, as a part of the Constitution. It appears to me that the gentleman can reach his object by moving an amendment to the report when it shall have been called up for the action of the Convention. But I think it is entirely unnecessary to send this subject back to the committee when they have already reported upon it unanimously. And therefore, in order to save time, I move to lay the resolution and amendment upon the table.

On this question Mr. CLARKE, of Henry, called for the yeas and nays, and they were ordered accordingly.

The question being taken by yeas and nays upon laying upon the table, it was agreed to, yeas 24 nays 10 as follows:

Yeas—The President, Messrs. Ayres, Cotton, Day, Edwards, Emerson, Gibson, Harris, Hollingsworth, Johnston, Palmer, Patterson, Peters, Price, Robinson, Scott, Seeley, Skiff, Solomon, Todhunter, Warren, Wilson, Winchester and Young.

Nays—Messrs. Bunker, Clark of Alamakee, Clarke of Henry, Clarke of Johnson, Gower, Gray, Hall, Marvin, Parvin, and Traer.

When Mr. JOHNSTON'S name was called, he said: With the permission of the Convention I will state that I would vote cheerfully for the resolution of the gentleman from Henry, (Mr. Clarke) were it not that the committee to which it relates have made their report, which is now before the Convention. I shall therefore vote to lay the resolution on the table.

The resolution was accordingly laid on the table.

Mr. PETERS offered the following resolution:

Resolved, That the Committee on the Judiciary be requested to enquire into the expediency of so amending the constitution as to vest the judicial power of the State in a Supreme Court, in District Courts, Courts of Common Pleas, Courts of Probate, Justices of the Peace, and such other Courts, inferior to the Supreme Courts, in one or more counties, as the General Assembly may from time to time establish, and classify, and limit said Courts as follows:

The Supreme Court shall consist of five judges, a majority of whom shall be necessary to form a quorum to pronounce a decision. It shall have appellate jurisdiction only in all cases in chancery, and shall constitute a court for the correction of errors at law, under such restrictions as the general assembly may by law prescribe. The Supreme Court shall have power to issue all writs and processes necessary to do justice to parties, and shall exercise a supervisory control over all inferior judicial tribunals in the State. The Supreme Court shall be elected by the electors of the State at large. The State shall be divided into four common pleas districts, of compact territory and bounded by county lines; and each of said districts consisting of three or more counties, shall be subdivided into three parts of compact territory, and bounded by county lines, and as nearly equal in population as practicable, in each of which one judge of the Court of Common Pleas, of said district, shall be elected by the electors of said subdivision. Courts of Common Pleas shall be held in each, by one of said judges, of the said subdivisions, as often as the general assembly may by law provide, and more than one court or sitting thereof may be held at the same time in each district. The District Court shall be composed of judges of the Courts of Common Pleas of the respective districts, and one of the judges of the Supreme Court, any three of whom shall be a quorum; and shall be holden in such subdivision at least once in each year. And the general assembly may for each district provide that said court shall hold three annual sessions, in not less than three places. The general assembly may, by law, authorize the judges of each district to fix the times for holding courts therein. The District Court shall have original jurisdiction in all cases of law and equity, and such appellate jurisdiction as may be provided by law.

There shall be established in each organized county a Probate Court, which shall be a court of record, open at all times, and holden by one judge elected by the voters of the county, who shall hold his office for the term of three years, and receive such compensation out of the county treasury as shall be provided by law.

A competent number of Justices of the Peace shall be elected by the electors in each township in the several counties, whose term of office shall be two years, and their powers and duties shall be regulated by law.

The judges of the Courts of Common Pleas shall, immediately after the first election under this constitution, be classified by lot, so that one shall hold office for the term of two years, one for three years, one for four years, and one for five years—the chief justice to be elected for five years; and at all subsequent elections the term of each of said judges shall be for a term of five years.

The judges of the Court of Common Pleas shall, while in office, reside in the district for which they are elected, and their terms of office shall be for five years.

The resolution was agreed to, and referred accordingly.

Mr. AYRES offered the following resolution:

Resolved, That the Committee on State Debts be requested to enquire into the expediency of annexing to that department, as an amendment, the following sections:

Section 2d. That the State shall never assume the debt of any county, city, town or township, or of any corporation whatever, unless such debt shall have been created to repel invasion, suppress insurrection, or defend the State in war.

Section 3d. The general assembly shall never authorize any county, city, town, or township, by vote of its citizens or otherwise, to become a stock-holder in any joint stock company, corporation or association whatever, or to raise for, or loan its credit to, or in aid of, any such company, association or corporation.

The resolution was agreed to, and referred accordingly.

Mr. SOLOMON offered the following resolution.

Resolved, That the Committees on the Legislative, Executive and Judicial Departments be requested to enquire into the expediency of declaring any voter twenty-one years of age and upwards to be eligible to any office in this State.

The resolution was agreed to, and referred accordingly.

Mr. PALMER moved that the Convention adjourn until to-morrow morning at ten o'clock.

The question being taken it was agreed to, upon a Division, as follows: Ayes, 16; Noes, 14.

The Convention accordingly adjourned.

TUESDAY, JANUARY 27, 1857.

The Convention met at ten o'clock, and was called to order by the President.

Prayer by Rev. Mr. Kynett.

The journal of yesterday was read and approved.

Petitions.

The PRESIDENT laid before the Convention two petitions—one from R. M. Wilson and fifteen others, and one from Alexander Story and forty-six others, who, being fully convinced, as they state, of the necessity of legislative action with reference to the observance of the Christian Sabbath, and also of the necessity of a constitutional provision to give validity to such laws, would therefore petition this body to incorporate provisions in the constitution upon which such laws may be based.

Mr. CLARKE, of Henry, moved that they be referred to the Committee on Bills and Rights; which motion was agreed to.

Resolutions of Inquiry.

Mr. GOWER offered the following resolution:

Resolved, That the Committee on Education and School Lands be instructed to inquire into the propriety of locating the State University and devoting the school fund entire to it. Also, that the State take all school funds, present and prospective, and pay semi-annually a per cent. thereon; that the Auditor and Treasurer make a pro rata distribution of the interest semi-annually to the counties; that the county judges draw the amount due their counties semi-annually and distribute to the school districts therein, all to be done by salaried officers, ex-officio, free of charge; that the principal be a perpetual fund, the interest only to be used.

The resolution was agreed to, and referred accordingly.

Mr. PARVIN offered the following resolution:

Resolved, That the Committee on the Right of Suffrage be requested to inquire into the expediency of inserting a clause as follows:

The General Assembly shall pass laws for ascertaining by proper proofs, the citizens who shall be entitled to the right of suffrage hereby established.

And further: In section 1 after the word "days" insert "and within two years paid a state or county tax, which shall have been assessed at least ten days before the election."

Also, add to said section 1, "Provided that electors otherwise qualified, between the ages of twenty-one and twenty-two years, may vote without the payment of taxes."

The resolution was agreed to and referred accordingly.

Mr. EDWARDS offered the following resolution:

Resolved, That the Committee on the Legislative Department be instructed to inquire into the expediency of reporting an amendment to the constitution, providing that the General Assembly shall not pass local or special laws in any of the following enumerated cases, that is to say:

Regulating the jurisdiction and duties of justices of the peace and constables.

For the punishment of crimes and misdemeanors.

Regulating the practice in courts of justice.

Providing for changing the venue in civil and criminal cases.

Granting divorces.

Changing the names of persons.

For laying out, opening and working on highways, and for the election or appointment of township trustees and supervisors, vacating roads, town plats, streets, alleys, and public squares.

Removal of county seats.

Summoning and empanneling grand and petit jurors, and providing for their compensation.

Regulating county and township business.

Regulating the election of county and township officers, and their compensation.

For the assessment and collection of taxes for State, county, township or road purposes.

Providing for supporting common schools, and for the preservation of school funds.

In relation to fees or salaries.

In relation to interest on money.

Providing for opening and conducting elections of State, county, or township officers, and designating the places of voting.

Providing for the sale of real estate belonging to minors or other persons laboring under legal disabilities, by executors, administrators, guardians or trustees.

The resolution was agreed to, and referred accordingly.

Mr. HALL offered the following resolution:

Resolved, That after this day resolutions shall not be in order, offered for the purpose of reference to standing committees, instructing them to inquire as to the propriety of adopting indicated propositions.

Mr. CLARKE, of Henry. Will not that resolution have to lie over a day under the rules?

The PRESIDENT. The resolution will have to lie over for a day. Resolutions are at any time in order, but we have a rule that no change of rules shall be made without one day's previous notice.

Mr. EMERSON. Will it not be in order to suspend the rules?

The PRESIDENT. It can only be done by unanimous consent.

Mr. EMERSON. I hope there will be no objection to a suspension of the rules. We have had considerable discussion here in regard to curtailing our expenses, and it seems to me that if gentlemen would notice for a moment, how much we are encumbering our proceedings with these resolutions, they would see that they are entailing upon the Convention an unnecessary expense. I am entirely willing that the committees should entertain all the propositions that may be handed in to them by the members of the Convention, but it does seem to me that there is no necessity for encumbering our proceedings with all the various suggestions that may be made by members from day to day. If gentlemen are in earnest with regard to the amendments they desire to offer, they will have an opportunity to present them hereafter in the Convention, when the subjects to which they relate shal come up in their regular order.

Mr. PARVIN. I would inquire if the resolution is now before the Convention?

The PRESIDENT. It is not, and it lies over under the rules.

Amendment of the Rules.

Mr. CLARKE, of Henry. I desire to call up the resolution to amend the rules offered by me on Saturday.

The resolution was then read, as follows:

"Resolutions of instruction to Committees shall lie upon the table one day before reference and be debatable. Resolutions, petitions and memorials praying or suggesting amendments to the Constitution shall be referred to their appropriate committees without debate."

Mr. CLARKE. The object I have in offering this resolution is this: Resolutions are offered here which are mere suggestions, and are in the nature of petitions to committees, and they should not be debated here. Any member has a right to make any suggestion, however absurd it may be, and to have it referred to a committee who may give it such consideration as they see fit. The great advantage in offering resolutions here at all is, where committees themselves are in doubt and need light upon a subject before they make their report, and therefore resolutions which are in the nature of instructions should lie over for a day and be debated.

Mr. TRAER. I have drawn up a resolution here in the form of order of business, which I was about to ask the unanimous consent of the Convention to present. I suppose it will be in order to offer it as a substitute for the proposition of the gentleman from Henry, [Mr. Clarke.]

Mr. CLARKE. I raise the question of order. I suppose if the gentleman's proposition comes in as a substitute, that the rules require it to lay over for a day.

The PRESIDENT. The Chair is of a different opinion, and thinks that the proposition of the gentleman from Henry, [Mr. Clarke,] being now before the Convention for consideration is open to amendment.

Mr. TRAER. I offer the following proposition as a substitute for that of the gentleman from Henry.

It was then read as follows:

Resolved, That the rules of order be amended by adopting the following order of business: After the Journal is read, the following order shall govern:

1. Petitions or memorials to be offered.
2. Resolutions.
3. Reports of Committees.
4. Communications on the President's table.
5. Reports in possession of the Convention.
6. Unfinished business.

And also the following additional rule:

Rule 8. All resolutions and reports of Committees shall lie over one day before being acted upon, except by unanimous consent.

Mr. TRAER. I think the proposition I have now offered covers the whole ground, and gives us a regular order of business.

Mr. PARVIN. I would ask the gentleman from Benton, [Mr. Traer,] to withdraw his substitute, and give notice that he will offer it to-morrow as an additional amendment.

The PRESIDENT. The Chair would enquire of the gentleman from Benton, [Mr. Traer,] whether he did not give notice at the last sitting that he would offer such a proposition?

Mr. TRAER. I gave notice yesterday, that I would offer an amendment in relation to this matter, but it covers rather different ground from the one I have now offered. I think it necessary that we should have some regular order of business, and it seems to me that the resolution which I have offered, providing for an additional rule, would attain the object which the gentleman from Henry, Mr. Clarke, has in view. Those subjects, especially, which are to be discussed, should lie over for a day, in order to give members of the Convention an opportunity to inform themselves in regard to them. With that view, I have moved the adoption of this additional rule. I believe it is a rule which has been adopted everywhere in deliberative bodies. The notice which I gave yesterday was, that I would offer an amendment to the rules, so as to require that a proposition should be read three times upon three different days, but I see in looking over the rules that such an amendment was not necessary.

Mr. HALL. Our body is not a very large one and I do not think that we should tie ourselves strictly down to rules. If petitions come here, they come here for a specific object, and they are naturally referred to the appropriate committees by common consent. I do not see the least necessity for any rule upon that subject. What is the object of the rule now proposed by the gentleman from Benton, [Mr. Traer,] that resolutions shall lie over for one day? It is as gentlemen say, to instruct the committees that have the subjects under consideration to which they relate, how to report. A committee, then, before it can report, will have to wait this discussion, and when they report the result of their deliberations to the Convention, it will be referred to the Committee of the Whole, where we will have this same discussion over again, and then when the matter is reported back again to the Convention by the Committee of the Whole, the discussion will be again renewed. The whole tendency of such a course of procedure will be to lengthen our sessions and make our discussions almost endless, reflecting no very great credit upon our labors here. I think it is the duty of this Convention to facilitate its business here as rapidly as possible and get before the Convention as soon as we can the reports of the Committees, that we may act upon them. Let us have reports from the committees, and do not let us send instructions every day to them. Let us untie their hands, so that they can bring in their propositions here, and gentlemen can then offer anything in the way of amendments they please. We shall have abundance of time consumed in the amendments to be proposed here.

There is another objection which I have to the adoption of this rule. Gentlemen who offer amendments to propositions, and send them to committees, do it without much reflection, as every one knows, who has heard these propositions read here. They go before the committees in some form, and the gentlemen who have presented propositions feel themselves committed to advocate and urge their acceptance before the Convention. Hence, every proposition will undergo the fullest discussion. Let us keep ourselves as free as we can, and not trammel ourselves with too many rules. They have a long list of rules in the Senate, and what is the experience there? They do not obey them. I saw an instance of this last evening in the Senate chamber during the few minutes I was present at their session. Bills were taken from the first reading to the final passage, without more than one or two persons, except the movers, knowing what they contained. I presume they passed as many bills last evening as they did the first two weeks of their session—they did it by relieving themselves from the trammels to which they were subjected by their rules. In an ordinary legislative body, they have a variety of things before them for consideration, but in this body we have a single purpose to attain, and it is, therefore, in my opinion, useless to embarrass our action by the adoption of such a rule as that proposed by the gentleman from Benton, (Mr. Traer.) I hope gentlemen will look at the matter in this light, and endeavor to simplify our proceedings as much as possible. We came here with a certain definite object in view. We have been here now some two weeks, without accomplishing a single thing. Not a solitary project is before the Convention yet for its adoption. When shall we be ready to perform the work which we were sent here to do? We came here expecting to have a short session. I am anxious, for one, to go to work, complete the labors before us, and submit the result of our deliberations to the people.

Mr. WILSON. I do not know how it is with other members of this Convention, but so far as I am concerned, I can say that I have presented no proposition, or asked for its reference to a committee, which I did not intend to support in the Convention. I have reflected more or less upon all the propositions I have presented, and I intend to give them my support. The reason why I am in favor of the proposed rule is, that committees may know in advance of completing their reports, the views of different members of the Convention. I believe that by the adoption of this rule we will facilitate the transaction of our business, and if this be so, it will obviate the objection of delay urged by the gentleman from Des Moines, (Mr. Hall.) I believe we will get along faster by having the different propositions before the committees, than to have them brought in by way of amendment to the reports of the committees, and then acted upon. We might then, in very many cases, be compelled to re-commit the reports to the committees. I should rather have the propositions before the committees, and let them act upon them before they make their reports, than to have them afterwards in the Convention.

In relation to this question of rules, it seems to me that neither this Convention nor any other deliberative body can get along without some rules to govern its action. The substitute which has been offered by the gentleman from Benton, (Mr. Traer) I think, is just such a rule as we ought to have in this body. So far we have been doing our business in a loose and careless way. We have had resolutions, reports of committees, and every species of business which has come before us, mixed up in great confusion, so that there has been no regularity at all in our proceedings. When we come here in the morning, our business should come on in regular order, and when we adjourn, it should go on in regular order, so that we may know what is the first regular business in order when we meet again. I believe that regularity in the order of our proceedings will greatly expedite the business before us, and I shall therefore support the proposition offered by the gentleman from Benton.

The PRESIDENT. The chair would ask in what the proposition of the gentleman from Benton (Mr. Traer) differs from that offered by the gentleman from Henry, (Mr. Clarke.)

Mr. CLARKE. My resolution simply provides, that resolutions and reports of committees shall lie over for one day, under the rules, before being acted upon.

The PRESIDENT. The chair inclines to the opinion that the proposition, except the last paragraph, offered by the gentleman from Benton, (Mr. Traer) cannot be received under this motion as a substitute to that offered by the gentleman from Henry, (Mr. Clarke.) The chair decides, therefore, that that part of the proposition which relates to the same subject matter, as that contained in the proposition offered by the gentleman from Henry, (Mr. Clarke) will be in order.

Mr. SKIFF. I move that the resolution be indefinitely postponed.

Mr. TRAER. If it be in order, as the chair has decided a part of my proposition to be in order, I will ask leave to withdraw it. If leave be granted, I give notice that I will present it to-morrow.

Leave was granted, and the question then recurred upon the resolution offered by the gentleman from Henry, (Mr. Clarke.)

The question was then taken and the motion agreed to upon a division as follows—ayes 17, noes 11.

Mr. CLARKE, of Henry, offered the following resolution:

"*Resolved* That the Committee on Incorporations be requested to report in favor of a general banking law in preference to a State Bank system, and not report in favor of both such systems."

Mr. SKIFF. I would like to hear the opinion of members upon this resolution.

The PRESIDENT. It is simply a resolution of instructions. The only question before the Convention is, shall the resolution be adopted?

Mr. SKIFF. I do not wish to make any remarks upon this subject myself, but I would like to hear the expression of others who have investigated this subject, whether we shall have State or Stock banks, or whether we shall have neither.

Mr. PARVIN. I move that the resolution lie upon the table. It refers to a subject which ought to be considered.

The motion was agreed to, and the resolution was accordingly laid on the table.

Mr. WILSON from the Committee on State Debts, to whom was referred the resolution directing inquiry into the expediency of prohibiting counties, cities, &c. from becoming stockholders in joint stock companies, have had the same under consideration, and have instructed the undersigned to report the same back to the Convention and recommend that no action be taken thereon by the Convention.

Mr. EMERSON. I move that the report be laid upon the table and that fifty copies of it be printed.

Mr. JOHNSTON. I would suggest to the gentleman that he had better say one hundred copies, as that number can be printed nearly as cheap as fifty.

Mr. EMERSON. I accept the suggestion and will make the number one hundred.

Mr. CLARKE, of Johnson. I am opposed to the printing of this report, but I rise now to ask the question, whether it is expected that Committees will report upon the various resolutions of inquiry which are submitted to them.—I did not think it would be required at their hands, and I supposed the object of passing these resolution of inquiry was to refer them to the Committees, so that they might have the benefit of the suggestions which they contained. I did not suppose it was understood that these committees would report upon the various propositions submitted to them. Now I am opposed to the printing of the report now made, because if printed it goes to the world as the opinion of this Convention, when in fact this Convention has not come to any conclusion upon this particular subject, and will not, at least until after we have had some discussion upon it. If we are intending to print all the reports upon the various propositions submitted to the committees we will have an enormous amount of matter to print. Although I have said nothing about economy up to this time, I hope my friends upon the other side of the question will remember the doctrine they advanced yesterday. I trust that this report will not be printed, although I shall be in favor of printing all the reports of committees, where the reports are designed to be incorporated in the Constitution.

Mr. WILSON. I wish to say in behalf of the committee that the reason why we reported this resolution back to the the Convention in this shape was, that a number of the members desired to have that subject come before the Convention, and we deemed this plan as good as any that could be, for getting this matter before the Convention. The member who submitted the resolution which we have reported back feels some interest in the matter, and therefore for the purpose of giving him an opportunity to get the matter before the Convention, we reported the resolution back in the shape we did. I shall oppose the printing of the report. It is now before the Convention.

Mr. EMERSON. I have no objection to the course suggested by my friend from Lee (Mr. Johnston), for if this report is to come before the Convention for their consideration, I, for one, desire that it should be printed. The gentleman says that he desires action upon it, and in order to proper action, I desire that this report shall be printed for the purpose of giving the members of this body an opportunity of examining the subject.

Mr. JOHNSTON. This is a very important measure, and it is one which should not be passed by lightly. I hope that the report will be printed in order to afford members an opportunity of examining and investigating the subject matter of the report.

Mr. CLARKE, of Johnston. Any friend of the propositlon, when the committee make their report upon this subject, can move it as a substitute, and then the subject is brought before the Convention. I call the attention of the Convention to another fact: one of the members of the Committee on Bill of Rights, I believe the gentleman from Lucas (Mr. Edwards) made a report here yesterday. and I moved to print one hundred copies of it, and I expect to make the same motion in regard to all the reports of standing committees which recommend the adoption of any article in the constitution. The Convention resolved to print the one hundred copies. A motion was then made to reconsider, and the Convention refused to print one of the reports of a standing committee. And now gentlemen want to print the report of another committee reporting against a resolution of inquiry, passed by this body, not an article to be contained in the constitution. It seems to me that it will not be very consistent to refuse to print reports of standing committees of this house, and then print reports of the kind now made.

Mr. WARREN. As one of the committee to whom this matter was referred, I wish to say a word. I think gentlemen are laboring under a great mistake in this matter. If we go on and have all the resolutions which are offered to committees printed, there will be no end to them. This was a resolution offered to the committee for their investigation, and we thought proper not to accept it. We are now ready to make a full report upon this subject, and when we do that the friends of this resolution can offer it as a substitute, and it will be in order.

Mr. HALL. This committee have decided that they will not report in favor of the propositions that were referred to them. After they have made this decision and rejected the proposition submitted to them, they give us back their old clothes. If every member of the Committee adopts the same plan, and reports for or against every distinct proposition, it will take us about three weeks to get through with that part of the work. We cannot adopt all the propositions that are offered, they are so contradictory in their character. If it be the fashion to send in reports refuting everything done in committee, and requiring the Convention to confirm every thing done there, then indeed we are placed in a most peculiar situation. I am opposed to any such course, and I am opposed to printing any such reports. It is enough for me that the committee have decided what they will do. I suppose they will do something which will satisfy every gentleman, and, no doubt, they will report to the best of their judgment a suitable article upon the subject of Incorporations. When they do that, then will be the proper time for gentlemen to offer their amendments. I am exceedingly anxious that the Convention should go to work, and I want to see the committees report something for our action, something affirmative.

Mr. WILSON. The action of this commmittee does not seem to meet the approval of the gentleman from Des Moines, [Mr. Hall.] I will say that the subject matter of this resolution has not properly come under the duties of the Committee on State Debts. I cannot see what the subscribing of stock by the corporations of cities and towns to joint stock companies has to do with State debts. It is an independent matter entirely, and has no business in the report which we will submit in relation to that article of the constitution, that being a matter upon which we are called especially to act. We deemed it proper, therefore, to send this resolution back to the Convention, and we could not properly refer to it in any way in our report on State debts. Therefore it is, as the gentleman from Des Moines, [Mr. Hall,] has termed it, that we have given back our old clothes to the Convention, and they may take such action as to them shall seem most proper. I am opposed to printing in this case, but I deemed it proper to make this explanation, inasmuch as an independent matter was referred to us, that the Convention should know upon what grounds we based our action.

Mr. HALL. If the report was not on the table I would move that it be referred to another committee. Members of the Convention think that the subject ought to be considered. Let us give it to another committee, and let them consider it. The report of the committee made by the gentleman from Jefferson, [Mr. Wilson,] was a very proper one.

Mr. CLARK, of Allamakee. I am anxious to facilitate the business of this Convention, perhaps, as much so as any gentleman here. I have the charity to suppose that every member entertains that feeling. I apprehend that we can gain nothing by jumping at conclusions, and precipitating business at this early stage of the Convention, before we have adopted any system of regulating and arranging our business. In regard to the motion now before the Convention, it seems to me that the committee have done all that could be required at their hands. It is true that it was not a proper matter, perhaps, to have been referred to that committee by that name, but this Convention having appointed that committee for a specified purpose, it did see fit to refer this matter to that committee by name, consequently, that committee is the committee of this Convention upon that subject. It is a special committee, and their report is a report in fact of the proper committee, as much so as it would be if this Convention were to appoint another special committee and refer the same matter to them.

Now if I am right in this position, then the next question arises as to the printing. I am opposed to the printing of the reports of this committee for the simple reason that the report contains no principles and facts which it is necessary to present to this Convention for their consideration. A refusal to print the report does not preclude any member of the Convention from introducing a resolution upon that subject embracing any matter that he wishes to have incorporated into the Constitution which we are about to form. When such a motion can be made in its proper order, then I apprehend will be the proper time to print the contents of this proposition. Now I am in favor of economy here perhaps as much as some men who talk more than I do upon the subject, and who have made it a kind of capital in this Convention. I wish to be consistent in that economy, and I do not wish to subject the State to the expense of printing reports which will have no tendency to throw any additional light before the members of this Convention.

Mr. HARRIS. I am informed that the Committee on Incorporations has this same subject under consideration. They have not yet come to any conclusion in regard to it, and I think the better course would be to refer this matter to that committee. If it be in order I move that this report be referred to that committee.

Mr. EMERSON. I withdraw my motion to print.

Mr. CLARKE, of Henry. I would suggest inasmuch as the Committee on Incorporations have this subject under consideration, that the Chairman of the Committee on State Debts have leave to withdraw his report, and that the whole matter be referred to the Committee on Incorporations.

Mr. CLARKE, of Johnson. I would move that the report be referred to the Committee on Miscellaneous Subjects. That committee has nothing to do, and the chairman of the committee is anxious to have something to do.

Mr. HALL. This is a proper subject to go before the Committee on Incorporations. Counties and cities are corporations, and the question is, whether we we will limit the power of the Legislature so as to prevent them from authorizing those corporations to create debts. I believe it is a subject entirely proper to be referred to that committee.

The question was taken upon the motion of Mr. Clarke, of Johnson, and it was not agreed to.

The question then recurring upon Mr. Harris' motion, it was taken and decided in the affirmative.

So the Convention agreed to refer the report to the Committee on Incorporations.

Mr. CLARKE, of Henry. In order that we may understand ourselves, I offer the following resolution:

Resolved, That it is not expected that Standing Committees shall report separately upon petitions, memorials and resolutions referred to them, except resolutions of instruction.

This resolution is intended merely to obtain an expression of the sense of this convention.

Mr. WILSON. I would ask if this resolution would bar committees from making reports on these resolutions of enquiry? Suppose it should be the sense of the Convention that committees are not expected to make reports of this kind, would that bar the committees from making these reports should they desire to do so?

The PRESIDENT. The chair has no doubt that the committees could follow their own course upon that matter, but if they should report upon these resolutions separately, the result would be that the Convention might be taken a little by surprise.

The question being taken, the resolution was agreed to.

Mr. WILSON made the following report:

The Committee on State Debts, to which was referred article seven, of the constitution, relating to State Debts, have had the same under consideration, and are unanimously agreed upon recommending to the Convention the adoption of the following articles, upon the subject of State Debts:

SECTION 1. The credit of the State shall not, in any manner, be given or loaned to, or in aid of, any individual, association or corporation; and the State shall never assume or become responsible for the debts or liabilities of any individual, association or corporation.

SEC. 2. The State may contract debts to supply casual deficits or failures in the revenue, or to meet expenses not otherwise provided for; but the aggregate amount of such debts direct or contingent, whether contracted by virtue of one or more acts of the General Assembly, or for different periods of time, shall never exceed the sum of one hundred thousand dollars, and the money arising from the creation of such debts shall be applied to the purposes for which it was obtained, or to repay the debts so contracted, and for no other purpose whatever.

SEC. 3. In addition to the above limited power to contract debts the State may contract debt to repel invasion, suppress insurrection, or defend the State in war: but the money arising from the debts so contracted shall be applied to the purposes for which it was raised, or to repay such debts, and to no other purpose whatever.

SEC. 4. Except the debts specified in the record, and third section of this article, no debts shall be hereafter contracted by, or on behalf of this State, unless such debts shall be authorized by some law, or for some single work or object, to be distinctly specified therein; and such law shall impose and provide for the collection of a direct annual tax, sufficient to pay the interest on such debt as it falls due, and also to pay and discharge the principal of such debt within twenty years from the time of contracting therefor; but no such law shall take effect until, at a general election, it shall have been submitted to the people, and shall have received a majority of all the votes cast for or against it at such election; and the money raised by virtue of such law shall be applied only to the specific object therein stated, or to the payment of the debt contracted thereby; and such law shall be published in at least one newspaper in each county, if one is published therein, throughout the State, for three months preceding the election at which it is to be submitted to the people.

SEC. 5. The legislature may, at any time after the approval of such law by the people, if no debt shall have been contracted in pursuance thereof, by law, forbid the contracting of any further debt or liability under such law; but the tax imposed by such law, in proportion to the debt and liability which may have been contracted in pursuance of such law, shall remain in force, and be irrepealable, and be annually collected, until the proceeds thereof shall have made the provision hereinbefore specified, and pay and discharge the interest and principal of such debt and liability.

SEC. 6. Every law which imposes, continues, or revives a tax, shall distinctly state the tax, and the object to which it is to be applied, and it shall not be sufficient to refer to any other law to fix such tax or object.

All of which is respectfully submitted,

(Signed) J. T. WILSON, Chairman.

On motion of Mr. WINCHESTER, the report was laid upon the table, and one hundred copies ordered to be printed for the use of the Convention.

Publication of the Debates.

On motion of Mr. TRAER, the Convention proceeded to consider the report of the Select Committee on Reporting and Printing, the vote adopting which was reconsidered on yesterday.

The question was upon the adoption of the report.

The reading of the report by sections was called for, and the first section, or resolution, was read as follows:

"That three thousand copies of the proceedings and debates of this Convention be published in book form, to correspond in size, appearance, and workmanship, with the debates of the Massachusetts Constitutional Convention, on good paper, each page of which book shall contain at least two thousand ems of solid matter.

Mr. TRAER moved to strike out the words "three thousand" in the first line.

Upon that question the yeas and nays were ordered.

The question being taken by yeas and nays, the motion to strike out was agreed to; yeas 32, nays 4, as follows:

Yeas.—The President, Messrs. Ayres, Bunker, Clark, of Alamakee, Clarke, of Johnson, Cotton, Day, Edwards, Ells, Emerson, Gibson, Gillaspy, Gower, Gray, Harris, Hollingsworth, Johnston, Marvin, Palmer, Parvin, Patterson, Peters, Price, Robinson, Scott, Seeley, Todhunter, Traer, Warren, Wilson, Winchester, and Young.

Nays.—Messrs. Clarke, of Henry, Hall, Skiff, and Solomon.

No motion to fill the blank being offered, the next section was read as follows:

"That it shall be the duty of the reporter to report at length, and accurately, the proceedings and debates of the Convention, to perform which, he shall employ at his own expense, and be responsible for the necessary corps of reporters; and that the report of each day's proceedings of the Convention shall be ready for delivery to the printer as soon as the same can be written out, and as rapidly as he may require the same.

No amendment being offered, the next section was read as follows:

That the reporter shall be allowed as a full compensation for his services the sum of three dollars per page; and the President of the Convention is hereby authorized from time to time, to furnish the said reporter with the necessary certificates on the Auditor of State for such sums of money as may be necessary to enable the said officer to meet his necessary expenditures, not at any time to exceed the amount of labor performed.

No amendment being offered, the next section was read as follows:

That A. P. Luse & Co. be employed to print and bind the proceedings and debates, and that they be allowed for said work the prices now paid the State printer for similar kinds of work.

No amendment being offered the next section was read as follows:

That it shall be the duty of the said A. P. Luse & Co., within thirty hours (unavoidable delays excepted) after the delivery of the copy of the proceedings and debates of each day, to place upon the desk of each member of the Convention a proof sheet of said days proceedings, &c.

No amendment being offered, the next section was read as follows:

That it shall be the duty of each member of the Convention at once to examine the said proof sheets and correct any errors that may be found therein; and the said proof sheets shall then be returned to the said printers to make the necessary corrections.

No amendment being offered the next section was read as follows:

That as soon thereafter as possibe, and not to exceed forty-eight hours after the return of said proof sheets, the said A. P. Luse & Co. shall print on a good quality of newspaper paper, twenty-five copies of each form of said proceedings and debates for each member for distribution, which said sheets shall be placed upon the desks of the members without delay, after which the said printers shall proceed to print the volume above provided for without delay.

Mr. CLARKE, of Johnson, moved to strike out the word "twenty-five."

Upon this question the yeas and nays were ordered.

The question being taken by yeas and nays, the motion to strike out was agreed to, yeas 24, nays 12, as follows:

Yeas—The President, Messrs. Bunker, Clark of Alamakee, Clarke of Henry, Clarke of Johnson, Cotton, Edwards, Ells, Emerson, Gower, Gray, Hollingsworth, Johnson, Marvin, Parvin, Peters, Scott, Seely, Todhunter, Traer, Warren, Wilson, Winchester and Young

Nays—Messrs. Ayres, Day, Gibson, Gillaspy, Hall, Harris, Palmer, Patterson, Price, Robinson, Skiff and Solomon.

The reading of the remainder of the sections was dispensed with.

The PRESIDENT stated that the question was upon filling the blanks caused by the adoption of the amendments striking out. The first question was upon filling the blank in the first section caused by striking out the words "three thousand."

Mr. TRAER moved to fill the blank with the words "fifteen hundred," and upon that motion called the ayes and nays which were ordered.

Mr. CLARKE, of Henry. I would ask if it is in order to name other numbers with which to fill the blank.

The PRESIDENT. It is in order, and the question will be taken upon the highest number first.

Mr. JOHNSTON. I was originally opposed to all this matter of printing these debates; but the suggestion made yesterday by the gentleman from Muscatine (Mr. Parvin) as to how far we are committed in this matter, is worthy of some consideration. If we are under an agreement in this matter, I think it better that we should understand our position, and learn how far we are committed. If we are pledged to any contract, I, for one, feel very much like standing to it, let it cost what it may, although the plan of printing these debates is very much against my convictions as to what is right and proper for us to do. I think the Convention should be fully informed on this matter before we come to any final conclusion.

Mr. PARVIN. I stated yesterday, when this question of a reconsideration was up before us, that in my opinion, the Convention had committed themselves to print these reports, by having employed a reporter and ordering the printing to be done in a particular way by these gentlemen in Davenport. I believed so then, and my vote was governed accordingly, and cast against the reconsideration; but a large majority of the Convention differed with me in opinion, and by their action decided that they were not bound by the contract that had been made, or which I supposed they had made. I stand, therefore, I think, freed from obligations, and at liberty to go back to first principles, if you please. I cared not one dime about having these reports printed when the question was first brought up, and I do not care about it yet. But I will go for printing fifteen hundred copies to be bound, and I will not go beyond that number. I consider myself released from the responsibilities I supposed this convention liable to, by their action of yesterday, and I will go with the farthest to reduce all unnecessary expenses, and will not vote for filling that blank with one single copy over the number moved by the gentleman from Benton (Mr. Traer)—that is fifteen hundred.

Mr. HALL. It seems to me the gentleman from Muscatine (Mr. Parvin) occupies rather a singular position to-day. I voted against taking this matter up again on yesterday, because that gentleman said that there was a contract which he considered binding upon this Convention. Now, if there was such a contract yesterday, there is one to-day, and we have not got rid of it at all.

Mr. PARVIN. The majority of the Convention by their action of yesterday have released me from that contract.

Mr. HALL. The majority of the Convention cannot violate a contract, nor make me violate it. I shall stand up to-day to what was the contract of yesterday, if it is for half a million. If the faith of this Convention is pledged, and we have so far committed ourselves as the representatives of the people, as to be in honor bound to carry out the action contained in the resolution we adopted the other day, then I say, stand by that action. I would like, with my friend from Lee (Mr. Johnston) to know in what condition this matter is. I saw upon my table yesterday a proof sheet of the proceedings of the first two days, published in the form indicated by that resolution. I judged from that, that the printer had commenced his work. I supposed that he had executed his bond, or was prepared to do so, and had made other preparations for carrying on this work, engaged his hands, procured the necessary materials, &c. If that is the case, then we ought to consider upon this matter a little before we do what as private citizens we could not do towards our fellows. I want some information upon this subject. The gentleman from Muscatine gets up to-day and overthrows all he said yesterday. He said yesterday that there was a contract; to-day he says there is none to bind us. Now, if there was a contract yesterday, I am for standing up to it, and not have one iota of that contract violated, at least by my consent.

I hope gentlemen who are acquainted with the facts of the case will inform us, and if we are not bound and committed then we can be at liberty to take other action. I suppose the gentleman from Johnson, [Mr. Clarke,] can give us as much intelligence upon this subject as any other member in this Convention. If we can reopen this question and preserve the good faith of the State of Iowa as represented by our action, I am ready to do so, and to act with gentlemen as my judgment may dictate hereafter, and not otherwise.

Mr. HARRIS. It was with the view that we might have an opportunity to examine this question and have the whole matter understood, that I voted for a reconsideration yesterday. I supposed that the motion, coming as it did from the other side—if I may be allowed to say so—indicated that perhaps there was no definite understanding as to what we were bound to do in this matter. I stated to this Convention at the first that I was in favor of having the proceedings of this Convention published in the newspapers. But after the matter had gone so far as it had, I supposed if the reconsideration was carried, the subject would be referred to a committee who would procure and report to us all the information that could be obtained upon the subject. I was a little surprised, therefore, at the motion to strike out without any further information being obtained in reference to this matter. Now I desire to know if we are bound, as the gentleman from Muscatine, [Mr. Parvin,] said yesterday. If not, I am in favor myself of going back to first principles. I am not in favor of having these debates published, further than to enable us to let our constituents know what we are doing here. I do not want to have our speeches sent to the country; I have no vanity of that kind. But I want to have this matter understood so that we may know how far we should violate contracts by opening this matter again. I would be in favor of having our peoceedings published in the newspapers, but I should not care to have any of these bound copies prepared for distribution.

Mr. CLARKE, of Johnson. I voted yesterday against the reconsideration of this subject, for the reason that I believed that this Convention, representing the people of the State, had made a contract with these gentlemen. I based my conclusion upon these facts: that at the opening of our proceedings here a committee was appointed consisting of the gentleman from Henry, [Mr. Clarke,] the gentleman from Des Moines, [Mr. Hall,] and myself, to obtain the name of a competent reporter; that we did so, and subsequently reported to the Convention the name of Mr. Lord as the person to be employed by us; that that report was adopted by the Convention, and that gentleman entered immediately upon the discharge of his duties; that the committee subsequently felt it to be their duty to prepare some plan that should give shape and form to this matter, and they drew up and presented a report with the assent of Mr. Lord our reporter, and Mr. Luse, the gentleman we recommended as our printer, specifying how this work should be carried on; that that report was adopted by this Convention, and these gentlemen, Mr. Lord, our reporter, and A. P. Luse & Co., our printers, have entered upon their work.

Now I suppose it is a well settled principle of law that if I offer a man so much to do a certain job of work, and he enters upon the performance of that work, it is a contract, and the courts of law will so hold it. If it be true that these gentlemen upon the adoption of this report, have entered upon the performance of this work, as we have evidence here, then can there be no doubt in the minds of every legal gentleman in this Convention, that this is a contract by which the State, or we as the representatives of the State, are bound. For that reason I voted against this reconsideration.

I supposed yesterday when this subject was brought and the motion to reconsider prevailed, that there must have been some proposition to do this printing for a less sum, as one of the grounds of objection to the report, was that the price paid for the printing was too high. But I now find that there has been no such proposition. Nobody has offered to do it for less. I am free to say, that as a practical printer, I know something about these matters, and no man can take this printing for less than is proposed here, with the extra trouble required of these gentlemen, giving us proof-sheets, keeping their forms standing until those proofs are returned, correcting their forms and then sending us corrected sheets of our debates. No one can take it at a less price and make a reasonable profit.

The proposition made here is to reduce the number of bound copies to be prepared for the State than the number—three thousand—proposed in the report of the committee. So far as that committee is concerned, I have only this to say; we deliberated much upon that subject. I first proposed the number three thousand, but after consultation with the gentleman from Des Moines, (Mr. Hall) we put it down to 2,500. And then again after consultation with other gentlemen not on the committee, we concluded to put it back to three thousand. And I think that that is not more than it will be found necessary to print. But I am willing, as a matter of economy—and poor economy I think it will be, too—to put the number of the bound copies down to two thousand, or even fifteen hundred. But I think every gentleman here must see that we are morally if not legally bound in this contract.

Mr. HARRIS. I would like to ask the gentleman from Johnson (Mr. Clarke) a question. There was something in this report about requiring the printer to enter into a bond with the Secretary of State. Has that requisition been complied with?

Mr. CLARKE. I am not advised whether the bond has been filed or not yet. It is here ready to be filed at any moment.

Mr. HARSIS. Has there been any negotiation between the committee and the parties to do this printing?

Mr. CLARKE. The report requires such a bond to be given by A. P. Luse & Co., as is given by the State Printer. The committee had nothing to do with that matter, but took it for granted that the bond must necessarily be such as would be approved by the State officers whose duty it is by law to attend to such matters.

Mr. PARVIN. I would ask the gentleman from Johnson (Mr. Clark) if he considers that we are bound to print three thousand copies of these reports?

Mr. CLARKE. As a lawyer I should say that we are bound to perform this contract as a whole. I suppose that the printer entered upon this job with the expectation that he was to print three thousand copies, and that his prices would have been somewhat different if he had understood that he was to print only fifteen hundred copies, because that would make, perhaps, considerable difference to him, as the profits of the job are governed to some extent by the extent of the work to be done. Any mechanic will do a large job cheaper in proportion than he will a smaller one. I think we are as much bound to print three thousand copies as we are bound to print any. I think this, however, that the majority of the Convention may over-ride that position, and that Messrs. Luse & Co. will yield, as they must be subject to the action of a legislative body. But I believe we are morally bound, if not legally, to do this work.

Mr. SOLOMON. I voted on yesterday in favor of a reconsideration, and I did so because I was dissatisfied with some portions, or fractions of the report. By reference to the yeas and nays taken upon the motion to strike out, this morning, it will be found that I voted in the negative, and I did so from legal considerations. When the proper time arrives I will offer my objections to this contract, and they will prove to be upon a point, perhaps, which will be deemed immaterial by most members. I refer to that little clause which enables the printers to place these reports upon our tables within thirty hours after the copy is delivered to him. I think he is relieved of his obligations to considerable extent by the phrase "unavoidable delays excepted." Now, I want to have it so changed as to compel him to place those sheets upon our tables by a given time, over thirty hours if you please, for unless it is so our twenty-five copies will be of but little use to us, for at this season of the year delays will occur which will be represented as unavoidable. That is the change I desire to see made, but I shall vote against changing the contract in any of its material features.

Mr. CLARK, of Alamakee. I voted yesterday for this reconsideration, for the reason that it had been suggested that there was something wrong about this arrangement. I did not believe so myself, but I was unwilling to cast a vote that would shut off opportunities for investigation if any other person felt dissatisfied. I believed then, as I believe now, that three thousand copies of these reports are not more than we shall need in this State.

So far as the obligations of this Convention are concerned under this contract with the persons who are to print these reports the question will be in the first place, whether any contract has been concluded. Now, I understand that as a proposition of law, when a person upon one side has made a proposition, and it has been accepted on the other side, that acceptance if it is made before the proposition is withdrawn, completes as a general thing, the contract. But in this case where the parties stand face to face, I apprehend to constitute an acceptance of the proposition made by the one party to the other, information of the fact should be conveyed to the former party, and if no objection be made to it, it would then become a valid contract. Now, whether bonds have been actually filed in this case in compliance with this resolution I know not, neither do I deem that a very material point, provided the party has entered upon the performance of this work with the knowledge and consent of this Convention.

Then, as to what is binding upon this Convention under this contract, there is another question. I believe this Convention can say, if we please, that we have altered our minds, and will not go on any further with the prosecution of this work; but we shall be liable morally, and I believe legally, for indemnification to the printers to the extent of any loss they may sustain in consequence of preparations they may have made to carry on this work, and I am not clear but what they may go further and claim as a part of the damages any profits that would have accrued to them out of this contract at the prices at which they covenanted to do this work. Of that, however, I am not certain, and I suppose it would depend to a great extent upon the fact, whether the parties to the contract are such as would be recognized in a court of law, and the contract itself was one that could be enforced; but I believe at any rate we are morally bound by this contract, and I hope the Convention will either stand up to it, or if they recede from it, make arrangements to indemnify those parties for any damages they may sustain.

Mr. EMERSON. From all the suggestions I have heard here from different gentlemen, I must say that my mind inclines to the belief that there is really a moral, if not a legal obligation binding upon this body in reference to this subject of reporting and printing. Now, I really supposed, judging from the quarter from which this motion to reconsider came—and in saying that I mean nothing invidious—that there was some information upon this sbject which could be obtained. I supposed that the mover of this reconsideration had learned from consultation with gentlemen capable of giving the information, that we were not bound in this contract. That I rather took for granted, and so acted accordingly. But such does not appear to be the case.

Now, after all the reflection I have been able to give this subject, it does appear to me that this body is at least morally, if not legally, bound by the original contract. Now, if I can be satisfied upon that point—and my mind is inclined to that opinion now—I would be the last one—no, I will not say that, but I would be among the last—who would violate any contract which is binding upon us either morally or legally.

I would prefer, if it was not for taking up so much time, the appointment of a committee to investigate this subject of reporting and printing, in order to give this body information of the condition we are in at the present time with reference to this subject of contract. And as I suppose that it will not take long for a committee to ascertain our true situation, I will submit the motion that a committee of three be appointed by the chair, to which this whole matter shall be referred for investigation, and that they be instructed to report to this Convention to-morrow morning at 11 o'clock.

Mr. ELLS. I voted to strike out "three thousand," not because I had changed my opinion since yesterday, of the importance and necessity of having that number of copies of these reports printed, but because I discovered from the result of the vote upon the question of reconsideration that members seem to think they had acted inconsiderately in what they had done, and would like to extricate themselves from their dilemma. And if a majority of this Convention take a misstep I am willing that they should have an opportunity to right themselves. I have no desire to force them to retain any position they regard as a false one. My own views are unchanged. I examined the question in the first place so far as to satisfy myself what should be done. I did not examine the cost, for I never examine questions of that kind in cases like this. I adopt the principle of David Crockett, see that I am right and then go ahead. I think the State of Iowa ought to furnish the funds for all our reasonable expenses. If it is right to print our debates at all, I think we should print enough of them to inform our people of what we may do, and that the State of Iowa ought to pay for so doing. That was the consideration that influenced me at first, and my opinion in that respect remains the same. But if the Convention think differently, as I find in the vote of yesterday, one side voting all together, even my friend from Des Moines, [Mr. Hall,] who joined in this report having been brought over, I am willing to submit to the desire of the majority. I still think, however, that independently of the contract with Messrs. Luse & Co., that we ought to print these debates, and print enough to supply all the demands of the community. If it is not worth printing to that extent then do not print it at all. It would be better to pay the reporter for the manuscript reports, and have it placed among our files. As for myself I do not care whether I have twenty-five copies of these sheets or not. All I want is to have a single copy to preserve. But I want the people to know what we are doing here, how we are agreeing, whether we are sound upon every question that comes before us. I do not wish to dodge any question myself, and I suppose no one else here desires to do so. I want to let the people know how every man here stands—let them know his votes and the reasons he assigns for those votes.

When this question comes up again, I shall vote for putting in "three thousand" again, if I can do so, although I voted to strike it out. I did so in order to bring this matter before the Convention again. As to the contract with Luse & Co., it is true that we are in good faith bound to carry out the contract, but we can pay him for damages, if that is considered necessary.

Mr. PETERS. I voted yesterday in the negative upon the motion to reconsider the subject of printing these reports, and I did so upon two grounds. The first was, that the matter having been referred to a committee, the statement of that committee satisfied me that they had given the subject due consideration. The second ground was, that a contract had been entered into by the Convention with these printers, by which the printers bound themselves, and agreed to print these reports according to the plan brought forward by the committee, and adopted by this Convention. I thought, therefore, it was an exhibition of bad faith on the part of this Convention to reconsider this contract, after it had been entered into. But upon examining this subject farther, I was led to enquire how and what we were to pay for the daily sheets to be laid upon our table. And as near as I can ascertain, I find that we are to pay these printers at the rate of about one dollar and forty cents per thousand ems, instead of seventy cents per thousand, as stated in this report. I shall, therefore, vote for the reference of this matter to a committee, in accordance with the motion of the gentleman from Dubuque, (Mr. Emerson.)

Mr. HALL. So far as the reconsideration of this matter is concerned, I look upon it as entirely unimportant. If we have made a contract with the printers—and I am very certain we have with the reporter—I would be the last person in the world to do anything to change that contract without the consent of the persons with whom we have made it. I do not think, however, they would make much by suing this Convention individually, and I do not know how else they can bring suit. I do not think there is any legal liability upon the part of anybody in this Convention. If there is a contract, it is without a responsible party to be amersed in damages, and that very fact would lead me to be the more careful in my action now. The very fact that these persons, who may have made the preliminary arrangements for carrying out this contract, may have gone to some expense, are dependent upon legal remedy, should make us the more careful. I would be more tenacious of their rights where they had nothing but our honor to depend upon, than I would could they appeal to the law.

But I am not able now to say positively whether there is any contract with them or not. It was passed on Friday last, and under our rules it could be reconsidered at the next meeting of this Convention, which was on yesterday. That rule was made for the safety of the members of this Convention. That they might have one day for reflection and repentance if they had done a wrong, and allow them to reconsider their course and take back what they did the day before. It was to guard against hasty legislation that that rule was framed. Now whether this resolution, occupying that position under the rules of this body, being subject to reconsideration and review at the next meeting of this Convention, would operate as a definite and complete contract I am not prepared to say at this moment. At least that cosideration should have some weight in settling that question.

Now I do not know as we would be any better off if we had this subject referred to a committee to report upon it to-morrow morning. I do not know how any committee composed of other gentlemen would be able to throw more light upon the subject than we have now. On the whole, however, I am willing to have it go to a committee to see what they would report.

We must at all events have our proceedings reported at the price agreed upon in that resolution—at three dollars a page. We have a contract in regard to that that has gone too far to be reconsidered. The employment of our reporter is a different question from that one of printing. The reporter was employed by this Convention on the first day it completed its organization and it has not been reconsidered and it cannot be reconsided now under our rules.—He had a right to act as an officer and employee of this Convention the day of his appointment, and the matter not having been reconsidered at the next meeting of the Convention, it is too late to do so now. And if this contract with the printers had lain beyond one day it would have been final and every one could put faith in it; consider the faith of the Convention pledged to carry it out. I merely make these suggestions without deciding upon them at all.

Mr. HARRIS. I would ask the gentleman from Des Moines, [Mr. Hall,] if the question concerning the printing is the only one that can be taken into consideration now?

Mr. HALL. I think that beyond doubt the question of reporting has gone too far to be reconsidered.

Mr. HARRIS. I would ask what would be the ratio of the reporting to the printing so far as the expense is concerned?

Mr. HALL. I cannot tell as to that.

Mr. SKIFF called for the previous question.

Mr. EMERSON asked if his motion to refer to a committee was before the Convention.

The PRESIDENT. The motion of the gentleman from Dubuque, [Mr. Emerson,] in the form in which he presented it, in the opinion of the Chair is not in order. It would be in order with a little variation, and under the previous question would be the first to be considered. It would be in order to move to refer this subject to a select committee of three.

Mr. PETERS. I desire to correct a statement that I made when up before. I was under the impression, and had been so informed, that the printers of these debates, under this contract, would get pay for two compositions, one for the bound book and one for these daily sheets. I have been informed by a member of the committee that reported on this subject that this matter had been considered by them and the printers would receive pay but for one composition.

The PRESIDENT stated that the previous question having been called and seconded, the first question was upon ordering the main question to be put.

Mr. CLARKE, of Johnson. I would like to answer the question of the gentleman from Appanoose, [Mr. Harris,] in regard to the relative cost of the reporting and printing.

Mr. SKIFF. I withdraw my call for the previous question for that purpose.

Mr. CLARKE. The cost of the reporting of a thousand pages at three dollars a page would be three thousand dollars. Upon further examination it has been ascertained that to print these debates in the syle of the Massachusetts debates a more costly paper will be required than was at first supposed by the committee, and the whole cost of reporting and printing three thousand copies will be between six and seven thousand dollars. The printing and binding will thus cost more than the reporting. If the volume is less than a thousand pages the cost will be less, if more, then the cost will be proportionably greater. We took the first volume of the Massachusetts reports, which we supposed would be about as much as all that this Convention would have to publish, and that contains about a thousand pages.

I have no particular objection to having this matter referred to a committee, but it would cause delay in this matter. Now in relation to the suggestions of the gentleman from Des Moines (Mr. Hall) as to the time in which this matter was open for reconsideration I have this to say. The Convention will remember that they were all in a hurry to have this matter set going, and the committee and I think the members of the Convention generally urged the printer to go to work with the understanding that the proof-sheets should be here on Monday evening, which was done. So that objection if legally a good one, is not morally a good one.

Mr. JOHNSTON. I was opposed in the first place to the printing of these debates, but I did not perhaps make my objections at the time when I should properly have done so. Subsequently my attention was called, by an officer of the state government, to the vast expense to the state which would be the result of this thing. When the subject came up I voted for the reconsideration, and in doing so I intended not to commit myself to any course, but merely to bring the subject before the Convention in the situation in which it now stands. I intended, if the subject could be properly brought up, to vote against the whole thing, and if I could not succeed in that, I would vote for the smallest number of copies to be printed that I could vote for. But while this debate was going on, the gentleman from Muscatine (Mr. Parvin) made a suggestion in regard to the matter which struck me as a forcible one, and that was that we were already responsible under a contract. Now, if I can satisfy myself that we have made a contract, I would vote for the highest number reported by the committee, even though the heavens should fall, in order that we might stand up to our obligations. But I have not learned from anything that has been said here to-day whether exactly there is a contract or not, and I cannot vote upon filling these blanks, or upon any other matter connected with this subject, without further consideration. I would prefer, therefore, that the whole subject should be referred to a select committee, or rather that it should be laid upon the table till to-morrow, that the Convention may satisfy themselves with regard to a contract having been concluded. If that meet the views of the Convention, I would move to lay this subject upon the table until to-morrow morning. I can satisfy myself in the meantime, and I suppose that others can.

The question being taken upon the motion to lay upon the table it was not agreed to upon a division as follows: ayes 16, nays 16.

The question recurred upon filling the blank with the number "fifteen hundred."

Mr. SKIFF. I do not wish to be captious in this matter. But it is now getting late and I think this debate has gone far enough, and I would therefore call the previous question.

Mr. CLARKE of Henry, moved that the Convention adjourn until to-morrow morning at 10 o'clock.

The question being taken the motion to adjourn was not agreed to.

Mr. PATTERSON. If it be in order I would move that this subject be laid upon the table until this afternoon. The motion to lie on the table was lost before on a tie vote, and I believe because members desired to have this matter disposed of to-day.

The PRESIDENT. The Chair would inform the gentleman from Lee, [Mr. Patterson,] that when the question was taken upon the motion to adjourn, the motion for the previous question was pending, and that motion should now be put.

Mr. EDWARDS. I move that the Convention adjourn till this afternoon at 2 o'clock.

Mr. SKIFF. I would ask if the motion to adjourn is now in order, tne Convention having just voted down a similar motion?

The PRESIDENT. The Chair regards the motion to adjourn till this afternoon to be a different motion from the motion to adjourn until to-morrow morning, and therefore in order at this time.

The question being taken, the motion to adjourn until this afternoon until two o'clock, was not agreed to, upon a division as follows: ayes 15, noes 16.

Mr. TODHUNTER. With the permission of the Convention I would state that I have been informed by Mr. Luse that so far as this contract is concerned he considers it binding upon him. He says he has made his necessary arrangements for type and other material and has some six or eight extra hands employed now. That is the way the matter stands with him now. If that is the fact, it seems that we are not only morally but legally bound by this contract.

Mr. CLARKE, of Johnson. I move to lay this whole subject upon the table for the present.

The PRESIDENT. The motion for the previous question having been made and seconded, it must now be put before the motion to lay upon the table can be entertained.

Mr. CLARKE, of Johnson. I trust the motion for the previous question will not be agreed to.

The question being taken upon the call for the previous question it was not agreed to.

Mr. MARVIN moved that the Convention adjourn until to-morrow morning at 9 o'clock.

The motion was not agreed to.

Mr. CLARKE, of Johnson, moved to lay the report of the committee on reporting and printing on the table until to-morrow morning at 11 o'clock.

The question being taken it was agreed to, upon a division as follows, ayes 20, noes not counted.

On motion of Mr. SKIFF

The Convention adjourned until to-morrow morning at ten o'clock.

WEDNESDAY JANUARY, 28th 1857.

The Convention met at ten oclock, A. M. and was called to order by the President.

Prayer by Rev. Mr. Kynett.

The Journal of yesterday was read and approved.

Resolutions of Enquiry.

Mr. GOWER offered the following resolution:

Resolved That the committee on incorporations be instructed to enquire into the propriety of engrafting the annexed bill in our Constitution, with such amendments as are deemed necessary.

SECTION 1. Be it enacted by the general assembly of the State of Iowa that ——— are appointed commissioners to open books, and receive subscriptions for the establishment of a bank in the city of ——— which bank shall be called the State Bank of Iowa, and as soon as the said commissioners shall have obtained subscriptions to the amount of $500,000, they shall then call a meeting of the subscribers in the city of ——— giving it at least thirty days notice, in five different papers published within the State of Iowa, of the time and place of such meeting, for the general organization of said bank, which shall be consumated by the election of six directors, from among said subscribers; and as soon as said organization has been consumated, they will then resign their trust into the hands of the newly elected officers of the bank.

SEC. 2. Be it enacted, that the bank situate in the city of ——— shall be called the main bank, and all other banks shall be branches thereof. The main bank shall only issue its notes to the branch banks, having inserted in each note the name of the particular bank for whose use they are intended, and in no case shall the main bank put in circulation any notes purporting to be issued by the state bank of Iowa, otherwise than through the branch banks.

Sec. 3. The main bank shall be divided into three departments, as

Firstly, The regular department.

Secondly. The issuing department.

Thirdly. The redemption department.

The regulating department shall be a board of control, consisting of three members, one of whom shall be elected by the legislature, one by the people, in general election, and one by an election to be held exclusively by the directors of the branch banks throughout the State—the directors of each branch being allowed to hold their meetings in their own banking house, to cast their votes—putting the name or names of their candidate so voted for in a sealed package, and sending it by mail, addressed to the President of the board of control, who shall open it in the presence of the whole board and count the votes, and the one receiving a plurality of votes shall be considered duly elected. The members of the Board of Control shall hold their term of office three years, one to be elected every year—the member elected by the Legislature being the President and the oldest member of the Board thereafter, according to the one term of his official service only. The duties of the Board of Control shall consist in the entire management of the organic operations of the main Bank and Branches; for the better and more impartial regulation thereof, they shall compose and have printed, a set of rules and regulations, applying in their effects to each and every branch of the main Bank alike. The Board of Control, or either of them, shall also have the power to appoint Inspectors, to visit all, or any one, of the branches, to inspect their books, papers and assets, generally; and report their standing to said Board, in writing—their visits being made at any time in which the Board of Control, or any member thereof, may deem fit, and without notice to the branch being so visited. And if it is shown in said report that the affairs of such branch are not in a sound condition, it shall be the duty of the Board of Control to call upon the executive officer of such branch to show cause why said branch should not be closed, and the assetts thereof taken possession of by the main bank, and its affairs wound up; and if the officer aforesaid shall not answer the call of the Board of Control, as aforesaid, or if they shall so do, but not give sufficient reason for the continuance of their business, it shall then be the duty of the said Board to take possession of the assets of such branch and dispose of them to the best advantage—using the proceeds, *Firstly*, for the redemption of its issues, *Secondly*, for the payment of depositors with the branch and *Thirdly*, for the payment of all other liabilities pro rata; and if any thing be left thereafter, the same shall be handed over to the stock holders, in proportion to their stock in said branch as paid in; but if there shall not be sufficient assets to meet the first, second and third class of claims against the branch, in that case the Directors shall be assessed in a like ratio with the amount of their stock subscribed, whether it is all paid in or not, to the amount necessary to liquidate the indebtedness of the Bank. If there shall not be enough assets to redeem all the notes of such branch, then, in that case, the Board of Control shall make an assessment upon each of the other branches, according to their capital, respectively, to make up the deficit, and if any branch shall neglect or refuse to comply with the requirement of the assessment, the Board of Control will then proceed to close up such branch in the same manner and to the same extent as the first.

The *Issuing Department* shall provide *all* the bank notes intended for circulation of the branches throughout the State, and disburse them to the branches, in accordance with the written order of the Board of Control—stamping upon each note the insignia of such department belonging to the great seal thereof—entering the number, letter, date and denomination of each note in a register kept exclusively for that purpose—keeping the registration of the notes of each branch seperately.

The *Redemption Department* shall have the possession of the specie and securities belonging to the Bank and to the branches, and provide a suitable fire-proof vault for security of the same, using the same only in the redemption of the bank note issues of the branches—the same having been issued from the Issuing Department aforesaid—which notes, the department will retain until duly required to be given up by a written order from the Board of Control, and endorsed by the Cashier of the Issuing Department.

Sec. 4. The salaries of the members of the Board of Control shall be ——— a year, and to be regulated entirely by the Legislature, but in no case to be decreased during their term of office. The salaries of the subordinate officers are to be regulated by the Board of Control, at their option.

Sec. 5. Branch banks must be organized upon the following plan, to-wit: Whenever any persons—numbering not less than twelve, two thirds of whom must be residents of the county in which it is proposed to locate the bank—shall wish to establish a branch bank, they must first get up an instrument of writing, in which they must state the names of the parties connected with it, their respective places of residence, business, and the amount of their present subscription, the place in which they wish to locate their bank, the name under which it is to be known and do business, the amount of its capital and the term for which it is intended that the charter shall continue; after which the application so arranged shall be forwarded to the Board of Control, whose duty it shall be to issue a permit authorizing the establishment of the bank, if they have published a notice in some paper in the place where it is intended to locate such bank, of such application having been made thirty days before granting such permit, and there exists no objection from any one to the creation of such bank—or if there are objections, but which have been overruled by the Board—the presentation of which to the Redemption Department, for safe keeping, will consummate the bank a branch of the State Bank of Iowa. Whenever the branch so created shall seek for bank notes for circulation it must then place in the hands of the receiving officer of the Redemption Department one-third the amount of the notes so required in gold and silver, as the said officer may require—this provision only extending to three times the amount of the capital of such branch. If any branch shall wish to obtain more notes than three times the amount of its paid in capital, it must then give to the receiving officer of the Redemption Department State or United States stocks, at the rate of five per cent. less than the ruling market value in New York City, at the time of such deposit, dollar for dollar of the amount of notes required for circulation; and if at any time thereafter, the stock so deposited shall fall in price three per cent. below the price at which it stood at the time of such deposit, the receiving officer aforesaid must then notify the executive officers of such bank that they must place in his hands more stock within ten days thereafter; and if they do not comply therewith, he must proceed to sell that in his hands, and apply the proceeds to the redemption of such notes, which notes must have stamped, or printed from steel engraved die, upon their face the words Relief Notes, by which they will be known from all others.

Sec. 6. All the notes so put in circulation by the branch banks shall be redeemed by the main bank only, but the branch banks must receive the notes of any and every branch in payment of any claims due such branch, if offered, whether the branch issuing them is solvent or not; but any branch so receiving such notes is not precluded from presenting the same, if it should choose to do so to the Main Bank for redemption; but in no case will a branch bank be allowed to make a deposit with the notes of other branches, for the purpose of obtaining circulating notes for its own use, either directly or indirectly. No branch bank shall issue or put into circulation any other notes purporting to be issued by such branch but those which it has obtained from the Issuing Department of the Main Bank in ———.

Sec. 7. The number of branches shall be limited to that of fifty, being properly distributed throughout the State—there not being more than three in any one city, or more than two in any one town, or more than one in any one village—these numbers to be increased only by an act of the Legislature, for the purpose of meeting the requirements of commerce and trade in any particular locality.

Sec. 8. The capital of each branch shall not exceed $1,000,000 in the cities nor less than $50,000. In the towns the capital of each branch shall not exceed $500,000 nor less than $40,000. In the villages the capital of each branch shall not exceed $100,000 nor less than $25,000.

Sec. 9. Each and every Stockholder shall be held personally responsible to the amount of his or her stock subscribed over and above the amount so subscribed for by him or her, in case it shall become necessary to collect the amount to liquidate all the claims against the branch to which they are Stockholders; but this liability shall not be enforced until after the property, both personal and real, of the Directors of such branch, and that of all the other branches, as above stated, has been exhausted in the payment of such claims.

Sec. 10. All taxes shall be assessed and collected of the banks in the same manner as they are of individuals; but when a branch pays its taxes upon its capital as assessed, the stockholders thereof shall not be assessed for taxes upon the stock so held by them of such bank.

Sec. 11. Any failure upon the part of any branch to comply with, or conform to, the requirements of this law, or any part thereof, shall be considered a forfeiture of its charter as such branch, and the assets, of all kinds whatsoever, shall revert to the Board of Control, the possession of which can be obtained if any resistance be shown by the officers or stock-holders of the branch so delinquent, by the issue of an order by the clerk of the court of , directed to the sheriff of the county in which the bank is located, or by the clerk of the supreme court of the State of Iowa, directed to any executive officer acting under him, or deputised by him for this special purpose.

Sec. 12. Any officer of any branch which has failed, or been closed by the Board of Control in consequence of improper delinquencies or outright frauds, shall not be eligible to hold office in any other branch bank within this State; and any branch violating this provision by the appointment of any such person, and persisting in the same after due notice having been given the officers thereof of the antecedents of such person by the Board of Control, it shall be deemed a delinquent branch, and as such be proceeded against by the Board of Control, in like manner, and to the same extent, as in other cases.

Sec. 13. If any branch shall wish to close its affairs, or to discontinue the circulation of its notes, it will be necessary for such branch to give the Board of Control due notice thereof, whose duty it shall be to advertise in two daily and weekly papers, published in the city of , of such intention, requiring the presentation of all notes of such branch at the redemption office, within two years thereafter, or all outstanding notes at that time will be barred from redemption at such office; and that the funds belonging to such branch will be handed to the receiver of the bank.

Sec. 14. The current expenses of the Main Bank shall be borne by the several branches, in proportion to their capital stock—each paying its allotted per centage, at the end of each six months, commencing on the first day of January of each year, in which expenses are to be included all payments for bank-notes and plates, together with all other expenses therewith connected or arising therefrom.

The resolution was agreed to, and referred accordingly.

Mr. TRAER offered the following resolution.

Resolved, That so much of the constitution as relates to the basis of representation be referred to a special committee of three.

The question was taken, and it was not agreed to upon a division, as follows: Ayes 11, Noes 12.

Mr. PARVIN offered the following resolution.

Resolved, That the Committee on Education and School Lands re requested to inquire into the expediency of making provision for the education of the children of blacks and mulattoes.

Mr. HALL. I move that the resolution lie on the table. The committee are ready to report upon that subject.

Mr. PARVIN. I hope that the usual course will be taken in referring this resolution. The fact that the Committee on Education and School Funds are going to make their report without considering the subject embraced in the resolution I have offered, is the very reason why I wish to have it referred to them. I ask for the Yeas and Nays on the motion to lay upon the table.

The yeas and nays were ordered, and the question being taken, the motion to lay on the table was rejected—yeas 15, nays, 21, as follows:

Yeas—Messrs. Ayres, Cotton, Day, Emerson, Gibson, Gillaspy, Hall, Harris, Hollingsworth, Johnston, Palmer, Peters, Price, Robinson and Solomon.

Nays—The President, Messrs. Bunker, Clarke, of Alamakee, Clarke of Henry, Clarke of Johnston, Edwards, Ells, Gower, Grey, Marvin, Parvin, Patterson, Scott, Seely, Skiff, Todhunter, Traer, Warren, Wilson, Winchester and Young.

The question then recurring on the adoption of the resolution.

Mr. HALL called for the yeas and nays which were ordered.

Mr. HALL. It appears to me that the reference of this resolution is entirely unnecessary. The committee on Education and School Lands are now ready to report. They make no discrimination upon this question at all in their report and do not put the blacks and mulattoes upon a distinct platform elevated above the whites.

The question was then taken and the resolution was agreed to, yeas—20, nays, 16, as follows:

Yeas—The President, Messrs. Bunker, Clarke of Alamakee, Clarke of Henry, Clarke of Johnson, Edwards, Ells, Gower, Grey, Marvin, Parvin, Scott, Seely, Skiff, Todhunter, Traer, Warren, Wilson, Winchester and Young.

Nays—Messrs. Ayres, Cotton, Day, Emerson, Gibson, Gillaspy, Hall, Harris, Hollingsworth, Johnston, Palmer, Patterson, Peters, Price, Robinson and Solomon.

Mr. CLARKE, of Johnson. I offer the following resolution:

Resolved, That so much of the Constitution as relates to the basis of representation be referred to a committee of five.

Mr. HALL. I do not see the necessity for the appointment of such a committee. I do not understand that the old Constitution furnished any basis of representation, but it authorized the Legislature, as soon as the government went into operation, to fix the basis of representation, which they have continued to do ever since that time. At present, I do not see any occasion for such a committee.

If the reports which may hereafter be made do not cover the ground embraced in the resolution, or if any contingency should arise in the course of our proceedings, rendering such a step necessary, it will be very proper to have such a committee appointed. I shall, therefore vote against the resolution, until the occasion arises which shal l call for the appointment of such a committee.

Mr. JOHNSTON. I rise for the simple purpose of making an explanation to the gentleman from Des Moines. [Mr. Hall.] The subject of basis of representation is before the Committee on the Legislative Department, of which I am a member. We have had some little difficulty in agreeing about the matter. The gentlemen from the new counties are rather disposed to think that they can do better with a Special Committee than with one of the Standing Committees. Although I am opposed to the proposition which the gentleman intends to present to the Convention, I am very anxious that he and his friends should be heard upon this subject.— It is an important question, and one which might well take up the deliberations of a Special Committee. I think there is no objection on the part of the Committee, which has that subject now under consideration to the reference asked for by the gentleman from Johnson.— [Mr. Clarke.] The Committee on the Legislative Department, to whom this subject was referred, although a majority of them are opposed to the proposition of the gentleman, are perfectly willing that the subject should be referred to a special committee, and they are desirous that gentlemen from the new counties should be heard.

Mr. HARRIS I do not see why gentlemen who wish to be heard upon this matter cannot accomplish their object just as well by presenting a minority report, as by the reference of this subject to a special committee. I do not understand that the mere fact of reports being made by a majority give any very great advantage over those made by a minority, where they represent separate interests. I do not see the necessity for the appointment of this special committee, and I shall vote against the resolution.

Mr. HALL. After the explanation of the gentleman from Lee, (Mr. Johnston) I am inclined to the opinion, that this subject should be taken from the Committee on the Legislative Department, and referred to a special committee. I think the Convention will find that it will facilitate their business very much if the reports that come from committees are unanimous. I am opposed to minority reports, from the results I have seen attendant upon them in other Conventions.

Mr. TRAER. This matter was fully discussed in the Committee on the Legislative Department, and as I understand the matter, the Committee have determined not to report upon this particular subject. This course was determined upon for the purpose of getting the views of some of the members from the new counties. We are not desirous of presenting a minority report. The object we have in view is the incorporation of a separate article in the constitution relating to this particular subject. I think this course necessary The gentleman from Des Moines (Mr. Hall) says, that there is nothing in our constitution which relates to the basis of representation. In the last clause of section thirty-one I find the following:

"And the general assembly shall also at every subsequent regular session, apportion the House of Representatives, and every other regular session the Senate for eight years."

The basis of representation there is the number of inhabitants. There are other views which some of the members of the Convention hold upon this subject, and it is for the purpose of getting them before the Convention that we purpose to have this matter submitted to a special committee. We only ask it as a matter of courtesy, and hope that gentlemen will be willing to grant us that favor. If it be not granted to us, we shall be forced to come in here with a substitute for the report of the committee, which will consume more time, than it will to refer this subject to a special committee. I hope gentlemen will be courteous enough to vote in favor of the resolution. I do not understand that gentlemen by so doing commit themselves to any particular principle, as the question is one of mere reference only.

Mr. PARVIN. I desire only to say a word in connection with this matter. The committee on the Legislative Department were pretty unanimous in their views in regard to the changes in that part of the Constitution. The committee could not agree with my friend from Benton (Mr. Traer) but they did agree with him and those who thought with him, that this matter should be placed in the strongest position before the Convention, by having a special committee appointed, to whom the subject should be referred. That committee will be composed of members from the new counties, and they will place this matter in a strong light before the Convention. Instead of having a minority report upon this subject, let the gentleman and those who act with him have the opportunity of referring this matter to a special committee. As at present advised, I am opposed to the proposition itself, but perhaps when I see the report from a special committee, I may be induced to change my opinion.

Mr. SOLOMON. I desire to alude to that portion of the present Constitution which this committee, I presume, propose to change. I understand the gentleman from Des Moines (Mr. Hall) to assert, that the present Constitution does not fix the basis of representation.

Let me read that part of the 31st section which the gentleman from Benton (Mr. Traer) did not read,—

"The number of Senators and Representatives shall, at the first regular session of the General Assembly, after each enumeration be fixed by law, and apportioned among the several counties according to the number of white inhabitants in each."

This, you will observe, fixes the basis of representation according to population. There is a desire on the part of some gentlemen and their constituents, of which I am fully aware, to inaugurate another principle in our Constitution as a basis of representation along by the side of this, and have them both go out together, and that new principle is one by which the new counties will have a better representation than they now have. I make this statement, that gentlemen may understand precisely the object of this motion.

Mr. HARRIS. This matter is to some extent a fight between the old counties and the new ones, and in order to have the whole State represented as far as possible, I move to amend the resolution by inserting "seven" in the place of "five."

Mr. TRAER. I accept the amendment.

Mr. CLARKE of Henry. I think I may vote for this resolution. If I do so, I shall do it under protest. I think we are establishing a bad precedent here, for every time there is a disagreement in a committee, those who are in the minority may come here and ask for a special committee to whom the subject of disagreement may be referred. Gentlemen can come here and express their views in a minority report before the Convention just as well as they can if they had a special committee of forty to whom the subject might be referred. But in this case, the Committee on the Legislative Department have requested that there might be a special committee appointed, and I shall vote for the resolution. I hope, however, the practice will not continue, for if it does, we shall never get through our business. It has been intimated here that a majority of the committee have made up their minds upon this matter, and it is for that reason the minority, not satisfied with the majority report, wish a separate committee. Why not take the usual course in such matters? Why not come in with a minority report, and then let both reports come before this body, because if we appoint a separate committee there may be a difference of opinion among them, and the minority will want a separate committee again, and so it will go on *ad infinitum*. Gentlemen who are in favor of this proposition can move to amend the report of the majority, then present their views in regard to this matter, and gain the end of their desires just as well as by having this separate committee appointed. So far as this one special committee is concerned, I have no particular objection to its appointment inasmuch as the Committee on the Legislative Department are willing that it shall be appointed, but I am opposed to establishing it as a precedent for the appointment of committees of a like character.

The question was then taken and the resolution was adopted.

Mr. WINCHESTER offered the following resolution:

Resolved, That until otherwise ordered the daily session of this Convention shall be at the hours of 9 o'clock A. M. and 2 o'clock P. M.

Mr. TRAER moved to strike out "nine" and insert "ten," which motion was agreed to.

The motion as amended was then agreed to.

Mr. TRAER. I would call up the resolution offered by me on yesterday.

The resolution was then read as follows:

Resolved, That the rules of order be amended by adopting the following order of business. After the Journal is read, the following order shall govern.

1st. Petitions or memorials to be offered.
2d. Resolutions.
3d. Reports of Committees.
4th. Communications on the President's table.
5th. Reports in possession of the Convention.
6th. Unfinished Business.

And also the following additional rule:

Rule 18th. All resolutions and reports of Committees shall lie over one day before being acted upon except by unanimous consent."

The question was then taken and it was not agreed to upon division, ayes 13, noes 14.

Mr. CLARKE of Henry, offered the following resolution, which, under the rules was laid over.

Resolved, That the Secretary be not required to enter the whole of any resolution, report, memorial or petition upon the Journal, but may enter the same by synopsis.

That he be required also, to furnish a synopsis of such voluminous reports, resolutions, memorials and petitions as have already been entered upon the Journals to be printed in their stead, unless otherwise directed by a vote of this Convention in particular cases."

Mr. SEELY offered the following resolution:

Resolved, That the Committee on the basis of Representation be requested to inquire into the expediency of reporting a system whereby there shall not be more than four organized counties included in one representative district; and whenever two adjoining counties have a population equal to one-half of the basis of representation fixed by law, they shall be entitled to one representative jointly; and when any one county shall have a like population, it shall be entitled to one representative.

The question was then taken, and the resolution was agreed to.

Reports of Standing Committees.

Mr. ELLS, from the Committee on the Preamble and Bill of Rights, reported that they had had the same under consideration, and had unanimously agreed to report the following amendments with a recommendation to the Convention that they be adopted:

Add to section two as follows: "And no privileges or immunities shall ever be granted, that may not be altered, revoked or repealed, by the General Assembly."

Add to section nine as follows: "But no person shall be deprived of life. liberty or property without due process of law."

Substitute for section ten as follows: "In all criminal prosecutions the accused shall have a a right to a speedy trial, before an impartial jury of the county or district in which the offence is alleged to have been committed, to demand the nature and the cause of the accusation against him, to be confronted by the witnesses against him, to have compulsory process for his own witnesses, and to have the assistance of counsel."

Add to section eleven the following: "Nor shall any persen be compelled in any criminal prosecution to be a witness against himself."

Add to sec. eighteen the following: "Private roads may be opened in the manner prescribed by law, but in every case, the necessity of the Road, and the amount of damages sustained by the opening thereof, shall first be determined by a jury of disinterested free-holders; and such amount, together with the expenses of the proceedings, shall be paid by the person or persons benefitted thereby, before said Road shall be opened.

The Committee have also under consideration the resolution offered by Mr. Solomon, and after duly considering the same, have unanimously agreed that it is inexpedient to recommend the incorporation of said proposition in the Bill of Rights.

On motion of Mr. SKIFF, the report was laid on the table, and one hundred copies of it were ordered to be printed for the use of the Convention.

Mr. CLARKE, of Alamakee, offered the following resolution:

Resolved, That the Committee on article fifth of the Constitution be instructed to take into consideration and report upon the propriety of so amending the same that the following provision, or its equivalent, shall be incorporated therein, viz:

1. There shall be a Court of Appeals, com-

posed of five judges, having appellate jurisdiction. Said judges shall be elected by the electors of the State at large, and shall be so classified that one of said judges shall go out of office in one year, one in two years, one in three years, one in four years and one in five years, from the time of their election, after which several times the said judges shall hold their offices for five years respectively, and until their successors are elected and qualified. Provision shall be made by law for designating one of said judges as Chief Justice. Three of said judges—one of whom shall be the Chief Justice so designated—shall be necessary to form a quorum to perform the business of said court.

Sec. 2. There shall be a Supreme Court having general jurisdiction in law and equity.

Sec. 3. The State shall be divided into three judicial districts to be bounded by county lines, and to be compact and equal in population, as nearly as may be. There shall be four justices of the Supreme Court in each district. They shall be classified, so that one of their number shall go out of office at the end of one year, one in two years, one in three years, and one in four years. After the end of their term under such classification the term of their office shall be four years.

Sec. 4. The Legislature shall have the same power to alter and regulate the jurisdiction and proceedings in law and equity as they have heretofore possessed.

Sec. 5. Provision may be made by law for designating, from time to time, one of the justices who is not a judge of the Court of Appeals to preside at the general terms of the said court, to be held in the several districts. Any three or more of said justices, of whom one of said justices so designated shall be one, may hold such general terms; any one or more of said justices may hold special terms, and be required to hold the Circuit Courts in their respective districts.

Sec. 6. The Judges of the Court of Appeals and Justices of the Supreme Court shall severally receive, at stated times, for their services, a compensation to be established by law, which shall not be increased or diminished during their continuance in office.

Sec. 7. They shall not hold any other office or public trust: all votes for either of them for for any elective office shall be void; they shall not exercise any power of appointment to public office. Any male citizen of the age of twenty-one years, of good moral character, and who possesses the requisite qualifications of learning and ability, shall be entitled to admission to practice in all the courts of this State.

Sec. 8. The classification of the Justices of the Supreme Court, the times and places of holding the terms of the Court of Appeals, and of the general and special terms of the Supreme Court, and also the times and places of holding the Circuit Courts within the several districts, shall be provided for by law.

Sec. 9. The testimony in equity causes shall ba taken in like manner as in causes at law.

Sec. 10. The Judges of the Supreme Court shall be the electors of the several judicial districts, and the Judges of the Court of Appeals shall be the electors of the State at large at such times as may be prescribed by law.

Sec. 11. The General Assembly may re-organize the judicial districts as the necessity of the people may require.

Sec. 12. The Legislature shall establish such other inferior courts as may be deemed necessary.

Mr. GILLASPY. I shall vote against the adoption of the resolution if it goes upon the journal and has to be printed.

Mr. HARRIS. We have established the precedent of printing the reports of the standing committees and resolutions offered by gentlemen for reference to the committees, and we certainly should extend the same courtesy in this case that we have in other cases. I would like to see the resolution printed.

Mr. HALL. I hope that the resolution offered by the gentleman from Henry (Mr. Clarke) will be taken up by unanimous consent and passed. I will vote with the greatest pleasure not to encumber our journals by publishing in full all the reports and resolutions that may be presented, and I hope the Convention will agree to take up the resolution offered by the gentleman from Henry (Mr. Clarke) and pass it.

Mr. CLARKE, of Alamakee. It does not make much difference to me, whether the resolution I have offered is printed or not. I am very confident that something similar to it will be adopted before we get through with the labors of this Convention. If it be not received and printed now, I shall move it as an amendment to the report of the committee on that subject, and I apprehend that I shall then have the right to have it printed. It is immaterial to me, whether it is printed now or upon the presentation of the report of the committee that have charge of this subject. I apprehend that the same course should be taken with this resolution, that has been taken with the other resolutions that have been offered in the Convention thus far, and I think, also, that the question of an alteration or amendment of the judicial system of this State is of more importance than any other subject that may come before the Convention, with the exception, possibly, of the question in relation to the Banking system. The present judicial system of our State is acknowledged almost universally not only by the members of the legal profession, but by every person who has occasion to become acquainted with its working from experimental knowledge, to be very defective, needing a thorough and complete reformation. I am, therefore, in favor of printing at some time this resolution or something similar to it. I am not tenacious about having this particular resolution printed, A majority of this Convention may not be in favor of the principles contained in it, yet I am confident that they will be in favor of some change in the present Judiciary system. It strikes me that the principles contained in this resolution should come before the Convention in order that they may consider the subject, and this is, certainly, a sufficient reason for its adopting and printing the resolution I have offered.

Mr. WILSON. I hope the Convention will adopt the resolution and refer it to the Committee on the Judicial Department, of which I am a member. Our report has not yet been perfected, and I shall be glad to have the views of all these members upon the subject presented for the consideration of the Committee, before we make our report. I am confident that the action of the committee will not be unanimous. I am not in favor of the plan proposed in the resolution of the gentleman from Alamakee, but I am disposed to stand by the present judicial system of the State with some slight modifications. I am willing, however, that the gentleman presenting this resolution should be heard, and that the matter should be referred to the Committee on the Judicial Department. I presume the question of printing is not to be considered now upon this motion. I shall be opposed to the printing of this and all other resolutions of the kind. Let the committee report upon them, and then if gentlemen feel themselves aggrieved, or think that the propositions should come before the Convention, they can then make their motions to print. I hope the resolution offered by the gentleman from Alamakee will be referred to the committee.—We have already had a very lengthy resolution in the shape of a law which will cover about as much legislation, as you generally find in Constitutions. It has been passed and referred to a committee. If we are going to object to the reference of these resolutions to committees I think we ought to have commenced then, for it covers more ground than all the other resolutions that have been introduced into the Convention. As for the objection raised by the gentleman from Des Moines [Mr. Hall] to spreading these resolutions upon the journal, I think we had better dispose of the one now before us and take up the resolution offered by the gentleman from Henry [Mr. Clarke] and pass it at once. I shall vote for the reference of this resolution to the Committee on the Judiciary Department.

Mr. BUNKER. I have uniformly voted for the reference of these resolutions to the committees. We adopted that system at the commencement of this Convention. In referring resolutions to committees, I do not feel, in any vote I may give for that purpose, that I am necessarily committed to the support of the measures which are embraced in them. Had I understood the matter in that way, I should have voted against a great many resolutions. Inasmuch as we have adopted the plan of referring resolutions to their appropriate committees, I think it would evince a want of courtesy to a member of the body to reject any resolution which he may see fit to offer, that is couched in respectful language. If we file resolution upon resolution, of the length they have been morning, unless there is some provision by which the labor and expense of spreading them upon the Journal may be saved, I shall change my course and vote against them all. I shall vote for this resolution under the belief, that we will make some provision by which we shall cease to spread resolutions at length upon the Journal.

Mr. EDWARDS. I think my friend from Alamakee (Mr. Clark) misapprehends the question. It is not whether the resolution as offered shall be printed as matter coming from a standing Committee, but the only question is, whether this whole matter shall be spread upon the Journal.

If it be spread upon the Journal, of course it will be printed with the Journal. Until the resolution offered by the gentleman from Henry (Mr. Clarke) is adopted, it strikes me, that as an act of courtesy, we ought to extend the same privilege to the gentleman from Alamakee (Mr. Clark) that we have extended to other gentlemen of this Convention.

Mr. YOUNG. The whole objection seems to be to the length of the resolution and to spreading it upon the Journal. I would suggest to the gentleman from Alamakee (Mr. Clark) that he withdraw his resolution for the present. I have no doubt that the resolution of the gentleman from Henry (Mr. Clarke) will pass, which will only delay this matter one day. The resolution of the gentleman from Alamakee appears to be pretty lengthy, and I think if we encumber our Journals with the resolutions in full, it will make a very large and unnecessarily voluminous volume. I am in favor of referring to their appropriate committees all the propositions which gentlemen may present here Resolutions may contain matter of great importance, and we are in duty bound to refer them to their appropriate committees. I do not want to cut off the gentleman from Alamakee from referring his resolution, but I would suggest to him that he withdraw it for the present.

Mr. WILSON. I move to amend the resolution of the gentleman from Alamakee by adding the following provision: "Provided, that the resolution shall not be entered at large upon the Journal."

Mr. CLARKE of Johnson. I hope the amendment will not prevail, for it raises a serious question as to the rights of every member of this Convention. I feel no interest in the fate of this particular resolution, but I take it to be the right of every member here to offer a resolution expressing his views or the views of his constituents, and to have that resolution go upon the Journal. The Convention may vote down his resolution, and they may take such action as they please, but I take it to be a Constitutional right, that every member upon this floor, representing the people of this State, shall have the opportunity of placing upon the record his particular views. If this Convention may, by a vote, say, that a resolution shall not go upon the Journal, it may also say, that a report of a Committee should not go upon the Journal; and the Journal of this Convention instead of being a true record of its proceedings will be just such a record as the majority shall from time to time deem fit to make. I say, that every member here has a right to offer his views upon every question in the shape of a resolution, and this Convention, unless they exercise a power, which in my opinion will be tyranny, have no right to exclude him from placing his views upon the Journal. I hope the gentleman from Jefferson (Mr. Wilson) will withdraw his amendment. The question is not, whether by the present course, we shall make a voluminous volume or not, but the question is, whether members shall have the right to place their opinions upon the record, so that they may be justified before their constituents and the people of this State. It seems to me, that the principle is a bad one, because the majority might prevent the minority upon this floor from being heard upon that Journal at all. If it can be done upon this resolution, it may be done upon every resolution which may be obnoxious to a majority of the members. The individual members of this Convention have a right in this matter, which the majority ought not to take away, if they could. I submit this question for the consideration of gentlemen, and especially those who compose the majority upon this floor.

Mr. HALL. I do not think that there is any authority which can control our action in this matter. If there be any power other than that we ourselves possess, I should like to know what it is and from what source it is derived. We are acting here in a primary capacity, and have the right to make our own rules, and establish such regulations as we think necessary for the dispatch of our business. I do not think that a member has an inalienable right to place upon the journal everything which he thinks proper to offer and claim to have it printed as a part of our proceedings. Now these resolutions have been offered and will probably continue to be offered. They are undoubtedly proper, but I question the propriety of making up a journal containing not only what we do, but every suggestion made in writing by members. It certainly is unnecessarily encumbering the journal, and will add nothing to the dignity of the Convention. I shall vote at the proper time to refer this resolution to the committee, but I move now to lay it upon the table for the mere purpose of taking up the resolution of the gentleman from Henry (Mr. Clarke), which I hope the Convention will pass.

We can then take up the resolution of the gentleman from Alamakee (Mr. Clark) and refer it to the Committee on the Judicial Department.

The question was then taken, and the resolution was laid on the table.

Publication of Debates.

The hour for the special order having arrived, the Convention resumed the consideration of the report of the Committee on Printing the Debates of this Convention.

The PRESIDENT stated the question to be upon the motion to fill the blank in the first resolution by inserting "fifteen hundred?' as the number of bound copies of the Debates to be published; upon which question the yeas and nays had been ordered.

Mr. CLARKE, of Johnson. I move to amend the motion by inserting "two thousand," instead of "fifteen hundred." After the adjournment, myself, in connection with the other members of the committee upon this subject, had a conversation with some of the members of the Convention, and with the printers; and while the printers were willing to submit to what a majority of the Convention may do, we agreed among ourselves that two thousand would be the proper and requisite number to be inserted in this blank. I trust that will meet the unanimous consent of the Convention as a sort of compromise upon this subject.

Mr. ELLS. I would move to fill the blank with the number "three thousand," and I believe the question must be taken upon the highest number first.

The PRESIDENT. The Convention having stricken out the number "three thousand," that motion is not now in order

The question was stated to be upon filling the blank with "two thousand."

Mr. TRAER. I would ask whether this matter was left in the hands of the Convention yesterday, or in the hands of the committee? The gentleman from Johnson (Mr. Clarke) speaks of of what the committee decided upon last night in regard to this matter.

Mr. GILLASPY. I desire to say that on Monday when this question of reconsideration came up, I was unwell and not in my seat. I was from the first, I am now opposed to having three thousand copies of these debates printed. I have been informed that there has been no particular contract made with these printers, and and that they will be satisfied with printing fifteen hundred copies. I heard this, but I do not recollect from whom. Now, if there had been a contract here, and the printers had gone on and commenced the work in good faith, I would have no disposition to break that contract, but would say that it should be carried out. But I have been informed that no definite contract has been made, and that the printers will be satisfied with printing fifteen hundred, and I shall vote for that number, though I would myself prefer to have only a thousand copies printed.

Mr. PALMER. I believe that the reduction of the number of these copies will make but little difference in the cost. I do not know what would be the difference, but it would be but the additional cost of paper and press work. The cost of composition is not changed at all by the number of copies printed. I think two thousand copies would not be too many to be printed and distributed through the State, and I shall therefore vote for that number.

Mr. WILSON called for the yeas and nays upon the motion to fill the blank with "two thousand," which were ordered.

The question being then taken by yeas and nays, the motion to insert "two thousand" was not agreed to—yeas 16, nays 20, as follows:

Yeas—Messrs. Ayres, Clarke of J., Cotton, Day, Edwards, Ells, Emerson, Gower, Hall, Harris, Johnston, Marvin, Palmer, Peters, Price and Solomon.

Nays—The President, Messrs. Bunker, Clark of A., Gibson, Gillaspy, Gray, Hollingsworth, Parvin, Patterson, Robinson, Scott, Seely, Skiff, Todhunter, Traer, Warren, Wilson, Winchester, and Young.

The question then recurred upon filling the blank with "fifteen hundred," and being taken, was agreed to.

The next question was upon filling the blank from which had been stricken the number "twenty-five" as the number of daily sheets to each member.

Mr. PALMER moved to fill the blank with the number "twenty-five."

The PRESIDENT. The chair is of opinion that the Convention having stricken out that number, it would not be in order to move to fill it with the same number.

Mr. HARRIS moved to insert "twenty-six."

Mr. PALMER moved to insert "twenty-four."

Mr. HALL moved to insert "five."

Mr. WILSON moved to insert "two."

The question was taken first upon filling the blank with the number "twenty-six," by yeas and nays, and it was not agreed to; yeas 6, nays 30, as follows:

Yeas.—Messrs. Clarke, of Alamakee, Gibson, Harris, Palmer, Robinson and Solomon.

Nays.—The President, Messrs. Ayres, Bunker, Clarke, of Henry, Clarke, of Johnson, Cotton, Day, Edwards, Ells, Emerson, Gillaspy, Gower, Gray, Hall, Hollingsworth, Johnston, Marvin, Parvin, Patterson, Peters, Price, Scott, Seeley, Skiff, Todhunter, Traer, Warren, Wilson, Winchester and Young.

The question then recurred upon filling the blank with the number "twenty-four."

Mr. PALMER. According to your decision the motion to fill the blank with "twenty-five" is not in order. I would merely call the attention of the Convention to the fact that when the proposition was up before us for supplying each member with twenty-five daily papers, it was urged in opposition to that number that we were to have a goodly number of these sheets of debates, and therefore twenty-five daily newspapers would not be necessary, and the motion to reduce the number to ten was carried. Now I find that the papers here do not publish reports of our proceedings at all—or if they do it is only a bare synopsis, that does not amount to anything. Now I am in favor of obtaining a report of our proceedings in some way and shape, and I think that twenty-four copies of these reports would not be too many for each member. I hope, therefore, the Convention will agree to fill the blank with that number.

Mr. EDWARDS. I desire to say in explanation of the vote I shall give, that I think the better plan to obtain this information would be to substitute papers for these sheets, and therefore I shall vote in the negative on this motion.

On the question, Mr. WILSON called the yeas and nays, and they were accordingly ordered.

The question being then taken by yeas and nays, upon filling the blank with the number "twenty-four," it was not agreed to; yeas 8 nays 28, as follows:

Yeas.—Messrs. Ayres, Clark, of Alamakee, Gibson, Harris, Marvin, Palmer, Robinson and Solomon.

Nays.—The President, Messrs. Bunker, Clarke, of Henry, Clarke, of Johnson, Cotton, Day, Edwards, Ells, Emerson, Gillaspy, Gower, Gray, Hall, Hollingsworth, Johnston, Parvin Patterson, Peters, Price, Scott, Seely, Skiff, Todhunter, Traer, Warren, Wilson, Winchester and Young.

The question then recurred upon filling the blank with the number "five."

Mr. HARRIS. I believe it is in order to move to fill the blank with a larger number, and I would therefore move to fill it with the number "twenty." And I would appeal to the generosity of those gentlemen who live in the thickly populated portions of the country, where their constituents have their daily papers, and, consequently, can be supplied with information in relation to the doings of this Convention. I am afraid those gentlemen do not understand the position some of us here are placed in; they do not recollect that our constituents do not have daily papers, but depend upon us here for the information they may get. The printing of these debates is to be done at any rate, as I understand, and there will not be much additional expense in furnishing us with twenty daily sheets of these debates.

There is a great anxiety upon the part of my constituents for information of our proceedings, and nearly every man of my constituents that I met before I came here, who was an intelligent and reading man, charged me to send him all the information I could with regard to the proceedings of this Convention, and I know they will be grievously disappointed if something of the kind is not done. What little additional cost these sheets may be, should be borne by the people, in order that they may have full information to pass understandingly upon what we may prepare here for their approval.

Mr. EDWARDS. I would enquire if it be in order to move to lay the motion of the gentleman from Appanoose (Mr. Harris,) upon the table?

The PRESIDENT. The chair is of opinion such a resolution would be in order.

Mr. EDWARDS. My object in submitting that motion is to test the sense of this Convention upon this subject, as I propose afterwards to submit a proposition to supply each member of this Convention with fifteen additional copies of the city papers. I am informed by one of the publishers of the city papers here that if this Convention will subscribe for a sufficient number of copies they will make arrangements to have the proceedings of this body fully reported and published in their papers. And I also understand that the parties we have engaged to publish our debates are not anxious to supply us with these daily sheets. I therefore move to lay the motion of the gentleman from Appanoose (Mr. Harris,) upon the table.

Mr. CLARKE, of Johnson. Perhaps it would be advisable before the question is taken on this motion for me, as a member of this committee, to make a statement upon this subject.

The PRESIDENT. The motion to lay on the table is not debatable.

Mr. MARVIN. Does not the motion to lay upon the table carry the whole subject with it? I am under the impression that is the practice both in the Senate and House of Representatives of the United States.

The PRESIDENT. The chair is of opinion that according to the usages and practice of parliamentary bodies in this State, a motion to lay an amendment on the table is in order, and does not carry the main subject with it.

Mr. EDWARDS. I will withdraw my motion for a moment to accommodate the gentleman from Johnson (Mr. Clarke).

Mr. CLARKE, of Johnson. In consultation with the printers of these debates, the committee learn that the supplying of these daily sheets or slips is going to delay the publication of the whole work to some extent, and the printers are very willing to surrender that portion of their contract. I perceive that there is some difficulty in getting information before the people, and I understaad that the number of copies we have decided to take of these daily sheets, if exchanged for our daily papers here, will enable the publishers in this city to pay for reporters in this Convention to prepare reports of our proceedings, and if these slips or sheets are cut off—and I think that as a means of giving information to the people, they will amount to but little more than detached sheets sent to few persons among our respective constituencies—if these slips are cut off I am willing to increase the number of daily papers, to be supplied to each member, and either have our editors make provision for reporting our proceedings for their papers, or do it ourselves. I think upon the whole, that is the best way to send information to the people, and for one, I am not willing to refuse them that intelligence, although my own constituents here would be able to supply themselves with it, either by attendance upon our sessions or through the city press. I think it would be a matter of economy to cut off these slips and have but a proof sheet or two furnished to each member for his correction and revision.

Mr. HARRIS. I was in favor of that plan from the first, and with the understanding that it will be adopted, now I will withdraw my motion to fill this blank.

The PRESIDENT. The gentleman from Appanoose (Mr. Harris) can withdraw his motion if no objection is made.

Mr. CLARK, of Alamakee. I object to the withdrawal of that motion. I am in favor of spreading information before our constituents by means of these slips or sheets. I was in favor of that from the first, and am yet, for several reasons. In the first place, I believe by this means this information will be conveyed more accurately and speedily than it can be done in any other form. In the next place, I believe it can be done cheaper this way than any other, for the reason that the printers of our bound reports have to set the type for the bound work and these slips can be printed from that type without additional cost for composition, besides they print upon these sheets nothing but the proceedings of this Convention, and that will be all we will have to pay for. But if we take our daily papers here, we will find that they will not have half a page devoted to the proceedings of this Convention. We will consequently have to pay for all the other matter contained in those papers, of which the greater portion will be advertisements. We will have to pay the usual price for the papers, while not one eighth part of it will be of interest to our constituents. All our constituents care for, are matters connected with this Convention, and they have no interest in the other matters usually contained in these papers.

I believe this is altogether the cheapest manner in which to obtain information to be distributed among our constituents. I believe this is the best way in which to obtain the facts connected with the proceedings of our Convention. Our constituents want it, and expect it, and will require it at our hands, and I believe these slips and sheets will prove to be the cheapest and most direct mode, and they will prove to convey the most correct information which we can obtain to give information to our constituents.

The PRESIDENT. The chair is of opinion, upon further examination, that the gentleman from Appanoose (Mr. Harris) can withdraw his motion to fill the blank with the number "twenty," upon a vote of the majority of the Convention.

Mr. PATTERSON. I move that the gentleman from Appanoose have leave to withdraw his motion.

The question being taken, the resolution was agreed to, and leave granted accordingly.

The question recurred upon the motion of Mr. Hall to fill the blank with the number "five."

Mr. CLARKE, of Johnson. I hope the Convention will agree to fill this blank with the number "two." If the Convention will adopt the idea which I have suggested of substituting daily papars instead of these sheets, two of these sheets will be enough.

Mr. CLARKE, of Alamakee, moved to amend the motion of Mr. Hall by adding the following proviso, to the clause in which the blank to be filled occurs:

Provided that any member shall be entitled to receive any number of those daily sheets not to exceed ten, by relinquishing an equal number of newspapers which he is now entitled by the rules of this Convention.

Mr. HALL. I will vote most cheerfully to increase the number of newspapers to any gentlemen who desire them. But I am opposed to voting any more of those slips or sheets than a merely nominal number, for I believe that we will not be able to get them here in time to be of any use to our coustituents. I do not want to send to any of my constituents one half of the debates that may occur here—to send it to them in broken doses. I believe, too, after further examination of the subject that those sheets will not answer the purpose that we first designed them for. I think, therefore, it best to relinquish all of those daily sheets or slips, except a few of them, and resort to the newspapers and thus give them sufficient encouragement to prepare all the report of our proceedings we will need for the purpose of distribution. And I am willing to vote aid to the newspapers of this city to do this, and to give members all the copies they may desire to any reasonable extent.

Mr. CLARK, of Alamakee. I suppose that no objection will be raised by any member of this Convention to permitting any gentleman who may desire to do so, to substitute those sheets for the daily papers we may be entitled to.

Mr. WARREN. I hope the gentleman from Alamakee [Mr. Clark] will withdraw his amendment, as we have already entered into a contract with the papers to furnish us with so many copies, and that contract cannot now be done away with.

Mr. CLARKE, of Alamakee. I do not see any difficulty about that at all.

Mr. HALL. I have just learned from the Secretary a fact which I suppose the gentleman from Alamakee [Mr. Clark] may not have fully understood, and that is that orders for those papers have already been sent off and those orders cannot now be recalled.

Mr. CLARK, of Alamakee. I should like to know for what length of time those papers have been ordered.

Mr. HALL. During the session of the Convention.

Mr. CLARK. Suppose that we should adjourn finally to-morrow, would those papers have any claim upon us beyond that time?

Mr. HALL. No, sir.

Mr. CLARK. And why would they have any more claim upon us if we were to inform the editors to-morrow that we did not want those papers any longer?

Mr. HALL. We could not do that for we have ordered them during our session, whether it be a long one or a short one. And the editors would have good cause to be surprised at any such action on our part.

Mr. CLARK. They would not be more surprised than I am at the action proposed here.—I understood when I voted for those papers that the reason more were not ordered was because we were to be supplied with those slips of debates, and now all I ask is that the Convention would stand to their own proposition in good faith.

Mr. GIBSON. I think the distribution of these slips would prove to be far the best plan for laying information before our constituents. I cannot see the advantage of circulating newspapers, because they certainly could not contain more of our proceedings than these slips will, and they will contain a great deal more that would be of any interest whatever to our constituents. If we send these slips to our constituents in the interior of the State they will be furnished with a journal of our proceedings, and if sent to any individual who takes an interest in this Convention they will be carefully perused and preserved. But we know that three-fourths of these daily papers are filled with advertisements and other matter not at all interesting to our constituents. It strikes me that the plan of distributing this information to our people by means of these slips or sheets as decidedly the best and cheapest. We have now placed ourselves under the necessity of having these reports published; the composition for the bound work is therefore to be paid for, and all the cost of these slips will be for press-work and paper. I would therefore move to fill this blank with the number fifteen.

Mr. GILLASPY. I am desirous of accommodating my friend from Appanoose (Mr. Harris) with all the information he desires for his constituents, and my vote will be governed only with regard to the cost of this information. If, in my judgment, the proposed number of these newspapers would cost more than these slips, I should vote for the slips. But my constituents feel no particular interest in the action of this Convention, except upon one question, that is the banking question. They are looking out for the dollars and cents in my district [laughter]. Now if I am called upon to vote down these slips in order to supply ourselves with the daily papers, I think at present I shall vote for the slips, because I believe they would be the cheapest and contain the most matter interesting to our constituents.

Mr. PARVIN. The argument used by the gentleman from Appanoose (Mr. Harris) is the only one that could induce me under any circumstances to vote for an increased number of these papers or slips. He represents that his constituents are a great way from here, and have no daily papers from which to derive information. And I have no doubt it would afford us all pleasure to accommodate delegates from such districts. But I do not believe these slips can be delivered to us here in time to afford much benefit to the constituents of the gentleman from Appanoose.

Mr. HARRIS. If the gentleman will allow me to interrupt him a moment, I will say that I have been from the first in favor of newspapers.

Mr. PARVIN. Then with regard to substituting newspapers for these slips. We have been here, I presume, one fourth of the time that we shall be in session, and by the time these papers can publish information of our proceedings, and we can send them to our constituents we will have left and gone, and the principal object, as I understand it, of sending out this information will not be accomplished. That object as I understand it is to let our constituents know what we are doing here, in time to allow them to give us any instructions they may desire to give us.

These papers cannot answer the same purpose in our case as they would with the Legislature. The Legislature has a long session before it, and time enough afforded to send information to their constituents, and have what instructions may be desired sent to them before they adjourn. But we will have completed our work and have returned home by the time our constituents can find out what we are doing, and let us know what they want changed in our action.

Now in regard to these slips, I am in favor of the least number that I can get the Convention to vote for. All I desire to have for myself is one copy to correct any errors there may be in it, and have it sent back to the printers. I shall certainly not vote for any increase for our papers as they are now filled. There has been so far nothing reported in our city papers of the proceedings of this Convention. The editors say they cannot afford the expense of making out these reports. Now if we had not already made our contract for ten daily papers I would not vote for having them sent to us. But few of them I think are worth the postage, with which the State is taxed to send to my constituents. Our proceedings have not yet been reported for them, and too much of the session of the Convention has passed to make it worth while for the editors to commence now to make out reports. I hope the Convention will vote neither for the papers nor the slips. The proceedings of this Convention will be published and bound in time to lay the information before our constituents before they will be called upon to vote upon the Constitution we may frame here. I hope therefore the Convention will take no more newspapers, and will vote for the smallest number of these slips.

Mr. TRAER. I have a proposition to make by way of a compromise. I would propose, that if the Convention have these daily reports, and also to take an increased number of newspapers, each member be allowed to select for himself, either three daily sheets of debates, or the newspapers. That will accommodate all parties, and is the manner in which this very question was settled in the Massachusetts Convention, where the same question arose.

Mr. EDWARDS. It seems to me the suggestion of the gentleman from Benton (Mr. Traer,) does not meet the difficulty under which we are now laboring. We are compelled to adopt one course or the other, to take these slips or the papers. If we take the papers, we are assured by the gentlemen who conduct them, that our proceedings shall be reported in full, and published in their papers. There is another reason why we should substitute the papers. They have been filled heretofore with the proceedings of the Legislature, but that body will adjourn to-day or to-morrow, and those papers can then be devoted to the proceedings of this Convention.

I differ with the gentleman from Wapello (Mr. Gillaspy) in one particular. My constituents have different views in regard to this Convention from those which, according to his statement, his entertain. I think his observations are altogether gratuitous about this matter. He says his constituents consider that we come here merely to act upon the subject of banking. Now my constituents expect that we will take other matters into consideration. And I have seen enough here to satisfy me that members of this Convention will present views upon other subjects than that of banking. I am as much in favor of retrenchment and a short session as any other member can be. But I know that no one can predict when this Convention will adjourn. That will depend upon the amount of business presented for its action.

Now I say the wisest course of policy will be to enlighten our constituents upon our proceedings here as soon as possible. It will not be determined until the schedule of the constitution is agreed upon, whether the vote upon it will be taken at the election in April next, in August, or at some other election. And assuming that it may be in April next, and that we may not be able to get home long enough before the election than to enlighten them upon our work by our own explanations. It is highly desirable to post our constituents upon the doings of this Convention in time for them to know how to vote, and the only mode we can do so is by sending them these newspapers which record daily our proceedings here. That I believe will be the most economical appropriation of our money that we can make in relation to this matter. The Convention has been in session now some eight or ten days, and only one sheet of our debates have been laid before us, and that contains the proceedings of only the first day, and part of the second day.

Now I differ with the gentleman from Muscatine, (Mr. Parvin.) I think if we adopt the paper instead of the slip system, our constituents will have a report of each previous day's proceedings, and can learn what we have been doing before we arrive at home. And if we do not provide some means for informing them before we return, it will be impossible for us to go before them, and post them with regard to our action here. My district consists of several counties, and is some seventy-five miles in width, and I cannot go before all my constituents and inform them what we may have done here. Therefore, as a matter of expediency and economy, we should adopt this system of informing our constituents through the daily papers, rather than by sending them these slips. I will vote for five of these slips as mere proof sheets, as that number will cost but little more than two, but I think we should devote the most of our means to taking these newspapers.

Mr WILSON. I desire to say one word in relation to this newspaper reporting. So far as my observation has extended, I consider the newspaper reporting in this city a humbug. I do not believe there is a man who has taken up these newspapers and read their reports of our legislative proceedings who can tell now what that legislature has done. The system of reporting that has been adopted here, amounts to nothing, or worse than nothing. A man may read three or four columns of these reports of the proceedings of the Legislature, and he cannot tell when he gets to the end, what the legislature has been doing. They tell us that House Bill number so and so, or Senate Bill number so and so, has been taken up, but do not give even the title of the bill. I suppose the same course of reporting the proceedings of this body will be adopted. They will say that the committee on the judiciary submitted a report which was laid upon the table, and ordered to be printed; that the committee on the legislative department, or some other committee, submitted a report which was also laid on the table, and ordered to be printed, and that is all that will be reported. Now, if we send this to our constituents they will not be able to find out a single alteration or amendment that we propose to make to the Constitution, and so far as enabling them to be informed of our proposed action here in time to send instructions to us, the whole matter will amount to nothing. I noticed the report of the proceedings of the two State nominating Conventions that were held here last week, and it was a bungling affair from beginning to end. There was hardly a motion reported correctly. It would be a useless expense to procure papers with such reports in, and our constituents would not receive the least benefit from them.

In regard to these slips or sheets of debates, I am in favor of taking two of them, and that, I think, is all that is necessary. I represent one county in which are published two weekly newspapers. I am a little more fortunate than some members here in that respect. I am happy to state that my constituents are a reading people, and take a great many papers, and are pretty well posted in regard to public matters. I think if we place this question upon the ground of expediency in benefitting our constituents, we will take but two of these slips, which can be sent to the papers, who will publish all of importance contained in them. I do not think the paper system would prove to be worth anything at all.

Mr. GILLASPY. I wish to correct the gentleman from Lucas (Mr. Edwards) with regard to what I said about my constituents. I said then, and I say now, that the great and absorbing question with my constituents, is the banking question. The people of my district supposed that there would be no very material changes in the constitution, except upon that one question. Hence I said what I did.

I differ widely from the gentlemen who have spoken in favor of these slips. I do not see how we can enlighten our constituents by sending them these slips of debates in broken doses. I have been a citizen of this State when we were called upon to vote upon the constitution, and none of their debates and proceedings were reported. I obtained my information concerning what we were called upon to adopt by leaving my plow on the day of election, and going to the place where the elections were held, and listening to stump orators, who explained the constitution to us. And that is the only way we can do it in the present case. We cannot do it by sending these slips to them, for one day's proceedings would be sent to one man, and the next day's proceedings to another. And as to the vote being taken upon this constitution before we can return home, I do not expect, neither do my constituents expect or desire to have this constitution submitted to them at the April election. I shall not vote for any such proposition here. And I undertake to say that the people of my district do not expect me to supply every man of them with a perfect copy of the constitution we may frame here, and all our debates and proceedings thereon, before they are called upon to vote upon it. They would be rather surprised to see the caravan leaving this city, and going from town to town leaving these sheets and proceedings. And if we were to do such a thing it would bankrupt the State of Iowa.

Mr. CLARK, of Alamakee. I do not understand gentlemen when they get up here and talk about our constituents receiving the proceedings of this Convention through these slips in broken doses. I understand that these slips are to contain a full report of the debates and proceedings of this Convention, and in far more perfect order and form than can be obtainrd in any other shape. We will be able to get much more of our debates and proceedings through these debates than we can get through the daily papers. Suppose that we decide to take ten or twenty copies of these slips. Every member will make out a list of those of his constituents to whom he desires to send these slips, and will continue to send them to these men so that when we get through here these constituents, scattered all over his district, will have a full record of the debates and proceedings of this Convention. Now when a member does not represent but one county, and has two newspapers in his county, two of these slips will answer his purpose perhaps, for he can send them to those papers, and they can publish their contents, and thus the information will be scattered all over the district. But when a member represents ten or a dozen counties, as I do, with an extent of territory of one hundred and fifty miles, and with eight or ten newspapers in that district, two of these slips will not be enough. And it is for that reason that I am in favor of allowing members to have these slips containing a full report of our proceedings, rather than the same number of newspapers. And it seems to me that it would be rather hard if a majority of this Convention should determine to send newspapers to their constituents, and not allow the minority to take the worth of those papers in slips if they prefer to do so. Now I admit that each member here is a better judge of the wants of his constituents than any other member can be. And I hope they will not deny me the same privilege of judging what is suitable for my constituents, but will permit me to take the amount of the price of the newspapers they may order in just such kind of matter as I may deem to be best adapted to the wants of the people I represent here.

Mr. GOWER. I have listened to the remarks here about enlightening our constituents, concerning our doings here. Now I should be most happy to enlighten my constituents, and I thought that sending two of these slips to the two papers in my county would be very desirable. I have also paid some attention to the remarks about the newspapers. And the broken doses in which our constituents would get this information has been referred to all around this hall. Now I do not desire to withhold this information from the people, and I desire them to have it in a perfect form, and I would like some way to be adopted for giving it to them that would be satisfactory to all the members of this Convention. I would make a suggestion, that I have not heard made by any other member here, which I think will settle the whole difficulty, and will prove to be as cheap, and will serve the purpose better than either these strips or the newspapers. I would suggest that we go on and complete our work here, or nearly complete it, and before we close our session appoint a committee to prepare an address to the people of this State, and in that address have embodied as the amendments and alterations we may propose to the present constitution. We can thus fully advise our constituents of all we shall have done here. We can have this printed in the newspapers of this State, paying them for it, if you please, and thus have it diffused all over the State. I think our people would obtain all the information necessary in that way, and it would be more intelligent to them than to receive these slips in broken doses, or to get the information through the papers of this city in an imperfect form. I do not want to back out from our contract with those papers that we have already ordered; but I do think there is force in the argument that our constituents would obtain this information in broken doses, either from these slips or from the newspaper reports.

Mr. HALL. I stated when I was up before that this matter of slips was impracticable, and now if every gentleman will make a personal application of this matter he will see that it is so. Would any member here prefer to put an advertisement into the city papers here to reach the 600,000 people of this State, or would he go to Davenport and have printed 600 or 900 slips to be sent to the people, six or eight to each county? He would of course prefer the newspapers, for he would circulate five times as many copies of his advertisement by that means than he could by the other. Nine hundred of those slips—25 to each member—is the highest number that has been proposed here. Now if you provide for the reports in these city papers they will exchange with the other papers in the State, and those papers will copy these reports and publish them, and thus all the people of the State will be informed. I am in favor of enlightening the people of the State, but I think we should do as the representatives of the people what we would do for ourselves if we desired to convey information to the people. Let us encourage the newspapers here. They say they cannot afford to make these reports now.—Let us extend our patronage to these papers and place them in a position where they can afford it, and thus this information will be radiated through the entire press of the State, and be placed properly and promptly before the people.

Mr. TRAER called for the previous question which call was seconded.

The question was upon ordering the main question to be put.

Mr. CLARKE, of Henry. I would inquire of the Chair what would be the effect of odering the main question to be put at this time?

The PRESIDENT. If the main question is ordered, then the first question would be upon the motion of the gentleman from Marion [Mr. Gibson] to fill the blank with the number "fifteen." The next question would be upon the motion of the gentleman from Alamakee [Mr. Clark] to amend the motion of the gentleman from Des Moines [Mr. Hall] by adding a proviso allowing each member to exchange his newspapers for an equal number of the sheets containing the debates of this Convention. The next question would be upon the motion of the gentleman from Des Moines to fill the blank with the number "five." Then upon the motion of the gentleman from Jefferson [Mr. Wilson] to fill the blank with the number "two," and then upon the report of the committee on reporting as amended.

The question was then taken upon ordering the main question to be put, and was agreed to.

The question was then taken upon the motion to fill the blank with the number "fifteen" and it was not agreed to.

The question was then taken upon the proviso allowing each member to exchange his daily news papers for an equal number of the sheets, containing the debates, and it was not agreed to.

The question was then taken on the motion to fill the blank with the number "five," and it was not agreed to, upon a division as follows—ayes 16 noes 18.

The question was then taken upon the resolution to fill the blank with the number "two," which was agreed to.

The report of the committee as amended was then adopted.

Miscellaneous.

Mr. TRAER moved that the Convention adjourn till this afternoon at two o'clock.

Mr. EDWARDS. I hope the gentleman will withdraw his motion, and permit us to settle this matter about the papers, and have it done with.

Mr. TRAER. I will withdraw my motion if that can be done now.

On motion of Mr. GILLASPY, it was

Ordered that Mr. Johnston of Lee county, be added to the Committee on Militia.

The PRESIDENT announced as the Select Committee ordered this morning to consider and report upon the subject of apportionment in this State, the following gentlemen, viz: Messrs. Traer, Solomon, Seely, Winchester, Wilson, Hollingsworth and Harris.

Mr. JOHNSTON. I suppose we cannot very well have afternoon sessions now, as several committees meet this afternoon, the Committee on the Legislative Department and the Committee on Incorporations among the number.

The PRESIDENT. The Chair would inform the gentleman from Lee, [Mr. Johnston,] that the Convention adopted a resolution this morning that the daily sessions of the Convention should commence at 10 A. M. and 2 P. M.

Mr. JOHNSTON. It will be impossible for members to perform their duties upon the committees and attend the sessions of the Convention in the afternoon.

The PRESIDENT. That order can be superceded by a special motion.

Mr. JOHNSTON. There is a resolution before this Convention in which I feel considerable interest. I refer to the resolution of the gentleman from Henry, [Mr. Clarke,] calling upon the Convention to express an opinion upon the subject of a State Bank, or a general banking system. It was intended, I believe, that that resolution should come up for discussion this morning. I am sorry the time this morning has passed away without that discussion. I suppose it is too late now to discuss it, and the Committee on Incorporations meet this afternoon. I desired that the resolution should go before them for their consideration this evening. I think that under the circumstances the gentleman had better call up his resolution, and let it be referred without discussion to the committee, who will consider the matter and bring the subject before the Convention in their report.

Mr. CLARKE, of Henry. I would suggest that it be made the special order for this afternoon, at two o'clock, as the Committee on Incorporations do not meet until four o'clock.

Mr. JOHNSTON. The Committee on the State Department meet at two o'clock.

Mr. CLARKE. We can meet here at two o'clock and discuss this matter for a short time and then have it referred to the committee in time for their consideration this afternoon. The object of the resolution is not to go into an elaborate discussion now, but merely to get a general expression of the views of the Convention on this matter. The time for discussion will come when amendments are proposed to the report that the committee may make on the subject. With that view I move that it be taken up and made the special order for two o'clock this afternoon.

Mr. PARVIN. As a member of the Committee on Incorporations I desired to hear this matter discussed in Convention, and with that view I yesterday moved that the resolution be laid upon the table till this morning. But as the matter stands now I would prefer to have the subject referred to the committee without discussion. I think with the gentleman from Lee, [Mr. Johnston,] that would be the better course, and that when we adjourn now, we shall adjourn to meet to-morrow morning at ten o'clock. There are so many committees who have their work to perfect, that we should gain no time by meeting this afternoon.

The question being taken on the motion to make the resolution the special order for this afternoon at two o'clock, it was not agreed to.

ADDITIONAL NEWSPAPERS FOR MEMBERS.

Mr. HARRIS offered the following resolution:

Resolved, That each member of this Convention be allowed fifteen daily newspapers in addition to those already ordered.

Mr. CLARKE, of Alamakee. I move to amend that resolution by adopting the following:

Provided, that any member be allowed to substitute for the same, an equal number of copies of the daily sheets of the debates of this Convention.

I deny to this Convention the right to dictate to any member what he shall take and what he shall not take: and they will be doing that, unless they adopt the amendment I have offered to this resolution. At the time the resolution was adopted which limited the number of papers we have already ordered, to ten for each member, the principle was distinctly avowed that the Convention would not dictate in what shape we should send the information of our proceedings to our constituents, and I now claim, as a right, that if this amount of money is to be expended in the publication of the debates and proceedings of this body, that each member shall be allowed to select in what form he will send this information to the people he represents.

Mr. BUNKER. As it seems to be expected that members will state what considerations regulate their votes here, it may be proper for me to state my position and the grounds for occupying that position. I voted against the reconsideration of the subject of reporting and printing our debates when that subject came before us the other day, for the reason that I believed that we would expend more of the people's money in discussing the subject, and thus extending the amount of our debates, than the whole matter we might retrench would amount to. It was for that reason, principally, that I voted against the reconsideration. To-day I have voted for taking the least number of these reports, because, having got into the question fairly by the reconsideration, I was desirous to save some portion of the money we were expending here in agitating the question again; and I think I shall vote against the newspaper proposition now, for the reason that I do not believe the voters of this State will desire any accurate information in relation to the constitution we may frame here, from any reports that can be, or may be published in the newspapers; and I think that before we adjourn we should order the publication of a very considerable dumber of the constitution we propose to be adopted, for general diffusion throughout the State, that the voters may see what we have done. These reports, if sent to them, would only enlighten them as to the opinion entertained by individual members here, but not as to what we may decide upon adopting in the constitution. I think the distribution of the new constitution throughout the State would enlighten the voters more than any number of newspapers we may decide to order for our use.

Mr. CLARKE, of Henry. I desire briefly to state my views upon this subject. I was opposed, as the Convention very well know, to the reconsideration of the reporting and printing of our debates, and when we voted upon the ordering of the newspapers, and also of these slips, I voted for the highest number, and believed that we ought to do so. I did not think that we were practicing very wise economy in bringing this subject up again for discussion, but that we were wasting more dollars than we would save cents. But now members having voted that we shall have only fifteen hundred of these bound reports, and having voted upon this matter of slips, that they will violate in another respect, the contract which has already been made with our printers, by cutting the number down from twenty-five to two, they turn round and vote fifteen daily newspapers into their own pockets—more than they have already ordered. I am for standing out openly upon this question, and shall call for the yeas and nays upon this resolution, that we may know who are for taking from the printer the contract for these daily slips or sheets, and then voting into their own pockets of the people's money, to the extent of fifteen daily newspapers.

The question was taken upon the amendment to the resolution, and it was not agreed to.

The question recurred upon the adoption of the resolution.

Upon this question Mr. CLARKE, of Henry, called for the yeas and nays, and they were ordered accordingly.

Mr. TRAER. I would ask the gentlemen who have refused to let us substitute these reports for newspapers, if they expect that they can force us to take these papers, whether we choose to do so or not? I understand that the object of this force work is to enable the papers of this city here to employ a reporter. Now I say to gentlemen here, that so far as I am concerned, if I cannot take these slips as I please, I will not take these papers that may be ordered at all. And I hope that all who voted with me will do the same. I think the Convention has no right to force us to do this thing. The resolution before us is to allow us to subscribe for fifteen daily newspapers each, in addition to those already ordered for our use. If the object is to put money into the pockets of the editors in this city, gentlemen better specify that those papers are the papers to be taken, or they may slip up after all. I think if gentlemen will act courteously in this matter, they will allow those of us who desire it, to substitute the debates for these papers. I think it would be a matter of economy to do so, as they will not cost so much as these papers. I protest against any such course as seems about to be adopted here. I will vote for this resolution, provided I can substitute these reports if I please, but not without.

Mr. GILLASPY. The gentleman from Henry [Mr. Clarke] seems to intimate that gentlemen here are talking one way and voting another. Now I do not intend to act inconsistently in this matter. I understood from some gentleman that if the number of bound copies of these debates was reduced below fifteen hundred it might injuriously affect our printers, and I voted for that number. But I understood that so far as these slips were concerned it made no difference to how low a number they were reduced. It was that consideration that influenced my vote. If I had supposed that by so doing we would violate any contract with our printers by which they would lose anything, I would have voted differently. I do not intend to do anything inconsistently, and I do not believe I have yet voted in any such way.

Mr. CLARKE, of Alamakee. I wish to enter my protest against this resolution, for I believe it is wrong in principle. When this question was up before the Convention the other day there was a proposition to furnish each member with twenty-five daily mewspapers, it was voted down, and the number limited to ten. I supposed therefore that it was settled by this Convention that that was the number of papers that we should take. I voted for that number with the understanding that we should have the privilege of taking a number of the sheets of our reports; twenty-five or some such number. Now I protest against this resolution for the reason that this Convention has once acted upon this matter and decided that the number of our papers should be limited to ten, and that there was then an understanding in this Convention that members should be allowed the privilege of having a certain number of these slips. That was the idea held out here I believe when the subject was up before, that we should have slips enough to make up twenty-five daily newspapers. That seemed to be supposed to be the requisite number of papers, provided we took nothing but the newspapers. Now the proposition is to allow each member to have fifteen additional newspapers. I protest against it and shall vote against it.

Mr. TODHUNTER. I do not wish to protract this discussion but there is one matter I would like to speak a few words about. Some of the members here seem to be dissatisfied with regard to the views of the majority. My friend from Alamakee, [Mr. Clark,] is dissatisfied because the majority of the Convention voted decidedly against his proposition. Now I think he ought to be satisfied with such a decided vote as was given upon his proposition, or if not satisfied, he should at least keep quiet. And there is the gentleman from Benton, [Mr. Traer,] who gets very much dissatisfied at the action of the majority, and flies off the handle very fiercely, and declares he will take none of these newspapers, no matter how many the Convention may order for each of its members. And the gentleman from Jefferson, [Mr. Wilson,] has made an attack upon the reporters of the papers of this city, which I think is very unwarranted, to say the least of it. He says the reports in those papers are bungling, and the whole system as there carried on is a humbug. He refers to the reports of the proceedings of the Legislature, and says he can make nothing of them; that they merely refer to House File No. so and so, and Senate File No. so and so, and that he cannot understand them at all, and that there is no sense in them. Now I would ask the gentleman to refer to the reports of the proceedings of any of the Legislatures and he will find the expressions "House File" and "Senate File" all through the reports. Now that is the way these matters really occur; those are the facts that actually transpire in the proceedings of the Legislature. Would he have the reporter falsify the facts, or should he not represent things as they really occur? I know that they appear like nonsense to those who have not sufficiently examined these matters. I confess that since I have been here I have been present in each House of our Legislature during their sessions, and have heard these very expressions, and many others used there, and I could not understand what was before the House at all. Now I think these remarks censuring papers and their reporters are uncalled for. And I must say also that I think some of our friends are getting unruly and a little contrary. [Laughter.]

Mr. CLARK, of Alamakee. With all due deferrence to my friend from Warren, [Mr. Todhunter,] I beg leave to inform him, and to inform this Convention also, that I hold myself responsible to my constituents alone for what I do here, so long as I do not violate the rules of this body. And I deny the right of any gentleman upon this floor, to mark out for me the course of conduct that I shall pursue. I have a right to be dissatisfied with the action of this Convention if I see fit to do so, and I have the right to express that dissatisfaction and to protest against that action; and I intend to exercise that right whenever my judgment tells me it is proper for me to do so. And as to being contrary, I say once more, that so far as my conduct here is concerned, I am answerable alone to my constituents and to no one else. And I say further that I shall decline to take any of these fifteen papers, let the Convention order them as they may.

Mr. HARRIS. I believe I have never yet, in any deliberative body of which I have been a member, called for the previous question. But I desire to have this whole subject disposed of without any further delay, and I therefore call for the previous question.

The call for the previous question was seconded, and the main question ordered to be put.

The question was upon the resolution ordering fifteen additional newspapers to each member.

Upon the question, Mr. CLARKE, of Henry, called for the yeas and nays, and they were ordered accordingly.

Mr. GILLASPY. I wish to state that I shall vote for this resolution for the benefit of my friends from the rural districts, and for no other consideration. [Laughter.]

Mr. TRAER. I hope the gentleman will give himself no uneasiness about the rural districts. [Renewed laughter.]

The question being then taken by yeas and nays, the resolution was not agreed to, yeas 16, nays 19, as follows:

Yeas—Messrs. Clarke of Johnson, Cotton, Edwards, Ells, Gibson, Gillaspy, Hall, Harris, Johnston, Marvin, Palmer, Patterson, Peters, Robinson, Solomon and Winchester.

Nays—The President, Messrs. Ayres, Bunker, Clark of Alamakee, Clarke of Henry, Day, Emerson, Gowen, Gray, Hollingsworth, Parvin, Scott, Seely, Skiff, Todhunter, Traer, Warren, Wilson, and Young.

Reports from Standing Committees.

Mr. TODHUNTER. I desire to submit a report from the Committee on the Executive, and I will state that it is the unanimous report of the committee, except the last section, to which the gentleman from Van Buren (Mr. Ayres) dissents.

The report is as follows:

The committee to whom was referred that portion of the constitution of Iowa regulating the executive department thereof, have had the same under consideration. and beg leave to make the following report, and recommend that the same be adopted:

Sec. 1. The supreme executive power of this State shall be vested in a Chief Magistrate, who shall be styled the Governor of the State of Iowa.

Sec. 2. The Governor shall be elected by the qualified electors at the time and place of voting for members of the General Assembly, and shall hold his office —— years from the time of his installation, and until his successor shall be qualified.

Sec. 3. There shall be a Lieutenant Governor, who shall hold his office —— years, and be elected at the same time of the Governor. In voting for Governor and Lieutenant Governor, the electors shall designate for whom they vote as Governor, and for whom as Lieutenant Governor. The returns of every election for Governor and Lieutenant Governor shall be sealed up and transmitted to the seat of government, directed to the Speaker of the House of Representatives, who shall open and publish them in the presence of both houses of the General Assembly.

Sec. 4. The person respectively having the highest number of votes for Governor and Lieutenant Governor, shall be declared duly elected; but in case two or more persons shall have an equal and the highest number of votes for either office, the General Assembly shall, by joint vote, forthwith proceed to elect one of the said persons Governor or Lieutenant Governor, as the case may be.

Sec. 5. Contested elections for Governor or Lieutenant Governor shall be determined by the General Assembly in such manner as may be prescribed by law.

Sec. 6. No person shall be eligible to the office of Governor or Lieutenant Governor who shall not have been a citizen of the United States, and a resident of the State two years next preceding the election, and attained the age of thirty years at the time of said election.

Sec. 7. The Governor shall be commander-in-chief of the militia, the army and navy of this State.

Sec. 8. He shall transact all executive business with the officers of Government, civil and military, and may require information in writing from the officers of the executive department upon any subject relating to the duties of their respective offices.

Sec. 9. He shall take care that the laws are faithfully executed.

Sec. 10. When any office shall, from any cause become vacant, and no mode is provided by the constitution and laws for filling such vacancy, the Governor shall have power to fill such vacancy, by granting a commission, which shall expire at the end of the next session of the General Assembly, or at the next election by the people.

Sec. 11. He may, on extraordinary occasions, convene the General Assembly by proclamation, and shall state to both houses when assembled, the purpose for which they shall have been convened; and when so convened, they shall have no power to legislate upon any subject save that suggested in the message of the Governor.

Sec. 12. He shall communicate, by message, to the General Assembly, at every regular session, the condition of the State, and recommend such matters as he shall deem expedient.

Sec. 13. In case of disagreement between the two houses, with respect to the time of adjournment, the Governor shall have power to adjourn the General Assembly to such time as he may deem proper; provided, it be not beyond the time fixed for the meeting of the next General Assembly.

Sec. 14. No person shall, while holding any office under the authority of the United States, or this State, execute the office of Governor or Lieutenant Governor, except as hereinafter expressly provided.

Sec. 15. The official term of the Governor and Lieuten't Governor shall commence on the— of — and on the same day every — year thereafter.

Sec. 16. He shall have power to grant reprieves, commutations and pardons, after conviction, for all offences except treason and cases of impeachment, subject to such regulations as may be provided by law. Upon conviction for treason, he shall have power to suspend the execution of the sentence until the case shall be reported to the General Assembly at its next meeting, when the General Assembly shall either grant a pardon, commute the sentence, direct the execution of the sentence or grant a further reprieve. He shall have power to remit fines and forfeitures, under such regulations as may be prescribed by law; and shall report to the General Assembly at its next meeting each case of reprieve, commutation, or pardon granted; and also all persons in whose favor remission of fines or forfeitures shall have been made, and the several amounts remitted.

Sec. 17. In case of the death, impeachment, resignation, removal from office, or other disability of the Governor, the powers and duties of the office for the residue of the term, or until he shall be acquitted, or the disability removed, shall devolve upon the Lieutenant Governor.

Sec. 18. The Lieutenant Governor shall be President of the Senate, but shall only vote when the Senate is equally divided; and in case of his absence or impeachment, or when he shall exercise the office of Governor, the Senate shall choose a President pro tempore.

Sec. 19. If the Lieutenant Governor while acting as Governor, shall be impeached, displaced, resign or die, or otherwise become incapable of performing the duties of the office, the President pro tempore of the Senate shall act as Governor until the vacancy is filled, or the disability removed; and if the President of the the Senate for any of the above causes, shall be rendered incapable of performing the duties pertaining to the office of Governor, the same shall devolve upon the Speaker of the House of Representatives.

Sec. 20. There shall be a seal of this State, which shall be kept by the Governor, and used by him officially, and shall be called the Great Seal of the State of Iowa.

Sec. 21. All grants and commissions shall be in the name and by the authority of the people of the State of Iowa, sealed with the Great Seal of this State, signed by the Governor and countersigned by the Secretary of State.

Sec. 22. A Secretary of State, Auditor of Public Accounts, Treasurer of State, Superintendent of Public Instruction, and Attorney General shall be elected by the qualified electors, who shall continue in office two years. The Secretary of State shall keep a fair register of all the official acts of the Governor, and shall, when required, lay the same, together with all papers, minutes, and vouchers relative thereto, before either branch of the General Assembly, and shall perform such other duties as shall be assigned him by law.

Sec. 23. Every bill which shall have passed the General Assembly shall be presented to the Governor; if he approve, he shall sign it; but if not, he shall return it with his objections to the house in which it shall have originated, which house shall enter the objections at large upon its journals, and proceed to reconsider the bill. If, after such consideration, a majority of all the members elected to that house shall agree to pass the bill, it shall be sent, with the Governor's objections, to the other house, by which it shall likewise be reconsidered; and if it shall be approved by a majority of all the members elected to that house, it shall be a law. If any bill shall not be returned by the Governor within ten days (Sundays excepted) after it shall have been presented to him, it shall be a law without his signature, unless the general adjournment shall prevent its return, in which case it shall be a law, unless the Governor, within ten days next after such adjournment, shall file such bill, with his objections thereto, in the office of the Secretary of State, who shall lay the same before the General Assembly at its next session, in like manner as if it had been returned by the Governor. But no bill shall be presented to the Governor within two days next previous to the final adjournment of the General Assembly.

On motion of Mr. HALL,

The report was laid upon the table, and one hundred copies ordered to be printed for the use of the Convention.

Mr. MARVIN, from the Committee on Education and School Lands, made the following report:

Your Committee to whom was referred the subject of Education and School Lands, have had the same under consideration, and after careful investigation and mature deliberation, the majority beg leave to report the following:

Section 1. The Educational interests of the State to include Common Schools and other Educational Institutions, shall be under the management and control of a Board of Education, which shall consist of sixteen members.

Sec. 2. No person shall be eligible as a member of said Board who shall not have attained the age of twenty-five years, and been two years a citizen of the State.

Sec. 3. The General Assembly shall district the State into sixteen Educational Districts, and one member of said Educational Board shall be chosen by the qualified electors of each district, and shall hold their offices for the term of four years, and after the first election under this constitution, the Board shall be divided by lot into two equal classes, and the seats of the first class shall be vacated after the expiration of two years, and one-half of the Board shall be chosen every two years thereafter.

Sec. 4. The first session of the Board of Education shall be held at the seat of Government, after which said Board may fix the time and place of meeting.

Sec. 5. The session of said Board shall be limited to twenty days, and but one session shall be held in one year, except upon extraordinary occasions, when, upon the recommendation of two-thirds of the Board, the Governor may order a special session.

Sec. 6. The Board of Education shall organize by appointing from their body a presiding officer, and the appointment of a Secretary, and other inferior officers usual in Legislative Assemblies. They shall keep and publish a journal of their proceedings, which shall be distributed in the same manner as the journals of the General Assembly.

Sec. 7. All rules and regulations made by said Board shall be published and distributed to the several Counties, Townships, and such School Districts as may be provided for by said Board, and when so passed, published and distributed, they shall have the force and effect of law.

Sec. 8. Said Board shall have full power and authority to legislate and make all needful rules and regulations in relation to Common Schools and other institutions of learning that are instituted to receive aid from the School or University funds of the State.

Sec. 9. Said Board may appoint a Chancellor, who shall have jurisdiction over all questions that may arise under the laws, rules and regulations of the Board, and from all decisions and judgments of said Chancellor, an appeal may be taken to the Supreme Court.

Sec. 10. The Board of Education shall provide a system of Common Schools, by which a School shall be organized and kept in each District at least three months in each year. Districts failing to organize and keep up a School, may be deprived of their portion of the School Fund.

Sec. 11. The Board of Education shall establish one University, which shall be located at some central point in the State, *Provided*, that until such time as such location may be made, and suitable buildings erected, said University shall continue as at present located.

Sec. 12. The University lands, and the proceeds thereof, and all moneys belonging to said fund shall be a permanent fund for the sole use of said University. The interest arising from the same shall be annually appropriated for the support and benefit of said University.

Sec. 13. The General Assembly shall encourage, by all suitable means, the promotion of intellectual, scientific, moral and agricultural improvement. The proceeds of lands that have been, or hereafter may be granted by the United States to this State, for the support of Schools, which shall hereafter be sold or disposed of, and the five hundred thousand acres of land granted to the new States, under an act of Congress, distributing the proceeds of the public lands among the several States of the Union, approved A. D., 1841, and all estates of diseased persons who may have died without leaving a will or heir, and also such per cent. as may be granted by Congress, on the sale of lands in this State, shall be, and remain a perpetual fund, the interest of which, together with all rents of unsold lands, and such other means as the General Assembly may provide, shall be inviolably appropriated to the support of Common Schools throughout the State.

Sec. 14. The money which shall be paid by persons as an equivalent for exemption from Military duty, and the clear proceeds of all fines collected in the several counties for any breach of the penal laws, shall be exclusively applied, in the several counties in which such money is paid or fine collected, among the several School Districts of said counties, in proportion to the number of youths subject to enumeration in such districts, to the support of Common Schools, or the establishment of Libraries, as the Board of Education shall from time to time provide.

Sec. 15. The General Assembly shall take measures for the protection, improvement, or other disposition of such lands as have been, or hereafter may be reserved, or granted by the United States, or any person or persons, to this State, for the use of a University, and the funds accruing from the rents or sale of such lands, or from any other source for the purpose aforesaid, shall be and remain a permanent fund, the interest of which shall be applied to the support of said University, for the promotion of literature, the arts and sciences, as may be authorized by the terms of such grant. And it shall be the duty of the General Assembly as soon as may be, to provide effectual means for the improvement and permanent security of the funds of said University.

Sec. 16. The financial agents of the School funds shall be the same, that by law receive and control the State and County revenue for other civil purposes.

Sec. 17. The money subject to the support and maintainance of Common Schools shall be distributed to the districts in proportion to the number of unmarried youths, between the ages of five and twenty-one years.

Sec. 18. The Board of Education shall each receive the same per diem and mileage as the compensation of members of the General Assembly.

Sec. 19. A majority of the Board of Education shall constitute a quorum for the transaction of business, *Provided*, no rule, or regulation, or law, for the regulation and government of the School System, shall pass without the sanction of the majority of all the members of the Board, which shall be expressed by the ayes and nays, on the final passage.

On motion of Mr. MARVIN,

The report was laid upon the table, and one hundred copies ordered to be printed for the use of the Convention.

On motion of Mr. SKIFF,

The Convention then adjourned until to-morrow morning at ten o'clock.

THURSDAY, JANUARY 29th 1857.

The Convention met at 10 o'clock, A, M., and was called to order by the President.

Prayer by Rev. Mr. Kynett.

The Journal of yesterday was read and approved.

Petitions.

Mr. WILSON presented the petition of Jesse Floyd and thirty-six others, citizens of Penn township, praying that the time of the meeting of the Legislature may be changed from the first Monday in December to the first Monday in January, and that the time of holding the elections be changed from the first Monday in August to the first Monday in October, which on his motion was referred to the Committee on the Distribution of Powers and Legislative Department.

Reports of Committees.

Mr. ELLS, from the committee on Education and School Lands, submitted the following minority report, which was laid on the table, and one hundred copies ordered to be printed for the use of the Convention.

The majority of the Committee to whom was referred the subject of Education and School Lands, having agreed to report in favor of a Board of Education, elected by districts, and clothed with exclusive legislative powers in all cases involving Common Schools, Colleges and Universities; also, in favor of a Chancelor's Court empowered to determine all questions arising out of the action of said board, or in any way connected therewith—the undersigned being unable to agree with said majority in their reasonings and conclusions, asks leave to make a counter report. Without attempting to discuss the details of said system of educational government embraced in said report, the undersigned would briefly state that he objects to the proposed amendments to the Constitution—1st. Because they assume to do that which properly belongs to the legislative department of the State; 2d. Because said Board of Education are clothed with powers, dangerous, as *precedents* to the liberties of a free and enlightened people; 3d. Because the system therein proposed could not be altered or amended without an amendment to the Constitution of the State. For these and other obvious reasons, the undersigned disagrees with the majority of said committee, and respectfully submits for the consideration of the Convention, the following, as Article 10, of the Constitution.

ARTICLE 10.

Education and School Lands.

SECTION. 1. The General Assembly shall provide for the election or appointment of a Board of Education, to be composed of twelve persons, who shall be the Trustees of the University, and shall have the general charge and control of education in the State. They shall have power to appoint a Secretary of the Board who shall be their executive agent, and perform such duties as may be imposed upon him by the Board of Education or the laws of the State.

SEC. 2. Knowledge and learning, generally diffused throughout a community, being essential to the preservation of a free government, it shall be the duty of the General Assembly to encourage. by all suitable means, moral intellectual, scientific and agricultural improvements and to provide by law for a general and uniform system of Common Schools, wherein tuition shall be without charge, and equally open to all. The proceeds of all lands that have been, or hereafter may be granted by the United States to this State, for the support of schools, which shall hereafter be sold or disposed of, and the five hundred thousand acres of land granted to the new states, under an act of Congress distributing the proceeds of the public lands among the several States of the Union, approved A. D. 1841, and all estates of deceased persons, who may have died without leaving a will or heir, and also such per cent. as may be granted by Congress on the sale of lands in this State, shall be and remain a perpetual fund, the interest of which, together with all the rents of the unsold lands, and such other means as the General Assembly may provide, shall be inviolably appropriated to the support of Common Schools throughout the State.

SEC. 3. The money which shall be paid by persons as an equivalent for exemption from military duty, and the clear proceeds of all fines collected in the several counties for any breach of the penal laws, shall be exclusively applied, in the several counties in which such money is paid or fine collected, among the several school districts in said counties, in the proportion to the number of inhabitants in such districts, to the support of Common Schools, or the establishment of libraries, as the general assembly shall, from time to time, provide by law.

SEC. 4. The General Assembly shall take measures for the protection, improvement, or other disposition of such lands as have been or may hereafter be reserved or granted by the United States, or any person or persons, to this State, for the use of a University; and the funds accruing from the rents or sale of such lands, or from any other source, for the purpose aforesaid, shall be and remain a permanent fund, the interest of which shall be applied to the support of said University, with such branches as the public convenience may hereafter demand, for the promotion of literature, the arts and sciences, as may be authorized by the terms of such grant. And it shall be the duty of the General Assembly, as soon as may be, to provide effectual means for the improvement and permanent security of the funds of said University.

Mr. GIBSON from the Committee on Future amendments to the Constitution submitted the following minority report, which on motion of Mr. Harris was laid on the table, and one hundred copies ordered to be printed.

The committee on amendments to the Constitution have had the same under consideration, and the undersigned beg leave to make the following Minority Report:

That in our opinion, it is inexpedient to submit the matter of amendment of the Constitution to the people once in ten years, unless the people so require, through their Legislature; and we therefore submit the following to be substituted in place of Section 2, in the Majority Report:

If, at any time, the General Assembly shall think it necessary, to revise or amend this Constitution, they shall provide by law for a vote at the next ensuing election for members of the General Assembly. In case a majority of the people vote in favor of a Convention, said General Assembly shall provide for an election of Delegates to a Convention to be held within twelve months after the vote of the people in favor thereof.

H. D. GIBSON,
TIMOTHY DAY.

Resolutions of Enquiry.

Mr. CLARKE, of Henry, offered the following resolutions:

Resolved, That the Committee on the Bill of Rights be instructed to report the following sections, or their equivalent:

1. That all elections ought to be free, and that all men having sufficient evidence of permanent interest with, and attachment to, the community, have the right of suffrage, and cannot be taxed or deprived of their property for public uses, without their own consent, or that of their representatives so elected, nor bound by any law to which they have not in like manner assented for the public good.

2. That no man, or set of men, are entitled to exclusive or separate emoluments, or privileges from the community, but in consideration of public services rendered by them; and in the same manner, no sect, class, or party of men, shall, as such sect, class, or party, be cut off, or debarred from the enjoyment of all the political and legal rights and privileges to which the citizens of the State are entitled.

Mr. HALL. I wish to ask the gentleman from Henry (Mr. Clarke) whether he intends to make it imperative upon the Committee to report these resolutions?

Mr. CLARKE. I do not intend to make it so.

Mr. HALL. I move that they lie on the table, and that they be printed.

Mr. CLARKE, of Johnson. I am opposed to the printing of these resolutions. If we do it in one case, we shall have to do it in all.

Mr. HALL. I withdraw my motion.

Mr. CLARKE, of Henry. I desire to change the word "instructed" at the commencement of the resolutions for "requested," so that they will read, "Resolved, that the Committee on Bill of Rights be requested to report the following sections. or their equivalent," &c.

Mr. CLARK, of Alamakee. I thought, when I offered a resolution yesterday, to refer certain matters to the Committee on the Judiciary, that the Convention had determined not to print any more resolutions, and would immediately adopt a rule to suspend the printing of such papers. The resolution which I introduced, and which expressed the wishes of the people of my district upon the subject to which it referred, was voted down, I suppose, upon the ground, that we would not print any more resolutions. But this morning I find that resolutions have been offered, and ordered to be printed. I would like to know what gentlemen mean by pursuing this course, and if they intend to apply this gag rule only to the thirty-fourth district. In presenting the resolution yesterday, which the Convention refused to print, I did it in obedience to the wishes of the people of that district, and I do not really understand why gentlemen should vote against printing it, and to-day vote in favor of printing resolutions introduced by other gentlemen. I would like to know what was the principle which led the Convention to reject the resolution offered by me yesterday.

Mr. HARRIS. I move that the resolutions be referred to the Committee on the Bill of Rights.

Mr. HALL. I wish to enquire whether the Committee on the Bill of Rights have reported?

Mr. CLARKE, of Henry. They have made a partial report.

The resolutions were agreed to, and referred to the Committee on the Bill of Rights.

Mr. CLARKE, of Henry, offered the following resolution:

Resolved, "That the Committee on Judiciary be requested to report in favor of electing all Judicial officers by the people.

Of dividing the State into four Judicial Districts, of a Supreme Court of four Judges, one from each Judicial District.

Of four Circuit Judges to hold Circuit Courts in each District, any one to preside.

That the Circuit Judges sit in Bank and constitute a District Court, having appellate jurisdiction from the circuits.

That no Circuit Judge shall vote upon an appeal taken from his own decisions.

That the General Assembly may provide by law for one of the Supreme Court Judges presiding in certain cases in the District Court, or for the District Judge of one District, sitting in certain cases on the Bench in another District.

That appeal shall be from District to Supreme Court.

That under certain circumstances provided for by law appeal may be directly from Circuit Court to Supreme Court."

The resolutions were agreed to and referred accordingly.

Mr. CLARK, of Alamakee. I would like to have that part of the Journal read which relates to the resolution I offered yesterday.

The Journal was then read, showing that the resolution referred to was laid on the table.

Mr. SKIFF moved to take up the resolution.

Mr. HALL. When the resolution was offered by the gentleman from Alamakee yesterday, I objected to its reference to the Committee on the Judiciary in view of the fact, that that Committee had already passed upon that subject and were prepared to make a full report. I thought the Convention sanctioned that idea by laying the resolution on the table. It was because the Committee had passed upon the subject and not from any want of respect to the gentleman from Alamakee (Mr. Clark) that I voted to lay his resolution on the table. I would oppose the reference of resolutions in all cases, where the Committees have reported. Are we to have these subjects referred over and over again to the Committees? If we do, when shall we have any thing reported from the Commitees, upon which we can rely. I acted against the resolution of the gentleman yesterday for the simple reason, that the Committee on the Judicial Department had reported.

Mr. CLARK, of Alamakee. I did not understand that the Committee on the Judicial Department had made any report, when I submitted my resolution yesterday. Even if they had made their report, I do not see that it would alter the principle involved. The Committee in submitting their report are not thereby discharged, and I understand it to be the duty of any member to move the reference of any proposition which he may see fit to offer, to the proper Committee. I am certainly taken by surprise in hearing the gentleman from Des Moines (Mr. Hall) say, that the Committee have sent in their report.

Mr. HALL. They have agreed upon the details of their report, although they have not yet sent it in.

Mr. SKIFF. It seems to me, that there will not be a great many more resolutions handed in. The gentleman from Alamakee appears to be very anxious to have his resolution go upon the record. A large number of resolutions fully as lengthy as his have already gone there, and I hope that the same courtesy will be extended to the gentleman in this matter that has been extended to other gentlemen.

The PRESIDENT. The pending question is upon the amendment of the gentleman from Jefferson, (Mr. Wilson) that the resolution should not go upon the Journal.

Mr. WILSON. I withdraw my amendment.

The question then recurring on the adoption of the resolution, it was agreed to, and the resolution was accordingly referred to the Committee on the Judicial Department.

Mr. GRAY offered the following resolutions:

1. *Resolved,* That when this Convention adjourn for the day, it will adjourn to meet during the remainder of the session in the Senate Chamber of this Capitol.

2. *Resolved,* That when the Convention remove from this room to the Senate Chamber, each member shall be assigned the seat and desk occupied by the Senator from his respective district unless an exchange may be made by agreement with another member.

Mr. GOWER. I have just been to the Senate Chamber and I find that a great unmber of our members have selected their seats. I do not see any reason why we should be controlled in the selection of our seats by the choice which our predecessors in the Senate have made. I am perfectly willing to have the seats assigned by lot, or in any other way gentlemen may choose to designate, but I do not care to be governed by the selection of somebody else.

Mr. WILSON. I hope the resolution will be passed. I know that several members were in the Senate Chamber last evening and talked over this matter of selecting their seats and putting their names upon them, but when it was suggested that a resolution of this character would be introduced, they took no farther action. I think the proposition suggested as equitable an one as could be adopted by this body, and by proceeding in this manner it will save time. The members who have selected their seats certainly have an advantage, which they would not have had, if the gentlemen who were in the Senate Chamber last evening had chosen their seats then.

Mr HARRIS. I am opposed to the resolution for the simple reason that I do not see why we should be bound by the choice which Senators have seen fit to make. If we are to have any rule about it, I would rather prefer numbering the seats and choosing them by lot. That is the course pursued by the House of Representatives of the United States. I would move, therefore, to amend the 2d resolution by striking out the words "the seat and desk occupied by the Senator from his respective district unless" and insert in lieu thereof the words "his seat by lot and that"

Mr. HALL. I think that the gentlemen who have anticipated this thing and selected their seats should give us all a fair chance. I will be perfectly satisfied as far as I am concerned, with the choice of the seat which the Senator from my district has made.

Mr. PETERS. I hope the plan of drawing the seats by lot will not take precedence of any other from the fact that if we take the seats of our predecessors in the Senate, I shall be thrown into the President's Chair, and I do not much care about occupying that position.—(Laughter.)

The question was then taken on the amendment of Mr. Harris, and it was agreed to, upon division. Ayes 16, noes 15.

The question then recurred on the adoption of the resolution as amended, which was read as follows:

"2. *Resolved*, That when the Convention remove from this room to the Senate Chamber, each member shall be assigned his seat by lot, and that an exchange may be made by agreement with another member."

Mr. PALMER. For my own part I prefer the resolution as originally stated. I would be satisfied with the proposition, that we occupy the seats chosen by the Senators of our respective districts.

Mr. EMERSON. I hope the resolution will pass in its present form. I think that these gentlemen who have been examining the seats of their predecessors in the Senate, and find that they occupied good ones, and, as a consequence, must suit them, should allow us all to have a fair chance in the distribution of these seats.

The question was taken, and the resolution as amended was agreed to.

Mr. SKIFF moved that the members now proceed to draw for their seats in the Senate Chamber by lot.

Mr. HARRIS moved to amend by allowing the Chair to determine in what manner they shall be drawn.

The PRESIDENT. The Chair is of the opinion that the seats could be better selected in the Senate Chamber than here.

Mr. TODHUNTER. I think that we had better do it here. As the majority have forced upon us this principle of gambling, we will try and play the game out as well as we can.

Mr. WARREN. I would suggest that the person drawing the first number shall have the first choice.

Mr. HARRIS. I think the better way to decide this matter will be to place the names of the members in a box, assign some person to draw them, and let members select their seats as their names are called. I will withdraw the motion I made a moment since.

Mr. CLARKE, of Johnson. I move that Messrs. Todhunter and Harris be appointed a committee to proceed to the Senate Chamber and number the seats, and the numbers can be placed in a box here, and the members can then proceed to draw.

The PRESIDENT. Will the gentleman from Johnson (Mr. Clarke) reduce his motion to writing?

Mr. CLARKE, of Johnson. I will do so, and offer it as soon as I have written it.

Mr. CLARKE, of Henry. With the permission of the gentleman from Johnson (Mr. Clarke) I offer the following resolution as a substitute.

"*Resolved*, That the Secretary prepare thirty-five slips of paper, numbered from one to thirty-five inclusive, and that members draw, and have choice of seats according to their numbers—number one having first choice, &c.

The question was taken, and was not agreed to upon division. Ayes 10—noes not counted.

Mr. CLARKE, of Johnson, then moved to amend the motion of the gentleman from Jasper, (Mr. Skiff) by adding thereto the following:

"And that Messrs. Todhunter and Harris be a committee to number the seats in the Senate Chamber, and that each member be entitled to the seat, the number of which he may draw."

The resolution as amended was then agreed to.

The committee appointed under the resolution then repaired to the Senate chamber to discharge the duty assigned them.

Mr. PALMER offered the following resolution:

Resolved, that the Committee on the Judiciary be requested to inquire into the expediency of incorporating into the article on the judiciary Department a provision abolishing all distinction between chancery and common law practice.

I do not care about its adoption, but desire its reference to the committee: I only desire to get the suggestion before the committee.

Mr. HALL. The suggestion has already been before the committee, and they have drawn up their report.

Mr. PALMER. I will withdraw the resolution, then.

Mr. PARVIN, from the committee on the Distribution of Powers and the Legislative Department, made the following report, which,

On motion of Mr. WILSON was laid on the table, and one hundred copies ordered to be printed for the use of the Convention:

1. The legislative authority of this State shall be vested in a Senate and House of Representatives, which shall be designated the General Assembly of the State of Iowa; and the style of their laws shall commence in the following manner: "Be it enacted by the General Assembly of the State of Iowa."

2. The sessions of the General Assembly shall be biennial, and shall commence on the second Monday of January next ensuing the election of its members; unless the Governor of the State shall, in the interim, convene the General Assembly by proclamation.

3. The members of the House of Representatives shall be chosen every second year, by the qualified electors of their respective districts, on the second Tuesday in October, except the years of the Presidential election, when the election shall be on the Tuesday next after the first Monday in November; whose term of office shall continue two years from the Tuesday next after the first Monday in November.

4. No person shall be a member of the House of Representatives who shall not have attained the age of twenty-one years; be a free white male citizen of the United States, and have been an inhabitant of this State one year next preceding his election; and at the time of his election have an actual residence of thirty days in the county or district he may be chosen to represent.

5. Senators shall be chosen for the term of four years, at the same time and place as representatives; they shall be twenty-five years of age, and possess the qualifications of Representatives as to residence and citizenship.

6. The number of Senators shall not be less than one-third, nor more than one-half the Representative body. The present Senators shall remain in office during the term for which they were elected, and shall be divided into two classes. Those Senators whose term of office expires on the first Monday in August, 1858, shall be one class, and those Senators whose term of office expires on the first Monday in August, 1860, shall be the other class; so that one-half shall be chosen every two years.

7. When the number of Senators is increased, they shall be annexed by lot to one of the two classes, so as to keep them as nearly equal in number as practicable.

8. Each house shall choose its own officers, and judge of the qualification, election and return of its own members. A contested election shall be determined in such manner as shall be directed by law.

9. A majority of each house shall constitute a quorum to do business; but a smaller number may adjourn from day to day, and may compel the attendance of absent members in such manner and under such penalties as each house may provide.

10. Each house shall sit upon its own adjournments, keep a journal of its proceedings, and publish the same; determine its rules of proceedings, punish members for disorderly behavior, and, with the consent of two-thirds expel a member, but not a second time for the same offence; and shall have all other powers necessary for a branch of the General Assembly of a free and independent State.

11. Every member of the General Assembly shall have the liberty to dissent from, or protest against any act or resolution which he may think injurious to the public or an individual, and have the reasons for his dissent entered on the journals; and the yeas and nays of the members of either house, on any question, shall, at the desire of any two members present, be entered on the journals.

12. Senators and Representatives, in all cases, except treason, felony or breach of the peace, shall be privileged from arrest during the session of the General Assembly, and in going to and returning from the same.

13. When vacancies occur in either house, the Governor, or the person exercising the functions of Governor, shall issue writs of election to fill such vacancies.

14. The doors of each house shall be open, except on such occasions as, in the opinion of the house, may require secrecy.

15. Neither house shall, without the consent of the other, adjourn for more than three days, nor to any other place than that in which they may be sitting.

16. Bills may originate in either house, and may be amended, altered or rejected by the other; and every bill having passed both houses, shall be signed by the Speaker and President of their respective houses.

17. Every bill which shall have passed the General Assembly, shall, before it becomes a law, be presented to the Governor. If he approve, he shall sign it; but if not, he shall return it, with his objections to the house in which it originated, which shall enter the same upon the journal and proceed to reconsider it; if, after such reconsideration, it again pass both houses, by yeas and nays, by a majority of two-thirds of the members of each house present, it it shall become a law, notwithstanding the Governor's objections. If any bill shall not be returned within three days after it shall have been presented to him (Sundays excepted) the same shall be a law in like manner as if he had signed it, unless the General Assembly by adjournment prevent such return.

18. No bill shall be passed unless by the assent of a majority of all the members elected to each branch of the General Assembly, and the question upon the final passage shall be taken immediately upon its last reading, and the yeas and nays entered on the journal.

19. An accurate statement of the receipts and expenditures of the public money shall be attached to and published with the laws at every regular session of the General Assembly.

20. The House of Representatives shall have the sole power of impeachment, and all impeachments shall be tried by the Senate. When sitting for that purpose the Senators shall be upon oath or affirmation; and no person shall be convicted without the concurrence of two-thirds of the members present.

21. The Governor, Secretary of State, Auditor, Treasurer, Judges of the Supreme and District Courts, Superintendent of Public Instruction, and Attorney General, shall be liable to impeachment for any misdemeanor in office; but judgment in such cases shall extend only to removal from office and disqualification to hold any office of honor, trust or profit, under this State; but the party convicted or acquitted shall nevertheless be liable to indictment, trial and punishment, according to law. All other civil officers shall be tried for misdemeanors in office

in such manner as the General Assembly may provide.

22. No Senator or Representative shall, during the time for which he shall have been elected, be appointed to any civil office of profit under this State, which shall have been created, or the emoluments of which shall have been increased during such term, except such offices as may be filled by elections by the people.

23. No person holding any lucrative office under the United States, or this State, or any other power, shall be eligible to the General Assembly: *Provided*, that offices in the militia, to which there is attached no annual salary, or the office of justice of the peace, or postmasters whose compensation does not exceed one hundred dollars per annum, or notary public, shall not be deemed lucrative.

24. No person who may hereafter be a collector or holder of public moneys, shall have a seat in either House of the General Assembly, or be eligible to any office of trust or profit under this State until he shall have accounted for and paid into the treasury all sums for which he may be liable.

25. No money shall be drawn from the treasury but in consequence of appropriations made by law.

26. Each member of the General Assembly shall receive a compensation to be fixed by law, for his services, to be paid out of the treasury of the State. Such compensation shall not exceed three dollars per day for the period of sixty days from the commencement of the session, and shall not exceed the sum of two dollars per day for the remainder of the session; when convened in extra session by the Governor, they shall receive such sums per diem as shall be fixed for the first sixty days of the ordinary session. They shall also receive three dollars for every twenty miles they travel, in going to and returning from their place of meeting, on the nearest traveled route.

27. No law of the General Assembly, of a public nature, shall take effect until the fourth day of July next after the passage thereof. If the General Assembly shall deem any law of immediate importance, they may provide that the same shall take effect by publication in newspapers in the State.

28. No divorce shall be granted by the General Assembly.

29. No lottery shall be authorized by this State; nor shall the sale of lottery tickets be allowed.

30. Every act shall embrace but one subject, and matters connected therewith; which subject shall be expressed in the title. But if any subject shall be embraced in an act which shall not be expressed in the title, such act shall be void only as to so much thereof as shall not be expressed in the title.

31. The General Assembly shall not pass local or special laws in the following cases:

For the assessment and collection of taxes for State, county, or road purposes;

For laying out, opening, and working on roads or highways;

For changing the names of persons;

For the incorporation of cities or towns;

For vacating roads, town plats, streets, alleys, or public squares;

In all the cases above enumerated, and in all other cases where a general law can be made applicable, all laws shall be general, and of uniform operation throughout the State.

32. No extra compensation shall be made to any officer, public agent, or contractor, after the service shall have been rendered, or the contract entered into; nor, shall any money be paid on any claim the subject matter of which shall not have been provided for by pre-existing laws, and no public money or property shall be appropriated for local, or private purposes, unless such appropriation, compensation, or claim, be allowed by two-thirds of the members elected to each branch of the General Assembly.

33. Members of the General Assembly shall, before they enter upon the duties of their respective offices, take and subscribe the following oath or affirmation: "I do solemnly swear, or affirm, (as the case may be) that I will support the Constitution of the United States, and the Constitution of the State of Iowa, and that I will faithfully discharge the duties of Senator, (or Representative as the case may be,) according to the best of my ability." And members of the General Assembly are hereby empowered to administer to each other the said oath or affirmation.

34. The General Assembly shall in the years 1856, 1862,1864,1866,1868, and 1875, and every ten years thereafter, cause an enumeration to be made of all the white inhabitants of the State.

35. The number of Senators and Representatives shall, at the next session following each period of making such enumeration, and the next session following each United States census, be fixed by law, and apportioned among the several counties, according to the number of white inhabitants in each.

36. The Senate shall not consist of more than fifty members, nor the House of Representatives of more than one hundred.

37. When a Congressional, Senatorial, or Representative District shall be composed of two or more counties, it shall not be entirely separated by any county belonging to another district; and no county shall be divided in forming a Congressional, Senatorial, or Representative District.

38. In all elections by the General Assembly the members thereof shall vote viva voce; and the votes shall be entered on the journal.

39. The annual salary of the Governor shall not exceed twenty-five hundred dollars; Secretary, Treasurer and Auditor of State, fifteen hundred dollars each; Judges of the Supreme Court, twenty-five hundred dollars each; Judges of the District Courts, two thousand dollars each.

Respectfully submitted,
J. A. PARVIN, *Chairman.*

Mr. WARREN called up the resolution offered by the gentleman from Henry, [Mr. Clarke,] yesterday.

The resolution was then read as follows:

Resolved, That the Secretary be not required to enter the whole of any resolution, report, memorial or petition upon the Journal, but may enter the same by synopsis.

That he be required, also, to furnish a synopsis of such voluminous reports, resolutions, memorials and petitions as have already been entered upon the Journals, to be printed in their stead, unless otherwise directed by a vote of this Convention in particular cases.

Mr. CLARKE, of Johnson. I gave my views briefly upon this question yesterday, when the resolution of the gentleman from Alamakee, [Mr. Clark,] was under consideration. The passage of such a resolution as the one now introduced would place it in the power of the Secretary of this body to make up such a journal as his own judgment dictated. If we are to keep a journal, it should be a full and complete record of what is done here. We should not leave it to the Clerk to say what has been done here, because members would be in danger of being misquoted; and there would be constant corrections made. I think that the adoption of the resolution of the gentleman from Henry, [Mr. Clarke,] would occasion more delay in our proceedings, than putting all these resolutions upon the Journal.

Mr EMERSON. I think the resolution offered by the gentleman from Henry, embraces too wide a range, and will not work well in practice. It is unusual in any deliberative body to pursue the course recommended in that resolution. I thought when the resolution was first introduced, that it referred merely to resolutions of enquiry, but as I find that it embraces a wider scope, I shall certainly oppose its adoption.

Mr. CLARKE, of Henry. I hope members will understand the resolution before they vote upon it. If it be adopted, any member if he desires it can appeal to the Convention to have his resolution or memorial spread upon the journal, and if a majority of the members are willing, they can vote to spread it at length upon the journal. If there be no such request, then the Clerk proceeds to make a synopsis of the paper, instead of placing it in full upon the journal. I think that these gentlemen who were so anxious to save expense, as they proclaimed themselves to be, when we wished to print the proceedings of this Convention in such a way that the people of this State might have them *verbatim et literatim*, should have the same principles in view now, and not encumber our journal with proceedings which one person in a thousand will never read, and relieve also the clerk of the labor which we are forcing upon him. As for myself, I have offered a number of resolutions, and I have always had some object in view in so doing. I say with the gentleman from Jefferson [Mr. Wilson,] I intend to stand by the principles of all the resolutions I have offered, and move them again in the Convention. They have been thrown out as mere suggestions to committees, and I do not care about their being spread upon the journal. I am willing that the Secretary shall give a synopsis of the resolutions that I offer for reference. The object I have in introducing them is not to spread them upon the journal, and I do not wish to make up a record for the future. If that be the object which gentlemen have in view in introducing their resolutions, then I am opposed entirely to spreading them at large upon the journal. I cannot conceive how gentlemen can be so anxious to have their resolutions go upon the journal, unless they have some object in view hereafter. Our work and our votes will be enough to go to the people, and I am entirely opposed to encumbering our journal day after day by spreading upon it these resolutions at length. That was the reason which induced me to offer the resolution now before the Convention. If I or any other member offer a resolution which gentlemen may wish to place upon the record, let them vote to put it upon the journal.

Mr. EDWARDS. The law requires that the Secretary keep a full and accurate record of our proceedings here, and that a copy of the journal be filed in the office of the Secretary of State. Aside from that consideration, if the resolution of the gentleman from Henry (Mr. Clarke) prevails, it will cause the members of this Convention more trouble and more difficulty than to pursue the course we are now doing. If it should be left in the power of the Secretary to make just such a synopsis of our proceedings here as he sees fit to make, I am satisfied that gentlemen will soon come in and say that they are not correctly presented upon the journal; and every day motions will be made to correct it. I hope the resolution of the gentleman from Henry will not prevail, and move its indefinite postponement.

Mr. HALL. I ask the gentleman to withdraw his motion for a moment, in order that I may offer an amendment to the resolution.

Mr. EDWARDS. I will withdraw then my motion for the present.

Mr. HALL. I would offer the following as a substitute for the proposition of the gentleman from Henry (Mr. Clarke)

Resolved, That resolutions offered merely for reference to Standing Committees shall not be entered at large upon the journal unless special instructions be given by the Convention to that effect.

Mr. WARREN. I now renew my motion to indefinitely postpone the whole matter.

The yeas and nays were ordered. The question was then taken and the motion was agreed to, yeas 21, nays 10, as follows:

Yeas—The President, Messrs. Ayres, Bunker, Clark of Alamakee, Clarke of Johnson, Clarke of Henry, Day, Edwards, Ells, Emerson, Gibson, Gower, Gray, Marvin, Parvin, Scott, Seely, Skiff, Traer, Wilson and Young.

Nays—Messrs. Cotton, Gillaspy, Johnston, Hall, Palmer, Patterson, Peters, Robinson, Solomon and Warren.

Mr. HALL. I wish to call up the resolution introduced by me two or three day's since, cutting off the introduction of resolutions. I think if we adopt such a rule, that we will greatly facilitate our business. The journal up to this time, I think, will make as large a volume as that of both the other conventions.

The resolution was then read as follows:

Resolved, That after this day resolutions shall not be offered for the purpose of reference to the Standing Committees, instructing them to inquire as to the propriety of adopting indicated propositions.

Mr. TRAER. I think it is unnecessary for us to adopt any such resolution, and I move that it be indefinitely postponed. We have decided this matter several times.

Mr. HALL. I do not know that this proposition has been offered or acted upon before. We have endeavored to cut off the printing of these resolutions, and to keep them off the journal. I now wish to cut off their being presented at all. The committees have mostly acted upon the subjects referred to them, and they have reported, or instructed their Chairman how to report. This is the case with the committee of which I am a member, and I presume it is the case with most of the committees. These resolutions, therefore, become unnecessary as these reports come in, and gentlemen who have propositions which they wish to present before members, can offer them in Convention by way of amendment. It appears to me that we ought to cut off their presentation now. Gentlemen have had two weeks time in which to offer them; and I think when we leave this room to-day, and go to the Senate Chamber, that we had better be prepared for some other kind of business.

Mr. EMERSON. I hope the resolution will prevail. I have considered the course we have been pursuing from the beginning as being unnecessary, and greatly encumbering our proceedings. I apprehend that the Standing Committees appointed by the Convention will readily consider any proposition that any member may hand in to them. It it is usual where a member desires to introduce a subject before a committee, for him to go before them and present his proposition. Committees generally dasire members to pursue that course. I have no doubt, if we had pursued that course from the beginning, that we should have proceeded in our business just as well; and committees would have paid just as much respect to the wishes of each member as they have done by the course we have pursued of referring all these resolutions to them. It seems to me, if any gentleman has a proposition which he desires either of the Standing Committees to consider, he has nothing to do but embody his proposition in writing, and request the committee to consider it; and I think I can safely say, that each of the Standing Committees of this body will give to any proposition, submitted to them in this way, the consideration it deserves. This course certainly would cut off the unnecessary encumbering of our journal with this matter. I hope that the resolution will prevail.

Mr. JOHNSTON. Is there any necessity for the double motion made in this case? I do not see the necessity of the motion made by my friend from Benton, (Mr. Traer) to indefinitely postpone this matter. It would save time to vote upon the resolution at once, because if the motion to indefinitely postpone be not carried, we shall then have to take another vote. I trust that we shall not have so many calls for the yeas and nays.

Mr. HARRIS. I desire to get rid of this whole matter. We have had the same resolutions, in not exactly the same language, it is true, but involving the same principle offered here, for two or three days, and I am anxious to put an end to this matter, one way or the other.

The yeas and nays were ordered.

The question was then taken, and the motion to indefinitely postpone was not agreed to. Yeas 9, nays 26, as follows:

Yeas.—Messrs. Bunker, Clarke, of Johnson, Clark, of Alamakee, Edwards, Gower, Harris, Johnston, Wilson and Traer.

Nays.—The President, Messrs. Ayres, Clarke, of Henry, Cotton, Day, Ells, Emerson, Gibson, Gillaspy, Gray, Hall, Marvin, Palmer, Parvin, Patterson, Peters, Price, Robinson, Scott, Seely, Skiff, Solomon, Todhunter, Warren, Winchester and Young.

The question then recurred on the adoption of the resolution.

Mr. CLARKE, of Henry. I voted against the motion made by the gentleman from Benton (Mr. Traer) for indefinite postponement, as I dislike this way of getting rid of a vote directly on the question itself. It is getting to be the practice in this Convention for gentlemen who are not favorable to propositions, to move an indefinite postponement of them, thereby forcing us to two votes. I prefer to meet questions right square in the face. I am decidedly opposed to the proposition made by the gentleman from Des Moines. (Mr. Hall.) I am not in favor of curtailing the rights of members here, and the resolution which I offered here to-day and which has been voted upon was not intended to curtail members of any of their rights, for if it had passed, any member who wished to present a resolution here and did not care about its going on the journal, could have had it left off. But if he desired to have it spread upon the journal at length, all he had to do was so to move, and the Convention as an act of courtesy would have granted the request. I believe it is not only the right but the duty of members to introduce resolutions and make suggestions to committees.

In the performance of my duties upon committees in which I am engaged, I feel myself under great obligations to gentlemen who have introduced resolutions, for the valuable suggestions which they contained. I shall vote against the resolution of the gentleman from Des Moines. (Mr. Hall.)

Mr. WARREN. I hope the resolution will prevail. I should like to know when there will be an end of this matter. Most of the committees have reported and their reports are here lying upon our table. The proper time in my opinion for gentlemen to present their various propositions will be by way of amendment, when the reports of committees come up for consideration there.

Mr. ELLS. I propose the following amendment, to insert between the words "Committees" and "instructing" the words "who have reported."

Mr. HALL accepted the amendment.

Mr. WILSON. I have but a word to say.—It seems to me if we are intending to cut off the right of members to have propositions referred to committees, that they had better be discharged as fast as they report. These committees are all standing committees of this Convention. They have been appointed to hold their places until the close of the sessions of this body, and now if any member desires to have any proposition, I don't care what it is, referred to a committee—and a majority of the members of this Convention when the proposition is introduced will permit it to go there—it is the duty of that committee to take the matter into consideration and report upon it. I believe that every member has a right to have his resolutions referred to the proper committees, and we have no right to enforce any gag law upon him.

Mr. CLARK, of Alamakee. I have but one word to say in addition to what has been said already. I hold that our constituents have a right to direct their representatives here to bring any particular matter before this Convention, either by petition or otherwise; and will this Convention by a resolution of this kind, say to the people, you shall not be heard here? It would be reversing the order of things, and making us the masters of the people, instead of the people being our masters. The very idea of having Standing Committees carries with it everything which needs to be stated on the affirmative of this question. They are to stand during the sittings of the Convention for the purpose of passing upon any subject which may be properly referred to them.

Mr. HALL. I understand that the object of these Committees is to get business presented before the Convention in its proper form for action by the body. They are Standing Committees, it is true, but after they have once reported they are useful only in cases where the Convention having considered the reports submitted to them, send them back with or without instructions, in order that they may give them a further consideration. Is there any very great danger that a member or his constituents may suffer injury, because gentlemen cannot have their resolutions referred to a committee? If a gentleman has any measure which he wishes to bring before the body, he can propose it by way of amendment to the report of the proper committee, when it is submitted. When are you to get business before the Convention if you allow these resolutions to be referred day after day to the committees, when most of them have already submitted, or are ready to submit, their reports? It is a matter of business entirely, and in that view I am opposed to the reference of any more of these resolutions to the committees.

Mr. WARREN. I hold in my hands the report of one of the Standing Committees. The reports of all the committees are to be printed for the use of the Convention, and if gentlemen who examine them have any objection to them they can move to refer them back to the committees, and ask them to make amendments.

Mr. WILSON. It seems to me that the gentleman from Des Moines, [Mr. Hall,] goes a great distance for his arguments. I do not presume that any member of this Convention will introduce a resolution which shall embody the same subject matter as is embodied in the report of a Standing Committee, and ask that the resolution shall be referred to the same committee. The intention of the mover of any of these resolutions is to get something new before the committee, something that is not embodied in their report, and for that reason I say that gentlemen ought to have the right to send their resolutions to these committees.

The question was then taken on the resolution as amended, and it was agreed to.

On motion of Mr. JOHNSTON, leave of absence was granted to Mr. Cotton of Clinton.

Mr. HARRIS, from the committee appointed to number the seats in the Senate Chamber, reported that they had discharged the duty assigned them.

On motion of Mr. SKIFF,

The Convention then proceeded to select their seats in the Senate Chamber, the Secretary placing numbers from one to thirty-five in a box and each member upon his name being called advancing and drawing therefrom the number of the seat to which he was entitled.

On motion of Mr. CLARKE of Johnson,

The Convention then adjourned till to-morrow at 10 o'clock A. M.

FRIDAY, January 30, 1857.

The Convention met at 10 o'clock, A. M. in the Senate Chamber, and was called to order by the President.

Prayer by the Chaplain, Rev. Mr. Kynett.

The Journal of yesterday was read and approved.

Amendment of the Rules.

Mr. CLARKE, of Johnson, gave notice that on to-morrow, or some subsequent day, he would ask leave to introduce the following amendment to the rules:

That all reports of the Standing Committees shall be read three times on as many different days, unless the rule be suspended by unanimous consent; and no report shall be read a third time and finally passed until all the reports of the Committees shall have passed a second reading.

Location of the Seat of Government, &c.

Mr. GOWER offered the following resolution:

Resolved, That the Committee on Miscellaneous subjects be instructed to enquire into the expediency of providing for the permanent location of the Seat of Government, the State University and the Deaf and Dumb, and the Blind Asylums.

Agreed to and referred accordingly.

Preamble and Bill of Rights.

On motion of Mr. EDWARDS, the Convention took from the table the report of the Committee on the Preamble and the Bill of Rights, and the same was made the special order for this afternoon, at 2 o'clock.

Reports of the Supreme Court.

Mr. PALMER offered the following resolution:

Resolved, That the Secretary of State be requested to furnish each member of this Convention with a copy of the reports of the Supreme Court of this State.

Mr. GOWER. I would like to ascertain if these reports are at all necessary to us in the discharge of our duties here? I would be happy to hear from some gentleman who is familiar with the contents of these reports, and can inform us of the importance of these works to the members of this body.

Mr. HALL. I hope this resolution will pass. I am sure if any member will examine the Constitutional questions which have already been decided in this State and inform themselves upon those subjects, they will reap more benefit from this work, than from almost any other we might obtain. We have had a great many judicial decisions under our present Constitution, and it is important that members should know what those decisions have been. There is no book which will prove so profitable to us in that respect, as these reports will prove.

Mr. GOWER. I have such confidence in the opinion of the gentleman from Des Moines (Mr. Hall), and as he thinks this work will be important to us and will aid us in the discharge of our duties, I shall not oppose the resolution.

Mr. EMERSON. I would be pleased to have this resolution amended, by adding a proviso thereto, also the recent decision of the Supreme Court in regard to city and county indebtedness.

Mr. HALL That decision, I believe, has not yet been printed.

Mr. EMERSON. Then I would have it printed for the use of this Convention.

Mr. WILSON. I understand that that opinion has been printed. If so, I will vote for the amendment; otherwise not.

Mr. EMERSON. I am not aware whether that opinion has been printed or not. But I would like to have it for the use of this Convention, whether it has been printed yet or not.

Mr. YOUNG. Does this resolution embrace all the volumes of our Supreme Court decisions or only one particular volume?

The PRESIDENT. The resolution says, "a copy of the reports," and in the opinion of the chair, embraces all the volumes.

Mr. HARRIS. I would enquire if there will be enough of these books to go all round, if we vote for them? We have ordered some other books of considerable importance and they fell short, and some of us did not get any.

Mr. EDWARDS. I would move to amend this resolution by inserting before the words "reports of the Supreme Court," the word "Clarke's", so that it will read "Clarke's Reports of the Supreme Court."

Mr. CLARKE, of Johnson. I will state for the information of the gentleman from Appanoose (Mr. Harris) that the State has taken 200 copies of the first volume of Clarke's Reports, and they have been delivered to the State. And an act has been passed by the last Legislature to take 200 more copies, and as soon as that act shall go into effect and be in force, there will be copies enough to supply the Convention. The second volume I expect to have here between the first and the tenth of next month, as the proof was read and the index prepared before I left New York City, some weeks ago.

Mr. PALMER. I understand that the State is possessed of some 400 copies of these reports, and that one branch of the Legislature, at its recent session, voted that each member should be supplied with a copy of the Iowa Reports. And they voted these reports to themselves when their session was about to close. I think that the reason and necessity for our having these reports is much greater when we are just at the commencement of our session, or rather at that stage of our proceedings when they will prove to be of some benefit to us. And I suppose it will be necessary that we should be supplied with these reports as soon as possible, as they will be of vast value to us in the business we are called upon to carry out. We wish to know all the decisions of the Supreme Court on those subjects that may have arisen under the present Constitution with regard to its construction. And it was with that view alone that I offered this resolution.

Mr. HALL. The object of the amendment as I understand it is to restrict us to Clarke's Reports. Now I do not know why we should call for the reports of those two years alone. The earlier reports, as every gentleman of the Bar knows who has examined the subject, contain the first and most important decisions arising under the Constitution. Those reports begin with the operation of the Constitution which we are now met here to revise and amend. And I would prefer to have those earlier reports—although I have them in my library at home—I want them here in order to obtain that kind of information, which, if we are furnished these reports will be read by gentlemen here and be of vast use to them. I hope, therefore, if we are to have these reports at all, we will be allowed them as far as they are published. There are two or three decisions made by the Supreme Court recently, which, to my certain knowledge have not been published and will not be published in the second volume, the Iowa Reports that are now being published. And I shall vote on the proper occasion to have those decisions published for the benefit of members here. One of them is in regard to the Mississippi river; and another in regard to Railroads, and both of them, I think, have an important bearing upon the interests of this State. I would like to see them published. As it is now, if we desire to examine them, we would be obliged to hunt over the manuscript and read them in hard writing, and perhaps find it very difficult to comprehend them.

Mr. CLARKE, of Johnson. The second volume of the Iowa Reports will contain decisions under the liquor law, involving a constitutional question, and also the railroad decisions, to which the gentleman from Des Moines (Mr. Hall) refers. The third volume will contain the decisions in the Mississippi case, but it will not be here in time for the use of this Convention. As to taking the prior reports, I have this suggestion to make: it may be possible that they are not in possession of the State. If the State has Greene's Reports and Morris's Reports, I have no objection to voting for them. But it would be well, perhaps, to ascertain if the State can supply us these reports, before we pass the resolution ordering them.

Mr. HARRIS. I suppose that if the State has not these reports already, it will not of course be forced to get for our use what it has not got.

Mr. PALMER moved to amend the amendment of Mr. Edwards by inserting after the word "Clarke's" the words "and Greene's."

The question being taken upon the amendment to the amendment, it was not agreed to.

The question recurred upon the motion to insert before the word "Reports," the word "Clarke's."

Mr. TODHUNTER. If that amendment is adopted, I shall certainly feel under the necessity of voting against the whole resolution. As has already been stated by the gentleman from Des Moines (Mr. Hall), the most important matter is not to be found in Clarke's Reports, and they would be of no advantage whatever to us. But the earlier decisions of the Supreme Court are certainly important to us in our labors here, and I should like to have them. I cannot vote for this resolution if the amendment is insisted upon and adopted, cutting off the only reports that will be of use to us.

Mr. EDWARDS. In reply to the gentleman from Warren (Mr. Todhunter) all I have to say is this: I presume nearly every lawyer already has Greene's Reports in his library, and is conversant with their contents. I do not, therefore, see the necessity of this Convention going to the expense of procuring additional reports, which every lawyer is presumed to have, and at least ought to have and be conversant with already. I think that all that it is necessary for us to obtain are the reports recently published.

Mr. HALL. I am not conversant with those reports, for one; and I never yet gave an opinion to a client in my life, when I could get hold of those reports, without examining them and learning what principles they contained bearing upon the case in hand. Other gentlemen may have a more tenacious memory and a more reliable judgment than I have. I always want the book before me in order that I may assure myself that nothing at least has escaped my recollection in regard to the principles presented in the case I am examining; and I think every gentleman will profit, or certainly have more confidence in his judgment and opinion, when he sees it before him.

Now, upon the subject of the importance of our having all the decisions of our courts under our present constitution: I think every gentleman will, upon reflection agree with me, that we should have them before us. This question of expense is a mere matter of moonshine compared with the benefit to be obtained, and I would ask the gentleman from Lucas (Mr. Edwards) if he can name a solitary decision reported in the last volume of those reports which has been printed, which embraces a constitutional question? Can he do it in regard to either of the volumes to be published?

The gentleman from Johnson (Mr. Clarke) is mistaken in regard to the publication of the railroad cases. The cases I refer to have not yet been published. I know that one or two decisions were made at the last term of the Supreme Court in regard to railroad bonds in the county of Lee that have not been published, and will not be during the session of this Convention unless by our order. I wish, and must, before these questions come before us for our action, examine those decisions and see upon what grounds our present law stands.

Mr. CLARKE, of Johnson. I did not refer to the recent decisions, but to the railroad case involving the constitutional construction of what is called just and equitable compensation for property taken for public uses. I refer to the decision of a previous term in the Dubuque Railroad case.

Mr. CLARKE, of Henry. I would state to the gentleman from Lucas, (Mr. Edwards) that the whole object of obtaining these reports, is to provide members of the Convention with the decisions of our courts, that we may look at them and see if there has been any conflict of law that we can provide against; to see if there has been any interpretation given by the Supreme Court that has worked unjustly or unevenly in any way, in order that we may provide in our Constitution against any unequal action of these laws. We know that conflict of laws exists in our State, and we desire to obtain the necessary information to enable us to remove the difficulty. The whole object of this resolution would be lost if this amendment is adopted. Let us have the whole of these reports, so that we can have all the decisions of the Supreme Court to enlighten us, or let us not have any. I hope the amendment will not prevail, but that the original resolution will be adopted.

Mr. GILLASPY. I am opposed to this whole matter. I am not a lawyer myself, and these reports will be of no benefit to me when I get them, unless I take them home with me, and sell them to some of our lawyers, which I have no desire to do. I was not sent here by my constituents to provide myself with these reports. And if the State of Iowa has two hundred copies of these reports to-day, then, certainly, every gentleman here can obtain them, examine them thoroughly, and return them to the State.

Mr. WINCHESTER. I am decidedly opposed to this Convention breaking up our State library. We have already voted ourselves a copy of the code, the acts passed by the last session of '55-'6, and of the Constitutions of the States. And for some of these books we had to send to Chicago, and was there only able to obtain twenty copies, not enough to supply us here, thus breaking up the assortment in the city of Chicago. We have voted ourselves several other incidentals, and I am not in favor of our adopting this resolution also. As the gentleman from Lucas (Mr. Edwards) has said, I suppose every lawyer of practice in this State, has already obtained and read Greene's Reports, and those who have not, can buy them. And those members of this Convention who are lawyers, and want those reports, have the same privilege with regard to Clarke's Reports, they can buy them for five dollars. I am opposed to our making any more appropriations to members individually, and I therefore move to lay this whole subject upon the table.

Mr. HALL called for the yeas and nays, and they were ordered accordingly.

Mr. CLARKE, of Johnson, upon his name being called, said: I desire to say, in explanation, that if this was a resolution purchasing reports from me, I should decline voting. And even though they are to be taken from the State, I do not feel at liberty to vote for them, and shall therefore vote for the motion to lay the whole subject upon the table.

The question being taken by yeas and nays, upon the motion to lay the whole subject upon the table, it was not agreed to—yeas 17, nays 19, as follows:

Yeas.—The President, Messrs. Ayers, Bunker, Clarke, of Johnson, Day, Gillaspy, Hollingsworth, Johnston, Parvin, Patterson, Seely, Skiff, Traer, Warren, Wilson, Winchester and Young.

Nays.—Messrs Clark, of Alamakee, Clarke, of Henry, Edwards, Ells, Emerson, Gibson, Gower, Gray, Hall, Harris, Marvin, Palmer, Peters, Robinson, Scott, Solomon and Todhunter.

The question was then taken upon the motion to amend, by inserting the word "Clarke's" before the word "Reports," and it was not agreed to upon a division, as follows; Ayes 3, noes not counted.

The question then recurred upon the adoption of the resolution.

Mr. SCOTT. I hope this resolution will be adopted. As I understand it these reports are now the property of the State, purchased expressly for the use of the State, and in my opinion they cannot be better appropriated than to the members of this Convention. We will probably need them more than any body of men who may follow us, and who will undoubtedly take them. If we appropriate them to ourselves as members of this Convention, they will be of practical utility to us, which they will not be to those who will come after us. I hope the resolution will be adopted, as I understand there will be no additional expense falling upon the State; and it is not assuming too much for us to assume that we have the right to take of the State the proper tools and implements to enable us to conduct properly our labors in this Convention.

Mr. YOUNG. The argument in support of this resolution seems to be that the State owns a large number of these reports, and we are entitled therefore to appropriate them to our own use. That argument I think is deserving of no consideration at all; has no weight, no foundation. The State owns a great deal of other property, and with the same propriety we can get up here and say, that because the State owns that property, it is therefore proper for us to appropriate it to our own use. We are asked to go on and appropriate six or seven volumes of these reports of the decisions of the Supreme Court, a thing that perhaps would be entirely useless to a great proportion of the members here from the fact that the very things we want to learn from them may not be in them. I understand that one volume of these reports has never been published, and that volume we cannot possibly get. And I also understand that two volumes of Clarke's Reports have not yet been published, and those volumes we cannot of course get at this time. I would be in favor of voting for anything that would aid the members of this Convention in their labors, but I am decidedly opposed to voting for anything to be sent to us hereafter when we have gone home.

I think this principle is altogether wrong and that it will become liable to censure, by carrying the principle out. And I think we will be setting a very bad example for those who may come after us, and which they will be likely to follow up. Now if gentlemen want to examine these decisions of the Supreme Court, they can get access to them in the State Library, and need not vote then directly for their benefit. Now for my part I would not give two cents for these reports after I get home, for I am not a lawyer, and they would be of no use to me. I am like my friend from Wapello, [Mr. Gillaspy,] in that respect. I do not think we would be doing justice to the State to appropriate these reports, merely because they happen to be the property of the State, to our own individual use. We might just as well appropriate any other property belonging to the State. If anything was to be gained by it for certain, then it would be another thing. But two of these volumes cannot be obtained until after we adjourn, and several of the others may not be obtained at all.

Mr. HALL. These reports are to be used for the benefit of the State in enabling us to perfect ourselves in that information that we need here to conduct our labors properly, and which is contained only in these volumes. And I wish gentlemen to recollect that at the time this Convention assembled, it was larceny for any member to take a book out of the State Library. A resolution was passed by the General Assembly before they adjourned, giving us the same privilege of using the library that they themselves possessed, but whether that resolution has gone into effect or not I cannot tell. Now I do not wish to take books of that kind out of the library for a length of time, the privilege given by the law being very limited, and running the hazard of the penalty myself. If I can get rid of that responsibility I desire to do so. It is no argument against this resolution that we can go to the library and get a book, or that all that will hereafter be published are not now published. Let us have the benefit of the information we can get now; let us use the means that lie before us. If gentlemen do not wish to take these books from the State, they can return them at the end of the session. I have no objection to that being done. But let us have these books now, that we may not run the risk of incurring the penalty of larceny by taking them from the State Library

Mr. CLARK, of Alamakee. Upon reflection I am in favor of this resolution. I am satisfied that the Convention needs these reports and various arguments are presented here against the resolution by members. They say they are not lawyers and therefore the books would be of no use to them. Now, that in my opinion is an argument in favor of the resolution. We are sent here by our constituents to prepare a Constitution which is to be the foundation of all law that is to be enforced in this State; and of all bodies of men that can be congregated in this State for any purpose whatever, this Convention should be the best posted in the laws of the State, and if any members here are not lawyers there is so much the more need, in my opinion, for their having these reports, that they may make themselves acquainted with the principles contained in these reports. Therefore, I am in favor of this resolution, and as has been suggested by the gent. from Des Moines (Mr. Hall) if any member who receives these reports should have any conscientious scruples about carrying them home with him, he can leave them here in the State Library when the Convention adjourns.

There is another reason why I am in favor of this resolution. I might be opposed to it if it was going to require the State to expend money to purchase these reports. But as I understand, the State is now in possession of them; they are State property, and purchased for the express purpose of being distributed among the men called upon to do the business of the State. And it seems to me that this Convention is a body, if there can be one, that should be provided with all these aids to make us understand the law, the better to fit us for preparing a proper foundation for all laws.

Mr. GILLASPY. I came here for the purpose of representing my constituents in preparing a Constitution, and I know law enough to enable me to represent them here, I think. They do not expect this Constitution to be made wholly by lawyers. Now, if this Convention is disposed to divide up the property of the State among themselves, I am in favor of taking my share of it, but I would prefer to take that share, not in these reports, but in some of the valuable lands this State possesses. She has some in my county which I would prefer to these reports. But I do not hold the opinion that because the State of Iowa has a little property, this Convention should divide it up among its members, and the lawyers ought to be well posted up in the principles of law contained in these reports, and if any of the members of this Convention should have these books, it should be those gentlemen who are not lawyers. But I intend to inform myself about questions that arise here which I do not understand, without voting myself the property of the State in the shape of reports of the decisions of the Supreme Court.

Mr. TRAER. I believe I have uniformly voted against all resolutions appropriating the property of the State for the members of this Convention, and I do hope, that this body will refuse to adopt the resolution under consideration. I think it is a perfect outrage that we should come here and simply because the State happens to have these books, appropriate them to our own use, when in in my opinion there is no advantage to result from our having them. I would refer gentlemen to the fact that there was appropriated to each one of us here a copy of the Code, and I would refer them to the further fact that a great many members of this Convention have disposed of that work and have the money for it in their pockets. And this is the way it will be with these reports. Members will not put them to any use here, but the result will be that we will all get fifteen or twenty dollars in our own pockets. Now, I am opposed to this whole system of plundering the public treasury of the State and appropriating the public property to our own use, and I hope the Convention will adopt a provision in our Constitution against any such thing being done in future. I think the action of the Legislature of this State at its last session was a perfect outrage, and if carried out will result in a system of stealing and plundering the public property that will land all of us who are in favor of it some where below par. I hope this resolution will not be adopted, but that this Convention will set an example of retrenchment in this matter, so that when we go home we may not be charged with stealing.

Mr. HALL. It may be possible that a majority of this Convention, or a large number of them are in favor of a proposition here that amounts to stealing. It may be that I come under that category. I am not yet advised about that matter; I have not yet discovered that rule of law, or of moral ethics that would make that term applicable to myself. Perhaps a different rule prevails in some other parts of this State from what prevails in the portion from whence I came.

Now I understand that these reports were published by the law reporter, and that the State subscribed—I think the gentleman from Johnson (Mr. Clarke) informed us—for four hundred volumes. That is a mode the State has adopted for encouraging and insuring the publication of the reports cf the decisions of the Supreme Court, rather than to make a direct appropriation from the treasury of the State for that purpose. But according to th idea that some gentlemen here seem to entertain of this matter, the State should open a book store for the sale of the volumes for which they have subscribed, and which stand piled up year after year, as we all know was the case with Green's Reports, and did no one any good whatever. Now I think that at proper times and upon proper occasions some method of distributing these books must be adopted. We must place them among the people and inculcate them among the people that they may learn and understand what our laws are. I have no doubt my distinguished friend from Wapello (Mr. Gillaspy) understands all the law that he ever needs to know, and that he feels himself competent to vote upon any question that may arise here, however intricate it may be, and I would be willing that he should have his portion of these books exchanged for lands if he desires, if he is that perfect in what these reports contain. But I must confess that I do not feel myself to be so perfect as that. There are questions that are continually arising in this State as it advances in wealth and population, that require thought and reflection. And I am aware that a system of judicial decisions has commenced, and which will increase with the growth of the State with which I am not perfectly familiar, for the reports of the Supreme Court have been in a measure kept back, and I wish soon to obtain that portion. This is all that I ask and all that this resolution requires.

If we wish to use the means to enable us to get this information, and if that is larceny and stealing, and plundering then I must let myself remain under that charge. But I shall know that it will be that kind of larceny which enriches our intellectual powers and conduces to the good of our constituents by increasing our ability to do good here. I wish to make my mind strong; my perceptions and observations clear. That is what I want, and I care not a feather for h miserable pittance these reports will cost, some ten or twelve dollars.—What I desire is the means of information.—These books were purchased for the purpose of extending that information, and yet they are now molding and rotting upon the shelves in our State House. Why not devote them to the purpose for which they were intended?—If gentlemen to whom they may be apropriated choose to sell them, they will at least fall into the hands of some one who will read them and the State at large will be so much the wiser, and will lose nothing in this way.

Mr. TRAER. I wish to state by way of explanation, that it was no part of my design in what I said to impugn the motives of any member here. I used the terms I did in a general sense only, and I do think that it is wrong for us to appropriate to our own use a thing merely because it belongs to the State. I do not think that argument is entitled to any weight at all. We might just as well go to work and appropriate the whole of the State library to the use of this Convention, because it belongs to the State. As regards this conscientious question of which the gentleman from Des Moines (Mr. Hall) speaks, I will say that I suppose all matters of conscience, and this among the rest, will be decided in the way gentlemen have been accustomed to consider such subjects. As I said before, I am opposed to the whole system, not only of this resolution, but of all the resolutions passed here appropriating the property belonging to the State without a law to that effect, or in compliance to the provisions of the law.

Mr. HARRIS. I did not intend to say any thing upon this subject; but after listening to remarks of gentlemen here, it strikes me that the reason for opposition to this resolution assigned by the geneleman from Benton (Mr. Traer) is hardly tenable when carried out to its full extent. He says we may just as well go on and appropriate the whole of the State library. Now I think the gentleman has not consulted the contents of that library very much, or he would not make that suggestion to this body. A great portion of its contents is composed of theological works, such as Clarke's Commentaries and Scott's Commentaries, &c., works, which I think would hardly be of so much service to the members of this Convention at this time as these reports would be. [Laughter.] I think, therefore, that that suggestion of the gentleman is not very well applicable to us at this time.

Mr. SOLOMON. I shall vote for this resolution because I am in favor of it. I deem it hardly necessary for me or for any other member of this Convention to state explicitly and in direct term that he does not vote for this resolution to accomplish any selfish end. I shall vote for the resolution because I deem these works necessary to our deliberations. And I get my authority for this measure from the act under which we are assembled here. We are here as a Convention of this State. For what purpose ? Why, sir, for the important purpose of revising and amending the Constitution of this State. That Constitution hus been the

Constitution of Iowa for ten years, and under that Constitution, the Supreme Court of Iowa has been each year making decisions, many of which have an important bearing upon the great questions we are called upon to consider here.

Now, sir, I know that many of us are lawyers, and have noticed these decisions, and have studied them. But as the gentleman from Des Moines (Mr. Hall) has already remarked we may not have the principles of those decisions clearly fixed in our minds at the present time. And I therefore deem it highly necessary, almost indispensable to a correct action upon the questions before us to which these decisions relate, that we should have these reports before us. I have Green's Reports in my library, but that library is 270 miles from this place, and I want those works here for my present use. What becomes of them after the Convention adjourns I care not. We came here for the purpose of revising the Constitution of this State, of amending an instrument that has been in operation in Iowa for ten years. And I might add to the arguments in favor of this resolution that as a member of the Committee on the Judiciary, questions have already been presented for my consideration in regard to the decisions of the Supreme Court, which have made me hesitate in regard to the report that we ought to send it here, and I do not know as I shall be prepared to report until I can see those reports. I suppose it is the same with other committees, and I shall therefore vote for this resolution.

Mr. CLARKE, of Henry. I would not make any further remarks upon this subject, but for the fact that the discussion has taken a direction which no gentleman here could have anticipated. Some reports have been made here impugning the motives of those who may vote for this resolution, which I consider highly improper. If I felt anywhere in my heart that I was supporting this resolution with any reference to my individual benefit, I should then feel like the gentleman from Benton, (Mr. Traer) that perhaps some one might accuse me of stealing and thieving, and perhaps I might regard that imputation as a just one. But we must consider that we come here to form a constitution for the benefit of the people of this State, and not for any paltry three dollars a day, and the little incidental matters that we may vote to ourselves here. We were called to meet here for a great public work, for the benefit of the whole people, and we know that the people of the State expect us to use all the necessary means to enable us best to fulfil the duty incumbent upon us. Now in order that we may compromise this matter, in order that gentlemen may not be forced to return home to their constituents, with the word "thief" pinned upon their backs, I will move, as a substitute for this resolution, "That the Secretary of State be requested to furnish all the members of this Convention, *who may require him so to do*, with a copy of the reports of the decisions of the Supreme Court of this State."

Mr. HALL. I shall oppose the amendment of the gentleman from Henry, (Mr. Clarke.) I want to see how many members here will refuse to take them. I want to try them, for I think they will not refuse their number of the volume of this work if the resolution is adopted.

Mr. EDWARDS. I rise for the purpose of explaining my position upon this subject, and to tell the gentleman from Davis, (Mr. Palmer) that I shall be compelled to oppose this resolution in its present shape, for the reason that I stated a few moments since that I think it is a useless expenditure to vote for Greene's Reports, for the simple reason that every lawyer already has those reports in his library, and should be well posted in regard to those decisions. Now as to the questions of constitutional law, I differ with my friend from Des Moines (Mr. Hall) in his opinion that we are above all the principles contained in these reports, and that by the alterations we may make in the constitution, we can declare those decisions a nullity. Now every advantage that members here could obtain from these reports, can be obtained only from Clarke's Reports, for we have not yet seen the decisions contained in them, and they might furnish us information with regard to some questions of constitutional law that might come before us here. Now if we are to vote ourselves all these reports, I am satisfied that with the time this convention will probably remain in session here, we could not become conversant with all the principles contained in them. All of us here, who are not lawyers, have not the time nor the disposition to examine so thoroughly as to enable us to fully comprehend, and be able to apply the principles of the decisions they contain.

Now so far as the remarks of the gentleman from Benton, [Mr. Traer,] are concerned, I must say that I think they are uncalled for. That gentleman, I am afraid, is not disposed to yield with that courtesy that should characterize members of a body like this, one to another. I have my peculiar notions, and I make my motions here to secure what I deem necessary, and I do it in good faith. If the majority vote down these motions, I yield out of respect to the opinions of that majority. I have no desire to set up my *ipse dixit* against the will of the majority here whenever my opinions happen to differ from theirs. And I think the insinuation of the gentleman from Benton, [Mr. Traer,] that if gentlemen of this Convention vote themselves these reports, their action in so doing will go forth to the world as of a character to brand them as a set of thieves, is entirely uncalled for. When questions of this kind arise here, I have no desire to manufacture capital for bunkum. I think there is a great deal of courtesy due from the members here to each other, and each should be allowed to enjoy his opinions without being taken to task for it.

Mr. TRAER. I am certainly at a loss to tell to what the gentleman from Lucas, [Mr. Edwards,] refers, when he speaks about being opposed to the will of the majority. I do not understand that we have any expression of the will of the majority in reference to the propriety of adopting this resolution. Now if I had had the extreme impudence—as I suppose the gentleman would call it—to get up here and read the majority a lecture, then it would be another thing. But I have not done so. I consider that every individual here has the right to express his opinions upon every subject that may be brought forward here. Now in regard to the expression I used here in reference to public stealing. I stated in my explanations a few moments since, that I used it merely as a general expression, and did not intend to apply it to any member here personally. But I can only say here that if gentlemen choose to take the expression home to themselves, and apply it, and the cap fits them, it is not my fault. I want that distinctly understood. And I want to be understood further with regard to pinning the word "thief," on the backs of gentlemen here. If anything is uncalled for here, it is expressions of that kind. I made no remark intended to implicate or impugn the motives of any gentleman. My only intention was to express my opposition to the general plan of appropriating the property of the State for the use of this Convention, or of any other body of men. As I said before I hope this Convention will adopt an amendment to the constitution that will effectually stop any practice of this sort in future.

Mr. JOHNSTON. I am very unwilling to enter into this debate; and I dislike exceedingly to disagree with my legal brethren. I feel all the *esprit du corps* that members generally feel, who belong to that ancient and honorable profession; and I would be glad to go with them upon this matter, but I cannot perceive any necessity for the adoption of this resolution. But I rose mostly to correct an impression made here in regard to the rules of the library. As I understand them they will permit any member of the Convention to take any book from the library, and use it for ten days, Now there are two hundred copies of the Supreme Court decisions in that library, and if gentlemen want them they can take them home for ten days, in which time they can inform themselves upon the subjects to which they may refer. I care nothing particularly about this matter; but I do not see the necessity of any such thing. I am opposed to the resolution because it presupposes that we are to have a session here much longer than I or any other member here anticipated when we came here. We are preparing for a session of three months or more here, by obtaining all these reports of the Supreme Courts of this State, and I hope, therefore, that the resolution will not be adopted.

Mr. CLARK, of Alamakee. Gentlemen labor under a great misapprehension here, I think, when they have the idea that members of this Convention must become familiar with every question or principle that may be contained in those three or four volumes. The object of obtaining these reports, as I understand it, is in order that we may become familiar with those principles of constitutional rights therein discussed, and every member here can do that in forty-eight hours if he has this work before him.

The question was taken upon the amendment of Mr. Clarke of Henry, to request the Secretary of State to furnish these books to those members who may ask them of him, and it was rejected.

The question was then taken by yeas and nays upon the adoption of the resolution, and it was agreed to, yeas 18, nays 15, as follows:

Yeas—Messrs. Ayres, Clark of Alamakee, Clarke of Henry, Ells, Emerson, Gibson, Gowen, Gray, Hall, Harris, Marvin, Palmer, Peters, Robinson, Scott, Solomon, Todhunter, and Warren.

Nays—The President, Messrs. Bunker, Day, Edwards, Gillaspy, Hollingsworth, Johnston, Parvin, Patterson, Seely, Skiff, Traer, Wilson, Winchester and Young.

When the name of Mr. CLARKE, of Johnson, was called, he said: I will ask to be excused from voting upon this question. I find that the vote I gave upon laying this resolution upon the table, may subject me to some imputation.

Mr. HALL. I do not see the necessity of excusing the gentleman from Johnson, [Mr. Clarke,] as his interest is too remote to be affected in any way by this resolution.

Mr. HARRIS moved that Mr. Clarke of Johnson, be excused from voting upon this resolution, which was agreed to.

County Indebtedness.

Mr. TRAER, offered the following resolution:

Resolved, That the Secretary of State be instructed to lay before this Convention a statement containing the amount of indebtedness of the several counties contracted for railroad purposes.

Mr. HALL. I would enquire if that information is within the possession of the Secretary of State?

Mr. TRAER. I do not know that it is, but I suppose he can get it in a very short time. Most of the counties that have contracted their debts can at once supply this information. I understand there is already some ten million of dollars of these debts contracted over the State. The question I understand will be up here with regard to prohibiting the contracting of State debts, and I desire to know the amount of these and other debts that have been contracted, and I thought this would be as good a way to obtain that information as any.

Mr. YOUNG. I do not think this resolution will get the information the gentleman desires. As I understand it, it only requests the Secretary of State to give information in regard to the counties that have already contracted these debts. Now some counties have taken a vote upon railroad stock and such like indebtedness, but that vote is a conditional one, and it will not properly constitute a debt until the condition is fulfilled. I do not think the gentleman can ascertain the full amount of this indebtedness without putting his resolution in some other shape. The county I have the honor to represent here voted a loan to a certain Railroad Company of $ 250,000 upon a condition which that company has not yet fulfilled. The county has not already contracted this debt, and it will only become a debt when this condition shall have been complied with, and under this resolution I do not think our county will come in for any indebtedness at all.

The question being then taken the resolution was agreed to.

Miscellaneous.

Mr. HARRIS. I would like to know what has become of the report of the Committee on the Bill of Rights. It was the first report sent in, but it has not yet made its appearance.

Mr. EDWARDS. The committee reported that they should make no amendments to the present article in the Constitution on the Right of Suffrage and by the consent of the Convention their report was laid on the table. I understand that the Secretary has taken the article in the present Constitution and attached it to the report of the committee, and that it will come up in its regular order.

Mr. HALL offered the following resolution:

Resolved, That this Convention will act upon the reports of the standing committees, in the order in which the committees were appointed.

Mr. JOHNSTON. I would like to understand from the gentleman the object of his resolution.

Mr. HALL. The standing committees, as I understand, are appointed in the order in which the various subjects, which they are to consider, stand in the present Constitution. First, the Preamble and Bill of Rights, and next the Right of Suffrage, and so on, and I think we had better consider the reports of the committees in this order.

Mr. CLARKE, of Johnson. I trust that we will not tie our hands by the adoption of this resolution. A majority can at any time take up any one of these reports; and I think that the passage of such a resolution as this is entirely unnecessary.

Mr. HALL. If we adopt this resolution, we will take up the reports in their regular order. First, we will consider the Preamble and Bill of Rights, but we can at any time lay it aside if we are not ready to dispose of it, and take up the next report in order. I think it of great importance that we should have regularity in our proceedings, and it strikes me that the course I have recommended would be the proper one for us to pursue in regulating our action here.

The question was taken, and the resolution was agreed to upon division—ayes 20; noes not counted.

Mr. HALL offered the following resolution:

Resolved, That Willis Connard be employed as paper folder in this Convention.

Mr. PARVIN. I do not see the necessity for the employment of any more paper folders or messengers, and I shall therefore vote against the resolution.

Mr. CLARKE, of Johnson. I will state that this lad has been employed in one branch of the Legislature, to the great satisfaction of its members. He is a cripple, and as we shall need additional assistance, I think we could not employ a more worthy messenger than this lad.

The question was taken, and the resolution was agreed to.

Mr. HARRIS. As there appears to be nothing else before the Convention, I would like to make a suggestion for the Convention to adopt. In looking over the list of Committees, it strikes me that there is one committee that ought to have been appointed, and that is a "Committee on Charitable Institutions." There is nothing of the kind mentioned in the old constitution, and unless that subject comes within the duties of the Committee on "Schools and Education," there is no provision now made for the consideration of this subject. I do not know that it will be necessary, but it occurred to me that this subject of charitable institutions should receive some little attention from this Convention. I hope, therefore, that a committee will be appointed to take this subject into consideration.

The PRESIDENT. Does the gentleman give notice that he will offer a resolution to that effect?

Mr. HARRIS. I made the suggestion in order that I might ascertain the sense of the Convention in relation to this matter, but I now give notice that I will offer a resolution for the appointment of such a committee.

Mr. CLARKE, of Johnson. I would suggest that we have a committee on "Miscellaneous Subjects," to which this matter might be referred. A resolution was passed this morning, which was referred to that committee.

Mr. HARRIS. It seems to me that this matter of charitable institutions should be referred to a distinct committee; but, however, if the matter can be sufficiently considered and treated by the Committee on Miscellaneous Subjects I have no objection. I give notice that I will offer a resolution of the character I have indicated, and in the meantime I will confer farther with members in regard to this matter.

Mr. ROBINSON. In looking over the list of Committees, I observe that Mr. Peters has not been placed upon any committee, and I move therefore, that his name be added to two of the committees.

The PRESIDENT. The Chair will remark in explanation of the omission of the name of Mr. Peters from any of the committees, that at the time the committees were arranged the gentleman from Delaware (Mr. Peters) was not in his seat.

Mr. ROBINSON. The member from Clinton, (Mr. Cotton) has had leave of absence for some time, and Mr. Peters might supply the place thus made vacant. I will therefore, offer the following resolution:

Resolved, That Mr. Peters be added to the Committee on the Preamble and Bill of Rights, and that he be also added to the Committee on Schedule.

Mr. CLARKE, of Johnson. The adoption of such a rule would change the rules giving the appointment of committees to the President.

Mr. HARRIS. I would certainly be as much pleased to see Mr. Peters upon the Committee as any other gentleman of this body, but I shall be opposed to setting aside Mr. Cotton for that purpose. Mr. Cotton assured me when he left town, that he should make all possible dispatch, and that he would probably be back before the Convention were half through their labors. I hope that we will do nothing which will reflect upon him in his absence, or show him any want of courtesy. I hope the resolution will not prevail. It will have the tendency to displace Mr. Cotton.

Mr. ROBINSON. I do not desire to displace Mr. Cotton; but I do not think it would be a violation of our rules to place another member upon one of the committees by a special vote.

Mr. CLARKE, of Johnson. I suppose that the adoption of such a rule is entirely unnecessary. It is merely sufficient to call the attention of the President to the fact of this accidental omission, and I move therefore, to lay the resolution upon the table.

The question was taken and the resolution was not laid on the table upon division— Ayes 6, Noes not counted.

Mr. TODHUNTER. I am informed that Mr. Cotton has had leave of absence, and is not expected to return under four weeks. If that be the fact, I think there will be no impropriety in passing the resolution.

The question was taken and the resolution was agreed to.

Mr. HARRIS offered the following resolution:

Resolved, That in addition to the number of Standing Committees already appointed, there shall be another which shall be the 13th on "Charitable Institutions."

The resolution was laid over, under the rules.

Reports of Committees.

Mr. CLARKE, of Henry, from the Committee on Incorporations submitted the following report which on motion of

Mr. TODHUNTER was laid on the table, and one hundred copies ordered to be printed for the use of the Convention.

The Committee on Incorporations having respectfully read and considered the several memorials and resolutions referred to them, together with Article 8 of the Constitution, would report said Article amended as follows, and recommend its adoption:

ARTICLE 8.

Section 1. No corporations shall be created by special laws, but the General Assembly shall provide by general laws for the organization of all corporations hereafter to be created, except as herein provided.

Sec. 2. Corporations may sue and be sued, and their property shall be liable to taxation in the same manner as natural persons; and the liabilities, powers, privileges, and duties of stockholders in corporations may be fixed and defined by law, subject to the provisions hereof.

Sec. 3. The State shall not become a stockholder in any corporation, nor shall it assume or pay the debt or liability of any corporation, unless incurred in time of war for the benefit of the State.

Sec. 4. No political or municipal corporation shall become a stockholder in any banking corporation, directly or indirectly; nor in any other corporation or corporations to an amount exceeding, at one time, two hundred thousand dollars; nor shall the bonds or other evidences of indebtedness of any municipal or political corporation be issued or granted, or its credit loaned, directly or indirectly, or pledged as security, to an amount in the aggregate exceeding two hundred thousand dollars, at any one time.

Sec. 5. It shall be the duty of the General Assembly to provide by law for the restraint of municipal and political corporations in regard to assessments, taxations, borrowing money, contracting debts, issuing bonds, and loaning their credit, so as to prevent, as far as possible, unnecessary burdens and unjust taxations and frauds.

Sec. 6. Subject to the provisions hereof, the General Assembly may pass a general banking law, under which corporations may organize for banking purposes.

Sec. 7. If a general banking law is passed, it shall provide, amongst other things, for the registry and countersigning, by an officer of the State, of all bills, or paper credit designed to circulate as money, and require security to the full amount thereof, to be deposited with the State Treasurer, in United States stocks, or in interest-paying stocks of States in good credit and standing, to be rated at their average value in the city of New York, for the thirty days next preceding their deposit; and also provide for the recording of the names of all stockholders in such corporations, the amount of stock held by each, the time of any transfer, and to whom.

Sec. 8. Every stockholder in a banking corporation or institution shall be individually responsible and liable to its creditors, over and above the amount of stock by him or her held, to an amount equal to his or her respective shares so held, for all of its liabilities; and in all cases where its stock shall be transferred, the liability of the transferer shall not cease, nor shall the liability of the transferee commence until the expiration of six months after such transfer shall have been duly recorded, as provided for by law.

Sec. 9. The General Assembly may also charter a State Bank with branches, to be founded upon an actual specie basis.

Sec. 10. If such a State Bank be established, the branches shall be mutually responsible for each others liabilities upon all paper credit issued as money, and the liabilities of stockholders shall be the same as those of banks organized under a general law—all of which shall be provided by law.

Sec. 11. It shall be the duty of the General Assembly, in case of its passing either or both of the banking laws herein provided, to provide also such other restrictions, and fix such other liabilities, and adopt such other guards and checks, as shall be conducive to prevent frauds on the part of banking institutions, its officers and directors, and to secure to the people of this State a safe and reliable currency.

Sec. 12. In case of the insolvency of any banking institution, the bill holders shall have a preference over its other creditors.

Sec. 13. The suspension of specie payments by banking institutions shall not be permitted and sanctioned.

Sec. 14. Every banking corporation or institution shall cease banking and close its business within twenty-five years from the time of its organization or creation.

Sec. 15. No bill, note, draft, check, or other evidence of debt shall be issued for circulation as money, except by banking corporations or institutions duly organized or created by law.

Sec. 16. But no general banking law, nor law creating a State Bank, nor shall amendments thereto, nor acts in repeal thereof, take effect until the same shall have been submitted, separately, to the people, at a general or special election, as provided by law, and shall have been approved by a majority of all the voters voting for and against it.

Sec. 17. Subject to the provisions hereof, the General Assembly shall have power to amend or repeal all laws for the organization or creation of corporations, or granting of special privileges or immunities, by a vote of two-thirds of the House of Representatives, and also of the Senate; and no exclusive privileges, except as in this article provided, shall ever be granted.

Sec. 18. No corporation shall hold any real estate hereafter acquired, for a period longer than twenty-five years, except such real estate as shall be actually occupied by such corporation in the actual exercise of its franchise, but the same shall escheat to the State for the benefit of the school fund.

Sec. 19. Private property shall not be taken by corporations for their use or benefit, without compensating the owner for the actual damage resulting to him or her in the taking, and the manner thereof.

On motion of Mr. HARRIS, the Convention then took a recess till 2 o'clock P. M.

EVENING SESSION.

Preamble and Bill of Rights.

The Convention re-assembled at 2 o'clock P. M., and was called to order by the President.

The PRESIDENT stated the business before the Convention to be the consideration of the report of the Committee on Preamble and Bill of Rights, which was made the special order for two o'clock.

Mr. HARRIS. I would inquire what would be the proper course to get clear of the consideration of this special order. There has been a great deal said about proceeding immediately to the business of the Convention, and finishing our labors as soon as possible. I certainly have as great desire to do so as any member here, but I wish to consider the subjects that are presented here in such a manner as will do them and ourselves the amplest justice. For one, I must confess I am not prepared to act upon the special order this afternoon. I believe the report of the committee, containing printed amendments, was only laid upon our tables this morning, and I had no opportunity of examining it until the recess. I desire to offer some amendments to it, and I would ask it as a favor of the Convention to let this matter pass by for the present and take up something else. I have no desire to be captious or cause delay, but I have amendments to offer which I think will be unanimously agreed to.

Mr. HALL. We have been here now almost two weeks, and I think it is almost time to take some action on the business before us. This morning we agreed to take up this special order at this time. I must confess when I heard that announcement that I breathed freer and easier than before, and I began to think that at last we should do something. We have been here long enough to do some business, and I hope that the Convention will not delay their work another hour.

Mr. HARRIS. I would inquire what would be the proper motion to get clear of the consideration of this question?

The PRESIDENT. The Chair is of the opinion that a motion to postpone the special order would be in order.

Mr. HARRIS. I make that motion then. If it would accommodate any gentleman better, I would name any particular time which he may suggest.

Mr. EDWARDS. I am in hopes that the Convention will not postpone the consideration of this special order. I concur fully in the remarks made by the gentleman from Des Moines, [Mr. Hall.] We have been here a considerable length of time, and this Convention should now take hold of something tangible and proceed to accomplish the work before them. No gentleman can premise, if we resolve ourselves into Committee of the Whole upon this subject, what time we shall finish its consideration. It may take us two or three days before we can perfect this article of the constitution, and this will afford the gentleman from Appanoose. [Mr. Harris,] ample opportunity to prepare his amendments.

Mr. HARRIS. I certainly supposed that the favor I asked would be granted, especially as this report, made the special order for this hour, was only laid upon our tables this morning; and there has been no possible opportunity for making preparation for discussion upon it, or offering any amendments to it. I did not suppose where amendments were sought to be offered in good faith, and which I believe the Convention should take considerable time to consider, that action upon this report would be pressed in such haste, especially as this is the first report that has been made the special order. When I ascertained that this report was made the special order, as soon as I had the opportunity, although it was a hurried one, I began to compare our Bill of Rights with the Bill of Rights in the constitutions of other States; and I suppose that was the reason why these constitutions were given to us, that we might have the opportunity of making these comparisons. Let me first read section fifteenth in the Bill of Rights of our own constitution:

"No soldier shall, in time of peace, be quartered in any house without the consent of the owner, nor in time of war except in the manner prescribed by law." That is good as far as it goes, but let us look a little further.

The fourth section of the article on the Bill of Rights in the Ohio constitution reads:

"The people have the right to bear arms for their defence and security; but standing armies in time of peace are dangerous to liberty, and shall not be kept up: and the military shall be in strict subordination to the civil power."

If gentlemen will take the trouble to compare these two provisions, they will see that the privilege allowed to the people to bear arms and keep them for their own defence, forms no portion of our present Bill of Rights. Will gentlemen say it is a sufficient reason to adopt the provision upon this subject reported by the committee because it is just like the one we now have? It is not a sufficient reason to me because the committee have reported the provisions of the present constitution, that we should agree to adopt what they have reported.

Again: Section twenty of our Bill of Rights says:

"The people have the right freely to assemble together to consult for the common good, to make known their opinions to their representatives, and to petition for a redress of grievances."

I will call the attention of gentlemen to section three of the Bill of Rights of the Ohio constitution.

"The people have the right to assemble together in a peaceable manner, to consult for their common good, to instruct their representatives, and to petition the General Assembly for the redress of grievances."

Gentlemen will see at once that there is a very great difference between these two provisions. The people of this State have a right to make known their wishes to their representatives, but they have no right to instruct them, as the people have in Ohio.

I have not had the opportunity of examining the whole of the report to see what amendments are needed. I have instituted this comparison between the Bill of Rights in Ohio and this State to show that there is need of amendment here. I hope that gentlemen, therefore, will give us sufficient opportunity to examine this subject, so that we can prepare such amendments as may be needed.

Mr. ELLS. I wish merely to say, that it will be impossible for us to make any progress in our business, unless we take up the reports in their order and discuss them. We are not obliged to dispose of this special order in one day, but we can progress to a certain extent, then report and ask leave to sit again. We must commence the discussion somewhere, and we ought to commence with the Bill of Rights, for that is the first subject in the constitution. If gentlemen are not prepared to discuss the whole bill, let them discuss that which comes first. I presume that every gentleman here is ready to act. If there are clauses that need amendment, you can amend them in Committee of the Whole. The Preamble and Bill of Rights are no longer in the hands of the committee, but they are now before gentlemen for discussion. When the report comes up for consideration, every clause is open to amendment; and I hope that this evening or to-morrow morning we will commence the discussion of this report in Committee of the Whole, and that members will all have the opportunity of freely expressing their views upon this question. I hope I may be always ready for discussion upon the Bill of Rights, for if there be any question which will excite the interest of the American people, it is the doctrine contained in the Bill of Rights. I am surprised that my friend from Appanoose (Mr. Harris) is not prepared to discuss the principles of the Bill of Rights at any time. I hope, therefore, that the Convention will not postpone the consideration of the special order, unless there be some reason given for such postponement more valid than any that has yet been given.

The question was then taken on postponing the special order, and it was not agreed to.

Preamble and Bill of Rights.

The CONVENTION resolved itself into Committee of the Whole (Mr. Edwards in the chair) and proceeded to consider the Preamble and Bill of Rights in the present constitution. with the amendments reported from the committee.

The Preamble and Bill of Rights reads as follows:

WE, THE PEOPLE OF THE TERRITORY OF IOWA, grateful to the Supreme Being for the blessings hitherto enjoyed, and feeling our dependence on Him for a continuation of those blessings, do ordain and establish a free and independent Government, by the name of the STATE OF IOWA, the boundaries of which shall be as follows:

Beginning in the middle of the main channel of the Mississippi river, at a point due east of the middle of the mouth of the main channel of the Des Moines river; thence up the middle of the main channelof the said Des Moines river, to a point on said river where the northern boundary line of the State of Missouri—established by the constitution of that State, adoptedJune 12th, 1820—crosses the said middle of the main channel of the said Des Moines river; thence westwardly along the said northern boundary line of the State of Missouri, as established at the time aforesaid, until an extension of said line intersects the middle of the main channel of the Missouri river; thence up the middle of the main channel of the said Missouri river to a point opposite the middle of the main channel of the Big Sioux river, according to Nicolett's map; thence up the main channel of said Big Sioux river, according to said map, until it is intersected by the parallel of forty-three degrees and thirty minutes north latitude; thence east along said parallel of forty-three degrees and thirty minutes until said parallel intersects the middle of the mrin channel of the Mississippi river; thence down the middle of the main channel of said Mississippi river to the place of beginning.

ARTICLE 1.—BILL OF RIGHTS.

1. All men are, by nature, free and independent, and have certain unalienable rights—among which are those of enjoying and defending life and liberty, acquiring, possessing, and protecting property, and pursuing and obtaining safety and happiness.

2. All political power is inherent in the people. Government is instituted for the protection, security, and benefit of the people, and they have the right at all times to alter or reform the same, whenever the public good may require it.

3. The General Assembly shall make no law respecting an establishment of religion, or prohibiting the free exercise thereof; nor shall any person be compelled to attend any place of worship, pay tithes, taxes, or other rates for building or repairing places of worship, or the maintenance of any minister or ministry.

4. No religious test shall be required as a qualification for any office or public trust, and no person shall be deprived of any of his rights, privileges or capacities, or disqualified from the performanee of any of his public or private duties, or rendered incompetent to give evidence in any court of law or equity, in consequence of his opinions on the subject of religion.

5. Any citizen of this State who may hereafter be engaged, either directly or indirectly, in a duel, either as principal or accessory before the fact, shall forever be disqualified from holding any office under the constitution and laws of this State.

6. All laws of a general nature shall have a uniform operation.

7. Every person may speak, write, and publish his sentiments on all subjects, being responsible for the abuse of that right. No law shall be passed to restrain or abridge the liberty of speech or of the press. In all prosecutions or indictments for libel, the truth may be given in evidence to the jury, and if it appear to the jury that the matter charged as libellous was true, and was published with good motives and for justifiable ends, the party shall be acquitted.

8. The right of the people to be secure in their persons, houses, papers and effects, against unreasonable seizures and searches shall not be violated; and no warrant shall issue but on probable cause, supported by oath or affirmation, particularly describing the place to be searched and the papers and things to be seized.

9. The right of trial by jury shall remain inviolate; but the General Assembly may authorize trial by a jury of a less number than twelve men in inferior courts.

10. In all criminal prosecutions, the accused shall have a right to a speedy trial by an impartial jury; to be informed of the accusation against him; to be confronted with the witnesses against him; to have compulsory process for his own witnesses, and to have the assistance of a counsel.

11. No person shall be held to answer for a criminal offense, unless on presentment or indictment by a grand jury, except in cases cognizable by a justice of the peace, or arising in the army or navy, or in the militia, when in actual service, in time of war or public danger.

12. No person shall, after acquittal, be tried for the same offence. All persons shall, before conviction, be bailable by sufficient sureties, except for capital offenses where the proof is evident or the presumption great.

13. The writ of habeas corpus shall not be suspended, unless in case of rebellion or invasion the public safety may require it.

14. The military shall be subordinate to the civil power. No standing army shall be kept up by the State in time of peace; and in time of war no appropriation for a standing army shall be for a longer time than two years.

15. No soldier shall, in time of peace, be quartered in any house without the consent of the owner, nor in time of war except in the manner prescribed by law.

16. Treason against the State shall consist only in levying war against it, adhering to its enemies or giving them aid and comfort. No person shall be convicted of treason unless on the evidence of two witnesses to the same overt act, or confession in open court.

17. Excessive bail shall not be required; excessive fines shall not be imposed, and cruel and unusual punishments shall not be inflicted.

18. Private property shall not be taken for public use without just compensation.

19. No person shall be imprisoned for debt in any civil action, on mesne or final process, unless in case of fraud; and no person shall be imprisoned for a militia fine in time of peace.

20. The people have the right freely to assemble together to counsel for the common good;

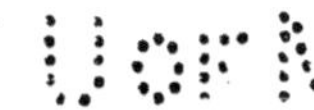

to make known their opinions to their representatives, and to petition for a redress of grievances.

21. No bill of attainder, ex post facto law, or law impairing the obligations of contracts shall ever be passed.

22. Foreigners who are or may hereafter become residents of this State, shall enjoy the same rights in respect to the possession, enjoyment and descent of property, as native born citizens.

23. Neither slavery nor involuntary servitude, unless for the punishment of crimes, shall ever be tolerated in this State.

24. This enumeration of rights shall not be construed to impair or deny others, retained by the people.

The amendments reported from the committee are as follows:

Add to section two as following:

"And no priveleges or immunities shall ever be granted, that may not be altered, revoked, or repealed, by the General Assembly."

Add to section nine as follows:

"But no person shall be deprived of Life, Liberty, or Property, without a due process of law."

Substitute for section ten as follows:

"In all criminal prosecutions the accused shall have a right to a speedy trial, before an impartial jury, of the county or district in which the offence is alleged to have been committed, to demand the nature and cause of the accusation against him, to be confronted by the witnesses against him, to have compulsory process for his own witnesses, and to have the assistance of counsel."

Add to section eleven the following:

"Nor shall any person be compelled in any criminal prosecution to be a witness against himself."

Add to section eighteen the following:

"Private roads may be opened in the manner prescribed by law, but in every case, the necessity of the road, and the amount of damages sustained by the opening thereof, shall first be determined by a jury of disinterested free-holders; and such amount, together with the expenses of the proceedings, shall be paid by the person or persons benefited thereby, before said road shall be opened."

The committee have also had under consideration the resolution offered by Mr. Solomon, and after duly considering the same, have unanimously agreed that it is inexpedient to recomend the incorporation of said proposition in the Bill of Rights.

Mr. ELLS. Mr. Chairman. Before proceeding to the discussion of the report, I wish to have a distinct understanding with the members of the Convention in regard to the rules of procedure. Now, we are all, probably, whether we have been in parlimentary bodies or not, quite rusty in our recollections of terms of address. I may call you Sir, Mr. Chairman, Mr. President, or Mr. Speaker, but it is all intended as being proper and right, and not disrespectful to the incumbent of the Chair. Again, it has been the practice in all parlimentary bodies of which I have any knowledge for the chairman of each committee by courtesy to speak first upon the bill reported by him, whether it be a majority or minority report, by way of explaining the reasons which influenced him to report the bill. Then all who are in favor and who are opposed to the bill, have a right to be heard before it can be taken out of the committee of the whole. Then in conclusion, when all have spoken who desired so to do, the gentleman who had the honor of first reporting the bill, has a right to reply by way of rejoinder, to the remarks which have been made. I now come to the consideration of the Preamble and Bill of Rights. By the appointment of the Pesident of the Convention, I had the honor of being placed at the head of the committee upon this subject, and I feel thankful to the gentleman who presides over our deliberations, for his kind consideration in placing me at the head of that committee. I regard it as one of the highest compliments ever paid to me, for I have a greater respect for those clauses which secure to the people, the free and full enjoyment of those God-given rights, than for all the other guarantees of the Constitution.

But to the question before us for consideration. The Committee who had in charge the Preamble and Bill of Rights were singularly unanimous in their conclusions; they were all desirous of maintaining the Bill of Rights in the present constitution, by the addition only of such provisions as would enlarge, and not curtail the rights of the people. They did not doubt that the people of Iowa had heretofore exercised all the rights which freemen may enjoy under any charter of liberty, but they did desire to put upon record every guarantee that could be legitimately placed there in order that Iowa not only might be the first State in the Union, unquestionably as she is in many respects, but that she might also have the best and most clearly defined Bill of Rights. Now, sir, as this is a discussion of principles as well as clauses, it is expected, of course, that a very wide range will be allowed to gentlemen in the expression of their opinions, and perhaps a good deal may be said that is not legitimate. I trust, however, that the utmost latitude will be allowed in a discussion of this character, and that if members deviate from the question, they will not be called to order for so doing.

It may be said that the people of this country have so long enjoyed the right of self-government that a written Bill of Rights in and of itself is not necessary for them; and as a consequence, is rendered almost obsolete. This is unquestionably true to some extent. But the history of the world teaches us the absolute necessity of guarding well the rights of the people; for power is always receding from the many to the few. The strong in intellect, and the strong in body, have ever domineered over their fellows. The annals of the world also furnish many instances in which the freest and most enlightened gov-

ernments that have ever existed upon earth, have been gradually undermined, and actually destroyed, in consequence of the people's rights not being guarded by written constitutions.

The British Constitution, that great bulwark of human freedom from which ours is mainly derived, is understood to be simply a recognition of the rights and privileges originally enjoyed by the ancient Britons, and by them deemed as old as the human race itself. When King John had usurped all the powers of the British government—had undermined every valuable institution in the land—had taken away from the people virtually the right of trial by jury—they arose in their might, and compelled him, at Runneymede, to charter their liberties; but in doing this, they solemnly declared that they were not asserting any new principles, or demanding any new rights; that all they asked was a recognition of old rights, and a remedy for existing abuses. Although we are deeply indebted to our British ancestors for a knowledge of many valuable rights, srill, as a people, we may justly pride ourselves on the rapid progress we have made in the development and rational exercise of natural and social rights, within the passt eighty years.

The Committee who reported the amendments to the present Bill, acting, as they conceived, up to the spirit and intelligence of the times, have inserted clauses in their report new to the Bills of Rights of most of the other States in the Union.

The first two sections of the present Constitution reads as follows:

1. All men are, by nature, free and independent, and have certain unalienable rights—among which are those of enjoying and defending life and liberty, acquiring, possessing and protecting property, and pursuing and obtaining safety and happiness.

2. All political power is inherent in the people. Government is instituted for the protection, security, and benefit of the people, and they have the right, at all times, to alter or reform the same, whenever the public good may require it.

The committee propose to add to the second section the following:

"And no privileges or immunities shall ever be granted that may not be altered, revoked or repealed, by the General Assembly."

These words, "privileges and immunities" are very broad in their signification. I hold that they cover all subjects of legislation that confer power upon any man, or any set of men. I take the ground that all power conferred is simply a grant, unless the term by which the power is conferred expressly stipulates, that it shall be a contract. Therein I differ, doubtless, with many gentlemen upon this floor, and I apprehend with some who will agree with me generally in most other matters.

Taking this view of the subject, it necessarily follows, that the General Assembly have the *right* to repeal all *grants* of power, (whether provided for in the Constitution or not) and should exercise that right in all cases where the powers granted have become destructive of the ends for which they were created, or injurious to the common welfare of the State. Notwithstanding this, I desire to have the power of repeal distinctly expressed in the Constitution. In thus expressing my own opinions, I wish it distinctiy understood, that I do not assume to speak for the Republican party, or any other party. Nevertheless, I am firmly of the opinion that a large majority of the intelligent people of this nation are with me in this opinion. I am aware, sir, that many very intelligent gentlemen hold to the old doctrine on this subject, which claims that all grants of power by the General Assembly become *vested rights*, and can only be reached by writs of *quo warranto*. This doctrine was earnestly contended for by the advocates of the United States Bank, when the opponents of that institution threatened to repeal its charter for alledged abuses. The enemies of that institution took the position assumed by me in this discussion. Since that day the new doctrine has been mooted all over this country; has divided parties, and has in fact been the means of exciting more discussion and investigation than any other question that has been agitated in this country, in relation to the powers of the general and State governments since their formation.

It seems like an absurdity, Mr. Chairman, to say, that the people have not the right to repeal obnoxious charters, when we assert in our National Declaration of Independence, that the people are the source of all power, and have the right to alter or abolish these forms of government whenever it becomes destructive of the ends for which it was created.

I therefore hope, Mr. Chairman, that our Bill of Rights will not only recognize the *right* of the General Assembly to *alter, amend or repeal* all *privileges* or *immunities* that may be granted hereafter by this State, but will make it imperative on the General Assembly to exercise the right whenever a case shall arise requiring it.

The next amendment proposes to add to section 9, as follows:

"But no person shall be deprived of life, liberty or property, without due process of law."

The committee transcribed that clause from the Constitution of the United States; and I apprehend that no member will object to its incorporation into our present Bill of Rights. The words "without due process of law," have a legal significance, as I understand, in all the courts. I am one of that class of men who believe that that clause in the Constitution of the United States, has been violated by the Congress of this nation in such a manner that we would be justified at this time, either by legal enactment or by incorporating provisions into our constitution, in protecting ourselves from its operation. I regard the Fugitive Slave Law as unconstitutional, because it does not give to man the right to defend his life and liberty by "due process of law." In this opinion, I expect to be at variance with my friend from Lee, [Mr.

Johnston,] and those who act with him. Now, the committee who have offered the amendment to this second section, did so from a desire that the Bill of Rights in the Constitution of this State, should be as strong, in this respect, as the Constitution of the United States. We have seen, Mr. Chairman, that Constitution violated again and again by the dominant party in the land, which rides rough-shod oves the necks of freemen. In common with a large majority of the people of this State, I desire to see our constitution contain every guarantee for freedom that words can express. If the words "due process of law," shall in time be recognized by our judicial tribunals to mean what they really do mean, "that no person shall be deprived of life, liberty or property, without a legal proceeding based upon the principles of the common law, and the constitution of the United States—that every man, when his life or liberty are imperilled, shall have the right to be tried by a jury of his countrymen. Then, sir, that infamous Fugitive Slave Law will become a nulity, and the American people will trample its odious enactments in the dust. It makes the very blood tingle in my veins, sir, when I think that such a law disgraces our national character.

The committee offer as a substitute for section ten of the Bill of Rights, which is in these words:

In all criminal prosecutions, the accused shall have a right to a speedy trial by an impartial jury; to be informed of the accusation against him; to be confronted with the witnesses against him; to have compulsory process for his own witnesses, and to have the assistance of a counsel"—

The following section:

"In all criminal prosecutions the accused shall have a right to a speedy trial, before an impartial jury, of the county or district in which the offense is alleged to have been committed, to demand the nature and cause of the accusation against him, to be confronted by the witnesses against him, to have compulsory process for his own witnesses, and to have the assistance of counsel."

The section we here propose as a substitute for section ten, gives an accused party the right to be tried before an impartial jury of the county or district where the offense is alleged to have been committed, where the witnesses live, where the facts are all known, and where he is likely to have a more fair and impartial trial, than if taken to a distant part of the State.

The Committee purpose to add to section eleven, which provides that "no person shall be held to answer for a criminal offense, unless on presentment or indictment by a grand jury, except in cases cognizable before a justice of the peace, or arising in the army or navy, or in the militia, when in actual service, in time of war or public danger," the following.

"Nor shall any person be compelled in any criminal prosecutions to be a witness against himself."

The committee recommend the addition of this clause to the eleventh section, because they wish, as I said before, to make the Bill of Rights as full and perfect as possible, and not because it has ever been infringed upon in this respect in this country. I have no doubt, if there were no provision upon the subject, that the common sense of the country and the humanity of the age would not compel a man to testify against himself in any criminal proceeding. It is best, however, to place this provision in the Bill of Rights, not only because it makes the instrument more perfect, but because it shows that the object we have in view is to protect every man in the enjoyment of the largest liberty consistent with his duties to civil government.

The Committee also propose to add to section eighteen which provides, "That private property shall not be taken for public use without just compensation," the following:

"Private roads may be opened in the manner prescribed by law, but in every case, the necessity of the road, and the amount of damages sustained by the opening thereof, shall first be determined by a jury of disinterested free-holders; and such amount, together with the expenses of the proceedings, shall be paid by the person or persons benefitted thereby, before said road shall be opened."

I shall leave to other members of the Committee to explain this section, as I have been so little time in the State that I am not correctly informed what your laws are in regard to this matter.

The Committee have not reported other amendments to the Bill of Rights, not because they believed it to be as perfect as it could be made, but because the sections to which they have proposed amendments seemed to be the only ones that rquired a radical change. We well knew that our action was not final, and that there were many gentlemen in this Convention whose wisdom would enable them to see more clearly than themselves what further was needed by way of amendment to the Bill of Rights. I certainly will go as far as the farthest to enlarge the meaning of this Bill of Rights and add new clauses to it, and use other language, if necessary to express more clearly, and define more accurately the rights of the people. But allow me to say again that I do not consider that we are conferring power upon the people by the Bill of Rights. I hold that every right contained in this bill, and every one contained in the Constitution exists in the people, and we are but simply embodying these ideas in a tangible form so that they can be read and understood.

Again, this section of the Constitution will probably be read more by the people than any other clause in the Constitution, and therefore it should receive the consideration of this Convention to a greater degree than any other subject which may be discussed here. It is true that the subject of corporations and charters is of great importance to us and to the people at large, but at the same tlme, I hold that the Bill of Rights is of more importance than all the other clauses in the Constitution put together, because it is the foundation and written security upon which the people rest their rights. I hope, therefore, that the members of this Convention will feel free to express their views, and state every thing which may suggest itself to them by way of objection to the amendments proposed by the committee. I do not claim that the Bill of Rights, as here reported, is perfect, and the gentleman from Appanoose (Mr. Harris) was correct in saying that time was necessary to digest and examine, not only this Bill of Rights, but all the other Bills of Rights in the Union and see if we cannot improve them. I do not wish to see this matter hastily disposed of, but hope the whole subject will be fully discussed, and treated in such a way as to be entirely satisfactory to the people of the State.

We are organizing new parties as well as forming a new Constitution, and it is well to understand now what basis we are establishing for our future action. Here is the place to do it, and if we are not harmonious and cannot act together, now is the time to know it.

I had intended, as chairman of the committee, to have said much more upon thie subject but I do not desire to take up the time of the Convention unnecessarily. I have simply stated what I believe to be correct positions upon this subject, and I will now leave the whole matter in the hands of the committee, claiming the privelege, however, of replying to the remarks which may be made in opposition to the amendments proposed by the committee, if I desire to do so.

Mr. CLARKE, of Johnson. As I understand the position of the question now, we have the whole Bill of Rights before us for consideration. We are not confined to the amendments reported by the Committee but for the purpose of getting at the matter in a tangible shape, I move that we take up the Bill of Rights as a whole.

The CHAIRMAN. The chair undestands that the Chairman of the Committee (Mr. Ells) who made this report claims the right, that is granted to the Chairman of a Committee in giving his general views upon the amendments proposed to the article on the Bill of Rights. The question before the Committee is, upon the first amendment proposed by the Committee to the second section.

Mr. CLARKE, of Johnson. My motion is this, that we take up the Bill of Rights section by section.

Mr. PARVIN. I undestand that the Committee have reported the whole of the Bill of Rights in the present Constitution with some amendments to a few of the sections, except the 10th section, for which they propose a substitute. These amendments have already been printed. The first section of their report is the first section, therefore, not printed in their report, of the Bill of Rights. I hope the suggestion of the gentleman from Johnson (Mr. Clarke) will be acquiesced in, and that we will proceed first to the consideration of that section.

The question was taken and the motion was agreed to.

Mr. WILSON. I wish to ask the gentleman whether he intended to embrace the Preamble in his motion? There should be an amendment to the Preamble, because it reads,

We, the people of the Territory of Iowa, grateful to the Supreme Being for the blessings hitherto enjoyed, and feeling our dependence on Him for a continuation of those blessings, do ordain and establish a free and independent government, by the name ot the STATE OF IOWA, the boundaries whereof shall be as follows.

When it should read, "We, the people of the State of Iowa, &c."

I move, therefore, to strike out the word "Territory" and insert in lieu thereof the word "State."

The question was taken and the amendment was agreed to.

The 1st section of the Bill of Rights was then read as follows;

"All men are, by nature, free and independent, and have certain unalienable rights—among which are those of enjoying and defending life and liberty, acquiring, possessing and protecting property, and pursuing and obtaining safety and happiness."

Mr. BUNKER. I move to strike out the word "independent" and insert in lieu thereof the word "equal," so that it will read,

"All men are, by nature, free and equal, and have certain unalienable rights—among which are those of enjoying and defending life and liberty, acquiring, possessing and protecting property, and pursuing and obtaining safety and happiness."

This may appear to be a very unimportant amendment, but it appears to me, that we should endeavor to get this Bill of Rights as near the truth as we can. The framers of our present Bill of Rights, no doubt, conceived that the word "independent" was perfectly applicable, but I do not think it is, from the fact, that a man is not in reality absolutely independent, although the equal of his fellow man. Webster says that the meaning of the word "independent" is not subject to control. My object in moving this amendment to strike out the word "independent," is simply to declare that men have certain equal rights, instead of declaring, that all men are independent. I wish simply to declare the great truth, that men are, by nature, perfectly equal in the use of whatever Nature's God has bestowed upon them. But I think the inculcation of the sentiment in the Bill of Rights, that men are absolutely independent would have the tendency to produce a false sentiment in the community. I believe that every action of this Convention may produce an influence for good or evil in all coming time. On the other hand, the expression of the idea, that men are, by nature, possessed of equal rights, contains the germ of that great idea, which embodies the sentiment of universal brotherhood, in which we feel that we are all equal in the exercise of whatever nature has bestowed upon us.

Mr. CLARK, of Alamakee. I cannot see the necessity for the suggestion by the gentleman from Washington (Mr. Bunker). The great idea, that all men are, by nature, equally free and independent, I apprehend is inculcated in the clause upon this subject, which we find in the present Bill of Rights. The section, as it now stands contains, it seems to me, every thing that is necessary, and you cannot make it more definite and broad than it is now. It comprehends every thing that we can claim by the laws of nature and Nature's God.

The question was, taken on Mr. Bunker's amendment and it was rejected.

Corporations.

The 2d section was then read as follows:

"All political power is inherent in the people. Government is instituted for the protection, security, and benefit of the people, and they have the right, at all times, to alter or reform the same, whenever the public good may require it."

To which the Committee proposed the following amendment.

"And no privileges or immunities shall ever be granted, that may not be altered, revoked, or repealed, by the General Assembly."

Mr. PALMER proposed to amend the amendment by adding the following:

"And that the State shall be liable to pay all damages which may be caused by such repeal, revocation or alteration, unless such privileges or immunities shall have been violated or abused by the person or persons to whom they may have been granted."

Mr. ELLS. For the benefit of the members of the Convention, I would like to read the definition of the word "privilege." Webster gives the following definitions:

"1. A particular and peculiar benefit or advantage enjoyed by a person, company or society, beyond the common advantages of other citizens. A privilege may be a particular right granted by law or held by custom, or it may be an exemption from some burden to which others are subject. The nobles of Great Britain have the *privilege* of being triable by their peers only. Members of Parliament and of our Legislatures have the *privilege* of exemption from arrests in certain cases. The powers of a banking company are *privileges* granted by the Legislature.

"2. Any peculiar benefit or advantage, right or immunity, not common to others of the human race. Thus we speak of national *privileges*, and civil and political *privileges*, which we enjoy above other nations. We have ecclesiastical and religious *privileges* secured to us by our constitutions of government. *Personal privileges* are attached to the person, as those of ambassadors, peers, members of legislatures, &c. *Real privileges* are attached to place, as the *privileges* of the King's palace in England."

The first definition embraces all we claim for the word "privilege."

Mr. SCOTT. I move to strike out from the amendment proposed by the committee, the words "by the General Assembly." If my amendment be adopted, the clause will then read:

"And no privileges or immunities shall ever be granted, that may not be altered, revoked or repealed."

I think there will be a double meaning or clashing in the terms of this article unless amended. It first says that all political power is inherent in the people. If it be, and they alone are possessed of political power, they are the proper ones to restrict or curtail their own rights, and not a portion of themselves, called the General Assembly. The objection which I have to the use of the words "General Assembly" here is, that if the General Assembly have the right to alter, revoke or repeal all the rights of the people, they have the right at their next sitting, to alter, revoke or repeal the constitntion which we are now making. I would reserve to the people of the State the right to alter and amend their chartered constitutional rights, and not leave it in the power of the Legislature to do so. The adoption of this clause would give to the General Assembly the right to make a new constitution. I would have that power reserved to the people, and not given to the General Assembly. I think gentlemen must take the same view of this matter that I do, when they give it the consideration which the subject demands.

Mr. CLARKE, of Henry. I would suggest that, perhaps, the words "by the General Assembly" should also be inserted after the word "granted," so that the amendment will then read, "and no privileges or immunities shall ever be granted by the General Assembly that may not be altered, revoked or repealed, &c."

Mr. PALMER. My object in offering the amendment I have proposed is, that we may not violate the constitution of the United States, which provides that no State shall pass any law impairing the obligation of contracts. I consider that the amendment proposed by the committee leaves the field open for such violation, without redress to the person or parties injured thereby. If that is the operation of the amendment, where will we find ourselves? We would say to a railroad company, for instance, that is a body corporate capable of contracting and being contracted with, come and contract with us, if you please, but beware, when you make that contract, what you do, for we hold in our hands the right to annul it whenever we please, and so far from your having redress we will "laugh when your calamity cometh." I think that we should not repeal or annul any contract, unless the party with whom we contracted shall have redress, or unless he shall have violated the contract on his part, by abusing his privileges, or in any other way; and I do not think this State desires to enter into any child's play here, by saying that they will make any contracts that they will annul or repeal at their pleasure, without the consent of those with whom they contract. I do not think it is the desire of the people of this State to do any such thing. Suppose that we make a contract with a corporation, for instance, and have it incorporated in our statute books, for the navigation of the Des Moines river. By that contract we say to them, build your boats with such a draft as will enable you to navigate that river, and with such proportions as will enable you to pass through the locks erected on that river; and when you shall have built those boats in pursuance of the contract, we claim the right to pull down all the dams on the river, and thus violate the contract; and we can do this thing in a year or a month, or less time, after the contract shall have been entered into, without your having any redress. Now, I ask, have we the right to ruin those persons who may have confided in our integrity, by thus going into operation under a contract? I think not. I think, as I said before, that this may lead to a violation of the constitution of the United States; and, therefore, I have offered this amendment. If any gentleman disagrees with me upon the grounds I have stated, I would like to hear from him, and see if he can convince me that this amendment is unnecessary; and if I am convinced of that, I would be as willing as any one can be, to vote against the amendment, though offered by myself.

Mr. CLARKE, of Johnson. I am in favor of the amendment of the gentleman from Davis (Mr. Palmer) provided the provision reported from the committee is to go into the Bill of Rights. But I beg leave to ask that gentleman a question. How are these questions to be determined? I understand his amendment to propose, that the party injured may recover damages: against whom? Against the State? Who is he to sue? If you give the right to repeal charters and destroy contracts, and intend to provide that the party to the contract so repealed, may have remedy in damages, you must provide a place where he may go to enforce his remedy, and a judge to determine his rights under that contract. If the gentleman will modify his amendment, and make it a little more explicit, I will vote for it, as I am in favor of the principle contained in his amendment, should the amendment reported from the committee be adopted. But now, the amendment provides that the party may recover damages, in case the contract has not been violated on his part; but where is he to go to have his remedy? He cannot sue the State, because a citizen cannot sue the State. Where is he to go, then, to get his damages?

Mr. PALMER. I will modify my amendment by providing that the State shall be liable to an action at law in any court of record in this State.

Mr. HALL. I believe that all these amendments are unnecessary. Perhaps I do not understand the meaning of them. But I understand from this amendment of the ommittee, that, first, the Legislature shall not pass a law that they cannot repeal again. If that be so, then I shall oppose the amendment, because it contains a principle too universal to need reiterated here. In the second place, if the amendment means that the State, when it makes a contract, shall also be at liberty to annul it, then I shall oppose it because I believe the State should be held to its contracts as much as a citizen would be. The idea that a State can repeal a contract at its pleasure would, if carried out here, give the State a character so grossly unjust that I cannot agree to it.

Besides, if it means that, then it is in violation of the constitution of the United States, and we would by passing it violate the oaths we took here to support that constitution. I will read from the tenth section of the first article of the constitution of the United States:

"No State shall enter into any treaty, alliance, or confederation; grant letters of marque and reprisal; coin money; emit bills of credit; make anything but gold and silver a tender in payment of debts; pass any bill of attainder, ex post facto law, *or law impairing the obligation of contracts;* or grant any title of nobility."

Now, I cannot consent to making a provision in the Constitution of Iowa, that the State may be capable of making contracts with its citizens, or the citizens of other States, and then say that they can violate that contract at their pleasure, by repealing the law creating it. There is a want of good faith in the whole thing—something which I know this Convention will never sanction. If this amendment is intended merely to assert that the Legislature shall have a right to repeal a law, when by so doing it would not repeal a contract, then there is no such provision at all. That right we have had a thousand years, in America and England, and it is a right that has never been denied.

There is an over-anxiety, I think, on the part of the committee to make our constitution more perfect than it was before. Now the constitution in this respect cannot be made more perfect than it is now, and by making amendments to it we shall only render obscure the provisions which are perfectly plain and obvious. I shall oppose all amendments that do not go to give the constitution more effect than it now has, and especially this one which will lead to the violation of our trusts. I would leave the constitution, in this particular at least, as it now stands.

Mr. WILSON. I think the proposition contained in this amendment clearly constitutional, and not in conflict with the constitution of the United States. Ohio has in her constitution the precise provision reported here by the committee on the Bill of Rights. New York has the same provision in her constitution. Now as the gentleman from Des Moines, [Mr. Hall,] has well said, the legislative departments of the States, and of the general government have always possessed the power to repeal any law which they may make. But it has always been held, and that doctrine was well settled in the celebrated Dartmouth College case, that those legislative powers could not interfere with vested rights, special privileges, or franchises, and could not repeal them unless there was some clause in the constitution warranting them to do so. And I would put this question to the gentleman from Des Moines: if the constitution of the State of Iowa says that the legislature of this State shall not grant any privilege or immunity, which may not be repealed by the legislature, I would ask whether the party receiving a grant from the legislature, does not also receive this constitution as a portion of the contract, and with the full knowledge that the constitution has retained in the hands of the legislative department a right to repeal the privilege or immunity granted? It gives notice beforehand to the parties entering into contract with them, and says: what we give you now we may take back again at any time. and you receive it at your own risk. I merely throw out this suggestion to correct the proposition of the gentleman from Des Moines.

I do not say that I shall support the proposition of the committee. But I am opposed to the amendment of the gentleman from Davis, [Mr. Palmer,] for I do not want to ingraft anything upon the Constitution of the State of Iowa, that will be liable to get the State into an innumerable number of law suits. I do not believe in having the State dragged into the courts of the State. I am opposed to this thing here, and if anything of the sort is to be done, let the legislature make the necessary provision for it.

Mr. CLARK, of Alamakee. I am in favor of the amendment to the Bill of Rights as reported by the committee, but I will not object to a proper amendment to their amendment. I am opposed, however to the amendment proposed by the gentleman from Davis, [Mr. Palmer,] and for the reason stated by the gentleman from Jefferson, [Mr. Wilson.] I do not believe it would be politic to make a constitutional law that will be the means of getting the State into law suits, the end of which no man can foretell. I believe that would be bad in principle. If the amendment would provide that the legislature which repealed the contract, or took away the franchise, should also provide some equitable means of causing damages to be paid, it would then be less objectionable.

The amendment reported by the committee, or some equivalent for it, I am in favor of. The history of our country has proven this fact: that corporate bodies with exclusive privileges have been growing upon us; have been intrenching themselves in the strongholds of our government; that they have been surrounding themselves with privilege after privilege, until they have come in fact to control the action of the legislatures of the older States of the northern part of our confederacy at least. And I am opposed to the principle that would allow our legislature to grant those privileges and those charters, and to create these corporations without having any power to put any limit upon them. They are represented to be creatures without souls, mercenary, grasping, over-reaching; in short, so many stepping stones to an aristocratic government, and opposed directly to the first principles of a republican government. I am in favor of putting some check upon this system, of having something incorporated into our constitution which would have a tendency to check this growing evil in our country. And I know no better way to do that than by allowing the legislature that creates these corporations the power of repealing, modifying or annulling them as the wishes of the people may require, so that when they are once brought into existence they may not be forever independent of the will of the people.

I do not consider the objections of the gentleman from Des Moines [Mr. Hall] as valid ones, and the gentleman from Jefferson [Mr. Wilson] has fully proved his positions to be untrue and fallacious. Now if we have a constitutional provision of this kind, whoever contracts with the State or takes a charter under a law passed by the legislature of this State, would do so subject to this Constitutional provision which becomes a part of the contract itself, and those persons who take a contract under this Constitution, take it with the express and implied agreement that they consider it subject to the restriction that is in the Constitution. That would be no hardship to them; they would do it with their eyes open, and knowing what they were about, and they are at liberty to accept it under these restrictions or let it alone. For these reasons I am in favor of some kind of provision in the Constitution that will bring these privileged classes of the communtity within the scope of legislative action.

Mr. HALL. I merely rise to make my acknowledgment to my distintinguished friend from Jefferson [Mr. Wilson.] I am happy to be corrected. But at the same that I make my acknowledgments I wish merely to make a suggestion to the gentleman, that when he has lived as long as I have, he will find himself more frequently in error than he considers himself now, and he will find then that he does not know so much as he thinks he does now. We are all very apt to have this opinion of superior knowledge at his time of life.

Now I neither know nor care what the Ohio Constitution contains. I know it does not express on the whole anything different from what our present bill of rights express. I know that that State, with this very clause in her Constitution existed forty nine years, during which time I lived under it for a longer time than the gentleman from Jefferson(Mr.Wilson)has been living in his majority and heard no complaint of it upon that score. I have lived ten years in Iowa under the present Constitution, and I have yet to hear the first objeciion from any source upon this subject. I believe in letting well enough alone.

Mr. WILSON. Shall I refer the gentleman from Des Moines (Mr. Hall) to the clause in the Ohio Constitution? It is as follows:

"And no special privileges or immunities shall ever be granted that may not be altered, revoked or repealed by the General Assembly."

Mr. HALL. That clause is modified by the word "special" which was inserted for a reason well known to those who are acquainted with the history of that State. Now, will the gentleman, as a lawyer, say that taken in connection with that part of our Constitution providing for the creation of corporations by general law, that clause woufd have favor in it? It is a mere dead letter. It would be well enough here under their system, but under the one we have adopted, and the one under which we have lived for the past ten years,and which has proved its efficiency here in every way, a system which has a tendency more than any other system ever invented by human genius to concentrate capital and esterprise, for the purpose of carrying on internal improvements. Under such a system as ours it would not operate beneficially. If we are to stand by that system then leave off encroachments in this manner. That is what has made the country, and will make a country. It is what we ought to look to, for all those great improvements, associated private enterprises should be encouraged in a form legitimate and proper. I am unwilling to put this State in a position where we cannot make a contract with any corporation under our Constitution without having it in the power of the legislature, at its next session, to violate it in such a way as would leave a blot upon the character of a private individual. Now I do not want to make this distinction between the government which we are to look to and respect, and the people and citizens under that government. I say that the contracts of this government should be enforced with the same rigid severity as the contracts of private citizens. We want no saving clauses—no protection against the fulfillment of our contracts. If we adopt this proposed amendment no person will trust us in a contract unless he gets some enormous price under it. Should a private citizen put such a provision as this in the contracts he might make, he would get no one to enter into them with him, except he could get some exorbitant price or privilege under them.

Mr. CLARK, of Alamakee. I find in the constitution of the State of New York, this provision:

"Corporations may be formed under general laws; but shall not be created by special act, except for municipal purposes, and in cases where, in the judgment of the Legislature, the objects of the corporation cannot be attained under general laws. *All general laws and special acts passed pursuant to this section may be altered from time to time, or repealed.*"

The experience of the State of New York satisfied the convention which framed the constitution from which I have read, that there was a necessity for some provision of this kind. Let us look a moment at the matter: It is true that to a certain extent our country has been enriched by the operations of private chartered companies. That is undeniable; and it is the policy of governments, and especially of ours, to encourage that kind of corporations which tend to enrich our country, and tend to make it prosperous so far as we can do so, without surrendering up her best interests to these incorporated companies. But the moment they step beyond the bounds calculated to protect and secure the interests of the State, we then pervert that which would be a blessing into a curse and a tyrant.

Now, I apprehend, there will be found no difficulty in this State in obtaining capitalists enough to engage in all the enterprises which the interests of the State may require, even with a clause like this in our constitution. Our capitalists are pretty shrewd in looking out opportunities for making money; and, I apprehend, no reasonable man will be afraid to invest money under a constitution of this kind, for they will have that confidence in the people of the country at large, htat will lead them to invest money in our works upon the pledge of our good faith. They will say, our charters will only be altered, repealed or taken away when we abuse our privileges and powers, or the interests for which those charters were granted have become injurious to the rights of the people. We will find no difficulty in getting capitalists to invest money in all proper works of internal improvement under such a constitution as this would be. I apprehend that capitalists who would invest their money under the constitution of New York will seek for investments for profits to be obtained soon, whereas, under our present constitution, I apprehend, there has been any quantity of charters granted in this State to men who have sought them, and who do not intend to use them for years, and only when they can make them profitable. This provision, therefore, will tend to have a beneficial influence in our State in this respect. For these reasons I am in favor of placing this provision in our constitution, and hope it will be adopted.

Mr. WILSON. The gentleman from Des Moines (Mr. Hall) has put a question to me which I am willing to answer. Before doing so, however, I desire to say I am glad I have arrived at that age when people know so much more than they do when they get as old as he is. I am sorry that he is forced to acknowledge that his wisdom and information are passing from him. [Laughter.] And I hope that I shall not be compelled, when I arrive at his age, to make the same humiliating confession. [Laughter.]

The gentleman wants to know if the Legislature can confer privileges upon any corporation or company under a general law which they cannot take away? I answer, yes. I say that under a general law companies may be organized and corporations formed whose rights cannot be interfered with under the general laws of the State, unless that right be reserved in the constitution of the State. I apprehend that nothing can be clearer than that corporations can be formed under the law as it now exists, and although the law may be repealed at the next session of the Legislature, the rights acquired under that law cannot be repealed, because they have become vested rights. Hence it would be necessary to make a provision of the constitution retaining the power to repeal the privileges so granted, by general law, or otherwise. Now, as I said before, I am opposed to the amendment of the gentleman from Davis. But I am disposed to favor the amendment reported from the committee, on the ground, solely, that the Legislature should hold in their hands the rights that may be granted by general or special laws to companies in this State, and I would lay down this proposition again, and I want every lawyer and other member of this Convention to consider it: whether, if this clause goes into the constitution of the State of Iowa, it does not become a notice to all parties acquiring rights under the acts of the Legislature of State, that those rights will be subject to repeal by the Legislature, and thus this provision will become a part of the contract between the company and the State.

Mr. CLARKE, of Johnson. I regard this as a very important question, and peculiarly important in connection with the position of this State with regard to the construction of internal improvements. It has so far been the policy of this State that all incorporations should be established under general laws, and so far as that policy is concerned, it meets my approbation. I grant the position of the gentleman from Jefferson (Mr. Wilson) to be true that as the law now stands under our present Constitution, corporations for railroads, or any other purposes organized under that law cannot lose their rights, and that is I think as it should be. But the gentleman argues that the legislature should have the power to do this, and beseech by this amendment to the Constitutoin to give them the power to take away those rights which have been honestly acquired, and under which they have entered upon these works. Now that very argument is to me an argument against this amendment.

Mr. WILSON. I do not seek to support any amendment, nor will I support any which will act retrospectively. That we cannot do.

Mr. CLARKE. I do not understand the gentleman as desiring that. Now what are the effects of this argument? All the railroads we desire, to make in this State are not yet made, and all the companies for railroad purposes are not yet organized under the general laws of this State, and may not be until after the adoption of the Constitution, we are now engaged in preparing. The principle of the gentleman is correct that any company organized under our Constituttion with this provision in it would receive as a part of their contract a notice of our right to alter, or repeal it at any time, or even to take away from them all the rights they may have acquired under those contracts. It may be that their road is half completed and their debts all contracted, but all will be swept away by this repeal, and for what purpose? Merely to place in the power of the legislature and the people of this State the right to violate these contracts. Now I say, that such a proposition is not reasonable, is not just, is not honest, and I concur with the gentleman from Des Moines (Mr. Hall) in saying, that if adopted, it would reflect disgrace upon the character of our State abroad, and it is not only the mere disgrace that would result from it, but it would be the utter ruin of every project of internal improvement now in course of contemplation.

Every member of this Convention knows that the great bulk of the capital used in the construction of works of internal improvement in this State is furnished, not by our own citizens, by the wealthy men of other States. And I ask gentlemen to consider how many of the capitalists of the States will put their money into these works with such a clause as this in our Constitution? If gentlemen want to kill off these works of internal improvement in their desire to strike at other corporations at the same time they are using the most effectual means to do so. I should regard this amendment to the Constitution as a death blow to every railroad corporation in this State. There are other corporations to be established in this State. I understand that this Convention has been brought about from the necessities of the people to have construsted, or have provided some kind of banking system. What that system shall be has not yet been determined. But whatever mode is determined upon it must a corporation and the funds must come from the States. Under such a clause as this in your Constitution how much banking capital will be furnished by the States? I undertake to say, not a dollar.—Twe effect of this provision therefore will be to effactually nulify the demands of the people in regard to the banking question. The arguments I have used have been directed mostly to the expediency and the policy of this provision.

There are other considerations which are as deeply embodied in this proposition as perhaps those I have noticed I am a stonished at the division in this Convention on this question. It is true this amendment is very general in its terms, and there may be adistinction between immunities and privileges and the term contract. But as a lawyer I think the term contract is fully implied in the amandment. This amendment would give the legislature power to repeal or destroy a contract. Now upon principles of common honesty I am not willing to place this power anywhere. The people of this State are represented in those contracts by their agents, and they are supposed to know what they are doing when those contracts are made, and the people, like individuals, should be responsible for their contracts.

There is another objection and that is this:—insert this amendment in your Constitution, and your legislature will be continually assailed with all kinds of propositions for incorporations or immunities or privileges, and in place of the legislature carefully considering and studying well what they are granting, they will grant them without care or consideration, relying upon this provision for power to repeal them when they become troublesome. The result will be that in place of doing good in any manner, great harm will be done.

Entertaining these opinions, I am opposed to this whole proposition of the committee to amend, and if it is to be adopted, I am in favor of something of the nature of the amendment of the gentleman from Davis, [Mr. Palmer.] I must insist that if this power is to exist in, and to be exercised by the legislature, the party injured should have the same mode of redress against the State, as he would have against an individual. There should be some consideration of propriety and common honesty in this matter if we would sustain our character abroad as a State.

Mr. HARRIS. Like my friend from Johnson, [Mr. Clarke,] I am certainly somewhat astonished at the divisions among us here upon this question. And especially am I astonished at the opposition of my friend from Des Moines, [Mr. Hall,] knowing as I well do the clause in the constitution of Ohio, which is nearly the same as the amendment proposed by the committee, and the same that I will offer myself when I get an opportunity, with the exception of the word "special" before the words "privileges and immunities." The doctrine taught by my friend from Johnson, [Mr. Clarke,] sounds very natural to me, though coming from one of those whom I have been accustomed in my political life heretofore to oppose. It may not be amiss perhaps, for me to say that in the political warfare in the State of Ohio, where I understand my friend from Johnson has had some political experience, and more than I have had, this question we have been contending over, was the main bone of contention for ten or fifteen years; whether the legislature should have the right to repeal immunities and privileges. Now I would invite the attention of the committee to this word "special" before the words "privileges and immunities." In this State I understand these immunities have been granted under general laws. This amendment, as I understand it, strikes at private and special corporations. And I speak of this class because I am more particularly acquainted, more conversant with them than with any other. The clause in the constitution of Ohio in which I most heartily concur was placed there in reference to bank charters, and with scarcely any reference to other subjects. The banks of that State, previous to the passage of the law which created the State Bank of Ohio, were all created by special laws; they were special corporations created by special enactments to give them existence. And when once they were placed upon the statute book, and had come in possession of their immunities, those immunities become chartered privileges, and the legislature could not affect them in any way whatever, and hence the difficulty arose which led to this clause being put in this constitution.

Now I am not prepared to pass an opinion upon the effect of the amendment of my friend from Davis, [Mr. Palmer.] But I know that it is considered by the best politicians of the country that great injury to the country has resulted in consequence of these special immunities, these soulless corporations, as the gentleman from Alamakee, [Mr. Clark,] calls them, that were placed entirely beyond the reach of the legislature, and were perfectly irresponsible to the community. Now I am in favor of placing some bridle upon them. I apprehend that there is no danger of any repeal of these immunities where the corporations are acting in good faith, and where the privileges granted them are not abused. It is only when they transcend the limits prescribed to them by the law that breathed them into existence that this provision would be taken advantage of by the legislature. And I say that if they do violate their contracts and see proper to step beyond the bounds assigned, where is the right to call upon us to allow them remedy for damages? If a man violate a contract which he has made with another, he has no right to come into a court of justice and ask to have the other party impaled in damages when that contract is declared broken. I understand that the person whose rights have been trampled upon, and not the person who tramples upon those rights is entitled to recover damages.

My friend from Johnson, [Mr. Clarke,] speaks of the danger of curtailing our internal improvements, of breaking down our system of internal improvements, if this provision is incorporated into our constitution. We find this provision in both the constitution of Ohio and in the constitution of New York, and we do not hear that those States are in any way retarded in their progress in internal improvements. And I do not think any such danger need be apprehended here. I know that danger has arisen from the want of such a provision as this, and that there is a necessity for some restraint being placed upon these otherwise irresponsible corporations. Hence I shall support most heartily the amendment of the committee, when it shall have been amended by inserting the word "special" before "privileges and immunities." But so far as the amendment of the gentleman from Davis, [Mr. Palmer,] is concerned, as I said before, I am not prepared to pass an opinion upon it.

And that was one of the subjects that I wished to examine when I moved to postpone the consideration of this report in Committee of the Whole; but I suppose the committee will rise without finally determining what will be done with this subject. I desire to examine the constitution of the United States, and see what that has to say upon this subject. My friend from Johnson says, we have no redress against the State; that, being the subjects of the State, we could not commence an action against the State. As to that, I do not know, and not being a constitutional lawyer, I am not prepared to give an opinion upon it, and cannot, at present, decide to support the amendment of the gentleman from Davis; but I am in favor of placing some restraint upon special corporations.

Mr. PARVIN. I did not intend to engage in this discussion at all; but I perceive from the remarks of gentlemen here, that there is going to be difficulty in examining the report of one of our committees, until we have the reports of all before us; for I understand that the Committee on Incorporations propose to have engrafted upon their report the same provision that is contained, in principle, in the amendment of the Committee on the Preamble and Bill of Rights. The Committee on the Legislative Department, in their report, propose to cut off much of this special legislation, and to provide that the Legislature shall provide by general law, for corporations that have heretofore been done by special acts. The gentleman from Appanoose (Mr. Harris) proposes to amend this amendment by inserting the word "special," so that it will stand the same as it is now in the constitution. This matter of privileges granted by special law will not be touched by this Bill of Rights; but if the Legislature step aside and give special privileges and create special corporations, they will have preserved to them the right to revoke those special privileges and corporations; and I hold that to do so would be right and proper. Is it right to allow one Legislature to grant special privileges and cut off future Legislatures from inquiring into what they have done? Under the operation of this provision there is, I think, no danger but what we will have corporations enough to go on with all the legitimate business provided for in those special acts. Therefore, when the gentleman from Appanoose (Mr. Harris) shall move his amendment, I shall vote for it. I would make this portion of our Bill of Rights precisely as it is in the Bill of Rights in the constitution of Ohio. I have heard of nothing wrong there, and think that nothing wrong will result from it here; and with the amendment of the gentleman from Appanoose (Mr. Harris) I shall certainly vote for the amendment of the committee. But I cannot see the propriety of the amendment of the gentleman from Davis (Mr. Palmer). I fear if it is adopted here and made a part of our constitution we will receive great trouble from it; that it will be injurious to the State without any good resulting to the individual.

Mr. CLARKE, of Henry. The views of gentlemen here upon this question seem, after all, to be very little in conflict. All recognise the necessity that has arisen in some of the States for providing some power to repeal acts of incorporation, of repealing certain special privileges and franchises. We do not find this provision in the constitutions of any of the States but Ohio and New York, so far as I have examined. But I think the gentleman from Des Moines (Mr. Hall) is wrong in supposing that there can be no possible necessity in the State of Iowa for such a provision as this. We know not yet what is before us. The past and the present are ours—but what contingencies may arise to call for such a provision as this in our constitution, none of us can tell.

The remarks of that gentleman in regard to opinions expressed here by the very able representative from Jefferson (Mr. Wilson) I think were entirely uncalled for. To be sure, that individual expressed his opinions here decidedly, as he has a right to do; and I regret that the gentleman from Des Moines (Mr. Hall) with his long experience and his age, has not yet arrived at that age of discretion where he can leave the individual alone who is expressing opinions, and consider the principle which is under discussion.

We—all of us—recognise the necessity, then, of some check upon these special corporations. The only difficulty or question is, can we put into this constitution a provision to operate as such a check, that shall not operate injuriously in some other direction? Every mind here recognizes the fact, that if the Legislature goes to work and repeals a law that they have passed, creating certain privileges and franchises, under which a company or an individual has commenced acting, and has acquired vested rights, then there is a wrong done to that company or individual; and we can only exercise wrong and have our consciences approve it, when the interests of the community demand it. Therefore the amendment of the gentleman from Davis (Mr Palmer) is founded in justice and right. Then arises the question concerning the impolicy of making the State a party to a suit at law, in courts of justice: and every mind recognizes the impolicy of that practice. Then we are brought to the necessity of having this clause in the constitution to protect the State. Now, though an old Whig, and standing here now as a Republican, I claim to be as democratic as any man dare be.

Now, I would propose, to reconcile all differences of opinion, that if this amendment of the committee is adopted, we connect with it a proviso, that the people of Iowa shall vote upon the necessity of any such repeal or amendment of corporated privileges and immunities. In that way we will throw around this provision a safeguard and check that will prevent, on the one hand, those corporations from becoming a perfect gangrene and cancer upon the body politic, and allow the Legislature to apply the knife to remove them, when the public good demands that the knife should be applied; and on the other hand, prevent the Legislature from doing unnecessary injury to any corporation, by providing that the people themselves shall decide whether the proposed repeal or amendment is desired by them. Now, say what we will, this is but the application of the knife, after all, and though necessary, we should at the same time guard against its improper use. And I, therefore, would submit, that in the consideration of this amendment of the committee, it be considered in connection with what I will myself offer when the opportunity arrives to do so.

I would suggest that the consideration of this matter, in this place, be indefinitely postponed, for it will be considered when we come to the report of the Committee on Incorporations. In that report the Convention will find that it is proposed that no corporations or privileges shall be granted, except the power of amending or repealing those rights be retained in the Legisla ture, and it is also provided that that repeal shall be submitted to the people, and receive their sanction, before it becomes of force. Now, I would offer as a substitute for the amendment of the gentleman from Davis (Mr. Palmer) the following:

"Provided, that in all cases where such revocation, repeal or alteration shall prejudice vested rights, it shall first be submitted to the people at some general or special election provided by law, and be approved by a majority of the voters voting for or against it, before it shall have effect."

Mr. HALL. The gentleman from Henry (Mr. Clarke) and myself will never be able to see alike. Of course we will differ. If we were both called upon to give a definition of what constitutes a principle, we would not get at the same thing—that is very certain.

Now this amendment, which he has proposed, is, to my mind, monstrous. We are called upon by it to constitute the people a high court of impeachment, to impeach corporations by their votes. Now, has it come to that? Shall we not provide something before we get to that, and have we not provided already? Have we not a judiciary department of this government, which stands as high as any other department of the government? and is it not made the peculiar province of that department to decide all questions of right and wrong between citizens of the State, and citizens and the State? Is it not already provided, that when a corporation, from a school or church up to a railroad, or any corporation, for any other purpose, shall violate its charter, the court shall test the violation of that charter, and according to their judgment decide the controversy? If the corporation shall not have violated its charter, and has not exceeded its rights and privileges, it ought not to be punished. If it has, then the punishment will be awarded. But what is proposed, now? It is proposed to take away from the judiciary this duty, and make Tom, Dick and Harry the complainant in the Legislature, and then let the people at their elections decide upon the rights of their citizens. We would unloosen every tie that holds society together—we would be trampling upon every right secured to us heretofore, by this powerful and noble arm of the government—the judiciary—and for one I never could consent to it.

Now let us come home to ourselves upon this subject of Incorporations. We have had ten years experience under the constitution as now in force. Will gentlemen point out to me one instance where that power has been abused? Will gentlemen say to me that society has suffered, or that they can see in the future any indications of an overshadowing power to crush out the liberties of the people under our present policy? Let well enough alone. I say that the present constitution has operated well in this respect. When we come to frame that part of the constitution in relation to corporations, we can guard this matter there, if necessary. But I am not prepared now to say that I would be willing that the Legislature should have the right to modify, or infringe upon, charters after they have been consummated under the laws of the land. But when we come to that part of the constitution, I will be prepared to express my opinion upon this subjeet.

Now, if we want to guard the people against incorporations, let us go directly to the point. I will vote for an amendment prohibiting the Legislature from ever granting any of the privileges spoken of here. But if we allow the Legislature to grant them, and individual rights are acquired, property invested, and time expended under them, then I would be the last man to say that the Legislature, without the intervention of the judicial power, should repeal those rights and destroy that property.

Mr. CLARK, of Alamakee. I am opposed to the amendment under consideration, from the reason that it recognizes a proposition which has no existence in fact. It recognizes the principle that a corporation may obtain a vested right under the constitution. I think that a proposition of that kind would be a nullity, and therefore I shall oppose its passage.

The question was then taken upon the amendment offered by Mr. Clarke, of Henry, and it was not agreed to.

Mr. CLARK, of Alamakee. I offer the following amendment:

"Provided that the Legislature that repeals or alters such law, shall provide by law for a fair and equitable compensation to any corporation or company which may be injured by such repeal."

Mr. WILSON. I hope that this proposition will meet with the same fate that the other did. It simply providesforrepeal, without making any reservation as to the action of these corporations, that they shall have some compensation.

Mr. CLARKE of Henry. I hope gentlemen will not pass this matter over hastily. I hear gentlemen crying out "question," "question," when we are considering one of the most important questions that can come before us. I think gentlemen should consider well what we are doing, for this amendment is one, which if passed, will affect vitally the interests of this State. In the first place we must suppose if the legislature wish to repeal a law giving special privileges to corporations, that it is on account of some mal-feasance or wrongful act. If a corporation be guilty of this, you are virtually providing by this amendment, that the Legislature cannot repeal the act of incorporation. The provision upon this subject is better as it stands now, to leave it to the individual who may be damaged to memorialize the Legislature for relief. I think if this whole matter were duly considered by members in connection with the question of incorporations, that they will perceive there is no necessity for incorporating here in the Bill of Rights that section which gives to the Legislature a very great power indeed, the power of chartering and repealing corporations at will.

I do not wish to speak here merely for the purpose of speaking. I want members to consider what evils may spring up by the adoption of the amendment here proposed. The Legislature meets to-day, the lobby goes to work and carries a law through the Legislature that provides for certain incorporated companies and under it these companies are all organized. Two or three sessions pass, and then somebody comes forward and says he is injured and that his property has been taken from him, and he claims proper renumeration by way of damage. A feeling is at once got up against the law, and an effort is made by the lobby to change it. Here, then, you will have a continual struggle between the corporation and the adverse party who is trying to procure a change or alteration in the law. The mischiefs that will grow out of such a state of things will have no end unless we provide some check for it. The check that I proposed, the Convention saw fit not to entertain. I leave it to the conscience of every man to consider if it is not absolutely necessary that we should throw some restraint around our Legislature, or else we should have a conflict eternally between those who are acting for companies and those who are acting adverse to them.

Mr. EMERSON. I rise not because I desire to take up the time of this Conventien with any remarks, but simply to say, that I am gratified that this controversy on the Bill of Rights has taken place. I do not know, if this controversy were to go on a little longer, but in the end I should have more friends upon a certain subject than I anticipated. I am glad to see that there is a feeling aroused here with regard to this subject of Corporations. I agree with my friend from Henry (Mr. Clarke) upon the necessity of carefully restricting corporations, but expect to vote against the amendment of the Committee, and all other amendments that have been introduced upon this subject, because I believe that the present provision in the Bill of Rights is sufficient for that place, but I now give notice, that when we come to act upon the subject of Corporations, that I will go as far as the farthest. I am for placing such restrictions upon them as will hold them, if possible, to the most rigid accountability. But to my mind, this whole controversy at the present time is unnecessary, save, that we get the views of the gentleman in regard to the subject of Corporations. This subject is one which does not legitimately belong to the Bill of Rights. It seems to be conceded here by every gentleman almost, with whom I have talked, that we are about to embark in the business of Banking in this State, under either special or general laws, most probably both. I for one think, that it will be the proper time when we come to consider the subject of Corporations, to throw around them those guards which are necessary to protect the people against their improper influences. With reference to the amendment of my friend from Henry (Mr. Clarke) to refer these matters to the people, and other indications I have seen here, I hardly know whether it will be necessary to have a Legislative Department hereafter. It seems to me that we might as well appoint some gentleman at Iowa City, perhaps the Governor, simply propose laws to the people for them to legislate upon and enact at the ballot box. I am glad to see my friends here in favor of the dear people, but in a representative government like this, it seems to me, that they cannot do all the legislation. I for one, as a member of this Convention, shall expect to take and carry home with me all the responsibilities that belong to my position, and I shall not in order that I may appear to be very frienly to the dear people, refer any matter to them to get clear of the responsibility myself.

I do not believe this is a purely Democratic form of government, and for one I do not believe in that pure Democracy, or rather the Iron will of the majority enact their laws at the ballot box. If that were our form of Government it would be unnecessary for us to be here to-day making a Constitution. We came here simply to protect the rights of the weaker, the minority if you please. Hence I am opposed as a general rule, to referring every thing to the people. It is right, however, to refer our work to the people, let them judge of it, and adopt it or not, as they please. I hope that we will not consume any more time in the discussion of these matters until we take up the report of the Committee on Corporations, and that we will vote down all the amendments that are now offered upon this subject.

Mr. GILLASPY. I came to this Convention with my mind made up on this subject, with a desire to re-adopt the article in the present constitution, that refers to this matter. If there should be any change made in regard to the rights of the General Assembly upon this subject, it should be that they should not have the right to interfere with any corporation which has been created under the general incorporation laws. I shall vote against all the amendments offered thus far to the Bill of Rights. We have had a fair illustration of Legislative action upon this subject of corporations in the doings of the General Assembly that has just adjourned. In my portion of the State, there is a corporation known to the people of this State as the "Des Moines Navigation and Rail Road Company," who have incorporated themselves under the general incorporation law as proscribed by the present Constitution. The State of Iowa has been represented in this matter by a Commissioner and Assistant Commissioners, and I might say that one of these Commissioners occupies the position to-day of Chief Justice of Iowa. They entered into a contract with a foreign corporation, and what do you see as a consequence here in the Legislature? Why, a general prejudice against corporations and especially a corporation the members of which all live out of the State; and the Legislature go to work and pass a law saying that that corporation does not exist in the State, that they have no contract with them whatever, and the consequence is, if they do not destroy the entire enterprise in which that company is engaged for the benefit of the whole State of Iowa, they will throw the matter into litigation, which will prove fatal to the contemplated improvements. My opinion is, if the Legislature has the power to set at naught all corporations of this kind which may be created, you will have to search a long time for men of capital, who will come to this State and associate themselves together in a corporation for the purpose of building our rail-roads. We need and must have many railroads in this State, but my judgment is, that you will find very few capitalists who will engage in enterprises of this kind, and be subject to the caprices of the General Assembly upon this subject. I undertake to say, that corporations for the violations of their rights ought to be held subject to the decision of the Courts. In other words, if they have done wrong, they ought to be tried before the Courts of the State and not before the Legislature; because that body is not the proper tribunal to judge of these acts.

But to return to the history of this Des Moines Navigation and Rail Road Company. This Company has been chartered over two years, and they have gone to work in the improvement of the Des Moines River. Mr. McKay, the Commissioner selected two years ago, resigned, and Mr. Manning was appointed by the Governor to take charge of the improvement, who entered upon the discharge of his duties and made a contract with this corporation the present winter. He made a report upon the subject to the General Assembly, and said, that that corporation was not violating any of the principles and privileges that had been granted to them by the laws of the State, but the General Assembly refused to print it. Such a prejudice had grown up in the minds of members, by the influence of a few intriguing gentlemen, that they refused to hear the agent of the State, who certainly ought to be the friend of the people and not of the corporation. The truth is, that he was a friend of the people, but they have said through the general Assembly, by a solemn act, that no such corporation existed, and that they were entitled to no privileges or immunities under the Constitution. I ask any gentleman upon this floor, if a project were started in his town or county for procuring a Bank Charter, would he take stock in it, if the General Assembly that should meet five years afterwards, were to have the right to say you must close up your affairs at once? I apprehend that not a solitary gentleman upon this floor would do such a thing.

With the views I have here expressed upon this subject, I shall vote against all the amendments to the present Bill of Rights, believing it to be just as good in that respect as we need have here.

Mr. CLARK, of Alamakee. I was educated as a democrat, and I was taught as a part of the Democratic creed that we were bound to repose confidence in the people at large, that the people were sovereigns, were capable of self-government, and that individually and collectively they were the bulwarks, in reality, of universal liberty. I was taught to believe that all of these great questions were always safe when they were left to the people. I am a little surprised, I must confess, when I find members upon this floor, who I supposed were educated in the same school with myself, now affirming that it is unsafe to trust the people, and that it would be no better than trusting to a mob. Gentlemen say that capitalists have no confidence in the people and will not come here to establish improvements, if you allow the people through their legislature to repeal those charters. I admit that this is a new doctrine to me as democratic doctrine. It may be correct democratic doctrine, but it is not that kind of Democracy in which I was educated.

Let us examine this question in regard to Banks for a moment. Does it require any great expense to go into the operation of Banking in this State under the general banking law? I apprehend not. They have in New York just such a provision upon this subject as we propose to have here. They have a general banking law in that State, and we find that a multiplicity of Banks have sprung up there in every part of the State, and if any inconvenience is experienced there from the operation of this law it is from the fact that there are too many banks established there already, and too many applications for the establishment of such institutions; notwithstanding they have this provision in the constitution to repeal their charters if they see fit.

Again, we find in the history of corporations in that State, that rail-road, plank-road, and all kinds of corporations flourished under the adoption of their constitutional provision upon this subject, and that they have experienced none of the inconveniences which gentlemen predict would follow in this State, if we were to pursue a similar policy. It proves most clearly that the old democratic doctrine upon this subject, that it was safe to trust the people, is the true doctrine after all. Why? Because it proves that capitalists have confidence in the people, and that they are willing to trust their privileges in their hands. Capitalists will have the same confidence here. But gentlemen tell us that capitalists from the Eastern States will not come here and invest their money if you incorporate such a provision, as is here proposed, in the constitution of this State. But I ask you if these capitalists, knowing that the inhabitants of this State come from Eastern States, will not have the same confidence that they have in the people of those States?

Let me here say, that I find that some of my Republican friends are leaning to this kind of doctrine. I am sorry to see it. Some of them seem to labor under the impression, if this provision is incorporated in the constitution, it will strike a fatal blow at our banking system. Let me tell you, so far as my experience is concerned, that there is no danger to be apprehended from that source. Take the constitutions of other States, where they have this same provision, and you will find that no evil results have followed from its adoption.

I have made these remarks for the purpose of

calling the attention of this Convention to the history of our country for a few years past; and I claim that that history demonstrates to us this fact, that no evil results have followed from the incorporation of such provisions in the constitutions of any of the States. It is manifestly clear to my mind, that the people should have the right to control those corporations, which may be established for their own profit, and that they should never surrender up such right, but should retain it in their own hands.—They should ever hold a supervisory power over them, and they should have the power to say that these institutions should cease, whenever they have accomplished the object for which they were created.

Mr. HARRIS. I wish to add the following as an amendment to the substitute:

"When the incorporators or persons concerned shall have not violated the terms of the law or charter, which created the privileges and immunities repealed."

If I understand the substitute it is this, that when any of these privileges or immunities shall have been repealed, the Legislature shall make provision to pay the damages in consequence of the repeal. The amendment I have offered, simply provides, that if the corporations themselves are the wrong-doers that they shall not be entitled to damages.

Mr. CLARKE, of Alamakee, accepted the amendment.

Mr. TRAER. I think this discussion is rather premature, and that it would be better to postpone this matter until the article on Corporations comes up for consideration. This Convention cannot possibly create any corporations. With a view of postponing this matter, I move that the Committee rise, report progress and ask leave to sit again.

The question was then taken on the amendment of Mr. Clarke of Alamakee, and it was not agreed to.

The question then recurring on Mr. Scott's amendment was taken and the amendment was not agreed to.

Mr. HARRIS. I ask to insert the word "no" before the word "special," so that it will read, "And no special privileges or immunities shall ever be granted, that may not be altered, revoked or repealed, by the General Assembly."

Mr. CLARKE, of Alamakee. I am opposed to the amendment for the reason, that there can be privileges which will be just as grievous in their nature, and which will be open to as much objections as have been urged against a general provision in the Constitution, which shall provide merely, that no privileges or immunities shall ever be granted that may not be altered, revoked or repealed by the General Assembly. If the amendment of the gentleman should pass, the Legislature could avoid its force by passing general laws for railroads and any other kind of public imporvements, and when the law was passed, they would be beyond the reach of any Legislative action. Some gentlemen seem to be laboring under the apprehension, that we can provide in the article on Corporations for every thing of this description. I do not think so, but I think there should be something in the Bill of Rights as a safe-guard for the people in their capacity as a people, I think the Bill of Rights is the proper place for a provision of this kind, in order to protect the rights of the people of the State.

Mr. WILSON. I am satisfied that there is a question here which will not be embraced in the report of the Committee on Corporations, but I want time for the consideration of the matter. The difficulty is this, that you simply provide in this article for a repeal of the general law under which corporations may be created in this State, and still the privileges which they gained will not be repealed by the repeal of the law. Unless there is a provision of this kind in the Constitution, the privileges which they get under the general law will be vested rights. For the purpose of looking into this matter a little further, I move that the Committee rise, report progress and ask leave to sit again.

The motion was not agreed to.

The question was then taken upon Mr. Harris' amendment and it was not agreed to.

Mr. PETERS moved to strtke out all of the Committee's amendment to section two, which is as follows:

"And no privileges or immunities shall ever be granted, that may not be altered, revoked or repealed by the General Assembly."

Mr. HARRIS. I wish to say a few words upon this amendment, before the Committee proceed to take a vote. I have no desire to take up the time of the Committee by talking for the mere sake of hearing myself talk, but I do think this is one of the most important questions that can be presented to us upon this Bill of Rights, if not, upon any question that may come up for consideration. I ask gentlemen this question, whether they wish to have the power retained in the Legislature of this State to control incorporated companies after they have been incorporated, other than by simply repealing the act under which they were incorporated. They may go on and incorporate a company under the general laws of this State, and they may next winter repeal the law and yet leave the company all the right, which it ever had. The amendment of the Committee made to the Bill of Rights goes back to the company itself, and says that the Legislature may have control in the matter. Here is an important question and one which we should very carefully consider before determining it. If you want these companies organized under a general law and leave them forever in existence, or so long as the general law may designate, notwithstanding its repeal, then vote against the amendment, but if you want to retain the power in the hands of the Legislature to reach these companies whenever they exceed their powers, amend the Bill of Rights so that these corporations may be reached. I ask the Convention to take this matter into consideration and not vote hastily upon this matter.

Mr. CLARKE, of Henry. It occurs to me, that there is not that necessity for this section in the Constitution, which may be appended on the part of some members. We can trust something to the General Assembly that shall come after us, and it will be very easy for the gentleman from Jefferson, (Mr. Wilson) and for others who may have the ambition to be in that body to suggest, or if they are not members of that body themselves, to make suggestions to their Representatives, which will enable them in passing charters to provide the people with a perfect safe-guard.

The question was then taken on Mr. Peter's amendment and it was agreed to upon division, ayes 19—noes not counted.

Mr. BUNKER moved that the Committee rise, which was agreed to.

The Committee then rose, and the President having resumed the chair, the Chairman reported that the Committee of the whole, to whom had been referred the report of the Committee on the "Preamble and Bill of Rights" had had the same under consideration, made progress therein and asked leave to sit again.

The report of the Committee was accepted and leave granted for them to sit again, to-morrow at 10 o'clock, A. M.

Smoking During the Session.

Mr. TODHUNTER offered the following resolution:

Resolved, That there shall be no smoking allowed in this Chamber during the sittings of this Convention, and that the Sergeant at Arms be required to strictly enforce this resolution.

The question was taken and the resolution was agreed to.

On motion of Mr. PATTERSON,

The Convention then adjourned till to-morrow morning at 10 o'clock, A. M.

SATURDAY, January 31, 1857.

The Convention assembled at ten o'clock A. M., and was called to order by the President.

Prayer by the Chaplain.

The Journal of yesterday was then read and approved.

Order of Morning Business.

The PRESIDENT stated that in the absence of any rule of the Convention upon the subject, he would make the suggestion that the order of proceeding in the morning of each day be, first, presentation of petitions and memorials; second, reports from standing committees; third, reports from select committees, and then the regular business of the day.

No objection being made, the order of proceeding as above indicated, was adopted.

Petitions and Memorials.

The PRESIDENT laid before the Convention the petition of James Hamilton and twenty-three others, citizens of Louisa county, praying for the incorporation into the constitution of the following provision:

"The legislature shall have power to pass laws regulating, restricting or prohibiting the manufacture and traffic in intoxicating liquors, and to that end may confiscate all liquors manufactured or sold, or held for sale in violation of its action."

Mr. CLARKE, of Johnson. I move to refer the petition to the Committee on the Bill of Rights. I would merely call the attention of the committee to that subject, and say that at the proper time I expect to propose an amendment to the Bill of Rights, giving the right to the people to secure the abolition of this traffic, when they think proper to do so.

The petition was referred to the Committee on Preamble and Bill of Rights.

Mr. CLARKE, of Henry, presented a petition of James Rice and fifty-four others, citizens of Delaware county, without distinction of party, praying the incorporation into the constitution of a provision that no person should be disfranchised on account of color.

Referred to the Committee on the Right of Suffrage.

Reports of Standing Committees.

Mr. CLARKE, of Johnson, from the Committee on the Judiciary Department, presented the following report of the majority of the Committee:

ARTICLE —.

Section 1. The Judicial power of this State shall be vested in a Supreme Court, Superior Court, District Courts, and such inferior Courts as the General Assembly may, from time to time, establish.

Sec. 2. The State shall be divided into four judicial districts, to be bounded by county lines, and as compact and equal in population and territory as may be; in each of which districts, at the first general election under the constitution, one Supreme Judge and three District Judges, who shall be residents of their respective districts, shall be elected by the people. The Supreme and District Judges so elected, shall be classified so that one Judge of the Supreme Court, and one of the District Judges in each district shall go out of office every two years. The Judge of the Supreme Court holding the shortest term of office under such classification, shall be Chief Justice of the Court during his term, and so on in rotation. After the expiration of their terms of office under such classification, the term of each Judge of the Supreme Court shall be eight years, and the term of office of each District Judge six years, and until their successors are elected and qualified

Sec. 3. The Supreme Court shall consist of the four Judges elected as required by the foregoing section, three of whom shall constitute a quorum. They shall hold their court at such time and place as the General Assembly may prescribe, and shall be ineligible to any other office in the State during the term for which they were elected.

Sec. 4. The Supreme Court shall have appellate jurisdiction only in cases in chancery, and shall constitute a Court for the correction of errors at law, in all cases that may be appealed from the Superior Court, under such restrictions as the General Assembly may, by law, prescribe; and shall have power to issue all writs and process necessary to secure justice to parties, and exercise a supervisory control over all inferior judicial tribunals throughout the State.

Sec. 5. The Superior Courts shall be held in each district at such time and place as the General Assembly may prescribe; shall consist of the Judges of the District Courts of that district, two of whom shall constitute a quorum; and the Judge holding the shortest term of office shall be the Chief Justice of the Court of his district, and so on in rotation.

Sec. 6. The Superior Courts shall have appellate jurisdiction only in all cases in chancery, and constitute a court for the correction of errors of law within their respective districts, under such restrictions as the General Assembly may prescribe; and shall have power to issue all writs and process necessary to secure justice to parties, and exercise a supervisory control over all inferior judicial tribunals within their respective districts.

Sec. 7. The District Court shall consist of a single Judge, and the District Judges of each district shall hold a court in each county alternately, at such time and place as the General Assembly may prescribe.

Sec. 8. The District Court shall be a court of law and equity, which shall be distinct and separate jurisdictions, and have jurisdiction in all civil and criminal matters arising in their respective districts, under such restrictions as may be prescribed by law.

Sec. 9. The salary of each Judge of the Supreme Court shall not be less than two thousand five hundred dollars, nor more than five thousand dollars per annum. The salary of the Judge of the District Court shall not be less than two thousand, nor more than four thousand dollars per annum: and the salary of no judge of either court shall be increased or diminished during his term of office.

Sec. 10. The Judges of the Supreme and District Courts shall be conservators of the peace throughout the State.

Sec. 11. After the year 1860, the General Assembly may re-organize the judicial districts, and increase or diminish the number of districts, or the number of judges of the Supreme or District Courts; but such increase or diminution shall not be more than one district or one judge of either court at a time; and no re-organization of the districts, or diminution of the judges shall have the effect to remove a judge from office. Such reorganization of the districts or increase or diminution of the judges shall take place every five years thereafter, if necessary, and at no other time.

Sec. 12. The Supreme and Superior Courts shall have the power to appoint the necessary clerk for each Court, and a reporter of their decisions. The other officers of the Court shall be provided for by law.

Sec. 13. The Judges of the Supreme and District Courts shall be chosen at the general election, and the term of office of each judge shall commence on the first day of January next after their election.

Sec. 14. The General Assembly shall provide by law for the election of an Attorney General by the people, whose office shall be kept at the seat of government.

Sec. 15. The qualified electors of each county shall elect, at such times as may be prescribed by law, one Prosecuting Attorney and one Clerk of the District Court, who shall be residents therein, and hold their several offices for the term of two years, and until their successors shall be elected and qualified.

Sec, 16. When any vacancy occurs in the office of Judge of the Supreme or District Courts, before the expiration of the regular term for which he was elected, the same shall be filled by appointment by the Governor, until it shall be supplied at the next general election, when it shall be filled by election for the residue of the unexpired term.

Sec. 17. The General Assembly may provide by law for the creation of a temporary court for the trial of any Judge of either the Supreme or District Courts, or any other State officer, who may be charged with incompetency or misconduct. If a Judge of the Supreme Court is a subject of the charge, four of the Judges of the District Court, selected from the respective districts, shall constitute a court to investigate the charge. If the complaint is made against a Judge of the District Court, or any other officer of State, the Supreme Court shall have original jurisdiction of, and constitute a court to investigate the same. The charge shall be made by petition, under oath, and the cause shall be tried by the Court.

Sec. 18. The style of all process shall be: "The State of Iowa;" and all prosecutions shall be conducted in the name and by the authority of the same.

W. PENN CLARKE, Chairman.

I concur with the majority report, except that I favor the election of Supreme Court Justices by the people of the State at large. That I favor the subdivision of the districts into four circuits; and that in each district four judges shall be elected—one from each circuit—three to form a quorum in the District Court. That a prosecuting attorney shall be elected in each circuit. That no judicial officer shall be tried for incompetency unless presented by a majority of the General Assembly.

R. L. B. CLARKE.

Mr. CLARKE, of Johnson, also presented the following report from the minority of the Committee on the Judiciary:

ARTICLE —.

Sec. 1. The judicial power of this State shall be vested in a Supreme Court, District Courts, and such other courts as the General Assembly may from time to time establish.

Sec. 2. The State shall be divided into four judicial districts, to be bounded by county lines, and as compact and equal in population and territory as nearly as may be, in each of which Districts, at the first general election under the constitution, one Supreme Judge, and three District Judges, who shall be residents of their respective Districts, shall be elected by the people. The Supreme and District Judges so elected, shall be so classified that one Judge of the Supreme Court, and one of the District Judges in each District, shall go out of office every two years. The Judge of the Supreme Court holding the shortest term of office under such classification, shall be Chief Justice of the Court during his term, and so on in rotation. After the expiration of their terms of office under such classification, the term of each Judge of the Supreme Court, shall be eight years, and the term of office of each Judge of the District Court, shall be six years, and until their successors are elected and qualified.

Sec. 3. The Supreme Court shall consist of the four Judges elected as required by the foregoing section, three of whom shall constitute a quorum, and they shall hold their court at such time and place as the General Assembly may, by law, provide. The Judges of the Supreme Court shall be ineligible to any other office in the State during the term for which they were elected.

Sec. 4. The Supreme Court shall have appellate jurisdiction only in all cases in Chancery, and shall constitute a court for the correction of errors at law, under such restrictions as the General Assembly may, by law, prescribe, and shall have power to issue all writs and process necessary to secure justice to parties, and exercise a supervisory control over all inferior judicial tribunals throughout the State.

Sec. 5. The District Court shall consist of a single Judge, and the District Judges of each District shall hold court in each county of such District, alternately, at such time and place as the General Assembly may, by law, provide.

Sec. 6. The District Court shall be a Court of law and equity, which shall be distinct and separate jurisdictions, and have jurisdiction in all civil and criminal cases, arising in their respective Districts, under such restrictions as may be prescribed by law.

Sec. 7. The Supreme Court shall have the power to appoint a Clerk and Reporter of its decisions. The other officers of the Court shall be provided for by law.

Sec. 8. The Judges of the Supreme and District Courts shall be conservators of the peace throughout the State.

Sec. 9. The salary of each Judge of the Supreme Court shall not be less than three thousand dollars per annum, nor shall the salary of each Judge of the District Court be less than two thousand five hundred dollars per annum. After the year 1860, the General Assembly shall have the power to increase the salaries of the Judges of the Supreme and Districts Courts: but the salary of no Judge of either Court shall be increased or diminished during his term of office.

Sec. 10. In case the office of any Judge of the Supreme or District Court shall become vacant, before the expiration of the regular term for which he was elected, the vacancy may be filled by appointment, by the Governor, until it shall be supplied at the next general election, when it shall be filled by election for the residue of the unexpired term.

Sec. 11. The Judges of the Supreme and District Courts shall be chosen at the general State election, and the term of office of each Judge shall commence on the first day of January next after their election.

Sec. 12. After the year 1860, the General Assembly may reorganize the Judicial Districts, and increase or diminish the number of Districts, or the number of Judges of the Supreme or District Courts, but such increase or diminution shall not be more than one District, or one Judge of either Court at a time, and no reorganization of the Districts, or diminution of the Judges, shall have the effect of removing a Judge from office. Such reorganization of the Districts, or increase or diminution of the Judges of either Court shall take place every five years thereafter, if necessary, and at no other time.

Sec. 13. The General Assembly may provide by law, for the creation of a temporary Court, for the trial of any Judge of either the Supreme or District Courts, or any officer of State, who may be charged with incompetency or misconduct. If a Judge of the Supreme Court is the subject of the charge, four Judges of the District Court, selected from the respective Districts, shall constitute a Court to investigate the charge. If the complaint is against a Judge of the District Court, or any officer of State, the Supreme Court shall have original jurisdiction of, and constitute a court to investigate the same. The complaint shall be made by petition, under oath, and the cause tried by the Court. In either case, the judgment of the Court shall not extend beyond deprivation of office, and ineligibility to hold any other office in the State, or either of them.

Sec. 14. The style of all process shall be: "The State of Iowa," and all prosecutions shall be conducted in the name and by the authority of the same.

Sec. 15. The General Assembly shall provide by law, for the election of an Attorney General by the people.

W. PENN. CLARKE.

Mr. WILSON, of Jefferson, concurs in this report, so far as it provides for the creation of two Courts, instead of three; but differs as to the mode of electing the Judges.

On motion of Mr. CLARKE, of Johnson, the above reports were laid on the table, and the usual number ordered to be printed for the use of the Convention.

Resolutions, &c.

Mr. HARRIS, in pursuance of previous notice, introduced the following resolution:

Resolved, That, in addition to the number of standing committees already appointed, there shall be another—which shall be the thirteenth —on "Charitable Institutions."

Mr. CLARKE, of Johnson. I do not desire to be very particular about these things, but this subject has already been referred to the Committee on Miscellaneous Subjects, which has nothing else before it, and I think it would be useless to take the matter from that committee, and appoint a new committee to consider it.

Mr. HARRIS. I do not wish to interfere with the business of any other committee, and was not aware that there had been anything of this kind referred to the committee on Miscellaneous Subjects. I still think, however, that the subject should be referred to a separate committee.

The question being taken upon the resolution, it was not agreed to.

Mr. EDWARDS offered the following resolution, which was agreed to:

Resolved, That the hours of meeting, for the Convention, shall be 9 o'clock, A. M., and 2 o'clock, P. M., each day, until otherwise ordered.

Mr. CLARKE, of Johnson, in pursuance of previous notice, introduced the following resolution, which was agreed to:

Resolved, That the following be added to the rules of this Convention:

The reports of standing committees shall be read three times on as many different days, unless this rule be suspended by unanimous consent; but no report shall be read the third time and finally passed, until all the reports of the committees shall have passed their second reading.

Preamble and Bill of Rights.

On motion of Mr. WARREN,

The CONVENTION then resumed the consideration, in Committee of the Whole (Mr. Edwards in the chair) of the report of the Committee on the Preamble and Bill of Rights.

The CHAIRMAN stated that when the Committee rose, yesterday, they were engaged in reading the Bill of Rights by sections as it stood in the present constitution. The second section would now be read.

Miscellaneous.

The second section of the Bill of Rights was then read, as follows:

2. All political power is inherent in the people. Government is instituted for the protection, security, and benefit of the people, and they have the right, at all times, to alter or reform the same, whenever the public good may require it.

Mr. SKIFF moved that the section be adopted.

Mr. CLARKE, of Johnson. I would ask, Mr. Chairman, if it be necessary to move the adoption of any section read here, or will it pass *pro forma*, without such a motion?

The CHAIRMAN. The chair does not consider a motion to adopt a section necessary. If no amendment be offered, the chair will consider the section concurred in as read, and order the reading of the following section.

Mr. SKIFF. Then I will withdraw my motion, if that is to be the understanding.

No amendment being offered to the second section, the third section was read, as follows:

3. The general assembly shall make no law respecting an establishment of religion, or prohibiting the free exercise thereof; nor shall any person be compelled to attend any place of worship, pay tithes, taxes, or other rates for building or repairing places of worship, or the maintenance of any minister or ministry.

No amendment being offered to the third section, the fourth section was read, as follows:

4. No religious test shall be required as a qualification for any office or public trust, and no person shall be deprived of any of his rights, privileges or capacities, or disqualified from the performance of any of his public or private duties, or rendered incompetent to give evidence in any court of law or equity, in consequence of his opinions on the subject of religion.

Mr. HARRIS moved the following amendment by way of addition to the section:

And no preference shall be given to any religious society, nor shall any interference with the rights of conscience be permitted; but nothing herein contained shall be construed to dispense with oaths or affirmations.

The question being taken upon the amendment, it was not agreed to.

No further amendment being offered to the fourth section, the fifth section was read, as follows:

5. Any citizen of this State who may hereafter be engaged, either directly or indirectly, in a duel, either as principal or accessory before the fact, shall forever be disqualified from holding any office under the constitution and laws of this State.

No amendment being offered, the sixth section was read, as follows:

6. All laws of a general nature shall have a uniform operation.

No amendment being offered, the seventh section was read, as follows:

7. Every person may speak, write and publish his sentiments on all subjects, being responsible for the abuse of that right. No law shall be passed to restrain or abridge the liberty of speech or of the press. In all prosecutions or indictments for libel, the truth may be given in evidence to the jury, and if it appear to the jury that the matter charged as libellous was true, and was published with good motives and justifiable ends, the party shall be acquitted.

No amendment being offered, the eighth section was read, as follows:

8, The right of the people to be secure in their persons, houses, papers and effects, against unreasonable seizures and searches shall not be violated; and no warrant shall issue but on probable cause, supported by oath or affirmation, particularly describing the place to be searched and the papers and things to be seized.

Mr. WILSON moved to amend by striking out of the clause "and the papers and things to be seized," the word "papers," and insert the word "person."

The amendment was agreed to.

No further amendment being offered, the ninth section was read as follows:

Trial by Jury.

9. The right of trial by jury shall remain inviolate; but the General Assembly may authorize trial by a jury of a less number than twelve men in inferior courts.

To this section the Committee on the Preamble and Bill of Rights reported the following amendment:

Add to section nine as follows: But no person shall be deprived of life, liberty or property withdue process of law.

The question was upon the adoption of the amendment of the committee.

Mr. SCOTT. I cannot see the propriety of making this addition to this section, as recommended by the Committee. All are guaranteed that right now by the Constitution of the United States. That guard has been thrown around by a power stronger than any we can exert in our Bill of Rights. I think it is unnecessary duplication to put this provision in here.

Mr. TODHUNTER. I would inquire from my friend from Johnson, (Mr. Clarke,) whether the Supreme Court has decided this question of a jury less than 12 in number or not. I think the question has been decided, and that such a jury was in contradistinction to the Constitution of the United States. If I am not mistaken the question arose in Madison County, in a liquor case, and one of the grounds of objection raised against the decision of the trial there was, that there had been a less jury than 12 called to try the case, and that number was unlawful and unconstitutional.

Mr. CLARKE, of Johnson. For the information of the gent from Warren, [Mr. Todhunter.] I will say that I have no recollection of the case to which he refers, but my present impression is that the Supreme Court has decided that the fact that a man is tried by a jury of less number than 12 is not a violation of the Constitution of the United States. I think that is decided in one of the liquor cases either from Davenport or Keokuk.

Mr. CLARK, of Alamakee. I hope the amendment of the committee will be adopted; we find the same provision it is true in the Constitution of the United States, but that, I think is one good reason why we should put it into our constitution, for it has had the endorsement of those very eminent men whom we are all in the habit of believing were desirous to secure and throw guarantees around the personal rights of individuals. And the fact that it is in the Constitution of the United States is no reason who it should not be inserted here. So far as I understand the weight of authority upon this point, this portion of the Constitution of the United States is regarded as having reference only to United States laws and Acts framed by Congress, and is designed to regulate their action, but has no bearing upon the Courts created by a State, or the manner in which they dispose of this subject. And I apprehend if it is necessary to incorporate it into the Constitution of the United States, it is equally necessary to have it in the Constitution of this State.

Mr. HALL. I suppose the Constitution of the United States is the law for that Government, but has no restrictive effect upon the States, whatever, in this particular.

The question being taken upon the amendment of the Committee, it was agreed to.

No farther amendment being offered, the tenth section was read as folloms:

Criminal Prosecutions.

"In all criminal prosecutions, the accused shall have a right to a speedy trial by an impartial jury; to be informed of the accusation against him; to be confronted with the witnesses against him; to have compulsory process for his own witnesses, and to have the assistance of counsel."

To this section, the Committee on Preamble and Bill of Rights, report the following, by way of amendment:

"In all criminal prosecutions the accused shall have a right to a speedy trial, before an impartial jury, of the County or District in which the offence is alleged to have been committed, to demand the nature and cause of the accusation against him, to be confronted by the witnesses against him, to have compulsory process for his own witnesses, and to have the assistance of counsel."

Mr. HARRIS. I move to amend this amendment, which otherwise I think would be a little objectionable if adopted, by inserting after the words "accusation against him," the words "and a copy thereof," and also to add a clause as follows: "provided this section shall not be construed to prevent the General Assembly from passing laws ordering a change of venue from one district to another," so that the section will then read:

"In all criminal prosecutions, the accused shall have a right to a speedy trial before an impartial jury, of the County or District in which the offence is alleged to have been committed; to demand the nature and cause of the accusation against him, and a copy thereof; to be confronted by the witnesses against him; to have compulsory process for his own witnesses, and to have the assistance of counsel: Provided this section shall not be construed to prevent the General Assembly from passing laws ordering a change of venue from one district to another."

Here the words are "in the county or district in which the offense is alleged to have been committed," and it may be construed that the criminal shall not be tried in any other county or district than the one he committed the offense in. I believe every person at all familiar with our courts, knows there are times when a change of venue is necessary to preserve the rights of citizens, and also the rights of the State.

As to my first amendment, to give the accused a copy of the accusation against him, I suppose no objection can be offered to tnat.

Mr. PARVIN. I have looked with as much scrutiny as I can to this section of the Bill of Rights, and to the substitute proposed by the committee, and I cannot come to the conclusion that the substitute is any better than the old section of the Constitution ; and in my opinion, in some respects it is not as good. It adds the words, "of the county or district in which the offense is alleged to have been committed." Now our laws have provided for all such cases as that, and there is no necessity for it here. In the amendment there are also to be found these words : "to demand the nature and cause of the accusation against him." Under the old constitution he is "to be informed of the accusation against him." I prefer the old section to the substitute proposed, and can see no necessity for changing it.

Mr. HARRIS. I would ask the gentleman from Muscatine, [Mr. Parvin,] a question. Will he contend that a man who has the right "to demand the nature and cause of the accusation against him," has also the right to have a copy of the indictment furnished him?

Mr. PARVIN. No sir ; but our laws have abundantly provided for that.

Mr. HARRIS. I was not aware of that.

Mr. PARVIN. Did the gentleman ever know a court to refuse a copy of the indictment when the accused asked for it?

Mr. HARRIS. I do not know how that would be. But I would not have a man depend upon the courtesy of the court for a copy of the indictment, but give him the power to demand it as a matter of right.

Mr. PARVIN. I believe a man has that right now under the old constitution, and that it has never been refused. I do not think the courts can avoid giving him a copy of the accusation if he asks for it. They are compelled to do so. I see no advantage in the substitute of the committee.

Mr. CLARK, of Alamakee. I am not particular about this amendment ; but I apprehend it will be necessary to give a man the right of demanding a copy of the indictment or accusation under which he is tried. I am in favor of this amendment for it contains a right which every man should have. He should have the right to demand this copy as a right, and not be compelled to depend upon the courtesy of the court to be furnished with a copy of the accusation against him. I certainly hope the amendment of the gentleman from Appanoose, [Mr. Harris,] will be adopted; but I am indifferent whether it is made to the original section or to the substitute of the committee.

Mr. HALL. I will go as far as any gentleman here to secure the rights of citizens, but while I do that I desire to look a little to the interests of the public. There are two sides to this matter ; and it strikes me that we are only producing confusion by this amendment to this section of the constitution. As that section now stands it provides abundantly for all the purposes for which it was made. This amendment of the gentleman from Appanoose makes it the duty of the court to give the accused a copy of the indictment and charges against him. Suppose now that a record should go to the Supreme Court that does not show that the accused ever had a copy of the indictment furnished him, a thing which would happen in frequent instances. The accused may perhaps, or his counsel may for him, waive the right of having a copy of this indictment when he is brought up for trial ; or if he receives a copy his counsel may cunningly contrive to secure the absence of the fact that he has received it, or even that he has waived his right to receive it, and upon that ground the Supreme Court might reverse the judgment of the lower court, and he would go unwhipped of justice. You would be giving a loophole through which the guilty may escape. You would be giving a new construction to the constitution under which we have lived for ten years without any objection being found with it.

Now as to the other objection; shall the defendant have the right to say whether the jury shall be selected from the district or county in which the crime is alleged to have been committed, or shall the people have the right to make that choice? If the people shall say the jury shall be taken from beyond the district, does not the defendant receive the benefit of it? Should the defendant have the right to call for this, it would be putting an enormous expense upon the county or district, at the mere caprice of the accused. I would say let the Constitution remain as it is, and under it a man is assured of an impartial trial. The tenth section of the present Bill of Rights secures to him an impartial trial, and does not leave any of those opportunities for quibbling that the amendment suggests. He may say that the constitution gives him the right to have a jury from the "County or District;" and if the jury shall have been empanneled from the County, he may claim that the jury should be taken from the District. Under the amendment offered by the gentleman from Appanoose, [Mr. Harris,] the accused may say that he will waive the right to a copy of the indictment, and keep that fact back when the case goes to the Supreme Court, and by that means he might get the judgment of the lower court reversed.

Mr. HARRIS. I would like to ask the gentleman from Des Moines, [Mr. Hall,] as I have much confidence in his legal knowledge, whether he is opposed to changing the venue, or to conferring the right to grant a change of venue. Cases certainly have arisen in practice within my knowledge, where the courts have held on to the causes, and tried them, although the accused have filed affidavits that they believed the courts were prejudiced against them. I would like to give the accused the right to get away from the courts in any particular District when there is a necessity for it.

Mr. WILSON. I can not conceive how the section in the old Constitution, or the substitute proposed by the Committee, can cover the ground laid down by the gentleman from Appanoose, [Mr. Harris,] and which he proposes to attain by his amendment. As to the objection of the gentleman from Des Moines, [Mr. Hall,] it seems to me the Supreme Court will not encounter the difficulty he has suggested. The substitute provides that the accused shall have the right to demand the nature and the cause of the accusation against him. The amendment provides that after the demand is made, he shall have a copy of the accusation furnished him. If it does not appear upon the record that the copy was furnished him, the Supreme Court would have no difficulty, for the presumtion would be that the accused had not demanded it. With the amendment of the gentleman from Appanoose, [Mr. Harris,] I would feel like voting for the substitute of the Committee.

In relation to the word "District," as I understand the reading of this provision, that word was not intended to mean a Judicial District rather than a Senatorial District. A Senatorial District may be composed of one County, while a Judicial District would be composed of several Counties. And if we divide the State into four Judicial Districts for the election of Supreme Judges, as has been proposed here, then there would be another kind of Districts. I understand this word "District" merely to refer to the Judicial District in which the offence is alleged to have been committed. That is my understanding of what is meant.

Mr. CLARKE, of Johnson. I am opposed to all these amendments. I think the objection to them all is, that they go too much into detail. If we were sitting here debating an act regulating the criminal practice of this State, these amendments would perhaps be proper. But we are here to frame a Constitution, to lay down general principles, to secure the rights of the people, and leave the details to be carried out by the General Assembly. I agree with the gentleman from Des Moines, [Mr. Hall,] that all these amendments will lead to a new construction of the Constitution, and open loop-holes for the escape of criminals, and create fruitful subjects of litigation. I apprehend there has been no complaint in this State, concerning this portion of our present Constitution, or that the country at large complains that the rights of citizens are not sufficiently guarded in this respect. If we go into all these details, we will make a Constitution as large as an ordinary law book, and create the most fruitful source of litigation that can be imagined.

Mr. GOWER. Is it in order to offer an amendment to the amendment of the gentleman from Appanoose (Mr. Harris)?

The CHAIRMAN. The chair is of opinion that the amendment of the gentleman from Appanoose is an amendment of the Committee, and a further amendment would not be in order.

Mr. TODHUNTER. I would suggest that the subject under consideration, by the Committee of the whole, is the report of the Committee on the Preamble of the Bill of Rights, and not the Preamble and Bill of Rights itself. A part of that report of the Standing Committee is the substitute they propose for the tenth section of the Bill of Rights. The gentleman from Appanoose (Mr. Harris) proposes to amend that portion of the report of the Standing Committee. The gentleman from Cedar (Mr. Gower) proposes to amend that amendment, thus proposing an amendment of the second degree, and consequently is in order. We are acting upon the report of the Standing Committee and not upon the old tenth section of the Constitution. If that is the fact, then there has been only one amendment offered as yet, and that by the gentleman from Appanoose, and the gentleman from Cedar, can offer an amendment to the amendment.

The CHAIRMAN. The chair still entertains the opinion that the amendment of the gentleman from Appanoose (Mr. Harris) is an amendment to an amendment. The Committee of the whole upon commencing their consideration of this subject, took up the Bill of Rights as it now exists in the Constitution, reading it section by section, and receiving such amendments as may be proposed as they go on with this reading, regarding the report of the Standing Committee in the same light as any amendment offered by individual members here. By adopting this course, they made the Bill of Rights in the present Constitution, the principal subject under consideration, and not the report of the Standing Committee.

Mr. CLARKE, of Henry. It strikes me, that the Committee, in their proposed substitute, have not given as broad a protection to the criminal as he has under the old Constitution. They have certainly limited his rights in their substitute. Under the old Constitution he has a right ts "an impartial jury." Here the Committee have provided that he shall have that right only in the county or district where the offence is alleged to have been committed. Now, I cannot for the life of me, see the object of this restriction. Before, the provision was as broad as it could be; it concerned the whole State, and we always have heen taught that the whole embraces the part. And if he has a right to an impartial jury, taken from anywhere in the State, then he would have that right in any district or county, whether the offence be alleged to have been committed there or not. Therefore I think the substitute of the Committee is not a good one.

And I would throw out another suggestion. In my limited practice the question arose as to whether a person indicted for a criminal offence had the right to have a change of venue, and the case taken out of the district. And upon application to the District Judge, he doubted his power to grant such an application. Now I would suggest to the legal profession whether it would not be well to have something here to settle that question, and give to the criminal the right to have a change of venue from one district to another.

Mr. PARVIN. This subject of the change of venue, I know has been decided upon in Muscatine county, and criminals have taken a change of venue to other counties. I think our laws provide amply for all this. Criminals can now change the venue if they desire, have a copy of the indictment and everything that is necessary. No evils have arisen under this portion of the old Constitution, and I hope no change will be made in it.

Mr. HALL. On this subject of the change of venue I would say a few words. I know that my brethren of the legal profession will almost all be in favor of it. But I have had more than twenty years experience, and have been engaged in the profession all my life since I arrived at manhood, and I have had some practice in the defence and prosecution of criminals, perhaps as much so as any other member of the bar in this State. And I can say one thing that the principle of changing venues has cleared more rascals and scoundrels than any other principle in our jurisprudence. It is the most powerful weapon of defense put in the hands of counsel. I can change the venue from pillar to post, and district to district, until I have tired out the witnesses, and thus ultimately get the criminal clear. I believe there are instances where a change of venue is just and right, and to wholly deprive the accused of that right would be unjust. But I believe experience and observation in cases that may arise from time to time should test this matter. But for this Convention to make an iron rule to control the matter, would, in my mind, be doing violence to our duty. I am unwilling to say one word upon that subject in the constitution, but believe the legislature will provide humane and proper measures for all cases of that kind.

Mr CLARK, of Alamakee. I do not see what the question of change of venue has to do with the subject before this committee. The substitute of the standing committee simply proposes to place a safeguard around the rights of persons accused of crime. Under the old constitution I apprehend the legislature might pass a law, should they see fit to do so, under which the trial of an offence committed in one part of a State should be taken to another part of the State; under which a man might be dragged against his will to some other county than that in which the offence is alleged to have been committed.

I am not very tenacious about the adoption of this amendment. Yet it was urged to some of the members of the committee, that perhaps this was one of the series of evils of which our forefathers complained, that they were dragged from the place where the offence was alleged to have been committed, and carried away from home. It seems to me that the gentleman from Henry, [Mr. Clarke,] takes a wrong view of this when he says it narrows the right given in the old constitution. The substitute reads: "In all criminal prosecutions the accused shall have a right to a speedy trial, before an impartial jury, of the county or district," &c. He shall have a right to demand a trial there, not that he shall be compelled to have a trial there. I do not think it interferes with a change of venue at all. It merely provides that the legislature shall not pass a law changing the venue, so as to take the accused against his will away from the county or district where the offence is alleged to have been committed.

It seems to me there is a misapprehension with regard to the meaning of the word "district." The substitute says "county or district." "District," then I apprehend, means nothing more than the particular county or district in which the court is sitting at the time, over which the court has jurisdiction. If that district is composed of a single county, then it will be that county; if there are two or three counties in that district, and the court is sitting to try all the causes in that district at that time it would apply to that. Does the term "district" mean the judicial district over which the judge may hold separate courts, or the simple district in which the court is then sitting? It seems to me there can be no difficulty in this matter. I apprehend that this substitute is merely intended to throw additional securities around the rights of the accused, and that that security may be abused—that the change of venue may be abused—is no answer to a proposition which has for its object the securing the rights of the accused. The right of the defendant to demand a trial by jury has been abused, and has enabled many persons to escape. But because it has been abused, is any person prepared to say that this provision should be struck out of existence? I think no one will say that.

Mr. SOLOMON. Upon an examination of the report of the committee, and after listening to the arguments offered upon this subject, I cannot see any change proposed by the report of the committee to the old constitution, unless it be that which may lead to further litigation. The old constitution embodies all that is requisite and necessary to defend the rights of the accused and protect the citizens of the State of Iowa, without the substitute of the committee.

Mr. PALMER. I am of opinion that the original section of the constitution is sufficient as it is. But if the substitute of the committee is to be adopted, I am in favor of the amendment of the gentleman from Appanoose, [Mr. Harris,] so that it shall not be misconstrued. It has been said here that our courts have doubted their right to grant a change of venue out of the district. If they have already doubted, this substitute would lead them still more to doubt, because it provides that the defendant shall have the right to a trial before an impartial jury of the county or district in which the offense is alleged to have been committed. And in construing this provision it might be said that because the constitution has provided how and where the defendant might be tried, it is intended that he should be tried there and nowhere else. Therefore I think if this substitute is to be adopted, the amendment of the gentleman from Appanoose should be attached to it.

Mr. CLARKE, of Henry. I would like to ask the gentleman from Des Moines (Mr. Hall) if I understand him to say, that as the law is now, the accused have the right of a change of venue from one district to another?

Mr. HALL. I do not recollect what the law is. It depends upon the Legislature to say whether he shall have that right or not.

Mr. CLARKE, of Henry. I understand the gentleman from Muscatine (Mr. Parvin) to say, that it is a settled question that they have the right to change the venue from one district to another. And the gentleman from Des Moines (Mr. Hall) argues against the adoption of the amendment of the gentleman from Appanoose (Mr. H arris) thatthis principle of the change of venue works great evil.

Mr. HALL. I said it might work a great evil and should be well guarded. I objected to putting an iron rule in the Constitution, and would leave the matter to the Legislature.

Mr. CLARKE, of Henry. We are introducing a clause here for the benefit and to protect those charged with crime. It is not to be supposed that any man charged with a crime is a criminal. We are to suppose that he is innocent until he is proven guilty. We are to throw guards around citizens and secure to them certain rights; not to protect criminals and allow lawyers to take advantage of certain provisions in the Constitution, by which they can screen criminals. It is to protect innocent people. Cases might arise where it would be necessary in order to secure an impartial jury and an impartial trial to change the venue out of the district.

It is true, as remarked by the gentleman from Davis (Mr. Palmer) that any court sitting here, putting a construction upon and getting at the intention of what this body desired in this provision, might say that it was our intention in altering the old Constitution to limit the jury to the district or county in which the offence is alleged to have been committed, and that the trial should be carried on there. The accused might get a change of venue from county to county in that district, but he could not go beyond it, because this Constitution has made no provision for an impartial jury out of that district. It appears to me, that if we pass this substitute without any amendment, it will go to the world that we intend to limit the trial before an impartial jury to the district in which the offence is alleged to have been committed.

As the Constitution is now, perhaps the gentleman from Muscatine (Mr. Parvin) is correct. I know that in my district, the question of a change of venue once arose and the Juhge doubted whether he had the power to allow the accused to take a change of venue from his district to another, but he would allow the accused go from one county to another in the district. That was only about a year ago, in the case of Mr. Trueslock tried in my district, applying for a change of venue from Henry county to some other.

Mr. CLARKE, of Johnson. I think my friend from Henry (Mr. Clarke) is mistaken in the bearing of that case. It came to the Supreme Court, and I was one of the counsel, and my recollection is pretty clear that the Judge below refused the application, because it was not upon sufficient grounds. It was upon that ground that the Supreme Court reversed the decision

The rule of practice is well settled in this State, that when the objection upon a change of venue is asked is against the Judge of that district, it cannot be changed to another district.

Mr. HARRIS. I would ask the gentleman from Johnson (Mr. Clarke) if the case has not been presented in the Supreme Court where the Judge has over-ruled objections to himself, upon the ground that they were not well founded. For instance, the affidavit of the accused sets forth that the Judge is prejudiced against him, and the Judge takes upon himself to decide that he is not prejudiced and refuses the application for a change of venue.

Mr. CLARKE of J. The law as it now stands, gives the Judge a discretion in the whole matter, whether the application is upon the ground of the prejudice of the people of this district, or the prejudice of the Judge, or the interests of the accused. My impression now, is this, that there has been a case in the Supreme Court where the Judge below refused the change of venue, exercising his discretion, and where the Supreme Court overruled that decision. But I think that there is no doubt that when there is sufficient reason to warrant change of venue, there is no difficulty in obtaining it.

Mr. TODHUNTER. I understand there is a discretionary power with the Judge, when the accused charges some other reasons than the partiality of the Judge, or of prejudice in the County. I would refer the gentleman to section 3272 of the Code, which reads:

"Such Court, in the exercise of a sound discretion, may grant such change of venue, and if the same is prayed for on the ground of objections to the Judge, such change must be awarded to some convenient County of an adjoining District; or if such change is prayed for on the ground of excitement and prejudice in the county, such change must be awarded to the nearest and most convenient county, where such excitement and prejudice does not exist."

Mr. CLARKE, of Henry. I want to be understood here, that my opinion coincides with that of the gentleman from Johnson, [Mr. Clarke.] I took that ground in the Court below, upon the application for a change of venue, which was refused, and I doubted the right of the Judge to refuse it. I am of the opinion that the accused has a right to have a change of venue from one District to another. I throw out this suggestion that gentlemen having more practice than I have had, may settle this question.

That question being settled, let us recur to the amendment of the Committee. If the substitute proposed by the Committee is adopted, then we unsettle that law. I think it is there settled that a criminal is not entitled to a change of venue from one District to another. "In all criminal prosecutions, the accused shall have a right to a speedy trial, before an impartial jury, of the County or District in which the offence is alleged to have been committed." It does not say "in the County or District," but "of the County or District." Now why should we change the language of the Constitution unless we mean something by it. Will the gentlemen of that Committee explain to me what they mean to accomplish by this amendment? If the Constitution is altered in any particular, how is it altered if not in this particular, and no other. It takes from the accused the right to a change of venue from one District to another, and confines him to the Ditsrict in which the offence is committed.

Mr. ELLS. It does not confi e him to that district, but gives him the right to demand a trial in that district.

Mr. CLARKE, of Henry. He has that right now. The venue must originally be laid there. The only question is, has he the right to demand a change of that venue? As I said before, we should protect those who are charged with crime. They have the right now to be tried in the county or district where the offense is alledged to have been committed, and the only question is, should we change the provision which gives them that right?

Mr. WILSON. Is there anything in the present Constitution, and particularly in section ten of the Bill of Rights, to prevent the Legislature from providing by law, that juries in criminal cases may be drawn from different counties?

Mr. CLARKE, of Henry. If the gentleman from Jefferson, (Mr. Wilson) will show me an instance of that kind for us to guard against here, I will attempt to answer his question by asserting the right in a provision to protect the accused in this Bill of Rights.

Mr. WILSON. It does not require any searching of records, but simply an examination here to see if there is anything to confine the Legislature to the county where the offense is committed.

Mr. CLARKE, of Henry. I do not suppose that there is or is not any necessity for that. We might be asked to put provisions in the Constitution to guard against any possible evil that might result from any kind of Legislation. To suppose that the Legislature would resort to any such absurdity is absurd in itself. If any gentleman here will show me that there is danger of a person charged with crime being dragged out of his county, Morgan fashion, to some other county, I would throw guards around him to protect him against that. But until that is done, I do not see why we should tear to pieces the old Constitution and make amendments to it. The only difficulty that I fear is, that by changing this clause of the Bill of Rights we will give rise to misunderstandings hereafter. Just see how gentlemen differ in their constructions now. Every man understands that under the old Constitution he has the right to a trial before an impartial jury in the county or district in which the offense is alleged to have been committed, and further, that he can get a change of venue under certain circumstances. I do not want to endanger that right, and mystify Judges in their construction of this portion of the Constitution. I shall, therefore, vote for the section as it now stands in the Constitution.

The question being taken upon the amendment proposed by Mr. Harris, to the substitute reported from the Committee, it was not agreed to.

The question being then taken upon the substitute, it was not agreed to.

No further amendment being offered to the tenth section, section eleven was then read as follows:

"No person shall be held to answer for a criminal offense, unless on presentment or indictment by a grand jury, except in cases cognizable before a justice of the peace, or arising in the army or navy, or in the militia, when in actual service, in time of war or public danger."

Which the committee propose to amend by adding the following:

"Nor shall any person be compelled in any criminal prosecution to be a witness against himself."

The question was taken and the amendment of the committee was agreed to.

Mr. SKIFF. I move to strike ont the word "navy." I do not believe that the State of Iowa has or ever will have any navy.

The question was taken and the amendment was not agreed to.

Mr. PALMER. I move to strike out the first clause in the section, that part of the old constitution which is retained, and insert in lieu thereof the following:

"All offences of a lower grade than felony, and crimes of which the penalty is, imprisonment for more than one month, shall be summarily tried before magistrates without indictment, presentment, or the intervention of a Grand Jury."

I see that in the discussion of this question of Grand Juries, in Conventions recently held in other States, it has been found expedient to provide that a Grand Jury be not required to find indictments in all cases of criminal prosecution. I think myself that it would be well to leave it to the legislature to say, whether a plan of a different kind should be adopted, that of dispensing with the Grand Jury altogether. I think the Grand Jury should be dispensed with as my amendment provides, in all minor offences. Under our present code our courts are encumbered with the trial of numerous offences of the most trivial character—cases which come before these courts by indictment. I believe that the least offences that can be committed against our laws are indictable by a Grand Jury, such as cases of simple affray, and assault and battery; and the courts are required to spend much of their time in their trial, at great expense to the counties in which these cases arise, without restriction, either by law or by the Constitution. I think that a plan might be probably devised to bring subjects of the greatest importance, in criminal prosecutions, before the courts without the intervention of a Grand Jury. But the amendment which I have offered does not provide for that question. The Legislature may, at their discretion, provide for a Grand Jury to find indictments in cases of felonies and the higher misdemeanors, and make provision that in all cases of criminal prosecution of a lower grade, that they shall be disposed of before a magistrate, without the intervention of a Grand Jury, or the necessity of finding bills of indictment. I think the adoption of such an amendment as I have offered would not take away the rights of accused parties. If they are aggrieved, or if injustice be done them by the decision of the courts below, they still have the right to take an appeal.

Mr. CLARKE, of Johnson. The suggestion contained in the amendment offered by the gentleman from Davis (Mr. Palmer) is well deserving the consideration of the committee. It is true, as the law now stands, that every offence known to our criminal code, is the subject of indictment by Grand Juries, and it perhaps would be well to limit this matter of indictment somewhere. For one, I am not prepared to say where the limit ought to be. This is a subject that might be properly referred to the Judiciary Committee to examine, and provide some rule in relation to it. I think the lower grade of crimes might be tried before a magistrate without the intervention of a Grand Jury, but with the right of appeal to the District Court. But, I am aware that in all trials before Justices of the Peace, injustice is very often done, and in a provision of the kind here proposed, there ought to be very strong restrictions to guard against any possible abuse.

I am not prepared to vote for or against the proposition of the gentleman from Davis, (Mr. Palmer) but I am inclined to think if the plan were properly carried out, that it might take a great deal of unnecessary labor from the District Courts, and save time and money to the people of the State.

I am aware, that in some States they are dispensing with Grand Juries to some extent, if not entirely. As I cannot make the motion here, I will move when the Committee rise, to refer this section, with the amendment of the gentleman from Davis, (Mr. Palmer) to the Judiciary Committee.

Mr. PALMER. I will withdraw my amendment for the purpose of offering it in the Convention.

Mr. TODHUNTER. I would suggest to the gentleman that he change the word 'magistrates' to 'Justices of the Peace.'

Section twelve was then read as follows:

No person shall, after acquital, be tried for the same offence. All persons shall, before conviction, be bailable by sufficient sureties, except for capital offences where the proof is evident or the presumption great.

Mr. PALMER. I move to insert before the word "acquittal" the words "and trial," so that it shall read

"No person shall, after trial and acquittal, be tried for the same offence, &c."

The question was taken and the amendment was rejected.

Habeas Corpus.

Section thirteen was then read as follows:

The writ of habeas corpus shall not be suspended, unless in case of rebellion or invasion, the public safety may require it.

Mr. CLARKE, of Johnson. I move to insert between the words "suspended" and "unless" the following;

"Nor shall it be refused when application is made as required by law."

The section as amended would then read,

"The writ of habeas corpus shall not be suspended, nor shall it be refused when application is made as required by law, unless in case of rebellion or invasion, the public safety may require it."

The writ of habeas corpus is a very important one, and it has always been looked upon as very sacred, to be guarded with the utmost care. I am aware that in some instances in other States, although not in this State, this writ has been refused, although it was applied for according to law. I am inclined to guard this writ and to make it secure to our citizens from innovation.

The amendment I have offered can certainly do no harm, and may do good.

Mr. PARVIN. I see no necessity for the adoption of such an amendment as this. We say that the writ of habeas corpus shall not be suspended, and the Judge is bound to grant it, if application be made for it according to law; and upon his head must rest the responsibility of a refusal.

Mr. HALL. I do not think the amendment offered by the gentleman from Johnson (Mr. Clarke) is necessary, for the section, as it stands, secures to every person the right to have this writ issued in cases that require it. Suppose an application should be made to a Judge, and he was prepared to decide, that even if the writ were granted, he would have to refuse the remedy prayed for. Ought we to provide in the Constitution that the Judge, in court, to whom this application is made, shall grant the writ absolutely under all circumstances? It strikes me, that this is not necessary. If I were the Judge to whom application was made for the writ, and the application itself showed, that I should be obliged to refuse the relief prayed for, why not give me the privilege of refusing the writ at once?

Mr. CLARKE, of Johnson. In reply to the gentleman from Muscatine (Mr. Parvin) let me say, that the provision, as it now stands, contemplates, that this writ may be suspended in certain emergencies. A military commander may suspend this writ. It was done upon one occasion in the history of this country. That is well enough so far. It is also written in the history of the country, that this writ has been refused, when applied for according to law.

I come now to the argument of the gentleman from Des Moines, (Mr. Hall.) Suppose that the writ is applied for according to law. The judge may be satisfied, in his own mind, that, upon a hearing, he cannot grant the relief prayed for, and upon the hearing the writ is refused, the party then has his remedy by appeal to a higher court, and he is placed in a position to have that decision renewed. Upon the other hand, if the privilege be given to the judge to refuse the writ, the party seeking it has a remedy, it is true, but by another proceeding, which may cause him great delay, and that is, a mandamus to compel the judge to issue it. Then arises another question. If it be in the discretion of the judge, the writ of mandamus may not lie, and hence the judge may refuse the writ of habeas corpus, and prejudge the case. The provision I have offered is intended to secure to every person who makes application for this writ, as required by law, the right to be heard, so that if, upon a hearing, his right to liberty is decided against him, he may have the right of appeal to a higher court, and have the decision of the judge reviewed, and not be put to the expense of suing out an independent proceeding, in order to get the writ of mandamus to compel the judge to do his duty.

Gentlemen of the Convention should give this matter their serious consideration, and see how sacred this writ is—the only writ by which every man may test his right to personal liberty. My object in offering the amendment I have, is to secure this right to every man who needs it, to protect his personal liberty, or at least give him the opportunity of presenting his case before the proper tribunal to determine his rights.

The question was taken upon the amendment, and it was not agreed to upon division. Ayes 14, noes 16.

The Military.

Section fourteen was then read as follows:

"The military shall be subordinate to the civil power. No standing army shall be kept up by the State in time of peace; and in time of war, no appropriation for a standing army shall be for a longer time than two years."

Mr. HARRIS. I offer the following as a substitute for this section:

"The people have the right to bear arms in defence of their persons, property, and the State, but all standing armies, in time of peace, are dangerous to liberty, and shall not be kept up. The military shall be in strict subordination to the civil power, and in time of war, no appropriation for a standing army shall be for a longer time than two years."

This is one of the amendments which I think are needed in the Bill of Rights, and to which I referred yesterday. It does not change, in effect, any thing in the present section, but adds more to it.

The question was taken, and the amendment was not agreed to.

Section fifteen was then read as follows:

"No soldier shall, in time of peace, be quartered in any house without the consent of the owner, nor in time of war, except in the manner prescribed by law."

No amendments being offered to this section,

Section sixteen was read as follows:

"Treason against the State shall consist only in levying war against it, adhering to its enemies, or giving them aid and comfort. No person shall be convicted of treason unless on the evidence of two witnesses to the same overt act, or confession in open court."

No amendment being offered to this section,

Section seventeen was read as follows:

"Excessive bail shall not be required; excessive fines shall not be imposed, and cruel and unusual punishments shall not be inflicted.

No amendments being offered to this section,

Section eighteen was read as follows:

Private Property.

"Private property shall not be taken for public use without just compensation."

To which, the amendment proposed by the committee was as follows:

"Private roads may be opened in the manner prescribed by law, but in every case, the necessity of the road, and the amount of damages sustained by the opening thereof, shall first be determined by a jury of disinterested free-holders; and such amount, together with the expenses of the proceedings, shall be paid by the person or persons benefitted thereby, before said road shall be opened."

Mr. HARRIS. I have an amendment to offer to this section, which it seems to me is of more importance than any other principle in this Bill of Rights. There appears to be such a disposition, however, in the committee to frown upon everything in the shape of amendments, that I think I will not offer it here, but wait and offer it when we consider this subject in Convention.

Mr. CLARK, of Alamakee. It may be deemed necessary to introduce an amendment of the nature of that proposed by the committee. In the old constitution of New York, they had a provision like the present one in our constitution, that "private property shall not be taken for public use without just compensation." The legislature, under that constitution, passed a law providing for the laying out of private roads, and and which continued in force some twenty years, there was not a county in the State, perhaps, that did not have more or less of these private roads. The question came up then, and was decided in the Supreme Court, a copy of which is to be found in the fourth of Hill. The Court held that the act authorizing private roads was unconstitutional, that all roads built under that act were a nullity, and that private property could only be taken for public, and not for private purposes. The Constitutional Convention which met in that State in 1846, adopted the same provision which we have here, "nor shall private property be taken for public use without just compensation," which forms the latter clause of the sixth section, and then they passed a seventh section, which read as follows:

"When private property shall be taken for any public use, the compensation to be made therefor, when such compensation is not made by the State, shall be ascertained by a jury, or by not less than three commissioners appointed by a Court of Record, as shall be prescribed by law. Private roads may be opened in the manner to be prescribed by law; but in every case the necessity of the road and the amount of all damages to be sustained by the opening thereof, shall be first determined by a jury of freeholders, and such amount, together with the expenses of the proceeding, shall be paid by the person to be benefitted."

In the decision of the Supreme Court in New York, to which I have referred, the Court held that private property cannot be taken for any other than public purposes, and then only by making just compensation. I believe it is a principle of eminent domain, recognized by the common law, that private property cannot be taken from a person even with just compensation, without his consent.

One point made in the New York decision was, that when the public good requires it, private property can be taken, but there was no principle in the common law that authorized the taking of private property for private purposes. The other point made, was, that when private property was taken, there shall be just compensation; and the Court says also that that provision is intended to protect the property of individuals from being taken for private purposes, even with just compensation.

If our Supreme Court hold in accordance with the ruling of that Court, under a constitution precisely the same in both States, I apprehend there will be a necessity for so altering the constitution of this State as to enable the Legislature, under proper restrictions, to provide for the opening of private ways.

Perhaps the necessity for opening such ways has not become a matter of very great necessity with us, but the time is coming when we shall feel such necessity; and therefore we should take such action now as will provide for such an emergency.

Mr. GILLASPY. I am opposed to the amendment of the committee to section eighteen, and I move to strike out the words "benefitted thereby," and insert in lieu thereof, the words "desiring the same," so that it will read:

"Private roads may be opened in the manner prescribed by law, but in every case, the necessity of the road, and the amount of damages sustained by the opening thereof, shall be first determined by a jury of disinterested freeholders; and such amount, together with the expenses of the proceedings, shall be paid by the person or persons desiring the same, before said road shall be opened"

If a man desires to establish a road for his own particular purposes, he is to be the party benefitted, and he should be required to pay the expense.

The question was taken upon Mr. Gillaspy's amendment, and it was not agreed to.

Mr. TODHUNTER. The provision that private roads may be opened in the manner prescribed by law, and that in every case the damages which are sustained must be first determined by a jury of disinterested freeholders, contemplates litigation. It contemplates an action commenced in some court having jurisdiction of the case. Suppose a man wants a private road made for his own benefit. He commences proceedings for the purpose of getting the road opened; and the question of the amount of damages sustained by him has to be passed upon by a jury, in a court having competent jurisdiction, before he can take the first step for opening his road. The individual who is opposed to the making of such road will take the case from one court to another, and keep the matter in litigation perhaps two years before the matter can be adjudicated upon. By the adoption of an amendment of this kind, endless agitation would arise, and the benefit aimed at by the party desiring a road, is not obtained. It seems to me, that here is a difficulty which ought to be considered by the gentlemen of this Convention. Under the present practice of opening roads of this character, you must make application to the County Judge, first, by petition giving notice in three places in the township, and posting one notice at the Court House door, how it is to be done. A Commissioner is then appointed for the purpose of viewing the premises. Before the final hearing, the party aggrieved may make application to the Court for his damages, and there are then three referees appointed for the purpose of ascertaining the amount of the damages, and return it to the Court. The Court then pass upon the question. This is the shortest course of settling the matter, it seems to me, because the individual desirous to do so, cannot put off the decision longer than three months.

Mr. CLARK, of Alamakee. There can be no difficulty, it seems to me, growing out of the amendment as it stands. The practice in New York is to have three road commissioners appointed for each town. If a party makes an application for a road to be opened, the Road Commissioners issue a precept summoning a certain number of jurors, disinterested freeholders, to go on and view the premises and ascertain whether the road is necessary, and they themselves assess the damages. There is no litigation growing out of this course. If the amendment be adopted, the process in this State for ascertaining the damages would be the same, except the Legislature might fix upon six or twelve men, instead of fixing upon three.

The question was then taken, and the amendment of the committee was rejected.

Mr. TRAER. I offer the following amendment

for the purpose of testing the feelings of the committee upon this subject:

Insert after the word "compensation" as follows: "first being made to the owner thereof. Such compensation shall be assessed by a jury without deduction for any benefits to any property to the owner," so that it will read as follows.

"Private property shall not be taken for public use without just compensation first being made to the owner thereof. Such compensation shall be assessed by a jury without deduction for any benefits to any property to the owner."

Mr. HALL. I hope the Convention will not disturb that article in the constitution which has already received the construction of our courts. We know what the law is, and what construction has been put upon it by the courts. I would say to the gentlemen who are so much in love with the New York system, that the decisions made in that State upon this subject, have been adopted in this State, under this clause of the constitution. No gentleman who looks at the decisions of the Supreme Court here, will object to the equitable mode they have adopted. Why make an alteration here, which may create great difficulty, and put the law in doubt for years to come. In two instances this question has been fully and satisfactorily settled; and I do not believe that any gentleman who will look at the decisions in these cases, will object to the principles they have settled.

Mr. CLARK, of Alamakee. I would inquire of the gentleman to what decisions he alludes?

Mr. HALL. I recollect one, which was the Burlington and Mount Pleasant Plank Road Company against Sater. The names of the parties in the other case, I do not now recollect.

Mr. YOUNG moved that the committee rise, report progress, and ask leave to sit again.

The question was taken, and the motion was not agreed to.

Mr. CLARKE, of Johnson. The construction which the Supreme Court, in the case of Henry vs. the Pacific and Dubuque Railroad Company, have put upon this clause, is this: First, That just compensation means the value of the property taken, without regard to the benefits derived; second, that the damages must be paid before the property can be taken. That decision completely covers the amendment proposed by the gentleman from Benton (Mr. Traer).

Mr. CLARK, of Alamakee. It does not touch the question decided in New York.

Mr. HARRIS. I would direct the attention of the gentleman from Johnson (Mr. Clarke) to section 538 of our Code, which reads as follows:

"Upon the filing of such claim, the court must appoint three suitable and disinterested voters of the couty, as appraisers, to view the ground, on a day fixed by the court, and report upon the amount of damages sustained by the claimant, after deducting therefrom the benefits he will receive from said road."

This section is evidently in direct conflict with the amendment offered by the gentleman from Benton (Mr. Traer).

Mr. CLARKE, of Johnson. The case which I have cited was the case of a railroad taking private property for public use. The constitutional question was raised as to the right of taking this property, when payment was to be made. The court decided, first, that the money must be paid before the property could be taken; second that the damages must be ascertained without reference to the benefit derived from the road.

Mr. TRAER. Does the fact, that the Supreme Court of this State have decided this question, make it unalterable? Cannot the next Supreme Court reverse that decision, and make another decision exactly the contrary?

Mr. CLARKE, of Johnson. It is certainly true, that one Supreme Court may reverse the decisions of another; but I will say this, that where a rule has been laid down and established, it is not likely that a succeeding Supreme Court will reverse it.

Mr. TRAER. If the Supreme Court have decided that persons are not to take into consideration the amount of benefit to be derived by the owner of the property, it certainly comes into conflict with this provision of the constitution, for it says, specifically, they are to take into consideration the benefit.

I desire to offer one or two additional reasons in support of the view I take upon this question. I see that in the constitution of Ohio they have this same provision, which I have offered here. It was considered necessary there to adopt such a provision, for the safety of private individuals. I would say, one difficulty in sustaining the position of the gentleman from Johnson (Mr. Clarke,) is this: that in cases where this questions comes up, and is submitted to a jury, that most individuals in communities, especially, where they have little experience in the matters of railroads, have the idea that a railroad passing any where within ten miles of them, is going to make them independently rich; and in nine cases out of ten, you cannot get, in such communities, a jury that will give a fair decision under the law, from the fact that they are in favor of railroad corporations. It appears to me, if the Supreme Court have decided this question, and that decision is open to be reversed hereafter, it will be better to establish, in the constitution, the principle I have advocated. If we establish it now, it does not interfere with the decisions of the supreme Court, which it only affirms. In other words, it makes that decision final. I understand the gentleman from Des Moines, (Mr. Hall) whose ability and experience I acknowledge, to say that the adoption of this amendment will open this question to litigation. I do not so understand it; but I understand that it will establish the principle beyond the reach of any further litigation, and any further interference. For that reason I am in favor of the incorporation of this principle into the constitution.

Mr. HARRIS. There seems to be a disposition in the committee not to entertain these amendments, and therefore, I am not disposed to make any remarks now. I have an amendment to offer, but I will not do so now. When the proper time comes I shall offer it in Convention, and shall insist upon its adoption.

The question was then taken on Mr. Traer's amendment, and it was not agreed to.

Miscellaneous.

Section nineteen was then read, as follows:

"No person shall be imprisoned for debt in any civil action, on mesne or final process, unless in case of fraud; and no person shall be imprisoned for a militia fine in time of peace."

Mr. PALMER moved to strike out the words "unless in case of fraud," so that it will read—

"No person shall be imprisoned for debt in any civil action, on mesne or final process; and no person shall be imprisoned for a militia fine in time of peace."

If there be a case where fraud is charged, the action will then take the form of criminal prosecution; and I can see, therefore, no necessity for retaining the clause here, "unless in case of fraud." In civil suits we never charge fraud, so, as the section now stands, it is rather inconsistent. If my amendment be adopted, it would still leave cases of fraud open to be punished by laws passed by the General Assembly and enforced in our courts, where criminal prosecutions are carried on.

The question was taken on the amendment, and it was rejected.

Section twenty was then read, as follows:

"The people have the right freely to assemble together to counsel for the common good; to make known their opinions to their representatives, and to petition for a redress of grievances.

Mr. CLARKE, of Johnson. I offer the following amendment:

To insert after the word "assemble," the words "in a peaceable manner;" and to strike out "counsel," and insert in lieu thereof, "consult," so that the section would then read—

"The people have the right freely to assemble together in a peaceable manner to consult for the common good; to make known their opinions to their representatives and to petition for a redress of grievances.

The question was taken, and the amendment was agreed to.

Mr. TODHUNTER. I move to amend the section by striking out the words "make known their opinions to," and insert in lieu thereof the word "instruct."

Mr. HARRIS. I would suggest to the gentleman that he had better not strike out the words indicated by his amendment, by adding "instruct" to what he proposesto strike out, it would make the language more harmonious.

The question was taken and the amendment was not agreed to.

Section twenty-one was then read as follows:

"No bill of attainder, *ex post facto* law, or law impairing the obligation of contracts, shall ever be passed."

Mr. HALL. At the suggestion of several members, I offer the following amendment. To insert after the word "contracts" the following, "or the right of property," so that it will read,—

"No bill of attainder, *ex post facto* law, or law impairing the obligation of contracts or the right of property, shall ever be passed."

The question was taken and the amendment was agreed to.

Mr. TODHUNTER. I move to insert after the word "contracts" the words "or their remedies."

The question was taken and the amendment was not agreed to.

Rights of Foreigners, &c.

Section twenty-two was then read as follows:

Foreigners who are or may hereafter become residents of this State, shall enjoy the same rights in respect to the possession, enjoyment and descent of property, as native born citizens.

Mr. CLARKE, of Henry. I move to amend the section by inserting after the word "foreigners" the following words, "and other persons not being citizens," so that the section would then read,—

"Foreigners and other persons not being citizens, who are or may hereafter become residents of this State, shall enjoy the same rights in respect to the possession, enjoyment and descent of property, as native born citizens."

On motion of Mr. SKIFF, the Committee then rose and the President having resumed the chair, the Chairman reported that the Committee of the whole, to which was referred the Preamble and Bill of Rights, with amendments reported by the Committee had had the same under consideration, made progress therein and asked leave to sit again.

Mr. CLARKE, of Johnson, moved that the Committee of the whole have leave to sit again, on Monday next, at 10 o'clock, A. M., which was not agreed to.

Mr. SKIFF moved that the Committee sit this afternoon, at 2 o'clock, which was agreed to.

Mr. JOHNSTON. I offer the following resolution:

Resolved, That the Committee on Miscellaneous subjects be instructed to inquire into the expediency of amending article twelve, by striking out section two."

The question was taken and the resolution was agreed to.

On motion of Mr. WINCHESTER, the Convention then took a recess till two o'clock, P. M.

EVENING SESSION.

The Convention assembled at 2 o'clock, P. M., and resumed in Committee of the whole, (Mr. Edwards in the chair) the consideration of the report of the Committee on the Preamble and Bill of Rights.

The question was, upon the amendment of Mr. Clarke, of Henry, to the twenty-second section of the Bill of Rights, to insert after the word "foreigners" the words, "and other persons not being citizens," so that the section would then read as follows:

"Foreigners and other persons not being citizens, who are or may hereafter become residents of this State, shall enjoy the same rights in respect to the possession, enjoyment and descent of property, as native born citizens."

Mr. SKIFF. I would suggest to the gentleman from Henry (Mr. Clarke) the propriety of modifying his amendment, so that it would read, "Foreigners and other persons, who are or may hereafter become residents of this State, &c."

Mr. CLARKE, of Henry. I will accept the amendment of the gentleman from Jasper (Mr. Skiff,) and modify my amendment accordingly.

Mr. HALL. I would ask the gentleman what other persons there can be but foreigners and native born citizens. The Constitution now provides for natives and foreigners. If there are any persons who are neither natives or foreigners, I should like to be informed of them.

Mr. CLARKE, of Henry. I do not know the gentleman from Des Moines (Mr. Hall) is aware of any other class. I wished there were no other but these two classes, and have long wished that there were none. But I am one of those who are not afraid of any citizens, whether native born or citizens by adoption. But unfortunately it happens that there are another class of people of our country whom we do not recognize as entitled to citizenship Now I say we should treat them at least with that magnanimity, occupying the position they do, that becomes us as a powerful State now making a Constitution intended to shield the rights of all. This provision is put in here to shield the foreigners. Why? Because there must be a necessity for it. Now the same necessity will extend to that other class of individuals. I scarcely dare name them for fear of shocking the sensibilities of the gentleman. But there is another class that we have cut off to a certain extent from all the rights and privileges guarantied to citizens, the elective franchise, &c.—Now I want that class to come in here under this article for the protection of the law, by amending it so that it shall read "Foreigners and other persons who are or may hereafter become residents of this State shall enjoy the same rights in respect to the possession, enjoyment and descent of property as native born citizens."

Mr. HALL. The gentleman has not answered my question, whether there are any besides those who are not born here and are native, and those who were not born anywhere else, that he desires to provide for. If there is any such class I would like to know it.

Mr. CLARKE, of Henry. The gentleman has not made a correct quotation from this section. It does not read "native born," but "native born citizens."

Mr. GILLASPY. I shall vote against the adoption of the amend't of the gentlemen from Henry (Mr. Clarke) and I do it for this reason: I do not intend by any vote I may give here to hold out inducements to that class, that the gentleman from Henry has a common feeling for, to come into this State. I am opposed to the whole thing, and would to-day vote for a proposition, if it was before this Convention, to exclude the negro forever from coming into this State.

Mr. HARRIS. I had not intended to say anything upon this amendment if it had not been urged with some pertinacity by the gentleman from Henry, (Mr. Clarke.) But I feel myself instructed by my constituents to use all the influence that I may possess in this Convention not only to not invite the classes he has in view—the colored population so numerons in the southern portion of this confederacy—to this State, but to do what I may in my weak way to prevent them from obtaining a settlement in this State. I feel myself instructed not only by my own political party, but by the great body of the party to which the gentleman belongs, and I should be recreant to the trust confided to me, if I did not so act here, and I shall oppose all amendments of this character.

And I will here state, in order that the gentleman may not be surprised when it comes, that at the proper time I shall propose an amendment to prevent those negroes not already here from becoming residents of this State.

Mr. HALL. I do wish the gentleman from Henry (Mr. Clarke) would answer my question. If by his amendment he means negroes, let him say negroes; if he means negroes and Indians, let him say negroes and Indians. Now I do not believe there is any law in this State prohibiting the colored people of this State from buying or inheriting property, and possessing it, the same as other people do. But there is a law against Indians purchasing, inheriting and possessing property in this State. Foreigners, persons who are aliens and not inhabitants, can inherit under our present Constitution, and I am in favor of continuing that privilege to them.

I do not intend to discuss this question.—There is nothing in the law of this State—I am very confident I should know it if there was—prohibiting the negro from buying and owning and inheriting property in this State. He certainly can do it unless there is a prohibition in the Constitution. There is no necessity for affirming that privilege in this Constitution. Under the decisions of our supreme court in repeated instances that a person who is not an inhabitant of this State or of the United States, cannot inherit property in this State. For instance, if a man from Germany comes here and acquires property, and dies here, leaving his children in Germany, that property would escheat to the State. That is the doctrine of the law in this State. Without a prohibiton in the

Constitution those persons would have all the rights of property after they became residents of this State, that other residents have. And I do not see the necéssity, unless the gentleman from Henry, (Mr. Clarke) wants to get the Indians here, for any such amendment as this. If that is what he wants let him speak out plainly and say what he means. Let him tell us whether he means the negro or the Indian, or both.

Mr. CLARKE, of Henry. The gentleman from Des Moines (Mr. Hall) seems to be very obtuse. He has not half the perception of the gentleman from Wappello (Mr. Gillaspy) who understood my meaning before I had well arisen from my seat, understood it almost instinctively.

Mr. HALL. He is from Kentucky, and smells a nigger instinctively. [Laughter].

Mr. CLARKE, of Henry. The gentleman from Des Moines (Mr. Hall) knows very well the effect of the amendment I have offered. We are making provisions in this Constitution, not merely to settle the rights of individuals as individuals, but those in corporations, bodies and classes. And to provide for the power of Legislatures, too. What we fix here is to be the governing principle under which our Legislature shall act. And what I propose is to place a provision here to take it from the power of the Legislature forever to make class legislation, to make laws respecting this kind of people that we do not recognize as citizens, and do not secure by these guarantees which others have, to take their property from them or dispose of it in any other way than they may dispose of the property of other citizens of the Commonwealth, in other words, it is putting them exactly upon the same footing as any gentleman in regard to holding property.

The gentleman from Des Moines, and others here, I know are very much shocked at the idea of having the negro put upon an equality with the white man. But there are certain things in which even they claim they are equal. If a negroe's life is taken by a white man the white man is hung, the same as he would be if he had killed a white man. We hold the white man and the negro equally answerable to our criminal law. But when we come to social privileges, gentlemen shrink from putting them upon an equality. Now my amendment is introduced to give all the same right to hold and inherit property in this State the foreigners have, and the same that is held by the citizens of the State. I do not care what class that provision may reach. If it reaches the Indian that would make no difference to me. We are called here to settle certain great principles. And if Indians acquire property here, I want them to be protected in that property. I want the same rules of property to apply to the negro and the Indian as applies to citizens and foreigners, who may come to this country. That is what I mean by my amendment.

Mr. GILLASPY. If the gentleman will so modify his amendment as to include those already here, whether negroes or Indians, and exclude those who are not here now from coming, I will vote for it. But I do not desire to give any vote here that may be an inducement to an influx of that kind of population in the State of Iowa.

Mr. CLARKE, of Johnson. There seems to be a "nigger in the wood pile' here. [Laughter]. Now I do not see any necessity for this amendment, and I am opposed to it because I deem it unnecessary as the law is now. If the gentleman from Henry (Mr. Clarke) desires to protect the rights of negroes, I think they are amply protected under this provision of the Bill of Rights as it stands now in the Constitution. They stand now upon the same footing as you and I do. They are already citizens so far as the right to acquire and have property descend to them is concerned. The amendment of the gentleman from Henry, tends to produce doubt and confusion where none now exists. The object of this provision of the Bill of Rights is to secure to those who are aliens the possession of inherited property in this State. Now to make a distinction in favor of one class who have already rights with white citizens in this respect, it seems to me is creating an unnecessary distinction and not promoting the object of the gentleman.

Mr. CLARKE, of Henry. I beg leave to reply to the gentleman from Johnson (Mr. Clarke) by saying that if our Courts and our Legislatures were always governed by the principles of that gentleman, and rules he has laid down there would be no necessity for it. But unfortunately such is not the case. And we find now that there are laws existing in this State of a class character, Legislating for persons as a class in relation to our schools, &c. There are laws upon our statute books exempting their property, personal and real, from taxation. Now Legislatures seem to think that they can dispose of negroes and their rights, legislating in regard to them as though they were in fact, cattle and not human beings. It is to prevent the Legislature from making this kind of law in regard to the property and rights of negroes that I offer this amendment.

Mr. HALL. I understand the gentleman from Henry [Mr. Clarke] claims that his amendment will give to the Negro and the Indian, and every other class of people who may see fit to come into this State, the right of purchasing, acquiring, possessing, and disposing of property, the same as is now enjoyed by the citizens of this State. I agree perfectly with the gentleman from Johnson, [Mr. Clarke] that at this time, and at all times, the Negro has the right of acquiring, and making disposition of property, and may inherit it, and transmit it to his heirs as I can, or any gentleman here can. That is the law now, and without a prohibition, they would naturally be entitled to this privilege under this constitution which we may make, as under the one now in force. I do not propose, nor do I desire, to put in any such prohibition in this constitution. But at the same time, I do not believe it is necessary to innovate in this respect upon the constitution now in force in this State, and which was adopted when this question was not quite so much agitated as it is now, and which was based upon the most just principles. I do not want to make them the special subject of constitutional law now. I do not want, in other words, to appear to boil over in their favor, and when the kettle is already full, I would be content, and not make the fire in their favor so hot that it will boil over. This amendment is unnecessary, unless the gentleman is fearful the courts will become unjust hereafter, or the legislature will become tyrannical, and pass laws to deprive them of the rights secured to them by this constitution. Now, if the legislature will violate the constitution, when it is so plain as it is now, the gentleman cannot make it so plain but what they will violate it. We must presume that the men who come after us will be honest, that the courts will be composed of men of integrity, and that our legislators will be men of common sense, and honesty, and will faithfully discharge their duty under the constitution they have sworn to support. We do not need any of this boiling-over process in favor of the negro.

Mr. MARVIN. I would like to ask the gentleman from Des Moines [Mr. Hall] if the heirs of a negro dying in this State, and leaving property in this State, if they live in another State, can inherit that property?

Mr. HALL. Yes, sir, they can.

Mr. TRAER. It appears to me that the whole matter here turns upon the meaning of the word "citizen," and I want to ask the gentleman from Des Moines [Mr. Hall] if a negro in this State is considered a citizen in the full sense of the word?

Mr. HALL. He is considered a citizen sufficiently to be protected in his property, as every man here knows. He can buy and sell, and dispose of property by will—which is only a mode of sale—and nobody but his heirs would inherit the property, if he had any heirs. His property would not escheat if he had any heirs.

Mr. TRAER. If a negro is considered a citizen, then I should hold that under this section of the Bill of Rights, he could buy, sell, inherit, and transmit property. It is true, as the gentleman says, that under our statute laws a negro can hold property. But is there anything in this Bill of Rights to prevent the legislature from framing an act to prevent the negro from holding property? If there is not then I hold that it is necessary to fix it so as to prevent the legislature from doing so. One gentlemen here gives notice of a proposition to prohibit the negro man from coming into this State at all. Now if the party to which that gentleman belongs should come into power in the legislature, we might have such a law as this amendment is intended to prohibit. I do not undertake to say those gentlemen would not be honest, but from the opinions indicated here, it appears to me if they should get the power they would pass such a law. And I consequently come to the conclusion that if the negro is not a citizen, the legislature would have the right to legislate in that way. And I therefore shall vote for this amendment, to prevent them from doing so.

Mr. GILLASPY. I do not intend to speak in this Convention for the Democratic party. I only speak for myself. And I do not intend that a gentleman from a rural district shall say that I speak for the Democratic party. (Laughter.)

Mr. TRAER. I had reference to the gentle- from Appanoose, (Mr. Harris) and not the gentleman from Wapello. (Mr. Gillaspy.)

Mr. CLARKE, of Henry. I would not rise again upon this question but from the fact that there certainly seems to be a misapprehension on the part of some who ought to take a different position upon this subject. I refer to the gentleman from Johnson. (Mr. Clarke.) I do not understand how it is here that when amendments are proposed to this Constitution, they are thrown aside without any sort of consideration as though they amounted to nothing. This seems to be done upon the ground that as we have got a pretty good Constitution as it is, we ought to let it remain as it is. But the gentleman from Des Moines (Mr. Hall) certainly knows that in many States of this Union legislatures have passed laws to prevent negroes from holding property. He certainly knows of the black laws of Indiana, Illinois, and other States of this Union which preclude the negro from holding property in those States. That is understood by us all.

Let us not make boy's play of this thing. I did not believe from the beginning that the gentleman did not understand this amendment. I did not wish to make a speech upon this subject. The gentleman from Des Moines knows what it reaches; the gentleman from Wapello, [Mr. Gillaspy,] knows what it reaches, and he is honest about it, and admits it. He knows what it means, and comes right out with it. He says—so far as men have acquired rights here now, I would preserve them ; I would not violate vested rights. But I would not put this into the constitution. Why? Because, he says, I do not wish to have anything here which can in any way encourage the negro to come to this State. He is honest in that. And let the gentleman from Des Moines imitate his honesty. The gentleman from Wapello is opposed to having this matter in the constitution, because he knows if it is there we should forever prevent the legislature from coming in here and enacting the black laws of other States. We should protect those who may come here, into this, by the blessing of God, our free community from those black laws, and in the enjoyment of such property as they may acquire. What do gentlemen think? What do they wish? Do they think it is possible for them to keep this class of men from our midst? Are these gentlemen who are so much in favor of the Kansas-Nebraska law—that Illinois slavery law—that they would violate all their pledges and guarantees, and carry into the whole of the territory of the United States, and black it all over with this cursed system of slavery? Are they who are so much in favor of having the negro as a slave, so afraid to allow him to come here as a free man? I desire to hold out to them some encouragement, that after they are freemen they can acquire property, and have the guarantee of the constitution of the State of Iowa to protect them in that property, and that no legislature of sham democrats coming here shall legislate their rights away from them, and say to their posterity, you shall not hold this property. That is what we want.

The gentleman from Des Moines (Mr. Hall) understands the full effect of this amendment. Oh, says he, it will encourage the negro to come here. I do not know about that; but if it were so, what of it? What in the name of Heaven has God made the great earth for—made Iowa capable of being inhabited,—made its soil conducive to the wants of man? I cannot conceive if it was not that man should live here and enjoy. He has held out inducements to them and to us to come here, and shall we cease to do justice and right because, forsooth, there may be encouragement for the negro to come here in our midst? Pass your black laws, and encouragement would necessarily cease for the negro to come here, and for the white man, too, for he would become worse than the negro. Let right and justice prevail. If the negro does come here let us guarantee to him his rights. Is it not better to endeavor to protect the poor and the feeble in our constitution, than the wealthy, and the powerful and the mighty? They can take care of themselves. But we are trying to throw a shield over the feeble and the weak, and to keep the oppressors from treading them down with their iron heels. We are to protect the blacks as well as the whites in their rights, and it is for that reason that I am in favor of this amendment; and I want gentlemen to understand that when the vote is taken here, I shall call for the yeas and nays upon it.

Mr. GILLASPY. I had supposed, from what knowledge I had of the course of the gentleman from Henry (Mr. Clarke) for the last three or four years, that he was a good Republican. Now, so far as I can judge of the position I occupy upon this question, it is in favor of the Republican doctrine as laid down by the constitutional convention of Kansas. Yet, when I uphold that same doctrine here, the gentleman flies off the handle, and is not willing that that doctrine should prevail here. Now, I desire to imitate here the course pursued by the people of Kansas in their Convention at Topeka. The constitution which they formed there being one which the gentleman from Henry, I have no doubt, would have been willing to have voted for if he had succeeded in ousting our representative from his seat in Congress. Yet that Constitution would have excluded the black man from breathing the free air of Kansas when it should have become a State. Now I am here to imitate the people of Kansas in their Topeka constitution, which I endorse with all my heart.

Mr. HARRIS. I have no desire to go into an extended discussion of this question; but I would make a few remarks, and first and foremost, in reply to the gentleman from Benton (Mr. Traer) I do not know as it would be a violent presumption—the gentleman from Benton seems to think it would—that if the Democratic party should chance to come into power, it would be honest, as other gentlemen are disposed to think their own party would be honest, in a matter of this kind; and while I would protest against the introduction of a party discussion here, I would say that I apprehend the Democratic party would not seek to give any advantage to the black population over the white, to say the least of it.

I am proud to think that the party to which I belong is the white man's party, and seeks to promote the interests of the white man. I believe that this country and this Government legitimately belongs to the white man, and when the two races cannot live together in harmony, upon an equality, I would give the ascendency to the white race. I will say with my friend from Wapello (Mr. Gillaspy) that so far as the rights of the black population and their descendants in this State are concerned, I will go as far as the farthest to protect those rights; but I do protest against holding out inducements to this class of people to come here. But the gentleman from Henry (Mr. Clarke) says if you fail to hold out encouragement to them, you will prevent the whites from settling here. It may be possible such would be the effect upon that portion of the white men, who, like the gentleman from Henry, seems to court the society and protection of the black rather than the white race; but I say that white men, so far as I understand the term white man, would desire to settle among us, and that would not prevent them from doing so; and I undertake to say, that so far as the gentleman's own party is concerned in the section of country from which I come, they are as anxious as I am, or any other gentleman upon this floor can be, that we shall make provision in the constitution to prevent the colored race from settling in this State. There are a few—a baker's dozen—whom we were in the habit of calling Abolitionists, before the Republican party came into existence, in my district, who would go with the gentleman from Henry. But so far as the bulk of the Republican party is concerned, they take the same position upon this question as the Democratic party; and if we would do injustice so far as encouraging the black race to settle in this State is concerned, then, I undertake to say, the gentleman's own party, in my portion of the State, would do the same injustice.

I may, perhaps, be a little prejudiced upon this question, but I must confess that the scenes I have witnessed in the settlements of the black population in Ohio, who have come from other States, have been such that I do not think any gentleman who could see those settlements, and witness the pauperism and degradation among them, would give any support to any proposition that would lead the same class to come here. I protest against making this State an asylum for the superanuated, the worn out and broken down of other States. Let them take care of their own paupers. I protest against making this State a hospital for them. The gentleman from Henry says we should protect the weak and oppressed. I am in favor of letting those who have worn these people out, take care of them. I do not wish to make this State a hospital for the worn out negroes of the South.

Mr. SKIFF. It seems to me we have got into a little unnecessary excitement upon this question. I do not see any mischief to result from this amendment. It reads: "Foreigners and other persons who may hereafter become residents of this State," &c. If it does no good or harm, if it does not change the meaning of this section at all, I do not see the use of fighting about it. My friend from Des Moines (Mr.Hall) does not want this amendment in here, because the clause is perfect as it is, and it would be superfluous. Now, if it would be superfluous, and gentlemen of the other side desire to have it in here, it would do no harm. I would like very well to see it here. I think, myself, it means something; or may, at all events, mean something. It may restrain the Legislature hereafter from doing what may be cruel and tyrannical. I am not altogether posted in all the laws of descent in this State. I want to have the constitution fixed so that if any person comes here, whether he has heretofore been a slave or not, and acquires property, he can have it descend to his posterity. The gentleman from Des Moines says that it is so now. Then, if we put this provision in here, it will do no harm, certainly. I hope the amendment will be adopted.

Mr. CLARKE, of Johnson. I regret, exceedingly, that the gentleman from Henry (Mr. Clarke) should be surprised at my position upon this question. I think that it is probable we do not differ so much in our object, as in our modes of getting at it. Suppose that we admit that all these black laws have been passed in the States to which the gentleman refers. We should look and see whether they have any such provisions in their constitutions as we have in ours. If I understand the argument of the gentleman, he seeks by this amendment in this section of the Bill of Rights, to prevent class legislation. Now, I think his amendment would not have that effect, and for that reason I am opposed to it.

This section now provides that foreigners who are, or may hereafter become residents of this State, shall enjoy the same rights as to the possession, acquiring, and descent of property as native born citizens. The gentleman seeks to amend by inserting after the word "foreigners," the words "and other persons." I beg leave to ask the gentleman if he does not know that there is at least one class in this confederacy, the negro, that is not held as persons. Now if his amendment is adopted, and the party he fears should come into possession of the legislature holding that opinion, they could still do what he fears, for they hold that the negro is not a person, and this amendment would have no effect but to produce confusion and uncertainty. The constitution provides that foreigners shall have the same right of property as native born citizens; and that, I undertake to say, includes the blacks as well as the whites.

Now, the practice in this State is notorious—I can point to a family of negroes in this town where the father died worth a considerable amount of property, which is enjoyed by his descendants the same as I would enjoy any of the property left by my father. Nobody pretended to say they were not the heirs, and had not the right to that property. The amendment of the gentleman from Henry will only tend to produce confusion where certainty now exists. When the proper time and place are presented for the consideration of this question, it is probable I shall vote with the gentleman, for at my time of life I have learned that we are all children of the same creator, and have rights here which should be preserved. But I do not want to run mad upon the subject, and at least jeopardise the interest of this class by putting in a provision here which will have a tendency to do more harm than good.

Mr. HALL. I would not have troubled the Convention with any further remarks upon this question, had it not been for the remarks of the gentleman from Henry (Mr. Clarke). I do not know why gentlemen here take the liberties with me that they do. It was no longer ago than yesterday that a proposition I was advocating was denounced as larceny and plundering, and today the gentleman from Henry tells me that what I say is untrue; that I am not candid, and he says I think the very contrary to what I say I do. That I think, is taking pretty broad liberties with me, and would authorise me to use expressions, perhaps, that would not be very palatable to ears polite—which I shall, however, refrain from doing.

Mr. CLARKE, of Henry. I was not aware that I used any such language. I wish the gentleman to state how I used it.

Mr. HALL. The gentleman said that the gentleman from Wapello (Mr. Gillaspy) was honest and candid in his expression of opinion here, and I was not.

Mr. CLARKE, of Henry. I referred to his expressing at once that he understood the operation of my amendment.

Mr. HALL. I must confess that I do not understand the amendment yet. I have not studied my geography enough to tell whether it means Hottentots, Negroes or Indians, or everything else, from the baboon up. I wanted the gentleman to say if he meant negroes, or if he meant the Indians, or both negroes and Indians. The gentleman understood me perfectly, I am sure, and so did everybody here.

Mr. CLARKE, of Henry. Will the gentleman allow me to explain?

Mr. HALL. I will give way for an explanation but not for a speech.

Mr CLARKE, of Henry. I will say, that I consider the colored people, the mulattoes and negeoes of this countrv as entitled to citizenship. That is my position. But there is a difference made and I want to provide for just that difference. You might honestly entertain a different opinion, and if you and your party had a majority in the Legislature, you might pass laws to cut off these negroes from holding property in this State. Certainly there can be nothing more explicit than that.

Mr. HALL. I understand that so far as negroes are concerned, there is now no prohibition against their holding property in this State and transmitting it to their posterity. And the gentleman from Johnson (Mr. Clarke) has asserted the same thing. And so far as that is concerned the gentleman's amendment amounts to nothing, and is useless

The gentleman went on, however, a little further and brought into this discussion subjects which I regret he did bring forward. He charged me, and perhaps those with whom I act, with whom I am politically associated. with being in favor of the institution of Slavery. The gentleman is a great deal more than mistaken upon that point. He charged us with being in favor of the extension of Slavery, of settling Kansas with Slaves. He is infinitely mistaken upon that point. That may do very well at the hustings, out of doors upon the stumps, but it ought not to be asserted here, for the assertion cannot be true. On the contrary, every person against whom he makes the charge, will assert in the most solemn manner, that the charge is totally and wholly unfounded. Then why make these charges here? Why throw this firebrand into this Convention? I do not wish to be uncourteous to that gentleman, nor do I want to be treated myself with a want of courtesy, when he knows I stand ready to contradict most flatly any assertion of that kind. Why did he assert it? I do contradict it in the most emphatic manner for myself and my friends.

The difference between the gentleman and myself is a difference, I have no doubt, honestly entertained by him, and I know it is honestly entertained by me. Now I do not believe it is possible in fact, though it may be put on paper, to put the negro upon an equality socially and politically with the white man. I believe an effort of that kind would be ruinous to both races, would inure to the injury of both. And I do not believe the people of this country are prepared, or ever will be prepared, to sanction the political and social equality of the two races. For that reason and not wishing to have a population of this kind in our community, not wishing to encourage the settling of this population here, when they must necessarily take this barren position, I would do nothing to encourage their settlement here; I would do nothing to bring them here, to make this country, as the gentleman from Appanoose (Mr. Harris) says, a hospital for the runaway and discarded negroes from the States where they are raised. That is the position which I took before. That is the position upon which I am willing to stand.

And I wish to say here once for all, that when the gentleman charges me or the party with which I act, or rather my friends here, for I did not come here as a partizan, with being in favor of the extension of Slavery, that I would do one act to encourage that extension, he will meet from me, and I presume from the rest, the most flat contradiction.

Now in regard to this question, there is but little in it. As was properly observed by the gentleman from Jasper (Mr. Skiff), there is no great harm in it. But I am opposed to anything that would disturb the Constitution as it now stands, unless there is a necessity for it. I would be opposed to admitting Indians here and calling them citizens, and putting it out of the power of the Legislature to keep them away. If they have the right to acquire property here, they have the right to come and remain here. The amendment opens the door to the Pottawatamies, the Sacs and Foxes, and all the western tribes of Indians to come into our State. If they have the right to purchase property here in any part of the State, no power can prevent them from coming here, and we can never make any effort to get rid of them. The gentleman's philanthropy goes a little too far. He is swallowing the whole of God's creation at a single gulp. His stomach is capable of taking in the whole human family. It is this we do not want to tolerate, and do not intend to tolerate. What would be the condition of our northern and western frontiers if the Indian had a right to come in and stay as long as he pleased, and claim the protection of the Constitution while he was here? You would bring a calamity upon those portions of our State, and upon the people of that part of our State. By this amendment you give the Indians the right to acquire and hold property in this State, and to remain here as long as they please. You would turn all the wild tribes of Indians loose among us in this State, and we never would get rid of them. I might vote for the negro but I would not vote for the Indian. I wanted the gentleman to put his amendment in such a shape that we might be able to tell how far this thing was to go. And the gentleman well knew what I meant, and what I wanted to know; and that was, whether he meant the negro, or the Indian, or both.

Mr. WILSON. It seems to me that this discussion has taken a range that is not warranted by the amendment proposed. Now as I read the section with the amendment proposed, the gentleman from Des Moines (Mr. Hall) and those who argue with him, are wholly mistaken as to the effect of it. The section proposed to be amended was as follows:

"Foreigners and other persons who are, or may hereafter become residents of this State, shall enjoy the same rights in respect to the possession, enjoyment and descent of property, as native born citizens."

Now the gentleman from Des Moines, (Mr. Hall) and the gentleman from Wapello, (Mr. Gillaspy) and the gentleman from Appanoose (Mr. Harris) have all treated this amendment as though it was an invitation to the negroes, and other classes to come into this State, and that they could not by any possibility be prohibited by the legislature if they had the power to prohibit them under the present Constitution from coming here. Now I apprehend that that is not the meaning of this amendment, and that no court would give it that construction. The meaning of it is this, and I think every lawyer and every honest court would be compelled to give it the same construction—taking it for granted that the legislature has now the right to prohibit them from coming here—if the legislature does not interfere with the right of such persons to come here and acquire property, they shall hold it after having acquired it, and the legislature shall not have the right or the power to deprive them of that property.—That is all, and there is nothing more of it. If the legislature under the present Constitution has the power to prevent negroes from coming into this State, the section under consideration as proposed to be amended will not interfere with that power, but simply says if you permit negroes to come here, they shall have the right to acquire property and you shall not have the right to take it away from them. It seems to me this is the legal force of this section as the amendment would make it. It is not a declaration that the legislature, if it now has the power to prohibit them from coming here, shall not continue to have that power. It appears to me that there is a misapprehension about this matter.

Mr. HARRIS. I would ask the gentleman who is the best capable of judging of the effect of this amendment, he himself, or the gentleman who offered it?

Mr. WILSON. I would say in reply to that, that the gentleman from Henry (Mr. Clarke) might have meant one thing, while by the language of his amendment he has arrived at another. A gentleman does not always give in the language he uses the exact thing he means. I am speaking of the language of the amendment of the gentleman from Henry, and not of what his intentions may have been.

Mr. CLARKE, of Henry. I would answer both gentlemen at the same time by saying that I believe that I have expressed just what I meant exactly, and I mean just what I have expressed. I have not said that this interferes with any power that the legislature might now have, nor with any other power that might be conferred by the Constitution which would enable them to prevent any class of men from coming into this State.

I would ask the gentleman from Des Moines (Mr. Hall) this question. Does the Constitution as it now stands prevent the legislature from prohibiting foreigners from coming into this State? It is no invitation to foreigners as it now stands, and gentlemen might just as well get out their pocket handkerchiefs and go to wiping the tears from their eyes for fear this amendment should invite the bog trotters of Ireland to come and settle in this State, as to go into such lamentations over the possibility of some of the inhabitants of Ethiopia coming here. This amendment is merely intended to state what is right, and that if men shall come here and become residents and obtain property, they shall hold that property secured to them by the same laws, and protected by the same laws under which the citizens of the State hold their property.

Mr. HALL. Will the gentleman allow me to ask him a single question?

Mr. CLARKE, of Henry. Certainly.

Mr. HALL. If the negro is a slave, leaving his family in a State where slavery is tolerated, should come here and acquire property, and dying leave it here, would not the children being slaves in Missouri for instance, or the slave mother in Missouri inherit that property under this amendment?

Mr. CLARKE, of Henry. So far as the laws and institutions of this State are concerned, they would. But the laws of Missouri would interfere. And I would state to the gentleman, since he asks me the question, and since he seems to be more afraid of the Pequods than of the Hottentots, that he himself had better prepare an amendment to my amendment, excepting the Indians.

Mr. TODHUNTER. I understand the gentleman from Benton [Mr. Traer] to ask the question whether negroes under the constitution, as it now stands, are to be regarded as citizens. I understand, according to decisions made in Connecticut, that negroes are citizens, so far as property is concerned, and are so considered in that State.

Mr. TRAER. I said my opinion was, that the right of the negro to hold and transmit property to this State, depended upon the fact whether they were considered citizens. If they are citizens, then they now have that right; if they are not, then they would not have it.

Mr. TODHUNTER. I hold in my hand the first volume of Bouvier's Institutes, and his definition of "citizen" is this:

"Citizens are native or naturalized. All persons born in the United States are not citizens. The exceptions are, first: Children of foreign ambassadors; secondly, Indians, and thirdly, in general, persons of color."

Here he excludes negroes from the technical meaning of the word "citizen." In Webster we find, under the fifth definition of the word "citizen," the same thing precisely, as follows:

"In the United States, a person, native or naturalized, who has the privilege of exercising the elective franchise, or the qualifications which enable him to vote for rulers, and to purchase and hold real estate."

According to the technical meaning here, they are not citizens. And there is nothing now in our constitution to prevent a legislature, with a majority like the gentleman from Appanoose, [Mr. Harris] and the gentleman from Wapello, [Mr. Gillaspy] from enacting a law to prevent them from coming here, and holding property in this State.

How, then, is the decision made by the Supreme Court of Connecticut, that they are citizens so far as holding property is concerned. But we have no assurance that the Supreme Court of Iowa would make such a decision. They certainly would not, if they had such men upon the bench as those who have expressed themselves here to-day. Then is it not right that we should make some regulation in regard to this matter in this constitution? The gentleman from Wapello [Mr. Gillaspy] says he is willing to protect all who are now here in their property, but not those who may come hereafter. Now suppose that there was a colored person here possessing an immense amount of property, and he was to die, and leave heirs out of the State, and those gentlemen were to pass laws to prevent them from coming into the State to get that property. They could do that under the present constitution. I think we should make some regulation in regard to this matter.

I am not opposed to including the Indians either. I understand that there was a delegation of Indians here the other day—I do not know whether the gentleman from Des Moines [Mr. Hall] was present or not—counseling with the Governor concerning the purchase of lands in this State, and they left a sum of money in the hands of the Governor for that purpose. I understand that there was a special act of the legislature, giving them the right to purchase lands in this State, and live upon them, and become citizens. Shall we not secure to them the privilege of holding this land after they shall have purchased it, the same as other citizens?

Before I close I will read the decision of the Supreme Court of Connecticut in regard to negroes being citizens, and entitled to hold property. It is as follows:

"Amy vs. Smiths 1, Litt. 334; Crandall vs. State 10, Conn. 340. Persons of color and Indians have some rights as citizens; they cannot in any sense be considered as aliens, nor can they be deprived of any of those rights which belong to American citizens, of holding property, of obtaining a patent for an invention, and the like; but they are deprived in some States of the right of voting for public officers, and of holding office."

Mr. CLARKE, of Henry. I shall defend this principle as strongly as I can, and I will go as far as any gentleman upon this floor, consistent with my views and those of my constituents. I intend that my course shall be in harmony with their views, if I know what they are. At the same time, I will freely express my own opinion upon every proper occasion, with regard to the rights of man everywhere. I observe that when men attempt to do a wrongful act, they are apt to take such a course as in the end will defeat the very objects they have in view. There is but one way to do a right thing, and if you depart from it, and attempt to accomplish a wrongful act in the name of the right, you will defeat the very object you had in view. Take this clause in question, which speaks of "foreigners and descendants of foreigners." Suppose a man from Africa were to come here? Would he not be a foreigner, and enjoy the rights of foreigners, as prescribed under the constitution; and yet you would exclude the negro born here, although he might be as intelligent as Fred Douglass. You would not include him, and allow him the privileges guaranteed by the constitution to the foreigner, and yet you would allow the African, as ignorant as the brute, to come here and enjoy the rights and immunities of citizens, so far as the holding of property is concerned.

But gentlemen tell us that the negro of this country is not a citizen. It will do for the people of Iowa to talk in that way, but it will not do for Missourians to do so. The citizens of slave states do not use that kind of language, and they do not act upon that hypothesis. The Supreme Court in Missouri has decided time and time again, that he is a citizen, and there is a case in point, that of Dred Scott, now before the Supreme Court at Washington, in which that very question has been decided over and over again in the courts in Missouri. The question of whether Dred Scott was a citizen of the United States, capable of bringing a suit and prosecuting his rights in the State of Missouri, was decided in his favor, and the Court decided unanimously that he was a citizen, so far as his right to sue was concerned. So all the laws you might pass could not keep a colored man out of this State, if he were a citizen of any other state, because the United States constitution would override our own in that particular. The constitution of the United States says that citizens of the United States shall be entitled to the privileges and immunities of the citizens of the several States. Do you wish to discriminate in this matter? Do you wish to say that a colored man coming from Missouri or Virginia, shall not have equal rights and privileges with one coming from Connecticut and Pennsylvania? My democratic friends would not be guilty of an act so inconsistent as that. Why this quibbling about these things? That clause of the constitution, if changed, would not strengthen the position of the colored man at all, and it will not give him any power which does not now exist. A colored man can come here and defy all the laws you may pass, because he claims to be a citizen of the Union, and standing upon that platform he may claim his rights. You may use physical force, but you cannot use legal force to expel him from the State.

Mr. CLARKE, of Johnson. This discussion has become a little more serious, than I anticipated when the amendment was first offered. I desire to offer a few suggestions, which I think may place this matter right before the minds of the Convention.

There are two classes of persons spoken of in the Bill of Rights; first, foreigners, and second, native born citizens. The object of the provision is to secure to foreigners the same rights in the acquisition and descent of property, which native born citizens have. These two classes are placed by this provision in juxtaposition to each other. The amendment of the gentleman from Henry, [Mr. Clarke,] if it means anything, amounts to this, that if any negro should die here having property and having heirs in Africa, that they may inherit his property. That is the effect of his amendment and nothing more. If any negro come here, acquires property and dies, if his heirs live in this country, under the decision of the court of Connecticut, and under the decisions of all the free states, they would not be aliens. The only effect of the amendment is to provide that aliens in Africa shall have the right to acquire the property which a negro in this State may leave at the time of his death. It does not seem to me that this is a matter worth quarreling about, as there is not a negro in this State, and probably will not be for the next fifty years, who will die here, leaving heirs in Africa. What was the object of the committee in reporting the article they have upon this subject? There was an immense number of Germans, Irish, Welsh and other foreigners, settling in the State, who had left behind them fathers, brothers, and sisters, and the object of the provision in question was to preserve to these connections the right to enjoy the property which might be left to them by their relatives in this State, just the same as if they were born here. I do not see that the negro question enters into this controversy at all, and this attempt to array party feeling upon this subject has really no application whatever. The practice in this State fully settles this thing. If a case of this kind should come before our courts for adjudication, they would look to that practice in determining that question. It seems that my friend from Henry, [Mr. Clarke,] has not that confidence in the integrity of mankind that he ought to have. I presume that every man occupying a judicial position is at least a man possessed of ordinary integrity and ordinary sense of justice. Whenever the courts make a decision upon this question, they will look at the practice, which under the present constitution and all the former laws bearing upon this question, and they will make no decision which will impair the rights of any of these parties. What do we understand by citizenship? Bovier gives two definitions of the word "citizen," and says first:

"A citizen of the United States is one who is in the enjoyment of all the rights to which the people are entitled, and bound to fulfil the duties to which they are subject. This includes men, women and children."

Here is the general definition of citizenship, and it takes in every man, woman and child, who lives in the States. They are all subject to the same laws and same obligations, and are required to perform the same duties; and in this respect the negro is as much a citizen as any member of this Convention. In a more limited sense, Bovier says that a citizen is one:

"Who has a right to vote for officers, for example, Representatives in Congress, and who is qualified to fill offices in the gift of the people."

These are the two definitions we have laid down by Bovier upon this subject of citizenship.

I find the following decisions in Connecticut Courts upon this subject: Amy vs. Smith, 1st Litt. 334, Crandall vs. the State, 10 Conn. 340:

"Persons of color and Indians have the same rights as citizens. They cannot, in any sense, be considered as aliens, nor can they be deprived of any of those rights which belong to American citizens, of holding property, of obtaining a patent for an invention, and the like. But they are debarred in some States of the right of voting for public officers, or of holding office."

This is the commonly received definition upon the question of the right of descent of property, in the case of colored persons, and it is one which would be as binding upon our Courts as any decision upon any other question. The question is, is a negro born here an alien? No gentleman will contend that he is. The question, then, is between aliens and citizens. If he be not an alien, his children enjoy his property just as much as the children of any of us here.

I make these remarks for the purpose of settling this question, and preventing any arraignment of party here, and creating any bad feeling upon a question which ought not to excite any such feeling. The time may come, when party may be arrayed against party here, but I desire to delay that time as long as possible.

The question was taken, and the amendment was not agreed to upon division. Ayes 8, noes not counted.

The twenty-third section was then read as follows:

"Neither slavery, nor involuntary servitude, unless for the punishment of crimes, shall ever be tolerated in this State."

No amendments were offered to this section.

Mr. WILSON. I offer the following, to come in as an additional section, so that in case it be adopted, the section which is now the twenty-fourth will become the twenty-fifth.

"Exclusive jurisdiction shall never be granted to the Government of the United States over any Territory embraced within the limits of this State."

I should never have dreamed of introducing such a section as this into the Bill of Rights, I freely confess, had it not been for the recent action of the General Assembly of this State; and in that action I have the strongest argument I can present in favor of the addition of the section I have offered. It seems, that the people of Dubuque wanted to get an appropriation from the Government of the United States to build a Custom House, Post Office, or some other public buildings, but the general government demanded at the hands of this State exclusive jurisdiction over the property which the government might purchase in that city for its use. The Legislature, in pursuance of that demand, passed a bill, giving to the United States exclusive jurisdiction over the property the government might so acquire in Dubuque. The passage of such a law as this, brings us right back to the doctrine of states-rights, in relation to which, some gentlemen of this Convention feel so deep an interest. If the Legislature of this State continue to pursue that course in legislation, we may have twenty or thirty, or more, places in this State over which the general government will have exclusive jurisdiction, so that if you issue civil or criminal process against a person in this State all that he has to do, to escape from the service of the process, by any officer of this State, is to step over the line upon the property which the United States may hold. No matter what crime he may have been guilty of, the moment he steps upon the property of the United States, although within the limits of this State, that moment he is beyond the reach of the process of the State. The Governor wisely and properly vetoed the bill, and although I have been no friend of the veto power, yet I must say it was very happily used in this instance. I wish to take away the power from from the Legislature to pass such laws in the future, as they passed in this case; and I hope the section I have introduced will be agreed to.

The question was taken, and the amendment was agreed to.

Mr. CLARKE, of Johnson. I wish to offer the following, to come in as an additional section:

"The right of the people to prohibit by law the manufacture and sale of intoxicating liquors, as a beverage, shall not be violated."

I do not propose to discuss the question, but I move the amendment now for the purpose of giving notice, that if it does not succeed in committee, I shall move it in convention, and when the proper time comes, I shall have something to say upon it.

The question was taken, and the amendment was not agreed to.

Mr. SOLOMON. I offer the following:

"The manufacture of or traffic in property, which is a production of this State, or a legitimate article of traffic with other States, or foreign nations, shall not be prohibited."

Mr. CLARK, of Alamakee. I do not wish to take up the time of this convention with any remarks upon this question, but I hope the amendment now offered will not pass here. I would myself be in favor of leaving the Legislature free, if such be the will of the people, to pass laws which would restrict the use and manufacture of any intoxicating beverage. It strikes me, that in the amendment now offered, there is a principle lurking, which will overturn that which, I apprehend, we are all in favor of supporting, the exclusion of slavery and slave property from this State.

Mr. TRAER. I rise to a point of order. I think it is unnecessary for this committee to entertain two propositions containing the same substance matter. Now the amendment of the gentleman from Des Moines, [Mr. Hall] and which was adopted before the recess, covers the same ground with the one now under discussion; and I do not think it necessary to adopt another, which will come in collision with it.

Mr. HALL. I had not the same idea in my mind when I offered my amendment, which was done at the suggestion of several distinguished men who are not members of this body. I suppose the amendment offered by the gentleman from Mills [Mr. Solomon] has a direct reference to a prohibitory liquor law, which the amendment I offered did not have, although it may have that effect to a certain extent.

Mr. TRAER. I do not wish to mis-interpret the gentleman from Des Moines, [Mr. Hall] but I think the amendment, now under consideration, covers the ground embraced in that offered by him.

The CHAIRMAN. The Chair is of the opinion that the amendment of the gentleman from Mills (Mr. Solomon) is in order.

Mr. CLARK, of Alamakee. If a provision of that description should be embodied in our Constitution, it will allow any person who holds property in any slave State, and recognizes the principle of chattel slavery, and where that species of property is held as an article of merchandise, to bing it to this State, and the legislature could pass no laws prohibiting it. If we are in earnest, when we say in the Constitution, in the first place, that all men are created equal and endowed with certain unalienable rights, if we mean all that, we certainly do not intend in the same instrument to adopt a principle which will recognize the right of man to hold his fellow man in bondage within the limits of this State. That such a construction would be put upon this amendment, if it should pass, there can be no doubt. It strikes me that it covers that description of property. It recognizes and allows the right to hold it in this State and prohibits the legislature from interfering with the right to hold any species of property, which is recognized as property in any State, thereby allowing the legislative bodies and Constitutional Conventions of other States to over-ride the institutions, legislative and constitutional enactments of our own State. I am, therefore, decidedly opposed to the introduction of the amendment offered by the gentleman from Mills. (Mr. Solomon.)

Mr. SOLOMON. I waited until all the other sections of the Bill of Rights had been passed upon, before I introduced this resolution of mine. I did it, knowing that there were certain gentlemen upon this floor who are in the habit of snuffing danger from the breeze from afar, and that they would, as the gentleman has done, try to pervert the meaning of the proposition I have introduced, and impugn the motives perhaps of its author. But my action and the place I have sought to give this proposition in the Bill of Rights must certainly clear me from any such charge. You will observe, Mr. Chairman, that I have waited until that proposition in the Bill of Rights has been adopted which says "neither slavery nor involuntary servitude, unless for punishment of crimes, shall ever be tolerated in this State." No matter what kind of regulations may be made by a declaration in the Bill of Rights in regard to property, along by the side of that provision, it could never have any efficacy in bringng slavery into this State. I regret that the gentleman from Alamakee (Mr. Clark) and others who think with him could not meet the proposition I have presented upon fair ground. I believe, and I think a majority of the party with whom the gentleman has acted, believe that such a regulation as I have proposed is demanded in this State. Laws infringing on the rights of the people in regard to certain articles of property were passed two years ago by the General Assembly. The very friends of those laws have now lost confidence in them, and to such an extent, that they have taken away a great deal of what was objectionable in them. I think it is the duty of this body assembled for the purpose of amending and revising the Constitution, to constitutionalize just such views as I have embodied in my proposition. Where a principle has become so well fixed, that no man in his senses will undertake to argue it before the public, it is unnecessary to incorporate it in the Bill of Rights. This is a question upon which there have been recent and frequent legislative enactments, not only in our own State but in other states of this Union, and it is for this reason I have introduced this proposition here. I know very well that the State in which the prohibitory system first originated has receded from its position, but it still remains upon our statute books. I desire to insert a clause in the Constitution which shall in a very few words put a quietus upon this question.

I do not wish to say any thing more upon this question at present, from the fact that if my amendment is voted down in Committee, I shall insist upon its adoption in Convention, and call the yeas and nays upon it, so that I may know where gentlemen stand upon this question.

The question was taken and the amendment was rejected.

Mr. CLARKE, of Henry. I offer the following amendment:

"Laws may be submitted to a vote of the people to decide whether they shall go into effect."

The question was taken, and upon division the amendment was not agreed to—ayes 15, noes 16.

The twenty-fourth section was then read as follows:

"This enumeration of rights shall not be construed to impair or deny others, retained by the people."

There being no amendments to this section, the question then recurred on the adoption of the Preamble and Bill of Rights as amended, and being taken, it was adopted.

On motion of Mr. CLARKE, of Johnson, the Committee then rose and the Chairman reported, that the Committee of the whole, to which had been referred the Preamble and Bill of Rights, with the report of the Committee upon the same had had the same under consideration, had made sundry amendments thereto and asked to be discharged from its further consideration.

The question was taken upon discharging the Committee of the Whole and it was agreed to.

The PRESIDENT. The report of the Committee of the Whole is now before the Convention, and is open to amendment.

Mr. CLARKE, of Johnson. Section eleven was passed by for the purpose of referring it to the Committee on the Judiciary, together with the amendment which the gentleman from Davis (Mr. Palmer) desires to offer in relation to offences of a minor character. I move that that section, together with the amendment be referred to the Judiciary Committee.

The question was taken and the motion was agreed to.

Mr. PALMER. I offer the following amendment to section eleven:

"All offences of a lower grade than felony and crimes of which the penalty is imprisonment for more than one month, shall be summarily tried before magistrates without indictment, presentment, or the intervention of a Grand Jury."

A member suggested that section thirteen be also referred to the Committee on the Judiciary.

The question was then taken, upon referring sections eleven and thirteen, together with the amendment of Mr. Palmer, to the Judiciary Committee, and it was agreed to.

Mr. HALL. I move to lay the report of the Committee of the Whole upon the table and make it the special order for Monday at 10 o'clock, a.m.

The question was taken and the motion was agreed to.

On motion of Mr. HARRIS, the Convention then adjourned till Monday, at nine o'clock, A. M.

MONDAY, February 2, 1857.

The Convention met at 9 o'clock A. M., and was called to order by the President.

Prayer by Rev. Mr. Page.

The Journal of Saturday was read and approved.

Reports of Committees.

Mr. CLARKE, of Johnson, from the Committee on the Judicial Department, made the following report, which was received and laid on the table, and ordered to be considered with the Bill of Rights:

The Committee on the Judicial Department to whom was referred sections eleven and thirteen of the Bill of Rights, with the amendment proposed by the gentleman from Davis, [Mr. Palmer,] have had the same under consideration, and beg leave to report the following:

Strike out section eleven and insert the following:

"All offenses less than felony, and in which the punishment does not exceed a fine of one hundred dollars, or imprisonment for thirty days, shall be tried summarily before a Justice of the Peace, or other officer authorized by law, or information under oath without indictment, or the intervention of a Grand Jury, saving to the defendant the right of appeal; and no person shall be held to answer for any higher criminal offense, unless on presentment or indictment by a Grand Jury, except in cases arising in the army or navy, or in the militia when in actual service in time of war or public danger."

Amend section thirteen by inserting between the words "suspended" and "unless," the following:

"Nor shall it be refused, when application is made as required by law."

Mr. SKIFF. I move that we take up the special order, which was set down for ten o'clock this morning.

The question was taken and the motion was agreed to.

Preamble and Bill of Rights.

The PRESIDENT. The report of the Standing Committee on the Bill of Rights as amended is now before the Convention for its second reading, and open to amendment.

Mr. CLARKE, of Johnson. I rise to make an enquiry of the Chair. Is this to be considered as a report of a Standing Committee or the report of the Committee of the Whole? The resolution which was adopted a day or two since, upon my motion, required that reports of Standing Committees should be read three times.

The PRESIDENT. The Chair regards it in its present shape as a report of the Committee of the Whole, or rather as a report of a Standing Committee revised by the Committee of the Whole.

The Preamble was then read as follows:

We, the People of the Territory of Iowa, grateful to the Supreme Being for the blessings hitherto enjoyed, and feeling our dependance on Him for a continuation of these blessings, do ordain and establish a free and independent government, by the name of the State of Iowa, the boundaries whereof shall be as follows:

Beginning in the middle of the main channel of the Mississippi river, at a point due east of the middle of the mouth of the main channel of the Des Moines river; thence up the middle of the main channel of the said Des Moines river, to a point on said river where the northern boundary line of the State of Missouri —as established by the Constitution of that State, adopted June 12th, 1820—crosses the said middle of the main channel of the said Des Moines river; thence westwardly along the said northern boundary line of the State of Missouri, as established at the time aforesaid, until an extension of said line intersect the middle of the main channel of the Missouri river; thence up the middle of the main channel of the said Missouri river to a point opposite the middle of the main channel of the Big Sioux river, according to Nicollett's map; thence up the main channel of the said Big Sioux river, according to said map, until it is intersected by the parallel of forty-three degrees and thirty minutes north latitude; thence east along said parallel of forty-three degrees and thirty minutes until said parallel intersects the middle of the main channel of the Mississippi river; thence down the middle of the main channel of said Mississippi river to the place of beginning.

State Boundary Lines.

Mr. EDWARDS. I rise for the purpose of making an enquiry. It has occurred to me that there is or has been a project pending before Congress for the purpose of attaching to this State a portion of Minnesota, lying upon the northwestern portion of our borders. If that should be the case, and Congress should conclude to make such disposition of the matter, what effect would the adoption of this preamble have upon the question?

Mr. HARRIS. I would suggest, and I am reminded of the fact by my friend near me, that since the adoption of the present constitution there has been a survey of the southern part of the State made, that may perhaps make some changes in the boundary lines there. I do not know whether the committee have had any action upon this subject, but I would like to have this matter definitely fixed and settled.

Mr. HALL. If the gentleman will look at the matter, he will find that the southern boundary line has been fully established. The old Sullivan line has been established as the north line of Missouri. There was some difficulty as to what points the line extended, and as to where the line was; and an amicable suit was, therefore, made between Iowa and Missouri. A survey was made, and that survey was established by the judgment of the Supreme Court of the United States. The line of Missouri has been irrevocably established; and I do not believe that anything is necessary to be settled here upon that subject.

Mr. GOWER. These remarks in regard to boundary lines bring to my mind a case which came under my own observation in Ohio. From 1832 till 1841, I resided in the northern part of that State, and during that time a difficulty grew up between Michigan, then a territory, and Ohio, in regard to the northern boundary line between them. For a long time they maintained a hostile attitude to each other, so much so, that they called out their forces to enforce revenue and other laws in the disputed territory. The matter was finally referred to Congress, where it was settled by their giving the disputed land to Ohio. It strikes me that we are in a condition precisely similar to that of Ohio and Michigan, and if this be so, I think it would be advisable to ascertain from our delegation in Congress what the prospect is of our obtaining this strip of territory on our northwestern border. If there be any prospect of getting it, let us send in a petition to Congresss to that effect. If there be not any chance of getting it, we had better then adopt our present line.

Mr. PALMER. I think probably that some proviso might be added to this preamble, to define the southern boundary, and provide for any additional territory that might be granted by

Congress. I move, therefore, that this Preamble be referred to the Judiciary Committee.

Mr. HALL. I do not see that this question can be settled any more definitely by a reference to the Judiciary Committee. I would vote most cheerfully for a reference if I thought it did. If gentlemen will look at the decision of the Supreme Court upon this question, they will see that our southern boundary is as irrevocably fixed as it is possible for it to be fixed; and they will see that that line is as distinctly marked as it can possibly be. What can be done to make it more certain? There was a thorough and accurate survey made, which was acquiesced in by the people on both sides of the line, and by the Legislature of our own State, and it appears to me that there is no necessity for the reference now asked.

In regard to the territory in the northwest, our line is just as perfect, the Sioux river being the northwest boundary of the State. It is a river which can be traced without difficulty, and when we get up the river to a certain parallel, we go east to the Mississippi river. That line has been established by a scientific corps appointed by the United States Government, and they have erected monuments along the line designating the boundary, and about which there can be no mistake. In regard to this strip of territory between the Sioux river and the Missouri river, there is a peninsula which Congress may or may not give to Iowa. It might be well enough to refer that subject to the Committee on Miscellaneous subjects, and let them make a proviso if Congress see fit to concede it to us, that we would accept it or not, as we shall choose.

There is no room for controversy, in my opinion, in regard to our boundary lines. There is not a quarter section in our State better defined, or whose monuments are more easily ascertained than those of the northern and southern boundaries of our State.

Mr. EDWARDS. The gentleman from Des Moines, [Mr. Hall,] has not answered the enquiry I made. He is taking it for granted that the present northwest boundary line of our State is defined. But the question I desire answered is this: Suppose after the adoption of this constitution defining the boundaries of the State, Congress should attach this strip of territory, now belonging to the territory of Minnesota, that lies west of the Big Sioux, to the State of Iowa, what effect would it have upon the State boundaries, and upon the State jurisdiction, if there be not some proviso placed here in the preamble that would cover such a case.

Mr. HALL. If Congress propose to attach this, or any other territory, to the State of Iowa, it would be for the State then to decide whether she would have it. Congress having the power to attach it, and Iowa having the will to receive it, there would then be a bargain, and it would become a part of the State, and become subject to our jurisdiction. If we should not see proper to receive it, they could not force it upon us. I think it is advisable, perhaps, to make some proviso in the miscellaneous subjects by which if Congress should propose to attach this territory to this State, we should say whether we will receive it or not.

Mr. WILSON. I propose to offer the following amendment:

To add to the section defining the boundaries, "The boundaries of the State may be enlarged by consent of Congress and the State."

Mr. HALL. I do not see any necessity for this amendment. We might just as well say that two men might make a bargain if they both agreed.

Mr. WILSON. The amendment I propose to offer I deem very important. The only power in this State after the adoption of the constitution, which can consent to accept additional territory, is the Legislature. Now, I put this question to the gentleman: if the boundaries of the State are defined in the constitution, can the Legislature, under that constitution, accept additional territory, and extend the State jurisdiction over it?

Mr. PALMER. I withdraw my motion.

Mr. HALL. I move to refer this matter to the Committee on Miscellaneous Subjects. I do not think that it comes properly under the question of boundary. It is very proper, perhaps, to have a provision of the kind incorporated into the constitution; but not in that part of it defining the boundaries of the State.

Mr. WILSON. It seems to me that this matter might be disposed of here, without another reference, and that this is the most proper place for it. It is a question which relates to the boundaries of the State, and if there is any change to be made in our territory, this portion of the constitution is the place where we should provide for it. I do not see the necessity for referring this subject as suggested by the gentleman from Des Moines (Mr. Hall) to the Committee on Miscellaneous subjects. I presume that we will all agree in placing this provision in the constitution somewhere; and as it relates to the boundaries of the State, it should be inserted in that portion of the constitution which defines the boundaries of the State.

Mr. PALMER. I think it would be better to refer this provision to the Committee on Miscellaneous Subjects, who can take this matter into consideration and report it in such shape as they may think proper.

Mr. CLARK, of Alamakee. I do not see any necessity, myself, for defining the boundaries of the State in the constitution at all. I observe that the constitution of several other States do not contain a description of their boundaries. A provision in the constitution defining them does not establish them any more positively, than they would be established without such a provision being placed there. Suppose we should say in this constitution, that the boundaries of this State shall be different from what they actually are—does it make them so? Suppose we should insert a provision in the constitution defining boundaries which would infringe on the rights of Missouri, Illinois or Wisconsin? Does it make our right of territory belonging to those States any more perfect? Does it enlarge our rights at all? Does it make, in any shape, our title of jurisdiction over such territory any more clear or perfect? I suppose that the boundaries of the State are upon record, and the place where those boundaries run are established by laws—laws over which this constitution can have no effect. The act of Congress, in fact, which provided for the admission of this State into the Union, established its boundaries, and I suppose that law will govern all others in this matter of boundary. I see, then, no necessity for defining the boundaries of the State in the Constitution at all.

Mr. GOWER. It strikes me that this matter should be investigated. I understand that word came from Washington from one of our Senators (General Jones) that it would be advisable for this State to make application for the territory in question; and the Legislature at their last session passed a joint resolution making application for it. It seems to me quite probable that it may be annexed to our State, and if so, why not make proper provision for its reception? So far as I have considered the matter, I concur with the gentleman from Des Moines (Mr. Hall) that the proper disposition of this matter would be to the Committee on Miscellaneous Subjects.

The question was taken on the motion of Mr. Hall, and it was agreed to.

So the amendment was referred to the Committee on Miscellaneous Subjects.

Bill of Rights.

Mr. CLARKE, of Johnson. I rise for the purpose of suggesting a question of order here. I understand the chair to have decided that the Bill of Rights is now before the Convention in the order in which it comes from the Committee. It seems to me that the proper mode of proceeding would be first upon agreeing to the amendments made to this report in Committee of the Whole. I understand the committee to have made some amendments. The usual mode, I believe, in parliamentary proceedings of this kind, is to take the question first upon agreeing to the amendments made in Committee of the Whole, and when that is done, then to go through with the bill, and make such amendments as may be deemed advisable.

The PRESIDENT. The chair is aware that that is the usual course pursued in Legislative bodies, in regard to bills reported from the Committee of the Whole, but the chair is rather inclined to regard this as a different matter from a bill in the Legislature, and to consider the report of the Committee of the whole as a revised report from a standing committee.

Mr. CLARKE, of Johnson. I take it that it is only a question of convenience and practice. We can obtain the same results either way.

The PRESIDENT. The chair thought that it would facilitate the action of the Convention to go right through with the report of the Committee of the Whole, which was the Preamble and Bill of Rights as it now stands, with sundry amendments. When we come to any action of the Committee of the Whole, we can then act upon it. The sections will be read in the order in which they stand, and amendments can be made thereto.

Mr. CLARKE, of Johnson. By this mode of proceeding, it seems to me, there would be nothing upon the journal which would show what amendments were made in Committee of the Whole. By adopting the course I suggest, the journal would show the amendments adopted in the Committee of the Whole.

The PRESIDENT. When the sections are read, to which the Committee of the whole have made amendments, the question will be stated upon such amendments.

Mr. CLARKE, of Johnson. I had intended to submit the motion upon agreeing to the amendments made to the report in the Committee of the Whole, but I will not press it.

The PRESIDENT. If it be the sense of the Convention the Secretary will now read the first section of the Bill of Rights.

The first section was then read, as follows:

"All men are, by nature, free and independent, and have certain unalienable rights—among which are those of enjoying and defending life and liberty, acquiring, possessing and protecting property, and in pursuing and obtaining safety and happiness."

There being no amendments offered to this section, the second section was then read, as follows:

"All political power is inherent in the people. Government is instituted for the protection, security and benefit of the people, and they have the right, at all times, to alter or reform the same, whenever the public good may require it."

Mr. ELLS. Mr. President, I propose to add to section second of the Bill of Rights the following amendment:

"And no special privileges or immunities shall ever be granted, that may not be altered, amended or repealed, by the General Assembly by a vote of two-thirds of the House of Representatives, and also of the Senate."

This amendment, sir, is different from the one reported by the Standing Committee on Bill of Rights. The word *special*, and the proviso of a two-thirds vote on repeal, have been added as a modification in order to meet the objections of the honorable gentleman who opposed the report of the committee in the discussion that took place in Committee of the Whole.

It might seem, Mr. President, that the subject had been discussed enough in Committee of the Whole, but deeming the principle contained in the amendment one of vital importance, I cannot let the occasion pass without making another effort to secure its incorporation in the Bill of Rights.

For myself, sir, I prefer the original amendment, but the fears of the gentleman that the power conferred would be liable to abuse, has induced me to offer the modification. I desire to see harmony in this Convention, and I will go as far as any gentleman honorably can to secure it.

The amendment offered is the same as that

adopted by the people of Ohio, in 1850-51, with the exception of the two-thirds proviso.

It is therefore no untried experiment, having been the organic law of that State for several years, and without any bad results so far as I have had the means of knowing.

Gentlemen tell us that we are going too far when we give the power of repeal to the General Assembly They are not willing to trust the representatives of the people. They seem to think the Legislature have no other desire than to distract the country and take away vested rights, as they call them. That is a most extraordinary position for gentlemen to assume who are a part and parcel of the body politic of the country; and who profess to believe in the doctrine of the largest liberty consistent with the requirements of civil society. They discriminate between the people and their representatives. That is strange doctrine to my ears. I had supposed that the representative was strictly the agent of the party or power represented; and that his duty was to conform his action to the will of those who authorized him to exercise the powers with which he was delegated.—That is the doctrine as I understand it of the Republican party.

It was the doctrine of the old Democratic party when that party was a true Democratic party, but her glory is departed, and I fear forever, under her present organization.

Mr. President, I have none of the fears expressed by some of the gentlemen upon this floor, that the people of this State are in danger of being ruined by the corrupt action of their General Assembly. I have no fears that the people by their representatives will ever do any act that will disgrace us as a State. I am well aware, sir, that there are such things as log-rolling, and bribery, but I shall be slow to believe that a minority, much less a majority of the representatives of the people of Iowa can be corrupted by those means. I have more fears of the corruption outside, than inside of our legislative halls. Yes, sir, those institutions which have neither bodies to be kicked nor souls to be damned, are far more liable to become corrupt than the people's representatives. And I may add, sir, that so far as my knowledge of the people of this country extends, such is the general impression. Money, sir, in this country exercises a power almost omnipotent. I think we can discover this influence upon the minds of men who are not themselves conscious of that influence—honest men naturally, who have been so long associated with special corporations, that the idea of making money has become part and parcel of their very nature, and the almighty dollar stands out before them larger than any other object. To guard against the influence of money, for in my opinion it is the most dangerous element of corruption in this country, I would throw around the people all the written safe-guards that I can do in the form of an organic law. I hope, therefore, that the principle contained in the amendment I have offered will be retained in the Bill of Rights. If the phraseology is not satisfactory to gentlemen, I am perfectly willing to listen to the suggestions of others in amending it in any way. I care nothing about the language, it is the principle that I wish to see recognised.

But I am told by gentlemen that the right of repeal will be provided for in the article on Corporations. It is true, it does appear in the report of that Committee as printed and lying before us. But in my opinion, the article on Corporations is the only place where that wholesome principle should be retained. I desire to see it inserted in the Bill of Rights, which defines the Rights of the people. I desire to see that broad doctrine recognised there, and I do not care how often it appears in other clauses. The people will read the Bill of Rights more than any other portion of the Constitution. When they read it, I wish them to see how cautious and careful were the men sent here to make a Constitution, in putting in plain English what they conceive to be the true, primary and original rights of the people.

Mr. PETERS. I moved to strike out the amendment proposed by the Committee to this section, and which the amendment of the gentleman from Scott (Mr. Ells) embodies and carries out a little farther. I did so, not beeause I doubted the principle contained in it to be a correct principle, not but what I believe the Constitution of the State of New York, and other States also, contained the same principles. I but apprehend it becomes our duty in amending the Constitution of this State, to adopt it to the wants and necessities of our people. The question presented here, in the light I view it, amounts to this, whether we intend to lay down general principles in the Constitution, which may give the Legislature the right to throw those clogs about Internal Improvements, which will restrict and retard their completion, until the Constitution can be so amended as to allow the Legislature an opporounity of assisting and encouraging them. I admit, the principle embodied in the amendment of the gentleman, t be generally correct, not that I am forced to admit that fact because the gentleman calls it a Democratic principle, or because it has been adopted in other States. I apprehend that what may be a correct principle generally, may not be proper and applicable to the condition of the people of Iowa, and may not be advisable to incorporate into her Constitution. If the condition of the State of New York, or other State, is precisely parallel to the State of Iowa, then we can get rid of a great deal of labor by simply adopting her Constitution as it stands, because it has received all the debate and consideration that is necessary for a proper understanding of the subjects contained in it. It is well known, that the population and wealth of this State have kept pace with the building of Railroads; and it is well known too, that in order to build these Railroads, it requires more money than the people of the State of Iowa can command within themselves for that purpose. The wants of the people of the State require some ten or fifteen millions of dollars, and perhaps more, to be invested in Railroads within the coming year. The capitalists who have this money to loan are very few in number in this country, and even in the civilized world. At the present day, there is perhaps a greater demand for the means of building Railroads in this State than have been required for years before, and consequently, the men who have this money to loan are looking to the action of this body and the Legislature, to the action of the people of this State generally, to see what will be their future course, and whether they intend to aid and assist these corporations, so that they can be able to carry out the objects and plans which they have in view. The amendment now under consideration, instead of aiding and assisting these men and giving them certain privileges, which would enable them to build these roads, reserves to the Legislature the right to take away from them at any time, the very privileges by which they are enabled to prosecute and carry to a successful completion, these works of internal improvement. I apprehend, that under these circumstances, no man having money to loan will invest in this State, but seek those localities, where rights of Corporations are best protected. The State of Missouri formerly adopted a course similar to that now proposed here by this amendment. They taxed railroads to an enormous extent and laid heavy burdens upon them, and the consequence was, that their Internal Improvements were suspended, until the Legislature seeing the necessity for pursuing a different policy, amended their laws upon this subject by adopting a more liberal policy than before. I am informed, and I have the very best information for my belief, that every railroad projected in this State must stop where it is, unless the companies are able to negotiate loans for money from abroad; and the capitalists to whom we must look for the means to carry on our Internal Improvements are watching the action of this body and the General Assembly, to see whether it would be safe to make an investment of their funds here.

Another proposition has been submitted here, to submit this question to a vote of the people. It has been charged that it is anti-Democratic to object to any such course. As I said before, I am not here as a party man, neither do I wish to draw party lines upon any question which may come before this Convention. I believe it to be my duty so far as my vote may go, to lay down such a fundamental law as the wants and necessities of the people require. I have no objection so far as the principle is concerned, of submitting any amendmendment or proposition to the people of this State. I do not question their intelligence, integrity or honesty, but I do not believe that the people of the State have any desire to become legislators in that capacity. I hope that the amendment proposed by the gentleman from Scott (Mr. Ells) will not be adopted. I would vote for any proposition to carry out the same principle in controlling the action of every corporation in this State, with the exception of those corporations which are created for the purpose of prosecuting the Internal Improvements of the State, but I shall vote against the amendment now under consideration

Mr. TRAER. I would ask the gentleman if this provision is incorporated into the Constitution, whether the effect would be to confer a power to report corporations already existing in this State? I do not understand so. I understand that under the corporation law of this State, now existing, no corporation existing under that law will need be affected by this provision, even if it is adopted and becomes a portion of our Constitution. I think the argument of the gentleman is of no force, so far as that is concerned.

Mr. PETERS. I will answer the gentleman by saying that I want to put all these corporations upon the same footing. I do not wish to grant exclusive privileges to any corporation, or class of corporations, which may have been formed before this provision is agreed to, if it should be adopted by this Convention.

Mr. CLARKE, of Johnson. I fought this matter on Saturday, when it was up then, and I should be very glad to accommodate the gentleman from Scott (Mr. Ells) by going for this proposition, if it did not contain a principle which seems to be abhorrent to every man's sense of natural justice. Now, if I were to get up here and make a proposition here by which you or I, or the gentleman from Scott (Mr. Ells) should have the right to make contracts and receive benefits under them, and then abrogate those contracts without having any compensation or damages to the party who may be injured by that abrogation, every man in this house would raise his hands in horror, and would say that I am destitute of those natural principles and the natural instincts of honesty which are believed to pervade the principles of every honest man. It seems to me the proposition of the gentleman from Scott is exactly the same in principle. His proposition is, that the State may make contracts through the agents of the people here, the General Assembly, and after those contracts have been made, and the parties have acted in good faith under those contracts, the State then shall have the right to repeal and nullify those contracts. If I understand his proposition, that is the amount and effect of it, and I do say as I said before, that it is at war with the common honesty of every man—with his sense of right and justice.

Now, I have no fear of the people; nor have I any fear of their representatives in the Legisture.

There seems to me to be here a spirit manifested to guard the people against—what or whom —of guarding the people against themselves; for the Legislature is but the people in a representative and collective capacity; they are but the agents of the people, authorized to act for them. If the people are discreet in their selection of their agents, the presumption is that the State, or the great mass of the people are not going to be wronged by the creation of corporations. If this amendment goes into the Constitution, and that Constitution is to be approved, then we should have in anticipation of its adoption and approval there will be scores and scores of irresponsible corporations passed, through the Legistature, or formed under the present corporation law. Every man who has a project in view, will seek to take advantage of the present law and Constitution so as to obviate and avoid the operation of the new Constitution, and thus the very thing that we are desirous to avoid, the creation of unnecessary and irresponsible, and irrepealable corporations, would be naturally the result of this amendment.

Now, I do not want to put the State in a position to do wrong, or to permit her agents to do wrong, nor do I want to give corporations for any purpose, whether for banking, internal improvement, or any other purpose, in a position to do wrong in order to give an advantag. There is no qualification here for this provision. It will reach every corporation created under a general law, it matters not for what purpose. For instance, the people of a religious society go to work and organize themselves into a corporation, for the purpose of securing the right to hold property. They proceed to build a church, and to procure other property connected with it. But under this provision they may in an hour, without a moments notice, without a trial or a complaint against them, have their rights taken from them, and so of all corporations of whatever character they may be. This is a dangerous power to place in the hands of the Legislature, or the people themselves, and a power, it seems to me, the people will not, and do not ask. Now, if this provision is adopted, and the idea I have suggested is carried out, and parties seek to incorporate themselves under the present law, we would have a rivalry and confusion in these corporations which may be disastrous to very many of them.

I notice another thing, and that is, that gentlemen fancy because a provision of this kind is inserted in the Constitution of New York, and of Ohio, it must necessarily be inserted here. Now, I must be excused for saying that I regard the Constitution of New York as one of the poorest in this Union. It is a conglomeration of everything, and the last one that we should take as a model for ours. But look at it in another point of view. The people of New York may insert a provision of this kind in their Constitution, when it would be improper for us to do so. The State of New York abounds in capital and wealth, which perhaps control public opinion and the country, and they can oppose and frown down every attempt to violate vested rights. But we are not in that position. We are a new people; we are a poor people, a poor State, and we look to other States, to people out of our own State for capital, with which to make our internal improvements, to create our banks, and carry on almost every department of industry. But it is proverbial that eastern, or English capitalists if you will, are fearful of the stability of western legislation. Put this clause into your Constitution, and that which they fear will become dread reality, and it will be proclaimed from one end of the Union to the other that the people of Iowa are so dead to natural justice that in their fundamental law, they claim the right to break contracts when they please, and when your agents go East to borrow money, that provision will be thrust at them, until they will blush with shame, and be glad to leave the precincts of the commercial emporium of the country. I do think this provision will be disastrous to every public interest in this State.

As to Ohio, she is a rich State, and has capital of her own, in her own borders. Neither New York nor Ohio are, however, patterns for us to follow upon this question. We do not occupy the same position that they do, but in the position of a new State, and we should frame such a constitution, and fundamental law, as will draw to us the capital, and wealth, and interest, and intelligence of the country. It is possible that this provision, if adopted, would not be abused. I admit that that is possible. But there is a charge that it will be abused, there is danger of it. And every man upon this floor knows how apprehensive capitalists are of these dangers.

But, perhaps, many words need not be wasted upon this matter here. If the Convention shall adopt the report of the Committee on the Legislative Department, we will not have any necessity for this provision, to meet the difficulty that gentleman seems to fear. I trust this will not be adopted. And I would throw out another suggestion, and that is, that if this provision is placed in the Constitution, there will be danger that it will defeat it before the people. Every section of the State is interested in the railroad projects spoken of here. And every man who expects these roads to bring a market to his own door, will vote against this Constitution, with this provision, for every one would realize, that as soon as it becomes a fundamental law in this State, no more corporations for internal improvement will be made, or enacted here. And if we desire that the money we have already spent shall be in vain, then adopt this provision, and I undertake to say such a howl will be raised about the ears of members, when they go home, they will be glad to flee from the public indignation.

Mr. HARRIS. Knowing the position of the gentleman from Johnson, [Mr. Clarke,] and recollecting the intimations he has thrown out here before, I did not seek the floor because I supposed I would bring a new argument against this proposition. But the gentleman will bear with me, if I say that every argument he has used here against this proposition, has fully convinced me that it is the more necessary that it should be adopted.

I rise to attempt to discuss this question with a great deal of reluctance, for the simple reason that I see many gentlemen in this hall, whose wisdom and experience I should, perhaps, take as lamps to my feet, attempting to fix our constitution, and our fundamental law, are arrayed upon the other side. But when I feel convinced that I reflect, at least, the sentiments of those I came here to represent, and that I shall, at least, have the approbation of my own conscience in what I shall do here, I cannot be deterred from taking the position I believe to be right, and which I believe will ultimately enhance the best interests of the community.

Now I do regret a little that the chairman of the committee [Mr. Ells, of Scott,] should indulge in a fling at the party to which I belong. He says it has lost its glory. Now as I claim to be ready to take the position of a forlorn hope, a rear guard of that party, I must say that, in my opinion, it has not lost its glory. And I believe that the principles maintained by that party are as true now as those professed by them in times past, when they were as hard pressed as they are now. I do not hold that any present success or expediency is an apology for a departure from well defined, and well settled principles of action, by which a party may claim to be governed, especially if they do not find a reason for so doing in its having become inpracticable, and improper to be put into operation.

What are the reasons assigned here why we should not engraft this provision here, and give the people the right to control the immunities their agents, the legislature, may grant. We hold the doctrine that the people are sovereign, that they are absolute sovereigns here, and that there is not, and ought not to be any appeal from the will of the people, when fairly, and honestly, and properly expressed. I am in the habit of going farther, perhaps, than some may be willing to do in this matter, and holding—not the doctrine that Kings can do no wrong—but that the people cannot, and will not do any injustice to those who may trust them. I believe there is a sense of honesty, and a sense of justice, pervading the great mind and heart of the American people, which will prevent and forbid them from doing an act of injustice to those who may trust them. I believe that honesty and justice constitute the very life blood, the main principle of our institutions. And if they are capable, and if they are just and honest, I do not see any necessity of such warnings as have gone forth here, that this is an unjust power to be entrusted to the people.

The main argument made here is, that capital is jealous, that the money mongers of the country are afraid to entrust their capital to the caprice and uncertainty, and injustice of the people, and that they will not dole out their precious gifts to the people, unless they can have their bond, with security, that any privilege, and any immunity that the people may have extended to them, shall remain like the laws of the Medes and Persians, unchangable and unalterable. Now my little experience has led me to conclude that there is more danger to the people themselves, and to the capitalists themselves, by attempting to fix these rights unalterably, than there is to have it understood in the bill, and in the bond, at the time; that when these immunities are violated, when the sovereign rights of the people are trampled upon by these corporations, by these privileged classes, then the people, through their representatives, shall have the right to cancel the bond, and take back those precious privileges thus trampled upon.

The first argument, and that made by the gentleman from Delaware [Mr. Peters] is that we are in great need of internal improvements, that we ought to have those internal improvements in this State, and his argument is only reiterated and amplified by the gentleman from Johnson [Mr. Clarke], who says that capital will not come here, and we will get no internal improvements, no railroads or other works, if we permit a provision of this kind to go into our Constitution. Now I have yet to learn that capital will not go where it can obtain the best interest, and my experience tells me that the capitalist of the east, the man of wealth in the east, that the gentleman seems to think have such a sacred notion of the fulfillment of obligations, will leave their markets there where they can get but six or seven per cent. and will come here and higgle for thirty or forty per cent., and that, too, in the face of the law.—Gentlemen know that to be true—they know that is the history of the matter: they know that the rapacious maw of the money lender is not satisfied with anything he can obtain, whether it comes within the purview of the law or not. I would ask you if the experience of some of the new States, of those which were once in our position, is not such in consequence of having granted those privileges which gentlemen have spoken of, has not been such as to prove that they would now be better occupying the position that Iowa does today, without a railroad completed within her borders, than to be as they now are in consequence of those immunities and privileges which they have extended to capitalists.

I would call the attention of the gentleman from Johnson to the State of Ohio. There was a magnificent system of internal improvement projected there, in the way of digging canals, and all these privileges, and vested rights were then given under a constitution like that the gentleman seeks to pass here. And the gentleman knows the mountain of debt, and the waste of public money, and the abuse of the confidence of the people, which have resulted from that policy, and millions of debt and interest have accumulated upon the people of that State in consequence of the extension of these privileges. The improvements that were projected, and for which debts were contracted, that Ohio has got to pay, have been thrown aside as useless. The State of Ohio is now woven over by a net work of railroads, built by private enterprise, under the very provision in the constitution of that State that is sought to be placed here now. That provision was placed in the constitution of that

State by the people, after a direful experience of its necessity, an experience that the gentleman would force upon the people of this State. The gentleman says that it is no reason for putting this provision in our constitution, because it is in the Constitution of New York, and the Constitution of Ohio, or of any other State. Now I say, that the experience of the people of Ohio, upon this question, is worthy of some consideration at the hands of this Convention. I venture to say, that the same system prevailed in Ohio previous to the adoption of this principle in her constitution, that gentlemen are attempting to fasten upon this State. They have been saddled with debt, with bank corporations, and corporations in every shape, all over Ohio, that the imagination could conceive. They endeavored for some ten, fifteen, or twenty years to obtain the privilege of having a convention to revise their *magna charter*, and they obtained it only after one of the fiercest and most severe political struggles that has ever taken place in any State in this Union. That convention was composed of the ablest men in the State, of both political parties, and after a session of five months, where these principles underwent a close and scrutinizing discussion and investigation, the one we seek to place in the constitution we are now framing, with a further guard upon our part of a two-thirds vote of the legislature, was placed in that constitution. And though they felt all the anxiety we feel here for railroad projects, and the advantages to be derived from them, that constitution was adopted by the people by an overwhelming vote. And permit me to say that that principle of the rights of the people to revise these corporations, and when the necessity arose, to wipe them and their abuses out of existence was one of the main principles that called that Convention together, and it was the principles upon which the opponents to the convention and to the constitution, when made, went before the people, and it was upon the adoption of that principle that the people of Ohio voted and ratified that constitution by an overwhelming vote.

But the gentleman from Johnson [Mr. Clarke] says that if it is put in here it will defeat this constitution; that every voter who desires a railroad brought to his door will vote against the constitution, on account of this provision. Why, sir, that is one of the very reasons that we should put it in here. There is a wild excitement, a mania in the community at this time for getting rich; an idea that every man is to become wealthy in consequence of some railroad project, some fancy scheme by which he is to have the privilege of using the money of somebody else: and it is for that very reason that we should insist upon this provision in the constitution, that we may be able to lop off some of the branches of this wild tree of excitement. I am as much in favor of railroads as any one can be. I think we in our part of the State stand as much in need of them as any other portion of the State.

But I understand that we are not only acting here for the present, but also for the future prosperity of the State, that we are to frame the institutions of this State in such a manner as will mete out justice to every class and interest in the State, and so frame them that we may confidently look forward to the future wealth and prosperity of our Commonwealth, rather than to those present emoluments and advantages which we may seek by inviting irresponsible money mongers and capitalists to come among us.

I insist that there is no danger of the injustice of the people, but that there is rather a greater danger to be apprehended from the abuses that corporations and capitalists may make, and from their being able to control the representatives of the people, and lead them to extend those immunities and those abuses, than that they will be called to account unjustly and have injustice done them by the people. There is no saying more true than this: that money is power. The gentleman understands that; any man in this community understands that, and they know the tremendous lever that every man of wealth, and that every monied institution is able to use on the community. And the history of the country does not afford an instance where great injustice has ever been done by the people, where they have claimed the right to overlook and review these things; that these immunities are not interfered with unless they have been abused; and after being abused, I hold that it would be right to interfere with them.

It was properly remarked by the gentleman from Jefferson [Mr. Wilson] the other day, that when an individual by his own bad conduct forfeits his liberty, or his life, we claim the right for the protection of the community to take it from him.

Now, I hold that the provision the gentleman seeks to put in or retain here, has only the tendency to continue the life of these corporations after they have by their bad conduct, by their malfeasance, forfeited their right to the protection of the community. The gentleman from Wappello (Mr. Gillaspy) referred the other day to the action of the present Legislature in the repeal of a certain law, in terminating a certain contract. He cited that as an act of great injustice that had been done to one of the great interests of the State.

Now I do not intend here to review the action of the Des Moines River Improvement. or the course pursued by the officers connected with that improvement. But I will say here that I believe that so far as the public officers in that matter are concerned, they are honest and capable of discharging the duties entrusted to them. I make no charges in that respect to them. But permit me to say in reply to the objection made to this provision, in consequence of the action of the Legislature in repealing those privileges, and immunities, that I was one of the members of the Legislature upon this floor four years ago, recommending, democrat as I was, the appointment as one of the commissioners to contract in regard to this matter of the present chief magistrate of this State, whig as he was, and I am not prepared to say that if those who entered into that contract had lived up to the contract made by that commissioner and his associates, everything would now be right.

I pass no opinion, whatever, in regard to these things. But permit me to say one thing here, and in saying it I arraign no individual, no man, no party whatever. But, I will say that the history of this work shows the common lot of all great public improvements that are superintended by the State, and that is, that while most of the grant to the Des Moines River Improvement has been frittered away, in one shape or another, the officers with the very liberal salaries given them have been able to rear their palaces that tower almost to the clouds, while the improvement remains very much the same as it was eight years ago when I first came to the State. This is the impression that has fixed itself deep and strong, and with an iron grasp upon the minds of the people, of almost the entire southern portion of this State, and can we wonder then that there is an enjoining sentiment coming up here from the other portion of the State? We cannot, and it is but just and reasonable to expect that it should; and yet I used what little influence I possessed with the members of the Legislature, from the portion of the country from which I came, and I believe I had some influence with them, to continue this work, to take no steps that might lead to the work being discontinued. I said, let it progress, let the lands, so far as they can do so, be devoted to the building of that improvement.

But, I do not care how much gentlemen talk upon this floor about this great wrong done by the Legislature in this matter. I do not care how much they may complain of the injustice that has been done to the Des Moines River Improvement. That will not do away the impression that is fixed and unalterable in the minds of the people, that the money has not been judiciously used upon that matter. It is a fixed fact. It has entered into the history of the country, and it will never be erased from it. I say this in reply to the argument used by my friend from Wappello, (Mr. Gillaspy) that the action of the Legislature upon this matter was a sufficient reason why we should not extend to the people , through their representatives, the privilege of passing in review the action of these mammoth monied institutions.

I say then, that the reasons that have been urged here, only afford additional and still stronger reasons to my mind why this amendment should prevail. Notwithstanding the fling from the chairman of the committee, in regard to the democratic party, I hold it to be the essence, the life-blood of that party, that the largest liberty compatible with free constitutional liberty in opposition to anarchy, should be extended to every class of the community. Gentlemen have said, they do not come here as partizans. I do not come here as a partizan, that is, simply to waste partizan words; but I apprehend that if I had not been a partizan, I would never have been honored with a seat upon this floor, and I apprehend that is the case with most gentlemen here. I think if they had not preferred an intention to carry out, so far as practicable, the principles and sentiments of the parties with which they were associated, they would not have been sent here to represent any portion of the people of this State. Then understanding, as I think I do, the sentiments of those who sent me here, I feel myself called upon to reflect, as well as I am able in my feeble manner, that sentiment, and give it an expression in the action of this body. I see men here whom I am proud to acknowledge and honor as leaders in my own party. Yet I feel satisfied that they are talking what would have been considered as rank heresy to the principles of the party, in the State of Ohio, when I was there ten years ago, and I feel called upon to make these remarks, and to come to the conclusion I have to separate from them upon this question.

I hope this amendment will be adopted, for I believe it is one of the most important provisions that can be placed into this Constitution. If you will permit the expression, I will say that there are not, perhaps, more than two or three propositions that come into this bill of rights, that may be regarded as practical propositions. Most all of them are more anxious, which we all acknowledge and approve, and which no man would attempt to remove, or would be willing to leave the people to do so. But here are one or two which become active, practical principles, with a life giving energy, and force in them, which it is highly important should be so considered and acted upon by this Convention, as to become of practical benefit to the people, and the State. Now the proposition in this section is a practical one which admits of legislative action. But gentlemen tell us that in regard to some of these principles, the courts have already acted, and concerning which, the courts have already given constructions, and have therefore done away with the necessity of further action upon these questions here. Why then should we meddle with these matters here now? For the simple reason that we are not here to codify the decisions of the courts; we are not here to place in the *magna charta* of this State the *ipse dixit* of any judge upon the bench. But we are here for a peaceable and amicable revolution, by which we seek to change somewhat, the institutions of our State, and we are not called upon to go back into the cobweb, and worm eaten systems that have prevailed heretofore, but to embrace in the Constitution which we shall present to the people for their approbation, such principles as we believe necessary to protect them in their right, and to the future prosperity of the State, without any regard to the opinions of the courts or individuals elsewhere.

I know that gentlemen of the bench, and gentlemen who have been long in the habit of depending upon these decisions, and of making decisions, precedents is everything. Present to them a principle of justice, fraught with the greatest consequences, to the community, they will resort to their books and consult their old musty records, to see if they have there a precedent. Present to them a principle or a question fraught with the greatest consequences to the well-being of the community, and they run to their library to seek for a precedent; if they find one, they say the principle is all right, but if there is not one there the principle must be wrong. But are we here to hesitate and doubt and tremble, simply because we have not the *ipsi dixit* from the bench in favor of what we want put in here? It was once said of the celebrated Manning, in one of the revolutions of England, when precedents and decisions of the courts and the former parliaments were thrust upon him, he said that a man in a revolution who depended upon precedent, was in the position of a man in a wilderness, who should claim that the king's highway was the best to be travelled, and he would therefore not stir a step, but remain where he was, in the desert and wilderness because he could not walk upon the king's highway. In a revolution a man must be his own precedent; he must make, not follow, precedents; and so far as precedents are concerned in this matter, that we are very much in the position of the man in the wilderness—we are not to depend upon the king's highway—we are not to hunt precedents, but to look for principles of justice and right to which we may give existence and vitality in this constitution, in order that we may best secure the best interests of the community. We are to examine and judge upon these matters ourselves, without any regard to the decisions that may have been made. We have the letter of the law as a guide: it is the only lamp that we have to our feet, and it should be our bulwark and protection, without any regard to any precedent or decision that may have been made heretofore.

I know that there is a prejudice in the minds of those who have lived long in the law, and have become wiser in its precepts, against any interpolation, against any change. Now, when I first came upon the stage of public life, there was an active warfare going on in the community upon what was called a law reform, for the purpose of tearing down the old worm-eaten system that had so long prevailed, and to get for the people something new and fresh, that should comport with the hearts and minds of the people. Did you find those old lawyers, grown gray in the jurisprudence of the country, supporting this reform? No, sir; they attacked it with all the ferocity of a tiger, preparing to pounce upon his prey. One of the Southern States had changed her constitution so as to enable her to elect her judges by the people. At that time that policy was denounced as outrageous and monstrous, and that it was submitting the rights of the people to the rabble and the populace, who are incapable of taking any account of judicial courts and matters which are expected to mete out to us our rights. But we have seen that law reform prevail and progress, and now the most growling opponent of the system has been forced to acknowledge that the people have placed as good men upon the bench as the executive or the legislature formerly did. Now a reform in the executive department is necessary; a reform in the legislative department is necessary; and we think that a reform in this matter is particularly necessary.

We know that the prevalent opinion is, that when one's rights have been extended they become vested rights, and there is no opportunity for us to pass them in review; there is no right, in consequence of abuses, to wipe them out; no right to take cognizance of the conduct of those concerned in it. Now, I came here expecting to act in accordance with the political principles which challenged the confidence and support of the political party with which I was connected when I was in another State, and it seems strange to me to find men who must have been upon the stage at that time, and acting with me, taking opposite grounds now. It is a part of the education of the gentleman from Johnson (Mr. Clarke) to oppose this matter—that does not surprise me. But the other gentlemen opposing it, I think must certainly have stretched their magnanimity a great deal more than could have been expected from warm partizans, as I know they have been. I hope this amendment will prevail, and that it will become a part of this constitution.

Mr. EDWARDS. I have but few remarks to present, and will endeavor to make them as brief as the nature of the case will admit. I regret that I am called upon to differ from the courteous gentleman from Scott (Mr. Ells), but the duty I owe to the obligation I have here, and to my obligation to the constituents whom I represent, requires, at my hands, that I should make some remarks upon this question. It appears to me that if this amendment should prevail, we would at once dam up and hedge in the future growing prosperity of the State. It is probable that this convention will incorporate into this constitution a provision prohibiting the State from becoming a stock holder in any of these corporations; that it will not directly foster any of the great public improvements of the day. Now, it seems to me, that if this State shall adopt a policy which shall disconnect her from all banking and other associations, she should adopt the most liberal policy that would invite foreign capital to come into our State and perform that which we refuse to do ourselves in a municipal capacity.

It is true, practically speaking, that if this amendment prevails, it might not operate injuriously, yet it may do so. It is well known by every gentleman, who has ever been acquainted with capitalists at the East, who have ever been engaged in railroads enterprises, that these money lenders are persons well acquainted with our laws upon this subject. They know more about this matter, and they understand better the relations that these incorporated companies sustain to the institutions of the State, than we ourselves do. It is their business to inquire into these matters. If a railroad company wish to borrow money, they go to the East for the pur pose of effecting a loan by giving mortgage upon their road. I ask you, if capitalists looking into the fundamental law of our State, should see there, in plain and unmistakable language, that it was left to the caprice of a subsequent Legislature to repeal their vested rights, would loan their money under such circumstances?

I regard the principle contended for by the gentleman from Scott [Mr. Ells] as a mere abstraction. It would place some gentlemen here, who have urged the adoption of the principle contained in that amendment, in a very contradictory position, because they will, no doubt, vote to reverse the prohibition in the constitution in regard to banking within this State.—They come in here, open the doors, and invite your Legislature to create banking corporations in the State. The position of the gentleman, and those who think with him, when they all agree that the State shall not engage, to any extent, in the prosecution of works of internal improvements, yet at the same time are anxious to have private enterprise and capital come among us to assist us in carrying on such works, appear to my mind to be the same as that related by the eccentric Lorenzo Dow in regard to the Calvinists, who invited all men to partake of the immunities and privileges of the Gospel, yet at the same time cut them off from their enjoyment by the irrevocable decrees of Deity.

> "You will and you wont,
> You shall and you shan't;
> You'll be damn'd if you do,
> And you'll be damn'd if you don't."

The gentleman uses another argument to sustain his position, and that is, in regard to the system of log-rolling, that is frequently practiced in Legislative Halls. The argument that he has made to sustain his position, I think we can use to sustain our side of the question. Let us see what the practical operation of this matter would be. Suppose there were three railroads running across the State of Iowa from east to west. Now, sir, two of these railroads, through jealousy or rivalry of the third, could, under a system of log-rolling, concentrate their force and unite their interests together against the weaker, and thus they might repeal the charter or act under which that company was incorporated. The gentlemen have made use of the argument, in order to carry their point, that if we did not incorporate into the constitution some provision of this kind, we would place ourselves in the power of the money lenders. They are endeavoring to raise a war between the people and the corporations. As I stated a while ago, the State has no direct interest as a stock-holder in these works of internal improvement. The people who are the source of fundamental law, and who give us our seats here are the owners and stock-holders. Why are gentlemen trying then to raise an issue between the people and the corporations? I do not view this matter of building railroads in the same light that other gentlemen do. I think it will be a very difficult matter to prosecute our internal improvements to a successful completion without they receive direct assistance from the State, and I take it for granted that every gentleman here will concede that these works will redound to the prosperity of the State, and the interests of the people at large. It is well known that there are two or three railroads already commenced in this state, that are already gasping for breath. The companies engaged in building them have been unable to raise the means abroad to prosecute these works, and hence they have been constrained to call upon the people of the counties, and individuals through the section of country where the roads are proposed to be located, but even with the funds raised in this way, they are unable to raise sufficient means to prosecute these works. I assure gentlemen—and I have had some experience upon this subject—that you cannot raise money for the purpose of prosecuting these works, until capitalists know that the people themselves require them. They have no data by which they can establish that fact, until the people themselves shall raise the means within themselves to build these railroads to such a distance that they will become paying roads, and until the people have expended such an amount, that they will feel a direct interest in regard to the prosecution of these roads to a successful completion. You can then obtain money from eastern capitalists by mortgaging the roads. The people, therefore, have a direct interest in regard to this matter, and the gentleman from Scott, [Mr. Ells,] and those who act with him are not making war against the great money lenders, from whom he apprehends so much danger, but against the interests of the people themselves. The adoption of the amendment he has offered will, in my opinion, blight the prospects and prosperity of this State for many years to come. I cannot see that any good could result from its adoption, but on the contrary, much harm may result from its enactment.

Mr. PRICE. I am opposed to going into a discussion upon this Bill of Rights, such as has been carried on in Committee of the Whole, and is now extended into this Convention. I think that we have embarked upon a sea of words, shoreless and fathomless; and it is high time we should come to anchor here. I would not launch my frail bark upon this ocean, if it were not that in this discussion upon the Bill of Rights, sentiments have been uttered and which have gone upon the record, from which at home and in the private circle of my constituents, I should be obliged to dissent. I have entirely different opinions and different conceptions of the Bill of Rights and of corporations, from what has been here suggested by gentlemen in the discussion of this question? What is a Bill of Rights? It is not a bill of particulars, but it is a bill embracing general principles of human freedom, founded upon, and having their origin in concessions wrung from King John at Runnymede, embodied and preserved in the great charter of one of the most powerful nations upon earth, and inherited by us as their descendants.

Now looking upon it in that light, I cannot see why the subject of Incorporations is dragged in here. It does not belong to this part of the constitution, and it has already been referred to the appropriate Committee, because we have a Committee on Corporations. My ideas of corporations are certainly very different from those of other gentlemen here. Leaving out those natural divisions which jurists have made, and speaking of those corporatians alone, other than those created for banking purposes, and what are they? They are mere associations of individuals, in order that we may secure the advantages and benefits which belong to associated strength, and to secure objects beyond the compass and power of individual effort.

Now I do not look upon corporations as mere monsters created for the purpose of tortures and fetters, in order that we may see how much they may endure, and yet be able to live and move. This is not my idea of corporations.—I look upon them as things of benefit, because really they have been of great benefit. They never invent or discover anything, but without their aid no great project in this or any other age, has ever been successfully accomplished.—What have they already done, and what are they now doing in this country?

They have levelled your mountains, bridged your rivers, annihilated time and space, they have dived deep into the bowels of the earth and dragged forth its hidden treasures in order that they may lay them shining at the feet of those who live and move upon its surface. It is such things as these that gentlemen desire to fetter and control. Why, I would legislate in regard to them so as to make them potent for good and imporent for evil.

But gentlemen are continually appealing to our fears of the danger to be apprehended from corrupt corporations. Why, they are things which have existed from time immemorial; from a period of time so long that the memory of man runneth not to the contrary, and in all that time they have subverted no people, they have ruined and destroyed no single government in which they have flourished, but all through they have scattered blessings far and wide in every land.

I desire not to go into a discussion upon this subject of corporations, but sentiments were uttered by the gentleman from Scott (Mr. Ells) which I cannot approve, and from which I desire to dissent here. The gentleman brought an enthusiasm to the subject, and if I may be pardoned the expression, a fanaticism, which I did not expect he would bring to a subiect of this character. I did hope he would discard all enthusiasm, all fanaticism, and every other ism, when talking of this plain subject of the Bill of Rights; and that to the discussion of this question he would bring a calmness and dignity of thought, commensurate with the subject itself; that he would manifest a desire to obey the laws of the country, rather than to trample upon them; that he would lay aside all political considerations as far as this question was concerned, and that he would not rise up in the discussion of this report and tell us that the glory of the Democracy had departed. Permit me here to say in reply, that the Democracy, like a certain plant, the more it is trampled upon the more successfully it flourishes.

As I remarked before, I am not disposed to go into a lengthy discussion upon this question of corporations here. I do hope,that the amendment proposed by the gentleman from Scott [Mr. Ells] will be rejected, and that this whole matter will be permitted to remain with the Committee on Incorporations, to which it has bsen referred.

Mr. CLARKE, of Henry. The position I occupied in regard to this amendment in Committee of the Whole, is well known to the members of this Convention. I thought something of the kind was necessary, but I was opposed to the amendment as it was first reported by the committee, because it gave unlimited power to repeal and alter general laws, creating corporations, and granting chartered privileges. My opinion is still the same. I am somewhat doubtful in regard to the great necessity, in this State, of incorporating this clause into our constitution. I confess, after listening to gentlemen here, and especially to the gentleman from Appanoose, [Mr. Harris,] that my doubts have increased. It is very difficult for me to imagine a case, where it may be necessary for the public good, that the Legislature should exercise their power. With all the guards, which, I believe, this constitution will throw around incorporations, and around the legislature, in the matter of granting special privileges, I think it will be very difficult for any gentleman to point out to us the time when it will be necessary to have recourse to such a provision, if placed in the constitution. If I could conceive, that in the future, the time might come, when any one of the corporations, existing in our State, would become a great evil, a great cancer upon the body politic, then I should be in favor of placing such a provision as this in the constitution. I will never favor the idea of any man, or set of men, acquiring "vested rights," which may be thrown into the face of courts and legislators, where the exercise of these vested rights may work a great evil in the community. I know that one great reason for the incorporation of this principle in the New York Constitution was the evil that grew out of the acquisition and exercise of "vested rights," as where, for instance, a corporation had acquired a vested right, by virtue of a charter, to build a bridge across a river. This was the case, I think, at Oswego, which grew to be a large city upon each side of the river, after the granting of a charter, and building of a bridge. And so also in the case of the bridge across the river which separates Allegany City and Pittsburg, and which, intended only to benefit, resulted greatly to the detriment of the people at large. If gentlemen can imagine any case in the future, where such an evil could possibly exist, and could not be reached by repeal of the laws creating it, or by the action of the courts, then I am in favor of the amendment.

The gentleman from Johnson [Mr. Clarke,] is

very much mistaken in regard to the effect of this provision, if it were incorporated into our constitution. I cannot look upon it as freighted with all the evil with which the imagination of the gentleman has endowed it. I find in looking over the constitution of the different States of this Union, the same principle incorporated in some ten or twelve of them. Some of them give a great deal more power to the legislature in terms, than is attempted to be given by this report under consideration. In Missouri, they are required, in every act, to incorporate the right of repeal, alteration, or amendment. If gentlemen will look into the acts of our own State, he will find that the same clause is incorporated, although we have nothing of the kind in our constitution. I think gentlemen have nothing to fear from an incorporation of this clause into the constitution, if we would adopt some provision guarding against hasty legislation. I expressed myself, the other day, as being willing to favor this amendment, if we would provide for a sober-second thought of the people, to say whether the law creating incorporation, should be altered, amended, or repealed. The chairman of the committee on the bill of rights [Mr. Ells,] suggests another amendment, that it shall require a two-thirds vote of the Senate and House to pass a law repealing, altering, or amending, all laws under which corporations organize or are created. This, I think, would be satisfactory to me, and, with such a check, I am not afraid of the passage of such a law. I do not believe it is possible that a case could arise, in all future time, in which a two-third vote of the House, and two-thirds of the Senate, would concur in passing a law repealing any act incorporating any institution of the State, or repealing any general law under which corporations might be organized, unless the same ought to be repealed, and their repeal would be demanded for the great public good.

There are other cases, which might arise, but which the law can guard against. If corporators, or stock holders, transcend their power, or do not comply with the requisites of the law, under which they were created and regulated, why then the courts can dispose of them. Every individual has the right to inquire into the acts of a corporation, and if he detects any thing wrongful, the courts are open to him for redress. It strikes me, whether this provision be adopted here or not, it can make very little difference. If it be incorporated, it will do no harm, and it may do some good. I, therefore, should incline to favor the admission of this clause into the constitution, believing that it can do no injury, and, perhaps, if we do not make such a provision, those who may come after us, may wish, at some future time, that there had been a constitutional provision for remedying an evil, which, otherwise, they cannot reach.

Mr. WILSON. I do not desire to detain the convention with any extended remarks, but I think it proper, at this time, that I should make some remarks upon this subject, in addition to those I made the other day. I will state here, that I am, by no means, an enemy to incorporations, but, on the contrary, I have the most kindly feelings towards them. I desire to see the internal improvements of this State carried on to successful completion. I am also favorable to the establishment of the banking system here, but while I am friendly to incorporations, I do not wish to be more friendly to them than I am to the private citizens of the State, and I do not wish to confer upon them a right of which they cannot be deprived by the same power.

It has been well remarked, that a private citizen may forfeit his life. If so, can gentlemen give me any good reason, why a corporation should not forfeit its life, if it transcends the law, and if it becomes oppressive. Here gentlemen may meet me, when I use the term oppressive, in regard to corporations, and say, that I am endeavoring to excite a feeling of antipathy against them. But this is not the case. I apprehend that if many gentlemen who appear to be the special champions of vested rights in corporations, would take a little more pains not to excite the people against them, there would be no danger of Legislative bodies interfering with their rights.

It has been represented by the gentleman from Des Moines (Mr. Hall) that parties injured by corporations have a remedy in the writ of *quo warranto*. I lay down this proposition that that remedy is totally inadequate to reach the evil, wherever the evil exists. I can bring a practical illustration of that doctrine in the case of the Railroad monopoly in the State of New Jersey. Tyrannical in the exercise of the power with which it is clothed, it has become an instrument of oppression, from which the people would be glad to find relief, but they cannot, and what is the reason? It has a life that the Legislative power of the State cannot take away, and, although you may sue out your writ of *quo warranto* against that corporation and bring it before the courts, what course has it to take? Merely to hold up its charter and say to them, that it has not transcended a single provision of that charter. However opprescive it may be, however it may have interfered with the State government, however much it may control the citizens of the State, no matter how great the tyranny it imposes upon them, all it has to do is to hold up its charter and say, "we have complied with the letter of our charter and your writ must be dismissed at the expense of the relator. The remedy by *quo warranto* for such cases as this is inadequate. We must have something else, and we must have a power, which will reach a corporation, although it may be following the strict letter of the act by which it was created, and yet under which it becomes oppressive. Whenever that time comes, that a corporation becomes oppressive to the people, it ought to be destroyed, and there is a crime for which we seek to take away its life, just as we seek the life of a private citizen when he transcends the laws of the State, by taking the life of his fellow-man. Every citizen has the right to life, liberty and the pursuit of happiness. He has a right to use his physical force, so that he does not interfere with the rights of others, but when he does interfere with those rights so as to deprive his fellow-man of his life, he forfeits his own life. So should corporations stand. Whenever they interfere with the rights of citizens, whenever they become oppressive, and as a consequence, the people demand that they shall cease to exist, let them cease to exist. But I apprehend that there will be no danger of their being interfered with by the Legislature so long as they keep within bounds.

Let me notice here a remark dropped by the gentleman from Pottawattamie (Mr. Price). He says, that corporations for a period of time so long, that the memory of man runneth not to the contrary, during which corporations have existed, that they have subverted no government. That may be all true, but let me ask the gentleman this question, whether moneyed corporations have not existed protected and upheld government, because they controlled that government to which they owed their very existence? I find in the history of almost every nation, that where corporations have existed, and where they have become so strong as to control the Legislative power of the government, that they have corrupted the Judiciary, and by by its corruption and by this control they have interested themselves in prolonging the government so long only as they could control it for their own purposes.

I claim that the Bill of Rights is the proper place for the insertion of the clause proposed by the gentleman from Scott (Mr. Ells), for it is where the rights of the people are set forth and defined.

The gentleman from Pottawattamie (Mr. Price) referred to the concession of the Magna Charta to the people of England at Runnymede. How was it gained? King John had arrogated to himself powers that his barons were not willing to grant him, and for the purpose of holding him in check, they rose against him and they incorporated in the charter which they wrung from him, the powers which they intended to retain in their own hands. The object of a Bill of Rights is to set forth and define powers which the people seek to retain within themselves, and they should always be contained in that instrument. If it be proper for us to say, that the Legislature shall have the power to interfere with, revoke, amend or repeal those acts of incorporation, or those special privileges which may be granted, is it not a power retained to the people? If so, does it not properly belong to the Bill of Rights? When the people say, that they will retain in their hands a power which may prevent rights from becoming vested in incorporations to such an extent, that they cannot be deprived of them, when they determine to retain in their hands that right. I say is it not proper to go into the Bill of Rights?

Another argument has been used against the adoption of this amendment, and it is this, that the article reported by the Committee on Corporations contains the same provision. I apprehend that any gentleman who will read the seventeenth section of the report reported by the Committee on Corporations, will come to a very different conclusion, as I shall attempt to show, when that report comes up. There is no such power retained in that section. The section says:

"*Subject to the provisions hereof*, the General Assembly shall have power to amend or repeal all laws for the organization or creation of corporations, or granting of special privileges or immunities, and may repeal the same by a vote of two-thirds of the House of Representatives, and also of the Senate; and no exclusive privileges, except as in this article provided, shall ever be granted."

So that article provides for the incorporation of special corporations. And under that article as reported by the Committee on Corporations when an act shall have been passed by the Legislature, no power will exist in this State that can deprive them of their rights.

Mr. CLARK, of Henry. If the gentleman will read the report of the Committee a little more carefully he will see that it does make such provision. The preceding section says:

"But no general banking law, nor law creating a State Bank, nor shall amendments thereto, nor acts in repeal thereof, take effect until the same be submitted, separately, to the people, at a general or special election, as provided by law, and be approved by a majority of all the voters voting for and against it."

Mr. WILSON. I do not see that it changes the principle one iota. They can only submit a law to the people for the purpose of repealing, revoking, or amending any chartered privileges, which may be granted by the Legislature, "*subject to the provisions hereof.*"

Does not this reach the case supposed by the gentleman? The few words that are appended to that section cover the whole ground for which I have contended.

Now, allow me to say a word in regard to the cry that has been raised here, that if we adopt this provision, we shall have no incorporations for internal improvements.

Ohio has such a provision in her constitution, and who does not know that since it was adopted, that thousands of miles of railroad have been constructed where, before that time, hundreds of miles only were constructed. But gentlemen say Ohio is a wealthy State. Where did that State get her capital? She got it from the European capitalists, who have sent their capital there for building railroads, and who did not allow this provision to interfere or stand in their way, although it is a much more stringent provision than the one which the Committee on Corporations propose to adopt. The provision in the Ohio constitution reads as follows:

"All political power is inherent in the people. Government is instituted for their equal protection and benefit, and they have the right to alter, reform, or abolish the same, whenever they may deem it necessary; and no special privileges or immunities shall ever be granted that may not be altered, revoked or repealed by the General Assembly."

A simple majority vote is sufficient there to alter, repeal or revoke a charter, but the amendment now offered by the gentleman from Scott (Mr. Ells) requires a two-thirds vote. We are offering here a greater safeguard than they had in Ohio, and yet that State has never experienced any inconvenience from the adoption of the clause in her constitution which I have read. No State in the Union has such a perfect system of net-work by railroad communication as the great State of Ohio, and yet the great majority of her railroads have been built since the adoption of her new constitution.

It has also been urged here, that if we adopt this provision, we will have no capital invested in banks. But I ask you how many banks have sprung up in Ohio since the adoption of the provision upon corporations in her constitution? From what quarter does this capital come? It matters not, whether it be home or foreign capital. If an investment is safe for home capital, it is safe for foreign capital, for foreign capitalists depend a great deal upon the home investments for determining whether it is safe for them to make an investment there themselves. It seems to me that all the theories that gentlemen can advance in support of their position cannot do away with the practical results that have followed the adoption of such a provision as this in other States. I am in favor of the amendment offered by the gentleman from Scott [Mr. Ells] and I believe the Bill of Rights is the proper place for its insertion. If I cannot get it incorporated there, then I shall move to strike out some portion of the article on corporations and insert it in lieu thereof.

Mr. HALL. I did not intend to say one word upon this subject when this discussion first came up, nor will I now detain the convention but a few minutes. I must confess that I was not before apprised of the unfortunate condition in which our State had been placed for the last ten years, from failing to incorporate in the Bill of Rights the provision now proposed by the gentleman from Scott [Mr. Ells]. If we are to believe gentlemen a tyrannical power may strike a death-blow through the Bill of Rights as it stands at present, at the freedom of the country, and there is a pit-hole at the end of every section, in which liberty is about to be buried. For one, I never heard a word of complaint from the people of any section of the State in regard to the present Bill of Rights. I believe that it requires no amendments whatever, and I believe that all this effort to amend in this convention is so much time thrown away.

The proposition now made, if I understand it, is intended to reach corporations. "No immunities or privileges shall ever be granted, that may not be altered, revoked or repealed by the General Assembly, by a vote of two-thirds of the House and also of the Senate;" or, in other words, all laws that grant immunities and privileges shall be subject to repeal by the Legislature. I wish to set the gentleman from Jefferson, [Mr. Wilson,] right in one point, and I do so because he has frequently taken the privilege of setting me right. The constitution of Ohio provides that "no special privileges or immunities shall ever be granted, that may not be altered, revoked or repealed by the General Assembly."

Can the gentleman say that no solitary road or work of internal improvement has been created by special charter since the adoption of that constitution?

Mr. WILSON. I will answer the gentleman by saying that the amendment we propose is precisely the same.

Mr. HALL. Then they have a general incorporation law there, which the Legislature cannot touch; and hence they must have gone on under that law in Ohio. So that fact, I think, answers the gentleman from Jefferson, [Mr. Wilson.] I oppose this amendment, because I deem it totally unnecessary, and a wanton violation of the principles which have governed us for the last ten years. A new feeling seems to have dawned upon the subject of corporations within the last ten or fifteen years. Under the old system the Legislatures of the different States granted acts of incorporation to special companies. The idea of a general incorporation law had never entered into the Legislative history, at least to no considerable extent. While grave Legislative bodies doled out to citizens associated together in one section of the state, such privileges as they desired, they withheld them from the mass of the people. This kind of legislation was partial in its effects, and in many instances was wrong and oppressive. Many of the States throughout the Union were engaged in the prosecution of extensive internal improvements at this time, but by reason of this system of partial legislation, they were at last driven to the necessity of abandoning them. Then it was that the people of the country began to look around and see how these great improvements could be made, from what quarter the capital was to come, and who the persons were that would furnish the means with which to build them; and the result was, that the policy of making these improvements was turned over from the States to associated private enterprise. In this State we have continued, and will continue doubtless, to look to private associated enterprise for the purpose of making our internal improvements. Her rivers are to be improved, her railroads built, and all her internal improvements are to be carried on by associated private enterprise. In the place of clogging or putting the least barrier in the way of the fullest success of these enterprises, I would prefer to cherish and encourage them in every honorable and legitimate way. Gentlemen have asked me if the position I take is democratic doctrine. I understand democracy to be that principle which does justice to all, protects all, and allows the largest possible liberty consistent with the public safety. It is that which puts no shackles or trammels upon the man in his individual or associated capacity, that is not absolutely necessary for the public good. It will protect the citizen individually, and it will protect him when associated with others, for a lawful and laudable purpose. When an attempt is made to take away his rights, it will not turn him over to the Legislative body, but to the Judiciary, the proper tribunal for ascertaining and passing upon rights of this kind.

Gentlemen in their arguments, in connection with this subject, have urged as a reason for the adoption of this provision in the Constitution, that the fact that the Legislature may make at some time an improvident bargain, and allow those companies to collect tolls, larger perhaps, than they would have done, if they had foreseen what was to have happened at the time their charters were granted. Now, will gentlemen say, after they have granted the right to a citizen, or an associated number of citizens, that they shall have the privilege of breaking their charter whenever they please, that after a company have invested their money, they shall have the right, at one sitting of the Legistature of taking away their rights—destroying their business, and forcing them to sell out. That would certainlv be unjust. There may be instances where the State may make a bad bargain, but it is no reason if she does why she should not fulfill her agreement, any more than in the case of indvidual parties, in similar circumstances.

I shall vote against this amendment, believing that it is entirely unnecessary to insert such a provision in the Bill of Rights. I do not believe there is any more necessity for the insertion of such a provision here, than there would be to insert a provision, that boys and cattle should not run at large.

The remarks of the gentleman from Johnson (Mr. Clarke) upon this subject, were very pertinent and appropriate. Capitalists are jealous and timid, and if they see the least possibility of a construction to be given to our laws, which will defeat the purposes which they have in view in lending their aid to internal improvements, they will be slow to engage in any enterprises of this kind; and the result will be that our good and noble system of internal improvements will be checked in its progress.

My desire is to give the largest liberty to associated, as well as individual corporators, in order that our State may still go forward in her march of improvement.

Mr. GILLASPY. I do not wish to make a speech, but I intimated the other day, that I should oppose this amendment, and therefore, I wish now to present a few reasons why it ought not to pass. The gentleman who introduced this amendment said, that those who arraryed themselves in opposition to it, were afraid to trust the people. I will say to the gentleman, that I am not afraid to do so, and if the gentleman will so modify his amendment, as to leave it to the people to say whether acts of corporations shall be repealed or not, I may be induced to vote for it.

I have gained the the reputation form the gentleman from Henry (Mr. Clarke) of being honest. I want to say now, that I have no fears of the people. I am willing to trust them, but I am not willing to trust all future legislation, upon this subject. Gentlemen may say this is a harsh remark, to apply to honorable gentlemen who may be sent here to represent the people, in their capacity as legislators, but I appeal to members upon this floor, if they do not know to their certain knowledge, that it is a great ambition at Washington, as well as elsewhere, on the part of members of Congress to be placed at the head of some of the most impórtant committees of Congress for the purpose of fleecing corporations. Why, if I were disposed to make money in that way, I would rather be chairman of committee on Patents, than President of the United States, so far as dollars and cents are concerned. If you incorporate this provision in your Bill of Rights, they will have at every successive session of the Legislature all the corporations, and every individual engaged in them thronging these halls, and for what purpose? Some individual, who has not as much ready cash in hand as he would like, will introduce a resolution of inquiry into the management of some corporation, and the expediency of declaring its charter null and void, and then the first train after that, the entire force of the corporation will be on hand. The first inquiry on their part, will be, "how much do you want."

I contend, that the adoption of such a provision as this, would present an inducement to corrupt the Legislation of the State; and I am opposed to placing in the Bill of Rights any such provision as this.

I have a single word to say in reply to the gentleman from the "Hominy Nation," or Appanoose [Mr. Harris] in his remarks about the Des Moines Improvement. He said, that it was a magnificent fund, which had been frittered away by the gentlemen having charge of it, and who had been enabled, from their fat salaries, to build fine houses, towering to the clouds. It is known to most gentlemen here, that I have been heretofore a member of the Board of Public Works. I was elected by the "dear people"—a word that sounds beautiful in this hall. I want to say, however, that I never built a house in my life, and that I live in the worst house in my town, so these remarks of the gentleman about the Board of Public Words cannot apply to me.

Mr. HARRIS. I said positively and distinctly that so far as the honesty of the Board of Public Works of the Des Moines River Improvement was concerned. I made no charge against any man. I suppose they were all honest, and discharged their duty faithfully, under the circumstances.

Mr. CLARKE, of Alamakee. In listening to the arguments which have been addressed by those who are opposed to the introduction of this principle into our Constitution, we should be led to suppose that we were not framing a

Constitution for the State of Iowa, but for eastern capitalists. The whole drift of the argument, so far as I have been able to learn, is to ascertain whether this provision, if placed in the Constitution, will please the captalists abroad, who wish to come here and invest their money in Internal Improvements.

Now it strikes me, that this is not the first enquiry which should be made, in a discussion of this question. The first and prominent question should be, what is for the best interests of the people of Iowa. Shall we make our own institutions, keep the reins of government in our own hands in order that we may be able to control foreign capitalists, or shall we surrender at once, at discretion, that power into their keeping?

In my opinion, it is the best policy and the safest course to retain that power within our own control. If so, then I wish to enquire for one moment what will be the best course to be pursued by this Convention upon that subject.

It is contended by the opponents of this amendment, that foreign capital will not seek investment here, if this provision be adopted. They assume that proposition without the first particle of proof. The history of the country proves the contrary to be true. I do not, for one, wish to retard or check Public Improvement, in the shape of Railroads, in any legitimate progress they may make, but I am unwilling to surrender into the keeping of any monied institution, the right to make our laws. I believe it should be retained by the people, and in such a manner that they themselves can control that matter. Upon what principle is it, that private interests shall always succumb to public interests? Is it not the principle, that the public interest is always paramount to the private. If that be the case, why should there be an exception made in favor of corporate bodies. Why should not our laws be so made as to reach corporate bodies, as well as private individuals?

Why corporate bodies should in reality be excluded from the general principle that their interests shall yield to the public interests, the gentleman upon the other side have failed to tell us. They say that capital has done wonders in the developement of our resources and the improvement of our State. It is true that capital is necessary for the prosperity of all countries. It has leveled mountains, bridged rivers, and performed the many wonderful things claimed by the gentleman from Potawattamie (Mr. Price) but can the gentleman point his finger to a single instance, where any corporation has ever acted from the impulse of generosity, or from a desire to benefit the public. It has rendered all this service, not for the benefit of mankind, but because it was absolutely necessary to perform it in order to reaeh the benefit which it intended to gain from the adoption of this course. Corporations are entitled to no gratitude, and no sympathy at the hands of the people, for the benefits which they have conferred upon us. I look upon them as necessary evils. They are dangerous in themselves, and they are so many stepping stones to aristocratic government, and just so many encroachments upon the rights of individual liberty. Every institution of the kind is chartered at the expense of individual rights. Institutions of this character may be tolerated to a certain extent, but I do claim that the power should be vested in the people to say that they shall be deprived of their charters, when they cease to be beneficial to the great interests of the community.

We have been also told by the gentleman from Pottawatamie, [Mr. Price,] in the course of this discussion, that the history of the world does not produce an instance where corporations have subverted a government; but let me tell the gentleman that it never becomes necessary for a corporation to do so. Money is all powerful, and when that power is combined with the other influences it can exert, it has the means of corrupting a government, and conforming that government to their interests. Consequently, it becomes their interest not to obstruct, not to trample upon the government, but to make it conform to their wishes. The history of our country proves that corporate bodies have taken that course.

It is claimed by some members upon this floor that if this provision is introduced into the constitution, that it will defeat it at the hands of the people. I claim it to be an argument in favor of the introduction of this provision here, that gentlemen should express a fear in the very infancy of this State, when corporate bodies have hardly been breathed into existence, that the people would not vote for a constitution containing a provision that reserved to them the right to control them. I ask you what would be the fate of the people of this State if we should neglect to incorporate such a provision into the constitution at this time, and the corporations should get firmly rooted in our soil. We must settle this question now, or before another revision of the constitution, those corporate bodies will settle that question for us.

It is claimed again by another member that if this provision is incorporated into the constitution, we shall have rivalry among her incorporated bodies, and that one or two will combine to destroy another. They say that by the adoption of this provision we will put a stop to public improvements and strike a death-blow at corporate bodies, and that there will be such a spirit of rivalry among them that they will devour each other. I believe that there is far more danger of their devouring the people than each other.

But gentlemen on the other side say that they have not unlimited confidence in Legislative Assemblies. If this be so, I claim it to be another argument in favor of our side of the question. The same argument was urged in Committee of the Whole upon this question, that legislative bodies might be acted upon by corrupt appliances. Money is all powerful, and it may induce a legislative body to pass a law which will favor a certain class of individuals at the expense of the community at large, and if the principle which gentlemen contend for upon the other side be correct, when such a law has once been passed, it is like the laws of the Medes and Persians, unalterable. I claim in view of this consideration that we should place in the constitution some kind of restraint, which will enable our legislative bodies to exercise control in these matters. If there may be committees in our legislative halls, who may be corrupted by corporate bodies, we shall lose nothing but may gain much by the incorporation of this provision into our constitution. As the constitution now stands, when once such a law is passed they have no necessity to try and wield future legislative action, for they have securely established their rights beyond the reach of legislative action.

Then again we are told that the adoption of this provision would work a great injustice to corporate bodies. I apprehend that no such result would follow from the adoption of this clause in the constitution, as proposed to be amended. If the constitution is adopted with this provision it becomes the fundamental law of the land, the supreme law; and our agents, the legislature, when they make a law allowing certain persons to form companies for corporate purposes, would conform it to that provision of the constitution, and which would thereby become a part of the law. That very provision of the constitution becomes then a part of the contract. The legislature say to the corporation when they give them a charter, that they shall have the power to alter, amend or revoke it. I ask you then if there is any injustice or wrong in this, when they themselves agree that such shall be the power reserved to the people? And so it is with this, as with all the other objections that have been urged against the adoption of this provision, the moment you come to apply the test of investigation to it, you see that it has no weight and force whatever.

But I have spoken longer than I intended already, and I must close my remarks by expressing the hope that the amendment now under consideration will prevail.

Mr. WINCHESTER. Before the vote is taken upon this question, I wish to make a very few remarks, as it may be proper and necessary for me, being a member of the Committee on Bill of Rights which submitted amendments here, to make an explanation in regard to the vote which I shall cast. The gentlemen of that Committee very well recollect that I opposed any changes in the Bill of Rights as it stands in the present constitution, as I considered them entirely unnecessary and uncalled for, but I gave way to the gentleman from Scott, [Mr. Ells,] the gentleman from Clinton, [Mr. Cotton,] and the gentleman from Alamakee, [Mr. Clark,] in order to allow them an opportunity to submit those amendments. I did not consider the objections to them as of sufficient importance to submit a minority report, but I shall vote against this proposition as it now stands. From what has already transpired in this Convention we may suppose there will be an endless number of propositions and amendments submitted which will simply alter the language of clauses proposed to be amended, without changing in the least particular their sense or meaning. But I am glad to see a disposition manifested here to vote down all propositions for amendment, where gentlemen do not absolutely make a change for the better. I came here not to tear into fragments the old organic law of this State, but to make a few amendments and changes which the wants of the people required and their necessities demanded.

It is a well settled principle that one Legislature has not the right to tie the hands of its successors. I deem that principle equally applicable to us as a body, and that we need not undertake to frame a constitution for succeeding generations. It was the universal remark in the section of the State that I represent, before I came here, that the old constitution was good enough, with a very few changes; for instance, in the provision relating to a banking system, in the time of holding our general elections, and the time of the meeting of our Legislature.

Now, I shall vote against everything which I do not deem absolutely necessary for the advancement of the interests of the State. As I said before, it is unnecessary to undertake to legislate for all coming time. However good a constitution this people may adopt, they will not be satisfied with it ten years hence. The people will clamor for a change. The universal Yankee nation is composed of a restless, energetic, and persevering people, ever eager for a change. I consider the physician most skillful who cures the present malady, instead of prescribing for a disease that his patient may contract at a subsequent period.

Mr. CLARKE, of Johnson. I desire to be heard before this vote is taken, and I understand that the chairman of the Committee on the Bill of Rights [Mr. Ells] desires to close the debate. I think that upon our side of the question, I ought to have the right of reviewing the positions taken by the gentleman from Appanoose [Mr. Harris], and the gentleman from Jefferson [Mr. Wilson], who have both in a special manner alluded to me. But as the hour is late, I will ask the permission of the Convention to defer my remarks till the afternoon session.

On motion of Mr. WARREN the Convention then took a recess till 2 o'clock, P. M.

Mr. CLARKE, of Johnson. I trust the gentleman from Appanoose [Mr. Harris] will excuse me for saying that his speech this morning, is not a new one to me. I have a very distinct recollection of hearing just that mode of argument some fifteen years ago in the State of Ohio, when, perhaps, he and I were battling upon opposite sides of this question. And I trust he will excuse me for further saying, that I think the character of his argument, by appealing to the prejudice against wealth and capital, is better suited to the stump than to a deliberative body like this, and that I like the omissions of his speech better than I do the commissions; and I am glad to see that even he, with all his hostility to corporations, did not attempt to confute the position I took in the outset, that this proposition was in violation of the natural instincts of common honesty. He tacitly admits that this proposition is a dishonest one upon its face.

Now, that this Convention may perceive the enormity of this proposition, I have placed the principle of it in another form of words, which reads, "the State shall have the right to violate its contracts at pleasure, and the injured party shall have no remedy or redress." This is the essence and principle of this proposition. Now I put it to this Convention to say, what gentleman on this floor would give a vote to a proposition of this kind? The proposition is that the Legislature shall have the power to destroy the immunities and privileges which it may grant. Now, what is meant by immunities and privileges? Why, sir, acts of incorporation; and the highest judicial tribunals, not only State, but national, have decided that these privileges and immunities are contracts, and the gentleman from Scott [Mr. Ells] proposes to put into the fundamental law of this State a proposition which will give the State the right to violate its contracts at its own pleasure. Now, let me inquire of the Convention, what is the State? It is but an artificial individual, but an aggregate of the people of this State, in a governmental capacity; and if it is right to give the State this power, then it is right to give it to every individual in the State. If the State may have the right to repeal and violate contracts, and the party injured shall have no redress, why is it not right that you and I, as individuals, shall have the same right? If these gentlemen are consistent they would amend the proposition so as to say that the individual citizen shall have the same right as they propose to give the State. They would then be consistent, and the monstrous proposition would go forth from this State that we will repudiate and nullify contracts.

Now, I am glad to see that the gentleman from Appanoose [Mr. Harris] did not undertake to justify this proposition as morally right. Now, if it is morally wrong, and shocks the common sense and honesty of every member of this Convention, that, it seems to me, ought to be an end to the proposition. But the gentleman has much to say about the indebtedness of the State —and he made here the bold proposition, that the new States had not been benefitted by their internal improvements, and he cites Ohio as an instance of his argument. Now, admit that Ohio is in debt—

Mr. HARRIS. I would beg leave to interrupt the gentleman by saying that he entirely misunderstands my argument.

Mr. CLARKE, of Johnson. I know that when the gentleman was commenting upon the old States he made the emphatic declaration that the new States had not been benefitted by the debts they had contracted for purposes of internal improvement. Now, I take issue with the gentleman, upon that position. While we admit that there may have been improvidence in these matters of internal improvement in the new States, I will say this, and the common experience of all men will sustain me in saying it, that the State of Ohio, the State of Indiana, and the State of Illinois have been benefitted ten fold more by their works of internal improvement, than the cost of those works have been. Look at Ohio, rising within a few years to be the third State in the Union. Look at the increase of her popnlation; look at her increased facilities for trade and commerce, and what is the cost of these internal improvements compared with the advantages? Without them, Ohio, to-day, would be what Virginia is, and what Missouri is now. Contrast the condition of Ohio, under this system of internal improvements, with that of the older State of Virginia, "the mother of Presidents." and we will see the effect of these internal improvements. And from this fact we should learn to encourage and foster those improvements, that the same results may follow here.

The gentleman from Jefferson [Mr. Wilson] uses another argument here in relation to the word "special." We are told that because Ohio has this provision in her constitution, we may safely put it in here. Now, I beg leave to call the attention of the gentleman to this fact. He is familiar with the contest in Ohio in relation to this question of corporations. He knows, as has been truly remarked by the gentleman from Des Moines [Mr. Hall] that the war was against special corporations, and it was to prevent them that this provision was inserted in that constitution, and if this clause ever comes under the consideration of the Supreme Court of this State, they will give it the interpretation it has received elsewhere. And the word "special" may have a meaning in it in Ohio, that it may not have in this State, because in this State we have never had any special corporations, or any worth speaking about. All our corporations now in existence have been organized under general laws, and in that respect they are not special corporations. In another respect, however, they are special corporations. Every corporation in this State, whether organized under a general law or not, is a special corporation, because the corporators derive a special benefit by virtue of their action under that law. Hence, under our constitution with this clause in it, and without any previous political history similar to that of Ohio, our Supreme Court would decide that this provision applied to incorporations organized under general laws, while in Ohio they would decide that it applied only to special acts passed by the General Assembly. Here, then, is a consideration worthy of thought, before this Convention decide upon this matter.

My friend from Appanoose [Mr. Harris] made another remark, which I suppose he meant but as a casual remark, but it amounted to the declaration that he wanted this constitution voted down by the people. That was, perhaps, a slip of the tongue. But if he does want the constitution voted down, I trust I may be permitted to say that I do not want any such thing. I want this Convention to make such a constitution as the people will approve, not by a party vote, but by a vote of all parties. I trust it will be so just and equal that it will commend itself to the public approbation; that men of all parties can meet and stand upon it as a common platform. Hence it is, that I oppose the insertion of this dogma into the constitution, because I believe it will have a tendency to perhaps drive our people back to old party lines and party organizations, and the question may be fought over in this Staie as it was in Ohio, after ten years' conflict, and in such a conflict the best interests of this State must suffer.

Now I come to another argument, and by the gentleman from Jefferson [Mr. Wilson]. He asks if a corporation may not forfeit its life, as a man may forfeit his life? Granted; but suppose we reverse this proposition. Suppose that it was asked here that the Legislature should have the right to hang a man without a trial, without a hearing, without a judge, and without a jury? I would ask the gentleman if he would not be shocked by such a proposition? and yet that is his argument. He argues that because a corporation may violate its charter, may violate the law, therefore the Legislature shall be the judge and the jury, and the executioner, and that, too, without a hearing. That is his position, and it is no more just than the propositions that these corporations shall be destroyed, as proposed by the amendment of the gentleman from Scott [Mr. Ells].

We have been told that injury has resulted from these corporations, and as an instance the railroad monopoly in New Jersey has been cited by the gentleman from Jefferson. Now what does that teach us? Not that there should be no incorporations, not that there should be no railroads, not that the Legislature should possess this arbitrary power. It does not teach us that; but it teaches us that the Legislature, the representatives of the people, should be careful in regard to the contracts they may make, and that is my object in so leaving this thing in the hands of the agents of the people, that they may be able to make fair and honest contracts. It is no argument against railroads that the people of New Jersey have made a bad bargain; it is no reason why a power should be lodged in the Legislature to destroy contracts and vested rights, because a Legislature may have made a bad bargain.

Mr. WILSON. If the gentleman will allow me to interrupt him, I will say that I have no desire to have my argument misrepresented. I did not cite the instance of New Jersey for the purpose of showing that we should have no railroads, I cited it to show that these corporations might keep within their charters and yet become burdensome and oppressive to the community.

Mr. CLARKE, of Johnson. I hove no desire to misrepresent any gentleman upon this floor. But if my conclusions were not the legitimate results of the gentleman's argument, then I have misapprehended it entirely. He cites New Jersey as an example of a monopoly existing that is grievous to the people of that State, and fearful that a similar state of things may result here; the Legislature are to have the power to repeal these acts of incorporation. That is the legitimate result of his argument. And it is just as honest and right to give the Legislature the authority to hang a man because he has violated the law, as to give them authority to destroy a corporation because it has violated the law. We have now in existence the very department of government whose duty it shall be to try all those matters, and to them we can look for a decision of the violation of the charters as well as to the commission of crime. It is their peculiar and legitimate sphere, and I see no reason for taking from them this power that we may give it to the Legislature, and endow it with judicial and executive powers. We aim to keep the Legislative, executive and judicial departments separate from each other, and not to give to the Legislature the right to try, condemn anq execute these corporations.

The gentleman from Henry (Mr. Clark) has a very amiable way of getting over this proposition. He is in favor of it because it may do good and can do no harm. Now I am opposed to it for the very reason that I think it can do no good and must work a great deal of harm. The first question for members to decide conscientiously is this; is this proposition morally right? No man upon this floor has, so far attempted to justify the morality of this provision, but all coincide that it is placing in the hands of the Legislature a power no man would trust himself with. Suppose it was proposed to pass a law giving to every man the right to violate his contracts and to judge of their propriety and justness. What would become of private rights and private property? And yet the State is but an aggregate of the people and should possess upon this matter no more right than belongs to every individual citizen.

This is the view I take of this proposition. I have my opposition to it first upon the ground that it is morally wrong, that it is placing a power in the hands of the Legislature that no man, individually, would take for himself. I oppose it secondly, upon the ground of expediency, that in our young State with the necessity we have for Internal Improvements, for capital of all kinds, for labor and associations of labor, this proposition strikes a vital blow at every combination of that kind. Gentlemen talk about corporations as if they were the only horrid thing to be dreaded. Now what is a corporation? It is nothing but a partnership, a kind of artificial person. And why do men assemble and congregate in these combinations? Simply because they have neither the wealth nor the capacity to do these things individually. No man will undertake to construct a railroad from Iowa City to Council Bluffs. Why? Because first he has not capital enough; secondly, he has not the ability to do it, to attend to and oversee the whole work. A capacity for this is beyond the power of any one man, and have four or five men get together and do it with their united means, and energy and ability. They stand in the position of so many individual men, and have no more nor less right than individual men, and it is no more right to apply this principle to them in the aggregate, than as individuals.

The gentleman from Jefferson (Mr. Wilson) says that Ohio has a similar provision in her Constitution, and yet she has been able to construct extensive works of internal improvement. Now I must differ with the gentleman a little.—I venture to say that long before any such provision was inserted in the Constitution of Ohio, the great bulk of their internal improvements was commenced, the outlines were fixed, and that they have been made under a different fundamental law from this. I would ask the gentleman if he can point to any considerable line of railroad that has been commenced in Ohio since this Constitution of 1851 has been in operation? But even admit that such is the case, I said this morning and I repeat it now, that Ohio occupies a different position from what our State does. She has her own capital and wealth at home, and that controls that State; and in all those questions of pecuniary interest they can contrive together and maintain their rights.—But we are in no such position, and an act may be done here that in Ohio or New York would be frowned down. The internal improvements of Ohio was planned under a different Constitution and a different system of law from what is now proposed here, and those that have been made now have been made with the understanding that the word "special" did not apply to incorporation under general laws, but to special corporations under special acts of the legislature.

Mr. WILSON. I would ask the gentleman from Johnson, [Mr. Clarke,] one question. Suppose this amendment should be adopted, can any law be passed under it that will have a retractive effect?

Mr. CLARKE, of Johnson. Certainly not.

Mr. WILSON. Very well, then the provision would not apply to corporations now in existence.

Mr. CLARKE, of Johnson. I do not say this amendment, if adopted, will affect corporations already formed. But I do say that the corporations already in existence are not one-tenth, no not one-fifteenth part of those which will be required to promote the true interests of the State. I would ask gentlemen to consider that not one-half of this State is yet settled, and from every town almost, and from every point of the compass, there are projects for internal improvement which will come under this provision. I fear there is a settled purpose in this Convention to prevent the creation of corporations for any purpose. Adopt this amendment of the gentleman from Scott, [Mr. Ells,] and you will have taken the first step to that end.

Let us look at the report of the Committee on Incorporations, and presume that it is adopted. The first thing I see in that report is this: that the Legislature shall pass no special act of incorporation. That is well enough. What next? "The State shall not become a stockholder in any corporation, nor shall it answer or pay the debt or liability of any corporation, unless incurred in time of war for the benefit of the State." What next? "No political or municipal corporation shall become a stockholder in any banking corporation, directly or indirectly," nor in any other corporation, except to a limited amount .What is the result? You tie up the hands of the State in its aggregate capacity, and you tie up the hands of every municipality, of every county and town, except to a certain extent. Who are to become your corporators to build your railroads? If it is done by you and I, and others, uniting our individual capacities together, then your legislature—after we have prohibited the counties and the towns taking stock, after we have prohibited the State from becoming a stockholder to help these works—can come in and take away our charters whenever they shall choose to do so. Where then is the encouragement for wealth and capital to come to Iowa, or for the citizens who have money to go into this work of making railroads, building churches, establishing libraries, and other public beneficient institutions? I say there is no encouragement, and the effect of this amendment will be to destroy all those works of benificence and public advantage.

Take it altogether I consider this the most perfect system to prevent the improvements of this State and to check its progress morally, politically and intellectually, that I have ever seen attempted anywhere. Believing this to be but the commencement of this thing, I oppose it here in the Bill of Rights where the fight has commenced, as I expect to do through its entire progress.

Mr. SOLOMON. It is true that four or five hours have dragged their slow length along in this debate, and I have no desire to add a small portion of another hour to it. But I feel that I ought to say something upon the subject in explanation of the vote I shall give after the debate which shall have preceded the vote. I voted in Committee of the Whole against this amendment, and I shall vote against it now for reasons stronger than I entertained for voting against it then.

I, and the Democratic party with whom I act, have been arraigned for a detraction from our former views. Perhaps we have fallen from our position in the advocacy of Democratic doctrines. But I do not look upon our position here in any such light. I feel that in supporting this amendment I am supporting a principle which has always been and ever will be a time-honored principle in the Democratic party. I am not surprised, however, at gentlemen who have left the Democratic party, clinging to these wrecks as the principal trusts in the belief they now profess.

Now I shall go against this amendment for the simple reason that I am opposed to the creation of all special corporate privileges. And I say that the man who casts his vote in favor of this amendment, who votes in favor of the annulment of a certain class of legislation, votes indirectly in favor of the establishment of these special corporations. Under the present constitution, under which we have lived so long, special corporations are prohibited. I will read to gentlemen from it: "Corporations shall not be created in this State by special laws, except for for political or municipal purposes." Now gentlemen insist upon the passage of this amendment to prevent injury to the people of the State of Iowa from mammoth monopolies in the shape of corporations. Now I ask gentlemen who take that position to cite me a single corporation of that kind now in existence. Can they do it? No, sir. Gentlemen have complained of the corporation known as the Des Moines River Improvement Company. Let me ask my friend from Wapello, [Mr. Gillaspy,] if that is a special corporation? It is not; it is a corporation established under a general law, not under a special law. Then this amendment would not apply even to a corporation of that kind.

I shall vote against this amendment because it is an implied assumption that corporations of this character may be established by the legislature, because if you give them the power to repeal and destroy such corporations, you give them impliedly the power to establish them. I want gentlemen to remember their positions here upon this question. I want gentlemen who vote for this proposition to remember when they come to cast their votes upon the other proposition, with regard to the power to create special corporations, to vote with us against it. And I pledge them they will find every Democrat upon this floor voting against having such corporations in this State. Now if they are so fearful of their privileges, I ask them to come forward then when they have an opportunity of showing their real colors, and vote with us against such corporations.

I yield to no gentleman upon this floor, or in this State, in opposition to special monopolies in the garb of corporations. Corporations are good things when they are organized upon correct principles, when proper safeguards are thrown around them. When some work of public enterprise is to be performed which requires a great amount of capital, corporations are a good thing. But in order to have a perfect security against bad corporations we must make the laws general under which they are formed

Now let us advert for a brief time to the difference between special and general acts of incorporation. What is that difference? Draw up an act incorporating a company upon as just and equitable principles as you can, and then at the bottom of the act say that all other corporations by complying with the principles therein embodied, may enjoy the same privileges. Here you have an act of general incorporation, and men in framing their charters of incorporation must confine themselves to this act and its correct principles. If they do not, and have their favorites which they wish to clothe with immunities and privileges, they will be estopped from doing so because their enemies and those they desire to compete with, can come together under the same act and enjoy the same privileges. That is the kind of corporations I shall insist upon in this State, and I will never cast my vote for anything that can imply my being in favor of anything else.

Mr. HARRIS. I would like to say a word further in regard to this matter. I have been handled without gloves so very roughly by my friend from Johnson (Mr. Clarke) I desire to say something in reply. I have been charged very seriously, if this charge come correct, that I did not defend this amendment upon the principle of its being morally honest; and it certainly becomes necessary that I should say a few words in order to extricate myself, if I can do so, from this charge. Now I say here, that it is upon principles of moral honesty that I take the position I do. I stand here in favor of this amendment upon the principles that no class of individuals when associated together in a corporate capacity are more entitled to immunities and privileges than as individuals they would be entitled to possess. And I understand it to be a principle in moral honesty—for that is the term used by the gentleman from Johnson—upon which I take my position here.

But lest I forget it, before I proceed to the main argument of the gentleman from Johnson, let me say a few words in reply to my friend from Des Moines, (Mr. Hall) to whom, as I said before, I concede much more learning and experience than I possibly could have in matters of this kind. But I find my opinions so diametrically opposed to his as they are at this time, I cannot surrender them for his opinions or the opinions of any one else. He comes up here and attempts to burlesque and ridicule the position we have taken by appealing to the history of the country since the present Constitution was adopted, and asks us to show him where the harm is that has arisen under it. He speaks of our regarding every section of the Bill of Rights we are about to amend, as a pitfall for liberty, and says from our complaints it might be supposed that those principles we wish to defend by it had been jeopardized in consequence of the Bill of Rights we have had.—And then he asks with an air of triumph, if such be not the case where is the danger to arise in consequence of failing to place amendments of this character in the Constitution?—Now that gentleman knows, as does every gentleman upon this floor, that the inauguration of a new era in the politics of this State has demanded the calling of this Convention, and that we are to have ushered in those corporations which have not heretofore existed under the old Constitution. And one word will reply to the whole argument of that gentleman, and that is, that as these corporations could not exist under the old Constitution, no harm could of course have resulted from the abuse of them. Such is certainly the fact. And the gentleman cannot be deceived by his own sophistry upon that pont.

And we are asked by my friend from Des Moines (Mr. Hall) why not place individuals upon the same footing in regard to contracts as we would place the corporations? Now I would ask that gentleman to say as a lawyer if the courts do not do it? But an incorporation, a body of men associated under an act of incorporation, have their charter directly from the legislature, and they are not amenable to the provisions of law that govern individuals. You cannot get out your writ of Injunction against an incorporation, and take them into court and shut them up in prison in consequence of the violation of the terms of their contract, because they have their charter from the legislature, and might say in reply to you, that they were not responsible to you, and when their charter had placed a padlock upon the mouth of the court, they would turn round and ask in triumph, why do you not take us into a court of justice, and not before the legislature of the State. Now I understand that you can take an indivual who has violated a charter made under laws regulating contracts in this State, before a court of justice, upon a writ of injunction. But your corporators acting simply under the privilege given them by the legislature will laugh you to scorn.

The gentleman from Wapello (Mr. Gillaspy) comes in here and tells you of the monstrosities committed by the last legislature. He speaks of what has been done at Sioux City and other places, and says that if this amendment prevails then you will have every incorporation in the market, and your legislature and your judiciary will become corrupted by them, and every class of men will be in the interest of these corporations, that is, every class who wish to use their money for the privileges they can obtain from the legislature. If that be true, it certainly does not present a very pleasant picture. If it be true, then we certainly should have the privilege of being in the market, and endeavor to buy off the legislature; let us have the privilege of buying them off as long as the others have the privilege of buying them on. If they have the privilege of buying up the legislature to obtain these privileges, do let us at least have the privilege of buying the legislature back again, and get clear of those vultures who feed upon the public. It is a poor rule that will not work both ways. I had not expected to present the question in this light and would not have done so but to meet the argument of the gentleman from Wapello, (Mr. Gillaspy.) It seems to me that it is a sufficient reply to him. If it is true that legislative bodies can be moved to do things they should not, in consequence of sinister arguments held out to them, is there any reason why we should not have an equal chance in the market.

But I will pass this matter and make a few remarks in reply to the position taken by the gentleman from Johnson [Mr. Clarke], and say no more upon this question, having said what I did in the former part of the day. Now while the gentleman attempts with such serious strictures to confute the position I have taken, he admits that so far as the political history of the matter is concerned, I am correct. He charges that I have taken this position, and virtually admitted it, for the purpose of having this constitution voted down. Now the gentleman is mistaken. I have no such motives, no such intentions; but I will say to that gentleman, and to other gentlemen upon this floor, that so far as the constituency I represent is concerned, if this provision is not in the constitution, I believe they will vote against it. The gentleman says this provision will have a tendency to draw old party lines, and throw parties back as they were in the State of Ohio, and this matter must be fought over again before the people.

Now, so far as what I said here this morning may resemble a stump speech, I said then what I believe to be just, and I say it yet, and whether it be a stump speech, or any other kind of speech, whether those remarks are fitting to be made in this hall or not, I must reiterate the same thing, and I trust that whenever I am called upon to speak in regard to the matter, be it a stump speech or any other kind, I shall advocate the same doctrine as I have here to-day. But permit me to call the attention of this convention to the attitude in which the gentleman places himself by referring to the political history of Ohio. He says he has heard the same speech I made this morning, and it is not new to him. He heard it some fifteen years ago in Ohio. I can tell him he did not hear it from me, but I have no doubt that others took that position, and what was the result? After one of the fiercest struggles--after one of the most violent political struggles that have characterized the political history of any State in this Union, this question was decided in the State of Ohio by an overwhelming majority against the position taken by the gentleman here. What, then, is the conclusion? Why that he is afraid to trust this matter before the people, for the reason that if the same discussion shall take place in this State, if the same information shall be disseminated among the people, presupposing that the people are alike honest here as in Ohio, then the same result would ensue. I can come to no other conclusion. The gentleman will not dispute that such was the position taken in Ohio, and that it was decided as I have stated. Then I did not urge this amendment for the purpose of having the constitution voted down—and I am not aware of having used any remarks that would justify the gentleman in coming to such a conclusion. I took a position in favor of the amendment because I believe it to be correct, because I believe it to be proper, because I believe it to be just, and further, I say that I believe it to be honest, whether the gentleman understands honesty as I do or not, I must say that I go for it because I consider it an honest provision. Then I would ask gentlemen of this body if he is correct in the construction he gives my remarks upon the effect of the internal improvements of Ohio, Indiana, Illinois, and other States?

I am charged with saying that the new States are worse off with, than they would have been without improvements. I certainly never thought such a thing as that, much less did I say it. I did say that those States would have been better off in the position of Iowa, without these privileges, all fastening a tax upon them that has been fastened upon the other States, than with all the benefits of these improvements by the debts thus created. And the gentleman will not dispute me when I say the enormous debt hanging over the people of Ohio at this time was for the purpose of creating a system of internal improvements, which has been entirely done away, and the canals then projected have become deserted thoroughfares and waste places. To be sure there are mills constructed on these canals where the locks are in repair, and in some places the reservoirs are used for fishing ponds. But farther than that they have become entirely useless, and it was under a system that the gentleman wishes to fasten upon this state that these things were done. Hence, when railroads were started in Ohio there was such an enormous debt upon the State for these canals, that they could not go into the market themselves as a State, but were compelled to rely upon individual effort. Now, however, the state is woven all over by railroads, for which she is indebted entirely to individual enterprise. Certainly then the remarks of the gentleman are not applicable in regard to what I said about State indebtedness. I spoke of the enormous debts of Illinois, which some years ago were so much as to greatly lower the credit of Illinois, in the market, and to bring her well nigh to repudiation. And I understand that the improvements that were attempted under the system creating this debt, have become a waste to a great extent. And for the railroads they have there now they are indebted to individual and to private enterprise, and not to the State as a corporate body.

The gentleman says that Ohio is wealthy, and that the wealth of that State commands the action of the Legislature, and gives that as a reason why we may not do here in this State what Ohio has done under this provision in her constitution. Now I would ask what Ohio has to make her wealthy that Iowa has not? We have the natural resources here, which if properly husbanded and cultivated, will make us one of the wealthiest States in this Union. And it is to prevent the fastening of these enormous debts upon the proprietors of that soil, which may result from these soulless corporations if they are left without any restraint or control whatever, that we wish to place this provision in the constitution.

There is one aspect in which this question presents itself to my mind, which seems almost ludicrous. One class of gentleman here say that this amendment amounts to nothing. It is true we have another very serious objection offered to it, that there is really no necessity for it. Then why are these gentlemen so seriously opposed to this provision, if there is no harm in it, if it amounts to nothing? Then here comes another class, who say it is fraught with great evil, very great evil, and hence they are opposed to it. Then here comes another class of gentlemen who are also opposed to it, but they say they are opposed to it because they are opposed to all special corporations; they are opposed to putting a bridle upon them, because they are opposed to all corporations. Now is that consistent, is that reasonable? Now for the very reason that I am opposed to these things in principle, is it that I am desirous to impose some restraint upon them.

Mr. SKIFF. It seems to me that this amendment will not do a great deal of good or a great deal of harm any way, as I understand the disposition of this body, it is that not very many special privileges shall be given to corporations; that the most of them shall be incorporated under general laws, and of course if you have a general law of incorporation, and a number of men want to incorporate under that law, this provision will not apply to them. That is the way I understand this thing, and I am inclined to think, that aside from corporations for municipal and political purposes, there will be no special incorporations granted by the legislature. So I care but little whether this provision passes or not. Consequently, I do not see that there is a great deal of use in taking up so much time in considering this subject. If it were to apply to corporations organized under general laws, I should be most strongly opposed to it. Now in regard to the instance of the effect of a monopoly, which has been cited by the gentleman from Jefferson, [Mr. Wilson,] that of the railroad in the State of New Jersey. The State of New Jersey, through her Legislature, granted special privileges to two or three railroads in that State. Those corporations were smart enough to get perhaps rather the start of the State. But that difficulty will not arise in this State; for I am confident that this Convention will put a provision in our constitution so that all railroad and other corporations, except for municipal and political purposes, and perhaps those too, shall be created under general laws. Then what is the use of all this contest here about this provision, when it will do no harm and will do no good. For instance, suppose we were to let down the bars and permit all associations of men to invest whatever they may have in the world, whether little or much, in these corporations, and they go to work to do this depending upon the good faith of the State. They know what they are going into before they form this corporation. Now, suppose that the Legislature, which as gentlemen say here, is so easily affected, can be bought up, bribed and lobbied, until they take away these charters of incorporation, without any ceremony, without allowing any time for appeal whatever. One Legislature has induced individuals to embark all their worldly goods and possessions in these enterprises, and then the succeeding Legislature can take it all away, we would then have to do as they have been compelled to do in the General Government, establish a Court of Claims where these persons can go and ask for relief and damages for the injuries they have sustained by this repeal of their charter of corporation. And that Court will be the greatest Court in the State, and it will be thronged night and day by applicants for relief. I think the State would most certainly lose more in that way, than it would by permitting these corporations to go on.

I suppose all corporations will be limited as to time. That I believe is the intention of the Committee on Corporations, to limit them to not over twenty-five years. Now that is but a short time in the life of a State, and these corporations cannot do a great amount of mischief, even if they were to get a good bargain of the Legislature. Then let them go on, and when their charters expire by their own limitations, if there is anything wrong it can be amended then, and not let the Legislature tear this work to pieces and set everything adrift again. If that was done they would go into something like a Court of Claims, and the interests of the State would suffer more by far in that way than they will by letting the corporations go on. But I say, and I will hold to this doctrine all the way through, that we should have none of these special corporations, none of this special legislation in regard to corporations, but they should all be placed upon a general basis, as we have it in our Code here: "Any number of persons may associate themselves and become incorporated for the transaction of any lawful business, including the establishment of ferries, the construction of canals, railroads, bridges, or other works of internal improvement; but such incorporation confers no power or privilege not possessed by natural persons, except as hereinafter provided." The manner in which this incorporation can be carried out can be prescribed. If they want to go into mining, to build a railroad, to go into manufacturing, or any other kind of business that is legitimate, let them do it. If they go into anything that shall be a nuisance, why nuisances can be abated according to law. In every State there is a law for the abatement of nuisances. And if a body of men establish an incorporation to do that which is a nuisance, that nuisance can be abated if it is a corporation. I do not see any great deal of good or harm in this amendment, unless the Convention intends to grant power to the Legislature to create special laws for incorporations. I shall not, therefore, oppose the amendment.

Mr. BUNKER. I thought I understood very well how to vote when this matter was first presented for our consideration. But I acknowledge I am getting somewhat into a fog now after hearing the different positions taken by gentlemen here. I do not rise to make a speech but merely to look at some points connected with this matter. I understand this word "special" in a different light from what some seem to understand it. It appears to me to allude to the simple franchise, the life of the corporation. I would like to ask some legal gentleman here—the gentleman from Des Moines, [Mr. Hall,]—if that is the legal construction that would be put upon it?

Mr. HALL. It alludes I suppose to special laws for incorporations.

Mr. BUNKER. Then if this amendment should be adopted, it would have no force, according to the interpretation of the gentleman from Des Moines, to any body or association of individuals who should incorporate themselves under our general corporation laws. If I was perfectly certain that would be the case, I should have no very great objection to this amendment. Still it might operate unfavorably. We might probably want some special corporations in this State, and it would interfere with their creation and establishment. If this amendment were so changed as to say that there should be no exclusive privileges granted, but what might be revoked, then I think I might vote for it.

Now, it seems to me that the gentlemen who have spoken warmly in favor of this amendment are looking back to some old corporations long past, something rather in the past history of the country, in which the policy was to grant exclusive privileges to companies, and they are fighting that thing, it appears to me, at all events. In relation to our ordinary corporations here, all that I can see about them is, that the Legislature confers upon a number of men—poor men, perhaps—authority to do what one rich man woald be able to do, independent of any act of the Legislature; and I do not see any reason why this company of poor men should not be protected by the law just the same as the rich man would be, who could act upon his own responsibility without any act of incorporation.

Mr. CLARKE, of Henry. I would like to offer a very few remarks before the chairman of the committee, the gentleman from Scott [Mr. Ells] shall conclude this discussion; and I will state that they are drawn out by the remarks of the gentleman from Johnson [Mr. Clarke]. I consider it a compliment, more especially in a body like this, to be called amiable. I believe if there were more amiable men in this Convention we would get along somewhat better.

Now, it seems to me that some of us are inclined to take positions much like boys in a debating school, and offer arguments for the purpose of discussing some abstract question that cannot be brought into any application at all, and cannot be of any particular benefit to anybody when decided. I think we should discuss all questions that come before us in such a spirit as will enable us to get at results that will be the most beneficial to the people that we represent in this convention; and there is certainly something in this amendment that has been proposed by the gentleman from Scott, [Mr. Ells]. I am more and more impressed with it as this discussion progresses, and if there is anything in it, I honestly want to get hold of it; if there is not, then I want to see it exploded. The amendment either ought, or it ought not, to go into this constitution.

The gentleman upon the other side have made

use of this argument, an argument with two branches to it. One is, that this amendment is unnecessary, because our laws are to be so framed by wise legislators that are to come after us, and we are going to put such very wise provisions in some other part of this constitution, that it will be useless to have this provision inserted here! Very well; if there is to be some provision incorporated in some other portion of this constitution, that will make this entirely needless, then I have nothing particular to say about the importance of this provision. The other branch is set forth in the arguments of the gentlemen from Des Moines and Johnson. If the argument of the gentleman from Johnson [Mr. Clarke] be correct, and gentlemen mean to *act* upon it here in their votes, then I consider a very important question presented for us to settle. That is, *whether the acts of incorporation passed by the Legislature which shall come after us and pass laws under this constitution shall have the force and the sanction of a constitutional provision!* That is the question. If we provide here for the legislature enacting laws creating a State Banking corporation, and also provide for their making general laws under which corporations may be organized, and have nothing in our constitution by which a succeeding Legislature may reconsider the acts of a previous one, to amend, alter and repeal them, then I would ask gentlemen if these acts of the Legislature would not have all the qualities of a constitutional provision, so far as persons acquiring vested rights under the provisions of those laws are concerned?

I care nothing about this talk of how our constituents will howl when we go home, if we put such provisions as this or that in the constitution. Such things do not effect me. I have no such constituents. If the gentleman from Johnson has, such howling will only betray their nature. I come here to make a constitution for *men* and not for creatures that "howl." I come here to settle principles that shall be fixed, and upon which our legislatures and our courts shall act hereafter, and the question presents itself to every man here, do you intend by this constitution so to fix these principles that when the Legislature shall have made general laws under which incorporations shall be brought into existence, or shall make special laws creating corporations, those laws shall be irrepealable, irrevocable and unalterable? That is the question for us to decide.

I say to the gentleman from Johnson [Mr. Clarke] when he appeals to my conscience, and urges upon this body the question of right and justice, that it seems to me he has looked but a little way into the ethics of this question. I think he has not looked into it so closely as into those legal propositions which come more properly within his peculiar province. I ask gentlemen here what is there that is not right and just in saying to men before they embark into any undertaking, under laws of incorporation, for any object that they must do so with this understanding: that at any time when the necessities of the people demand it, these acts of incorporation may be altered and repealed? If we were called upon here to make an *ex post facto* provision, if we were asked to clothe the Legislature with the power to strip men of the rights which in another part of the constitution we agree to protect, then the moral dissertation as to the honesty and justice of the proceeding might come with something of force. But we are merely saying that when the Legislature that comes after us shall make laws to establish corporations, and men come here whether from the East or over the water, with their bags of glittering gold, which gentlemen have been shaking before our longing eyes, if you invest your money in our midst, you must do it with this understanding: that when the good of the people demands it, this law under which you propose to make your investment, under which you go into banking operations, under which you start a railroad, may be altered, amended or repealed. If you are willing to trust to the enlightened sense of justice of this community, to their moral sense, and embark in enterprise and risk your capital among us, with this understanding, then you can do so. If you are not willing to do this, then you can return to your homes, or go to a more favored land, where they have no such awful provision in their constitution, as that the people may do what is right when it is necessary. The pictures the gentleman has so feelingly drawn of the desolation to ensue from this provision, of our railroads left unfinished, or not begun, of our prairies overgrown with rank grass, and perhaps with the buffalo and wild Indian returning to roam over them again, as in days of yore, are all delusions, and will never exist, except in the luxuriant fancy of the gentleman entertaining them.

As the gentleman from Jefferson [Mr. Wilson] remarks, "stubborn facts prove the contrary." I will read to this Convention similar provisions from the constitutions of different States of this Uuion, upon this subject. New York has this provision in her constitution:

"Corporations may be formed under general laws; but shall not be created by special act except for municipal purposes, and in cases where in the judgment of the legislature, the objects of the corporation cannot be attained under general laws. *All general laws and special acts passed pursuant to this section may be altered from time to time and repealed.*"

Florida has this provision in her constitution:

"No act of incorporation shall be passed or altered, except by the assent of two-thirds of each branch of the Legislature."

Ohio has this provision in her constitution, and I wish gentlemen to notice that Ohio provides for the repeal or alteration, or change of general laws for the creation of corporations:

"Corporations may be formed under general laws; *but all such laws may, from time to time, be altered or repealed.*"

The second section of the Bill of Rights in the constitution of Ohio is as follows:

"All political power is inherent in the people.

Government is instituted for their equal protection and benefit, and they have the right to alter, reform, or abolish the same, whenever they may deem it necessary; *and no special privileges shall ever be granted that may not be altered, revoked or repealed by the General Assembly.*"

This principle occurs twice in the constitution of Ohio.

In the constitution of the State of Michigan I find the following:

"Corporations may be formed under general laws, but shall not be created by special act, except for municipal purposes. *All laws passed pursuant to this section may be altered, amended or repealed.*"

And here is a provision from the constitution of the State of Missouri—perhaps not very good authority here, in some respects:

"No corporation, except for political or municipal purposes, or for the purpose of education or charity, shall be created, *unless the bill creating the same shall contain a provision that the charter of such corporation may be repealed and annulled by a majority of the houses of the General Assembly.*"

In Texas there is this provision in the constitution:

"No private corporation shall be created, unless the bill creating it shall be passed by two-thirds of both houses of the Legisla.ure; *and two-thirds of the Legislature shall have the power to revoke and repeal all private corporations by making compensation for the franchise.*"

This, in my opinion, is the wisest provision in any of the constitutions.

In the constitution of Wisconsin is the following provision:

"Corporations without banking powers or privileges may be formed under general laws; but shall not be created by special act, except for municipal purposes, and in cases where, in the judgment of the Legislature, the objects of the corporation cannot be attained under general laws. *All general laws or special acts enacted under the provisions of this section, may be altered or repealed by the Legislature at any time after their passage.*"

And now I come to the constitution of the youngest State in the Confederacy. A constitution framed when they had all the lights of all the constitutional provisions that preceded, and we find this provision incorporated into the constitution of California:

"Corporations may be formed under general laws; but shall not be created by special act, except for municipal purposes. *All general laws or special acts passed pursuant to this section may be altered from time to time, or repealed.*"

Now I am not tenacious about the adoption of the amendment of the gentleman from Scott [Mr. Ells], but I am tenacious about having the principle of the amendment incorporated somewhere in this constitution. I am in favor, also, of some check upon this power of repeal and amendment, but, as I said before, I am not tenacious about what exact form that check may assume. I want a check against party legislation, and that, I think, is necessary. All of us have to trust something to the people, for what are we, except what we derive from the people? And what are Legislatures and corporations but what the people permit them to be.

Gentlemen have passed encomiums here upon corporations; very good. We all understand it. We know they are beneficial. But, we know also, that in certain times and places they have so accumulated power, and so used it, that the people have regretted that they had not that control of them, that would enable them to force them into proper channels, and compel them to do what was right and just. Now, are corporations made for corporations sake, or for the benefit of the people? I would ask gentlemen, what are Railroads made for? Take away the people and what are they? So far as they are a benefit to the people, they are a blessing; but if they get into the hands of persons who use them only for the benefit of corporations, and injurious to the people, they are a curse. Should there not be some power short of a revolution, to rectify them, when they fail to be a benefit to the people? Is it not wiser that we should here put a provision in this Constitution for an emergency that may arise, though it has not yet, than to leave this thing entirely unguarded? We are yet in our infancy, and do not know what will come to us in the future, but we find those who have gone before us inserting this provision in their Constitutions.

And as I said before, which the gentleman from Johnson [Mr. Clarke] considers an "amiable" suggestion, certianly this provision can do no harm, and if I understand the argument of that gentleman, and the gentleman from Des Moines (Mr. Hall) it may be absolutely necessary. Now the provision is so far limited that it requires a vote of two-thirds of each house of the legislature, before any corporation can be repealed, and with that limit, can gentlemen conceive that the time will come when a repeal or alteration will be made of these special laws, even that incorporating a State Bank, or of general laws under which corporati ns may organize unless the exigency of the case shall imperatively demand it. And if gentlemen are fearful of that, why not go to the full extent of the check I proposed to this Convention? If they are afraid that capital will not be invested here under such a provision as this now is, and if they have not confidence in the intelligence and honesty of the people, why not say, that after the legislature shall have passed any law repealing, or amending any general law or special act, under which corporations are organized, it shall not have effect until the same shall have been submitted to the people at some general or special election, and received the sanction of a majority of the votes at said election? In that way, they will protect all interests alike, and with such a provision as this, if capital is invested in their internal improvements, do you suppose that the people of the State of Iowa are going so far in a spirit of spite and caprice, as to destroy themselves and their own interests in order to make a sacrifice of incorporations? Does any gentleman anticipate that any such contingency can possibly arise in the affairs of this State. We can throw checks about the exercise of this power, and I think it proper we should do so, but I also as firmly believe that it should be retained in the hands of the people.

I do not look upon the legislature in the light that some gentlemen do. I look upon the legislature in the light of the most direct and practicable reflection of the people. They stand here as the people; they come from the people; they come up here to express the wishes of the people. But, when they get here in a body they are more available, it is true, for purposes of corruption than are the whole masses of the people. There is not a member here who will question that.

They know how this thing is done. They have been in the halls of the legislature, and know how bills are got through there. The fears of the gentlemen may have some foundation, when they suppose that legislators may be worked upon by their own prejudices, by popular excitement, and by influences even less honorable than those. And thus they may hastily repeal the charter of some institution which we may provide for here, or some general law, under which all our corporations are organized. But if there is a provision here, that before that act of repeal shall go into effect, it must go before the Governor, and even after he shall have approved it, it shall go before the people at large, and be discussed in every school district throughout the State, and the people must come up deliberately and deposit their ballots for or agains it, can gentlemen believe that any great wrong is going to be done. If so how in the name of God, can you permit it, provision of the Constitution, or no provision? If the people of the State of Iowa are so lost as to what is right and just, do you suppose that a Constitution on paper is going to restrain them? not at all. I say then, that there is no possible chance, short of a revolution, for the rights of corporators to be infringed, or justice to be outraged, by the legislature, with a provision in this Constitution containing the restraints I have indicated.

I am in favor of the principle of this amendment; but I am willing to consult with gentlemen as to where it shall be placed. But let us place it in this Constitution somewhere. Let us not do as the gentleman from Johnson [Mr. Clarke] would lead us by his argument to do, to throw this provision aside, as something that will defeat our Constitution if inserted. I believe it is necessary for us to incorporate it in our Constitution, or I believe the very reverse will occur to what the gentleman has prophesied. I believe, if you leave this provision out entirely of the Constitution, the people will send others here to draft another for them, with that provision inserted, for I do not believe the people of Iowa will consent, at this day, with all the lights from every Convention similar to this, to have a Constitution without this provision incorporated in it.

Mr. SKIFF. I would ask the gentleman if he understands that this amendment referring to special corporations and privileges will have any effect on other corporations? Suppose that there is a general law for incorporations, and persons incorporate themselves under that law, and afterwards this general incorporation law is repealed or altered, does the gentleman understand that this provision will affect the rights of those who have incorporated themselves under that general incorporation law. Will this repeal with this provision take away any of their rights under that general law?

Mr. CLARKE, of Henry. The Legislature may go to work and pass a general law. After it has gone into effect, they may see some defect in it, by which some undue advantage is given to corporations. The people may, in such a case, wish to amend the law. Questions have sprung up in the court, in regard to the power of the Legislature to make amendments affecting the rights and powers of corporations in such a case, after the corporation, for whose benefit the act was passed, or under which they organized, acquired certain vested rights. I suppose if we pass a general banking law without any provision in it setting forth that the same may be repealed, modified or amended, granting to certain individuals, upon complying with its requisites, the right to incorporate themselves into companies, that they may acquire vested rights under it, just as much as they would under a special law of any kind.

Mr. SKIFF. Then suppose the provision is inserted in the Constitution, that the Legislature may have the power to repeal, amend or alter any law under which a corporation was established, does it take away any of the vested rights of the corporators? Every man who goes into a corporation, does so with the understanding, that the Legislature may repeal or amend the charter under which it is organized, and no injustice is done.

Mr. ELLS. Mr. President. After the able arguments that have been offered in favor of the amendment, it would hardly seem necessary for me to make any further remarks. I have listened with the greatest pleasure to the discussion upon this subject, and if nothing else were gained, I shall be satisfied with having offered an amendment that elicited so much thought and expression of sentiment. There seems to be no difference of opinion about this principle on the part of the majority of the committee. The difference of opinion seems to be as to the proper place for placing this clause in the constitution. I do not propose to contend very strongly that this provision should be placed in the Bill of Rights, if it can be secured in any part of the constitution where it will be equally beneficial. I think, however, the Bill of Rights ought to define the rights of the people, and to place the proper restrictions upon the powers of the Legislature. It stands there in the beginning like a sentinel guarding the gates of a city; and it is a warning to all who come there that unless they give the sign-manuel, they cannot enter. I prefer, therefore, to see all rights that are reserved or declared, placed in that bill. I am surprised that gentlemen here who profess to believe in the broad doctrines contained in this amendment, opposing it, and giving no valid reasons for their opposition.

They say that they have provided in another place for this same good. If they have, why not vote for it here as well as there? I would vote for it in both places if they desire to have it so. I cannot understand their motives, although I do not impugn them. Neither can I understand their reasons for placing this provision in one part of the constitution and not in the other, to exclude it from the Bill of Rights, and place it in the article on Corporations. I can, however, understand the action of the gentleman from Johnson, [Mr. Clarke,] for he is consistent, having given notice that he "will oppose it all through." He believes the principle of repeal is morally wrong, and so believing, he is right in manfully battling against it.

I will now notice his position in this matter. I think he is radically wrong in the first view he takes of the question. He tells you that charters are contracts. If they are contracts, the Legislature has no power to interfere with them. If they attempt it, the act of doing so is in and of itself inoperative, because the constitution of the United States protects contracts and renders them inviolate. The gentleman is therefore running no risk, and he is endangering no right by allowing this amendment to be placed in the Bill of Rights. But, sir, I deny the position he takes in *toto*. I deny that any grant of power by the Legislature to any man or set of men is a contract, unless it is expressly stipulated in the terms of the grant. A mere right of way for a railroad is certainly no contract, no consideration being given therefor. The granting of corporate powers to a banking company is not a contract for the same reason. The doctrine contended for by the gentleman was mooted years ago, and long since settled by the common sense of the people of this country. Some of the most eminent jurists of the nation have changed sides upon this question within the last twenty-five years. This sir, is an age of change, and I hope of progress; but that all change is not progress is evident from the fact that only a few days since the members of the Committee instructed me *unanimously* to report to the Convention this amendment, and ask for its adoption. And now, sir, one of that same Committee has gone over to the opposition, leaving me so far as he is concerned, to fight this matter out single handed. "Call you this backing your friends?" If so, I confess I do not understand it. [Laughter.] So it is not at all marvellous that men change their opinions in twenty years, if they can do it in twenty hours, and still be consistent in doing so. [Laughter.]

Again, the gentleman from Johnson, [Mr. Clarke,] objects to the amendment for another reason. He boldly asserts that it contains upon its face an immoral principle. Now, sir, I think the gentleman equally wrong here. The amendment provides that no special privileges or immunities shall be granted by the Legislature that may not be altered, revoked or repealed by the same power. What is there immoral in this principle, I would like to know? If parties accept a grant of power they do so with the law attached thereto, that defines the conditions upon which that power is granted. Of course the parties take it altogether and must abide by the consequences. I know of no reason why corporations should not suffer for wrong-doing as well as individuals. If a citizen does wrong your criminal laws will reach him. Not so with your corporations. The only punishment you can inflict on them is to deprive them of the power to do further injury; and the most effectual way of doing that is to repeal their charters.

The next position which the gentleman from Johnson, [Mr. Clarke,] took was, that the adoption of the amendment would destroy the credit of the State, and discourage men from investing their capital here; and being a Buckeye, he tells you that he saw a similar battle fought in that State when she adopted her new constitution, but he does not pretend to say that the effect of it was to discourage the investment of capital in that State. He tells you further that Ohio is so rich that she is able to build all her works of internal improvement without foreign aid. The history of that State, sir, is written out in bitter experience by her own citizens, as any man who owns property there and pays taxes can tell you. Is it not the fact that taxes there have been raised as high as eighteen to twenty mills on the dollar to pay her current expenses, and the interest on the money she has borrowed to build her internal improvements? This same question that is now under consideration here was discussed in Ohio in 1850 and '51, for the Constitutional Convention sat there a portion of those two years, and the same arguments were used in that Convention against the adoption of this clause, that have been offered by the gentleman from Johnson, [Mr. Clarke,] and yet that Convention, largely Democratic, almost unanimously voted in favor of it, after a very full and lengthy discussion. The great battle there was in regard to the Banking power, but there was a compromise effected, by which that question was submitted to the people and by them approved. Ohio is, and always has been a prosperous State, and her prosperity has in a great measure been owing to the fact that she enjoys good credit abroad, and has commanded money at low prices in all the markets of the world, where men go to borrow money. That clause in her constitution, which we are now discussing, has never rendered her credit less valuable than it was before. I apprehend if we insert here the clause proposed, the effect of it will be more apt to create respect for a people who are jealous of their rights and liberties, than to impair their credit in the least. The State of Ohio has learned many bitter lessons in regard to corporations. There is a community in that State that was cursed for nearly thirty years by one of these irresponsible institutions that have so often sprung up at various times in this country. I allude to the Granville Bank. The history of that institution would be sufficient to convince any man, if he had any power in making laws and could exercise it, that it was best to prevent such institutions from becoming operative, and if they did so, to provide for their destruction.

In order that I may not be misunderstood, permit me to say, sir, that I do not war against banks or corporations of any kind. I only want to guard and protect the people against the *abuses*, and not against the *uses* of those institutions. I did not come here to throw obstacles in the way of wholesome legislation in favor of corporations. No, sir. I came here to assist in preparing the way for good and wholesome legislation in favor of chartering companies. I came here to represent that side of the question. But knowing as I do by bitter experience the tendency of monied institutions to abuse the confidence reposed in them, I must be excused for being quite zealous in my efforts to guard the people as well as the corporations. The case of the Granville Bank illustrates the view I take of this question. At an early day in the history of Ohio, a colony from New England settled in the central part of that State, by purchasing a township of land, and laying out a village, which they named Granville. Money being very scarce in that early day, an artful, keen Yankee lawyer conceived the idea of getting up a bank there in the woods, and issuing paper money. In order to effect his object he applied to the General Assembly of that State for a charter for a Library Association, to be called the "Granville Alexandrian Library." He represented to the Legislature that the Granville people were a colony from New England, that they were a reading people and liked good large libraries, and thought more of their books than of anything else in the world; and that they wanted a charter to enable them to purchase books, and to distribute them among the people. The gentleman being an old and experienced lawyer drafted the act of incorporation in the usual form, but very ingeniously inserted a clause giving to the corporation the power to "make all needful rules and regulations for the government of their institution, and to dispose of their property in any manner they saw proper, for the benefit of the institution." The bill passed without opposition—no one suspected for a moment that they had done anything more than was necessary to enable the Association to perform its corporate duties. After the Legislature had adjourned, an article was published in the village newspaper informing the people that the Legislature had granted a charter for Banking purposes, and inviting them to take stock in the institution. The stock was taken, and notwithstanding the remonstrances of the people of the State, they commenced Banking.—It was said that when the officers met for the purpose of issuing notes, every silver dollar they had was laid on the crown of a hat and did not cover it. Like many others of its kind, it turned out a wild cat affair, in which the people were sufferers to an immense amount by its failure. In about fifteen years after, this same Bank charter was resurrected, new officers were elected, and operations were again commenced. With all the knowledge the people of Ohio had acquired in regard to Banking charters, vested rights and the right of repeal, they were not able to stop that institution from issuing another batch of paper money, and again cursing the country with its lying promise to pay. I was living in the State at that time, and am quite familiar with the history of this institution. To guard ourselves against the effect of the second issue, we applied for a writ of *quo warranto*. The case came up for hearing before Lane, Chief Justice of our Supreme Court. The case was ably argued on both sides. The Chief Justice in one of the most elaborate opinions ever delivered by any Judge, decided that the charter contained Banking powers, that they were perpetual and could not be reached by the Court, or by the Legislature, and that they could only be taken away for mal-feasance in office. As long as the charter did not require them to have any amount of gold and silver on hand, we could not reach them. We were then compelled to submit to another explosion, that worked disastrous results all over the State. With this experience, sir, I feel fully justified in doing all that I can honorably, to guard against any possibility of our being surprised in this State by any hasty action of that kind on the part of the Legislature. I wish to deprive the Legislature by a single blow, of the power to create special corporations. And I will vote for a clause of that kind when it comes up in proper order, but I do desire, as I said before to place this power in that part of the constitution defining the rights of the people. I am not willing that it should be placed there simply as a precautionary measure. I want it to stand out clear and bold, as a right belonging to the people, independent of the Legislature or any other power. If, sir, they are the source of all power, and contain within themselves the elements of sovereignty and self-government, let us say so; say that with them rests the responsibility, and leave it there.

As to the credit of Ohio, which has been so much discussed here by the gentleman from Johnson (Mr. Clarke), I must be pardoned for again alluding to it.

Mr. President, I have yet to learn that Ohio ever had a bad credit. I have always understood that the paper of that State stood as high as that of any other State in the Union. If that be so, then the argument of the gentleman against this clause, as impairing the credit of the State, falls to the ground, for, by parity of reasoning, if the paper of Ohio sells in market at par value, while she has this clause in her constitution, I may fairly argue, that if our state places it in her constitution, that her credit will stand equally fair in the market. But, sir, I hold that the credit of Ohio does not depend alone upon the fact that she has this clause in her constitution. Nor will Iowa, if we should decide to incorporate it into the constitution we are now forming. No, sir; the noble young State which I have the honor in part to represent, rests her fame upon a far different foundation. She, sir, is regarded abroad as one of the soundest States in this Union, and the people have a reputation for energy, morality, intelligence and integrity, that does not require any constitution to endorse. Since she enjoys such a credit, I wish her to sustain it, and in order to do so, she must have the best fundamental law in the land, most clearly defined, and if possible in advance of any other State in this Union.—That is my wish, sir, and that is what brought me here, and if I can aid and assist in bringing about such a result, even by some compromise, I am willing to do so. I will compromise as to time and place, but I will compromise nothing as to principle. I would be glad to have those gentlemen who stood up in times gone by for the principle we are now discussing, come up and give us the benefit of their wisdom. If they desire modifications or amendments, why not offer them?

Again: we are told by the gentleman from Johnson [Mr. Clarke] that if we insert this clause in the bill there is danger of the Legislature repealing the charters of all the corporations in the State, and he even went so far in his argument, as to imagine that the religious institutions of the country were in danger of losing their corporate privileges. I am glad, sir, that the gentleman has some respect for the religious as well as the banking institutions of the country, for the one class has souls, and the other has none. It is marvelous, however, that the gentleman can see this question only in one light. He says that the Legislatures are corrupt—not to be trusted—that if we give them this power they will repeal all charters. Will they, sir, be more likely to repeal a good charter than to create a corrupt one? And if a corrupt one, ought it not to be repealed? I, sir, have no fear of the Legislature interfering with an institution that does not transcend the powers conferred upon it by its charter; but I do fear the action of corporations that hold themselves entirely independent of the people and the power of repeal. The experience of thirty years has made me very cautious in this particular, and I hope that this convention will deliberate long upon this matter, before they reject a proposition so wholesome in itself, and so honorable to the convention and to the State.

The gentleman from Johnson, [Mr. Clarke,] tell us again, that he is very much afraid we shall fall back upon the old party issues, if we incorporate this clause in the constitution. If, sir, we do fall back upon old party lines, the gentleman will most certainly find himself in strange company—not where he found himself twenty years ago. I apprehend that the gentleman and his new associates would be hardly willing to call me a hale fellow well met in this matter. [Laughter.]

As I said before, Mr. President, we are here for the purpose of making an organic law for the State and not to advance any party or any particular set of principles except those which legitimately belong to the functions we are called upon to exercise. I am therefore willing to concede everything as to form and place, but nothing as to principles. Relying on the sober second thought of the convention, I trust the amendment will prevail.

Mr. EMERSON. I offer the following amendment to the amendment:

To strike out "by the vote of two-thirds of the House and also the Senate," and insert the following:

"Except corporations for works of internal improvements," so that it will read—

"And no privileges or immunities shall ever be granted which may not be altered, revoked or repealed by the General Assembly, except corporations for works of internal improvement."

I will detain the convention but a moment. I offer this proposition for the reason that I do not believe in the present state of internal improvements in this State, it would be proper to include works of internal improvements in this connection. I have had something to do, within the last few months in trying to raise money for railroad purposes, and I can fully appreciate the great difficulties experienced in obtaining money for objects of this kind. In operations of this kind you must commence by counting by millions, and millions are counted by only a few persons, either in this or any other country. If we should incorporate into our constitution a clause that would give to the Legislature the right of repeal, not only of the law, but all the privileges granted thereby, it does occur to me, from what experience I have had in procuring money in the market, that we may fold our hands, with reference to the building of railroads in this State. I am not willing by my vote to bring about such a result, and as a consequence, I hope the amendment will not prevail. So far as corporations other than railroads are concerned, I will support the proposition reported by the committee as cheerfully as any man in this Convention.

The question was taken, and the amendment of Mr. Emerson was rejected.

Mr. PALMER. I offer the following amendment:

"The State shall be liable in an action at law in any court of record, or otherwise, in the State for all such damages which may be caused by any such alteration, revocation or repeal, unless such privileges or immunities shall be violated by persons or corporations to whom such privileges and immunities shall have been granted."

Mr. ELLS. There seems to be an impression on the part of some members that the State of Iowa cannot be sued for any wrongful act of her officers or her Legislature. This is an entire mistake. The State can be made to answer in damages in the Unied States Court, to any citzen of any other State, and this amendment of the gentleman from Davis (Mr. Palmer) is therefore entirely unnecessary. It is nothing uncommon for a State to be sued in the United States Courts. Suppose there were a swamp in the neighborhood of this city covering fifty acres of lands, which the State is anxious to have drained. A charter is granted by the Legislature to a company, who agree to drain it for the use of the land for fifty years. They commence their operations, but it is ascertained when the water is reduced below the water level, that the health of the country becomes materially impaired in consequence thereof, and the Legislature repeal the charter. I ask, in such a case if the parties who had expended money there, would not have the right of action against the State and ajust claim to be indemnified in every particular for the damages they would sustain by the repeal of their charter.

The question was taken on the amendment of Mr. Palmer and it was rejected.

The question then recurring on the amendmend offered by Mr. Ells, the question was taken by yeas and nays with the following result:

Yeas.—14 Nays—19.

Yeas. The President, Messrs. Ayers, Clark, of Alamakee, Clarke, of Henry, Day, Ells, Gray, Harris, Marvin, Parvin, Robinson, Scott, Seely, and Wilson.

Nays. Messrs. Bunker, Clarke, of Johnson, Edwards, Emerson, Gibson, Gillaspy, Gower, Hall, Johnston, Palmer, Patterson, Peters, Price, Skiff, Solomon, Todhunter, Traer, Warren and Young.

So the amendment was rejected.

There being no other amendment offered, the next section was read as follows;

Religious Tests and Competency of Witnesses.

No religious test shall be required as a qualification for any office or public trust, and no person shall be deprived of any of his rights, privileges or capacities, or disqualified from the performance of any of his public or private duties, or rendered incompetent to give evidence in any court of law or equity, in consequence of his opinions on the subject of religion.

Mr. CLARKE, of Henry. I move to amend by adding the following:

"Nor in consequence of his belonging to any particular sect, class or party of men."

Mr. HALL. I move to amend by adding "Negroes, Indians, Knaves, and Fools."

Mr. CLARKE of Henry. I presume the gentleman offering that amendment has some personal interest to secure in attaching the two latter classes to Negroes and Indians; if so I have no particular objection.

The PRESIDENT. Does the amendment of the gentleman from Des Moines (Mr. Hall) receive a second?

The amendment not being seconded, the Chair ruled that the amendment was not in order and stated the question to be upon the amendment offered by the gentleman from Henry (Mr. Clarke).

Mr. GILLASPY. I suppose, Mr. Chairman, that the people of the State of Iowa sent the members of this Convention here to make a Constitution, which would provide for the white race first. But to my utter astonishment, upon the second or third day of our deliberations, a proposition was offered by some gentleman to provide for the education of the blacks and mulattoes, before he had ever said a word about the whites.

I am opposed to the amendment, now before the Convention, and shall vote against it. I shall oppose every thing of the kind that may be offered, which would hold out any inducement to the blacks and mulattoes to come into this State. The gentleman from Henry (Mr. Clarke) seems to be very tenacious about this matter, and does not move in any thing, unless there is a "nigger in the wood-pile," connected with it.

Mr. SKIFF. I shall feel myself called upon to vote against this amendment, although I have no very serious objection to it. I hope to see in the article on the Right of Suffrage a section incorporated submitting to the people the question, whether colored persons shall be permitted to vote and hold office. This course has been pursued in some other States, and I hope this Convention will adopt the same course now, submitting this question so the people, as a seperate matter, for their decision.

Mr. HALL. I notice that the gentleman from Henry (Mr. Clarke) has a great idea of sticking in this "nigger" question upon every possible occasion, and I know that he puts his gloves on before he touches it. I want the gentleman to handle it without his gloves. I want him to come plainly out and say what he means. If we are to incorporate into our Constitution such a provision as this, I want it to define in so many terms the class of persons it is intended cover.

I look upon this amendment as broad enough to cover all the classes I named. Idiots and insane persons are a class of people, and as I understand the gentleman's amendment, it will cover them, as it will persons who have been convicted of infamous crimes, and who may have served their time in the penitentiary. If the gentleman means to include all these classes let him come out and say so in distinct, and unequivocal terms. I am in earnest upon this question.

Mr. CLARKE, of Henry. I am very glad to hear from the gentleman's own lips, that he is in earnest upon this question. I have no doubt that otherwise we might have supposed that he was joking, and disposed to treat this matter with ridicule. The gentleman speaks of the member from Henry as though he came here for the purpose of looking after the rights of negroes. Standing here, as I do, with my whole heart echoing to the sentiment of the gentleman from Appanoose [Mr. Harris], that "we came here to seek after the principles of eternal truth and justice, and to incorporate them into our constitution." I know no such beings as "negroes and Indians." I came here not to insert anything in our constitution recognizing any difference in the classes of men. I came here to establish principles that are eternal, and I can assure the gentleman from Des Moines [Mr. Hall] that I am, ever have been, and ever shall be in earnest when questions of principles are under discussion; and the gentleman's sneers, and his cries of "nigger," will not influence me any more than the passing of the idle wind.—What is the declaration to which I seek to append my amendment?

It starts out with the declaration that every man shall be judged by the character which he has established in the community, and that no particular test of religious belief shall be required as a qualification for any office of public trust, and that no person shall be deprived of any of his rights, privileges, or capacities, or rendered incompetent to give evidence in any court of law or equity in consequence of his opinions on the subject of religion. I wish to carry out that principle in full, and if any poor, down trodden creature belonging to the human family receives a benefit from it, God be praised. It is for this reason I wish to set forth this principle in the constitution, that somebody may be benefitted who might otherwise have his rights denied to him. What necessity is there for spreading out all this declaration of human rights here, if you do not carry it out to its full extent? Is any man here afraid that his rights as an American citizen, and as a citizen of Iowa, may be taken away from him, that we declare these principles and spread them out here upon parchment? If it be not right to deprive me of my rights on account of my religious belief, it is not right to deprive me of them because I come from any particular place or country, or because I have a particular hue to my skin? Gentlemen must recollect that we are not acting here in the capacity of legislators, but we are settling great and eternal principles, no matter who derives benefits from them when they are settled, and no matter who may be injured by them, if injury results therefrom. We must believe, if the principle be correct, that nobody will be injured. God established principles, and man makes laws, and when these laws come into conflict with principles, they ought to fall. I am one of those who believe in the correctness of the Democratic Republican institutions of our country. I believe in the spirit of Democracy and Republicanism, and I might almost say that it is my religion. I believe that it is the very spirit and essence of christianity itself; and as I once said, which at the time was deemed almost blasphemy, but I am not afraid to repeat it here, I believe that Jesus Christ was the first great Democrat of the world. If the gentleman from Des Moines [Mr. Hall] would meet this question manfully, and show me wherein the principle I ask to be incorporated into the constitution is wrong, then I would listen to him patiently, and consider well his reasons. But no; that gentleman, as I think, very undignifiedly and ungenerously endeavors to carry this question by crying out "niggers;" and the gentleman from Wapello [Mr. Gillaspy] also gets up and says there is "a nigger in the wood-pile;" and whenever these gentlemen can see that the negro is going to get any advantage from any principle which we ask to be incorporated into the constitution, they accuse us of desiring it because of the benefit that may result to the negro. Now, my object is not to secure any particular amount of advantage to that class of the community; but it is to prevent my fellow citizens, in their prejudice and madness, from trampling upon all principle and making laws which would work injustice to their fellow men. Let us strike right now, and trust ourselves to a declaration of principles, let the results follow where they may. We need have no fear of the issue. Why, do gentlemen know that you find none of these distinctions in any of the constitutions of the New England States, with the exception of Connecticut? If the gentleman from Appanoose [Mr. Harris] and the gentleman Wappello [Mr. Gillaspy] are so afraid of encouraging negroes to come in here, allow me to tell them that they need be afraid no longer! Cheer up, dear friends; there is really no danger of their wandering in the midnight hour, taking possession of the State and expelling the whites, as you may learn from the fact that Connecticut, the only State in New England that has any provision in her constitution recognizing distinction in classes, has a greater number of negroes in proportion to her population than all the other New England States put together!

It is not from any desire of asking or inviting negroes into our State, that I submit the amendment now under consideration. I tell you, I care not whether another negro comes into the State of Iowa, or crosses the Mississippi. I would not ask or invite negroes to come, but I would, so help me God, spread upon our constitution principles that every man, wherever he may be on the whole face of the earth, may say, there is a land were I can go and have my rights and my liberty secure. I am proud that I dare to be an American citizen, in the fullest sense of the term, alive to all the principles that are set forth in the Declaration of Independence. Who occupies the proudest position. I accused of being the friend of the negro, or the man who is a worse slave than any negro upon a Southern plantation, and who cowers down before a vitiated public opinion, and belies the principles that are spread upon that immortal instrument. I stand here, prouder this day, than any of you, who are ashamed to be considered the friend of the negro. Let us do right, though the heavens fall. Spread out the declaration upon your constitution, that no person shall be deprived of any of his rights in consequence of his belonging to any particular sect, class, or party of men, and it will be a declaration of which you may well be proud, and you may say that we stand here in the consciousness of our own strength and ability to protect ourselves under all circumstances. No matter who avail themselves of the privilege, throw open your doors and bid the world come! And still by our penal code, and by our laws we can prevent "knaves and fools," who seem to enjoy the especial patronage and protection of the gentleman from Des Moines [Mr. Hall] forever from enjoying the rights and privileges of American citizens. Make laws that shall punish individuals for the offences they themselves commit, but make no laws that shall punish individuals for the offences of their fathers. You have no laws of primogeniture. You suffer me not to reap the honors of my fathers; why then punish me for their sins or their misfortunes? Why because of my connection with any sect, class or party of men, ostracise me, and shut me out from the rights and privileges enjoyed by my fellow men. Can you not stand upon principles so broad that they shall underlie all humanity, and so firm that they can be handed down and form a constitution for those that shall come after us? Can you not trust to the legislature to make laws for the punishment of offenders of every class of society, without incorporating into the constitution a clause, that shall make exceptions in regard to certain classes? No, let these things regulate themselves, and let every American citizen stand here as God made him, knowing that as soon as he acquires property and reputation, that the constitution is about him as a shield to guard and protect him; and if he fails in his duty that the laws of the country are about him to punish and correct him.

It is for the reasons I have now given that I wish to amend the fourth section of the Bill of Rights, by the amendment I have offered. If my amendment be adopted, the section will then read:

"No religious test shall be required as a qualification for any office or public trust, and no person shall be deprived of any of his rights, privileges or capacities, or disqualified from the performance of any of his public or private duties, or rendered incompetent to give evidence in any court of law or equity, in consequence of his opinions on the subject of religion, nor in consequence of his belonging to any particular sect, class or party of men."

I do not ask you to declare if a man is convicted of an infamous crime, that he shall no longer have the elective franchise, or be in a position where he can fill office in the State. You have a penal code which, by its provisions, regulates all this matter. I do not ask you to make any exceptions in regard to any particular class of men, but I only ask you to establish this principle, that the Legislature shall make no law ostracising a whole class, sect or party of men, or deprive them of rights belonging to any other citizen, on account of their belonging to such class, sect or party.

Mr. GILLASPY. I only rise for the purpose of asking the gentleman a question which I hope he will be good enough to answer, and it is this, whether the amendment he offers embodies the principles of the late Republican party?

Mr. CLARKE, of Henry. I speak for myself only. I am not the mouth-piece of the Republican party, nor the exponent of their views or principles. If the Republican party has any principles that are in conflict with those I have uttered here, then I am not of the Republican party.

Mr. HARRIS. I do not rise to make a speech, but having been publicly referred to by the gentleman from Henry, [Mr. Clarke,] I desire to make an explanation. He says that he bases his position upon principles that I have advocated upon this floor. I am not aware of having advocated any such principles as he presents here, and I hope that in this respect, the gentleman and myself will not be regarded as having opinions in common with each other. The mania which the gentleman has upon this particular subject is very well known here, and therefore I will not take unkindly any allusions which the gentleman has made to myself in his remarks. So far as honesty in this matter is concerned, I have surely shown no disposition to shrink from a full and thorough discussion of this question. The gentleman says that his Republicanism, embracing as it does the notions he has advanced here to-day, is a part of his religion, but I must say that I cannot worship at that shrine. I expect to show, when the proper time comes, that I am a better friend of the negro than the gentleman himself, so far as the promotion of the interests of that class is concerned, but it is not by the mingling the two classes, the negroes and the whites together, but in seperating and keeping them apart.

The PRESIDENT stated the question to be upon the amendment of the gentleman from Henry, [Mr. Clarke.]

Mr. HARRIS. What became of the amendment of the gentleman from Des Moines?

The PRESIDENT. The amendment not being seconded, could not be entertained.

Mr. HARRIS. I will second the amendment.

The PRESIDENT. The amendment is not now before the Convention. The gentleman from Appanoose, if he desires it, can offer it himself as an amendment.

Mr. HARRIS. I will offer it then. I move to amend the amendment by adding the words "except Indians, negroes, knaves and fools."

The PRESIDENT. Does the amendment receive a second?

Mr. HALL. I will second the amendment.

The PRESIDENT. The question is now upon the amendment to the amendment.

Mr. HALL. I may have misunderstood the gentleman from Henry, [Mr. Clarke,] but I understood him as advocating the amendment which I offered. He certainly said nothing against it. If so, I hope he will vote for it. He did not say that his intention was not to include negroes and Indians, and he did not prove or go into an argument to show that persons who have been in the Penitentiary did not form a class in the community, nor that idiots and lunatics did not form another class. These persons have always in Legislative action been regarded as forming a class in the community, and they will probably be always regarded as such. I think that the amendment I proposed covers the whole ground, and embraces all the classes I named. The difference between the amendment I proposed and the one which the gentleman from Henry offered, is simply that one defines the classes by name, is open, frank and honest, while the other does not so define them, and is covert, insinuating and cowardly.

Now the gentleman is unwilling to believe—and I do not blame him for it—that his proposition covers the two last classes named in the amendment I offered—knaves and fools. The words of the gentleman's amendment would certainly include the three or four classes I have named. The convict from the Penitentiary will say that he belongs to a class, and will find in the constitution reasons why he should have these rights.

My object in advocating and first proposing this amendment was to drive the gentleman to use plain English. If he will use language that cannot deceive, I am willing to meet him in argument. If the majority here see fit to incorporate such a provision into the constitution, I desire that it may speak truly and in unmistakeable language what it means. I want no covering up of the tracks, so that gentleman can say that it means one thing in one section, and something entirely different in another section of the State, so that the gentleman from Henry cannot go into his own county and claim that abolitionism is the great feature in it, and then go to another portion of the State and say that there is no abolitionism in it at all. I want the amendment to speak out plainly what it means, so that when the proposition comes up, the people shall see how to vote without the least shade of doubt.

Mr. ELLS. Mr. President. I shall vote against the amendment offered by the gentleman from Appanoose, (Mr. Harris) specifying the classes that are to be benefitted by the operation of the amendment of the gentleman from Henry (Mr. Clark). I shall vote against it, because I am not willing to deprive any class of persons of the right to testify in our courts of justice. In my opinion, Sir, the credibility of a witness should be the test, and not his color or condition.

If he were a convict from the Penitentiary, I would hear him, and if his testimony was corroberated by circumstances, I would give it the consideration it deserved and no more.

I am unwilling that this Constitution shall contain any language which shall convey the idea that we are legislating for a class of any kind.

I want the amendment of the gentleman from Henry (Mr. Clarke) to cover all classes of people in the State, I care not who they are. The amendment struck me as being proper, for this reason, that there are some narrow-minded, bigotted, Justices of the Peace in the State, who, in place of administering justice according to forms of law, will seek to gratfy their private predudices, if there be not some act restraining them in the exercise of that narrow-minded feeling. I should like, therefore, to see the Constitution so broad as to prevent such officers from doing any acts of this character. I have met with such men in my practice in Ohio, and I have always found them to be the meanest class in society—men at war with the broad principles upon which their own government is based, and upon which they as citizens rest, and by which they are maintained and upheld in society.

The gentleman from Des Moines (Mr. Hall) tells us, that he would like to see us meet the question now presented, by the amendment offered by the gentleman from Appanoose (Mr. Harris). I, for one, Sir, am willing to meet that question at any time the gentleman and his friends will afford me the opportunity. I have nothing to conceal upon that or any other subject.

I desire, Sir, to see this Constitution made acceptable to the people, and respectable in the eyes of the world, and I should exceedingly regret to see any class of legislation brought to bear against the weaker classes of society, in any form. I go for the principle, that every man should stand upon his moral worth, I do not care what his complexion or creed is. It is the man, and his moral worth, not his place and dignity that I would respect. I would say to the gentlemen from Des Moines (Mr. Hall) that when he denounces the whole negro race as immoral, and unworthy of credit, he does them great injustice.

I have seen, Sir, as much moral worth under a dark, as I have ever seen under a white skin, and that two among that degraded class, called negro slaves.

In the slave States they allow colored men to testify. They do not administer the corporate oath to them, but allow them to make their statement, and let that statement go upon the strength of their moral character.

My friend from Pottawatmie (Mr. Price) who has resided many years in slave States, will bear me witness, that in nine cases out of ten the mere statement of a slave would be credited in a court of justice where the testimony of a white man of the lowest class would not be.

There is another view of this subject to which I wish to call the attention of the Convention; it is this: If you destroy the competency of colored citizens of Iowa, as witnesses in our courts of justice, you do, in effect, violate the constitutional right of white citizens, in all cases when the testimony of a colored person is necessary to the defense of their lives, liberty or property. It is well, therefore, Mr. President, for us to ponder and deliberate long, before stultifying ourselves by incorporating into our organic law, a principle of proscription at war with our most cherished rights and the humanity of the age.

Mr. GILLASPY. I have no desire to make a speech, but only to make a single remark in reply to the gentleman from Scott, [Mr. Ells.] I was born and raised in a Slave State, and it is the first time I ever heard that a negro was a competent witness, and that he was better and a more honest witness than a white man. If the position of the gentleman be correct, he had better have a law passed to send the whites down to the Slave States, for he says a white man must take an oath, whereas a statement of a negro is worth just as much.

Mr. PARVIN. My object in rising now is simply to make an explanation, so that I may place myself right upon the record. I do not consider that we express our views as to the competency of black men to testify in this country, by voting for or against this amendment. Whenever that question comes up I am ready to meet it. I say here that no honest man has any thing to fear from all the testimony coming before a jury of his country. Let all the evidence which parties have to present come before a jury, and they will decide what is right. A case was tried in the county which I have the honor to represent, where a black man sued a white man, and where the testimony of another black was offered in evidence, but the Court decided that his evidence was inadmissable. The case was carried to a higher court on that ground, but the court sustained the decision made below. This admission of the testimony of the negro is not a boon granted to him, but it is an act of justice to the white man. If the question of the competency of the black man depended upon the adoption of the amendment offered by the gentleman from Henry, [Mr. Clarke,] I would vote for it, but believing that it does not, I shall vote first against the amendment of the gentleman from Appanoose, [Mr. Harris,] and then against that of the gentleman from Henry, [Mr. Clarke.] Under our present Bill of Rights, the Legislature have a right to pass a law permitting the black man to testify, and no one pretends to say that they have not the right to pass such a law. In voting against the amendment of the gentleman from Henry, I do not wish to be understood that I am opposed to the black man giving testimony. As I said before, an honest man has nothing to fear from all the testimony which can come before a jury. But, believing that the amendment of the gentleman from Henry has nothing to do with this question I shall vote against it.

Mr. GILLASPY. Do I understand the gentleman from Muscatine, [Mr. Parvin,] to say that every man who votes against this amendment is dishonest?

Mr. PARVIN. I said no such thing. But I said that an honest man has nothing to fear from testimony. I do not say that an honest man might not think that a negro ought not to be allowed to testify. But I do say that none but a dishonest man will feel afraid of their testimony.

The question recurred upon the amendment proposed by Mr. Harris to the amendment of Mr. Clarke of Henry, to add the words "except negroes, Indians, knaves and fools."

Upon this question the yeas and nays were ordered, and being taken the amendment to the amendment was not agreed to, yeas 1, nays 33, as follows:

Yeas—Mr. Harris.

Nays—The President; Messrs. Ayres, Bunker, Clark of Alamakee, Clarke of Henry, Clarke of Johnson, Day, Edwards, Ells, Emerson, Gibson, Gillaspy, Gower, Gray, Hall, Johnston, Marvin, Palmer, Parvin, Patterson, Peters, Price, Robinson, Scott, Seely, Skiff, Solomon, Todhunter, Traer, Warren, Wilson, Winchester and Young.

The question recurred upon the amendment of Mr. Clarke of Henry.

Mr. CLARKE, of Henry. I desire to make a verbal amendment in the first part of the section by striking out in the first line after the words "public trust," the words "and no person shall," and inserting "nor shall any person;" and then add my amendment to the end of the section so that the whole section will then read:

"No religious test shall be required as a qualification for any office or public trust, nor shall any person be deprived of any of his rights, privileges or capacities, or disqualified from the performance of any of his public or private duties, or rendered incompetent to give evidence in any court of law or equity, in consequence of his opinions on the subject of religion, or in consequence of belonging to any particular sect, class, or party of men."

Mr. HALL. The proposition of the gentleman from Henry, [Mr. Clarke,] is in the first place entirely too broad to meet my approbation under any circumstances, in any portion of the constitution. And I believe it is broad enough to include all the classes mentioned in the amendment which has just been voted down by an almost unanimous vote. As I supposed at the first it is a broad net and intended as such for the purpose of testing the question whether there should be a provision in the constitution, fastening upon the people of this State the unalterable necessity of negroes—I use the plain and popular expression—being permitted under all circumstances and without limitation to give evidence in our courts of justice. I understand that the citizens of this State are composed of white people. And I believe it is not the policy of this State to do any one act, however trivial, however seemingly unimportant it may be, that may invite this class of population here, and after they get here give them all the rights of citizens. In that respect, therefore, I must consider this proposition as one of doubtful policy, exceedingly doubtful. I would consider it as tending to invite this black population to come to our State, thereby tending to increase a class of population of which we have already more than is desirable.

There is another point of view in which this should be considered, and which presents another objection to my mind to this proposition, I refer to the trials in our courts of justice in relation to property, the questions concerning the possession of property or something connected with the possession or enjoyment of real estate. All who are in the habit of attending our courts and justice trials are aware that but few of the multiplicity of trials there reach beyond a few days, or perhaps two or three weeks. Now we have in this State a system of taking depositions, and there are very few trials of any importance in which this kind of evidence is not relied on to a great extent, in consequence of the constant changing of our inhabitants, and the increase of trade between this and the States south and east of us. You have therefore to resort to depositions to test your cases, and to elicit truth and obtain justice. It is a notorious fact, especially in the southern portion of this State, that we have a large trade with Missouri, and some considerable trade with Kentucky. And it is a common thing in the investigation of transactions in connection with this commerce and trade to send to those States, and even to more remote States for the purpose of procuring testimony.

Gentlemen talk here about justice and about right, and go into abstractions, forgetting completely the practical application of their principles. Theory alone will never answer; it is always delusive; it never can be adhered to in society. Let us put this proposition to a practical test, and see what its consequences will be. Suppose that a man living in St. Louis is transacting business with a citizen of this State, and a difficulty arises between them. Testimony is sent for to St. Louis, and the man there has a great many slaves whom he can compel to give just such testimony as he pleases, and their testimony is sent on here. What can you tell of the character of these witnesses? It may be such that none of us in this State would be willing to allow a single penny of his property to depend upon it. There may be such testimony there as would be entitled to credit, but that would not be likely as a general thing, and we are called to act upon general principles. There is not a man here who would be willing to have the negroes in this State called to prove a contract with another person. It is said in answer to that objection, why, what harm would be the result, if this class of testimony is called, as the jury would not give them any weight or belief? I will say that there is this objection: you invite the committing of perjury for the purpose of sustaining the glorious principles of freedom, according to the views of the gentleman from Henry, [Mr. Clarke.]

Now, I have lived a good many years, and have lived all my life in states where negroes were prohibited from giving testimony, and I have never known that any one failed to obtain justice in consequence of this kind of testimony not being received. I have never known an instance of oppression or wrong to the black man when his testimony would have given him a better remedy than he otherwise had, nor have I known of an instance of the rights of white men suffering for want of this testimony; I have never heard of a man losing a dollar in consequence of excluding this testimony. Now, is this a privilege which it is necessary to confer upon the black man? Are you really conferring a privilege upon him when, in nine cases out of ten you cannot make a jury believe him when you bring him up? Do you confer a privilege upon a man by allowing him to be sworn before a jury that are so prejudiced against him—if you choose to consider it prejudice—that they will not believe him, and you merely stamp a want of credibility upon him by bringing him forward, and thus arousing their prejudices against him. I have seen but two instances of black testimony being introduced into courts of justice, and I confess that my experience has been adverse to that testimony. Those witnesses have not been believed, and one that I heard was not entitled to belief, and any man who would have sworn as he did, should have been tried for perjury. I do not consider that man a wise legislator who does not act according to the prejudices of the people—if you call these things prejudices. It is a prejudice of centuries standing, that is deeply imbedded in the minds of the people. The gentleman from Henry may have escaped from or released himself from these shackles of prejudice; but I have not. They are still operating upon my mind, and I should not tell the truth to say that such was not the case. Why should we open the door to this class of testimony merely to gratify an abstract proposition? Now where is the necessity of changing this constitution from what it now is, and thus proclaiming to the world, as has been proclaimed upon this floor, and will stand upon the archives of this State to all coming time, that negroes are as good as white men? Why should we undertake to do that which we cannot do? The gentleman says he has found as honest a heart under the skin of a black man, as under that of a white man. Now I have never seen nor felt under the skin of a black man, and have found no such thing. I was educated where there were but few of this class of people, and I have learned but little about them; and I wish to know but little about them. So far as the welfare of the black population of this State is concerned, I have as deep a feeling and sympathy for them, and am as deeply anxious to see their condition bettered as any gentleman upon this floor; and I will go as far as the farthest to do anything that will be substantially beneficial to them, and do no injury and wrong to the rest of the people; but I cannot become a slanderer and libeller of my own race and the race of my fathers for the purpose of elevating the negro. I will never attempt to drag down the white race to the very dregs of degredation that the negro is in, for the purpose of making the two races equal. If I were to do anything it would be to endeavor to elevate them and lift them up, if they are susceptible of it. But we cannot do it here; we cannot do it by marks of printer's ink upon paper. You cannot legislate a poet; you cannot change the condition of a race of men by merely saying so. You have not the wand of a wizard to elevate these people and make them different from what they are now. This is all a mere matter of speculation. It is a crusade upon a subject that can do no good whatever. Then will not gentlemen let the constitution remain as it now is? No evil has been suffered, no inconvenience has resulted to us from the operation of the present constitution. Everything has passed along smoothly without a complaint or murmur anywhere. Then why this change?

I have no harsh epithets to apply to any gentleman here, and I want that understood now and hereafter; and however much the gentleman from Henry [Mr. Clarke] may work himself into a frenzy to denounce me and other gentlemen, he shall not provoke from me those fruitless and ungentlemanly epithets and taunts that he throws out while in that state of excitement, and which, but for that excitement, he would not use.

The PRESIDENT. The chair begs leave to suggest that he considers the gentleman from Des Moines [Mr. Hall] and the gentleman from Henry [Mr. Clarke] are about equal in this matter, and the chair begs both of them to indulge no further in these personalities.

Mr. HALL. I was not aware shat I was indulging in any personalities.

The PRESIDENT. The chair alludes to the remark of the gentleman from Des Moines in saying that the amendment of the gentleman from Henry [Mr. Clarke] was cowardly.

Mr. HALL. I was, perhaps, wrong in using that expression. I thought the gentleman was skulking behind one thing while he really meant another, and I only wanted to bring the gentleman out in his true colors. I only called his amendment cowardly in comparison to what it would have been, had it expressed really what it was intended to accomplish.

The PRESIDENT. The chair is of opinion that the remark of the gentleman from Des Moines was provoked by the remark of the gentleman from Henry [Mr. Clarke] in reference to honesty. The chair noticed that remark at the time it was used, and would have called the gentleman to order, had that course of remark been persisted in.

Mr. CLARKE, of Johnson. I shall support the amendment of the gentleman from Henry (Mr. Clarke) because I think the present condition of the laws in this State requires it. This question has been raised here in consequence of the decision of the Supreme Court in the case of Motts vs. Usher and Thayer, 2 Iowa Reports 82. That is the same case alluded to by the gentleman from Muscatine [Mr. Parvin]. In that case a negro sued white persons, and upon the trial the white men offered the testimony of a negro against the negro who had sued them. That testimony was excluded, and in consequence of that exclusion they lost their case. An appeal was taken to the Supreme Court; but that Court held that under our present laws a negro could not testify in any case, and as a consequence of that decision, the General Assembly at it late session provided for the testimony of negroes being received, but to what extent I am not informed, whether only to cases where negroes are parties, or where one of the parties to a case is a negro, or to other cases, I do not know. But, whatever may be the extent of the law upon that subject, I understand that one of the great parties of this State has arrayed itself against it.

Now I am in favor of putting it beyond the power of any Legislature to exclude negroes from testifying, where it may be for the benefit of the negro, and for the benefit of the white man also. Now, let me suppose a case. Here is my friend from Lee [Mr. Johnston] who is a much larger and better looking man than I am. Suppose he were to commit an assault upon me, and do me a serious bodily injury in the presence of no other person than a negro. I may perhaps be maimed for life and disabled from supporting my family. I bring an action against him to recover damages. The only witness I can bring forward is a negro; he cannot testify and consequently I am able to obtain no redress, and your system of law settles the question.

Now, I am not willing to be placed in such a position. I am willing, at least, that the negro shall be a witness, leaving it to the jury to say, as they would say of your testimony or mine, how much they will believe of it. If the negro should not be a man worthy of belief, then the jury would attach no importance to his testimony, and my injurer would pass unscathed, and I should be the sufferer.

Now, as an act of justice, aye, justice to the negro and to the white man, I want this thing here. Thousands of instances may be cited which would come home to every man. My friend from Muscatine [Mr. Parvin] is not willing to vote for this amendment, but is willing to leave the subject to the Legislature. Now, suppose that the party arrayed against this proposition obtains the power in the Legislature and the law of the last session is repealed, and the matter would rest as before. Now I want this as a matter for the protection of the white man, and I should suppose gentlemen would support it upon that ground alone.

I differ with my friend from Des Moines (Mr. Hall) upon this question; and I am sorry to differ with him now, after acting together so much as we have done in this Convention. His argument is based, if I understand it, upon two grounds: he fears if we permit negroes to testify that southern slaves will be compelled to commit perjury; and the othe assumption is, that the negro does not possess that natural integrity common to the white man. Now, I am not legislating here to prevent the slaves of the south, of Missouri and Kentucky, from being compelled to commit perjury. I think in discerning natural rights, it is rather too much for us to go upon the assumption that one class of people, whether black, brown or white, do not possess natural integrity. I was born where there were many of the negro race, and I know something about them, and I say that as a people they possess as strong integrity as any other class, and standing in this position, why should they not be permitted to testify when the interest of the white man requires it, leaving their creditability to be determined upon by the jury, as that of every other witness is at this time? I think the negro slave, even, would be willing to tell the truth, upon oath. If the counsel in the case is anxious to know whether a deposition from abroad is that of a negro or a white man, the counsel can put that question, and then he can go before the jury and expatiate loud and long against their believing it, because it is the testimony of a negro. Thus nobody will be hurt by it.

But I do conceive that this provision will secure an important right, not to the negro but to the white man. We are not dragging the white man down to a level with the negro, but it is protecting ourselves and giving to each citizen the right to protect himself. I think the gentleman is mistaken in that.

I regret that whenever questions of this character are brought up here, instead of their being met as they should be, insinuations are thrown out about negro questions, negro philanthropy, &c. The world is presumed to be progressive, and it is progressive, and I have progressed somewhat with it, and at my stage of life, I have come to the conclusion that we should look upon these matters as questions of natural right and duty, and not have them met with sneers and jests. If it is not fair and right to do this, let us have that shown us, so that we may know how far it is unfair and erroneous. This is not a mere question for the benefit of the negro. I do not care three pins for the negro, as far as that is concerned, and would not undertake to benefit him more than it is my duty to act for the benefit of all God's creatures. I am for benefitting my own race by this proposition.

On motion of Mr. CLARKE, of Alamakee, the Convention then adjourned.

TUESDAY, February, 3, 1857.

The Convention met at 9 o'clock, A· M. and was called to order by the President.

Prayer by the Chaplain.

The journal of yesterday was read and approved.

No petitions, memorials, reports of standing or select committees being presented,

The PRESIDENT stated that resolutions were in order.

Debates furnished to Members.

Mr. MARVIN offered the following resolution:

Resolved, That each member of the Convention be allowed three additional copies of the daily reports of this Convention.

Mr. MARVIN said: My object in offering this resolution is that we may be enabled to furnish each newspaper in our different counties with a copy of the debates that they may have an opportunity to examine them and prepare for publication such a synopsis as would be interesting to their readers.

Mr. HARRIS. I move to amend the resolution by striking out "3" and inserting "8" which will give us ten copies each, and that will enable us to send one copy to each paper in my district, and to each of the prominent points in my my district. I would take it as a great favor if the gentleman would extend that privilege to me, and I have no doubt other members similarly situated, would also regard it as a favor.

The question being taken upon the amendment to the resolution, it was agreed to upon a division as follows, ayes 14 noes 9.

The resolution as amended was then adopted.

Correcting the Proofs of Debates.

Mr. CLARKE, of Johnson. I would make a suggestion on the subject of correcting the proof sheets of these debates which are furnished us. The report of the committee on debates, which was adopted by the Convention, provided for a committee to superintend the publication of these debates. I am not advised whether the chair has appointed that committee or not. If not, I would suggest that it would be well for the committee to be appointed now, and then that committee, or some member of it would make it a duty to read these proofs. That is necessary, for I have perceived on looking over the proof sheets that have been already furnished, that there are some typographical and other errors, the correction of which in future could be attended to by some member of this committee.

The PRESIDENT announced the following gentlemen as members of that committee:

Messrs. Clarke of Johnson, Traer and Solomon.

Preamble and Bill of Rights.

The Convention then resumed the consideration of the report of the committee of the whole upon the Preamble and Bill of Rights.

Religious Tests and Competency of Witnesses.

The PRESIDENT stated the question to be upon the amendment of Mr. Clarke of Henry, to the fourth section of the Bill of Rights, by striking out of the second clause the words "and no person shall" and inserting " nor shall any person," and adding to the section the words "or in consequence of belonging to any particular sect, class or party of men."

The section as proposed to be amended was read as follows:

No religious test shall be required as a qualification for any office or publict trust, nor shall any person be deprived of any of his rights, privileges or capacities, or disqualified from the performance of any of his public or private duties, or rendered incompetent to give evidence in any court of law or equity, in consequence of his opinions on the subject of religion, or in consequence of belonging to any particular sect, class or party of men.

Mr. CLARKE of Henry. At the suggestion of some gentlemen I will further modify my amendment. There was a question raised yesterday by the gentleman from Des Moines (Mr. Hall) which I propose to obviate entirely, so that every gentleman here can vote with the understanding that those who have been convicted of infamous crimes shall be excluded from giving testimony. I have therefore modified the amendment I propose to come in at the end of the section, so that it shall read "or in consequence of belonging to any particular sect, class or party of men; but persons convicted of infamous crimes shall be liable to such disabilities as the laws may provide."

The PRESIDENT. It would not be in order for the gentleman to modify his amendment without unanimous consent. He can move it as an amendment to his amendment.

Mr. CLARKE of Henry. Then I move to amend my amendment by adding thereto the words "but persons convicted of infamous crimes shall be liable to such disabilities as the laws may provide."

The question being taken upon the amendment to the amendment, it was agreed to.

The question then recurred upon the amendment as amended.

Mr. WILSON. I wish to offer a few remarks in explanation of the vote I shall give on this amendment. I understand that the intention of the mover is simply to reach the object of determining the competency of such persons as his amendment embraces to give testimony in courts of justice, and that I can endorse. The last legislature repealed the black laws of this State, and removed the disability from negroes and mulattoes in giving testimony in courts of this State, and thus the matter rests on the provision of the present Constitution, which I believe covers all the ground necessary. I am not exactly satisfied with this amendment; I think it is too broad. And another thing: while I am prepared and shall hold myself in readiness to defend the action of the last legislature in the repeal of this law, I do not feel willing to place this provision in the Constitution at this time, and for this reason.

The Democratic State Convention passed a resolution denouncing that repeal; the Republican State Convention passed a resolution endorsing it, and thus an issue has been made before the people between the two great parties of this State. Now I do not feel willing to place in the Constitution that provision under the present circumstances. We have the advantage at present in an act of the legislature, which I do not think the legislature will dare to repeal even if the Democracy should get the power. And inasmuch as we have the issue on the subject already, I am not in favor of placing a thing in the Constitution that will tend to divide the people of this State into party divisions when called upon to vote upon this Constitution. I hope we shall be able to determine upon a Constitution here upon which the people can all unite. If I find a spirit manifested here to prevent our doing so, then I may be prepared to go further than I am now. But I want to get a better Constitution for this State than the one we now have; to make one containing the amendment which the people have demanded. If I cannot get all I want without endangering what the people desire, then I shall take the best I can get. I shall therefore vote against this amendment.

Mr. PALMER called for the yeas and nays upon the amendment and they were accordingly ordered.

The question being then taken by yeas and nays the amendment was not agreed to, yeas 11 nays 22, as follows:

Yeas—Messrs. Bunker, Clarke of Henry, Clarke of Johnson, Ells, Gower, Gray, Scott, Seely, Skiff and Traer.

Nays—The President, Messrs. Ayres, Clark of Alamakee, Day, Edwards, Emerson, Gibson, Gillaspy, Hall, Harris, Johnston, Palmer, Parvin Patterson, Peters, Price, Solomon, Todhunter, Warren, Wilson, Winchester and Young.

Mr. CLARKE, of Henry. I offer the following amendment to come in at the end of the fourth section:

"Nor shall any person be rendered or held thus incompetent to give testimony in consequence of his or her belonging to any particular sect, class, society or party."

Mr. HARRIS. I would raise a question of order, that this amendment is not in order, as this Convention has just voted down substantially the same thing.

Mr. CLARKE, of Henry. I contend that this amendment is a very different one from the other. The first amendment I offered proposed to carry out all that is contained in the fourth section and qualified only by the subject of religion, to all classes, sects and parties of men.—The section now says that no person shall be deprived of any of his rights, privileges or capacities, or disqualified from the performance of any of his public or private duties in consequence of his religious belief. My amendment would have provided that no man on account of his belonging to any particular sect, class or party, should be deprived of any of his rights, privileges or capacities, or disqualified from the performance of his public or private duties. That amendment gentlemen considered too broad and it was voted down. The one I now propose relates solely to the competency of an individual to give testimony, in consequence of his belonging to any particular sect, class, society or party.

Mr. HARRIS. I still contend that the amendment is not in order, and I call upon the chair to decide.

The PRESIDENT. The chair is of opinion that the amendment is in some respects different from the one just voted down, and therefore it is in order.

Mr. CLARKE, of Henry. The Chair having decided my amendment to be in order, I will proceed with a few remarks that I desire to offer. As I said before, gentlemen objected to my former amendment as being too broad. Now if this principle is correct when applied to religious belief, I cannot see why, nor where it is too broad when applied to man as a class, or party or society. My idea was that no man should be deprived of his rights and privileges in this State, or rendered incapable of discharging his duties here because he was a Catholic, for instance. Gentlemen who have been haranguing all over the State in regard to Know Nothingism, who have spoken of the Know Nothing party as one desiring to restrain a large portion of their fellow-creatures, because they belong to a particular sect, now start back with holy horror from the proposition I offered, and are not willing that it shall go forth to the world that that sect shall be protected in all their rights and privileges in this State. They shrink back from it, and some of them get up here and say, oh, if you will narrow it down so that they will be permitted to testify, I will go for it; but it is so broad now I must go against it; but if it be so worded that they shall be permitted to testify in courts of law and of equity, then I will go for it. Now I like to see men stand up to a principle when it amounts to something. They can stick their principles into resolutions; they will come forth before the world and resolve that they will do great things, but when the moment comes for them to do and to act, then they back down. Now I want to see them assert the principles of their resolutions in their votes.

It is true that the Republicans in their last State Convention have declared before the world that it is a correct principle that men shall not be deprived of their right to give their testimony in courts of justice, on account of belonging to any particular sect, class or party of men. It is true that another party in this State have assumed the reverse of that position. Now because parties have arrayed themselves upon different sides of this question, shall we who are here framing a constitution for the whole people of the State, say we are debarred thereby from expressing in that constitution what is right in principle? Now in order to accommodate some of the gentlemen here who are afraid to go for this principle to its full extent, I have offered this other amendment, covering only the ground that no person shall be deprived of his or her right to testify in courts fo law or equity on account of belonging to any sect, class or party of men. I want to put it out of the power of any legislatrue hereafter to pass any law saying that any man or class of men shall be deprived of any of these rights; shall be subjected to any of these disabilities. Legislatures have so declared, and I believe bills have been passed, wherein it has been declared that those who belong to secret societies shall have certain disabilities attached to them. That thing may occur again.

I would ask gentlemen why this section has been placed here in the Bill of Rights at all? Why is it that we find here the declaration that "no person shall be deprived of any of his rights, privileges or capacities, or disqualified from the performance of any of his public or private duties, or rendered incompetent to give evidence in any court of law or equity, in consequence of his opinions on the subject of religion?" Can gentlemen point me to a statute in this State whereby in a single instance any man has been deprived of any privileges or rights, or been rendered incapable of discharging his duties, public or private, in consequence of his opinions on the subject of religion? If that has not been done, why not throw this whole section out entirely? If the reasoning of gentlemen is good in regard to this amendment, then it is correct in regard to this whole section. They cannot point to a single instance where the Legislature of this State has ever attempted to deprive any man of any of his rights on account of his religious belief. This provision then is not based upon any action of the Legislature of this State, but has reference to the action of the Legislatures of other States, whereby men on account of their peculiar religious belief, on account of not believing in a God, or not being orthodox, or being Quakers, or something of that kind, have been deprived of their rights and their oaths in a court of law, or of holding office in the State. And in order to prevent our Legislature thereafter from passing any law rendering them thus incapable, this provision was inserted in this constitution.

Now if that be a reason for incorporating this section here, then let me ask gentlemen, who say they are ready to stand by the action of our late Legislature, why they will not support the provision I have submitted? It comes close home to them, for they have the fact before them that a Legislature in this State has been so lost to the principles laid down in the constitution, that they did pass a law declaring that a whole class of men, without any regard to their character for truth and veracity, or their standing in community, should be deprived of their oaths in a court of justice. Is not that enough for every man of us here to show us the necessity of the provision I ask to have incorporated into our constitution? But gentlemen spring up here and cry out—"oh, there is a nigger in this matter; there is a nigger under the fence; you have reference solely to a negro being deprived of his oath in a court of justice; you are a friend of the negro, and therefore you come in here with this amendment.

Now I will say that I am not particularly the friend of the negro. I am a friend of the whole human race, and if the negro belongs to one branch of the human family, then in that sense I am a friend of the negro. But so far as my own individual feelings are concerned, perhaps I should say it with shame, there is probably no man who has a greater repugnance naturally to that race than I have; and no man would be more rejoiced than myself if there was not one of that particular race on this continent; and there is no man who would go farther to remove them than I would, if it were practicable. For I tell you that as I look forward to coming events, and the final consummation of this thing; as I look into the future and see the amalgamation, or perhaps what is worse, the growing antipathy, hating and strife of the races, and the whole body of evils that the most vivid imaginations of gentlemen upon the other side can conceive of, it fills my mind with as great a horror as is possibly felt by them. But God in his inscrutible providence has permitted this thing—I cannot see why, and I must not ask wherefore. It is here and we must meet it. And in establishing the principles of this constitution shall we depart from what is correct, from principles of truth and justice—to which the gentleman from Appanoose, [Mr. Harris,] has referred here —shall we depart from them because, forsooth, in the declaration of these principles, negroes may partake of the blessing?

Gentlemen say if you incorporate this provision in the constitution you will so make it that never hereafter can a Legislature pass a law that shall deprive negroes giving testimony in our courts of justice? Why that is just what I desire to accomplish. The Legislature should never be allowed to do such a thing; there is no necessity for it to be done. And yet a gentleman who occupied the highest judicial position in this State at one time, gets up here before this Convention, and when we might naturally suppose that he would bring to the consideration of this question all the knowledge and information that he has had an opportunity to acquire in his position, and which his long practice of law might have given to him, and that he would give us correct ideas in regard to the legal workings of this provision; we find him on the contrary attempting to make men shrink from the discharge of their duty here by calling their attention to some wonderful danger threatening them in the distance, by referring them to Missouri and Kentucky, and imagining some case where some "border ruffian" might come here in our courts of law, and having sued you or me, might then return home, and then come back to Iowa furnished with the testimony of all the negroes on his plantation, for our legal destruction and pecuniary ruin. Coming from such a gentleman as he, it struck me with perfect astonishment that such paltry balderdash could be employed to deter members from voting for a proposition founded on truth and justice. Does not the gentleman know that we are not now fixing the rules of testimony and evidence for the State of Missouri and the State of Kentucky? We are not endeavoring to render legal the evidence of negroes in Missouri and Kentucky, but to establish principles in regard to the matter, for our courts here in the State of Iowa. The negroes of Missouri and Kentucky must continue to remain subject to all the disabilities that their own peculiar institutions throw about them. We are only saying so far as the inhabitants of this State are concerned, what shall be the rule of evidence here. That is all we propose to do.

But the gentleman says this amendment would be opening the flood-gates to perjury! Now if the gentleman will show how this will be done—if he will give the instance where it can occur, then I might listen to his objections. But it is only a bugbear thrown out here to deter us from giving our honest votes. We have come here to form a constitution, and in this Bill of Rights we are pretending to place before the people of this state an enunciation of those rights that we propose to be secured to each individual in this State, and to declare that all the people shall be protected in their rights. I propose here a plain proposition, that no class of men shall be prevented from giving their testimony in a court of justics on account of constituting that class. For instance, look at the operation of a law upon the statute book preventing negroes from giving testimony in the courts of this State. That law was once upon your statute book, and may be placed there again. What, then, would you have? You would have every man in this State who has negro blood in his veins, at the mercy of every robber and plunderer who may choose to deprive him of his property. How was it in the State of Ohio under a similar law? I have been told by the chairman of the Committee on the Preamble and Bill of Rights (Mr. Ells) that while that law was in force in the State of Ohio, armed bodies of men actually took property from negroes—took their horses from them, and otherwise robbed them openly—and there was no law that would reach them, because the law must have testimony that is admitted to be of force, before it can proceed to punish. There were living witnesses of these transactions, but the law would not receive their testimony, and these colored men whose testimony would have been believed and credited in any court of justice were forced to see their property stripped from them without any means of redress! Now I would ask gentlemen what kind of constitution this would be if it permitted such a state of things? An instance came under my own observation, where a white man went into a barber's shop and gave him a counterfeit five dollar bank note. The barber detected it just as the man left, and followed him into the street, and presented it to him again; but the man did not know him—had never seen him—had never been in his shop—did not know the bill, and had never had it in his possession! The barber undertook to satisfy him by relating the circumstances connected with the transaction; but no, he knew nothing about it, and could not be brought to recollect anything about it it or the man. Yet everybody believed the barber, for they knew him to be an honest and upright man. He went before a justice of the peace to obtain redress; the justice asked him if there was any one present in his shop when the transaction occurred. The barber told him that there was nobody but a black boy. He now asked if there was any white person present. No; there was no one but this black boy. He was told *that was no evidence!* And there was nothing left for those who believed the barber, but to invite the fellow who passed the counterfeit note upon him, to leave town. They could connect him in a round about way with bills of a similar description; that is, a white witness had seen him have a similar bill in his possession. This was enough to satisfy the people that he was guilty, and they ordered him to leave. But the barber had to lose the amount of the bill, and what is worse, the white scoundrel with a black heart went unpunished.

Now, I would ask if these men, if this class which we have now in our midst, are to be protected in their rights? And as was well remarked by the gentleman from Johnson (Mr. Clarke), shall we—the white people of this State—be deprived of their testimony, under all circumstances, if we may wish it? I have so narrowed down my proposition that it does not now apply to anything except the giving of testimony in courts of justice. This is not a party question—I do not wish it to be a party question—it should not be a party question. I have not urged it as a party question. I have urged, as a matter of mere justice, not only to this particular class of people, but to the whole community, that this provision should be incorporated into our constitution in order that no future Legislature shall be able to disturb that principle. If there is any necessity—I wish gentlemen to think of this thing—of our incorporating any principle in the Bill of Rights, there is certainly a great necessity of incorporating this principle here, because it has once been outraged! And when I hear gentlemen say that the law as it now stands permits of this class of our population giving testimony, and they are willing to leave this matter to the Legislature, what can I think? I think that these gentlemen had better sweep away the whole Bill of Rights, and leave everything to the Legislature. I will be bound, that this is almost the only instance that has ever occurred in the State of Iowa where the most common and ordinary principles of right and justice have been actually outraged by legislative enactments, and where we absolutely need the incorporation of some such provision in the Bill of Rights to prevent future legislatures from again committing the same outrages. Yet gentlemen who are willing to slide over other provisions, and vote them in because they have been voted in before, shirk the question of incorporating this principle in the constitution, because they fear the "dear people" will not vote for it, or it may lead to a party struggle! When some members can forget what is behind them "on the record," and shall cease to hear the "howling" of their constituency, and to see dire phantoms shaking sticks at them in the distance, and can give their minds to the contemplation of principles and measures to be incorporated into our constitution, I think we shall be able to get along faster in the discharge of our duties. As for myself, I say here that I will do what is right, what my judgment tells me is right, and what I believe to be necessary, and I will trust the people to look at it in the same light. And if they do not, I will tell you what I do believe: I have confidence that they will give me the same endorsement which I gave the gentleman from Wapello (Mr. Gillaspy) the other day, that I *mean* to be honest and to do what is right. But if I were continually to look back after the character of my record, or forward to see what the people are going to say, I should be afraid of this: that my constituents might with propriety say that their representative here thought more of gaining their applause, than of settling correct principles in the constitution. From some such cause, I fear, gentlemen seem determined to give this matter the go-by, and have said here that they are "willing to leave this question to the Legislature!" Now I will say to those gentlemen, they may slip over this proposition—they may record their votes against so self-evident and manifestly just a proposition as this embraced in my amendment, and they will learn what the people will in future say of them in connection with this subject. If gentlemen wish to look upon it in that light, I would ask them to reflect.

Gentlemen tell me that there is already an issue between the Democratic party and the Republican party, as it is called, although it is but a poor party at best, and thank God it is hardly a "party," and I hope the time will never come when it will be a drilled and organized party. Gentlemen tell us that the Republicans are arrayed on the one side and the Democrats on the other side, the one sustaining the principles in the repealing law of the late Legislature, and the other opposing it. And yet Republicans are afraid to stand up here and incorporate this principle in the constitution. Now, how will that appear to the people? Let gentlemen reflect how they are going to stand up before their constituents, if they intend to take the Republican position upon the act passed by the late Legislature.

Now let us look at this matter. I have asked two gentlemen—prominent men in the Democratic party—as to what their action would be provided they should obtain a majority in our General Assembly, and I wish Republicans to reflect upon this thing. Let each one ask his next neighbor, who like the gentleman from Appanoose (Mr Harris) and the gentleman from Des Moines (Mr. Hall) hold that my amendment and the law that has just been passed by the General Assembly, would be opening the doors to perjury, &c., and that only evil must result from allowing this class to come in indiscriminately and testify; ask them what will be their action, provided—it is an almost inconceivable thing—but provided they should ever get the majority in both branches of the General Assembly of this State? I would ask Republicans to listen to me. It is proclaimed already here on the floor of this Convention, that if the Democrats should get the ascendancy in our General Assembly, they will certainly re-enact the black laws—they will re-enact the law depriving blacks of the right to testify in our courts of law and equity! and I would ask if it is not better to settle this question by a provision in the constitution, if the principle involved is right and just, than to have it before the people dividing them into parties, and to have it the subject of conflicting legislation hereafter? Suppose that the next Legislature is Democratic, and they go to work and re-enact these black laws, as they say they will if they get the power? Then suppose that there is a re-action, and the Republicans come again into power, and those laws are again repealed—what a state of useless contest and confusion will that lead to! I am willing to meet this question upon the threshold. If it is to be a question to go before the people and become a subject of party strife, I will tell you how I want it to go before them. Not in connection with local questions, or bank laws, or something of that kind, or any political question that may be agitating the public and dividing parties; but I want it to go before them by itself, when party spirit shall not be called upon to decide it. I want it incorporated into this constitution, and have it go before the people and be discussed without party feeling, and voted upon without party distinction. Now is the time and here is the place to settle this question, and the argument of the gentleman from Jefferson (Mr. Wilson) that it is already before the people, and the parties have arrayed themselves upon it, is one great reason why I would insist upon my amendment, and take it away from the parties, for it does not belong to them.

The gentleman from Des Moines (Mr. Hall) speaks of me as being peculiarly friendly to the negro—as being very anxious at every opportunity I can get to insert some provision here for their particular benefit. I tell that gentleman that I stand here distinct from any party—the representative of no party. I stand here by myself, at this time, having been elected to my seat by votes of the Democratic party as well as of the Republican party. The gentleman who run against me in my district was known as an old third party man, as a freesoiler, and he received the votes of the ultra men in that district, who did not consider me ultra enough to represent the constituency of Henry county, and I suppose the gentleman will wonder how ultra a man must have been to have satisfied them, if I did not. But no matter about that. I stand here in favor of those principles that I consider right and just, without any reference to their bearing upon any party under God's heavens: and I would ask Democrats just as freely as I would ask Republicans, to stand up here in support of those principles which no man has attempted to deny at all, by any argument—no! not one!

The gentleman from Des Moines, [Mr. Hall,] calls this an abstract principle, and says that abstract principles will never do any good here. He wants to satisfy me that this can never be a practical question. "Oh, no," says he "this is not practical; come in here with something practical. This principle of yours may be correct as a general principle, but when you come to apply it as a practical question, it will not work." That is what they call my amendment in substance. No gentleman has got up here and attempted to show as that the principle is not correct. But they want to make exceptions to it, and while they ask those exceptions to be made, they acknowledge the principle to be right.

Mr. GILLASPY. I would ask the gentleman if it was generally understood in his district before his election, that he advocated the principles that he advocates here?

Mr. TODHUNTER. That is a leading question. [Laughter.]

Mr. CLARKE, of Henry. It is much too leading. I would say in reply to the question that those of my constituents who knew me, knew, I believe, what my principles were, and what principles I had lived up to all my life; and those principles were to do whatever I thought was right, as near as I could, and sticking to those principles I considered right, whether they affected God, man or the devil.

Mr. GILLASPY. With the permission of the gentleman I would ask him another question. Was not he the nominee of the republican convention of Henry county?

Mr. CLARKE, of Henry. I was.

Mr. GILLASPY. That is all.

Mr. HARRIS. Before the gentleman takes his seat, I would like to ask him a question. He has made some charges here in regard to the democratic party in relation to Catholics. I would ask the gentleman if he was not a member of what is known as the American party, that proposed certain disabilities in relation to the Catholics?

Mr. CLARKE, of Henry. I am willing to answer any question that gentlemen can propose to me, that is at all germain to the question now before us. I wish the Convention to understand that no proposition I offer here is intended merely to excite discussion. I make no proposition with any disposition to create any agitation or anything of the kind. I say that there are certain principles upon which all of us should unite. As the gentleman from Johnson, [Mr. Clarke,] said, we are in a progressive age, and the time will come when every gentleman who takes a position adverse to the principles I advocate here—not because I conceived it in my wisdom,—will find how far he has mistaken the true position. And I ask every gentleman to look into his own bosom and see if he has not a consciousness that the time is soon coming when the real principles of democracy are going to be embraced by the American people to their full extent.

Mr. HARRIS. I asked the gentleman a question a few moments since, and I simply want an answer to it. If the gentleman wishes to know why I ask the question, I will simply say that I was informed by a gentleman of integrity that he was a member of the so-called American party.

Mr. CLARKE, of Henry. What has that question to do with this discussion?

Mr. HARRIS. It has this to do with it. The gentleman has made certain charges against the democratic party, and has called upon us to say if we intended to stand up to certain positions we had taken in regard to Catholics?

Mr. SCOTT. I think as the gentleman from

Appanoose, [Mr. Harris,] is himself in favor of not allowing a certain class to testify, it is not proper for him to urge an answer to his question.

Mr. HARRIS. I only desire the gentleman to give an answer to my question.

Mr. CLARKE, of Henry. I am satisfied that the remarks to which the gentleman from Appanoose, [Mr. Harris,] alludes, had their force and their desired effect. They have caused a fluttering among gentlemen here. I regret that I cannot accommodate the gentleman from Appanoose quite yet. If he will talk with me in private I will give him all the information he may desire on that or any kindred subject. But as what I have been, or may now be, is foreign to the subject now before us, I shall decline answering his question.

I have only to say now in conclusion, that I wish every gentlemen here to consider what he is doing before he votes against my amendment. I believe there is a majority for the amendment, from the very fact that a former Legislature passed a law which excluded a whole class from our courts of justice as witnesses, and that a subsequent legislature sent here by the people, considered the operation of that law unjust, and working badly for the interests of the people, and they repealed it. And certain gentlemen have proclaimed here that in certain courts that law shall be re-enacted and re-placed upon our statute books. Now it behooves us, standing here as we do, forming a constitution for the people of the State, to forever settle this question upon principles of justice and right. That is all I ask. I do not ask anything because one and the other of the political parties have taken positions upon this question. I would appeal to no man as a republican, or as a democrat, upon this subject. I only appeal to the conscience of every man here, and ask him, am I demanding anything of you but to sustain a correct principle, when I ask you to vote for this amendment? If that is so I hope and trust that gentlemen will vote so that this vexed question may be settled here and taken entirely from the political arena. I am so well satisfied of the correctness of this principle, that I believe if it is suffered to go into party politics, whichever party takes the ground that it is right for the Legislature to ostracise any class of individuals, will be finally defeated; and that any party which takes the reverse position, and will stand upon the broad principles laid down in this section throughout, will eventually triumph. But not for that reason would I have it go into party politics; not for that reason would I want the republicans as a party to array themselves upon the side of the principles I have incorporated into my amendment. I care not for mere party success and triumph. The mere triumph and success of party should influence no man. But the success of the principles upon which his party is based should be the glory and triumph of every man, if the principles of his party be correct. Now I say this, that the true democratic party, the Jeffersonian democratic party, has for its very basis the principles which I wish to have incorporated into this section. The triumph of that principle ought to be hailed by every true democrat with as much joy as by any true republican. It should not be made a party question at all. I ask, therefore, a respectful consideration of the amendment I have offered, and the support of this Convention to make it a part of our constitution.

Mr. WILSON. I think the gentleman from Henry, [Mr. Clarke,] has taken a pretty extensive job on his hands this morning. He seems to have determined on lecturing friends and foes. It seems to me that while the gentleman has been carrying his lectures to the extent he has carried them, if he had looked a little deeper into the subject he has been discussing, he might have discovered some other ground for his position. I do not think his remarks in relation to Catholics apply to his amendment, or his intention in offering the amendment. I am satisfied it is intended to apply to persons of color; that is his object. And so far as his proposition is concerned, I have indicated my position in my former remarks.

Now I have a question to ask the gentleman from Wapello, [Mr. Gillaspy.] I want to know if by the system of catechising he has carried on here, he intends to draw the party lines in this Convention? I want to know if I am to understand him as standing here upon the part of the democracy, seeking to draw party lines in this body?

Mr. GILLASPY. I do not intend to speak for the democratic party, but only for myself. So far as my own desires are concerned, I desire upon this negro question to draw the party lines; I want to see who is in favor of the negro testifying and having all the privileges of the white man: in other words, of bringing the white man down to the level of the negro. I want to put all who are in favor of that upon the record.

Mr. WILSON. I want to ask the gentleman one other question. When he goes home from this Convention does he expect to hold the republican party responsible for the answers given by the gentleman from Henry, [Mr. Clarke,] to his question?

Mr. GILLASPY. I do not expect to hold myself responsible to any member of this Convention for what I may say or do after I go away from here.

Mr. WILSON. I see that the gentleman is not willing to answer the question. He asked the gentleman from Henry if he was the nominee of the republican party. Now I want to know if he expects and intends to make that a handle to use against the republican party when he goes away from here, and when this constitution is submitted to the people? I shall be better prepared to vote when I understand that matter.

Mr. GILLASPY. I hope the gentleman will not be alarmed. I am only an humble individual from the State of Ohio; I am only a private citizen at home. I am sorry the gentleman is alarmed at anything I may ask the gentleman from Henry (Mr. Clarke.) The gentleman from Henry and myself are particular friends, and I accord to him that honesty he is willing to accord to me.

Mr. WILSON. I suppose the gentleman intends his remarks to be taken with some gratification. He is a private citizen at home—when he is not in office—which latter position I believe he has occupied most of the time for several years past. (Laughter.)

Now I wish to state another reason in addition to what I have already stated why I shall vote against this amendment. The gentleman from Wapello (Mr. Gillaspy) seeks by catechizing the gentleman from Henry (Mr. Clarke) to hold the Republican party responsible for the positions assumed here by that gentleman.—Now I wish to say this: that it was the understanding in my county during the canvass, that both the candidates, my competitor having been nominated by the Democratic party and supported by the old line whigs, democrats and Know Nothings in opposition to myself, and also myself as the candidate of the Republican party, occupied the ground that we would not advocate any change of the old Constitution in relation to the races. That was the understanding in my county, and I do not feel willing at the present time to betray the understanding of the people of my county. And there is one other reason why I shall vote against this amendment, and that is that the gentleman by the amendment he proposes, will establish a principle in direct conflict with the principle he has been advocating, and that is a recognition in the Constitution of this State of a distinction between different classes so far as giving testimony in courts of justice is concerned. It amounts to a declaration that the legislature now has the right to exclude a portion of the people of this State from testifying in courts of justice. Now I do not believe in any such doctrine. I believe that wherever there is a man, whether he be black or white, who is capable of telling the truth, he is a proper person to introduce in a court of law or equity to give testimony. And I will remark here with the gentleman from Muscatine (Mr. Parvin) that no honest man need fear the testimony.

I am prepared to sustain the action of the last legislature in that respect; but am unwilling to go with the gentleman from Wapello in making this a party question. I am unwilling in relation to this Constitution which is demanded by the great bulk of the people, to make a party issue here, and divide the people of the State in relation to their fundamental law. By drawing the party lines many democrats will be compelled to follow in the wake of their leaders. I believe it is proverbial in relation to the Democratic party that the lay members always follow their leaders. That I believe is a proverb that no man here will attempt to refute.

That party has an organization which will bring their members square up to the position of their leadersat any time.

Mr. GILLASPY. Does the gentleman from Jefferson (Mr. Wilson) believe what the gentleman from Henry (Mr. Clarke) said awhile ago, that he received Democratic votes against the Democratic candidate in Henry county?

Mr. WILSON. Certainly I do; I have no reason to dispute his word.

Mr. GILLASPY. Then does the Democratic party always follow its leaders?

Mr. WILLSON. I believe there were two candidates in Henry county; Mr. Clarke, and a Mr. Howe, as Freesoilers.

Mr. GILLASPY. Was not there a Democratic candidate.

Mr. WILSON. There was a third candidate who was a know nothing, and the mass of the Democratic party voted for him, just as they did in my county.

Mr. GILLASPY. I understand differently; I understand from a reliable gentleman from Mt. Pleasant that the gentleman who ran as the Democratic Candidate never was a Know-Nothing.

Mr. WILSON. I know it is very difficult to get men to own that they have ever been Know-Nothings when they are canditates for office.

A Member. Particularly Democrats. (laughter.)

Mr. WILSON. Yes, particularly democrats.

Mr. PATTERSON. I would ask the President if he decides that the amendment now proposed by the gentleman from Henry [Mr. Clarke] is in order. It seemed to me when it was read to embrace the same subject matter as the one that was voted down this morning. I know that the same speeches have been made upon it. I think this whole debate with the amendment is out of order.

The PRESIDENT. The chair is of opinion that the amendment now proposed is a different proposition from the one offered before, and therefore that it is in order.

Mr. WILSON. I am sorry that the gentleman is becoming uneasy. I should not have pursued the course I have but for the course of members upon the other side, members of the Democratic party. They have commenced this thing, and I am only following their lead in the matter.

I do not know as I have anything farther to add upon this subject. My vote upon this proposition will be the same that it was upon the other for the reasons I have already stated. I am not willing to go with the gentleman from Wapello [Mr. Gillaspy] and draw party lines in regard to this Constitution. Neither am I willing here, whatever my private views may be, to prove false to my position as it was understood during the canvass in my county; I am willing to stand up to that, but not to go beyond it.

Mr. HARRIS. I do not wish to detain the Convention but a moment, and I will endeavor to be as brief as possible. Now, it so happens, that I offered an amendment to this same section when in Committee of the Whole, and if I am not very much mistaken, the gentleman from Henry (Mr. Clarke) himself, voted against it. The amendment which I offered in committee was to the effect that no preference or advantage should be given to any religious society, and that the right of conscience should not in any manner be interfered with, and nothing herein should be construed to dispense with oaths and affirmations. It was voted down, and I do not know of any other vote that was given for it but my own. The member from Henry (Mr. Clarke) would make us believe, that the amendment he offered was in relation to persons belonging to religious societies and organizations. He then turns around and asks us whether we are going to face the music in regard to the catholics, and when I asked him whether he had ever been a member of any Native American Organization, he refused to answer. And yet we are charged upon this side with seeking to gain an unfair advantage, and with attempting to do something which will place the opposite party in a false position. I do not seek to draw the party lines, as far as this matter is concerned, but I wish to present what is fair and right, and if the Republicans upon the other side of the question see proper to support my view of the matter, I shall have no objections.

So far as allowing colored men to give testimony is concerned, I will say here in answer to the gentleman from Jefferson (Mr. Wilson) that we will hold the Republicans responsible, so far as they shall endorse that proposition. As to the fluttering which the gentleman from Henry [Mr. Clarke] sees among those who hold different views from his own, I have not seen it. As far as I am concerned, I have no objections to going upon the record in every solitary instance where I may be called upon to vote, and I think I have shown some evidence of my willingness to do so, upon the various occasions upon which I have been called to vote.

My object in rising was simply to remind the Convention of the proposition which I submitted in Committee of the Whole, and which was voted down. If the proposition of the gentleman from Henry (Mr. Clarke) has any reference to religious organizations, placing them all upon an equality, why then, certainly, those gentlemen who voted against my proposition must face about or else vote down this proposition. If it does refer to persons of color, then I am opposed to the whole thing.

Mr. EDWARDS. I desire before the vote is taken upon this question to place myself right upon the record. I do not think that there is such a thing, as "discretion being the better part of valor." I regret exceedingly the course that has been pursued by the gentleman from Henry, (Mr. Clarke) although I agree with him in regard to the principles that he expresses.

We are told in sacred writ, that there are things that may be beneficial but not always expedient. I understand that one of the great objects for which this Convention was called, was to take into consideration the subject of Banking, and a few other questions of as nearly important character, and therefore, I am opposed to encumbering the Constitution with those matters, which may cause its rejection by the people.

Even if the Legislature that has just adjourned had not removed the disability from colored persons giving testimony in courts of justice, I would not have been willing to have incorporated a provision upon this subject in the constitution, upon the ground of expediency. There is such a thing as recognizing the opinions of those who may disagree with us. There is a prejudice existing in the community, whether it be well or ill founded, against that unfortunate race of people I do not know whether it is because the Northern wing of the Democracy is tied body and soul to the car of southern slavery and because of the loaves and fishes they expect to get from that alliance, or whether it is because they are governed by principles which they believe to be right, but they do hold to the doctrine that the unfortunate colored man has no right to enjoy any privileges in this land, that we boast of as being the "land of the free and the home of the brave." I say that I am not willing, upon the grounds of expediency, to recognize in the constitution the right of the colored man to give testimony in the courts—not desiring to shock the moral sensibilities of those who entertain prejudices against that unfortunate race of people—but so far as the principle is concerned, I cordially endorse the law enacted by the Legislature upon that subject. I endorse the principle for other reasons. I believe the people are capable of self-government. If the Democratic party fulminate the doctrine from time to time, when they meet here in Convention, that they act for the greatest good to the greatest number, and then falsify their declarations, by their acts in deliberative assemblies, I cannot help it. I say I cannot help it, if they falsify their declarations, and do legislate partially and for a portion of the human family.—It is a mockery upon their lips when they declare they act for the greatest good to the greatest number. I can state an instance by way of illustration, which came within my own recollection. Some two or three years ago, and you will all doubtless recollect the circumstances, a Methodist preacher residing in the State of Missouri, "clothed with the livery of heaven to serve the Devil in," came to Indianapolis and made affidavit that a colored free man residing there, was a slave of his who had escaped from services, and he brought several white men as witnesses from Missouri to establish that fact. The unfortunate colored man was incarcerated in prison for a period of four months, and was put to the expense of sending to Georgia for the purpose of procuring the testimony of his old master, that he was free. This old master came in person, recognized him as soon as he saw him, and with tears coursing down his cheeks, clasped him to his bosom—but not until this affecting interview took place did this Methodist preacher relinquish his grasp. If that negro man had been allowed to offer the testimony of colored persons to prove his identity, he would have established the fact clearly before the court that he was a free man.

There was another case in an adjoining county to where I resided, where justice failed to be meted out because of the exclusion of the testimony of colored persons. A white man committed a rape upon a colored woman, who was thereby socially, morally and physically ruined forever, but the brute in human form who had committed the offence, was permitted to go unpunished, because of the law which refuses the evidence of colored persons to be given in courts of justice. When these Democrats profess that they are willing to trust the people, I say to them that they distrust the people, and the courts and juries of the country when they say they are not capable of deciding the question of the credibility of a witness.

I can see no harm that would result from permitting the testimony of colored men to be given in evidence in our courts; but gentlemen on the other side have availed themselves of the opportunity, and have stigmatized the gentleman from Henry, and all who are connected with the Republican party, as being the especial friends of the negro.

The gentleman from Appanoose (Mr. Harris), a little while ago asked the gentleman from Henry (Mr. Clarke) if he belonged to what was called the Know Nothing party, and the gentleman from Wappello (Mr. Gillaspy) put a question of the same character. I assure the gentleman from Appanoose [Mr. Harris] that when I was nominated by the Republican party for a seat in this convention, the Democratic party ran against me a man who had been all his life a Whig, and who had been an avowed Know Nothing leader in the county of Lucas. The Democratic party is ready to fuse with any party if thereby they can gain a triumph. But a short time before this fusion of the Democrats and Know Nothings, of which I speak, the Know Nothing party was the most formidable party in the State, against whom the Democrats were then arrayed in opposition. Then, with the latter, it was the cry of persecution for religion's sake, and all their influence was exerted to put down the Know Nothings. But when, by the force of circumstances, another party sprang into existence, which bid fair, in view of the imminence of the peril which threatened the liberties of the country, to become the most formidable party at the North, then it was that the Democracy directed their energies and their whole battery against the Republican party, and they commenced at the same time wooing and courting the Know Nothings.

Mr. HARRIS. As the gentleman has referred to me, I would like to ask him a question, and I hope he will take it kindly, because I have the best feeling in the world for him. I desire to know of the gentleman whether he was not at one time a member, and one of the leaders of the Native American party in Lucas county.

Mr. EDWARDS. Yes, I was; and I glory in the fact. If I were a member of the Know Nothing party, which the gentleman and his party have denounced in such unmeasured terms, it comes with an ill grace for them to take a leading man of the "dark lantern" party—a man who had been arrayed against them in word and deed upon every possible occasion, before he was nominated—and run him against me. But what does the past election show, in relation to the Democrats in affiliating in other places with the Know Nothings? Why, in the city of Boston they took up Mr. Appleton and ran him against Mr. Burlingame, and they did the same with Washington Hunt in one of the Congressional Districts in New York. The great principle which binds the Democratic party together is the adhesive power of public plunder. They are banded together and drilled to obey the behests of their leaders, and the moment a man has the courage to stand up and declare for principles they apply the lash to him and endeavor to whip him into the traces. They will not allow a man to think and act independently for himself; and he must unhesitatingly subscribe to what they dictate and lay down as the doctrine of the party. The gentleman from Henry [Mr. Clarke] gets up here and expresses his opinion as an independent freeman, as he has a right to do, and they ask him if he is the exponent of the Republican party. I cordially endorse the position taken by that gentleman, but thank God, the Republican party has no leaders, and it is governed by those holy principles which they believe will promote the honor, glory and welfare of our common country We expect to stand steadfast in the maintainance of those cherished principles which are so dear to us all, in despite of the sneers and taunts that may be indulged in by gentlemen on the other side.

Mr. GILLASPY. I do not desire to take up the time of the convention in making a speech, but I merely wish now to say a few words in reply to my friend from Jefferson [Mr. Wilson] and my friend from Henry [Mr. Clarke.]

In the first place let me make a single remark in regard to the amendment offered by the gentleman from Henry, [Mr. Clarke.] The gentleman offers an amendment that I undertake to say applies solely to the colored race, and he makes a speech in which he attempts to make this Convention believe that it only applies to Catholics.

I am proud to say here to-day that in the County of Wapello I was the especial friend in the days of Know Nothingism, of what were termed by that party, the "damned Irish Catholics." I was proud then, and I am to-day, to declare myself their friend, and I have always so declared myself in all the Democratic Conventions I have attended. I came here to represent exclusively the interests of the white race, and I am in favor of retaining the word "white" exclusively in every part of the constitution, and I hope that this Convention, in every thing they may do here, will look to the interests of the white race alone. It is in very bad taste for the gentleman from Jefferson to insinuate that I am desiring to draw party lines here. I ask the members of the Convention, whether if up to the time the gentleman addressed his interrogatories to me, I had ever said a single word upon this floor, intended to draw the party lines. One thing I see this morning, that my Republican friends have discovered that they have not drawn the party lines as strictly, and which they now desire to do. They put forward a leading member of this Convention, the gentleman from Henry, [Mr. Clarke,] who has occupied a high place in the Republican party in the State of Iowa, and who was the candidate of that same party in my district for a seat in Congress, to draw the party lines in this Convention, and he catechises the gentleman from Muscatine, [Mr. Parvin,] and the gentleman from Jefferson, [Mr. Wilson.] These gentlemen say that the amendment of the gentleman from Henry is proper and right; and they endorse the action of the Legislature in passing a law upon this subject, but they are afraid to put it into the constitution. I dare the Republican party to engraft this principle upon the constitution, and I say to them here if they do it that my county, believing that the white man is better than the negro, will give a thousand majority against the constitution.

The gentleman from Henry county comes here endorsed by the Republican party of his county, and he rises here upon this floor, and draws the party lines, saying to his republican friends you must support this measure. The gentleman from Jefferson says that this question was an issue between the republican and democratic parties, made so by their respective State Conventions that met in this city, and he seeks to draw the party lines upon this subject, and he wants the Convention to understand by his insinuations, that the gentleman from Wapello is desiring to draw them. So far as I am individually concerned, I do not pretend to speak for the democratic party, because I have never claimed to be a leader of that party, and to my knowledge I have never been recognized as such. I am not one of those who follow in the wake of party leaders, but I follow only the time-honored principles of the Democratic party. I have ever done, and ever expect to do this. If the gentleman will change his amendment and apply it to the race that the gentleman, and the party to which he belongs, were willing two years ago to disfranchise, I will support it. I would as soon be willing to extend privileges and immunities to the Catholics, the Germans and Irish, as any other people on the face of God's earth. If the gentleman desires to draw party lines here —I am the last man willing to do so—I will be found acting with the minority, the democratic portion of the Convention, and I will go home to my constituents, and hold the gentleman from Jefferson, [Mr. Wilson,] and the gentleman from Henry, [Mr. Clarke,] and the republican party responsible for every vote they may give here. I know that the gentleman from Jefferson county is shaking in his boots in view of this responsibility. I know that the people of Jefferson county—and I have known them as long as the gentleman himself has—are not prepared to endorse the doctrine that the negro is as good, or perchance better, than the white man. I dare gentlemen here to incorporate into the constitution the amendment of the gentleman from Henry. If they want to see the constitution defeated, let them insert this provision so repugnant to the free people of Iowa, as it ought to be to every man in the country. If the negro is to be placed upon an equality with the white man, by the adoption of the amendment now proposed here, it will defeat the constitution in my judgment; and it shall be, when submitted to the people for their votes, if it can be by any influence which I may exert.

Mr. HALL. I regret exceedingly, Mr. Chairman, the course which this discussion has taken, and that the firebrand which it seems has been prepared on the part of some gentlemen was not kept out of this hall yet a little longer. Now sir, my constituents sent me here for the purpose of amending and revising the present Constitution, and putting it in a shape which would be more acceptable to the wants, condition and interests of the people than the one we now have. If I know the feelings of that portion of the State which I have the honor to represent upon this floor, I know that there is a very small number of the people there who would be willing to hazard the labors of this Convention by provoking a controversy here upon the local surface topics of the day. I did not come here, as I have had already occasion to say, to force into this Constitution any political opinions of my own. I did not come here for the purpose of making it a Constitution of the Democratic party, or the Constitution of any other party, but I came here to make the amendments which public opinion has long since pointed out; and to discuss as fairly and clearly as I was capable of doing, the various questions which would arise in our deliberations here. I happened to have the honor of being a member of the Convention that met in this Capitol twelve years ago, it being the first Convention that was called by the people of the then Territory of Iowa. There were seventy-three members in that convention elected from a population not exceeding 70,000. In that Convention I think I heard not one word or syllable in favor of a proposition, that has now apparently become so vital, if we are to believe the assertion of gentlemen; and a gentleman who now occupies the position which everybody did then, can now say nothing but what is termed balderdash, and he must be subject to taunts and reproaches for his position by gentlemen upon this floor. And so it was in the second Convention; there was not a member who offered this proposition at that time. There was not any considerable number of citizens in this State then who desired that this feature should be incorporated in their fundamental law. If it were spoken of at all, gentlemen as members of the Convention, and as citizens, were willing to leave the question to be decided by the Legislature. They had sufficient confidence in the representatives of the people who were to be elected under the new Constitution, to leave this question to them without the distracting elements of agitation that even then existed to some extent. It seems that a new light has dawned upon the State, that new ideas have opened up, and a distracting element has been thrown into our deliberations; and gentlemen who compose the majority here are to be driven into the party traces and lines in order to incorporate this distracting element into the fundamental law of our State. I am opposed to this proposition, believing that it will produce most mischievous results and work an irreparable injury to the best interests of the State. I should look upon it as a public calamity if measures of this kind should be introduced into this Constitution, which would inevitably tend to defeat it whenever we shall be ready to submit it to the people. It would be in my opinion not only a public calamity to the State, to introduce this controversy into our deliberations at this time, but it might have a tendency to demoralize the public sentiment of the people. I agree with the gentleman from Jefferson [Mr. Wilson] and the gentleman from Muscatine [Mr. Parvin] who both occupy the same position, that it would be safe enough to leave this matter in the hands of the Legislature. I appeal to gentlemen as candid men, if there be not enough division of public sentiment upon this matter to leave it an open question to be decided by the Legislature hereafter. It seems to me there is, and the people will be better satisfied if the matter is so left. It strikes me that no gentleman will have cause of complaint if this matter is so disposed of. I concede the right of the gentleman from Henry [Mr. Clarke] coming from the county he does, and having passed through the canvass he has, to carve out and worship his beautiful Gods in ebony when he has made them, but I ask gentlemen who are differently situated to leave this question to the Legislature. Let us act upon the propositions that the people sent us here to consider. Let us go back two days before this question came up in its present shape, and let us act as we acted then. I am certainly content to stand upon the ground then occupied. The gentleman from Henry [Mr. Clarke] and other gentlemen upon this floor speak with great emphasis in regard to the duty enjoined upon them of maintaining and upholding the great leading principles of eternal truth contained in this amendment. We have all lived so far without having in our Constitution such a principle incorporated, and we have seen no evil consequences resulting from its omission in that instrument. I do not believe all the tales of wo, and all the legends of wrongs which gentlemen relate here in regard to the negro race. It is utterly impossible for any human institutions to exist without injustice sometimes resulting from the maintainance of the laws. Innocent men have been condemned to the gallows, and been sent to the penitentiary for offenses they never committed; and they have been sometimes compelled to pay debts which they never owed, and I might cite numberless instances in society where the innocent man may be made to suffer, but does that afford any argument against the laws which punish the murderer, the felon or thief, or make the debtor pay his debt?

As to the doctrine of Know Nothingism, I would not allude to it, had it not been dragged more than once into this discussion. I do not believe the gentleman from Henry will deny the fact, that within the last two years he united with that party.

The gentleman from Lucas, (Mr. Edwards) most proudly asserts upon the floor, that he was a member of that organization. If I understand the doctrines and objects of that party, they sought through the political action of the country, to disqualify a large portion of people from the enjoyment of the very rights which these gentlemen are so strenuously urging should be provided for in this constitution. They were willing to say that with regard to foreigners, the term of naturalization should be extended to twenty-one years; that the foreign-born citizen shall not be eligible to office; and that he should be a proscribed man all his life. These very gentlemen who were in favor of placing these restrictions upon foreigners are now most eloquent in asserting a doctrine, that shall establish an equality apparently, not only for the foreigner, the Catholic, but also for the negro.

Mr. EDWARDS. So far as I am concerned upon this question of Know Nothingism, I will state this, that no man in my section of country ever heard me express, publicly or privately, but what I was satisfied with the laws of Congress upon the subject of naturalization. I took the position that I did not wish them disturbed, and all I asked was that those States (Indiana, Illinois, and one or two other States) that had annulled the laws of Congress upon the subject of naturalization, should alter their constitutions, so as to conform to the laws of Congress upon this question.

Mr. HALL. If our constitution as it now exists was not in conformity to the acts of Congress upon this subject, I should certainly vote to make it so, but I will never unite with any party that will undertake to compel the people of Illinois or any other State, to follow a certain line of policy. Let the people of Illinois make a constitution to suit themselves. They are just as capable of making a constitution to suit themselves as we are to make one that will be adapted to our wants. That is all I have to say upon that question.

The gentleman from Henry [Mr. Clarke] has attempted to dragoon his own party into making this a party question, and has attempted to force the Democrats in this Convention to say that they would make it so. I do not desire that this matter should be made a party question, and it shall be made so only because a majority of this Convention force it upon the minority. It has not been made a party question in this

Convention so far, as the most distinctly shows. There has been nothing before the Convention yet upon which the party lines have been drawn. Gentlemen have voted, so far upon their own conceptions of what is right, and I should regret to see any other policy adopted. I should regret to see anything introduced here that would prove an element of discord and destruction into our deliberations, and be the means of defeating the great work we have in view.

I believe the question now under consideration will be perfectly safe in the hands of the Legislature. A law has already been passed by that body making the evidence of Indians and negroes admissible in our courts of justice. If the people are dissatisfied with the action of the Legislature upon that subject, why, they can send back their representatives with instructions to repeal that law. If this testimony becomes a public calamity, if it should be found upon trial to be improper, and demoralizing, ought not the people to have the power to send back their representatives with instructions to repeal it? If, on the other hand, it proves beneficial and answers the ends which gentlemen here seem seem to think it will, ought not the people to have the privilege of saying through their representatives that they will retain it? Is there any violation of principle here? If there is, then gentlemen and myself have very different ideas of what violation of principle consists in. I propose, then, to leave this question just where it has been in years past—in the hands of the Legislature.

Mr. CLARK, of Alamakee. I believe I was never acsused of being an Abolitionist or Know Nothing. I became, however, in the days when Know Nothingism flourished, a member of that organization, and yet there were certain principles that I avowed that led me to incur their displeasure. One of those principles is involved in the question that is before this body to-day. I was induced, a short time ago to cast a vote here against my own convictions of what was right, and in favor of what I deemed to be merely a question of expediency. Since that time, from the course this discussion has taken, and the disposition which has been manifested here, I have become satisfied with a fact that I knew well before, that it is unsafe to abandon principle for the sake of expediency, for there is a law pervading all nature that in the end will make it safer for mankind to obey the great eternal principles of right, and let expediency take care of itself. This has been demonstrated within two hours in this Convention. Let us shape our course, then, in accordance with the dictates of truth and justice, and not of expediency. If we adopt the amendment of the gentleman from Henry, the Democratic party will undoubtedly array itself against us, and make use of the question as a party issue. If we defeat it, that party will equally array itself against us, and they will say "you call yourselves the Republican party, in all the elections you profess great sympathy for the rights of your downtrodden brethren, but when you come into a convention for the purpose of forming a constitution which will secure equal rights to all mankind, you back out of your position, you do not carry out the principles you profess, and you are therefore hypocrites."

I say to gentlemen, let us show by our actions that we mean what we say. Now, gentlemen rise here and ask what shall we do? Shall we abandon principle and be governed by what we deem to be a question of expediency, or shall we stand by those principles and let popularity take care of itself? I am in favor of standing up to principles, and that conclusion leads me to another inquiry.

What is right upon this question?

I have listened with a great deal of attention to the arguments that have been adduced against this amendment, and to my mind I have not found one valid objection against it. In the first place, I ask gentlemen to tell me upon principle, why the colored man should be singled out above all other men, and why he should be made the exception to the general rule, that allows any other man to testify in the courts of justice in this State, and permits his credibility to go to the jury for what it is worth. I, for one, am opposed to the principle which I have seen manifested here—one which grated harshly upon my feelings—and it is that feeling of revenge, hatred and malice, which is shown by a certain class of men here against a man because he is colored. When they have exhausted all their arguments against this proposed amendment they wind up with—"why he is a nigger."

I suppose the Great Father of all mankind created the colored as well as the white man.—The very first principles laid down in our Bill of Rights recognizes the rights of the colored man just as much as they do those of the white man. It does not say that all white men are endowed by their Creator with certain unalienble rights, &c. Will we be consistent in carrying out that principle in the Bill of Rights, or will we adopt a principle that will give the lie to it?

I am one of those, although I have never been an Abolitionist, who believe that the negro by nature is just as good as the white man. It is true, that we find that the negro in this country, as a general thing, is degraded, but I think I can show from the history of the country that that degredation is owing, not to any defect in his nature, but to the unnatural position which, through generations the negro race has been compelled to occupy in the world. If I understand the history of the world, there was a time when this same race was on a level with the rest of mankind, and when, in fact, they excelled in the arts and sciences. For some reasons, after this period, the Christian world became the vultures that preyed upon the flesh and sinews of this race of people, and traders repaired to the coast of Africa, and with their gold and silver stirred up the different tribes to intestine wars, for the purpose of securing captives—and this has gone on from generation to generation, so that, with all the demoralizing influences exerted by such a system as that of the slave trade, it is no wonder that you find the African the ignorant and degraded being that he is. But you may take the history of any other people in the world where they have been oppressed and ground down for ages, and you will find that the same results will follow. If you look to Holy Writ, for example, you will find that the Israelites, who were once God's chosen people, known throughout the world at one time for their intelligence and enterprise, and for all that makes a race noble and elevated, after they had been carried into captivity, and were again restored, were perhaps, the most ignorant and degraded people upon God's earth. Look, for example to Greece, the nurse of the arts and sciences. Even in our boasted day of progress and refinement, we have not been able to reach the wonderful perfection in the arts and sciences to which she attained. But where is she now, and in what condition are her people? We find that disaster overtook that fair land; that her people were conquered and subdued; led into captivity and held in bondage generation after generation, until now they have become vicious, barbarous and degraded. From these examples, and others which might be adduced, if I had time, it is evident to my mind that the degradation of the negro is not owing to his color, but to the unnatural position which he occupies in our country.

The question arises here now, whether we, who profess to be free, and declare that all men are created free and equal, shall extend freedom to this down-trodden class among us, or whether we shall help to crush out the last lingering, remaining principle of intelligence and integrity, which now remains in their bosoms, whether we shall join hands with the oppressor of our fellow men, or whether we as men shall imitate and copy the example set us by our ancestors. It strikes me, that any man when he reflects upon this question for a moment, will not hesitate as to the course he should pursue, if he is governed by principle and rises superior to all prejudice and party considerations.

While we cast reproaches and stigmas upon the black man, we ourselves are slaves to the very worst principles that ever emanated from the breast of man; slaves to a preducice unfounded in principle, and unfounded in reality except from the fact of its growing out of the unnatural position in which we find a certain class of men. Is this the right and manly course for freemen engaged in a holy cause for the emancipation of the whole human family.

Some of my friends upon the other side are struck with horror at the idea of allowing a negro to testify in a court of justice. I am surprised to see manifested here, a feeling that does not exist in any other part of the world, not even in some of the slave States. I am surprised to see that prejudice exhibited by gentlemen, against color that does not exist elsewhere, Go into the Southern States, where slavery exists in all its force, and you do not find this prejudice existing against color, but you find that an amalgamating and an unmistakable bleaching process is going on there. If my recollection does not prove treacherous as to his history, I think that if a former Democratic Vice President of the United States, were here to day he would hiss down with scorn and contempt the feeling against the African race that is manifested by some members of this body, because he reared a family, the offspring of a black woman, whom he took to Washington with him, when he was acting as Vice President.

Mr. GILLASPY. Do you endorse the action of that gentleman?

Mr. CLARKE. No, neither do I condemn him.

Mr. GILLASPY. I do.

Mr. CLARKE. You have a right to do so. I challenge the gentleman to give a reason upon which he is authorized to condemn it. If you travel into Europe, you will find that prejudice against color does not exist there. A man is there weighed by the position he occupies in society, by his moral worth, and not by the color of his skin. A few years ago, in France, so the current history goes, when Louis Philippe was on the throne, at an exhibition for prizes at a College where a son of his was a student, a full-blooded negro received the first honors of his class, and carried off the palm of the day. How was Douglass received in Europe—I do not mean Steven A., but Fred. Douglass! With open arms and a most cordial welcome, and he was universally respected and admired for his moral and intellectual worth.

Let us come back for a moment to our own country, and let us take the question as we find it presented here. I was born and reared in a State which was once a slave holding State—New York. If I am not greatly mistaken, they have never had any thing upon their statute book which prevented a colored man from giving his testimony in courts of justice. I am informed that none of the slave-holding States ever had such a law upon their statute books. New York is an old State, and I would ask gentlemen if any inconvenience has been experienced there from allowing colored persons to testify? If there were any evil resulting from such a course, it would be felt in a State where slavery had once existed and perished, leaving the victims of that cruel institution among the people. Look at the State of Illinois. She once had a black code, but the intelligence of the age has swept it away. I say to gentlemen on the other side, if they undertake to thrust this principle upon us as a party issue, I shall not shrink from it. They are behind the age in which they live, if they think that in this enlightened State of Iowa they can make capital out of that issue. I do not wish to make party issues here, and since I have been in this Convention I have been very cautious in the remarks I have made to prevent such a result. But if this issue is to be thrust upon us, if it is the design of gentle men on the other side to compel us to make this issue, I say, let us take it, and meet it openly and boldly, and if they can make capital out of it, they are welcome to it with compound interest. Then the question arises, is it our duty as members of this Convention to adopt this principle in our Constitution? We are told that there is no necessity for it. Can gentlemen prove that this is the case? What have we upon our statute book in relation to this subject:

"Every human being of sufficient capacity to understand the allegation of an oath, is a competent witness in all cases, both civil and criminal, except as herein otherwise declared. But an Indian, a negro, mulatto or black person, shall not be allowed to give testimony in any case wherein a white person is a party."

Those who are opposed to the amendment now under consideration, claim the right to have the Constitution remain precisely where it was when this law was passed. They say if the good sense of the people require that the law shall be modified, or if they require it as it now stands, that they will so make it. The same argument if carried out, would strike directly against the provision, that declares all men are created free and equal, and endowed with certain unalienable rights &c., and it would strike out every section in the Bill of Rights and our Canstitution, and we would leave the laws of our State in the hands of our Legislature, without any safe-guard thrown around the individual liberties of man. I am unwilling, for one, to adopt this principle. I believe it is our duty in making a Constitution which is to be the foundation of all our laws, to frame it in such a manner as to protect the rights of every human being, the negro as well as the white man.

I was a little surprised at another remark made by gentlemen in opposition to the amendment. They ask this Convention if they are willing, by permitting a negro to give his testimony in the courts to place him upon a level with the white man. I tell gentlemen that governed by the law of human kindnees, and actuated by a desire to discharge our duties to the best of our ability, we should endeavor, as far as in us lies, to raise the negro up to a level with ourselves. What is it that makes the great mass of American citizens so much more enterprising and intelligent than the laboring classes in Europe? It is the stimulant held out to them by the character of our institutions. The door is thrown wide open to all, and even the poorest and humblest in the land may, by industry and application, attain a position which will entitle him to the respect and confidence of his fellow-men. This is the sole cause of the difference between the great mass of our fellow-citizens and those of European countries; and we are in duty bound to extend to a certain extent at least that same fostering care to the unfortunate black man. I will not put this question upon the ground that it is for the benefit of the white man, although it will undoubtedly prove so. It will work for the benefit of the white man in two senses, one suggested by the gentleman from Johnson, [Mr. Clarke,] and in still another. The negro is an inhabitant of this State. We have not the power to disfranchise and expel him from the State. Is it for the interests of the white man to pass laws which shall forever shut the door against him and deprive him of the chance of rising in the social scale, or is it for our interests to remove the restrictions within which he is confined, and allow him within safe and proper guards, to assume the position of a man among his fellow-men?

Again, the passage of such a provision as this is an imperative duty which the colored man has a right to demand at our hands. I ask gentlemen by what principle of justice, law and reason, they can come into this Convention and ask us to refuse placing in the constitution a provision guaranteeing to the colored man the right of giving his testimony in courts of justice, when they claim that right for the foreigner. Bear in mind that these unfortunate colored men are citizens by nature and by those immutable and eternal laws of right which override all human legislation.

Again I ask what right have we to so shape our constitution that our Legislative bodies may pass a law which will disregard the constitution of the United States. There is a provision in the constitution of the United States which guarantees in the first place that each State shall have the right to declare for itself who shall or shall not be citizens. That right the State detains in its hands. When the States assembled in Convention to form a constitution they never surrendered their right, and in the exercise of that right there are several States of this Union that recognize colored men as citizens. Now the constitution of the United States under which we now live, says that the rights and immunities of the citizens of the several States shall be secured in all the States. If that be the case, I ask you what right we have as a Convention sitting here to form a constitution, to deny that the Legislature may pass a law disfranchising the colored citizens of New York or Massachusetts, and thereby violate the constitution of the United States.

Mr. HARRIS. I rise to a question of order, and it is this, that the gentleman is discussing the question of franchise, a subject which is not now before the Convention.

The PRESIDENT. That is a matter for the Convention to determine. The Chair is of the opinion that the gentleman from Alamakee, [Mr. Clark,] is in order.

Mr. CLARK, resuming. I ask gentlemen to pause and seriously consider whether they are willing to leave this an open question? Are they willing to leave it in such a shape that our Legislative bodies may pass a law that shall violate the constitution of the United States, and disfranchise the citizens of other States, who have a right to come here and claim the privileges of citizens. When gentlemen talk here about discouraging the emigration of colored men to this State, what do they mean? Do they mean to be understood as avowing the principle that they design to make laws that will prevent them from coming here? They have no right to make such laws, for the constitution of the United States secures to colored citizens who may be citizens sf other States, the right to come here and demand at our hands all the privileges and immunities which are guaranteed to the citizens of the State. Will they in the face of that principle say that they are in favor of enacting laws that will exclude from this State colored men? I am not in favor as an individual of the emigration of blacks to this State, and I am opposed to it so far as I can do so legitimately and properly. The question is not whether we can or will exclude them, but it is whether we will obey the principles contained in the constitution of the United States, and extend to this people the right to come here, and recognize as belonging to him those immutable privileges, which the very first clause in the Bill of Rights declares in broad terms is guaranteed to them.

The challenge has been thrown out by the other side, that if we adopt this provision they will make it a political question. It is already a political question outside of the Convention, and I have no doubt, from what has been said here to-day, that it will be made a political contest when the question of the adoption of this constitution is submitted to the people. A republican legislature has endorsed this principle. Now I ask gentlemen, as the question is now before the Convention, shall we as a republican majority sustain the principle which we in our hearts endorse, or shall we refuse to support it simply because we do not deem it expedient to incorporate it into the constitution? What will be the effect of such a course upon the politics of the State, and what will be the argument used by the members of the other party, who are always ingenious in new devices and inventions? If we reject this proposition they will say that although the Legislature, in their wisdom and integrity, carried out the principle which we believed, that we played the hypocrite by shrinking our duty in this respect, leaving the Legislature to look out for themselves. It is not a party question in its legitimate sense, and it can only become so by parties traveling out of their duty as American citizens. If the Democratic party are willing as a party to array themselves against this principle—which has been a democratic principle from the days of Jefferson to 1854—let them do it. I challenge them to do it if they dare, and I will meet them upon that issue.

I wish to say once more that we live in a progressive age. In other States where this same question has been under consideration, they have adopted the principle now opposed by gentlemen on the other side, and even in the States where they had "Black Laws," the people have risen in their majesty, and through their Legislatures, have expunged them from statute books: and this has been done by democratic majorities. I ask the members of that party here who threaten to make this a party question by what right they assume to change democratic principles, and demand that men shall wheel into the ranks and quietly submit to disown a principle which was so long sanctioned by their party. If gentlemen want to try another experiment upon the same principle they adopted and carried out in the Kansas and Nebraska bill they will never have a better chance than the present. I shall vote for the amendment as it is now submitted to the Convention.

Mr. WILSON. I desire to say a few words which I deem necessary after the speeches made here this morning, and which have gone upon the record. I regret that the gentleman from Wapello, [Mr. Gillaspy,] has endeavored to give the character to our discussions that he has. I thought there was dignity enough in this body to forbid anything of the kind. I regret to hear any gentleman use the phrases upon this floor that that gentleman used. It reminded me of boys with chips on their shoulders, daring each other to knock them off. I thought we were here to discuss and consider principles of constitutional law and government. And yet he gets up here and talks about "the gentleman from Jefferson trembling in his boots." And he says that if this amendment is incorporated into the constitution he will go before his constituency with it and get a thousand majority against the constitution. Now if the gentlemen is satisfied that he can raise a thousand majority in Wapello county against this constitution if this provision is incorporated in it, then, in that case, he can put his mind at rest concerning his county, and come over to Jefferson county and see what kind of a majority he can raise against it there. And I now invite him, if this amendment is incorporated into the counstitution, to come into Jefferson county and work against it. I will guarantee that he shall be well taken care of, and we will then see, to use his own elegant language, who will "tremble in his boots."

I have already given my reasons for voting against this amendment. I have said that the position of both of the candidates for seats in this Convention in my county was, that so far as the races are concerned, we would permit the present constitution to remain as it is. And I gave an additional reason for voting against it, which I think should have force upon the minds of some gentlemen here. I said that I opposed the amendment upon the same ground that the gentleman from Henry, [Mr. Clarke,] seeks to enforce it, and that is that it creates the very distinction with respect to the races, that the gentleman seeks to obviate by its adoption. I hope that I am understood, and that no gentleman will again attempt to dragoon me into measures which may result in the defeat of the constitution. I do not care whether the constitution results in benefit to the republican or the democratic party, or whether it injures both parties. All I ask is that the constitution we may adopt here and send to the people shall be one that shall advance the best interests of the State to the greatest degree. That is all I ask, and I do hope that we will not draw party lines and make party issues in connection with this constitution. But if party issues are forced upon us, and this provision is incorporated into the constitution, and in that shape is sent to the people, I guarantee to the gentleman from Wapello that Jefferson county will give a majority in favor of the constitution, if it contains no worse provision.

Mr. GIBSON. I have thus far said nothing upon this subject, and I do not now propose to discuss it at any length. I regret exceedingly that this discussion has taken the range it has. I do not like to see the time of the Convention consumed in such a manner. We have been engaged nearly a week upon this one question.—I supposed it would have been settled this morning. But it seems that the gentleman from Henry [Mr. Clarke] has brought forward the same subject again in such a form as, under our rules, allows him to do so, and the same discussion is continued, so far as I can judge, that arose upon the proposition we voted down this morning. I regret that this has been done, but as it is so, I would say a few words in relation to the subject.

There was a large majority in the district I have the honor to represent here, who voted against the call of this Convention, and they did so for the very reason that they believed this very question would be brought up; they feared that party issues and lines would be raised or drawn, and the whole object of the Convention be thus defeated. Every gentleman here is aware of the fact that this whole State has for the last year or two been in a condition of political excitement; that political influences have been operating to secure certain results. The whole political world has been, and is, as it were, completely upturned. This being the case, a large majority of my district, at least three to one, voted against calling this Convention, not because they desired no change in our Constitution, but because they feared the course that would be pursued here. There are amendments that can be made to this Constitution that they consider right and absolutely necessary. But they feared the very crisis we have now reached would take place in this Convention, and thereupon they voted against it. Rather than have such a state of things they preferred to let the Constitution remain as it was.

I do not stand here, Mr President, as the representative of a mere party. It is true my political views and opinions are well known, and I am not ashamed of them. I act with the great Democratic party when they act rightly, and I think that is pretty generally. But there was no political issue raised in the election, and I had no formidable opposition for the seat I now have the honor to occupy. Whether that fact is to be regarded as a compliment to myself, I cannot say. I have therefore full liberty to express my views as suits myself upon what I conceive to be right.

I am opposed to the amendment of the gentleman from Henry. I am opposed to anything that seeks the objects which I believe this amendment is intended to accomplish. My constituents are opposed to it, and I believe the Republicans in my district are opposed to it. I was in the town of Knoxville in my district when information reached there of the passage by the late Republican Legislature, of the bill giving to negroes, mulattoes and Indians the right to testify in our courts, and the universal expression of opinion from all parties, without distinction, was that it would never do. The strongest Republicans in Marion county, those who stood front in the ranks of the party, were opposed to the bill, and said that such a measure would sink the Republican party into oblivion. I make these few remarks that I may stand right upon the record. I am opposed to the amendment and shall vote against it.

Mr. GILLASPY. I desire to state here to this Convention that in anything I have said upon this floor, I have not intended to convey any impression but of the very kindest feelings towards every member of this body. I do not intend that any man shall surpass me in kindness and liberality, for I consider that the highest trait of a gentleman.

Now I would say to the gentleman from Jefferson [Mr. Wilson] that as he thinks everything will be right in his county even if this amendment should be incorporated in the Constitution, if he will come up to Wapello county we will give him a hearty reception, and he may try what he can accomplish there. I have no desire to go to Jefferson county, as I believe there are enough there to take care of this question. But I would say another thing to the gentleman from Jefferson, and that is that he was the first upon this floor who insinuated that party lines were sought to be drawn here. And he sought to convey the impression that that was being done by myself. Now all I said was that as one individual I wanted the party lines to be drawn when the vote came to be taken upon this question. Now, I know that some of my Republican friends have been somewhat refractory upon this subject, and are unwilling to take the position occupied by the gentleman from Henry [Mr. Clarke], and I know also that gentlemen of the Republican party have been outside of this Convention and have called upon the citizens of Iowa City to endeaver to whip the members of that party into the traces in order that the party lines might be drawn here. Now is there anything unusual or surprising that knowing this as I do, I should say that so far as I was concerned, I was willing to see those party lines drawn here?

I come here as the Representative of a people who desire but one or two changes in the present Constitution, and with those changes I desire to see it adopted by the people at large.—And I think if the Constitution is changed in but two particulars it will meet with but little opposition. I want to see the old provision in relation to banking thrown out and another put in its place; I want a provision that the judges of the supreme court shall be elected by the people. What is all that I o r my constituents desire.

Now I would ask the gentlemen of the Republican party, if they desire to incorporate into this Constitution the new issue raised by the action of the late legislature, when it must do one of two things; either thwart the will of the people or defeat the Constitution? I hope they will not desire any such result as that. I hope they will consent to leave this subject to the legislature. Now to my mind I think if this provision is placed in the Constitution, it will defeat it. The people have not desired this matter to be incorporated here, though in the part of the state from which I came, we charged the doctrine upon the Republican party, and as the gentleman from Marion [Mr. Gibson] says, they denied it, and said it was not a principle in the great Republican party. Now I hope gentlemen will not put this provision in the Constitution until the people of the State of Iowa have spoken for or against it. I hope we will not hazard this Constitution which the people are looking to us to form for them. I hope we will form such a Constitution as in the language of a member of Congress from this district "will do them proud to adopt." I trust this matter will be kept out of this Constitution, and that it will be left to the Democratic and the Republican parties to decide outside of this Convention, and to the legislature to treat as they may see proper.

Mr. CLARKE, of Johnson. I have no desire to prolong this discussion, and as it is a question affecting human rights, I should be contented with what I have already said, and and give now a silent vote. But as a member of the Republican party, and having my views of the doctrines of that party, I desire to say that I should consider myself false to the principles of that party if I did not vote in favor of the proposition now before us. I wish to say in the outset that so far I have given no vote and spoken no word from mere party considerations, and I expect the time will come during the session of this Convention when I, and perhaps every other member of this Convention will be called upon from convictions of duty, to vote differently from what a majority of their political friends may do.

I understand that there is one principle which is the basis and foundation of the Republican party, a principle which commends itself to every mind, and without that principle that party would never obtain my sanction and support. I believe that principle to be one that is incorporated into the Declaration of Independence, that all men are created free and equal; that all men have the same natural rights. That I understand to be the fundamental principle of the Republican party, the foundation stone upon which the party rests; without that foundation stone I believe the party would have no basis whatever. Now what is the proposition of the gentleman from Henry [Mr. Clarke]? It is to incorporate into our Constitution that principle virtually to which I have alluded. It is to say that no man, whatever may be his complexion, wherever may be his birthplace, whatever may be his political views, shall be rendered incompetent to testify because of that complexion or those views.

That is the plain proposition, and I ask the republican members at heart, of this Convention, if that is not the foundation stone of the party to which they belong? If it is not then I am mistaken in the doctrines and positions of the republican party, and when I am convinced of that then I for one shall have to seek other associations and other companions in political life. But this is my view of it.

Under our present Constitution, this right is not secured to every human being in the State. The gentleman from Jefferson [Mr. Wilson] says that under our present Constitution this right cannot be taken from the people, and yet by a solemn decision of the Supreme Court, the highest court in this State, it has been decided that the negro cannot testify, that the law as it then stood, was so framed that a negro cannot testify, even though placed upon the stand as a witness for a white man against a negro. Now, I say, standing here as I do, in a Convention assembled for the purpose of defining and establishing natural rights, that it is our duty to act upon this question. I take issue with the gentleman from Wappello, [Mr. Gillaspy] who says that he is here only to represent the white people of the State of Iowa. Now I stand here as a delegate to represent, not the white people of Iowa City, not the Republican party alone who elected me, but as the representative of my district, and of every human being in it. I should be false to my feelings, false to my party and false to my God, if I consented to have the franchises of the meanest or weakest of God's creatures denied. I understand my position here to be a higher and nobler one than merely to represent one class or sect, or one complexion, to the exclusion of any other portion of God's creation within our boundaries. We are making a Constitution here, not alone for the government of the white people of Iowa, but to govern all in our community, of all different complexions, climes and nativities. We stand here, not to provide protection for the strong alone, but for all alike. Entertaining this view of our duties here, I would appeal to gentlemen to lay aside all their prejudices. They will excuse me I trust, when I say that their arguments against this proposition, have been based entirely, not upon moral, political and natural rights, but upon prejudice; and they will excuse me, if I say further, that such arguments are, in my judgment, to say the least of it not becoming this age and generation.

Now, occupying the position I have indicated, and in the present uncertain state of the law upon this subject, I am unwilling to take the position of the gentleman from Jefferson (Mr. Wilson) and say that I will leave it to another tribunal to be decided upon—another field of contest. It is not our place to leave questions of natural rights to be fought out in a political conflict in which at one time, the one side, and at another time, the other side will have the ascendency, and in which these natural rights of men are bandied about like foot-balls among boys. This is the place, and now is the time to meet this issue and to decide this question, and for one I am glad this discussion has arisen and progressed thus far. I am glad that our reporters here are taking down the words and principles, and declarations of the members of this Convention. I, for one, am willing to have these speeches go before the people, and depend upon them for my justification for the votes I may give here.

It is true that in the present case, a Republican Legislature have passed an act settling this question, so far as they can settle it. But while that is true, it is also true that one of the great political parties in this State have arrayed themselves in direct opposition to that act; they do not consider the right there bestowed, as a right of a certain class of the population; they go back behind the doctrine of mere legislation; they go back to natural rights and natural capacities, and declare that the negro is so dishonest, so destitute of integrity by nature, that he is not competent to be admitted to testify in this State, although the interests of the white population may require it. In this state of things, another conflict may strike down this law, and in that conflict, this question will not be brought into direct issue; this is not one of the questions that are made a direct issue. The conflict is decided upon other issues, and upon those the party opposed to this act may obtain a majority in our General Assembly, and then this law will be repealed.

Now I want to come to a practical proposition. Suppose that this law should remain in force for two or three years, and then a Democratic Legislature should be elected? What will be the result? Men will have acted under this law, negroes will have witnessed agreements and contracts, have been present at the making of contracts. If this law is then repealed, every man upon this floor may have his rights, his home, his very hearthstone placed in jeopardy, by such repeal. Now I am unwilling to bring such a state of things upon this State. If it is right to have this privilege conferred upon a class by a law, then let us put it in here, and have no question about it presented to the people to divide them. It is upon conviction as a matter of duty that I am in favor of this proposition. I am convinced that it is required by the beaming intelligence and onward progress of the age. Whenever this battle has been fought in any State the intelligence and virtue of the people have stricken down these men of prejudice and class proscription.

We are not here merely to legislate. We are sitting here as a convention assembled to make a constitution. If we are men of like intelligence and virtue with those who preceded us in forming a constitution, we should seek to secure in this constitution something that the people had not secured to them before. The gentleman from Des Moines [Mr. Hall] says that we have had two conventions in this State for the formation of a constitution, and in neither of those conventions was this question raised. That is true. I do not want to make party speeches, or arraign men here as partizans. But it is a notorious fact that in the days of those conventions, the Democratic party was the party of equal rights, and not a party of class legislation and prejudice; and that was the reason, perhaps, why this question was not raised in those conventions. But there has been, not a progress, but a going backward in the position of this party during the last five years. It was formerly a party with "free trade and sailors' rights" inscribed upon their banners. And if there was any one thing about the Democratic party of which I was proud, although I was opposed to the party, it was that it had emblazoned upon its flag "equal rights to all." But during the last five years that principle has been stricken down; this motto has been erased from its escutcheon, and therefore it is necessary for this question to be raised at this time. But we are told that this provision will demoralize the people; and the gentlemnn from Wapello (Mr. Gillaspy) threatens that if this provision is inserted in here, this constitution will be defeated before the people. Now let me say to that gentleman, that the first question with me here, is not whether the people will approve or disapprove of my work. The first question is, what are my convictions of right and justice towards my fellow men; and under those convictions I intend to vote, and after my votes have been given, and the constitution has been submitted to the people, should they disapprove of it, I will at least have the consciousness that I have done my duty in the sight of heaven.

But I have no fear of the defeat of this constitution. And I tell gentlemen now, plainly, that if the mode of argument used before the people is the same as that assumed here to-day, the Republican party, or the champions of this question, have nothing to fear from the result. I am willing to go before the people upon this question, and appeal to their virtue and natural sense of justice, and their intelligence, and in that contest I have no fear of the result. I think, and honestly, too, that if this provision is not put in here, there is greater danger of the defeat of this constitution, than there would be if it be placed here. I believe the people are marching onward, and progressing upon this doctrine of human rights, as well as upon other questions. And in this christian age, I believe now is the time to meet this question, not—as the gentleman from Wapello insinuates almost every time he gets the floor—for the purpose of dragging down the white man to the level of the negro, but to lift up those who are below us. And that, I have always been taught to believe was one of the noblest doctrines of God and man.

I am in favor of lifting up, not the black man alone, but every man who, by misfortune or misconduct, has fallen below that standard of virtue and morality which should be the standard of every man.

Let us look at this matter as a practical matter. Let the law stand as it now stands; let the constitution be uncertain as to what are the rights of any portion of the population of the State of Iowa, and what will be the result? We are not called upon to act for those who may come hereafter; to hold out inducements for blacks to come here, but to act for those who are now here and hold property, and have a right to be heard in this chamber. And yet, what are we asked to do? To throw around them a bond of slavery infinitely worse that the bonds which bind men in the Southern States. And I would make another statement. I believe I am correct in saying that in some of the Southern States of this Union, even slaves have been permitted to testify, and who has ever been injured by it?

All men who have ever investigated this subject, concede that integrity is one of the traits of the negro character—they are ranked high in that regard by every man who has made him his particular study. It is said that they are not to be trusted like other men. I say that as a race they stand for integrity as high as any other class of people. If they did not possess natural integrity of heart, slavery could not exist in this country at all. In the South the masters trust everything to their slaves—their lives are in their hands—and they trust them because of their conviction of the integrity of the negro. Compared with other slaves, taking into consideration their degraded condition, larceny and other crimes are less frequent there than in our own free and enlightened State.

I wish to call the attention of my Republican friends to this position. I say we are in danger of losing all the moral influence of the Republican party, unless we take a high and noble stand upon this question. It goes back to the very first principle—that of equal rights and civil liberty—and I ask them, I appeal to them, that upon this question which I must regard as a very important one, they will so act that the Republican party shall stand before the people upon high moral grounds. I, for one, mean by every vote I shall give, to endeavor to obtain for them that position, and if stricken down here, I will at least attempt to justify that position before the people of my district and of this State.

On motion of Mr. WARREN the Convention then took a recess until 2 o'clock, P. M.

EVENING SESSION.

At 2 o'clock, P. M., the Convention re-assembled, and was called to order by the President.

The CONVENTION resumed the consideration of the report of the Committee of the Whole on the report of the Committee on the Preamble and Bill of Rights.

The PRESIDENT stated the question to be on the amendment of Mr. Clarke, of Henry.

Mr. PETERS. It is with no desire to prolong this discussion that I rise to address the Convention at this time. I have been influenced by the contrary feeling, and that has led me to keep my seat during the long debate we have had in relation to this subject. I was in hopes that gentlemen would get through with what they might have to say, and that we could come to some final action that should wear, at least, the appearance of progress.

But I know that there has been a petition presented here from citizens of Delaware county, and I desire to correct any misapprehensions that may be entertained in regard to it.

Some time ago there was a suit in my district in which I was engaged as prosecutor, against two white men and one negro. The negro we succeeded in convicting of, and punishing for larceny. The white men, however, escaped, in consequence of the fact that, under the Code, we could not introduce the evidence of the negro against his accomplices in the transaction This matter created some excitement in the place, and a petition was talked of, and finally got up, to ask the Legislature to so change the statute as to allow negroes the right to be heard as witnesses in our courts of justice. At the time this movement was on foot, during the session of the General Assembly, there were two petitions circulated, and some man, before the petition was sent down to this body, saw upon it the names of five or six men, who afterwards told him they signed that petition supposing it was addressed to the General Assembly, and not to this body. From the general impression which I have received from my conversation with different persons in my district, in relation to this matter, I am satisfied that the men who signed that petition, or at least those belonging to the Democratic party, did not intend to petition for any alteration in the constitution of this State, so as to allow negroes the rights of citizenship, but supposed they were petitioning the Legislature in relation to the statute upon the subject of testimony.

Now the amendment offered here, I understand, will have the effect, not only to give negroes the right to testify, but also give him every right of citizenship which a white man enjoys in this State, while the arguments brought forward here all seem to be directed to the sole object of allowing nogroes to testify in courts of justice.

Mr. CLARKE, of Henry. Does the gentleman from Delaware [Mr. Peters] understand the amendment as going further than to allow negroes to testify?

Mr. PETERS. Most certainly I do.

Mr. CLARKE, of Henry. It certainly is not intended for any such object. The section, as it now stands, reads as follows:

"No religious test shall be required as a qualification for any office or public trust; and no person shall be deprived of any of his rights, privileges or capacities, or disqualified from the performance of his public or private duties, or rendered incompetent to give evidence in any court of law or equity in consequence of his opinions on the subject of religion."

Now I propose to amend by adding—

"Nor shall any person be rendered or held thus incompetent to give testimony in consequence of his or her belonging to any particular sect, class, society or party."

My amendment relates only to the giving of testimony; nothing else.

Mr. PETERS. I have not changed my opinion upon hearing the amendment read again. At all events I can put no other construction upon it than I did, and do not see what other construction can be put upon it. Be that as it may, however, in the debates upon this subject, I have heard no man argue that the present law was unconstitutional. That law, passed by the late legislature, gives to negroes the right to testify in our courts of justice, and I believe without any qualification. Now, if we are to put this clause in this constitution, by which the legislature is required to put every man upon the same footing, I see no reason why the negro should be placed in any higher position than foreigners and others. So long as the constitution now allows the negro to give testimony, I see no good reason to alter it, and give him more privileges, or make the provision more explicit or clear than it already is.

I trust that the debate upon this subject has already gone as far as it will go: it has certainly gone as far as it should go, I think. I hope the old constitution in this respect will be adhered to.

Mr. BUNKER. The gentleman who has just taken his seat (Mr. Peters) has argued to show that the present constitution confers the right upon all classes in this State to give testimony. I cannot see then, that this amendment can do any harm if his position be true.

I was led myself to believe, upon looking over this constitution, it was all that was necessary. We have, in the first section of the bill of rights, declared that "all men are, by nature, free and independent," and have the right to acquire and defend property, and to pursue and obtain safety and happiness. Now, if that declaration be true, I do not see that this amendment can do anything more than to make a practical use of what we have already declared to be the fact. But it would appear that a necessity for this amendment of the present constitution grows out of the fact, that notwithstanding this constitution protects the rights and property of every human being in the State, yet former legislatures have disregarded that provision of the constitution, and the courts have sustained them in doing so, and the testimony of a certain class has been ruled out of our halls of justice, on account of their constituting such class. I regard this, therefore, as pre-eminently a practical question.

Now this amendment seems to be argued upon the one side as if it was inviting into our State somebody different from those that are already here; some Hottentot from Africa, or something of that kind. I do not understand it in any such light. I take it to mean, that the present inhabitants of Iowa, or those who may hereafter become inhabitants of this State, shall be protected in their rights, and be allowed to go into our courts, and by their evidence obtain protection for their persons and property against wrongs that may be committed against them by other persons. Hence I regard this, as I said before, as pre-eminently a practical question, and one which is worthy of our consideration.

I recollect a case in the State of Indiana, where I came from, that a question came up involving principles very similar to this one, and where it was supposed that the provisions of the constitution were amply sufficient, and that every person in the State was abundantly protected, let their opinions upon the subject of religion be what they might. A notorious scoundrel, counterfeiter and forger, of the name of McCracken, was brought up in one of the courts for forgery. The only witness, upon whose testimony it was possible to convict him, was a man of unimpeachable character, and one who stood high in the community. But, unfortunately, owing, perhaps, to the inconsistencies he saw, or conceived he saw in the religious world, he had become a confirmed atheist. And under this constitution, the judge decided, when he was brought up to testify, that, notwithstanding the provisions of the constitution of the State upon the subject, inasmuch as that constitution required an oath of the most solemn appeal to Almighty God, there would be an inconsistency in the man taking that oath, when he did not believe in a God. This witness was questioned as to his views of a God. He said he did not know whether there was one or not; there might and there might not be a God. He was then questioned in regard to his belief in a future punishment. He replied that he knew nothing about it; there might and might not be a place of future punishment. But when questioned as to whether perjury should be punished, he answered promptly, that it should be. And yet his testimony was ruled out, and in consequence one of the most notorious scoundrels went unwhipped of justice. I heard afterwards that he had been arrested in some other State, where he paid the penalty of his crimes. This matter caused a general excitement throughout the State, and at the next session of the legislature the member for the county in which I resided introduced a bill by which the construction placed upon the constitution, concerning that matter, was done away with, and every man was to be allowed to come into court and testify. An excitement was got up in certain sections of that county, and at the next election that member was set aside, because he went for that law. This was twenty-five years ago. But at this time, in that State, under their present constitution, all cases of this kind that can occur are abundantly provided for.

Now I believe that the convention that framed our present constitution, considered that they had met every point in which a human being could be outraged, whether in his person or his property, and that they had provided for his going into court and obtain his remedy. And yet the legislature passed a law disqualifying one whole class from going into court and testifying, and hence the necessity for this provision, to make secure what the delegates, who framed the present constitution, believed they had secured.

Methinks, Mr. President, I can see the shade of Jefferson standing by your side, with one hand resting upon the shoulder of his grand-child, and the other holding the Declaration of Independence, from which he reads to his democratic followers the declaration: "We hold these truths to be self-evident that all men are created free and equal." He turns and points to his great grand child; it is true there is blood upon her bosom, and her hair is dishevelled; and he says to his professed followers here, "This is my grand-child, the fruit of my loins; she was met in the streets by a demon in the form of a white man who violated her person, and rendered her miserable and an outcast forever. Will you give her the protection she is entitled to by all the laws of right and justice? Will you, who claim to be the defenders of the doctrines which I have laid down here, will you come up here and, by your action in this convention, prevent the possibility in the future of this my own child being prevented from going into a court of justice, and claiming its protection against her chastity being outraged by any one with impunity?" And what will they, who look up to this apostle of liberty as the founder and exponent of their party and creed say to this appeal? Let their acts here proclaim to the world that they at least live up to the creed they profess.

Mr. CLARKE, of Henry. Whatever may be the fate of the amendment I have offered, I shall never regret having submitted it. The speeches made this morning by the gentleman from Alamakee, [Mr. Clark,] and the gentleman from Johnson, [Mr. Clarke,] should certainly compensate us for all the time that has been expended in the discussion of this question. But knowing that there is a desire among members to look into this subject a little farther, to look at its legal effect, perhaps its political effect—I will submit the motion that the further consideration of this section be postponed for the present, and that we proceed with other sections of the Bill of Rights.

The PRESIDENT. The gentleman can perhaps attain his object equally as well by withdrawing his amendment for the present, with the understanding that he will be allowed to offer it again at some other time.

Mr. CLARKE, of Henry. With that understanding I will ask leave to withdraw my amendment.

The question being taken upon granting leave to withdraw the amendment under consideration, it was not agreed to.

Mr. CLARKE of Henry. I now renew my motion to postpone the further consideration of this section and the pending amendment for the present.

Mr. JOHNSTON. I have taken no part whatever in this protracted discussion, but have sat patiently and listened to, and have been very much entertained and instructed by what I have heard. But I do hope that the Convention will not now postpone this matter. We have had it thoroughly discussed in Committee of the Whole, and also in Convention, nearly every member upon either side having made speeches thereon. We have sat here now two weeks, nearly three, and we have progressed as far as the fourth section of the Bill of Rights, the first article in the constitution. Now I see no reason why every member upon this floor should not have his mind made up upon this subject. I am ready myself to vote upon this question; I presume, Mr. President, you are ready to vote upon it, and every gentleman who has spoken upon it has announced his readiness to vote, and how he will vote. I know the question is an important one; but it has been ably and thoroughly discussed, and I trust the vote upon it will be taken now.

The question was then taken by yeas and nays upon postponing the further consideration, for the present, of section four of the Bill of Rights, and the amendment thereto offered by Mr. Clarke of Henry, and it was agreed to, yeas 18, nays 14, as follows:

Yeas—The President; Messrs. Bunker, Clark of Alamakee, Clarke of Henry, Clarke of Johnson, Edwards, Ells, Gower, Gray, Marvin, Parvin, Scott, Seely, Todhunter, Traer, Warren, Wilson and Young.

Nays—Messrs. Ayres, Day, Emerson, Gibson, Gillaspy, Hall, Harris, Johnston, Palmer, Patterson, Peters, Price, Skiff and Winchester.

Duelling.

Section five was then read as follows:

"Any citizen of this State who may hereafter be engaged, either directly or indirectly, in a duel, either as principal or accessory before the fact, shall forever be disqualified from holding any office under the constitution and laws of this State."

No amendment being offered to this section, Section six was then read as follows:

Uniform Operation of Laws.

"All laws of a general nature shall have a uniform operation."

Mr. EDWARDS moved to amend by adding the following:

"And the General Assembly shall not grant to any citizen or class of citizens privileges or immunities, which, upon the same terms, shall not equally belong to other citizens."

Mr. JOHNSTON. Will the gentleman be kind enough to explain the object of his amendment?

Mr. EDWARDS. Certainly; its object is contained in a nut shell, and is merely this: It is to prevent the General Assembly from granting any privileges or immunities to any citizen or class of citizens, that it would not be willing to grant to any other citizen or class of citizens upon the same terms. It is to prevent the Legislature from granting exclusive privivileges to any class of citizens.

The question being taken upon the amendment it was agreed to.

No further amendment being offered to section six,

Section seven was read as follows:

Freedom of Speech.

"Every person may speak, write and publish his sentiments on all subjects, being responsible for the abuse of that right. No law shall be passed to restrain or abridge the liberty of speech or of the press. In all prosecutions or indictments for libel, the truth may be given in evidence to the jury, and if it appears to the jury that the matter charged as libellous was true, and was published with good motives and for justifiable ends, the party shall be acquitted."

No amendment being offered to this section,

Section eight was read as follows:

Right of Search.

"The right of the people to be secure in their persons, houses, papers and effects, against unreasonable seizures and searches shall not be violated; and no warrant shall issue but on probable cause, supported by oath or affirmation, particularly describing the place to be searched, and the person and things to be seized."

No amendment being offered to this section,

Section nine was read as follows:

Trial by Jury.

"The right of trial by jury shall remain inviolate; but the General Assembly may authorize trial by a jury of a less number than twelve men in inferior courts."

The following amendment had been made in Committee of the Whole, to add the words:

"No person shall be deprived of life, liberty or property without due process of law."

The question, being taken the amendment was concurred in.

No further amendment being offered to that section:

Section ten was read as follows:

Criminal Prosecutions.

"In all criminal prosecutions, the accused shall have a right to a speedy trial by an impartial jury; to be informed of the accusation against him; to be confronted with the witnesses against him; to have compulsory process for his own witnesses, and to have the assistance of a counsel."

Mr. CLARKE, of Henry. I move the following as a substitute for that section:

"In all criminal prosecutions, and in all cases involving the life or liberty of an individual, the accused shall have the right to a speedy and public trial by an impartial jury, to be informed of the accusation against him, and have a copy of the same; to be confronted with the witnesses against him, to have compulsory process for his own witnesses, and to have the assistance of counsel."

Mr. JOHNSTON. I would be glad if the gentleman from Henry, [Mr. Clarke,] would point out the difference between his proposed substitute and the old section.

Mr. CLARKE, of Henry. The difference is in this: My amendment contains the words "and in all cases involving the life and liberty of an individual;" the words "a public trial;" and also secures to the accused a copy of the accusation against him. I will state here that I find that last provision in other constitutions. It was also suggested by other gentlemen upon this floor while we were in Committee of the Whole, and I have drawn it up in the form I thought would be most acceptable.

Mr. SKIFF. I would suggest to the gentleman from Henry the propriety of inserting after the words "and to have a copy of the same," the words "when demanded," so as to obviate the objection raised by the gentleman from Des Moines, [Mr. Hall,] while we were in Committee of the Whole.

Mr. CLARKE, of Henry. I accept the amendment, and will modify my amendment accordingly.

The question was then taken upon the substitute as modified, and it was agreed to.

Section eleven was then read as follows:

"No person shall be held to answer for a criminal offense, unless on presentment or indictment by a Grand Jury, except in cases cognizable before a justice of the peace, or arising in the army or navy, or in the militia, when in actual sarvice, in time of war or public danger."

The following substitute for this section had been reported from the Committee on the Judiciary:

"All offenses less than felony, and in which the punishment does not exceed a fine of one hundred dollars, or imprisonment for thirty days, shall be tried summarily before a justice of the peace or other officer authorized by law, on information under oath, without indictment or the intervention of a Grand Jury, saving to the defendant the right of appeal; and no person shall be held to answer for any higher criminal offense unless on presentment or indictment by a Grand Jury, except in cases arising in the army or navy, or in the military when in actual service in time of war or public danger."

The question being taken upon the substitute it was adopted.

Section twelve was then read as follows:

"No person shall, after acquittal, be tried for the same offense. All persons shall, before conviction, be bailable by sufficient sureties, except for capital offenses where the proof is evident or the presumption great.

No amendment being offered:

Section thirteen was read as follows:

Writ of Habeas Corpus.

"The writ of habeas corpus shall not be suspended, unless in case of rebellion or invasion the public safety may require it."

The Committee on the Judiciary had reported the following amendment:

Insert between the words "suspended" and "unless" the words:

"Nor shall it be refused when application is made as required by law."

The question being taken the amendment was adopted.

No further amendment being offered:

Section fourteen was read as follows:

The Military.

"The military shall be subordinate to the civil power. No standing army shall be kept up by the State in time of peace; and in time of war no appropriation for a standing army shall be for a longer time than two years."

No amendment being offered to this section, section fifteen was then read as follows:

"No soldier shall, in time of peace, be quartered in any house without the consent of the owner, nor in time of war except in the manner prescribed by law."

No amendment being offered:

Section sixteen was read as follows:

Treason.

"Treason against the State shall consist only in levying war against it, adhering to its enemies, or giving them aid and comfort. No person shall be convicted of treason unless on the evidence of two witnesses to the same over act, or confession in open court."

No amendment being offered:

Section seventeen was then read as follows:

Excessive Bail, &c.

"Excessive bail shall not be required; excessive fines shall not be imposed, and cruel and unusual punishments shall not be inflicted."

No amendment being offered:

Section eighteen was read as follows:

Private Property.

"Private property shall not be taken for public use without just compensation."

Mr. HARRIS. I move to add to this section the following:

"First being made to the owner thereof; such compensation to be assessed by a jury, without taking into consideration the advantage arising therefrom."

The section will then read—

"Private property shall not be taken for public use, without just compensation first being made to the owner thereof; such compensation to be assessed by a jury, without taking into consideration the advantage arising therefrom."

Mr. WILSON. I move to amend the amendment by inserting after the words "first being made" the words "or secured to be paid."

Mr. HARRIS. I accept the amendment.

The question was upon the amendment as modified.

Mr. HARRIS. I would like to have the attention of the convention for a few moments upon this question. It is one in which I feel a great deal of interest. And I do not believe that gentlemen, who have properly considered the effect of the constitution as it now stands, and the operation of the amendment I have proposed, can vote against my amendment. We are told, that in construing this section, the Supreme Court have decided that the law, as it now stands in our code in relation to this matter, is a nullity, and that you cannot take into consideration the benefits arising to the individual from the profits accruing to him from the rest of his property, in consequence of the use of that taken for public use. If that be so, then the Supreme Court have legislated in this matter, and all I propose is, that we shall take out of their hands and put into the constitution, the law as it is. The decision of the Supreme Court, I understand, was made in reference to some railroad laws, of which, however, I do not know the provisions. I would call the attention of gentlemen to section 538 of the code, in relation to the establishment of county roads, as one which has wrought grievous hardships in some cases. I know one instance where it has done great injustice, and it is to prevent such injustice in future, that I desire to incorporate this provision into the constitution. Section 538, of the code, in relation to the establishment of county roads, and claims for damages, is as follows:

"Upon the filing of such claim, the court must appoint three suitable and disinterested voters of the county as appraisers to view the ground, on a day fixed by the court, and report upon the amount of damages sustained by the claimant, after deducting therefrom the benefit he will receive from said road."

Now I may be asked the question, if the claimant does receive any benefit from the establishment of the road in question, why shall not that benefit be taken into consideration? Because others receive the same, perhaps more, benefit from the road than he does, and they are called upon to pay nothing for that benefit. Perhaps the claimant does not wish to have the road, while his neighbors decide that it must be made, and have none of their land taken for the road, yet are benefitted by it more than the man whose land is taken. If you take his timber for the purpose of building bridges, or for any other purpose, the whole neighborhood are benefitted thereby, yet their property is not taken, they have to pay nothing, while he is compelled to bear the whole expense himself.

Now I wish to state to the convention one instance which occurred under my own observation, in the town where I live, in reference to the establishment of a State road. There was a poor widow woman, with a large family of children to support, who owned a small piece of land, of ten acres I believe. There was a State road planned to run immediately in front of the door of her house. She had no use for the road, it was no benefit to her. On the other side of her house, within some ten or fifteen feet from the line of her property, there was a spring of great benefit to her. But certain parties who lived farther back desired the road to go there, and it was so decided, and compelled her to make some forty rods of fence, and threw the spring into the public way. Yet the commissioners decided that it was a benefit to her, and refused to pay her any damages, while those who lived farther back, received all the benefits without paying anything for it. Now in my capacity as county judge, in my county, I have been compelled in three instances, in the execution of the law, to do positive injustice to private parties. I believe it was left to the legislature to construe this section of the constitution, and I could not conceive how the law could be in opposition to the constitution, because it was left to the legislature to say how this compensation should be made. And I therefore felt myself called upon to do what I believed to be wrong and foul injustice to private parties. Now it is my object to get clear of this difficulty. But gentlemen say that the supreme court has decided that the law in the code is of no force. Then, if they have done that, there is nothing wrong in putting the provision in here. But the trouble is now, that another supreme court may reverse this decision, just as easily as the first court made it. Their decision was a mere matter of opinion, and not final. They can do it without difficulty. And if I was on the bench, and was called upon to construe that section of the code, I should say that it was not contrary to the constitution. I think that the bench, who have already construed this section, have decided wrongly. And I think, besides, that gentlemen will find that this decision was made upon a railroad law.

Now I want to put this matter beyond a doubt. I know that precedents and decisions of the supreme court are considered sacred by some gentlemen here, especially those who have become wise in the practice of the law. I wish to have something here besides precedents; I wish to have the letter of the law in this matter, that cannot be trampled upon.

Mr. WILSON. I understand there is some misapprehension in the minds of some members in relation to the amendment to the amendment which I offered, and which was accepted by the gentleman from Appanoose, [Mr Harris.] The amendment to the amendment provides that the compensation instead of being paid immediately, may be secured to be paid. That is, if it is necessary to take a right of way, to take private property for public use, instead of waiting for a jury to decide the amount of compensation for such property before it can be used, it will only be necessay to secure the amount so that the person shall have whatever amount may be afterwards decided to be the compensation due him. That is the effect of the amendment I proposed, and it seems to me that there can be no doubt about its propriety.

Mr. PALMER. This question has been up before; and it has been said that our supreme court has decided that the section should be construed in a certain way; and if we want to know what that section is to mean, we can go to the decisions of the supreme court and there ascertain. Now I think if there is a provision in the Constitution which is so uncertain as to require the solemn decision of the supreme court to decide what it means, we should add a few words to explain it. We do not want to go to the supreme court to ascertain what our Constitution means; we want to see it in the Constitution itself, and not require the supreme court to legislate. It is a known fact that not only our courts of record have misconstrued this section of the Constitution, but that our legislature has misconstrued it and enacted a law in open violation of this section of the Constitution. I think it will do no harm here to add a few words to the old section so as to ascertain the meaning of it and make it plain to every one what this section does mean. It is true that gentlemen learned in the law, know what the section means, or what it has been construed to mean by our Supreme Court, and the Supreme Courts of the States. It is also true that the courts of several States have disagreed as to the construction of a section similar to this. For instance, some courts have construed this section to mean that if private property be taken for public use, the owner of the property may be compensated in part or in whole by the benefits conferred by the use to which his property is put. Now our Supreme Court has decided, and very properly and judiciously, I think that that is not the meaning of this section. Some courts have said that the benefits conferred may be offset against constructive damages in consequence of taking the property: while others have decided that compensation would be made for the intrinsic value of the property. Now I am in favor of some such amendment as that proposed by the gentleman from Appanoose [Mr. Harris], although it is not exactly worded as I would like. But I will vote for it rather than to have none.

Mr. CLARKE, of Henry. On account of some supposed ambiguity in the amendment which I do not really think exists, I would ask the gentleman from Appanoose [Mr. Harris] to accept the following:

"As soon as the damages shall be ascertained by a jury, who shall not take into consideration any advantages that may result to said owner on account of the improvement for which it is taken."

Mr. HARRIS. I accept the amendment.

Mr. WINCHESTER. I object to the amendment principally upon the ground that it contains too much legislation. I hear it frequently said when a proposition is submitted here, "let it pass, if it does not good, it will do no harm." I do not consider that a sufficient reason for adopting any amendment, for by pursuing this course we will soon encumber our new Constitution with a multiplicity of words. I hope the amendment will not pass.

Mr. TRAER. I am decidedly in favor of the amendment. The argument brought up here, that the Supreme Court has decided this question will have very little force with me. I repudiate the whole idea of gentlemen coming here and bringing up the decisions of the Supreme Court to control the action of this body. According to my understanding, this Convention is superior to the Supreme Court; or in other words, we stand here in regard to the Supreme Court in the position of creator to the creature, and we have a right to make and unmake that court. I understand that that court decides questions not according to right and equity, but according to the law and Constitution. When a question comes up in the Supreme Court they decide whether it is according to the law and evidence, and according to the Constitution under which that law is enacted. Here is a principle of right involved in this question, and I undertake to say, that the Supreme Court in this State have never decided that question of right, and therefore I am in favor of placing this provision in the Bill of Rights, so it will be distinctly understood in what form this question will come up.

It is said by gentlemen, that this amendment is entirely unnecessary, but the very fact, that it has been necessary to bring up the question before the Supreme Court of Iowa shows that either the Legislature which passed the law did not understand the provision in the Constitution or else they passed an unconstitutional law. We propose by this amendment to place this question in such a light that it can be distinctly understood. I think the amendment of the gentleman from Appanoose [Mr. Harris] places this matter in a very correct light, and provides a remedy for cases where injustice might be done. In view of the fact, that injustice has been done under the present law, I think it is proper and just that this amendment should go into the Bill of Rights. With that view of the question, I shall vote for it.

Mr. PETERS. I desire to say but a single word upon this question. The construction given to the present law by the Supreme Court is well known throughout the State. I presume that there is no lawyer in the State, or any individual who is likely to have a railroad pass through his farm who does not understand that his rights are well guarded. The Supreme Court of Wisconsin under a Constitution precisely similar to our own have made this same decision, until it has become the well established law of the State.

Mr. TRAER. I wish to ask the gentleman this question. Is there any thing in the Constitution that will prevent our Supreme Court from reversing their decision?

Mr. PETERS. I think that they will be likely to follow the pattern set them by other courts throughout the United States.

Mr. TRAER. When there is a question open here, I think it will be well for this Convention to settle it, and do away with the probabilities of that decision being reversed.

Mr. HARRIS. This question was discussed to a very great extent in Ohio five years ago, as in very many instances great, and grievous injustice had been committed by the location of railroads. There was one instance of this kind near Columbus, which at the time was much commented upon, and which I presume had something to do in the passage, by the Constitutional Convention, of the provision which they adopted upon this subject. I recollect the circumstances of this case very well, as it gave rise to a long litigation in the courts. The party to whose case I refer, owned some two hundred acres of land, which was worth some three hundred dollars an acre, in the line of the railroad running from Columbus to Cleveland, which run one side of his land for some three-quarters of a mile.

The commissioners who were appointed to assess the damages, took into consideration the very same principle which you find in our present code, and they decided, in consequence of the location of the road, that he was not entitled to any damages while one of his neighbors, who had a fine farm, and who was benefitted just as much as himself, was not compelled to give the right of way. He had the whole right of way to give, because the Commissioners decided that he was not entitled to damages, in consideration of the benefits to the property of the owner, arising from the location of the road. Other cases arose which gave rise to the adoption of the following provision in their new Constitution:

"Private property shall ever be held inviolate, but subservient to the public welfare. When taken in time of war or other public exigency, imperatively requiring its immediate seizure, or for the purpose of making or repairing roads, which shall be open to the public, without charge, a compensation shall be made to the owner, in money; and in all other cases, where private property shall be taken for public use, a compensation therefor shall be first made in money, or first secured by a deposit of money; and such compensation shall be assessed by a jury, without deduction for any benefits to any property of the owner."

It seems to me, that this provision carries out the same principle which we should adopt in this State.

Mr. SCOTT. Before the vote is taken upon this amendment, I desire to express my views briefly upon it. There may be many reasons urged why it should not pass. You must recollect that one-half of our State is not yet supplied with roads. As the case now stands, roads pass over the broad prairies, and little damage is sustained by the owners of the land through which the roads pass, but on the contrary they are greatly benefitted by the building of these roads. If this amendment be adopted, would not every one whose land had been touched by a road bring in his claims for damages, and have jurors appointed to ascertain and assess his damages, when in fact he sustained none. I do not object to the principle contained in the provision, for I think it is probably the correct one, but in view of its practical operation, it would not be advisable for us to adopt it here. I am fearful that the result would be, that a great many claims would be presented for damages by parties, when in fact they had no just claims. There is no real damage done by taking any portion of the land for a high-way, and the settlers who desire the road opened are comparatively few and less able to pay the damage which may be sustained. I think that the view of the matter I have presented is worthy, at least, of a little consideration at the hands of the Convention.

I think that the adoption of the amendment now under consideration will have the effect to retard the opening of roads in the newer portions of the State, because the settlers who desire to open these roads are comparatively poor, and they will hesitate a long while before building them, if they are to be required to pay to the individual owners of the land the damages which they may claim, and which may be assessed by the jurors.

Mr. GOWER. I would suggest to the gentleman from Appanoose, that he add the following to his amendment:

"Unless the public exigency shall require it."

The section as amended will then read:

"Private property shall not be taken for public use without just compensation first being made or secured to be paid to the owner therefor, as soon as the damages shall be ascertained by a jury, who shall not take into consideration any advantages that may result to said owner, on account of the improvement for which it is taken, unless the public exigency shall require it."

Mr. HARRIS. I accept the amendment.

Mr. GILLASPY. I had intended to vote for the single proposition of the gentleman, but it is now so complicated that I cannot understand any portion of it.

The question was then taken on the amendment of the gentleman from Appanoose (Mr. Harris), by yeas and nays, and it was not agreed to. Yeas, 9. Nays, 23, as follows:

Yeas. Messrs. Ayers, Clark, of Henry, Day, Gibson, Harris, Marvin, Palmer, Seely and Traer.

Nays. The President, Messrs. Bunker, Clark, of Alamakee, Clarke, of Johnson, Edwards, Emerson, Gillaspy, Gower, Gray, Hall, Johnston, Parvin, Patterson, Peters, Price, Scott, Skiff, Solomon, Todhunter, Warren, Wilson, Winchester and Young.

Mr. CLARKE, of Henry. I hope that we will not preceed until we fully understand the question before us. I will ask for another reading of the section just as it stands with all the amendments.

Mr. WILSON. Would it be in order, now to offer the amendment of the gentleman from Appanoose (Mr. Harris) before he accepted the amendment of the gentleman from Cedar (Mr. Gower).

The PRESIDENT. In the opinion of the chair, it would be in order.

Mr. WILSON. I would move the amendment then, as originally proposed by the gentleman from Appanoose, (Mr. Harris) which would make the section read as follows:

"Private property shall not be taken for the public use without just compensation first being made or secured to be paid to the owner thereof, as soon as the damages shall be assessed by a jury, who shall not take into consideration any advantages that may result to said owner on account of the improvement for which it is taken."

Mr. GOWER. It appears to me that the last clause here is unnecessary. In all matters of improvement every one has to suffer something for the general good; and in our public roads we must take into account that there are benefits as well as injuries received. I consider that the amendment I suggested a while ago, would cover all the ground necessary.

Mr. CLARKE, of Henry. I desire to make a few remarks for the consideration of the Convention upon this subject. The provision here proposed to be incorporated into the constitution is no new principle in Iowa. It is one which has been acted upon by your Legislature, and it is one upon which there has been a great deal of dispute in the courts. Before the law was passed upon this subject I had a little experience bearing upon this matter. It was a case where a plank road was surveyed through a man's farm, cutting it diagonally, and under the law there were three men appointed to assess the damages. The sheriff then selected from the county just such men as he saw fit to put upon the jury. They commenced selecting the jury, the sheriff striking off names, and the other party striking off, until they had selected the three men who were to assess the damages; what did they do? They allowed to the person claiming damages merely a nominal sum, hardly a fraction of what any man would have said the real damage was, because, under the law, that was not to be taken into consideration. I suppose that the necessity of incorporating a provision into the law that they should look to the question of real damage, was evident to the Legislature, and thus you find nearly this provision in the present Code of Iowa, and the same necessity must present itself to the mind of every man here for incorporating it into the constitution, so that jurors shall not, in assessing damages, look forward to what may be the benefit to the individual, for by thus doing they may bring him in debt to the contemplated improvement—a case which actually occurred, as I am informed, in a sister State.

Now it is to establish the rule of assessing damages that we ask for the incorporation of this provision here, so that jurors shall assess the real damages, and not assess the benefits that may accrue from the building of the road. I ask gentlemen if the benefits that result from the building of a road through a man's farm do not accrue as well to the man whose farm lies adjoining, and through which the road may not run? I think if jurors shall take into consideration in assessing damages, the benefits that may accrue, then we ought to have some law by which those benefits shall be equalized, so that my neighbor, whose farm is not touched by the proposed improvement, shall not reap all of the benefits and none of the damages, and I all the damage, while I pay for the benefits. The principle proposed here is founded in justice and good sense; and I think we can trust something to the good sense of juries, that they will look and carefully assess the damages to the individual, so that he shall get the full damages to which he is entitled.

If jurors are laboring under the idea, that they are to take into consideration the remote benefits that may possibly result to the individual, you have no reliable rule upon which to assess the damages. I ask gentlemen if it be not a correct principle, where a person's property is taken for the benefit of these corporators that they shall pay him the just damages that may result to him from the taking of his property? I have that confidence in the future of Iowa, and in the great value of her internal improvements, as to sincerely believe that every great railroad project started here, will prove valuable, and that the company can afford, whenever a road is demanded by the wants of the people, to pay the damage assessed by the jury of the men of Iowa, regulated by this rule which the gentleman from Appanoose [Mr. Harris] wishes to incorporate into this constitution. It will establish the rule for the future; and for that reason, believing that it is a correct principle, and one upon which we have commenced to act, I am in favor of incorporating it into the constitution.

Mr. GOWER. I wish to say that the amendment I offered here a while ago, is incorporated into the constitution of the State of Maine.—It is a rule which has been in operation there for a great many years, and it has worked well.

Mr. EMERSON. My idea in regard to the matter now before the Convention is this: that the value of the property taken shall be determined without regard to the enhanced value that the improvement may give it. Let me suppose by way of illustration, that a railroad it about to pass through my land, which is worth $10 per acre, but so soon as it is understood that this improvement is to be made, the value of that land is increased to $20 per acre. I think it would be unjust in such a case to compel the road to pay the enhanced value of that land, because that enhanced value grows out of the contemplated improvement. I suppose every gentleman here has seen something of this kind in his own neighborhood. I do not want the road to pay for the enhanced value which it would give to the land through which it is to pass, but I would like to see the property valued at the price it was worth in its original state, before the improvement was contemplated.

Mr. HALL. That is just exactly what the law now provides for. The Supreme Court has settled the question in that way.

Mr. EMERSON. If that is the law at the present time, that is all I want, and as a matter of course there is no necessity for offering any amendment to meet the views I presented.

Mr. MARVIN. There are probably a good many men called upon to appraise damages, who may not be aware of this decision of the Supreme Court. Why then object to adopting this amendment, and placing it in our Bill of Rights where everybody can see it.

Mr. HALL. Everybody understands what "just compensation" means. The matter cannot be made more plain and distinct than it has been made by the decision of the Supreme Court.

Mr. CLARKE, of Henry. And yet there is a little misapprehension about this matter. There happens to be a law that the gentleman from Des Moines, [Mr. Hall,] has not referred to, which is of equal authority with his decisions of the Supreme Court. He has referred everything to the decision of the Supreme Court. It seems to be the "omnium gatherum" with the gentleman from Des Moines, [Mr. Hall,] from which he obtains all his wisdom and intelligence to settle every question that comes up. The law of Iowa upon this subject is this:

"The jury shall then proceed to examine the ground and may hear testimony, but no argument of counsel, and shall set apart by notes and bounds a quantity of land convenient and suitable for the purpose intended, and assess the damage occasioned to the owner thereby.

"In estimating the damage *no deduction shall be made for any benefit* that may be supposed to result to the owner from the contemplated work."

Gentlemen talk here as though they were perfectly ignorant of the existence of this law. I am astonished to think that they object to the incorporation of this provision into the constitution upon the ground that it would tend to retard the improvements of the State. The gentleman from Dubuque, [Mr. Emerson,] is certainly right in the position he assumed. We ought to incorporate some such principle as he suggested and have it forever settled, for now the decision of the Supreme Court is founded upon the statute law, and that may be changed by the next Legislature. These corporations may become very powerful, and may so work upon the next Legislature as to induce them to change this rule. It is to settle this principle and not leave it a matter of mere statutory regulation, that the gentleman from Appanoose, [Mr. Harris,] has made his suggestions to amend the section. I conceive that the amendment offered by him embodies the correct principle, and I do not believe any valid objection can be offered against it. Nobody has complained of it as it stands upon our statute book. Why not then incorporate it into the constitution, and have the matter forever settled?

The question was then taken by yeas and nays

upon the amendment with the following result, yeas 17, nays 16.

Yeas—Messrs. Ayres, Bunker, Clark of Alamakee, Clarke of Henry, Day, Ells, Gibson, Gillaspy, Gray, Harris, Marvin, Palmer, Parvin, Seely, Traer, Wilson and Young.

Nays—The President; Messrs. Clarke of Johnson, Edwards, Emerson, Gower, Hall, Johnston, Patterson, Peters, Price, Scott, Skiff, Solomon, Todhunter, Warren and Winchester.

Mr. CLARK, of Alamakee. I offer the following as an additional section:

"Private Roads may be opened in the manner prescribed by law, but in every case the necessity of the road, and the amount of damages to be sustained by the opening thereof, shall first be determined by a jury of disinterested freeholders; and such amount, together with the expenses of the proceedings, shall be paid by the person or persons benefitted thereby, before said road shall be opened."

I offer it for the reason that there can be at present no private roads established in this State. That question has been already settled in New York and in some other States. Under our present constitution nothing in the shape of roads but public highways, can be established against the will of the owner of the soil through which they are to pass; but if it is desired by the people of the State that the right may be reserved to them of establishing private ways, it is proper to do so, and I would like to secure to the people the right to open such roads.

Mr. CLARKE, of Henry. I would be glad to have this proposition receive the consideration of the Convention, and I wish to make a single suggestion in regard to the matter. If, as the gentleman from Alamakee states, there is no way in which private roads can now be opened, and a constitutional provision is required in order to enable the Legislature to legislate upon the subject, it is certainly a matter which we ought to consider, and not pass over lightly. I do not know whether the gentleman is correct in his position or not. I would like to have gentlemen who have had more experience than myself upon this subject explain this matter to the Convention, so that I may vote intelligently upon this question. I do not want to pass this matter over in a hurried manner, because it may be of the very greatest importance.

Mr. WARREN. I know the fact that private roads are opened every year, but whether it is done according to law I do not know. I am opposed to legislating upon this subject here, because we are sent here to frame a constitution, and not to pass legislative acts.

Mr. CLARK, of Alamakee. I wish simply to say to the gentleman that this question came up some ten or twelve years ago in the Supreme Court of Kentucky, in regard to building a railroad through a certain city. It was contended there that they had the right under the constitution to build it as a private way, but the Supreme Court decided that they could not, and they went on further to say that it was a public way. If gentlemen will turn to the fourth of Hill's Reports, they will find that the Supreme Court of New York decided that they could not under the constitution establish private roads. If private roads are opened in this State, as the constitution now stands, the Supreme Court of this State would unquestionably hold the same doctrine.

Mr. WILSON. I shall vote against this proposition. I cannot see any necessity for opening private ways, if all ways can be opened and made public. It would be better to adopt the policy of opening public highways, than to adopt the proposed course. The provision is, in my opinion, wholly unnecessary.

Mr. CLARK, of Alamakee. I did not mean to say that these private roads were considered as public ways. The Supreme Court of the State of New York have defined in the third of Hill's reports what private roads are. They hold railroads, and plank roads to be public ways, because they open up public thoroughfares. A public road, according to the decision of that State, must be a road established for public purposes, communicating with a public highway established for public purposes, and not a way leading from a public highway to a person's dwelling for his convenience merely.

Mr. CLARKE, of Henry. The gentleman will find by referring to the constitution of New York, the following provision:

"Private roads may be opened in the manner to be prescribed by law; but in every case the necessity of the road and the amount of all damages to be sustained by the opening thereof, shall be first determined by a jury of freeholders, and such amount, together with the expenses of the proceeding shall be paid by the person to be benefitted."

Mr. CLARK, of Alamakee. That provision was inserted in the constitution after the decision of the Supreme Court was made.

The question was then taken upon the amendment of Mr. Clark, of Alamakee, and it was not agreed to—yeas 9; nays 24; as follows:

Yeas—Messrs. Bunker, Clark of A., Clarke of H., Day, Ells, Gray, Marvin, Seely and Traer.

Nays—The President, Messrs. Ayres, Clarke of J., Edwards, Emerson, Gibson, Gillaspy, Gower, Hall, Harris, Johnston, Palmer, Parvin, Patterson, Peters, Price, Scott, Skiff, Solomon, Todhunter, Warren, Wilson, Winchester and Young.

Section nineteen was then read, as follows:

"No person shall be imprisoned for debt in any civil action, on mesne, or final process, unless in case of fraud; and no person shall be imprisoned for a militia fine in time of peace."

There being no amendments offered to that section, the twentieth section was then read, as follows:

"The people have the right freely to assemble together, to counsel for the common good; to make known their opinions to their representatives, and to petition for a redress of grievances."

The amendments proposed by the Committee of the Whole, were—

To insert after the words "assemble together," the words "in a peaceable manner," and to strike out the word "counsel" and insert "consult," so that the section will read—

"The people have the right freely to assemble together in a peaceable manner, to consult for the common good; to make known their opinions to their representatives, and to petition for a redress of grievances.

The question was taken, and the amendments were rejected.

The twenty-first section was then read, as follows:

"No bill of attainder, *ex post facto* law, or law impairing the obligation of contracts shall ever be passed."

The amendment proposed by the committee of the Whole, was to insert after the word "contract" "or right of property."

Mr. HALL. I offered this amendment at the suggestion of several gentlemen, as I stated in the Convention the orher day, from the fact that there was now no constitutional protection against the rights of property being impaired by the Legislature. I believe the amendment is a proper one, and I hope gentlemen will not vote against it because they imagine they smell something in it intended to affect the prohibitory liquor law.

Mr. PARVIN. I wish gentlemen would consider well before they vote upon this proposition, whether it does not prevent the Legislature from passing any prohibitory liquor law. I do not know that the gentleman who offered it intended any such thing, but it occurred to me when it passed the Committee of the Whole, that it had a direct tendency that way. I am well satisfied with the section as it now stands, as I think it will protect a citizen in all the rights of property which are necessary to be protected. I do not wish to see anything inserted here, that will prevent the Legislature, if, in their wisdom, they see proper, from passing any prohibitory liquor law, that shall declare certain property, in the shape of whisky, confiscated. I shall certainly vote against the amendment.

Mr. WILSON. I am opposed to the incorporation of such a provision as this into our constitution. Suppose the community wish to get rid of any nuisance in which there is property? They would not have the power under a provision of this kind to provide for its abatement.—Every gambler has certain devices which are his property; but under this provision the Legislature cannot interfere with them. It is even questionable whether, under such a provision, the Legislature can pass an act fining a man for the commission of a criminal offence—because you may interfere with the rights of property. This doctrine may go a great ways, and we ought to pause and consider this matter well before we vote for the adoption of such a provision. In my opinion, it will completely tie the hands of the Legislature in relation to all these respects.

Mr. GILLASPY. I shall vote against the proposition, but if I thought it would tie the hands of the Legislature from passing a prohibitory liquor law, I should vote for it.

Mr. CLARKE, of Henry. I will not be so ungenerous to the gentleman from Des Moines [Mr. Hall] as to accuse him of coming to the consideration of this question with his "gloves on," but if he smells a "nigger" every time I get up to make a motion, I smell whisky every time he offers an amendmen. "I want the gentleman to come right out plainly and tell us" whether it is whisky and lager beer he means. [Laughter.] The gentleman recognizes property in these articles. and he wants us to insert a provision of this kind, that the Legislature shall make no law impairing the right in that property, and that the owner of it may sell and traffic in it in any manner he pleases. If the provision in question does not mean that, it does not mean anything. Now gentlemen understand the matter, and seeing the gentleman stripped of his gloves, can vote, having a correct view of the question, as it stands fully presented in all its nakedness.

Mr. HALL. I did not dream when I first presented the proposition that it would assume the shape it has. I think this amendment is necessary. As, between the gentleman and myself, we are perfectly agreed, he may take the "nigger," and I will take the "whiskey," (Laughter,) though I think the gentleman can smell whiskey as far as I can.

But I would seriously refer to this subject, in answer to the gentleman from Jefferson, [Mr. Wilson.] I understand it to be one of the common maxims of law, that you cannot make a contract, that is illegal, and enforce it. I undertake to say, that this amendment does not interfere, and could not be made to interfere with the right of the legislature to pass salutary prohibitory laws upon any subject. If a man had liquor here, which was property under the law of the State, while it was so held, it could not be confiscated. I will vote against any laws, that will suddenly deprive a man of that which was previously held as property.

Mr. WILSON. After this constitution shall have gone to the people, and been accepted by them, can any law in this State stand, which comes in conflict with its provisions?

Mr. HALL. Any law of this State, that should prohibit all future dealing in ardent spirits, could be made perfectly consistent with the constitution. But it could not confiscate ardent spirits, where they had been previously recognized as property, and we could not then declare, that they were not property. We could say, that all liquors held after the passage of the law shall not be considered as property. As I stated at the outset, whether the amendment I offered prevails or not, I made it at the suggestion of several gentlemen who stood high in the community, and my judgment concurring in their views, I offered it. I have simply done what I conceived to be my duty, and I now leave the matter in the hands of the convention.

The question was then taken upon agreeing to the amendment of the Committee of the Whole, by yeas and nays, and it was not agreed to. Yeas 7; nays 26, as follows:

Yeas.—Messrs. Emerson, Gillaspy, Hall, Harris, Peters, Price and Solomon.

Nays.—The President, Messrs. Ayres, Bunker, Clark, of Alamakee, Clarke, of Henry, Clarke, of Johnson, Day, Edwards, Ells, Gibson, Gower, Gray, Johnston, Marvin, Palmer, Parvin, Patterson, Scott, Seely, Skiff, Todhunter, Traer, Warren, Wilson, Winchester and Young.

Section twenty-seccond was then read as follows:

"Foreigners who are, or may hereafter become, residents of this State, shall enjoy the same rights, in respect to the possession, enjoyment, and descent of property, as native born citizens.

No amendment being offered to this section, Section twenty-third was read as follows:

Slavery, or Involuntary Servitude.

"Neither slavery nor involuntary servitude, unless for the punishment of crimes, shall ever be tolerated in this State."

Mr. WILSON. I move the following as a substitute for this section:

"There shall be no slavery in this State; nor shall there be involuntary servitude, unless for the punishment of crime."

Now, according to the present section, the presumption is clear, in fact the declaration is direct, that slavery may exist in this State, provided it is as punishment for crime. I wish to change the phraseology of this section, so as to declare that slavery shall not exist in this State under any circumstances; and that involuntary servitude, and not slavery, shall be the punishment of crime.

The question being taken upon the substitute it was adopted.

Prohibition of Intoxicating Drinks.

Mr. SOLOMON offered the following to come in as section twenty-four.

"The manufacture of, or traffic in, property which is a production of this State, or a legitimate article of traffic with other States, or foreign nations, shall not be prohibited."

Mr. CLARKE, of Johnson, offered the following as a substitute for the proposed section:

"The right of the people to prohibit, by law, the manufacture and sale of intoxicating liquors, as a beverage, shall not be abridged."

Mr. CLARKE, of Henry. I would suggest to the gentleman from Johnson, [Mr. Clarke,] to incorporate with his provision a clause, making constitutional the submitting of such law to the people.

Mr. CLARKE, of Johnson. I cannot do that.

The question was upon the substitute for the proposed section.

Mr. PALMER. I wish to state why I shall vote against any proposition relating to the manufacture and sale of intoxicating liquors, whether prohibitory or not. I think the incorporation of such a provision here would be the most effectual mode that could be adopted to defeat all the other amendments we may adopt to this constitution. I think the subject is one that should not be dragged in here, if we desire to have our other amendments adopted by the people.

Mr. EDWARDS moved to lay the proposed section and substitute upon the table.

Mr. GILLASPY. I shall vote against laying this subject upon the table, because I want every gentleman here to vote directly upon this proposition. I call for the yeas and nays upon the motion to lay on the table.

The yeas and nays were ordered accordingly.

The question being then taken by the yeas and nays upon the motion to lay on the table, it was agreed to—yeas 21, nays 12, as follows:

Yeas.—Messrs. Ayres, Bunker, Clark, of Alamakee, Clarke, of Henry, Day, Edwards, Emerson, Gibson, Gower, Harris, Marvin, Palmer, Patterson, Scott, Seely, Todhunter, Traer, Warren, Wilson, Winchester and Young.

Nays.—The President, Messrs. Clarke, of Johnson, Ells, Gillaspy, Gray, Hall, Johnston, Parvin, Peters, Price, Skiff and Solomon.

Exclusive Jurisdiction of the United States.

The following section, to come in as section twenty-four, was adopted in Committee of the Whole, on motion of Mr. Wilson;

Exclusive jurisdiction shall never be granted to the government of the United States over any territory embraced within the limits of this State.

The question was upon concurring in the action of the Committee of the Whole.

Mr. PETERS. I find in the Constitution of the United States, that congress shall have exclusive jurisdiction over such districts and places ceded by, or purchased of the several States. Now, what the effect of this section would be, I cannot tell; perhaps it would prove to be in direct conflict with the Constitution of the United States, or have the effect of prohibiting the government of the United States from purchasing any such territory in any of the States.

Mr. WILSON. I will explain the effect of this provision as I understand it. The seventeenth clause of section eight of the first article of the Constitution of the United States, provides that congress shall have power "to exercise legislation, in all cases whatsoever, over such district (not exceeding ten miles square,) as may, by cession of particular States, and the acceptance of congress, become the seat of government of the United States, and to exercise like authority over all places purchased, by the consent of the legislature of the State in which the same shall be, for the erection of forts, magazines, arsenals, dock-yards, and other needful buildings."

This section provides that Congress shall have "exclusive legislation" over all such portions of territory. What I wish by having this section adopted, is to secure to the State of Iowa, in all her civil, and inall her criminal processes, the right to go upon this property of the United States, for the purpose of serving those writs, and to say that unless we can have that right guaranteed to us by the general government, we will not consent to any purchase being made by the United States, within the territory of this State. There is no provision in the Constitution of the United States, or in any of the statutes of the general government, by which persons having committed a breach of the law of the State, and escaping to this property of the United States, can be reclaimed by the authorities of the State. Now, if we grant to the government of the United States this exclusive jurisdiction, then a person committing a crime in our State, may escape to this property and remain there forever, or until his friends can provide him a way to escape, and we can never reach him. I would rather that this State should never receive a dollar from the general government, than that we should give up this doctrine of State rights. I would lay down this proposition, that unless the general government would consent to permit us to send our officers with our writs upon her property, the government of this State should never consent to her purchasing any property in this State. I would have this placed in our Constitution, and if the general government would not consent to that, then I would say let us have no appropriations from the general government, but let us sustain our State rights.

Mr. HARRIS. I would ask the gentleman from Jefferson [Mr. Wilson] if he ever knew of an instance in any of the States where this difficulty, he proposes to provide against, has occurred.

Mr. WILSON. I am not able to refer the gentleman to any instance, but I know this, that the last legislature of this State granted to the United States, this very privilege in regard to property purchased in Dubuque, and the Governor vetoed the bill, and I think very properly too. If an asylum of this kind was afforded to criminals in this State, they will soon find it.

Mr. HALL. I do not believe there is any necessity for this section. The Constitution of the United States contemplates that the government of the United States may want these possessions as places for arsenals, post offices, custom houses, and such institutions. And our legislature has memorialized Congress, over and over, again, for the purpose of obtaining appropriations to build such institutions in this State. Now, although I do not speak positively, and I am not in the habit of doing so in regard to law, I do not think that in any instance, when an offence has been committed within the limits of a State, have the courts of the United States decided that the State processes could not extend to this property of the United States.

Mr. WILSON. I am informed by the gentleman from Mills [Mr. Solomon] that some three instances of the kind have occurred in the State of New York.

Mr. HALL. I would as soon trust my own recollection in relation to this matter, as that of the gentleman from Mill, or any other gentleman; and I undertake to say, that the practice has been the reverse of that, and that the processes of the State Courts extend over these possessions of the United States, and criminals can be arrested there under those processes. The United States reserved this right, in order to retain the right to try, and punish persons who shall commit offences within the limits of this purchased territory. If the crime is committed off the premises, then the State punishes, and can go to this property and bring the criminal away. But, if the offence is committed within the territory that is ceded; if, for instance, a soldier commits a crime within this territory, then he is amenable to the laws of the United States. I am sure there is no necessity for putting a provision of this kind in our Constitution. The legislature can exercise their discretion in this matter when they make the cession. The Governor has vetoed the bill passed by the last legislature. I have not seen the bill, and therefore cannot say whether he has acted correctly, and properly or not. But I do not believe the Governor has gone so far as to desire to retain on the part of the State the entire jurisdiction over this territory proposed to be ceded. I think we are called upon to act a little in the dark in this matter.

Mr. SOLOMON. I desire to state in explanation of the information I gave the gentleman from Jefferson, [Mr. Wilson] and to which he referred, that I do not, as I can, refer to the cases of which I spoke to him, by their titles. I asked him if it was his design to secure to the State of Iowa concurrent jurisdiction with the United States, in this territory, and I understood him to say that such was his object. In reply to that, I said that cases had arisen in the State of New York where the State had been deprived of this jurisdiction. But, as the gentleman from Des Moines [Mr. Hall] has intimated, the offences occurred within the limits of the territory ceded to the United States.

Mr. WILSON. I desire to make one remark, in reply to the gentleman from Des Moines [Mr. Hall]. I think there is a very important principle involved here. I will put this question: Suppose that the State of Virginia issues a writ for a person having committed a criminal offence, who had escaped to the district of Columbia, and to that portion of it which she had ceded to the general government, could that writ be served upon that person there? It could not be. Then if the legislature of Iowa should grant the government of the United States exclusive juriidiction over certain lands within this State, does not that grant of exclusive jurisdiction stop the writs of the State as soon as it reaches the limits of that cession? If the offence is committed within the State, and off the lands ceded to the government of the United States, and the criminal escapes to that ceded territory, what is the result? The State has no jurisdiction over that territory; the general government cannot try the offender, because there is no law of the Uniied States which he has offended, and there is no law providing for the delivering up of this fugitive from justice, and the criminal would thus go unpunished. Therefore, I say it is not right to allow this thing in our State. The question of State rights is involved here, and we ought, as a State, to interfere here, and stand by our rights, by declaring that throughout our borders all processes of the State, both civil and criminal, shall reach all rffenders against the laws of the State, whether on this ceded territory or not. I say that is but right, and I do not see how any gentleman, who is in favor of sustaining the doctrine of State rights, can vote against this provision.

This provision can by no possibility, do any mischief. When the legislature of this State comes to act upon a proposition to give the government of the United States the right to purchase lands within our borders, all it has to do under this provision, is to notify the general government that this State cannot give exclusive jurisdiction to the United States, over these lands. Then the terms can be agreed upon; and whatever the terms may be, we, as citizens of this State, under this provision of the Constitution, can rest content that all our rights are secure. But, I am not willing to leave it open as it was before.

Mr. BUNKER. I would ask the gentleman from Jefferson, [Mr. Wilson,] if he knows of any instance where any difficulty of this kind has arisen in the District of Columbia, where Congress has exclusive jurisdiction? Is that District in fact a "city of refuge" to which offenders may flee and be beyond the reach of State processes?

Mr. WILSON. As I have already remarked, I am not prepared now to give any particular instance in reply to the gentleman's question. But I know this much, that unless this place of refuge is guarded by some such provision as the one under consideration, it may be created to an infinite injury. And I know further, that the tendency of all rogues and all men who wish to escape the serving process, is to those places of refuge, and once they get there, they are safe. I want to retain our own rights in the premises.

Mr. EMERSON. The recent act of the legislature in reference to the custom house, post office, &c., in the city of Dubuque, would seem to settle this fact; or rather the fact has been settled long since. The Constitution of the United States seems to settle the fact that if the State of Iowa at any time sees proper to grant to the United States any portion of her Territory for purposes such as erecting arsenals, dock yards, custom houses, &c., the Constitution requires that in order that the government of the United States can accept that grant it must also have complete jurisdiction over that portion so ceded or sold. This amendment permits this consideration: if it is put in this bill of rights, we cannot hereafter cede Territory to the United States simply because the United States will not receive it under the restrictions we have placed upon it. The government of the United States not only will not receivee it, but it cannot receive it.

And as an evidence of that position, I will state that the Secretary of the Interior of the United States was written to in order to ascertain what kind of bill the United States would accept; what should be its provisions; and the Secretary drafted such a bill as the United States could accept under this provision of the Constitution of the United States, and sent it on here, and that was the bill passed by the legislature and vetoed by the Governor of this State. This proposition then, in my opinion, entirely sets aside any probability of our hereafter having any of those improvements by the United States within the limits of the State of Iowa.—Now if members are ready for that, if they think that the best mode to sustain this great principle of state rights we have heard spoken of here, then they can vote for this section.

Mr. SOLOMON. The gentleman from Dubuque [Mr. Emerson] speaks of the inability of the government of the United States to accept any grant of Territory under this proposed provision. Will he refer me to that portion of the Constitution which entails this inability upon the United States to receive these grants except on certain conditions.

Mr. EMERSON. I would refer the gentleman from Mills [Mr. Solomon] to the eighth section of the first article of the Constitution of the United States.

Mr. SOLOMON. I do not find that inability there, according to my reading of it. It says, "Congres shall have power to *exercise exclusive legislation*, in all cases whatsoever, over such district (not exceeding ten miles square), as may by cessions of particular States and the acceptance of Congress, become the seat of government of the United States, and to *exercise like authority* over all places purchased, by the consent of the Legislature of the State in which the same shall be, for the erection of forts, magazines, arsenals, dock yards, and other needful buildings." Now I understand the gentleman to interpose this objection to the proposition of the gentleman from Jefferson, [Mr. Wilson,] that if we adopt that proposition, all the cessions we can make must be of such a character under this provision as to prevent the United States from accepting them.

Mr. EMERSON. So I understand from the letter of the Secretary of the United States.

Mr. SOLOMON. The gentleman places his objection upon some correspondence that has taken place. Now though that may be the policy and decision of the Secretary of the United States, I do not consider that it is at all clear that this provision of the Constitution of the United States makes it so. "The Congress shall exercise exlcusive legislation, &c.," now we may retain concurrent jurisdiction over this property even after it is ceded to the United States. By means of our Legislature we can absolutely secure the right to extend our proceses into that ceded territory. I cannot see that the objection of the gentleman is sustained by the provision of the Constitution to which he refers.

Mr. HALL. I wish to read from an act of Congress in reference to grants of this character, passed March 2, 1795, and still in force. It is found in Story's Laws of the United States, chapter 105, and is as follows:

"An act relative to cessions of jurisdiction in places where light-houses, beacons, buoys and public piers, have been, or may hereafter be erected and fixed.

Sec. 1. Be it enacted, &c., That where cessions have been, or may hereafter be, made, by any State, of the jurisdiction of places, where light-houses, beacons, buoys, or public piers, have been erected and fixed, or may, by law, be provided to be erected or fixed, with reservation, that process, civil and criminal, issuing under the authority of such State, may be executed and served therein, such cessions shall be deemed sufficient, under the laws of the United States, providing for the supporting or erecting of light-houses, beacons, buoys, and public piers.

Sec. 2. That where any State hath made, or shall make, a cession of jurisdiction for the purpose aforesaid, without reservation, all process, civil and criminal, issuing under the authority of such State, or the United States may be served and executed within the places, the jurisdiction of which has been so ceded, in the same manner as if no such cession had been made. [Approved March 2, 1795.]

Now, States sometimes put in these restrictions in their acts of union. But it seems to me that while this act of Congress is in force there is no necessity for anything of this kind in our constitution.

Mr. HARRIS. It seems to me that no difficulty having arisen in any State from the escape of these criminals to these ceded territories of the United States, and especially as the District of Columbia, spoken of by the gentleman from Washington, [Mr. Bunker,] has not, under the circumstances surrounding it, become a "city of refuge," there can be no necessity for this provision in our constitution. And if I read the constitution of the United States aright, we must cede this exclusive jurisdiction with the territory. And yet another thing; all those difficulties have been provided for by the law read by the gentleman from Des Moines, [Mr. Hall.] Now I do not wish to come in here and get up questions of nullification. I am disposed to support the constitution of the United States; I have come here for that purpose, and have taken an oath to do so. I do not think this involves the question of State rights at all. I do not recollect of seeing any similar provision in any constitution of any other State. It strikes me we are getting very smart just at this time.

Mr. WILSON. However smart we may be getting, it is evidently necessary and proper that whenever we do discover anything that is right and appropriate we should lay hold of it and preserve it. The argument presented by the gentleman from Dubuque, [Mr. Emerson,] is completely overturned by the law read by the gentleman from Des Moines, [Mr. Hall]. The gentleman from Dubuque says, that the United States cannot have exclusive jurisdiction over this ceded territory. And yet by this very statute of the United States we find that the Congress of the United States can accept these sessions upon certain conditions. Congress has passed a certain statute in relation to this matter. But have we any guarantee that that statute will remain in force? I ask gentlemen if there is no danger that this statute may be repealed for the purpose of consolidating the power of the general government? And are we to be deterred from adopting this provision because there is nothing of the kind in the Constitutions of other States? I grant that Iowa would be the first one to do this thing, and I believe it would be a credit to her some day that she had taken the first step to preserve her rights in this respect. We have no reason to believe that the general government will not some day, whenever they may deem it advantageous to themselves, repeal this statute. Besides, this statute does not extend to custom houses: it only refers to arsenals, dock yards, hospitals, forts, &c.

Now, the amendment reported by the Committee of the Whole will cover the whole ground. I am in favor of it, and I believe we ought to concur in it. There is certainly nothing in the provision of the Constitution of the United States that would prohibit the government of the United States from agreeing to this thing. She may agree that we may have jurisdiction over the ceded territory so far as our writs are concerned; or she may agree to do without the territory. And I say again, that I would rather to-day that it should be determined forever that the State of Iowa shall never have a single custom house, post office, or other government building within her limits—that not a dollar of the money of the general government shall be expended here than to relinquish the doctrine contained in this section. And I say to the gentleman from Dubuque, that I would rather have the buildings in his city stopped where they are than to give up this doctrine. I believe the State of Iowa ought to be jealous of this matter; she ought to watch every step taken by the general govenment, and hold in her own hands the power to prevent the consolidation of the general government so far as law is concerned. I believe this is a proper step in that direction. If we are to give up the right to serve our own writs upon the property of the United States we might as well give up all our rights as a State, as to give up this, the most material one, affecting the jurisdiction of our State within her own limits. For one I am not willing to do this thing. And I do not believe that gentlemen, if they will properly reflect upon this proposition, will be willing to do so. It takes nothing from the United States that she should have, and secures to us what is necessary to carry out our laws.

Mr. WINCHESTER. If there is any honor to be derived from the incorporation of this provision in our Coustitution, I have no objection, if it is so incorporated that the gentleman from Jefferson, [Mr. Wilson,] shall have it all to himself. But I am not afraid of Uncle Sam taking undue advantage of his children. I shall vote against this proposition for the same reason that I shall vote against every thing that I do not consider absolutely necessary to be incorporated in our Constitution.

Mr. PETERS. I have been somewhat surprised since I occupied a seat in this Convention to learn that the Legislature of Iowa is exceedingly in danger of becoming corrupted, and that every safeguard must be placed in this constitution to prevent it. I have been informed here that not only our Legislature, but the Congress of the United States are corrupt, and not to be trusted, and that the decisions of the Supreme Court of this State, borne out by the decisions of almost every Supreme Court in the Union, and upheld by well-settled principles of law, are liable to be reversed by the Supreme Court that may come hereafter. And then the United States are going to create an asylum for scoundrels, to which they may flee and escape from justice. Now, while I continue to have that confidence which I have always entertained in the Legislature and judiciary of our State, I am unwilling to put anything in the constitution of the State of Iowa that can come in conflict with the constitution of the United States. I apprehend that the United States can only purchase lands pursuant to the provisions of the constitution of the United States.

The effect of this amendment is simply this: To say that the United States shall never acquire from the State of Iowa one single inch of territory. As for the difficulty apprehended concerning the serving of the writs of the State upon this ceded territory, I think this provision is wholly unnecessary, because there has never any difficulty of the kind arisen. I hope the amendment will not be concurred in.

The question being then taken by yeas and nays, upon concurring in the section adopted in Committee of the Whole, it was decided in the negative—yeas 9; nays 23; as follows:

Yeas—The President, Messrs. Clarke of H., Scott, Seely, Solomon, Traer, Warren, Wilson and Young.

Nays—Messrs. Ayres, Bunker, Clark of A., Clarke of J., Day, Edwards, Emerson, Gibson, Gillaspy, Gower, Gray, Hall, Harris, Johnston, Marvin, Palmer, Parvin, Patterson, Peters, Price, Skiff, Todhunter, and Winchester.

Leases of Land.

Mr. CLARKE, of Henry. I have a section which I propose to have inserted here, and I will state to the Convention, that I have copied it, in substance, from the constitution of the State of New York. The occasion of its being introduced there was the occurrence of the anti-rent difficulties in that State. I think the provision must commend itself to the mind of every member of this body. It is as follows:

"No lease or grant of agricultural lands, reserving any rent or service of any kind, shall be valid for a longer period than twenty-five years."

Mr. HARRIS. Is not the principles of this proposed section contained in a section reported by the Committee on Incorporations.

Mr. JOHNSTON. No, sir.

Mr. CLARKE, of Henry. The section the gentleman refers to, does not cover this matter.

Mr. SKIFF. I would move to amend this proposed section by striking out "twenty-five," and inserting "twenty," so as to limit the lease or grant to twenty years.

Mr. CLARKE, of Henry. I accept the amendment.

The section as modified was then adopted.

Common Law.

Mr. CLARKE, of Henry. I have another section which I will offer, and I ask for it the consideration of the legal profession here. The question has been raised as to how far the common law extends and prevails in this State. I propose to settle that matter definitely by the insertion of the following section in our constitution:

"Such parts of the Common Law as are not repugnant to this constitution, and the statutory laws of this State, shall be, and continue, the law of this State, subject to such changes and alterations as the General Assembly may make therein."

The question was upon adopting the section as a part of the Bill of Rights.

Mr. HALL. I doubt the propriety of adopting this section. I know that there are such provisions as this put in the constitutions of other States, and perhaps properly enough when they have a common law of their own. But we are not old enough yet to have any common law of our own. I am afraid that this provision, if adopted, will lead to confusion, and therefore I shall vote against it.

Mr. CLARKE, of Henry. I would like to have some other gentlemen give some opinions upon this matter. The gentleman from Des Moines, [Mr. Hall] has given, I think, rather a hasty opinion in reference to this provision. I do not think that it would lead to any more confusion than we are certainly in now, in regard to what is common law, and that is the only question that could be raised. Every Judge upon the bench, and the gentleman himself, if he should ever occupy that position again, would certainly be appealed to, and the common law, as understood on either side, would be presented and argued, and he and they would be called upon to form some idea of what it was, and give an opinion in the premises. I do not suppose that common law is to be considered as custom merely, grown up in Iowa; but I suppose our common law here is the same as it was in New York at the time their constitution was adopted, and the same that it is in Illinois, Indiana, Wisconsin, Michigan, and other States. You will find the same provision incorporated into the constitutions of other States when they were young as we are. Our common law is not merely the common law of Iowa, but the common law of the country, as we received it from our English ancestors. Every one understands that, when he quotes the common law in our courts of justice. But the question is, how far is it recognized and binding here? I want to give it a constitutional recognition and force.

I am surprised at the view taken of this matter by the gentleman from Des Moines [Mr. Hall] by supposing that we must be a state for a certain number of years before we have a common law. The very moment Iowa was organized she had a common law, and the same common law that they have in New York and New England, only modified by the peculiar circumstances by which we were surrounded, and applicable to us, as those circumstances would admit. Custom may have modified it to some extent; but where it is unmodified, it is the same common law as they have in New England, New York, Ohio, Indiana, and other States. It is to that common law to which I wish to give a constitutional recognition. If it is not proper to do so, I should like to have some gentleman explain why it is not, and give his reasons.

Mr. CLARKE, of Johnson. The fact that this provision has been inserted in the constitutions of some other States does not enhance its value in my estimation. As I understand the decisions of the Supreme Court, the common law is now in force in this State, so far as it is applicable to our institutions. The proposition of the gentleman from Henry [Mr. Clarke] only affirms what our courts have already offirmed, with this addition to that proposition, that the Legislature has the right to change it. That is the law now; that right now exists. We gain nothing, therefore, by such a proposition in our constitution. I am opposed to putting abstract propositions in our constitution, unless they are calculated to secure some important right, or restrict the action of some department of the State. This does nothing of the kind.

The question being taken on the proposed section, it was not agreed to.

Miscellaneous.

The last section of the Bill of Rights was then read, as follows:

"This enunciation of rights shall not be construed to impair or deny others, retained by the people."

No amendment being offered to this section—

The PRESIDENT announced that the Preamble and Bill of Rights had passed its second reading.

Mr. BUNKER. I would inquire if this article is now open to amendment?

The PRESIDENT. This article cannot be finally acted upon until all the other reports of the standing committees have passed their second reading.

Mr. JOHNSTON. I would inquire what is the present position of this Bill of Rights? If we are to discuss all these questions in Committee of the Whole, and then discuss them again in Convention, and then, after having passed the article through its second reading, we can still propose amendments, and the whole variety of questions involved in this article are to come up again, there is no use in our having gone thro' the course we have followed. Now I desire to lock the door at some time to future amendments. It cannot be done now, I suppose, because one amendment to the fourth section was reserved for future action.

The PRESIDENT. The chair considers that this report, embracing the subject of the Preamble rnd Bill of Rights, has now passed its second reading.

Mr. JOHNSTON. According to parliamentary usage, the Bill of Rights must have passed its second reading pefore it went into Committee of the Whole. According to the practice of the Legislature, it is necessary that a bill be read a second time before it can be referred to the Committee of the Whole.

The PRESIDENT. A bill is considered upon its second reading until it is ordered to its third reading.

Mr. JOHNSTON. Is the Bill of Rights open to amendment in its present shape?

The PRESIDENT. Those sections that the Convention has acted upon cannot now be modified in the particulars wherein they have been acted npon, except by means of a reconsideration.

Mr. HARRIS Do I understand the decision of the chair, that those portions of this Bill of Rights which the Convention has acted definitely upon, cannot now be reached except by motion to reconsider?

The PRESIDENT. That is the opinion of the chair. All sections not acted upon in any way, are still open to amendment.

Mr. BUNKER. My understanding of the rule of proceeding here is that when we get through the Bill of Rights upon its second reading it will be laid upon the table, and when taken up again for final action, it would be in order to offer amendments to any portion of it.

The PRESIDENT. The Chair is of the opinion that this report has passed its second reading now. If it was a bill in a legislative body, a motion that it be engrossed and ordered to its third reading would now be in order.

Mr. BUNKER. I was under the impression that a resolution had been adopted by which the reports upon the different portions of the constitutions, when respectively passed their second reading, were to be laid upon the table until all had passed their second reading.

The PRESIDENT. According to that resolution, no report can be read a third time until all have passed their second reading. It would be in order, however, to submit a motion to order a report to be read a third time on some future day.

Mr. CLARKE, of Johnson. My idea of the

effect of the resolution referred to is, that these several reports shall be perfected upon their second reading, and then be laid aside. It might perhaps be necessary in going through the several articles, to correct inaccuracies in the preceding articles, remove inconsistencies, &c., to do which it might be necessary to refer all these reports to a committee on revision, to be examined in order to have no conflict between them. The object of ordering any report to its third reading is that we may go on with other reports, and not find ourselves still considering that report upon motions to reconsider, in which as much time might be consumed as in passing it through its second reading.

In relation to the position of the present report, I suppose that as a part of it is still unacted upon, the only disposition we can now make of it is to lay it upon the table, and to-morrow or on some subsequent day, we can take it up and act upon it then, though that portion of the report which has been already acted upon cannot be now amended. I beg leave to remind members that this Bill of Rights is perhaps the most important part of this constitution, and though we have passed some two or three days upon this subject, I do not think that time has been misspent, but that the light drawn out by that discussion will be of benefit to the convention hereafter.

Mr. PARVIN. As this is the first part of the business we have gone through with, I think we should fix some method of proceeding, so that we may have some understanding in regard to such matters hereafter. I suppose that after a report has gone through its second reading, a motion to order it to its third reading would, if carried, cut off all amendments, except by general consent.

The PRESIDENT. It would have that effect, unless the report be referred again to some committee.

Mr. PARVIN. Then here is an amendment of the gentleman from Henry, [Mr. Clarke,] to this fourth section, which has not been acted upon yet, and I suppose the way to reach that amendment would be to let this report lie upon the table at present. Undoubtedly when the report is taken up again, it would be open to amendment as it is now. I am as anxious to get through as any person can be, but so far as regards this Bill of Rights we cannot get through with it because there are some amendments proposed to it which we have agreed to postpone for the present.

Mr. CLARKE, of Johnson. I move that this report, together with the amendments that have been made to it, be printed for the use of the Convention. We have adopted quite a number of amendments to this article, with some one or two of which I am dissatisfied because I do not know what they are, and I do not know what will be their effect. I want to see them and examine them before we pass upon them finally. This is an important part of the constitution; a wrong word here in any one section of this Bill of Rights may cause confusion in the legislation of the State for years to come. And I would prefer to see those amendments in print before I am called upon to act finally in regard to this portion of our constitution. I voted against one amendment offered by the gentleman from Henry, [Mr. Clarke,] which was adopted a few moments since, in relation to leases of land, because I was not prepared in my own mind to support it. It is now in this Bill of Rights, and as I understand it, it affects the right of a man to dispose of a certain kind of property in a certain manner beyond a given number of years. I think we should fully understand all that is in this part of the constitution. I desire to make a constitution that will last at least during my life.

Mr. HARRIS. I do not believe the gentleman can effect any desirable object by having this article with the amendments printed. As I understand the decision of the chair, no portion of this Bill of Rights upon which we have acted, can be reached now except by reconsideration. And if it is printed the time for reconsideration will pass before we get it before us again.

Mr. CLARKE, of Johnson. I withdraw my motion to print.

Mr. BUNKER. I understand that no final action has been taken upon this article yet, and that any section that has not been acted upon is still open to amendment.

The PRESIDENT. That is the opinion of the Chair.

Mr. BUNKER. Then I offer the following as a substitute for the first section of the Bill of Rights:

"All men are by nature equally free and equally dependant upon each other; are possessed of certain inherent and inalienable rights, among which are those of enjoying and defending life and liberty, and pursuing and obtaining safety and happiness."

Mr. CLARKE, of Johnson. I move to lay this article and all its amendments upon the table, subject to the order of the Convention.

The question being taken the motion was agreed to.

Report of Committee on Incorporations.

Mr. CLARKE, of Henry, from the Committee on Incorporations, made the following report:

The Committee on Incorporations to which was referred the resolution of Mr. Gower, at a time when they had matured the plan of the report heretofore submitted by them, would farther respectfully report:

That the act for a State Bank and branches, annexed to said resolution, meets with the approval of the committee in all its main features, so far as the provisions extend; but after providing suitable restraints and limits within which laws may be formed, the details of special enactment fall more legitimately to the province of a legislative body than to this Convention.

They would for this reason deem it inexpedient to engraft into the constitution the bill annexed to said resolution, with or without amendment.

On motion of Mr. CLARKE, of Johnson,

The report was received and laid upon the table.

On motion of Mr. WINCHESTER,

The Convention then adjourned.

WEDNESDAY, February 4, 1857.

The Convention met at nine o'clock, A. M., and was called to order by the President.

Prayer by the Chaplain.

The Journal of yesterday was read and approved.

Petitions.

Mr. PARVIN presented the petition of Chas. Jackson, and 32 other colored men, asking that negroes may have the right of suffrage; which was read and referred to the Committee on Right of Suffrage.

Mr. TODHUNTER presented the petition of John G. Deakin, and 84 others, citizens of Des Moines and Jasper counties, asking for a change of the second section of the eleventh Article of the Miscellaneous Provisions, which restricts the size of counties within certain limits; which was referred to the Committee on Miscellaneous subjects.

Order of Business.

The PRESIDENT. There being no reports from Standing or Select Committees, the first business in order will be the consideration of the report of the Committee on the Right of Suffrage.

Mr. CLARKE, of Johnson. I move that we take up the report of the Committee on the Bill of Rights.

Mr. WILSON. I would suggest to the gentleman from Johnson, [Mr. Clarke,] that the member from Mills, [Mr. Solomon,] who desires to be present when the question is taken upon the section he proposes to insert, for which the gentleman from Johnson, [Mr. Clarke,] proposed a substitute, is not now in his seat.

Mr. CLARKE, of Johnson. I will not urge my motion then.

Mr. CLARKE, of Henry. I move to take up the report of the Committee on the Distribution of Powers and the Legislative Department.

Mr. JOHNSTON. I would like to know if there is any good reason for not taking up the subjects in the order in which they appear in the Constitution?

Mr. HALL. Can this report on the Legislative Department be taken up without a suspension of the rules, which require us to consider the reports of Committees in a certain prescribed order?

The PRESIDENT. It would require a suspension of the rules in order to entertain the motion made by the gentleman from Henry, [Mr. Clark.]

Mr. JOHNSTON. I want the President and the Convention to understand that I make no objection to this course.

If it will accomodate any gentleman upon this floor, I am willing to take up and consider these reports out of their order.

Mr. CLARKE, of Henry. I wish to say to the gentleman from Lee [Mr. Johnston] that in regard to the report on the right of suffrage I have a proposition upon that subject which I wish to present to the people as a distinct question, and which I am not yet prepared to submit to the Convention; and that is one reason why I wish not to take up that report now. And besides this, there is a member not in his seat who is anxious to be present when we take this report under consideration.

Mr. JOHNSTON. I have no objection to the motion of the gentleman.

Mr. TRAER. I hope the motion for taking up the report on the Legislative Department will not prevail. I think that we had better postpone that report until the special committee appointed sometimes on the Basis of Representation are ready to report. I should like to consider that subject before we take up the report of the Committee on the Legislative Department.

Mr. CLARKE, of Henry. I have no objection to taking up the report of the Committee on Incorporations; but I presumed the Convention would prefer considering the other at this time.

Mr. HALL. My only desire is to take the course which will best facilitate the business of the Convention. We have passed a resolution without a dissenting voice to take up the business of the Convention in the order in which the committees were appointed.

Mr. TRAER. I desire to ask if that resolution will interfere with the motion to lay the report of the Committee on the Right of Suffrage upon the table. I understand the Chair to have announced that that report is the first in order. I would enquire of the Chair if a motion to lay that report upon the table for the purpose of taking up some other report would be in order?

The PRESIDENT. The Chair considers the report of the Committee on the Right of Suffrage to be now before the Convention. They can dispose of it by laying it upon the table, proceeding to its immediate consideration, or disposing of it in any other manner they may desire.

Mr. HALL. If there is any good reason, as was observed by the gentleman from Lee, [Mr. Johnston,] why we should depart from the rules which we have adopted, it will be entirely proper to do so. I do not believe this Convention will gain anything by a hop, skip and jump through the different articles of the constitution, discussing one for a short time, and without finishing it, then proceeding to the consideration of another. I do not believe that is the proper course for a deliberative body like this to pursue. If we proceed in the regular order and dispose of each subject as it comes up, we will be more likely to have a correct and intelligible understanding of what we have already done and what we are to do. If we adopt the course recommended by the gentleman from Henry, [Mr. Clarke,] we shall be likely to consume more time than in any other way. There is another reason why we should adhere to our regular order, and that is this: If we follow the order in which the Convention assigned its business, we will be better prepared to discuss and act upon the questions as they come up; but if we are to have no regularity in our mode of doing business, we shall never know when questions are to be presented, and as a matter of course, we will not be so well prepared by study and reflection to act upon them.

Mr. HARRIS. It will be borne in mind that the report of the Committee on the Right of Suffrage was the first report presented here. The committee were unanimous in making it, and gentlemen who are not satisfied with it, have had abundant opportunity to prepare themselves with the objections and amendments which they might desire to make to it, when it should come up in its regular order for consideration.

Mr. CLARKE, of Henry. The gentleman from Des Moines [Mr. Hall,] has raised a question here in regard to the rules, that are to govern us. It appears, that this body did pass a resolution upon this subject, but it is merely a resolution expressing the sense of the convention; and it is not one of our standing rules. There was no notice given, as I understand, of the offering of such a resolution. It was passed, I think, some time when I was not present, or else I was not cognizant of the fact, when it was offered. I made the motion to postpone action upon the report of the Committee on the Right of Suffrage, and take up in lieu thereof the report of the Committee on the Distribution of Powers and the Legislative Department, for the reason that some time since, a resolution was passed postponing action on the fourth section of the report on the right of suffrage, and I do not think if that report is now taken up, that a discussion upon it at this time would be profitable. The proposition which I intend to submit upon this subject, I hope will come up in such a shape as will meet the approbation of the gentleman from Des Moins, [Mr. Hall.]

Another reason for deferring the consideration of this report until some future time is, that one of our members, who desires to be present when we take it up, is now unwell, but will probably be with us in a day or two.

Mr. HALL. Why not take it up, and refer it to a special committee, or dispose of it in some way?

Mr. CLARKE, of Henry. Very well. I will agree to be satisfied with such an arrangement.

The PRESIDENT. The chair is of the opinion that the resolution offered by the gentleman from Des Moines, [Mr. Hall,] and which was passed by the convention, is binding upon us so long as it remains unrescinded.

Mr. CLARKE, of Johnson. I hope that we will proceed in the regular course of business which our rules have prescribed. I am in favor, therefore, of taking up the bill of rights, and disposing of it now. I move, as a substitute for the motion of the gentleman from Henry, [Mr. Clarke,] that we take up the bill of rights.

Mr. JOHNSTON. I would enquire of the gentleman from Henry [Mr. Clarke,] whether he is now prepared to present the proposition upon the question of the right of suffrage, which was postponed a few days since at his instance.

Mr. CLARKE, of Henry. I am not ready.

Mr. HALL. I do hope, that this convention will act upon this report in some form. If there is to be a new report, with material alterations from the former one, I do not want it to be sprung upon us. I do not wish gentlemen to come in here and offer material and radical changes in this article, which we may not be prepared to meet. I hope the convention will at least take up this question, and consider it now, and if there are any radical changes proposed to the report, it can then be referred to a select committee, if the convention shall deem proper to do so.

The PRESIDENT. The decision of the chair is that the first business in order is the report of the Standing Committee on the Right of Suffrage.

Mr. SKIFF. I move that that report be referred to a select committee of five.

Mr. HARRIS. I do not wish to take the wind out of the sails of the gentleman from Jasper, [Mr. Skiff,] but I move that the gentleman from Henry, [Mr. Clarke,] be appointed chairman.

Mr. SKIFF. I do not propose to impose any obligations upon the President, but let him appoint his own commiitees.

Mr. EDWARDS. I see no necessity for the motion of the gentleman from Jasper, [Mr. Skiff,] to refer this article of the constitution to a select committee. It appears to me, that a standing committee having made a report upon this subject, the best way to dispose of this matter would be to bring it before the convention or committee of the whole. If gentlemen are anxious to expedite the business of the convention, this is the course we should pursue. If we should refer this matter to a select committee, and they should make a report differing from that of the standing committee upon this subject, it will only have the tendency to prolong the session of this convention. I cannot see that any advantage will be gained by such a course. If the gentleman from Henry, [Mr. Clarke,] desires to submit any proposition, by way of amendment to this report, he can do it in convention, or in committee of the whole.

Mr. SKIFF. I will state briefly the object I had in making the motion I did. And allow me here to say that I fully concur with the suggestion made by the gentleman from Des Moines, [Mr. Hall.]

If there are any radical changes to be proposed to this article, it is well enough to refer them to a select committee, whose report can be printed and laid upon our tables. I think this course will expedite the business of the convention more than the offering of amendments here on the spur of the moment, and taking delegates by surprise.

Mr. EDWARDS. Let the committee report as they may, every gentleman can then offer his peculiar propositions, by way of amendment, to the various sections as they come up.

Mr. HALL. I understand, that there is a portion of this convention who probably were not represented upon that committee, and there is a proposition to make a radical change upon this matter of the right of suffrage. I am the last man who would wish to deprive those gentlemen from the opportunity of offering propositions embodying their views upon this subject. I may wish myself to offer my views in the shape of amendments, and I do not wish to debar any gentleman from having the same privilege. I want to know in advance what the contemplated changes in the report are, and for that reason I shall vote to refer this report to a select committee.

Mr. CLARKE, of Henry. If the gentleman from Jasper, [Mr. Skiff,] will allow me, I would like to modify his motion so as to refer the fourth section of the first article of the Bill of Rights to the Select Committee.

The PRESIDENT. The Chair is of the opinion that the motion would not now be in order.

Mr. PALMER. I believe we passed a resolution that the different articles of the constitution should be referred to appropriate Standing Committees. Can we refer this matter to a special committee, unless we reconsider the vote by which that resolution was passed?

The PRESIDENT. The Chair is of the opinion that the rule would not preclude the reference of any article or part of an article to a special committee.

Mr. GILLASPY. I am opposed to the appointment of this select committee, for it will certainly lead to procrastination. It was expected by the people of Iowa that the labors of this Convention would have been concluded in at least two weeks and a half We are now in the middle of the third week, and nothing is done yet. It does seem to me that every gentleman upon this floor is as well prepared to dispose of the article on the Right of Suffrage at this time, as he would be a week hence. I have no disposition to choke off or gag discussion upon the subject of the petition which came in here this morning. I am willing that those who favor the extension of the right of suffrage to the negro should make the most they can out of it, make a report upon that subject and spread it upon the record. But I am opposed to consuming all the time in order to accommodate a "nigger in the wood-pile," to use the expression of the gentleman from Henry, [Mr. Clarke. I am just as well prepared to-day, so far as I am concerned, to take up the several reports in the order in which the committees stand, as I will be a week hence. But gentlemen come here and say that they are not prepared to take up and consider propositions. If any gentleman wants to strike out the word "white" in the report on Right of Suffrage, and make a speech upon it, if he is not prepared to do so to-day in Committee of the Whole, he can do in Convention when the report comes up there for consideration. I believe if we mean to accomplish anything, we ought to proceed according to our rules, and take up the reports in the regular order.

Mr. CLARKE, of Henry. Will the gentleman from Jasper, [Mr. Skiff,] amend his section so as to include the fourth section of the Bill of Rights?

Mr. SKIFF. I am willing to accept the amendment.

The PRESIDENT. The Chair would state that the report of the Committee on the Preamble and Bill of Rights is not now before the Convention.

Mr. WARREN. I will ask the gentleman if he will not amend his motion so as to provide for three additional members of the committee. It is a matter in which my constituents feel some interest, and I know that they require some change in regard to the right of suffrage. I hope the gentleman will amend his motion so as to make the committee consist of eight instead of five.

Mr. SKIFF. The Standing Committee upon this subject have already reported in favor of the right of suffrage as it now stands in the constitution. If there should be three additional members appointed upon the committee, there might be a minority report. The present committee have reported unanimously upon this subject, but if there be three more added it would involve the necessity of making a minority report. I think, therefore, that I will not accede to the request made by the gentleman for an increase in the number of the committee.

Mr. EDWARDS. I think gentlemen misconceive the facts in the case. The Standing Committee that reported upon this subject and recommended the adoption of the article in the constitution as it now stands, are not unwilling to entertain any reasonable proposition to amend, that may be offered. I am satisfied with that portion of the constitution as it now exists, but I am not unwilling to have any gentlemen, when that matter comes up, propose any reasonable amendment. It appears to me that it will expedite matters to consider the various reports in the order in which they stand. If this matter goes to a Select Committee, they may not agree, and we may have both majority and minority reports. It appears to me that the most rational mode for this Convention would be to take up the reports of Committee in their order, and as the gentleman from Wapello, [Mr. Gillaspy,] says, dispose of them at once.

Mr. HARRIS. Being a member of the committee that made the report on the Right of Suffrage, I desire to make a single remark. I hope this matter will not be referred to our committee again. It was said by the gentleman from Lucas, [Mr. Edwards,] that the committee would not be inflexible in the maintainance of their opinions as reported, but so far as my opinions are concerned, there is little probability of their being changed upon this question. I have joined in making this report, and I do not want to be under the necessity of making the same report over again.

Mr. CLARKE, of Johnson. I wish to explain the position I occupy upon this question. I shall vote for referring this matter to a special committee, for this reason: The standing committee upon this subject have made their report. It is well known, that a large number of persons in the community are in favor of submitting the proposition of the gentleman from Henry [Mr. Clarke] to a vote of the people. I am willing that the subject shall go to a select committee, and they may, perhaps, report in favor of submitting this proposition to the people. For the purpose of giving the friends of the measure such an opportunity, I shall vote for a reference of this to a select committee.

The question was then taken on the motion of Mr. Skiff, to refer the report of the Committee on Right of Suffrage, to a select committee, and it was agreed to, yeas 18, nays 14, as follows:

Yeas—The President; Messrs. Bunker, Clark of Alamakee, Clarke of Henry, Clarke of Johnson, Ells, Gower, Gray, Hall, Harris, Parvin, Price, Skiff, Seely, Todhunter, Traer, Warren, and Wilson.

Nays—Messrs. Ayres, Day, Edwards, Emerson, Gibson, Gillaspy, Johnston, Marvin, Palmer, Patterson, Peters, Solomon, Winchester and Young.

The PRESIDENT then announced the following named gentlemen, as members of said committee.

Messrs. Skiff, Hall, Clarke, of Henry, Price and Marvin.

Legislative Department.

The PRESIDENT. The next business in order will be the report of the Committee on the "Distribution of Powers, and the Legislative Department." This report is now upon its second reading.

Mr. JOHNSTON. I see no necessity of reading this report, if we are going into Committee of the Whole. There are very few changes from the article upon this subject in our present Constitution.

Mr. HARRIS. I hope the report will be read.

The report, as heretofore published, was then read.

Mr. CLARKE, of Johnson. I confess, that I am not prepared to act upon this report, this morning. After sitting in this Hall for six hours a day, and discharging the duties which have devolved upon me in the Committees of which I am a member, I have not had the time to read and investigate this report; and I apprehend that other gentlemen are placed in the same situation. I move that the report be laid upon the table, and made the special order for Friday afternoon.

If that motion be agreed to, I will then move to take up the report of the Committee on the Executive Department, which does not involve so important qnestions as this. I hope that the report on the Legislative Department will be put over to Friday, as it embraces the questions of taking the census and ousting the present legislature, and a good many other questions which are important, and which many of us may wish to consider and reflect upon before taking action upon them.

Mr. JOHNSTON. I have no objection myself, to this report being laid upon the table, provided that we proceed to some other business I do not know that I ought to insist upon taking up this particular article in the Constitution, because I was one of the members who reported it, and therefore have had better opportunites of examining it, than other gentleman. I do trust, that if it be laid upon the table for the present, we will take up something upon which we can act. But the same objection may arise in regard to taking up the report of the Committee on the Executive Department, and we will have no end to this interminable delay.

The question was then taken, by yeas and nays, on the motion of Mr. Clarke, of Johnson, to lay the report of the Committee on the Legislative Department, on the table and make it the special order for Friday next, and it was agreed to.—Yeas, 18—Nays, 14.

Yeas,—The President, Messrs. Bunker, Clark, of Alamakee, Clarke, of Henry, Clarke, of Johnson, Ells, Gower, Gray, Marvin, Parvin, Peters, Scott, Seely, Todhunter, Traer, Warren, Wilson and Young.

Nays—Messrs. Day, Edwards, Emerson, Gibson, Gillaspy, Hall, Harris, Johnston, Palmer, Patterson, Price, Skiff, Solomon and Winchester.

Executive Department.

The PRESIDENT. The next business in order is the report of the Committee on the Executive Department.

The report, as heretofore published, was then read the second time.

Mr. PETERS moved that the convention resolve itself into a committee of the wnole upon the consideration of this report.

Mr. SKIFF. We have tried one report in committee of the whole, and I consider that our time was thrown away. I shall hereafter be in favor of taking up these matters, and disposing of them in convention, in the order that we reach them.

Mr. PRICE. I move to postpone the further consideration of this report until Monday next, and that it be made the special order for that day. As one of the Committee upon the Executive Department, I feel considerable interest in the provisions incorporated in this report. Besides, it appears to me, that the report upon the legislative department comes naturally first in order, and should be first disposed of. I believe the report upon the legislative department has been postponed until Friday next. There are changes to be made in this article reported by the committee upon the executive department, which do not correspond with the report of the committee on the legislative department, and should that report be agreed to, the report of the committee on the executive department may not correspond with it. I believe, too, that the chairman of the committee on the executive department, [Mr. Todhunter,] is unprepared to take action upon this report to-day. I, therefore, move that it be postponed until Monday next, and be made the special order for that day.

The question being taken, the motion to postpone was agreed to, upon a division, as follows—ayes 15, noes 7.

Order of Business Resumed.

Mr. GILLASPY moved that the convention adjourn,

The question being taken, the motion to adjourn was not agreed to.

Mr. PARVIN. I do not know but what the gentleman from Wapello, [Mr. Gillaspy,] was right to move to adjourn, if we have nothing to do. I would like to go back to the beginning, and take up the bill of rights.

The PRESIDENT. A motion to take up the preamble and bill of rights would be in order.

Mr. GILLASPY. The gentleman from Muscatine [Mr. Parvin,] stated my position exactly. I want to be doing something, and if there is nothing for us to do here, I want to adjourn, that I may go about town and see what is to be seen.

Mr. CLARKE, of Henry. I do not understand what gentlemen mean by crying out that we have nothing to do, or that we are doing nothing here. Most of us happen to be upon committees, that have work to do. My attention has been directed almost exclusively to the business of the committees with which I am connected. If other gentlemen have had nothing to do upon their committees, and have had time to examine these reports, they have had some advantage over me, and I presume many other members of this body. The fact is, the first time I have had to examine these reports has been this morning, while following the secretary as he read them. And I think that in that we have gained something. We have had an opportunity this morning to examine these reports. And if we go on and take them up, and read them, one after another, and then make each one the special order for some particular day, we have then something in view, to which we can look forward. We can then calculate, that we will take up such or such a report upon such and such a day, and we can examine that report and prepare ourselves for its consideration. I know there are members upon this floor, and I am among the number of them, who desire time to examine these matters. I wish to be prepared to consider them when they come up for deliberation. If I can get hold of the materials with which to prepare myself for a proper discharge of my duty here, I want to do so. I cannot say as the gentleman from Wapello, [Mr. Gillaspy,] has said, that I am prepared to vote upon every question that may be presented. The gentleman may himself present some proposition here which will take every one completely by surprise, and I may be as unprepared to act upon it as the gentleman from Des Moines [Mr. Hall,] has sometimes said he was upon propositions presented by myself and others.

In looking over these reports, as they are read at the secretary's desk, each one may discover some new question in which he is interested, and perhaps some ideas may be called up which will be new to this body in relation to the subject embraced in the report. The humblest member of this body may thus be enabled to throw out some idea that may be taken hold of, and incorporated into this constitution, and prove to be of great benefit to the people of this State. We are not therefore losing time in listening to these reports, and considering them as they are read.

I trust the suggestion of the member from Muscatine, [Mr. Parvin,] to take up the bill of rights, will not be pressed at this time, but that we will go on and take up the next report, and read that. And if any gentleman suggests that he would desire to have it postponed, and made the special order for some future day, I will vote with him. If there is one mind here not prepared to act upon any report, even if all the rest of us say we are prepared to proceed with it, I think it is due to that one, to give him an opportunity to prepare himself. If we allow him that opportunity, he may be enabled to throw out some suggestion here that the rest of us will be glad to receive, and incorporate into this constitution. For this reason I hope we will proceed as we have commenced, and go through the consideration of these reports one after another.

Mr. GILLASPY. I do not desire to say one word upon this floor to offend any friend. What I said about our doing nothing was not intended to offend any gentleman upon this floor. I will, however, take the liberty of saying this; I presume the difference between the gentleman from Henry [Mr. Clarke,] and myself is about this. When these reports have been laid upon my table I have taken them to my room at my hotel, and examined them carefully at night. I suppose the gentleman from Henry [Mr. Clarke,] has left all of his, except the bill of rights, and perhaps the article on the right of suffrage, and gone every evening he had an opportunity to hear Horace Greeley, the New York lecturer. Now I am, in my own opinion, as able to decide now upon the principles contained in the reports under consideration as I would be a week hence, not but that the wisdom of members of this convention may throw out some suggestions that would be of value. But I have examined these reports, and am prepared now to act upon them. I do not desire to drive any member of this convention to the necessity of acting upon matters he has not considered and examined. But if gentlemen are going to take weeks and months to examine these reports, I shall be opposed to it, and shall be in favor of some measures being taken to force them to examine them when they ought to do so.

Mr. PARVIN. I do not wish to proceed to the consideration of any subject, until members are prepared to act upon it. But I want to act upon something, and be doing something.

I would say here, that I have just learned, for the first time in my life, that it is a crime, or a misdemeanor for any one to attend the lectures of distinguished men. I had intended myself, as an humble individual, to hear that distinguished man, Horace Greeley, lecture here in this city, but chance alone prevented me from doing so. I suppose, according to the gentleman from Wapello, [Mr. Gillaspy,] that I must think that chance saved me from the commission of some great crime. But it was only chance, I assure this convention, that prevented me from hearing him, for I fully intended to do so.

At the suggestion of several gentlemen here, I will withdraw my motion to take up the bill of rights, or rather I will not make the motion I indicated, a few moments since, and which I proposed to make.

Mr. HARRIS. If it be in order, I would move to take up the report of the committee on future amendments to the constitution. That report has been before us for some time, and I suppose there will be little to do with it. It was the second report made to this convention, I believe.

The PRESIDENT. The next report in order, is the report of the committee on the judicial department.

Mr. GILLASPY. I wish to say that my remarks were not intended to apply to the gentleman from Muscatine, [Mr. Parvin.]

The PRESIDENT. As there is no motion before the convention, no debate is in order at this time, except for the purpose of personal explanation.

Mr. GILLASPY. I desire to make a personal explanation. As I said, my remarks were not intended to apply to the gentleman from Muscatine, (Mr. Parvin.) Neither do I think that I said it was, or that I so regarded it, a crime to go and hear a lecture. What I said was only for the benefit of the gentleman from Henry, (Mr. Clarke.)

I move that the convention now take up the bill of rights, and proceed to act upon it. I am satisfied that no member upon this floor can give for an excuse, that he is not familiar with the subject, and, therefore, not prepared to act upon it.

Mr. CLARKE, of Johnson. I would move that the convention resolve itself into committee of the whole upon the majority and minority reports of the committee on the judiciary department.

Mr. HARRIS. I shall be opposed to going into committee of the whole upon the reports of the committee on the judiciary. That is a matter that I feel some interest in, but I have not examined it, and I am not prepared to act upon it yet. It has been upon our tables but a short time, and I have not had an opportunity to examine it as I desire to do.

The question was stated to be upon the motion of Mr. Gillaspy to take from the table the Preamble and Bill of Rights.

Mr. HARRIS. I trust the motion of the gentleman from Wapello (Mr. Gillaspy) will prevail, rather than that the Convention should go into the Committee of the Whole on the Judiciary Department. The subject of the Judiciary is perhaps the most important subject that will come before us, and should receive a careful examination, which I have not been able to give it yet.

Mr. WILSON. I hope the motion of the gentleman from Wapello (Mr. Gillaspy) will not prevail, for the reason that I believe a further postponement of the article on the Bill of Rights will be a saving of time. I believe if it is taken up now, we shall consume more time in discussing it than we shall gain by taking it up for consideration. I am satisfied that the same questions, which occupied so much of our time on Monday and Tuesday, will arise again if it be taken up now. I am satisfied, also, that all the members of this convention are not prepared to act decisively upon those questions at this time. I hope, therefore, that the motion to take up that subject will not prevail; but that it will be permitted to remain upon the table.

There are three or four reports upon which we certainly are prepared to act. If members are not prepared to act on the report upon the Judiciary Department, there is the report of the Committee on State Debts, the report upon future amendments to the Constitution, and the report of the Committee on Incorporations. I suppose most members are prepared to pass on one or the other of those reports. I can see nothing in the report of the Committee on State Debts that we cannot pass upon now. Neither do I perceive anything in the report of the Committee on Amendments to the Constitution that we may not consider now. I think we would save time by not taking up the report of the Committee on the Preamble and Bill of Rights.

Mr. SOLOMON. Although I am aware that it is looked upon as presumption in the young members of this convention to bring forward their notions about matters before this body, still I feel inclined to give my reasons for voting for the motion of the gentleman from Wapello [Mr. Gillaspy]. I think a mistake has been committed this morning in reference to these matters, and that the policy which has been pursued by the Convention exhibits a kind of unreadiness to proceed to business. A resolution was passed several days since to the effect that we would proceed with the business before this convention in a certain order. We adhered to that resolution up to this morning. Members of this convention being aware of the nature of that resolution, expected that, in accordance with it. we would proceed to the consideration of the report of the Committee on the right of suffrage, as being the next in order. With that expectation, I apprehend, the majority of this convention are better prepared to take up that report; for when the report of the next committee is taken up, there is a general expression of unreadiness to consider it. And this is the reason: no gentleman has been looking forward to its being considered now. Let us go through with the report of the Committee on the Bill of Rights, and then we will be prepared for the one next in order. I think all our difficulty has arisen from making this change in the order of business.

I differ with the gentleman from Jefferson [Mr. Wilson] in the opinion that we will gain time from the postponement of this report of the Committee on the Preamble and the Bill of Rights. I do not believe such would be the case. I am well aware that there are two parties in this convention, upon the questions that have engaged our time and attention for some days past. I am aware that there is a disposition upon the part of one of these parties to strike out the word "white" in the present report of the Committee on the Right of suffrage. And I am equally well aware that there is a disposition upon the part of the other party not to consent to that.

Now, this question is reduced to a nutshell—more so than any other one that can come before this Convention. And I think we are better prepared to take up and pass upon that matter than we are upon any other before us. I am ready, for one; and I presume we are all ready, from the fact that it embraces a subject more fully and earnestly discussed than any other subject that can be presented, and one that entered more largely, perhaps, than any other, in the recent campaign, which has resulted in our being assembled here. I think we would lose time by postponing this matter; for while we were delaying this Convention, members would be loading themselves with long speeches which they would come in here and claim the privilege of delivering.

Mr. WILSON. I wish to correct one thing the gentleman from Mills [Mr. Solomon] has asserted here. I presume that in his remarks about parties, he refers to the Republican and Democratic parties. Now I do not know where he gets his authority for saying that there is a disposition upon the part of one of those parties, as a party, to strike out the word "white," where it occurs in the article on the right of suffrage. But I know this, that he is ahead of time, speaking beyond the book, when he says any such thing as that. Those having charge of that matter have determined that subject among themselves. Whenever the gentleman undertakes to speak in that way for the Republican party, he speaks without authority, and I desire to correct him now.

Mr. HALL. If I was not mistaken in understanding the gentleman form Henry, [Mr. Clarke] he desired to have the fourth section of the bill of rights, with his amendment, referred to the select committee that has been appointed this morning. I would therefore suggest that we take up the bill of rights from the table, for the purpose of moving that reference. I think we have exhausted a sufficient portion of our time upon that part of our Constitution, although I am willing to agree to this reference in consequence of the suggestion made this morning, by the gentleman from Henry, that he believes a proposition can be drawn up, that will be acceptable to all the members of this convention. If that can be done, we shall save time by agreeing to the reference. I am willing to meet gentlemen half-way. Perhaps it would be better to take the bill of rights from the table, and make that reference, and we can then proceed with our other business.

Mr. HARRIS. I am willing to vote for the motion to take up that subject, with that understanding.

Mr. WILSON. I will also support the motion to take the bill of rights from the table, with the understanding it is to be done for the purpose of making that reference.

Mr. EDWARDS. I am just as anxious as any member upon this floor, to transact the business we were sent here to do, that we may return home as soon as possible; and I would suggest to the convention that we take up the report of the committee on incorporations, for the reason that that is the most important question that can come before this convention for its consideration. It will require a longer time, closer attention, and more consideration to dispose of that question than probably any other; and the quickest way, the best way to expedite business would be to go into committee of the whole upon that question, and then interchange opinions upon it. It is a subject that cannot possibly conflict with any other portion of the constitution.

It has been suggested by a friend near me, that we should not go into committee of the whole, for the reason that when we did so the other day, we made sundry amendments to the report then before us, which were not concurred in. It is for that very reason, that I think we should go into committee of the whole, in order that our journals may not be encumbered with all these useless amendments. Just suppose, that all the business we transacted in committee of the whole had been transacted in the convention; onr journals would have accumulated to an enormous extent. When in committee of the whole, we have interchanged opinions, and given gentlemen time to reflect; and when we came into convention where all our proceedings are spread upon the journal, we can pass upon the subjects before us more expeditiously. If we can dispose of this report of the committee on incorporations, I am satisfied that the rest of the business of the convention remaining to be done, can be got through with in a short time. This is the most complex, and interesting question that can come before us, and we will gain time by going into committee of the whole, and interchanging opinions upon it there. If the gentleman from Wapello [Mr. Gillaspy] will withdraw his motion to take up the bill of rights, I will move to take up the report of the committee on incorporations for the purpose of referring it to the committee of the whole.

Mr. BUNKER. It seems to me, that we are getting into unnecessary difficulties. If I understand the resolution adopted the other day, on motion of the gentleman from Des Moines, [Mr. Hall] it was that we should take up the reports of the standing committees, in the order in which the committees were appointed. Whenever a report comes before this body, if I understand anything of the effect of the rule, that report is subject to the disposal of the convention, and they may lay it upon the table, refer it to a select committee or dispose of it in any other way they see proper; and then the next report comes up in its order, and so on through the chapter. I think there is no difficulty about the matter if we follow this course.

Mr. GILLASPY. I desire to say to the gentleman from Lucas, [Mr. Edwards] that if he can give me any guarantee that the convention is prepared to go on with the report he has referred to, I will withdraw my motion. I only desire to go to work. But, I am satisfied that this convention is prepared to act upon the bill of rights.

Mr. CLARKE, of Henry. I apprehend that there is no objection at all to the motion of the gentleman from Wapello [Mr. Gillaspy] to take up the report of the committee on the preamble and bill of rights, with the understanding that the fourth section, and the pending amendment to it, be referred to the select committee. After that has been done, I would enquire of the chair if it would then be in order to move to lay upon the table, all the reports that precede the report of the committee on incorporations, and take up that report and act upon it?

The PRESIDENT. That can be done if the convention will agree to it.

Mr. JOHNSTON. Can any portion of the bill of rights be referred at the present time to the select committee?

The PRESIDENT. No motion to refer can be made, until the report of the committee on the bill of rights be taken up.

The question being then taken, upon the motion to take from the table, the report of the committee on the preamble and bill of rights, it was agreed to.

Preamble and Bill of Rights.

The PRESIDENT stated the pending question to be upon a substitute for the first section of the bill of rights, offered by the gentleman from Washington (Mr. Bunker).

Mr. CLARKE, of Henry. I would now move that the fourth section, with the pending amendment, be referred to the select committee, to which was referred the report of the committee on the right of suffrage.

Mr. JOHNSTON. I move that the tenth section of the bill of rights, as amended by the convention on yesterday, be also referred to the same committee.

The PRESIDENT. The pending question is upon the substitute offered for the first section.

Mr. BUNKER. I think we can dispose of that substitute without any difficulty. I would like to have a vote upon it, though I do not know whether any gentleman will vote for it, but myself or not.

Mr. JOHNSTON. With the consent of the gentleman from Washington, (Mr. Bunker) I will include in my motion to refer, the first section, with his proposed substitute.

Mr. BUNKER. I am willing to have that done.

Mr. CLARKE, of Henry. I will modify my motion so as to include the eighteenth section also. The motion will then be, that sections one, four, ten and eighteen, with their amendments, be referred to the special committee.

The PRESIDENT. The chair would suggest that to avoid confusion, it would be better to refer the whole report to the committee.

Mr. HALL. I will move to refer the whole of the report upon the preamble and bill of rights, to the select committee already appointed.

Mr. CLARKE. of Henry. I think that select committee will have too much to attend to. if this report be referred to them, in addition to the report of the committee on the right of suffrage, which has already been referred to them. I therefore move, that this report be referred to a select committee of three, to be appointed by the chair.

Mr. HALL. There has been a select committee already raised this morning, and that article of our constitution in relation to the right of suffrage has been referred to that committee. The subject referred to that committee embraces everything that pertains to the question so much discussed before this Convention while considsidering the Bill of Rights, and particularly the subject embraced in the amendment of the gentleman from Henry, [Mr. Clarke.] I am opposed to taking up these matters and dividing them and referring them to three or four special committees. Let all the matters pertaining to this subject be referred to the committee already raised. A new committee I think would be unnecessary and uncalled for. If we have this new committee, we will but have a Pandora's box opened in our midst, and cause a discussion which will last all next week.

Mr. TODHUNTER. I understood that this fourth section was to be referred to the select committee upon the right of suffrage. What made that impression upon my mind was the remark of the gentleman from Appanoose, [Mr. Harris,] that while he had no desire to take the wind out of the sails of the gentleman from Jasper, [Mr. Skiff,] who moved the appointment of that select committee, still he wanted the gentleman from Henry, [Mr. Clarke,] appointed chairman of that committee.

The PRESIDENT. That was in reference to

another report. No action has been had upon this report. The question is upon the motion of the gentleman from Des Moines, [Mr. Hall,] to refer this report to the select committee already raised.

Mr. HALL. I do not see the necessity of raising a new committee for this report. It does appear to me to be splitting this matter up too much, and opening the door for diverse reports upon this subject. I do not understand that there is any great division of sentiment in this Convention, or any difficulty to reconcile, upon any other than this one subject. That question arises perhaps more evidently and directly in the article in regard to the right of suffrage. This fourth section, which has drawn forth so much discussion, was laid upon the table yesterday on the motion of the gentleman from Henry, [Mr. Clarke,] with the partial promise that an amendment would be hereafter submitted that would obviate all the serious differences brought out by that discussion. And a remark to the same effect was made this morning, when the special committee upon the report on the right of suffrage was ordered, and it was understood then that this fourth section should be referred to the same committee. That committee can agree upon the one report, and we shall have the one subject before us divested of all other matters before the Convention. But if we divide this matter, and have it committed to separate committees, we will open a vast field of discussion, and we cannot tell when it will terminate I have no other desire than to progress in the business of the Convention, and I think it would facilitate business here by having this whole subject referred to the committee now raised, and thus let us get rid of these questions if we can.

Mr. PARVIN. I cannot agree with the gentleman from Des Moines, [Mr. Hall.] Here are two separate and distinct propositions. The report of the committee upon the right of suffrage has been referred to a select committee. Now if we burden that committee by referring to them the report of the committee on the preamble and bill of rights, they will have more than they ought to attend to. I think we should have a select committee upon the bill of rights. Both of these committees can report separately, sooner than one committee can, upon both subjects. I hope the Convention will refer this matter to a separate and distinct committee.

Mr. SKIFF. I am not very particular whether this matter is referred to the select committee on the right of suffrage or not. I shall vote for that reference, however, for the reason suggested by the gentleman from Des Moines, [Mr. Hall.] I have but a word to say in reply to what has been said by the gentleman from Mills, [Mr. Solomon,] in relation to the motives which induced me to move, in the first place, for a special committee upon the right of suffrage. I do not want to strike out the word "white" in our constitution. I want to have that matter referred to the people at large, and leave it to them to say whether "citizens" in the full sense of the term, shall have a right to vote. If they shall say, let them vote, I will agree to it; if not, I will agree to that. I shall vote upon that question as I see proper, and I want everybody else to do the same.

And I would here take occasion to say to this Convention, that if any member wishes to present his views to the select committee on the right of suffrage, I hope that he will hand them in soon in writing, that we may be able to make our report as soon as may be.

Mr. WILSON. The reference now proposed will, I imagine, affect more particularly the proposition submitted by the gentleman from Henry, [Mr. Clarke,] than any other. And it seems to me that courtesy requires that we should raise a special committee upon this article, and that he should be the chairman of that committee. The proposition in question was brought forward by him; he has taken a more active part in it than any other member of this body. And I think it is but due to him that a committee be raised and he be appointed chairman of it, as he would be according to parliamentary usage, being the member who moved the reference.

Mr. HARRIS. It is certainly very evident to every gentleman here that the gentleman from Henry, [Mr. Clarke,] is perhaps more radical than many of his republican friends. And it seems that upon some of the propositions he has brought forward, he has not received the support of the party to which he belongs. He has his particular notions and sentiments, and having taken the course he has, it does seem to me that it is nothing more than fair and right that he should have this committee appointed.—The right of suffrage is a separate matter from this. And if he differs upon this subject from those on that committee which we have already raised, as is most probably the case, it would be treating him with no more than courtesy to give him the opportunity he desires of having a new committee appointed.

Mr. CLARKE, of Henry. I am really moved by no consideration such as gentlemen seem to suppose, in moving for this new select committee. If my motion, as it was made originally, to refer the fourth section of the bill of rights to the committee already appointed, had been suffered to pass as I made it, I would not have moved for this separate committee. But when the gentleman from Lee, [Mr. Johnston,] moved to refer other sections of that article to the same committee, and the gentleman from Des Moines, [Mr. Hall,] moved to refer the whole bill of rights to that committee, I saw at once the necessity of having another special committee. The whole report of the committee on the right of suffrage has been referred to the select committee already appointed. And now the whole report of the committee on the preamble and bill of rights, with all the amendments we have passed upon, is to be referred to a select committee. If it be referred to the same committee as the other report, we would be putting upon that committee the duties of two standing committees to perform. For that reason I think it would be better to have a special committee to which this matter can be referred, but not because I desire to be made its chairman, or to have my particular ideas reiterated by it. I am willing to concur with any gentleman I may meet upon that committee, and agree upon such a report as the majority of the committee may decide upon.

Mr. PATTERSON. I would ask the names of the gentlemen appointed upon the select committee on the right of suffrage.

The PRESIDENT. That committee consists of Messrs. Skiff, Hall, Clarke of Henry, Price and Marvin.

Mr. PATTERSON. It does seem to me that that committee will be capable of examining this matter also, so that we may avoid the necessity of having two or three separate reports.

The question was upon the motion of Mr. Hall to refer the preamble and bill of rights to the select committee on the right of suffrage.

On this question Mr. HALL called for the yeas and nays, and they were ordered accordingly.

The question being then taken by yeas and nays, the motion was not agreed to, yeas 12, nays 21, as follows:

Yeas—Messrs. Ayres, Day, Emerson, Gibson, Gillaspy, Hall, Johnston, Palmer, Patterson, Peters, Price, and Skiff.

Nays—The President, Messrs. Bunker, Clark of Alamakee, Clarke of Henry, Clarke of Johnson, Edwards, Ells, Gower, Gray, Harris, Marvin, Parvin, Scott, Seely, Solomon, Todhunter, Traer, Warren, Wilson, Winchester and Young.

The question recurred upon the motion of Mr. Clarke of Henry to refer the report of the committee on the preamble and bill of rights to a select committee of three.

Mr. HALL. I move to amend that motion so as to refer the fourth section of the Bill of Rights with the amendment of the gentleman from Henry, [Mr. Clarke,] to the Select Committee on the Right of Suffrag.e

The PRESIDENT. The chair doubts whether it would be strictly in order to refer one section of a report to a Select Committee. The gentleman from Des Moines, [Mr. Hall,] can move to refer the whole report with instructions to the Committee to consider particular sections of it.

Mr. HALL. I understood that on yesterday the gentleman from Henry, [Mr. Clarke,] proposed a material modification of the fourth section of the Bill of Rights, and that section with the proposed amendment was laid upon the table, and the Convention proceeded to consider the remainder of the Bill of Rights. We have, this morning, taken that section with the pending amendment from the table and it is now before the Convention for their disposal.

The PRESIDENT. The Convention took up the whole report of the Committee on the Preamble and Bill of Rights.

Mr. HALL. I desire to move to refer the fourth section of the Bill of Rights, with the amendment proposed by the gentleman from Henry, (Mr. Clarke,) to the Select Committee upon the Right of Suffrage. Does the chair decide that such a motion would not be in order?

The PRESIDENT. The chair says that he doubts whether a motion of that kind would be in order. The chair thinks that at all, events, to refer a section of a report to a Committee would be an awkward way of doing business, and would create confusion.

Mr. HALL. That is very true. I voted this morning to raise the Special Committee already appointed for the express purpose of referring this report to that Committee, and I understood that such was the intention generally.

The PRESIDENT. The chair would inquire of the gentleman if he could not attain his object by moving to refer the whole report to the Committee, with instructions to consider a particular section?

Mr. HALL. That will do just as well. I therefore move that the report of the Committee on the Preamble and Bill of Rights with the amendments thereto, be referred to the Select Committee on the Right of Suffrage, and that they be instructed to examine and report upon the fourth section of the Bill of Rights, together with the amendment of the gentleman from Henry.

Mr. CLARKE, of Henry. I would move to amend that motion, so as to refer the report to a Select Committee, with instructions to consider and report upon the fourth and tenth sections.

Mr. HALL. If the gentleman is disposed to insist upon having a Select Committee appointed, I suppose the vote the Convention has already given, is sufficient to indicate their willingness to gratify him; I will therefore withdraw my motion.

The question recurred upon the motion to refer the Bill of Rights to a Select Committee, with instructions to consider and report upon the fourth and tenth sections.

Mr. BUNKER. I would move to instruct the Committee to report, also, upon the first section with the substitute I have submitted.

Mr. CLARKE, of Henry. I will modify my motion so as to include the first section.

The question was then upon referring with instructions in relation to the first, fourth, and tenth sections.

Mr. HALL. I beg leave to say, that I would not have voted for raising the first Committee, had I not supposed this whole matter would have been referred to that Committee. It was with that understanding that I voted for that Committee. I will not say that the gentleman from Henry, (Mr. Clarke,) has acted in bad faith towards me, but I certainly understood him to acquiesce in that proposition. I do not want to take this thing in broken doses. I do not want to have it divided up and brought in here upon separate dishes; I want it in one stew, all at once, and be rid of it.

Mr. CLARKE, of Johnson. I am opposed to referring this whole Bill of Rights to this Select Committee, for the reason that the gentleman from Mills, (Mr. Solomon,) offered an amendment concerning the prohibition of articles of traffic, for which I proposed a substitute, both of which were laid upon the table. I wish to have that matter disposed of by this Convention, I do not care how, provided I get their action directly upon it. I am opposed to this way of blinking matters by laying them upon the table. Now if this whole report is referred to the Select Committee, we cannot act upon this matter until the report comes back again. I am inclined to differ with the chair in his decision that a particular section of a report cannot be referred to a Committee, and I may perhaps take an appeal from that decision. The effect of referring the whole report would be to delay the settlement of any portion of this Bill of Rights until the report comes back again. I am willing to refer the first, fourth and tenth sections to this Select Committee. But the proposition of the gentleman from Mills, (Mr. Solomon,) to which I offered a substitute, has no connection with this other matter. It is entirely disconnected from it, and I want to have it acted upon by the Convention in some way. I understood the chair to express a doubt about his decision, and not to have finally so decided. It may be true that this would create a little confusion and inconvenience, but I think the Convention has a right to retain a part of this report in their provision and send the rest to a Committee. If the whole report contained but a single subject, then, perhaps, the decision of the chair would be correct. But such is not the case; the report embraces several separate and distinct subjects, and I think, therefore, we can separate them, refer one or more, and retain the rest in our possession to be acted upon here.

Mr. CLARKE, of Henry. If it would meet the views of the gentleman from Johnson, [Mr. Clarke,] I would include in my motion of instructions to the Committee, the proposition of the gentleman from Mills, (Mr. Solomon,) together with his substitute.

Mr. CLARKE, of Johnson. That would not answer my purpose, because the Committee would probably do as the Convention has done, evade the matter.

Mr. JOHNSTON. I have no doubt that the chair is right in his decision upon this question of reference. I presume this report of the Committee on the Bill of Rghts occupies the same position that a bill, with its different sections, does before a legislative body. And it would be something unusual to refer a section of a bill to a Committee, and retain the remainder of the bill for action. I think in this matter the gentleman from Johnson (Mr. Clarke,) is wrong.

Mr. CLARKE, of Johnson. I do not regard this in the light of a bill; if I did I should be wrong.

Mr. JOHNSTON. It is anologous to a bill.

Mr. MARVIN. I am convinced that a portion of the members of this body do not know how to act in this matter, and therefore I move to lay this whole subject upon the table. If that motion prevails then I will move to reconsider the vote by which a Select Committee on the Right of Suffrage was ordered. Should that also prevail, I have a proposition to submit with regard to this subject, which I think will meet the views of the gentlemau from Henry. (Mr. Clarke.)

Mr. CLARKE, of Henry. With the permission of the Convention, I will state that I concur with the gentleman from Johnson, (Mr. Clarke,) in his opinion in regard to the unfairness of blinking questions, to which he refers. I am very desirous that my young friend from Mills, (Mr Solomon,) and my friend from Johnson, would have a direct vote of the Convention upon their two propositions. I do not think it proper and right, or, at least, not proper treatment towards any gentleman who offers a proposition here, to lay it upon the table, and there let it sleep the sleep that knows no waking. I think that would be begging the question. And I do hope the Convention will so act that the sense of the Convention can be taken upon the two separate propositions of those gentlemen. I desire to place myself upon the record in regard to both of those propositions.

The question being then taken, upon the motion to lay upon the table, it was not agreed to.

The question then recurred upon the motion to refer the Bill of Rights to a Select Committee of three, with instructions to confine their attention to the first, fourth and tenth sections.

Mr. CLARKE, of Johnson. I move to amend the motion so as to include in the instructions the eighteenth section of the Bill of Rights. Several amendments were offered yesterday to that section and adopted, and I apprehend they are not just in the shape they should be in, to go into this Constitntion; and this Committee, or some other, should examine them and put them into proper shape.

Mr. CLARKE, of Henry. I will accept the amendment.

The question was then taken upon the motion to refer with instructions in relation to the first, fourth, tenth and eighteenth sections and it was agreed to.

The PRESIDENT announced as the members constituting that Committee, Messrs. Clarke, of Henry, Harris and Wilson.

Mr. EDWARDS moved to take up the report of the Committee on Incorporations.

The PRESIDENT. That would require a suspension of the rules, which can be done only by unanimous consent, as there is no rule providing for such suspension.

Mr. SKIFF. I trust we will proceed to consider the reports in their regular order.

Judicial Department.

The PRESIDENT stated that the next business in order, was the consideration of the majority and minority reports of the Committee on the Judicial Department.

The two reports were then read as heretofore published.

On motion of Mr. EDWARDS,

The majority and minority reports of the Committee on the Judiciary Department were referred to the Committee of the Whole, and made the special order therein, at two o'clock this afternoon.

On motion of Mr. TRAER,

The Convention then took a recess until two o'clock, P. M.

EVENING SESSION.

The convention met at two o'clock P. M., and was called to order by the President.

The PRESIDENT stated the business before the convention to be the consideration in committee of the whole of the majority and minority reports of the committee on the judiciary department.

Judicial Department.

The Convention accordingly proceeded to consider these reports in committee of the whole. (Mr. Johnston in the Chair.)

The CHAIRMAN. The subject before the committee of the whole, is the report of the majority of the committee on the judicial department, which is now open to amendment.

Mr. CLARKE, of Johnson. As chairman of the committee upon this subject, it may be, perhaps, proper for me to state the substance of these reports, and show the radical difference that exists between them. The committee will perceive, that there is no difference in the minds of the committee as to the number of judges, and the manner of electing them. Both reports provide for a supreme court of four judges, and for dividing the State into judicial districts, in which these judges shall be elected—one judge of the supreme court, and three judges of the district court in each district. These reports also concur in the salaries of the judges, and in reporting and providing for a temporary court for the trial of officers of the State, who may be charged with misconduct and incompetency. In all these respects these reports concur. The radical difference between them is this. The majority report provides for the creation of three courts; first, a district court; second, an intermediate or appellate court, which is the supreme court of the district, and which consists of the district judges of that district; and third, the supreme court, which would be analogous in this State to the court of appeals in the State of New York. The minority of the committee are opposed to the three courts. They recommend, first, a district court; second, a supreme court, leaving the system as it now stands in the present constitution, with the exception, that the mode of electing the judges is different. This is the radical difference between the two reports. The question to be decided then is, whether there shall be two courts or three, or in other words, whether our system shall remain as it is at present, or whether there shall be created a supreme court for each district. As this is, perhaps, the main question, and the first to be determined, for the purpose of bringing it directly before the convention, and having an expression of opinion upon it, the details of both reports being so similar, I move to substitute the report of the minority for that of the majority. I suppose it will be understood, that a vote of this committee substituting the report of the minority for that of the majority, will be considered as an expression of the committee upon that subject. It seems proper, in the first instance, that we should determine the question, whether we should have two or three courts; and I know no other way of raising that question than by moving to substitute the minority for the majority report. I make that motion then for the purpose of bringing that question before the committee.

Mr. PARVIN. I find in looking over these reports, that from a committee composed of five members, we have four different reports, two separate and distinct reports, with a disclaimer attached to each, showing that there are four different opinions in regard to these reports. I prefer the minority to the majority report, but I prefer the present judiciary system to either of the systems now presented; and in order to test the minds of the committee in regard to this matter, I move that the article on the judiciary, in the present constitution, be substituted for the reports of both the majority and minority.

Mr. HARRIS. I think there are some changes that the gentleman from Muscatine (Mr. Parvin) would like to see made in the present system, especially in the election of judges. I was about to offer a substitute, which I think will meet his views.

Mr. PARVIN. We can take the old system, and make such amendments as may be needed.

Mr. CLARKE, of Johnson. I raise the question of order, whether the motion of the gentleman from Muscatine is in order, (Mr Parvin.)

The CHAIRMAN. The chair does not think that his motion is strictly in order.

Mr. WILSON. I would ask whether the minority report would not be the first in order?

The CHAIRMAM. In the opinion of the chair, the majority report would be the first in order, but the question now before the committee is upon substituting the minority for the majority report.

Mr. HALL. I suppose the gentleman from Johnson, (Mr. Clarke,) made this motion for the purpose cf having the committee decide whether they shall have two or three courts. I suppose it is the intention of the gentleman to take up the minority report, and pass over that of the majority, for the purpose of testing the sense of the convention upon that question. If this plan be adopted, it will leave the question sufficiently open for gentlemen to determine in regard to all the propositions submitted, and it will bring up every thing which gentlemen can desire to submit in this discussion. With that view, I hope gentlemen will not embarrass the matter by any technical questions, but allow this question of two and three courts to be submitted to the consideration and judgment of the committee.

Mr. CLARKE, of Johnson. I am not particular as to the manner in which this question is disposed of. I thought if we decided this main question of difference between these two reports it would save the necessity of examining them both at length, and perhaps leaving us, at the end, just where we started. The details of either of these reports may not be perfectly satisfactory to members, but my object in making the motion I did was to settle the question of the radical difference between the two; and then, after that question was settled, we could take either of these reports and make such amendments as the convention might deem proper.—As the question, whether we should have two or three courts, was a matter of great difference in the minds of the Committee, I did not suppose the motion I made would pass without some discussion. I am free to say, that if the State were ten years older, I would be in favor of the report made by the majority. I think that with our present population, wealth, and amount of business, it would be an unnecessary burthen upon the people to provide for three courts; and I believe for the next ten years to come, two courts will be sufficient in this State. With the view of providing for a third court in future, if it shall become necessary, the minority report leaves the necessity of establishing another court hereafter, to the Legislature to determine.

I trust that members will express their opinions upon this subject, so that we may vote understandingly upon this main proposition. I do not care in what shape it comes up, but I wish to get an expression of opinion from the Committee of the Whole upon the difference between the two reports.

Mr. EDWARDS. It appears to me from the position in which the Convention stands, that we are much divided upon this question. There are some gentlemen who favor the majority report, others again, who favor the minority report,and still others who favor the system as it exists in the present constitution. It seems to me, that the shortest way to dispose of this matter would be for the gentleman from Johnson [Mr. Clarke,] to withdraw his motion; adopt the suggestion of the gentleman from Muscatine [Mr. Parvin] and substitute the article on the judiciary in the present constitution. That will bring up the whole subject, and discussion can then be had upon all these systems—the present, and those proposed by the majority and minority reports.

Mr. HARRIS. I was intending to offer a substitute, based upon the present system as it now stands, for both of these reports, but I understood it was out of order.

The CHAIRMAN. The chair understands that the Committee on the Judicial Department have presented both a majority and a minority report. The majority report, in the opinion of the chair, would have the preference. The gentleman from Johnson [Mr. Clarke] moves to substitute the report of the minority for that of the majority, for the purpose of giving it the preference.

Mr. PARVIN. Would a substitute be now in order?

The CHAIRMAN. An amendment to the amendment would be in order, but not a substitute for a substitute.

Mr. PARVIN. I will wait until the question is taken upon the proposition submitted by the gentleman from Johnson [Mr. Clarke]. If his motion be voted down, I will then make my motion.

Mr. CLARKE, of Johnson. It seems to me that the gentleman would gain nothing by that course. If he is in favor of the two court system, it seems to me that he ought to vote in favor of my proposition: for if that prevails, the question of having three courts is disposed of; then when the minority report comes up, if he prefers the system as it now exists, all he has to do is to propose it by way of amendment. He gains nothing by voting down my proposition and moving his, because the same question would then come up. While I concur with him in having two courts instead of three, I should be found arrayed against other provisions of his plan; and he would therefore be dividing the friends of the two court system by the plan he proposes. If he is in favor of two courts he ought to vote with me, but if he is in favor of the three court system, he should vote against my plan.

Mr. PARVIN. In looking over these reports, I think the convention will find that they can amend the present article easier than they can amend the minority report.

The CHAIRMAN. The question presented here is, whether the minority report shall be substituted for that of the majority. Having settled that question, it would then be in order for the gentleman from Muscatine to offer his substitute.

Mr. HARRIS. I have looked over these two reports very carefully, but as yet I have been unable to come to a satisfactory conclusion in my own mind. I think a majority of the members here would prefer the present system to either of the systems now reported by the committee. I do not wish to vote for either of these propositions.

Mr. SKIFF. It seems to me that this question has been rather suddenly sprung upon us. If we are to adopt this minority report without any discussion, and it is to be considered as a test question, why we might just as well rise, report progress, and go into convention. The minority report, I understand, is the only thing that is now before the Committee, and before this question is taken, I would like to hear members of the Convention express their opinions; and I would myself like to have the privilege of saying a few words.

I am in favor of the three court system reported by the majority; and I can give my views for preferring that system in a very few words. I think the present system works a great hardship upon the suitor, unless he has the good fortune to live somewhere in the vicinity of the Supreme Court.

Mr. TRAER. I rise to a point of order. I would ask if the gentleman from Jasper is in order in discussing the merits of either of the reports presented by the Committee on the Judiciary? The question, as I understand it, is upon substituting one report for another.

The CHAIRMAN. The chair thinks that the gentleman from Jasper is in order.

Mr. SKIFF. My reasons for favoring the report of the majority, I will briefly state. A suitor, for instance, who lives somewhere near the capital of the State, where the Supreme Court holds its sessions, can take his case from the District Court where it is tried, directly to the Supreme Court, with very little expense; and the same attorney who attends the District Court can follow the case to the Supreme Court, with very little additional expense. But this would not be the case with suitors who live at a distance from the capital where the Supreme Court holds its sessions. The attorney who manages a case is supposed to know more about it than any one else can; and although generally, when a case is taken to the court of last resort, it is the practice to authorise some one else to manage the case, yet it is important, if it can be done, to have the attorney, who managed the case at the start, attend to it in its progress from one court to another, and be ready with his counsel and advice to co-operate with the counsel who tries the case before the court of last resort. If we have four districts, as proposed in this majority report, and the judges of these districts hold a court in bank for the correction of errors in cases that may arise on trials in the districts, many cases that now go up to the court of last resort will be tried at some point in these districts. The Judges who try these cases, although they may be very profound lawyers, are liable to make mistakes in deciding questions upon the spur of the moment. If they can have an opportunity to correct their errors, as is proposed by this majority report, a great many cases that are now taken to the court of last resort will be stopped in this intermediate superior court. By the adoption of the system proposed by the majority, the Supreme Court reports would be less voluminous, from the fact that in the superior courts, matters which have been decided over and over again would not be considered of consequence enough to report.—The decisions of the Court of Appeals of the State of New York, are those which govern in the determination of legal matters, and that will be the case here. The cases only in the third court, the supreme court, (which is analagous to the court of appeals in New York, would be reported.

The business of the present Supreme Court in this State has been accumulating for many years past, and all the cases that come up, are, as a matter of course, reported. In a short time our reports will be very voluminous, and every one who desires to know what the law is, will have to wade through a great deal of unimportant matter to find what he really wants. I think that under the plan proposed by the majority, a large amount of the business that now goes up to the Supreme Court will be disposed of in these intermediate courts; and if this be true, we shall have a smaller number of reports, and what we do get will contain what we actually want. The bar in that case will be better supplied than they will be by having a large library of unimportant decisions.

I am opposed to retaining the present system, and am in favor of the plan proposed by the majority of the committee.

Mr. HALL. Being a member of the committee that agreed to the minority report, which is now before the committee of the whole, I desire to say a few words. I am aware, that there are many gentlemen who will object to that report, and I am aware also, that some gentlemen of the profession, to which I belong, will object to it. I beg gentlemen, before they oppose this report, to consider this matter a little, and learn precisely, and definitely, what they are doing. I know that the judiciary, which is a high and co-ordinate branch of the government, is looked upon by some members of this convention, and by many people of the State, as a matter of no comparative consequence, and they seem to think that they can get along as well with almost any kind of a judiciary, and that it needs no care and attention. But gentlemen who entertain that opinion, perhaps forget that the entire property of the State, that millions upon millions of property, now invested here, and which is constantly increasing, as the State increases in population,—all the property of the State undergoes the inspection and judgment of the judiciary in this State, at least once in thirty years. They forget, perhaps, that the judiciary is the guardian of the lives and property of every person in the State;—they forget the dependence which every human being, within reach of the process of the court, has upon it, for the maintenance of his dearest and most precious rights. I do say, without fear of successful contradiction, that the judiciary is the most important branch of government, and while gentlemen come here, and are anxious, that the legislature should be so constituted, that every person shall be immediately represented by some one who lives in his vicinity, or neighborhood, and who will be familiar with his wants, I say that they lose sight of a still greater blessing, when they deny to the humblest individual the protection which the judiciary may throw as a shield around him. I exceedingly regret—and my experience teaches me that that regret is well founded—that you cannot carry your court nearer than you do to the home of every citizen, that you cannot carry justice into every neighborhood, and have the law expounded in all its truth and force at the door of every person who has just cause of complaint, for which he seeks redress at the hands of justice.

Now I ask gentlemen to look for one moment and see in what condition the Judiciary system of this State is placed. A little more than twelve years ago I had the honor of having a seat in the Convention which was called to form a new constitution for this State. We had then some sixty thousand people, but neither wealth nor property. There were not means or credit enough then in the State Treasury to pay for the candles and stationery which the Convention used; and the members came here, paid their own expenses, received no pay for their services, but took scrip to be paid in the future, when the Treasury might be in a condition to redeem it. That was twelve years ago, and a judiciary that would answer the purposes of the State at that time, will not meet our wants at this day. Since that time our population has increased from sixty thousand inhabitants to some six hundred thousand; and with this great increase of population we have had a corresponding increase in wealth, commerce, and all the arts of civilization. Yet with all these great changes in our midst, we hear gentlemen say that the present Judiciary system is sufficient for our wants, and needs no revision. In 1850, Illinois had no larger population than Iowa now has. They held their convention and modified their judiciary system, which had been a great source of annoyance to the people for years; but looking only to the changes then demanded, and to the state of things then existing, they neglected to establish a system which should meet the wants and requirements which an increase in the population and wealth of the State would demand in the future. Every intelligent man now in that State sees and regrets the great mistake the convention made in not enlarging the judiciary, so as to make it sufficiently comprehensive to meet the wants and exigencies of the present time. I have conversed with the most intelligent men of this State, and they concur with me in the opinion that the new impulse and activity which have been given to commerce in consequence of the introduction of railroads, have created a necessity here for a change in our present judiciary system.

What is the system which we now propose, and what is the great innovation at which gentlemen appear so much alarmed? The first argument in favor of the plan reported by the majority, is the fact that arrangements may be made by which the judges will interchange with each other in holding the District Courts. In the election of judges we may have a variety of talent, adapted to the different requirements of the bench. For instance, in one place a member of the bar may be elected Judge, who is distinguished for his ability to try chancery causes, while in another a lawyer who is noted as being a good commercial lawyer may be elected; and still again, a Judge may be selected who has been long known as a good real estate lawyer. Here, I think, a great advantage may be gained under the system I have recommended, by detailing these various judges to try the causes in that branch of the profession with which they have rendered themselves familiar, and in which they have gained their distinction as lawyers. If, at some point in the circuit, important chancery business arises, let the judge who is familiar with practice in that class of cases, hold his court there, and if at some other points in the circuit, commercial and real estate cases arise, let them be tried by the judges respectively who shall be most familiar with that class of cases. This system has been tested in some of the States, and the wisdom and the practicability of the plan have been so fully demonstrated, that objections to the system are no longer urged. This feature of the working of the system I consider renders it a decided improvement over the present system; and the committee, I believe, were fully satisfied upon that point.

The next argument in favor of the proposition is, that when these officers have gone their rounds, at the spring and fall terms, they shall then meet at some convenient central point in the district within their jurisdiction, where writs of error shall be taken, when the courts shall have adjourned. These three judges meet then, investigate the decisions which have been made, and render such judgments as they believe the laws of the State require. An investigation takes place in the vicinity of the courts where the trials are held, where every suitor can attend, see and hear for himself the state of his case, which will make it more convenient and less expensive for him than to send him to the capitol.

This course would save the suitor time and money; and a large majority of the decisions of that court will remain without an appeal being taken from them by writ of error.

There is another argument that may be urged in favor of the adoption of this system, and which gentlemen of the legal profession will regard as important. As was justly said by the gentleman from Jasper, [Mr. Skiff,] important questions are often sprung upon the judges, which they have to decide upon the spur of the moment. The cases are numerous in which a judge has to postpone decisions in cases of exceedingly great importance, and examine them under advisement. This has been done in many cases by the judge in the county where I am now practicing at the bar. Under the plan now proposed, instead of taking them home for advisement, he will take them to this superior court, where they will be re-argued and examined, and the cases be finally disposed of.

This superior court would dispose of a great many incidental questions, which would arise during the progress of the trials, and which can be settled there on the spot. Important cases, involving intricate questions, would be taken to the supreme court, which I would have irrevocably established at the State capitol. I would give this court a character and tone which should command the utmost respect of the people for its decisions.

The adoption of this system will involve no additional expense—not a dollar—as far as the salaries of judges are concerned. This system proposed by the majority, then, offers to the people a convenient and gratuitous court, without money and without price, and all the expenses that would be incurred would be only those for stationery, fuel and lights during the time they are holding their sessions. If this system will tend to facilitate and dispatch business, bring justice nearer home to the suitors, and cheapen litigation, why do gentlemen object? Simply because it is a new and untried system in Iowa. Wherever they have formed new constitutions recently, with the exception of Illinois—and they are now regretting there that they have not made the change—they have established this intermediate court; and, indeed, in some of the States one of the principal objects in calling the conventions to change their constitutions was to accomplish that result. Finding their old systems totally inadequate to perform the duties which the increase in population and commerce had devolved upon the courts, the people demanded a change in the system, which should amply provide for the accumulating business.—Under these circumstances, and with the examples before us, of our sister States that have adopted this system, it strikes me that gentlemen ought not to object to its introduction into our prosperous and flourishing State.

The gentleman from Johnson, [Mr. Clarke,] said if the State was ten years older, he would favor this system. I do not understand what the gentleman means by that expression. There was a time when I could have understood that argument, but I cannot now. It reminds me of an anecdote I once heard of a negro and a traveler on horseback. The traveler inquired how far it was to a certain place. "Why," said the negro, "I'll tell you: Wid your hoss, you is ten miles off; wid Massa John's hoss you'd be only four miles off, but if you was on de railroad, you'd be dare now." [Laughter.] And so it is with Iowa. I tell you that she is already ten years in advance. [Renewed laughter.]

Gentlemen can estimate what this State will be ten years hence, when the railroads already projected from the Mississippi to the Missouri will have traversed the State, and how large will be her cities, and what will be the extent of her commerce. With this increase of population and commerce, there will be, as a matter of course, a corresponding increase of business in the legal tribunals of the State. If we can calculate from the past, the business and commerce of the State will have increased with such unprecedented rapidity, that the two courts proposed by the minority report will be found totaliy inadequate to perform the business devolving upon them; and even with the addition proposed by the majority report, I am fully persuaded that the Legislature will be called upon in a very short time to establish superior courts in the cities.

I ask gentlemen, in view of the considerations I have presented, not to turn a cold shoulder upon the system recommended in this majority report, but weigh well and carefully the merits which this system presents, over that presented in the minority report, and which I think must strike with force the mind of every reflecting man. It is a system which, as I have already said, will bring justice home to all; pervade every corner of the State, and its influence will be felt every where. We will have then, a judiciary, to which every citizen, no matter how humble, may appeal with confidence for a redress of his injuries. Confidence in the judtciary is what the people want, and it should be our great aim to give them that confidence, by giving them a court to which any citizen can apply, with the certainty that he shall have his rights secured, without unnecessary delay and expense. I would ask gentlemen to consider well, the system now proposed by the majority report, and weigh well its advantages before acting upon the various systems, that are, and will be proposed in the course of this discussion. I would vote for enlarging the system as now proposed by the majority, rather than cut it down in the least.

It may not be improper for me, before I sit down, to say a single word in regard to the supreme court.

Both of the reports agree upon the necessity of having four judges for that court. That number was selected, bocause it was believed that four was the best possible number to constitute the highest court of the State. The idea of having an odd number of judges, to my mind, is perfectly fallacious. If you have three judges and there is one dissenting, and two concurring in the opinion, the decision is regarded as worthless, and is never considered settled, because the decision of the Judge below, with that of the dissenting judge above, offsets the opinion of the two judges above. If you have four supreme judges, and they are equally divided, then the decision of the judge below would be affirmed; and if there are three to one, then the decision would acquire additional strength.

I think this number of judges is the best possible number that we can have, and that it will give more character to the decisions when made, than any other number that can be devised.

It is perhaps, not proper at this time, for me to examine the other questions embraced in this report, but I supposed it was not out of order for me to allude briefly, to this question of the number of supreme judges. I shall therefore, with these remarks, calling the attention of members to this subject, to which I desire they will give their careful deliberation, refrain from saying any thing more at present.

Mr. HARRIS. I feel great reluctance in attempting to discuss the best plan of a judicary system, especially in view of the fact that I shall feel compelled to dissent entirely from the views expressed by the gentleman from Des Moines,

(Mr. Hall.) His experience as a lawyer, and the position he has occupied upon the bench, certainly entitle his opinions to great weight at the hands of the convention, and where I can do so, without surrendering my own convictions of what is right, I would certainly yield my own pre-conceived opinions to his better judgment, or that of any other gentleman upon this floor, who has had the same experience, and whose opinions are entitled to the same weight as his are. I must confess, that I have not had much experience, practically, under any other system of judiciary than the present, but I have made some little examination and comparison of other systems, and have especially observed the workings of that presented by the majority report. I believe, that so far as the practical operation of the systems is concerned, there is very little difference between the plans recommended by the minority and majority reports, except that one has two courts and the other three, the third court being a supreme court in the district. I understand that both reports propose to divide the State into four judicial districts, with three judges to each district. It is proposed by the majority report, that these judges shall come together, after trying causes separately in their respective jurisdictions, for the purpose of hearing and deciding cases that come up on appeal; and it is urged by the friends of the system, that in this way the litigants will have the combined wisdom of these judges in the decision of their cases. The gentleman from Des Moines, (Mr. Hall,) in the course of his argument, said, that this system would bring justice nearer home to the parties. I cannot see how that result will be accomplished, unless you propose to have more courts; and I do not see why you could not just as well let one judge hold the court as to have the work divided up among three. He says, that one judge, who may have been a good commercial lawyer, will have charge of all cases that may arise relating to that branch of the law; and that another judge, who may be a good real estate lawyer, will dispose of all the business involving the titles to real estate; and that there may be another judge, whose attention has been particularly directed to chancery cases, to whom all equity cases will be transferred; so that, in this way, each of the judges may have the disposition of those cases which may arise in that branch of the legal profession, with which he has been the most familiar. But I would ask the gentleman, is there any assurance, that the litigants will have the services of the judge, to try the cases which he is particularly qualified, by study and experience, to dispose of? I apprehend, that all the cases will be placed upon the calendar, and that the judge, whose turn it is to hold a particular term of the court, must have jurisdiction of, and try the cases as they are presented at that term of the court; and a party, therefore, might not command the services of the judge for a case in that particular department of the law for which he is the best qualified, without it was called up for trial at the term in which this judge shall hold court.

A very serious objection to this proposed system would be, that in a case where there was much feeling among the parties involving a good deal of responsibility on the part of the Judge, who should decide it, there would be a scramble among the Judges to escape the responsibility and throw it upon other Judges. If a suitor does not happen to like a particular Judge, who is upon the bench, he will make affidavit for a continuance, in order that his case may be tried by some other Judge; and this difficulty will often arise in the working of this system. I cannot see how it is, that this system will tend to bring justice any nearer home to a suitor, than under the present system, provided you secure the services of good and competent men, in whose decisions the public will place confidence.

One argument which the gentleman from Des Moines, [Mr. Hall,] urged was this, that parties in cases where they were not satisfied with the decisions made in these district courts, could take them up to the Supreme Court of the District, where the three Judges meet together, for the purpose of hearing all cases of appeal. But what would be the result in this case? Would the contested cases stop there? Would not the parties still continue to appeal? I agree with the gentleman from Des Moines, [Mr. Hall,] that the Judiciary is the most important branch of the government, and I believe it is essential that every man should have the means placed within his power of obtaining justice at the hands of the legal tribunals of the country. It was remarked by one of the most distinguished Judges of Ohio, that courts were really more essential for the purpose of putting an end to litigation, and letting men know what their rights are, than for any other purpose. My experience teaches me, that where parties rush into litigation, they are very apt not to rest satisfied with the decision of one court, but they will take their cases through all the courts they can. If a party commences a suit in a Justice's Court and is beaten, his counsel, through feeling or chagrin in consequence of his defeat, may advise him to take an appeal to the District Court; and if beaten there, he will then go to the Supreme Court, where his case must stop, and he can get no farther. If you should establish a dozen courts, and if the suitor has that privilege, he will be very likely to take his case through them all; and when he gets to the last court, if he is the winner he may have the glorious satisfaction of running his hand into his pockets and taking his last dollar to pay the attorney. I am inclined to think, that the results I have pictured would follow under the operation of the system here proposed.

What are the objections urged against the present system? Gentlemen say that it does not afford means sufficient to give every man justice. Permit me to ask, wherein is the system that now exists, inadequate to meet our present wants and requirements? But gentlemen say, by way of objection to our present system, that we do not secure the services of men who are qualified to disposee justice upon the bench, and be able to give satisfaction between the parties. If that be the case, I do not see how the fault can be remedied by the system proposed by the majority report, because it will be left for the people to select their Judges as they now do.

I do think, that there is one objection to the present system, which can be easily remedied, and that is the compensation now paid the Judges, which is inadequate to secure the services of the best men upon the bench. I would increase that compensation to an amount sufficient to command the services of the best men in the State. I think that when parties have had a fair and proper trial before an impartial jury, that the case should stop there; and I would not be disposed to go farther. If the case is not well conducted in behalf of either of the litigants, it is the party's own fault in not securing an attorney qualified to manage it. I would have the Supreme Court considered as a court for the correction of errors merely. If the number of Judges is not now sufficient, I have no objection to increasing their number to five; and in my opinion, it would be cheaper to increase it to seven, than to adopt the system now presented. Certainly as far as the settling of principles of law is concerned, a court of errors established under the present system, with the proper modifications, will be quite as good as that recommended by the report of the majority.

The gentleman from Des Moines, [Mr. Hall,] has referred to the workings of the judiciary systems of other States, modelled upon the plan which the majority have here presented. I have conversed with gentlemen in whose judgment I place the utmost reliance, in regard to the workings of the system in some of the States to which the gentleman referred, and they all assured me that they were desirous of getting clear of these systems, and adopting a simple system like our own.

I have prepared a plan of a judiciary which I desire to present to the committee, and in which I have incorporated the present system with such amendments as I deemed the exigencies of the State required. One change I propose in the present system is the election of a district in the place of a county prosecutor, for the simple reason that criminal prosecution, in a great majority of the counties in the State is now but a mere mockery, and is entirely inadequate to meet the ends of justice. Let me say one word before presenting my plan, in regard to the number of the Supreme Court judges. Some gentlemen prefer to have five judges, while others again think that three are sufficient. For the purpose of securing the services of the best men, I am more inclined to favor the idea of having five than three judges. With the permission of the committee, I will now read the plan which I have drawn up, and which is as follows:

ARTICLE —. JUDICIAL DEPARTMENT.

Sec. 1. The judicial power of the State shall be vested in a Supreme and District Court, and such inferior courts as the General Assembly may from time to time establish.

2. The Supreme Court shall consist of a Chief Justice and two associates, two of whom shall be a quorum to hold court.

3. The judges of the Supreme Court shall be elected by the electors of the State at large, qualified to vote for members of the General Assembly, and shall hold their courts at such time and place as the General Assembly may direct, and hold their offices for six years, and until their successors are elected and qualified, and shall be ineligible to any other office in the State during the term for which they may be elected.. The Supreme Court shall have appellate jurisdiction only in all cases in chancery, and shall constitute a court for the correction of errors at law under such restrictions as the General Assembly may by law prescribe. The Supreme Court may have power to issue all writs and process, necessary to do justice to parties, and exercise a supervisory control over all inferior tribunals and the judges of the Supreme Court shall be conservators of the peace throughout the State.

4. The District Court shall consist of a judge who shall be elected by the qualified electors of the district in which he resides, at the general election, and hold his office for the term of five years, and until his successor is elected and qualified; and shall be ineligible to any other office during the term for which he shall be elected, except Supreme Judge. The District Court shall be a court of law and equity, and have jurisdiction in all civil and criminal matters arising in their respective districts, in such manner as shall be prescribed by law. The judges of the District Court shall be conservators of the peace in their respective districts. The boundaries of the several judicial districts shall remain as at present fixed until they shall be changed by law.

5. The qualified voters of each judicial dictrict shall, at a general election, elect a district attorney; and the qualified voters of each county shall, at a general election, elect one district clerk, who shall be residents therein, and who shall hold their respective offices for the term of two years, and until their successors are elected and qualified.

6. The judges of the Supreme and District Courts and District Attorney shall each receive after the first term for said offices, under this constitution, as their only compensation, a salary to be fixed by law, which shall neither be increased or diminished for the term for which they shall severally be elected.

7. The salary of the Supreme Judge for the first term shall be two thousand dollars; that of the District Judges one thousand five hundred dollars, and that of District Attorney one thousand dollars.

8. The style of all processes shall be "The

State of Iowa," and all prosecutions shall be conducted in the name and by the authority of the State of Iowa.

I have now presented my views upon the judiciary system, as embodied in the plan here presented, which I hope will receive due consideration at the hands of the committee. I will make but a single remark in conclusion. So far as the salaries of the judges are concerned, a majority of the members with whom I have conversed, expressed it as their opinion that the sums I have named are too small. I have made the salaries of the Supreme Court Judges the same as agreed upon by the General Assembly, and for the district judges $300 more than the sum named by them. I thought that there should be as great a disparity as that between the two classes of judges ; but I am not particular as to the compensation of these officers. If you give them all $2000, it will then make the amount we pay the judges 1500 or 2,000 dollars less than by the system proposed by the majority.

Mr. CLARKE, of Henry. I would ask the very careful consideration of the committee to the question now before them. It is a question involving, not the settlement of any particular article or any particular section of an article of the constitution, but it is a question in regard to the establishment of a system of judiciary for the State. I do not propose in my remarks to enter very fully into all the details and minutiæ of the two systems proposed by the committee on the judiciary. When the committee shall have decided which of the two reports they will take up and consider, it will then be time enough to enter into an examination of those details which have already been alluded to by gentlemen in the course of this discussion. The gentleman who first addressed you, the chairman of the committee on the judiciary, stated to this convention that he was in favor of the system proposed by the majority as a general plan, and I wish every gentleman here to recollect his remarks. He stated that he was in favor of that system as a principle, and if the state were some ten years older, he would be in favor of its adoption. This I consider a full endorsement of the majority report. We must all recollect that we live at a period when the past affords no criterion for the future, and when we may confidently predict that the accumulation of business in our courts within the next five years, will be greater than it has been within the last twenty years. If gentlemen will reflect for a moment, they will be satisfied that such will unquestionably be the case. We should, therefore, occupying the position we do at this time, having assembled at great expense to the state to remodel our present constitution, make such changes in our judicial system as will be demanded for the great increase of business in our courts in the future. Why not then provide now for the future wants of the state in this respect, rather than incur the great expense which may be entailed upon us ten, nay five years hence, in finding a judiciary system that should be adequate to meet the wants and necessities of the state at that time?

The only serious objection I have heard urged by gentleman, against the proposition made by the majority, is the additional expense, that they apprehend will be incurred by the State.

The objection which was raised by the gentleman from Appanoose, [Mr. Harris] that it would allow lawyers to indulge in a little sharp practice, I consider a very trivial one; for it would be impossible to establish any system that would prevent lawyers from doing those things of which the gentleman so much complains.

The system proposed by the majority committee is no innovation, no new and untried system, but it has been practically treated in other States of the Union, and it is therefore the embodiment of an actual experience. Another object is its complexity. Why is your State divided into counties, townships, and again subdivided into school districts? It is done, in order that you may more conveniently carry on the whole machinery of the government. As well might gentlemen complain of the complexity of this political machinery, as of that of the judicial system which we propose here, and which divides and simplifies our proceedings, instead of making them more complex. The system which we propose, is modelled upon that of the United States, and comprises a supreme court, district court, and a circuit court, and it is under this form, and upon these principles, that I wish to have it presented before this body.

Bnt the committee have given these courts a little different name, and they have classified them under the heads of a supreme court, superior court and district court.

By the system we propose, you will have four judges in a district, which is to be composed of a certain number of counties. Here are to be four districts in the State, and each of these districts is to be sub-divided into circuits, and the district judges of each district will hold court in each county alternately. These same udges, you will bear in mind, are to be called together at some convenient point in their district, and hold a court in bank, to hear and decide cases on appeal, and writs of error from the circuit courts.

These economical gentlemen here, will recollect, that by the adoption of this system, we provide for no additional salaries, and impose no additional expense upon the people. What is the object in providing for this second, or intermediate court? It is, that, the four judges acting together, three of whom shall constitute a quorum, shall form a court to which appeals and exceptions in the first instance may come from these different circuits.

Under the present system, I would ask gentlemen if a majority of the cases that come before the Supreme Court are not such as arise upon some simple question which could be decided by the intermediate court which we propose without the unnecessarry expense and delay now incurred? Here is the gentleman from Appanoose (Mr. Harris),—and I am surprised to hear him arguing against the system we propose

—living at the extremity of the State. Suppose now that he has some case where the amount involved does not exceed two hundred dollars. There has been some mistake made by the judge on the trial, and he cannot get a new trial there. The only relief for him is to make out a bill of exceptions and come with it to Iowa City, for argument before the supreme court; and his client will have to bear the expense thereby incurred, for simply arguing a motion for a new trial. I ask gentlemen who live in the remote portions of the State, if they have not suffered wrong and injustice many a time rather than put their clients to the expense of carrying their cases up to the Supreme Court? In all such cases as this under the system proposed by the majority, your appeal would be taken to the court in bank in the district where the case originated, and your case would be heard by the judges whom the people have selected as being candid and upright men, and well qualified to discharge the duties devolving upon them; and this hearing, too, would be granted without any additional expense.

These four Judges come together at some central point in the district, and form a court: but the Judge who has made the decision from which the appeal is taken, is not allowed to have a vote in the matter. The other three judges are then ready to hear the case; the lawyer comes before them and argues the case, and three judges can decide upon the question, without the party appealing being subjected to the expense of taking it up to the Supreme Court. I ask you how many of the cases that go up to the district court in the first instance, would ever be taken up to the Supreme Court? Those cases only would be taken up to the court of last resort, which were of very great legal importance, or in which large interests were involved. Unless a lawyer has several cases arising in the same term of court, in which he can file a bill of exceptions, he cannot afford to come to Iowa City to attend to the terms of the Supreme Court. In the district court he will, perhaps, get new trials in a large portion of his cases, and he is satisfied, and unless the other cases in which he is less fortunate, are of sufficient importance, he will not take them up to the Supreme Court.

The same reason will prevent him from going on with trivial cases, that prevail with him now. All the important cases, that may arise, and in which principles of law are involved, will find their way to the supreme court; and these are the cases that we desire should be taken there, these alone we desire to see in our books of reports.

The gentleman from Appanoose (Mr. Harris,) seems to entertain the idea, that we should have laws to prevent litigation! For my part, I would give to the people the cheapest, and the most speedy judicial system that could be devised, and I claim that every man who feels himself aggrieved, has the right to seek for redress in courts of justice, and no obstacle should be placed in his way; and justice should be brought as near home, to every man's door, as circumstances will permit.

I do not know that this system we propose will meet with much favor at the hands of this body. I know that it will not with the judiciary themselves, and with a majority of the bar, but I am satisfied, that the wants and requirements of the State demand such a system, and that the change, if not made now, will be eagerly demanded a few years hence, even by the very parties who have now arrayed themselves in opposition against it. I have consulted with several gentlemen of the profession here, and especially with the gentleman from Des Moines, (Mr. Hall,) in regard to the proposed change; and they all concur in the opinion, that the necessity for an alteration, in our present system, is imperatively demanded. I am told, by other gentlemen, that before coming to this body, they were appealed to by their constituents to give them a district court, to relieve the supreme court from the mass of business now accumulating upon its calendars, and to simplify, and make easier, judicial proceedings. I would say here, that the committee do not regard the report, which they have submitted, as perfect in all its details; and they desire to hear any suggestions from gentlemen that may improve and perfect the system. A majority of the committee are perfectly willing to let the number of supreme court judges remain as they are, to have but three, if a majority of the convention should so desire. They are also in favor of having the State divided, at this time, into only three districts, and have four judges in a district, three of whom shall make a quorum. By the adoption of the system proposed, we should get rid of a great number of what are now called prosecuting attorneys, for this system supposes that the State will be divided into districts, and these again divided into circuits, with only one prosecuting attorney to each district. If that system be adopted, and we have only the same number of supreme court judges that we now have, with three districts subdivided into four circuits, it would lessen the expense of the judiciary system to the people.

And again, in regard to this matter of salary: I think the majority of the committee would be willing to have the legtslature limited in this matter, from two to five thousand dollars for the Supreme Court, and from fifteen hundred to three thousand for the District Court Judges. I did not listen as attentively to the argument of the gentleman from Des Moines, [Mr. Hall,] here to-day, as I would have done, but for having heard his argument before the Judiciary Committee. I suppose the gentleman from Des Moines, stated to this Convention, that after a great many experiments in New York they have finally resorted to nearly this system here recommended. Their system is much more complex, and enters more into details, but by examining it you will find that the judicial system of New York is pretty much the same as this. I believe, we at this time, should establish a judicial system in view of what we are to be, rather than what we are now. And I would ask gentlemen to reflect one moment upon the fact that there is no State in the whole Union that will eventually support as great a population to the square mile as this same State of Iowa. Now do not let us cramp those who are to come after us. Do not let us, for Heaven's sake, act upon the reason suggested by the gentleman from Johnson, [Mr. Clarke,] that because we are not so great now as we will be ten years from now, we should not adopt a judicial plan suited to a great and populous State. Let us not cramp ourselves in so small vesture and raiment that bye and bye we will be compelled to rip the seams and enlarge.

Mr. CLARKE, of Johnson. What is the population of New York, at this time, compared with ours?

Mr. CLARKE, of Henry. I do not recollect what the present population of the whole State of New York is. I can only tell the gentleman this; that if he will reckon the number of judges in the State of New York, in proportion to the population, he will find that there are not more judges, in proportion to their population, than we propose now, in proportion to our population.

Mr. WILSON. In New York they have, in all, thirty-two judges, if I am not mistaken.

Mr. CLARKE, of Henry. I do not recollect about that. But gentlemen will understand, that the different municipalities in New York have their different courts. They have the local courts; they have their county courts, with certain jurisdiction; they have their recorder's courts in every city, and a large proportion of the business of the State of New York is done in these local courts. And cases that involve important principles are commenced in these local courts, and carried up until they reach the highest tribunals. I do not care which way the gentleman may take it. I will take him upon the other horn of the dilemma. If the judicial business of the great State of New York, with all its great and important interests, can be carried on with such a system, with so few judges, as the gentleman mentions, it certainly must be a system which works most admirably. I wish we could get one like it. I do not think the same amount of work can be done as expeditiously, as promptly, and as cheaply, under any other system, as under one that divides the labors in the way we propose here. The principle of a division of labor is well understood by us all. This system divides up the labor, and takes a large amount of it to settle in the district where it originates. Here is a gentleman from Council Bluffs. Suppose you have a district court there. You take the judge who holds the court in Council Bluffs, and associate him with the other three judges, and take before them all the cases that go up on appeal, or error, in that district. Does not every gentleman here believe that nine cases out of every ten, that should go before the court in bank, would be there disposed of, or be sent back for a new trial, and go no farther? Then if that be the case; if these courts act as a sort of sieve, and everything they catch is kept out of the supreme court, certainly there is so much saved to the people in time, trouble and expense.

Mr. WILSON. I wish to submit a few words by way of explanation, as to my position, as a member of the committee on the judiciary department. The gentleman from Johnson [Mr. Clarke] has placed me in a position a little different from that which, in fact I occupy, in relation to this report of the minority of the committee. I differ from the majority and the minority both, though my name is on the minority report. I am opposed to increasing the supreme court to four judges, as suggested by the gentleman from Johnson. I am in favor of retaining the three judge system, as we now have it.

I will here remark, further, that there are other details in the minority report, to which I am opposed, one, for instance, is that of fixing the salaries.

Now, I wish to submit a few remarks in relation to the two systems proposed, the three court and the two court systems. I am in favor of keeping the judicial system of the state as nearly in its present position as possible. I am in favor of that, in the first place, because I believe the people in the State have not demanded the change proposed. I am free to say, that I have, myself, heard no complaint of the present system. I did not hear that question mooted at all, until I came to the capital. I wish to examine some of the reasons suggested here, by the gentleman from Des Moines, [Mr. Hall] in relation to the system of three courts. He takes the position, in the first place, that such a system would cheapen litigation in this State. I cannot see it in that light, and any gentleman acquainted judicial proceedings must at once come to this conclusion; that every case involving rules of property, will go to the highest court in the State. Every case involving questions, aside from mere questions of practice, will go to the supreme court. This intermediate court will act as a kind of seive to divide these cases, involving more questions of practice, from cases involving great and leading questions, whether in relation to property or otherwise. Farther than that, I do not believe litigation will stop in this superior, or intermediate court; and this whole difficulty may be caused by the legislature. If the legislature will give us a practice act for the law side of the court, and a practice act for the chancery side of the court, that difficulty will be done away. We never have had a practice act in this State, and it is a thing that we very much need, and I hope the legislature will give it to us soon.

Now let us look at this matter in another light. As we have our courts organized at present, the great difficulty in the different districts is, that the same question has been decided differently in different districts. A question may arise in the first district, and a decision made in regard to it. The same question may arise in the second district, and be decided in the opposite manner, and so on throughout the State, and you may obtain as many different decisions as there are different districts in the State. That is the difficulty we all feel now. Now suppose, that instead of having these different decisions in the district court, you create four superior courts throughout the State, you will have the same multiplicity of decisions in those courts as in the courts below, in proportion to the number of courts. The decision of the superior court for the first district, will be no authority in the second district, and the decision in the second district will be no authority in the third district, and so on. In order to obtain a decision that will be authority throughout the State, and will be recognised by the profession, and by the courts, as authority, you are driven into the highest court in the State to obtain it. In that view of the case, this doctrine of cheapening litigation falls to the ground.

The gentleman says farther, that you will be giving these judges more to do, and will pay them no more for doing it. That may be true. But will the gentleman pretend to say, that there are no other costs connected with courts, except the salaries of the judges? This majority report provides for clerks and other officers for these courts. Take the clerk of your supreme court, for instance; I suppose his fees in each year will amount to two thousand dollars, or two thousand five hundred dollars. You will have about the same number of cases in your superior courts that you now have in the supreme courts, and you propose to have four superior courts in the State. Now multiply two thousand five hundred dollars by four, and you will see the increase of costs in clerks' fees alone, and the parties in courts have to pay those fees.

And while the gentleman is arguing that parties because of the distance to the supreme court from the locality where the litigation has commenced, will take their cases to these immediate courts, I will ask whether this superior court coming in, and deciding the questions partially, does not prevent a man going any farther, who would otherwise go to the supreme court? Men who are not able to pay the costs of litigation cannot go to the supreme court. A poor man may have as important cases of litigation as a rich man may have, but by the time he gets through the superior court his money is gone, and he is deprived of the benefit of the supreme court of the state. I cannot look at it in any light that is not reprehensible, especially at the present time, with the present population and with the present amount of litigation. It seems to me that it is a cumbrous system, not adapted to the wants of our people, a system that they have not demanded, and I take it that when a people need anything they demand it, and that is the best argument I can present against this thing, so far as the people are concerned.

There is another thing I desire to notice. I refer to the division of the state into four districts. I do not remember the number of organized counties in this state, but there are nearly a hundred of them. That will give to each district at least twenty-five counties; the districts in the west would probably have more, and the districts in the east probably not so many. In order to carry out the beautiful system that the gentleman from Des Moines, [Mr. Hall,] has presented, that of having a chancellor for the chancery cases, a good land lawyer for your land cases, and so on through the different departments of law and equity, you might have to wait until your judge traveled entirely around the district before you could have your case tried. The system is defective in this respect, that is if we are to attach any weight to the argument of the gentleman from Des Moines. In a district of twenty-five counties it may take a judge two years to get around under the system proposed, and you would have to wait in order to have the superior attainments of that judge in his particular department, until he could make his circuit and try your case. That argument, I take it for granted, will not recommend itself to the approbation of this convention, and it falls to the ground. You must take your judge as you find him, and try your case when it is called, unless you have a good reason for continuing it. Because the judge is not able in this particular department would not be a very good cause for a continuance.

There is one other reason against the adoption of this system at the present time. I find in the report of the committee on future amendments to the constitution a provision that the Legislature may at any time submit propositions for amending the constitution to the people.—Now, if the people think, after continuing the present judicial system of the State for a time, that it will not work, and that they must have more courts and more costs, they will instruct their members of the Legislature to present that proposition to them for them to pass upon. But no gentleman will pretend to say that it is necessary now to adopt that kind of a judicial system in this State.

I am in favor of reducing the number of judges in this State. I believe that thirteen judges —ten district judges and three supreme judges—can do all the business of the State, and do it well. There is not a district judge in this State who has business enough to keep him employed as he should be. Some of our district judges—I presume the majority of them—have, probably, business enough to occupy their attention from two to four months in the year: very few of them will go beyond that. I am in favor of reducing their number so that each district judge will be occupied at least eight or nine months in the year. We should then have better judges, their decisions would be in better shape, and there ould be fewer appeals from the district courts to the supreme court, if we would only give our judges enough to do, and keep them at their proper work all the time.

There is another thing that I might throw out here, in connection with the complaints that gentlemen make in relation to appeals to the Supreme Court. I believe that a majority of the cases brought up from the district in which I reside, to the Supreme Court, are submitted on written argument. Now, I know that that course requires more labor on the part of the lawyer. It is more trouble to him to sit down and write out his argument, and put it in such a shape as will commend it to the due consideration of the supreme judges than it would be to come up here with his brief, and present his arguments orally. I know that; but he can do it, nevertheless; and it would be better for the interests of his client, than for him to come up to the Supreme Court and argue his case orally, provided you have the right kind of men upon the bench. If you have not, then it matters little whether your arguments be written or oral. Instead of the lawyer coming up from a remote portion of the State, he can submit his case upon a written argument; and he need not put his client to the expense of paying his board and travelling expenses; unless he has many cases at the same time, and then he can divide the expenses among his clients; and that need not be so much of a consideration, perhaps, as when he has but one or two cases.

That does away with that objection; and I believe if we would, as a profession, devote ourselves a little more closely to the hard work that belongs to us, we would hear much less complaint about the remoteness of the Supreme Court from us. I am satisfied that lawyers can do a great deal more than some of them do now, and when they come in here and plead for cheap litigation, I am satisfied they can apply the present system of practice, and make it quite as cheap as the one proposed by the majority of the committee.

I have nothing more to submit to the committee of the whole upon that subject. But inasmuch as the gentleman from Des Moines, [Mr. Hall,] has made a very feeling appeal to the members of the Convention not to turn the cold shoulder, as he terms it, upon the most important and exalted department of the State, I would make an appeal to the convention, also. (By the way, he made one suggestion which I cannot say I can fully comprehend, and which, I think, shows that the gentleman has a very strange idea about the matter. He says that all the property of the state passes through the courts every thirty years. He may refer to county courts, but I imagine that remark could not apply to other courts.) I would also appeal to members of the convention to preserve the present judicial system of the state, with, perhaps some slight modifications, until the people of the state demand a change. And while we have listened day in and day out to appeals from members of the Convention and more particularly from the gentleman from Des Moines [Mr. Hall] in relation to innovations, and have heard his well known cry "let well enough alone, let well enough alone," permit me to say the same thing now, and ask the convention to "let well enough alone. Whenever we have presented any amendment to the present constitution, we have been met with some musty old statute, or some old decision dragged out from the State library, and the cry has gone up loud and long "let well enough alone," "do not innovate upon the present constitution of the State." I would use the same language here now. And I tell the gentleman the people would prefer the old system, and that he should "let well enough alone."

Mr. CLARK, of Alamakee. I am in favor, Mr. Chairman, of "letting well enough alone," unless it can be made better; but when it can very easily and readily, then I am not so much in favor of "letting well enough alone." I do not agree with my friend from Jefferson [Mr. Wilson] in some of the remarks he has submitted to the committee. Now he says he is willing to alter the judicial system of the State, when the people demand it. I do not know how it may be in his district; I do not undertake to speak of the sentiments of the people there. But I think I understand something about the wishes of the people in the northern portion of the State. And I not only speak of my own district, but I think I state the feeling of some other districts, when I say that in relation to this matter there is but one opinion there, and that is for a change, and a radical change in our present judicial system. I shall, therefore, upon the principle the gentleman has himself laid down, most certainly go for a change, as the people in my part of the State have demanded it.

The next question then is, what is the best change that can be made to suit the wants and convenience of the people of this State? For upon the judicial system, as has been well remarked here, depend the efficacy of our laws. Laws are good for nothing without courts to adjudicate, to construe and to administer them. If it is necessary to have courts, it is necessary to have able courts; to have courts accessible to the people, to which they can readily go. I for one, am not so very much afraid of the spread of litigation among the great mass of the people, as gentlemen seem to be who have spoken in opposition to this majority report. My experience among my people has been that they are not so anxious for litigation; they are very cautious of lawsuits, and enter into them but as a matter of last resort. There are exceptions to this rule, as to all others. But as to lawyers advising their clients to take their causes up from one court to another, I must say that I have had no such experience. But I am not able to speak upon that subject to any great extent. I apprehend no danger in that respect, however, from this change.

But the principle objection urged by those who oppose this majority report, as I understand it, is that it will enhance the expense; that we are not far enough advanced in population and business to warrant this extensive change. I believe this to be an error—that it is wrong. That system is in itself pure, which, in any profession or business, increases the facilities and thus diminishes the expenses attendant upon that profession or business, whatever it may be. We have, I believe, fifteen district judges in this State, and they are required to do the present business of the State. I am prepared to say that twelve judges, under a proper system, can do all the district court business that is now done in those fifteen districts, and find ample time to sit in bank and decide all appeals from justices of the peace and districts, in addition to other business that is now done by fifteen judges. If I am correct in this position, then certainly the expense does not increase, but diminishes. In the State of New York, with nearly or quite four millions of inhabitants, they have eight judicial districts. and four judges in each district. These four judges do all the business of the circuit courts, which we call district courts, and they also sit in bank and hear all appeals from justices of the peace and county courts. Such a system adopted here, where we have not a million of inhabitants, would necessarily reduce the number of judges—perhaps not in the same ratio, for there is more territory, but they would be reduced to some extent. Under the old system in New York the same number of judges did not perform the same amount of business they now perform, for they could not do it. It is the perfectness of the system which enables that amount of business to be accomplished.

Now adopt this same principle here, and bear in mind, if you please, that this majority report of the committee does not bind down the convention to the number of four judicial districts. They can take the number two or three, as they may deem best, giving to the legislature the power to increase the number of these districts as the necessities of the people may require. We can adopt this system with such modifications as this convention in their wisdom may consider necessary. Say that the number of judicial districts is reduced from four to three, and then we will have twelve judges who, I think, will prove amply sufficient to do all the business now done by fifteen judges. There will then be a saving of expense of at least three judges. Then again, instead of having so many appeals from one court to another, I would have all cases arising before justices of the peace end with the circuit or district court sitting in bank, and not allow those trifling cases to go to the court of last resort. We can arrange the system so that there will be no difficulty upon the score of litigation. Have it so arranged that the causes shall not be taken from this circuit court, sitting as a court in bank, without the consent of the judges. There is no difficulty about this matter, no fear to be apprehended from it.

I have practised some four or five years in the State of New York under their present system, and I have had some little experience under that system, I think. And there is no use in telling me that the people of New York are tired of it. No inducement, strong enough, could be held out to them to persuade them to go back to their old system. They have taken a step in progress forward in the judicial system of their State, that they never will retrace. Instead of retracing, they will rather progress.

There is no difficulty in carrying out this system in this State. It has this advantage in it; it brings our cases, as it has been remarked, home to ourselves, in each part of the State. People, near the capitol, may not experience any inconvenience from the present system; but in the remote parts of the State, we have no appellate court from the district court, except at the capital of the State. If the capital should be at Fort Des Moines, the supreme court will be some three hundred miles from the north-eastern portion of the State. The gentleman from Jefferson (Mr. Wilson,) says, that that difficulty can be obviated by sending the cases up with written arguments. That was the practice in New York under their old system, and it was practiced until the people grew tired of it. In order to practice this written argument system, you must have an attorney at the capital, and in nine cases out of ten he will neglect to investigate the cases confided to his care, as they should be investigated before they are presented to the court. On the other hand, if you depend upon written argument alone, it is doubtful if you can place an argument upon paper, that will attract the attention of the court to the different points of the case in the same effectual manner as can be done by having the assistance of counsel, who is acquainted with the history of the case, and has his professional pride at stake. The system has been tried, and has been abandoned so far as it is possible to abandon it.

Now, with this system, three or four judicial districts in the State, you will have a kind of supreme court sitting in bank within a few days travel of each individual, and cases can be brought before that court, from justices of the peace, county courts, or the district courts, with readiness, facility, and cheapness. There is no difficulty, that I can conceive of, in this matter; it is all plain and right.

The gentleman from Jefferson (Mr. Wilson,) argues, that the cases would not stop at this superior court, or court in bank, but would go on to the supreme court. The experience of the State of New York proves, that not one case out of ten, probably not one out of twenty, passes their supreme court, which is the court in bank, to the court of last resort, which is there called the court of appeals. At the time when this new system went into practice, the reporter of the State of New York had made out some twenty volumes of reports in about six years, and then the court of last resort had on hand business enough to fill two volumes of the old supreme court reports, cases which had been dragging along for years, like cases in the old chancery court in England. For the time during which Barbour had made his twenty volumes of reports, the court of appeals had made six volumes of reports, comprising the cases from the old supreme court, together with all the business that had gone up from the circuit court sitting in bank, to the court of last resort. As a consequence, the people are satisfied with the change. Now, under this system, you will have three or four judges sitting in bank, after having performed their duties as circuit or district judges, upon all the cases appealed from them, which they are sitting at *nisi prius*. It will not be a court possessing all the authority of a court of last resort sitting at the capital, but in many cases, I apprehend, it would be as good as that court.

There is another objection made to this new system, that of the log rolling of the judges of the courts below. It is said they would have a pride in sustaining their own decisions in the circuit. But if the judge, who has made the decision, from which there is an appeal, is excluded from the court in bank, there can be but little danger on that score. He will have little opportunity or need of urging his own opinions, for he knows that if he is not sustained where he should be, there is a remedy beyond that court, to the court of last resort. That objection, therefore, is thus entirely done away. There is nothing of that kind experienced where this new system has gone into practice.

So far as I have heard an expression of opinion upon this subject, the people feel, in the remote districts of the State, the inconvenience of the present system. Suppose that our State should continue to increase in population, wealth and business, in the future, as it is now doing. Suppose that we have our justice courts, county courts, and district courts, multiplied, as must necessarily be the case, and we have but one court of appeal, and that is at the capital of the State. How long will it be before that court is flooded with business? It will be impossible for them to do the business that will come before them. There is a great hardship experienced already by those who have small cases, or have but little means to carry on their cases, in the district courts. The district judge, in these matters which are so small, that they will not warrant the taking them, at enormous expenses, to the court of last resort at the capital, becomes a little king in his district. His decisions are omnipotent, and you must submit to them. Besides it is natural for a judge, especially if he be a man of strong feelings and passions, to have those passions and feelings enlisted from the time those cases are called, to the time of their final trial. He lives in some particular portion of the district, and has his little clique of favorites from that portion of the district. And in all these cases which will not warrant their being taken to the court of last resort, this favoritism affects the judge, and warps his mind, and leads him to render a decision which he would not otherwise have given perhaps. If we had a more speedy remedy, a court near at hand, where we could go for redress, this fact of enormous expenses, and great delays, would never be presumed upon, and the favorites would never attempt to presume upon the friendship or feelings of the judge. In some parts of the State, that thing has been felt, and at this day is a crying evil. Taking all these things in connection, it works a great hardship upon the people, to say that they shall have no redress for wrongs, except at the capital of the State.

I am decidedly in favor of some system different fiom the present system. I am not tenacious about the particular system, so that there be incorporated into that system a principle which will remedy the evils which are complained of. I do not care whether it is called a superior court, or a supreme court, or a court of appeals, or a supreme court, with its branches, so that it embodies this principle. The present system I believe to be imperfect, inadequate, and one that does not meet the wants and wishes of the people at the present time. And I am surprised when I hear gentlemen say here, that there has been no demand made for this change. I certainly understand that one of the changes demanded by the people, in calling for this constitutional convention, was a change in the judicial system of this State. But even if there had been no such demand, if we, sitting here, could conceive of the necessity of such a change, even prospectively, it is our duty to make it. And so far from being a draw back, a dead weight upon the constitution, when submitted to the people for their approval, I am satisfied that it will be the means of adding a large amount of votes to it, at least in the portion of the State from which I come. It is true, perhaps, that the banking question absorbs more of the attention of the people than any other question that led to the calling of this convention; but, second to that, I place the desire for a change in our judicial system. For these reasons I am in favor of the change.

On motion of Mr. TRAER, the committee then arose.

The PRESIDENT having resumed the chair,

The CHAIRMAN of the committee of the whole reported that that committee had bad under consideration the majority and minority reports of the committee on the judicial department, had made progress therein, and asked leave to sit again.

Mr. CLARKE, of Johnson, moved to lay the report of the committee of the whole upon the table.

Mr. CLARKE, of Henry. I would like to move that the majority report be referred back to the majority of the committee on the judiciary for further consideration.

Mr. CLARKE, of Johnson. I think that would raise the whole discussion again. We had better agree upon the principles we will adopt, whether that of three courts, or of two courts. When that is decided, we can then refer this matter to the committee again.

Mr. CLARKE, of Henry. I would enquire of the chair, if laying this subject upon the table, would prevent me from submitting my motion to refer?

The PRESIDENT. It would.

Mr. CLARKE, of Henry. I would like to state to the convention my position in regard to this matter, and my reasons for desiring this reference.

Mr. CLARKE, of Johnson. The gentleman can explain as well to-morrow as to-day.

The PRESIDENT stated the question upon laying the report of the committee of the whole on the table, subject to the order of the convention.

Mr. HALL moved to amend the motion, so that the report of the committee of the whole be received, and leave granted them to sit again to-morrow morning.

Mr. CLARKE, of Johnson. I accept that motion in lieu of the one I submitted.

The question being taken upon the motion as modified. it was agreed to, and leave granted accordingly.

On motion of Mr. CLARKE, of Johnson, the convention adjourned.

THURSDAY, FEBRUARY 5th, 1857.

The Convention met at 9 o'clock, A. M., and was called to order by the President.

Prayer by the Chaplain.

The PRESIDENT. The first business in order is the consideration of the report of the Committee on the Judiciary.

Mr. PARVIN. I move that the reports be referred to the same committee with instructions to report the article in the present constitution with amendments, providing for the election of judges by the people, and re-districting the State.

Mr. HARRIS. Into how many districts?

Mr. PARVIN. Not to exceed ten.

Mr. HARRIS. I think that number too small.

Mr. PARVIN. If the motion I have made prevails, the gentleman can move to amend in this respect.

Mr. CLARKE, of Johnson. I hope the motion will not prevail, and that we will decide the main question presented by these reports, and for that purpose, it seems to me, that the motion now pending in Committee of the Whole is in just as good a shape as we can have it.—The moment we decide the question whether we shall have two or three courts, we can go to work and perfect the details. If this whole subject be referred to the committee with the instructions recommended by the gentleman from Muscatine [Mr. Parvin] we shall have to discuss the whole subject over again, which we had up yesterday afternoon. While the matter is fresh in our minds we had better decide the main question, whether we shall have two or three courts, and then leave the details to be perfected afterwards.

Mr. PARVIN. It does appear to me that the object of the gentleman from Johnson [Mr. Clarke] would be attained sooner by voting for the motion I make than for any other If we should vote in favor of his motion to take up the minority report, the convention may then refuse to consider it, and take up the article in the present constitution. I hope gentlemen will see that my motion will bring the Convention to a direct vote, whether we shall have a court of two or three judges.

The PRESIDENT. The chair is inclined to the opinion that the motion made by the gentleman from Muscatine [Mr. Parvin] is not strictly in order. The Convention directed yesterday that this matter should be made the special order for this morning.

Committee of the Whole.

On motion, the CONVENTION then resolved itself into Committee of the Whole, Mr. Johnston in the chair.

The Judicial Department.

The CHAIRMAN. The question before the Committee of the Whole is the consideration of the majority and minority reports of the Committee on the Judicial Department. The question before the committee is the motion made by the gentleman from Johnson [Mr. Clarke] to substitute the minority for the majority report.

Mr. PETERS. As the discussion upon this subject was cut short yesterday, by adjournment, I propose to answer some of the objections which have been urged against the system proposed by the committee in the majority report. It has been urged here by the gentleman from Jefferson [Mr. Wilson] that we should vote against any change in the judicial system of the State, upon the ground that there had been no demand for such change on the part of the people. For one, I would say that in the county where I reside, there was no one subject which assisted more in bringing about a revision of the constitution than a change in the judicial system; and I think there is no one question—not even excepting the banking question—in which the people feel a deeper interest, than in this change now proposed by the majority of the committee on the judiciary.

I am not surprised, I confess, to find gentlemen residing near, and having railroad communication with the capital, satisfied with the present system. That it works hardship on the part of those living remotely from the capital, is evident. As the system recommended by the majority approximates closely to the judiciary system of New York, it has been said that there has been great complaint on the part of the people of that State against the present system. I apprehend that you will find some persons objecting to the most perfect system that could be devised.

Although I never resided in the State of New York, I have been a constant reader since I have been in this State, of three papers published in the city of New York,—two of them I consider to be good authority here,—the Tribune and Herald,—and I never heard, through this source, one word of complaint against the present judiciary system of that State. I do not believe that any serious objections exist on the part of the people, or the members of the legal profession of New York, against their judiciary system.

Gentlemen again urge as an objection against the system proposed by the majority, that it will tend to increase the expenses of litigation in this State, by the creation of a new court. I apprehend, that so far as the expenses of this court are concerned, they will be very trivial. For instance, there will be twelve judges of the superior court in the State. Placing the salaries of the judges at two thousand dollars a year—and they ought to be established at that rate, if their services are worth anything—we will have a court which answers, to a great extent, to the present supreme court, without any additional expense, with the exception of the light and fuel which will be necessary for the use of this court. The expenses of these judges are paid by the districts, as those are now paid the district judges. Under this system the judges of this intermediate court form a court in bank to decide cases on appeals; consequently, the amount of salary necessary to create a court for that purpose, outside of the district system, would amount to twenty thousand dollars a year. The gentleman from Jefferson [Mr. Wilson] objects to the system on account of the provision in relation to the clerks of the court.

I am willing to offer an amendment in that respect, by which I would make the clerk of the district court, in the county where the superior court was held, the clerk *ex efficio* of the superior court, which would save the expense to which the gentleman objects. I think, however, that the salaries paid to those judges should be in proportion to the amount of their labor; and if the district judges are to hold terms of the superior court, they should have, in my opinion, more compensation than if they are simply to hold district courts; and the clerk, too, should have more compensation, for the additional services which might be devolved upon him. But, this question of expense is a very trifling objection to the system. The great advantage in the establishment of this court would be, that we should have within our reach, a court of competent jurisdiction to which we could take up cases on appeal, without being subjected to the expense and trouble of sending them up to the supreme court at the capital. A great advantage that will be derived from the establishment of this superior court will be, that it will produce a uniformity in the decisions of the courts in the several districts of the State, in the place of the diversity of opinion which now exists in the different districts. I am in hopes, that the report of the majority committee will be adopted, with such amendments as the convention may see fit to make.

Mr. PALMER. I desire briefly, to express my opinion upon the question now under consideration. I am rather inclined to favor something like the present judiciary system, if we can by continuing such a system, devise some plan by which to relieve the supreme court of its labor, either by increasing the number of judges, or constituting some other district court, which may perform all the duties which the majority of the committee on the judiciary contemplate shall be performed by the superior court which they propose to establish. I see no necessity for three judges holding courts in each county of a district alternately, for I can see no good that will result from it. The gentleman from Des Moines [Mr. Hall] enlarged at considerable length, upon the benefits that might be derived from the difference of qualification in these three judges for trying different classes of cases. For instance, he says, that one judge may be better qualified to try chancery cases, another common law and statute law cases, and still another, criminal cases. Let us see what the practical operation of this would be. Suppose the three judges are elected for the district, as the gentleman proposes, and the best qualified to discharge the duties of common and statute law goes his rounds, and in due time, another judge comes along, who holds a court for which he is the best qualified, in which most of the criminal cases will be tried, and afterwards the equity judge comes around to try the chancery cases. Now, this course of proceeding will necessarily involve some delay, because the cases will have to be postponed until that judge comes around, who is best qualified to try these particular cases.

After they complete their rounds, I understand from the reading of the majority report, that these three judges are to hold a superior court for the hearing of cases on appeal. I do not know whether it is proposed that all three shall sit and hear every case, or not. Perhaps it is understood, that when a case comes up before the superior court, in which one of these three judges has rendered judgment below, that this judge will step off the bench, and leave the other two judges to decide the case. Suppose he does so, and the superior court then holds its session. The cases are called up for trial, and the first one in the calendar is a chancery case, which has been tried by the judge below, who is supposed to be best qualified to try such cases. This chancery judge accordingly steps off the bench, and he will step outside of the bar and converse with the outsiders about shooting turkeys, and deer perhaps, while the judges who are best qualified to try common law and statute, and criminal cases, will proceed to hear the chancery case.

The two judges who are supposed to be the least qualified to try this chancery case are the very judges who will have to try it, while the judge best qualified to try it, will have to leave the bench. And so it will be with the other judges, they will have to step off the bench when the cases come on which they respectively are best qualified to try. I think that the system will not work well in that respect.

I would have no objection to adopting some plan by which a system somewhat similar to the present district courts could be retained, and if necessary, that a certain number of these districts might constitute a district for a superior court, and let each Judge hold the courts in his district as he does now. This would perhaps be a good modification of the present system. It might be so arranged that these districts could be so constituted that the supreme court could hold a term in each of them yearly, to dispose of the cases that came before them; and if it were necessary to increase the number of Supreme Court Judges for this purpose, let it be done. But it will be argued, probably, that the Supreme Court should hold its term at the Capitol where the State Library is. I think that if the superior court can hold its terms in these separate districts, the supreme court can do it just as well there.

I think the change proposed by either the minority or majority reports would not be acceptable to the people in the section of the State where I reside. I have heard no suggestions made there in regard to the necessity of a radical change in the present Judiciary system. The only change I have heard mentioned was in regard to the manner of electing Prosecuting Attorneys; but I believe either of the systems proposed by the committee would entail upon us the necessity of electing a Prosecuting Attorney in every county the same as at present. It would be impracticable to have but one State's Attorney in each of these districts, for he could not follow all of the three Judges and attend all the courts in the District. Many of the new counties feel the necessity of some change in the manner of electing the Prosecuting Attorneys. In the new counties many times there is hardly a man to be found who is capable of performing the duties of a Prosecuting Attorney as they should be performed. In the older counties the good Attorneys prefer not to accept this office as the salary is small, and they can make more money by defending than by prosecuting criminals. The people in my part of the State desire that the districts shall be made sufficiently large, perhaps the size of our present judicial districts, where one prosecuting attorney shall be elected in each of the districts, and that he shall receive an annual salary sufficiently large to compensate him for his time and make it an object for him to devote himself to that office and that alone, and that he shall follow the judge wherever he holds his courts, for the purpose of attending to the interests of the State. In this way they think the interests of the State will be more beneficially subserved than they are at present. Under the plan I have suggested sufficient compensation would be allowed to obtain the services of a well qualified prosecuting attorney in each district; but as long as we retain the present plan of electing prosecuting attorneys in each county, I think there will be great cause of complaint. Between the two reports on the Judiciary, the majority and the minority, I would prefer the report made by the majority of the committee. I shall not vote for the motion of the gentleman from Johnson [Mr. Clarke] to substitute the minority for the majority report. I cannot say that even the majority report satisfies me, and I would prefer some plan similar to the present system of District Courts.

Mr. CLARKE, of Johnson. As the author of this minority report, I desire to present my objections to the report of the majority, and to answer some of the positions which the gentleman from Des Moines, [Mr. Hall,] has taken in favor of that report. The gentleman seems to be surprised at the remark I made, that if the State were ten years older, I should be in favor of the system reported by the majority. It is conclusive, to my mind, that a system which will suit a population of three millions is too cumbersome and burdensome for a population of half a million. As I remarked before, it is only a question of time, and if our courts were overborne with business and inadequate for the litigation of the State, and if it were necessary to create an additional court, I would favor the system proposed by the majority and favor as I expect to some years hence, an intermediate court between our present District and Supreme Courts. I think that the time has not yet come, when we can impose such a system upon the people. There has been no demand made by them for a charge in this respect, and I think it is, therefore, the safest plan to leave the necessity for the establishment of this court to the future action of the people. I may say here, that the report of the minority proposes to leave it an open question, and gives to the Legislature the right to establish this court if it shall be deemed necessarry, and this discussion will call the attention of the people to this subject. If the next or any other succeeding Legislature shall find that this court is demanded and is absolutely necessary, they can establish it and put it into practical operation.

My first objection to this majority system is, that it will not only add to the expenses of litigation, but it will tend to create delay in legal proceedings. The gentleman says, that the majority report provides for no extra expense for Judges, and that offers a gratuitous court. It is true that the Judges are to have no additional pay for this increase of labor, but there will be additional costs attending the establishment of this court, to which the gentleman has not referred. If cases are taken from the Districtto the Superior Court there must be transcripts made, writs issued and process served. There are various expenses attending the removal of cases from one court to another, for it is not contemplated by the gentleman from Des Moines, [Mr. Hall,] or by the majority report, that the original papers shall be taken from the District to the Superior Court.

I think there is nothing in the argument of the gentleman, that the lawyers will take charge of their own cases at this Superior Court. I believe that this court, if established, will be attended by a body of lawyers, just as the Supreme Court is now attended, who will take the papers of a case, and argue it before that court.

There is another question to which I wish to refer in this connection. Under the present system, if a case is decided at the spring term, there is usually time enough to bring it up before the Supreme Court at the ensuing June term, and so if a case is decided at the fall term there is time enough to bring it before the Supreme Court the ensuing winter term. Under this Superior Court system between the term of these District Courts and the term of this Superior Court, there will not be time enough to take the cases up on appeal, and consequently a great many of them will be compelled to lay over some six months, a delay which will very often prove a serious injury to the parties. In this length of time witnesses may be removed by death, or may go out of the reach of parties, and although the party seeking a new trial may succeed in reversing the decision made below and a new trial may be ordered, still, when the time comes around for re-hearing of his case, he may find himself helpless in consequence of the absence of his witnesses. But suppose the decision of the court below is reversed, the other party in the place of allowing it to go back may take it up to the Supreme Court. There is a delay of another six months, which must create an additional expense, because the party losing has to pay the expenses of all these courts. The position of the gentleman from Delaware, [Mr. Peters,] has no force in it for this reason. Suppose you substitute or make the clerk of this Superior Court the clerk of the District Courts. Why, you will have to pay him as much for his services as you would a new man who might be appointed clerk. The salaries of these clerks will be fees regulated by law. There is nothing in the argument that you obviate the expense of a clerk of the Superior Court by making the clerk of the District Court clerk of that court.

But there is a still greater objection to this system than the objections I have mentioned, and it is one which I apprehend the gentleman from Des Moines, [Mr. Hall,] has overlooked. The time will come, if it has not now, in which judges of the district court will be unable to perform the duties devolving on them as judges of the superior court. In all the populous counties of this State, it has now become necessary to hold three courts a year, spring, summer and fall terms; and in some of the counties—and if I am not mistaken, it is so in Dubuque—they have four terms a year. In my own district we have three counties, Linn, Johnson and Washington, in which the law provides that three terms shall be held a year. In the counties of Linn and Johnson it takes two weeks at least to hold each of these terms; and by the time the judge has gone through with these three terms, one in February, one in July, and one in November, I desire to know what time he will have to meet the other judges for holding this superior court. This is the case in all the river counties, or if it be not so now, the increase of business will very soon demand three terms of the district court a year, and where then will these judges obtain the time to hold this superior court? If I am right in this supposition, and you adopt this majority report, in what position will you be placed? The constitution compels these district judges to hold a court which they have no time to hold, and the legislature will have no power to substitute other judges to perform the duties of that court. This, to my mind, is a strong objection to this system. The minority report obviates that difficulty, and leaves the whole question of the establishment of this intermediate court to the legislature to decide, when this court shall be demanded by the people. If this court shall be found necessary, the legislature can create it, and they can impose its duties upon the district judges for the time being, or they can substitute other judges.

Another objection which I have to this system is, that this superior court is the supreme court of the district, and its jurisdiction and power extend no farther. The decisions of this superior court in its own district makes the law for that district, not only in relation to the questions of practice, but in relation to questions of constitutional rights and private property. The decisions of the superior court are to that district what the decisions of the supreme court are to the State, and you will have, as they have in New York under this much vaunted system, conflicting decisions in the different districts of the State. If any gentleman will look at the decisions made by the superior court under the code of New York, involving perhaps questions of property, they will find that in different parts of that State there are different rules of law; and it is the experience of every lawyer with whom I have conversed upon this subject, that the establishment of this court has produced confusion in the decisions made. And I think if we establish this system here, that the same results would follow. Take for instance, this much mooted question of a prohibitory liquor law. Suppose that no decision had been made by the supreme court, regulating this matter. The judges in one district may decide it to be constitutional, while the judges in another district may decide it to be unconstitutional. Here we have parties acting under a different rule of conduct in different parts of the State, and yet the parties on both sides will be acting in accordance with the law; and instead of making the law certain you will render it uncertain. Such has been the result in New York, and I think it affords a very strong objection to the system proposed to be established here.

It seems to me that the gentleman from Jasper [Mr. Skiff] is entirely mistaken when he argued in favor of the system reported by the majority, that it would lessen the bulk of the decisions and reports of the Supreme Court. If you adopt this system, and if the decisions of the superior court are to be the law in the districts, why it follows as a matter of course, as it has followed in New York, you will have two sets of reports, one set of reports of the Superior Courts showing what the law is in the district, and another set of reports showing what the decisions of the Supreme Court are, so that this system instead of reducing the number of reports, which is so great a tax upon lawyers, must inevitably increase the number. If gentlemen will refer to New York, they will find that Barbour's Supreme Court Reports under this system have reached the 23d volume, and they are publishing them at the rate of three and four volumes a year. When you endeavor to find out what the law is by the Supreme Court reports of that State, you have to commence with the first reports and go through them all to find out how many contradictory decisions there are, and you have to get the decisions of the higher courts to know how many of these decisions have been overruled. It is now an exceedingly difficult matter to find out what the law is there. I remember a recent case in point in the county of Linn where I was employed upon one side. I went on and argued my case, referring to a decision made in the superior Court of New York, which I considered bore strongly in my favor, and I felt myself perfectly safe. When I had concluded my argument the lawyer upon the other side, who was a little better versed upon the decisions of that court than I was, cited as authority another volume of these reports, which entirely upset the position I had assumed. I contend that the establishment of this system here will tend to produce the same confusion and uncertainty in the bar, that now exists in New York; and its effect will be not only to mislead the bar and the people, but we will have a different system of law in operation in different parts of the State, or in other words, we will have a wheel within a wheel, or rather four little wheels running inside of a big wheel.

Another argument that has been used in favor of the establishment of this new system, is that it will do away with expense to which lawyers and their clients are subjected in coming to the Capitol to attend the terms of the Supreme Court. In regard to this matter, I would say, that if a majority of the Convention wish to make the Supreme Court a traveling machine, I shall make no objection. I agree upon this subject with the gentleman from Des Moines [Mr Hall] that the Supreme Court should have a local habitation as well as a name; that not only the legislative but the judicial power of the State should be established at the Capitol. But this argument about the expense of parties coming to the seat of government, I consider is entitled to but little consideration. Parties do not come here to watch their cases through this court, and no lawyer wants his clients here, buzzing about his ears The cases are presented upon transcripts, and the lawyers have no use for the attendance of their clients, and require no suggestions from them. This expense of appealing cases has to be made somewhere. If parties who have cases in the District Courts deem it necessary to take them to the Supreme Court, and if their necessities are such that they cannot stay and watch the cases, will they not follow the Supreme Court wherever that court is held, so that instead of the expense of following their case once to the Supreme Court, you double that expense under this proposed system.

I concur with the gentleman from Des Moines [Mr. Hall] in saying that this question of a judicial system is one of the most important questions that can come before us, and it ought not to be passed over lightly. It is one which should receive the careful consideration of the Convention, because this department of the State, in its operations, comes home, not only to the pockets, but to the dearest rights of every man in the State.

I would not tie the hands of the legislature upon this subject, nor would I prevent the people from increasing the number of judges. I propose, therefore, in the minority report to leave this an open question, and I ask if this is not the safest plan, as we are situated at present? Suppose we adopt the system proposed by the majority, and it becomes a part of the constitution, and it is found—as I think it will be—that these district judges cannot perform the duties assigned them—what will you do? You will have to amend this constitution, either by putting the people to the expense of calling another convention, or providing some other way for remedying the difficulty. It seems to me unnecessary, therefore, to adopt this system of the majority at this time. This subject may be safely entrusted in the hands of the people, and if the prophecy of the gentleman from Des Moines [Mr. Hall] be fulfilled, then ten years hence, perhaps sooner, I shall be found with him, in favor of creating such a court as this.

Another subject has been referred to in this discussion, which it seems to me is hardly involved in the question of whether we shall have two or three courts, to which I have endeavored to confine my remarks, and that is in relation to the manner of electing these district judges. As gentlemen have given their views upon this question, I claim the indulgence of the committee for presenting my views, also, upon it as briefly as I can.

It is well known that we now have upon the bench many judges of the district court who are entirely unfitted for the station—incompetent to perform their duties satisfactorily to the people, and the result has been that the districts have been cut up in order to displace the judges with whom the people were dissatisfied. In two districts the territory has been so cut up that the district judges are left but three counties each, while in other districts where there is a great amount of business, population, and wealth, the judges are overloaded with work. When these districts are small and narrow, there may be no person in them qualified to fill the place of judge with credit to himself and satisfaction to the people; but in a large district where you elect three judges instead of one—and this is a point upon which the gentleman from Des Moines [Mr. Hall] and myself agree—the people have a better opportunity for the selection of competent judges. For instance, if you throw three districts into one, you may take a section of country that has no good lawyer in it, and unite it with another section that has good lawyers in it, and by that means get three good judges, or two good judges, with one poor judge. If they can get two good ones, and one poor judge, that will be worth something, because it will be better to have two good judges in a district, than to have only one judge, and he a poor one.

I desire to suggest another consideration in connection with this question. I regard the minority report upon this subject as really providing for what is equivalent to an additional court. For instance, if the people should happen to select in a district one good, and two indifferent judges, the action of the competent judge, who understands legal distinctions and rules of law, and who has a clear legal mind, will have an influence in correcting the decisions of his colleages in the district.

If one indifferent judge should get into a district the members of the bar can always manage that he shall be in a position where he can do little harm.

Every lawyer knows, if one of these judges should be a very indifferent lawyer, that he can always, as a matter of safety to his client, manage to throw his cases over. It is true, this course may devolve a little more labor upon one judge than upon another. But that is not the question. The question is, whether we can devise a system which shall give to the people a choice of judges, a chance to elect good judges, and if they make a failure, to give them a chance to obviate the evil without bringing their cases to the supreme court. I think under the system reported by the minority this can be done.

The gentleman from Des Moines [Mr. Hall] argued that under the operation of the system proposed by the majority, if one judge was a good chancery lawyer, another a good commercial lawyer, and another a good criminal lawyer, they respectively would have referred to them for their decision the cases belonging to that department of the law for which they were peculiarly qualified. But this result would not follow, because if the parties do not agree to let their cases go before these judges in this manner, they can insist upon a trial in due course of law, and they must have it.

There is another suggestion which I wish to make here. As has been remarked by some members, there has been no special demand for an alteration of the judicial system. So far as I know, the only point raised in my own district in regard to this matter, was the election of supreme court judges by the people. But, even admitting that, I suppose that we have a right to act upon questions which were not mooted during the canvass, because there are many questions which have not been made subjects of public discussion. I understand our duty while sitting here, is to make such a constitution as shall secure a stable government, and protect the right of every man in the enjoyment of his life, liberty and happiness.

While I do not think there is any thing in the argument, that we should not act here upon questions which have not been discussed among the people, I do not wish to run into the other extreme and burden the people with a system which will be entirely new, and which may tend to defeat the Constitution; or in other words, I do not wish to incorporate into the Constitution a system, which, from its novelty and cumbersomeness, would make our work in vain. I do not wish to present a system that would not meet the approval of the people, and be open to the objection of increasing the expenses of litigation. In the first place, I prefer the system presented by the minority, to the present system, because I think it will give the people an opportunity of selecting better Judges. I am free to confess, that the idea of limiting the districts and throwing three Judges into one district, was the prominent object I had in view in presenting this minority report. I want to rotate out of office these District Judges, and I wish to give the people a chance of making a better selection of Judges than they now have. I know that there is a universal complaint against some of the Judges for incompetency; I do not blame the Judges. The fault is with the people, in the first instance, because they have no right to expect to secure a person of the proper talent and capacity to fill the office of Judge unless they pay him a proper compensation. I would provide a remedy, if possible, for this evil. One of the best Judges of the District Court in my district, acknowledged to be so on every hand, has been compelled within a short time past to resign his seat. Shortly before his resignation, I wrote to him, urging him in the most earnest manner to wait and see the action of this Convention. In reply, he said that he was unable to live upon $1000 a year, and he had been compelled to go into other business in order to support his family and provide something for the future. I hope that this Convention will fix the salaries of these Judges at $2000 a year, so that we may secure the best men in the State for the Bench; and in order to effect that result I wish to give the people a chance to rotate out of office the present Judges and get better ones in their stead.

In the hope that the views I have here presented will meet with due consideration at the hands of the Convention, I will say nothing further upon this question at present.

Mr. HALL. I desire to submit a few remarks upon this question, and I promise gentlemen I will not detain them long. The subject now before us is one upon which a great deal could be said, and upon which every gentleman here has formed opinions based upon his own personal experience. While I do not arrogate to myself the experience or capacity which other gentlemen have, yet I think I have that kind of experience which will enable me to speak with some degree of confidence as to the necessity for a change in the present judicial system of our State. Having practiced law in this State for eighteen years, a part of the time when it was a territory, I have had a good opportunity of observing the nature, character, and practical operation of the judicial system of this State. My experience has taught me—to which I am willing to bear testimony here—that the judicial system of this State was most wofully neglected by those who made the present constitution, and by the course which has been pursued since by the legislature; and I am not alone in this opinion.

The judiciary I consider to be the most important branch of the government; and it should be nursed with the greatest care, and watched with more scrutiny than any other department of the government; but instead of this we have seen it most shamefully neglected and rendered inadequate to meet the wants and requirements of the people. Those persons who appeal to the judiciary for protection, and who have causes of complaint for which they seek redress, are but a small fraction of the people. They are turned away from the courts where they have sought redress, without being able to obtain that satisfaction which they demanded. The uncertainty of the law is enough to deter any honest man from appealing to the tribunals of the country for justice. I say now, without the fear of successful contradiction, that the judicial system of this State has become almost a term of absolute reproach. I ask gentlemen here who are not members of the legal profession, have you that confidence in the judicial system of this State, that you would risk the decision of an important right there without apprehension and occasion for alarm? Do the legal tribunals, to which the citizen should always look with the most perfect confidence, afford you the proper safeguards for the protection of your property? I undertake to say that there is not a gentleman here, who has ever reflected upon the subject, who can rise in his seat and say that he has that confidence in that branch of the government, that he would be willing to entrust to its determination his most important rights, with that unshaken reliance which he should entertain?

If I desire anything sincerely, it is to elevate the character of that department of the government, and place it in such a position that it shall receive that confidence from the people to which it is entitled. I think that the plan proposed by the majority of the committee would remove the reproach which, to a very considerable extent, is now cast upon the judiciary of this State. This proposition is simply to establish an intermediate court to be held by three judges, who pass in their rounds through the districts, and who, by that means, know the suitors, and the circumstances under which the litigation was commenced, and who constantly associate and mingle with the people; and when they meet together to hear cases in appeal, they have an opportunity to investigate and correct the errors which may have been committed in the hurried trial of cases upon the circuits. And herein lies the great advantage of having this new court. A judge sitting upon the circuit, however honest and capable he may be, may make in a hurried moment a wrong decision, which often subjects him to the imputation of a want of integrity and judgment: and I would give him by this system an opportunity for further reflection and study, so that he may amend his decision, if made under erroneous impressions of what the law really is. Will not this be a very great advantage to the judges themselves, and to the people at large? To my mind there is nothing more certain than that such a system will inspire confidence among the people towards these judges, and bring about a better state of things than now exists. My experience in regard to judicial matters, as I said before, may be of little worth; but although it may conflict with that of other gentlemen, and particularly with that of the gentleman from Jefferson, [Mr. Wilson,] yet such as it is, I beg leave to state it. I concede that my observations may have been confined within a very narrow circle. My experience is so limited that although I live in a county adjoining to that where the gentleman from Jefferson, [Mr. Wilson,] resides, and although I have practiced in that county for ten years, and live only eighteen miles distant from him, I have never heard of the gentleman as a lawyer, until I came to this convention. I state this in justice to the gentleman, that what I say may not be considered as entitled to as much weight as the remarks he has made upon this question.

My experience, as far as it has gone, is that where a party has an opportunity for a double argument, it tends to secure a better administration of the law, and a greater certainty in the law. If a case is once argued before the superior court, and if it be then taken to the supreme court, it goes there with the light of all the learning which the superior court can shed around it. Cases would then go from this superior court to the supreme court, after they were fully and completely argued, and after full investigation and examination by this superior court, from which the supreme court would derive a very great advantage and benefit. This would be the effect of it—the necessary result; and you would thus give increased confidence in, and weight to, the decisions of the court. There would be no hurried decisions there; none given without deep consideration and deliberation. And hence you would restore to that court the confidence which it has now I must say—and gentlemen of the bar will bear me out in what I say—to some extent lost; and the want of which has shaken the judicial system of the State as it now stands.

I wish to answer, and in all kindness, the argument of the gentleman from Johnson, (Mr. Clarke.) The gentleman says, that if you establish these district courts, you have four wheels within a wheel; one district judge will decide the law one way, and another will decide another way; and he asks, what will be the result? Now that is a thing that cannot be avoided in our judicial system. But the way the matter stands now, you have fifteen districts in this State, and the decision of each judge is the law in his district, until the supreme court interferes. The gentleman has fifteen wheels within a wheel, while I have only four. I, at least, have the decisions uniform in a portion of territory embracing one fourth of the State, while the decisions of a judge now are only recognized over one fifteenth of the State. To that extent we diminish and decrease the conflict of decisions. Under the system we propose, the supreme court, which is now the regulator of the fifteen districts now established, would then be the regulator of but four districts. As four is to fifteen, so has my system the advantage over the other.

Now in regard to the expense of coming to the seat of government, which my friend from Johnson (Mr. Clarke,) seems to think of so little moment. He has always resided at the capitol. Since we have been a State, the supreme court, for some years, sat in five places in the State. For two or three years it was held in Burlington, and the business from the first judicial district, including Washington county, was done in that place. I know, and there is not a member of the bar in that district who will not agree with me, that it was a convenience to the people there; it cheapened justice, and enabled many, who could not afford to go to the capitol of the State, to be heard in that place. The manner of holding the court there, we all know to have been a popular one. And so it was all over the State; wherever the court was held, it was felt to be a convenience.

But there was an evil attending it, and this convenience, in my opinion, did not overbalance the evil. It was true, that at Burlington there were respectable libraries, and matters were very well investigated; at Ottumwa there was no library at all; at Fort Des Moines there were but few libraries. The necessity and advantage of these libraries must be evident to every one. But the evil attending that plan grew out of the want of libraries. The result was, that the court could not investigate business at several points. It was a supreme court on wheels, going from pillar to post. Consequently the decisions of that supreme court, as every gentleman knows, failed to carry that weight they should have done, and the confidence of litigants in them was diminished. You cannot have a supreme court that will give as uniform decisions, and bestow such investigation upon the cases before them, as is necessary to secure confidence, where it goes about the State on wheels, as when it is stable and fixed in some one place.

I recollect a very distinguished man, a member of the bar, who came from Illinois to practice in this State—Mr. Cyrus Walker. His policy was to ascertain what books his adversary was going to use in the case, and then he knew in advance the argument he would have to meet. Now let me be acquainted with the character of the library that a member of the bar is going to use, and I can tell you very nearly the conclusions that will be reached in regard to the law, unless the library is very complete and varied. His mind will be made up from the authorities, commentaries and decisions his library contains. If he has the court decisions, and commentaries upon the law of the State of New York, he will bring them forward, and from them draw his arguments. If his authorities are drawn from Pennsylvania, then Pennsylvania practice and decisions will be his guide; if of Massachusetts, then that State will be his guide. Yet those States, in many decisions, conflict with each other; the same rule and policy that govern in one do not in the other.

Now our supreme court should be so situated that it can have a general and universal library, where they can examine all these different decisions, and adopt those which they deem best adapted to the condition of this State. But this cannot be when the supreme court is traversing the State on wheels. You cannot give uniformity and character to its decisions under those circumstances. And hence I would have the supreme court hold its sessions at the seat of government, and at no other place.

One word in regard to another point. The gentleman from Jefferson (Mr. Wilson,) tells the convention that if lawyers would work as they ought, they would prepare written arguments for their cases before the supreme court. Now my experience has been such as to lead me to believe that no case of mine is safe without both written and oral argument. Let the lawyer prepare a rigid written argument, and then elaborate upon that in an oral argument before the court. In my opinion, no case can be well investigated without both kinds of argument. These investigations require a great deal of time, and a great deal of labor, and the court should have ample time and opportunity to make that investigation, and go carefully through their deliberations.

Now in this system I propose to take from the supreme court all the trash and rubbish, all the unimportant cases, a vast number of which now claim their attention, and distract their deliberations; by means of this superior or intermediate court, I bring this superior court home to the people. The gentleman says that his clients do not come to the seat of government here, on their appeals. Mine do, very often. Even if they are told that it will do no good, they come here out of anxiety. I had several here during the last term of the court, and they remained here one or two weeks. And this is no uncommon thing as far as my experience goes.

This, however, I do not consider an argument one way or the other. But I think we should act a little upon that principle, which has passed into a proverb, and endeavor to give such a character to our tribunals as will lead the people to have confidence in them. Our primary, and principal object should be to do justice, though the heavens fall, and not look at the expense or the price. Let us endeavor to make a system as convenient and practicable as possible, so as to secure to our decisions the highest tone and character, and the greatest certainty in the expounding of the law.

I have no desire to detain the convention, and will make but one remark farther, in relation to an error that my friend from Appanoose. (Mr.

Harris,) my friend from Davis, (Mr. Palmer,) and the gentleman from Jefferson, (Mr. Wilson,) have fallen into. I spoke of the advantage this court would secure of dividing cases in different branches of the law. I illustrated my meaning by supposing that one judge may have distinguished himself as a land lawyer, another as a commercial lawyer, and another as a chancery lawyer. Now these things do occur, and I referred to an instance which, if it had occurred here, would be productive of benefit. If it did not occur, we would at least be as we are now, and lose nothing. I said that if a chancery trial was coming on before a judge of this term, and I had not as much confidence in him as the judge who was to try the next term, I would have a feeling in common with the counsel on both sides, and we might, if we desired, have the case continued, and thus secure the benefit of the chancery judge. If we did not do it, we would be as well off under this system as under the old one. But gentlemen have taken up my idea, and treated it as if I intended that it should be a part of the system, and parties were to have a chance of compelling this contingency. I spoke of it in no such light; I had no such intention; and I do not see how I could have been understood in that manner.

Mr. HARRIS. I had not proposed to trouble the convention with any farther remarks upon this subject. But I would like to ask my friend from Des Doines (Mr. Hall,) a question in regard to a point to which he has not spoken. This superior court, as I understand it, is intended for the correction of errors of the courts below. Suppose that a case taken up there on appeal is reversed, and goes back for a new trial. The judge who tried it before, of course cannot try it again, and it is tried by one of the judges who reversed it above. Still there is dissatisfaction, and it goes back again on a writ of error, and is again reversed, and again sent below for a new trial. It is tried again, and again an appeal is taken. But there is but one judge now to appeal to, and if he reverses it, there is no one left to try it again. Now, to use a ludicrous, but I think an expressive illustration, is not this something like a puppy pursuing his own tail, and never catching it? And would not this thing sometimes be the result of this system?

Mr. HALL. That would depend very much upon circumstances. If the judges were all pettifoggers, and the lawyers ditto, then it might happen; but not otherwise. I mean no disrespect to the gentleman, for I have the kindest feelings, and entertain the highest respect for him. I will take the case he supposes: Here is a decision brought up from the circuit court to this superior court, and it is reversed. I am for the defendant upon the appeal, and if I am not satisfied, I sue out my writ of error and appeal to the Supreme Court, and pass it right on. If they reverse it there, it goes back to the district court.

Mr. HARRIS. In that case it goes through three courts instead of two, as is the case now.

Mr. HALL. Certainly.

Mr. HARRIS. Then I do not see how this new system renders litigation cheaper.

Mr. HALL. Let those who dance pay the fiddler.

Mr. HARRIS. That is just the way I thought it would be.

Mr. HALL. This additional court costs the State nothing. If the client is satisfied with its decision, he can go back to the district court; if not, then with a little additional expense he can take his case to the Supreme Court. But I argue that a large portion of the cases would go no further than that superior court.

Another member here argues that this would produce delay in the trial of cases. I claim that it would not, in the aggregate of cases.—There may be a few cases delayed for a few months, but as a general thing it would not produce delay. To the great mass of suitors it would prove a benefit, by facilitating the final disposition of their cases, instead of delaying. This superior court will be held at the close of the circuit or district court; and experience teaches us that not more than one case in six or eight, that are decided in this superior court wherever this system is adopted, would go to the supreme court. The State of Virginia has a similar system. If gentlemen will examine the working of that system there, they will see that only one in six or ten cases finds its way to the supreme court, while the rest are disposed of conveniently and speedily; and gentlemen only beg the question when they present these instances of delay, as an argument against my view of this matter. I hold that it would afford facilities for litigation that parties do not have now; that it would cheapen litigation, and above all, strengthen the confidence of litigants and the people in the system under which justice is to be administered. It would strengthen that confidence—I am satisfied of it. It has done so in other states, where this system has been tried, and it would do so here. It would certainly render the administration more secure and more certain, and make the decisions of the court more uniform; and they will, in consequence be received with more confidence by the people throughout the State, and by members of the profession generally.

Mr. PETERS. I hope the Convention will pardon me for taking the floor upon this subject. I have sat here listening to the arguments which have been offered so far, and have failed to discover any good reason against the proposed change in the judiciary. I agree with the gentleman from Alamakee [Mr. Clark] that this change was demanded by the people, and was but second to any other that led to the call of this convention. I have, so far, heard no good and valid objection, in my opinion, to the system proposed by this majority report. If gentlemen will show me that by this change a delay in the litigation of the State will be caused, then I may oppose it. But I do not believe there could be framed a system more prolific of delay than the present one. I know that upon the docket of the county I represent, there are cases which have been there for five years, and no one can tell how much longer they will remain there.

As regards the question of expense attending this matter, I believe it is the duty of this convention to give every man in this State, who has a cause to bring into court, or already there, that system which will afford him the most speedy and adequate remedy. I do not believe that can be afforded him under the present system.

It is urged by gentlemen here that to create another court, composed of the judges of the district, will be to require them to do what they have not time to do. The argument is, that there is now so much business in some of the districts, that some of the present judges cannot attend to it all; and consequently, if we create another court, and do nothing to take from them a part of the business they have now to do, it would increase rather than diminish their labors. Now, I do not admit that by increasing the number of courts you consequently increase litigation. This superior court would have no more business than the necessities of the people would require. For instance: I do nct suppose that more than five or ten per cent. of the cases originating in the district court are taken to the supreme court. And if gentlemen cannot show me that the establishment of a court of competent jurisdiction, to hear appeals in every district of the State, thus furnishing the parties with a court nearer home—that this will not be cheaper than going to the capital with their cases—then, in my opinion, so much of this argument falls to the ground.

So far as the cost to the State is concerned, in creating this additional court, that would not weigh one feather with me, in the vote I should give upon this question. I do not care what the cost is to the State, so that it is within reasonable bounds. I wish to give to the people an opportunity of trying their causes somewhere within their reach.

This change has been objected to further upon the ground that no demand has been made from the people for it. Now, if the declaration of some four or five gentlemen upon this floor, that such demand has been made by the people, does not prove the fact, then I would suggest to those who doubt it to take the affidavits of those gentlemen.

I was a practicing attorney, residing at the capital of the State, I should personally feel desirous that all the causes in the state should come to the capital for trial, for I should suppose that I had a good location to obtain practice.

It is urged further, that parties are unable, after going through the district and superior courts, to carry their cases further, and consequently, justice will be denied some of them in that way. Now, I do not believe that the profession generally are so miserly as gentlemen would insinuate. For my part, if I was engaged in a case where I believed that justice was on my side, I would find means some way to prosecute that case before a court that I considered competent to give a correct decision.

I do not believe it is the policy of this State to hold on to an old system which is burdensome to the people, and which prevents them from seeking their remedy, because the tribunal to which they desire to go, is so distant that they are unable to reach it. I believe the old system has this effect, and that the people residing at a distance from the capital, are anxious for a change in this system which will bring justice nearer home to them.

Mr. WILSON. I had not intended saying anything further upon this subject, until I heard the remarks of the very amiable gentleman from Des Moines [Mr. Hall]; but in justice to myself I will submit a few remarks in reply to some which have fallen from that gentleman.

I know that he is a very amiable gentleman, and not at all in the habit of arrogating to himself anything which does not belong to him. And while he may have all the knowledge in the world at all necessary for the discussion of subjects that come before this body, I do not suppose that it is at all necessary for him to have any particular knowledge of myself. I am happy that he carried his statement farther, and informed the convention that he once had a very extensive practice in the county I have the honor to represent. And I am also happy to inform the convention that that amiable gentleman has no practice in that county now.

I do not know why it is that the gentleman from Des Moines [Mr. Hall] has adopted the practice of singling out members of this Convention for his attacks. Certainly every individual member here has a right to express his opinions. And yet, from the very commencement of this session, that gentleman has singled out, for his personal attacks, those who happen to run counter to his views. I have heard of the gentleman even beyond the limits of this State, so that he is not so unknown an individual as he makes me out to be. I heard of the gentleman in Ohio—I do not know but what he practiced law there at one time. But I only knew him by a title which he received there, and by which, I believe, he was generally known; the beautiful cognomen of "Civic (Kivic) Wreath" Hall. [Laughter.] That was the way I came to hear of that gentleman in that State. Now, all these things entitle that gentlemen to my respect, and he has my profound respect. And if he has a right to arrogate to himself full knowledge of anything that is necessary for our discussion here, and to consider it presumption on the part of an humble individual like myself, and particularly of a young man, to run counter to his views, I have no objection to offer.

There is one remark of the gentleman in relation to a "court on wheels," which I wish to notice. He says, while the supreme court was traveling the State on "wheels"—to use his own expression as nearly as I can—its decisions sunk into disrepute. Such may have been the case. I read some portions of the decisions of the supreme court of this State before I came here, and I have read some of them since. I am not aware, however, if the decisions of the court during that time sank into disrepute, they were raised to a very high standard above what they then held, while the gentleman from Des Moines was upon the supreme bench. I have yet to learn that his decisions are held in any higher esteem.

I would remark further, in connection with that argument, that if that is a valid objection to the old system of this State, I would ask if it is not a valid objection to the superior court that the gentleman is urging this convention to adopt? You divide this State into four districts. and you place your judges on "wheels" to traverse the several districts all the time. They have a large territory to travel over, and a vast amount of business to attend to; and when they meet as a bench in the superior court, I ask if they are any better prepared to make decisions than was the old supreme court while it was traveling the State on wheels?

And, as has been well remarked by the gentleman from Johnson [Mr. Clarke] in relation to the reports of the State of New York—and I apprehend no lawyer will dispute the statement, there are no reports in the United States, held in so low repute as the circuit court reports of New York. It is a complaint among the profession everywhere, that those reports are not worth anything. The law is unsettled under that system; and by adopting this system, your courts will be no better prepared to make decisons than was the court under the old system.

The gentleman from Des Moines speaks of libraries. It may be as difficult under this new system to find in some of the districts, the necessary libraries to enable the court to make just and respectable decisions, as in some of the districts under the old system.

Again, it has been urged here, that the cases going up to the superior court will be heard by the two judges who have not taken part in the court below. But, you have nevertheless the judge who made the decision below, and who is influenced by that principle of pride, which influences every man in matters of even less importance, using his influence to have his decision sustained, though he may use it indirectly, and perhaps not intentionally; and suppose the case should be reversed, and it should be sent back to the district court to be tried again, and again taken back to the supreme court, as is frequently the case. You will have two judges upon the same bench who have sat upon the case in the court below, and you may go on and carry your case up the third time, and every judge in the superior court has sat upon it, and you have no one to try the case.

Now, I ask what is the necessity of this thing, and why are members attacked personally, because they are not willing to fall in with the views of the gentleman from Des Moines [Mr. Hall] in relation to the judiciary of the State? I say this proposed system will prove burdensome, and will unsettle the law of the State. We have been laboring under difficulties, since the present system was adopted, and particularly since the code came into existence, to get the system of practice settled; and now by this new system we will have to go through this whole matter again, and wait for years to come to fix the practice to the little extent that has now been done. The minds of the people have been harmonized to the present system; and the legal profession are harmonized to it. The people are not expecting this change, and they will reap no benefit from it. I say, therefore, that we ought not in haste to make this change.

Now in connection with the remarks of the gentleman from Des Moines in relation to written and oral arguments. I prize oral arguments probably as highly as the gentleman does; I know they are very beneficial and effectual. I used the argument, however, in reply to those gentlemen who spoke of the distance of some portions of the State from the capital where the supreme court is held. I said that neither party would have the advantage if they would agree to submit their cases upon written arguments. If the supreme court should be removed to Fort Des Moines, the future capital of the State, it would then be in the central part of the State, and the trouble and distance will be divided among the people of the State. That will prove as beneficial to the people of the state as to divide it into four judicial districts, and perhaps then have to go to the seat of government with every important case.

I think these views are entitled to some respect, and should not be met by ridicule because some gentleman has had "eighteen years experience." Some persons can live a great while, and have a great deal of experience, and not amount to much after all. And when a man has arrived at the time of life that the gentleman from Des Moines has, and uses his self-claimed experience to cry down the opinions of others, it is an evidence that he has lived but to little purpose, having failed to learn the requirements of common decency. I desire to treat the opinions of all men with respect. But it does seem to me that when a man is so lost to that sense of courtesy due to members of this body, as to single out members for personal attack, his opinions are not entitled to more weight than they will probably receive in a body of this kind. Such a man must have narrow views and contracted ideas. I do hope this question will be discussed in a manner and with a spirit suitable to this body.

Mr. PALMER. I did not misunderstand the gentleman from Des Moines [Mr. Hall] in his former remarks. I understood him as saying, in support of this measure contained in the majority report, that it had one incidental advantage over the other one, and that was that we might have a diversity of talent among the judges; and my argument was in answer to that. That was one of his arguments, and it was with that understanding I replied to it. Now we have had some further information from th gentleman from Johnson [Mr. Clarke] of the design of this project of having but four districts in the State, and that is, that at present we have too small range for obtaining legal talent to supply the bench. So far as that is concerned, I have no objection to allowing the judges to be chosen from any part of the State if it be necessary to obtain the required legal talent, or if the people will be benefitted thereby. I am willing to go to Dubuque, or Muscatine, or Burlington, if it be necessary for the benefit of our State, for all our judges. But does our experience teach that such a plan would benefit us? Experience is the best lamp to light our steps in our course here. We have had experience in choosing our supreme judges by the legislature, when we have had the whole State to select from. We have had experience in electing our district judges from particular districts of the State. And what has been the result? I have frequently heard it remarked—and I do not refer to it for the purpose of disparaging the judges of our supreme court—that on the average the districts in this State have been as well supplied with legal attainments and talent upon their benches as the supreme court. It is possible that we may have had judges upon the supreme bench not so well qualified to fill the station as we might have obtained. It is also possible that we may have had judges in the districts not so competent for the stations they occupied as others might have been. Yet on the average I think it no disparagement to our supreme judges to say, we have had equal talent in the districts of the state as upon the supreme bench. At least that is the case so far as my experience goes. I believe that the district from which I come has been well supplied with tolerably good lawyers for judges, and we have not had to resort to the river towns for our judges.—But perhaps gentlemen will say they do not desire us to go there for them. Now I say that when a system which restricts us to half a dozen counties or more for the selection of our judges, works as well as a system which gives us the whole range of the State, that objection cannot be urged as an objection to small districts.

So far as regards the question of the comparative expenses of the two systems, I do not think this is a case where we should take into consideration small changes, or small variations in the amount of expenses, though it is true we might take into consideration a large increase of the expenses of our judicial system. But I do not conceive that the adoption of either of these plans is going to increase or diminish the expenses very much, from what they are now under our present system. I am in favor, as I said before, of the present system with some slight variations.

Mr. SOLOMON. As one of the members of the Committee on the Judicial Department, from whom this report came, it may be proper for me to say a few words upon this subject, although it is one that admits of almost any degree of explanation without any certainty of arriving at any definite conclusion. There is one point of view, however, in which this matter can be considered, that I think, has escaped the observation of members here. An extensive view has been taken of the Superior Court, its character, its bearing upon the people, and also upon the judiciary of the State. The same view has also been taken of the Supreme Court under the system proposed.

Now, it may perhaps be best for me to confine my remarks, from my inexperience in the practice, to that court with which I am alone acquainted: the District Court. I do think that the system proposed in the majority report will have a very great tendency to strengthen the character of our District Courts. And as that is the very commencement of litigation, the first court to which resot is had by litigants, I think an object of this kind is very desirable. Let us see how it would have this tendency, by comparing this system with our present one. In the first place, we are confined to narrow limits in the selection of our District Judges. This system enlarges the limits from which to make the selection, and consequently we have a wider field of talent from which to choose. Not only would it do that, but after we have selected our Judge we have the advantage of this meeting together judicially, for the purpose of taking a candid, fair, and impartial review of the various decisions made. Although from my inexperience, I know my opinions are not entitled to much weight, yet I do think that this would have a tendency to strengthen the legal ability of these Judges after they have been selected for their respective offices.

Let us consider for a moment some of the causes of error in our District Courts, in which alone I have practiced. So far as my experience goes, two of the great sources of error in a District Court are the prejudice of the Judge, and undue haste in rendering a decision. This is the case in the District Court in the county where the cause first arises; where the Judge is surrounded by the influences of the several litigants, the parties of their friends, and where all the influence of the lawyers on the several sides is brought to bear upon the court. Now what does the attorney who takes the appeal desire? If he desires nothing more than justice he appeals for the purpose of obtaining a correct decision. He seeks nothing more nor less than a removal from these causes of error. All we have to ask ourselves is this question: Will a removal of the case to this intermediate Court, to this Superior Court, remove these sources of error? Prejudice cannot certainly reign there to the same extent as in the District Court. There is no necessity for haste in rendering the decision. You have then your paper lawyer, and your practical lawyer upon the bench.

Let me say by way of explanation that when this question was first proposed by the distinguished gentleman [Mr. Hall] who has urged it here with so much ability, I was myself opposed to it, from the fact that I thought it was an unnecessary expense to the people of the State.

But I favored the majority report so far as to enable it to come in here, with the express understanding that I should be allowed to dissent from it in my vote and otherwise, if I thought proper to do so. But I confess that, notwithstanding the advantage my young friend from Jefferson (Mr. Wilson) may have obtained of the gentleman from Des Moines (Mr. Hall) in personal matters, I am convinced conclusively, beyond a doubt in my own mind, of the propriety and strength of the position of the gentleman from Des Moines in regard to his plan.

I find my reasons chiefly in this, and I assigned them in the committee. One of the greatest objections to the jurisprudence of the land, both of the States and of the United States, arises from the fact that our judges are too apt to be mere paper lawyers who are placed upon the bench with large salaries, and for long terms, and who never look outside the channel of Peters', and other reports. This is my objection to the supreme court. We live in a day and age of progress. The philosophy of a practical jurisprudence ought to be brought to bear upon the rules of property, and it ought to be brought to bear as a check, in connection with this long array of old and respected decisions. This then would give to this intermediate court—although its position and title of superior court would indicate that it was inferior to the supreme court—one thing which in my opinion would be superior to the other. It would furnish a ready means to litigants of obtaining a new hearing and a speedy hearing, in a court where this prejudice cannot exist.

And here let me say that in many cases clients desire to take their cases up to a superior court from mere prejudice against the judge below.—And if litigants do take up their causes on account of this prejudice, it is better that they should be met at as early a period in the path of appeal as possible. It is chiefly for this thing that the proposed system is better for the jurisprudence of the country. When, however, these two reasons have not prevailed in the District Court, but there is absolutely an error in law, then when you take your case up to the superior court, and it fails to recognise and establish your position as a correct one, you are still not denied your appeal to that other court, which for distinction I will term the paper court.

Now let me say, that besides these reasons which have occurred to my mind, I have another one which pertains to myself particularly, and which may perhaps account for the difference between the distinguished member from Johnson [Mr. Clarke] and myself, upon this question. That gentleman lives about 275 feet from the supreme court of the State of Iowa, while I live about 275 miles from it. I have frequently felt myself aggrieved by decisions of the district court, and have three or four times presumed to take appeals from them. Once or twice my opinions have been sustained by this indescribable power in the distance; and once or twice they have not sustained me. Yet I was not convinced that I was not right, when they failed to sustain my position. The reason was this: I was present at the trial in the district court, knew all about it and the force of the points which I raised. But the court to which I appealed was at so great a distance that I had to depend upon some other person to conduct my case, and he could not feel the same interest in it as I did, and he could not also understand the exact bearing of the points I could have presented to the court. These reasons pertain to my section of the country, and it is an additional reason why I wish to have some other intermediate court which is nearer to us. It may be said to me by members that I will be brought nearer to the supreme court of this State in consequence of the operation of a law lately passed, providing that the Capitol of the State should be removed to Ft. Des Moines, and the supreme court will be held there. That I admit would be more satisfactory to me. But there is an old adage that "there is many a slip between the cup and lip." It is whispered around, as I have heard, that there are opinions held by those who are high in power, and have the power to do or not do as they may see proper; and there may be a slip in this case.

Now, with this view of the subject, I should not know how to justify myself before my constituents, with this uncertainty and contingency before me, if I did not vote for this intermediate court. The present system works an absolute injury to my section of the country. The best of men stand back there in complete awe of the law, but they have very little respect for our district judges; and in consequence of the inordinate expense attending it, they have but little possibility of reaching the supreme court. And let me say to gentlemen here, who bring forward the old argument against this new proposition that it has not been demanded by the people of the State, as regards my section of the country at least, that I think is not exactly true. I know that I was frequently asked during the canvass, if I would not favor some judicial system by which my people would be brought nearer to the higher courts of the State. And I pledged myself to go for such a change. I feel, therefore, for that reason compelled to vote for this proposition. And I support it also because I believe it to be right; that it will make a better district court to commence with. And if we are not satisfied with the earlier canvass of our opinions and views by this superior court, we can still go up to the capital.

Mr. CLARKE, of Johnson. I think I can demonstrate to the gentleman from Mills, [Mr. Solomon,] that I do not practically live nearer the supreme court than he does. I have not for some time argued a case orally before the supreme court, as I have become convinced that it is not the better plan, especially in any case which involves an important principle, or an amount of property. And so, if he will adopt the practice of writing his arguments as I have, he will be just as near the supreme court as I am.

There have been one or two intimations that in the views I have suggested here upon this subject, I have been influenced by my position here at the capital. I regret these personal allusions, especially as it seems to be understood that the capital is to be retained here but for the present. I desire to say to those gentlemen, and to this convention, that when I entered this Hall as a delegate to this convention, I laid aside my professional character. I am not here acting as a lawyer, or with any view to my interests as as a lawyer. I am acting here as a representative of a portion of the people of this State, and upon this subject as upon others, my only question is, what is best, and for the benefit and prosperity of the people. That is the way I look at it.

Mr. SOLOMON. I had no design of imputing any selfish motives to the gentleman from Johnson, [Mr. Clarke.]

Mr. CLARKE, of Johnson. I did not understand the gentleman as intending any such imputation.

Mr. GOWER. I think we must have a very bad case here, when we have so much disagreement among our judicial doctors, with regard to the reports of the judiciary committee, now under consideration. I must say that all this has not recommended either of these reports to my mind. I have looked over carefully the constitution of the State of Maine, in which State I lived for thirty years; and I think no more power is given to the legislature by the sixth article of that constitution, than is given by our present constitution to our legislature. And I heard much less dissatisfaction with regard to the judiciary in Maine, than I have heard here. I do not doubt that under our present constitution, with some slight amendments, we may have as good a judiciary as they have in that State.

I was not of the opinion when I came here that my constituents desired much of a change in our judiciary. I did hear some suggestions made in favor of the election of the supreme judges, at the end of their present term. I think there is a propriety in having the supreme judges try the State officers, &c. And probably district prosecutors would serve the ends of justice better than county prosecutors. But I do not now see the necessity of further changes than these.

Mr. CLARKE, of Henry. Will it be in order now to move that the report of the majority of the Committee on the Judicial Department be recommitted for their further consideration?

The CHAIRMAN. It would not be in order to submit such a motion in the Committee of the Whole.

Mr. HARRIS. Gentlemen have quoted old adages here, and I think of one which I consider pretty true, "a lean dog for a long race." I think if the committee now rise and members go to dinner, they will come back this afternoon not quite so long-winded. I therefore move that the committee now rise, report progress and ask leave to sit again.

Mr. CLARKE, of Johnson. If there are any gentlemen here who desire further discussion of this question, I will not object to the committee rising. But if we can decide this main question now I think we should settle it. Let us settle this question now, and then these details can be determined hereafter.

Mr. HARRIS. I will withdraw my motion for the committee to rise.

Mr. CLARKE, of Henry. I cannot consent that the vote demanded by the gentleman from Johnson, [Mr. Clarke,] shall be taken at this time, without some explanation in regard to these two reports. I think it would be unfair to the majority report, to have a vote taken at this time. I desire when the committee rise to make a motion that the majority report be referred back to the majority of the judicial committee for their reconsideration; and for this reason: That report was made out and not submitted to the members who are supposed to compose that majority. I think that no one of that majority concurs in that report. So far as I know, it does not meet the views of any one of that majority. I believe if the majority of that committee are allowed to make their own report, and put themselves upon paper, and not be put there by a gentleman who comes here before this convention and attacks the very report he has drawn up as the majority report, the convention will then understand the merits of this question much better than they do now.

Mr. CLARKE, of Johnson. I would ask the gentleman from Henry, [Mr. Clarke,] what there is in the report that is not in accordance with the instructions of the majority of the Committee? I understand the gentleman as casting a serious imputation upon me as chairman of the Judiciary Committe.

Mr. CLARKE, of Henry. This is just the state of facts; when we met in Committee to compare our views upon the system that we should report, I understood that we would each yield somewhat in order to bring a unanimous report before the Convention; to which amendments might be offered by any member of the Committee. I would ask the chairman of the Juidciary Committee if such was not the understanding?

Mr. CLARKE, of Johnson. I will answer that question when the gentleman answers mine.

Mr. CLARKE, of Henry. I can say that such was my understanding. I had no idea that there were to be two reports made. If I had supposed there were to have been two reports, I should have endeavored to have had my views represented in one or the other. But I am not fully represented in either! And I understand that other members of the Committee are in the same position. Even the gentleman uniting in the minority report, [Mr. Wilson,] says he does not concur in it! I was taken perfectly by surprise when I first learned there were two reports, and I was obliged to go to a member of the Committee to learn which one I was supposed to be on.

Mr. WILSON. I will say that the minority report was submitted to me, and I appended my disclaimer to certain portions of it, and it was made with that disclaimer.

Mr. CLARKE, of Henry. At all events, I saw nothing of the majority report until it was in the hands of the Secretary. And then, upon looking it over hurriedly, I put a disclaimer to it, which shows that I did not concur. Now, this is putting us in a false position. I do not complain that the chairman of the committee *intended* to do anything that was wrong. But I say, that there was a misunderstanding about the matter. I certainly conceded points in the committee, which I would not otherwise have done, because I supposed there was to be but one report. I understand from the gentleman from Des Moines, [Mr. Hall,] that such was also his expectation. And this would have prevented the discussion of these two systems. We would then have had but one report, while we are having a discussion now concerning the preference between two reports. I suppose the gentleman from Johnson, [Mr. Clarke,] understands me perfectly now. I make no charges against him. I merely say that these two reports put us in such a position, that I must beg of the committee not to pass a vote at this time, but permit the committee to rise, that we may refer the majority report to the committee again, for their further consideration.

Mr. CLARKE, of Johnson. I desire to set myself right upon this matter before this Convention. It is true that there was a radical difference between the different members of the Judiciary Committee. The gentleman from Des Moines, [Mr. Hall,] and the gentleman from Henry, [Mr. Clarke,] were decidedly in favor of this three court system, while the gentleman from Jefferson, [Mr. Wilson,] and myself were equally decided against it. And the gentleman from Mills, [Mr. Solomon,] for the purpose of enabling the majority report to be made, sided with the gentleman from Des Moines, and the gentleman from Henry, leaving himself free to act as he might think proper, when the matter came up before the Convention. But the vote was taken upon every proposition contained in this majority report, and the chairman was instructed to make out a report in accordance with that majority vote. I appeal to the gentleman from Des Moines, [Mr. Hall,] if such was not the case? And Iwould ask him further, whether that majority report contains anything that did not receive this assent of the majority, and if it was not also submitted to him before it was made to the Convention?

Mr. HALL. I do not believe that there were any two upon the Judiciary Committee, who were satisfied to be bound down to any particular report. But we did the best we could. The report, as made for the majority, is one that I agreed to. But had I known that there was to have been a minority report, I probably should have sought to have had the majority put into a little different shape. All the members of the Committee will recollect that I begged of them not to have a minority report, for I apprehended this very difficulty would arise and create confusion and consume time unnecessarily. I said I would yield a great deal for the purpose of having but one report, and I was not aware until the two reports came in here, that there was to be a minority report.

Mr. CLARKE, of Johnson. That is true; we will admit that. The gentleman from Des Moines, [Mr. Hall,] did desire that there should be but one report. But I felt, and I suppose the gentleman from Jefferson, [Mr. Wilson,] felt the same, that the majority had no right to dictate to us, and that if they had their views and opinions presented, we also had the right to present ours. There were difficulties with regard to the details in the minds of the minority as well as of the majority. But our only object was to bring the two systems before the Convention and leave individual members of the committee the right to act as they thought proper in the Convention. That was the understanding through this whole matter.

The gentleman from Henry, [Mr. Clarke,] claims that this report was made without his knowledge. The fact is, that it was the fault of the gentleman himself, for he was generally the last member that came to the meeting of the committee, and once or twice he was not present at all. I think it is with a bad grace that he comes in here and casts imputations upon me, because this report was made by a member of the Committee who was adverse to it. It is well known that I had no desire to make this report, but my position as chairman of the Committee compelled me to do so. If he had had any desire to make this report, he certainly had the opportunity to do so. But I understood, that neither the gentleman from Henry, nor the gentleman from Des Moines, desired the labor of preparing ti, and hence, it was put upon me.

Mr. CLARKE, of Henry. The gentleman from Johnson. [Mr. Clarke,] will still insist upon misunderstanding me. I repeat that my understanding in the committee was, that there was to be but one report. We talked that matter over and I certainly conceded many things to accomplish that object. But when I saw the two reports in the hands of the Secretary and not till then, I put my disclaimer to the one which I was told, was supposed to be the report of myself and the gentlemen from Des Moines and Mills. If I had agreed to the presenting of this report, I would not now ask this reference. But my point is this: that since the gentleman from Johnson comes in here and attacks this report, which purports to be the report of the majority, we should, at least, have the privilege of putting ourselves upon paper as we wish to be understood, without making any concessions at all! And I can assure the Convention that it will not take up much time, for the maajoriiy of the committee have determined upon the report they desire to make, one, too, which differs materially from the report presented here for that majority. It is only to enable us to have our opinions properly expressed before the Convention, that I desire to have this done. Otherwise no one could conceive how it could be, that we, of the majority could make this report, and then come in here and vote against it! I ask the gentleman from Johnson, if it would not seem strange without the explanation I have made? I owed it to myself to make this explanation, to show that while this appeared here as the report of the majority, we entertained views in regard to the judicial system which should be adopted, entirely different from this. I make no charges against the gentleman from Johnson. I do not say that he misrepresented us for the purpose of placing us in a difficult position. But I do say that he has not as clearly set forth our views in that report, as we can set them forth for ourselves. If I had understood that he was making out a report for us alone, I should have given him some intimations of what I desired embodied in that report. But I understood that he was trying to express the views of all the members of the committee in the report, so as to produce harmony and unity upon the matter, and I had no wish, or thought to overlook him. But it so happens that in drawing up the majority report he has not expressed the opinions of the three members who are supposed to constitute that majority. And when I looked at these two reports, I hardly knew which one I was expected to support, for each contains some things that I am in favor of and much that I am opposed to. I do not mean to insinuate that the gentleman desired, or intended, to misrepresent us. But I must say that we are not fairly represented in this report, and therefore ask that it may be recommitted to us that we may make out our own report.

Mr. HARRIS. I do not think that this delay is productive of anything, except, perhaps to get up a misunderstanding in the Clarke family. I therefore move that the committee now rise, report progress aud ask leave to sit again.

The question being taken, the motion to rise was agreed to, upon a division, ayes 17—noes not counted.

The PRESIDENT having resumed the chair—

The CHAIRMAN of the Committee of the Whole reported that the committee had had under consideration the subject referred to them, had made progress therein, and asked leave to sit again.

The report of the Committee of the Whole was received, and leave to sit again granted accordingly.

On motion of Mr. HARRIS,

The Convention then took a recess until 2 o'clock, P. M.

EVENING SESSION.

The Convention met at 2 o'clock, P. M., and was called to order by the President.

Order of Business.

The PRESIDENT. The first business in order is the consideration of the report of the Committee on the judiciary department.

Mr. CLARKE, of Henry. I wish to submit a report from the majority of the committee on the judiciary.

Mr. JOHNSTON. I understand that we have one report from the majority of the committee upon this subject already, and the reception of another will lead to worse confusion than that in which we are already involved. I suppose what the gentleman is really endeavoring to effect is to secure the adoption of some proposition like that contained in the report of the majority, which is now before the committee of the whole. The great features of both the minority and majority reports have been very ably and fully discussed in committee of the whole, and I presume there is not a single gentleman in the convention who has not made up his mind fully upon this subject. I am anxious to have a vote taken upon this question. I am satisfied that four-fifths of the members of the convention are in favor of the two court system. Let us terminate the difficulty in which we are now placed, by agreeing to take up the minority report, and then gentlemen can make such amendments to that report as they please.

I hope the gentleman from Henry [Mr. Clarke] will not press his motion now. Indeed I do not think it is in order to receive another report from that committee.

Mr. PARVIN. As a matter of courtesy to the gentleman from Henry, I move that his report be received. It is rather singular that after the majority of the committee have made their report, they should come in and deny that it is theirs, and ask to make another. I hope, however, that as a matter of courtesy to the gentleman from Henry, and to the gentlemen who profess to form the majority of the committee, they may have the privilege of presenting their report.

My preference is for the present system with such amendments as may be deemed necessary, and I trust that the convention will come to the same conclusion.

Mr. JOHNSTON. I wish to ask one question. In what situation will we be placed, provided we receive this report? Of the two reports from the majority of the committee which one will we regard as the true and correct report? Is the majority report that has already been submitted to be withdrawn?

The PRESIDENT. The chair so understands it.

Mr. CLARKE, of Henry. If I understand it, the two—minority and majority—reports are signed by our chairman. If the gentleman from Lee [Mr. Johnson] will refer to the printed report of the majority, he will find that it reads—

"Mr. Clarke, of Johnson, from the majority of the committee on the judicial department made the following report."

Now when we come to consider this matter, we find that this is not the report of that gentleman for he disowns it. And when we come to discuss it, we find that the gentleman from Des Moines [Mr. Hall] and the gentleman from Mills [Mr. Solomon] and myself, who are supposed to concur in making that report, do not, in fact, so concur. Therefore, the majority of the committee have made a report in which they do agree, and which they propose to submit as a substitute for the supposed majority report that has been already presented.

The PRESIDENT. The chair is of the opinion that this is a matter for the convention to determine.

Mr. JOHNSTON. If the majority of the committee have certainly agreed that the report they now propose to present is their report, I hope that the convention will consent to its reception, and that no obstacles will be thrown in the way of its consideration. I trust the convention will consent to a withdrawal of the former report.

Mr. GILLASPY. I have been a listener here, and have not troubled the convention with any remarks upon the subject of the judiciary. The object I have in rising now is to inquire if the committee are allowed to withdraw these two reports upon which we have been occupied all the morning, whether we will have to go through the same routine on this substitute. If so, I desire to make a single remark upon this subject before this course is taken. We, who are not members of the legal profession, have been appealed to by the gentleman from Des Moines [Mr. Hall] and the gentleman from Jefferson, [Mr. Wilson] to weigh and consider this matter well before we cast our votes.

I desire to say that the people I have the honor to represent upon this floor do not desire any great radical change in the judicial system of the state. The universal expression among them is that the present judiciary system is well enough as it is at present, and the only change needed is that the supreme court judges should be elected by the people. Notwithstanding the able arguments presented here by the gentlemen from Des Moines [Mr. Hall], from Appanoose [Mr. Harris], from Jefferson [Mr. Wilson], from Johnson [Mr. Clarke], from Henry [Mr. Clarke], and the no less able argument of the gentleman from Allamakee [Mr. Clark], in favor of a change in our present judicial system, I am not prepared to change my mind upon this subject. I shall do my duty here as a representative of the people of my county, and in accordance with their wishes vote against the report we have had before us, and also against the proposition now proposed to be submitted; and I shall vote for the present system.

Mr. TRAER. I think that in order to save time, the best thing we could do would be to vote upon something like the proposition made this morning by the gentleman from Muscatine [Mr. Parvin], and decide in the first place, whether we will agree to take up the article as it stands in the present constitution, and amend it, or take up the two reports of the judiciary committee. I believe that a majority of the members of the convention will vote for the present system; and I think that all the time taken up here in discussing these reports is lost; as I do not think that the convention will adopt either of them, nor adopt the proposition of the gentleman from Henry (Mr. Clarke), after it is presented.

Mr. CLARKE, of Henry. All I have to say is that the majority of the committee have made their report, and they desire to be heard. I offer it here in convention, and I wish to say to members that in my opinion the system now reported differs very materially from the majority report that has heretofore been made. It makes no innovation upon the old system, but merely provides that the judges shall do a little more work than they now do, at the same salaries. It leaves all the provisions for carrying the system into effect to be arranged by the people themselves through the legislature. In that respect it differs very materially from the report now before the convention.

The PRESIDENT. The chair would say to the gentleman from Henry (Mr. Clarke) that his proposition might be submitted in committee of the whole. It would be in order for him there to move it as a substitute for the majority report. The chair considers the report of the majority of the committee as the basis of our action here.

Mr. JOHNSTON. Does any one object to the withdrawal of the former report of the majority of the committee?

The PRESIDENT. The chair understands that two gentlemen have objected to it.

Mr. JOHNSTON. I would inquire what can be gained by the objection? It will only place matters in worse confusion.

Mr. GILLASPY. I object to the withdrawal.

Mr. JOHNSTON. We shall gain time by consenting to a withdrawal of the former report.

Mr. CLARKE, of Henry. If it would meet with the wishes of the Convention, the committee would ask leave to withdraw their former report.

Mr. TRAER. Will it be in order to withdraw the report after it has been referred to the committee of the whole?

The PRESIDENT. It can only be done by the unanimous consent of the convention.

Mr. TRAER. This matter, as I understand it, is in possession of the committee of the whole, and not of the convention. The committee of the whole have had some action upon it, reported progress and asked leave to sit again. They did not report it back to the convention at all.

Mr. TODHUNTER. I have taken no part in this discussion before, in consequence of my ill health, and I only desire now to make a single remark. It seems to me that we will get into difficulty again, if the course that some gentlemen recommend is pursued.

It appears that this judiciary committee, five in number, submitted a report here, but who were its authors, we are unable to tell. They all deny its authorship now, and there are none left willing to father it, for it is not what they wanted, although it purports to be a majority report. I believe they have all abandoned it, except my friend from Johnson, (Mr. Clarke.) They now come in, and ask the privilege of withdrawing their report, which has undergone such rigid scrutiny here, and submitting another in its place. During the time it have been in the convention, this report has been pretty severely criticised, and they see that it does not meet the views of the convention; and now they want to back out of their position, and present another report entirely different from their former one. It seems to me, before allowing these gentlemen to submit another report, we ought to have some assurance on their part that they will not disown that, too, and ask to present still another one. So far as I am concerned, I have no particular objection to allowing these gentlemen to withdraw this report, but I am inclined to think that we will get into the same difficulty again, in which we are now involved, because I am satisfied from what I have seen and heard, that there is a disposition on the part of members of the Convention, to adopt the present judiciary system with very little alteration, that of the election of Supreme Court Judges by the people, and one or two other changes. It matters not to me, what the plans of these gentlemen may be, or how anxious they are to set themselves right upon the record. As I look at the matter they cannot do so, because their report sets out by stating that it is the report of the majority, and then it is signed by Wm. Penn Clarke, Chairman, with the following attached:

"I concur with the majority report, except that I favor the election of Supreme Court Justices by the people of the State at large. That I favor the subdivision of the districts into four circuits; and that in each district four judges shall be elected—one from each circuit—three to form a quorum in the district court. That a prosecuting attorney shall be elected in each circuit. That no judicial officer shall be tried for incompetency unless presented by a majority of the General Assembly.

R. L. B. CLARKE.

This shows that it was a majority report, and that the gentleman from Henry [Mr. Clarke] assented to it with the exception above noticed. It seems to me that they had not better get upon the record with another report, for by so doing they may get placed in a worse position than that in which they now are.

Mr. HALL. I do not believe that there is a gentleman in this convention who will object to this new report being substituted for the former majority report.

It is unpleasant for the majority of the committee to acknowledge the fact that the report already presented does not contain their views, but they believe that they can submit a report that will be more satisfactory to themsolves. I stated this morning, and I state again now, that I was anxious as a member of the committee on the judiciary, to have only one report. I did not rely upon the fact of having a minority report. I was willing to compromise, and do any thing to prevent the confusion which has followed this presentation of two reports. If I am driven to the necessity of standing upon the majority report, as one of that majority, I would be glad to place myself upon the record in as favorable a light as possible. Certainly no gentleman will object to that. I consented to the report which has already been presented with the expectation that whatever defects and errors it contained would be corrected in committee of the whole, or in Convention; but a different course has been pursued, and it is but an act of justice to the majority of the committee, that they should now have the opportunity of placing themselves right upon the record, and perfecting the system as they desire. I do not consider that it makes any difference whether the majority of the convention are opposed to the system we report or not, it is but justice to ourselves that the committee should have the privilege of making a report which embodies their correct views. If the matter be re-referred to them they are ready to report *instanter*.

Mr CLARKE, of Henry. I think the gentleman from Lee [Mr. Johnston] for the courtesy extended to us. I am taken entirely by surprise at the course pursued by gentlemen here in relation to the report which we have offered.—Ater full explanations of the condition in which we stood, and when it must have became evident to the mind of every gentleman that they were considering a report which was not the report of the majority; and when that majority came forward and stated that they had come to a different conclusion from that which was set forth in the report, I did suppose that the Convention as a matter of course, would permit us to withdraw the former report, which was not ours, and receive another in its stead which is. I did not suppose that it would give rise to any discussion, but that without appealing to magnanimity, every gentleman here having even an ordinary sense of what was due from man to man and always proper, would at once consent to the acceptance of the report which we proposed. I hope the Convention will unanimously accept of the report of the Committee which we now offer, and if it does not meet the approbation of the majority, I will most cheerfully yield my own preferences and abide the result.

Mr. HARRIS. It occurs to me after the explanations that have been made, that there is nothing which will implicate the motives of any gentleman here. It is clearly a misunderstanding between those parties, and they have been taken by surprise. After the statements that have been made, it seems to me that this committee ought to have the privilege of withdrawing this report, and present another report which shall embody their views upon this subject.

The PRESIDENT. The chair is of the opinion that these reports are not now before the Convention, but they are still in the possession of the Committee of the Whole. They are not yet reported to the Convention, and the chairman, when the committee last rose, reported that they had had these reports under consideration, made progress therein, and asked leave to sit again.

Mr. HARRIS. I would inquire of the chair if the proper course to relieve ourselves of the difficulty in which we are placed, would be to go into Committee of the Whole.

The PRESIDENT. The chair would say that the gentleman can attain his object by moving, if the Convention resolve itself into Committee of the Whole, that the committee rise and report back these reports to the Convention.

Mr. HARRIS. I move then, that the Convention resolve itself into Committee of the Whole?

The motion was agreed to, and the Convention resolved itself into Committee of the Whole on the Judicial Department, [Mr. Johnston in the Chair.]

The CHAIRMAN. The question before the committee is upon agreeing to the motion made by the gentleman from Johnson (Mr. Clarke) to substitute the report of the minority for that of the majority of the Committee on the Judiciary.

Mr. HARRIS. I move that the committee rise and report back to the Convention, without amendment, the two reports on the Judiciary now before them for consideration.

The motion was agreed to, and the President having resumed the chair. The Chairman reported that the Committee of the Whole, to whom had been referred the reports of the majority and minority of thecommittee on the Judicial Department had instructed him to report the same back to the Convention without amendment.

Mr. CLARKE, of Henry. I move that these reports be referred to the Standing Committee on the Judiciary.

The question was taken and the motion was agreed to, and the reports were referred accordingly.

Mr. CLARKE, of Henry, immediately submitted the following report from the majority of the committee on the Judiciary which was then read:

Report of the Judiciary Committee.

Section 1. The judicial power shall be vested in a supreme court, district courts, circuit courts, and such other inferior courts as the General Assembly may establish.

Sec. 2. The supreme court shall consist of a chief justice and two associate justices, two of whom shall be a quorum to hold court. They shall be elected by the people of the State at large, and shall hold their office six years, (except as herein provided,) and until their successors shall be elected and qualified. The salary of each shall not be less than two thousand dollars nor more than five thousand dollars per annum, to be fixed by law, and not changeable during their term of office.

Sec. 3. The State shall be divided into three judicial districts, to be bounded by county lines, and as nearly equal in population and territory as may be, and each of said districts shall be subdivided in the same manner, into four divisions, called circuits.

Sec. 4. There shall be twelve district judges, who shall also be circuit judges, one of whom shall reside, after his election, in each of the said circuits; shall be elected by the people of the districts at large, and to hold for four years, (except as herein provided,) and until their successors are elected and qualified; and shall have each a salary of not less than one thousand dollars, nor over three thousand dollars, and not changeable during their term of office.

Sec. 5. At the first election of judicial officers under this constitution—which shall be at the first general election after its adoption—they shall be so classified, under provisions of law, that one of the supreme court judges shall go out of office every two years, and one of the district judges in each district shall go out of office every year, and their successors shall be elected for the full terms. The justice of the supreme court having the longest term at the first election shall be chief justice; and after the expiration of his term, the justice longest presiding shall be chief justice. And in each district the judge elected for the longest term shall be presiding judge, and after the expiration of his term, the judge longest presiding shall be thus designated.

Sec. 6. The resident judge in each circuit shall hold the courts therein, except when otherwise provided by law, and the circuit court shall be courts of law and equity, having jurisdiction in each, over all matters, civil or criminal, arising in their respective circuits, under such regulations as the law may provide.

Sec. 7. The district courts shall be composed by the meeting of the circuit judges in each district in bank, at such times and places as shall be provided by law; any three of whom shall constitute a quorum to hold a court; but no judge shall vote, or join in an opinion, in a case which was tried before him in the circuit court; nor in which he may be or may have been interested; nor in which he may be, or may have been connected as attorney or counsellor at law. The General Assembly may make provisions for justices of the supreme court, and judges from another district, to sit upon the bench of the district courts in cases where it may be necessary, or for the good of the public.

Sec. 8. The district courts shall have exclusive jurisdiction in all matters arising in the circuit courts of their respective districts, and brought up on appeal or writ of error, in such manner as shall be provided by law, except in cases where the law may provide for their going directly to the supreme court.

Sec. 9. The supreme court shall have appellate jurisdiction in chancery, and constitute a court for the correction of errors at law, in all cases coming from the district courts; and in such cases from the circuit courts as the law may provide; and shall have the right to appoint its own reporter and clerk.

Sec 10. There shall be a clerk of the circuit court elected in each county where a term of such court shall be appointed by law to be held, who shall also be clerk of the district court in those counties where said district courts shall be appointed by law to be held.

Sec. 11. Each of said courts shall exercise a supervisory control over all inferior courts within the limits of their respective jurisdictions and be conservators of the peace therein, they shall have power to issue all usual writs and process, and to enforce the same.

Sec. 12. No judicial officer, provided for herein, shall be eligible to any other office during the term for which he shall be elected; except that district judges shall be eligible to the office of justice of the supreme court; and their term of office shall commence the first of January next after their election, but in cases of a vacancy the same may be filled by appointment by the Governor, until it shall be supplied at the next general election, when it shall be filled by election for the residue of the unexpired term.

Sec. 13. It shall be the duty of the General Assembly to make such provisions by law as shall be necessary for the carrying into effect of this article and to provide for a regular system of practice in all the courts of the State. To provide for the election of an Attorney General, to reside at the capitol, and for the election of Prosecuting Attorneys in each circuit, in lieu of the Prosecuting Attorneys in the several counties, and to prescribe their powers, duties, terms of office and salary.

Sec. 14. The style of all process shall be, "The State of Iowa;" and all prosecutions shall be conducted in the name and by authority of the same.

Sec. 15. After the year 1860, the General Assembly may re-organize the judicial districts, and increase or diminish the number of districts, or the number of judges of the supreme or district courts: but such increase or diminution shall not be more than one district, or one judge of either court at a time; and no re-organization of the districts, or diminution of the judges shall have the effect of removing a judge from office. Such re-organization of the districts, or increase or diminution of the judges shall take place every five years thereafter, if necessary, and at no other time.

Sec. 16. The supreme court, with one district judge from each district, to be selected as shall be provided by law, shall form a court for the trial of all impeachments, except in cases where a justice of the supreme court is upon trial, when the court shall be composed of the district judges, a majority of whom shall constitute a quorum. Incompetency shall be a ground for impeachment in a judicial officer; and all impeachments must be found by the General Assembly.

R. L. B. CLARKE,
J. C. HALL, and
D. H. SOLOMON, Committee.

Mr. SKIFF. I move that the report be laid upon the table and printed.

Mr. CLARKE, of Johnson. I would inquire what has become of the minority report?

The PRESIDENT. It was referred with the former report of the majority to the Committee on the Judiciary.

Mr. CLARKE, of Johnson. As a member of that Committee, I submit upon my own responsibility, the same minority report that was submitted before. I do this upon my own responsibility. that there may be no misunderstaning about the matter. The gentleman from Jefferson, [Mr. Wilson,] is at liberty to endorse the report or not, as he may think proper. If I understood the report from the reading of it, these gentlemen have very materially changed their views in a short time, and that there may be no farther misapprehension about the matter, I move the minority report upon my own responsibility. I am now prepared to support the motion of the gentleman from Jasper, [Mr. Skiff,] to print this majority report, as I confess I am anxious to see it.

The question was then taken upon the motion of Mr. Skiff, and it was agreed to.

So the report was laid on the table and ordered to be printed.

Mr. JOHNSTON. What is the next order of business?

The PRESIDENT. The report of the Committee on Militia would come up next in order.

Mr. SKIFF. I would say, as Chairman of that Committe, that they have not yet agreed upon any report.

The PRESIDENT. That being the case, the report of the Committee on State Debts will be next in order..

The report of the Committee on State Debts was then taken up for consideration and read the second time, as heretofore published.

On motion of Mr. JOHNSTON, the Convention then resolved itself into Committee of the Whole, upon this subject. (Mr. Gray in the chair.)

The CHAIRMAN. The Clerk will now proceed to read the report by sections for amendment.

Mr. WILSON. I beg leave, as Chairman of the Committee on State Debts, in submitting this report, to say that I do not deem it advisable to make any explanations of the report. I consulted with a majority of the members of the Convention before drawing it up, and the several matters set out in the different sections, seemed to meet with the views of members so universally, that I do not deem it necessary now to explain the reasons that induced the Committee to make it. If there are objections made to the sections as we shall progress in its reading, I shall feel at liberty to answer them as well as I can.

The first section was then read as follows:

"The credit of the State shall not, in any manner, be given or loaned to, or in aid of any individual, association, or corporation; and the

State shall never assume, or become responsible for, the debts or liabilities of any individual, association, or corporation."

There being no amendments offered to this section, the second section was then read as follows:

"The State may contract debts to supply casual deficits or failures in revenues, or to meet expenses not otherwise provided for; but the aggregate amount of such debts, direct and contingent, whether contracted by virtue of one or more acts of the General Assembly, or at different periods of time, shall never exceed the sum of one hundred thousand dollars; and the money arising from the creation of such debt, shall be applied to the purpose for which it was obtained, or to repay the debts so contracted, and to no other purpose whatever."

Mr. GOWER. I move to strike out the words, "one hundred thousand dollars," and insert in lieu thereof, "three hundred thousand dollars."

Mr. WILSON. I hope, that the motion of the gentleman from Cedar will not prevail, and that the section will stand as it was reported by the committee.

This matter of a State debt was fully discussed by the committee, and I believe different members of the committee took some little pains to ascertain the views of persons residing in different portions of the State in relation to this matter, and after consultation and as full investigation of this question as we could make, we came to the conclusion to recommend the sum that is named in the article on State Debts in the present constitution. We came to that conclusion from various considerations. In the first place, we could not see any real necessity for the State incurring any debt at all, but in order to prescribe some limit, we concluded to settle upon the amount named in this section. We took into consideration the fact, that the annual revenue of the State, with the one hundred thousand dollars indebtedness which the State might contract, would be sufficient to enable the State to carry on any improvement, until a proposition for an increase of the debt could be submitted to the people, for their action.

It has been suggested, that it would be better to increase this sum, say to five hundred thousand dollars, for the purpose of enabling the State to erect her capitol buildings at the seat of government. In relation to this, I have simply this remark to make. I am opposed to leaving this matter in the hands of the legislature. I believe the better plan for this State to adopt—and the experience of other States will bear me out in this—is to determine what her buildings and their probable cost will be, and then submit the plan together, with the cost to the people, for them to adopt or reject. If the section in the report of the legislative department be adopted, which provides "that no extra compensation shall be made to any officer, public agent, or contractor, after the service shall have been rendered, or the contract entered into, &c., it will compel the contractors and the legislature to carry out precisely, the plan agreed upon by the people.

I am opposed to the principle of State indebtedness *in toto*. I believe, that one of the best things that this convention can do, will be to prevent the State from incurring any debts at all. There cannot be any difficulty, in my opinion, in the way of the State getting any amount of money that is required to carry on the improvements which she may desire to make. The people who pay the taxes ought to say whether money shall be borrowed, and what amount of indebtedness the State shall incur. Under the provision reported here, the State is not confined to an indebtedness of one hundred thousand dollars, but she may incur a greater debt, only the people must sanction it. Unless it is referred to the people, the legislature can only incur an indebtedness, on the part of the State, of one hundred thousand dollars, and that sum, I believe to be sufficient. I believe that beyond that amount, the legislature should leave it to the people to determine, whether a State debt shall be contracted or not.

Mr. PARVIN. I consider that the clause in the present constitution, upon this subject, has been the salvation of our State. I am satisfied that the mania for building railroads has prevailed so extensively in this State, within the last five or six years, that without such a clause in our constitution, we would have been in debt, at least, a million of dollars. Every person of any reflection at all, must regard such a thing as a great calamity to the State. While I am in favor of putting a restriction of this kind in the constitution, yet I think it is unnecessary to confine it to so low a sum as that named in the present constitution. That sum was large enough at the time this provision was adopted, but three, four, or five hundred thousand dollars would not be so much now, perhaps, as one hundred thousand dollars was at that time. Cases might arise, in which it will be necessary to run the State in debt; and I do not think it expedient to submit the question to the people every time they wish to contract a debt for over one hundred thousand dollars. I will go with the gentleman from Jefferson [Mr. Wilson] for restriction, but I will vote to increase the sum to over one hundred thousand dollars. I will propose to fill the blank with three hundred thousand dollars.

The CHAIRMAN. The motion to strike out, is the only one that can now be entertained.

Mr. GILLASPY. The gentleman from Muscatine, [Mr. Parvin] in my judgment, made a very appropriate remark, when he said that the clause in the present constitution, in relation to State indebtedness had been the salvation of the State. I do not believe that our salvation is complete yet, consequently, I believe it is the duty of every gentleman upon this floor, but of course he will judge for himself what his duty is, to support this provision as it came from the hands of the committee. The people of the

State, I believe, are almost crazy upon the subject of speculation.

This Convention is about to adopt a provision here, that will allow banking in the State of Iowa. My opinion is, that if we increase the amount of this restriction, the next general assembly will not adjourn until they have made appropriations for various purposes to the full amount that they are allowed to contract debts by the constitution. If we adopt a provision here of that kind, it would be hailed with acclamation by every broker in the State, and the bonds of the State would offer the best security for banking that could be possibly presented, and by that very inducement you could persuade every body in the community to sign petitions asking the legislature to make appropriations for building a new capitol, asylums, and various other public institutions. What would be the result of all this? Why, the issue of bonds upon the treasury of the State, which the speculators might buy up for the purposes of banking. I undertake to say, had it not been for the provision in the constitution upon this subject, that the people ere this would have voted appropriations for railroads of upwards of ten millions of dollars. Every gentleman upon this floor will readily come to that conclusion if he will examine the act passed by the legislature four years ago memorializing Congress for a grant of the public lands. It was thought then that they would be unable to obtain these appropriations, and from what I saw and heard here in this capital, I have no doubt that had it not been for this provision in the constitution, that there would have been a log-rolling system got up here, and by one act they would have voted ten millions of dollars.

If you make the restriction three hundred thousand dollars, the State will run in debt to that amount, or if you increase the amount to ten millions dollars, five years will not elapse before the State will be in debt to that amount. This old dilapidated building would not be sufficient, and you would be obliged to build a magnificent capitol, a splendid asylum in one county, and a new university building in another, and so the expenditure would go on, and there would be no end to it.

I hope that the provision reported by the committee will be adopted. I believe that the people demand it, and I know that my constituents desire to have a restriction of this kind incorporated into the constitution. If the people desire to go into debt, they can do so by their own vote, but I would not have the state incur a debt beyond the amount prescribed here, through the influences that may be exerted in the legislature.

Mr. TRAER. I am surprised at the remarks of the gentleman from Wapello [Mr. Gillaspy]. I have so much confidence in his judgment, that I supposed he would favor an amount larger than that fixed in the present constitution. If I recollect rightly, a certain gentleman, when we were discussing the propriety of an adjournment to some other place, talked about paying ten or fifteen dollars a day for his board, and it seems to me he should evince the same liberality now upon this matter.

Mr. GILLASPY. If the gentleman will examine the reports of our proceedings, he will find that I referred to board by the week. The remarks I made were in allusion to the remark of the gentleman from Scott [Mr. Ells] when he said that board could be had in first class hotels at Davenport for seven dollars a week. When I pretend to be liberal, I design to take the money out of my own pockets, and not out of the State Treasury.

Mr. TRAER. I do not know that this matter about paying board has anything to do with this question.

I wish to remark here, that if the gentleman will take up the last message of the executive, he will find that the total indebtedness of the State amounts to $128,000. It appears to me, that when the constitution provides that the indebtednes of the State shall not exceed, in the aggregate, the sum of $100,000, and when the executive tells us that the State has incurred a debt of $128,000, we had better amend the constitution so as to give the officers of State an opportunity of meeting the ordinary expenses of the government.

I have taken considerable pains to ascertain the views of gentlemen in different parts of the State upon this question of State indebtedness, and I find very few who are not decidedly in favor of enlarging the amount beyond that now prescribed in the present constitution. It seems to me that the same argument which the gentleman applies to sustain his position might be brought to bear on the opposite side of the question.

I know that it is necessary to place some limit in the constitution, and it will not do to give the legislature full power to go as far as they should deem fit. In making a provision of this kind, we should take into consideration the exigencies that may arise under this constitution. It is evident to every one here that the natural resources of Iowa for agriculture and commerce will combine to make it a wealthy State, and we should not, therefore, cramp the hands of the government, as we should by placing in the constitution the restriction reported by the committee. When the present constitution was formed, and when that restriction was placed in it, the State was in a very different situation from that in which she is now placed. When the state government was first organized, there were but a few inhabitants then to pay the taxes necessary to pay the interest upon the debt which was then created. Now, our population has greatly increased, and our wants are increasing every day. There is no doubt that we will soon be called upon to erect public buildings for the use of the State, and I would ask gentlemen how they can be erected with such a clause as that on State indebtedness contained in the present constitution? I am aware that the gentleman from Jefferson (Mr. Wilson), in whose judgment I place a great deal of reliance, says that we can submit the question of the necessity of an increase of the State indebtedness to the people. Is it necessary for this State government to cramp her hands in such a way that they will have to submit this question to the people? I think not, and I think we had better, in framing this constitution, provide for the public exigencies which may arise hereafter. I am opposed to this idea of getting the General Assembly to legislate for us, and then submitting their action to the people. We should then have propositions to be submitted to the people almost every day. I am in favor of striking out the words "one hundred thousand dollars," in this section, and inserting a larger sum.

Mr. GIBSON. Being a member of the committee on State debts, I feel it my duty to say to the Convention, that I heartily concur with the report that has been submitted. I believe it is the wish of that portion of the State that I represent, not to have the constitution changed in this respect. They believe that an indebtedness of $100,000 is an amount sufficient for the state to contract at any one time. This being the case, as I before remarked, I heartily concur in the report.

The gentleman from Benton [Mr. Traer], it seems to me, takes a very singular view of this question. He undertakes to prove to this committee, that it is necessary to increase this indebtedness, and what reasons does he assign? The most prominent is, that it appears by the recent message of the Governor, the state is now in debt $128,000; but I do not consider it as any argument further than this: that it places the Governor and his Republican legislature in a beautiful predicament; for the chief executive of this State, before entering upon the discharge of the duties of his office, has to take an oath to support the constitution of the State, and that constitution forbids the State from contracting a debt which, either singly or in the aggregate, shall exceed one hundred thousand dollars a year. The gentleman from Benton now tells you that the Legislature has made appropriations which fasten a debt upon the State of twenty-eight thousand dollars over the amount presribed by the constitution. I do not see what object the gentleman can have in bringing forward this fact in order to show that this State ought to have more liberality, so far as State debts are concerned, for it places the legislature and the governor in a very unpleasant predicament, to say the least of it. I shall leave it for the gentleman and his republican friends to relieve themselves from it in the best way they can.

Mr. TRAER. If the gentleman will examine the record he will find that one branch of the Assembly was Democratic.

Mr. GIBSON. If that were the fact it would not alter the case at all. If the legislature through some mistake made appropriations by which the State contracted a debt of one hundred and twenty-eight thousand dollars, is it not the duty of the chief executive of the State to guard against such legislation by the exercise of the power entrusted to him? Why did he not do it in this case?

Another reason the gentleman urges for increasing the sum named in the report is, that the State will be called upon to build a State capitol, and other public buildings in a short time.

Mr. SCOTT. I would ask the gentleman for what object the sum of twenty-eight thousand dollars was appropriated?

Mr. GIBSON. I am not dealing in items, and I suppose the report upon the subject of appropriations will show for what purpose this twenty-eight thousand dollars was appropriated. It is not a matter to which I wish to refer, and should not have done so, had I not been induced to do so by the remarks of the gentleman from Benton [Mr. Traer]. That gentleman says that we will be required to build a state capitol in a short time, and how are we to build it, he asks, unless we borrow money? This, it seems to me, would be very singular economy. If you, Mr. Chairman, were about to undertake an enterprise, what would we think of you, as a financier, if the first question you asked was, where shall I borrow the money to commence this speculation? Would it not look more like a prudent and safe course, if you should apply your own resources, and not go to borrowing money from others? If you wanted to put up a dwelling, would it be proper economy, even if you had credit, to borrow five thousand dollars for that purpose, and incur a debt to that amount? If you were able to commence and complete a building from your own resources, why, that would be a safe and prudent business operation. If the legislature will provide the ways and means, independent of a State debt, to build a State capitol, then I have no objection, but if they cannot do it, rather than fasten a debt upon the State, I would put up with an inferior building.

With these views I shall vote for the proposition as it comes from the hands of the committee.

Mr. WILSON. I wish to submit my views briefly upon this subject. I will state that this question of building a new State capitol, asylums, and other public buildings, was fully discussed by the committee before they agreed upon their report. It was with a view to the necessity of erecting these various public buildings, that the committee reported this sum of one hundred thousand dollars. We wished to prevent, if possible, the legislature from commencing a set of buildings that would cost to complete them from one to two millions of dollars. We wanted to have it understood before they were commenced, how much they would cost, and then let the people pass upon that question. Some states have commenced erecting their public buildings without limiting in the first place, the amount of expenditure, and the consequence has been, that it has cost more to complete them than was originally intended.—This was the case with the building of the new state house in Ohio, and it was found before its completion, that it would cost from four to five millions, an expense which the people of the State never contemplated should be incurred by the State. If you increase the amount of State indebtedness to three hundred thousand dollars, I ask you whether that will be sufficient, of itself, to cover the probable amount that these buildings will cost? You may commence building your capital, blind and deaf asylums, and before they are completed it will be found that three hundred thousand dollars will not be sufficient to complete them, and operations will have to be suspended until the question is submitted to the people. I think the best plan is to submit this question to the people in the first place, and let them determine what the buildings and their cost shall be, and then make the necessary provision accordingly, and not permit the legislature to go on and make such appropriations as they please. I believe with the gentleman from Wapello [Mr. Gillaspy], that at the very first session of the legislature after the adoption of this constitution, they will provide for the consumption of the entire amount, even if you increase it to three hundred thousand, or five hundred thousand dollars.

The terms "debt or liability" in this clause do not mean warrants that the State may issue upon the treasury. The State may issue her warrants upon the treasury even beyond the amount specified.

Mr. TRAER. Does the gentleman mean to put the same construction upon the present constitution?

Mr. WILSON. I do. I cannot see how the term "debt or liability" can mean anything but a bonded debt. The state may draw her warrants upon the treasury, but if there is no money there, they cannot be paid, and those who hold them will have to wait.

Mr. TRAER. Allow me to read the first part of the section upon this subject in the present constitution:

"The General Assembly shall not in any manner create any debt or debts, liability or liabilities, which shall singly or in the aggregate, with any previous debts or liabilities, exceed the sum of one hundred thousand dollars." I don't understand that this means issuing the bonds of the State.

Mr. WILSON. The only construction that can be placed upon that article in the Constitution is, that it applies to the bonded debt of the State, and for that reason I hope the provision will be adopted just as it came from the hands of the committeee. I do not believe that $300,000 will be sufficient to cover the objects which have been named by the gentleman, and you would have to increase the sum to a still greater amount. If we are compelled to run the State in debt in order to meet the exigencies of the government, why not wipe away the restriction entirely, in order that the legislature may have full play?

Mr. PARVIN. I do not understand what a debt means, if the gentleman is correct in the proposition he has laid down, that the State may run in debt just as much as she please, draw her warrants upon the Treasury and sell them in the streets to the highest bidder. I do not wish to see such a state of things, and I want this constitution to mean just what it says, that this State shall never go into debt, or be liable beyond a certain amount, unless the question is first submitted to the people as provided for in this second article.

Mr. TRAER. I wish to ask the gentleman from Jefferson, whether as Chairman of the Committee on State Debts, he intended to put the same construction upon the article in the report, that he does upon the article in the present Constitution, that this $100,000 meant only a bonded debt, and had no reference to warrants drawn upon the Treasury?

Mr. WILSON. That is the only construction I put upon either of the articles.

Mr. TRAER. I wish to ask the gentleman another question. Suppose we incorporate into the Constitution a provision preventing the State from running into debt, what is to prevent the State from running into debt for putting up State buildings, and issuing her warrants?

Mr. WILSON. There is just this about it.—I presume in relation to debts contracted by the State, that parties will take the same position that they would in contracting with individuals. They will endeavor to ascertain in the first place, whether the parties with whom they contract can pay. Before making a contract for the erection of public buildings, you will have to determine when the payments are to be made. If the State cannot create the debt and meet the payments, then as a matter of course, no contract will be made.

Mr. TRAER. I am a little apprehensive, that the gentleman by pursuing this course will get into the same difficulty in which some of our counties have been involved. In the place of making a contract in the manner the gentleman speaks of, they went on and erected their public buildings and issued warrants upon the treasury for the payment of the expenses thus incurred; and the consequence was, that those warrants have depreciated in some cases 25 per cent. I apprehend that the State will be placed in the same position if the gentleman's construction of this provision be correct; and they would have the power to go on and build a State House, issue warrants for the expenses incurred, and the consequence would be, that you might run the State millions of dollars in debt.

Mr. WILSON. I would ask the gentleman from Benton this question: Suppose the estimated expenses of the State for two current years should be $300,000, and the probable amount of taxes during the years, should be $300,000. I ask whether the legislature would not be authorized to make appropriations to that amount, and have warrants drawn upon the treasury for the same.

Mr. TRAER. My understanding of the matter is simply this: that the legislature, under the present constitution, would have no power to make any appropriations beyond the one hundred thousand dollars, over and above the revenue estimated for the next two years. If they exceed this limit it would be unconstitutional.

Mr. WILSON. I would ask the gentleman from Benton, whether these warrants, when they go out are not debts? If they are issued to the amount of three hundred thousand dollars, do they not exceed the sum prescribed in the constitution?

Mr. TRAER. I contend that the Legislature have no power to do that. If they make such an appropriation it is an unconstitutional act. If the legislature see fit to go on and make provision for building a State house, and issue warrants, which, according to the gentleman's construction would not create a debt, the banks would catch them up, and consequently they would raise the money to pay for the building of the State House, and yet the gentleman says the State would not be in debt a dollar.

Mr. WILSON. During the past session of the legislature a bill was introduced, and which passed the senate, appropriating one hundred thousand dollars for a lunatic asylum. Now, the estimated receipts of the treasury for the next two years, I understand, will be something over three hundred thousand dollars. I ask any gentleman of this convention, whether the legislature have not the constitutional right to pass appropriations for this asylum, and other public buildings to the full amount of three hundred thousand dollars, and draw warrants upon the treasury for that amount, although the money has not yet been collected? I think that there can be no question at all about it. It is not to be presumed, that the legislature will go on and make appropriations beyond the probable receipts, but the State has a right to anticipate her revenue.

Mr. EDWARDS. I think the gentleman from Jefferson [Mr. Wilson] puts the wrong interpretation upon his own report. I think that the true meaning of the section is, that the legislature connot contract a debt beyond the amount of one hundred thousand dollars, whether it be a bonded debt or not. If he is right in his position, that it applies alone to a bonded debt, I see no difficulty in making some compromise about this matter, that will be satisfactory on all sides. My own opinion is, that the gentleman is wrong in his construction, and that according to the article he has proposed, the State cannot contract a debt of any description beyond one hundred thousand dollars. Suppose there were three hundred thousand dollars in the State Treasury. The legislature at one session may expend this sum and an additional sum of one hundred thousand dollars, a portion of which might be for incidental expenses, and a portion might be bonded debt.

It appears to me, if at the time our present constitution was adopted, the sum of one hundred thousand dollars was considered a proper limit for State indebtedness, that at this time the amount proposed by the gentleman from Cedar, [Mr. Gower] would not be too large an amount. I am distinctly opposed to the proposition contained in the fourth section, which provides, that expenses of this character shall be submitted to a vote of the people. I am opposed to going back to the barbarous days of ancient Greece, when the whole people met for the purpose of making laws for their government. Ours is a representative form of government, and we are not compelled to look to ancient, and different forms of government for models upon which to shape our conduct. If the system be adopted, of submitting all acts passed by the legislature, to the people for their action before they become the laws or the land, the expenses of the State would run up to an enormous extent.

If the committee shall settle upon the amount of three hundred thousand dollars, as the limit of State indebtedness, I shall move to strike out the fourth section, which proposes, that all questions of this character shall be submitted to the people before they become laws.

Mr. PALMER. I am not willing to vote for striking out separately. I do not know but what I might be induced to vote for the striking out, if the number to be inserted was included in the motion. I do not like to make a blank until I have some idea of what it is to be filled with. I suppose it would be proper to move to strike out, and fill up at the same time, and unless the motion is put in that way I must vote against it.

The question being then taken upon the motion to strike out the words "one hundred thousand," it was agreed to upon a division—ayes, 18—nays, 9.

The question was then upon filling up the blank.

Mr. SKIFF moved to fill the blank with the words, "five hundred thousand."

Mr. WINCHESTER moved to fill the blank with the words, "two hundred and fifty thousand."

Mr. PARVIN moved to fill the blank with the words, "three hundred thousand."

The CHAIRMAN stated that the question would be first taken upon the highest number.

Mr. SKIFF. My object in moving to insert the number "five hundred thousand" is, that it is the number that I have always favored. I have conversed with persons well acquainted with affairs of this kind, and my opinion has been confirmed. It has been suggested here by some members, that we should throw off limitations entirely, and let the legislature run at large in this matter, and go into debt as much as they please. Now, I am not willing to agree to that. I am in favor of having the State limited in this matter, but I do not desire to have it limited to the small amount now fixed in the constitution, of one hundred thousand dollars. We want to build a State House, and some asylums for the unfortunate, the deaf and dumb, the blind, and the still more unfortunate, the insane; but in our present cramped condition we cannot do it.

Now, although we may levy a tax upon the people to build these institutions, and not run into debt at all, still I do not think it is good policy, or just and right, that the present generation, this year or next, should pay out their money for benefits that will be enjoyed altogether by posterity. If those to come after us are to derive the benefits from these institutions, let them pay for them. Our money is worth more than the six or ten per cent. the State would pay for a loan. If we authorize the State to go into debt to the amount of five hundred thousand dollars, and issue her bonds, bearing interest at ten per cent, those bonds can probably be sold at par, and this money can be obtained, and our charitable institutions, and the State house, can be built, and the burden will not be felt. It is not for the purpose of having bonds issued, upon which men can go to banking, or for anything of that sort. As soon as all these works are accomplished, I am in favor of having the State without any debt at all. I do not want the bonds of Iowa offered for sale, in England, Germany, New York, California, and everywhere else they can be sold. I want to have the State of Iowa out of debt as soon as possible. But I think it is only good policy, and right and just, to authorize the State, at this time, to go into debt to the amount of five hundred thousand dollars, and I trust the limitation will not be put down lower than that sum.

Mr. WILSON. I hope this amount of five hundred thousand dollars will be voted down. And I perceive there is a misapprehension in the minds of some members I have conversed with, in relation to my position upon this matter. I will state that my position is this; the State can issue her warrants to the full extent of the probable amount of her revenue for the coming year, whether two, five, or even ten millions of dollars, without coming within the operation of this article of the constitution. But should she exceed that revenue, then she is creating a debt within the contemplation of this article.

Mr. CLARKE, of Henry. I think I appreciate fully the remarks of the chairman of the committee on State debts, and understand clearly his position, and his idea of the State running into debt. As I understand him, his idea was this; that the State might now go on and make appropriations, when there was even nothing in the treasury, in anticipation of the incoming revenue. Say that the revenue should be three hundred thousand dollars, and the State should make appropriations for five hundred thousand dollars. Then she would have gone into debt the one hundred thousand dollars allowed by this constitution, besides having the three hundred thousand dollars of the revenue, and the other one hundred thousand dollars would be held in abeyance, because it would be to that extent, that the State would have exceeded her constitutional power. Now if there is any necessity for the State to go into debt beyond the sum of one hundred thousand dollars, we should have the amount of this limit placed at a higher sum. For instance, the State has negotiated for the erection of an asylum, and made an appropriation of one hundred thousand dollars. Suppose that the excess of annual revenue of the State, over and above expenses, should not be one hundred thousand dollars, that is, that the current expenses of the State should consume more than all the revenue, then this appropriation of one hundred thousand dollars for this asylum would exceed the amount fixed by the constitution as it now stands, for the limit beyond which the State may not go into debt. And as the State has engaged in these works, and as it may need a greater extension than afforded by this limitation, I can see no possible danger in increasing it to the full amount proposed by the gentleman from Jasper, (Mr. Skiff.)

And I would state farther to this committee, that owing to some unfortunate circumstances connected with the management of our school fund, the suggestion has been made, and it has met with decided approbation in all quarters, that the State itself shall absorb the school fund. Gentlemen will understand the object of this; it is to put the school fund in a situation where it will be forever safe. And if the State borrows the school fund, there is a debt at once of two hundred and fifty thousand dollars. We must therefore increase the limits, in order to enable the State to carry out this idea. The question for us to consider—and I would put it to the chairman of the committee (Mr. Wilson,) if it be not so—is, whether it would not be better for us to establish a reasonable limit within which the legislature may act in making these appropriations, and within which the bonds of the State may be given, and a debt secured at once, than to place the legislature in a position where they are called upon from the necessities of the case, to make an appropriation which will exceed the revenue of the State more than one hundred thousand dollars; and thereby forcing them to exceed their constitutional limits, or let the State suffer in her most vital interests! Most certainly, no man will pretend to say, that if the general assembly should make an appropriation that would exceed the constitutional limits here fixed, any citizen of the State would wish parties, to which the State should become thereby indebted for these improvements, to lose this amount; but would rather desire that the State should pay it. It would become a debt of honor, and all we seek to do is to make what would be a debt of honor, a bonded debt from the beginning. We desire to allow the State sufficient scope to carry on these works of charity, generosity, humanity, that are demanded by the inhabitants of the State, and to let them be carried on economically, without being cramped. That is the question; whether the bonds of the State shall be issued at once for funds to carry on these works, or whether the legislature shall be forced to go beyond their constitutional limits, and have the honor of the State only pledged for the payment of the debt.

I shall vote for the largest amount that has been mentioned here.

Mr. GOWER. I think there is much in the arguments in favor of filling this blank with a high number. Should the State borrow the school fund, both present and prospective, that will, I suppose, at once, create a debt of some three hundred thousand dollars. Other expenses will necessarily arise, which will probably require something beyond what the constitution now allows. We have all along been fully up to the limit prescribed by the constitution, and according to the remarks of some gentlemen here, it seems that we have already exceeded the constitutional limit. Gentlemen have referred here to so many objects, which need the care and encouragement of the State, that it seems to me the sum of five hundred thousand dollars is as small a sum as we should insert in this section. I am as much in favor of keeping out of debt as any one can be, but I do not wish to cramp the State. I have no desire to throw a debt upon posterity, but I think the public good really requires that some material change should be made in this portion of the old constitution.

Mr. CLARKE, of Henry. I will state that I find upon examination that the school fund exceeds three hundred thousand dollars.

Mr. CLARKE, of Johnson. I have but few words to say upon this subject, and I should not say these words did I not conceive that there was a very radical difference of opinion in the minds of the members of this convention as to the nature of government, and what it is proper for us to do here. I understand it to be a well settled axiom, to which all parties agree, that the people are the source of power; that all political power comes from them. We are sitting here by virtue of that power, and are to make a government to be carried on by virtue of that power. We are to make a representative government in which the public voice is to be expressed, and through which the people are to act. This proposition is what? It is a proposition to tie up, not the hands of this government, but the hands of the people. We are called upon to put a check, not upon the government, but upon the people themselves. If there must be a check, I am willing to give the government a very large latitude here. I shall vote, perhaps, to make the sum to be inserted here five hundred thousand dollars, for the simple reason that five hundred thousand dollars now is not larger, in comparison, than the one hundred thousand dollars which we had ten years ago, when the present constitution was framed and adopted. I hope we shall make a constitution here under which the government shall be established, and under which it will be enabled to work so that in ten years we shall not find ourselves, as we are now, under a government so cramped as to be inadequate to the wants and necessities of the people. I can conceive of many things which will call for the expenditure of money, that are vital to the protection, happiness and prosperity of our people. There are many matters far more important than that of building a State House, or any kind of institution. And I do not desire, when the time comes and the emergency arrives, to have this constitution so arranged as to stand in the way of the progress and prosperity of the people.

Now I am afraid that some members of this convention are not so willing to trust the people after all. If the people send foolish men here to represent them and make laws for them, who will spend their money for them unnecessarily, it is their business, not ours. We are not sent here to guard and watch the people, and place a check upon them and prevent them from acting for their own good. And yet it seems to be the idea of many members of this convention that unless we so check the government we are not doing our duty. I shall vote for the largest amount here, for I believe the time will come in less than ten years, when circumstances will arise that will require this State to go into debt to the amount now named. If those circumstances do not arise, then the debt need not be incurred, and no harm will be done.

Mr. JOHNSTON. I differ *in toto* from my friend from Johnson, [Mr. Clarke,] when he says we are not sent here to place limitations and restrictions upon the future action of the legislature. I think that is our business, and I think it is highly important that we should do so, if we are to believe the half that has been said in this hall about the rascality and villainy of the legislature. I regret that the sum of one hundred thousand dollars was stricken out of this section. I am in favor of that sum, and think it is amply sufficient for all our purposes. My reason for thinking so is this: Gentlemen will recollect that this State is growing and progressing rapidly, and if they will look at the last report of the auditor, they will find for the next two fiscal years the estimated amount of receipts over the estimated expenditures is two hundred and fifty thousand dollars, which added to the one hundred thousand dollars which the state would go into debt under this provision as it was reported, would afford over three hundred thousand dollars for the expenditure of the State every year for these extraordinary objects. The rate of taxation now is forty mills on every one hundred dollars. That can be changed at any time, and if the State desires to raise a larger amount of money by taxation at any time than it now raises, it can easily do so. There has never been a time in the history of our State when it was so important that some restrictions should be placed upon the subject of state indebtedness, than the present. The people are all wild, all crazy upon the subject of making money. We all deem ourselves rich, or soon about to be. Probably two years hence it will be otherwise. And I tell you, gentlemen, that this is the sheet anchor of the security of this State, and we ought to cling to it.

I believe with the gentleman from Jefferson, [Mr. Wilson,] that the true interpretation of the words "debt or liability," is a bonded debt. It is so considered by all the lawyers with whom

I conversed during the session of the legislature just adjourned, except Mr. Cloud of Muscatine. And if gentlemen will observe the article reported for our consideration by the Committee on State Debts, they will perceive that it is in a much more contracted form than the old constitution. The old constitution says "debt or debts, liability or liabilities," while the provision under consideration says "the credit of the State shall not, in any manner, be given or loaned to, or in aid of," &c. That provision could not be interpreted as the gentleman from Benton, [Mr. Traer,] interprets it. And I say again that there never has been any time when it was more necessary to throw these restrictions about the legislature than it is now.

Mr. TRAER. I will state to the gentleman from Lee, [Mr. Johnston,] that I have not put any construction upon this repart. I have only stated the construction of the gentleman from Jefferson, [Mr. Wilson,] and I asked him if he put the same construction upon this report that he did upon the old constitution. I put no construction upon it at all.

Mr. GILLASPY. I would ask to whom the State would execute her bonds if she borrowed this school money?

Mr. CLARKE, of Henry. Having endorsed the gentleman from Wapello, [Mr. Gillaspy,] as one of the honest members here, I must see that my endorsement is kept good. And lest the convention should suppose that the gentleman was indulging in a quiz, and was not perfectly honest, in my opinion, in the question he put to me, I will give an answer to it. I will say that if the State should borrow the money of the school fund, it would not have to give their bonds to any one. Under the enlarged powers proposed to be given in this constitution, the State would merely borrow the money and be debtor to the school fund for the amount it would receive, which would be about three hundred thousand dollars. And the sums additional to that, that would be coming in annually from the United States and sales of lands, would soon increase the fund to five hundred thousand dollars. And that can be appropriated to such works as they may see fit. Now as the gentleman has expressed such confidence in "the dear people," and in their integrity and good intentions, he certainly can have no objection to their taking charge of this fund and appropriating it for the general good, constituting the state a debtor to the school fund, and paying the interest upon it, instead of having it as it is now.

Mr. HALL. So far as I am concerned personally, I am not particular whether this sum is put at $100,000, $200,000, or $300,000, provided the section contains the principle I stand upon, to have the interest upon the indebtedness of the State not become oppressive upon the people. I believe it would be better to have the amount increased beyond $100,000, if for no other purpose than to get rid of these very questions upon which gentlemen here and elsewhere disagree. It is a fact that this State has gone into debt more than the Constitution directs and authorizes. Gentlemen upon the one side say that it means a bound debt, while gentlemen on the other side contend that the Constitution did not distinguish between the two kinds of debt, but that if the money is owed it is a debt. Now I do not believe that the Constitution refers particularly to a bonded debt; I believe it means any debt that draws interest. This provision was intended to prevent an addititional burden being put upon the people in the shape of interest, by way of a bond or anything else. Now it makes no difference whether you draw a warrant upon the treasury to bear interest after a certain date, or whether you give a bond bearing interest. The two things are the same in principle. A simple warrant not drawing interest would not be a debt within the meaning of the Constitution; if it draws interest it would be a constituttional debt, whether it is a bonded debt or not. Now our State has been in this condition, and I would be willing to give it a little morelatitude in this matter. There is now a permanent debt against the State of $100,000. And there are other liabilities which I suppose this provison of the Constitution may be construed to embrace. I do not think there can be any harm or danger resulting from extending this limit, and I shall therefore vote to extend the limit to $200,000, as about what is called for by the necessities of the State at this time.

Mr. PATTERSON. I voted to strike out the sum $100,000, believing that a majority of the Convention were in favor of extending the limits herein prescribed. But I am opposed to the sum of $500,000, and shall vote for the lowest sum that can be agreed upon here. I am satisfied that if we go up to $500,000, or a million of dollars, I believe that the State would reach the amount at once, as soon as the debts can be contracted.

Mr. GILLASPY. I desire to say to the gentleman from Johnson, [Mr. Clarke,] and the gentleman from Henry, [Mr. Clarke,] that to my mind, they have said more about "the dear people" than I have done, or any other gentleman upon this floor, and yet they are throwing out insinuations here, of gentlemen upon this floor being afraid to trust "the dear people." I think this comes with bad grace from gentlemen who talk so much about their willingness to trust the people, and then when they come to vote show that they are not disposed to trust the people. I will just call the attention of gentlemen to the fourth section of this report, where they can perceive that the report has left everything to the people that is proper and right. We say we are willing to trust the people to contract such debts as are absolutely necessary, but before such debts shall be contracted they shall be presented to the people in such a manner as to let them understand the object of the debts to be so contracted. I am willing the people should vote $20,000,000 if they think proper, for any object of internal imorovement in this State, provided they do it understandingly. I have as great confidence in the people as any other member can have. And while I say that I am willing to trust the people, I desire also to show by my votes that I am willing to trust them. I undertake to say that the fourth section extends over the broadest possible ground, and covers every contingency that may arise in the progress in this State.

And I will say for the benefit of the gentleman from Benton, [Mr. Traer,] while I am up, that we have very high authority for the position taken by the gentleman from Jefferson, [Mr. Wilson,] and the gentleman from Lee, [Mr. Johnston,] in regard to the proper construction of the provision of the Convention as it now stands in relation to debts and liabilities. I understand that after the delivering of the message of the Governor to the General Assembly, the trustees of the State University memorialized the Legislature to make an appropriation of $100,0000 for their use, and it was not considered, if they had made it that it would have been a violation of the present Constitution of this State. That, I think, should be authority enough for the gentleman from Benton.

Mr. HARRIS. There seems to be a diversity of views in regard to this matter, and it may be well enough for me to state the reasons for the course I propose to pursue when the question comes up for action. If I understand the message of his Excellency, Governor Grimes, to the last Legislature, I endorse it to a very great extent. There are some things in it I do not concur in, but I concur in all the monetary portion of it. I understand him to take the ground of no more State indebtedness than we can possibly get along with. That I agree to; I believe it is just as detrimental for a State to go into debt and incur the necessity of paying a large amount of interest, as it is for an individual to do so. And with our revenue system, regulated as it is, which was so fully explained by my friend from Lee, [Mr. Johnston,] I cannot conceive of any necessity for the State going into debt more than the present Constitutional limit, the sum of $100,000. And when the proper time shall come I will vote to retain that sum of $100,000, which was stricken out of this section. I should not feel willing to go home to my constituents without at least being placed upon the record as in favor of retaining that sum. However, I did not get up simply to tell how I shall vote, for that could be understood by all when I come to vote.

But there is another idea in connection with this matter to which I desire to call the attention of the committee. In referring to the indebtness of the State at this time, it is stated to be some $128,000. And gentlemen seem to suppose that because that is really a fact, it must have been legitimately incurred, and that perhaps there has been no needless expenditure of the money of the State in creating that amount of indebtedness. Now, I have only to say that my impression is, that it has not been properly created, and that there have been, perhaps, some expenditures which should not have been made. I do not propose, however, to speak as to what particular matters were not necessary. But I believe that the affairs of the State could have been conducted in such a manner as not to violate the Constitution, as I believe it has been violated, if that amount of indebtedness really exists. I believe that all the means necessary to carry out the proper and legitimate purposes of the government could be raised without any infraction of the Constitution. So far as the necessity of creating any State debt is concerned at this particular time, I am not disposed to go farther than is necessary to carry on the government, and if I may be allowed the expression, keep the wheels of State well greased.

So far as this idea of creating and erecting these public buildings and other public improvements are concerned, of which gentlemen have spoken so much here, it is to prevent that I am opposed to allowing the State to incur this amount of indebtedness. I think if there is any subject which should properly go before the people for them to act upon, to consider like the democracy of olden time, to sit upon as a jury, if you please, it is this very system of entering upon these public improvements. So far as erecting the State Capitol and other public buildings is to be considered, I understand that there are ample provisions already made to enable the State to get along for fifty years to come, and to have as good accommodations as we have here, without incurring any indebtedness whatever. And it is only when the wealth of the State and the amount of the tax paying property of the State have become such that the amount of revenue can be increased without saddling indebtedness upon the State, that it should be considered proper to embark upon this system of internal improvements. I do not think that there is any necessity, at present, of creating a State debt of more than $100,000. I certainly consider the remark of the gentleman from Lee, [Mr. Johnston,] that the people of this State have become wild upon the subject of speculation and getting rich, a remark that every gentleman here can fully endorse.

As for this idea of the State assuming this school fund, and giving bonds, upon which interest is to be paid, I am opposed to it entirely. And I believe the idea is only mooted as something which may be done for the purpose of creating a basis for a banking system. If we cannot have banks without making the indebtedness of the State the basis of that banking system, then I am opposed to having any banks. I know that so far as the people I represent here are concerned, if there is any one provision of the Constitution with which they are entirely satisfied, and which they would, under no circumstances, have changed, it is the one in reference to State indebtedness. I know they would frown upon any attempt to change that provision, more than they would upon any other change that could be made in the Constitution. And I believe gentlemen will find it so all over the State whenever the sovereign people come to express their opinion in regard to the matter.

Mr. TRAER. I have no desire to make any speech upon this subject. But I wish to say a few words in reply to the gentleman from Wapello [Mr. Gillaspy]. In speaking of his authority for his side of the question, he referred to the opinions expressed by the gentleman from Jefferson, (Mr. Wilson), and the gentleman from Lee (Mr. Johnston). Now I have no disposition to cavil at their decision in regard to this matter. I have the utmost confidence in their judgment; still I must say I am not inclined to give up the position I took before, that the constitution of the State has been violated. And I will read a statement from the message of the Governor in answer to the position taken by gentlemen that nothing but bonds create a State debt within the meaning of this constitution. And I will show that the state is already in debt over and above the amount which the constitution specifies shall be the limit. In summing up and giving a detailed account of the indebtedness of the State, the Governor says:

"There were outstanding, unpaid auditors' warrants due on the first Nov., 1857, amounting to	$11,567 64
There are bonds of the State due first of January, 1857, . . .	71,442 00
Due to the School Fund, Sept. 15, 1859, ...	5,000 00
Due to the School Fund July 15, 1866, . . . :	40,000 00
Total indebtedness, . . .	$128,009 64

Now there is an amount of $71,000 that this State owes on her bonds. A great portion of that debt I suppose was contracted before the present constitution was formed, or soon afterwards.

Mr. HALL. That has been paid already.

Mr. TRAER. That may be, but how has it been paid? By contracting another debt—and the violation of the constitution remains the same.

I am much obliged to my Democratic friends here for coming forward and supporting the action of the legislature and the executive, and I hope they will not go out of this convention and endeavor to make capital against the party to which I belong, by citing the action of the present executive of the State, as they tried to do before I came here.

Mr. WINCHESTER. I desire to say in support of my motion to fill this blank with the words "two hundred and fifty thousand," that I have heard the people in my district say more about this question of State indebtedness than any other question, except that in regard tobanking. It was the prevailing opinion among them that the sum to which the State has heretofore been limited, might, perhaps, bear increasing to two hundred thousand or two hundred and fifty thousand dollars. Consequently, I shall vote for the amount I have named, and no greater amount. I believe that the revenue of this State will increase from this time forward faster in proportion than the actual necessities of the State.

I think it would be well, however, to authorise the contracting of debts to the extent I have named for the purpose of building the necessary charitable institutions in this State. That was my object in proposing the amount I have proposed here.

Mr. PALMER. I would ask the gentleman from Benton [Mr. Traer] how he makes out that the Democrats have violated the constitution in relation to State indebtedness?

Mr. TRAER. The gentleman misunderstands me. I said that I was glad that the Democrats have endorsed the action of the Republican party. And the gentleman from Wapello [Mr. Gillaspy], the gentleman from Lee [Mr. Johnston], and the gentleman from Appanoose [Mr. Harris] have cited their action as good authority for their proposed action here. I am glad they have committed themselves, so that they cannot go out from this convention and charge this upon the Republican party as a Republican measure.

Mr. GIBSON. I charge it upon the Republican party, and do not justify the course they have pursued. I would leave it with the Republican party to give their own explanation.

Mr. HARRIS. I did not before understand that the gentleman from Benton [Mr. Traer] was the keeper of the reputation of the governor. Now, if I know anything about the history of parties in regard to this matter, we are not to be suspected of getting upon the Republican platform. And I suspect if his Excellency was called upon to express his private and individual views in regard to this matter, it would be found that they have undergone some change. And so far from our getting upon the Republican platform, if the Republican party has ever had any platform, in reference to State indebtedness, his Excellency has got upon the Democratic platform. And not only upon that question, but upon other questions. And hence we are not estopped from speaking with respect to his Excellency, or the Republican party, so far as the position of the Democratic party in regard to State indebtedness is concerned.

Now, I understand that so far as this portion of the constitution is concerned, which has been aptly termed by the gentleman from Lee [Mr. Johnston] the sheet anchor of the State, it has been and is yet a Democratic measure. I only regret that some of those whom we had a right to look to for support, and who ought to have been the pillars of the democracy in this matter, are disposed to become a little loose in their notions about it. I understand that the sentiment of the Democratic party of this State is against State indebtedness, and if there is any other party that has a sentiment against State indebtedness, they are but endorsing the old Democratic doctrine. I do not understand, therefore, what right the gentleman from Benton has to catechize us, as to how we shall speak about the Republican party, or his Excellency, or any body else, in regard to this matter of State indebtedness. It gives me pleasure to agree with any gentleman, with whom it might have been reasonably supposed I would disagree, upon any question; and I do not understand that I thereby place myself under any bonds, or that in consequence of so agreeing, I am not to have the privilege of talking about the position of either of the parties in this State. I do not understand that I commit anybody but myself in this matter. Nor do I think I should be debarred from referring to his Excellency, because he is understood as differing with us in politics. I will say, however, that so far as this, and some other questions, perhaps, are concerned, I regard him as occupying the Democratic platform.

Mr. BUNKER. I do not believe there can be very much capital made out of this little matter, any way you may take it.

Mr. HARRIS. I had no desire to make any capital out of it, but only to reply to what I thought was an improper insinuation.

Mr. BUNKER. We have provided in a section of this report that we have already passed over, that the State shall never go into debt by embarking her capital in any internal improvement whatever. We have excluded from our constitution the provision that has got many of the older States into debt, and hence I cannot conceive that there is any danger of involving the State very seriously in debt. We have cut off all the means to do so. There is nothing left but the erection of the public buildings of the State for which money can be expended. So far as I am concerned, I am not anxious to raise the amount to which the State may become indebted above the sum of one hundred thousand dollars, if that will meet the necessary expenses of the State, without our taxes becoming oppressive to the people.

It has been said that the state has already transcended the limits prescribed by the present constitution. Now, if my memory is correct, the very first legislature under the present constitution contracted a debt of nearly one hundred thousand dollars, and that debt has been hanging over the State ever since. At the present time the indebtedness of the State appears to be a little over one hundred thousand dollars. In view of these circumstances, and in view of the fact that there is a project for turning the school fund over to the State, making the State responsible to the fund for the safe keeping thereof—though I do not know what will be done—I think I shall vote to authorise the State to contract an indebtedness of perhaps three hundred thousand dollars, or five hundred thousand dollars. But I do not think there is any scarecrow in this thing, or any political capital to be made out of it in any way.

Mr. SCOTT. I hope the motion to fill this blank with the words "five hundred thousand," will not prevail. And I will say that however much I may have been impressed at one time with the propriety of enlarging the limit here prescribed for the amount of indebtedness the State shall be permitted to incur, yet upon further investigation of the subject, I am satisfied that one hundred thousand dollars is sufficient for all necessary purposes. It has been the pride of our State that its demands upon its citizens have been comparatively light as compared with other States. Our taxes have been small, and I trust the expenditures of this State will never exceed, to any great extent, the amount of revenue derived from the taxes imposed upon the people of this State. And I hope gentlemen will take into consideration the fact that whatever amount of indebtedness the constitution may permit the State to contract, will certainly be contracted and that speedily. It will surely speedily become a burden and incubus upon the tax-payers of this State My opinion is that if we were to fix this limit as high as twenty millions of dollars, the legislature would in five years bring the State into debt to the full amount of the limitation. Now the object of this amount of indebtedness which the State is to be allowed to incur, as I understand it, is to provide a contingent fund to draw on. When this constitution was formed one hundred thousand dollars was supposed to be a sufficient contingent fund to meet all the exigencies that might arise. But so soon as the matter was determined that we might incur an indebtedness of one hundred thousand dollars, the whole of it was absorbed almost immediately, and we went up to the highest point we could reach. And if it could be put up to any amount, however high, we would soon reach that amount. So that for the purpose of a contingent fund in case of neeessity, one hundred thousand dollars is as good as ten million dollars. For if you were to put in a provision here that the State shall be allowed to incur an indebtedness of ten millions of dollars, the State would soon reach that sum, and the amount left for contingencies would be no greater than it is now.

There is another view of this matter which I hope members will take, and that is, that should any contingency arise where it would be absolutely necessary for the State to have more means than this section now provides, this report has abundantly provided for that matter, by allowing the legislature to submit a proposition to the people for whatever expenditure might be desired, and thus appropriations could be made, if the legislature saw fit, for all those charitable institutions desired, and for whatever other purposes might be considered necessary. I see no necessity for raising this amount at all, and shall certainly vote for the lowest amount possible.

Mr. SOLOMON. I wish to state briefly the reasons which will influence my vote upon this question. I shall vote against enlarging the amount to which the State may become indebted under the present constitution. And if any gentlemen will introduce the proposition here, I will vote with him against allowing the State to create any indebtedness at all, even to the extent of one dollar. And I will go further and say that any indebtedness created by the officers of the State, engaged in the creation thereof, beyond the amount the constitution may prescribe, shall be paid by that officer. And I take this position because of my thorough conviction that the State should never go into debt at all. I wish a similar provision had been in our present constitution, that our officers might have been taught not to have gone beyond the limits of one hundred thousand dollars, which, it has been said upon the other side of the house, has been already done. My own opinion is that if such is the case, this State does not owe that amount, that the amount of indebtedness which has been created beyond the one hundred thousand dollars allowed by the present constitution, is illegal and void. But I am willing that the restriction should remain as it is in the present constitution, for I am pledged to my district to go for that. But I will never consent to go beyond that sum. I go for the State being prohibited from using its credit for any purpose. I would keep the State out of debt entirely.

The question being then taken upon filling the blank with the words "five hundred thousand," it was not agreed to, upon a division as follows: ayes 8, noes 14.

Mr. CLARKE, of Johnson, moved to fill the blank with the words "four hundred thousand."

The question being taken, the motion was not agreed to.

Mr. CLARKE, of Henry, moved to fill the blank with the words "three hundred and fifty thousand."

The question being taken, it was not agreed to.

The question then recurred upon the motion of Mr. Parvin, to fill the blank with the words "three hundred thousand."

Upon a division, the motion was not agreed to, as follows, ayes 12, noes 15.

The question then recurred upon the motion of Mr. Winchester, with the words "two hundred and fifty thousand."

Upon a division, as follows, ayes 16, noes 11, the motion was agreed to, and the blank filled accordingly, allowing the State to incur an indebtedness of two hundred and fifty thousand dollars.

Mr. CLARKE, of Johnson. I move farther to amend the section by adding to it the words, "and any debt created beyond that amount shall be void." If I understand the arguments of gentlemen upon this floor, it is conceded that the present restriction in our constitution has been violated, and the State now owes a debt beyond the amount of one hundred thousand dollars, which is the limit prescribed by the present Constitution. I would beg leave to ask this practical question: Of what value is this restriction, if there is now a debt contracted beyond the constitutional amount? and what is proposed to be done about it? Do we propose to repudiate all of this debt above one hundred thousand dollars? Does anybody propose that we should do that? Would the people of this State sanction and tolerate such a proposition for a moment? and if they did, would not the State be disgraced everywhere in the eyes of the world? It seems to me that, practically this restriction does not amount to anything. If the legislature, or the officers of the State, can go on and violate this constitution, and establish a debt beyond the limits prescribed by the constitution, and that debt is considered a valid one, then this restriction does not amount to anything. Now, in order that the people may understand, and that every man who deals with the State shall know the full consequences of his act, I propose making this restriction so strong, that the whole world shall know and understand it. Practically, I do not think this restriction will amount to anything; but in order to make it as plain as possible, I propose to amend it by declaring, that any debt contracted beyond the restriction placed in the constitution, shall be considered as null and void.

Mr. TODHUNTER. Would that provision have a retrospective action and effect.

Mr. CLARKE, of Johnson. Oh, no.

Mr. TODHUNTER. If it did, I am afraid we should be defrauded out of the forty thousand dollars which the governor has secured from the superintendent of education.

Mr. PARVIN. I can hardly think that the gentleman from Johnson [Mr. Clark] is in earnest in offering this amendment. I hold that if we employ agents, and they go beyond the amount to which they are restricted by the provisions of this constitution, we should hold them responsible, and not make the individuals with whom they deal, suffer for their wrongful acts. I believe in paying all our debts, and not repudiating one single dime of it, but hold our agents responsible for any thing of this sort that may be done. I hope, therefore, that the amendment of the gentleman from Johnson [Mr. Clarke] will not prevail. If our legislature runs us into debt beyond the limits prescribed by the constitution, let us pay that debt, and not repudiate it. I have practiced many years, in my dealings, upon this principle, that if a man cheats me once, it is his fault; but if he cheats me the second time, it is my fault.

Mr. PALMER. I am in favor of the principle contained in the amendment proposed by the gentleman from Johnson, [Mr. Clarke] but I think it would come in here rather out of place, and may conflict somewhat with some of the sections that follow. I have drawn up an amendment to come in after this place, as an independent section, containing the same principle that the gentleman from Johnson desires to embody here. It is as follows:

"Any contract made, or entered into, shall directly, or indirectly, increase the State debt above the limit prescribed by this article, shall be null and void."

Mr. CLARKE, of Johnson. I will withdraw my amendment, and permit the gentleman from Davis (Mr. Palmer) to offer his amendment, at the proper time.

No farther amendment was proposed to that section.

Mr. HALL. I move to insert in this place the following amendment, as a new section:

"That all losses to the government, school, or university funds of this State, which losses shall have been occasioned by the mis-management or fraud of the agents, or officers, controlling or managing the same, shall be audited by the proper authorities of the State, and the amount so audited shall be a permanent bonded debt against the State in favor of these respective funds, upon which six per cent., annual interest shall be paid, for school and university purposes; the amount of liability so created shall not be accounted as a part of the indebtedness authorized by the second section of this article."

I have appended this section to this report believing this to be the proper place for it. I look upon the university and school funds of this State as a dear trust confided to the State, and I believe the State should be held responsible, if her agents, by fraud or mismanagement, abuse and lose these funds.

The amendment I have proposed will only hold the State responsible, the same as an individual would be if he had the management of these funds. I think the trustee, whether individual or State, should be held responsibile. I wish to place the State in the same position towards the benificiaries of these funds, as an individual would occupy. I consider this trust as the most sacred of all trusts that can be confided to any people. The beneficiaries of this school fund are never adults; they are ever children, and can have no voice, control or management, nor should they have it. But this fund should be cherished with the utmost care, and we should be exceedingly careful about how we act, lest the funds be lost, wasted or squandered. I think a proposition of the kind I have offered will render the people a little more watchful. If they are to be taxed to pay the interest of all losses, they will certainly be more careful to see that this property is placed in safe hands, and properly protected. I do not think this proposition will be any way unjust towards the tax paying portion of the State. Most of them have children to educate, and will receive a benefit in the advancement of the cause of education which this provision will secure.

Mr. GOWER. I would offer an amendment, that the interest shall be ten per cent., and paid semi-annually.

Mr. HALL. I will accept that amendment.

The proposed section, as modified, was then adopted.

Section three was then read as follows:

"In addition to the above limited power to contract debts, the State may contract debts to repel invasion, suppress insurrection, or defend the State in war; but the money arising from the debts so contracted, shall be applied to the purpose for which it was raised, or to repay such debts, and to no other purpose whatever."

No amendment being offered to the third section—

Taxes to pay Debts.

Section four of the report was then read as follows:

"Except the debts specified in the second and third sections of this article, no debt shall be hereafter contracted, by, or on behalf of this State, unless such debt shall be authorized by some law for some single work or object to be distinctly specified therein; and such law shall impose and provide for the collection of a direct annual tax to pay, and sufficient to pay the interest on such debt, as it falls due, and also to pay and discharge the principal of such debt, within twenty years from the time of contracting thereof; but no such law shall take effect until at a general election it shall have been submitted to the people, and have received a majority of all the votes cast for and against it at such election; and all money raised by authority of such law, shall be applied only to the specified object therein stated, or to the payment of the debt created thereby, and such law shall be published in at least one newspaper in each county, if one is published therein, throughout the State, for three months preceding the election at which it is submitted to the people.

Mr. HALL. I move to amend the first line of the section by striking out the words "specified in the second and third sections of this article," and insert the words "herein specified." I make this motion because a new section, which now stands as section three has been adopted, while the one that is here referred to as number three is now number four.

The question being taken the amendment was agreed to.

Mr. PALMER moved to amend by striking out the words "to pay and" after the words "direct annual tax," so that it will then read read "the collection of a direct annual tax sufficient to pay the interest on such debt, &c.

The amendment was agreed to.

No farther amendment being offered,

The next section was read as follows:

"The legislature may, at any time, after the approval of such law by the people, if no debt shall have been contracted in pursuance thereof, repeal the same; and may, at any time, by law, forbid the contracting of any further debt, or liability, under such law; but the tax imposed by such law, in proportion to the debt and liability which may have been contracted in pursuance of such law, shall remain in force, and be irrepealable, and be annually collected, until the proceeds thereof shall have made the provision hereinbefore specified, to pay and discharge the interest and principal of such debt and liability."

No amendment being offered to this section,

The last section was read as follows:

"Every law which imposes, continues, or revives a tax, shall distinctly state the tax, and the object to which it is to be applied; and it shall not be sufficient to refer to any other law to fix such tax or object.

No amendment was offered to this section.

Mr. PALMER offered the following as an additional section;

"Section ——. Every contract made, or entered into, which either directly, or indirectly, increases the State debt, above the limit in this article prescribed, shall be null and void."

Mr. HARRIS. So far as preventing the State from incurring indebtedness, I am disposed to go as far as any one possibly can. But I am not disposed to repudiate. If any means can be devised by which the officers of the government, and the members of the general assembly, who create the debt, shall be held accountable and amenable, I should have no objection to vote for it. But, say gentlemen, private parties will not suffer, for the constitution will constitute a notice to them. Now every man does not know what the constitution is. And that is not all. They cannot tell how far the State has gone in her appropriations already made, and, in that way, they may advance money upon the credit of the State, which may make the indebtedness of the State beyond the amount prescribed by the constitution. I cannot vote for a provision which will lead to a repudiation of the debt thus incurred in good faith. Now if any provision can be devised, by which you can indemnify those that may enter into contracts with the State upon the faith of the State, then I will have no objection to it.

The only argument that seems to be used here is, that because we have fixed a limit, and the State has gone beyond that limit, we shall place the limit so high that the State cannot reach it. Now I do not know what we can do in this matter, except to say that the State may incur a certain amount of indebtedness, and shall go no farther into debt than that amount. We are to suppose, that we elect honest men to the legislature; they are sworn to support the constitution of the State of Iowa. Now if by mistake, or otherwise, they exceed the limits prescribed in this constitution, and persons are thereby led to pay money upon the faith of the State, I am not disposed to repudiate. If your agent goes beyond what you authorize him to do, you do not therefore become relieved of your responsibility. You, perhaps, have some claim upon your agent, but the party with whom your agents contracts looks to you for his claim to be made good. I am willing to go as far as any one to hold those accountable who contract debts beyond the limits set forth in the constitution, but I cannot go for repudiation.

Mr. CLARKE, of Johnson. This proposition brings us to the practical effect of this thing, and brings the gentleman from Appanoose, (Mr. Harris,) who has spoken so loudly against State debts, in just the position I desired to get him in. If we mean, by this article, to give the broadest notice to the world, that a debt beyond this amount is not to be paid, then here is a practical way of accomplishing that purpose. This puts every man, who may come into a position to contract with the State, to the necessity of going to the books of the State, with paper and pencil, and footing up the various amounts of indebtedness, and the interest upon that indebtedness, to see if he can enter into a contract, and be supported by the constitution. Such a requisition as that I consider to be impracticable.

It seems strange to me, that the gentleman from Appanoose, (Mr. Harris,) who is so fearful of State debt, is unwilling to say, that those who are parties to creating a State debt beyond the limits of the constitution, shall suffer the consequences of their acts. There is no practical benefit in this restriction, if the party who becomes a *particeps criminis* in this violation of the constitution, can still come to the State, and claim that they are bound to pay him. There is no safeguard, or check in this thing, so far as it is practically concerned. Now if we have State agents, who deem that the public interests require it, or that exigencies demand it, this restriction will not restrain them, they will incur these debts, and they will be paid as they have been paid here or elsewhere.

Mr. WILSON. Why did not the bill appropriating one hundred thousand dollars for the benefit of the lunatic asylum pass the house of representatives?

Mr. CLARKE, of Johnson. I cannot tell why, more than I can tell why the house of representatives ordered certain maps of one of our book sellers of this city, and refused to pay him? Did they find out that they were going into debt beyond the limits of the constitution?

Mr. WILSON. Was not the argument used that they were going beyond the constitution?

Mr. CLARKE, of Johnson. I cannot say. If this restriction is to be placed upon the people through their agents, I want it to mean something. I want the legislature. and the parties who are contracting with the State, to understand that if they do violate the constitution in this respect it shall be void. And not allow the parties to come before the legislature with constant applications for the passage of bills for their relief. And I think the amendment of the gentleman from Davis, [Mr. Palmer,] is the very kernel of this whole matter. Without it, this section is not worth the paper it is printed upon.

Mr. PALMER. I do not know that the section I have offered is absolutely necessary to render void contracts made in violation of this article. But I thought it might be of some service in notifying the world that we did not hold ourselves responsible for any debts contracted in violation of this article. Suppose the indebtedness of the State shall amount to two hundred and forty thousand dollars. A contract is entered into which will increase the indebtedness to three hundred thousand dollars or four hundred thousand dollars. Would that contract be entirely void under this article as it now stands? The section I have proposed would make the whole contract void. Without my provision, it might be construed that the amount of ten thousand dollars would be good, and only the excess be void. While I would make the whole contract void, I suppose that all the indebtedness over the constitutional limit would be pronounced void by any competent court, if the question is ever raised.

Mr. HALL. If I thought the gentleman from Davis, (Mr. Palmer,) was correct in his position, I would vote against this amendment. If I thought the State could not, in anticipation of its revenues, provide for the expenses of building its charitable institutions and State House, I would vote for some clause that will authorize them to do it. I do not believe that this article of the constitution was ever intended to reach any such questions. I would have an article in the constitution that would prevent the legislature from creating any funded debt, so as to prevent the State from being taxed for the payment of interest on money borrowed. Wherever they do create a debt which encumbers the State in the payment of interest, I would make it void; but I would not tie up the hands of the State to such an extent that she could not go on and anticipate her revenues for the purpose of erecting her charitable institutions and other public buildings.

Mr. GILLASPY. I have no fear, neither do I believe that any other gentlemen ought to entertain any fear, that this State is going to make fraudulent contracts, or contracts that she ought not to make. We should say by the adoption of this amendment that Iowa was going to be dishonest, and make fraudulent contracts. I do not believe any such thing, and I do not believe that this Convention should prejudice the State in this way. I am opposed, therefore, to the proposition of the gentleman from Davis, [Mr. Palmer.]

The question was then taken upon Mr. Palmer's amendment, and it was rejected upon a division, ayes 4, noes not counted.

Mr. HARRIS. I move that the committee rise, and that they ask leave to be discharged.

The motion was agreed to.

In Convention.

The committee then rose, and the President having resumed the Chair—

The Chairman reported that the Committee of the Whole had had under consideration the report of the Committee on State Debts, had instructed him to report the same back to the Convention with sundry amendments, and asked to be discharged from the further consideration of the same.

Leave was granted, and the committee were discharged.

The PRESIDENT. What action will the convention take upon the report of the Committee.

Mr. CLARKE, of Johnson. I move that the report be laid upon the table.

The question was taken and the motion was agreed to.

On motion of Mr. TRAER,

The Convention then adjourned till to-morrow at 9 o'clock A. M.

FRIDAY, Feb. 6, 1857.

The Convention met at 9 o'clock, and was called to order by the President.

Prayer by the CHAPLAIN.

The journal of yesterday was read and approved.

Reports of Special Committees.

Mr. TRAER submitted the following report from the Special Committee on the Basis of Representation, which was laid on the table and ordered to be printed.

Mr. President—The committee to whom was referred that part of the constitution relating to the basis of representation, have had the same under consideration, and have instructed me to report the following section as an amendment to the article on legislative department, as reported by your standing committee. Insert after section 36 as follows:

Section 1. The House of Representatives shall be based upon the several counties of the State in the following manner: Provided, that no representative district shall contain more than four organized counties, and shall be entitled to one Representative. Any district containing one or more counties, and having a number of inhabitants equal to one-half of the ratio fixed by law, shall be entitled to one Representative, and any one county containing in addition to the ratio fixed by law, a fraction of one-half of that number shall be entitled to one additional Representative. Provided farther, that no floating district shall hereafter be formed.

Sec. 2. At its first session under this constitution, and at every subsequent session, the General Assembly shall proceed to fix the ratio of representation, and also to form into districts as above provided, those counties which will not be entitled to a Representative singly under the provision of the preceding section.

All of which we respectfully submit,

J. C. TRAER, Chairman.

Mr. Solomon dissents from the above in the fact that he prefers a strict county representation, which will secure at least one member to each county.

First Messenger—James Hawkins.

Mr. SKIFF. I desire to make a simple statement. I dispatched just now one of our messenger boys to the Post Office for my mail matter; but he came back with the information that our mail messenger, Mr. Hawkins, would not let him have my letters. I move, therefore, that Mr. Hawkins be dismissed.

Mr. PARVIN. Will the gentleman from Jasper state whether any reasons were assigned for this refusal?

Mr. SKIFF. He sent the boy back saying that he would attend to his own business. I do not think that a messenger has any right to treat the members of the convention in this manner. If we have messengers or other officers, they should treat us with courtesy.

Mr. HARRIS. The punishment the gentleman from Jasper proposes may be a little too harsh, and I think he had better modify his motion so as to provide for a reprimand from the President. I have been treated myself somewhat discourteously by the principal messenger.

Mr. SKIFF. If the gentleman from Appanoose will move a resolution to that effect, then I will not press my motion.

Mr. HARRIS. I move then, that Mr. Hawkins be reprimanded by the Chair, and informed what his duties are.

Mr. WARREN. I myself have sent to the Post Office, and this messenger has refused to let the boy I sent, have my mail matter. I think that some person more responsible than this young man, should occupy the position he holds.

Mr. SKIFF. I dislike to treat this young man harshly, but I do not like, when I send a messenger specially to the Post Office, to be treated in this uncourteous manner.

Mr. CLARKE, of Johnson. Let us at least be just. If this boy has done anything wrong, he ought to be punished in some way; but it may be a question whether he deserves to be dismissed, without being at least heard. Perhaps this lad, being the oldest we have here, has taken it as his part of the duty to attend to the Post office, the most important of any of the duties devolving upon the messengers. I understand from the other boy, that he was at the Post Office getting all the mail matter, and he may have thought it his duty to keep it in his charge, rather than entrust it to a smaller boy. Acting as a body here, let us learn the facts fully and endeavor to do what is just. I do not wish to screen this boy from punishment if he has done wrong.

Mr. PARVIN. I second the motion made by my friend from Appanoose, [Mr. Harris,] that this messenger be reprimanded by the President.

Mr. YOUNG. If the messenger is responsible for the delivery of the mail here, and goes to the Post Office for it, I do not conceive that he has any right to give it up there to any one else. Here is the proper place for its distribution. This messenger is responsible for the delivery of this mail, and the other boys have nothing to do with it. I think the motion of the gentleman from Jasper, [Mr. Skiff,] is altogether unnecessary.

Mr. HARRIS. I am always disposed to act kindly where gentle measures are sufficient to answer the purpose. It would probably answer the object of the gentleman as well, if this messenger is informed by the President what his duties are.

Mr. EDWARDS. I would not like to see this boy expelled; but I have heard a great deal in regard to his impertinence, and I can bear testimony to it, in some respects, myself. I hope that he may be reprimanded, as it will do him good.

Mr. HALL. I move to lay the subject upon the table for the present.

The question was then taken and the motion agreed to.

Miscellaneous.

Mr. CLARKE of Johnson, asked leave of absence for Mr. Traer till Tuesday next, which was granted.

Mr. TRAER. I move that the consideration of the report of the Committee on the Legislative Department, which was made the special order for this morning, be postponed till next Tuesday. The reasons I have for making this motion are these: I expect to be away, as the Committee are aware, to-morrow and Monday, and I am very anxious to be here when that report is considered; another reason I have for postponing the farther consideration of this report is, that I desire to offer the report of the Special Committee on the "Basis of Representation" which I submitted this morning as an amendment to the report of the Standing Committee, which was made the special order. I hope, therefore that it may be postponed till Tuesday next, and then both of these reports can be considered at the same time.

Mr. HARRIS. I hope that the motion made by the gentleman from Benton will prevail.—This matter of representation is one in which he takes a great deal of interest; and knowing his anxiety upon this subject, I hope that the Convention will extend this courtesy to him.

The question was taken and the motion of Mr. Traer was agreed to.

Mr. TRAER. I now move that we take up the report of the Committee on State Debts.

The question was taken and the motion was agreed to.

State Debts.

The PRESIDENT. The Secretary will now proceed to read the report of the Committee on State Debts by sections, with the amendments reported by the Committee of the Whole.

Section 1st was then read as follows:

"The credit of the State shall not, in any manner, be given or loaned to, or in aid of any individual, association, or corporation; and the State shall never assume, or become responsible for, the debts or liabilities of any individual, association, or corporation."

There being no amendments offered to this section, the second section was then read as follows:

Limits of State Indebtedness.

"The State may contract debts to supply casual deficits or failures in revenues, or to meet expenses not otherwise provided for; but the aggregate amount of such debts, direct and contingent, whether contracted by one or more acts of the General Assembly, or at different periods of time, shall never exceed the sum of one hundred thousand dollars; and the money arising from the creation of such debts, shall be applied to the purpose for which it was obtained, or to repay debts so contrated, and to no other purpose whatever.

The amendment made by the Committee of the Whole to this section was to strike out "one hundred thousand and insert in its place two hundred and fifty thousand.

Mr. CLARKE, of Johnson. If the yeas and nays are called I shall vote for two hundred and fifty thousand dollars, but I want a still larger sum. I will move to amend the amendment by striking out two hundred and fifty thousand, and inserting in lieu thereof five hundred thousand, and upon that I call the yeas and nays.

The question was then taken by yeas and nays, and the motion was not agreed to, yeas 8—nays 23, as follows:

Yeas—The President, Messrs. Bunker, Clarke of Henry, Clarke of Johnson, Ells, Gower, Skiff and Young.

Nays—Messrs. Ayres, Clark of Alamakee, Day, Edwards, Emerson, Gibson, Gillaspy, Gray, Hall, Harris, Johnston, Marvin, Palmer, Parvin, Patterson, Peters, Price, Scott, Solomon, Traer, Warren, Wilson and Winchester.

Mr. PALMER. When this question was under discussion before, I said that I would not object to a small increase of the State indebtedness; but gentlemen are putting a very different construction upon this whole article, from what I have put upon it. It seems, that several gentlemen upon this floor, whose opinions are entitled to great weight, consider this section to include only the bonded indebtedness of the State. I do not so understand it. I think if we are to put this construction upon it, and it is to go forth to the world as the construction of the convention that framed the article, it will be a violation of what I consider to be the spirit and intent of the whole article. I think there are various ways of increasing the indebtedness of the State, without making it a bonded indebtedness. I desire that the State shall be limited in some manner. I believe, that the school fund may be, and probably has been, obtained, under the action of the last legislature, without increasing the bonded indebtedness. I would ask the gentleman from Johnson (Mr. Clarke) if that is not the case.

Mr. CLARKE, of Johnson. I do not concur in the construction put upon this section, by the chairman of the committee, (Mr. Wilson). I think that the language of the report is broad enough to cover any indebtedness; consequently I do not agree with that gentleman in the construction he has given to the language there used.

Mr. PALMER. If this question should ever be raised before the courts, I do not think that they will put the construction upon the article, which has been put upon it by some gentlemen upon this floor. However, if there be any latitude given to the construction of this clause, I shall go for the least amount of indebtedness. If gentlemen put such constructions upon this section as to make it discretionary with the State to create indebtedness beyond the amount prescribed, provided, they do not create a bonded indebtedness, then I shall change my vote a little from what I at first intended.

Mr. HARRIS. I would ask what the question is?

The PRESIDENT. It is upon agreeing to the amendment made in committee of the whole, to strike out the words, "one hundred thousand," and insert the words, "two hundred and fifty thousand."

The question was then taken by yeas and nays, and it was agreed to—yeas, 18—nays, 14, as follows:

Yeas—The President; Messrs. Bunker, Clarke of Henry, Clarke, of Johnson, Clark, of Alamakee, Edwards, Ells, Gower, Gray, Hall, Marvin, Parvin, Patterson, Seely, Skiff, Traer, Winchester and Young.

Nays—Messrs. Ayres, Day, Emerson, Gibson, Gillaspy, Harris, Johnston, Palmer, Peters, Price, Scott, Solomon, Warren and Wilson.

The following amendment, made in committee of the whole, on motion of Mr. Hall, was then read as section three:

"That all losses to the permanent school, or university funds of this State, which shall have been occasioned by the mismanagement, or fraud of the agents, or officers controlling and managing the same, shall be audited by the proper officers of the State, and the amount so audited shall be a permanent fund against the State, in favor of their respective funds, upon which ten per cent. interest, payable semi-annually, shall be paid for school and university purposes. The amount of liabilities so created, shall not be accounted as a part of the indebtedness authorized by the second section of this article."

Mr. CLARKE, of Johnson. I concur in the main with this provision. I think the gentleman from Des Moines (Mr. Hall,) urged the adoption of this amendment upon the ground that the State was a trustee for this fund, and as a trustee she ought to be responsible for it. While I concur in that view, I see no reason why the State, as a trustee, should pay any higher rate of interest than any other trustee. In our courts, a trustee is liable for no higher rate, than the legal rate, six per cent. I move, therefore, to strike out "ten per cent.," and insert "six per cent."

Mr. GOWER. I am willing that the State shall assume the school fund, but I am not willing that she shall assume all losses that may arise to the university, deaf and dumb, and blind asylums, and other public institutions. I look upon the school fund as a most sacred possession, to be guarded with the utmost care.

Mr. SKIFF. The amendment of the gentleman from Johnson (Mr. Clarke,) meets my approbation in part. I would prefer, that the same rate of interest should be established here, as would be in the case of any other person borrowing money of the school fund. The State puts men into office to control and manage this school fund, and I think it is proper for the State to make this fund good at all times. When we borrow any money of the school fund we have to pay ten per cent annually; and whenever any officer, controlling either the school or university fund, shall squander it, the State should assume the loss, and pay ten per cent. annually. If an amendment would be in order, I would move to amend the amendment of the delegate from Johnson, (Mr. Clarke,) so that it shall read "ten per cent. annually," instead of "six per cent. semi-annually."

Mr. CLARKE, of Johnson. The gentleman from Jasper is evidently laboring under a misapprehension. This is not a proposition to authorise the State to borrow of the school fund. This proposition is based upon the idea, that this State is a trustee for this fund, that she holds it for the minors of the State; and I can see no reason, in case her agents should prove faithless in the discharge of their duties, and squander this fund, why the State should pay any higher rate of interest, than any other trustee in the same position would. I desire to be just to this fund as well as to the State; and it seems to me, that if the State guarantees the principal of this fund, with such rate of interest, as is provided for in the cases of other trustees, she is doing as much as ought to be required at her hands.

Mr. SKIFF. I wish to make a simple explanation of this matter, as I understand it. If I employ any one to manage certain funds which are entrusted to my care, and he squanders them, I am obliged to make those funds good to the depositors. The State is, to a certain extent, the trustee of the common school and university funds. If the State selects improper officers to manage these funds, and they should squander them, I would have the State make up those losses, and pay ten per cent. interest, just as any individual would be compelled to do under like circumstances.

Mr. CLARK, of Alamakee. I am opposed to placing this provision in the constitution, upon the ground that has been previously taken by some members of this Convention, in regard to other proposed amendments to the Constitution; that is, that we shall be legislating too much here. I believe that the Constitution should lay down certain general principles of fundamental law, but not attempt to curtail the right of legislative action, farther than is necessary to secure individual rights. This principle has been contended for strenuously by members who now urge the adoption of this provision. I am opposed to this special legistation upon questions, which, more properly, should be left by the Constitution to our legislative bodies.

Then again, I am opposed to this provision as a matter of principle. I do not believe that the State should become responsible for any losses to these funds, in consequence of the fraud or mismanagement of its agents. I do not believe that we should incorporate such a provision in the constitution, unless we provide here the whole legislative machinery of putting safeguards around these funds. They should be the subject of legislative enactment, and the legislature can put around them such safe-guards as they see fit. They can make their agents liable, and provide by law for ample security. If this provision be adopted as it is now offered, it will extend to all the funds in the State, which are now, and will continue to be, under the control, to a certain extent, of the counties. It seems to me that it is not right to make the State liable for any losses to these funds, which are sustained in consequence of any fraud or neglect of these officers, when those losses may be all provided for by putting ample protection around these funds, by an act, which will require such security as will always guard against loss. It is an unsettled question yet, in the case of treasurers and tax-collectors, where money which they have collected has been stolen from them, or has been lost without their fault, whether these officers would be liable for this money. It seems to me, it would be more proper that there should be a provision in the constitution, to protect against that class of losses, than against this class of losses, where the State has the power of protecting itself against them.

But gentlemen say that this provision is intended for the benefit of minors and persons who have no voice in the legislative department of the State. Although they have no voice in reality in this respect, yet their guardians have, and they are interested, and in reality, feel the responsibility when they are called upon to act. Consequently, those persons for whose benefit this fund is intended, have in reality a voice here, through both their natural and legal guardians. The minors' interest will always be protected, although they have no voice here. It is true, that literally speaking, the benefit to result from the fund is intended for minors; but when we look at this question in its true light, we find that they are represented here by that class of persons, who will protect that fund, because every guardian is under a natural obligation to protect the rights of his ward. That obligation leads him directly to adopt those measures which will assist him in carrying out the obligation which rests upon him. For these reasons, I am opposed to the incorporation of any such principle in our constitution as is now proposed.

Mr. HALL. I did flatter myself that this proposition would meet with the favor of this Convention. But so far as the principle was concerned, I hoped it would be the unanimous voice of the Convention, to make the State responsible to the rising generaion for a faithful and honest keeping and application of its school funds. I indulged the hope that every member of the Convention would be willing to adopt a provision, requiring the State, which the General Government has made a trustee to carry out her benevolent designs for the education of the youth of the State, to assume the same liabilities in regard to that fund and its beneficiaries, that would be required in the case of private individuals. I did entertain the expectation that we would take a position here, that would tend to elevate the tone and character of our institutions, and make our State Government respected and honored by the people for its honesty and integrity, and thus set a worthy example for them to follow. It strikes me, in making our fundamental law here, we should endeavor, as far as we can, to adopt those great principles of national right and justice, which exert such a powerful influence in shaping and moulding the character of any people. And in view of this consideration, I ask gentlemen to adopt this provision, and declare here in the Constitution, that the school fund in the hands of the State, shall be guarded with the same care as it would be if it were in the hands of individuals; and that the State shall be subjected to the same responsibilities. I supposed, when I introduced this provision, that this would be the uniform feeling of the Convention, I felt that there was a necessity for such a provision; that the mode of managing the school fund was at present intolerably defective; that it had been carelessly and indifferently managed, and that great losses had already accrued to the fund. The simple proposition now made is, that if the State shall manage the fund so as to lose any portion of it, it shall assume the loss. I think this is a just and equitable proposition; and I did hope it would receive the universal sanction of the Convention.

So far as the amount of interest is concerned, I first proposed *six* per cent. annually, but accepted the amendment offered by the gentleman from Cedar, [Mr. Gower,] making the interest ten per cent., and payable semi-annually. I do not believe it is necessary to pay the interest semi-annually, and I hope the section will be changed in that respect; but I shall insist upon the payment of ten per cent. interest annually.

Mr. YOUNG. I wish to offer an amendment to provide that the rate of interest "shall not be less than six per cent." That will leave it in the power of the Legislature to make provisions according to the necessities of the case; and if they see fit to raise the interest to ten per cent. they can do so.

Mr. WILSON. It seems to me that this section reaches back, and includes all the defalcations that have already taken place.

Mr. CLARKE, of Henry. I would ask of the gentleman who introduced this proposition if it was his intention to have it to cover all the cases of defalcation which have hitherto occurred?

Mr. HALL. That was not my design.

Mr. CLARKE, of Henry. I am in favor of this proposition even if that construction be put upon it. If an agent of the State has caused a loss to the school fund through his mismanagement, whether by misfortune or other causes, the State should make it good, and preserve the fund inviolate and undiminished. The State should not allow it to be squandered and dissipated through its own agents. I do not see how this provision can work any injustice to any portion of the State, because the people all derive a direct benefit from the school fund, more direct than through any other fund, which they are called upon to supply even by direct taxation.

Mr. JOHNSTON. In regard to this matter of interest, I would say that the sum of ten per cent. is not fixed in the old Constitution. The interest accruing to this loan fund can be regulated by the Legislature, and they can establish such rates as they please.

The question was then taken upon the amendment of Mr. Clarke, of Johnson, to strke out the words "ten per cent.," and it was agreed to.

The question was then taken upon the amendment offered by Mr. Young, to fill the blank with the words "not less than six per cent," which was agreed to.

Section four was then read as follows:

"In addition to the above limited power to contract debts, the State may contract debts to repel invasion, suppress insurrection, or defend the State in war; but the money arising from the debts so contracted, shall be applied to the purpose for which it was raised, or to repay such debts, and to no other purpose whatever."

No amendment being offered thereto,

Section five was then read as follows:

Raising Taxes.

"Except the debts specified in the second and third Sections of this Article, no debt shall be hereafter contracted, by, or on behalf of this State, unless such debt shall be authorized by some law for some single work or object to be distinctly specified therein; and such law shall impose and provide for the collection of a direct annual tax sufficient to pay the interest on such debt, as it falls due, and also to pay and discharge the principal of such debt, within twenty years from the time of contracting thereof; but no such law shall take effect until at a general election it shall have been submitted to the people, and have received a majority of all the votes cast for and against it at such election; and all money raised by authority of such law, shall be applied only to the specified object therein stated, or to the payment of the debt created thereby; and such law shall be published in at least one newspaper in each county, if one is published therein, throughout the State, for three months preceding the election at which it is submittted to the people."

The amendment of the Committee of the Whole to this section, was to strike out in the first line, the words "the second and third sections," and insert between the words "debts" and "specified" the words "herein before."

The question was taken, and the amendment was agreed to.

No further amendment being offered,

Section six was then read as follows:

Repeal of Tax Laws.

"The Legislature may, at any time, after the approval of such law by the people, if no debt shall have been contracted in pursuance thereof, repeal the same; and may at any time, by law, forbid the contracting of any further debt, or liability, under such law; but the tax imposed by such law, in proportion to the debt and liability which may have been contracted in pursuance of such law, shall remain in force, and be irrepealable, and be annually collected, until the proceeds thereof shall have made the provision herein before specified, to pay and discharge the interest and principal of such debt and liability."

Mr. WILSON. I beg leave to call the attention of the Convention to the last clause of this section. It seems to me, by the only construction which I can give it, that this law could not be repealed, or this annual tax could not be collected until this debt was paid, although the State might be able, through other sources and with other means, to discharge the debt.

I move, therefore, to strike out all after the word "until" and insert the following: "the principal and interest are fully paid," so that it would then read,—

"But the tax imposed by such law, in proportion to the debt and liability which may have been contracted in pursuance of such law, shall remain in force, and be irrepealable, and be annually collected, until the principal and interest are fully paid, &c."

The question was taken and the amendment was agreed to.

There being no other amendments offered to this section, the seventh section was read as follows:

"Every law which imposes, continues or revives a tax, shall distinctly state the tax, and the object to which it is to be applied; and it shall not be sufficient to refer to any other law to fix such tax or object."

There was no amendment offered to this section.

Certain Debts not Binding.

Mr. CLARKE, of Johnson, offered the following as an additional section:

Sec. 8. Every contract made or entered into which, either directly or indirectly, violates the provisions of this article, shall be null and void.

Mr. PALMER. The section now offered by the gentleman varies a little from that offered by myself in committee of the whole. I shall favor its adoption, and I hope it may prevail. Some members seem to entertain the idea, that if this article be violated by contracting a greater debt than is herein prescribed, still the contract is good and valid. I do not look upon constitutional provisions in this light. I consider it useless to put restrictions into the constitution, if they may be violated, and such violation can be held as law in spite of the constitution. I believe that the article as it stands in the present constitution of this state, has virtually been violated. Let every person understand that if he loans this State any money, in violation of this article, the State and the people of the State, do not hold themselves responsible for the repayment of that money.

I think that if any officer of this State violates this provision, by borrowing more money than the constitution allows him to borrow, he is, perhaps, liable, in law, individually, for the amount, and the State will not be liable. I think it is more necessary that this provision under consideration should be inserted in the constitution since the discussion which has taken place upon this subject. Refuse to insert this provision in this article, and it will go forth to the world through our debates that the convention refused to do so, upon the ground that this article might be violated with impunity. If our courts in deciding upon this question should have any doubts upon this subject, they might refer to the debates to ascertain the sense of the Convention in refusing to insert such a clause; and they would there find that some gentlemen understood that debts contracted for an increased amount beyond that herein set forth, would be still binding upon the State, and the decisions of the courts would perhaps be made in accordance with such understanding.

Mr. PARVIN. I cannot concur with some gentlemen, who have expressed their views upon this subject; neither can I see in those views much good morality. I consider that where the agents of this State go beyond their constitutional right, the innocent dealer should not be the sufferer. It cannot be supposed that every man with whom the State deals, knows everything about its constitutional law and its requirements. I hold that this responsibility should rest upon those who negotiate these loans, and exceed their authority in making them; and I hold that the state should be responsible to the innocent holder of these bonds, and the innocent purchaser should not be the loser. I am opposed to any such amendment as that offered here, as it will throw the responsibility where it ought not to rest—upon the innocent contractors, and not upon the State. Let the State be responsible, and let the state hold her agents responsible, for going beyond the limits which we here prescribe.

Mr. TRAER. There is one point upon which I would like to have some light before I vote. As I understand the amendment, it will apply to all debts contracted contrary to the provisions of this article in the constitution. There is a difference of opinion, as I understand it, upon this subject between gentlemen who are good judges of law, and upon whose opinions I am accustomed to place great reliance. I understand the gentleman from Des Moines [Mr. Hall] to say that if the State should issue her orders upon the treasury, payable one day after date, or payable at sight, they would not be included within the debt contemplated in this section. I desire to know before I vote upon this question, whether this repudiation, which is contemplated, is going to reach debts of that kind; or whether it is intended only to reach debts of a bonded character. If it is contemplated that this State will repudiate the payment of her orders drawn upon the treasury, I shall oppose the amendment. If it is only contemplated to reach bonded debts, contracted in violation of the constitution, I shall be willing to vote for it.

There is one objection, however, which I think may be urged against this amendment, and that is, that its adoption will open the way for litigation. There being a variety of opinions as to the construction to be put upon this part of the constitution, the question may arise, what is a violation of it? A man may honestly hold the opinion, when he has bought up bonds of the State, that they are not issued in violation of this provision in the constitution; and yet when the courts consider that matter, they may decide that they are issued in violation of it, and consequently the innocent purchaser would be the sufferer.

I desire to know more about this subject before I vote; and I would be glad to hear the expression of other gentlemen upon this subject.

Mr. HARRIS. Since this question was mooted yesterday, I have given it some little attention. I have not been able to satisfy myself that the conclusion to which I then came was incorrect. I wish gentlemen to bear in mind that when parliamentarians so sharp as my friend from Johnson [Mr. Clarke] are seriously opposed to any measure, they load it down under the guise of friendship, with such amendments as will make it odious to its friends, and by that means accomplish indirectly what they could not do directly. It seems to me, that I can see that kind of pretended guardianship for the State treasury, in the anxiety of the gentleman to get this amendment fastened upon the constitution.

It does look to me as if it really meant repudiation, if the agents of the State should exceed the jurisdiction that might be given to them. As I said before, if you can contrive any method by which you will make the agents of the State either civilly or criminally liable, for any mismanagement on their part, I will go as far as any gentleman in supporting it. I hope that those gentlemen who are in favor of leaving the constitution as it now is, so far as the subject of State indebtedness is concerned, will not be frightened from their propriety by this sharp practice of the gentleman from Johnson [Mr. Clarke.]

Mr. CLARKE, of Johnson. Perhaps the definition of the word "sharp," down in the "Hairy Nation" has a different signification from what what it has here. If it bears the same signification there as here, it seems to me that it is uncourteous ever to use it in a body of this character. It is true that I am opposed to this whole section, and for the plain and simple reason, that I regard it as clap-trap, a tub thrown to the whale, the people. I am opposed to it principally for the reason that it will result in no benefit and have no effect. If the Legislature disregard it, the people are bound to pay the debts legally contracted. Yet while I am opposed to this section, and while I submit to the voice of the convention in placing it here, I desire to have it improved, if it can be.

A question has arisen here as to the meaning of the word "debt," and it has elicited nearly as much discussion as that in the discussion in the Massachusetts convention upon the word "loan." Yet it is a question to be considered, and if we look at section two of this article, we will see that there is some ground for a difference of opinion upon this question between legal gentlemen upon this floor. Section two provides, that

"The State may contract debts to supply casual deficits or failures in revenues, or to meet expenses not otherwise provided for; but the aggregate amount of such debts, direct and contingent, whether contracted by virtue of one or more acts of the general assembly, or at different periods of time, shall never exceed the sum of two hundred and fifty thousand dollars."

If I owe a man a sum of money, it matters not to me whether it is in the shape of a note bearing interest, or whether it is an account, which bears interest after six months. It is a debt in both cases. The word debt, as used here, applies, it seems to me, to every kind of indebtedness, for which the State may become liable. I think there is a question here which does leave room for litigation, if we should insert in this constitution, as has been suggested by some members, a provision by which the State may be sued. I think the word debt applies to the indebtedness of the State in any shape or form; and standing here without limitation or qualification, I think such would be the decision of our courts

The object of this provision is not to repudiate. I suppose if even a debt were illegally contracted, public opinion would say pay it. But the object is this: If the agents of the State violate this provision of the fundamental law, where it says that such contracts shall be void, why it follows, as a matter of legal consequence, that so far as they exceed their authority, they cease to be our agents, and would themselves be personally liable under their contract. If this would be the legal construction of this provision, it seems to me that it effects the very object which the gentleman from Appanoose (Mr. Harris,) said he had in view in his arguments upon this subject, to act as a check upon the State officers, and make them liable in case they exceed their authority. I understand it to be a well settled principle of law everywhere, that if an agent of a State makes a contract, which exceeds his authority, and the party contracting has no notice of it, the principal is discharged from liability, and the agent makes himself personally liable. If you want to tie up the hands of the State officers so that they shall not exceed a certain amount of indebtedness, then declare here what will be the legal effect of this provision. Allow me to say, I am not seeking to defeat this proposition.

Mr. HARRIS. If the amendment should be so modified that any contract shall be void, made by a party who shall know that the debt created by that contract will increase the amount of State indebtedness beyond the limit prescribed by the constitution, then I would have no objection to it.

Mr. CLARKE, of Johnson. Will not the putting this provision in the constitution be a notice to the parties, that they must keep within certain limits in making contracts with this State?

Mr. HARRIS. It might be sufficient if he had possession of the State archives to see what had been already contracted.

Mr. CLARKE, of Johnson. He can have them if he desires. Now if this article is to go into the constitution it should be made effective. It is charged, and avowed upon this floor, that the present article of the constitution has been violated, that a larger amount of indebtedness has been incurred than the constitution authorizes. Then what is the effect of such an article in our constitution? Do our people save a single dollar by it, or are they protected from the burden of indebtedness? Not at all. Then if gentlemen are so anxious to protect the State from these burdens, let them do that which will accomplish their object, and not merely throw a tub to the whale, not merely put in something that is of no account, except to enable them to cry out to the "dear people"—see what we have done to protect you.

Mr. WILSON. Suppose this amendment is adopted, and the legislature goes on and creates a debt that exceeds the limits prescribed in the constitution, and orders an appropriation to pay the excess; where will the responsibility rest?

Mr. CLARKE, of Johnson. I will tell the gentleman where the responsibility will rest; it will fall upon the proper parties, in this way: If the legislature does pass a law increasing the amount of State indebtedness beyond the limits prescribed in the constitution, the State officers, if they are honest in the discharge of their duties, will refuse to pay the appropriation thus made. And then the party contracted with can sue out this writ of mandamus to compel the officer to audit his account, and the question will be brought before the courts, and tested practically as it should be.

Mr. WILSON. Another question; suppose this amendment is not adopted, and we do not provide in the constitution, in so many words, that all such debts shall be void, but merely provide that the State shall not contract debts to an amount exceeding two hundred and fifty thousand dollars. Then suppose the legislature does contract a debt of three hundred thousand dollars. Would not the effect be the same? Will the amendment now proposed make this article any stronger than it would be without that amendment?

Mr. CLARKE, of Johnson. I will answer the gentleman by referring him to the facts as they are said to exist under our present constitution. It is argued here that the amount of State indebtedness now exceeds the limitation prescribed in the present constitution; yet no officer has acted so as to bring the matter before the courts for their decision. But if you put this amendment in the constitution, and make the officer a *particeps criminis* in the act, he will hesitate before he acts as he has now done.

Mr. WILSON. But is there any difference in the legal effect of the two propositions?

Mr. CLARKE, of Johnson. I think there is a difference in this way: This amendment will be a notice to the world, and especially to the officers of the State, who are disposed to be honest, and to live up to the constitution, and will lead them to refuse to pay, and thus force the other party to sue out a writ of mandamus to test the matter.

Mr. WILSON. Is not the provision, that the State shall not contract a debt exceeding two hundred thousand dollars a notice to all the world?

Mr. CLARKE, of Johnson. Certainly: but the officers of the State will be likely to argue from the past, and say, no complaint was made before, and we will pay this time.

Mr. HALL. I do not believe this amendment is at all necessary, and I would not say one word upon the subject, if we could leave the constitution in the same condition in which it now stands. The gentleman from Benton, (Mr. Traer,) and others here, most confidently assert, that the present constitution has been violated. Now I really do not know whether it has been or not. I would be unwilling to make such an assertion until I knew all the facts involved, and the manner in which the liability, that now exists, has been created.

As to this amendment, if it is to have the effect claimed for it by the gentleman from Johnson, (Mr. Clarke,) I shall most certainly oppose it. We have been in the habit of making our appropriations two years in advance, and there has never been a time when there was money enough in the treasury to meet all those appropriations. The legislature passes a law which creates a liability against the State, though the time for the payment of the money has not arrived. There never can be a liability against the State, unless as authorized by the legislature of the State, acting under the constitution. Whenever they pass a law authorizing the creation of a debt against the State, the constitution goes along with that law, and you have to decide whether there is a conflict between the law and the constitution, and the constitution must be the controlling and governing law.

But here is a provision proposed, which gentlemen say will have this effect: if the legislature make appropriations at any time, or make contracts by which the liability to be created against the State, will cause the total amount of the indebtedness of the State to exceed the sum of two hundred and fifty thousand dollars here provided for, then the whole contract is void. Or to illustrate the matter in another way: if the State, speaking through its legislature, should come to the conclusion that it would be a proper policy and a wise measure to build two or three or more of the charitable institutions, which this State so much needs, and which would prove so beneficial to the State, and they enter into a contract by which they agree that buildings to cost half a million of dollars shall be erected, there will be a contract exceeding the amount here prescribed, which the State in the progress of these improvements will be called upon to meet. This amendment, it seems to me, will prevent the State from doing any such thing as that. There may perhaps be a debt of two hundred and fifty thousand dollars already against the State, funded and paying interest. And you will be prevented from anticipating the resources of this State, and creating liabilities for the future.

It is this tying down the hands of a great and growing State, like the State of Iowa, and putting shackles upon what would otherwise become a giant, that I consider as totally unnecessary. I do not apprehend any danger of any very mischievous violation of the constitution. There may be a technical violation, an accidental, an unwitting violation of it, but not a *bona fide* violation. And there has not been—I assert for the honor of my State, that there cannot have been—a wilful violation of the constitution. If the legislature has passed the boundary assigned them by the constitution, it has been accidentally done, as bodies and individuals are all liable to do. But I am not afraid to trust our legislature with this matter as it now stands. I do not want this cramping section to go into the constitution, and I hope the convention will not adopt it. This article is well enough as it stands, and sufficiently binding; and the attention of the world is sufficiently called to it.

Mr. WILSON. It seems to me that the wording of this second section settles this matter at once. It reads:

Sec. 2. The State may contract debts to supply casual deficits or failures in revenue, or to meet expenses not otherwise provided for; but the aggregate amount of such debts, direct and contingent, whether contracted by virtue of one or more acts of the General Assembly, or at different periods of time, shall never exceed the sum of two hundred and fifty thousand dollars; and the money arising from the creation of such debts, shall be applied to the purpose for which it was obtained, or to pay the debts so contracted, and to no other purpose whatever.

Now suppose the state should go on and contract, as the gentleman from Des Moines, [Mr. Hall,] has suggested, to a greater amount than there is money on hand to pay; she has a perfect right to do so, because she bases her contract upon the probable amount of her revenue. If at the end of the year, or of the series of years, through which the contract runs, the revenue should prove insufficient to pay the liabilities under this contract, the State may then contract a debt to the amount of two hundred and fifty thousand dollars, over and above what may be derived from the revenue. But she cannot go beyond that revenue except for that amount of two hundred and fifty thousand dollars. I think that is the effect of this second section, and the amendment supported by the gentleman from Johnson, [Mr. Clarke,] will be wholly without effect.

Mr. MARVIN. I would ask if it is the intention of the supporters of this amendment to make it compulsory upon the State to repudiate? It strikes me that such is the drift of the argument, to prevent the people from paying any debt that may be contracted beyond the limits here prescribed.

Mr. GILLASPY. I certainly supposed that this question was settled yesterday, in Committee of the Whole. Not being possessed of the legal ability of some other gentlemen upon this floor, I was, for one, satisfied to depend upon the opinions of those gentlemen, as to the legal and proper construction of the report of the committee as amended, and of the present constitution, and also as to what was a funded debt.

But I only rose to perform a duty to the honorable and distinguished gentleman from Benton, [Mr. Traer,] and to return to him the thanks of myself and the democratic party, for the incessant attacks he has been making upon the Governor of this State and the late General Assembly. I do this with feelings of the utmost kindness towards the gentleman.

Mr. PALMER. It appears to me that the arguments which have been brought forward here against this amendment, might be made with equal propriety and force in favor of inserting a clause in this article, providing that all contracts made in violation of this article shall be binding and of full force; and that the article is only intended as a guide to the State officers, as merely directory, and not compulsory and imperative. That is the way I look upon the matter.

The gentleman from Muscatine, [Mr. Parvin,] and other gentlemen here, argue that if we declare all contracts void which may be made in violation of this article, we may inflict great hardships upon some innocent creditors of the State. That may possibly be so. But I consider that if persons loan money to the agents of the State, it is their duty to look at the record. Hardships exist and occur in the common transactions of life. If a private individual purchases an estate of another party, he purchases it at his own risk; in other words, he is bound to learn what the records are. The public records are considered in law as a notice to him. If there is a mortgage on the estate, or a judgment against it, the buyer is bound to ascertain that fact. If he buys it without examining the records, he must abide the consequences. It would be only carrying out the same principle in transactions with the State, that now exists with regard to transactions between individuals.

The question then recurred upon the amendment, which was read as follows:

"Every contract made or entered into, which either directly or indirectly violates the provisions of this article, shall be null and void."

Upon this question, Mr. CLARKE, of Johnson, called for the ayes and nays, which were ordered accordingly.

The question being then taken by yeas and nays, the amendment was not agreed to, yeas 13, nays 18, as follows;

Yeas—The President; Messrs. Bunker, Clarke

of Henry, Clarke of Johnson, Ells, Emerson, Gower, Palmer, Peters, Price, Scott, Winchester, and Young.

Nays—Messrs. Ayres, Clark of Alamakee, Day, Edwards, Gibson, Gillaspy, Gray, Hall, Harris, Johnston, Marvin, Parvin, Patterson, Seely, Skiff, Solomon, Traer, and Wilson.

Mr. SOLOMON. Before passing from this subject, I would like to give my reason for voting in the negative. I did so because I believe the constitution has the same validity and vitality without this provision as with it. I believe the judiciary can intercede and prevent the violation of the constitution, as was done in the State of California lately.

On motion of Mr. CLARKE, of Johnson,

The article reported by the Committee on State Debts, as amended by the convention, was then ordered to be engrossed and read a third time.

Order of Business.

Mr. HARRIS moved that the convention take up the report of the committee on incorporations, which was agreed to.

The Secretary then proceeded to read the report, as heretofore published,

Mr. CLARKE, of Henry, informed the convention that the printed reports, that had been previously distributed, were not correct. The correctly printed reports were printed on but one side of the page.

Mr. HARRIS, moved that the report be referred to the committee of the whole, and be made the special order for this afternoon, at 2 o'clock.

Mr. CLARKE, of Henry. I move to amend that motion, so that this report shall be made the special order for Wednesday next. I have been requested to make this motion, by gentlemen here, who wish to examine this subject carefully, and prepare themselves to consider it at some stated time.

Mr. HALL. I would make one enquiry, and that is, whether gentlemen here expect to live to be as old as Methusaleh? We are asked to put off to the fourth week of our session, the consideration of the most important question that can come before us, when it will be discussed for a week or ten days. I think this is all wrong, and I hope the motion to make this report the special order in committee of the whole this afternoon at two o'clock will be agreed to.

Mr. CLARKE, of Henry. I take the same position in regard to this matter to day, that I took in regard to another motion the other day. That is, that when any gentleman asks for further time to examine any question, no matter how well prepared I myself may be to consider it, I will be willing to accede to his request. That is the reason I have submitted this motion. As for myself, I am as well prepared now to go into committee of the whole, upon this report, as I will be at any other time. It is not for my own gratification that I make this motion, but I do so at the earnest request of members of this body, who desire to have the consideration of this matter postponed until next Wednesday.

Mr. GILLASPY. It is well known here, that I took the ground the other day against postponing matters that come before us for consideration. I am anxious to go home, but if we continue to postpone every subject that comes up here for the consideration of this convention, we will never do anything. I had supposed that every gentleman here was prepared to consider this subject.

I must confess, however, that no two lines of this report, in the copies laid upon our tables, correspond with the copy read by our Secretary. I consider such printing as this, a great outrage upon members of this convention. I have examined the report which was laid upon my table, and have read it carefully; but the one read by the Secretary contains different provisions, and an additional section, from the one I have examined. Now, if the State is expected to pay for this kind of printing, and members are to take such specimens of reports home with them, there to examine them, and try to come to some correct conclusion as to what should be their action upon them, I should like to know it now. I am opposed to any such thing. I have examined this old report, and endeavored to prepare myself to act upon it, but it seems I did not have a correct copy. If any gentleman has a correct report, I should like to get hold of it.

Mr. CLARKE, of Henry. The gentleman can have the copy I have.

Mr. GILLASPY. I am much obliged to the gentleman from Henry (Mr. Clarke) for his kindness. I will examine the report and be ready to act upon it by two o'clock this afternoon. I hope this subject will not be postponed any longer than till this afternoon. I think that we should have been through by this time and ready to go home. But if we are to postpone every report that comes before us, till some future day, we will not get away from here until grass-growing time. I am opposed to the motion of the gentleman from Henry. He is too kind, and too amiable a gentleman. He seems to be willing to take the responsibility of making this motion to postpone, to oblige some other gentleman upon this floor. If I were in his place I would let them make the motion for themselves.

Mr. ELLS. I am one of those who desire this postponement, and for this reason: I consider this article of the Constitution as the most important article that remains unacted upon, and one in which the people of the State take more interest than any other. I want time to examine it and deliberate upon it. I find there is difference of opinion among those who are in favor of a banking system. I think we should be allowed opportunity to consult upon this matter. I came here as much for the purpose of preparing a provision of the Constitution to authorize the legislature to pass banking laws, as for any other purpose. I confess I am not prepared to vote upon the provisions of this report. I am of opinion now that I shall support the main features of it, but there are some features here to which I object, and I want to have time to examine further and see if I am right in my opinions upon this subject. I hope, therefore, that farther time will be given for this question.

It may be that the gentleman from Wapello [Mr. Gillaspy] has business to transact at home of more importance to him than the work before this Convention. If so, I have no doubt he can be excused from attending here. I think we can get along without him. [Laughter.] But I think we should so do our work here that the people of the State may be satisfied with it. What is our private business in comparison with the framing the fundamental law of this State? Let us do that well, and not complain of the length of time it may require.

Mr. HARRIS. I must say with my friend from Wapello (Mr. Gillaspy) that my cogitations and calculations in regard to this report have been completely upset by what I learned concerning it this morning. I find that the printed copy laid upon my table does not contain as many sections as the one read by the Secretary. But still I am not disposed to be quite so sharp in my strictures as that gentleman seems disposed to be. The mistake may have been unintentional upon the part of the printer. I do not know how that may be.

I made a request the other day to have a report postponed, and stated that I was entirely unprepared to consider it at that time. I urged the postponement as trongly as I could, but my arguments did not seem to have much effect upon gentlemen here, for my request was not granted. and I suppose gentlemen can prepare themselves as well to consider this report now, as I could the other day to consider the one then before us. Besides, if we go into Committee of the Whole, there will be a great deal of discussion, and all the points will be considered in every view in which they can be presented.

Mr. GILLASPY. I will say to my friend from Davenport [Mr. Ells] that I have business at home of far more importance to me than the three dollars a day that I get here. However, I will say that I came here to do the business of the State, and to discharge what I conceived to be my duty, and to endeavor to meet the expectations of the people of the State, and particularly those who sent me here, And I undertake to say that, so far as I know the expectations of the people all over the State, it was the universal opinion that this Covention would get through their work here at the farthest, within three weeks from the time it assembled here.

I do not expect to have to ask the convention to excuse me in order that I may go home and attend to my business there. I represent a constituency that have a deep interest in the action of this convention; and not only in that, but also as to the money that the delay of this convention is going to draw from their pockets. Hence, I am in favor of progressing as rapidly as possible; and it does seem to me, if gentlemen would pay more attention to the business of this convention, and let outside matters alone, they would be better prepared to act when subjects come up here for their consideration, and not get up here and ask for the postponement of matters that have been before committees where they have made speeches upon them and have examined them.

Mr. ELLS. I wish to know a little concerning the opinions of those who sent me here, in regard to this report. I intend to return to Davenport to-morrow, if I have an opportunity. I have sent over one of these reports already, and I want to know what my people think about it. It is a little stronger than I expected it would be, and I want to consult with them about it. I want time to consider this subject before I am called upon to act here in regard to it.

Mr. CLARKE, of Henry. I will say in explanation of the fact of this report being brought in here in this imperfect state, that it was made out in a great hurry, a portion of it being written out here while the business of the convention was going on. It was handed to the printer with directions that a proof should be furnished, and also that it should be printed only on one side of the sheet. That was not done, from some cause, and there were also found some typographical and other errors in the printed copies brought up and distributed. It was shown to the printer, and he at once offered to set up the type and reprint the report, without any extra charge to the State. The gentleman from Wapello [Mr. Gillaspy] can therefore relieve his mind from any anxiety in this particular.

In regard to his other remark advising me to leave to other gentlemen, who desire this postponement, the responsibility of the motion, I will say that I do not consider that there is any great responsibility involved in the matter.— There are certain gentlemen here who, no doubt, can discharge their duty to their consciences, and to the people of their respective districts without much trouble or preparation. And they are those who have nothing to do but to come in here and vote against amending the constitution in any particular. They are one idea men, and that one idea is to stick fast to the old landmarks. Such gentlemen do not need much time or preparation, so long as they have a copy of the old constitution before them. All they have to do is to turn to any particular article in it, and find out whether the one reported by the committee is exactly like that one, with every "t" crossed, and every "i" dotted, as in the old constitution. If it is not, they can then vote against it. But other gentlemen here are not so happily situated. Some of us represent constituencies who desire and expect that changes will be made; and we desire to give some examination and deliberation to all propositions made here for such changes in the present constitution. We desire to be prepared to defend and advocate them, if they are worthy; and if they are not, to oppose them and prevent their adoption.

It is due to ourselves and to the people at large, and not merely to those gentlemen who ask for this postponement, that we should allow every member here full time to prepare himself to act understandingly upon every report that comes before us. I have too much confidence in gentlemen to refuse this request. If they come to me and say they are not prepared to consider any particular subject, and want further time for deliberation, I will not charge that they are influenced by any ulterior design, that is not proper, much less will I insinuate that they are only desirous to increase the time for which they will receive their three dollars a day! I believe we are all as anxious to go home as the gentleman from Wapello [Mr. Gillaspy]; but we will not get home any sooner by attempting to drive these matters through in a hurry. More obstacles will be thrown in the way by members who have not examined these matters, and matured their opinions upon them, than if we allow them time to get ready, and come in here and vote without discussion.

Now in regard to the reference the gentleman from Wapello (Mr. Gillaspy,) has made to outside matters, which gentlemen may attend to here. I do not think it is courteous, or kind, for us to attempt to follow every member about the city, and see how he uses up his time, whether attending lectures, or doing anything else, when he is not required to be present upon committees, or in convention. It is an espionage which is simply unmanly and contemptible. I think all such references as these are improper, and out of place, and I trust they will cease. If gentlemen say they are not prepared to act in regard to any matter before us, no charge that they have been misspending their time should be made here, and go upon the record. Let every man stand by what he says himself. If he says he is not prepared, let that be the end of it.

The motion I have submitted, is simply a motion to make this report the subject for consideration on a particular day. If the gentleman from Wapello is prepared to consider it now, then he need not devote any more attention to it, until it again comes up, but attend to something else. If any gentleman is not prepared, then he can prepare himself in the meantime, and perhaps then be able to vote without discussion, or discuss it with benefit to others.

Mr. MARVIN. I should be decidedly opposed to postponing this report, had all the members been furnished with correctly printed copies of it. I do think that some of us have reason to complain that we have been furnished with imperfect copies of this report, while others have had corrected copies. Indeed, I have been unable to obtain several reports that have been made. They were not on my desk, and when I enquired for them, none were to be had. It seems to me, that when the committee discovered that this printed report was full of errors, and had been laid upon our tables in that shape, and we had been conning them over, and preparing ourselves to act upon what we thought was the subject to be considered, they should have made the corrections, and furnished us with perfect copies before this time. And again, I suppose it is in the power of every member here to speak an hour or two hours upon every question that comes up; that takes up much more time than is at all necessary. And I would suggest, that perhaps it would be better for members to give merely a synopsis of what they have in their minds, and not tell us all they know every time they speak.

Mr. HALL. I am one of the most accommodating men in the world, provided I can be accommodated myself. (Laughter.) Now if gentlemen wish to check this work of constitution making, I am willing to adjourn for two or three months, and go home, and then come back again. But I am unwilling to lose my time for gentlemen to undergo a schooling, during our deliberations, and thus extend our session. Let us adjourn, and go home for one, two, or four weeks. I do not care how long, even if it be six months, if it is necessary. But while we are here, I do not like to be continually postponing all these matters upon which we are to act. I hope this convention will proceed regularly with its business. If we progress slowly, let us at least do something. I hope this report will be made the special order for this afternoon, and let us go on with it as well as we can. Its consideration will take up time enough at the best.

Mr. CLARKE, of Johnson. I am willing to divide the responsibility of asking the postponement of this subject, with the gentleman from Henry, [Mr. Clarke,] and the gentleman from Scott, [Mr. Ells]. While I am as anxious that this Convention should adjourn at the earliest possible period, and perhaps I am making as many and as great sacrifices in attending here, as any member upon this floor, I am free to confess that I prefer to sacrifice my own interests to the object of discharging my duty here properly. And I am also free to confess that I am not now prepared to act upon this subject, for the simple reason, that we are kept here from early morning till late at night, and when I leave here, I am too exhausted and worn out to examine these reports. It is very easy for gentlemen upon the other side to act upon this matter, and press subjects to a consideration, for whatever may be the shape of the Constitution we send out they can leave this hall and say to the people, whether justly or not, that they are not responsible for it.

Now, I do not misstate the fact, when I say that this question of corporations had more to do with the calling of this Convention, than any other question that may come before us. And the majority here should consider well upon it, for while gentlemen upon the other side are pressing us to its consideration and saying they are prepared to act, they have openly avowed, from time to time, their opposition to all banks. And their organ in this city, comes out here with instructions to them upon the subject. They may, therefore, well assert to us, that they are prepared to vote now, because they will vote against this report. But it is not so with the majority here, who are in favor of it; and they require cautious and prudent investigation to enable them to make such provisions as they would be willing to sustain before the people.

I am not disposed to be hurried into this thing; I want to know what I am doing. I do not feel like saying whether I will vote for or against this provision. Perhaps I may change my opinion in regard to some portions of it. And I desire to say once for all, that it is not very material whether we sit here ten days longer, or twenty days. But it is a matter of importance that we should make such a Constitution, that, if approved by the people, it will contain principles and provisions that will advance and promote their interests and happiness. I think if we should shorten the length of our daily sessions here, so as to have more time to deliberate and compare our views with one another, and have time to go to our rooms, as the gentleman from Wapello [Mr. Gillaspy,] says he does, and examine these reports, we would make faster work than we do now, by meeting at 9 o'clock and adjourning at 12 o'clock, or after, and meeting again at 2 o'clock and sitting until five for six o'clock. I think the three dollars a day I earn here is the hardest earned money I have made for many years. I go home at night fatigued physically and mentally, and I think the State has no right to require this of me. I want an opportunity afforded to all members here, to compare their views upon this matter, so that they may be able to act systematically and understandingly.

Mr. GILLASPY. I do not desire to be considered captious upon this question, and I want to say now, once for all, that I do not intend by any remarks I may make, to wound the feelings of any gentleman here. I am one of those who always intend to act courteously and respectfully to every one, if I know how. But it does seem to me that this question of postponement turns upon one point alone. The gentleman from Henry [Mr. Clarke,] says that he has been requested to move that this report be postponed, and made the special order for Wednesday next. The gentleman from Johnson [Mr. Clarke,] says he is willing to favor that motion because the gentleman from Scott [Mr. Ells,] desires it. And the gentleman from Scott says he desires it that he may be able to go home and consult his constituents about it. All I have to say to that is, that if the people of Scott county will send a representative to this convention who has not lived long enough in the county to understand their opinions and wishes upon this most important question, then the wheels of this convention ought not to be clogged to accommodate Scott county alone.

I want to say for the benefit of the gentleman from Johnson, [Mr. Clarke,] that I stand here responsible only for what I say myself, and not what the newspapers of this city, or of any other portion of the State may say. And I want to say further, for the benefit of the gentleman from Johnson, that I have always been a bank man. I am in favor of a well-regulated system of banking. My democratic constituents are in favor of such a system, and I am in favor of giving them the right and opportunity to go into banking, if they see proper to do so. And I believe the party to which I belong have always been willing to consult the sentiments and wishes of the people.

I have no desire to hasten this matter unreasonably. But here we are now on the Friday of the third week of our session; and here is a matter that has been referred to a committee, consisting of a majority of the party of the gentleman from Johnson, [Mr. Clarke,] and the chairman of that committee, [Mr. Clarke of Henry,] is a member of his party. They have had this matter in committee, and have examined and matured it there, and have brought this plan forward for the action of the convention. It does seem to me that at the end of the third week of our session, gentlemen ought to be prepared to take up some of the reports of our committees, and act upon them, unless it is to be expected that we are to stand still here till the gentleman from Davenport, [Mr. Ells,] can go to Scott county and consult the views of his constituents upon this question. However, if that is the sense of this convention, I will submit.

Mr. HALL. I wish to make the record correct in one matter, by stating that our average daily sessions have been between four and five hours. Now I do not think that is excessively laborious upon our part, and I do not think gentlemen need complain here for want of time for preparation. I think if we only remain in the convention five hours a day, and allow nineteen hours out of the twenty-four, for preparation and other purposes, we are very liberal to ourselves.

The gentleman from Johnson, [Mr. Clarke,] appeals to his party here in regard to this matter. He wants members to go into caucus, or something of that kind, to settle the disposition to be made with the minority upon this floor. Whether they are to be retained at will as prisoners here or not, will depend upon how the majority may feel about the matter. Now this may be right in the estimation of the gentleman from Johnson, [Mr. Clarke]; but if he was in our place, he would doubtless think it wrong, and would take the ground that gentlemen should vote upon their convictions of duty, independent of all ties of party. But if it is to be understood that we are to be ruled over in that way, I should be glad to know it, in order that I may be satisfied whether or not this is to be a party convention, in which the views of the minority are not to be consulted or regarded. I would like to know in advance how this will be. I do not know that that information would alter my course at all here, but it would alter my present judgment and impressions in regard to the subject.

I am anxious to go on. If gentleman are not

ready, then as I said before, let us adjourn over until Monday week, and go home and see our constituents.

Mr. EDWARDS. It appears to me that the time of this convention is taken up too much in the settlement of preliminary questions. If we wish to facilitate the action of the convention, let us take up our business in order, go into committee of the whole, compare views there, and then we will be prepared to act when we come into convention again. I am just as well prepared to go into committee of the whole upon this report this afternoon, as I should be a week hence, if we should postpone it that long. Now, if we go into committee of the whole, and compare views upon this subject—and this is one of the questions upon which we will probably deliberate several days—I venture to say we can dispatch it in a shorter time, than if we were to postpone it. I can see no good reason for a postponement at this time.

Mr. CLARKE, of Johnson. There are special orders for Monday and Tuesday of next week, and that is the reason we propose Wednesday.

Mr. BUNKER. If I am not mistaken, we have a special order for to-morrow, one for Monday, and one for Tuesday. Now, if we take up this subject this afternoon, we must interfere with the special orders for Saturday, Monday, and Tuesday, or else drop this subject without having made any progress in its consideration. It is not probable that we will get through with this subject of incorporations in one evening. It is most likely that it will occupy this convention, in committee of the whole, for two or three days. It appears to me, that it would be but throwing away this afternoon to consider this report during that time. And even now, from the time this motion to postpone was first made, we have occupied nearly an hour in discussion. Certainly this is not a very great economy of time. If the motion had been adopted at once, and the time had been fixed for the consideration of this subject, we could have gone on, and taken up other reports, in their order, upon which we were prepared to act this afternoon. For instance, there is the report of the committee on amendments to the constitution, upon which every member is now prepared to act, that could probably have been disposed of this afternoon.

Mr. WINCHESTER. I would enquire what is the special order for to-morrow morning? I was not aware that there was one.

Mr. CLARKE, of Johnson. There was some reason for making the others special orders for Monday and Tuesday.

Mr. WILSON. My impression now is, that the report of the committee on the judiciary department was assigned for consideration to-morrow.

Mr. JOHNSTON. It was merely ordered to be printed, but not made the special order for any day.

Mr. YOUNG. Is there any special order for to-morrow morning? If we cannot have to-morrow to consider this report of the committee on incorporations, I shall vote to make it the special order for Wednesday next. If we can, then I will vote for making it the special order this afternoon.

The PRESIDENT. The chair is not aware of any special order for to-morrow.

The question was upon the motion to postpone the further consideration of the report of the committee on incorporations, and make it the special order in committee of the whole for Wednesday next.

Upon this question, Mr. GILLASPY called for the yeas and nays, and they were ordered accordingly.

The question being then taken by yeas and nays,

The motion to postpone was not agreed to, yeas, 11—nays 19, as follows:

Yeas—The President, Messrs. Bunker, Clarke, of Henry, Clarke, of Johnson, Clark, of Alamakee, Ells, Gower, Gray, Scott, Traer and Wilson.

Nays—Messrs. Ayres, Day, Edwards, Emerson, Gibson, Gillaspy, Hall, Harris, Johnston, Marvin, Palmer, Parvin, Patterson, Peters, Seely, Solomon, Warren, Winchester and Young.

Mr. CLARKE, of Johnson, moved that the report be made the special order for to-morrow morning.

Upon this motion, Mr. HALL called for the yeas and nays, and they were accordingly ordered.

Mr. TRAER. I hope the gentleman from Des Moines [Mr. Hall] will withdraw his call for the yeas and nays. We are certainly taking up time uselessly in calling the yeas and nays upon unimportant questions.

Mr. HALL. If this matter is postponed until to-morrow morning, we will have nothing left us to do this afternoon, and we may as well spend our time in taking the yeas and nays.

The question being then taken by yeas and nays, upon the motion to postpone until to-morrow morning, it was not agreed to—yeas, 9—nays, 21, as follows:

Yeas—The President, Messrs. Bunker, Clarke of Henry, Clarke, of Johnson, Clark, of Alamakee, Ells, Gower, Gray and Wilson.

Nays—Messrs. Ayres, Day, Edwards, Emerson, Gibson, Gillaspy, Hall, Harris, Johnston, Marvin, Palmer, Parvin, Patterson, Peters, Scott, Seely, Solomon, Traer, Warren, Winchester and Young.

The question then recurred upon the motion of Mr. Harris to make the report the special order in committee of the whole, this afternoon at two o'clock, and being taken was agreed to.

On motion of Mr. EDWARDS,

The Convention then took a recess until two o'clock, P. M.

EVENING SESSION.

The Convention assembled at two o'clock, and was called to order by the President.

Incorporations.

The Convention then proceeded to consider in committee of the whole [Mr. Traer in the chair] the report of the Committee on Incorporations.

Mr. CLARKE, of Henry. I desire, Mr. Chairman, to say in regard to the report now before this convention, that the committee who made it are desirous that every section and provision of it should be considered carefully and critically by this committee; and they court suggestions by way of amendments to it. They are not at all tenacious in regard to this report. They do not consider it a particular "bantling" of theirs at all. They have endeavored to take advantage of all the lights to be obtained from the various provisions in other Constitutions upon this subject; from suggestions made to them while acting in committee, and from resolutions sent to them for their consideration, to make out a report that would embrace all the best features for constitutional restrictions in reference to incorporations. And without attempting, too far, to legislate in the matter, they have especially endeavored to lay before this Convention certain constitutional provisions, which shall operate as beneficial restrictions upon the legislature in their enactments of banking laws for the State.

I will say, that I believe each individual member of that committee desires to stand here perfectly free, as any member of this body, to make any suggestions, to move any amendments, or to take any position in regard to this matter that he may deem advisable, and as his own convictions of right and duty may suggest. No member of this committee considers himself as bound by this report, and they, therefore, are prepared to enter upon its consideration, with the same freedom as any other member of this body.

I, therefore, propose that this committee now proceed to consider this report, by sections, so that any member here may have an opportunity to make such suggestions, in regard to each section, as he may think proper.

Miscellaneous.

The first section of the report was then read as follows:

"No corporations shall be created by special laws, but the general assembly shall provide by general laws for the organization of all corporations hereafter to be created, except as herein provided.

Mr. PALMER. I move to amend this section by inserting before the word "provided" the word "otherwise," so that the clause will then read, "except as herein otherwise provided."

The question being taken, the amendment was agreed to.

No further amendment being offered to that section,

Section two was read as follows:

"Corporations may sue and be sued, and their property shall be liable to taxation in the same manner as natural persons; and the liabilities, powers, privileges, and duties of stockholders in corporations may be fixed and defined by law, subject to the provisions hereof.

Mr. HALL. I move to amend the first clause of this section by striking out the word "their" before "property," and inserting "the;" also insert after the word "property" the words "of all corporations for pecuniary profit;" so that portion of the section will then read "Corporations may sue and be sued, and the property of all corporations, for pecuniary profit, shall be liable to taxation in the same manner as that of natural persons."

The question being taken, the amendment was agreed to.

No further amendment being offered,

Section three was then read as follows:

"The State shall not become a stockholder in any corporation, nor shall it assume or pay the debt or liability of any corporation, unless incurred in time of war for the benefit of the State."

No amendment being offered to this section,

Section four was read as follows:

"No political or municipal corporation shall become a stockholder in any banking corporation, directly or indirectly; nor in any other corporation, or corporations to an amount exceeding, at one time, two hundred thousand dollars; nor shall the bonds, or other evidences of indebtedness of any municipal or political corporation be issued or granted, or its credit loaned, directly or indirectly, or pledged as security, to an amount in the aggregate exceeding two hundred thousand dollars, at any one time."

Municipal Corporations Holding Bank Stock.

Mr. HALL. It seems to me that there should be an amendment made to this section, authorizing municipal corporations to become interested in the payments of debts that may be due them by banking corporations. I would, therefore, move to insert after the words "indirectly," where it first occurs. the words "except for the payment of debts due them." This will then authorize municipal corporations to receive bank stock for debts due them.

Mr. CLARKE, of Henry. That amendment will defeat the whole object of this provision; for, if it is adopted, then all that municipal corporations would have to do, would be to get the banking corporations in debt to them, and then receive bank stock in payment of those debts.

Mr. HALL. If they should get banks indebted to them in any way, and they could not get paid except with bank stock, it would be very unjust to deprive them of this opportunity of being paid.

Mr. CLARKE, of Henry. Let them have the stock sold, and receive the proceeds.

Mr. HALL. Why not let them receive the stock, and sell it afterwards?

Mr. CLARKE, of Henry. They might prefer to hold it, and thus defeat the object of this provision.

Mr. SCOTT. I do not exactly understand the object of this amendment. If the gentleman from Des Moines (Mr. Hall,) will explain it more fully, perhaps I may be persuaded to go for it. But I do not fully understand the object of it at this time.

Mr. HALL. My object is to authorize both political and municipal corporations to receive, if necessary, bank stock in payment of debts due them from banks.

Mr. WILSON. It seems to me that this would be a very dangerous amendment to put in here, because, under it, a county could, at any time, become a stockholder in banks, and engage in banking, and then the same liabilities would attach to the county, as an artificial person, as to a natural person: and it would thus become responsible for double the amount of stock held by it. All the county would have to do, would be to get the bank in debt to it, then take their stock in payment, and go on with the banking operations. It would be better to have the stock sold, and the proceeds given to the county, for it would get as much for it before, as after it had become a stockholder, and had assumed the responsibilities attached to the State.

Mr. HALL. I do not apprehend any such consequences from this amendment as gentlemen suggest may result from its adoption. I think that when you authorize corporations to sue and be sued, to create debts and become creditors, you should not deprive them of any of the facilities for collecting debts that a natural person has. I do not think they would necessarily become stockholders in these banks. They might hold the stock without occupying the relation of stockholder; hold it merely as property to be disposed of. However, I will withdraw my amendment for the present.

The amendment was accordingly withdrawn.

City and County Indebtedness.

Mr. SKIFF. The first part of this section reads as follows:

"No political or municipal corporation shall become a stockholder in any banking corporation, directly or indirectly; nor in any other corporation or corporations to an amount exceeding, at one time, two hundred thousand dollars"

I was in hopes this convention would submit this matter as a separate clause to the people, and let them vote upon the proposition, whether or not cities and counties should be permitted to take stock in any corporation. There is at present quite a rage for counties to embark in these railroad and other corporations. And it has become a question, whether this matter may not have a deleterious effect upon the interests of cities and counties who engage in it. Our governor, in his message, has called the attention of the people of the State to this subject. And since that message has become pretty generally read, the people have began to think about the matter, and a great many, who were before in favor of voting loans to railroad companies, have had their opinions somewhat modified. I would prefer to have this portion of the section amended, so as to have submitted to the voters of this State, as a separate clause, whether or not municipal corporations shall be permitted to take any stock whatever in incorporations for internal improvement. I bring this matter forward with a view of getting the opinions of members here upon this subject. I, therefore, move to strike out all after the word "indirectly," where it first occurs, to the word "dollars" inclusive. There is no power now conferred upon municipal corporations to vote loans.

Mr. MARVIN. If this section is left in the shape proposed by the gentleman from Jasper (Mr. Skiff) it would leave to the legislature the power to grant this privilege to cities and counties. If the gentleman wishes to prevent cities and counties from issuing their bonds, a clause to that effect should be inserted here.

Mr. SKIFF. At the suggestion of the gentleman I will modify my amendment so as to strike out all of the words "corporation or corporations," so the section will then read "no political or municipal corporation shall become a stockholder in any banking corporation, directly or indirectly, nor in any other corporation or corporations." If the people desire to have their municipal corporations take stock, I would let them have that privilege. But I would submit the question to the people, where it will be thoroughly canvassed by them, and the voters of the State will perhaps vote more understandingly upon this subject than we would here. I am not fully apprised of the views of the people upon this subject. It is a new subject, and I would be unwilling to vote here that municipal corporations might or might not take stock, for I do not know exactly what the people think about it. I would rather have the question submitted to them for their decision.

Mr. GOWER. I observe that the fifth section of this report reads as follows:

"It shall be the duty of the General Assembly to provide by law for the restraint of municipal and political corporations in regard to assessments. taxations, borrowing money, contracting debts, issuing bonds, and loaning their credit, so as to prevent, as far as possible, unessary burdens and unjust taxation, and frauds.

Now if we adopt this amendment as moved by the gentleman from Jasper [Mr. Skiff] all that will be left of the fourth section will be "no political or municipal corporation shall become a stockholder in any banking corporation, either directly or indirectly, nor in any other corporation or corporations." There it stops. It seems to me that the fifth section will cover all that will be left of the fourth section, and we had better strike out the fourth section entirely.

Mr. JOHNSTON. There appears to be some indisposition on the part of this committee to go into an examination of this report of the Committee on Incorporations. As one of the members of that committee I beg leave to say that this matter was brought before the committee by a resolution of inquiry referred to them by the Convention. The committee came to no definite conclusion upon this subject. They were divided among themselves, and their report has been brought here that the committee might receive the suggestions of members of this Convention.

The object of this section as is well known to members of this body, is to restrict county or State loans to an amount not exceeding two hundred thousand dollars, for railroad purposes. That is really the intention of this section. So far as I am myself concerned, I believe this system of city and county loans is a great evil and should be restricted. It is of very little consequence, I presume to my colleague [Mr. Patterson] and myself, because the people of the county of Lee have already contracted a debt of four hundred and fifty thousand dollars, and that is as much as they will desire to have. It is for gentlemen who live in new counties, where no loans of this kind have been voted, to give us their views upon this subject.

I have not clearly made up my mind how I shall vote upon this question. If it were entirely a new question, if no loans had been made by any counties, I believe I should take ground against the whole system. But as some counties have involved themselves to some extent, and as other counties desire to come forward and carry out the plans of internal improvement, for which these loans were made, it may perhaps present itself to us with more claims for favorable consideration. It would be well for delegates from the several counties to give us their views in relation to this subject.

The proposition of the gentleman from Jasper [Mr. Skiff] as I understand it, is to keep the matter out of the Constitution and submit it as a separate clause to the people. If so, he should move to strike all out after the word "indirectly" where it first occurs. That would then leave this other question an open one.

I have nothing special to say upon this matter. I desire to hear from the other members of the convention, and I am willing to go as the majority of those who come from new counties may desire. We have done our duty so far as voting loans in the old counties is concerned, and therefore do not feel particularly interested in this matter.

Mr. HARRIS. I am, perhaps, one of the members that the gentleman from Lee [Mr. Johnston,] wishes to hear from upon this matter.

I must say that the doctrine advocated in the message of Governor Grimes is not new to me. It is rather an old-fashioned notion that I have entertained for a great many years. I am very much in the position of my friend from Lee as to what I should do in this matter. This question has been discussed a great deal in the part of the State from which I came. But there has never been any occasion yet to test the real feelings of the people in regard to this matter. It has its advocates and its opponents, but I have no good information by which I can tell which side has really the majority. I would myself, in any county, vote against any stock being taken by the county in these corporations; but I would much prefer to let the matter go to the people for them to decide upon it. I am myself prepared to vote at any time against these loans, but I am not prepared to say that the majority of my constituents feel as I do about it. Individually, I am opposed to such a thing, but I would prefer to have it in such a shape that we could practically test the wishes of the people upon it.

Mr. AYRES. Standing here, Mr. Chairman, as a delegate from Lee county, and Van Buren county, in part, it matters very little, as my friend from Lee [Mr. Johnston] says, with my constituents, what action shall be taken in relation to the matter now before us, as we are already deeply in debt. But inasmuch as I am a representative of Van Buren county, in part, where a definite expression has been given upon this question, I feel it to be my duty to my constituents to state my disapprobation of this section as it now stands. I feel inclined, not only as the representative of Van Buren county, but as an individual, to oppose the latitude given by this section to public indebtedness.

If it be in order, I would move an amendment to the amendment; to strike out all after the word "corporations," to the end of the clause; and also strike out all after the word "indirectly," where it last occurs, so that the section will then read:

"No political or municipal corporation shall become a stockholder in any banking corporation, directly or indirectly, nor in any other corporation or corporations; nor shall the bonds or other evidences of indebtedness of any municipal or political corporation be issued or granted, or its credit loaned directly or indirectly."

I am one of those who have had their fingers scorched with this thing of county and city indebtedness, and whenever anything is proposed which can place a public debt upon the county where I live, I feel it my indispensable duty to urge my fellow citizens to vote against it. I was formerly a citizen of the State of Pennsylvania which became deeply involved in debt, and the tax to pay simply the interest upon that debt was almost unendurable. When I came to this State I hoped to be free from anything of the kind. But I perceive an effort here to place me in a similar position to that in which I was placed in the State of Pennsylvania.

It may be said that there can be but little danger to be apprehended from counties taking stock in corporations of this kind. But I regard it as only a different form of public indebtedness. And I will say just here, that before I was elected to the office which I have now the honor of holding, I was told by individuals who were deeply concerned in the matter of railroading, that it was their object and design to have the constitution so framed by this convention, that they might have an opportunity at the next session of the legislature, of getting the State to assume all these county debts, and thus fasten upon the State as a public debt, all the debts of the counties. Gentlemen here, who have made the calculations, may perhaps be able to tell what those debts amount to at the present time. I have been told that the amount is about eleven millions of dollars. Who here desires to see such a debt cast upon the State? I do not, for one.

Mr. JOHNSTON. I understand that these debts of cities and counties now amount to about six or seven millions of dollars.

Mr. AYRES. I have made no calculations myself. But I have been informed since I have been here that they amount to about eleven millions of dollars. And who know but in a single year from the present time, these debts may not be increased to six or seven millions more.

Mr. JOHNSTON. Six or seven millions is amply sufficient.

Mr. AYRES. So I think myself. And for these reasons I think it would be well to adopt the amendment I have indicated. My object is to prevent the loaning of the credit of the counties and cities, as well as their taking bank stock.

Mr. HALL. I would state to the gentleman from Van Buren, [Mr. Ayers,] that I have drawn up an amendment, which, perhaps will meet his views fully as well as the one he has offered, and I think the gentleman from Jasper, [Mr. Skiff,] will accept of it. I propose to strike out all after the word "indirectly," where it first occurs and insert the following:

"And no county or other political or municipal corporation, shall in any manner become stockholders in any corporation; provided that cities having a population of five thousand inhabitants, and a taxable property exceeding two million dollars, may become stockholders and loan their aid to incorporations for internal improvement, to an amount not exceeding ten per cent. on the assessed value of property for State and county purposes."

Mr. HARRIS. Does that amendment cut off counties? We are not much troubled with city corporations up our way.

Mr. HALL. I would state that since these projects for building railroads have engaged the attention of the people of this State, and the rest of the country, it has been my good or bad fortune to have some little connection with some of them; and I have had some little opportunity of witnessing the effect of this kind of subscriptions upon these improvements. These projects flourished to a considerable extent in Ohio prior to the adoption of their present Constitution. They saw the evil as we see it here now, and put a provision in the Constitution against it.

If counties could subscribe stock in railroad and other internal improvement corporations, and could get the benefit of the stock that they subscribed, and a full consideration for the debt which they created against the people of their respective counties, there would be no great objection to the system. But the whole system is one, which to my mind, must in the end prove ruinous: I can see no escape from that result. County subscriptions, in most instances where they are made in this State, will become a total loss to the counties, and the people must, for a long time, be taxed to pay the debt thus created. This must flow from the very conditions of things; from the very necessities of the case.

Let us suppose an instance. Here is a railroad about to be built. The people along the proposed line of the railroad are not people of much wealth, and cannot subscribe, individually, a very large amount for the purpose of constructing this road. And if they had to build this improvement by private subscription, to be raised within the State, the task would be a hopeless one, one that the most sanguine person would abandon in despair. But another expedient has been resorted to, and that is to get the people of the counties along the line of this projected road, by a vote, to enact a debt against their respective counties; in other words, to get the counties' promises to pay fifteen, twenty, or thirty years after date, and in this manner create a debt against each county, for which it receives an amount in stock of the railroad company, dollar for dollar, equal to the amount of bonds in issue. Now, where a private stockholder subscribes he pays for his stock, dollar for dollar, in the currency of the county. Yet the bonds of the counties are received by the company at par, the same as money is received from the other stockholers.

The money received from the private stockholder can be used at once to buy materials and pay for labor upon the road. But they can do nothing with the bonds received from the counties, so long as they hold them as bonds, and they must resort to the eastern market and sell them; endeavor to find somebody who, looking at the interest, which is generally from eight to ten per cent., will be willing to invest his money in them. The agent of the road hunts up a broker, and shows the bonds to him. He looks at them and sees they are county bonds. What will you sell them for? Says the agent; What will they bring? Why, says the broker, from sixty-five to seventy, perhaps seventy-five cents on the dollar. The bonds are sold, and the broker is paid one or two, or more per cent. for selling them. The average of the sales of the bonds of the counties of this State is not more than sixty-five cents on the dollar. Thus a very considerable percentage is eaten up in negotiating these bonds, and about sixty-five cents, perhaps not over sixty cents goes into the treasury of the company, for every dollar of the bonds issued by counties, while for the stock subscribed by individuals they receive dollar for dollar. Thus by this county subscription, forty per cent. is added to the cost of the road, over and above the actual means the company obtain for its construction; you issue forty per cent. more stock than the road actually costs. A man is a fool who takes stock in a railroad company, when county stock, which realizes only sixty cents on the dollar, is received upon an equality with his stock for which he pays the par value in money.

And you never can have a stock-built road in Iowa while this system is continued. The result is that you get just enough of county stock and private subscriptions to start the matter going. The counties are liberal in their subscriptions, for every voter looks to having the road go through his own property and increasing its value, and he is therefore willing to vote almost any amount to get the road built. The road goes on in its construction. Nominally one-half enough is raised to build it, while in fact only about one-third enough is realized. When that is used up, a mortgage is made upon the road, which includes in its expense of construction all the county bonds that have been issued. Bonds are issued upon that mortgage, and sold generally for about seventy or eighty per cent. The means of construction then include what has been realized from the sale of the county bonds, and also that obtained upon the railroad bonds secured by this mortgage. We then go on and complete the road. We have the road, it is true; but there is a mortgage on it, which, as soon as it is due, is foreclosed, and perhaps the road is sold to satisfy it. That has been repeatedly done in Illinois and Ohio, and will continue to be done, until all the roads built upon this kind of stock are swallowed up entirely, and the mortgagees of the stock will become the owners of the road, and not a picayune will be left with which to pay the interest upon the stock which the counties obtained for their bonds.

I think this certainly will be the result in Iowa. We are building a road from Burlington west. Des Moines county has issued her bonds for one hundred and fifty thousand dollars worth of stock; and other counties have done the same thing. What is the result? The road has been mortgaged, and we must pay the interest upon that mortgage semi-annually, for upon a failure to pay, the mortgage will be foreclosed, and the whole road will be sold out; and Des Moines county will find herself indebted to the amount of one hundred and fifty thousand dollars, for which she will receive no return. We look forward to that result. We say now that the road is cheap enough, if we do lose all we have subscribed; but when the people are called upon to pay, it will take a great deal to make them think so then.

Now when we see that this system requires this enormous sacrifice, in order to enable the road to use our bonds, we should take some step to stop it. There will be enough of indebtedness incurred by the time this constitution goes into effect. And I do hope, therefore, that we will allow no counties to take stock hereafter. We may give the privilege to the cities, because they are compactly peopled, and when the tax-collector stares you in the face, you will be cautious how you incur this indebtedness. I am willing to allow cities to go into debt to the amount of ten per cent. upon their property. But I would prohibit counties from doing so in future.

Mr. EDWARDS. My mind is not fully made up in regard to the course I shall take upon this question, especially when I see gentlemen who represent counties upon the river, where they have commenced a system of railroads, and where they have already incurred indebtedness to a very great extent, going against this provision. I know that this policy presents many difficulties to our view; and yet I know that there are many benefits to be derived from it also. I could name many counties within my own knowledge, where they have derived benefit from the adoption of this principle. If a road is a paying one, the county contracting the indebtedness for building it, will derive a benefit from it. I know of several counties in the State of Indiana that contracted indebtedness for building railroads, and before their bonds became due, the roads paid large dividends, and the counties disposed of their stock at a large premium. I have known cases on the other hand, of counties taking stock in roads that did not pay, where the stock greatly depreciated, and could not be sold for more than twenty-five dollars on a one hundred dollar share. I have conversed with a great many citizens from the counties, where they have suffered this kind of loss, especially those that were far distant from market, and the universal expression of opinion has been that they could afford to lose what money they had invested in the road for the sake of having it built. They said the facilities for getting to market, and the rise in real estate would amply compensate them for all the losses they had sustained in consequence of the depreciation in the stock. In my section of the State the people are anxious to have the road that runs through the county represented by the gentleman from Des Moines, [Mr. Hall,] extended still farther west, but what the feelings and views of the people are upon this question of taking stock, I am not prepared to say. If the road should be a paying one, it would be for the interest of the people in that county to make this connection with the road at Burlington, at as an early day as possible.

Another consideration which has prompted the people where I live to build this railroad, and is used as an argument in behalf of the counties taking stock, is the fact that in my county about one-half of the land is owned by non-residents, a class of men who contribute nothing to the advancement and prosperity of the State. While the pioneers who have settled the State have done much in developing the resources and increasing the value of the lands of the State, these non-residents have done nothing in this respect; and this mode of county subscriptions is the only way to reach them, and make them pay their proportion towards those improvements, which will contribute so much to the interest of the State. There is much force in that view of the question.

I would prefer, as an individual owning lands in my section of the State, rather to pay my proportional part of the cost of building a railroad, than to become a private stockholder in a road, to build up the interests of these non-residents. If the State, as we have already agreed, is not to take any interest in any incorporated company, and if we are to prevent any county from aiding in the prosecution of these works of internal improvement, then the question is narrowed down entirely to this, whether we shall have railroads or not. If the people, individually, have the means to invest in these roads, the companies may prosecute them.

Some gentlemen have intimated, that if this question of county indebtedness were left to the people to decide, they would have no objection to the incorporation of this provision in the constitution. If it should be found necessary to leave this question to the people, it appears to me, that the question then comes directly before them, whether the counties will take stock or not. That appears to me to be the proper mode of leaving the question. The people of Jasper county are the proper judges to decide whether they will take stock in the Dubuque railroad; and so it is with the people of any other county in regard to any other contemplated road. And then if a county should decide in favor of taking stock, and the road should prove a paying one, and should declare a dividend, there would be no difficulty in negotiating this stock at fair rates. The question comes up, when we make our investigations, whether it will be a paying stock or not.

If we should adopt this principle of county indebtedness, I think that we should establish a system of graduation. I think that rich and populous counties should have the liberty of taking more stock than counties that are sparsely settled. I think, for instance, that the county of Lucas, that has only four thousand inhabitants, should be restricted to an indebtedness of one hundred thousand dollars; while the populous county of Van Buren should be allowed to take three hundred thousand dollars or more. Some graduation principle should be established in this matter.

Mr. GILLASPY. It was not anticipated by my constituents or myself, that this question would come up in this convention. I was among the first in my county, when the question first came up, to support the principle of allowing counties to take stock; but after considerable reflection upon the subject, I have become satisfied that it is wrong. If this system were to be commenced anew in this State, I should oppose it entirely; but I do not believe that we, of the eastern part of the State, should now come up and decide this question for the people of the western counties. I shall, therefore, be governed in my vote by the feelings of gentlemen who live immediately west, upon the two projected railroads, the Burlington and Missouri Road, and the Keokuk and Des Moines Road. The people of my county have voted upon the question of the Burlington and Missouri River Road; but I doubt whether they will vote one hundred thousand dollars to the Keokuk and Des Moines Road. I am not instructed in regard to this matter, and in the absence of any instructions I shall go for striking out two hundred and fifty thousand dollars, and inserting one hundred thousand dollars; and I would leave it to the people of the western portion of the State to decide this matter for themselves, as the people of the eastern portion of the State have already done. We have already voted four hundred thousand dollars to the Burlington and Missouri Road, and I am disposed to favor the three counties represented by the gentleman from Lucas, (Mr. Edwards,) lying immediately west of the counties I represent, and allow them to vote upon this matter as they shall see proper. While we of the eastern counties have voted large sums for railroad purposes, I am not disposed to close the doors against the people of the western portion of the State.

The gentleman from Lucas (Mr. Edwards,) seems to think that the people of the western counties will be disposed to vote appropriations, in order to tax non-resident owners of land. I know, that in a great many counties upon the Dubuque and Sioux City Road, as well as upon the Lucas Air Line Railroad, and upon our own road, there are large tracts of land owned by speculators and non-residents; but I do not believe that three-fourths of them are. If the people of the western counties desire to vote this stock in order to make non-residents pay a fair proportion towards building these roads, I shall be inclined to leave it an open question for them to determine for themselves, as we have already determined it in the older counties.

Mr. GOWER. I understand the proposition is that a city of five thousand inhabitants containing two millions of taxable property may assess ten per cent. upon it for aiding incorporations and works of internal improvements. Is there not something exclusive in this? Are there not cities of less than five thousand inhabitants that may desire some of these advantages? It seems to me that there would be great impropriety in adopting provisions of this kind, and that it would be better to confine the assessment to a per centage on the amount of property, and not take into consideration the number of inhabitants.

I wish to refer to another matter, and that is, in regard to counties issuing bonds and taking stock in these corporations. I have no doubt of the correctness of the remark made by the gentleman from Des Moines, [Mr. Hall,] that they do not usually bring over sixty-five or seventy cents on a dollar. When the necessary expenses of transacting the business are deducted, they do not often produce over sixty per cent. The expenses of converting these bonds into cash, together with the discount, would amount to forty cents on the dollar. In the county where I reside, they voted fifty thousand dollars to the Lyons Central Road, under conditions that the road was to be commenced and prosecuted according to certain specified terms. During the progress of that work, our county issued bonds to the amount of thirty thousand dollars. They failed, however, to complete the work, and we have been taxed two or three years to pay the interest upon our bonds. Although we have been paying this money and have no road, still we congratulate ourselves that we have made money, and are satisfied that the issuing of these bonds for the building of this road was a good operation. Now I ask if we would deprive these western counties, that are just as anxious as we are to build roads, from making money in the same manner that we of the eastern counties do. It seems to me that this is a matter which we should duly consider. It would certainly be exclusive to confine assessments to cities of five thousand inhabitants. The best thing we can do is, unless we are prepared to allow all corporations the privilege of making assessments, to submit the question to the people, whether they will have these assessments or not.

Mr. HALL. I wish to explain the reason why I suggested the amendment to confine the assessments to cities. The fact is notorious to every gentleman that the credit of cities is better than that of counties. For instance, the bonds of the city of Burlington sell readily for ninety cents on the dollar, while county bonds sell at less than seventy cents on the dollar.

Mr. EDWARDS. If the gentleman from Des Moines will withdraw his substitute, I think I can offer an amendment that will meet the case.

Mr. HALL. I will withdraw it.

Mr. EDWARDS. I would move to strike out all after the words "corporation or corporations," and insert, "provided it shall not exceed ten per cent. upon the taxable property of any city or county," so that the section will then read:

"No political or municipal corporation shall become a stockholder in any banking corporation, directly or indirectly; nor in any other corporation or corporations, provided it shall exceed ten per cent of the taxable property of any city or county."

Mr. GIBSON. Living in the interior of the State, I wish to make a few remarks in relation to this matter. We have not voted a debt upon ourselves, as some of those counties have that are situated nearer the river. It strikes me that it would be wrong to prohibit those counties from becoming stock-holders in works of internal improvements, if they see fit to do so. It occurs to me, that it would be wrong even to restrict them to the ten per cent. upon the taxable property of cities, counties and towns. If the people of a county, city or town, desire to subscribe stock to any railroad, or loan their credit for that purpose, they certainly ought to have that privilege. A proposition was submitted by the gentleman from Jasper [Mr. Skiff,] but which, as I understand, is now withdrawn, to submit, as a separate clause, to be voted upon by the people, whether or not they will have this provision in the constitution, allowing counties to become stockholders in works of internal improvements.

This seems to me to be altogether unnecessary. It has been urged by some gentlemen that even our State cannot contract indebtedness of over one hundred and twenty-five thousand dollars, under the present arrangement, and that it would be bad policy for a county to take that amount or more, as some counties have already done. You will find a provision reported in the constitution, that the State may become a stockholder in corporations for certain purposes, to any amount, provided the people vote in favor of it. It seems to me, that we ought to give the same privilege to counties that we do to the State, and leave the people of the respective counties to determine this matter for themselves.

In making these remarks, I do not wish to be considered as being either in favor of, or opposed to, the system of counties taking stock. In certain cases I might be opposed to it, and then again in others, I might favor this principle; and, therefore, I desire to leave this question to the people of the respective counties to determine for themselves. I will vote against any proposition here, giving any authority to county officers, or a county judge, to take stock without the express will of the people. But it seems to me that it would be doing no injustice to anybody if we allow the majority of the people of any county, if they desire to do so, to vote for taking stock in railroads. I am not in favor of any county taking stock in any banking corporation, because such a corporation is evidently established for pecuniary gain. But this is not the case, to the same extent, at least, with corporations for railroads; for these roads, when completed, are intended to benefit all the people of the counties through which they pass, whether they have stock in them or not.

It has been truly said, that in some of the counties a large portion of the land is in the hands of non-residents, who will be greatly benefitted by the enhanced value of their property, caused by the building of these roads. I ask, should we not tax those lands for the building of these internal improvements, which so materially enhance the value of all real estate? This being the case, without entering upon an elaborate argument upon the subject, I will say in conclusion, that I favor the proposition of giving the people of the counties the privilege, in some shape or other, of becoming stock-holders in works of internal improvements.

Mr. GRAY. I have given some consideration to the amendment of the gentleman from Lucas (Mr. Edwards) and I must say, that it does not meet my approbation. It seems to me to be far more objectionable than the provision reported by the committee. From the report of the auditor, it seems, that under this amendment, the different counties in the State might be able to contract a debt of something like seventeen millions of dollars. The policy adopted by the convention that framed our present constitution, I regard as eminently right and proper, and I am unable to see any objection to State indebtedness, that does not apply with equal force to county indebtedness.

I heard it stated last fall, that three counties in the north-west had voted four hundred thousand dollars each, in aid of railroads. I find, upon reference to the statistics, that they contain in the aggregate six thousand nine hundred inhabitants, two thousand and a little fraction over to each county; making a debt of almost two hundred dollars to each person, man, woman and child in these counties being three times the amount that drove Mississippi into bankruptcy.

I think, that, the public mind is carried away with a kind of mania upon this subject of county indebtedness, which may lead, if not checked, to disatrous consequences. and which may seriously affect the prosperity of the State. Our policy should be, therefore, to restrict the exercise of a passion, which may become dangerous, which is liable to abuse, and may involve us ultimately, in ruin.

Mr. HARRIS. I do not propose at this time, to enter into an elaborate argument upon this question, for the reason, that it has been discussed by those who hold the same views that I do, and who are better acquainted with the wants of these counties than I am. I refer especially to my friend from Des Moines (Mr. Hall) But there is one view of this question to which I invite the attention of the Committee for a single moment, and which was barely hinted at in the course of this discussion. It strikes me that there is a clear distinction between having the question, whether the principle of county indebtedness shall become the policy of the State, determined by the people of the whole State, or by the people of each county, separately, for themselves. It strikes me, that gentlemen are involving themselves in difficulty, when they say that there is no necessity for submitting this question to the population of the whole State to determine, because we can refer it to the counties to determine, individually, for themselves. Let me suppose, to make my meaning clear, that in the district represented by my friend from Lucas, [Mr. Edwards] his own county has taken one hundred thousand dollars worth of stock, and Monroe county refuses to take any. They cannot build the road which is to pass through Monroe county, without benefiting it as much as it will Lucas county. The result is, you saddle a debt of one hundred thousand dollars upon the people of Lucas county, for the purpose of building a road, which will prove as great a benefit to the people of Monroe county as to the people of Lucas county. I ask, therefore, whether it would be just to the people generally, to inaugurate a system which will work so unfairly.

Here is another case, that I may present, by way of illustration. The gentleman from Lee [Mr. Johnston] says, that they have voted in that county four hundred and fifty thousand dollars for railroad purposes, desiring to build roads farther west, to the Missouri river. While Lee county has voted this large tax, Van Buren county refuses to vote any tax, although the road passes through that county, and will benefit them as much as it will Lee county. Davis county too, has voted for the same purpose a tax of one hundred and fifty thousand dollars, for the purpose of building a road, which will benefit the people of Van Buren county as much as it will the people of that county. It strikes me, from the illustrations I have here given, that gentlemen will see that the principle of allowing each county to vote upon this question will work unfairly. It strikes me, that there is a a wide difference between allowing the people of the counties, and allowing the people of the State, generally, to vote upon this matter.

So far as the people of my county are concerned, the question has been canvassed to such an extent, that I do not believe they would vote a dollar under any consideration. But I represent two other counties, and I am informed by gentlemen who ought to know something of the matter, that they would be ready to vote a large amount of county indebtedness. That is the position in which I am placed in regard to this matter.

As I said when I was up before, so far as my individual sentiments are concerned upon this matter, I am always ready to act. I was called to act upon this question when I first became a voter in Ohio. I saw the workings of the system there, and I think that the experience of the people of that State ought to teach us a lesson. The system worked somewhat differently there from what it did in Indiana, if I may judge from the remarks of gentlemen here who have referred to the history of that State in connection with this question.

Those counties in Ohio in which were large and populous cities, upon the line of railroads, sold their bonds readily, and at a premium very often; while counties upon the same line of road that were sparsely settled, and had no large cities within their limits, found it a difficult matter to sell their bonds at all, and if they did sell them it was only at a very low rate. Take, for instance, the road from Columbus to Cleveland. The bonds that were taken by Franklin county, having within its borders the city of Columbus, were sold before the road was constructed, and the county made a large per centage upon them. Other counties that had taxed themselves to a greater extent than Franklin county for building the same road, had difficulty in selling their bonds at all, and when they did sell them it was at a ruinous rate of discount.

In this State the counties on the river, especially those counties in which there are large towns, would have no difficulty in selling their bonds; but when you get back into the rural districts, as my friend from Wapello, (Mr. Gillaspy) calls them, whenever you fasten a debt of one hundred thousand dollars upon any one county, it will prove, in my opinion, a great drawback upon its future advancement and prosperity. I believe if this State of things should continue twenty years will not elapse before every tax-payer in the state, and especially in the counties where they have no large cities, will curse and execrate the memories of those who saddled a tax of that kind upon them.

Mr. PATTERSON. I am in favor of the proposition now under consideration, and I am opposed to the idea of excluding counties taking stock in railroads in case they see proper to do so. Although it may prove a detriment to some counties, it will prove a blessing to others. So far as my county is concerned, I think we have created a debt for railroad purposes sufficiently large already, and I do not think that I would be willing to increase it. But my friends and neighbors west of me, in Van Buren county, when they wake up to a sense of what is for their interest, may desire to take stock; and I am willing, therefore, to include them in this grand project. I should feel unwilling to vote for any proposition that would exclude Van Buren, or any other county, from taking stock in the road that will pass through their county. I hope that the amendment offered by the gentleman from Lucas [Mr. Edwards] will pass.

Mr. AYRES. As I represent Van Buren county, I would like to relieve the gentlemen who are fearful of laying any restrictions upon that county in this respect. She has twice voted down the proposition to take stock. So gentlemen need not be fearful of laying any restrictions upon Van Buren county.

Mr. MARVIN. The people of the county that I represent have now a proposition before them to raise money for railroad purposes, upon which they will be called to vote next April. A great deal of interest is manifested there upon both sides of the question, and the subject is being thoroughly discussed among the people. When they shall wake up to a sense of their true interest in this matter, I believe it will be perfectly safe to trust them to vote upon it. It strikes me that it would not be exactly popular to call in the State, in the first instance, to decide whether certain localities shall determine what indebtedness they shall incur for railroad purposes. There may have been cases, where the people have voted upon this question without a full understanding of what they were doing; but with the discussion now taking place upon this subject all over the State, I believe the people will fully appreciate what is for their best interests, and vote accordingly. I am aware that the gentleman from Linn [Mr. Gray] may suppose that he has all he wants; but unless the people of Jones county vote a tax, the people of Linn will lose a very important branch, which is to connect them with Dubuque. The people of Linn county may have, therefore, a direct interest in Jones county voting a tax for that purpose. I believe that it is safe, under existing circumstances, to leave it to the people of Jones county to vote upon this matter. And I believe it is safe to leave it to the people of any other county to vote a tax upon themselves for railroad purposes.

I see no impropriety in certain counties that have a small population voting a large tax upon themselves, or those who may come after them. If I were in a new county that had four thousand inhabitants, with an immense unoccupied country around it, I would much sooner vote a tax upon it than if it were a large and populous county. The very fact that men from different parts of the Union have bought up large tracts of land in every neighborhood, and are waiting for the people to make improvements that will enhance the value of their lands, is the very reason why I would tax the lands in the localities.

Mr. EMERSON. I am opposed, Mr. Chairman, to this whole system of county and city indebtedness; to the ten per cent. proposion; to the two hundred thousand dollars restriction proposed by the committee, and to all other propositions which allow cities and counties to incur a debt for purposes of internal improvements, either with or without a vote of the people. While I am in favor of, and fully recognize the right of government to tax the people for the legitimate support thereof, I deny that the power exists anywhere to tax for any other purpose. The taxing power would never have been conferred on the Government, if Government could have existed without the surrender of that right.

Now, sir, it is said by members, that couties and cities may, by a majority vote of the citizens of such municipal corporation, contract debts, take stock, or loan their credit to railroad projects, thereby subjecting the people to grievous and unlimited taxation. Now, sir, I hold that that mode of taxation is not necessary to the support of Government, and hence is wrong in principle and practice; that it is an unrighteous exercise of power over the dearest rights of the minority; that you compel the minority against their will to embark their means in railroad projects, in the success of which they have no confidence, nor in the honesty or capacity of the projectors to carry the work forward.

It is urged by the friends of this measure, that as railroads benefit all, hence it is right and proper to tax all for their construction. Now, if this doctrine proves anything, it proves too much; for if correct in regard to railroads in this State, it is equally true in regard to roads extending through other States to our eastern border; I suppose it will be conceded by every member upon this floor, that Iowa owes much of her present prosperity to the net work of railroads approaching us from the East. Yet, I apprehend no gentleman will contend that this State, either by cities or counties, should have taken stock in those projects, in order to secure their construction. Again, we all derive a common benefit from the labor of others in the improvement of the country. Will gentlemen contend that we should therefore make common cause, and improve the country by county and city taxation? A case involving the principal now under consideration, has recently been decided in the fifth Judicial District of New York; in which case the court held that the taking of stock in, or loaning the credit of municipal corporations to railroad projects, by a majority vote of the electors thereof was void. And the court further held that the legislature did not possess the power to confer such right upon the electors of municipal corporations.

When this question of taxation for railroad purposes first came up in Dubuque, I opposed it; but I was met with the argument, "look at Ohio, see what this policy has done in developing her resources and making her one of the wealthiest States in the Union." I did not believe, at the time, that this policy had wrought such results for Ohio, and this belief was fully sustained by what followed in that State. In 1851 she revised her constitution, and incorporated the following clause in it, which proves in clear and unmistakable language, that she repudiated this whole doctrine of taxation for railroad purposes.

"The General Assembly shall never authorize any county, city, town or township, by vote of its citizens or otherwise, to become a stockholder in any joint stock company, corporation, or association whatever; or to raise money for, or loan its credit to, or in aid of any such company, corporation, or association."

The people of that State had suffered greatly from the system of taxation for railroad purposes, and here you have the result of their experience embodied in this clause of their new constitution. It is an example which it would be well for us to follow, rather than rush recklessly into a system as yet untried in this State.

But, Mr. Chairman, as I feel quite indisposed, I will defer making any farther remarks until a future occasion, when I hope I may able more fully and clearly to show that the adoption of the priuciple, now contended for by gentlemen upon the other side, would result in the most mischievous consequences to the interests of the State and the people at large.

Mr. PALMER. I believe it is understood, that we have adopted in the seventh article of this constitution, a provision prohibiting the State from contracting an indebtedness exceeding in amount two hundred and fifty thousand dollars. Now it appears to me, that if we allow the counties separately to contract debts to any amount they choose, we might as well leave out that provision in the seventh article. That prohibition is intended to prevent public indebtedness. Shall we go on, in the very next article, and introduce a section, which shall sanction the principle of allowing counties to incur indebtedness to any amount? There being no restriction upon the counties, except in the aggregate, they might, under such a section, as is here reported by the committee, increase the indebtedness of the State to the amount of ten millions of dollars. I was once disposed to encourage this county subscription for railroad purposes. But I admit that my views have been changed somewhat upon this question. I am opposed to the principle from other considerations than the fact that it creates a public debt. What is the object of a constitution? Is it not our object, in framing a constitution, to protect the minority? And was not that the object in adopting this restriction in the seventh article? We get together and say, that in order to protect the weak, we will adopt this, as a fundamental rule in our constitution, that those who are in power, although they come into power by the will of the majority, shall not oppress or wrong the minority, by entailing upon them a debt to which they did not consent. We propose to adopt this as a principle with regard to the State as a whole. But it is now proposed, in the section before the committee, to reverse that order, and say that the counties may do that which we will not allow the State to do. This question was argued ably by the gentleman from Dubuque, (Mr. Emerson,) and the reasons he advanced to support his position were, I think, conclusive. Suppose the project of submitting the question of incurring a debt in certain counties shall be submitted to the people, and a bare majority vote in favor of incurring such a debt. The minority, although they voted against the proposition, will be compelled to submit to a tax upon their property to pay this indebtedness. I think that this principle is wrong. I think it should be left to individuals, if they wish to secure the benefits of public improvements, to subscribe to these improvements themselves, and not fasten a debt upon others, who do not wish to have anything to do with such projects.

The gentleman from Wapello (Mr. Gillaspy,) said he had understood, that in some of the northern counties the people voted county subscriptions to railroads, for the purpose of taxing the lands of non-residents. I say that non-residents should be compelled to bear a proportion of that debt; but I think that if the people should vote a tax upon the counties for that purpose, they will defeat the object they had in view. Suppose they do contract a debt? Why the very fact of a contemplated improvement will have the effect to enhance the value of the property of the non-residents; and they will immediately sell out at a great profit, and the real burthen of the improvement will after all be borne by the permanent residents. It will have exactly the contrary effect to that which I understand the voters of these northern counties had in view.

The gentleman from Cedar (Mr. Gower,) has said, that in his county they had incurred a debt for a railroad which is not completed; and yet they had reaped a great benefit from it, because their property had been raised in value by the contemplated improvement. If they have reaped a little benefit from the system now, they have not yet seen the bitter end. I think that counties that have incurred indebtedness of this kind, will, in the future, bitterly regret the steps they have taken.

Mr. HALL. I do not believe all the citizens

of Cedar county are as well satisfied with, and reconciled to their condition as their representative here seems to be. I know very well that while I had the honor of a seat upon the supreme bench, they were fighting these bonds, and trying to get out a writ of mandamus against them. During the last session of the supreme court they had a suit for refusing to pay principal and interest upon these bonds. As long as they can stave them off they may laugh; but when the time comes for them to pay, they will not laugh quite so much.

There are many lights in which to view this subject of county indebtedness. I suppose that many gentlemen felt as I did when we first started upon these internal improvements, and began to look around for means to carry them on. We studied the example of Ohio and other States, in regard to this matter of city and county indebtedness. I took hold of the matter with others, and advocated county subscriptions. I went through the country and made speeches, and used the strongest arguments of which I was capable, and made the most forcible appeals I could think of, in favor of this system of subscribing stock by counties. All the counties along the line, so far as the first section of the road extended, have subscribed. Des Moines, Henry, Jefferson and Wapello counties, have subscribed liberally to our road. But I must say that there were some things connected with this matter of county subscriptions, that never accorded entirely with my judgment, as being entirely right. I felt a great deal like the gentleman from Dubuque [Mr. Emerson,] that in a matter where the rights of man to life, liberty and property are concerned, we did not adhere strictly to that principle, when by a vote of the people of the county in spite of me, and when I was resisting them, and had no desire to go into this enterprise, they would place an encumbrance upon my property, and make me engage in that business without my consent. There was something in that a little odious to my sense of right, and a little inconsistent with my idea of liberty, which I conceive to be using one's own as he pleases, and enjoying it without interruption.

If this demand upon me and my property was for the purpose of securing to the people the right of enjoying liberty and property, it would then be well enough, and I would be equally interested with others to secure a proper enjoyment of what I possessed. I would be willing to contribute my proportion of the means necessary to protect any citizen in the enjoyment of what he possessed, for this is a duty which government imposes upon us all. But when a majority of the citizens of a county desire to go into a partnership, to form themselves into a corporation and subscribe capital for speculating enterprises, for purposes of gain, is it right to allow them to take a portion of my property and put it into that speculation without my consent? This is an encroachment upon my idea of liberty, which I could never reconcile. And I have always contrived some way to waive that question when I was arguing for these contributions, and say, it was too abstract for the occasion, or something of that sort.

Now I do not think any gentleman here has the right, or that all of them, or the majority in the county where I live, have the right to take one dollar of my property and devote it to any purpose, except to sustain the great principles and objects of municipal government. They have no right to take it and invest it in a mercantile business; that would be monstrous. Now I may not want to engage in railroading, or in a mercantile business, but may prefer to keep what I have, and use it as my judgment may dictate. But here comes up a system which has crept on us, and declares that by a vote of the people this thing shall be done. But, it is said, you live in a republic; do you not believe that the majority should rule? No, sir; I do not believe that the majority should rule under these circumstances. I believe that liberty consists in the fact that I shall be free from this rule of the majority, and that no human power shall touch me or my property, but for the sole purpose of supporting the government. I agreed to that when I came under the government. And this is an argument which when fairly presented no man can answer upon principle.

And how is it in this matter? Must we bow to the dictates of the majority, and submit to what they may determine? I suppose that in some of the counties one-fourth of the population have never contributed anything of any amount to the purposes of government. And yet they can under this system involve all we possess, and then leave the county, and leave all this tax to be paid by those who remain there. This tax and this debt necessarily falls more directly upon the real estate of the county, than upon anything else. A man who has real estate in one of these counties cannot escape the consequences of this debt in which he has been involved without his consent, and his property must remain under, as it were, a perpetual mortgage. There may be men in a county, who never had a cent of property subject to taxation, and will never be called upon to discharge one iota of this debt. They come up to another man, who, in consequence of his industry and success in business, has got a few hundred acres of land. They propose to him to subscribe for a railroad. He says that he does not want to invest his money in an enterprise of that kind. The others say they are the majority, and he must contribute what he has; for they have nothing; he must contribute for their benefit.

Now I hold that doctrine is a wrong one, and will produce disastrous results to the State. In place of doing good, it will work mischief in proportion to the importance of the principle it violates. Could there be any assurance from any quarter that you would get anything for this, there would be some little consolation in it. You might say to a person, it is true we take your property without your consent; but you will get it back again in some shape. But that security and assurance cannot be given here.

The very thing itself—the process and mode of transacting this business precludes the idea that improvements of this kind can be profitably built upon this subscription of stock.

I make a distinction between cities and counties, because I know that Burlington city bonds sold for ninety seven cents on the dollar, while Des Moines county bonds sold for only 76 cents. Yet each received one hundred dollars worth of stock for every one hundred dollars of bonds, and they stand as equals in that respect. Now you cannot obtain private subscription for the purpose of building these roads. And the only way to use this principle is to get enough to induce capitalists to come in and buy the road after it has got into debt, and then they will get private subscriptions to complete it. That has been the result in regard to some of the roads in Iowa; but I hope it will not be so in regard to all.

We say about our road that the advantages derived from it are so great that we can afford to bear this great reduction in its nominal value, and we can pay a dividend on all the stock issued. But it would have cost some 40 per cent less, if it had been built by cash subscriptions, and we will have to pay dividends on forty per cent. more stock than we would have been obliged to do, had it been built entirely by cash subscriptions. In Illinois I believe no county can subscribe more than fifty thousand dollars. They have no other limit in their Constitution, but I think they have fixed the amount of population before a city can go into debt. They build roads fast enough there. But every dollar subscribed to the St. Louis, Alton and Chicago road by the counties along the line of the road, was sunk in two years after it twas commenced.

Gentlemen here have alluded to Ohio. I am aware that this kind of stock was subscribed in Ohio, and while the excitement was up they sold that stock and got the money for it. But those who bought it have since had to lose money on it. And some of the roads have been abandoned and torn up.

Our true policy would perhaps be to step back to a principle that is right. But we have gone too far to recede, and it would be a calamity to those counties who have become involved in this thing, to prevent the other counties from coming up to their aid with a liberality equal to that of those who have already subscribed to these roads. My judgment rather inclines to the opinion that we ought to take a medium course. I think we should leave this question an open one. I hope we will take some course that will at least be a medium one, and not crush out those counties who have already been so liberal in their subscriptions, and have been so, with the expectation that the western counties would come up to their aid whenever it might be necessary.

Mr. EDWARDS. The gent from Des Moines (Mr. Hall) appears to me to take a very curious position here. He made one of the strongest and most elaborate arguments against this system *in toto*, and then he says that he would be willing to adopt a clause imposing a restriction upon these municipal corporations. Now if a thing is wrong at all, it is wrong altogether. If the principle is wrong as the gentleman has set forth, then it is wrong to restrict the counties to any amount at all.

There lived a few years ago one of the master spirits of the age; DeWitt Clinton of New York, who projected a canal across the whole length of that State. He wrote to Mr. Jefferson in regard to it, and Mr. Jefferson wrote in reply that in his opinion the work could not be completed within one hundred years. But they both lived long enough to see that stupendous work completed, and Mr. Jefferson wrote to Mr. Clinton that he had been one hundred years behind the age.

Now there are large and expansive minds in all communities, and there are also narrow, contracted minds. And when any great enterprise is projected, there are more or less sticklers and croakers, who have been, and always will be, opposed to every enterprise of internal improvement. It is their nature and constitution to be so. There are men in every community who aid the advancement and prosperity of the country, and yet who have not one tenth part of the means of those others who endeavor to strangle those enterprises in their infancy.

I differ with the gentleman from Des Moines [Mr. Hall] in regard to the principle he has laid down in his argument here. I hold that in our political, as well as in our social relations, we are individual and integral parts, making up the whole. And especially under a republican form of government like ours, I contend that the majority ought to rule. There are always individuals in every community to oppose railroad projects of any kind. But if a project is presented to the people of a county, and a majority say they will take stock in it, for the purpose of expending it in their midst, to establish a work of internal improvement, not only to enhance the value of their lands and their property, but to give them a communication with a market, it benefits the man who holds back as much as it does the man who drives on. And I say that any man who constitutes an integral part of the whole community, is socially and politically bound to add something to the common good, to make some sacrifice for the general good. I hold that if a project is submitted to the people of my county, and a majority of my neighbors believe that it will be for the interest and advancement of the majority, the minority ought to submit, because it must benefit the minority in like proportion to its benefit to the majority.

Suppose I live in a county along side of my friend from Van Buren (Mr. Day). He is worth one hundred thousand dollars, and I am worth only ten thousand dollars. He takes no more stock than I do, but he is benefitted ten times as much as I am, for he has ten times the property to be benefitted by this improvement. That would be the result when you build roads by subscription. Now, I say, when every man is taxed according to the *ad valorum* system, each one should be willing to yield something to the general good. These railroads are exceptions to the general rule, because they can be built upon no other system. There are two classes of citizens, and only two classes that are benefitted by railroads. I make that assertion without fear of contradiction. They are the farmers and the land holders. I care not whether a railroad passing through a country, pays a dividend or not. When it is completed it will enhance the value of the land of a man who lives near it, one hundred or two hundred per cent.; it will give him increased facilities for getting to market, and increase the price of his produce. All these benefits and many others, are for the general good; and therefore, I think the principle of the gentleman from Des Moines, [Mr. Hall,] falls to the ground.

Mr. HARRIS. The gentleman from Lucas, [Mr. Edwards,] says that the majority ought to rule. Suppose that he and Judge Johnston and my friend Day here, lived in one county. He and Judge Johnston are worth ten thousand dollars each, and Mr. Day is worth one hundred thousand dollars. They conclude that it would be a fine thing to get Mr. Day into a speculation, if they can get him to put in all his property. They are the majority, and can overrule him. Are the majority bound to rule in that case?

Mr. EDWARDS. I stated most distinctly that railroads were exceptions to the general rule.

Mr. HARRIS. What distinction can the gentleman make, to compel a man who owns one hundred thousand dollars worth of property to be taxed by a vote equally with one who is worth only five thousand dollars? The majority can rule as well in the one case as in the other.

Mr. EDWARDS. If I understand the gentleman he draws a distinction between railroads and other projects. I know the principle would not hold good in banking institutions, I do not know what the wishes of my constituents are upon this question. I have no means of obtaining a knowledge of their wishes. If I knew them I would cordially acquiesce in them. The course I shall take here will be determined by the position that gentlemen in this convention may take. I am perfectly willing that the gentleman who represents Des Moines county, [Mr. Hall,] and who lives at the eastern extremity of the road, should build the road they propose to run through our section of the country. And I am willing that the people of Keokuk, Burlington, &c., should have incurred a debt; for if they get the railroad started, they will soon send it along to us. If a majority of this convention are not willing to adopt the system, so as to restrict the counties to a certain amount, I am perfectly willing that the people living along the river should construct the railroads for us. We will content ourselves for some years longer with trudging along after the old fashion in our mud carts.

Mr. HARRIS. I think I can make myself intelligible to the gentleman from Lucas [Mr. Edwards.] I should like to know the difference between half a dozen men meeting in a caucus, and a majority of them deciding that they will form a corporation and compel the rest to put their property in, and the taking a vote of the people to compel a man's property to be taxed against his will, when his property may amount to more than that of all those who may have voted this tax for these roads?

Mr. CLARKE, of Henry. If no other gentleman desires to speak upon this subject now, I will make a few remarks in regard to the views of the committee on incorporations upon this matter, it having been discussed to considerable extent in the committee.

There are but few persons in this State who now defend the principle they started out with, of allowing cities and counties to take stock in these railroads. I opposed it from the first, and voted against it. I did so upon the same principle suggested by the gentleman from Appanoose [Mr. Harris.] I did not acknowledge that it was good democratic republican doctrine, for the majority to vote money out of the pockets of the minority, for any purpose but the general purposes of government. But there are other things we must not overlook. We are considering the institutions and interests of the State at large, and this matter must be considered and treated as a State policy. This system having been inaugurated in this State, and these railroads having been commenced, they are now, as we may say, crystallising out into the interior of the State, from the east to the west, and from the south to the north, in every possible direction. The counties along the river have taken stock, and become interested in these roads. A road has been built to this city from the river. This county, in taking stock, contemplated that the western counties would take stock, as the road was extended in their direction. At the west there are large portions of territory, some organized, and some unorganized into counties. In process of time they may wish to be upon exactly the same footing with the other counties, and to be allowed the privilege, if it be a privilege, of taking stock in these railroads, as was expected of them when the older counties took their stock.

And another thing; I think that by putting in a restriction here against counties taking any stock at all in railroads, we may perhaps embarass the operation of these different companies. It is, in my opinion, a mere matter of policy with us, whether we will allow them to do so or not. If we do allow it, then I submit to this convention, whether the restriction proposed by the committee is not a better, and a more equitable restriction to meet the object in view, than the one proposed by the gentleman from Lucas [Mr. Edwards.] The county I represent would, under the restriction he proposes, be allowed to take four hundred thousand dollars of stock; Lee county could take six hundred thousand dollars, or eight hundred thousand dollars, and so with other counties. We must also observe this thing: This is a constitution we are framing; not a law which can be amended or changed at any time, but a law that will run on for years to come. And in the coures of six, eight, or ten years, these counties will double in population and wealth, and there would be practically no limitation to the amount of subscription that would be taken under the proposed amendment. Some counties which now do not take ten thousand dollars of stock, could perhaps in five years take one million dollars.

Now the object of a restriction here is to prevent the whole State, as a community of counties, from becoming embarrassed in this matter. The majority of the Committee on Incorporations, concluded that some limit should be placed in the constitution, within which the people of the counties might go on and take stock in these corporated companies, and have all the counties of the State upon a perfect equality. So far as that goes, it is certainly a democratic principle, to allow the new counties to occupy the same position as the old ones in regard to internal improvements.

I am somewhat surprised at the position of the gentleman from Des Moines [Mr. Hall.] I had certainly supposed that upon this question he occupied entirely different ground from that he has taken here to-day. However, he has a right to define his own position, and I am glad he has done so. I know that not a great while since he occupied a different position. I know that the people of this State will, in the future, endorse his present position, that this is a great and growing evil, and should be checked. But I do not believe with the gentleman from Des Moines, that because this system of cities and counties taking stock has been gone into to a very unwise and injudicious extent, it is going to operate disastrously to the different communities who have embarked in genuine, well-organized railroad corporations. I believe the railroads of Iowa, when completed, will be good-paying investments; and if the different counties which have taken stock, should not be in some way defrauded—if the railroad is not sold out under foreclosure, or some such operation, the people of those counties will eventually derive a revenue from their stock, which will in a measure relieve them from taxation. I believe railroads can be so managed in this State, as not necessarily to defraud the people. But that such will be the case in the future, we have no guarantee, and this is thus far one reason why the committee have proposed this restriction.

Mr. JOHNSTON. This is one of the most important questions that can come before us for consideration. The discussion which has taken place this afternoon has been of a suggestive character at all events, and will call the attention of members of this body to this subject. And as I understand there are several members who desire to say something upon this subject, and as I may want to say something myself, I will now move that the committee rise, report progress and ask leave to sit again.

The question being taken, the motion was agreed to, and the committee rose.

The PRESIDENT having resumed the Chair,

The CHAIRMAN of the Committtee of the Whole reported that the Committee had had the subject of Incorporations under consideration, had made progress therein, and asked leave to sit again.

The report was received, and leave granted accordingly.

Mr. SKIFF moved that the Convention adjourn.

Mr. CLARKE, of Johnson. I would move that the Convention adjourn until to-morrow morning at ten o'clock. For the last two mornings we have adjourned to meet at nine o'clock, and have not met until ten o'clock.

Mr. JOHNSTON. I hope this motion will not prevail. I know that we do not meet till ten o'clock, but like a great many others, I desire to be right on the record.

The question being taken, the motion was agreed to, and

The Convention adjourned until to-morrow morning at ten o'clock.

SATURDAY, February 7th, 1857.

The convention met at ten o'clock A. M., and was called to order by the President.

Prayer by the Chaplain.

The journal of yesterday was read and approved.

Committee of the Whole on Corporations.

The convention resumed the consideration in committee of the whole on the report of the committee on corporations, (Mr. Traer in the chair.)

The CHAIRMAN. The question pending before the committee of the whole is upon the adoption of the substitute offered by Mr. Edwards for the amendment of Mr. Skiff, to the fourth section.

The proposed substitute reads as follows:

"No political or municipal corporation shall become a stock-holder in any banking corporation, directly or indirectly; nor in any other corporation or corporations, except to an amount not exceeding ten per cent. upon the taxable property of any city or county."

Mr. HALL. I desire to move a substitute for the fourth and fifth sections of the report of the committee. I wish to say before offering it, that I am not entirely satisfied with it myself, but I propose it in order to test the sense of the convention upon the subject, embracing, as it does, principles which I regard as highly important, if we are to adopt any system whatever.

The CHAIRMAN. Does the gentleman from Lucas withdraw his substitute?

Mr. EDWARDS. I would like to hear the proposition of the gentleman read.

The substitute of Mr. Hall was then read as follows:

Sec. 4. Counties, cities, towns, and all other political and municipal corporations, are prohibited from taking stock, or in any manner becoming interested in any bank or banking institution, authorized by the laws of this State.

Sec. 5. For the purpose of aiding works of internal improvement that shall pass through counties, or terminate within any county of this State, such counties, and towns, and cities, within the same, may be authorized to take stock to create debts, by a vote of the property holders residing in such county, city, or town, who are charged with an annual tax for county and State purposes, of not less than five dollars, or who are the owners of real estate in said county, town and city, of the value of two hundred dollars.

Sec. 6. The general assembly shall provide by law the manner and mode by which counties, towns and cities may create corporate debts for internal improvements under the fourth and fifth sections of this article; but no debt shall be authorized, or permitted, which shall at any time exceed the sum of two hundred thousand dollars for any county, city or town, nor shall said debt in any case exceed ten per cent. upon the taxable property in such county, city or town, to be ascertained by the assessment for State and county purposes.

Mr. EDWARDS. I could subscribe to a portion of the substitute, which the gentleman from Des Moines proposes. But it appears to me, that the phraseology of his substitute is too complex. For instance, he does not alter the reading of the report, where it names two hundred thousand dollars as the limit for taking stock. This substitute embraces that same provision, and yet allows each county to make an assessment as high as ten per cent. upon property which may exceed the sum of two hundred thousand dollars.

There is another principle embraced in the substitute, which I do not believe is correct, that all persons who do not pay a tax of five dollars shall not be allowed to vote upon this question of indebtedness.

Mr. HALL. The proposition, which I have presented, contains two or three principles, which I deem essential and of the highest importance, when viewed in connection with this question of county indebtedness. One is, that when a debt against the corporation of a county, city or town is to be voted for the purpose of internal improvements, no person shall have the right to vote who does not pay a tax of five dollars. That provision is intended to exclude men who own no real property, who are transient in their character and position in society, of which class there are a great many in all communities. Another provision is, that a a person who shall own real estate to the value of two hundred dollars shall have the privilege of voting upon the question of creating this indebtedness for railroad purposes. Certainly those persons who have to pay the taxes that are levied, and pay the interest on the debt, are the persons most capable of judging as to the propriety of creating an indebtedness. The city of Burlington has been for the last six or eight years occasionally voting loans. We voted one hundred and seventy-five thousand dollars, which were expended in the Burlington and Peoria Railroad. We have voted five to ten thousand dollars at a time for plank roads, and various other local improvements. We also voted, first, seventy-five thousand dollars to the Burlington and Missouri Rail Road, and then another loan of $75,000 more; and also various sums for city purposes. It became obvious to every tax payer, and to the best part of the community there, that the system was wrong, and this last winter they memorialized the Legislature to the effect that they considered it essential to the safety of the city against debts, that all matters of this kind should be referred to the property holders. Hence, I have incorporated in this amendment the principle that persons who own property, and those in whose hands it may be hereafter, and who may be taxed for the payment of interest, and ultimately for the principal of such debts, shall be the persons to say whether it is right and proper to create it.

The next principle I have incorporated in my amendment, is the principle contained in the section reported by the committee. As to the amount of the debt I have named, that can be easily changed to meet the wishes of the convention. I have adopted the idea of the committee, and provided that no county shall create a debt of this kind exceeding two hundred thousand dollars. If it shall be the will of the convention to increase or diminish that amount, they can do so, with the principle of limitation clearly established. In the next place, in order to limit the new counties, where roads are now being projected, I have inserted the provision, that they shall in no instance create a debt, which shall be greater than ten per cent. upon the amount of the taxable property of the county. I have presented this plan, in order to get the sense of the convention in some shape upon this subject.

Mr. EDWARDS. If the gentleman from Des Moines will alter his substitute, so as to make it bear more equally upon the various counties, I would be willing to accept it, in lieu of my proposition. As the substitute now stands it would make a very great disparity between the various counties. I understand it to limit the indebtedness of all counties to two hundred thousand dollars; and the new counties are restricted to ten per cent. upon taxable property. I think that this is too great a disparity. The wealthier and more populous counties, like Dubuque and others, are able to incur a larger amount of indebtedness than the smaller and newer counties. I would ask the gentleman to modify his proposition, so as to allow the older counties to take a larger amount than he names. I am willing to restrict the new counties to the amount proposed by his substitute. I will, however, withdraw my substitute in the hope that the gentlemen on the committee, may modify the substitute so as more fully to meet my views.

Mr. CLARKE, of Johnson. So far, I have taken no part in this discussion, and do not propose to do so at this time. I was adverse to the report of the committee on incorporations upon this subject, the first time I saw it, and the discussion so far has only tended to increase my objections to it. The main objection I have to it is, that there is too much legislation in it, and that we are undertaking to do what comes more properly within the province of the General Assembly. I rise now to enquire, whether a substitute could be offered for the whole report.

The CHAIRMAN. The chair is of the opinion, that a substitute would be in order.

Mr. CLARKE, of Johnson. I have prepared a substitute, not because I have any personal convictions as to my own ability or skill upon the subject, or because it meets entirely my own views, but because I think it contains less legislation than the proposition now under consideration. The main idea, which ought to pervade this convention in making constitutional provisions, upon the subject of incorporations is the safety of the people; and in the substitute I have prepared, I have looked more to that end than I have to the details of the system.

Mr. EDWARDS. I rise to a point of order. The gentleman from Johnson proposes a substitute for the whole report. I ask if it would be in order to receive that substitute, until we have gone through with the whole of this report, section by section? When that is done, I apprehend it will then be in order for the gentleman to offer his substitute.

Mr. CLARKE, of Johnson. I am inclined to concur in the opinion of the gentleman from Lucas (Mr. Edwards). But the difficulty is in getting my proposition before the members. I would be glad to have it printed, as well as the proposition of any other gentleman, which is offered in the shape of substitute. I regard this subject as the most important one that we will have to discuss here; and I should like to see the views of gentleman presented here in the shape of propositions. I thought, at the first sitting of the committee, that I would wait until they had finished the discussion, and then offer my proposition in convention as a substitute; but I concluded that it would look, perhaps, too, much like egotism then to offer it. I would prefer to get it in some shape before the committee, that members may have the opportunity of comparing it with the report of the committee. I do not desire to express any views upon the general proposition now under consideration until I have an opportunity of presenting my substitute.

The CHAIRMAN. The chair would state, that in his opinion, the substitute proposed by the gentleman from Johnson (Mr. Clarke) is in order. The substitute offered by the gentleman from Des Moines (Mr. Hall) has not received a second.

Mr. SKIFF. I second it.

The CHAIRMAN. The question then will be upon the adoption of the substitute offered by the gentleman from Des Moines [Mr. Hall).

Mr. JOHNSTON. It is perhaps, best not to be too technical about this thing. I would like to hear the proposition of the gentleman from Johnson [Mr. Clarke] read, for information.

The CHAIRMAN. The chair supposes it will be in order to read it.

The subtsitute proposed by Mr. Clarke, of Johnson, was then read as follows:

ARTICLE—

Sec. 1. Corporations may be formed under general laws, but shall not be created by special act, except for municipal purposes, and in cases where, in the judgment of the General Assemly, the objects of the corporation cannot be obtained under general laws. All general laws, and special acts, passed pursuant to this section, may be altered or repealed, saving to parties the rights acquired under the same.

Sec. 2. The State shall not become a stockholder in any corporation; nor shall it assume or pay the debt, or liability of any corporation, unless incurred in time of war, for the benefit of the State.

Sec. 3. No political or municipal corporation shall become a stock-holder in any banking corporation, directly or indirectly; but such corporations may become stock-holders in corporations for the construction of works of internal improvements within the State, upon a vote of the citizens of such political or municipal corporation, under such restrictions as the general assembly may provide.

Sec. 4. It shall be the duty of the General Assembly to provide by law, for the restraint of municipal or political corporations in regard to assessments, taxation, borrowing money, contracting debts, issuing bonds and loaning their credit, so as to prevent, as far as possible, unnecessary burdens, and unjust taxation and frauds.

Sec. 5. Banking institutions may be provided for, by a general law under the following restrictions:

First. All bills, notes, or other paper, evidence of debt, that may be issued for circulation as money, shall be based upon the stocks of the United States, or the stocks of interest-paying States, deposited with the proper officer of State, at the rate of not less than one hundred and twenty dollars, for every one hundred dollars of paper so issued, which may be increased or diminished, as the said stocks may increase, or diminish in value.

Second. All paper of any such institution, intended to circulate as money, shall be registered in the office of the proper State officer, and counter-signed by such officer.

Third. In case of the insolvency of any banking institution, the bill-holders shall have a preference over all their creditors; and the General Assembly may provide for the conversion of the stocks, deposited by such institution, into money, and the redemption of its bills.

Fourth. The suspension of specie payments, by banking institutions, shall never be sanctioned by law.

Fifth. Upon the failure of any banking institution to redeem its bills, or other paper, issued to circulate as money, such institution shall forfeit its rights; and it shall be the duty of the proper legal officer, to commence proceedings in the manner prescribed by law, to close up its business, and liquidate its indebtedness; and such institution shall have no power, after such failure, to redeem, or to transfer its property.

Sixth. The issue of any bills, or other evidences of debt, intended to circulate as money, by any banking institution, without being secured and countersigned, as hereinafter required, shall be deemed a forfeiture of all its rights, by such institution.

Sec. 6. Any person, or body of persons, who shall issue for circulation as money, any bill, or other evidence of debt, without the authority of law, shall be deemed guilty of felony, and punished as provided by law.

Sec. 7. The State shall be responsible to the proper parties, for all stocks deposited with the proper officer, as the basis of paper, intended to circulate as money.

Sec. 8. The General Assembly may limit, by law, the amount of real estate which any banking institution may hold, at any one time, and the period of time for which it may hold the same.

Sec. 9. The word "corporation" as used in this article may be construed to mean any individual, association, or company, having or enjoying rights and privileges, by provisions of law, not possessed by every individual or partnership.

Mr. CLARKE, of Johnson. I do not desire to press this substitute upon the committee now. I only desire to present it at the proper time for the action of the convention, and I hope it may prove a compromise measure upon which the convention may unite.

Mr. ELLS. I move that it be printed.

Mr. HALL. If this way of transacting business be introduced, we will never get anything decided.

My objections to this substitute, especially to one branch of it, are so great, that I could not for a moment think of tolerating it. We did not come to create banking institutions; and I will never consent, while I sit here, to incorporate into the constitution in any shape and form, the provisions of this substitute. Let it lie on the table without printing. We may have forty other propositions of the kind laid before the Convention, which we would have to print, if we consent to the printing of this.

The CHAIRMAN. The chair has not entertained the motion of the gentleman from Scott [Mr. Ells] as the committee have not the right to order anything printed.

Mr. HALL. Let us decide upon some principle, which will govern us. After we have done that, it will then be no great trouble to manage the details, when we come to the banking portion of the report. Let us decide upon some principle which shall govern us.

Mr. PARVIN. If I understand from the reading of the substitute of the gentleman from Johnson, [Mr. Clarke], the section that refers to legislative action, and counties and cities taking stock in any other than banking institution, the object of the gentleman would be accomplished by striking out in the fourth section of the report, all after the word "indirectly," in the second line. I should certainly be opposed to the substitute upon the ground that it creates a bank or banks under a general banking law.

The CHAIRMAN. The chair would remark to the gentleman from Muscatine [Mr. Parvin] that the substitute offered by the gentleman from Johnson, [Mr. Clarke], is not before the committee. The question is upon the substitute offered by the gentleman from Des Moines [Mr. Hall].

Mr. PARVIN. I desire to make a few remarks in regard to the substitute offered by the gentleman from Des Moines. He proposes that persons may be allowed to vote upon this question of taking stock in railroads under certain restrictions. The individual who owns property to the amount of two hundred dollars, or the individual who pays a tax of five dollars, may vote upon this subject; but the poor man, who has just as much sense as the rich man, is forbidden by this restriction from voting for these objects. This sounds like strange doctrine, coming from the gentleman from Des Moines, and it appears to me that this is carrying out the principles of squatter sovereignty with a vengeance. I know many men who have not a dollar in the world, who are just as capable of judging what is right and proper upon these subjects, as one who owns millions of property.

I am at a loss to know whether we should restrict counties at all, in this respect. We have forbidden the State from taking stock in corporations, over a certain amount, which, in my opinion, is right and proper. But when we come down to counties and cities, the case is very different. No railroad can pass through a county without benefitting every person in it, in some degree. A railroad may pass through one section of a State, and not benefit other portions of the State; and hence, we have forbidden the State from taking stock for railroad purposes over a certain amount. I live in a section of the State where we have voted loans for railroads, and the people there wish to vote more. I do not, therefore, as a delegate from that section, intend to vote against this principle of county indebtedness, although I think the whole principle is wrong. The children of the present generation, will, in my opinion, have occasion to regret that their fathers were no more wise in the policy they pursued; for I fear that by inviting these railroad companies among us, we are placing ourselves, in some measure, in their power, and that we are creating a monopoly that will wield an influence over our cities and counties, that we will in due time have occasion to regret. Notwithstanding my objections to counties and cities incurring an indebtedness for railroad purposes, as a matter of principle, still, I would not prevent their taking stock in these corporations, if they so desire.

I cannot vote for the substitute of the gentleman from Des Moines, for the reason that he says only those who own property shall vote for loans to railroads. If you carry out that doctrine still farther, you will have property qualifications staring at you on every question that may come before the Legislature; for the same reasons as urged for requiring such a qualification here, may be urged in regard to every other proposition.

I have reflected much upon this subject of universal suffrage, and I have examined with some care that provision in the constitution of Connecticut, which declares that no man shall vote unless he can read and write, and have come to the conclusion that we ought not to place any restriction upon the right of a man to vote upon any subject. I would not restrict the right of a man to vote because he cannot read and write, or because he does not hold property. I would let every man, at all times, go up to the ballot-box and deposite his vote, whether he be rich or poor, ignorant or learned.

Mr. HARRIS. The remarks of the gentleman from Muscatine (Mr. Parvin) will save me the necessity of expressing my views at length, as I intended to do, upon this substitute of the gentleman from Des Moines [Mr. Hall]. When my friend from Des Moines announced this morning, that he was intending to offer a proposition that would be a compromise of this whole matter, I felt greatly relieved; because, as I said to the committee on yesterday, I felt some little regret that I was under the necessi- of occupying the position I did, and giving the vote upon this question that I should feel compelled to give. Hence, I did entertain the hope, that some proposition would be presented by the gentleman from Des Moines that would be a compromise of this matter, and by which we would leave the majority the right to exercise their judgment and discretion in this matter; and at the same time not impose upon them the necessity of saddling upon a respectable minority, taxes that they were not disposed to incur. But I must say that the substitute meets my most unqualified disapprobation, more so than the report of the committee itself.

It has been very truly said by the gentleman from Muscatine (Mr. Parvin), that the grand feature in this substitute is the recognition of the property qualification. There is one point in connection with this matter, to which I wish to call the attention of the committee, and which was not presented by the gentleman from Muscatine.

In this country, property is constantly changing hands; and the man of wealth and position to-day, may become a pauper to-morrow. I cannot see that any security is afforded by confining the right of suffrage in connection with this matter, to the property holders, or to the individuals who pay taxes. Have we any assurance that the man, who to-day holds no position in society, and who would be excluded from exercising the right of suffrage under this provision of property qualification, although he may be a man of intelligence and sagacity, will be a poor man for twenty years to come, during which time this tax may have to be paid? Certainly not; because the children of the poor men of one generation, are the rich men of the next.

I know it is said, that without some restriction of this kind, you throw wide open the door to the laborers who seek for employment upon these internal improvements, and who vote for raising taxes for this purpose, simply that they may, by that means, have employment. But I can see no distinction between this class and those who, under the property qualification vote for these taxes, because they are both benefittted by the building of these roads. It was very properly remarked by the gentleman who last addressed the committee, that we frequently find that men who do not own a dollar in the world, are persons of greater information and better qualified to determine what will be best calculated to advance the interests of the community at large, than many a millionaire, who, in point of intellect, would fall far below the other. My observation does not teach me that the most intellectual and sagacious men in the community are the most wealthy.

I cannot support this proposition to impose a property qualification in this matter of voting a tax for railroad purposes. It meets my most unqualified disapproval, more so than anything that has been presented to the committee in connection with this matter. The more I think about the proposition to give one portion of the community the right to impose burdens upon another class, against their will, for other purposes than those that are necessary for the support of the Government, the more I am confirmed in the sentiments which I have ever entertained, that you have no right to impose a tax only as it becomes necessary for the actual support of the government.

Mr. EDWARDS. I would inquire of the gentleman if he believes it to be a correct principle for a majority of the people in a school district to vote a tax upon the minority for the purpose of erecting a school house, and educating the children of the district?

Mr. HARRIS. Yes sir. I cannot see that there is any parallel between the case of levying taxes for school purposes, and levying taxes for railroad purposes. I advocate the policy to the full extent, of compelling the man of property, whether he has children or not, to pay taxes to educate the children of his poor neighbor. I make a great distinction between the voting to levy a tax for building school-houses, and employing school-masters for the education of the children of the poor man, and voting to compel a man to pay a tax and burthen himself with a debt, for the purpose of making money for a corporation. I apprehend, that there is no gentleman here, who will undertake to say that under our institutions, the majority in a county or State would have the right to impose a tax upon the minority, for the purpose of entering into manufactures of any kind, for establishing a corporation for a paper mill, a grist mill, a cotton mill, or woolen factory. And yet these would be corporations established for making money out of the community, just as railroad corporations are. You might say, that they would be corporations established for the benefit of the farmer, as they might increase the price of his wool and grain, the same as a railroad would increase the price of property, in the section of the country through which it passes. I apprehend, that there is no gentleman here who will stand up and say that the majority have the right to force the balance of the community to come in, as associates and partners, in any manufacturing establishment. I cannot see, from whence the right is obtained, on the part of the majority, to compel the minority to come in as associates in railroad or any institutions, other than municipal corporations. This is the view in which this question presents itself to my mind, and I will now close by again declaring that I am strongly opposed to the substitute of the gentleman from Des Moines [Mr. Hall].

Mr. GILLASPY. I only desire to say that I am opposed to the proposition of the gentleman from Des Moines, [Mr. Hall,] and shall vote against it. I think it attacks one of the great principles of right that every American citizen should be proud to sustain, and that is, the principle of the right of suffrage. I recollect very well that I was a voter in this territory when I was not worth a dollar, yet I believe I was just as competent to discharge that duty then as I am to-day. It is on account of that feature in the proposition of the gentleman from Des Moines, that I shall be compelled to vote against it.

And I want to say that I do not concur with the honorable gentleman from Muscatine, [Mr. Parvin.] I do not believe in the doctrine of *universal* suffrage. That is a very broad term. And I would have been glad if the gentleman had had the frankness and candor, when he commenced defining the broad question of universal suffrage, to have gone through with it, and not stop after he had said "the rich and poor." Why did he not go on and say that the mulatto, the negro, and the Indian had the same right in his opinion as the white man? Why stop after referring to the white race? Why did he not put himself upon the record by saying exactly what he means, when he talks about universal suffrage?

Mr. PARVIN. I refe.red distinctly in my remarks to the limits set down in the present constitution as being what I meant. And I will put myself on the record to that effect, whenever I have an opportunity.

Mr. GILLASPY. I do net understand that the doctrine of universal suffrage is laid down in the old constitution; if it is so, I have never seen it. If the gentleman will show it to me, I shall be pleased to have him do so. As to the putting himself upon the record, I hope he will put himself upon the record and say, the negro, the mulatto, and the Indian have the right to vote.

Mr. PARVIN. The old constitution does not say that.

Mr. GILLASPY. Neither does the present constitution say anything of the kind. The gentleman cannot get out of it in that way.

Mr. HALL. I desire to offer a few remarks at this stage of the discussion. I assure gentlemen that I will not vote for any proposition in this constitution, that will authorize or inculcate the doctrine of universal suffrage, when that phrase is applied to the kind of voting that robs men of their property without their consent. Why, sir, the veriest agrarianism that was ever yet inculcated by the philosophy of the most chimerical mind in the world, never went beyond that. Talk about the right of suffrage! when they are voting the property of a man into a speculation against his wishes and his consent! Talk about the right of suffrage? Why, it is the highest prerogative of government to do such a thing as that; it is the worst kind of despotism that claims that power over man and his property. The ordinary taxing power in the government is bad enough, and is always looked upon with jealousy. But to make a man go into a private enterprise and speculation without his consent, to have him forced into it by those who have no individual interest in it, and contribute nothing to it, is something with which the right of suffrage has nothing to do. It is nothing but agrarianism from beginning to end.

We should approach this subject with great caution, and meet it and bridle it at the very first step we can, if it is to prevail at all. It is argued here that it is a natural right of the majority to vote money out of my pocket, and put it into a business, where I do not want it to go. I would ask where do you find any natural right for that? I beg gentlemen to turn to the Bill of Rights, which was adopted a few days ago, and see how far this fallacious right of universal suffrage is there embodied. The very first section reads:

"All men are, by nature, free and independent, and have certain unalienable rights, among which are those of enjoying and defending life and liberty, acquiring, possessing and protecting property, and pursuing and obtaining safety and happiness."

Now, I would ask how much protection a man has for his property, when you say that the right of suffrage will allow the majority to take it rrom him, and if they please, divide it among them, and divide, you may as well say, the property of all the citizens throughout the county every Saturday night? Is there any right of suffrage in that? No, sir, it is the trampling down a great right and privilege, which is guaranteed to every American citizen.

As I said yesterday, we have entered into this matter of county and city indebteness, while under a state of excitement. The several counties of this State have involved themselves, from eight to twelve millions of dollars, already in this indebtedness. The question before us now is, shall this system go on; shall it be continued without restriction? Shall we still go on under the principle that the majority of any county, without reference to the interest they may have in any enterprise when completed, shall decide whether the enterprise is worthy the assistance of the county, and how much the county shall involve itself in carrying it on?

There is no doctrine of the right of suffrage involved in this matter. There are two sides to this question. I stand here as a property-holder, and claim to be protected, in the enjoyment of that property, by my government. That is one side of the question. On the other side comes up a dozen men, who, perhaps, have been in the State barely long enough to acquire a residence, who have no interest in the State, and who have never contributed anything to the support of the government; and they say to me—here is a project we want to have you enter into, so that we may have some work to do. Now I do not want to do any such thing. But a vote is taken, and they vote a portion of my property to the carrying on of the enterprise, because it gives them work to do. They decide that it is a profitable investment, and also decide how much I shall give to afford them business and employment. Now in France the government has to furnish this employment to the people; it has to open work-shops, and furnish a certain amount of the pay for the purpose of keeping a certain class of people in employment, fearful that, unless they are furnished with this employment, they would become revolutionists, and overturn the government. And yet there is not a reflecting man anywhere, whether in France or elsewhere, who does not condemn that policy as a bad one, and one which must ultimately prove fatal to the government which attempts to bolster itself up by this means.

Now, if you adopt the principle I have suggested here, and let only those men who pay the money, decide whether or not a project is a feasible one, you at least guard the rights of property to that extent. There will be no injustice done to those who contribute nothing; it is no attack whatever upon the elective franchise. The object of government is to protect men in the enjoyment of their property, and not to dispossess them of it when they have acquired it. The right of suffrage has no application whatever to this matter now before us. I am sure that those who desire to act rightly upon this subject, will see, after a few moments reflection, that this right of suffrage, when applied to this matter of creating a debt against a political or municipal corporation for the purpose of private speculation and individual enterprise, has no application to the matter at all.—There is no analogy between the two principles.

I hope the convention will examine this subject carefully, before they decide upon it. As I have said before, this matter has been experimented upon, and we have felt in my section of the country, the results of it. And I understand that it was the feeling of every reflecting mind in the city and county where I reside, that this restriction should be placed in our Constitution. I know the Governor of the State, who resides in the same city with myself, actually drafted or indicated the plan of the bill, which was passed by the legislature, to allow those who have to pay this tax, the exclusive right to impose it. Had those who have to pay the taxes, voted to impose it, there would not be that complaint there now is. But our people have borne it as long as they can, and have shielded themselves this year by legislative action.

I think if we permit this thing at all, this restriction is absolutely necessary. As I said on yesterday, this matter will not bear the test, when weighed by the principles in the bill of of rights, which we have already sanctioned.—This thing will not stand that test. I am unwilling to open the door wider now than is necessary, to enable us to secure ourselves in what has already been done. We have the wolf by the ears, and dare not let go, and it is dangerous to hold on much longer. We must adopt the best plan we can. The eastern counties have involved themselves, by voting those loans, with the expectation that when the roads progressed to to the west, they would come forward and help us. But if the western counties are cut off from giving us this aid, the enterprises we have engaged in must fail; the counties already engaged or embarked in them must suffer loss, and the improvements must fail or be greatly delayed. The very fact that you have stock worth to the companies but sixty or seventy cents on the dollar, which is quoted at par, forever cuts off the idea of carrying on these roads by private subscription. If these improvements are to be carried on, I am of the opinion that some measure, just and fair to all, should be adopted, by which future subscription be obtained upon proper terms. But I do not want, in the name of conscience, to have this idea of the right of suffrage brought in here.

Now, to illustrate my argument. The Burlington and Louisa railroad is completed nearly to the line of Jefferson county, or nearly through Henry county. We want an additional loan from that county. This company may throw in six hundred or eight hundred votes there, and overwhelm the vote of the county. This very thing has been done in Illinois, where the citizens of a county were voted down by the hands working on the railroad there. Now I want to so guard this matter in our Constitution that, if these debts are to be voted against the property of the county, those who own the property shall have the privilege of doing it.

Mr. WILSON. It seems to me that if we are to stand by abstract principles of justice in this matter, we must go farther back than this proposition appears to go. It seems to me we shall have to go back to the first section of the article upon the right of suffrage, and instead of saying that "every white male citizen of the United States, of the age of twenty-one years, who shall have been a resident of the State six months next preceding the election, and the county in which he claims his vote, twenty days, shall be entitled to *vote at all elections* which are now, or may be hereafter authorized by law," we should make it read "in all elections no person shall be entitled to vote unless he possesses ——— dollars worth of taxable property." The principle of the proposition of the gentleman from Des Moines [Mr. Hall] is good for nothing unless it can be carried to that extent. I cannot conceive how you can hold elections upon any subject, or for any purpose whatever, without involving to a certain extent, the question of taxation. And if gentlemen are going to stand by the groundwork and principle in this case, they must provide a property qualification to be applied to every election.

I have been somewhat surprised at the position taken by the gentleman from Des Moines, and I know that my constituents will be quite as much surprised as I am, when they come to read his speeches here. I remember very well when the gentleman was in the county I have the honor to represent here, endeavoring to get that county to take an additional one hundred thousand dollars worth of stock in the Burlington railroad company. The county of Jefferson had already voted the sum of one hundred thousand dollars, and the cry came up from the company that the road could not progress without an additional one hundred thousand dollars. And I am very confident that the position occupied by the gentleman from Des Moines, at a public meeting held at the court house in Fairfield, was very different from his position here to-day. I well remember that he told our people that it was a good investment, that the stock in the company would be a good paying stock, and that the people would never have to pay a dollar of their bonds, but the dividends of the road would pay the interest upon the bonds, and bring revenue into the treasury. I did not believe it at the time, and I opposed it, and it was voted down in our county. And it does seem to me that the speeches we have heard here to-day will present a strange contrast when they come before my constituents, to the speeches made in the county at that time.

I am opposed to the substitute of the gentleman; and I cannot for the soul of me, see why a man should have to pay five dollars tax, or be possessed of two hundred dollars worth of taxable property, before he shall be allowed to vote upon this subject. Now if a man pays one cent of tax, he pays just as much, in proportion to his ability, as any other man. And when the tax is imposed, it cannot be told who are to pay it. The poor man of to-day may be the rich man of to-morrow. The men who pay no tax, and according to this substitute would not be allowed any voice in creating this debt, may to-morrow have to bear the burden resulting from that debt. I cannot tell why this provision should not be applied to all matters of taxation; to our school tax, for there we vote to tax one man for the benefit of another man's children.

So far as the doctrine of subscriptions to incorporations for internal improvements is concerned, I have this to say, that I believe the principle to be a wrong one, and if it were a new question in this state, I should have no hesitation in coming to the conclusion that it would be our policy in this convention to prohibit it entirely. But under present circumstances, I do not believe it would be good and wise policy for us to do so: I believe it would be a death blow to this Constitution when it goes before the people, if we were to place a total restriction in it, aside from the injustice of the doctrines of the proposition of the gentleman from Des Moines. Many of the men who will vote upon this Constitution are poor men, men who pay no taxes at all. And yet these men are just as jealous of their right of suffrage as rich men can be. And if you submit a Constitution to them, containing a property qualification, every one of them will vote against it, and your Constitution will be voted down. I believe the proposition of the gentleman from Des Moines is wrong in principle, and I believe it will be wrong in practice, and disastrous in its results upon the fate of the new Constitution.

Mr. CLARKE, of Johnson. As I understand the question now before the committee, the substitute of the gentleman from Des Moines [Mr. Hall,] is a substitute for a motion of the gentleman from Lucas [Mr. Edwards,] whose proposition is a substitute for a portion of the fourth section.

The CHAIRMAN. The substitute of the gentleman from Des Moines, is a substitute for the fourth and fifth sections of the report of the committee on incorporations.

Mr. CLARKE, of Johnson. I will state here that when this substitute is disposed of, I shall propose a substitute for the fourth section myself, which I will read now for the information of the Convention:

"No political or municipal corporation shall become a stockholder in any banking corporation, directly or indirectly; but such corporations may become stockholders in corporations for works of internal improvements within the State, upon a vote of the citizens of such municipal corporations, under such restrictions, as to the mode and amount of subscription, as the General Assembly may prescribe."

Mr. BUNKER. I do not know but I ought to make an apology for the opposition I made on yesterday to going into committee of the Whole upon this subject of incorporations, on the ground that I was not fully prepared to act upon this subject, and wished to have it postponed until Wednesday next. I do not know, however, but what I was as well prepared to go into committee of the whole, as others who refused to agree to the postponement, because they said they were fully posted upon this whole matter. At least I judge so from the course of the discussion here, and I do not know but that I should make an apology for opposing going into the committee of the whole. I have heard gentlemen who professed to be fully prepared to act, get up here and speak upon all sides of the subject. We have had very beautiful and forcible speeches upon all sides of the question, intended, I suppose, to enlighten the minds of those, who, like myself, were not prepared to act upon it. We have had both sides presented in all their force, by the same gentlemen. There are a few, however, who appear to take one side distinctly and clearly.

The gentleman from Dubuque [Mr. Emerson,] took one side of the question definitely and clearly. I would only remark in relation to the position he assumed here yesterday, that if the abstract principle is worth anything, it will go a great deal farther than he carried it. We could not levy a tax upon the people for their benefit; for he and others would step aside and say, this property is mine and secured to me, and the public shall not tax my property for the common benefit. And so with regard to municipal taxation and regulations; the tax laws of the State; the common school fabric; he may step aside and say, I do not want your protection; I do not want your government extended over me, for I will place myself upon my natural rights, my inherent rights, and refuse to be taxed to support any governmental fabric. And so you can go on. And if you follow up that abstract principle you will destroy every principle of social government. I cannot see any distinction in this matter, or if there is one, it is a distinction without a difference. You may say you have an inherent and natural right to tax men to sustain the common school fabric, to construct roads, and build school-houses, and all this thing; but you have no inherent right to tax people to construct for them works of internal improvement, because it will yield a profit to some, who may not pay a portion of the tax which is levied to build these works.

I regard this matter merely as a question of expediency. This question has been submitted to my county a number of times. I have generally voted against it myself, but I voted for the last proposition, because it was presented upon a different basis from that which the previous propositions occupied. I would be willing to let the people themselves judge of what they deem to be for their common benefit. I do not think it is proper for this Convention to exercise a dictatorial power over the people and say to them, you shall not do this or that thing, which you as a community may desire. We have here just agreed to a clause by which we have conferred unlimited power upon the State of Iowa, to contract any amount of indebtedness for any object, by submitting the matter to a vote of the people of the State. No opposition was made in this Convention to that clause. If that is right, it appears to me that it is equally right in principle for the people of a county to enjoy the same privileges as a community, that we have so freely conferred upon the people of the State as a community.

The gentleman from Des Moines [Mr. Hall,] travels off into the bill of rights, in order to ascertain something about this matter. I believe we have not finally acted upon that bill of rights yet. I have offered a substitute for the first section, which the gentleman quoted, which substitute was was referred to a special committee, which will report, I hope, in favor of it. I do not believe the first section of the bill of rights speaks the truth at all. I believe it is a falsehood, and not a truth, and hence I offered the substitute for it which I did. This subject may not properly belong to this discussion, but as the gentleman quoted that section, I will give my views upon it.

That section declares that "all men are, by nature, free and independent." I hold that to be absolutely false, that there is no truth in it at all. All men are not independent; yet this clause means, if I understand it, that all men who ever were, or ever will be, are by nature, free and independent. According to my view of this matter, every human being is forced into this world without his knowledge or consent. I have had some little experience of this matter of being introduced into the world, and as far as I am familiar with it, a man is forced into the world a perfectly helpless creature, and without the aid of his fellow-beings, would not live a single day. He is perfectly dependent upon his fellows for his very existence.

The gentleman quotes the property qualification in this section, which is, "All men, &c., have certain inalienable rights, among which are those of acquiring, possessing, and protecting property." He says that all men have an inherent right to acquire, possess, and protect property. Now I passed over that matter in my substitute, because I believe no man has an inherent right in property, except just so far as it is given or conferred upon him by the divine principles of grace. And I think that the principles of grace and the principles of nature are very similar. I believe you have an inherent right of property, just so far as you do to your fellow-man as you would have him do to you; and there your property right ceases. I do not believe that, if by some extraordinary hook or crook, you or I should come into the possession of all the property on this continent, either you or I would have any natural or inherent right to famish and starve any member of the human family that may be upon this continent, and to hold this property as an inherent right from the great Creator. Our property right, when we carry it beyond the principle, of doing to others as we would have them do to us, is simply a legal right. I do not propose to interfere with that legal right at all, and I have luded to it merely as connected with the marks of the gentleman from Des Moines [Mr. Hall].

I hope those gentlemen who pressed this subject to a consideration in committee of the whole, will come out and let us know which side they are really on. I cannot make out where they are. I think I shall vote for allowing the counties some privilege to act for themselves.

Mr. SOLOMON. Before the vote is taken upon this question, I would like to say a few words; and I shall endeavor to speak directly to the question which has been before us for the last hour, without referring to that other question, whether we should allow the counties to proceed in this matter.

So far as I can understand it, the proposition before us is, whether we will restrict the right to vote upon this matter of county debts by a property qualification. I will confine my remarks to that point, as the discussion seems mostly to have been directed to it; and I must say that, however much I may dislike to differ from the distinguished gentlemen who offered this proposition, a gentleman upon whose sagacity and ability we all so much rely, to keep us from error in framing this constitution, yet I must beg leave to differ from him, and dissent *in toto* from his proposition. I think it is wrong in principle, from the ground work to the top. I think it is radically wrong; and not only that, I do not see a single ingredient in the proposition which would have any direct tendency to bring about what the gentleman would consider a desirable result.

Let us examine the gentleman's proposition a little. It is this: to confer upon a certain class of citizens in each county the right to vote upon this question; and that class upon which the gentleman would confer this prerogative is to be selected solely with reference to their possession of property. If they possess property enough to pay a tax of five dollars, or if they own two hundred dollars worth of real estate, then they can be allowed to vote upon this question; that is to say, the gentleman makes the possession of property the criterion of the right to vote. Now, there is a distinction between the possession of, and the right to, property. Does the gentleman mean that both, or only one, of these things shall be required to entitle a citizen to vote? Does the gentleman mean that the mere right, without possession, to two hundred dollars worth of real estate, shall not entitle a man to vote? If he has an interest in that property, and if this interest is the ground upon which he shall have a right to vote this debt upon the property of the county, why not permit this right to confer the power to vote, as well as permit the possession of the property to confer that power? And if the right to the property confers this power to vote, then that privilege would be conferred upon persons who are not residents of the county in which the vote is taken. One-half, if not two-thirds, of the owners of the real estate in the district I represent, are non-residents of that district. Will you confer this right to vote upon all, or only upon the residents in the county or district, and allow them to exercise this prerogative over the property of those who are not residents therein? If you do this, then the object which the gentleman says he has in view, will not be reached, for the property of persons not in the county would be confiscated to this public project without their consent, and even without their knowledge; not only without their votes, but without their personal influence at the polls. The proposition is then imperfect in its operation, even if the principle upon which it is based were a just one.

I do not see why there should be any limit in this case. I think that the effect of these improvements, upon the future prosperity and character of the county, is as much worthy of consideration, as their effect upon the property of individuals in the county. If that is so, then have not I, who may have just come into the county, and may not be worth the proposed amount, just as deep an interest in the future character of the county, as the man who owns property sufficient under this proposition to be entitled to vote? Certainly I have. I have a pride in the matter. I desire to have my county hold out inducements to persons to come there and settle, and increase its wealth and prosperity; and I may be just as capable of judging of these improvements to induce this settlement, as the man who owns a large amount of property, and I think I ought to have the privilege of expressing that judgment at the polls. It is said, that if you allow this voting to be done in the counties, without respect to property qualifications, you would substitute in the place of non-resident land-holders, voters who have come in, but do not possess the requisite property interest in the matter. That, I think, is but just. If men, who have invested their gold in these lands in our new counties, will not come in themselves and assist in the formation of society, and the developement of the counties, then the elective franchise should fall upon those who do go there, whether they are able to buy property or not. That is the way I look at it.

I have commenced life in a new county, where there was no society, where there was almost the opposite of society, in a Mormon village. I expect always to live there. And I do not desire to see men, who from misfortune in business or otherwise, have not been able to acquire this property qualification, deprived of this right of franchise, without some better reason than the gentleman from Des Moines (Mr. Hall,) has yet offered. I shall say nothing farther upon this subject; but close without saying one word in reference to the propriety of allowing counties the right to vote at all upon this matter.

Mr. SKIFF. I know very well, that the position taken by the delegate from Des Moines, (Mr. Hall,) upon this question, is a little unpopular; but I do not see any very great objection to it. It seems to touch some delegates here in rather a tender spot, some who are young men, and do not desire to have any property qualifications applied to them. In ordinary cases I am myself opposed to any property qualification for voting. But here is an extraordinary occasion; I think, a very extraordinary occasion. If a number of my neighbors and myself are going to incorporate ourselves for manufacturing purposes, for instance, our articles of incorporation state that each one of us shall have a vote according to the number of shares that we may hold. That is the manner of incorporations, whether for banking, or any other kind of business. Now it seems to me, that if the citizens of a county desire to embark in internal improvements, and invest their property in an incorporated company, some provision of this kind should prevail, in order that this matter should not be controlled by a class of voters totally irresponsible, so far as pecuniary matters are concerned; for instance, that class of persons to which the delegate from Des Moines (Mr. Hall,) has alluded, the laborers upon railroads, who only desire to have as many works of internal improvement going on as we can possibly have, in order to make the price of their labor higher. They are interested in the matter only in this way; this is the only light in which they view it. But that is not the light in which the tax payers of the county look at this question. They look upon it as a proposition to take part of their property to build works of internal improvement.

This matter then is not one that may be considered as coming under the ordinary course of voting. The building of a court house in our county is something that should be decided by the ordinary mode of voting, it is something in the ordinary course of political organization. The election of our officers is something in the ordinary course of things; so is the building of school houses in our school districts. And if there is a man there who has no children to be educated, but monopolizes most all the property in the district, I say stick the tax right on him just as strongly as you please, and make him pay it. And I do not care if you make him help support the school after the school house is built.

But I do not believe it is right, or in the ordinary course of govermental purposes, for you to take a part of my property, or my neighbors' property, and put it in incorporations for works of internal improvement, and force us along in the current, against our wills, unless a majority of those, who are situated as we are, say that we shall do so. I would not have every man vote upon this matter, whether interested in it or not, and who votes for it merely because it will give him a good job of work. I know how this matter will sound before the people, and it may operate badly against me. But if my constituents prefer somebody else to represent them, why, all I have to say, is, that they may lose more than I will. I do not care two coppers about being in another deliberative body. I am perfectly independent in this matter, and I suppose other gentlemen here are just as independent as I am.

These are my sentiments, and I shall vote for something like the proposition of the delegate from Des Moines, if I have an opportunity, because I believe it to be right.

Mr. MARVIN. I had not proposed to take any part in this discussion, and I shall say but little now. I did not suppose the proposition of the gentleman from Des Moines (Mr. Hall,) would meet with sufficient encouragement to require much opposition. His proposition is one that I have been called upon to meet in many ways since I have entered upon active life. It has been urged here in favor of this proposition, that if something of this kind is not adopted, a railroad company may import sufficient laborers into a county to impose just what tax they please upon the people of that county. But may not that occur in other elections? May there not be members upon this floor to-day, who hold their seats by means of these imported voters? I do not say there is; but there is equal danger to be apprehended from that source in the one case as in the other. Now if there were any means, under a democratic government, of subjecting these imported voters to a certain ordeal, I would be willing to vote for it. But there is not. We know that many elections have been carried by these imported voters, and we may look forward to the time when, perhaps, our institutions may be changed by just such voters.

Now you propose to place a restriction upon persons who vote upon this question, and that that restriction shall be, the payment of taxes to the amount of five dollars. Let us examine the practical working of this proposition. For instance, I have a superanuated old man for a neighbor, who is worth one hundred thousand dollars, or five hundred thousand dollars. He has, like a miser, hoarded every dollar he could obtain, and the county has never been benefitted by it. He will not vote for improvements of any kind, because he will be called upon to pay out some of his cherished gold. Near him lives another man, who possesses eighty acres of land, worth perhaps one hundred dollars. But he has a clear head and a strong arm, worth more to the county than the one hundred thousand dollars of the other man. Well, you say that this man, whose children will perhaps be called upon to pay the tax thus imposed, shall not have a voice in the imposing that tax, because he has not two hundred dollars worth of real estate, while you give the right of voting to this tottering old dotard! That is not republican doctrine, as I understand it.

I have no desire to prolong this discussion. I merely desired to state to the convention, as briefly as possible, the position I occupy, and my reasons for that position. While I am in favor of leaving this subject to the people, I would rather strike out all the provisions relating to it, than have property qualifications attached to this subject. I cannot separate this proposition from the principle of the right of suffrage. You may just as well extend this property qualification to every other kind of voting as to this. If you propose to build a bridge, or a school house, this principle would apply just as well to that, as to this matter. Therefore if you restrict the right of suffrage in the one case, you should, to be consistent, restrict it in the others.

Mr. SCOTT. I would ask the gentleman from Des Moines (Mr. Hall,) if it is absolutely necessary that a special guarantee and privilege should be placed in our constitution, in order to allow a few rich individuals of a city, or county, to take stock in these railroads? I should suppose that they might be able to take stock just as well without this constitutional provision as with it. I may be mistaken; if I am, then I may be shown that there is some necessity for this substitute, the gentleman has proposed. If I am not mistaken, then I cannot see the object of this proposition.

Mr. HALL. I consider that this matter of railroads has just about as much to do with our municipal institutions as the fifth wheel has to do with the efficiency of a wagon. I do not consider that it pertains to the legitimate operations of government. In whatever belongs to the legitimate operations of government I would go for giving every person the right of suffrage—the rich and the poor equally. In that matter I will go as far as the farthest. But I will also go as far as the farthest to let every individual do with his own as he pleases. I would let him subscribe stock to those railroads, or refuse to do so, as he might choose. It is this freedom to do either the one or the other that he may please, that I am contending for. I am seeking to prevent the majority from subscribing for the minority without their consent; or at least, I would have those who authorise the subscription to be those who are themselves to be affected by the debt they may authorize to be created. I would not have this tax imposed by those who will have none of it to pay.

Gentlemen talk here as if it was a part of the legitimate business of government to build railroads. In that I think they are mistaken. This is a new idea; and gentlemen did not learn it from the old Democratic party, whatever they may have learned from their new Republican party. The idea that I can be forced to contribute my property for something that is not for the protection of the life, liberty and property of the community, is a violation of all the principles of freedom, and an unwarranted encroachment upon the rights of man. And if it is to be incorporated in our system of government, in any way, let us at least guard, check and limit it; let us confine it in some way, that we may have a good jury and some challenges, when we are to be tried and have our property taken from us. Let us have a partnership matter of it, and have it so that if a man proposes to take our property for this debt, he shall also become a partner in the affair.

And I tell gentlemen, that if this proposition, or the principle contained in it, is not popular to day, the time is not far off, when the people of this state are being taxed millions of dollars for her debts, when taxes are being levied upon the people of this State beyond what any other State may have to bear, they may think of this proposition, and may regret that they did not adopt this check, or put this bridle upon this question of imposing debts upon the different counties by a mere vote of the majority. Look forward a little, and see where this matter will lead you, if you adopt the principle that the property of the minority is subject to the will of the majority, without any constitutional restriction or restraint whatever. Where will you stop? Is this a constitutional government? Have we laws instituted to protect every man in all his rights? We seem to have everything at loose ends here.

Now, I understand democracy differently from what some gentlemen appear to do here. It is not the blind following of the will of the majority. It is liberty regulated by law; liberty first fixed by constitutional regulations, and then protected and guarded by law. I understand liberty to consist in my enjoying my property and other rights, without the encroachment or interference of government, any farther than is necessary to carry out the great principle of protecting and preserving the rights of all. Government has no right to try to make me rich; it has no power to make me rich, and can give me nothing unless it takes from some one who has it. If it does it at all, it must do it at the expense of somebody else. It is powerless in itself for any such thing. A man is best off when he is free to live and use his property as he pleases, restricted only by those regulations essential to the peace and order of the community, and the protection of the rights of others. That government is the best which is regulated by those principles best calculated to preserve the rights of all, and infringe upon the rights of none, except so far as the legitimate objects of government may require.

Talk to me of the elective franchise! of the right of suffrage inherent in every man to vote my property away! to take my means that I have accumulated and devote them to any purpose against my will! I do not care how miserly a man may be. It is his privilege and his right to be so. The right of suffrage, indeed! The right to vote property out of a man's pocket against his consent, for purposes of private speculation, and to make other men rich! There is no right about it, except the right of the robber, the right of the highwayman and the pirate; nothing more nor less than that, and if this principle is to be recognised here at all, I shall go as far as I can to restrict and limit it.

Mr. HARRIS. I would ask the gentleman from Des Moines [Mr. Hall] if he can make any distinction between the right of the majority to vote away his property, when that majority consists of property holders, and when they consist of those who do not hold property?

Mr. HALL. There is no distinction in principle; but there is a vast distinction in the security that is given a man that his property shall not be improperly used. I would rather have my rights of property depend upon men who are equally interested with myself, than upon men who have nothing to lose, but everything to gain. It gives me a better tribunal before which I must go; I have more assurance of safety and protection in the enjoyment of my property, because I get at least all the security they give themselves. That is the reason why I think it is better to have the property holders vote upon this question, than to have everybody come in and vote. I have some assurance that the project in which my property is to be invested will be a wise and proper one, and one in which I will be less liable to loss.

Now, one word in regard to the remarks of the gentleman from Jefferson (Mr. Wilson). He is remarkable for his historical recollections. He recollects things about me that I do not recollect myself; that I have been ignorant of all my life. He hunts up his recollection for a quarter of a century back. Now, I have never, on the stump or elsewhere, advocated the principle of county subscription, except when I felt that the project was a safe and proper one, that it would be profitable to all who invested their means in it. I appropriated my own individual means to it, and urged it upon the people as a matter of policy. I was unsuccessful in Jefferson county, I admit. But as to advocating this doctrine as an abstract principle, I am very confident I never did it anywhere. I hesitated long before I engaged in that enterprise. But whether I advocated this principle or not, I do not feel myself bound, in the position I hold here, by declarations I may have made in times past, and under other circumstances. I admit that I am frail, and as apt to be wrong and inconsistent as other men; but I shall endeavor, as far as possible, to do what is right while I am acting in this convention.

Mr. PARVIN. I do hope that this Convention will take no steps backward in this matter of the right of suffrage. I had supposed that the principle of requiring a property qualification for voting had long since passed away, not to be introduced again either in this body or any other, at least in the State of Iowa.

Now, let us look at the practical operation of this proposition. The gentleman proposes here that no person shall be allowed to vote upon this subject without he possesses a real estate property of two hundred dollars assessed value, or pays a tax amounting to five dollars.

Mr. HALL. I merely put those amounts in to complete the proposition, and get the principle before this Convention. I will not promise to vote for those amounts myself. All I desire is to assert the principle that if a vote is to be taken upon giving the credit of cities to these works of internal improvements, the owners of property shall be the persons who shall decide the question.

Mr. PARVIN. Very well; this sum of two hundred dollars is just as good as any other to illustrate the principle. We will suppose that there is a man in one of the new counties who owns not quite land enough to be worth two hundred dollars. He is anxious to have a railroad built through that county to enhance the value of that land. He is willing to work hard to pay his tax. But he is not worth quite enough to entitle him to vote to have the road. There is another man who has just two hundred dollars worth of land, who lives by the side of a millionaire. And he can go to the polls and vote while his neighbor, with nearly the same amount, and with an equal interest, cannot vote. And the man worth a million of dollars can vote no more than the one worth just two hundred dollars. I use this illustration to show the inconsistency of this principle, when practically tested. Now, if you wish to establish a property qualification, let it be a just and strict property qualification, and graduate it from two hundred dollars up, or it will not be a strictly property qualification in practice.

I am opposed to this property qualification in any shape. I rejoice that I can vote as well as my neighbor, who has ten times as much property as I have. It is a right that is inestimably dear to every citizen.

Now one word more.

I desire to allude to another subject. I had not intended to do so, but as I am speaking, I will refer to it briefly. I know that my friend from Wapello (Mr. Gillaspy) intended nothing wrong in his remarks, for his heart is in the right place all the time. But when he alluded to the remarks I made about universal suffrage, he forgot to mention that what I said was in reference to the qualifications now required by our present constitution. It may be that I shall vote for something different from that, if the opportunity is presented to me. But I assure you, gentlemen of this Convention, that I am not afraid to put myself upon the record, whether I shall be able to sustain myself before the people or not.

But the gentlemam from Des Moines (Mr. Hall) says that if you allow a man without property to vote upon the question of these public improvements, his vote will counterbalance the vote of a man who has property.

Mr. HALL. I deny that they are public improvements; they are not owned by the public when made. but they are private property.

Mr. PARVIN. I suppose the gentleman means the private property of the county. The county gives her bonds and receives her stock, upon which she expects to receive dividends. The men who are not property holders do not vote for the purpose of taking property from the property holders, but, as they believe for the best interests of the county. I know how this matter has operated in the city and county of Muscatine, where these loans have been voted. I know that to some pretty considerable extent, those men who have no property, have voted against these loans, because they did not want to pay taxes for improvements which were no benefit to them, inasmuch as they had no property to be enhanced in value.

I hope the Convention will pause before they impose any such restriction as this, of a property qualification, upon the rights of any man to vote.

Mr. CLARKE, of Johnson. I was in hopes we would have been able to take a vote upon this question before adjourning this morning; but as the discussion seems to be taking a wide range, I move the committee rise, report progress, and ask leave to sit again.

The question being then taken, the motion that the committee rise was agreed to.

In Convention.

The PRESIDENT having resumed the chair:

The CHAIRMAN of the Committee of the Whole reported that the committee had had under consideration the subject referred to them, had made some progress therein, and asked leave to sit again.

The report of the Committee of the Whole was received, and leave granted accordingly.

Mr. SKIFF moved that the Convention adjourn to meet on Monday morning at ten o'clock.

Upon this question Mr. GILLASPY called for the yeas and nays, which were ordered.

The question being then taken by yeas and nays, the motion was not agreed to—yeas 5; nays 28, as follows:

Yeas—Messrs. Bunker, Clarke of Johnson, Ells, Skiff, Traer.

Nays—The President, Messrs. Ayres, Clarke of Henry, Clark of Alamakee, Day, Edwards, Emerson, Gibson, Gillaspy, Gower, Gray, Hall, Harris, Johnston, Marvin, Palmer, Parvin, Patterson, Peters, Price, Robinson, Scott, Seely, Solomon, Warren, Wilson, Winchester, and Young.

On motion of Mr. HARRIS,

The Convention iook a recess until 2 o'clock this afternoon.

EVENING SESSION.

The Convention met at two o'clock P. M., and was called to order by the President.

The Convention then resumed in Committee of the Whole, (Mr. Traer in the Chair,) the consideration of the report of the Committee on Incorporations.

The CHAIRMAN stated the question to be on the substitute offered by the gentleman from Des Moines [Mr. Hall,] which was read.

County and City Indebtedness.

Mr. EMERSON. I propose now, Mr. Chairman, to finish the remarks, which I was prevented by indisposition, from completing on yesterday. I had then, I believe, called the attention of the committee to the precedent set us by Ohio, in adopting a provision, in her constitution of 1851, which declares that the General Assembly shall never authorize counties, cities or towns, by vote of the people, to become stockholders in any joint stock corporations. Gentlemen have referred us, with an air of great satisfaction, to Ohio, as being a State where the taxation of counties, for railroad purposes, had served to develope the resources and wealth of the State. But we find that, as soon as the opportunity came, the people, through their convention for a revision of the constitution, put a final estopper upon the principle of county and city indebtedness, to be incurred for the purpose of taking stock in railroad projects. The people of Ohio, at one time, were completely carried away by this mad idea, that in order to have a system of railroads at all, it was necessary for the cities and counties to incur indebtedness. It only required a few years experience, however, to teach them that the principle was wrong in itself, and one which, if carried out to its ultimate consequences, must inevitably end in ruin to their best interests.

Gentlemen in the course of this debate, have acknowledged that the principle of county taxation for railroad projects was all wrong. Yet, they say, as we have already allowed some counties to take stock and incur an indebtedness for railroads, we must not deprive other counties of the same privilege. Acknowledging that the principle is wrong, and that the results growing out of its adoption, will, in the end, prove disastrous to the best interests of the State, yet they come forward, and, in this enlightened day tell us that the way to cure an evil is to increase it. A very strange doctrine indeed!

It seems to me, sir, that this is not the proper place to consider and entertain questions of expediency; that we have a higher duty to perform; and that duty is, to lay down the great fundamental principles, which will guard the minority against the unjust encroachments of the majority. Holding, as I do, sir, that the primary object of a constitution, is to throw guards and checks around the several departments of government, to define and limit their action, and to guard and protect the inalienable rights of the people against abuses, it seems to me this is the wrong form in which to consider questions of mere expediency.

I desire, gentlemen, to consider the general proposition I have advanced, as bearing upon this question. I wish now to examine a few of the positions taken by gentlemen upon the other side in the course of this discussion. The gentleman from Lucas [Mr. Edwards,] referred to the great work of New York, the Erie Canal, of which De Witt Clinton was the originator. He told you that Mr. Clinton addressed Thomas Jefferson upon the subject, and because Mr. Jefferson did not view the contemplated improvement in the same light with Mr. Clinton, that therefore it was conclusive in the premises, that his position with reference to county and city indebtedness was right. All I have to say to the gentleman is, that I do not arrive at the same conclusion from the premises, that he does. I suppose there is not a member of this Convention who is opposed to internal improvements; hence, there can be no controversy on that point. The only question, and the practical question for us to decide, is in reference to the propriety or impropriety of counties and cities running in debt, loaning their credit, and issuing their scrip in bonds, for the purpose of carrying on these improvements. That is the question which we have now to consider and determine.

Gentlemen admit, and they say they are desirous of incorporating a provision into the constitution, that the State shall never assume debts contracted by municipal corporations. Why do this, if the principle of county taxation be all right, and if there be no danger resulting from the adoption of this principle? Why do gentlemen come to the conclusion to put such a restriction upon the State? It is simply because they fear the dangerous tendencies of this principle. They abandon all their chimerical notions of expediency. They see that these municipal corporations are running wildly into debt, and that the next thing will be, a cry for the State to assume their debts. And, therefore, in order to keep the State clear from embarrassment, they declare their willingness to incorporate a provision in the constitution, which shall prevent her from assuming these debts.

There is not a gentleman upon this floor who will say that the principle of city or county indebtedness will add one cent to the aggregate ability of such city or county. If this be true, why contend for the principle? The reason is obvious; it is to force men against their judgment and will, to embark their hard earnings in wild schemes of speculation.

Mr. EDWARDS. I would like to enquire of the gentleman what system they adopted in the growing city which he represents here, in reference to grading and paving the streets?

Mr. EMERSON. I will snswer the gentleman with the greatest pleasure, because I am aware that there are certain gentlemen upon this floor, who have begged the question by introducing questions of a character similar to this. The gentleman has probably failed to understand one thing, which I think is very vital to this question. I do not believe that the gentleman in all his experience, has ever found an instance when it was necessary to raise means for the opening of streets, alleys, &c., that it followed as a necessary consequence that every dollar thus raised would be managed by an irresponsible corporation, over which they had no control.

Mr. EDWARDS. I would ask the gentleman if the same principle is not involved in both cases, that of taxation by cities and towns for rail road purposes, and that of taxation for opening streets alleys, &c?,

Mr. EMERSON. By no means; because in the latter case the limits in which the money thus raised is to be expended, are well understood; the persons who control and manage the funds are under the direct supervision of the electors of such municipal corporation.—But in the case of railroads, as I before remarked, the funds raised are handed over to a separate and distinct corporate body, in the which you have no voice, or at most a very partial one.

Mr. EDWARDS. I would ask the gentleman if it be not a condition, when the money is voted for railroad purposes by counties, that it should be expended within their respective limits.

Mr. EMERSON. I admit that such is the law in regard to counties, but not so with cities. But while it is true that the money so voted is required to be expended within the county, yet it is equally true that the stock thus taken, forms a part of the general stock of such railroad company. Another objection I have to the system which the gentleman favors, is that there is no limit within which the appropriation can be confined. Let me suppose a case, by way of illustration, for the benefit of my friend from Lucas [Mr. Edwards] to show the dangers that may result from the adoption of the policy which gentlemen are so strenuously urging here. Suppose that in the county where my friend resides, it is proposed that the county shall take one million dollars worth of stock in a rail road project; that this is five hundred thousand dollars more than the aggregate value of all the property in the county; and that there are two hundred and one voters in that county. Of these two hundred and one voters, one hundred vote for, and one hundred against the proposition. The remaining voter walks up and deposites his vote for the proposition. What is the consequence? Why, this one man mortgages the county for five hundred thousand dollars more than it is worth.

I rejoice that I am here to-day to record my vote against any provision that can by any possibility work such mischievous results.

The case I have supposed is not entirely imaginary; it is a practical illustration of the effect that will legitimately follow from the adoption of the principle now urged by the gentlemen upon the other side.

I desire to notice briefly the amendment offered by the gentleman from Des Moines [Mr. Hall] which has been regarded as a little anti-Democratic and anti-Republican. The difficulty lies behind the amendment offered by my friend from Des Moines. The principle contended for here, is not only anti-Democratic and anti-Republican, but against all right. Hence the necessity of the property qualification grows out of the fact that you propose to submit to the ballot box a question that is wrong in itself; therefore in order to be consistent, you are compelled to adopt a wrong principle in order to carry it out.

Mr. EDWARDS. I would like to put a practical question to the gentleman. Suppose that in this State, the cities and the counties are prohibited from engaging in the prosecution of works of internal improvement. And, suppose further, that the general government had not provided for the Dubuque railroad, by making a grant of a million acres of land; what resources would be left to you for prosecuting that work, and how long would it take to complete it?

Mr. EMERSON. In answer to that question I would say that the general government was not like my friend from Lucas [Mr. Edwards,] if I understand his proposition. It took care of the rights of every individual throughout this broad land. The general government did not launch out into the broad sea of a general distribution of property, but did what a provident government ought to have done. It provided that the alternate sections retained after making the grant should be sold for two dollars and fifty cents an acre, double the price they were offering it at before, and consequently no loss was inflicted upon any one in the community. Those who stood at the helm of the general government carefully protected the rights and interests of all.

Again, sir; if cities and counties become interested in these corporations, they can never have their interests well attended to, because it is the business of no one in particular to watch and guard their interests; or rather it is every body's business, and we all know that what is everybody's business is nobody's business. In this way their interests are more likely to suffer than the interests of individuals, for, in the latter case, each one looks out for his own interests. That argument alone is, I think, sufficient to prove that cities, towns and counties should be kept out of these schemes for internal improvements.

I have noticed that the only argument used in favor of this proposition is, that in order to do away with the evils resulting from the wrongs already committed by some of the counties, you must allow all the rest of the counties to do the same wrongful act. Now the gentleman may as well say that as the evil of slavery exists in fifteen of these United States, the way to cure that evil is to extend it over the whole thirty-one States. I have endeavored to present my views upon this subject, and will therefore yield the floor without further remarks.

Mr. PETERS. I desire to say a few words upon this subject. I regret that I cannot agree with my colleague, the gentleman from Dubuque [Mr. Emerson,] in the opinions he has expressed upon this subject. I am somewhat surprised to hear the arguments that gentleman has brought forward here, knowing as I do, the peculiar position he occupies, as one of the board of directors of the Pacific and Dubuque railroad company. He has had these county, city and town bonds in his hands for sale, in order to obtain money to carry on this road; and yet he comes forward in this convention, and tells us that railroads are not furthered by the counties and cities taking stock in them; that there is no necessity for this aid in order to forward the improvements of the State.

Now I will start out with the proposition that the railroads of the State are as necessary to its growth and prosperity as her other institutions. I would ask the gentleman if the city of Dubuque had refused her assistance to the Dubuque and Pacific railroad company, if the county of Dubuque had also refused her assistance, and if the government of the United States had not made that magnificent donation of public lands, would that road to-day have had one shovel-full of earth removed from it, instead of now having thirty miles built? They could not have raised any private subscriptions in the city for that purpose. I am surprised when the gentleman gets up here and says that the aid of the city and county of Dubuque, amounting to one and a half million of dollars has not been productive of one iota of benefit.

The gentleman has drawn a figure here to demonstrate what he seems to consider the principle involved in this question. He has pictured three or four men combining to vote away the property of another man. Now I would like to draw another picture. Take the county of Webster, situated two hundred and fifty miles from the Mississippi river. What would their land be worth without the prospect of some of these internal improvements being built there? I venture to say there is not a man here who would pay the tax upon the whole of the land in the entire county for it, but for the fictitious value caused by the inception of a road to enable the people there to get to market. Suppose, for instance, that twenty men go into that county, and each of them buys a section of land, and settles upon it. The rest of the land there is taken by eighty others, non-residents, upon speculation. Now this property is not worth a dollar to these eighty men, or anybody else, unless it is increased in value by some system of internal improvements. These eighty men who are not residents,—with the anticipation that, if improvements were built, others would come in there and buy their lands at an enhanced price on which to settle—say to the twenty men who are settlers there, you must start a railroad here, and while you bear the burden and the heat of the day, we will stand back and speculate upon the advantageous results of your labor. They will, therefore, compel these men to build this road and use their means and resources for this purpose, and the eighty men will receive eighty per cent. of the advantages to be derived from the road. Now I want to know if it would be contrary to any particular principle of right and justice to say to these eighty men, you must come in and share equally, and bear your proportion of the burdens and expense necessary to build this road?

Mr. EMERSON. Will the gentleman state to the Convention where he obtains the right for these twenty men to declare that these eighty men must become stockholders in this road?

Mr. PETERS. I mean to say that I get it from the very necessities of these twenty men to have this road built.

Mr. EMERSON. But where do they get the right to compel the others to aid in the work?

Mr. PETERS. I will answer the gentleman by referring him to a portion of his own argument. And I would ask him by what right he, or any other railroad corporator, or any body of corporators, can say to me, move your building from this ground, for we want to build this railroad along here? No reason can be given except that it is necessary for the public good.

Mr. EMERSON. Is the gentleman opposed to this right being exercised by a railroad company?

Mr. PETERS. I am not; because it is necessary for us to restrict some of the rights of the people, in order to protect the people in the enjoyment of the rights which they possess naturally, and would not be able to enjoy otherwise. The public good requires it, and I contend that that principle applies in both cases.

Mr. EMERSON. Do I understand the gentleman to say, that the right to locate and build a road, carries with it the right for the majority to compel every man in the county or city to become a stock-holder in the company? Does that follow from the principle, that it is right to take private property for the public good?

Mr. PETERS. I think I have illustrated my views as nearly as I can, by the case of the county of Webster. My idea is, that when the necessities of the people require it, it becomes the duty of every man, owning property in a given district, to lend his aid towards advancing the general interests of the community.

Mr. EMERSON. I want to understand if the gentleman claims, that because there is a principle recognised in this State that, for the purpose of building roads, highways, &c., private property may be taken, upon a jury assessing the damages to which a person may be entitled, by the removal of his house or passing through his land, it follows from this that it is right for the majority of the county, in which you may reside, to tax you to any amount they may see fit, for the purpose of aiding particular corporations?

Mr. PETERS. So far as the general principle of the right of taxation is concerned, I do not know where it would stop, without some constitutional limit being placed upon it. If there was no constitutional limit, I do not know but what the people might run this State into debt to almost any extent whatever. I do not know, but upon the question of voting taxes for the building of school houses, if there was no constitutional restriction, they might erect school houses, to pay for which, it would be necessary to mortgage every dollar of property in the district for double its value; and so far as I can see, the argument used by the gentleman applies with equal force to the one case as to the other.

Mr. EMERSON. The gentleman has not yet answered my question. I want him to tell me how he can connect the two propositions, the one, that of taking private property for the public good; and the other, that of taxing the people of the county to pay for the buildingof railroads.

Mr. PETERS. I can only refer the gentleman to the right of corporations to take private property for corporate purposes, for which I believe the gentleman himself voted.

I do not know as I have much more to advance upon this matter. As I said at the start, I believe railroads to be essential and necessary for the well being of the State, and I would be glad to see any measure, which I thought safe and prudent, adopted as the fundamental law of the State, that will have a tendency in any manner to aid and encourage these improvements. The opponents of this principle, before they can convince me that it is improper for counties and cities to take stock in these roads, must show me that it is possible to raise these means in some other way. If there are other means, within the reach of the people, whereby they can accomplish the same object, then their arguments would come with some weight and force. But without other means, this expedient must be resorted to, or the improvements of the State must stop where they now are. There are now four lines of railroads contemplated through this State, each of which has received from Congress a grant of land, and perhaps in that way they have received sufficient to start them, and in time, perhaps complete them. But I do not want to place any restriction in this Constitution, to prevent the building of any other road that the people may desire, and which they would be willing to aid and assist by this means. I do not want to prevent the counties, in future, from aiding roads that may be hereafter projected, as they have heretofore aided those already in progress. I would place all railroads upon an equal footing in this respect, and while we give the right to counties to loan their credit, I would be in favor of restricting that right to a certain per centage upon the property of the county. But, I do not think it would be good policy, to say these counties shall not exercise that right at all.

Mr. CLARK, of Alamakee. We, of this convention, are here in a primary capacity, representing the people in that primary capacity. When we come to frame a constitution, it is necessary that we should enquire what rights the people have, in their individual capacity. I apprehend that when the people come together in their collective capacity for the purpose of forming a fundamental law, upon which to base their social fabric, they do not carry into that association any other rights or privileges than they had in their individual capacity by the laws of nature.

Suppose that there are one million of inhabitants in the territory comprising the State of Iowa. They meet together for the purpose of framing a social compact, and providing a form of civil government. They all meet together in a body; they carry into that body, collectively, no more right than they possessed individually, before they went into that convention. That is the way I understand this matter. We are here in a representative capacity, the same as the people in their collective capacity. Then it becomes necessary to enquire, for a moment, what rights the community has as individuals; what their natural rights are, for those are all that can be brought into this body. These individual rights are nothing more than the right of every man to protect his life and liberty, and acquire, possess and enjoy property. These are all their rights, and they cannot be used so as to infringe upon any of the rights of any of the rest of the human family. Now, if my position is right, then we have only this enquiry to make—how far have we the right, in our collective capacity, to trample upon, and disregard individual rights? In order to form a social compact, to frame a constitution for civil government, when the people meet in their primary capacity for that purpose, they have to surrender certain of their personal rights, in order to establish a form of government, that will be effectual and beneficial. In other words they surrender some of their natural rights in exchange for that protection which is thrown around them by a united form of government, which must derive its strength and efficiency of action from the consent and support of the multitude. Now, all the rights not surrendered in this compact, are retained by the people, and they must be protected in them.

If I am right in this, then the next enquiry is, what rights are those thus retained by the people, and which must be protected under this compact? In order to ascertain this, we must consider what was the object of the compact. It was for the purpose of forming a government. And it may be fairly inferred that all the rights necessary to be surrendered up under that compact for forming a government, were surrendered into the keeping of that government, which that convention instituted; but I apprehend it would not be just to infer that any other rights were surrendered. The object of that compact was to form a government; and the object of the government was to protect these individuals in those natural rights which they retained, and did not surrender for the purpose of forming that government.

If I am right in this position, then we will proceed one step farther. The question then arises—how far may private or individual rights or property be infringed upon for any purpose? I understand it to be a general principle of common law, even in monarchical governments, independent of any republican notions upon this subject, that private property can only be taken for public uses. And you can only take the property of individuals because the interests of the community are paramount to the interests of the individual. But the use must be a public use, common to all under the government, and in which all are to have equal rights. I apprehend that that does not give authority for the taking of private property in any case for private corporations. I believe if you establish the principle, that private property may be taken for any other than public uses, you establish a principle that will, in the end, subvert the government, which was intended to protect individual rights.

Now it was a pretty nice question, and one in dispute for some time, whether railroads should be considered as public thoroughfares, so far as to come within the principle of eminent domain. The courts of Kentucky decided that such a road did not come within that principle; that it was a private concern, and was not a public road, and private property could not be taken against the will of the owner for the benefit of the road. That case went upon appeal to the supreme court, and they came to a different conclusion, so far as to allow the road to take private property in order to locate the road.

I allude to this for the purpose simply of ascertaining where the line must be drawn. Now granting, for the sake of argument, that a railroad is so far a public road that it comes within the law of eminent domain sufficiently to enable the road to go across private lands by giving just compensation therefor—and I believe no court ever went beyond that—it by no means carries with it the conclusion, that the position taken by members of this convention in favor of the proposition before us is correct in principle. There is this difference, they claim that the majority has the right to govern, and control the minority. Now although the majority may have the right to control the minority upon all questions pertaining legitimately to the government, the moment you carry that principle farther, you make the government an engine of oppression and wrong, and you thus subvert the first principles upon which our government was intended to be based.

Now it is said, that when the majority vote a tax upon the community, upon themselves and all the rest, for the purpose of building a railroad, they do it because it is for their interest; and as it is also for the interest of the minority, the majority are consequently voting, not against, but in favor of the interests of the minority. Now does not that very proposition take from the minority that right which underlies all other rights, that of judging for themselves what is for their interest? The minority has just as good a right to judge what is for their interest as the majority has. And it will not do for those who urge this proposition to say that the majority must be the judges of this matter, because when they judge of their own interests, they judge also of the interests of the minority. That argument will not do, for it takes from the minority the opportunity of judging what is for their own interest; and the moment you deny them this right, you strip them of their manhood, their identity, and their individuality; you disfranchise them, and trample upon all their rights as individuals. Carry the principle out to this extent, and you make the government of the majority the greatest despotism upon earth. It seems to me that a proposition in itself so palpably antagonistical to all the doctrines upon which republican principles are based, should never have found an advocate in any deliberative body. The idea that the majority shall take the property of the minority, and say how it shall be used, and for what purposes the private property of individuals shall be used, is altogether wrong. I do not care how many the minority may consist of. It may consist of but one person, yet the majority has no right to control, or dictate to him the manner in which he shall manage, or dispose of his time, money, or influence; provided that time, money, or influence, is not used so as to encroach upon the rights of his neighbor. It will not do to say in this case that there is a great necessity which overrides their rights, that the necessity of these railroads, at the present time, overrides the principles upon which our government is founded.

I am aware, that at the present time, it would seem that two thirds of the people of this State are almost crazy. There seems to be a mania prevailing here. If this constitution was not to be submitted to the people for two or three years from this time, I would not care what kind of provision you should have in the constitution, so long as you submit this provision as a separate article; for within three years from this time, this proposition of allowing the majority of the people of the counties to mulct all the people of that county in a heavy debt, and saddle upon the minority the necessity of paying a part of that debt, will be as unpopular as it is popular to-day. This mania has now gone beyond the bounds of reason and prudence. Every nerve has been strained, and every inducement brought to bear, to stimulate this mania for railroad improvements. And as true as is that law of nature, that everything must find its level, so true will this thing react upon itself, and those who originated it.

I cannot concur with those who press this question upon us, and claim that the necessity for building these railroads overrides all other rights. I deny the proposition; it has no foundation in truth and justice. I hold, in the first place, this principle to be correct: that wherever there is a demand for a railroad, wherever the population in a community is such as to make a railroad a money-paying institution, when it is built, there will be means found to build that railroad, without trampling upon the first rights cf mankind. There is no necessity for this thing, in my opinion, and it will never do to say there is any necessity in this case that can warrant or justify such a proposition as this; to say that the ends will justify the means.

Now I will grant, for the sake of argument, that it may be for the interest of this State that this principle should be allowed to a certain extent, so far as it can be done consistently, and within proper limits. But the moment you go beyond that, you work against your own interests and depart from the true principles of policy which should control the government.

I believe the safer way would be to leave these internal improvements to private enterprise. The capitaliststs of the East are keen for making money, and they are continually looking out for opportunities of investment. They have their agents here in this State, and as soon as the interests of the community demand a railroad sufficiently to make it a paying project, they will find the means to accomplish that purpose. If they do not do that, then I apprehend the argument of the other side defeats itself. If you are to build railroads that are not money-paying concerns, because a few counties in the West, with half a dozen men in each, favor the road, and half that number are opposed to it, then the matter is different from what I had supposed it to be, and it must be considered an argument against it. This proposition not only endorses the principle that the majority may convert the property of the minority to their own use, against their will, when it is beneficial to the minority, but also when it is not beneficial to them, and when it will involve the county, and all those engaged in the operation in a speculation that will prove ruinous.

These are my views upon the right of the people thus to impose a tax or allow a law to be made which will compel the minority to embark in a private enterprise against their will. You cannot view this in any other light than as a private enterprise, got up for private purposes. I do not care if the county owns all the railroad that is in the county, it is a private concern; it is not a public road in that sense of the word which would authorize the establishment of such a road at the expense of individual rights. The road is a private enterprise; and if you establish the principle that the majority in a county can compel the minority in that county to embark in such an enterprise, you can carry out the principle and compel the minority to establish banking institutions, or institutions for manufacturing, or any other private purpose. If the principle can be applied to the building of railroads it can be applied to anything else. And the moment we adopt that principle, we strike at the very foundation of republicanism that underlies all free government, and which is the principle that the majority can only rule so far as it is necessary for the existence of government. Government is intended to protect the minority in those inalienable rights which the God of nature gave to man at his birth. The moment you go beyond that and launch out upon the principles advocated here to-day, and overstep those bounds, and establish the principle that the majority can compel the minority to contribute funds for purposes of internal improvement of a private nature, because the majority are in favor of it, you sweep away the only landmarks for the protection of the rights of the minority. It would effectually trample down the bulwark government is intended to establish, and make the majority a despot of the most cruel and irresponsible character, that has ever existed upon the face of the earth. Those forms of government which are despotic have always been oligarchies or aristocracies. Where the despotic government has been lodged in ths nands of many individuals there have alwaye been more outrages and oppressions, than where it has been vested in the hands of one man. In the former case the responsibility is divided up among so many individuals, and so many are interested in upholding the power of Government, that they have more power, strength and influence to carry out their oppressive measures.

than in the latter case, when one man has the sole control of the government.

Now, having noticed at some length the proposition of the committee, I will for a moment notice the substitute offered by the gentleman from Des Moines [Mr. Hall], and more especially that part of it which requires a property qualification to entitle a person to vote upon this question of county and city indebtedness. I am aware that it may be thought that enough has been said about that matter. Yet I will ask leave to call the attention of members of this Convention for a moment to that subject.

I cannot subscribe to the doctrine contained in that substitute. I believe it is wrong in principle. I admit that if the proposition was to fasten a debt upon those who were tax-payers of the county at the time the vote is taken, there might be some plausibility in it. But such will not be the effect of this proposition if it is placed in this constitution. For those very persons who, under this provision, would to-day be deprived of the privilege of voting upon this question, yet when the full consequences of the vote thus taken began to be felt, might be the very persons upon whom the greater portion of this burden would fall, while the posterity of those who would now have the privilege of voting this debt, would be entirely freed from any portion of the burden. There is no just ground, I apprehend, upon which such a proposition can be sustained for a moment.

Let us look at it in another light.

There would seem to be some plausibility in this substitute, if the fact of my being entitled to vote, gives me the right to vote a tax upon my own property. But my having one million of dollars of property would give me no right to vote money out of the pocket of another person, or to impose a tax upon the property of another person, which might not consist of more than one thousand dollars. There can, consequently be no right based upon property in this respect.

Again, this is a new matter. We are a young State, and changes are occurring in the condition of our people from day to day. A man may come into this State to-day and not be worth more than is absolutely necessary to pay his expenses in coming here. He settles in a new county and proposes to make that his future home. Now he may not be worth two hundred dollars in real estate. But are the muscles and the mind he brings with him to be measured against mere dollars and cents? Why, sir, in my humble opinion, the mind that can conceive, and the will that can execute what may be conducive to the future benefit of that community for all time to come, should weigh more in the scale, with reference to the right to vote, than millions and millions of worthless dross.

The next view of the question that presents itself to my mind is this. I am clearly of opinion that this proposition is wrong in principle, and cannot be presented in any shape that would make it right in practice. And with regard to the principle of creating county and city indebtedness for purposes of internal improvement, my friend from Dubuque (Mr. Emerson) says it is wrong in principle and should be abandoned. He says with apparent plausibility that if that practice is wrong in principle, why continue it? Now, I am opposed to continuing a wrong practice; I am in favor of doing all in our power to restrain this practice. But as I said awhile since, we are in the midst of a mania upon this subject. If we were now discussing this question for the first time, and the proposition was to give the counties and cities the right to vote these subscriptions to corporations for internal improvements I would vote against it. But we find this practice looked upon with favor by a large majority of the people of this State, and they have to a great extent, in the eastern portion of this State, engaged in this practice. If that is the case, we have not the power now to lay the axe at the root of the evil. All we can do is to restrain it. Under our present constitution this right is conceded without limit. Now I propose, so far as I can do so by my vote, to restrain this practice, and confine it within the narrowest possible limits that I think would be endorsed by the people.

I shall vote for a provision in this constitution to allow the people of the counties to impose a debt upon themselves to a certain extent for the simple reason that I have not the power to prevent them from doing so. for without such a provision the people would be at liberty to reject the Constitution and retain the privilege of ruining themselves if they please, by following out this mania to its fullest extent. That reason will induce me to vote in such a way as will impose the greatest restraint upon the action of the peope in this respect, and not defeat the Constitution entirely.

And I would suggest another idea here in regard to this matter. In that portion of our Constitution which has been ordered to a third reading, we have provided that the State shall not have power to impose a debt upon the State of more than two hundred and fifty thousand dollars, either directly or indirectly. Now, this provision before us, with all the restrictions proposed to be placed upon it, will allow the people of this state to create a debt which in the aggregate will amount, perhaps, to between fifteen and twenty millions of dollars. Suppose that a majority of the voters in each county in this state shall decide to take the privilege conferred on them by this provision, and create a debt of one hundred thousand dollars or two hundred thousand dollars, or even five hundred thousand dollars each; we will find that the state will eventually have a debt imposed upon it, from which to extricate ourselves, will require all our ability. What would be the inevitable result of incorporating in this Constitution the provision that the majority in any county may cotrol the purses of the minority? Why the counties in which the majority have settled upon the people this debt, having become burdened with it, will perhaps endeavor to throw off that debt, and they will go into our legislative halls and compel the minority there to make these a debts a State debt, either by passing a legislative enactment providing for an amendment of the Constitution to that effect, or for a Convention to amend the Constitution so as to require the State to assume these debts. And in this way we will be paving the way to do what we have declared in another part of the Constitution shall not be done—that is, that the State shall never incur an indebtedness over the amount of two hundred and fifty thousand dollars—and increase the debt of the state to an amount which, if it could be placed before members here, would scare the most insane into their senses. I think the people demand some right and privilege of this kind in order that they may subscribe to these incorporations for internal improvements. I will vote for that, but at the same time I wish to confine it within the narrowest limits that I can get the people to agree to.

MR. ELLS. Mr. Chairman, I propose to occupy the attention of the committee for a short time, in reply to some of the arguments of the gentlemen who have discussed the amendment proposed by the committee, and also the amendment to the amendment, proposed by the gentleman from Des Moines [Mr. Hall]. The gentleman from Dubuque, [Mr. Emerson] and also the gentleman from Alamakee, [Mr. Clark], object to the amendment of the committee, authorising municipal corporations to take stock in railroad companies, because they say it authorises the violation of a moral principle. Now, sir, I cannot, for the life of me, see how gentleman can detect in the action of the citizens of a county voting in favor of taking stock in a railroad, the violation of any principal involving moral turpitude. The amendment proposes to allow townships, counties, and municipal corporations the right take stock in railroad companies, provided a majority of the voters of said corporations, at some general election, decide in favor of said subscription. Here is a direct appeal to the people themselves, who are left free to vote for or against the proposition. But, say gentlemen, "suppose a large *minority* vote against the proposition, because they do not want their property incumbered with a heavy debt—what right have the majority to force the minority into such a measure?" Such an act, they say, is nothing short of absolute despotism, and ought not to be tolerated; majorities have no right to oppress minorities—the law is made to protect the minorities and not the majorities.

Now, sir, I deny that laws are made for any such purpose. The law is made to protect all the citizens of a community alike, the majority as well as the minority. And in settling all questions that are legitimate subjects of legislation the will of the majority is of necessity the will of the whole people, and must be obeyed. If the minority are dissatisfied with the action of the majority, they have but one way in which to relieve themselves, and that is to become the majority and repeal the obnoxious law. It is upon this foundation that our whole social fabric rests. Any other rule of action would lead to anarchy and confusion. Let me illustrate by a single example: Suppose I am the owner of real estate in a corporation; a meeting is called of all the members of the corporation and a majority decide to levy a tax. I am one of the minority. When the tax gatherer comes to collect the amount due from me, I refuse to pay on the ground that I voted against the levying of the tax. What sensible man is there in the community that would not say that I was either a knave or a fool to assert anything so utterly absurd? And yet that is just the position gentlemen place themselves in when they assume that the rights of the minority are greater than those of the majority. But in saying that, I do not impute any unworthy motives to the gentlemen; far from it, I know they are as anxious to serve the rights of all as I am, or any other gentleman on this floor.

Having disposed of that objection, I come to the next question, in order of arrangement. Is it expedient to authorise counties, townships and municipal corporations to take stock in railroad companies? And if so, to what amount? If this question was presented to me, for the first time, in a convention to form an organic law for the government of the people, I should most assuredly decide against it, as I should against the whole credit system, including banks, and all other institutions that tend to give to property and labor a fictitious value. I make this declaration here, in order that I may not be misunderstood. But while I avow this, I am as sensible, as any other gentleman can be, of the utter hopelessness of ever seeing these United States go back to a policy so much at variance with the wild spirit of reckless speculation so rampant in the land.

Of all the schemes of internal improvement that have been introduced into this country, that of railroads, in my humble judgment, is best calculated to promote the happiness and advance the prosperity of the people. Commerce has been, unquestionably, one of the greatest civilisers of the world. What she has been to nations, railroads will be to states. When our national railroad system shall have been fully completed, the people on the Atlantic coast will become almost next door neighbors to those on the Pacific, and those on the extreme north with those on the extreme south, thus making us one people, with a common interest, and bound together by the holy ties of a common brotherhood. The facilities offered by railroads for inter-communication between the north and the south, will do vastly more to remove the jealousy now existing between the two sections, and ultimately destroy that infernal curse, African slavery, than any other single agency in our country.

Again, sir; there is another important consideration which should have great weight, in determining our action on the subject under consideration. It is this: the railroad system, projected in this State, contemplates several lines of roads running parallel from east to west, through the State, nearly equidistant from each other. These roads have all, or nearly all, been commenced on the eastern border of the State; many of the counties on the Mississippi river have taken stock in some one of them, and several interior counties have done the same. I am informed—for I was not in the State at the time—that when those counties and cities voted to take stock in these roads, it was the understanding that other counties along the line would do the same; and thus furnish the means to carry forward these important works of internal improvement. The good faith thus pledged, the people are anxious to redeem as fast as the means are needed for completing these works. All they ask is, that no obstacles be thrown in the way to prevent their doing so.

The gentleman from Dubuque [Mr. Emerson,] opposes the committee's amendment, because he prefers that the railroad enterprises should all be constructed by private individuals. No one, I apprehend, would differ with the gentleman in this view, or advocate any other agency, provided, private companies could and would undertake and push forward these works. Now, sir, although the roads projected through the western portion of the State are not of doubtful utility, still, they are not so promising of rich dividends as some others, and, consequently, capitalists will not as readily invest in those roads as in some others. Yet, notwithstanding this, the roads must be constructed in order that the resources of the country may be developed, and find their way to the eastern and southern markets. The lands of the several counties have been purchased with this expectation—many of them at high prices—prices utterly ruinous to the purchasers, unless these expectations are realized. Again, sir, many of these lands are held by non-residents, who, like the dog in the manger, will neither eat themselves nor permit others to do so; in other words, will neither improve the lands nor sell at fair prices to those who will improve them. The only way you can compel these land-sharks to contribute their proportion to the building up of the country, by the construction of railroads and erection of school-houses, is to permit the people of these counties, in their corporate capacity, to levy the necessary taxes for the one, and sell their credit for the other. Nor is there anything wrong in this, for it is a well-settled principle that he who takes equity shall return equity.

I therefore hope that this amendment will prevail; and at the proper time I shall vote for authorizing the people, in their corporate capacity, to take stock in railroad companies. But, at the same time, knowing how prone mankind are to purchase largely on credit, where the pay day is indefinitely distant, I shall go for limiting the amount of indebtedness. My judgment inclines to one hundred thousand dollars, as the maximum for a single corporation; but I am willing to meet gentlemen at a higher figure, if necessary to effect a compromise.

I will now notice, Mr. Chairman, the amendment offered by the gentleman from Des Moines [Mr. Hall,] which prescribes a property qualification for those voting to take stock in railroad companies. Had a proposition of that kind come from some of those gentlemen who have come down from old federal ancestors, I should not have been at all surprised, however much I might have regretted it. But that that gentleman, claiming, as he does, to hold his patent of democracy almost by divine right, himself one of the legitimate descendants of the old democratic school—so utterly democratic as to have come almost literally out of the ground—for him sir, at this late day in the history of the world, to offer such an amendment, in such a convention as this, is certainly one of the most extraordinary developments of the tendency of the *new* democracy that has yet come to light. I had hoped sir, that one of his own political associates would have called him to account for standing up here in his place, and putting on record these old federal dogmas, that characterized the Hamiltons, the Ameses, the Adamses, seventy years ago; dogmas then repudiated by that great apostle of American democracy, Thomas Jefferson, and by his noble compeers, and ever since regarded by the true democracy of this country with utter loathing and abhorence.

It is said, Mr. Chairman, that men change, but principles never. I believe this is true, sir, and think I see around me, in the action of some gentlemen, most painful evidence of the truth of that dogma. As evidence of this, only a few days since, when the Bill of Rights was under consideration, I offered an amendment securing to the people, through their representatives, the right to repeal by a two-thirds vote, any special privilege or immunity; expecting, of course, to receive the cordial co-operation of the old line democrats in this Convention. But, sir, how stood the record? When the yeas and nays were called, there were found ten of those old liners voting against that cardinal principle of the old democratic party, and only four sustaining it. And one of that four, I am happy to say, was the gentleman from Appanoose [Mr. Harris,] who battled manfully for that time-honored principle. I did expect, when I came up to this Convention, that a portion of the Republicans would not vote with me for the incorporation into the Bill of Rights of a principle so broad as this; but I did not expect to see my old brothre democrats repudiate their own professed principles; much less did I expect to see the honorable gentleman from Des Moines [Mr. Hall, stand here and advocate the most odious features of the old federal doctrine, and in the bitterness of his heart almost spit upon what he is pleased to call a wild and lawless democracy; as though any man had claimed here that a democratic government was anything else than a government of law and order. I had supposed, Mr. Chairman, that democratic governments, especially, were instituted for the purpose of protecting man, and property as an incident to man. That, sir, was old democratic doctrine; but the gentleman tells us in his argument that property is the object of protection, and that you must guard it against the suffrages of that class of men who have no interest in the soil. Truly we have fallen on strange times. It is very evident, sir, to my mind, that property has become the ideal of worship to many gentlemen who are utterly unconscious of its influence. Indeed, sir, the "almighty dollar" seems to stand out in such bold relief before their imaginations, that everything like private right sinks into insignificence.

I said, sir, that I did expect that one of the gentleman's own political rriends would have called him to account for thus uttering his federal dogmas. I am reminded by the gentleman from Dubuque [Mr. Emerson,] that he did condemn and denounce the sentiments to which I have alluded. It is true, sir, that the gentleman did give the matter a passing notice, but concluded by saying, that it was only using one evil to cure another; and that he himself would vote for the property qualification for voting, if the power to take stock was conferred on municipal corporations—thus evincing the same distrust of the popular voice that has been so boldly avowed by the venerable member from Des Moines [Mr. Hall.] Again, sir, the gentleman from Dubuque [Mr. Emerson,] took occasion to read us quite a homily on political consistency, in his speech the other day. It has been truly said that a man is never more inconsistent than when attempting to prove his consistency. The gentleman himself is an excellent illustration of the truth of this maxim. When the amendment to the Bill of Rights was under consideration the gentleman favored us with his views of the doctrine of repeal, endorsing it as a principle, but declined to sustain it; and actually voted against it, because he feared it would injure the credit of our railroad companies in the money market. Truly sir, man is a short-sighted animal, and never more inconsistent than when claiming to be consistent.

Mr. CLARK, of Alamakee. The gentleman from Scott (Mr. Ells,) assu mes that I, and those who acted with me, took the position, that it was wrong for corporations to be allowed to take stock in railroads. No such position has been taken by any one here; no one has raised an objection to any set of men forming themselves into an association for building railroads. The question is, whether ten men, or one hundred men, or any number of men, have a right to coerce one tenth of their number into a corporation for that purpose. I apprehend that even my friend would not contend for that right. If one hundred men have not the right to coerce five men into an enterprise of this kind, and if a corporation has not that right, I ask you where do counties and towns derive that right? For certain purposes, counties and towns are corporations; they are formed for specific ministerial purposes, and none other. If one hundred men have not the right to coerce five men into a private enterprise, I ask you where is the principle that will allow a corporation, when formed for ministerial purposes, to coerce a minority of that corporation into a private enterprise of this kind?

Mr. HALL. As I offered the amendment, I desire to offer a few remarks by way of closing the discussion. When I offered the amendment, as I had occasion to say before, I inserted nominal sums, and stated, at the same time, that I did not know as I should vote for every detail. My object was merely to test the question of principle involved in this matter, which was, that those who were compelled to contribute their property for building a railroad, should have the power to say whether they would contribute it or not. The proposition which I supported, and which is contained in my amendment, deprives persons, who are not tax payers, of saying whether the public shall become a partner in a private enterprise. For offering this proposition, gentlemen have seen proper to assail me, as one advocating the odious doctrine of property qualification, in connection with this question. Although I have not studied the docarines of Jefferson,Hamilton, Adams, and others, as fully as the gentleman from Scott, [Mr. Ells] yet I have studied another book, which is the law of Moses, in which I was taught in my infancy, and in which the gentleman will find written down, that no man shall covet his neighbor's house, or any of his possessions.

Now is there any right of suffrage in this proposition, any natural right of man, which is to be taken away from him, because he cannot take money out of other people's pockets for the purpose of putting it in his own? Is the proposition I have presented connected at all with the right of suffrage? Does it take away from any man a solitary privilege to which he is entitled, or any voice in the matter of government, of municipal law or regulations? Does it take away from him any thing that belongs to him, politically or naturally? If I understand this question at all, I can say to the gentleman from Alamakee, [Mr. Clark,] that the young man with stout arms and well-trained mind, who comes here, would find them to be of little account, if what he gains by the exertion of his industry, is to be voted away from him as fast as he acquires it. It is to afford a stimulus to industry, that I would have man as little restricted, and as little taxed, as possible. I would give him a full voice in saying whether he shall be taxed, when you seek to tax him for purposes other than the support of the government. It is a good conservative principle, which I wish to see incorporated into the constitution. It leaves the power in the hands of those, whose business it is peculiary, to decide whether they will vote a tax upon themselves; and it asserts the independence of man over himself, and over his own property; it asserts the dominion of man to make such disposition of the property he has acquired, as he pleases. Is it wrong to provide, that a man, without property, shall have no voice in saying how those, who have property, shall dispose of it? What right has a man, who has no property, and who contributes nothing to the support of government, to compel me to make a disposition of my property in a certain manner?

The supporters of this doctrine use very', singular logic, and I shall have to hear more of argument, and less play upon words, before I can sanction the principle they advocate. If this omnipotent majority are to be the sole judges of this matter, why does the gentleman from Scott [Mr. Ells,] want to limit them to voting upon a debt of two hundred thousand dollars? Why not follow this doctrine out, and vote away every title of property a man may own, if the majority so wish it? Adopt this principle, and you at once sink back into barbarism. I admit that the majority must govern, but it must be under constitutional law. That is American doctrine—that is the American principle.

The great and vital principles which protect man in all his dignity, would be of very little consequence, if it was not for the inherent aspiration for acquisition of property, which exists in the minds of men. Protect a man in the enjoyment and disposition of the property he acquires, and you at once give security to commerce. It is this protection, which has stimulated industry, and made the American name respected and honored by all the world. Deprive him of this protection, and you paralyze the arm of industry, and strike a deadly blow at every manly and honorable enterprise, for a man will not labor, unless he can enjoy the fruits of what he earns.

We come here, and say in our constitution, that the State shall not incur a debt of over two hundred and fifty thousand dollars, and you will not allow the people to vote upon internal improvements, and borrow money for that purpose, unless they vote separately upon every project that may be submitted to them. You will not put different schemes together in one log-rolling measure, and let them be voted upon, and by this means you keep the State of Iowa out of debt. Yet while you limit the State in this manner, you are willing to let towns and cities vote upon this subject of incurring indebtedness by persons who are not responsible. I ask gentlemen, who are opposed to imposing a debt upon the State for this purpose, if they will not place around the hundred small communities that are scattered all over this fair State, some guards and checks against the imposition of a debt upon them, as upon the one large community, the State. Let us go farther, and limit this matter of indebtedness, so that no overwhelming debt will be imposed upon the people to crush them by an endless taxation.

If we allow counties to incur indebtedness, and if you allow people to be burdened, in another capacity, and not in their capacity as a State, let those who must bear the burthens, and who contribute the money, determine the matter for themselves.

An argument has been adduced here, in the course of this discussion to which I wish briefly to allude, and it is this: that there is a class of people, enterprising and industrious, who have not yet acquired, but who will acquire property subject to taxation; and you prevent them from voting a debt against that property if you deprive them now of the privilege of voting upon the question of indebtedness on the part of cities and towns for the building of railroads. I am inclined to think that that class of people will most likely, when they get property, thank the framers of the constitutution for having thrown around them such a safe-guard as is proposed here. They have then something to be taxed, something that will bring the question home to them, whereas, before they had not. There may be many instances in which men of no property could exercise this right judiciously, but there can be no rule upon the subject. I judge in relation to this matter from what I have known of the general feelings of the community. I can illustrate by referring to the condition of the county of Lee, adjoining the county where I reside. If you had left this question of indebtedness to the majority of the property holders there, they would never have voted four hundred and fifty thousand dollars for railroad purposes. But there were a large number of workmen engaged on the railroad, say four or five or six hundred men; and there were populous towns that looked to these public improvements, and the expenditure of money for future labor among them; and all this influence was brought to bear, and they succeeded in carrying the question. I recollect of one precinct which never gave more than four hundred votes at ordinary elections, that gave nine hundred and forty-three votes upon this question. I speak of this by way of illustration.

I say, then, leave this question to be settled by the property holders, the tax-payers, the persons who are to be taxed for the expenses of building these improvements. I assert that the great principle of the right of suffrage is not involved in the proposition I have submitted, but it is merely a mode of ascertaining the wishes of those persons in a community as to whether or not a certain enterprise shall be carried out, for which they are to be taxed. The right of elective franchise is no more involved in this question than it would be in a corporation where the man who owns a hundred shares casts a hundred votes, and the man who has but one share, casts one vote. This very principle is recognized in all corporations for pecuniary profit. The parties interested vote according to the property they hold in the corporation. We should leave this matter to those whose business it is, and let them decide it for themselves.

I will modify my amendment by striking out the amounts of taxes and property, and inserting the words "assessed for taxes for county or State purposes." The amendment will then read:

"The same may be authorized by a vote of the property holders residing in said city or town; and who are the owners of real estate assessed for county or State purposes."

Mr. CLARKE, of Henry. Before the vote is taken upon this amendment, perhaps it would be well for me, as chairman of the committee on incorporations, to say a few words in regard to it.

There is one little incident connected with this debate, which appears to me to be somewhat peculiar. The gentleman from Muscatine [Mr. Parvin] in the course of his remarks upon the amendment of the gentleman from Des Moines (Mr. Hall), made use of the expression "universal suffrage." The gentleman from Wapello (Mr. Gillaspy), who seems to be as keen on the scent of a negro, as any well trained bloodhound that ever run through the everglades of Florida, immediately thought he could discover something covert in the expression, and called the gentleman to account. He asked him to define his position, and tell what he meant by universal suffrage! Sir, I fear the time will soon come when gentlemen who are assembled in convention for the purpose of amending a free American constitution, and who shall happen in the course of their discussion to make use of the expression that "all men are born free and equal;" or if they go further and say they are "endowed with certain inalienable rights, among which are life, liberty and the pursuit of happiness," will be called to account for it. Gentlemen will ask them what they mean, and demand a definition of their positions! And if those questions are asked, perhaps gentlemen will define their positions, by saying that they use those expressions "according to the definition put upon them by the present constitution!" Great God! may the time yet come in Iowa, when a citizen of Iowa can get up, and proudly say, I am in favor of UNIVERSAL SUFFRAGE, and not be called upon to define his meaning, by saying he means "universal suffrage according to the present constitution."

I wish that every man could stand here as free and independent as I am upon this question. I wish that every man could say, I am in favor of universal suffrage, and like me, not be called upon to account for the expression. Sir, gentlemen must come up to my position, if they wish to be consistent, else the time may come, when, if they should happen to use the expression "equal and exact justice to all men," they will have to add the modern democratic definition "except negroes."

Now I am not at all surprised at the position of the gentleman from Des Moines (Mr. Hall) upon this subject. I am not at all surprised at the introduction of a principle here, by that gentleman of the nature of the one before us for consideration, and I expect gentlemen entertaining his views will go even further in extending and applying the principle of this amendment. I expect that they will desire to give this principle of property qualification an extension and application beyond the mere question of voting upon subscriptions to railroads and the issuing of bonds. I know the position the gentleman from Des Moines occupies upon this question. I know that the city of Burlington has already made application for a provision in her charter to restrict any one from voting on this question within the limits, except they own property. The gentleman occupies this position at home, and I expected he would occupy it here.

The arguments of the gentleman in favor of this principle are such as to fully commit him to its application to any other question. We must believe that if there did arise other questions besides this to which this principle could be applied, the arguments of the gentlemen would be urged with equal force and power, for its application, and let me say that the gentleman from Jasper, [Mr. Skiff] took up the argument of the gentleman from Des Moines, (Mr. Hall), and carried it out to its legitimate results; for it applies with equal force to raising money for court houses, school houses and the employment of teachers in the several school districts and to every occasion where taxation will follow as a remote result, even, of the vote given; and I suppose the time may come when the gentleman from Des Moines, and others of his school, who can come in here, and take the position that men shall be deprived of the elective franchise, because they are not of the exact color of the gentleman, will also take the position that certain men shall be deprived of the right of elective franchise because they have not so many dollars, or so many acres of land. Why not carry the principle out to its full extent and be consistent throughout? Will Republicans tell me how a qualification of property is any worse than a qualification of color? As for me I go for "universal suffrage." Except the gentleman from Davenport, (Mr. Ells) and the gentleman from Clayton, [Mr. Scott] I must say that I consider myself the only consistent man in this body upon this question. I stand here in favor of "universal suffrage," without property qualification or any other qualification of that nature. I would let every man belonging to and having a permanent interest in our community, vote according to the intelligence God has given him.

The gentleman seems to act upon the supposition that poor men must, from necessity, vote to plunge the country into debt by the issuing of their bonds for stocks in these railroad and other corporations. Now I consider such is not the case. A poor man, though almost starving from poverty, may be the man most anxious to keep the county or city of his residence out of debt. In this country most of the young men have but little besides their hands and brains with which to commence life; and they look to the future for their wealth and property. They will take, therefore, as much interest in the future welfare of the community in which they live, as a man who may have a few more dollars and cents now than they have.

This subject of property qualification, is a subject that never meets with approbation in any community, where it is discussed. It is an old, antiquated idea, entirely abandoned and obsolete, and only renewed here by the gentleman from Des Moines, because of his peculiar ideas of its beauty and appropriateness. I had supposed from the definition of his position given by the gentleman on yesterday, that we were to have his entire support in opposition to allowing municipal corporations to take stock at all. Under the present constitution municipal corporations can take stock, and the provision here does not propose to take away that right, or to sanction it, but leave it as it is at present, entirely in the hands of the legislature. The legislature, under the present constitution can, if they see fit, enact a law saying that counties shall not take a single dollar's worth of stock. The section for which this is offered as a substitute, only provides, in effect, that if the legislature does not interfere, and counties do take stock, they shall not go beyond two hundred thousand dollars.

The gentleman from Des Moines, in speaking of this matter, has likened our position to that of a person who holds a wolf by the ears, where it would be difficult to hold on and dangerous to let go! And when the gentleman, after committing himself so fully against the practice of corporations taking stock, turned round and attacked this provision as one wholly and entirely opposed to it, and gave his illustration concerning his position, I was also reminded of a story, of two neighbors who went out to hunt cattle. After going some distance they came upon the trail of a bear, and one of them, who was an old bear hunter, was anxious to go in pursuit. The other thought it would be dangerous and impolitic, and said he should go home. The first one, being a keen hunter, kept on after the bear, and came up with him just as he was backing down a tree. Without thinking of the result he ran up and caught Bruin by the fore paws, and then he had him, sure enough. It did not require much time for consideration to convince the hunter that he had got into a tight place. He had the bear, that was certain, but how long could he hold him? The bear was getting more and more furious, and had led the hunter round and round the tree until it became evident that he must soon let go, unless he could contrive some way to kill the brute or obtain assistance to capture him. He at length set up a shout of distress in hopes his neighbor would hear him and come to his assistance.

And I will say here that we, of Henry county have had something like such a shout as that come up from Des Moines county. I have heard them shouting for help, and crying out that the city and county would be borne down with debt if we did not help them. I was opposed to this bear hunt—this county going into debt—from the first, and was willing, when I came up here, to put a provision in the constitution to prevent other counties from getting into the same difficulty.

But to my story. The old hunter shouted, and shouted until he was nearly spent, when his neighbor came to his assistance, and proposed to dispatch the bear at once. No, says the hunter, it is nothing more than fair, that I should kill the varmint as I caught and held him. You take hold of his paws, while I kill him. His neighbor did as he was asked, whereupon the old hunter traveled off and left him, saying: you would not come and help me when I was in this condition, and I will now let you hold the bear a while; it will be difficult to hold on, but dangerous to let go.

Now, I was induced, by the cries of distress in this county stock matter, to come in here with a report, as a kind of compromise, which, I acknowledge, was against the principles I have always entertained upon this subject. I did this, hoping we could unite upon it. But, what does the gentleman from Des Moines [Mr. Hall] do, after getting me to take the bear by the paws? He very coolly marches off and leaves me in that position, while he is out of the scrape. It is well known, that the gentleman was on the stump urging the people of the counties to take stock in these enterprises. He was foremost in the hunt. He got himself in a tight place. I came to his assistance in this report, and he has left me holding the bear. But, this morning he comes to the rescue, but with such a pack of ill looking curs at his heels, that I am more afraid of them, than of the bear; for now the gentleman, with other things, comes in with his property qualification, and wishes us to incorporate that principle in the constitution, in regard to counties taking stock in these improvements.

Now I ask gentlemen to examine, rather, the provision in the report of the committee. We do not propose to make this system of indebtedness constitutional, but propose that if the people do exercise this power, it shall be within certain limits. We leave it where the present constitution leaves it, and allow the legislature to place such restraints about its exercise as they may see fit. Do not gentlemen remember, that when I proposed to insert a provision in here, to allow citizens to make use of such testimony as might exist, leaving witnesses to stand upon credibility, they told me to trust the people through their legislature. I reply to them now. Let this matter be left to the people, up to a certain amount. Do not be afraid of the people. This provision merely says, that the people shall not go beyond two hundred thousand dollars, and then leaves it to the legislature to place what restrictions they see fit upon the exercise of this right to even that extent.

Mr. WILSON. I wish to submit a remark or two here. I do not know but what the gentleman from Des Moines [Mr. Hall] may find himself in a difficulty with his proposition. While I have no objection to my friend from Wapello [Mr. Gillaspy] getting after members here, whenever he happens to get scent of a negro, or thinks he detects something of that kind. I am a little surprised that he does not question his friend from Des Moines. There is certainly a negro in his proposition, [laughter] for he says that all persons assessed for State and county taxes shall have the right to vote upon this question, and a negro, whether he owns property or not, is a person.

Mr. HALL. I will only say, if a negroe's property is to be taxed, he should have something to say about it.

Mr. WILSON. I would like to know if a proposition is submitted for a county to take stock in a railroad company, is the gentleman in favor of giving negroes who hold property in that county a right vote?

Mr. HALL. We have no negroes in our county with property.

Mr. WILSON. There are negroes in some counties who have property. Does the gentleman intend to give these negroes the right to vote where they hold property?

Mr. HALL. What does my proposition say?

Mr. WILSON. The proposition says "any person."

Mr. HALL. Then it explains itself, and there is no need of asking me about it [laughter].

Mr. WILSON. Then we have the gentleman upon the record in favor of negro suffrage. It is strange that such a proposition as this should have escaped the notice of the gentleman from Wapello [renewed laughter].

Now, I am opposed to this property qualification in any respect. But, if the gentleman means by his proposition to include negroes and indians, let him come out and say so, that we may know what he means [continued laughter].

Mr. GILLASPY. "The gentleman from Wapello" seems to put a great many gentlemen to considerable trouble. I will say to the distinguished gentleman from Jefferson [Mr. Wilson] that "the gentleman from Wapello" will ask questions at such times as he sees fit.

I dislike very much, when I claim to be but an humble representative upon this floor, to come in collision with the great leader of the republican party in this convention. Now, he [Mr. Clarke of Henry] has not made a single speech here, but what he has been after the negro, and I have only been after the gentleman from Henry. [laughter] I should almost be inclined to think, from the way he talks, that he is dissatisfied with his color, and is angry with his God, because he made him with a white skin.

I asked the gentleman from Muscatine [Mr. Parvin] what he meant by the doctrine of "universal suffrage." He is not quite so honest and out-spoken, as the gentleman from Henry, for he [Mr. Parvin] said he meant by universal suffrage, the doctrine laid dow in the present constitution.

So far as the proposition of the gentleman from Des Moines [Mr. Hall] is concerned, I believe I was the second man upon this floor, to say he was opposed to it. I do not know, nor do I care whether there is a negro in it or not. I am in favor of allowing the rich and the poor, the Irish and the dutch, in a word, all white male citizens of the State of Iowa, who shall have attained the age of 21 years, and been in the State six months, the right to vote upon all questions. I thought, I made myself sufficiently understood upon the proposition this morning, and I thought it was not necessary to ask the gentleman from Des Moines any questions about it, as I understood it sufficiently, when read from the Secretary's desk, to know I was opposed to it. If the gentleman from Jefferson [Mr. Wilson] wishes to have the proposition apply to negroes, he can move such an amendment to it.

Mr. HALL. I am not so familiar with the scent of a negro, as some other gentlemen here seem to be, and I may sometimes get upon the scent of one and not know it. I find we have here scented gentlemen upon this floor, who can scent a negro as far as it is necessary.

The question, whether my proposition would include negroes or not, would depend upon how it includes or embraces the right of suffrage. I contend that the principle of the right of suffrage is not contained in my proposition, and as it is now worded, I do not think there is any sign of a negro in it.

Mr. WILSON. The opinion of the gentleman may differ from the opinion of others, as to the right of suffrage being in his proposition. But he has got a negro in there, and cannot get him out. [laughter].

Mr. HALL. I can amend my proposition before a vote is taken upon it.

Mr. JOHNSTON. I am a member of the committee on incorporations, and had intended to make some remarks upon the subject before this committee. I have been heretofore prevented, by the frequent remarks of others, but I would like to have the opportunity afforded me to do so. As there is no probability of coming to a vote now, I move that the committee rise, report progress, and ask leave to sit again.

The question being taken, the motion was agreed to.

In Convention.

The PRESIDENT having resumed the chair,

The CHAIRMAN of the committee of the whole reported that that committee had had under consideration the subject referred to them, had made some progress therein, and had instructed him to ask leave to sit again.

The report was received, and leave granted accordingly.

State Historical Society.

The PRESIDENT stated that he had been requested to announce that there would be a meeting, for the formation of a State Historical Society, in the Supreme Court room, this evening at 7 o'clock, and the members of the convention were respectfully invited to attend.

On motion of Mr. TRAER,

The convention then adjourned until Monday morning at ten o'clock.

MONDAY, Feb. 9, 1857.

The Convention met at ten o'clock A. M., and was called to order by the President.

Prayer by the Chaplain.

The journal of Saturday was read and approved.

No petitions or memorials were presented, or reports made from standing or select committees.

Order of Business.

The PRESIDENT. The report of the committee on the executive department was made the special order for this morning. It is for the convention to determine, whether we shall proceed with that special order, or take up the report of the committee on corporations.

Mr. CLARKE, of Johnson. The report of the committee on corporations was laid over at the suggestion of the gentleman from Lee, [Mr. Johnston.]

Mr. JOHNSTON. I move, that we proceed to the consideration of the special order.

Mr. PRICE. I would remark, that the chairman of the committee on the executive department [Mr. Todhunter,] is unwell, and upon that account I would prefer to have the consideration of this special order postponed.

Mr. PARVIN. I would prefer myself to go on with the report of the committee on corporations, until we get through with it. I move, that the consideration of the special order be postponed for the present.

The question was then taken, and the motion was agreed to.

Committee of the Whole on Corporations.

The Convention then resumed, in Committee of the Whole, [Mr. Bunker in the Chair,] the consideration of the report of the Committee on Corporations.

City and County Indebtedness.

The CHAIRMAN. The question before the committee is upon the substitute offered by Mr. Hall to the fourth and fifth sections of the report, providing that any vote creating county or city indebtedness for purposes of internal improvement, should be decided by voters paying a tax of five dollars, or owning two hundred dollars worth of taxable property, &c.

Mr. HARRIS. I should like to make a few remarks, especially as in conversing with members, I find that my remarks, of the other day, were not understood exactly in the sense I intended. I find that I am understood by some as favoring an entire prohibition, and by others as being in favor of letting the matter stand just as it is in the present constitution. The latter was the sense in which I intended my remarks to be understood. When I spoke about being opposed to the whole subject that was then under consideration, I referred especially to the amendment that was offered by my friend from Des Moines, [Mr. Hall.] Notwithstanding I may place myself in a position, which has been charged upon some others, that of being upon both sides of a question, I am always open to conviction; and I have taken some pains, since the committee rose, to obtain some information in regard to the manner in which railroads are built, and the credit, which it is necessary they should have, in order to build them.

I am free to confess, that if I could be convinced, that this prohibition upon counties and cities incurring indebtedness for railroad purposes, would have a tendency to suspend railroad operations, and prevent the further building of these roads in this State, then I would hesitate long before I would place this prohibition upon them. I am deeply interested in this question of building railroads, and I desire to take that course, which will secure their completion as rapidly as the business of the State may demand; and at the same time protect, as far as may be, the credit of the State. I am assured by some gentlemen, who, I have reason to think, know more about this matter than I possibly can—as I have never been connected with any railroad project—that to attempt at this time to deprive counties and cities of the right to take stock in roads, would prove an effectual check upon improvements of that description. If that would really be the result, then I am not prepared to do it. From the very best information I could obtain, I had not supposed that this matter of county and city indebtedness was very effectual in securing the completion of these works, for the simple reason that the bonds of these counties, cities, and towns, when they incur an indebtedness of this description, go into market at a very depreciated value. I am told by gentlemen, who have engaged in enterprises of this kind, and who have the means of knowing, that notwithstanding these bonds go into the market at a depreciated value, yet they go there as collateral security for loans to construct these works.

I am not disposed to favor this fourth section, as it stands reported from the committee, much less do I favor the proposition presented by my friend from Des Moines, [Mr. Hall.] If this fourth section can be so amended, as to meet the objection that I make to it, then I have no hesitation in saying, that I am prepared to support this report, as it came from the hands of the committee. I have looked over it with some care, and I have tried, so far as my opportunities would permit me, to scrutinise its provisions thoroughly; and notwithstanding there are some things in it that I would not be disposed to favor, I find that gentlemen who go with me upon other things which I regard as of more importance, would favor those portions to which I take exceptions. I did not come here expecting to get every thing I wanted; but with the expectation of compromising, for the purpose of securing certain great ends in the adoption of amendments to our present constitution.

I took the trouble to procure a report of the Auditor this morning, in order to make some comparisons, and ascertain what the results would be, in fixing a certain amount of indebtedness upon any county. For instance, you fix the indebtedness, that any county may assume, at two hundred thousand dollars, and it would seem to me, that the report as it now stands, is simply an invitation to every county to take railroad stock, and run its indebtedness up to that amount. I have no disposition to invite, by anything in the constitution we are forming here, any counties to take that amount of indebtedness. The Auditor's report shows, that the assessment upon the county of Dubuque is fourteen million dollars, and it will be seen that two hundred thousand dollars indebtedness would not be two per cent upon that amount. While, if you take the county of Lucas, which has an assessment of only one million three hundred thousand dollars, two hundred thousand dollars of indebtedness would be little over fifteen per cent.

I shall propose to amend section four so as to provide that the indebtedness of any county shall not exceed five per cent. upon the valuation of the county, until it shall run up to the amount of two hundred thousand dollars. I find that the sum of five per cent. upon the valuation of Dubuque would give seven hundred thousand dollars, a sum which that county could not be expected to take; whereas if you take the county of Lucas, an assessment of five per cent. upon a valuation of one million three hundred thousand dollars, would give sixty-five thousand dollars. Take the county of Decatur, which is in my district. I understand that the citizens there have proposed to take a loan of three hundred thousand dollars. An assessment of five per cent. which will give Des Moines three hundred and fifty thousand dollars, will only give seventy-five thousand dollars to Decatur. It appears to me that we all have a common interest in saying how far any county shall be permitted to go in a matter of this kind. It is a fact, known. I believe, to every merchant who visits an eastern city for business purposes, that the credit of every other merchant from his section in that market has a tendency, more or less, to affect his own credit. And the same principle applies in the case of counties.

Suppose the county of Lucas—as I understand she talks of doing—takes a loan of two hundred thousand dollars. My opinion is that just at this time that amount of indebtedness upon Lucas, with its present valuation, would be ruinous; and her bonds would sell in the market for not more than forty or fifty per cent.; certainly at greatly depreciated rates. And if this be the case, does not every gentleman see, that her credit will affect the credit of the bonds of every other county in the State, that are in market; and that it will ultimately affect the credit of the State at large? I hold that we have a common interest in this matter, and that as a matter of protection to ourselves, we should not permit counties to incur an indebtedness at these ruinous rates, which will have the effect of destroying the credit of the State. You might not hesitate to take my note for ten dollars at ten per cent.; but if I were to offer it for twenty thousand dollars, without any interest whatever, you might well stop, and hesitate before accepting it. I hold that the same principle which applies to individuals holds good with reference to States and counties. We all have a common interest in placing some limit upon this indebtedness. It does not affect simply the interests of the particular counties that may incur an indebtedness, but it affects the interest of every county in the State, desirous of negotiating its bonds in the market. Hence I hold that some limitation of the kind I have suggested, should be required; and with such an amendment, I would not hesitate to support the report of the committee.

Notwithstanding my views have undergone some change, I am not yet prepared to say that State or county indebtedness is a blessing. All my political education has led me to the conclusion that such a thing is to be shunned and deprecated as much as possible. I live in a part of country that is remote from railroad facilities, and I am free to say, that if I thought we were to be deprived of railroad communication, I would at once leave my home and go where I could, at some period of my life, enjoy the advantages and facilities afforded by such a communication.

As I said before, I have since our last adjournment, taken some little pains to inform myself as to what result the action of the Convention upon the subject of railroads, would have upon the credit of the State and counties. While I believe that some restriction of this kind is necessary, to prevent the reckless incurring of indebtedness, on the part of counties, to an amount which it may not be possible to pay, I am not, after more mature consideration of the matter, disposed to shut down the gate entirely upon this system. I repeat again, that I believe we ought not to leave entirely to individual counties to say to what extent they will run a debt.

There is another view of this matter, which I wish to present for the consideration of the committee. Take my county, which I suppose from the best information I can get, has a valuation about this time of two million dollars. Suppose that we take stock in any railroad that may be projected there, and we put the bonds upon the market to the amount of five or ten per cent. upon our valuation. The great probability is, that we could not get for our bonds more than forty or fifty cents on the dollar. If we curtail our indebtedness to one hundred thousand dollars, and put our bonds upon the market, we could sell them perhaps at seventy-five, eighty or even ninety cents on the dollar, getting nearly par value for them. By incurring a smaller amount of indebtedness, you are saving the county several thousand dollars in the way of interest, and when the time comes for cancelling the bonds, you are saving a very large amount upon those bonds. That being the case, it seems to me that, as the dictate of mere prudence and safety, we should put some limitations upon this matter of indebtedness, and place the smaller counties in the same position we would the larger counties, that is, in such a position that they shall not be permitted to go into market at ruinous rates of discount, thereby affecting the credit of those counties that are able to pay.

Mr. EDWARDS. I rise for the purpose simply of correcting any wrong impressions that the remarks of the gentleman from Appanoose [Mr. Harris,] placed here upon the record, might produce. I did not desire, in the remarks I made last week, to place myself upon the record as advocating the policy of my county subscribing two hundred thousand dollars in the Burlington and Missouri railroad, because at home, as an individual citizen, I have always regarded that amount as beyond our means. I have contended, that a subscription of one hundred thousand dollars would be as much as the people of my county would be prepared to take. I rejoice to find, in the case of my friend from Appanoose, [Mr. Harris,] that a "change has come over the spirit of his dream," since last week, and that this morning he is disposed to pursue a different course of policy in regard to our system of railroads. If I could only believe that my hardshelled brethren from Van Buren county were made converts also, I would be satisfied, let the question go as it will.

Upon the question of taking stock in the railroad that passes through our county, the directors of that road made a proposition to us, that if we took two hundred thousand dollars, the company would agree to pay all the taxes, that is, the interest which we would have to raise by direct taxation for the purpose of meeting the interest on the bonds, upon condition that we would allow the company to have the dividends that might be declared upon the stock. It is probably known to all the members of this Convention, that this road is one to which the general government has made an appropriation of land, a small item, however, compared to that made to the Dubuque and Missouri road. Our road will perhaps realize about three hundred thousand acres, while the Dubuque and Missouri road will realize something over two million acres. Our road, running from the point and in the direction it does, east and west, will, in my opinion, be a paying road; and especially with this amount of land, which we regard as worth at least two million dollars, we might take two hundred thousand dollars in stock and never be required to pay one cent of interest by way of taxation. The company may assume that, yet at the same time, if they should fail to meet the interest upon the bonds as they become due, notwithstanding the contract existing between the county and the company, we would be bound, as a county, to pay that taxation.

In regard to the position occupied by the gentleman last week, in attempting to place an entire prohibition in our Constitution upon counties taking any stock at all, as sheer madness and folly at this present period in the history of our state. Take away the railroad improvements from the state, and in what condition would you place her? I know that the same objections could not be raised, so far as the eastern counties are concerned, or those bordering upon the Mississippi, but as far as the interior of the state is concerned, this question of building railroads is a matter of very great necessity to them. The interior counties of the state are all absorbed in the construction of these roads, for upon them depends their very existence. If you were, by a prohibition here, to say that the people of the counties should not take any stock at all in them, I tell you that in less than one year, your lands there will depreciate more than one hundred per cent. Because there are four railroads in the state that have been provided for with grants of land donated by the General Government in aid of their construction, I am not willing to be governed by a narrow policy and cut off my other neighbors, who may desire to have railroads.

I regard the three tiers of counties running from Muscatine westward, as being perhaps the best tier of counties in the state, and might be truly called the garden spot of the state. I understand that they contemplate running a road from Muscatine west through the counties of Mahaska and Marion; and if they can, by private enterprise, by individual and county subscriptions, prosecute this work for their local advantage, I would not be governed by a narrow, contracted policy, which would cut off my neighbors from the advantage of having this railroad. If the counties of Muscatine, Mahaska and Marion, should embark in this enterprise, and it should prove disastrous to their interests, it has nothing to do with the faith and credit of the counties that I represent. Men must act in those matters according to the best lights and judgment they possess; and if they are disposed to embark in railroad projects that may turn out to their disadvantage, it is their own fault. I will not take stock in any railroad, unless it bids fair to be a paying one; neither will I vote to tax myself or my neighbors for the purpose of taking stock in it, unless I believe it to be advantageous to do so. So far as our railroad is concerned, I believe it would be a paying one from the beginning; and I believe that if we are ever called upon to pay the interest upon the stock that we may subscribe, the counties through which it passes will derive a benefit from these subscriptions.

The other day I referred, by way of illustration, when speaking upon this question of taking stock in railroads, to the experience of Indiana. After the system which that state had inaugurated had broken down, and she had refused to embark in internal improvements, and had left it to the counties alone, I knew several counties, as I then stated, that realized large benefits by taking stock in these railroads; while on the other hand I knew counties that were actuated by a spirit of jealousy and rivalship, and were as anxious and desirous to have railroads as their neighbors, that embarked in these enterprises without examining whether the improvement was called for, or whether it would be a paying or profitable investment, and as a consequence they suffered greatly. But even in that instance, that is the very worst phase you can put upon these county subscriptions. I assert boldly that in every county where they have lost their entire stock, if the simple and naked question were left to the people there, whether they should have a railroad or not, even if they sustained this loss, they would not hesitate a moment in saying—let us have the railroad.

That is the very worst phase you can put upon that matter. But when gentlemen come here and harangue loudly and long about principle, about a mere abstraction in opposition to improvements, that will redound so much to the interest and welfare of the people at large, I say they are taking ground against their own best interests, and pursuing a course which will tend to retard the growth and prosperity of the state. I hold that every man, in consequence of the principle of association which binds communities together, is mutually identified in interest and feeling with his neighbor. If I have five neighbors, who for want of proper information and interest in the development of the public prosperity, steadily oppose the voting of any tax for building railroads, while there is a majority of their neighbors upon the other side, who are anxious to favor every movement designed to promote the prosperity of the state by means of these public improvements, I assume upon every principle that socially and morally should bind us together in a community, the interests of the majority should prevail upon this question of taxation.

If I were to go to the polls and vote for a system of taxation that would promote my individual interests without benefitting my neighbors, that would be another phase of the question.—But gentlemen upon this floor have endeavored to pursuade us that railroad corporations have no other interests but those of a private character. I think that they take a wrong view of this question. There is no man, I care not how narrow and contracted his views may be, if he should live a long distance from market, who does not really believe that railroads are a public benefit, although he may have no interest in them, either directly or indirectly. If a farmer could get upon a railroad where I live and go in one day down to Keokuk, a distance of one hundred and fifty miles, transact his business, and then be able to return home the next day, he would save some six or seven days time, which he could devote to his farming purposes, and which would be worth far more to him than the amount of his railroad fare.

It needs no argument to prove that a railroad is a blessing to the whole community, not only in the facility it affords the farmer for getting to market, but in the increased value which its construction gives to the real estate in its vicinity. The farmers and the land-holders are, in fact, more benefitted than the stockholders themselves. No individual who subscribes to the stock of a railroad, does so with the expectation that it will pay him as well as an investment of money in other enterprises. I could loan every dollar that I have, in my section of country, at forty per cent., upon the very best security; and yet, at the same time, I am willing to subscribe for all the stock I can afford to take, for I regard the future benefit that may arise from the building of the road, as above the consideration of forty per cent. that I might realize for my money for a year or two to come.

I regard the position taken by the gentlemen from Dubuque and Van Buren as a narrow and restricted policy; for they place themselves in an isolated condition, and array themselves against the prosperity and advancement of their neighbors.

I know that counties and individuals may take stock in railroads which, if not well located, may prove to be a bad speculation. But should we, for this reason, pass a prohibition here, that will effectually exclude counties from taking stock, and by which we should be deprived of having any railroads at all? Such a policy as that would defeat every cherished enterprise, tending to promote the growth and prosperity of our new and flourishing State.

Mr. HALL. In again speaking upon this subject, I do not propose to detain the Committee any considerable length of time. I propose, however, to examine in as brief a manner as I can, some of the arguments that have been advanced by gentlemen in the course of this discussion, and separate, as far as I can, what my judgment tells me is principle, from that which is policy.

Now, so far as the question of policy is concerned, I believe it is conceded by every gentleman that there should be some restriction made here in regard to this matter of indebtedness. But we differ as to the character of that restriction. Some gentlemen believe that the restriction should be limited, that the power of the people, when they act under this constitution, should be curtailed as much as possible. The extent to which this limitation should go, is a question of policy, and that question of policy, in my judgment, should depend upon the correctness and truthfulness of the great principle upon which the whole subject is based.

Now, as a matter of principle,—and when I say principle, I mean the effect which it is going to have upon the rights of the individual citizen, as one member of this government—it is a question how far you shall infringe upon a right, that is conceded to be a natural one, and how far you shall invade that which belongs naturally to man, for the purpose of government. That is the proposition which we are discussing here; and it makes no difference, in this question according to my judgment, whether this proposition is enforced by a majority of the people, or by the officers elected by the people, because the effect is the same upon the individual, come from whatever quarter it may. It is a matter of no consequence to me, or any other citizen, if our property is taken from us, whether it is done by the majority or the minority—we are deprived of our property in either case, and the consequences are precisely the same. I say, that wherever you place this power, it is a mistaken and fallacious idea, to assert that I must submit to have my property taken from me, because the majority of the people say that it shall be taken from me. It is no more right, than to say I must submit to have it taken in any other manner that the majority may devise. The consequence is precisely the same, and the great right, which I should be allowed to retain unmolested, is equally invaded. The thief, no matter in what way he may deprive me of my property, is still a thief.

The principle which I maintain, is the inherent right of man to enjoy and acquire his property. It is a matter of duty that I shall contribute my share in proportion to the amount of property I possess towards an economical support and maintenance of the government in consideration of the protection it agrees to afford me in the enjoyment of what I earn and accumulate. But I am not to be restricted in my right to earn property, nor of the enjoyment of it, after I have accumulated it. It is the first great object of government to protect man in the enjoyment of his rights to life, liberty and property. Whenever a government authorizes any tribunal, the majority or the minority, the courts or the legislature, to take the earnings of a citizen for that which is not necessary, and does not pertain to his protection, and is not necessary for the support of the government, they trample upon and invade this great right.

Then I say, if this new course of policy, which has sprung up here, within the last few years, and which is establishing monopolies and corporations throughout the country and creating a large indebtedness, which will be a perpetual tax against the people of these particular communities, is to be tolerated at all, it should be restricted. It is conceded by all here that the majority should not have unlimited power to vote these debts, and mortgage the property of the minority; and that there is a point beyond which they should not go. They all concede the necessity of such a limitation, but the difficulty is to determine where that limitation should be placed.

Now, I may be wrong, and I may err in judgment, in regard to this matter; but to my mind, the great benefits which gentlemen have depicted here as likely to result from the building of railroads, cannot, in the nature of things, flow from the system which we are now attempting to fasten upon the people of this State. A county or a State can no more make itself rich by borrowing, than an individual can. A person may, while he is using the money he has borrowed, and while he is rioting with other people's money, appear to be prosperous and wealthy, but when the pay-day comes, in nineteen cases out of twenty, he will be unable to meet his liabilities, and he will be in a far worse condition than if he had pursued a straight forward course of honorable application and industry, and by which alone he can secure prosperity and happiness.

You place a debt of five hundred thousand dollars upon a county, and the bonds, according to the usual rates in this State, would bear interest from seven to ten per cent., say eight per per cent. on the average. That would create a debt of forty thousand dollars interest every year: and you have to collect this amount of the actual currency floating through the county. You take it from the county, and send it to the owners of these bonds, and you thus create a drain from a county, once a year, of forty thousand dollars. I say that there is no county in the State that can have a drain of this amount of the currency circulating within its limits, without feeling the consequences in every branch of business. It will produce a scarcity of the circulating medium as often as this drain takes place.

When you come to foot up the aggregate amount of liabilities, to which the people of this State will subject themselves under this system, you will find it to be enormous. The result will be, that the tax payers will have to pay rent upon their land, and upon their property, to the bears and bulls of Wall street, to the Barrings and Rothschilds of Europe, to whom these bonds have been sold; and in paying this annual tax, they will have to contribute more than the petty dynasties of the continent of Europe pay to their reigning princes. They become absolutely tributary to the moneyed interests of this and other countries, and they will have to pay a heavier tax, than any European monarch levies upon his subjects.

Let us look at this question in the light of political economy. Take the county of Des Moines, in which I reside. Suppose we vote one hundred and fifty thousand dollars tax; there is twelve thousand dollars to be raised every year from the tax-payers to pay the interest on this debt, besides the expenses of assessment and collection. It will be conceded by every gentleman, that this money cannot be legislated into existence; you cannot, by a constitution and laws, make this money. The strong hand of labor will have to produce it. It will have to be dug from the earth, worked out in your mechanics's shops, and by the laborer's strong arm. This money proves a dead loss, as it were, for it goes out of the county and State to eastern cities, or to Europe. In less than five years, let me tell gentlemen, that in the majority of cases, the very interest, the very taxes which you impose upon the people, by this system, would build the roads, and the people would then own them. It appears to me, that you might as well undertake to raise oranges profitably in a hot house in a northern climate, as to advance the interests of the State and people by inaugurating a system of building railroads, by this forced and artificial way of raising money. It is like an artificial stimulant introduced into the human system, which makes a man feel, at the time, as if he were endowed with more strength and vitality, but when a re-action takes place he will find himself prostrated, and all his boasted strength gone.

We are, in my opinion, going too far in incurring this indebtedness for railroad purposes. We are here as representatives of the people of the State making a constitution, that shall last for years, a primary law that shall serve the people for a long time to come. We ought to scrutinize well this proposition, and guard it with restrictions that will prevent disastrous consequences to the people. In what position are the people of Europe placed? They are laboring under an enormous national debt, the interest of which they have to pay; and the result is that the laborer is ground down to the dust, and nearly four fifths of all that he produces goes to the tax-gatherer. The same evil consequences may follow here, if we load ourselves down with an indebtedness, upon which we will be required to pay a heavy interest. This will be the effect of the unrestricted action of the majority, in different counties, when urged on by these dreams of wealth, by this Utopian doctrine, that we can legislate and vote ourselves rich. I say this result will come upon us, as certain as darkness succeeds light. It is a mistake to suppose, that you can by legislation, legislate great prosperity upon a people, and make it perpetual. If you could perpetuate this prosperity, if you could so arrange it, that there would be no pay day, and no demand made for the money that we could not meet, I would go with gentlemen who favor this system of indebtedness, to the fullest extent; but experience teaches me, that such is not the case.

One restriction, which I propose by my amendment is, that the question, whether or not this tax for railroad purposes shall be levied, shall be left to the property holders themselves, upon whose property this tax will be assessed. I thought, when I offered it, that this would be a solitary restriction, a just and obviously natural one. But I was immediately assailed, by gentlemen who charged me with seeking to interfere with the elective franchise.

In this connection, I desire to read an extract from a work of some celebrity, and I will say to gentlemen that they cannot find any author, of character, respectability, and reputation, who assumes positions differing from those here laid down. Gentlemen may talk about Jefferson or Hamilton, or any body else they please; but they cannot find in any one of their writings, any place where they assert doctrines so wild and dangerous to the institutions of this country, as those that they themselves have advocated and enunciated here.

I desire to call the attention of gentlemen to the extract, which I shall now read from Walker's Introduction to American Law, as I think it bears most appropriately upon the subject now under consideration.

"The true nature of our boasted *liberty* and *equality* is often mistaken by some, and misrepresented by others. We have seen that civil liberty is liberty protected and restrained by law; and that civil equality is only an equality of rights and obligations, as determined by law. In this view, both are so mutually dependent upon each other, that neither can exist without the other. But this is true only of liberty and equality as above defined; for an absolute equality of condition is incompatible with any degree of liberty. What is it to be born free, and to live free, but to have the capability of carving out our own particular fortunes, for ourselves, and thus differing indefinitely from those around us? It would require more than a Nero's despotism to reduce all men to a strict level and keep them there. Even the most abject of slaves will differ in condition. Inequality of condition, therefore, is the natural offspring of civil liberty and equality of rights. But how often has this great truth been lost sight of! We need not go to the ostracisms, the persecutions, and the banishments of ancient Greece and Rome, for examples. We need not even go so far back as to the reign of terror in France, when the guillotine was employed in the name of liberty, to bring about an absolute equality. We may find alarming indications of the same spirit at home, under the magic name of equality, the abominable doctrines of agrarianism are beginning to be openly avowed; and unprincipled demagogues are industriously sowing the seeds of jealousy and disaffection between the rich and the poor, the intelligent and the ignorant, the illustrious and the obscure. These distinctions they would have abolished, not by the regular results of free and generous competition, but by the combined force of numbers, *trampling down to superiority;* miserable paradox. To compel freemen not to differ in condition! To enforce equality in a land of liberty!"

Now I want to know what right is invaded in this matter, if we do not allow a man to vote who lives in the community without contributing one cent towards the support of the government that protects him—a man who, if I may be allowed the expression, is a pauper upon the rest of the community for the very protection afforded his person? What right has he to say that his rights and privileges are abused, if his voice is not heard in a matter of peculiarly pecuniary interest; a matter affecting property, and property alone, affecting the real and personal estate of those who hold it? What wrong do you inflict upon him, if he has no property to put in the common fund; what wrong is there done in saying that he shall have no voice in the disposition of that fund? Is it a right inherent in him to vote upon this question? It would seem so from some arguments used by gentlemen upon this floor. But to my mind the right, if he claims and exercises it, is but the right of the highwayman; nothing more nor less. It is true the degree is different, but the principle is the same. He has no right to say how the property of the community shall be disposed of, when he can claim no more than the highwayman, as a matter of right.

A person who has property to be affected, has a right to be heard when laws are to be made or carried out affecting that property. And as laws affecting property are made and carried out by the same departments, I would not invade the right of suffrage of any man in the least respect, when the question is upon the election of members to a legislature, or the appointment of executive officers, whose action may affect his person or his property. I would have the poor man enjoy all the privileges that the man of wealth or talent enjoys, where he is equally interested. All political rights that pertain to his relations towards society should be awarded to him. I would make those privileges stronger, secure them more firmly, if possible, in the case of the humble, than the powerful and wealthy. But when you come to the disposition of that which industry and ability has accumulated and brought together, I would have each individual as free to use his own as he pleased, so far as may be practicable for the public good; and nothing but the most pressing public necessity would lead me to infringe upon those rights.

I did not intend or suppose that the amendment I offered, could not be improved. I have not vanity enough to suppose that any proposition I could offer, would be perfect. If there are defects in this one, I have invited gentlemen to make suggestions by way of amendment or improvement. But they have not seen proper to do so. I shall support the principles of my amendment, as far as I can. If the counties are to be allowed to vote this indebtedness to an indefinite extent, I would leave it to the property holders to say who should give that vote.

There is an error in political economy in regard to the value and extent of property. It grows out of the condition of society and the times of the present day. We know that at this time prices are ruling high. There is a wild fanaticism prevailing now upon the subject of suddenly growing rich. The price of real estate has gone up to an extent which cannot possibly be maintained for any considerable length of time. Towns are being laid out all over the State, and lots are sold at speculative prices to an inordinate degree. We cannot by legislation continue this state of things forever. We cannot change the result, perhaps, let us make this constitution what we will. But there is a future, and every man knows that these prices cannot be maintained; we know that this matter of property rising one hundred per cent. in a single year cannot last long; there must be a reaction. And if we look about and see how the debts, now being contracted in this State, are to be paid, we will find that there will be a vast deficiency; we will find that the exchequer will not bear the burden cast upon it. And instead of inviting, encouraging and extending this wild scheme of speculation all over the country, we should put some salutary restriction upon it, so as to check it at some point.

I have no desire to detain the committee long by this discussion. I merely wish to present briefly my views upon this proposition. I shall vote for restricting the counties to the greatest extent in this matter. I think the sum of two hundred thousand dollars is enough for any county to subscribe, I do not care how much taxable property there may be in it. We know the amount of taxes levied upon the several counties, is according to the amount of property in them. We know that it is as large in small counties, in many instances, as where there is a larger population. I know that it is as large in our county, as in other other counties with larger populations. It is no privilege to increase the taxes; we all desire to prevent that. It is only when the public mind becomes excited, when strong inducements are held out to them to engage in these enterprises, that this feeling is prevalent for voting these subscriptions. If we were to limit the amount to one hundred thousand dollars in each county, until the people began to pay the interest upon it, I do not believe we would be called upon from any quarter to increase the amount. We must, from necessity, even under the most favorable circumstances, pay the interest upon these debts for two or three years, while the roads are being constructed, and when they go into operation, it is probable that the dividends will be paid in stocks, until everything is provided for the road; and for three or four years this tax must be collected. If the counties will pay one or two years' taxes they wlll not want to take more stock. We are now already in debt I believe some ten or twelve millions of dollars, and before this constitution can go into effect it will reach twenty millions, if we do not place some check on it now.

Mr. EDWARDS. I have listened with a great deal of attention to some four or five speeches made by the gentleman from Des Moines, [Mr. Hall] and I confess that he is a perfect enigma to me. His arguments present a problem to me, which is beyond my power to solve. He has made four elaborate arguments before this Convention to prove that this principle is wrong in conception and practice throughout. He has argued both long and loud to show that this principle will prove disastrous in its consequences, and at the same time he holds up those who are opposed to prohibition as in favor of the largest limits in this matter. Now I do not believe that there are three gentlemen upon this floor who are opposed to the principle of prohibition; all are in favor of proper restrictions.

That gentleman argues to show that this thing is wrong in principle, and must prove disastrous to all those counties who may be engaged, to any extent, in taking stock in railroads and other improvements. And yet that gentleman, perhaps more than any other in the state, has used all his powers of persuasion, and all his reasoning faculties, and a large amount of industry and energy to convince the people that they should subscribe stock, in their capacity of county corporations, to those railroads. But now his whole speech from beginning to end is a kind of "good God and good Devil" affair, as if he knew not what kind of hands he should fall into.

Mr. PRICE. I perhaps might be pardoned if I refused to mingle in this debate. I represent a constituency not very deeply interested in this matter. They have two great roads secured to them by donations from Congress, and aid in other directions, which are to cross from river to river, connecting one great artery of commerce with another which is navigable for two thousand miles above my district. With all this in favor of the district I represent, I do not know but that it would be my policy, so far as interest is concerned, to advocate some restrictions which can defeat the introduction of railroads or other improvements to any greater extent than they have been introduced already. But suppose I should take that position, and sacrifice what I and other members must deem the great principle of the prosperity of a state; what would be the effect if it should be adopted and put in practice? Why these two, or rather four great contemplated roads, would become so many monopolies in this state.

Now having at our command these four great roads, giving that particular section of country bordering on the Missouri river, all the advantages accruing from the construction of these roads, we care but little, or might care but little, about the interests and prosperity of the remaining sections of the state, should we be desirous to consult our own interests only. But I am not disposed to take that view of the subject. I am not disposed to follow those, as my counsellors, who, having stepped upon the path of progress, surround themselves with phantoms of doubt, despondency and despair, afraid to advance a single step farther. What would be the result of a course of policy of that character, as Iowa is now situated, with railroads just piercing the state from the east, and others going on; with cities springing up at every step, both in reality and prospectively? Now what shall be the policy of Iowa in regard to railroads and other public improvements? Shall we put a stop to it now? Why, sir "there is a tide in the affairs of" states, as in the affairs of men, "which taken at the flood leads on to fortune." What shall be the policy of Iowa now? She stands midway between the east and the west, on the great highway from the Atlantic to the Pacific. Will you make her a desert? Will you say to those capitalists who are disposed to embark in the construction of railroads, as they approach this state,—pass around us; leave us a desert; let our cities be deserted; tear up these iron ribs on our railroads so far as they have been constructed; beat them into plowshares, but not for use here at home, for the husbandman of Iowa goes upon the principle that he will expend no labor except an immediate reward follows it; he will never turn a furrow to the sun to clothe this boundless prairies with golden harvests waving in the light of day? Shall we follow this policy, or the other, and the most liberal policy, of putting no restrictions upon these railroads?

Let them go from river to river and from ocean to ocean, and in their going I do not care what the tax may be to bring the road to the poor man's door. The poor man's muscles must provide the strength to load these railroads and bring the articles of commerce and produce to and from market.

Much has been said here about rights and privileges. Now there is no principle more strongly established in this country than that the majority must rule. We can get along with no other principle than this. It is the basis of republican governments, and would to God it was the basis of all governments. Majorities must rule in everything connected with this government. I differ with the gentleman from Des Moines (Mr. Hall) in regard to the question he has touched upon, that of who shall have a voice in the assessing of taxes upon property. I differ with him very materially upon this subject. However inconsistent it may seem, I can say that I have ever found, as a general thing, that those who have the least of taxes to pay are generally those who complain most bitterly of the burdens of taxation, and if you leave this question to poor men, in nine cases out of ten, they will vote against the construction of railroads It is the poor man who is generally opposed to this thing, though as I conceive, blinded to his interest. It is the rich man who is in favor of it generally, because it increases and adds to the riches he now has.

I am opposed to leaving this matter to be settled by property holders alone, although according to the gentleman from Des Moines, (Mr. Hall) these railroads are private matters and with private interests involved, yet they become public matters in so far as all the public are interested in their construction. The masses are jealous of their rights, and when you come to take the question upon the matter of taxation, so far as railroads are concerned, you make a public debt, and the massess should not be shut out. They would look upon such a course with jealousy and distrust, and finally with contempt. They would despise this sort of thing. I will not say it is anti-Democratic to shut them out, because my modesty and respect for the great attainments and experience of the gentleman from Des Moines (Mr. Hall) would forbid my intimating upon this floor that he would suggest anything anti-Democratic. But I say that the man who in this age would expect the the country to prosper, at the same time throwing every restriction and imposing every conceivable fetter upon the railroads, would be like the man who would stand upon the brink of a great river waiting for the ford to come to him, instead of going himself to the ford; for as sure as he continues to stand there he will perish upon the brink, never being permitted to cross to the promised land and enjoy its prosperity and advantages.

Mr. CLARKE, of Johnson. I had not intended take part in the discussion upon the question before us; but I find it has been conceded upon all sides of the chamber, that this is a general question, involving the question of internal improvements. And, I desire to say in the outset, that I shall not place myself in the position of either the gentleman from Des Moines [Mr. Hall] or the gentleman from Alamakee [Mr. Clark]. In other words, I shall not argue that the principle of authorising counties to take stock, is morally and politically wrong, and at the same time announce my determination to vote for that principle.

Upon this question, as well as upon every other that may come before us, and in every vote that I shall give, I shall endeavor to vote upon moral considerations; and if I entertained the same views as to the justice of this matter as the gentleman from Des Moines [Mr. Hall] I should be emphatically opposed to the principle.

I am opposed to the 4th section of this report, as well as to the proposition of the gentleman from Des Moines, for two reasons, and one of the reasons applies to both propositions. The proposition of the gentlemen from Des Moines descends to legislation. If it is adopted we will be fixing in the constitution a matter which, with propriety, should be left to the Generaly Assembly, who are the agents and servants of the people.

The gentleman from Des Moines proposes to limit the right of counties, by saying they shall take so much stock, and no more, in support of these improvements. The inadequacy of that proposition, the certainty that it will not work well, has been amply demonstrated by the gentleman from Appanoose [Mr. Harris]. He has shown you, that two hundred thousand dollars to some counties would be a mere trifle, while to others it would be a great deal too much. If you place this limitation in the constitution, what will be the effect of it? While some counties would be limited, and prevented from doing what they might desire to do, in aid of the construction of these works of internal improvements, other counties would be permitted to do all they are able, and all they desire.

But there is another objection to this section. I refer to the last clause of it, and would call the attention of the convention to it. It is as follows:

"Nor shall the bonds, or other evidences of indebtedness, of any municipal or political incorporation, be issued, or granted, or its credit be loaned, directly or indirectly, or pledged as security to an amount, in the aggregate, exceeding two hundred thousand dollars at any one time."

Here is a door opened for evasion, and if this section is adopted, it will defeat the very object the committee have in view. These counties could loan their credit at one time for two hundred thousand dollars. Then if they desired to take six hundred thousand dollars worth of stock, or to loan their credit to that amount, all they would have to do under this provision, would be to take two hundred thousand dollars to-day, two hundred thousand dollars more to-morrow, and the other two hundred thousand dollars the next day: and they would not be loaning their credit to more than two hundred thousand dollars at any one time. I think, therefore, this provision of the report will not have the effect the committee desired, or intended it should have, for it would open the door to judicial construction, and will only make the matter more difficult, than to have no restriction here at all.

I am opposed to placing any limits at all upon these counties; and for this simple reason, that I apprehend that the people, the source of all power, are fully competent to determine this matter for themselves. They know full well their own ability to assist; they can judge whether the projected work is going to pay; and it is, for them, and not for us, to judge what the amount of their investments shall be.

Now, to the general question. I take it that nobody upon this floor doubts, that internal improvements are a necessity. They are as essential to the success and prosperity of a people, as are our school houses and our bridges, or any other work of improvement which we now construct. To say you will not have internal imprcvements is to say, that you will place Iowa in the position of a desert island, surrounded by oceans for miles around, to cut off all communication between her and the world. We are compelled to have them, for if we do not, we will cease to be a part of the world, so far as things are in this age.

We have declared that the State of Iowa, as a State, shall not construct these works. I acceded to that proposition, not because it met my judgment, or because I entertain the views of government which have been expressed by other gentlemen upon this floor. I consider that the great object and purpose of government is of a higher and more benificent character than would appear to be the views of some gentleman here. I think the object and purpose of government is to do something more than merely to protect the physical man; and I think it should also be the object and duty of government, to do something more than to protect mere acres of land, or mere dollars and cents. I think the true object and purpose of government should be, to promote the morality and the intelligence, as well as the physical condition of man.

Now, if my views of government could prevail, I would have this government educate every child; I would have it build every road; I would have it construct every bridge; I would in fact, have it do everything which would conduce to the general happiness and welfare of the people. When a government does that, it will have attained its perfection, and not till then. But I am aware, that in this age, there are entertained far different views and opinions concerning the object and purpose of government. Our friends upon the other side, particularly, hold more narrow views as to the duties of government. Let me say to them, that entertaining the views they do upon this subject, they ought not to have passed over the bill of rights as they did; for, if I mistake not, the form of this principle, the basis of the right of the people to act upon the subject we are now considering, is alledged in the bill of rights. I word it in this way:

"All men are, by nature, free and independent, and have certain inalienable rights, among which are those of enjoying, and defending life and liberty, acquiring, possessing and protecting property, and the pursuing and obtaining safety and happiness.

"All power is inherent in the people. Government is instituted for the protection, security and benefit of the people, &c."

And I think that whatever secures and protects, and benefits the people, is an object and purpose of government. As I said before, we must have internal improvements; that is conceded upon all hands, and we have gone a step farther, and said that the government of Iowa, as a State, shall not make these improvements.

Now what is the next step? If the people, as an aggregate whole cannot make these improvements, then they must be built by the people in their smaller municipal capacities, or by them individually. That is the question and the only question, for us to determine.

It has been announced here with evident self-satisfaction by the gentleman from Des Moines, [Mr. Hall] repeated by the gentleman from Dubuque, [Mr. Emerson] and reiterated by the gentleman from Alamakee, [Mr. Clark] that it is not right in principle that the people of the counties should, by a vote ol the county, take stock in these roads. Now if I could not convince myself that it was right, I would take a different position upon this question from what they do; I would vote against this thing entirely. But I take the broad ground here, openly and boldly, that this thing is right; right morally as well as politically. What is a municipal corporation? It is an organization of the people. For what purpose? To enable them to enjoy rights they cannot enjoy individually—to do that which they cannot do individually? Certainly not. The gentleman from Alamakee says we do not take with us into a government any more rights than we possess naturally. I admit that. But has not every man a right to use his property as he may consider best, subject only to this exception, that he shall not use it to the injury or prejudice of his neighbors? I suppose every man has the right to make a railroad over his own land. If he chooses to dig a canal through his land or to make bridges over his streams, he certainly has a right to do so, and when he comes into one of these municipal corporations, which is a limited government, he takes with him that right, and that right then becomes the right of the government. We are all assembled together there. Why? The necessity of protection, the necessity of improvement, and the necessity of that aggregation of power and wealth which one man does not possess, binding us together in the shape of municipal corporations.

I say that corporations have the same rights morally and naturally which every individual of the aggregate possesses.

How is this question to be disposed of? Like all questions. A municipal corporation is but a partnership, in which the majority control the business of the concern. This principal is admitted in every department of the State. What is a school district but just such a corporation? Why it organized? Because it is inconvenient for every man to have a school in his own house, for that would be an unnecessary and needless expense. Hence the school district is organized: men come together and say, by virtue of law, we will send our children to one school; we build a school house, and in order to have each man pay his proportion, according to equity and justice, they levy a tax and in the language of the gentleman from Des Moines, [Mr. Hall] and the gentleman from Alamakee, [Mr. Clarke] they take the property of their neighbors to build a school house. Now do gentlemen consider this morally wrong? If so I ought to realize it and complain of it. I have been for years paying taxes for which I have derived no benefit as an individual, except so far as there has been a common good to the people, of which I am one. I have no children to educate, and yet I am yearly paying taxes for school purposes. And yet, if there is any force in the argument of the gentleman from Des Moines, I should be the first one to cry out against it. But I say the children should be sent to school; it is a natural right which they have, and in this way we may confer upon a body politic the right to do that which it would be inconvenient or impolitic for us to do individually.

The position of both these gentlemen, (Messrs Clark and Hall) it seems to me, strikes at the very foundation of government. Let us carry out their principle. We are taxed for county and state purposes. For what? Is it to promote my welfare and prosperity, individually? No. I could live without a government; the gentleman from Des Moines could live without a government. It is for the good of the whole people. For what is the money thus raised, expended? In punishing the vicious and criminal; not because they have done wrong to the gentleman from Des Moines, or to me, individually, but because they have done wrong to the body politic—to the great whole, and it is right that we should be taxed for that purpose, and that our property, to use the language of the gentleman, should be taken away from us for that purpose. It is done for the common good.

Are not internal improvements made for the common good? Does not every citizen derive benefit from them? Gentlemen assume here that nobody is to be benefitted by these improvements, except those who hold stock and receive dividends upon it. No gentlemen who favor this matter here, does so for the benefit of themselves alone. They contend for these improvements because they are a benefit to all the community. How is it so? Place the millionare to which the gentleman from Alamakee (Mr. Clark) referred upon a desert island, with all his property around him, but entirely without access to the world, and what would his million of dollars be worth to him? Not more than the sand upon the seashore, unless he can by it be placed in a condition to communicate with the word, where he can get the luxuries and delicacies of life, and so it is with the state. Let her raise ever so much of corn, wheat, oats, hogs, sheep and cattle, and be cut from the world, and of what value is all that to her? None at all!

Those who have been in the state of Iowa, as long as the gentleman from Des Moines, (Mr. Hall) and myself, can look back to the time when farmers were hawking their beef and pork through the streets here, and could find no purchasers. That furnishes one reason, one argument, why we should have internal improvements. It is to enable the people of Iowa to convey their products to market and enable them to obtain from that market that which is necessary for their enjoyment and happiness. And if this is necessary, then it becomes a great public necessity to construct these roads.

And is it not right, and just, and proper, that every man who is to derive benefit from these internal improvements, should contribute his fair proportion to their construction? It appears to me there is no principle more just and equitable, than that every man, who is to derive a benefit, should at least contribute something to obtain that benefit.

Now the experience of every man upon this floor, the experience of the gentleman from Des Moines, [Mr. Hall] as also my experience, is that, in a country like this, railroads cannot be constructed by individual means. I am situated like the gentleman from Des Moines, I have canvassed my own county; I have gone into the country among the farmers and urged upon them the necessity of railroads, and I have had them stare at me, when I pointed out to them the advantages and blessings these roads would bring to them, as if I had been talking wonders to them. I have gone to the richest farmers in the county, and could not get a dollar of them.

There is another view of this matter; another reason why I consider it just and equitable. I would call the attention of western members to the fact that there are millions of acres of land in this State owned by these capitalists that gentlemen have talked about here; men who are not here to improve their land, who do not plow and plant it, who do not build bridges or erect houses, by which the value of property would be increased, and the conveniences of life secured. By taking stock in the manner proposed, by counties, you make the non-resident land holder, who holding his land from cultivation, at high prices, pay his fair proportion of the expense. Are not they benefitted by it? Suppose there is a section of land of which you own forty acres, while the rest is owned by non-residents. The moment you improve your forty acres, and put a house upon it, that moment the whole section is enhanced in value. And so the moment you open a railroad along the lands of these non-residents, it increases doubly and trebly in value, and they derive a benefit from it. And there is no mode of reaching these men except in this way, to make them pay for these improvements in proportion to their property. This course, then, must commend itself to the approbation and sense of justice of every man.

My friend from Des Moines [Mr. Hall] has favored us with a wonderful hobgoblin this morning. He tells you that by this system you will be saddling the people with twenty millions of debt. Well, suppose we admit that that is so. You must admit that the people individually have not this money that they can take from their busines operation, from their agricultural, mechanical and mercantile pursuits, with which to build these roads. It follows as a necessary consequence, that whether these roads are built by county subscriptions or individual subscriptions, the money must be borrowed. And I beg leave to ask the gentleman where is the difference between the people in their aggregate capacity borrowing twenty millions of dollars, or doing it in their individual capacity? It is a debt for which their property is liable; it is still the same burden to which the gentleman refers. It matters not how, or where that burden rests, it is still a burden. There is, then, no difference in principle. We gain nothing by saying that these counties shall not take stock in these roads, if it is to be done by the people individually. The same amount of interest must be paid in the one case as in the other. The only advantage in taking this stock by county instead of by individual subscription is, that in that case you are able to reach the man who does not live here; while in the other case the non-resident landholder gets the benefit of your money and mine; he folds his hands in security and says, I will let the gentleman from Des Moines, the gentleman from Alamakee, and the gentleman from Johnson put in their money and build these roads; and the moment the line is even laid out, that moment my land, instead of being worth one dollar and a half, or two dollars an acre, will be worth five or six dollars an acre. That is the operation of this thing; the result of this policy will benefit nobody but property holders, who will not bear any of the burden, perhaps loan us their money for building these roads at ten per cent. interest, and thus will receive, not only ten per cent. as interest, but also fifty or one hundred per cent. more in the enhanced value of their lands.

In this view of the case, I say we have the right to take this stock in this way. The argument of the gentleman from Dubuque (Mr. Emerson) and his illustration, are fallacious. He says that three men have no right to take the money out of his pocket to build these railroads; that no three men have the right to agree together and say, here, we will take Mr. Emerson's money and use it as we please. The illustration does not meet the case before us. The argument of the gentleman would have some point in it, if the minority were not benefitted by these improvements. I concede to the gentleman, that if the voting to take these county subscriptions only benefitted the property of those who so voted, and resulted in injury to those who voted against it, then the moral objection which the gentleman raises would have some force in it. But railroads are like the sun of heaven, benefitting all alike, and the minority, though they refuse to take stock voluntarily, when the improvement is made, derive benefit from it equally with the majority, and to the same extent, so far as they have property to be increased in value by the work.

Mr. EMERSON. If the enterprise should not turn out to be a profitable one, what would then be the result?

Mr. CLARKE, of Johnson. Then all would

share the same fate. It would be in this as in every other thing—the result perhaps, of a bad judgment. But shall no public enterprise be taken hold of for fear it may turn out to be unprofitable? Is that to be the argument? Go back to the remotest ages of the world, and you will find that there has never been a project undertaken for the common good of mankind but what there was some doubter somewhere, who was afraid it would not be successful. If that is to be the criterion, you would stop all progress in the world. These things may turn out badly; but we have the judgment of the people to guide us in this matter; and, I apprehend, the gentleman from Dubuque (Mr. Emerson) is not one to doubt the judgment of the people. The government rests upon that judgment, and we are here as the result of that judgment; whether we have been well judged or not, time will determine.

The position of the gentleman from Des Moines [Mr. Hall] that no man had a right to take money out of his pocket, with his vote, without occupying the same position as a highwayman, is not a correct one. I think there is such a thing, at times, as benefitting people against their will. And I would say to the gentl man, that if the majority should take twenty dollars out of his pocket, and put forty into it, I do not think that he would be injured by it, or have any reason to complain of it. That is the effect of these internal improvements. I have no doubt the gentleman himself has been enriched by the contemplated railroads throughout the State. I have no doubt but his connection with a railroad has increased the value of his property treble the amount he has ever paid towards the construction of that road. I know that has been my experience. I know the little I have contributed either in time or in money, has been trebly repaid to me in the enhancement of the value of my property. And I would say that that is the experience of every man.

Mr. EMERSON. Will the gentleman permit me to ask him a question?

Mr. CLARKE, of Johnson. I would prefer to have the gentleman ask me his questions when I have concluded my argument.

Look at the benefit these railroads have been to my own city here, as an illustration of this principle. The gentleman's own city of Dubuque is another illustration of the same thing. And I undertake to say that as soon as these contemplated railroads began to assume a form and shape, and it was reduced to a certainty that they would be built, the property in both his county and mine doubled and trebled in value what it was before, and I undertake to say, that if you were to-day to take from the town of Dubuque, and from Iowa City, the increased value of property these proposed railroads have caused, it would pay all the taxes assessed for railroad purposes. And I undertake to say that the people of Johnson county and of Iowa City, are paying no more taxes to-day on account of these railroads, than they would have had to pay for the population, wealth and labor they brought here, had that population, wealth and labor been brought here without these railroads.

And I say, that as a general thing, railroads bring with them the means of building them. They bring with them the labor and capital, and they furnish a market for products of all kinds. And you may go to our farmers now, who, three years since, were fearful of this thing, and you will find that they have a ready market for their corn, wheat, pork, and produce of every kind, and they can go home with the hard cash in their pockets for all that they can raise. Gentlemen have truly remarked here, that everything now sells at an enhanced price, and a price that makes up doubly and trebly what these railroads have cost.

I believe every class in the community is benefitted by works of internal improvement; unless, perhaps, it is the class to which the gentleman from Des Moinas [Mr. Hall,] and myself belong. While any article of produce has increased in value, I do not know that lawyer's fees have increased. But I believe we are the only class now suffering from this renovated state of things.

I take issue with the gentleman from Dubuque, [Mr. Emerson,] who says this principle is wrong. I think it is right, because it makes every man bear his proportion or the public burdens. That is the principle of our government. We have no classes here, and seek to have none. We seek to give every man the same blessings and privileges the rest enjoy, and I think it is but right that every man should bear his full part of the public burdens.

In this respect I come to notice the position of the gentleman from Des Moines [Mr. Hall,] as to the right of the poor man, without property to vote upon the subject of taxation. If my views of government are correct, that it is the duty of government to promote the welfare of the people in every respect; to furnish them with facilities for market and commerce, and provide the means of education, and develope their moral and intellectual, as well as their physical faculties, then upon this question of taxation every man has a natural right to be heard; because the poor man, though he may have no acres of land, no dollars in bank, has yet an interest in this matter, and that interest is, that it furnishes him with his daily labor and means of subsistence; and he contributes to the support of government by his person, if he has not wealth with which to do so.

But let us look at this matter in another light. Suppose that here is a man of genius and intellectual power, who has spent his all for some great public good. That man yesterday was rich; but he invested all he was worth in what he supposed would promote the public good, and now he is not worth a dollar. Every man recognizes his integrity of character; every man admits his intellect and trusts his judgment. And yet, having lost his all in endeavoring to promote the welfare and prosperity of the public, the gentleman from Des Moines would deprive him of his vote upon this question. I cannot sanction a principle of this kind, nor can I hardly think the gentleman himself does. Looking at this subject in the light in which I view it, I think the humblest man in the land has an interest in the construction of these internal improvements, and pays just as much as the rich man, because the rich man pays no more than he has the ability to pay, and the poor man pays that. The poor man with nothing pays nothing; and the rich man only pays in proportion to what he has.

I differ with the gentleman in another view of the subject; that is, as to the doctrine of the natural rights of man in property. And the views which you, Mr. Chairman, gave to the Convention a few days ago, struck me as correct. I take the broad position that man has no natural right to property; his right is an acquired right. If I read my Bible aright, I learn that man came naked into the world; he did not come in clothed, with his pockets filled with gold and silver, and he himself placed upon so many acres of land, and told that that was his natural and unalienable right, of which no man could rightfully deprive him. I think that property is an acquired right, and that we take it subject to this limitation, that we shall use it, not for our own good solely, but for the good of our fellowmen. That is the charter of right under which every man holds his property. In that view I think the poor man has just the same natural right to vote upon this question, as has the rich man.

Now if the proposition of the gentleman from Des Moines shall be voted down, I propose to offer a substitute for this section as follows:

"No political or municipal corporation shall become a stockholder in any banking corporation, directly or indirectly; but such corporations may become stockholders in incorporations for works of internal improvements within the State, upon a vote of the citizens of such municipal corporation, under such restrictions, as to the mode and amount of subscription, as the General Assembly may prescribe."

I propose to recognise the right of the people to take this stock, but leave to the legislature the limitation of that right, both as to the mode and amount, to be determined by the agents of the people, the General Assembly. It seems to me this is a proper subject for legislation. We shall want to change the rule from time to time. What may be the proper amount to-day may not be the proper amount a year hence. As our towns and cities and counties increase in population and wealth, and as new projects are started, we may want to increase or diminish this amount. Leave it then subject to the action of the people, and I think it will be safe in their hands.

Since this discussion commenced, the suggestion has been made—perhaps not upon this floor, but by individual members—that we should leave this question as it now stands, and say nothing in this constitution about it. I desire to say a word or two upon that subject, and I would call the attention of western members to what I am going to say upon this point.

I am opposed to leaving this question as it now stands in the constitution, because if we do we may find ourselves subject to a sudden check upon this subject. The condition of the law in this State at this time, in regard to this question, is very uncertain and undefined. I think the gentleman from Des Moines, [Mr. Hall,] will not differ from me when I say that municipal corporations possess no power but what is conferred upon them by law. Our present constitution gives to counties and towns as municipal corporations no right to take stock in these works of internal improvement. And it is conceded upon all hands that there is nothing to sanction this thing of taking stock in railroads, except a decision of the Supreme Court, made by two out of three judges. I do not disparage that bench when I say, and I think the gentleman from Des Moines will concur with me in saying it, that that decision has never met the approbation of the bar. It was well known that that decision was made under influences different from what should be felt upon the bench. It was well known that one of the judges who made that decision, was an officer in a railroad company, and was anxious to establish this principle for the benefit of his own town. It was well known that the other judge who concurred in that decision, wanted to have a railroad in his own district. And there was but one perfectly disinterested man upon that bench, and he decided against the principle.

I remember when this subject of counties taking stock was first broached. We began to feel the necessity of it. The late Judge Carlton, than whom no better lawyer was ever in this State, with myself gave this matter a thorough investigation, for the benefit of the county judge. And we came to the conclusion that there was no power given to the counties to take stock. And one fact which led us to come to that conclusion was, that at the time of the adoption of the code, it was proposed to give to the counties that power, and it was defeated in the legislature. I think that it is the opinion of the bar that if we ever come to test this question in the present supreme court they will decide that this whole thing is illegal, unless they should be restrained from doing so by the decision to which I have referred. This question must yet come up for decision. It was before the supreme court at the present term in a case from the county of Lee. But the main question was not decided, for the reason that there were other errors upon which the decision was made. It was also before the court in a case from Cedar county. But the court waived that question for reasons I will not name. But there is a case in this county in which the question will be raised, and I am one of the counsel in that case.

And I would call the attention of western members to the fact, that if this court should decide that it is not legal to take this stock in railroads, they would bring our internal improvements to a dead stand for a long time.

Hence the only means, in my judgment, for the construction of these works, is to recognize in this constitution the right of municipal corporations to take stock, and when that is done the right is secured.

The exercise of this right, the limitation to be placed upon it, is altogether another question. I do not want to limit it, because I do not want to tie the hands of the people in regard to this subject. I want to leave them free, through their agents, to do as they think best. I think it is safe in their hands, and I therefore trust the proposition of the gentleman from Des Moines will not prevail. And in view of the present condition of the law in this State upon that subject, I trust, if that proposition is voted down, we will place in this constitution some recognition of this right, and leave its limitation, and the necessity for controlling it, to be determined upon by the General Assembly.

The recognition of this right cannot interfere with the progress of this State. If the people do not use this right wisely, and run into debt to the amount the gentleman from Des Moines [Mr. Hall,] has anticipated, and all the dangerous consequences he fancies he can foresee, should have come upon us, the people will have done it. They are the source of all power, and I think will be able to get along with it.

I think gentlemen are mistaken in saying that poor men, men who own no property, would vote this tax upon the rich. My experience has been the very opposite of that. I have had a great deal to do in my own county in this matter, and I have generally found wealthy men, men of means, the first to step forward to sustain the project of this county taking this stock. They do it because it is equitable, and every man pays in proportion to his means, and he derives benefits in proportion to his means. I do not think there is danger of the people voting for projects that cannot be sustained. I find that in several counties this project of taking stock has been voted down. The county of Washington voted down two or three projects of this kind. The county of Keokuk voted down a project of this kind. And in the county of Lee they had to join two or three good measures together in order to carry another through.

There is no danger in leaving this to the people, because they will follow the lead of the wise and the experienced, who are the first to take hold of this matter, and in every county control public opinion upon the subject. If the project is not a feasible one, they will take a stand against it, and, in nine cases out of ten, the masses of the people will abide by their judgment.

These are my views upon this subject. I look upon incorporations as beneficent things, and not the monsters which gentlemen represent them to be. I think they are designed and calculated to aid in promoting the public good. And the history of our own country establishes the fact that they have been useful and beneficent to a much greater extent than they have been hurtful. I undertake to say, that to-day, without these corporations, these organizations for the construction of works of internal improvement, our government, instead of being the greatest and purest government upon the earth, would be in a very different condition.

And now one other remark. I think these corporations, instead of being hurtful, instead of injuring and oppressing the people, instead of endangering the perpetuity of government, have the very opposite tendency. I believe that every railroad that is made, tends to strengthen and perpetuate this union, and the State governments. I believe that every dollar that is invested in these works of internal improvement connects the holders of that capital, as it were with a chain of gold, to the support of the government. And I think the perpetuity, and the successful and prosperous destiny of this government will be enhanced, and increased, just in proportion as you stretch these iron ribs from one end of the continent to the other. I do not believe that all these dangers are to be apprehended that gentlemen would have us believe. It is not the policy, it is not the interest, of these incorporations to destroy the government, nor to sap its foundations; but it is their interest to support this government in every wise and beneficent purpose. And I undertake to say, that the men who make these railroads, and invest the largest amount of capital in them, will always be found standing up in support of this government in every emergency that may arise.

Mr. PRICE moved that the committee rise, report progress, and ask leave to sit again, which was agreed to.

The PRESIDENT having resumed the chair:—

The CHAIRMAN of the committee of the whole reported that the committee had had under consideration the subject referred to them, had made some progress therein, and asked leave to sit again.

The report of the committee of the whole was received, and leave granted accordingly.

On motion of Mr. SKIFF—

The convention then took a recess until two o'clock P. M.

EVENING SESSION.

The convention met at two o'clock P. M., and was called to order by the President.

The consideration of the report of the committee on corporations was then resumed in committee of the whole, [Mr. Bunker in the chair.]

Mr. JOHNSTON. I expressed a desire, on Saturday evening, to submit some remarks in relation to the subject now under consideration before the committee, because I was a member of the committee on incorporations, and because my constituents were deeply interested in this question. I came here this morning prepared to carry out that intention, but the time of the convention has been occupied by other gentlemen, who have very ably and eloquently discussed this question, and who have anticipated to a great extent the arguments which I intended to use. I desire that the convention shall make as rapid progress as they can with their business, and I shall therefore refrain from speaking at great length upon this question, as it is a matter of more importance to my constituents to know how I vote, than what I may say.

I rise now, for the purpose of suggesting to the gentleman from Des Moines, [Mr. Hall,] that he withdraw the substitute he has offered for the fourth and fifth sections of the article before us, a proposition which I may say, if it becomes necessary, I shall both speak and vote against. I ask the gentleman from Des Moines [Mr. Hall,] to withdraw his proposition, in order that I may move to strike out all after the word "indirectly" in the second line of the fourth section. I desire to leave this question just as it was in the old constitution. I shall make this motion if I have the opportunity, because, in the first place, I desire to have as few changes in the constitution as possible; and in the second place, I desire that all loans, which may be voted under this constitution, shall stand exactly upon the same footing as loans voted under the old constitution. I know, that my friend from Johnson [Mr. Clarke,] has referred to a manner in which this question may be settled; but I have no fears of the decision of the Supreme Court. The chair will recollect that no votes were taken in any county in this State, until the Supreme Court had decided that counties had a right to take stock. It was that decision that induced these votes. And I do not believe that any Supreme Court can be found, that would, under the circumstances, reverse such a decision, the effect of which would be to plunge the whole State into bankruptcy, and irremediable ruin.

If the gentleman from Des Moines will withdraw his substitute I will make the motion to amend I have indicated.

Mr. HALL. I will withdraw my substitute under the circumstances.

Mr. JOHNSTON. I now move to strike out all after the word "indirectly" in the second line of section four, so that the section will then read as follows:

"No political or municipal corporation shall become a stock-holder in any banking corporation, directly or indirectly."

This will leave the whole question of county indebtedness just as it stands in the present constitution.

Mr. CLARKE, of Henry. Would it be in order to offer a substitute for the portion proposed to be stricken out.

The CHAIRMAN. In the opinion of the chair it would be in order.

Mr. CLARKE, of Henry. I will state to the convention, that upon consultation with different members, I have drawn up a substitute for the section as reported by the committee. It embraces the limitation suggested by the gentleman from Lucas, [Mr. Edwards.] I therefore offer the following as a substitute for the portion of the fourth section proposed to be stricken out by the gentleman from Lee, [Mr. Johnston.]

"Nor in any other corporation or corporations, directly or indirectly, to an amount exceeding two hundred thousand dollars; nor shall the bonds, or other evidences of debt, of any municipal or political corporation, be issued or granted, or its credit loaned, directly or indirectly, or pledged as security for the benefit of any banking corporation; nor for any other corporation or purpose whatever, to an amount in the aggregate exceeding two hundred thousand dollars. But no municipal or political corporation shall give bonds, or become indebted in any manner, to an amount exceeding in the aggregate five per cent. on the value of the taxable property within such corporation, which value shall be ascertained by the last State and county tax lists."

The idea of placing a restriction upon this matter of corporation indebtedness, mainly grew out of the fact, that capitalists abroad lose confidence in the safety of their loans, where they do not know to what wild extent corporations may go in issuing bonds. It was this idea that first suggested the thought of placing some restrictions in the constitution. And if it goes forth to the world that there is a constitutional restriction, I do not care if it be five hundred thousand dollars, only that there is a limit, beyond which a county or municipal corporation cannot go, the result will be, that their bonds will command a higher price in the market than they otherwise would. It makes a great difference to a county, whether its bonds are quoted at eighty-five or ninety cents on the dollar, or only at seventy-five cents. The gentleman from Dubuque, [Mr. Emerson,] who, I understand, has negotiated such bonds, knows this to be true. I am confident that a majority of this convention do not wish to deprive the counties, and other municipal corporations, of the right of taking railroad stock. We will, in fact, make it better, and more advantageous, for those counties who do take it, if we impose some constitutional limit, beyond which they cannot incur indebtenness. The limit suggested by my proposition is two hundred thousand dollars, if the taxable property of the county will admit of it; I also provide, that in the smaller counties, where they have not that amount of taxable property, they shall only be allowed to issue their bonds to the amount of five per cent. of the valuation of their property. It will be seen, I believe, that the proposition I have read expresses the views of a majority of the members of the convention, who have spoken upon this subject during this discussion.

Mr. JOHNSTON. I prefer to take the course I have indicated, and if my motion does not prevail, then I will have no special objection to the motion of the gentleman from Henry, [Mr. Clarke.] It would probably expedite the business of the committee, if we should first take the vote upon striking out, and then he could offer his amendment afterwards.

Mr. CLARKE, of Henry. I will withdraw my substitute for that purpose.

The question was then taken upon the motion made by Mr. Johnston to strike out, and it was agreed to.

Mr. CLARKE, of Henry. I will now offer the substitute, which has already been read by the clerk.

Mr. CLARKE, of Johnson. Do I understand the gentleman as offering a substitute for the amendment?

Mr. CLARKE, of Henry. I intend to offer it as a substitute for that portion of the section which has been stricken out.

The substitute was then read.

Mr. CLARKE, of Johnson. It seems to me, that it raises the question we have been discussing, that of limitations upon this right of voting county subscriptions, and consequently I shall be compelled to vote against it.

The question was then taken upon adopting the substitute offered by Mr. Clarke, of Henry, and it was not agreed to, upon a division; ayes 9, nays 13.

Mr. CLARKE, of Johnson. I offer the following substitute for the section as amended:

"Sec. 4. No political or municipal corporation shall become a stock-holder in any banking corporation, directly or indirectly; but such corporations may become stock-holders in corporations for works of internal improvements within the State, upon a vote of the citizens of such municipal corporation, under such restrictions, as to the mode and amount of subscription, as the general assembly may prescribe."

The question was then taken and the substitute was not agreed to.

There being no other amendments offered to this section,

Section 5, was then read as follows:

It shall be the duty of the General Assembly to provide, by law, for the restraint of municipal and political corporations, in regard to assessments, taxations, borrowing money, contracting debts, issuing bonds, and loaning their credit, so as to prevent, as far as possible, unnecessary burdens, and unjust taxation and frauds.

Mr. SKIFF. I move that this section be stricken out. It is totally unnecessary, as the preceding section now stands.

Mr. CLARKE, of Henry. With regard to this section, I will state to the gentleman, that he will find it in nearly all the constitutions of other States, where the principle of requiring the legislature to make general laws, under which all these corporations shall be organized, is also incorporated. It is well enough to have such a section as this in the constitution. It shows, at any rate, the sense of the people, expressed in their constitution, by which they instruct the General Assembly to restrain municipal corporations from borrowing money, contracting debts. and loaning their credit, so as to involve the people in a system of grievous taxation, and unjust and unnecessary burthens. You will find this provision incorporated into the constitutions of the oldest States of the Union.

The question was then taken upon the motion to strike out, and it was not agreed to.

Mr. SKIFF. I move to amend the section by striking out the word, "shall" and inserting in lieu thereof, the word "may," so that it will read:

"It may be the duty of the General Assembly to provide by law, &c.

The question was taken, and the motion was not agceed to.

Mr. PALMER. I move to strike out of the sixth line, the words "as far as possible," so that it will read

"It shall be the duty of the General Assembly to provide, by law, for the restraint of municipal and political corporations, in regard to assessments, taxations, borrowing money, contracting debts, issuing bonds, and loaning their credit, so to prevent unnecessary burdens, and unjust taxation and frauds."

The question was taken, and the motion was agreed to.

There being no other amendments offered to the section,

Section 6, was then read as follows:

Banking.

"Subject to the provisions hereof the General Assembly may pass a general banking law, under which corporations may organize for banking purposes.

There being no amendments offered to this section,

Section 7, was then read as follows:

Basis of Banking.

"If a general banking law is passed, it shall provide, among other things, for the registry and countersinging, by an officer of the State, of all bills, or paper credit. designed to circulate as money, and require securit y to the full amount thereof, to be deposited with the State Treasurer, in United States stocks, or in interest-paying stocks of States in good credit and standing, to be rated at their average value in the city of New York, for the thirty days, next preceding their deposit; and also provide, for the recording of the names of all stock-holders in such corporations, the amount of stock held by each, the time of any transfer, and to whom."

Mr. EDWARDS. I desire to offer the following amendment, to come in at the end of the section:

"The proper officer shall require for every one hundred dollars of bills, countersigned and registered, an amount of stocks equal to one hundred and twenty dollars, to be deposited."

If we are about to embark in banking, in this State, I presume that every gentleman upon this floor has a preference for the system by which it shall be carried on. So far as I, myself, and the people whom I represent, are concerned, we would prefer a State bank. with branches; for the simple reason that past experience, the best of all teachers, has shown us, that the purposes of commerce and trade are better subserved under such a system, than under a system of general banking.

In my opinion a system under which we will have a parent bank, with branches interwoven, and connected together, in their operations and machinery, will impart a greater degree of confidence to the public mind, than any other system we can possibly devise. A bank founded upon a proper basis, with its various branches, and with the supervisory care of the legislature over the whole, will, in my judgment, meet the wants of the people of this State, better than any system of general banking, especially where each branch is responsible for the misconduct of each other branch. The system I favor, has an advantage in this respect, that it is for the interst of the parent bank and all its branches to keep a supervisory control over all the branches, and see that they are properly controlled and managed.

Another advantage that a bank with branches would have over a system of general banking is that it can be made a safe depository of the trust funds of the State. A well regulated system of State Banks, carries credit and confidençe wherever their bills are circulated, from the fact, that there is a parent bank, with branches linked together.

I have discovered since I came here that the minds of gentlemen are very much divided upon this question, and I am satisfied, from what I have seen, that the constitution will be left open for the purpose of establishing a system of general banking and a system of a State Bank with branches also. If then we are to go into both systems, the great duty which this convention will be called upon to perform, will be the protection of bill-holders. I am opposed to this idea of legislating in our constitution. I have confidence in the experience, integrity, and judgment of our future legislators, that they will be abundantly qualified to regulate these matters in detail; but as I have seen a disposition in this report and in the propositions of other gentlemen that have been made to the convention, to enter upon a system of legislation to some extent as connected with this question, I feel it to be a duty devolving upon me, and a most important one, to guard and protect the great mass of the bill-holders. It is with this view that I have offered an amendment, which I regard as a very vital part of this banking system. I say that it should be our object and aim to protect the bill holders in every particular. The point I propose to secure by the amendment I have offered, has been the very point in which the system of banking has heretofore proved disastrous to the people.

I recollect that a few years ago, a system of general banking was established in Indiana, upon the very basis reported by the committee here, requiring the parties interested to deposite stocks of the United States and interest paying stocks of other states, upon every hundred dollars of which they were entitled to issue a hundred dollars in bills, registered and countersignen by the proper officers of state. It would appear at the first blush, that all solvent stocks of States rated at their average valuation, thirty days before they were deposited, would be safe; that the interest accruing from these stocks, and the faith and credit of interest-paying states, would be a sufficient guarantee for the protection of the bill holder in the redemption of the bills. But there is an important point to be taken into consideration here. While things go on prosperously and swimmingly, this system may prove a safe one, but suppose a monetary crisis should overtake the country, and some of the states should fail to meet the interest upon their stocks, as is frequently the case, what would be the result? Why, confidence would be lost in these isolated, independant banks, for the want of credit; a rush would be made upon them, and they would be unable to meet the demands of the bill holders by the payment of specie. In such a crisis a large amount of stocks would be suddenly thrown upon the market, as was the case in Indiana, and there would not be capital enough in the State to purchase them up, at even their actual value. The result in Indiana was, that in the short space of six 'months the auditor of the state was compeled to throw into the market some ten millions of dollars of stocks, and they were sold under the hammer to the highest bidder, from twenty to thirty per cent below their actual value; and the currency of the free state banks were quoted at a discount, ranging from twenty to thirty per cent., at about the amount which the bonds were sacrificed at a forced sale.

If you adopt the provision I have offered here, requiring the individuals or corporations who may seek to avail themselves of the privileges of the general banking system, to deposite one hundred and twenty dollars in state stocks for every one hundred dollars of bills counter signed and registered, you protect the bill holders beyond any possible contingency of loss; and if you protect them and furnish a sound circulating medium that can always be converted into gold and silver, there would then be no objection to this system of banking. I would regard it as being beneficial to the best interests of the State and designed to promote the various branches of industry and commerce. A banking system, if it be only established upon judicious principles, is a safe system; but if it be not established upon a sound and correct basis, the people will lose confidence in it, and it must go down.

I will state for the information of the committee, that after this disaster had overtaken the banks in Indiana, to which I have referred, the Legislature required, in the bank charters which they granted, that they should file an additional security of twenty per cent; and we find all the banks that availed themselves of this amendment to the banking law, are now in a healthy and prosperous condition, and the people have confidence in them. The security of the bill holders I regard as a vital point, the most important point that we should secure. If this be secure, I shall have no objection to embarking in a system of general banking.

Mr. CLARKE, of Johnson. I will suggest to the gentleman, that in place of his amendment, he insert before the words "their average value," the words "twenty per cent. below," so that it will then read—

"If a general banking law is passed, it shall provide, amongst other things, for the registry and countersigning, by an officer of the State, of all bills, or paper credit designed to circulate as money, and require security to the full amount thereof, to be deposited with the State Treasurer, in United States stocks, or in interest paying stocks of States in good credit and standing, to be rated at twenty per cent. below their average value in the city of New York, for the thirty days next preceding their deposit; and also provide for the recording of the names of all stockholders in such corporations, the amount of stock held by each, the time of any transfer, and to whom.

Mr. EDWARDS. I have no objection. I will accept the amendment.

Mr. HALL. I do not intend to discuss this question of banking, for I admit my ignorance of the whole subject.

I propose to strike out from section six to section nineteen, inclusive, and insert a section in place of section seven.

The CHAIRMAN. The chair is of opinion that a motion to strike out this section would not be in order while there is an amendment pending to it.

Mr. HALL. I will not insist upon it at present.

Mr. SKIFF. I feel a great interest in this question of banking, and I will detain the committee but a short time in what I have to say. I shall oppose the amendment of the gentleman from Lucas (Mr. Edwards) for just one reason. If the gentleman will examine the report of the committee thoroughly, he will find that bill-holders are already secured by this report. It provides that before any one can issue and circulate bank paper, he shall deposit with the proper State officer a certain amount of good stocks; and in addition to this each corporator shall be individually liable to an amount equal to the stock which he may have. I think, then, that the bill-holder is already safe by this provision.

I wish now to state my views in relation to the two kinds of banks proposed—the State bank and the general banking system. I hope when members of the Convention come to vote upon this subject, they will come to the conclusion that they will have only one kind of banks. If we are to have a State bank, I do not want any other system of banking; and so if we are to have free banks, I do not want to have any State bank. My reason for it is this: in case there are two kinds of banks, there will be a conflict and a spirit of rivalry between them, that will tend to injure them both. The same results would attend a clashing of interests in this matter, as in any other kind of business, only it would be more injurious to the public. Competition, to a certain extent, is healthy; but when you allow two systems of banking in a State, there will always be a run made by one class of bankers upon the other, so that it will invalidate, to a certain extent, the credit of them both, and render it less trustworthy. I hope the Convention will weigh this matter well, and come to the conclusion to provide for only one class of banks.

My preferences are decidedly in favor of the free banking system, as it seems to me to be the most democratic. I do not use the word democratic in a party sense, as I do not intend to have any thing to do with party, inside of these halls. I believe this system is more democratic, because it allows any person, who will furnish the requisite securities, to go into banking, just the same as you would allow any person to go into merchandizing, to establish a foundry, to undertake farming, or carry on any branch of legitimate business. A system providing for a State bank with branches, is nothing more or less than a monopoly, which, according to my views, is anti-democratic, and to which I am decidedly opposed. Let banks be established, where the wants of the community demand their establishment. If, in a certain community, they need a bank, it should be established there and should not be placed under the control of officers, a part of whom are elected by the people, and a part by the legislature. I do not desire to place banking under the control of the State, any more than I do business in merchandizing or farming.

These are the views which I entertained, and expressed in the meetings of the committee on incorporations. I subscribed to this report, because I did not like the idea of presenting both a majority and a minority report. We had enough of this manner of settling questions in the reports made upon another article in the constitution.

I am opposed to the amendment of the gentleman from Lucas, and shall support the report of the committee just as it stands. I am also opposed to the plan proposed by the delegate from Des Moines, [Mr. Hall] which is not now directly before us. He wishes to leave this question entirely to the action of the legislature.

I think that we have examples enough to establish the fact, that we are certainly in the line of safe and illustrious precedents, when we place something in our constitution to guard these banking institutions. We are here, with no lobby influence about us, no bankers electioneering to get us to establish this, or that system of banking. If we were sitting here in the capacity of legislators, we should be beset on every hand, and our lobbies would be filled; and although we might consider ourselves in no danger from bribery, men might come and approach us in such a manner, that we might, unconsciously to ourselves, do what was not right. But we are not placed in a position surrounded by such influences. Parties interested, do not come around us, for they know that we cannot charter a bank, and give the State anything like a banking law; we can merely provide here, the foundation for such a law. Consequently, I think that we are better prepared to judge what is best for the interests of the people, than if we were sitting as a legislature. That is the reason why I am opposed to leaving this matter to the legislature. I am in favor of placing wholesome restrictions around this portion of the constitution.

This is all I have to say upon the subject of banking, at present.

The question was then taken upon Mr. Edwards amendment, and it was agreed to.—yeas, 15—nays not counted.

Mr. ELLS. I move to amend the section in the 5th line, by inserting after the word "deposited" the following:

"In case of the depreciation of said securities, or any portion thereof, to the amount of ten cent. on the dollar, of the stocks so depreciated, additional stock to that amount, shall be given by such bank or banks."

Mr. CLARKE, of Henry. I will say in regard to this amendment, and the other that has already been adopted, that these questions came before the committee. They thought it was going too far into legislation, to incorporate all these matters; the proper place for them, they considered, was in the banking laws themselves. The object of depositing stocks, is for security; and no banking law will be made under this constitution, without the legislature making provision, that the stocks shall be made, and kept secure. The amendment certainly adds very little to the section, and there is no particular objection to it.

Mr. ELLS. My object in offering it here, was to prevent the possibility of its being overlooked at the proper time.

Mr. JOHNSTON. As one of the members of the committee on incorporations, I wish to make a few remarks in regard to these several amendments.

As the chairman of the committee has properly observed, these subjects were all before the committee; but they were omitted upon the ground that they would be going too much into detail. The truth is, as the section now stands, it is a little objectionable on that ground. The amendment offered by the gentleman from Lucas [Mr. Edwards], and the suggestion of the gentleman from Scott [Mr. Ells] were based, as they say, upon the laws of some of the other States. There is no such provision in the constitution of Indiana. It was contained in the general law creating banks. The banks of Indiana and Illinois are now undergoing a renovation and purification, and the experience of those two States should teach us a lesson that should prevent us from following in their footsteps. I think that the better way is for us to leave all these matters of detail to the legislature. I am not willing to go as far as my friend from Des Moines [Mr. Hall] and leave this subject wholly to that body. I would throw around the system a few general restrictions, but I would not go into detail. The very amendment proposed by my friend from Scott [Mr. Ells] and also the amendment by my friend from Lucas [Mr. Edwards], have been found, in the experience of Illinois and Indiana, within a few years past, not to work well. The legislature of Illinois this winter passed a law, or were about amending their old banking law. I rely more upon a law passed by the legislature than upon restrictions contained in a constitution, from the fact that this banking law, whatever it may be, must be submitted to a vote of the people, and thoroughly discussed throughout the State. I think the fewer amendments we adopt to the report of the committee the better. I mean fewer amendments in detail.

Mr. PARVIN. I shall not vote for the amendment of the gentleman from Scott, [Mr. Ells,] as I do not believe such a requirement as he demands is necessary. While I am not in favor of restricting the legislature too much, there are some limits, I think, that ought to be placed in the constitution, beyond which the legislature should not be permitted to go. To throw the door wide open in this respect would be, as the gentleman from Des Moines [Mr. Hall,] suggests, very bad policy. I am opposed to the amendment offered by the gentleman from Scott, for the reason, that it goes too much into legislation. The amendment of the gentleman from Lucas, which has just been adopted, is more appropriate. It provides that banks must deposit twenty per cent. over and above the amount of their paper issued. A banker pays one hundred dollars in specie, gets one hundred dollars in state stocks, which he deposits, and upon which he gets interest. In addition to this, he issues eighty dollars, in notes, and he thus receives interest upon one hundred and eighty dollars, for every one hundred dollars that he has invested.

If I could have such a banking system as I wished, I would have no basis but that of specie for I think that this system is fraught with many evil consequences. We can see the effects of such a system in our sister state of Illinois. I believe with a banking system based upon a specie basis, and a provision that the individual stockholders shall be firmly bound, we could get exchange upon New York for one-half less than we now pay for it. We cannot now get exchange upon an eastern city for less than two per cent.; but I have no doubt if we had a State bank, properly guarded, that we could get it for one per cent or less, and there would be a clear gain in this respect of over one per cent.

There are many reasons why a banker should not be allowed to issue dollar for dollar. This may do when the country is in a flourishing condition, and until there comes a crisis in financial affairs. In establishing restrictions, therefore, for a system of banking, we must make provision guarding against such a crisis. Whenever such an event happens, stocks will depreciate; and hence the necessity of a restriction, fixing the amount of bills to be issued at twenty per cent. below the amount of stocks. If a State bank goes down, and fails to redeem its notes in specie, by the time the stocks are disposed of for money, and the note-holders are paid, the twenty per cent. will be exhausted. I look upon this as one of the evils of banking, place it upon the best footing you can.

I have no fears in this matter as regards the banker, he will always take care of himself. Our care should be to extend protection to the bill-holder. When a bank fails, as a general thing, the loss does not fall upon the banker, or the rich man, who handles hundreds of thousands of dollars; but it falls upon the laboring man, who never holds but a small amount of bills at a time in his hands. When the bank first fails, his money cannot be redeemed, and he is not able to hold it until the stocks, which the State holds, can be disposed of; consequently, he goes to the broker and sells the bills he may have for what he can get. The broker holds his bills until provision is made for their redemption. The loss, then, falls mostly upon those who are least able to bear it.

I should greatly prefer the establishment of a State bank with branches, to any other system. I believe, if we should have such a bank, instead of going to the brokers and paying three per cent. a month, which a man has to do now—and persons have been compelled to pay even higher than that for the last year or two—that we could get money for ten per cent. per annum.

Another advantage which such a system would have, over that of general banking, is, that we would have a paper currency which would be considered current abroad, an advantage which a local bank under the general banking system, can never have. We have abundant evidence of this fact in the history of banking, as it has been managed in other States. In all my experience, I have never yet seen notes that were issued under a general banking law, that would go at par any great distance from home. But with a good State bank and branches, I believe that their notes would readily circulate in the other States and be considered perfectly safe. I have no idea that the Convention will establish a State bank or a general banking system; but they will leave it, as it is proper, perhaps, that we should do, to the Legislature to say which of the two systems they will choose, with a provision, that whatever action that body may take shall be submitted to a vote of the people for their approval.

For these reasons, hastily thrown out for the consideration of the Convention, I cheerfully concur in the amendment of the gentleman from Lucas [Mr. Edwards,] but shall vote against that offered by the gentleman from Scott, [Mr. Ells.]

Mr. ELLS. I rise for the purpose of putting the gentleman from Muscatine [Mr. Parvin,] right in this matter, so far as I am concerned. My object is to furnish the people with a safe and reliable currency, convertible at all times into gold or silver, by presenting at the counter of the institution that issued it. If I thought the removal of the present restriction on banks would result in the establishment of a system of banking by the legislature, without requiring a specie basis, I most certainly would oppose the whole system at the out-set, preferring to endure the present evils, rather than "fly to those we know not of."

The State bank-branches of Ohio (there being no parent bank,) are, by the provisions of the charter, all liable for each others issues. There is an annual tax levied for the purpose of creating a "safety fund" to meet any defalcations. This system is based on specie, while that of the general banking law is based on State stocks; both are required to redeem their currency in gold or silver, upon presentation at their counters, within banking hours, or forfeit their chartered privileges. These are the systems that the people of this State are demanding at our hands; anything short of this they will repudiate. Consequently, the fears of the gentleman from Muscatine [Mr. Parvin,] are without just cause.

If we were a legislative, rather than an organic body, and were creating a banking system for the people, I should oppose the establishment of a State bank system. All experience in the older States prove that the direct and legitimate tendency of that system is to create moneyed monopolies.

I am aware that honorable and intelligent gentlemen, on this floor, entertain different views of these two systems, and prefer to leave the whole question to the wisdom of the general assembly; and it illy becomes me to distrust the wisdom, integrity, and patriotism of the people's representatives; hence I shall, at the proper time, vote for leaving the two systems in their hands.

Mr. HALL. I agree to some extent with the gentleman from Scott [Mr. Ells]; but I am unwilling to tie up the hands of the legislature in regard to the particular mode by which a banking system shall be regulated. I am satisfied, that the legislature, which will be elected under this constitution, and elected, too, after this question has been fully discussed and considered, will come here better qualified, than we can possibly be, to judge what kind of a banking law should be passed. I am not very familiar with the banking systems of other States: but I do know that the system in Indiana—which is clogged with guards and checks, such as we are here attempting to throw around our system—has proved to some extent a failure. The system adopted in Ohio has served them better. I believe, from the best light I can get, that this system of banking upon State stocks, as originally designed and undertaken in these States, has proved, to some extent, a great mistake; and I do not believe, that the bill-holders can be indemnified for any losses they may sustain under any such system.

I presume gentlemen here know the fact that there have been failures in Illinois and Indiana, within the last few weeks, of a number of their banks, based upon State stocks, and whose notes were countersigned by the comptroller, bank commissioner, or the officer whose duty it was to countersign their bills. There may be stocks enough, which, carefully and prudently managed, may be converted into money, sufficient to redeem their issues; but many persons, who hold these notes, are unable to wait for their redemption, and are obliged to sell them at a great sacrifice. I have known such paper to be sold as low as sixty cents on the dollar. There are a great many persons, who will be compelled, upon the failure of a bank, to sacrifice their notes by selling them to the brokers at a loss of from ten to fifty per cent., although the bank has perfectly good securities. Every person in the community knows this to be the fact.

You can only make a banking system safe and reliable, in my opinion, by placing it upon a specie basis. The poorer class of people, who have but a few dollars of money at a time, cannot wait, in case of the failure of a bank, until its securities are converted into money. If you sell these securities at a forced sale, at the end of ten days after such failure, you cannot sell them for half enough to redeem the paper of the bank. These stocks have to be taken to the cities, where such things are sold. If you put them up in a place where there is no money to buy stocks, you will find great difficulty in selling them at par value.

I am unwilling to tie the hands of the legislature upon this subject of banking, for in my opinion they will be abundantly qualified to arrange and perfect a system that shall be well guarded in every respect, and shall prove most acceptable to the people when it is submitted to them for their approval. The subject will be thoroughly discussed by them, and every proposition that may be submitted to the people will be scrutinized carefully in every respect, by all classes of the community; and by those especially who are engaged in monetary transactions, or in business operations, that require the facilities offered by a good banking system. I am unwilling to endorse any system here by which we shall restrict the legislature in the provisions they may make in regard to a system of banking. With my present views, I would strike out the seventh section entirely, and leave the whole subject open. If there can be a good banking system established, I am not afraid to give the legislature full scope over the matter. If, after a full discussion, they should say, let us have a State bank, I would give them the power to submit the question to the people; or if they should decide in favor of a general banking law, I would give them the same power to submit that system, also. But I do not believe they should submit these two propositions together. One or the other of the systems should have precedence, and I would let the legislature submit to the people, whether they will adopt it or not. I do not wish to trammel the legislature in this respect at all. Let us give them the fullest scope and power to make as perfect a system as possible.

The eighth section of this report, which makes every stock-holder in a banking corporation individually responsible, and liable to his creditors over and above the amount of stock held by him, equal to the amount of his share of the stock, I consider to be a salutary one.

Sections fourteen and fifteen also, which provide that every banking corporation shall cease banking within twenty-five years after its organization, and that no bills shall be issued for circulation as money except by corporations duly organized, I regard as salutary; at least no harm can result from their adoption.

Mr. SOLOMON. I do not rise for the purpose of making a speech upon the general question of a banking law, for I feel unable to discuss it; I rise merely to indicate the reasons which will govern me in my vote, for or against the amendments that may be proposed. I have voted against the amendments already proposed, and I have done so without any reference to their character at all. I have done so for the very reason urged by the gentleman from Des Moines, [Mr. Hall], that I am not willing, by any vote or act of mine in this Convention, to place myself or my constituents in a situation, in which we should be considered as at all committed in favor of any system of banking. I expect that I am, upon this question, an old fogy; and I expect that my views will be disapproved of by a large majority of the members of this Convention. I know that my views met with opposition in my district, and I know that much was said by those who were in favor of a banking system. But there is one other little fact I know, and which I have the best reason for knowing, that this opposition came from those who did not support me. I would be willing to vote for such an amendment as was suggested by the gentleman from Des Moines, [Mr. Hall] awhile ago, to strike out all the sections in this report, from section six to section nineteen, with an additional amendment that when the question of banks is submitted to the people for their decision, some time, say six months, should elapse between the passage of the law by the legislature, and the voting upon it by the people.

I do not consider the points which are urged here by the committee, as the dangerous points in banking; I consider that there is another thing more dangerous to the community at large than these. I take it, that they are aiming, in their provisos and conditions here, to secure at all times and as speedily as possible, the convertibility of bills of credit into gold, a worthy object indeed, but one which is entirely above and beyond the power of any legislative enactment.

The want of this convertibility is not the great danger resulting from the banking system in my opinion. The great danger is, and it is one which you have all noticed and felt—the moral effect of having too much money among the people. My great objection to a banking system is, that too much of that which passes for a circulating medium is not money, that it consists of mere empty, void promises-to-pay, coming from some quarter, we know not where, but tending to inflate the money market, and create an unhealthy excitement in the public mind. We are surrounded by all kinds of banks, and if we do not have any of our own, we are flooded with the bank paper of other people, the character of which we do not know.

Let me suggest in regard to that basis of banking which seems to have been favored in this community, that I look upon the State stock system as delusive a dream as ever the South Sea Bubble was. I may be mistaken in this; but when the proper time comes for me to express my views upon this matter, I shall give my reasons more fully than I feel disposed to do at present.

I have great respect for the gentlemen who have made this report on corporations, and I have no doubt that they have reported what they deemed to be the best plan extant. I believe that the very nature of this system of banking is such, that if you establish any system, an hour may create a change in the public mind, inducing a desire for something else. I look upon banking as nothing more or less than a series of tricks of adroit swindlers, invented by ingenious financiers, to rob the laboring man of the fruits of his labor. I look upon it as invented for no other purpose; and I look upon it as a degraded position for a state to occupy, if she gives her aid and credit in breathing the breath of life into the nostrils such monsters as this.

When the proper time comes, as I intimated to this convention the other day, I shall insist upon it as a matter of principle, that the power of issuing paper money shall never be granted by this State, and upon that question I intend to call for the yeas and nays.

Mr. GILLASPY. I do not profess to understand the banking laws of this country. I had supposed, at the commencement of this Convention, when we had appointed the committees upon the various subjects embraced in our constitution, that this convention would, to some extent, adhere to the reports of those committees; but I find a disposition to the contrary shown here.

I believe that there are sufficient guards and checks contained in this report of the committee on incorporations. I have never, in all my life, been able to examine a banking law of any kind or character. But there is a saving clause in this report, to the effect that no banking law shall become operative until it has been submitted to, and approved by the people of this State. I believe we are endeavoring to steer between two great and dangerous snags—as I would have said when I was boating upon the Mississippi. We must prepare a provision to confer upon the legislature power to frame a banking law, such as will, on the one hand, induce capitalists to come to this State for the purpose of going into banking, and, on the other hand, guard the people against wrong. Now, I myself am not able or prepared to indicate what such a law should be, but I have the utmost confidence in the people I have the honor to represent here, and I have more confidence in the people of this State than I have in the General Assembly. I believe that when the legislature passes a banking law and submits it to the people, they will discuss and examine it until they understand it. If it is proper and right, they will adopt it; but if it is not so, if it is a law under which bankers can swindle the people, they will vote it down.

I want to prepare a constitution here that will permit banking, for I think a large portion of the people are in favor of it. I have no objection to the proposition laid down by the committee to allow the passage of a law providing for a State bank, and also for general banking. But I do not want to go into detail in this constitution, for fear we will defeat the object the people desire.

I will say to my young friend from Mills (Mr. Solomon) that I hope before we get to issuing paper money in this State, the railroad from Burlington will be completed to his county; and if he finds himself overburdened with money, if he will send it to Wapello, I will dispose of it for him. My people are not troubled with too much money—their great trouble has been that they have not had half enough of it.

Mr. SOLOMON. If the gentleman from Wapello, (Mr. Gillaspy) will promise, upon the honor of a man, to redeem in specie every dollar of this paper money we send to him, I will promise to send it to him.

Mr. GILLASPY. I will not promise that; but I will promise to give it a good circulation. [Laughter].

The question recurred upon the amendment submitted by Mr. Ells, which was as follows:

To insert after the word "deposited," in the fifth line of section seven, the words—

"And in case of the depreciation of said securities, or any portion thereof, to the amount ten per cent. on the dollar of the stocks so deposited, additional stock to that amount shall be given by such bank or banks."

The question being taken, the motion was not agreed to.

Mr. HALL moved to strike out the seventh section.

Mr. CLARKE, of Henry. Before the question is taken upon this motion to strike out this seventh section, I would call the attention of the Convention to the eleventh section of this report, which should be considered in connection with the one under consideration. That section reads—

"Sec. 11. It shall be the duty of the General Assembly, in case of its passing either or both of the banking laws herein provided, to provide also such other restrictions, and fix such other liabilities, and adopt such other guards and checks as shall be conducive to prevent frauds on the part of banking institutions, its officers and directors, and to secure to the people of this State a safe and reliable currency."

By this all the details of legislation are left to, and conferred upon, the General Assembly. The committee in the seventh section meant merely to provide for the character of securities, and nothing more. And if you look to the character of stocks mentioned in that section, which may be deposited under a general banking law, you will find that they are to consist of "United States stocks, or interest-paying stocks of States in good credit and standing, to be rated at their average value in the city of New York for the thirty days next preceding their deposit."

The gentleman from Des Moines (Mr. Hall) objects to thus fixing the kind of security, that there might be a fluctuation in the market, &c. Now there is hardly any fluctuation in the stocks of the nature required by this section. The people have, in the very nature of this stock, the greatest security they can have, and that is all we wish to effect.

Suppose the gentleman from Dés Moines desires to go into banking. He has one hundred thousand dollars in gold, which he puts in his vaults. There it draws no interest, but if, instead of that, he buys United States Stocks to the amount of one hundred thousand dollars, he will have interest upon that amount, and then he can issue eighty thousand dollars in bills, having deposited twenty per cent. more than that amount in the State Treasury. At the same time he must have at least thirty thousand dollars in specie in his vaults. No banking law will be passed in this State without requiring at least this proportion of specie. In other words, the stocks will be the security, the basis will be specie.

I think this stock security is the best feature of this provision; and another thing, every general banking law we may consult shows that if the value of these stocks should depreciate, they must be made good. The gentleman says he has great confidence in the legislature, and they will, of course, not omit such a palpably necessary provision as that.

Now, is it not a great deal more dangerous to leave this an open question to be settled by the next legislature, and then be unsettled again by the succeeding legislature, than it is for us to say here what shall be the quality and character of the security to be given? Certainly it would be. Suppose our next legislature should say, as we propose to say here, that this security shall consist of United States or interest-paying State stocks. There is no constitutional provision to prevent the next legislature from providing that railroad stocks may be received as security.

If gentlemen, after understanding the effect of this section, choose to strike it out, they can do so. But if that is done, it seems to me that it would be better to strike out the whole matter, and put no restriction upon the legislature at all. In my opinion it would be far preferable to fix the character of the stock beyond the action of all future legislatures, in order to give stability and confidence; and that the people may rest satisfied that when we do have a banking law, it shall not be altered to admit any other kind of stocks, for the benefit of wild-cat operators.

Mr. EDWARDS. I hope the motion of the gentleman from Des Moines [Mr. Hall,] will not prevail. And while I am up I desire to answer some arguments presented by other gentlemen upon the other side of this question. Ever since this Convention has been in session, whenever any proposition has been before us for consideration, gentlemen have risen in their seats and stated that they did not know the wishes of their constituents upon that question; that they had heard no expression of opinion from them upon the subject.

But the question now presented to us is one, I opine, in regard to which they have heard the opinions of their constituents. I presume there are but few gentlemen upon this floor, who will not admit that we were sent here for the purpose of removing from our constitution the prohibition against banking. The gentleman from Mills [Mr. Solomon,] tells you that he is opposed to all systems of banking. And I presume that when we go out of committee of the whole into Convention, and the ayes and nays are called, we will all be able to show our positions upon this question, whether we are in favor of being placed upon the record for removing this prohibition or not.

When the majority of twenty thousand of the people of this State voted for the purpose of calling this Convention, I understood that the ostensible object was to remove that prohibition now in the constitution, and to devise ways and means for some system of banking. While the gentleman from Mills is denouncing paper money and the system of banking, let me call his attention to one fact to which he alluded. That fact is this: notwithstanding we are prohibited in Iowa from issuing paper money, we have just as much bank paper here as any State of the Union where banking is allowed, and we are cursed with as worthless shinplasters as any State in this Union. And gentlemen are every day breaking the law here by circulating these shinplasters. If we should fix up a sound circulating medium for the people of this State, it would drive out of the State this worthless trash that we now have among us. The fact that we have no banking system of our own, is the very reason that all this wild-cat money from distant States is brought here and circulated among us. If we had a sound, safe and reliable circulating medium of our own, under our own control, we would be able to protect the people from the vast amount of worthless trash now brought here for the purpose of circulation among us,

So far as the question is concerned of whether or not we are to have a banking system, I think that has been fully determined. I am satisfied that a large majority of the Convention will go for removing this prohibition from the constitution.

The next question then is, shall we put any restrictions about banking in this constitution? I would prefer a State bank with branches. But

I am satisfied that a large number of gentlemen here are in favor of a general banking law also. I cannot see, with the gentleman from Jasper, [Mr. Skiff,] that the two systems of banking would necessarily conflict with each other. I think the experience of other States proves rather the contrary. The fact is that if they are carried out judiciously, they are instruments of blessing to the people; if they are not sufficiently guarded upon all points, they may prove disastrous. If well conducted, instead of paying three per cent. a month as we now have to do for our money, we would be able to get it for ten per cent. a year.

Some gentlemen say that if we adopt this provision, requiring the deposit of one hundred and twenty thousand dollars of stocks for every hundred thousand dollars of bills issued, we will defeat the very object we have in view; for capitalists who own these stocks would never engage in a system of banking under such a restriction. Now I think gentlemen are mistaken in viewing this matter in this light. In the first place it is presumable that these stocks will draw from six to eight per cent. interest.—Whether or not the paper issued by these banks is secured by their being deposited, they will still draw that interest. When they are deposited with the proper officer of the State they will draw that interest. And the banks can, by a system of exchange, make other interest, and I believe they are allowed by that system of exchange, to charge more than the legal rate of interest. They would get from ten to fifteen per cent. for exchange, besides the interest upon these stocks thus deposited, making in all from fifteen to twenty per cent. So there is that inducement for men to engage in banking, even under this provision, and experience proves that such is the case.

Several gentlemen who have spoken upon this question say that they have had very little experience in regard to banking. I do not claim to be conversant with banking, but I have had some experience in regard to the matter. I have had some experience, in a legislative capacity, in reference to framing laws concerning banking, and if my views are worth anything upon that subject, I am willing to give them here.

I have a duty to discharge to my constituents and I shall express my views here upon this subject. I care not what laws you may pass, or what details you enter into. The point I propose to guard is the main point, and with that point guarded, whatever the law may be, the thing is secured. In Indiana a banking law was passed under their constitution. The gentleman from Des Moines [Mr. Hall,] spoke about the long list of details in this report. Now if I understand the difference between general provisions and details, there are many details in the constitution of Indiana upon this subject. Some of them are as follows:

"The stockholders in every bank or banking company shall be individually responsible to an amount over and above their stock, equal to their respective shares of stock, for all debts or liabilities of said bank or banking company."

"Holders of bank notes shall be entitled, in case of insolvency, to preference of payment over all other creditors."

"No bank shall receive, directly or indirectly, a greater rate of interest than shall be allowed by law to individuals loaning money."

But the point we propose to guard in this constitution was not guarded in the Indiana constitution. And the effect was that there were influences brought to bear upon the legislature of that State by capitalists, which proved the necessity of such a provision in the constitution. The system that was adopted went down. At the next session of the legislature, when we were convened, there was not a man in either branch, together with the governor and lieutenant governor, who did not admit that if there had been engrafted in the constitution, the provision I proposed here, the system of general banking would have gone on smoothly, and there would have been no disastrous result. They amended the banking law by inserting the very provision I have offered here. What was the effect of it? All those banks that applied for incorporation under that law, and filed their additional securities, are getting along well, and no danger can be apprehended from them. And the free banks of Illinois have labored under the same difficulties, as did the free banks of Indiana before they were broken up.

Now I care not what details the legislature may go into; if you will guard the bill-holders against the possibility of loss, the system will work well. Under the laws of Indiana, and perhaps of Illinois, there was no want of detail. But a regular system of wild cat banking was established. A man could deposite his stock, establish his banking house, and issue his bills from some village out on the prairie, beyond the reach of railroads, and where the people could not reach it. He, at the same time, would be living in the city of New York. If this was a legislative body, and I a member of it, I would urge a provision in the law, that no banker should have his bills registered and issued, unless he had his banking house in some prominent locality in the State. He should have his banking house there, and keep his regular business hours, and also keep on hand a certain amount of gold and silver for the redemption of his bills. I understand that in Indiana several individuals, who had some of these bills they wanted to have redeemed, rode around trying to find the place where the banking house purported to be located. They would be told that it was at a certain place—go there, and it would be at another place, and so they went around over half of the State trying to find it. I would have such a provision here, that the legislature would be beyond the reach and power of capitalists who desire to get bills passed to suit themselves.

Mr. HALL. When I was up before, I gave, principally, the reasons which induced me to move to strike out this seventh section. That section reads:

Sec. 7. If a general banking law is passed, it shall provide, amongst other things, for the registry and countersigning, by an officer of the State, of all bills, or paper credit, designed to circulate as money, and require security to the full amount thereof, to be deposited with the State Treasurer, in United States stocks, or in interest-paying stocks of States in good credit and standing, to be rated at twenty per cent. below their average value in the city of New York, for the thirty days next preceding their deposit; and also provide for the recording of the names of all stockholders in such corporations, the amount of stock held by each, the time of any transfer, and to whom.

That section indicates the general character of the banking law the legislature shall pass, and it can pass no other than that. Now I want to take off these shackles from the legislature. I do not want to limit the legislature, or the people, by saying that they shall not pass a general banking law without such and such limitations. If they should see fit and proper to pass a general banking law upon a specie basis—which I believe to be the only true principle of banking, if there is any true principle—I would not prohibit the legislature from doing so. And there is no necessity of both bases if you adopt a good specie basis.

I want to get rid of this restriction of the legislature to a particular kind of general banking law. I want them to have the same liberty of action, in regard to that system of banking, as any other. Is this the only kind of system that can possibly be adopted, or thought of, that can promote the public good? It seems to me we should leave this matter open to the legislature, and it is for that reason that I moved to strike this section out. I think all restrictions, as to the kind of banking system to be adopted, whether it be a State bank or general banking, should be left to the legislature. I would leave the door open, so that they can do one thing or the other, or both. I do not want to confine them, and say they shall grant just this kind of charter, and no other. That is my position, and in that I think I am pursuing a course which will procure the adoption of a good banking law, if one can be made. They will have all the lights now shining, and hereafter to shine, to lead them on to a proper adjustment of this matter.

I am half of the opinion that this State stock system will be exploded before we can have any legislation upon this subject. And I should feel very foolish and flat if we should adopt a system which the whole world will condemn as fallacious and good for nothing. I would have the way open for the legislature to pass a banking law upon a specie basis alone, or a basis, part specie and part stock, as expediency may dictate, and experience prove to be the best.

In regard to this eleventh section, which the gentleman from Henry [Mr. Clarke,] has read, I look upon it as mere moonshine. It is just like what every mother says to her boy when he goes to school. "Joe, be a good boy; don't fight; keep your clothes clean, and come right straight home at night." And then the boy goes away, fights three times as much as he would otherwise do, tears his clothes all to pieces, and comes home as dirty as a hog. (Laughter.) This is all the good that will result from the piece of advice contained in this eleventh section, "To adopt such other guards and checks as shall be conducive to prevent frauds on the part of banking institutions." That is all gratuitous advice. They will be sure to do that if they can. If they cannot do it, it is useless to put this in here. This is gratuitous advice; means nothing, and does no good.

Here is the sixteenth section, that has more in it than all the rest.

"Sec. 16. But no general banking law, nor law creating a State bank, nor shall amendments thereto, nor acts in repeal thereof, take effect until the same be submitted, separately, to the people, at a general or special election, as provided by law, and be approved by a majority of all the voters voting for and against it."

Now I am decidedly in favor of that section, that when such a system has been submitted to the people, and they adopt it, it shall stand without amendment until the people change it themselves, because if we do not close up that door, the legislature might one year make a law of a certain description, and then the next year make one entirely different from it. I think we can disperse with the seventh, ninth, tenth and eleventh sections entirely The rest are well enough, and can do no harm.

Mr. CLARKE, of Henry. I would like to ask the gentleman from Des Moines [Mr. Hall,] whether, or not, the security, that is provided in this section, is not over and above and distinct from the specie basis, which every bank must have.

Mr. HALL. I would rather see the gold and silver than the bonds.

Mr. CLARKE, of Henry. My question is this; whether or not the security of State stock, which is required by this section, is not over and above the specie basis of which the gentleman speaks? Is it not a security beyond the specie basis?

Mr. HALL. I am well aware of one thing, that if I desired to get up a system here that would be wholly impracticable, I would vote for this system. But I am not for that; I want to get up a system that will be practicable, and go into operation upon the fairest terms, and with the best prospects of success. Any person, who is at all conversant with banking, knows, that if you adopt this plan, you cannot have a good system of banking. If we put this restriction upon the stocks of requiring twenty per cent. more stocks than there are bills issued, the capitalist will take his stocks to Illinois and Indiana, where he can use them for their full value, and we will not be able to get them here.

I am not begging the question whether stocks would be proper or not. But I do not want to fasten the general banking law down to the stock system absolutely. I want to give the legislature an opportunity to adopt either the specie or the stock basis, or a basis composed partly of specie and partly of stocks. I think that would be far better than any other provision we could adopt here.

As to this eighth section I regard it as an unnecessary clog upon banking. However, it is not proper to speak of that now.

Mr. PARVIN. I desire to say one word with regard to this specie basis. I certainly did not intend to be understood, as the gentleman from Scott [Mr. Ells,] understood me. I maintain, and I think I can do so without fear of successful contradiction, that these bonds, and not the specie, are the real basis of banking.

I do not intend to intimate that a banker would go into banking without a dollar in his vaults to redeem his notes. But I maintain that the basis of his banking is this State stock. It is true that he must have some specie to redeem his notes. But if you will search the country through, you will find that most all banks having one hundred thousand dollars of notes in circulation will not have more than five thousand dollars or ten thousand dollars in specie on hand. Specie is not the basis of their banking; it is these State stocks. And whenever they fail to redeem their notes in specie, these stocks are sold to redeem the notes. I do not mean that a man will go to banking under this system without a dollar of specie; but it is not the specie that is the basis of his banking, but these State stocks.

Mr. GIBSON. I had not intended to say anything upon this question. But perhaps it is due to myself that I should say a few words. I am in favor of striking out this seventh section for various reasons. I believe it to be wrong in principle, wrong in theory, and wrong in practice. In the first place it is going too much into detail; it is assuming to legislate too much. It seems to me, with all due deference to other members of the convention, that they consider themselves more competent, and better prepared, to get up a banking system, than any other body of men can be. Do this convention think that there is more talent, more wisdom, and more discretion here, than can be found in any other body of men who could be got together in this State? I, for one, do not think so.

While I am in favor of a banking system, I am not in favor of this convention going into the details of that system. I am willing that this convention should provide that the legislature should act upon this matter, and that before this section takes effect, it shall be submitted to the people, for their acceptance or their rejection. This seems to me to be a sufficient guard to be placed in here.

It is a very common remark of gentlemen upon this floor, that they do not know, and are not familiar with, the different systems of banking. Nor do they know what will be the wants and the wishes of the people two years hence, or four years hence, or six years hence. Under these circumstances are we going to lay down the precise basis, in our preliminary action here, upon which the legislature shall act, and provide that they shall act in no other way? I presume that the next legislature will contain as much wisdom, as much intelligence, as much discretion, as does this convention. And I am not willing for us to assume all the wisdom of the State to ourselves, and leave nothing to their wisdom and discretion. I rather think that whatever the legislature may lack, if it should lack anything, this matter will be safe in the hands of the people, who have to pass upon any law concerning banking before it can go into effect.

I am opposed *in toto* to the ninth section, which provides for the establishment of a State bank and branches. I believe such a thing would be wrong. I think it would be creating a monopoly, and should not be tolerated in the State of Iowa. I am in favor of a general banking law, by which all are placed upon a perfect equality, as regards entering into the business of banking, under which every individual, or association of individuals, by complying with the requirements and conditions of that law, may incorporate themselves for the purpose of enjoying all the benefits and privileges of banking. I am decidedly opposed to creating a State bank by special act of the legislature, conferring certain chartered privileges upon certain individuals, and denying them to others.

This is not equality. Gentlemen here have spoken of democracy; I do not consider this to be demecratic. The doctrine of democracy is the greatest good to the greatest number. This would not meet the doctrine.

The eleventh section strikes me as rather amusing than otherwise. We say in that, to the legislature—now you may frame a banking law, but be very careful in doing so, to prevent fraud; make it all right and secure. Now what does that look like? It looks as if we thought there was danger that the legislature would be reckless and extravegant, and not careful of the interests of the people of Iowa. It is just as my friend from Des Moines, (Mr. Hall) has said, like the advice of a mother to her child. It seems to me that it is, to some extent, reflecting upon the character of the members of the legislature, to incorporate such a provision as this in the constitution. To say the least, it is implying that they may not carry out the wishes, and guard the interests of their constituents in that respect.

I would like to see this report so changed as to give the legislature the right to pass a general banking law. Let them fix the basis of that law as they may think best, and before it takes effect let it be referred to the people of the state for their apppoval. That would be all the guard necessary for us to throw around this matter.

Some considerable time must pass before we can possibly have banks in this state. The public mind mind may undergo a great change before then. This constitution will not be submitted to the people before August. Admit that it will be adopted. A legislature will have to be elected and that legislature must provide a banking law according to these provisions, which must be submitted to the people for their approval. All this routine will probably take two years. Is this convention prepared to say that they will tie the hands of the legislature, and say that they must and shall legislate upon certain things, and incorporate certain provisions in any banking law they may pass? I think we should not do that.

If we are to have a banking law in this state, then suffice it to say, that it will be sufficiently safe to trust it in the hands of the next legislature. If this is done the people will consider it at the next election of members of the general assembly. This matter will be canvassed thoroughly in the different counties in the state. The legislature would come up here directly from the people, understanding fully what kind of banking law they wanted. If they did not understand it, or if they incorporated provisions in that law which were odious and wrong, the people would hold them to an account, and would vote it down.

I consider these preliminary details to be all wrong and unnecessary. Not only that, but I believe it to be cumbering up this portion of the constitution, when it should be free and unencumbered.

Mr. WILSON. I am opposed to the motion of the gentleman from Des Moines [Mr. Hall] to strike out this seventh section. I believe it ought to be retained in this article just as it was reported from the committee. I think there are very good reasons why it should be retained here. In the first place it determines and fixes the basis of banking in this state, and determines for all future time, at least while this constitution shall remain in force, what the basis of free banks shall be. Taking this section in connection with section thirteen of this report and we find that all the safe-guards are provided for this system that have been urged by gentlemen who oppose the seventh section.

Section thirteen provides that "the suspension of specie payments by banking institutions shall never be permitted and sanctioned."

Now I take it, that although the banking basis of free banks will be the stocks of the United States, and state stocks deposited by these bankers with the proper officers of the state, yet they will be compelled, in order to secure to themselves the rights and privileges to be enjoyed under the general banking law of this state, to provide for the redemption of their paper at their counters at any time, in specie. If they fail to redeem it when presented, their houses will be closed and their business stopped.

This section simply determines the basis of their operations; that it shall be either United States stocks or the stocks of interest paying states in good credit and standing. If that is taken as the basis I would ask if the bill holder is not just as secure as if they had specie, dollar for dollar, lying in the vaults of their banks? This restriction which is contained in this section provides that these stocks should be taken at their average value in the city of New York for the thirty days next preceding their deposite. I take it stocks of this character will be marketable and will always be considered good, as an investment. A man is always willing to invest his money in United States stocks, even if the money market is tight, because he considers them a good and secure investment. And so it is of the stocks of interest paying states, because they are on long time, and bring a good rate of interest in return.

Then the use that can be made of these stocks as a basis for banking, will be an inducement for men to invest their capital in banking, because their banking basis is bringing them in a return as well as the other departments of banking. There is no department of the business that is not remunerative. We create in this way an advantage, not only to the people, by giving them a secure basis, but also an advantage to the stockholders themselves.

I am unwilling to leave this matter entirely to the legislature. I am unwilling to do so at the present time for this reason: the people of this State are anxious to have banks established in the State. If you were to cut off all restrictions, and the next legislature should assemble, under the excitement now existing in this State upon this subject, and pass a banking law, I do not care if it should be full of defects, the probability is that it would be passed by the people. The people are anxious to have a banking law, and their cool, deliberate judgment would not operate now, as it would if banks had existed here before.

I am not willing to go with the gentleman from Des Moines, [Mr. Hall] and permit wildcat banking to spring up in this State. We all know that the money power of this country is almost, if not quite, as great as the power of the people. The people have to contend against that power in their legislatures, in their elections, and in short, everywhere, when the interest of the money power can possibly come in conflict with the interests of the people. I am for affording them some security against the exercise of this power. I believe the better course to be, to place some restrictions in the constitution. We find that the citizens of this State are now contending over this very matter. We have found the necessity for a banking institution; we have found that it is necessary to have a paper circulating medium.

The necessities of the community demand this; the necessities of commerce demand it; the necessities of all our business departments demand it. We have found springing up all around our borders a species of wild-cat banking. Nebraska has flooded our State all over, with a currency in which I have never had any faith. Every bank in the western States seems to have sent their paper here, and particularly those which have no credit at home. Even the city of Burlington has flooded the State with her shin-plasters, which have no basis whatever; none in the world. Let her repudiate the shin-plasters presented at her counters, and that moment we will have a crisis. I have no doubt but what the people of Burlington are honest, that they do not intend to do any injury. The people take these bills because they are presented for circulation, and they need something for a circulating medium. I believe the only plan is to secure a solid and firm basis, before this paper is put into circulation.

I will advert to another matter, inasmuch as it has been noticed by some gentlemen here, though it is not germain to the proposition now before the convention. I refer to this matter of establishing a State bank. If there is any question upon which my constituency differ, I believe it is this question of banks. I believe nine-tenths of them are in favor of banking; a portion of them are in favor of a State bank, and a portion are in favor of general banking. I am in favor of leaving the choice to the legislature, and let them say whether either or both systems shall be adopted, and I am willing that question should go to the people. I am also willing that a State bank should be established upon a specie basis, and I am pleased to find in this report another thing, which does not seem to meet with the approval of the gentleman from Des Moines, [Mr. Hall] and that is the tenth section, which reads as follows:

"If such a State bank be established, the branches shall be mutually responsible for each others liabilities upon all paper credit issued as money, and the liabilities of stock-holders shall be the same as those of banks organized under a general law—all of which shall be provided for by law."

I believe if a State bank is established in this State, all the branches of that institution would be responsible for each others issues. I have seen the effect of that in the State of Ohio, where all the branches of the State bank are liable for each others issues. A branch of the State bank was situated in the town where I resided—the Licking county branch. Through the financiering of its cashier that branch failed. But the paper of that bank, after the comptroller had taken possession of all its property, circulated just as freely as the paper of any bank in the State, and was taken by the people without objection. It was redeemable at the bank in Columbus, and all you had to do was to present your bills there, and you would receive the specie for them. I believe the best portion of this report is this provision, making these different branches responsible for the issues of all of them.

I do not know as I have anything farther to add in relation to this matter. There are some other features in this report which I shall move to amend at the proper time. There is one thing, in particular, in the seventeenth section that I am not pleased with. But as to the general features of the report, in relation to the two systems of banking, I am in favor of them.

I will, however, say a few words in reply to some remarks of the gentleman from Marion [Mr. Gibson]. He says he is not in favor of a State bank, because it would be a monopoly. Now I will say, that if the people are in favor of a State bank, I am willing for them to have it, and so far as I am personally concerned, I believe it to be the better system of the two here proposed.

Mr. EMERSON. I desire to be clearly and distinctly understood to be opposed to any alteration of the present constitution in reference to the subject of banking, believing, as I do, that if we go on and establish a system of banking in this State, we will be injured and not benefitted thereby. Holding these views as I do, I yet feel pretty well satisfied of one fact, and that is, that this constitution, if we should be so fortunate as to frame one, will inaugurate a system of banking in the State of Iowa. And while I feel that there will probably be no particular mode proposed here that I shall feel called upon to vote for, yet looking at it as I do, that some system will be presented to the people for their action, I feel called upon to do all I can, so to restrict that system as to prevent some of these evils that belong, as I believe, to all systems of banking. In doing that, I am not afraid, as some of my friends upon this floor seem to be, of making this constitution too long, nor am I afraid of too much detail. All that I am afraid of is that there will not be enough of detail.

Now I have all my life seen the working of this system of leaving to the legislature to get up provisions necessary for banking institutions, and such provisions as will prevent banks from entailing losses upon the community. And the result has been—which I suppose no gentleman will deny—one failure after another continually. This has been the case throughout this broad land, from the commencement of this system of banking in the United States to the present day.

If we must have banks, I hope that the friends of banks and banking, will at least meet me and assist me in throwing around whatever system may be adopted, every safeguard that the wisdom of this Convention can invent and devise.

With reference to this seventh section I had prepared an amendment to it which I understand was adopted before I came into the Convention to-day, rating these stocks at twenty per cent. below their average value in New York at the time they are deposited. I understand my friend from Des Moines, [Mr. Hall,] to express a preference for a specie basis over the stock basis. Now I had prepared a substitute to section thirteen, which I will read for the information of the Convention. It is as follows:

"All bills, notes, or checks, issued and circulated as money, shall be at all times redeemable in gold and silver; and on the failure of any bank or banks so to redeem in gold and silver, their bills, notes or checks, on demand of the holder or holders thereof, shall be deemed a forfeiture of all the rights, privileges and immunities granted to such bank or banks; and no law shall ever be passed sanctioning the suspension of specie payments."

And I do not know as it would be out of place, in order to pave the way for what I desire to say, to read a substitute I have prepared for section eight. It is as follows:

"The officers and stockholders of every corporation or association for banking purposes, issuing bank notes or paper credit to circulate as money, shall be individually liable for all debts contracted during the time of their being officers or stockholders of such banking corporation or association."

It will be perceived that my object is, if possible, so to guard in this constitution whatever system may be adopted, that we will at least put at a distance some of those frauds that have been practiced upon the people from the commencement of banking to the present time. I know no other way to do so than to put these guards in the constitution. The experience of other States certainly proves conclusively to every gentleman upon this floor, that it will not do to leave this matter to legislative bodies. This system of lobbying has become a little too powerful in its influence upon legislatures everywhere, and it might be just as powerful here, if we were differently situated. But we, in this Convention, are not surrounded by any of this outside pressure. I think if ever there could be a set of men in this State in a condition to settle these matters judiciously, this body ought to be able to do so. It is not that we are any more honest or capable than would be the next legislature that might meet in this capital; but it is simply because we are not surrounded by the circumstances usually attendant upon legislative bodies in such cases.

I have another amendment that I should like to read for the information of this Convention, and upon its adoption I believe more depends than upon anything else we may adopt. I propose to amend section fifteen by adding to it so that it will read as follows:

"No bill, note, draft, or check, shall be issued for circulation as money except by banking corporations duly organized under, or created by law. And no bank shall ever make, issue, or put in circulation as money of their own, or any other bank, any note, bill or check of a less denomination than five dollars."

As that question is not now under discussion I will leave it now for some other time.

The seventh section being amended as I now understand it to be amended, I shall be disposed to vote for it, with the expectation of having the friends of that section act with me hereafter, in inserting these other restrictions and necessary guards in the constitution upon this subject.

Mr. PETERS. I desire to state that I shall feel bound to vote for every proposition that may come up in this convention that will have a tendency to throw a safeguard around the rights of the people, against these corporations for banking purposes. And I believe that with all the wisdom of this convention, and with all the wisdom of the legislature that will follow this convention, and with all the honesty of "the dear people" thrown in, we will come about as near making an honest bank when we get through, as if we had undertaken to make an honest devil. That is my opinion of the system of banking.

Mr. HALL. All I contend for is contained in the simple proposition that if the legislature, that is to meet after us, should prefer that persons going into the business of banking, should, in place of buying stocks and depositing them with the State, put their money there and not make this extraordinary profit, they shall have the right to say so. And for that reason I have moved to strike out this seventh section. Do not bankers make profit enough any way? Must you put a provision in this constitution, that will, at least, delay the bill-holder, in case of a failure of the bank, though he may be ultimately paid? Does not everybody know that persons holding small amounts of these bills will lose on them? It cannot be otherwise. And if the legislature hereafter, and the people, are disposed to say that persons who wish to go into banking, instead of taking one hundred thousand dollars in specie and buying stocks to that amount, and make that stock the basis of their operations, shall take that amount of specie and make that the basis, I would let them have the opportunity to say so.

I am, in regard to what the gentleman from Jefferson, (Mr. Wilson) has said about the city of Burlington, a good deal in the condition of a Dutchman of whom I once heard an anecdote. A person with whom he was conversing, for some reason or other commenced abusing him. The Dutchman took it all very quietly, and paid no attention to it. The man then commenced abusing the Dutchman's wife. To that the Dutchman paid no more attention than he had done to the abuse of himself. He then abused the Dutchman's daughters; but that failed to excite any more attention, than the abuse of the Dutchman and of his wife. Finally, the man, seeing that what he had already said could not make the Dutchman mad, and noticing a horse which the Dutchman seemed to regard with evident satisfaction, said, "That horse of your's is good for nothing; it can't pull a bit." The Dutchman bristled up at once, and cried out—"Mein Got! I will not stand dat! you haf abuse me; you haf abuse mein frau, and you abuse mein shildren, and I haf not care, but, by dam, I will not haf mein horse abuse!" [Laughter.] And so it is with me. I have been abused here, but I have not deemed it worth my while to notice it; but I cannot stand having my city abused.

The gentleman from Jefferson [Mr. Wilson] speaks entirely without information, when he says that the city of Burlington has gone into banking. We have simply done this: we have borrowed twenty-five thousand dollars in gold, which we have distributed among the three banking institutions in that town. Orders have been issued, but never so much as they have of this gold. Those orders have been taken and used among our citizens as currency. These banks hold this specie and pay six per cent. to the city as long as they have this gold in their possession. But there is not a dollar of that money out, and there has never been a time but what a man could take these orders to the treasury and get the gold for them. I know something about this, and I do not want my horse, or rather, the city of Burlington, slandered. [Laughter.]

Mr. WILSON. I had no intention of abusing the horse of the honorable member, but his statement presents a singular state of affairs. The city of Burlington is anxious to have the use of twenty-five thousand dollars. She borrows it in gold, and must pay some interest, for men do not lend their money without receiving some interest upon it. The city of Burlington, instead of circulating that gold, deposits it in three banks there, and they pay her for it at the rate of six per cent. interest. Then the city of Burlington issues her paper, and the banks of Burlington are in partnership with that city, to send this paper all over the country. If the gentleman is so anxious to get down to a specie basis, and if he reflects the wishes of his constituency, why did not the city of Burlington, when she borrowed this twenty-five thousand dollars in gold, put that in circulation? If there is no advantage to her in this paper, why is it issued instead of having the gold put in circulation? As I said before, let the banks of Burlington refuse this paper, when presented to them for redemption, and it goes down all over the State.

Now, one word in reply to an allusion made here in regard to a specie basis. I want to know when a bill-holder is safest; when there is a hundred thousand dollars in United States stocks in the hands of the Auditor of the State, or when there is a hundred thousand dollars in cash in the hands of the banker? You may require a banker to have in his vaults a dollar in specie for every dollar he issues in paper; but you cannot always look into his vaults and see that he meets the requirements of the law. If you are going to have this banking system, let the security be placed in the hands of an officer of the State.

In relation to a state bank, you may provide for a specie basis, and for investigation of them, and provide for other security. You may not require them to have dollar for dollar to redeem their notes, but you may require them to give additional security, and then they must have specie enough on hand to redeem their notes, when presented. I believe it is safer to have part of the security in the hands of the officers of the state, than to have it all in the hands of the banker.

Mr. CLARKE, of Henry. It seems to me that the gentleman from Des Moines, [Mr. Hall] will persevere in really misunderstanding this matter of security. I suppose the gentleman will admit that no such thing as banking would be carried on in this state unless upon some sort of credit system. No banker could go into the business of banking and make anything, when he issues dollar for dollar for the specie he has in his vaults, and keep that specie there all the time. How much better would he be off, to issue bills in this way than if he loaned out his specie? None at all. Then the gentleman must suppose, that in case banking is founded upon a specie basis, the banker must have some advantage in some way, by issuing more paper than he has specie in his vaults. If he does that, then how much shall he be allowed to issue? Suppose it is one half more than he has specie; that is, for every one hundred thousand dollars of specie he is allowed to issue one hundred and fifty thousand dollars in paper, would the people of this state be as safe with such a banking institution—and I would throw around this system we are inaugurating every check we can to save the bill holder harmless—as they would be if that banker was required, if he had one hundred and thtrty thousand dollars in specie, for instance, to lay out one hundred thousand dollars in United States stocks, and deposite it with the officer of the state, and put the other thirty thousand in specie in his vaults? In that case the banker gets one hundred thousand dollars in stocks, and it draws interest. If he was to put that in his vault, it would be better to him there, than his gold; but if he puts it in the hands of the auditor of the state, he is placing it entirely beyond his control, in the keeping of one who is the trustee of the people. He would not put one hundred thousand dollars in gold there, for that could not be required, and never was heard of. By this section he would be required to deposite the one hundred thousand dollars worth of stocks for the benefit of the people, and the officers of the state would be the trustees; but the interest accruing upon the stocks would belong to the banker.

Then what does he do? For his one hundred thousand dollars worth of stocks he is allowed to issue eighty thousand dollars' worth of bills. What does he gain by that operation? For his one hundred and thirty thousand dollars he is drawing interest upon one hundred and eighty thousand—fifty thousand above his original capital, and this he is permitted to do by this system of paying stocks and depositing them with the proper officers of the State.

Now what do gentlemen wish? Do they wish us to throw upon the Legislature the whole matter, and permit capitalists to come here and lobby in our legislative halls, and enact the same scenes that have been enacted so many times in other states? Do they wish this constitution to go down to the people in such a form as will permit a wild-cat system of banking to be introduced into this state? Are the members here who have been the champions of the "dear people" and contending for the specie basis system —are these members here, who claim to be opposed to "soulless corporations," who claim to be against granting "monopolies" and allowing the monetary power of the country to get such a foothold as will enable them to crush out the liberties of the people—are these men, the very ones who will now, when we wish to incorporate into our constitution a provision that will forever secure the people under any institution or system of banking that may be established in this state—are these the men to oppose it, and say—leave it open to be decided in the halls of our Legislature that there may be done here in our midst what has been done by the legislatures of Michigan, Indiana, Illinois, Ohio and other states? Shall we have our state flooded with wild-cat issues, based upon fancy stocks, and moon-shine bonds?

This is the question for us to determine and this day is shown to the people of this state who are the true defenders of their rights against these "soulless corporations," and these "monster monopolies" that are considered so dangerous to their best interests.

I stand here to defend this seventh section. Strike it out, and I will vote against your banking system. It may be possible that some gentleman here wish to accomplish that object. I believe that there may be those in this convention who desire to have this constitution presented in such a shape that the people will vote against it. But I wish to guard against any such result. I wish to throw every constitutional check in our power, about the system of banking which may be inaugurated by its provisions. I want to so frame this constitution that the legislature can never come up here and pass laws permitting banks to be established upon the basis of rail road bonds, or county bonds, or upon any fancy stocks, that may be got up and sent to this state for the purpose. I want to so frame this constitution that the legislature can never establish a general banking system, except upon a sound and secure basis, of United States stocks and state stocks of good standing.

I do not stand here as a champion of bankers, but to defend the rights of the people, here at the very threshold, when we are about to inaugurate this new system in our midst. This seventh section is the principal provision in this whole report, that will best secure that object. We say to the legislature, we will permit you to frame a banking law, but under certain restrictions and subject to the higher law. When the convention assembled formerly, to frame a constitution, they were so jealous of the people, and of the legislature, that they took from them the power to make any banking law at all. But the interests of the State now demand that a banking system should be introduced, and the legislature should be permitted to frame a law for that purpose.

Now while we say that we will put a provision in the constitution that shall forever protect the rights of the people in this particular, and be a law to all coming legislatures, that they shall not provide for any other basis upon which banks shall issue currency, except such as we prescribe here, the gentleman from Des Moines, [Mr. Hall] who was in the former convention, is for opening the flood-gates, to let all this matter go before the legislature, for them to do as they may think fit. I demand that this restriction shall be thrown about this system. It is not a new provision: it has been acted upon elsewhere. It is no innovation, but has been tried heretofore, with beneficial results, wherever it has been carried out in its true spirit, meaning and intent.

Mr. HALL. It is a fortunate thing, that we here know so much more than any other body of men who can come after us, and that we are so certain of that, that we are not willing to trust any body of men who may hereafter be assembled in this State.

Now, in the convention of 1844, in which I had the honor of a seat, we authorized banking in this State, as I am willing to do now. I hope the gentleman from Henry [Mr. Clarke] will recollect that hereafter, and make no other misstatements upon that point.

Mr. CLARKE, of Henry. I stand corrected upon that point. I supposed the gentleman was in the convention which framed our present constitution.

Mr. HALL. My history seems to be quite familiar to gentlemen here, and yet they do not know anything about it. They make it as they go along. I do not believe any of these gentlemen have told the truth about me, since I have been here. [Laughter.]

Now, the gentlemen from Henry, [Mr. Clarke] gets up here and says, that the system which this seventh section proposes is the one, and the only one, that can give us safe banking institutions; and he claims to support this section as the extraordinary friend of the people, and that all who oppose it are their enemies. Now I will concede all that to him except the last clause.

Now let me give a little history, and I will try and not err as much as the gentleman has. I can recollect when Illinois State stocks were worth only forty cents on the dollar, and you could buy them even for thirty-seven cents on the dollar. I can recollect when Indiana State stocks were not much better than Illinois stocks; and Ohio State stocks were down to seventy and sixty-five cents. I can recollect when those State stocks were in as bad repute as the wild-cat banks of Michigan and other States, to which the gentleman has referred. I can recollect when the State stock banks in those States were down to forty and fifty cents on the dollar. Now, knowing these things, and having lived to see and experience all their operations, can gentlemen expect by mere words, to make me believe that I do not know any such thing? Can they expect to make me believe that the State stock system is to be maintained in all coming time precisely as it stands now? Can they expect to make me believe that this seventh section contains all the wisdom that can be brought to bear upon this subject? I am very sorry the gentleman has made the broad declaration that he will go against everything else that may be proposed, because there may something happen at some day to make the gentleman sorry that he committed himself so soon.

Now, I want to leave this matter to the legislature. I believe there will be some honesty left among the people of this State after this convention adjourns, besides what may be here.

I believe that there is some sagacity among the people of this State besides what may be in this body; and I expect to know about as much the next year, and the year after, as I know to-day. I expect to be just as capable then to judge upon this subject when it comes before me, as one of the people, for me to vote upon it, as I am here now.

I would be as unwilling as the gentleman from Henry can be, to see any system of banking introduced into this State which would not be a good and proper one. But gentlemen will not scare me with all their talk about wild-cats, and wild-cat banking. It happens to be my turn now, to have a little confidence in the people, and to ask the gentleman if he is afraid of the sagacity and judgment of the people, when they come to decide upon a banking law. Is this the way he shows his confidence in the people, in their future legislatures, the representatives of the people? Surely he must believe, judging from his course upon this question, that the people cannot judge of this matter at all, and that future legislatures will not be honest, nor have any sagacity whatever. Now, I have some confidence in the legislature, and in the people, at least sufficient to say that it is possiule, nay, probable, that some other system will be developed that will be fully as safe, and quite as secure, as the one proposed in this seventh section.

That section is a contradiction in itself. The State banks may be put in operation, but it does not provide any security for them. Does the gentleman want to get up one system that will be secure, and one that will be insecure? He avers that the only possible way to secure bill-holders is to have these State stocks; and yet there is no provision here, that says one word about State stocks, in relation to this State bank.

The old adage is, "that what is sauce for the goose, is sauce for the gander." Let us take away this State stock basis from the one system, or put it into the other also.

Now about this State Bank. This idea here about a State bank is altogether bogus. The State has nothing to do with a State Bank. It is a bogus idea altogether, and only calculated to deceive men by holding out the notion that the bank has the endorsement of the State, when the State is not responsible at all. You obtain your banking capital for both of these systems from the same sources, and the bill-holders should be secured under the one as well as under the other. The gentleman's own report proves that what he has asserted here is totally unsound, all mere flashy talk.

I have heard many men say, and I believe it to be true, and I would be willing to wager any amount upon it, that they could take twenty thousand dollars and break every State bank in Illinois; and take fifteen thousand dollars and break every state stock bank in Indiana, for there is not specie enough in these banks to enable them to redeem that amount of bills.

Mr. PALMER. How is it in Ohio?

Mr. HALL. I do not know anything about Ohio. I have been so long away from that state that I shall refer the gentleman to the gentleman from Jefferson, [Mr. Wilson,] for information upon that point.

Mr. WILSON. I can furnish the gentleman with some other information from that State besides that of banking.

Mr. HALL. No doubt of it. I know the gentleman is running over with information. [Laughter.] We have had some specimens of his information, and if it affords gratification to the gentleman to continue in that line, and the members of the Convention desire to hear him, I have not the least objection. I say that this state stock banking system has not the confidence of the moneyed world. It is not enough for them to know that the bills will be ultimately paid. They want to know that they will be redeemed with specie. I do not believe that any system of banking can be sound and safe to the bill-holder, so that he shall be secure against loss, unless there is a specie basis at the bottom.

The question was then taken upon the motion to strike out section seven, and it was not agreed to.

Mr. CLARK, of Alamakee. I move, that the committee rise, report progress, and ask leave to sit again.

The question was taken, and the motion was agreed to.

In Convention.

The PRESIDENT having resumed the chair,

The CHAIRMAN reported that the committee of the whole, to whom had been referred the report of the committee on incorporations, had had the same under consideration, made sundry amendments thereto, and asked leave to sit again.

The report of the committee was received and leave granted accordingly.

Limiting Debates.

Mr. ELLS. I offer the following resolution:

Resolved, That no member shall be allowed to speak more than twice upon any one subject, nor more than twenty-five minutes at any one time.

Mr. PATTERSON. I move to amend by inserting "fifteen" in the place of "twenty-five," so that no member shall speak more than fifteen minutes.

The PRESIDENT. As this is a resolution changing the rules, it will have to lie over for a day.

The resolution accordingly lies over.

Adjournment sine die.

Mr. GILLASPY. I offer the following resolution:

Resolved, That this convention adjourn on the 19th instant *sine die.*

Mr. CLARKE, of Johnson. I move that the resolution lie upon the table.

Mr. JOHNSTON. Upon that question, I call the yeas and nays.

The question was then taken upon the motion to lay upon the table, and it was agreed to—yeas, 16—nays, 14, as follows:

Yeas—The President, Messrs. Bunker, Clarke of Henry, Clarke of Johnson, Clark, of Alamakee, Edwards, Ells, Gower, Gray, Harris, Marvin, Palmer, Parvin, Scott, Wilson and Young.

Nays—Messrs. Ayres, Day, Gibson, Gillaspy, Hall, Johnston, Patterson, Peters, Robinson, Seely, Skiff, Solomon, Warren and Winchester.

On motion,

The convention then adjourned till to-morrow morning, at 10 o'clock.

TUESDAY, Feb. 10th.

The convention met at 10 o'clock A. M., and was called to order by the President.

Prayer by the Chaplain.

The journal of yesterday was read and approved.

Petitions.

The PRESIDENT presented the petition of H. C. Blake, and thirty-three others, praying for the adoption of some constitutional provision for the amendment of the laws by the General Assembly for the observance of the Christian Sabbath, which,

On motion of Mr. SKIFF, was referred to the committee on miscellaneous subjects.

Order of Business.

The PRESIDENT. On Friday last, the report of the standing committee on the legislative department was made the special order for this morning. It is for the convention to determine, whether they will now take up the special order, or proceed with the consideration of the report of the committee on incorporations, which was before the convention yesterday.

Mr. HARRIS. I move, that the special order be postponed, and that we take up the report of the committee on incorporations.

The question was taken, and the motion was agreed to, upon a division; ayes 14, nays 7.

Limitation of Debate.

Mr. MARVIN moved to take up the resolution offered by the gentleman from Scott [Mr. Ells,] yesterday, limiting the time for speaking upon any subject, which was agreed to.

The resolution was then read as follows:

"*Resolved*, That no member shall be allowed to speak more than twice upon any one subject, or more than twenty-five minutes at any one time."

Mr. PALMER moved to amend by striking out the work "subject," and inserting the word "motion" in lieu thereof, but there being no second, the motion was not entertained.

Mr. SKIFF. I would like to offer a substitute for the resolution, so that after a subject has been discussed in committee of the whole, no member should be permitted to speak for more than twenty minutes.

Mr. MARVIN. It is evident, that time must be taken up in discussion in convention as well as in committee of the whole. We are all of us becoming, more or less, uneasy, and anxious to bring our labors to as speedy a close as possible; and it is evident that unless we have some restriction of the kind now proposed, the session will be greatly prolonged. I am not in favor of applying any gag rule; but it must be evident to all lookers-on, that too much time is spent in discussing questions here, after they have once been thoroughly discussed in committee of the whole. We are as ready to vote after questions have been fairly placed before the committee of the whole, and sufficient discussion has been had upon them there, as we would be, after spending several days more in long discussions upon them in the convention.

Mr. WILSON. I do not think that such a rule as gentlemen suggest here can be applied in committee of the whole. If a member gets out of order there, the only way, as I understand it, by which you can get him in order, is for the committee to rise. You may adopt a rule requiring members to confine themselves to twenty minutes; but will such a rule apply to the committee of the whole? It seems to me, that such a rule would be of little avail, unless we abandon the idea of going into committee of the whole.

Mr. MARVIN. This is a new idea, that members are not subject to our rules, when in committee of the whole. I will grant, that we have no right to punish members in committee of the whole; but every member is honorably bound to obey the rules of the body when in committee of the whole, as much as when in convention. I have seen nothing in parliamentary law to the effect, that a member has a right to take all the liberties he pleases in committee of the whole. The gentleman from Jefferson [Mr. Wilson,] takes the position, that we cannot bring a member to a strict account, in committee of the whole, unless the committee rise. I should think that every member would feel himself as much bound by the rules, in committee of the whole, as when in convention. I may be mistaken, however, in this respect.

Mr. HARRIS. I would inquire whether the hour rule, as applied for a number of years in the House of Representatives of the United States, does not apply indiscriminately to the House, whether sitting as a House or as a committee of the whole? I do not understand, that there is any distinction made by their rules in this respect.

Mr. ELLS. I move to lay the resolution upon the table. I offered it with a view of expediting business; but perhaps it is too early in the session to adopt a resolution of this kind. My object in offering it was, more particularly, to give gentlemen a little warning, that it would be called up and acted upon, at some future time.

The question was taken upon the motion to lay upon the table, and it was not agreed to.

Mr. JOHNSTON. I understand that the rules of parliamentary practice require, that a person shall speak but once upon a question. There is, therefore, no necessity for the adoption of such a resolution as that now proposed. I find the following general rule, in reference to this subject, in Cushing's Manual, which, gentlemen will see, is very strict:

"The general rule, in all deliberative assemblies, unless it is otherwise especially provided, is, that no member shall speak more than once to the same question; although the debate on that question may be adjourned and continued through several days; and although a member who desires to speak a second time, has, in the course of the debate, changed his opinion."

Mr. WILSON. I wish to call the attention of the gentleman from Lee [Mr. Johnston,] to the following language, in the same authority, on page 155.

"In a committee of the whole, every member may speak as often as he pleases, provided he can obtain the floor; whereas, in the assembly itself, no member can speak more than once."

Mr. SKIFF. I move to amend the resolution by adding at the end the clause,

"After such subject has been once considered in committee of the whole," so that the resolution will then read:

Resolved, That no member shall be allowed to speak more than twice upon any one subject, or more than twenty-five minutes at one time, after such subject has been once considered in committee of the whole.

Mr. CLARKE, of Henry. I certainly favor the amendment of the gentleman from Jasper. [Mr. Skiff.] I know that there are certain individuals in this body, who seem determined to put on the steam and drag us right through to the end. I have no objection myself to every man putting on as much steam for himself as he desires, or limiting himself to as few minutes in speaking, or remaining as taciturn as he pleases. I will not quarrel wilth any gentleman for remaining quiet; neither will I quarrel with any gentleman for occupying as much time as he wants in giving his opinions.—Nobody has ever heard me make any complaint about "long-winded speeches." It is getting to be the habit with some, to quarrel with members of the Convention for speaking upon the various questions as they come up. I have heard this complaint continually, and I think this resolution has originated in some such feeling as that.

This is a deliberative body, and we should be allowed full and ample time for the discussion of the important principles embodied in the reports of the various committees. I claim it as a privilege and right to hear the gentleman from Lee (Mr. Johnston) or the gentleman from Benton (Mr. Traer) or any other gentleman, express their views freely and fully when they rise here to make a speech; and I am opposed to hampering or restraining any member in the expression of his opinion, especially in Committee of the Whole, where we ought to have perfect freedom, governed by Parliamentary rules, perhaps, but certainly by none other. I claim that we will lose nothing, but on the contrary gain much, by the discussion which we had yesterday. The adoption of such a rule as this, is a very poor compliment to the gentlemen who have addressed the Convention. For my part, I desire all the light I can get upon the various questions that arise here; and I am glad to hear the various suggestions that are made by gentlemen who participate in the discussions. I am inclined to the cpinion that if we leave discussion perfectly free, we shall conclude our labors much sooner than if we attempt to force an early adjournment, or cramp our action and stifle discussion by the adoption of such a rule as the one now proposed.

The question was then taken upon the amendment offered by Mr. Skiff, and it was agreed to.

The question then recurred on the resolution of Mr. Ells as amended

Mr. HARRIS. I move to amend the resolution so that the limitation of time for speaking shall apply both to the Committee of the Whole and the Convention.

The PRESIEENT. In the opinion of the Chair the amendment would not be in order.

Mr. JOHNSTON. I move to lay the resolution upon the table.

The question being taken the motion to lay on the table was agreed to.

The PRESIDENT. The next business in order is the consideration in Committee of the Whole of the report of the committee on Incorporations.

Committee of the Whole.

The Convention then resumed, in Committee of the Whole, (Mr. Bunker in the chair) the consideration of the report of the Committee on Incorporations.

Basis of Banking.

The CHAIRMAN. When the committee last rose, the seventh section of the report was under consideration, amended so as to read as follows:

"If a general banking law is passed, it shall provide, amongst other things, for the registry and countersigning, by an officer of the State, of all bills, or paper credit designed to circulate as money, and require security to the full amount thereof, to be deposited with the State Treasurer, in United State stocks, or in paying-interest stocks of States in good credit and standing, to be rated at twenty per cent below their average value in the State of New York, for the thirty days next preceding their deposit; and also provide for the recording of the names of all stock-holders in such corporations, the amount of stock held by each, the time of any transfer, and to whom."

Mr. GOWER. I desire to say a few words upon this question of banking. A large majority of the people of the county where I reside, are in favor of a sound and judicious system of banking, and my views upon this subject were well known, when I was elected to a seat in this body. After I was elected, in order to get as much information as I could upon this subject, I wrote to several acquaintances at the East, whom I had known when I was living there, and who had been engaged for a long time in banking, to aid me with their suggestions in preparing a suitable plan for a banking system. I knew that in answering my letters they would have no interest in giving me erroneous views, and I was satisfied that they would advise me correctly and truthfully. As early as November last I received information from persons engaged in that business, and in whom I have the fullest confidence, that they were in the possession of facts relating to the banking laws now in existence sufficient to convince them that general banking laws as now framed would not succeed; and all that I have seen since, in relation to the working of this system, has confirmed me in that opinion. Among others with whom I corresponded was James Monroe, No. 1 Wall street, who concurred in this opinion. I thought that this gentleman was as competent as any one that I knew, to draft a bill upon this subject, that might serve us; and the plan I presented awhile ago, and which has been printed, was prepared by him. He has had much experience in banking business.

Mr. GILLASPY. Where is his place?

Mr. GOWER. At No. 1 Wall street.

Mr. GILLASPY. I do not want anything to do with him if he hails from that quarter. [Laughter.]

Mr. GOWER. I intended to have this plan printed at my own expense, and furnished to the members at a very early date; but it so happened that the press was crowded, and it was not until after the committees were formed, that I discovered an opportunity of getting it before the Convention. I then introduced it in the shape of a resolution, and it was referred to the Committee on Incorporations. This morning I see a printed copy of it before me in the Debates, and I do not think it is necessary for me to give a synopsis of its leading features, as members have it all before them, where they can examine it at their convenience.

The CHAIRMAN. Does the Chair understand that the gentleman offers his proposition as a substitute for section seven?

Mr GOWER. I do not wish to offer it now. My object in presenting it in the first place was to get it before the Convention, and to have its merits compared with the other systems that might come before this body. I do not wish to offer it now, if it will produce confusion.

From the information I have been able to obtain, I think that a system of State banking upon a specie basis, is the true plan, where all the branches will be connected together, and all equally bound for the redemption of the bills of each other. It is evident to my mind, that if people cannot associate together for this purpose, and be responsible to each other, they have no reason to believe that the people will have confidence in them.

But I have no desire to detain the Committee by making any extended remarks upon banking at this time, and I will therefore submit the question.

The CHAIRMAN. The Chair would remark, that if there be no motion made to amend the seventh section, the eighth section will now be read.

Liability of Stockholders.

The eighth section was then read as follows:

"Every stockholder in a banking corporation or institution shall be individually responsible and liable to its creditors, over and above the amount of stock by him or her held, to an amount equal to his or her respective shares so held, for all its liabilities, and in all cases where its stock shall be transferred, the liability of the transferrer shall not cease, nor shall the liability of the transferee commence until the expiration of six months after such transfer sh ll have been duly recorded as provided by law."

Mr. CLARKE, of Johnson. I move to strike out this section, and I make the motion for two reasons; first, I think the effect of this provision, if adopted, will be to destroy the negotiable and marketable character of the stocks of these banks. Stocks, in order to be valuable, and in order that they may command a par value in the market, must be negotiable and must have a market value; they must pass as an article of merchandise. My second reason for striking out the section is this, that by the adoption of this provision you exclude from your banking institutions all the trust funds of the State. Trust funds will never be invested in banking stocks, where they most generally are, or where they ought to be, under a good banking system, if the trustee cannot destroy his liability with a transfer of his stock. It seems to me, the effect of such a provision as this eighth section will be to depreciate the character of bank stock, not only here, but in the commercial marts of the country.

For these reasons, I move to strike out this section.

Mr. WILSON. I offer the following amendment: to strike out all after the word "liabilities" in the third line, and insert the following lines: "created during the time that the person sought to be charged was a stockholder in such banking incorporation."

The section would then read:

"Every stockholder in a banking corporation or institution shall be individually responsible and liable to its creditors, over and above th amount of stock by him or her held, to an amount equal to his or her respective shares so held, for all of its liabilities created during the time that the person sought to be charged was a stockholder in such banking corporation."

Mr. CLARKE, of Johnson. I would enquire if that motion be in order. I would prefer to strike out the whole section, and if the motion I make fails then I would have no objection to amending the section.

The CHAIRMAN. The Chair is of the opinion that a motion to amend takes precedence of a motion to strike out.

Mr. CLARKE, of Henry. It is due to this Convention to state the reasons that operated in the committee for the incorporation of this section in their report. For my part, one of the strongest reasons that induced me to favor the adoption of that section, was the very one now given by the gentleman from Johnson, [Mr. Clarke,] for going against it. To my mind one of the greatest disturbing causes to the finances of this country, is the system of stock-brokerage that prevails in New York, Philadelphia, and other large cities. There is no system, perhaps, that is so productive of evil to the great financial interests of the country at large. No matter what it is that they can get hold of, to throw into the market, whether it be the paper of a company organized under a general or special banking law, or whether it be stock of a company to dig coal out of mountains five hundred miles away from any railroad communication; or whether it be stock of a company to take copper from mines on the far-off shores of Lake Superior; or whether it be for the issue of money in the distant territory of Nebraska; no matter what it is, if it can only be designated "stock," it is rushed into Wall street, and is there shoved up by the bulls, and pulled down by the bears. But I will not go into details. Every gentleman knows the workings of this system and the evils resulting therefrom.

I ask the members of this body what are gentlemen seeking to introduce into this State? Are we going to launch forth into this system of stock speculation? Are we instituting a banking system here for the purpose of making their stocks negotiable? Is that the object of the gentleman from Johnson [Mr. Clarke]? Is that the object of the Republicans upon this floor? If so, it is not the object of the people, so far as I know their wishes, to have what a scribbler in one of the daily papers sneeringly calls "a safe paper currency for a circulating medium." And that is the object which we should have in view. Whether we attain that object or not, the future must develope; but we should go honestly to work for the accomplishment of that object, and that object alone. One of the very reasons, therefore, why I would support the provisions of this section restricting the transferrability of this stock, and fixing the liability of the stockholders, is, that it would destroy their negotiability, so that they would not be made a common circulating medium through the country, and be transferred from one man to another the ease of a promissory note. If gentlemen here wish to afford this facility to the stockholders in corporations, of throwing their stocks into Wall street, to be run up by the Bulls and pulled down by the Bears, and thus make our banking system a prey to the stock-jobbers, why, then, support this proposition of the gentleman from Johnson [Mr. Clarke]. But on the other hand, if you really wish to have a safe circulating medium for the people of this State, then put all the constitutional restrictions you can around the system you are about inaugurating, and still have it practicable.

I look upon the whole banking system as a great evil; but I look upon it as a necessary one, demanded by the necessities of the people. I am for throwing around it every constitutional restriction that the wisdom of all past constitution makers have devised. In looking over the constitutions of our sister States, what do we find? We find that Massachusetts, Pennsylvania, New Jersey, New York, Delaware, Maryland, Louisiana, Alabama, Mississippi, Ohio, Indiana, Illinois, Wisconsin, California. Missouri, Texas—have all spread upon their constitutions the most stringent restrictions upon corporations; and in most of these States, we find that they make the stockholders of banking institutions individually liable.

The gentleman from Johnson [Mr. Clarke] must have some superior knowledge which he seems anxious to afford us the benefit of, upon every question that arises. As Supreme Court Reporter, nothing can be started here but he informs us that the Supreme Court have either so decided it, or are going so to decide it. The Supreme Court are all in all with him. We need not make a constitution, but take one complete in all its provisions from the Reporter of the Supreme Court.

I tell you, Mr. President, were I standing here acting as the agent of men who wished hereafter to embark in a certain loose species of banking, and wild-cat speculations, I could not make a better stand and argument for them, than the gentleman from Johnson makes in regard to the striking out this section. I do not impute to him any such motives, but I say that he occupies a position that a champion of bank men would occupy were he standing here attempting to carry through this convention such a measure as that.

I have seen too many operations of this kind. I can remember very well the scenes through which New York had to pass, before she adopted her present system of banking. I know very well what other States have witnessed in the assembling of bank men in the lobbies of their legislatures, to carry through the special privileges which they desired. And I know too well that it has been found too late in other States after corporations have grown superior to the legislature to restrain them, because the constitution had not thrown around that department the restraints that prevented the granting of exclusive privileges without the power of repeal, under which they acquired vested rights.

I stand here now with all these lights of the the past, determined, as far as in me lies, irrespective of any party objects, to do that which will be the best for the interests of the bill-holders, under any system of banks which we may see fit to institute. I am aware that many an honest man goes into the legislature with the right impulses, and determined to perform his duty to his constituents in this matter of granting exclusive privileges to corporations. But what is too often the result? Why, a few leading cunning men of the party gather around him, and say to him, "Oh, we must understand each other, or we cannot act together! Here is a great party that is watching our every movement, and we must take and maintain our position! Now let us get together, in "caucus," and take a stand upon the questions that may come up, and if we move at all, move in one solid phalanx against the common enemy!" And so they caucus in regard to this and that matter, until the poor man is bound fast by caucus arrangements and resolutions, and he casts his vote for measures which he would never have thought of supporting had it not been for this pressure of "caucus" and working of party machinery.

I tell you, Mr. President, and gentlemen of the convention, that many a bill is carried through the legislature by the manœuvring of the wire-pullers and these caucus arrangements, moved only by the hands of two or three designing men, which otherwise would never have cursed the statute book or the people. And it has thus been very often the case that a majority of a legislative body have been made to grant special privileges to corporations through the evil practices and chicanery of a few cunnning and designing men. Gentlemen may say that none of this caucussing has taken place here. Well, then, we who stand here free from any such influences, should do our duty—do what is right—act honestly in this matter, and let the only questions with us be, what is right and proper, and what is it the pleople expect at our hands?

The committee which had the subject of corporations under consideration entertained diverse opinions; one gentleman of that committee was entirely opposed to banking institutions, while others again, although as a matter of principle, opposed to the system of banking, yet looked upon it as a necessity demanded by the times; while still others entertained more favorable views in regard to the matter. The whole subject of banking was thoroughly discussed, and particularly in relation to the individual liability clause. The principal objection that was raised against the incorporation of such a clause in the banking system, was this: where stock holders are made individually liable, and the time comes when their liability may be fixed upon them, then it is made to appear that John Doe or Richard Roe own the whole stock, and the responsibility is thus shifted from the real stock-holders, upon some party who cannot be found. I ask gentlemen if this is not, after all the great objection to this system—this facility with which the stock can be transferred?

Let us examine the matter a little farther. Here are twenty men who wish to associate together in a banking corporation under a general banking law. Being well acquainted with each other they meet together and agree upon their whole plan of organization, what the amount of their stock shall be, and how much each shall put in. The association is thus organized by these individuals, each man relying upon his neighbor's honesty and integrity. They go on for the space of two years. I will suppose then that individual owners of stock sell out, and transfer, until a majority of it gets into the hands of a few designing scoundrels, who, after getting as much of its issues afloat as they can, again sell out and transfer the stock, swamp the concern, and leave the people with hands full of rag promises-to-pay. Here, then, is a corporation having their stocks in the negotiable shape of which the gentleman from Johnson (Mr. Clarke) speaks. A convenient method by which swindlers can get a banking corporation into their own hands, establish a credit for its paper in New York, and then when their stock is all transferred, and the time comes for the bubble to burst, they get out of the way, and are no where to be found.

That is also the great objection which is urged against the individual liability clause, and against which I wish to guard. Perhaps we have not gone far enough. If it be so, I think it would behoove gentlemen, who wish to place proper checks around this system, to come in here with amendments that would effectually accomplish that result. I for one, in behalf of the people of the State, would thank gentlemen for any such suggestions. If they would show in what respect the provision we have reported is not strong enough to secure the public against fraud, and in what manner it can be amended to give it more effect, I would be very grateful to them for the suggestions. But instead of this we have the proposition of the gentleman from Johnson to strike out the main security provided for in our report. The committee thought it would not even be sufficient that every stockholder who entered into a banking company should understand that he was to be responsible to the amount of his stock for all its liabilities, over and above the stock.

But further; we say by another provision, "we are not going to give you a chance to transfer your stock in such a way that you can be prepared for an emergency, slip out of the concern and let John Doe and Richard Roe bear the burden. If there is any body to be charged with responsibility, we want to fix it upon the real parties. Neither are we going to have it so arranged that you can in view of a failure, go and sell your stock, get its full nominal value, and defraud the purchasers by shirking the liabilities of the concern upon them. We wish to guard against both these things;—fraud against the bill-holders and fraud against the assignees of the stock. We do not intend you shall go on for a course of years, have your plot all arranged for a bank with a good outside appearance, but all hollow within; and negotiate and sell your stock in the market, thus defrauding the purchasers, and cheating the people also."

The provision intended to effect this purpose, which we recommend for the adoption of this Convention, may not be a suitable one. We deemed it necessary to incorporate some provision into the constitution, in order to prevent, if possible, the fraudulent operations to which I have referred; and we finally came to the conclusion that if we required that in all cases of transfer the liability of the original stock-holders should continue for six months after such transfer was made and publicly recorded, in all human probability parties desiring to secure, use, or transfer said stock, for the purpose of fraud, could not accomplish their object.

"Why," says the gentleman from Johnson, [Mr. Clarke,] "who will ever buy and sell bank stock, or who would ever dare sell or buy it under such a provision in the constitution? Here are twenty men engaged in banking. Will they dare to sell their stock to twenty other men and let them go on with their concern, when their liabilities shall run for the next six months after such transfer?" I asked a gentleman of this city, one of his constituents, who said that he intended to go into banking, what would be the effect of incorporating the individual liability clause into the constitution, with such a provision effecting the transfer? In reply, he said that if he were a banker and stock-owner, and wanted to transfer his stock in order to protect himself, he should demand some security. The introduction, therefore, of this individual liability clause into the constitution, with such a qualification respecting the right of transfer, would merely involve this necessity, that when I wanted to transfer my stock, I should require of the transferee security for the next six months, and thus while protecting myself I should incidentally protect the bill-holder.

But, say gentlemen, if you adopt this provision of individual liability, you will drive from the State eastern capital. Gentlemen are constantly referring to these wonderful capitalists who live somewhere "in the east." We have been taught that the wise men of old came from the east, and gentlemen seem to suppose that all capitalists must come from the same quarter; and therefore we must, in the opinion of these gentlemen, make such a loose system as will induce these wonderfully wise capitalists to bring their treasures and lay them at our feet; in other words, furnish us with their own paper for a currency, on their own terms. We shall have to depend servilely upon them, and therefore we must refrain from passing any provisions which will have the effect of preventing them from coming here with their capital to pluck and defraud the people.

Mr. President, for myself, I want it to go forth to the world that if bankers come here at all, they shall be hedged in with such restrictions and liabilities that they cannot commit frauds upon the public without fear of punishment. I do not want to establish a system of banking here, which, by a sudden and great influx of circulating medium, shall create a sudden rise in real estate, which again by its decline shall react upon every other interest and upon banks themselves, and thus cause panic, confusion and distress. I would prefer to throw such wholesome restraints around the whole system, as would rather tend to keep these wonderful moneyed men from coming here, if they are to come, with a view of plundering our citizens. I would prefer a system of banking conducted by our own citizens, who will engage in it as a legitimate business, just as the gentleman from Van Buren, [Mr. Day,] engages in farming, or just as any other gentleman here engages in any particular branch of business; engage in it as a business whose legitimate object shall be to afford facilities to the great public, rather than to supply stocks to be peddled in the market.

We are making a constitution for the people of Iowa, under which citizens of this State, and not the capitalists of Wall street, are to engage in banking. I want such a system that men, who will make it their business, shall not engage in it merely because the stocks shall be negotiable in Wall street or anywhere else. I would prefer even such a system as they have in some of the States, where the banks are established on a firm and secure basis, and are entirely owned and controlled by persons in the immediate vicinity where the banks are located. There are some places in Virginia where the same planters in a neighborhood have owned a bank for a long period of years. The Bank of Winchester, I think, has been owned for years by the same persons, and it will probably be owned by their descendants for years to come. They do not send their stock abroad, to have it floating through the market as negotiable paper. You cannot even go there and purchase the stock dollar for dollar. Such a system I desire to see established here—a system under which men may engage in banking as a regular and legitimate branch of business, without gambling risks to themselves or danger to the community, which the negotiable stock system entails.

The remarks I made yesterday with reference to the seventh section, will apply with equal force to this section. As I said before, by referring to the constitution of the different States I have mentioned, gentlemen will find that the provision we have here submitted, is incorporated in nearly all of them; and to strike out this principle here would certainly be saying to the world that we are opening wide our doors for a mad influx of wild-cat corporations.

Mr. CLARKE, of Johnson. I have no desire to indulge in a personal controversy with the gentleman from Henry [Mr. Clarke,] upon this question. Be my position what it may, whether as the organ of the Supreme Court, or as the organ of anybody else, whatever I say here, I say upon my own individual responsibility. I will dismiss the subject by saying, that if the intelligence and capacity of the gentleman from Henry were at all equal to his arrogance and presumption, he would be a very useful man upon this floor. He has announced before, and he has announced to-day, that unless he can have his way in the making of this constitution, he intends to vote against it. Whether he shall have his way, whether this constitution shall be the sole offspring of his mind, whether we shall concede that he has all the intelligence, wisdom and policy that are necessary to constitute a constitution-maker solely in himself, is a question upon which we may differ, without at least disparaging the gentleman's high estimate of himself. I suppose that we have met here to deliberate, to compare minds with each other, so that the result of this comparison of minds and deliberations may produce a constitution, which will promote and secure the rights and well-being of the people of this State. And I think it is a little out of place for the gentleman to announce in advance, that if he is not allowed to have his way, he will vote against the constitution. And I think it is equally out of place, equally improper, and equally wanting in respect to the members of the convention, for any gentleman to attempt to play the demagogue upon this floor. It may do in another forum; it may do upon the hustings; but here it is entirely out of place.

I am glad that the gentleman from Henry has announced, in advance, that he regards banking institutions as evil, and that he is so disposed to frame the constitution, that we shall not have what the people sent us here to obtain for them. I believe it will be conceded by every gentleman upon this floor, that the subject of banking was the leading cause which induced the people to vote for calling this convention, and for placing us upon this floor. They did not send us here to so alter the constitution that an impracticable scheme might be devised, which should hold out the "word of promise to the ear, but break it to the heart." They did not send us here to devise a banking system; and during the whole canvass, I venture to say, the people never expected us to provide in the constitution for a banking system. All they sent us here to do was to remove the restrictions in the present constitution, and to make a constitution which would permit banking.

The gentleman from Henry now takes the broad position, that banking institutions are an evil. If I thought so, I would not occupy the position of that gentleman. I would have the integrity and firmness to say, that I would not vote to create an evil. I would have told the people so in the canvass. If that gentleman had avowed that doctrine in the county of Henry during the canvass, I venture to say, that he would not to-day have been dictating to us, or manifesting his arrogance upon this floor.

I desire the convention to understand that the gentleman is opposed to banks. If he is honest, and opposed to banks, and believes them to be evil, why is he so desirous of incorporating in the constitution such restrictions as he has named? He says that he wants to make a system of banking, if we have one, that will shut out the capitalists of the east; and he wants whatever banks we have, owned solely and entirely by the people of Iowa. He has found a model bank at Winchester, in the State of Virginia—the last place I should suppose that the gentleman would go for a model—an old town, almost as dead as are now the cities of Sodom and Gomorrah; a place where there is no business, no life, and where, as the gentleman says, the stock of this bank is handed down from father to son for generations. This is the model which the gentleman has produced for the young, flourishing, and growing State of Iowa. Beautiful consistency for the gentleman to point us to Virginia as a model for us to follow! A State, too, which the gentleman so especially hates. I undertake to say, that any one of our private bankers, in this State, will do more business in banking, in one week, than they will do in this model bank of Winchester in a year. And this is the model which the gentleman would have us follow! If we are going to tie the people of Iowa down to such a system of business, such a system of commerce and agriculture as they have in Virginia, I am mistaken in the character and duty of this convention.

If we have banks, it is conceded by every man that the capital to establish these banks must come from somewhere else than from our own State. The very object of creating banks here is to bring in capital to facilitate our commercial and agricultural operations. What do we gain, if these banks must be held and owned solely by our own people? Would not the natural result be to draw from every department of industry the capital necessary to set these banks in operation? Our object should be to provide such a banking system that people will bring in capital here, and thus enhance our business facilities. Without capital, there can be no business. The very object and purpose of this convention was so to arrange the constitution, that capitalists might come in here—I care not from what quarter they come—and give us the benefit of their capital. I am not so terribly alarmed, as some gentlemen are, at the mention of this name—Wall street. I think capital can be used advantageously here, whether it comes from Wall street, or Chesnut street. It is the capital we want here; and it is but just and fair that we should offer it legitimate means of operation.

I am just as anxious as any one to have safe and stable banking institutions, and I think it is the duty of this convention to look to the safety of bill-holders; whatever system we should adopt we should have reference to that alone. As to the minor details, and the other departments of banking, I do not care a farthing, nor in my opinion is it our business to interfere.

The question arises, will this eighth section, the pet of the gentleman from Henry, promote the interests of banking institutions, and will it offer an inducement to bring capital here, with which to establish banks? Or will it have the contrary effect—as the gentleman argues it will have, and by his vote designs it shall have—of preventing capital from coming here?

I shall say nothing now upon the question of

individual liability, for I do not wish to enter upon an extended discussion of that subject. I think the mind of every member of the convention is made up in relation to that question. My objections to this section is, that it provides, in case of a transfer of stock, to make the transferor liable for six months after the date of his transfer. I take the position, that such provisions would keep out of the banking institutions the trust funds of the State. Go into New York and Ohio, and you will find that a large portion of the banking capital of these states are trust funds, held for minors and widows, or capital invested in those institutions as a matter of safety. The holders of these funds are in the habit of attending the meetings of the board of directors, watching the operations of these banks, and relying upon the provisions which the law has thrown around these institutions; and they feel that their money is safe. I say that such a provision as this, contained in the eighth section will keep out of our banking institutions all this class of funds, and in place of having this capital here as a basis of the business operations of the state, every trustee will lock up his money in his iron safe; every widow who has a dollar will tie it up in her old stocking, and hide it in a corner of her house; and the result will be, that there will be thousands upon thousands of dollars kept out of our banking institutions.

Another objection I have to the adoption of this provision is, that the stocks of your banks would not be par value stock in the markets of the world. The gentleman from Henry avows that he does not want them to be rated at their par value. Can there be a more effective method, by which to destroy your banking institutions, than just such a restriction as the gentleman would place upon these stocks? Would it not be just as reasonable to require that every man who should sell a horse that he owned, should not be relieved of the responsibility of that sale until after six months had elapsed, as to require such a provision in the transfer of stocks? Stock in a bank or any other institution, is just as much property, as a horse or any other article of personality. Why this restriction, then? These stocks are property, honestly acquired, paid for with money, and bought in good faith. Why should we throw around this article of property and merchandise a restriction, that a man may not sell it and be relieved of his liabilities, until six months after such transfer?

The inevitable tendency of such a provision would be to destroy the negotiable character of your stocks in the market. They have to go there, and if they have not standing and character, they are no better than any other species of property, without character and standing.

And not only that; the effect of this provision will be not only to destroy its negotiability, but to place the bank stock of the country in the hands of irresponsible persons. Every man who holds bank stock will be a man of straw—he will have nothing but his bank stock. It is like individual liability. It is a thing perhaps devised by the gentleman from Henry [Mr. Clarke], in the fertility of his imagination, to make this individual liability doctrine more offensive and worthless than it now is. I say that no responsible man would ever be found to own one dollar of this stock. It would produce the very result the gentleman says he desires to prevent. It will throw all your stock into the hands of irresponsible men, in the hands of the capitalists of the Easts and the sharpers of the country, who own no real estate, and have no tangible property that the sheriff could lay hold of; they would prove to be but men of straw.

I am interested in this matter of banking institutions. The people want banks because they are necessary to their business and their prosperity. And I want to make a constitution which will enable them to have that which is for their good. I do not think this convention possesses all the wisdom of this nineteenth century. I think it is possible that the legislature coming after us will have quite as much wisdom as we have. I do not think that the people have exhausted all their judgment of selection, in choosing this body; or that when we dissolve, no body of men equal to us in intelligence, patriotism and wisdom can be found. I believe that our successors in the legislative halls will be equal to us in all these qualities. I certainly trust they will.

The gentleman did not undertake to show that this would keep out of the banks of the country the trust funds of the country, which will increase with every year. He did not undertake to show that this will affect their negotiability and marketable value. This is the ground upon which I place this matter. But instead of that he makes an appeal to the convention to oppose my motion, because I fill the humble position of Reporter to the Supreme Court. He says that I am always quoting the decisions of the Supreme Court. Now, several members have asked me what their decisions were, and I have answered them. And the gentleman from Henry has taken this occasion to make a demigoguical appeal to the Convention. The manliness and generosity of that position I leave with him to enjoy.

Mr. CLARKE, of Henry. The gentleman from Johnson, [Mr. Clarke] takes exception to some remarks that I made here, and perhaps the remarks I did make had rather more warmth in them than I was conscious of myself. I must believe so from the effect they produced.

The gentleman seems to imagine that I am possessed of something of what he calls "arrogance." I do not know whether the gentleman uses that word in the same sense in which it is generally used by ordinary persons. It may be that when I address this convention, I address them with something of vehemence and something of earnestness. I claim to be an earnest man. I claim to say what I believe, and to believe what I do believe with all my heart. And if other gentlemen have the same feeling and the same opinion about me that the gentleman from Johnson seems to entertain, I sincerely regret it.

I do believe, if I know my own heart, that there is no man more willing to listen to the candid, impartial, unbiassed opinions of their fellow men, and give them due weight and consideration than myself. I will be behind no man in courtesy. I will receive from no man a kindness that I am not willing to return again. I will receive from no man a polite attention that I will be unwilling to bestow upon him.

I would ask what have been the acts of arrogance I have exhibited here? Have I ever come in here when any committee has made a report, and offered as a substitute for that report a report drawn up by myself? Have I offered to this Convention *my own individual gettings-up as a substitute for the report of five gentlemen* who have given it due consideration and been selected for that purpose? Arrogance! Have I stepped beyond the sphere in which my duties have called me to act? Have I taken upon my own shoulders the labor of any committee, and come forward here with my individual efforts, and asked this convention to give them the place of the report of this committee? I will leave it to this convention to decide the question of arrogance between the gentleman from Johnson and myself. As for intelligence and moral honesty, let our words and our acts be our best witnesses.

I stand here defending the report made by the committee, of which I am chairman. When I said that this was our report, did I not also say to this Convention, that every individual member upon that committee, claimed to have his own ideas, and to retain the right to come here and move amendments to this report, if he should see fit to do so? I certainly said that. Was there any thing of arrogance in that? I told the Convention that they could look upon the report merely as the index to our minds, after examining all the information that came before us in relation to the subject upon which we were called to act. And in my last remarks I stated that I would thank any man in this Convention to assist us, by any suggestion or amendment, to carry out the great idea of that report. Was there any thing of arrogance in that? The object of all the members of that committee, as I understand it, was to introduce a system here for safe banking for the people, and not for the benefit of monopolies and swindlers. We wanted to introduce a system that would allow of banking, but not of swindling.

The gentleman gets up here now, and says that I did not answer his great argument in favor of his motion; which is, that the money of the widow and of the orphan might be invested in these bank stocks, if we can only take away this principle of individual responsibility. My God! what an investment that would be for "widows and orphans!" A general banking law without any individual liability! A banking system with a specie basis, and no certain stock securities, when we would have the old sandy-hill operation gone over again, of filling vaults with coppers and paying them out to bill-holders, when they demand their specie for their paper, copper by copper, at the rate of fifty dollars a day, to keep from breaking.

Has not this old specie basis been already exploded? Shall we have this basis here, and see the bags of specie mounted upon wheels, and rolled from vault to vault all over the State? A pretty kind of banking system that would be for us to adopt, to enable the "widows and orphans" to invest their money! And when the banks broke, what a wonderful privilege it would be for these "widows and orphans" to have their money invested in these stocks.

It seems to me that if the gentleman from Johnson would use some of that wisdom which he does not accord to me—but which of course he must possess himself, else he could not judge so acutely of it in regard to others—he would see that if we provide here for a perfectly safe banking system under a general banking law, and make each stockholder individually liable, we would thereby provide in every bank, the best kind of a savings institution. Every bank organized under this law would be a savings bank, in which the gentleman, if he happens to be a trustee for any of these "widows and orphans," can most safely deposit their funds upon interest, and thus relieve himself of that grievous burden. As wonderful as it may seem, the system we propose here will afford an opportunity for the safe investment of all the funds that may be left by deceased persons for their widows and orphans. They can be deposited in these institutions, and they will be the safest institutions that can be provided, and interest will be allowed upon these deposites.

Does not the gentleman know that this is the system in vogue here now? Does not the gentleman from Jasper [Mr. Skift] allow interest after a certain time upon all deposits made with him? Is this not the best system? If you adopt a system in which the bankers would rather issue their own notes for circulation, and not use the money deposited with them, a system in which the negotiability of the stocks is more important than the bills, they would say, we cannot allow you interest upon your deposits, but you can invest your money in *our stocks*.

The gentleman has said so much upon this question, and has accused me so much of arrogance, that I will put the question in this way. If I am arrogant in this matter, it must be because I have claimed to myself superior wisdom over sombody else, over this convention, and over all similar conventions. Now, I find in the constitution of New York this provision:

"The stock holders in every corporation and joint stock association for banking purposes, issuing bank notes, or any kind of paper credit, to circulate as money, after the first day of January, 1850, shall be individually responsible, to the amount of their respective share or shares of stock in any such corporation or association, for all its debts and liabilities of any kind, contracted after the said first day of January, one thousand eight hundred and fifty."

In the constitution of Ohio is this provision:

"Dues from corporations shall be secured, by such individual liability of the stock-holders, and other means, as may be prescribed by law; but, in all cases, each stock-holder shall be liable, over and above the stock by him or her owned, and any amount unpaid thereon, to a further sum, at least equal in amount to such stock."

In the constitution of Indiana, is this provision:

"The stock-holders in every bank or banking company, shall be individually responsible to an amount over and above their stock, equal to their respective shares of stock, for all debts, and liabilities of said bank or banking company."

Illinois has the following provision in her constitution:

"The stock-holders in every corporation, or joint stock association, for banking purposes, issuing bank notes, or any kind of paper credits to circulate as money, shall be individually responsible, to the amount of their respective share or shares of stocks, in any such corporation or association, for all its debts and liabilities of every kind."

In California and other States, the same, or similar provisions can be found in their constitutions.

Mr. YOUNG. There is a clause in the Indiana constitution, requiring this individual liability. I want to know if any person was ever benefitted by that provision, or ever got any more on account of it? And there is another question I should like to ask, concerning the provision in the constitution of the State of New York. I would like to know if there has ever been any bank established under that provision in the State of New York?

Mr. CLARKE, of Henry. Plenty of them.

Mr. CLARK, of Alamakee. A hundred of them.

Mr. YOUNG. I think not one. There may have been some evasion there, but we attempt to guard against these evasions in a subsequent section here.

Mr. CLARKE, of Johnson. Will the gentleman from Henry [Mr. Clarke] allow me to ask him a question?

Mr. CLARKE, of Henry. [After a pause.] I will not. If the gentleman will be so uncourteous as he was to my friend from Dubuque [Mr. Emerson] on yesterday, as to refuse to answer any question from him, a gentleman much his senior, I will not answer any question he may put to me while I am upon this floor.

I submit to this convention, that I have not assumed any wisdom, superior to the wisdom of those who framed the constitutions of New York, Ohio, Indiana, Illinois, Texas, California and other States, which have provisions in them similar to this one. I have been humbly content to take their wisdom, and their reasons for this provision. I have been contented to be guided by that light in my course here: and I would ask this convention if there is anything of arrogance in that? And if I stand up here to manfully contend for that principle, believing that it is right, am I doing anything more than it is my duty and right to do?

The gentleman accuses me of arrogance. I believe that I have nothing of arrogance in the sense in which I understand that word. But, if I should get up here, and should raise my voice upon any question counter to, and in opposition to, the wisdom of all the conventions that have assembled in the different States, to form constitutions, then I should think I might be chargeable with something of arrogance. Whether the gentleman himself, may be correctly accused of that or not, I leave to his own conscience to determine. But so far as our positions are concerned before this body, I am not fearful of any verdict that may be rendered against me, when our record upon this matter, or upon others, shall be made up.

I occupy the position of five members of the committee, who took this matter into consideration and reported this section. I arrogate nothing to myself superior to the wisdom of the others of the committee, or to the wisdom that guided the conventions which framed this same provision in the constitutions of other States. If the gentleman occupies a different position, I think he is not entitled to throw stones. I stand upon this section, believing it will be efficacious in securing, if possible, the rights of bill-holders, under the system we are about to inaugurate in this State.

Mr. WILSON. I offered an amendment to this section a while since, but we have had two or three lengthy speeches, and I do not know as my amendment has been noticed much. I wish to present my reasons for offering that amendment. Section eight reads as follows:

"Every stockholder in a banking corporation or institution shall be individually responsible and liable to its creditors, over and above the amount of stock by him or her held, to an amount equal to his or her respective shares so held, for all its liabilities, and in all cases where its stock shall be transferred, the liability of the transferrer shall not cease, nor shall the liability of the transferee commence until the expiration of six months after such transfer shall have been duly recorded as provided by law."

My amendment is to strike out all after the words "for all its liabilities," and insert "created during the time that the person sought to be charged was a stockholder in such banking incorporation." The principal reason that induced me to offer that amendment was this. I believe the true policy, in relation to corporations of this kind, is to bring them as near to the nature of a partnership as possible; for after all they are but partnerships. If five persons enter into a partnership, all debts contracted by that partnership can be enforced against the partners individually. You have first to exhaust the partnership property in payment of their debts; if that is not sufficient you can then resort to the property of the individual partners as individuals.

Now when men associate in corporations for banking purposes, I can see no reason why they should not be held to their own contracts to the same extent as persons in ordinary partnerships. If five men enter into a corporation for banking purposes, and they engage in that business, create debts and liabilities of any character, I cannot see why those five men should not be held responsible for all the debts and liabilities so contracted, in the same manner as partners in any other kind of partnership. There is no reason why that should not be done. If you provide that the stockholders shall be individually liable to double the amount of their stock, as this section provides, for all the debts contracted while they were stockholders in the corporation, you necessarily compel, not merely the directors of the institution, but every stockholder to look into, and investigate and examine the contracts before they are made by that institution. Every man becomes interested in the matter. He does not depend entirely upon the directors of the institution, but it is his peculiar interest, in connection with his pecuniary affairs, to look into the contracts made by that institution.

If they prove disastrous, and the property of the institution is not sufficient, then why not make each individual stockholder liable for the contracts he entered into as a part and parcel of that partnership? Is there anything unjust in this? Do we seek to affix any responsibility to him that would not apply to a man in an ordinary partnership? He is not liable for any debts contracted after he has ceased to be a stockholder. It is then thrown upon others, and it falls upon those who enter into contracts to create liabilities. But so far as he is one of the contracting parties, I do not see why he should not be held responsible for his own acts and those with whom he is associated.

I am not so completely wedded to any particular scheme that I will not vote for anything else but my own proposition. I will vote for my own views first. If I cannot get them, I will vote for the best I can get, upon the principle that half a loaf is better than none at all.

I hope that hereafter, instead of lengthy personalities, such as we have had here, and which are certainly not very agreeable to the Convention, we will confine ourselves a little more closely to the matters before us. I think we can get along faster, and do away with the necessity of having resolutions of adjournment, and cutting off debates, introduced here. I think such a course would be more satisfactory to ourselves as well as to our constituents.

Mr. CLARK, of Alamakee. I will say, in the first place, that I am very sorry that this bone of contention has been thrown in among the Clarke family. I am pained at the ill-will and disregard of the interests of that family, which I have seen exhibited here this morning by two of its members. [Laughter.] Now I do not believe that the charges made pro and con, by each of the members, about arrogance, are really true. For if you take the family as a whole, I believe they will be found to be a very modest and unassuming class of men, [renewed laughter] and for the credit of the family I hope that hereafter we will not have so much of this thing.

As to the question before the committee—this eighth section—I am individually in favor of something of the kind, though I am not very particular as to the exact phraseology of the section. I believe, as has already been urged here, that something of the kind is necessary. I believe that good faith towards the bill holders of the community at large, requires that we should adopt a provision of this kind. It would be giving to the people, who take the issues of this bank, additional security and protection which is not afforded in any other shape. While it will do that, I do not believe it will materially retard capital from being put into banking operations. I believe at least the honest portion of the capitalists will not be affected by any such provision. If they intend faithfully to redeem their issues and meet their liabilities, they can have no serious objections to amply securing their creditors for any amount of liability they may create.

I do not believe it will have the effect that has been contended for by those who oppose this section, to drive the substantial capitalists out of the business of banking. I believe, if they are honest, they will intend to redeem their bills to the last dollar. And if they intend that, they can have no objection to place their liabilities in that condition, which will satisfy the community that the institutions which issue these bills, and announce these liabilities, are perfectly sound and solvent, and that the bill-holders will be safe and secure. It is for their interest to do so; it is the interest of every stock-holder to make the credit of his institution as strong and permanent as it possibly can be. And every safeguard that can be thrown around these institutions, to insure confidence in them, is beneficial to the stock holder.

I am opposed to the principle, which has prevailed heretofore in most States in relation to banking, of allowing men to go into banking associations, and taking a certain amount of stock. They may be worth millions of dollars outside of that stock. They put that stock into the bank, and paper is issued upon it, and they reap the benefit of it. People outside of that institution have confidence in its solvency, in consequence of the position and wealth of the stock holder, aside from his interest in that institution. The community take these paper issues, to an extent they would not do, but for the position and character of the individual stock holder. But when anything befalls that bank, that individual stock holder, who is worth his millions, and who, individually, would be considered responsible to any amount, steps aside, and gets clear of all the liabilities of the institution. I do not believe such a system can be maintained upon principle or expediency.

That such a provision as this has been adopted in the constitutions of other States, that it is in the constitution of the State of New York, that there has been a banking system in operation under that provision for years past, that these banks are flourishing and multiplying, and daily issuing their paper, all this is in itself a complete refutation of the argument that such a provision here will drive capitalists out of banking in this State. The gentleman from Mahaska [Mr. Young,] has asked if any banks in New York have gone into operation under such a provision as this. I can tell the gentleman that they have, and that every dollar of paper issued in that State, by any bank, since the first of January, 1850, has been issued with this liability attached to it, in consequence of this provision of the constitution of the State of New York; and it can be issued in no other way. Has it had the effect of retarding the business of banking there? Most clearly not; and if not, then I contend that it will not have that effect here.

I am in favor then of incorporating some provision of this kind into our constitution. I believe that it is safe, that it is just to the community, and to all engaged or interested. I believe, in fact, that something of this kind is expected by the people. I know this question was canvassed a great deal in the southern part of this State. There are not a few there who take the position that banks of every kind are anti-democratic, and directly in conflict with the best interests of the community. And many others take the position that if we are to have banks, all the guarantees, and checks, and safeguards, should be thrown around them, which the ingenuity of this convention can devise.

I do not see, for my part, what injustice can be done to any one, what injury will be sustained by any one, in consequence of a provision of this kind in our constitution. I am in favor of it, though, as I said before, and as the gentleman from Jefferson [Mr. Wilson,] has said, I am not so wedded to this particular provision that I will not yield, if the majority of the convention are opposed to it. I will fall back upon the next best thing, that can be adopted, if I cannot get this.

I am in favor of placing in this constitution all proper safe-guards about the bill-holder. Gentlemen will not frighten me from this position with the charge that we are legislating in the convention. We are here peculiarly exempt from many of the temptations and influences to which legislative bodies that come after us, will be exposed. I am not aware that any moneyed influence has been exerted, or brought to bear, upon any individual in this body, to affect his judgment, or his free action, in relation to placing our banking institutions upon a safe basis.

If we adopt a constitution without any of these checks and safe-guards, and leave the legislature to establish a system of banking with just such checks and restrictions as they may see fit to adopt, the first legislature that assembles under this constitution, will be beset by agents of these moneyed institutions, and the whole influence of the lobby, and of the capital intended to be devoted to banking, will be brought to bear upon that legislature. If we adopt this provision, then the legislature will stand free of all such influences, and will be more likely to act judiciously upon this subject.

Many men in this State, who are in favor of banking institutions being established here, if the prohibition is simply removed from our constitution, and the legislature is allowed to enact just such laws as they may see fit in regard to this matter, will vote against this constitution upon that ground, when they would vote for it if it contained proper safe-guards. This provision will recommend this constitution to the people when it is submitted to them for their adoption or rejection.

I do not believe this day, that, as anxious as the majority of the people are for some system of banking in this State, a constitution would be adopted by the people of this State, without some safe-guards being thrown about the bill holders, to secure them against worthless issues of banks that the legislature might be induced to incorporate, if this matter was kept entirely to them.

For these reasons, I am in favor of some kind of check, some kind of safe-guard, in the shape of deposits, and a provision rendering the stock holder individually liable. At all events it can do no harm, and I think it will do good.

Mr. SKIFF moved that the committee rise, report progress, and ask leave to sit again.

The question being taken, the motion was not agreed to.

Mr. PALMER. It seems to me, that if we were to discuss the questions before us, our speeches would be shorter, if not less frequent. The question at issue is the motion made by the gentleman from Jefferson, [Mr. Wilson,] which I do not consider as bringing before us the whole of this section eight. The question presented by that motion is, whether we will strike out the latter clause of that section, and insert what is proposed by him. The clause proposed to be stricken out, provides that the transferer of stock shall be liable for six months after the transfer, and the transferee shall not be liable for six months after that transfer. Now it appears to me that that clause should be stricken out, if something better can be substituted. It is not right, for one thing, that the stock holders in a bank should be liable for what is done after they cease to be stock-holders. Nor is it right to exempt any stock-holder from liability for six months after he becomes a stock-holder. For that reason I am in favor of striking that clause out. We would not impose such liabilities upon private partners, in firms for other business, for it would be unreasonable to impose such restrictions upon them as is here proposed to be attached to banking.

The question was then taken upon the amendment of Mr. Wilson, and, upon a division, it was agreed to; ayes 15, noes 10.

The question then recurred upon the motion of Mr. Clarke, of Johnson, to strike out the section as amended, and, being taken, it was not agreed to, upon a division; ayes 7, noes not counted.

Mr. TRAER moved that the committee rise, report progress, and ask leave to sit again.

The question being taken, it was not agreed to.

No further amendment being offered to the eighth section,

Section nine was then read as follows:

State Bank.

"The general assembly may also charter a State Bank with branches, to be founded upon an actual specie basis."

Mr. CLARKE, of Johnson. I move to amend this section by adding, after the word "specie," the words "or of the stocks of the United States or of interest paying states," so as to make this section conform to the provisions of the seventh section in relation to banking under a general law.

I do not know exactly what is meant by this idea of a State Bank. I presume it is not intended that the State shall own all the stock of this bank, but the bank will have something of the character of what is now called the Indiana State bank. As I understand it, the state does not own the stock of that institution, but, as under the general banking law, these banks are secured by stocks of other states. If that is the idea of the committee who made this report, I see no reason for having it upon a different basis than that of banks under a general law.

Mr. HALL. I would suggest to the gentleman from Johnson, [Mr. Clarke] to modify his amendment so that it will read "or on stocks as authorised by the seventh section of this article, or both."

Mr. CLARKE, of Johnson. That will accomplish the object I have in view, and I will accept that in lieu of my amendment.

The question being then taken the amendment was agreed to.

Mr. TRAER. I move to amend the section by striking out the word "state" in the first line of this section, so that it will read:

"The General Assembly may also charter a bank with branches, to be founded upon an actual specie basis, or on stocks, as authorised by the seventh section of this article, or both."

Mr. GOWER. I would move to amend the section so that it shall read that this state bank shall be called the "Bank of Iowa," instead of the "State Bank."

Mr. PARVIN. I am sorry that the pruning knives of members are so sharp this morning. They seem to be cutting and slashing all around. I do not think we are to have a banking system, with proper securities around them, without the action of the legislature. I am glad that we are not to do that here, I think the legislature will be better enabled to do this, after this measure shall have been discussed and examined by the people, than we are, at this time. The legislature is left free to adopt either or both of these systems, as they may think proper. The gentleman from Johnson, [Mr. Clarke] does not wish the state to own stock. If he will look at the third section of this report, he will find that the state is prohibited from owning any of this stock. This provision here is only to enable the state to have some control over this bank; this striking out will confine the legislature to one system of banking, and that is what I object to. Let us leave both systems as the committee have reported, and when the legislature meets, if they see proper to establish the general banking law, they can do so. I am not any prophet or the son of a prophet. But I think that by the time the legislature comes to act upon this matter, the general banking law of Illinois will be in disrepute. And that is the system, I believe, which the gentleman from Johnson [Mr. Clarke] desires to see established here.

Mr. CLARKE of Johnson. By no means.

Mr. PARVIN. I am glad to hear that. But I do not know what system he would have. I would allow the legislature a choice in this matter We can throw certain restrictions around any law that may be passed, and I think this body have signified their intention to do so by refusing to strike out this eighth section, and I trust the convention will never strike it out, for it is the sheet anchor of our banking institutions, and one which will hold amid the storms and gales which we may feel sure we will have.

I hope that the convention will refuse to strike out the word "state" and not restrict the legislature to any one particular system, when, by the time they meet, a large majority of the people will be opposed to that system.

Mr. TRAER. I think my friend from Muscatine, (Mr. Parvin) is mistaken in the question before the committee. I do not understand that the motion is to strike out the section under consideration. I made a motion to strike out the word "state" because it appeared to me to be a contradiction of terms. We say in one section of this article, that the state shall never take stock in any banking corporation. And it seems to me that this idea of calling this a *State* bank, when the state has no part or parcel in it, is a contradiction of terms. I therefore moved to amend the section in that respect. I think the naming of this institution is a matter which should be left entirely with the stockholders. I would therefore, leave this matter of the name an open question, and only provide by general principles for certain restrictions, to be thrown around this system. The same provision in this report is in the constitution of the State of Indiana, with the exception of the word "state," and the words, "upon an actual specie basis." I think it would be just as well to leave out this word "state," for if it is necessary to have it called by that name, there is no doubt that the stock holders and general assembly will give it that name. So far as the matter of fact is concerned it cannot be properly called a *State* Bank, because the state has no interest in the bank.

Mr. GOWER. I think there is same propriety in giving a name to an institution of such importance as this promises to be. If it is to be the bank of the State of Iowa, it should bear the name "Iowa," upon it. And I think it better so to amend this section as to have it read, "The Bank of Iowa," and that I consider just as proper as it would be to allow any company or association to fix upon the name.

Mr. HALL. Most people are willing to wait until a child is born before they proceed to name it. And I am willing to wait until I can learn the sex of this child before I proceed to give it a name.

The question being then taken upon striking out the word "State," it was not agreed to.

Mr. SKIFF. For the purpose of testing this question, I move to strike out this section.

Mr. CLARKE, of Henry. I would like to give my reasons for the vote I shall give. I therefore move that the committee rise, report progress and ask leave to sit again.

Mr. GIBSON. I hope this committee will rise. I wish to offer a few brief remarks upon this question. I feel that this is a matter of great interest, and it is perhaps too late now for me to give the opinions I entertain upon this subject.

The question being taken upon the motion that the committee rise, it was agreed to, upon a division, ayes 12, noes 11.

In Convention.

The PRESIDENT having resumed the chair,

The CHAIRMAN of the committee of the whole, reported that the committee had had under consideration the subject referred to them, had made some progress therein, and asked leave to sit again.

The report was received and leave granted accordingly.

On motion of Mr. SKIFF

The convention then took a recess until two o'clock, P. M.

EVENING SESSION.

The convention met at 2 o'clock P. M., and was called to order by the President.

Committee of the Whole.

The Convention then resumed the consideration of the report of the Committee on Incorporations, in Committee of the Whole, (Mr. Bunker in the chair.)

The CHAIRMAN. The question pending is upon striking out the ninth section, in relation to the establishment of a State bank and branches.

Mr. GIBSON. I propose to make a few remarks upon this question, but I will not detain the Convention at any great length. I am in favor of striking out this section, and I will state briefly my reasons why I am in favor of the motion now pending. This section provides that the General Assembly may also charter a State Bank with branches, &c. Now if I understand this matter correctly, we have already provided that the legislature shall pass a general banking law. To this I have no objection; and, I will go as far as any gentleman to make that banking law secure. I am willing that gentlemen shall incorporate any thing in this constitution that will strengthen that general banking law, by which the people may be made perfectly secure; but it strikes me that it is unnecessary and uncalled for, to have two systems of banking in our State. It seems to me that with two systems there would be endless confusion and discord. But this is not the only reason I have for striking out this section. I believe it to be wrong in principle, and therefore, that this section ought not to be retained in this article. As I understand it, it clothes the legislature with authority to charter a State bank and branches. If I am correct, then this charter is to be given to a certain company. Certain individuals will ask the Legislature to be incorporated in a banking company, and they will get their charter directly from the legislature. What is the universal practice in these cases? Is not the very first movement, on the part of the persons desiring an act of incorporation, to have engrafted in it such provisions as they desire? It is true, that it has to undergo the examination of the Legislature, but we have all heard a great deal about outside influences. I will not say that the Legislature is liable to be influenced by them; but from the remarks of gentlemen generally here, we would naturally come to the conclusion that there is some danger of these outside influences being brought to bear upon the legislature. Have not gentlemen said here that companies would present themselves before the legislature, and by the aid of their money, and by other influences which they could exert, buy up that body, and get them to pass just such a bill as the company required? If this is to be the case, then are not the people in danger? I do not say that such a result will follow; but for fear that it might, I would strike out any provision in the constitution, under which these corporations could go on and effect such a result.

Again, as I understand this provision, it would give to these favorites of the legislature exclusive privileges over the masses. They could be incorporated by special act of the legislature as a state bank, and have privileges which would be denied to the mass of the people. Why is this? Cannot a general banking law provide just as great safeguards, as a special act of the legislature? Could not a company incorporate themselves under a general banking law, and make just as good and safe a bank, as under a special act of the legislature? But the very object of this provision, as I understand it is, that they shall have certain privileges guaranteed to them by the legislature, which are not guaranteed to the mass of the people; and to this I am particularly opposed.

The name of a State Bank carries a falsehood upon its face. You are aware, Mr. Chairman, that we have already passed a certain provision, with very little objection, that the State shall not directly or indirectly become a stock-holder in any corporation whatever. This being the case, it forever excludes the State from being a stock-holder in any bank. Then why call it a "State Bank," when the State can have no interest in it, and cannot have a dollar invested in it? Why, gentlemen say, it gives the bank a character abroad. How? By practicing a falsehood and imposition upon the people, and making them believe that the State of Iowa is responsible for the notes of that bank, when the fact is, that she is not. If the State is not responsible, and the people are aware of that fact, in what respect would such a bank have greater credit, than would banks established under a general banking law?

As I before remarked, there can be a general banking law that can be sufficiently guarded. I am not now discussing what those guards shall be; they will no doubt come up at the proper time. I venture to say that there can be a general banking law, which will and can be sufficiently guarded, to secure the bill-holder against any loss whatever; and by so doing, we will avoid the necessity of establishing these special privileged classes among us, which would be, in fact, monopolies.

I wish to make a single remark in relation to these State stocks, although it is a subject not now under immediate consideration; yet as we are giving a wide scope to members in Committee of the Whole, I may venture to digress a little from the question now before us. I would say, by the way of suggestion, that so far as State stocks are concerned, as a basis for banking, I think they are rather unsafe. True, they may be good this year, but have we any assurance that they will remain good for five years to come? They may, and they may not, continue good. It strikes me, then, that it would be safer to introduce, to some extent, the real estate basis for banking. If we had such a basis as that, estimating the real estate at a fair valuation, and then taking one-half of that valuation as a basis for banking, there would not be any possibility of a failure. We are all aware that lands in this State are advancing and increasing in value every year from fifty to one hundred per cent; and with such a security there would be no possibility of failure, such as might arise in the case of banks with securities founded upon State stocks.

There is another point in connection with this question, to which I wish to allude. Banking companies are regarded by some persons as not very honest. I do not intend here to express my opinion, whether they are or are not. The probabilities are, that they are as honest as the times will admit. But with a certain amount of specie basis to bank upon, and with the amount secured by real estate, admitting that a banking company are not honest, and that every dollar in the vaults is liable to be squandered by them, the bill-holders would still be perfectly secure. They would be secured by real estate pledged or mortgaged to double the amount of the paper issue, which would certainly secure the redemption of the bills.

I am in favor of striking out this ninth section, because I believe it is a provision anti-republican, and anti-democratic in character. I do not use these terms in a partizan sense, but in their general signification. I am opposed to any law, that will give any chartered company privileges that we would refuse to the mass of the people. I want this matter of banking left free to all, so that when we leave here with our constitution ready to be submitted to the people, our constituents will not say that we have made any distinctions, or that we have given certain chartered privileges to a few, which we denied to the many. These are substantially my objections to this section of the report.

Mr. HARRIS. Being as ignorant, perhaps, as any other gentleman upon this floor, of the whole system of banking, having never, in any business of my life been called upon to investigate the different systems upon which it may be conducted, I did not intend to trouble the convention with any remarks upon this subject. But feeling somewhat flattered in looking over the debates of the convention, to see that my name has appeared there less frequently than the names of many gentlemen upon this floor, I would like to call the attention of the committee for a few moments to one particular section reported by the committee on corporations.

It is well known to every gentleman with whom I have ever had any particular intercourse, politically or socially, that I am not to be regarded as being the special and avowed friend of banking. As it is settled, however, that this state is to embark in some kind of banking, I should regard the striking out of the section now under consideration as a dire calamity to the people of this state. It is objected that some special act will be required on the part of the legislature to create a state bank and branches; and that such a system will become a special monopoly and, as such, will be opposed to the spirit and letter of our democratic institutions. So far as the question of monopoly is concerned, I have only to say, that when my person or my property is made secure it matters not to me, whether it is made so by a monopoly or private individuals, or a law that places all individuals upon the same footing in society. I am as strongly opposed to monopolies—those grinding corporations, that crush out the liberties of the laboring masses, as any man upon this floor. If a corporation, or any institution, protects the masses in their rights, and secures them in the enjoyment of their property, it matters not to me whether it is called monopoly, or whether it goes under the name of a free democratic banking institution. Such things as democratic banks I think will be very hard to find; but as was said by the gentleman upon my right, [Mr. Gibson] I do not use this term in any partisan spirit.

I was one of those that entertained serious objections to the present banking system of Ohio when it was put in operation there. It has been noticed, no doubt, by the gentlemen of this convention, that however much other parts of the country may have suffered in consequence of the explosions of the banks, the people of Ohio have suffered no losses from their banks for the last twenty years. I believe nothing has occurred to derange the currency of that state since the crisis of 1837. The present banking system of Ohio has been in operation since 1845. They had then just recovered from the awful calamities that were visited upon the people in consequence of the crash of 1837, created by the Granville or red-dog and wild-cat banking system, which flooded that state with such a vast amount of worthless paper.

The objection is taken by the gentleman who last addressed the committee [Mr. Gibson] that if we should impose upon the people a system which should be called the state bank, the state would not become responsible for the redemption of a dollar of their issues. Will the gentleman permit me to inform him that the banking institutions of Ohio have been in operation since 1845, the paper of which I presume the gentleman would prefer to that of the banks under the general laws of Indiana or Illinois, and at the same time the treasury of Ohio is not responsible for the redemption of one dollar of that paper? Then why is it called the "State Bank of Ohio," the gentleman will, perhaps, ask?

It is so called for the simple reason that it is. to a certain extent, under the control and guardianship of the State authorities, and the banking system is so interwoven together, as the gentleman from Henry told you, that the State bank and all its branches are responsible for the issues of each other. If any one of these branches fail, the paper must be redeemed at the counters of the other branches. Then gentlemen ask, are those banks which are solvent and prudent to be made responsible for the conduct of those that are irresponsible? By no means, but before they are permitted to go into operation, they were under the necessity of furnishing such securities, and placing them in such a shape, that when they failed to discharge their debts, and were under the necessity of closing their operations, the means they had placed there for security, should become available to those that were under the necessity of stepping in to discharge the duties which they had agreed to perform.—That is what I understand to be contemplated by the State Bank of Ohio, with its branches; and that is what is contemplated by the establishment of such a banking system in this State, if one should be created.

As I said before, I will not undertake to discuss the provisions of any banking law that might be framed here, because I must at once confess my ignorance as to the details of any of the systems of banking; but I only speak from that general information which is accessible to every other gentleman upon this floor.

One word upon this subject of real estate security, as the basis for banking, to which the gentleman from Marion. [Mr. Gibson] referred. I understand that something of that kind was projected in New York, and that it was no trouble at all for gentlemen who desired to start a banking institution in any part of that State, to get pine hills or tamarack swamps that would hardly sell for a dime an acre, and estimate them at such a high valuation per acre, that they could secure any amount of stocks as capital necessary to put their banks in operation. These banking institutions would flourish most beautifully for a time, until the day of reckoning came, and then their real estate would be placed under the hammer, and perhaps the whole amount of lands placed in security would not sell for a sufficient amount to pay the cost of the appraisement. And such, I apprehend, would be the result here, of requiring real estate securities as a basis for banking.

One gentleman here (Mr. Gower) has mentioned Wall street as the source to apply for information in regard to banking. I do not propose to spend any time in discussing such a question, but I would simply say that I would as soon think of going to Paris to acquire the best information necessary to correct extravagance in dress, or of going to the "London Times" for the best information as to the extent of the naval and military power of the United States, as to think of going to Wall street to obtain information on the subject of banking. I do not know very much about Wall street; but if I have any correct information of the men that operate there, they are, as a general thing, simply pirates upon the moneyed interests of every State in the Union. In the piratical warfare they carry on, it is their business to place the banking institutions of the country in such a position that they can attack one after another, as a well disciplined army would attack the outposts one after another, of a hostile country, that was not well secured.

I have information, directly from a gentleman concerned in banking in Ohio, to the amount of two hundred thousand dollars,—and I have no reason to doubt the correctness of his statement —that the difficulty which occurred in the moneyed circles of the country two years ago, through an attack upon the banks of Indiana and Illinois, created under free banking laws, was brought about by a preconcerted and well planned movement of the brokers of Cincinnati and New York. When the question was asked them, why the banks created under these general banking laws were attacked, in place of the State bank of Ohio, and the State bank of Indiana, the answer was, because we were not strong enough to overthrow either of those systems, but we could attack in detail the other banks, and when we had destroyed the credit of one, we knew we had to some extent, sapped the confidence of the people in them all. It would not do to attack the State bank, unless we were prepared to overthrow the entire system, and that we did not desire to do and could not have accomplished it if we had desired it.

I believe it is true that the failure that occurred in the monetary affairs of this country two years ago, was simply owing to the manœuvring of brokers.

I am convinced that where you leave any system of banking to stand or fall by itself, you will find that the brokers of Wall street will attack the banks in detail, whenever it shall suit their purposes. Hence I am disposed in this matter, to allow the greatest liberty in banking; yet so far as my feelings and preferences are concerned, I wish to have a system under which banks will be formed for the protection and security of each other.

I came here pledged to no particular system of banking. The people I represent know very well my preconceived opinions and prejudices against banking institutions, and I apprehend that there are many men in my district, who themselves are in favor of some kind of a banking system, who supported me, under the impression that so far as my private opinions and feelings were concerned, I was opposed to banking *in toto*. They knew, however, that I was aware that the majority of the people of this State, and a majority of those whom I represented, were in favor of some kind of banking; and they knew, also, that I have ever worshipped at the shrine of popular sovereignty, not precisely in the sense in which that term has been used in the recent canvass, but in its fullest and broadest sense; the sense in which it was used by our honored President in his opening address. It is a well settled axiom with us, that the "people are sovereign and the source of all power." and it was well known to my constituents, that I endorse that doctrine to the fullest extent.

This is, and must be, a government of the majority. I do not hold that the government will always act right and wisely; but I hold that there is sufficient wisdom, integrity and intelligence, when the sober, second thought prevails, to correct the errors into which they may have hastily and inconsiderately fallen. I believe that it will be as safe, in attempting to establish any particular system of banking, to leave it with the legislature that shall come fresh from the people, as to leave it with this Convention. I believe that we should leave it with the legislature entirely, to say what the details of a banking system shall be; and that we ourselves shall not in this matter, go farther than to lay down certain cardinal, general principles that shall inure to the benefit of the people at large.

There are two things to be considered in the creation of any banking institution. The first and important consideration should be the security of the bill-holders; and when you have secured that, then you can make the system practicable and beneficial, so that capital will seek investment in that direction. I was at one time the advocate of the adoption of the principle of "individual liability," in the strictest sense of the term, in regard to the banks created in Ohio in 1842; but when it was ascertained that you made a man liable for all the debts of the concern, when his stock did not, perhaps, reach a hundredth part of the capital, moneyed men would not make an investment in such institutions; and hence the scheme was found to be impracticable. I believe, as I said before, that the first consideration should be to make the bill-holders secure; and when you have done that, you make the system as practicable as may be, for the accommodation of those that are operating under it.

It is certainly well understood by every gentleman upon this floor, that no man will invest money in banking—and there is certainly a great desire on the part of the people of this State that capitalists should invest their money in banking institutions here—unless he can make a profit by it. I am not jealous of the profits that a banker may make, so that I can obtain money from him at as reasonable rates as I can in any other way, and at the same time be secure in what I hold. I would just as soon pay a banker in this community a large interest, from the profits of which he might build his fine house, as to pay the interest that the people of this State have been paying ever since Iowa has been a State, upon the worthless trash that has been circulated here, and which has enabled many a moneyed man of Wall street to build him a splendid palace.

I am in favor of letting this provision stand here, as it has been reported by the committee. I am in favor of the individual liability clause as it stands here. When I spoke of that principle a few minutes since, as established in Ohio, I referred to the provision there which made each man responsible for the whole amount of the stock. That is a different provision from the one herein contained.

Mr. GOWER. Gentlemen will recollect that a short time ago I made a motion to strike out the words "State Bank," and insert "the Bank of Iowa" in its place, and that we had a vote upon it.

It was objected to upon the ground that it would require special acts of the legislature to create these institutions. I do not desire to make any extended remarks upon this subject, but I would be glad to have the secretary read the plan for a banking system, which I submitted to the convention some time ago, and which has been printed. It will be perceived that the bill makes general provisions which can be easily applied all over the State. I will ask for the reading of the plan instead of making a speech upon this subject, as it embodies completely and fully the views I entertain upon this question of banking.

The CHAIRMAN. If there be no objection, the paper referred to by the gentleman from Cedar will be read.

There being no objection, the Secretary then read the following:

"*Resolved*, That the committee on incorporations be instructed to inquire into the propriety of engrafting the annexed bill in our constitution, with such amendments as are deemed necessary:

Sec. 1. Be it enacted by the General Assembly of the State of Iowa, that ——— are appointed commissioners to open books and receive subscriptions for the establishment of a bank in the city of ———, which bank shall be called the State Bank of Iowa; and as soon as the said commissioners shall have obtained subscriptions to the amount of five hundred thousand dollars, they shall then call a meeting of the subscribers in the city of ———, giving at least thirty days' notice in five different papers published within the State of Iowa, of the time and place of such meeting, for the general organization of said bank, which shall be consummated by the election of six directors, from among said subscribers, and as soon as said organization shall have been consummated, they will then resign their trust into the hands of the newly elected officers of the bank.

Sec. 2. Be it enacted, That the bank situated in the city of ———, shall be called the main bank, and all other banks shall be branches thereof. The main bank shall only issue its notes to the branch banks, having inserted in each note the name of the particular bank for whose use they are intended, and in no case shall the main bank put in circulation any notes purporting to be issued by the State Bank of Iowa otherwise than through the branch banks.

Sec. 3. The main bank shall be divided into three departments, viz:

Firstly—The Regular Department.

Secondly—The Issuing Department.

Thirdly—The Redemption Department.

The Regulating Department shall be a board of control, consisting of three members, one of whom shall be elected by the legislature, one by the people, in general election, and one by an election to be held exclusively by the directors of the branch banks throughout the State—the directors of each branch being allowed to hold their meetings in their own banking house, to cast their votes—putting the name or names of their candidate so voted for in a sealed package, and sending it by mail, addressed to the President of the Board of Control, who shall open it in the presence of the whole board and count the votes, and the one receiving a plurality of votes shall be considered duly elected. The members of the board of control shall hold their term of office three years, one to be elected every year—the member elected by the Legislature being the President, and the oldest member of the board thereafter, according to the one term of his official service only. The duties of the Board of control shall consist in the entire management of the organic operations of the main bank and branches; for the better and more impartial regulation thereof, they shall compose and have printed, a set of rules and regulations applying in their effect to each and every branch of the main bank alike. The Board of Control, or either of them, shall also have power to appoint inspectors to visit all, or any one of the branches to inspect their books, papers, and assets generally; and report their standing to said Board, in writing—their visits being made at any time in which the Board of Control, or any member thereof, may deem fit: and without notice to the branch being so visited. And if it is shown by said report that the affairs of such branch are not in a sound condition, it shall be the duty of the President of the Board of Control to call upon the executive officer of such branch to show cause why such branch should not be closed, and the assets thereof taken possession of by the main bank, and its affairs wound up; and if the officer aforesaid shall not answer the call of the Board of Control, as aforesaid, or if they shall so do, but not give sufficient reason for the continuance of their business, it shall then be the duty of said Board to take possession of the assets of such branch, and dispose of them to the best advantage—using the proceeds, Firstly, for the redemption of its issues; Secondly, for the payment of depositors with the branch; and, Thirdly, for the payment of all other liabilities, *pro rata;* and if anything be left thereafter, the same shall be handed over to the stockholders, in proportion to their stock in said branch as paid in; but if there shall not be sufficient assets to meet the first, second and third class of claims against the branch, in that case the directors shall be assessed in a like ratio with the amount of their stock subscribed, whether it is all paid in or not, to the amount necessary to liquidate the indebtedness of the bank. If there shall not be enough assets to redeem all the notes of such branch, then, in that case, the Board of Control shall make an assessment upon each of the other branches, according to their capital, respectively, to make up the deficit, and if any branch shall neglect or refuse to comply with the requirements of the assessment, the Board of Control will then proceed to close up such branch in the same manner and to the same extent as the first.

The Issuing Department shall provide all the bank notes intended for circulation of the branches throughout the State, and disburse them to the branches in accordance with the written order of the Board of Control—stamping upon each note the insignia of such department belonging to the great seal thereof—entering the number, letter, date, and denomination of each note in a register kept exclusively for that purpose—keeping the registration of the notes of each branch separately.

The Redemption Department shall have the possession of the specie and securities belonging to the bank and to the branches, and provide a suitable fire-proof vault for the security of the same, using the same only in the redemption of the bank note issues of the branches—the same having been issued from the Issuing Department aforesaid—which notes the department will retain until duly required to be given up by a written order of the Board of Control, and endorsed by the cashier of the Issuing Department.

Sec. 4. The salaries of the members of the Board of Control shall be ———, a year, and to be regulated entirely by the legislature; but in no case to be decreased during their term of office. The salaries of the subordinate officers are to be regulated by the Board of Control, at their option.

Sec. 5. Branch banks must be organized upon the following plan, to wit: Whenever any persons—numbering not less than twelve, two-thirds of whom must be residents of the county in which it is proposed to locate the bank—shall wish to establish a branch bank, they must first get up an instrument of writing, in which they must state the names of the parties connected with it, their respective places of residence, business, and the amount of their present subscription, the place in which they wish to locate their bank, the name under which it is to be known and do business, the amount of its capital, and the term for which it is intended that the charter shall continue; after which the application so arranged shall be forwarded to the Board of Control, whose duty it shall be to issue a permit authorizing the establishment of the bank, if they have published a notice in some paper in the place where it is intended to locate such bank, of such application having been made thirty days before granting such permit, and there exists no objection from any one to the creation of such banks—or if there are objections, but which have been overruled by the Board—the presentation of which to the Redemption Department, for safe keeping, will consummate the bank a branch of the State Bank of Iowa. Whenever the branch so created shall seek for bank notes for circulation, it must then place in the hands of the receiving officer of the Redemption Department one-third the amount of the notes so required in gold and silver, as the said officer may require—this provision only extending to three times the amount of the capital of such branch. If any branch shall wish to obtain more notes than three times the amount of its paid in capital, it must then give to the receiving officer of the Redemption Department, State or United States stocks, at the rate of five per cent. less than the ruling market value in New York city, at the time of such deposit, dollar for dollar of the amount of notes required for circulation; and if at any time thereafter, the stocks so deposited shall fall in price three per cent. below the price at which it stood at the time of such deposit, the receiving officer aforesaid must then notify the executive officers of such bank that they must place in his hands more stock within ten days thereafter; and if they do not comply therewith, he must proceed to sell that in his hands, and apply the proceeds to the redemption of such notes, which notes must have stamped, or printed from steel engraved die, upon their face the words Relief Notes, by which they will be known from all others.

Sec. 6. All the notes so put in circulation by the branch banks shall be redeemed by the main bank only, but the branch banks must receive the notes of any and every branch in payment of any claims due such branch, if offered, whether the branch issuing them is solvent or not; but any branch so receiving such notes is not precluded from presenting the same, if it should choose to do so to the main bank for redemption; but in no case will a branch bank be allowed to make a deposit with the notes of other branches, for the purpose of obtaining circulating notes for its own use, either directly or indirectly. No branch bank shall issue or put into circulation any other notes purporting to be issued by such branch but those which it has obtained from the Issuing Department of the Main Bank in ———.

Sec. 7. The number of branches shall be limited to that of fifty, being properly distributed throughout the State—there not being more than three in any one city, or more than two in any one town, or more than one in any one village—these numbers to be increased only by an act of the legislature, for the purpose of meeting the requirements of commerce and trade in any particular locality.

Sec. 8. The capital of each branch shall not exceed one million dollars in the cities, nor less than fifty thousand dollars. In the towns the capital of each branch shall not exceed five hundred thousand dollars, nor less than forty thousand dollars. In the villages the capital of each branch shall not exceed one hundred thousand dollars, nor less than twenty-five thousand dollars.

Sec. 9. Each and every stock-holder shall be held personally responsible to the amount of his or her stock subscribed over and above the amount so subscribed for by him or her, in case it shall become necessary to collect the amount to liquidate all the claims against the branch to which they are stockholders; but this liability shall not be enforced until after the property, both personal and real, of the directors of such branch, and that of all the other branches, as above stated, has been exhausted in the payment of such claims.

Sec. 10. All taxes shall be assessed and collected of the banks in the same manner as they are of individuals; but when a branch pays its taxes upon its capital as assessed, the stockholders thereof shall not be assessed for taxes upon the stock so held by them of such bank.

Sec. 11. Any failure upon the part of any branch to comply with, or conform to, the requirements of this law, or any part thereof, shall be considered a forfeiture of its charter as such branch, and the assets, of all kinds whatsoever, shall revert to the board of control, the possession of which can be obtained if any resistence be shown by the officers or stock-holders of the branch so delinquent, by the issue of an order by the clerk of the court of , directed to the sheriff of the county in which the bank is located, or by the clerk of the supreme court of the State of Iowa, directed to any executive officer acting under him, or deputised by him for this special purpose.

Sec. 12. Any officer of any branch which has failed, or been closed by the board of control in consequence of improper delinquencies, or outright frauds, shall not be eligible to hold office in any other branch bank within this State; and any branch violating this provision by the appointment of any such person, and persisting in the same after due notice having been given the officers thereof of the antecedents of such person by the board of control, it shall be deemed a delinquent branch, and as such be proceeded against by the board of control, in like manner, and to the same extent, as in other cases.

Sec. 13. If any branch shall wish to close its affairs, or to discontinue the circulation of its notes, it will be necessary for such branch to give the board of control due notice thereof, whose duty it shall be to advertise in two daily and weekly papers, published in the city of , of such intention, requiring the presentation of all notes of such branch at the redemption office, within two years thereafter, or all outstanding notes at that time will be barred from redemption at such office; and that the funds belonging to such branch will be handed to the receiver of the bank.

Sec 14. The current expenses of the main bank shall be borne by the several branches, in proportion to their capital stock—each paying its allotted per centage, at the end of each six months, commencing on the first day of January of each year, in which expenses are to be included all payments for bank notes and plates, together with all other expenses therewith connected or arising therefrom.

Mr. GOWER. As I observed this morning, I have been in constant correspondence, since November last, with gentlemen in whom I have great confidence, in relation to this question of banking, and the plan that has just been read was drawn up by one of these gentlemen in accordance with my suggestion.

I do not feel willing to trust this question wholly to the legislature; neither do I believe that it is advisable for us to introduce into our constitution all the prohibitions upon this subject, which we can find in every other constitution of the Union. I notice that there is a disposition, on the part of some gentlemen, to look over the constitutions of other States, and embody in our own, whatever of prohibition, upon this question, they can find in them. I do not think that that course will materially assist us. We need here a good system of banking, one which will induce capitalists to make their investments here, and one with which the people of the State will be satisfied. I think if we go to work with that end in view, restrict the general system, and deprive us of every thing else, it will not serve us at all. I think that the great object for which we were convened here, was to provide for the establishment of banking in this State. I am confident that this was the wish of the people of my district; and it has been my great aim, in the discharge of my duties here, to accomplish that object.

Mr. EDWARDS. I understand the question to be upon striking out the ninth section. I wish, upon that motion, to offer a few remarks in addition to what I presented upon a previous occasion, when I compared the relative merits of the two systems of banking. I came here instructed by my constituents to go, first, for a provision in the constitution favoring the system of State banks. Upon my arrival here, and after an interchange of views with different members of the convention, I found that there were several members who favored the general banking system, or in other words, what is called the free banking system. I have made no effort, nor has it been my desire, to prevent the gratification of the wishes entertained by these members of the convention, who are the especial friends of the free banking system, in having it submitted to the legislature. While I shall extend that liberality, in a spirit of compromise, to those who are the especial friends of that system, I hope that they will be actuated by the same spirit of liberality, and allow the friends of a State bank to have the same right in the constitution of leaving it to a future legislature to say whether they shall establish both systems, or either.

My experience in the history of banking, is, that the system of state banks is preferable to that of a general banking system; and the reasons for this preference I assigned on yesterday. If state banks are established on a proper basis, they will have a more extended character and credit than it is possible for individual banking associations to have.

Objections have been made here to-day by several gentlemen who are the friends of free banks, to the name which has been given by the committee, that of *State Bank*. Gentlemen have gone so far as to say that it was a fraud upon its face, and that it would be practising a fraud upon the people of the country, if the issues of such a bank should go out with the name of "State Bank," upon their face. I do not look upon this matter in the light that many gentlemen do. It is true that the state is not a stockholder in these banks; but if gentlemen will examine the laws in other states, the only light we have to guide us in this matter, they will find that the state is to some extent connected with these state banks. I have before me a copy of the charter of the State Bank of Indiana. It is true that the state does not own a dollar of the stock; yet, at the same time, the General Assembly of that state elect four directors upon the part of the state, who exercise an especial guardianship over that bank. This board of directors, elected on the part of the state, cannot be stockholers in that bank. They should be men of character and standing, who should be subjected to no invidious reproaches, and who could have a controling guardianship over such a banking system in order that the rights of the bill-holders should be properly protected. Under this system of banking, there is another officer who is responsible to the state, and that is the commissioner, whose duty it is to examine into the condition of these banks, and report to the governor their standing and condition; and if they should, any of them, be found to have violated their chartered rights, he is then required to proceed against them immediately.

The state is also connected with this system of banking in another way, as it has been managed in other states. All the funds that are collected by the county treasurers are deposited in the various braches of the state bank, in different sections of the state, only the proper officer at the seat of government drawing warrants upon these deposites. These banks become, then, the depository of the trust funds of the state. There is nothing wrong, then, in terming this bank, with its branches, the "State Bank." I would not care by what name you call it, whether it be as the gentleman of Cedar [Mr. Gower] suggests, the "Bank of Iowa," or whether it should be something else. "A rose under any other name would smell as sweet." I do not see how it would injure any one, to call it the "Bank of Iowa," the "State Bank," or any other name we may choose to give it.

The great object with all legislative bodies that have passed laws upon this subject of banking has been to create and establish banks with guards amply sufficient to protect the bill-holders. That should be the object which they should always have in view, when passing laws upon this subject. As I have said on previous occasions, I care not what the details of any law upon this subject may be, if you will only find a system that will be safe and secure for the bill-holders.

The committee on yesterday made an amendment to the report, which, I believe, provides everything necessary to secure the bill-holder. If you desire to have the bill-holder protected, you must have sufficient securities; and I think that the security that we have required here, by which bankers shall deposite one hundred and twenty dollars in United States or state stocks for every one hundred dollars issued, which issues are registered and countersigned, that is a sufficient guaranty against any probable losses that might occur on the part of the bill-holders.

A great deal has been said here to-day in regard to the individual liability clause,and permit me to say, that I regard it as one of the greatest humbugs that the ingenuity of man has ever devised. I have never yet heard of a single instance, where full and sufficient protection has been afforded to bill-holders, by the incorporation of such a clause as this in the charter of any banking institution. Gentlemen will recollect that last year, I think it was, a large amount of Georgia money was put into circulation here, which had emblazoned upon its face: "secured by individual liability." But the bubble soon burst, leaving a large amount of worthless paper in the hands of the people of this state. I ask you what security did this individual liability clause afford in that case? An individual liability clause was inserted in the very laws that created state banks in Indiana. What effect followed the introduction of this principle there? There was not a responsible man in the community who held stocks and expected to do honest and legitimate banking, who would file the stocks in his own name. The stocks were invariably filed in the names of irresponsible persons. These men were sharp enough to know when a bank was about to fail, and if there was any possibility or prospect that they would be called to an account, they would see that these stocks should pass into the hands of irresponsible persons.

You can never throw protection around a banking system by this individual liability clause. It carries fraud upon its face, and is calculated to deceive the people. But if the law requires that the basis shall be sufficient, then you secure protection to the bill-holders at the very fountain-head, and you remove all danger from the imposition of a worthless system upon the people. I care not so far as this state bank is concerned, whether it shall be based upon stock securities, or whether it shall be established upon a specie basis. So far as I am concerned I would prefer the specie basis. I believe, with a system of a state bank and branches, such as I have advocated, that we can amply secure the protection of the bill-holder, as under such a system it will be for the mutual interest of each branch to so conduct its affairs—and it is made the duty of the Board of Directors on the part of the state to see each branch properly conducted—that it shall not impair the credit of any other branch in the state. I think that when you institute a comparison between the two systems of banking, you will come to the conclusion that the system of a state bank is preferable to that of the general banking system, but for the purpose of compromising this matter I am willing to provide that it shall be left to a future legislature to say whether they shall establish both systems or either.

I hope the section now under consideration will not be stricken out.

Mr. ELLS. I have not troubled the Convention with any remarks of mine upon this subject. I desired not to do so, until I had heard what gentlemen had to say in favor of the two systems of banking provided for in this report. My own mind being fully made up in favor of a general banking law, I nevertheless desired to hear all that could be said in favor of a State bank and branch system.

I have listened to the arguments of gentlemen with a great deal of pleasure, and I trust with some profit. Still I am unshaken in my judgment in favor of a general banking law; and have lost none of my fears of the evil tendency of the other system. The report, as it now stands, leaves it optional with the General Assembly to charter one or both systems. Looking upon the State bank and branch system as a species of monopoly, liable to all the abuses that any system can be, and at the same time capable of being so conducted as to conceal its evil workings, I cannot but hope that the constitution will be so amended as to put it out of the power of the legislature to inflict so much evil on the country.

I am aware that a defective system of banking, in the hands of honest and upright men, may be so conducted as to be comparatively harmless. Such, for instance, as the State bank and branch system in Ohio. The branches of that system are principally composed of the old solvent banks that existed before the State bank system was introduced. The gentlemen who conducted these old banks were principally men of real wealth, well known to each other as honest and upright financiers. They had confidence in each other, and formed themselves into a banking co-partnership, and placed the whole system under the management of a "Board of Control," elected by the stock-holders of the several banks. This Board of Control countersigned and issued all the bills of the several branches, and kept up a vigilant supervision of all the transactions of the entire institution; but notwithstanding this, several of these branches failed and utterly exhausted all of their available means; and thousands of dollars had to be contributed by the solvent branches to make up the deficiency.

Now, sir, if a system of banking can only be kept solvent by the most vigilant conduct of a Board of Control, constantly on the alert to detect fraudulent practices, what may we not expect, when neither the Board of Control nor the officers of the various branches care for anything more than to fleece the people and feather their own nests?

Let us examine a little into the details of this system. The charter requires that the issues of the branches shall never exceed an average of three dollars in currency for each dollar of coin in their vaults; that at the end of each quarter of the year the cashier of each branch shall make a statement under oath, showing the amount of coin on hand, the amount of paper in circulation, &c. It also provides that the branches shall each be responsible for all the indebtedness of the other branches; and the stockholders individually liable, if you please. These are all the guards you can throw around the system for the security of the bill-holder. Suppose all this has been done by a set of swindlers who intend to flood the country with their issues and then burst up. Is there, I ask, any way to prevent them from accomplishing their purposes, or having done so, any way in which the honest bill-holder can indemnify himself for the loss of his property or labor given in exchange for the State bank paper? None, sir, none. Again sir, a loose and unguarded system offers temptations for speculators so strong, that many honest men are led astray by their ambitious desires to increase their wealth, and thus is ruin brought on the country. But, say gentlemen, the Ohio system has been in practical operation for about fourteen years, and, notwithstanding the failure of several branches, is still a good and solvent institution.

This was the statement of the gentleman from Appanoose, [Mr. Harris,] if I understood him correctly. Now sir, if my memory serves me right, the gentleman is not correctly posted in this matter. That system has been in operation only since 1851 or '52, and was adopted under the new constitution.

Mr. YOUNG. It was not adopted under the new constitution, but was in operation before.

Mr. ELLS. I do not think I am mistaken. My impression is that the question of bank or no bank was submitted as an outside question when the new constitution was adopted.

Mr. YOUNG. The system was in operation before, and the people only continued it under the new constitution after it was adopted.

Mr. ELLS. I had supposed the banking system of Ohio came in with that vote of the people upon the separate question of bank or no bank. If I am mistaken, no matter; let it go. Admit that the State bank and branches were not made up of new banks. The system was then conducted by honest men who knew each other, and they merely changed their charters and obtained new ones. All the banks knew each other. The bank at Columbus knew the bank at Zanesville, and the bank at Chillicothe, and these banks knew the character of the bank at Columbus; and hence they were willing to become bound for each other, in the same way that honest men are willing to endorse for each other. There was no experiment there; nothing hidden and unknown. They were willing to join in partnership for the benefit of the people of the State at large, and for themselves individually. As I said before, a board of control to have the management of the whole system, was created; and they were honest men, enabled to keep the system in successful operation, because they had the means to do it and intended to do it. But suppose that instead of being honest, they were dishonest men; they had the opportunity to swindle the community out of millions of dollars if they had desired to do so. And where is your safeguard, gentleman from Appanoose, [Mr. Harris]? Where is your safeguard, gentleman from Jefferson, [Mr. Wilson]? There is none. And there is no way to reach them for their dishonest acts, except to make it a penitentiary offense and punish them.

You cannot protect the bill-holder, except by giving him the certainty of receiving dollar for dollar for his bills. With honest men, this system will be a good one, but not with dishonest. But on the other hand the system we advocate, of having the banks based upon United States stocks, and the stocks of interest paying States, worth dollar for dollar in the market, this system is made perfectly safe by having those stocks placed beyond the control of the banker engaged in this business. These bankers, under this system, give up their securities, and place them in the hands of a third person—a State officer—to be held as a pledge for the honesty of their conduct.

Now, gentleman tell us that the legislature will place around this system all the safeguards it is necessary to have. I thought so myself at first. But I have heard gentlemen upon this floor, who have been members of our General Assembly, say that the legislature are not to be trusted, that they are corruptible to a greater or less extent. Now if that be the case, I am unwilling to trust them with the power to create a system that will in the end swindle the people. But gentlemen say in answer to that, the system that may be adopted is to be voted upon by the people, and they will reject it if it is a bad one. I wish that was a correct position. I am not one who will distrust the people; say they are dishonest and ought not to be trusted. The gentleman from Appanoose, [Mr. Harris,] says truly that the people of this country have been in the habit of paying from twenty-five to thirty per cent. for money upon which they have been speculating. This thing has now reached a point where this high rate of per centage cannot be paid, and the borrowers be able to indemnify themselves by buying land or going into other business. Hence it is that the people desire a banking system so that they may obtain money at less rates than is now given. That is the case in Davenport and in my county; and I suppose it is the same all over Iowa. The people have gone on until they have reached a point beyond which they cannot go safely. And unless they can obtain money at less rates, there will be a general break up all over the State. Now that fact contains the germ of the whole spirit of this matter. Suppose that the legislature should charter a bank under either system proposed here, and the form of the charter should be an unsafe one. I will place this matter upon the hypothesis that the system is not a good one. If it is presented to the people in their present state of feeling, even if the system be a bad one, they will vote for it. They will say, it is at least better than the Florence bank, or the Exchange bank, and thus they will compromise and take a bad system, rather than have no banking system. Now I wish to keep from the people any alternative of that kind.

Now, sir, I ask gentlemen to ponder well, and not act recklessly upon this matter. I believe that a State bank and branches will result in disastrous consequences to the State, if it is put into operation. With the other system we have safeguards furnished us, securities pledged, which the system of State bank and branches does not afford us. It is like pawning your watch for money. The one who advances the money on your watch knows he is safe, for if you never come back for your watch, he can dispose of that and remunerate himself. And so in this matter of general banking: the securities required to be deposited are sufficient for the purposes, and thus confidence is given, and confidence is everything. Confidence is said to be a plant of slow growth, and so I believe, especially in Iowa, where gentlemen say so much about having no confidence in the people. Then if confidence is a plant of slow growth, let us commence to cultivate that plant, and be careful in doing so, that we do not destroy that which we intend to create. Because that system has been successful in Ohio, and has secured the good opinion of the gentleman from Jefferson [Mr. Wilson], and the gentleman from Appanoose, [Mr. Harris], do not let us stray from the path of duty and safety, and act so as to ruin, not only the republican party who are responsible for the action of this Convention, but also the State of Iowa itself; for when you destroy the credit of the State, you have, in effect destroyed the State itself. I prefer to hold on to the one system, provided we guard it carefully and make it as it should be; then we may go home to our constituents with a clear conscience and present them with a clean record, and say to them, gentlemen, we surrrender the trust you have reposed in us, and it is now for you to do what remains to be done.

This view of the banking question, in my humble judgment, is worthy of all consideration. Just think of it, gentlemen, for a moment. Can there be any doubt about the people accepting an unsafe system of banking, while groaning under their usurous burthens of taxation? Why, sir, a gentleman sent me several thousand dollars to loan at twenty-five per cent. and take good real estate security. The money was placed in the hands of a broker, who soon effected a loan on first class security in our city. I was surprised at the result, but my astonishment was increased when the borrower informed me that he was saving five per cent. by the operation, for with the money he would take up a note on which he was paying thirty per cent. interest per annum. These cases are so common in Davenport that borrowers give their notes with two and a half per cent. per month written on the face of the paper; and such, I am credibly informed, is the case all over the State. Now, sir, it is not at all marvelous that wealthy gentlemen, like the gentleman from Des Moines [Mr. Hall], who have money to loan should prefer banks of deposite and exchange to banks of issue.

There is another objection to the State Bank and branch system, that I will notice. It is this: Once established, it becomes a monopoly in the hands of the stockholders. No one can enter the institution without the consent of the stockholders. To illustrate: Suppose the gentleman from Des Moines, [Mr. Hall], and myself should enter into copartnership for some speculative purpose, and invest ten thousand dollars in business. The gentleman from Appanoose [Mr. Harris] offers himself to come in and take a share in the concern. We have the power to say whether he shall be allowed to come in or not—we can control that matter. We decide that we do not want him. He is an honest man, and will prevent us from doing something we want to do. But the gentleman from Wapello [Mr. Gillaspy] is the right kind of man—just the one we want—we will take him and leave out the other one. This I consider the way matters may be conducted under this State banking system. Of course, gentlemen will understand me as merely imagining the case I have stated, without having any reference to anything else.

But under the general banking system every man who can buy ten thousand dollars worth of stocks, can engage in banking. If he loses, it is his misfortune and not his crime. The other system has all the disadvantages of this system, and none of its advantages. That is the reason why I support one system and not the other.

Mr. HARRIS. I plead guilty to having no particular affection for the Republican party, but I have no desire to make capital here.

Mr. WILSON. The gentleman from Scott, [Mr. Ells] is mistaken as to the time of this banking system being passed in Ohio. It was passed in the winter of 1844 and 1845. At the same time there was passed a law organizing the State Bank, and the independent banks of that State. The gentleman is mistaken as to the separate vote of the people of Ohio upon the question of banking. The only side vote submitted to the people at that time was in relation to the license question. The clause in relation to banking was embodied in the constitution itself, and voted upon as a part of the constitution.

Mr. ELLS. I recollect now. It was submitted to the people in the constitution. But there was so much talk about submitting it to the people separately that I thought such had been the case.

Mr. WILSON. In 1840 the Legislature of Ohio passed a law amending the law creating independent banks, and provided that the banks in question, if they accepted the terms of that law, should be held liable according to the terms and conditions of that law. There was a difficulty grew out of that, and the law was considered in the Supreme Court for a time—whether under the old or new constitution I do not recollect—to be unconstitutional. But that, I think is decided differently now. The law creating the State Bank provides for a Board of Control; and instead of these men issuing their bills as they may see proper, the bills must all pass under the hands of the President of the Board of Control, and be signed by him as president of the State Bank; and the branch banks issue none except so signed by him.

The gentleman from Appanoose [Mr. Harris] was also at fault about the banks of Ohio. He says there has been no difficulties there since 1847. The banks of Germantown, Massillon, Circleville, Urbana, Granville, and I do not know how many others, have gone down since the period to which he has referred. These banks were not connected with the State Bank; two or three branches of the State Bank have also gone down, but the bill holders have not lost their money. If the branch bank failed to comply with the law, if it failed to redeem its notes when presented, the Board of Control took possession of the assets of the bank, and closed up its business. It is also provided, under that law, that a certain portion of the profits of the branch banks shall be set apart annually, as a fund to meet the failure of any or all of them. If a branch bank goes down that fund is resorted to; if it is not sufficient to redeem the notes of that branch, then the Board of control levy contributions upon the rest of the branch banks sufficient to redeem the circulation of the one that has failed. They then make arrangements with some banking house for the redemption of these notes as they are presented, and in this way they are fully redeemed. The Board of Control go on in the meantime and sell the assets of the broken branch bank, refund to the sinking fund of each of the other branch banks, what has been used in the redemption of these notes. That system has worked well heretofore, and no bill-holder has lost anything by these failures.

And I say here, that though the Licking branch bank failed in 1850, I have received one of its notes since I have been in this State. It was in circulation, and was received as current money. The reason of that was, that the redemption of it was secured.

The Board of Control has a right to investigate the affairs of a branch bank at any time. They may send without notice, to the officers of the bank to make a return at any time, and if they are endeavoring to play the game to which the gentleman from Scott [Mr. Ells] referred, of sending specie from one branch to the other, the attempt to defraud will at once be detected. As yet no difficulty has occurred under that law in Ohio.

There is another provision in this report as it has now been amended, which I think will render this matter more secure, and do away with the objection of the gentleman from Scott. It is that portion that provides that the legislature may require that the basis shall be part stock and part specie. And the legislature may pass a law for a State Bank, which will be just as secure as any general banking law would be.

I am free to say, that if the legislature goes on and passes an act for a State Bank and branches which I do not think perfectly secure, I will exert all my influence to defeat it, when it comes before the people. I hope all these banking laws will be submitted to the people for their approval or rejection. I believe that under these provisions as now amended, a system of State and branch banks can be established as secure and as safe as any other system. And I hope the people of the State will have an opportunity of selecting between the two systems, or adopting them both as they may see proper. I believe a majority of my constituents are in favor of a State Bank; I judge so from conversations I have had with them upon the subject. If a majority of the people of the State want a State Bank and branches, let them have them. If they do not want them, let them vote them down. At least, give them an opportunity to take both systems, or either, as they may deem best.

Mr. ELLS. The gentleman from Jefferson [Mr. Wilson], says that the people of his district would prefer a State Bank and branches. Now it is a fact that the people at large believe that the State will be responsible for the issues of a State Bank; that the State is a partner in the concern. And it is that belief which gives credit and character to this State Bank system all over the country. Go wherever you will, and you will find that the people think the State is responsible for the issues of these State Banks. And the very name carries that impression with it at the first sight. The taking the name of a State Bank and not being a State bank, carries upon its face a lie, as many other shin-plasters do.

I want to call the attention of the committee

to another fact. I had hoped that gentlemen would reply to that feature of my argument, in which I endeavored to show that the State bank system was liable to the objection that dishonest men could take possession of it, and control it, and swindle the community, and you could not help yourselves. The gentleman from Jefferson [Mr. Wilson,] tells you that the branch of the State bank of Ohio, at Newark, was a failure, and so it was. And if every other branch of that State bank had been managed in the same way, the whole system would have been a failure. A man, by the name of A. J. Smith, took possession of that bank. He was regarded as the best financier in Ohio. It is true the Granville bank had gone down while he was connected with it, but it was believed that the failure of Benjamin Rathbun, of Buffalo, had caused the failure of that bank. It turned out afterwards, however, that Smith was in fault there. He went on in the same way with the bank at Newark. Judge Swan, and other honorable men, were overreached by him because he was backed up by honest men in Newark. But when Mr. Smith got possession of the bank, he loaned out its money to Tom, Dick and Harry. If all the rest of the branches had been conducted in the same way the State would have lost a million of dollars. If a system is rotten in part, it is a bad system to which to trust. A man may be a pretty good man, but if he has one bad leg he will not do for a foot race, where two good legs are required. However dishonest the actors may be in the system I have advocated here, it has two good legs, a good secure foundation. The gentleman from Jefferson [Mr. Wilson,] admits that his system has one defective leg, and the only way to prevent the whole body from becoming affected, was by lopping that leg off, and trust to the good leg that was left.

Mr. WILSON. I wish to say this, that I suppose it is impossible for any set of men to devise a system for banking, or any other kind of business, in which you could not find some scoundrels. The gentleman from Scott [Mr. Ells,] points to one in the person of the cashier of the Licking County Bank, A. J. Smith, who, he says, loaned the money out to Tom, Dick and Harry. But you could break down any system of banking in that way. There are objections that can be urged against every system of banking. You cannot devise any system that will be perfect. While the gentleman has found one rotten branch in the State Bank of Ohio, under the general or free banking system of Indiana, you will find that nearly all are rotten. Now I do not say that such is the necessary result of the free banking system. I believe you can frame a general banking system, so as to guard against the rottenness of the Indiana system. And I believe you can devise a State bank under the Ohio system that will be sounder than ever that was.

Men may rail against banking institutions as loud and as long as they please. But you may take these men in a community that cry out loudest and longest against banks, and it is more than probable that you will find that they have made a hundred dollars out of banks where they have lost ten. Men lose once in awhile, and they feel the loss. But they forget to take into account the many times they have made money, by having the means to use, which banks have furnished them. We can only make a system as perfect as we are able to do, and then take our chances with the rest of the community.

Mr. PARVIN. I acknowledge, Mr. Chairman, that there is great difficulty, even more difficulty, in devising a proper system of banking than in devising a system for any other kind of business that may come before us. It is for that very reason that I do not wish to establish any particular system by this constitution, but have the two systems presented to the people, and let them choose that which they may prefer.

I think no stronger argument could be adduced, to show the necessity of establishing a State banking system, than that brought forward by my friend from Scott, [Mr. Ells.] He mentions a case where a bank became rotten and corrupt through bad management, but its issues were redeemed entirely, because the branches of the bank were compelled to sustain each other. Now I wish to guard against loss by this very system, by which each branch will be bound to support and assist the others. According to the gentleman's own argument, if this system had not been in operation in Ohio great loss must have ensued to the bill-holders; whereas they lost nothing. The gentleman from Scott brought forward several objections against the system of State bank and branches advocated by the gentleman from Jefferson, (Mr. Wilson.] He supposes that if there are ten branches of a State bank, they will all combine to cheat the community. Now that is not a supposable case. I might just as well suppose that the gentleman would steal a horse, as to suppose that ten different branches of a State bank would combine to cheat the public in the way he supposes. The gentleman from Scott says they might combine to transfer their specie from one branch to the other, and in that way elude the State officers. That was fully answered by the gentleman from Jefferson.

I did not expect that the details of a system of a State bank and branches would be brought forward here. I do not wish, in this constitution, to throw too many checks about this matter, merely sufficient to guard the community, and leave the legislature to carry out the details. What kind of law they will pass I cannot tell. My idea of a State bank and branches, in which the State is not to be a stock holder, is merely to let the State have a controlling influence in the bank in such a way as to guard against any loss to the note-holders. I would have a board of control, which I suppose would have the right, certainly they should have the right, to send any of their agents at any time, wherever they suspected anything wrong in any branch, without giving any notice, to examine and see if it had the amount of specie on hand which the charter required them to keep. This would prevent them from carting the specie about from branch to branch when the examination was to be made. Suppose a board of control have the right to send one of their agents in this way, whenever they think proper to do so. This would require the same amount of specie to be kept on hand at all times, so as to be secure whenever the examination might take place.

The gentleman from Scott [Mr. Ells] says the branch bank might issue ten or twelve dollars in paper to every dollar of specie in their vaults. This might be prevented by providing that the parent bank should be the only one to issue notes. It is not intended that every branch shall have the right to issue their own notes, but that they shall be first issued by the parent bank, or the board of control, and then the proper amounts sent to the different branches for the wants of the communities in which they may be situated. This would guard against over issues and cheating.

When this is done, and a fund is set apart to meet any contingencies that may arise, if a branch fails, and everything belonging to the bank is sold, and the individual stock-holders are held responsible, I cannot see how, under any circumstances, there can be any loss to the bill-holders, for certainly all these securities cannot fail to accomplish that object.

We must look a little to the history of the past in these matters, to judge of what the future will bring forth. The light of the past must be our guide to the future. What is the history of the general banking systems of our sister States? Ask those who have held the notes of four or five of those banks for months past. They have greatly depreciated, and it is with difficulty that they are circulated for any amount. Gentlemen say that it was because some of the stock deposited as security was California stock, which had been declared illegal. That is one of the evils to which the system is liable. It is proposed here to have these stocks to be thus deposited, appraised at their average rate in the city of New York for thirty days previous to their being deposited. But we cannot tell how much they will depreciate afterwards. They would be sure to depreciate if we were to have a financial crisis in the country like those of 1837 and 1841. We cannot guard against those things. If there is nothing to derange public confidence in the credit of a bank, there would be no danger. But we must guard against other times when these financial convulsions come upon the country. These State stocks are not sufficient for that. They cannot be immediately converted into specie. A remark made by a gentleman here the other day, appears to me to have a great deal of weight in it: that those who lose money by these suspensions, are not those who have a great deal of money; but they are the laboring classes who cannot keep their money until these bonds are sold to redeem his notes. The wants of their families require them to sell their notes to a broker at a great loss, and he holds them until these stocks are sold, and then has them redeemed.

I insist upon it that a specie basis, with proper provisions to keep the specie in the banks, is the best and safest that can be adopted. My friend from Lucas, [Mr. Edwards,] says that this matter of individual liability is the greatest humbug ever started. I do not think so. But grant that such is the case for sake of argument. Just as quick as a man who has this individual liability resting upon him, sees that a bank is going to fail, he will sell out his stock to some man who is irresponsible, and that of course would be a humbug. But the provision here proposed is that the man who sells his stock shall be liable for six months after he disposes of it. That difficulty is therefore fully guarded against.

The gentleman from Scott, [Mr. Ells,] says we are paying a high rate of interest now. And why is it? Because the banks of Illinois, Nebraska and all around us, based upon these state stocks alone, are at a large discount, when compared with specie, and we must pay these high rates on account of their depreciation. Give us a good State bank and branches, properly secured so the note-holders will be safe, and we will be able to get our money at ten per cent. Now although I am strongly in favor of a State Bank system, and although I know that a large majority of my constituents are in favor of it also, I do not desire to have this Convention decide this matter so that we will have no system but the State bank system. I would give the legislature the opportunity to adopt either system they may choose. If you say here that the legislature shall grant but this free banking system, I prophesy that there will be an amendment to the constitution before many years.

Mr. HALL. I think it would be desirable for us to adopt some system that would be acceptable to the people, and which, when adopted and put into operation, would answer their expectations. I would look upon it as a calamity and a misfortune, if, in our deliberations here, we should adopt some system the people would not sanction, or which, if sanctioned by them, would be found impracticable. If there is any truth in what writers say upon this subject, it is rather a delicate question we have to settle. I am rather fearful that when we come to act upon the system we are now advocating here, it may not prove all we expect it to be.

It is the easiest matter in the world to put in the constitution, or in a law authorizing banking, provisions that will make the bill-holder ultimately safe, and secure to him in the end the payment of his notes. That is a very easy matter; and I think the provisions reported here by the committee on incorporations are abundantly adequate, so that so far as that is concerned I should be perfectly willing to go home to my constituents upon it. But there is one thing, which I think members of this Convention are overlooking; that is that that security will not of itself create a banking system for this State. We must look further than that; we must have another ingredient which is quite as essential as that, and that is to provide that these bills can at all times be convertible into gold and silver, when presented at the counter of the bank. Your banking system will not be worth a straw, if you have it so that the banks can suspend specie payment at any time. You must provide such a system that the public will have complete confidence that their bills will be redeemed. The fact that they will be ultimately secure will not be sufficient. You must provide a system that will secure the redemption of the bills at any and at all times. These two things must go together.

But it does seem to me that we may go so far, in this matter of requiring securities to be deposited, as to prevent our securing at the same time something which will enable us at all times to convert our bills into gold and silver. We may so contrive the system that nobody will engage in it. You require one hundred and twenty thousand dollars worth of state stocks—which cost the person who is to engage in the business of banking one hundred and twenty thousand dollars in money—for every one hundred thousand dollars worth of notes that he issues. Now you must have, besides this one hundred and twenty thousand dollars in stocks, at least thirty thousand dollars in specie, to give the public confidence that the bills will be redeemed when presented at the counter of the bank. You thus require a man to invest one hundred and fifty thousand dollars in specie, before he can get one hundred thousand dollars of bills in circulation. I was told not six months ago by a gentleman from St. Louis, who has been engaged in banking in St. Louis and also in Illinois, that he could take twenty thousand dollars in specie, and go into the system of private banking, and make more money than any man could by engaging in the system of state stock banking. It is true he could get his interest upon his stocks. But in private banking a man could make by the increase of interest over what the law allowed him, more than the interest upon the state stocks would amount to.

It is quite possible that while introducing a system of banking here, it may turn out as it has in other States. The trouble with these institutions is, that we do not and cannot, with this enormous outlay, have the security that must be there with a capital that can always be converted into gold and silver when needed. Where but little specie is kept in these State stock banks, there is always danger. This man told me that he would take twenty thousand dollars or thirty thousand dollars in bills to break every one of these banks. For that reason, I proposed on yesterday to strike out this seventh section, and leave the legislature free to act, aud not chain them down to one particular form in the constitution. It was from no hostility to banking that I did that. As this seventh section is now left, I shall be forced to go for a State banking system. I do believe that before this matter can be acted upon by the people, the whole State stock system of banking will be repudiated. Now, I want to go home to my constituents with a system of banking that will be agreeable to them, and can be applied to actual practice in this State.

The next thing will be to open the door to the State Banking system. Now, I am willing to have both. Let the legislature have the charge of this matter; let them combine them together or adopt either alone, as they may choose. They should not be held down with that stringency which affects them under other circumstances. You must combine security with convertibility into gold and silver, for all bills that are to be issued. If you do that, you will have a sound banking system, and not till then.

Mr. CLARKE, of Henry. Before the vote is taken upon the motion to strike out this ninth section, I wish to present some suggestions to this committee. I am more particularly led to do so, from the remarks made by the gentleman from Des Moines [Mr. Hall], the other day, in the debate upon this report. He said that he considered the report of the committee inconsistent with the position I took in defending the system of general banking, from the fact that I had inserted here in this report, a section which authorizes the legislature to charter a State bank with a specie basis.

I stated to the convention at the time this report was first taken up, that the committee had compromised their views in order to unite upon a report; but that each individual member of that committee stood perfectly free to propose such amendments to this report as he might see proper. My own views in regard to this matter are these: I disagree partially with gentlemen who occupy either side of this question, especially with those who oppose the State banking system, as being so rotten, as not to be trusted, &c. I believe that system can be made equally as safe as the other. With the same provision requiring stock securities, I can see no difference between the two systems in that particular.

But we have commenced here, as will be perceived, by reference to the first section of this article, on the principle that in this state there shall be no special privileges or immunities. Here we have resolved to agree, that hereafter the legislature shall give equal rights to all; to have no monopolies, no exclusive privileges; that none but general laws shall be passed; that all who desire may have the privilege of banking or going into a corporation of any other kind. We started off, I say upon that principle. My attachment to that principle leads me to rather incline towards the system of general banking. I think it is equally safe with the other and affords us all the circulating medium we may need. The great objection I have to this other system is, not so much the want of security to the bill-holders, as because it is a departure from the principle which we laid down in the first saction.

We must create something like a monopoly to have a State Bank; you can make nothing different out of it. Look at it: at the first setting out, we will say that there are to be twenty branches. How are they to be formed? By associations of individuals in different parts of the s'ate. They get together and you have commissioners, to settle the principles upon which you are to start. You start twenty different branches, and the stockholdere in each one of these branches knows all the rest. They are all satisfied and they start off equal. Now what are you going to do after this? Suppose that in another part of the state, there are others who want to come together, and form a branch. Upon what principle are you going to allow them to do so? Must you not get the general consent of all the other branches? If you do not, but allow all to come in who choose to associate together, and form a branch bank, then you will have this result: after these twenty branches have been established, there will be fifty more concerns started, one-half or nine-tenths of them honest, perhaps, while five are corrupt institutions, and they will force themselves upon the other twenty without their consent, and force them to stand sponsors for their frauds. We certainly do not desire to have such a state of things as that; in fact we could not if we would. No banks would ever organize under such terms.

What then shall we do? If you provide preventions against their coming in in that way, then you make these twenty branches first instituted, perfect monopolies; and no other branches can be got up, and organized without their consent, in some way obtained. That system, seems to me to be objectionable, either one way or the other.

I think we are here a pretty fair representation of the people at large. Here are some representatives afraid of the moral effect of money. Some are afraid of banks of any kind, and will not trust them at all. They are as suspicious of them in any guise as the old rat was of the cat after she had wallowed in the meal. Now others are in favor of banks, and believe them to be right in principle. Others are opposed to them on principle, but believe the necessities of the state, situated as we are, connected with other states, which have banking institutions, are such as to lead them to consent to this evil. Now I stand in the latter class. Others are in favor of a free banking system because it has operated well where they formerly lived; they like it in all its features. There is still another class who are opposed to that system because they regard it as rotten to the core. They want a state bank system because it has worked well in some other states.

And how will it be when this matter is presented to the people? You will find them divided among themselves, even as we are divided. One of the candidates for the legislature will mount his horse, and ride around, and spout his ablest in favor of a State banking system; while his opponent is stumping it around the same district, proclaiming that the State banking system is rotten and hollow, and that the free banking system is the only right one. They will then come together in the general assembly, and you will have the fight over again there, and if they do not destroy themselves like the Kilkenny cats, they may get up a compromise, as we have done, and pass a law providing for both of these systems of banks. Some now here may be in that legislature; perhaps the gentleman from Des Moines [Mr. Hall,] would be there, and he would so frame the bill as to give inducements to engage in the system he desires, and not in the other, and there would not be the same care and fairness, as though we confined them to one. There will be a great rush into State banking. Suppose there are even fifty branches provided for; they will soon be all organized. Then the other system also is put into operation, and banks are started everywhere. Will they operate as a check upon each other? Look at your check system in Indiana; it has nearly ruined every bank in the State. The brokers of Cincinnati had the control of them, and they are always fighting against each other, and never operate as a check, except as a check to each others success.

What then is the result? If you have fifty branch banks in the State, you unite the interests of the fifty banks under one institution, and all the concentrated influence, strength and power of these fifty branch banks, will be used against the other banks of the State. If this is so, you may be sure it will be reciprocated. Instead of favoring each other, and helping each other along, they will adopt the project suggested by the gentleman from Des Moines [Mr. Hall]; the State banks will take some thirty or forty thousand dollars, of the bills of the other banks, and endeavor to break them. Many of us have seen that plan carried out, and thus know how it is done. I know when the real estate security system was first started in New York; in many instances the old banks came down upon the new banks by a concert of action, drew all their specie from them, and closed them up before they had been in operation six months. Under the exciting state of public opinion some of those men, who organized these free banks, served terms in the penitentiary, for obtaining mortgages from farmers under false pretences, and depositing them as security, a thing which would never have been done, but for the failures thus forced upon them.

Now while I do not oppose the State bank system on the ground that it is not a safe system, I ask gentlemen to pause a moment before they set both systems afoot. I would prefer that we should adopt the one, or the other, and throw around whichever system we may select all the guards and checks we can. I am perfectly willing, if gentlemen wish it, to have both systems submitted to the people, and let them choose which they will have. We are all of us satisfied of this one thing; as was said the other day by the gentlemen from Dubuque, [Mr. Emerson,] the people are so anxious to have some banking system, that they will take almost any that may be presented to them, rather than have none at all. Our first great danger to be feared is over banking.

Let us not then do anything to induce or foster a banking mania. Let us not then introduce two distinct systems of banking, to act as competitors, and inspire, and keep up a mad spirit of rivalry. In this respect the State is in the condition of a man long deprived of his accustomed food, ready and sharp-set for anything—is it policy to engorge and surfeit it? Should we not rather supply the diet cautiously and sparingly? I do not want the time to come, when every one-horse town in Iowa will have its branch bank, and its two or three free banks, whose main business would be to issue bills to their full limit, and practice sharp tricks upon each other.

You may rest assured, if you place this permission in your constitution, the next legislature, which sits here after it is adopted, will make provisions for both systems of banking. Let us vote in regard to this question just as we would were we establishing these two systems in our midst to-day.

Mr. HALL. I wish it to be understood, that I agree with the gentleman from Henry [Mr. Clarke,] in his views upon the general banking system. I believe that system is preferable to the State bank system; but I shall support the other, because I believe that the proposition in relation to a general banking law is so bound down by restrictions that it will be entirely impracticable.

Mr. CLARKE, of Henry. I think the gentleman from Des Moines errs in his calculations in regard to the practicability of furnishing securities under this general banking law. If you start a bank with a capital of one hundred and fifty thousand dollars, you deposit in vault say thirty thousand dollars in specie, and deposit with the Auditor one hundred and twenty thousand dollars in State stocks, upon which you draw interest. You issue one hundred thousand dollars in bills, upon which you also receive interest. The thirty thousand dollars in specie, besides other deposits, is retained as a fund to redeem the bills when presented. You draw interest, therefore, upon two hundred and twenty thousand dollars, with only one hundred and fifty thousand dollars capital.

Mr. HALL. The one hundred and twenty thousand dollars in state stocks will only draw interest of five and six per cent. A person can take one hundred and fifty thousand dollars in gold and silver and do better than he can with interest on his state stocks.

Mr. CLARKE, of Henry. Under our present system those gentlemen who get two and three per cent. a month, would be very glad to have the system reported, and which I trust we are about to adopt, entirely defeated. Sir, I trust that one result of our inaugurating a system of banking institutions, will be to cheapen the interest upon money. If I did not think so, why most certainly I would be opposed to the incorporation of any provision for a banking system into our constitution. If a man can draw interest on two hundred and twenty thousand dollars when he has only a capital of one hundred and fifty thousand dollars, he can afford to let me have money at much less rates than he otherwise could.

Mr. HALL. No man has ever yet been so benevolent as to take his money from a profitable investment, and put it in any business where it will be less profitable. If a person can take one hundred and fifty thousand dollars and make more money with it in some other way than by investing it in state stocks for banking purposes, he will use it in that way.

Mr. CLARKE, of Henry. I have submitted this question to a banker, and he says that he can afford to go to banking under this section.

Mr. HALL. The gentleman may have made the remark but he will never do so.

Mr. HARRIS. The remark has been made in the course of this discussion, that we were supporting this system of banking to make it impracticable. I have no such intention. The majority of the people desire some kind of a banking system, and however ruinous it may prove to their interests, they have the right to demand the establishment of banks. I believe it is our duty, as representatives of the people, to secure them in their rights, as far as possible. I am in favor of establishing some kind of a banking system, and I wish to so arrange the matter that the Legislature shall have the opportunity of choosing the system best adapted for securing the bill-holder. I certainly have no intention to support anything here that is impracticable, for I profess to be sincere in my action here.

Mr. ELLS. I desire to make a few remarks upon this question. There has been a great deal said about the failure of banks in Indiana, as though it was owing to the fact of their being based upon state stocks. This is not the case. The failure in Indiana resulted in consequence of the inferior quality of the stocks deposited with the state, and not from the fact that they were state stocks. All kinds of wild cat stocks had been deposited, and when the failure took place, and the real value of the stock was ascertained, the currency of those banks was worth in the broker's offices in Cincinnati exactly what the stocks were worth in that market; thus showing that the stocks fairly represented the currency, and the currency the stocks.

The gentleman from Des Moines, [Mr. Hall,] claims that capitalists prefer private banking to banks of issue, because they can make more money by so doing. It is true that where capitalists have the entire control of the money market, and can impose their own terms upon borrowers, as they are now doing in this State, their profits are enormous. But once establish a good system of banks of issue, and these same capitalists would at once embark in the enterprise. And the rate of interest would come down on first class paper to ten per cent. per annum. There are many reasons why capitalists will engage in general banking; and not least among these is the destructability of paper money. Gentlemen may not be aware of the fact, but it is nevertheless true, that these banks that have a large and widely extended circulation, make thousands of dollars per annum by the destruction of their bills by fire and flood, and in various other ways. One fact in illustration: when the charter of the old Dayton Bank in Ohio expired, it was put up at auction, and Mr. Beckell, one of the stock-holders, paid a bonus of several thousand dollars for the profits arising from this source alone. That was a small institution; larger ones realize in proportion.

Mr. SOLOMON. I will detain the committee but a few minutes, with a remark or two, not by way of argument for or against either of these systems of banking, for it is well known that I am decidedly opposed to them both. I do not know that I have any right, having placed myself upon the record as being opposed to the issue of paper money, to engage in this controversy, which may terminate in a Kilkenny fight. It has certainly been very amusing to me to hear the criminations and recriminations indulged in by the friends of the different systems; and they have disclosed the wrong and enormity of their respective systems in such an unmistakeable light, that I feel perfectly satisfied, if this disclosure should continue on for two or three days longer, and the debate should be placed before the public, that the people would agree with me in prohibiting the establishment of either of these systems.

Let us look, for instance, at the debate which has sprung up this morning. Gentlemen have decided against the propriety of continuing the liability of stock-holders for six months after the sale and transfer of their stock. The argument of those who contend against the incorporation of such a requirement into the constitution, amounts to this, as well as I could understand it: that if you embody a provision of this kind in a bank charter, it will have a deleterious influence upon banking. What was the reason alleged? Why, gentlemen say, it will have a tendency to prevent responsible men from engaging in banking, because that class of men will not form themselves into a corporation for the purposes of banking, unless they can have the privilege of turning their backs upon that corporation at any moment they see proper. I ask you what kind of an argument is that, to come from the friends of banking? Does it not say to the world at large that the sagacious man, the man who values his property for what it is worth, will not go into banking unless he has the privilege of giving it up at any moment? And if he has such a privilege, what then is the condition of the poor bill-holder? The man who lives in a brick house, perhaps upon the corner opposite the bank, or in the immediate vicinity, can step across to the bank and make his exchange at any moment; while the laborer who lives for instance, at Glenwood, while your bank is at Iowa City, does not enjoy that advantage. He cannot afford to retain the paper which he holds, until the six months roll round, but in the meantime he has to sell it at a depreciated value and get what he can for it. So much for that disclosure in regard to that system.

I shall vote against this ninth section, from the fact that even if the legislature should determine that these two systems of banking could exist in our State, there would be a continual jealousy and prejudice existing between them, such as we have already seen manifested here in some degree, by the advocates of the two systems. If we are to have either of these systems. I should prefer the general banking system, from the fact that I believe there will be less outside pressure exerted upon the legislature, in framing laws for the establishment of this system, than there would be in the case of the other, which I consider a more exclusive system of monopoly. If banks are created under a general banking law for the State, there will be no single man, or set of men, expecting to derive peculiar privileges under it. This will be so in the very nature of the case, because you cannot frame a law of that kind so as to clothe any individual or set of individuals with privileges and immunities, which every other citizen in the State may not have. In other words, your legislature in framing that law will go to work and frame a law, the best in their wisdom for the operations of any particular bank, protecting and guarding carefully at all times the interests of the people. When they get it prepared, all they have to do to make it general is to say, that this law upon being complied with by any person or set of persons, shall confer banking privileges. These are the reasons why I prefer that system of banking to the other.

Mr. SCOTT. I did not design saying a word upon this subject, which I cannot be expected to understand very well; but I consider it my duty to this convention and to my constituents, if I have a preference between the two systems, to clearly and distinctly declare it. So far as my own observation has extended, I have been led to the firm conviction, that State banks, as they have heretofore existed, were comparatively safe; while local banks, under the general banking system, were comparatively unsafe and unsound. I think if we are to judge by the past we will all come to this conclusion, that State banks have been safe and sound, and that local banks, no matter under what general laws they may have been formed, have universally been subject to some defects, miscarriage or failure.

The gentleman from Mills [Mr. Solomon] said that he was opposed to State banks because they created a monopoly, that they gave exclusive privileges to certain individuals, which they did not give to others. So far as the practical operations of these two systems are concerned, I cannot see those points of distinctions which the gentleman sees so clearly. Under this system, we have the main bank, which may be called the State bank, or by any other name. The gentleman from Mills, the gentleman from Wapello, and the gentleman from Appanoose, by complying with the terms required by the legislature, of advancing a sufficient amount of basis in specie or stocks, can demand at the hand of the State, through the legislature, a charte for a bank, which will become a branch, and part of that State bank. They have this right then to establish a bank, and their petition is no more likely to be denied than the petition of any one else. The State bank may start five branches, and augment their branches in number as the increased demand for banking facilities may require. They may be added one after another, as I understand it, and each bank will have a distinct charter under which it may act. What is the difference between the two systems, if under both systems any man or set of men may petition the legislature for a charter, and under that charter create a bank? I cannot see any difference between the workings of the two systems in this respect; although I consider that in other respects there is a wide difference in the merits of the two systems.

I do not think, as I said at the outset, that banks chartered under the general banking system, are as safe as those established under the State bank system. I do not know but what banks chartered under the State bank system may be unsafe, but experience teaches me that they are safe.

My constituents desire and expect me to advocate the establishment of a State bank, and among them there are a great many who have lived under and experienced the workings of that system of banking. So far as my instructions have gone, they have uniformly been to do what I could to establish a State bank with branches, whose paper will be the same in every part of the State, and which we can recognise at first sight as being good. We shall then have but one bank with its branches to watch. If, under the general banking system, my friend from Mills should get up a bank in his county, and I should get up one in Clayton county, my constituents would not know whether his bank was good, and so his constituents would not know whether my bank was good. The faces of bills in distant counties would never become so familiar as the face of bills of the State bank, and they would never pass current among the farming population. This is one reason why I advocate the issue of State bank bills, that they afford an assurance to the bill-holder that they are good.

The other system, so far as it has been practiced, has proved not so safe for the community at large, from the fact that it does not give that stability and permanency to our currency that the State bank system does.

The question was then taken upon striking out the ninth section, and it was not agreed to, upon a division—ayes 8; noes 21.

Mr. EDWARDS. I move that the committee rise.

The question was taken and the motion was not agreed to, upon division; ayes 10; noes 12.

There being no other amendments to section nine, section ten was then read, as follows:

"If such a State bank be established, the branches shall be mutually responsible for each others liabilities, upon all paper credit issued as money, and the liabilities of stock-holders shall be the same as those of banks organized under a general law—all of which shall be provided for by law."

Mr. HALL. I move to amend the section so that it will read—

If such a State Bank shall be established, the branches shall be mutually responsible for each others liabilities upon all paper credit issued as money, and the liabilities of stock-holders shall be the same as those of the banks authorized under this article by general law—all of which shall be provided for by law.

Mr. WILSON. I would move to amend the section so that it would read—

If such a State Bank shall be established the branches shall be mutually responsible for each others liabilities upon all paper credit issued as money, and the liabilities of stock-holders shall be the same as those provided in section eight of this article—all of which shall be provided for by law.

The question was taken, and the amendment was agreed to.

Mr. EDWARDS. I move to strike out the latter part of the clause, "all of which shall be provided for by law."

The question was taken, and the amendment was agreed to.

Mr. TRAER. I move to strike out all after the word "money," so that the section would then read—

If such a State bank be established, the branches shall be mutually responsible for each others liabilities upon all paper credit issued as money.

I think that the clause I propose to strike out here is entirely superfluous, from the fact that we have provided security for banking in the ninth section. We have, in the first place required not only an actual specie basis, but we have required State stocks as a security, and in addition to that, we make stock-holders mutually liable. It appears to me that it is unnecessary to have any more liabilities. I do not think that this convention wish to establish a system that will act as a bar upon all banking. I think that we should stop somewhere in this matter of securities.

Mr. CLARKE, of Henry. I would suggest that section eight makes all the provision necessary for the liability of stock-holders. It reads thus:

"Every stockholder in a banking corporation or institution, shall be individually responsible and liable to its creditors, over and above the amount of stock by him or her held to an amount equal to his or her respective shares so held, for all of its liabilities; and in all cases where its stock shall be transferred, the liability of the transferer shall not cease, nor shall the liability of the transferee commence until the expiration of six months after such transfer shall have been duly recorded as provided by law."

In my opinion there is no necessity at all for the section we are now considering.

The question was then taken upon the amendment offered by Mr. Traer, and it was not agreed to, upon a division; ayes 14; noes not counted.

There being no other amendment offered to that section—

Restrictions, &c.

Section eleven was then read as follows:

"It shall be the duty of the General Assembly in case of passing either or both of the banking laws herein provided, to provide also such other restrictions, and fix such other liabilities, and adopt such other guards and checks as shall be conducive to prevent frauds on the part of banking institutions, its officers and directors, and to secure to the people of this State a safe and reliable currency."

Mr. HALL. I move to amend the section by adding the following:

"All frauds that may be committed by persons, having control or management of any bank or banks, established under this article, which shall materially affect the credit of such bank or banks, or diminish the capacity of such bank or hands to redeem their notes, on presentation, shall be punished as felony, and it shall be the duty of the General Assembly to provide by law for such punishment."

I think that such a check as I have proposed would be the best we could devise. I want to hold the penitentiary before these rogues, about whom we have heard so much to-day.

Mr. CLARKE, of Henry. I hail all such suggestions as that, and bid them welcome as an addition to the report, if they are not drawn up too strong, and do not enter too much into legislation. I would suggest to gentlemen who in their opposition to this section find ridicule more convenient than argument, that they will find the principles contained in this section embodied in the constitutions of some of the oldest States in the Union; and it is from that source I derived the idea of incorporating it into our own constitution.

The superior wisdom of the present day, perhaps, has discovered, that it is not necessary, under our present legislation, that there should be any constitutional provision prescribing what the duty of the general assembly shall be, in providing restrictions and guards for preventing frauds on the part of banking institutions. But other States have imagined that it did add some strength and force to incorporate such provisions in their constitutions. You will find provisions in the constitutions of Virginia, Connecticut, New York, Ohio, Indiana, and other States, similar to that which has been scouted at by gentlemen who pretend that it will have no effect, and is of no importance. This constitution is not to be the expression of the will of a few men here, but it is intended to express the sense of the whole community, and be a governing principle for the legislatures that may come after us. We wish it to go out to the world—by the adoption of this provision, as the sense of the people—that the legislatures that come after us, shall provide and preserve such other restrictions and guards for preventing frauds, in addition to those already provided in the constitution, as shall be deemed necessary for the protection of the people.

Mr. SCOTT. I rise to a question of order. The question is not upon striking out the eleventh section.

Mr. CLARKE, of Henry. I am advocating the adoption of the whole section, and the adoption of the amendment offered by the gentleman from Des Moines, [Mr. Hall.] I will go as far as any man in placing restrictions around banking institutions, and saying here in the constitution, that the legislature shall hereafter make these institutions as safe and reliable as possible.

Mr. EDWARDS. The adoption of an amendment as broad as that of the gentleman from Des Moines, I think, would virtually defeat the creation of any bank. Unavoidable and uncontrollable circumstances might arise where the credit of money might be depreciated, and where no suspicion of fraud could be entertained. To make a case of that kind felony would be, to my mind, ridiculous.

Mr. PALMER. I am in favor of the amendment, and I hope it will pass.

Mr. CLARKE, of Johnson. I call for a division of the question.

The CHAIRMAN. In the opinion of the chair, the question is not divisible.

Mr. GILLASPY. I am heartily in favor of the amendment, and it is decidedly the best thing that has been offered here to-day. I am satisfied that it will meet with the views of every citizen of my county. The people are honest there. We desire to have banks established among us, properly and honestly conducted, and if they are not, we want to punish them.

Mr. SKIFF. I am not only opposed to this amendment, but the section also. I am opposed to this section for the same reason that I was opposed to the fifth section, which reads:

"It shall be the duty of the general assembly to provide by law for the restraint of municipal and political corporations in regard to assessments, taxations, borrowing money, contracting debts, issuing bonds, and loaning their credit, so as to prevent, as far as possible, unnecessary burdens, and unjust taxation and frauds."

I moved to strike out that whole section, but the committee did not agree with me.

I think, that by this eleventh section—which says,

"It shall be the duty of the general assembly, in case of its passing either or both of the banking laws herein provided, to provide also such other restrictions and fix such other liabilities, and adopt such other guards and checks as shall be condusive to prevent frauds on the part of banking institutions, its officers and directors, and to secure to the people of this State a safe and reliable currency"—

We lay the foundation for two kinds of banking, which, as I look upon it, are diametrically opposed to each other. If you establish two systems of banking in this State, you will produce a confusion and clashing of interests, which will result in great detriment, in my opinion, to the best interests of the community. It is impossible that they should run smoothly and harmoniously together I do not believe that it is right for us to impose upon the legislature any such duty as is here provided in this section.

Mr. SOLOMON. I shall vote for the amendment, but not for the section. I think it is our duty to provide comfortable retreats for bankers in their declining years.

Mr. WILSON. I hope the amendment of the gentleman from Des Moines will not be adopted, I do not wish to impugn the motives of that gentleman, nor shall I do so; but I am satisfied from the line of argument the gentleman has pursued that he has proposed this amendment more by way of burlesque upon the section, than any thing else. I am prepared to vote for striking out that section, although I can appreciate the motives of the gentleman from Henry in introducing it. I believe it to be an unmeaning section, so far as its effect is concerned, and I am not in favor of incorporating into the constitution any thing, which I do not consider necessary. I am in favor of placing certain guards and checks around the banking institutions, which may be established in this State, but I do not regard this section as providing any such check. It simply directs the legislature to do certain things, but whether they will comply with the direction, we do not know, and we cannot force them to a compliance with the direction we give. I hope the section will be stricken out. I certainly think the gentleman from Des Moines might just as well, and with as much propriety, have moved to amend the section by adding to it the penal code of Iowa.

Mr. HALL. I did not offer the amendment by way of burlesque. I am sincere in believing that this amendment if adopted will prove the most salutary of any that has yet been offered. If these bankers commit these frauds, they should be made liable to prosecution, and if found guilty, sent to the penitentiary, as other people are.

Mr. TRAER. It strikes me that the adoption of such an amendment would be incorporating statutory law in the constitution. In a legislative body I might be disposed to vote for such a clause in a law chartering banks; but I cannot vote for such a provision to be incorporated in the constitution. If it will have to be a part of the constitution, we had better have all the preliminaries arranged here, the issuing of the warrant, and all the usual preparations for a trial. Such a provision as this would have no force under the constitution, if the legislature refuse to enforce and execute it. I think it will be well to leave this matter to the legislature to be acted upon hereafter. I think that there should be some distinction between statutory and constitutional law.

Mr. HALL. The gentleman is correct in one thing, that it is necessary for the legislature to carry out this provision. We cannot fix the penalty here, and for that reason it is made their duty to pass a law in accordance with this provision. Another part of this constitution, as reported, requires them to take an oath to support and sustain this constitution. Whether they would carry out the provisions of this constitution, I do not know. I want the principle established here, of affixing a penalty to the frauds, which banks are committing everywhere.

Mr. WILSON. The gentleman from Des Moines yesterday submitted a motion to strike out all of this report, from the seventh to the nineteenth section inclusive, and he argued earnestly and forcibly in support of his motion, that these sections contained too much statutory law. Now he comes in and argues in favor of incorporating provisions in the constitution, which are nearer legislative enactments and statutory law than any thing which we find in this article as reported by the committee. I suppose the gentleman has been converted since he made that motion yesterday and is in favor of legislating in the constitution.

Mr. HALL. I did make a motion of that kind but the chairman ruled me out of order. Upon reflection I withdrew it and did not renew it. The gentleman's recollection of things that transpire here must be exceedingly defective.

Mr. WINCHESTER. I move that the committee rise.

The question was taken, and the motion was not agreed to.

Mr. GILLASPY. I have no doubt the gentleman from Benton, [Mr. Traer] believes, that if he were a member of the legislature, he would be in favor of the passage of such a law as this; but there are influences exerted there which might modify his opinions in this respect. I believe this is the proper place and time to incorporate such a provision as this into the constitution, and let it stare people in the face who want to go to banking. It certainly can do no harm to pass it here, and no honest man should fear the result. My constituents are in favor of a provision of this kind, because they have been told by friends of free banking institutions and of the state banks also, that banking was a scheme by which men were going to combine and deceive the people, and that bankers would invariably steal. I am in favor of incorporating a provision in the constitution declaring that if they do steal they shall be punished for it. I hope gentlemen will vote for the proposition of the gentleman from Des Moines.

Mr. SKIFF. I would like to have it apply to farmers as well as to bankers [laughter].

Mr. TRAER. In reply to the gentleman to Wapello, I will say that it may possibly answer to have such a restriction in the county where he lives, but in our region of the state we generally suppose all men are honest until they are proved dishonest; and I must confess that I have learned for the first time this evening that bankers are any more dishonest than any other class of individuals. With regard to the reference the gentleman has made to my vote, if I should happen to be in the legislature, I wish to say in the first place that it is not very probable that I shall get into the legislature. In the next place if I should happen to get there, I am inclined to think, that I should do as I pleased, so far as these questions are concerned. There might be means brought to bear in the legislature that might have some influence with the gentleman from Wapello; but I wish to disclaim that they would have any over myself. I profess to be honest and in earnest in what I say; and I believe, if we are intending to incorporate such a provision as this in our constitution, as the gentleman from Jefferson said, we might just as well incorporate at once the whole penal code of the state. We are intending only to establish in the constitution general principles, and let the legislature carry out the details. I have the utmost respect for the gentleman from Des Moines, and I have no doubt that he offered this amendment with the best motives; but holding the opinions I do upon this subject, I cannot vote for it, and yet I must be granted the privilege of being at least considered honest.

Mr. GILLASPY. I entertain the highest opinion for the gentleman from Benton, as an honest man. I only referred to the fact that charges had come from that quarter of the convention that banks were dishonest. I noticed in the commencement of this convention that the gentleman put himself down as a banker. I wish to give the gentleman notice, that in the county I have the honor to represent, we are not issuing Nebraska money, and we never expect to issue it. I understand, that the gentleman is carrying on a branch of the Nebraska Bank, and if there has been any gentleman that has charged him with being dishonest, the charge has come from his friends and not from me. I contend that the amendment offered by the gentleman from Des Moines can do no harm, and if it would be proper and right to place such a provision in the statute book, it would be proper and right in the constitution.

Mr. TRAER. As to being engaged in the Nebraska Bank, I do not know that it would be any disgrace to me if I were. I believe that gentlemen here are generally anxious to get that kind of money. But I disclaim having any connection with it in any shape or manner. It is true that I am connected with a house that has something to do with it, but I myself, personally, have no connection with it.

Mr. GILLASPY. The explanation is entirely satisfactory.

Mr. EDWARDS. I move that the committee rise.

The question was taken and the motion was not agreed to.

Mr. CLARK, of Alamakee. I am opposed to this amendment for several reasons. The principal reason why I am opposed to it is, that it cannot be found in the constitution of any other State, and I apprehend it never will be. It is ascertaining and defining the nature and grade of crime. It is classifying and establishing the crimes which should be made a part of the penal code, and it is carrying out in detail the classes and grades of crimes which never yet entered into any part or principle of a constitution. The object of a constitution is to secure and lay down those general principles, that shall pertain to all mankind; and it was never intended that it should go into detail, so far as classifying and defining crimes and punishments, or their nature, is concerned. In other words, the constitution is designed to protect the weak against the strong, the few against the encroachments of the many, to protect the rights of the minority against the majority. It is a defensive, protective instrument, laying down general principles, which shall be guides and boundaries to legislative action, and it does not intend to supercede the necessity of a legislative body by carrying out in detail every principle which it lays down.

Now to say in our constitution that a banker who has committed fraud, by which a person may have been injured in his security, shall be deemed guilty of felony, is adopting in this constitution a principle which should properly be left to a legislative body to establish by law, and which may be repealed, altered or modified. If this new principle be incorporated into the constitution and the legislature obeys it, if a man, for instance, who is connected with a bank does anything, which could by any possibility be made to assume the appearance of fraud, and by which the bill-holder would be injured by the deception to the amount of only six cents, he would be declared guilty of felony. And yet you put other men in responsible places throughout the State, and do not purnish them with the like severity if they are guilty of deception—men, too, who may hold just as responsible positions, and whose fraudulent acts may be just as detrimental to the public interest, as the fraudulent acts of bankers.

I look upon this amendment as a measure or principle, which is intended to be hostile to banking institutions. It is offered here as a burlesque upon this principle of banking, and is not intended to throw any safeguards around the system; but rather to defeat the object of those who desire to establish a system that will subserve the best interests of the public. I look upon the amendment in this light, and I shall certainly vote against it, and I hope the Convention will reject it.

Mr. CLARKE, of Johnson. This amendment raises a very serious question, upon which I am not now prepared to vote. I should like to amend this amendment, and as it is now very late, I move that the committee rise.

The question was taken, and the motion was agreed to.

In Convention.

The PRESIDENT having resumed the chair,

The CHAIRMAN reported that the Committee of the Whole had had under consideration the subject referred to them, had made some progress therein, and asked leave to sit again.

The report was received and leave granted accordingly.

On motion,

The convention then adjourned till to-morrow morning at 9 o'clock.

WEDNESDAY, February 11, 1857.

The convention met at nine A. M., and was called to order by the President.

Prayer by the Chaplain.

The journal of yesterday was read and approved.

Petitions—Blacks giving Testimony.

Mr. PARVIN. I hold in my hand a petition, or rather a protest, signed by Henry O'Connor, and one hundred and ninety-eight others, of Muscatine. It seems that a mistaken impression has gone abroad with regard to the action of this convention. These memorialists state, that they understand that this convention is about to adopt a provision in the new constitution, excluding blacks and mulattoes from giving testimony in our courts of justice, and also excluding them from holding property, thus overturning the action of the last legislature in regard to that portion of our population. This mistaken idea originated, probably, from the fact that the amendment to the bill of rights, in relation to those subjects, moved by the gentleman from Henry, [Mr. Clarke,] was rejected by the convention. But, so far as I know, those who voted against that amendment, or the most of them at least, myself for one, expressed their unqualified approbation of the course pursued by the late legislature, in removing the disability in regard to receiving the testimony of negroes in courts of justice. The rejection of that amendment was therefore no indication that we intended to incorporate anything in our constitution to prevent blacks and mulattoes from testifying in the courts of justice in this State.

The principle embodied in that amendment of the gentleman from Henry, and in the legislation of the last general assembly, commends itself to all. I am happy to state that, upon looking over the list of names upon this petition, I find, among others, some of the oldest democrats of Muscatine; men whom I have known since I have been a resident in this State; whose heads have grown grey in the service of the democratic party, and who, to this day, endorse all the leading opinions of the democratic party, having worked and labored zealously for the election of Mr. Buchanan. I state this to show that this action of the people is not confined to the republican party. They protest against anything being done here that shall do away with the rights secured to the blacks of this State by the action of the last general assembly.

I stated here the other day that I believed this principle was so firmly fixed in the minds of the people of this State, that no party of men would dare, even if they had the power, to reinstate the disability which the late legislature removed. And if this protest be any criterion of the feelings and wishes of the people of this State, at this time, I warrant that those, who shall undertake to overthrow the legislation of the last general assembly in this respect, will find that even success will prove as fatal as the Kansas-Nebraska bill proved to the democratic party in the north. The principle of that legislation is so just and righteous, not only on account of the blacks, but also on account of the whites, that the people will never sanction the disability being again brought into force. I felt myself under obligation to make these remarks, knowing, as I do, many of those whose names I find attached to this petition.

I move that this petition be referred to the special committee upon the bill of rights.

Mr. HALL. I wish to make one remark in reply to the remarks of the gentleman from Muscatine, [Mr. Parvin,] from which the inference at least might be drawn that the democrats in this convention are in favor of shrinking from this subject in our constitution. Now there is not a democrat in this body who would be willing to have a restrictive clause in the constitution concerning the right of negroes and mulattoes to testify. It is all gammon to intimate that any democrat here wants any such restriction in the constitution.

Mr. SCOTT. Does the gentleman speak for the party?

Mr. HALL. I have said what I have said. The others are here, and can speak for themselves, and say whether I have misrepresented them. No one has proposed, or will propose, any such restriction here. They are willing to leave the constitution in that respect as they found it, and permit the legislature to act as they deem best upon this subject.

Mr. PARVIN. I did not understand fully the first part of the remarks of the gentleman from Des Moines, [Mr. Hall.] But I understood enough of the latter part of them to know the position he claims for his party upon this subject, and I am glad to hear it. I stated that it was a mistaken idea that the Convention were about to adopt any restriction of this kind. I learned yesterday, for the first time, from this protest, that such an apprehension is abroad, and for that reason I said what I did this morning. I certainly did not intend to intimate that any one here desired to place such a restriction in the Constitution. All those who spoke against the amendment of the gentleman from Henry, [Mr. Clarke,] and I think every republican who voted against it—and I do not know but some democrats—said they endorsed the action of the late General Assembly, but did not consider it necessary to incorporate this principle in the constitution. I am glad to learn that no democrat here desires to have any provision inserted in the constitution to prevent any class of persons from testifying in courts of justice.

Mr. HARRIS. It has seemed to be nothing very uncommon, during the progress of our discussions, for flings to be made, in some shape or other, at the democratic party. Now I did not come here to war upon any party. But when such threats and insinuations are thrown out, as have been by the gentleman from Muscatine, [Mr. Parvin,] I think it is at least due to members to say that we are prepared to appreciate the warnings the gentleman has given us, especially when he says if we do thus and so we will find another Kansas-Nebraska act. Now it strikes me that such threats as these are not deserving of much weight, especially after the backing down of the republicans since the late presidential election, and their abandonment of the only plank in their platform, the Topeka constitution, prohibiting blacks from entering the territory. Since the doctrine of the democratic party upon that subject has been endorsed by the American people, I can see no use in holding such a lash over us. I apprehend that there has been no abandonment by the democratic party of the principle contained in the Kansas-Nebraska act. And yet there is not a republican upon this floor who will vindicate in the constitution of Iowa, the principle contained in the Topeka constitution. I therefore see no necessity for insinuations of this character, especially since we do not provoke a war of this kind. But I undertake to say that if it is provoked we are ready to meet it any time.

The petition was then received and read.

The question being taken upon referring it to the select committee upon the bill of rights, it was agreed to.

No reports were received from standing or select committees.

Incorporations.

The Convention then resumed, in Committee of the Whole, (Mr. Bunker in the chair,) the consideration of the report of the Committee on Incorporations.

Restrictions, &c.

The question was upon the following amendment proposed by Mr. Hall on yesterday:

Add to section eleven the following:

"All frauds, that may be committed by persons having the control and management of any bank or banks, established under this article, which shall materially affect the credit of such bank or banks, shall be punished as felony, and it shall be the duty of the general assembly to provide by law for such punishment."

The question being then taken, upon a division, the amendment was adopted; ayes 12, noes 11.

Mr. CLARK, of Alamakee, moved to strike out section eleven as amended.

The question being taken, upon a division, the motion was not agreed to; ayes 12, noes 13.

No further amendment being offered to section eleven,

Preferred Creditors of Banks.

Section twelve was then read as follows:

"In case of the insolvency of any banking institution, the bill-holders shall have a preference over its other creditors."

Mr. HALL. I move to insert after the word "bill-holders" the words "and depositors," so that those two classes of creditors may be upon an equality.

Mr. SKIFF. It seems to me that the amendment of the delegate from Des Moines [Mr. Hall] will entirely destroy the object this section was intended to accomplish, which was to make a distinction between bill-holders and depositors. The depositors generally reside in the neighborhood where the bank is situated. The bill-holders are scattered all over the country, wherever the bills circulate, and consequently they are not able to secure themselves so readily as depositors can. I supposed that it was the intention of this section to give the bill-holders this advantage over the depositors. If we adopt the amendment proposed, and say that "the bill-holders and the depositors" shall have the preference, who else can be found interested in the matter? I think the committee intended to discriminate between these two classes of citizens.

Mr. WILSON. It seems to me if this amendmont is adopted, that we will destroy the whole system, so far as the committee have passed it. The committee require the depositing of one hundred and twenty dollars worth of stocks with the proper State officer for every one hundred dollars of bills issued. For what was this intended but to secure bill-holders? If we place depositors upon the same footing with the bill-holders, what will be the result? There may be deposites enough in the bank to amount to the whole circulation, and you thus reduce the basis of security to 50 or 60 cents on the dollar instead of one hundred and twenty cents, which the committee desired to provide; and cut off one half of the security intended to be afforded to the bill-holders. I am opposed to anything of that kind. Let the depositors stand upon their own footing. If they are willing to deposit and run the risk of getting their deposites back again, let them do so. But do not let them avail themselves of the security we propose to provide for the benefit of the bill-holders. If they are willing to let banks use their money by paying interest upon it, let them do so, and take their own risks. I am opposed to letting them come in and take one half of the security we provide for bill-holders.

Mr. HALL. It is a principle which I have upheld all my life, that the most sacred of obligations is that imposed upon one who is made the trustee of the property of another. And I believe if we give the bill-holder a preference over the depositor, who makes the bank a trustee, we will be doing that which will violate the first

principles of right. If I deposite my property with my landlord for safe keeping, by no act of his can he destroy my right to that property. He cannot sell it; he cannot give it away; he can do nothing with it to destroy my right to it, so strong is the law protecting me in my property. But when I deposite money in a bank, it may mingle with other money there so that I cannot identify it. But is the convention prepared to say, that in consequence of that fact, another class of creditors of a less sacred character, shall come in and take my property and divide it up among themselves, merely because it is of such a character that I cannot identify it exactly? Your statute books have always characterized as a fraud, and your code now makes it a punishable offence, should a banker do just exactly what this convention are seeking to do in this section. If I deposite my money with a man as a sacred trust, and he disposes of it in some other way, you send him to the penitentiary for that offense. Yet the Convention proposes to make just such an act as that a rightful act. Now if a man deposites his money in a bank, you cannot change the nature of his property. If the banker runs away or fails, the deposite is still the property of the depositor, the only difficulty being to identify it. If a man places money in my hands for safe-keeping, and I become bankrupt, should not he, of all others, be paid? Shall the other creditors take his money and convert it to their use, merely because he cannot clearly identify it?

Mr. SKIFF. I would ask the delegate from Des Moines, [Mr. Hall,] if he places the bill-holder and depositor upon the same footing, what preference is given; over what other class of creditors do those two classes have the preference? What other class of creditors would be left?

Mr. HALL. If there is a deficiency in the means of the bank to meet all the applications against it, the bill-holders and depositors should be the first paid. If there are no other creditors, then no harm is done any one. But I would not take all the money and other means of the bank to pay the bill-holder, and let the depositors go unpaid.

Mr. SKIFF. The delegate from Des Moines evidently considers the depositor as entitled to our first consideration; and I think he would be a little more consistent if he moved an amendment to give him the preference over the bill-holder.

Mr. ELLS. There is one reason why I shall vote against this amendment of the gentleman from Des Moines, [Mr. Hall.] I have obtained some little knowledge of the banking business in my time, and my experience has been that bankers always regard depositors as the gentleman from Des Moines would regard them, and if a bank is about to fail they always endeavor to secure the depositor, and pay no particular attention to the bill-holder. They look upon the depositor as having stronger claims to their care and regard. I would therefore leave them to the care of the banks, and allow them to settle their accounts in their own way, while we endeavor to secure the bill-holder, who is not upon the spot to take care of his own interests.

Mr. CLARK, of Alamakee. The object of providing a banking law is to accommodate the public, and to create a currency for the community at large, and all the checks and safeguards we throw around these institutions are for the benefit of the public. We require a certain amount of specie to be kept on hand by the banker to redeem his bills when presented; we require security to be given that the bill-holder may be protected against loss. In fixing these checks, the interests of the depositors never come in question.

We have provided here that one hundred and twenty dollars of United States stocks, or the stocks of interest paying States, shall be deposited for every one hundred dollars issued. That is intended to secure the bill-holder, and for no other purpose. Now if the depositor is to come in and claim to be equally entitled to the benefit of this security, no additional security is proposed for the bill-holder. Suppose that a bank issues one hundred thousand dollars in paper, and receives upon deposit one hundred thousand dollars. The security of the bill-holder as required by law is not increased thereby; no claim for him is established upon the money deposited; the banker can pay it out at any time, while the security deposited for the benefit of the bill-holder is beyond the control of the banker, and it is proposed to give the depositor an equal claim to its benefit. This amendment interferes directly with the principal means of security we propose for the bill-holder.

Now I do not agree with the gentleman from Des Moines, [Mr. Hall] in relation to the nature of the interests of a trustee in this case. Suppose there is a bank established for the purpose of affording a currency, a circulating medium for the community. It is true that an individual may deposite his money in that bank, as he may deposite it any where else he pleases. He deposites it where he has confidence. If he deposites his money in the bank, if he makes a special deposite, he has the right to draw that very money from the bank again. He does not become a creditor and the bank a debtor in that case. The bank occupies the relation of bailee to the depositor, who has a right to draw that very money or replevy it from the bank. The relation of trustee does not exist in that case. It is true the depositor would not be likely to obtain interest on his deposit, as his money would only be deposited there for safe keeping. He would have the right under that special deposite, to replevy that same money again, and it would not be used to satisfy the bill-holder even if it remained there. If the money was placed there as a general deposite, and he draws interest upon it, he becomes like any other money-lender in the state. It would be just as reasonable to say that any money-lender in the state shall have the privilege of coming in here and dividing up the security deposited for the redemption of the bills, as to say that a man who deposites his money for the purpose of drawing interest upon it shall be allowed that privilege. The depositor deposites his money at his own peril, and must rely upon the responsibility of the banker to whom he entrusts his money.

That the banks do not become the trustees of of the money, is a question that I think has been well settled. You will find a case in 19 Wendell's New York Supreme Court Reports, in which the court says that when there is a special deposite made in a bank, that bank does not become the debtor of the depositor, but simply the bailee; while the depositor is the bailor, and has the right to replevy the same identical money he has deposited. If the money is lost through the fault of the bank, the law that governs bailor and bailee applies here. It is an established doctrine, that when the bank has the right to use the money deposited, the person who loans the money—the depositor—becomes the creditor of the bank and the bank becomes the debtor. The relation of trustee is not created in either case, whether as general or special depositor of money. In the one case the relation is that of creditor and debtor, and in the other it is that of bailor and bailee. The principle of trust does not arise in either case. I am opposed to the amendment.

Mr. HARRIS. I do not know any thing about the principle upon which these things are conducted. But it seems to me that the section we are now discussing would not be worth a bundle of straw with this amendment. As I understand it there is always a set of doubtful depositors hanging around these institutions, and upon the slightest intimation of insolvency, they step in and draw all the specie before the bill-holders are aware that there is anything rotten in the concern.

Mr. MARVIN. I sincerely hope this amendment will be rejected. I have always noticed that those living in a village where one of these banks is located, if they do a heavy business, make a practice of depositing their surplus funds in the bank, while the bill-holders, who are scattered all over the country, cannot secure themselves in times of financial difficulty. In case of the depreciation or fluctuation of any of the paper circulation of the country, you will find every business man in the community, as soon as he gets ten or twenty dollars of this money, deposite it immediately, and the deposites may in some cases amount to sufficient to drain the bank of all the valuable funds in its possession.

Men are ready, when there is any doubt about any portion of the currency of the country, to deposite all they can get of it in the bank so as to make it debtor to them, so that if the bills thus deposited should become depreciated, they will have a lien upon the bank and take possession of all the available funds of the bank, and the poor man, the laboring man, the man of small means, suffers on account of the very men who, perhaps, have been the cause of breaking the bank. I cannot go for this amendment. I would rather strike out the entire section, and let each take his chance with the rest.

Nr. TRAER. I am inclined to look upon the amendment proposed by the gentleman from Des Moines, (Mr. Hall) in a somewhat different light from that in which it seems to be viewed by others here. It stikes me that, in considering this question, we should look somewhat to the security of the bank. It seems to me that the security of the bill-holder depends, to a considerable extent, upon the chances that these banks will be able to sustain themselves. In providing for the establishment of a banking system, it will be noticed that the object always in view is the security of the bill-holder. For that purpose it has been provided that certain securities shall be deposited, but no calculation has been made to secure funds on hand to redeem the bills when presented. Now my experience leads me to consider the man who, as my friend from Jones (Mr. Marvin) says, deposites every day his ten or fifteen dollars, in a bank of that kind, as the man who upholds it. For instance, suppose a bank is established here in Iowa City. The company deposite, with the Secretary of State, one hundred and twenty thousand dollars worth of stocks, and issue one hundred thousand dollars worth of bills. No provision is made here to require the company to keep specie on hand sufficient to redeem the bills they may have presented to them at any time, and they have been obliged to invest so much in stocks that they do not feel like investing more than they can in any way avoid. What then does a bank depend upon to redeem its bills as they come in? My experience is that its main dependece is the special deposites made in it, because they are generally of gold or silver, or the issues of other banks, for which gold and silver can be got at any time, and this is used to redeem its own bills when they are presented.

Now is it right and just that in case this bank fails, these special depositors, who have furnished the means for the redemption of its circulation, should be cut off, while the bill-holder is secured, though he has done nothing to support the institution, and comes in and takes that which actually belongs to the depositor? The gentleman from Jefferson, [Mr. Wilson,] says that if you allow the depositor to come in upon an equality with the bill-holder, you take away one-half of the benefit of the security deposited with the Secretary of State for the bill-holder. I do not look upon this matter in any such light at all. The fact of the matter is, that the security deposited with the State officer is not to be affected in the least. In every banking institution you will always find means on hand, either in gold and silver, or in bills upon other banks, or securities for money loaned, more than enough to pay the depositors if they have a preference over other creditors. And the securities deposited with the State officer can be used to redeem the bills of the bank.

I wish to say in this connection, that I look upon this matter of depositing stock securities with the State officer as of but secondary importance. The main thing is to keep a sufficient amount of funds on hand to redeem the bills as they come in. The fact of there being securities deposited with the State officer is not sufficient to give confidence in the bank. Let it be understood, or let the impression get abroad in the community, that a bank has not a sufficient amount of funds on hand to redeem its bills as they come in, and a run upon that bank will be the consequence. I therefore claim that it is no more than justice that the special depositors at least, the men who deposite every day in a banking institution, and thus assist in keeping up its credit, should at least be placed upon an equality with the bill-holder.

Mr. SKIFF. I would ask the gentleman from Benton, [Mr. Traer,] as a banker, what other creditors a bank has besides its depositors and its bill-holders?

Mr. TRAER. Has the gentleman never heard of a banker borrowing money upon which to carry on the banking business? The gentleman asked the question of me as a banker, and I ask the question of him as a banker. I undertake to say that there are a great many ways a bank can get into debt, besides to its depositors and its bill-holders. I do not think his question has any force in it; and if it had, it does not affect this matter at all. We found the claim of the depositor upon the fact that he is entitled to that which actually belongs to him.

I suppose a distinction may be drawn between special depositors, who place their money in the bank merely as a place for safe-keeping, and draw it out from day to day as they deposite it, and time depositors who take certificates for their deposites to draw interest after a certain time. In the one case the bank affords a place of security for the special depositor; in the other case the bank is the debtor, just the same as if it had given a note to the depositor for the amount so deposited on time.

Mr. YOUNG. It does seem to me that the adoption of the amendment of the gentleman from Des Moines, [Mr. Hall,] would destroy the entire effect of this section. As I understand it, there are but two classes of creditors of banks, bill-holders and depositors. The committee have undertaken to make a distinction between the two classes, and to give the preference to the bill-holder over the depositor, which I think is nothing but what is just and right. If I have money to deposite, and place it in bank, that is a business transaction over which I have complete control myself. But it is very different with the bill-holder. When a man is a depositor if he deposite in a bank, he is very apt to live in the immediate vicinity of the bank. But it is different with the bill-holder. When the bank issues its bills and circulates them through the country, they go into the hands of every man. And the poor man, the laboring man, who holds in his hands five, ten, or twenty dollars of these bills, is not so well able to keep thoroughly acquainted with the condition of the bank, as the depositors who live in its immediate vicinity.

The gentleman from Benton, [Mr. Traer,] speaks of special depositors. I do not know much about the terms used by bankers. But he and the gentleman from Jasper, [Mr. Skiff,] both of them bankers, differ upon this subject. They are, however, individual bankers. I hope we will be able to fix upon something different from our present system of individual banking. I do not want to injure them. But we have nothing to do with them here. We are not called upon to make any provision by which they can come in and charge thirty, forty or fifty per cent. for the money they loan, as they do now. We are to decide upon a system aside from them entirely. It is said that the men who go to our individual or private banker now and borrow money, get money that that very banker has himself borrowed and given his note for to some other banker. So it is said here. I never heard of it before, but I have no doubt such is the case. I can well understand how men, who call themselves bankers, may go east and borrow money at six or seven per cent., and come here and loan it out for thirty and fifty per cent. That, I think, is a very common thing. It has been the practice in my part of the State, and I doubt not gentlemen from other districts know about it there.

I think if the amendment proposed by the gentleman from Des Moines [Mr. Hall,] is adopted, we may just as well strike out the entire section. I have been a depositor in banks, whenever I have had an opportunity, all my life. And I would be willing to give the bill-holder a preference over me, and run my own risk as a depositor.

Mr. WILSON. As I understand it, the primary object we have in view, in providing ways and means to establish banking in this State, is to secure to the people a circulating medium of their own. That being a primary object, I wish to ask this question: is it not just and right; does not equity demand at our hands, that in the establishment of an institution for the purpose of creating a circulating medium, the securities we connect with that institution should be appropriated first to the redemption of this paper thus put into circulation? It is not our object to built up a set of institutions in this State merely to afford facilities for the depositing of money. Private banks all over the State furnish that facility now to business men. The gentleman from Benton, [Mr. Traer,] furnishes the citizens of Benton with that facility now, and the gentleman from Jasper, [Mr. Skiff,] furnishes the citizens of Newton with that facility now; and so it is throughout the State. That is all provided for now. Our business men are probably satisfied with the means of deposite, and security and safety they now enjoy.

But the people of this State are not satisfied with our circulating medium. They ask us to provide them with another. And I say, that if we provide them with that medium, the security we devise for its being rendered safe and secure, should first be appropriated to the redemption of the paper we hereby authorize to be put into circulation. That seems to me to be a good principle, and one which cannot be overthrown. The relation between a banker and a depositor is merely that of a private contract; just the same as if a man should come to me, not being a banker, and place money in my hands for safe keeping.

Mr. TRAER. With the permission of the gentleman from Jefferson (Mr. Wilson), I would say that I do not think he understood my argument exactly. My argument was this: that in making this distinction between the bill-holder and the depositor, you would simply deprive the bank that circulates these notes, of the benefit of these deposits to be used in their redemption. The gentleman has truly said that you can deposit your money with the private banker. I venture to say that if you were to put the question to every private banker in the State of Iowa, the majority of them would tell you that, individually, they would be in favor of this section, as the committee has reported it. And why? Because it would place this matter in such a condition that no man, who has money to deposit, will deposit it in these banks, where he knows he would come in second in case of any failure. He wants to be secured, by at least equal justice, and an equal chance to get his money. The result would be to drive depositors away from banks of issue to private bankers.

I say, in order to make these banks of issue secure, in order to give them every facility for redeeming their paper, in order to make the bill-holder safe, it is necessary for the banks to have these deposits. It is one of the great safeguards of banking institutions to have these deposits, so that they can redeem their paper upon presentation. And without these deposits, no bank could succeed and redeem all its notes at any time, unless it kept in its vaults at least fifty per cent. of its capital in specie. I say, therefore, this amendment is right, in order to induce special depositors to deposit their money in these institutions. If you take that away from them, you take away one half of the security they possess.

Mr. WILSON I undertake to say that a person going to a bank to make a deposite, does not take into consideration the amount of money that bank has on hand, so much as the confidence the community have in the banker. If the manager is considered a good financier, and the establishment is considered a sound one, the man will put his money there; and not because he himself is placed upon an equal footing with the bill-holders in the payment of the debts of the bank.

The provision we seek to make simply provides that the bill-holder shall be a first class creditor—a preferred creditor. Suppose that a bank uses the deposits for the redemption of its bills; in so far as the banks use them for that purpose, it leaves so much of these bonds, that have been deposited for the security of the bill-holders, a surplus for the payment of other debtors. After the bills have been redeemed by these deposits, the depositor can fall back upon the stocks which have been given by the banks for security. You simply provide that these funds placed in the hands of the State officer for the redemption of notes shall be applied at all events to that object, unless in the meantime the bank sees proper to provide other ways and means of redemption—by the use of deposites, for instance. That is all we propose—to give the bill-holder the first claim upon the security deposited by the bank.

Mr. TRAER. I would ask the gentleman from Jefferson, [Mr. Wilson] one question. Suppose there were two banking institutions in his town, one of them a bank of issue with a restriction of this kind; the other a private banking institution, known everywhere to be perfectly responsible. Now I would ask the gentleman in case he had money to deposite, in which institution would he rather deposite it; where he knew he would have an equal chance with all other creditors, or in the one where he would come in as second in settling up its affairs, should it fail?

Mr. WILSON. My deposite would depend entirely upon the confidence I had in the two banks.

Mr. CLARK, of Alamakee. There is another objection to this amendment to which I would like to refer. The object of requiring by a constitutional provision, the deposite of one hundred and twenty dollars of stocks with the proper officer of the State for every one hundred dollars of paper issued, is to put a check upon dishonest bankers, restraining them, placing it out of their power to issue any larger amount of bills than in proportion to the securities they have deposited. If the amendment proposed by the gentleman from Des Moines [Mr. Hall] is adopted, it will place in the hands of every banker the power to be dishonest. We can never frame a provision to regulate or ascertain the account between a bank and its depositors. Under this amendment the bill-holder would be entirely at the mercy of the depositor and the banker. Suppose that I am a depositor in a bank. There may be false accounts kept between me and the banker, and no man but ourselves need know it. The bank goes down, and I come in and claim that I am entitled to so much as my deposite, and that I must be put upon an equal footing with the bill-holder. No one but the banker and myself can tell whether my claim is a correct one, or a false one. In this way this amendment sweeps away the whole protection intended to be placed around the bill-holder, by requiring this deposite of stocks with the State officer. It places in the power of the bank by a system of false accounts with its depositors, to defraud its bill-holders of every dollar of that security. It opens the door to the greatest frauds, and thereby prevents us from accomplishing the very object we had in view by incorporating this section into this report, which is to control the issues of the banks and prevent the dishonest practice I have indicated.

Mr. HALL. Ever since commerce arose and prospered in the world, certain principles and practices in connection with it have grown up and obtained the force of law. These principles have been modified as we progressed, and as society changed and civilization increased. It was a principle inaugurated in common law that persons in the incipient stages of insolvency, could pay one class of creditors and refuse to pay others; have the claims of one class preferred and settled over those of the rest. This principle has been strongly condemned by the best minds and ablest jurists in England and in America. It was looked upon as immoral and wrong. Yet it became a principle of law, and has been adhered to. The world progressed; assignments became more frequent, and wrong and injustice became more powerful, until the legislature in some States, and the courts in others, overruled this unjust and wrong principle, and established the doctrine that a debtor should not make assignments to certain creditors over others, except under certain circumstances. This State passed a law some years since in which it was declared, that such an assignment should be of itself a fraud, that any assignment by which one creditor was preferred over another, should be void and treated as a fraud. We have been living under that principle some time, and I have yet to hear a man call it unjust.

In the case under consideration, here are creditors who have contributed to the fund that is ultimately to be used for the payment of the debts of the bank. Shall we say that one class of these creditors, where each have contributed equally to the funds of the bank, shall be paid fully and the other class cut off entirely? That is so palpably contradictory to natural justice, that it can hardly get a just mind to sanction it.

It is true that in the settlement of estates there is a class of preferred creditors; but they are those who secured to the person in his last sickness that attention and those comforts, which otherwise he would not have had. That is an entirely charitable provision, and submitted to as such.

As I said before, this matter of trust has always been considered the most sacred of the obligations imposed upon a human being. But it seems to me that a man forgets that he has any soul at all when he comes to talk about banks. They forget that there is anything like honesty and justice in the matter, or rather they forget honesty towards one class, while they attempt to be over-honest towards another class. They do not seem to view this question in all its bearings. If a man deposites his money in a bank for safe keeping, is he not as much entitled to be paid as the person who received the bills of the bank in circulation? I am answered that these depositors generally live close to the bank, and they can take care of themselves. Then so far as they are concerned, the amendment I have offered will have no effect. It is not for the class who are sure to take care of themselves, but for those who cannot take care of themselves, that I offer this amendment. If a bank is solvent, and able to pay its debts, this provision will be of no use. It is only when the bank proves insolvent, when its resources are not adequate to meet its liabilities to redeem its issues and its deposites, that I desire to have this provision made.

These two classes of creditors present themselves to be paid the amount due them. One class says, we had confidence in the bank, and received these bills in exchange for the property we possessed, and we ought, therefore, to be paid. The other class says, we have put actual gold and silver into this bank to be kept until we called for it, and we, therefore, ought surely to be paid. Now I ask gentlemen how, as a matter of justice, they can distinguish between these two classes, and say that the one is more meritorious than the other? I cannot see how it can be done. It seems to me that you trample upon a principle of natural justice, the very moment you undertake to make a distinction of this kind. It seems to me that it would be introducing a principle in regard to banking institutions, that could not be supported and upheld in the ordinary pursuits of life, between man and man. You cannot establish and uphold the principle that the man who has a negotiable promissory note, shall have a preference over the one who has a simple account. There was a principle of this kind at one time, but it has been long since abandoned as unjust—as grossly unjust.

Why, then, establish this favoritism? Is it by way of bribe to bill-holders to catch votes in favor of this institution? Is it by way of giving confidence to the people in these bills, by giving a fictitious security to them? Why are the means confidingly placed in the vaults of the bank, to pay off debts they were never intended to pay? Is this justice? Is this according to the character in which we would have our government presented to the world? I do not pretend to know much about the operation of this banking business. But I do pretend to know something, to be able to discriminate something, as to what is just, and right, and honest. Why should the depositor, who is as much a creditor of the bank as any one can be—why should he lose all, when anything is to be lost, and the bill holder lose nothing? Can gentlemen reconcile this thing upon any principle of right and justice? Can they give any good and sound reason for establishing this principle, to be applied to this business of banking alone?

As has been remarked by the gentleman from Benton [Mr. Traer], men will not deposite in these banks of issue, if this provision is applied to them. You will cripple these institutions, destroy their efficiency by this provision. This odious distinction will prove an injury to the very institution you profess a desire to build up. You will be doing injustice to the institution itself, as well as to the community. As the gentleman has clearly shown the bill-holder will be less secure and safe with this provision than he will be without it, for by making this distinction you destroy that principle of mutual interest which is best calculated to give confidence in any institution.

Mr. CLARKE, of Henry. I must say that I

Mr. SOLOMON. I will not detain the committee at any great length upon this question. I can appreciate fully the motives of the gentleman who offered this amendment. I appreciate the motives which appear to prompt that gentleman in his efforts to protect equally all the creditors of the favored institutions, which it seems to be the desire of the majority of the convention to inaugurate in this State. While I appreciate the justice of the gentleman's motives, I cannot support his proposition. I am glad, however, he has introduced it, from the fact that it has caused the friends of these institutions to show them up in all their deformities, and to indicate the liability to imposition to which the public are subjected from them. The gentleman's motives are correct, but his proposition will not secure his object. The difficulty with us is this, I apprehend; we provide, as a safeguard for *bona fide* holders of bills of credit, which are issued by these institutions, that certain securities shall be filed in a certain way. In making this provision, we provide that a certain amount over the amount of bills issued shall be deposited. That excess is only sufficient, I apprehend, to secure these bill-holders intact, to wind up the concern, and to pay the expenses necessarily incurred in so doing. If that be all that these securities can do, the attempt to secure other very large amounts, with the same securities, would of course fail, and work injustice to that very class, which we all desire to protect. If the gentleman will so alter his proposition, as in some way or other, I do not know how it can be brought about, to force these banks to have on deposit only such amounts of available assets, over and above their securities, as would pay off the bill-holders at any time, then I would favor his proposition.

The question was then taken on Mr. Hall's amendment, and it was rejected.

Mr. HALL moved to strike out the whole section.

The question was taken, and the motion was not agreed to.

There being no other amendments to the section—

Suspension of Specie Payments.

Section thirteen was then read as follows:

"The suspension of specie payments by banking institutions shall never be permitted or sanctioned."

Mr. TRAER. I move to strike out the words "be permitted" at the end of the first line, and insert "by law," so that the section would read,

"The suspension of specie payments by banking institutions shall never be sanctioned by law."

Mr. PALMER. I am opposed to the amendment, and I would be in favor of making the section stronger, if possible.

Mr. TRAER. I think it is uselcs to retain the words I propose to strike out. If the bills of a bank are in circulation, and if, when they are presented for redemption at the counter, they have not the specie on hand, the bank is bound to suspend. I think it is useless to have this clause in the section, unless the State will furnish the means to redeem the bills.

Mr. PALMER. I would make it a suspension, and not an absolute failure.

Mr. TRAER. The suspension of specie payment is a thing which only the bank can control. We can control the legislature by saying, that they shall not sanction it by law; and that is the only thing we can do.

The question was taken, and the amendment was not agreed to.

There being no other amendment to this section—

Term of Bank Charters.

Section fourteen was then read as follows:

Every banking corporation or institution shall cease banking, and close its business, within twenty-five years from the time of its organization or creation.

Mr. WINCHESTER. I move that this section be stricken out.

The question was taken, and the motion was not agreed to.

There being no other amendments offered to this section—

Only Banks to Issue Paper Money.

Section fifteen was then read as follows:

No bill, note, draft, check, or other evidence of debt, shall be issued for circulation as money, except by banking corporations, or institutions duly organized or created, by law.

Mr. HALL. I offer the following substitute for the section:

Except as provided for and authorized in this article, no bill, note, draft, check, or other evidence of debt, shall be issued by any person or persons, body corporate, or association of persons, in this State, which shall be intended to circulate as money, or enter into the circulating medium of this State, or any part of the State, as currency. And the General Assembly shall provide by law a penalty of fine and imprisonment for all violations of this section.

Mr. CLARKE, of Johnson. I desire to offer the following proposition, which, in fewer words, conveys the same idea, and which I will ask the gentleman from Des Moines to accept:

"Any person, or body of persons, who shall issue for circulation as money, any bill, or other evidence of debt, without the authority of law, shall be deemed guilty of felony, and punished as may be provided by law."

Mr. HALL. I will accept that in lieu of my proposition.

Mr. CLARKE, of Johnson. I have but a single word to say in favor of the proposition I have offered. The section as it now stands, is, perhaps, designed to attain the same object, but it seems to me that it does not effect it. It says that,

"No bill, note, draft, check, or other evidence

of debt shall be issued for circulation as money, except by banking corporations or institutions duly organized or created by law."

This is a mere direction, and a violation of the provisions of the section is not pronounced a crime. If we are to have a general banking, or a State Bank system, I want it distinctly understood, that if any man takes the responsibility of issuing bank paper without the authority of law, he commits a crime, and is to be punished for it. By the amendment I have offered, we declare it to be so; but as the section now stands, there is no crime attached to the offense of issuing paper without authority of law.

Mr. WILSON. I think the gentleman from Johnson [Mr. Clarke] is lost in a fog. The section is not, in my opinion, a mere direction. Suppose the gentleman from Johnson, after banking institutions had been established in this State, should issue his note, check or draft, without authority of law, for the purpose of circulating as money, and he should refuse to pay such paper upon presentation, I ask whether the party injured could go into Court and make him liable? The note is wholly void. The Constitution says, that a note, draft, or check, shall not be issued for circulation as money, except under certain prescribed regulations, and that banking institutions only shall issue this kind of paper. If the gentleman from Johnson issues any other, it will be void.

Mr. CLARKE, of Johnson. What good does it do the poor man, if the man who has committed this imposition upon him, and has reaped the fruit of his imposition, is not punished? Does it prevent others from doing it? I want to reach the man who commits the imposition.

Mr. WILSON. The gentleman virtually admits that his legal proposition is a bad one. The Legislature may provide what penalties shall be attached to the offense of issuing paper as money without the authority of law. They may provide that the person who issues the notes shall be sent to the penitentiary. I go for leaving this matter to the Legislature; and I do not think that we should establish a penal code in the Constitution.

The question was then taken on the substitute offered by Mr. Clarke, of Johnson, and it was agreed to, upon a division; Ayes, 14; noes, 12.

There being no other amendments to this section—

Submission of Banking Laws to the People.

Section sixteen was then read as follows:

"But no general banking law, or law creating a State Bank, nor shall amendments thereto, or acts in repeal thereof, take effect until the same shall have been submitted, separately, to the people, at a general or special election, as provided by law, and shall have been approved by a majority of all the voters voting for and against it."

Mr. WILSON. I move to amend the section in the second line, by striking out the words, "or acts in repeal thereof," so that it will then read—

"But no general banking law, or law creating a State Bank, nor shall amendments thereto, take effect until the same shall have been submitted, separately, to the people, at a general or special election, as provided by law, and shall have been approved by a majority of all the voters voting for and against it."

Mr. CLARKE, of Henry. I would suggest that if we give to the Assembly the power to repeal the acts under which corporations go into existence, they may do a great injury; and, therefore, some checks should be placed upon the exercise of that power. Hasty legislation may work great evil, and we should provide, therefore, the same means and method for giving effect to a repeal of any general banking law, or law creating a State Bank, that we do to the establishment of the law itself. I would require, therefore, if the Legislature should go on and repeal or amend a banking law, that the question should be submitted to the people, so that in case of unjust or hasty legislation, the corporation interested might have the opportunity of going before the people, presenting their case to them, and having a vote upon it; if the public good demanded the sacrifice, then the sacrifice should be made. I concur in the view that power over this subject ought to be given to the Legislature; but it ought to be so restricted that great injustice should not be done, at any time, to those acting under the laws.

Mr. PALMER. I think this matter is sufficiently provided for in section seventeen, in which it is provided that no repealing act upon this subject shall be passed but by a vote of two thirds of the General Assembly.

Mr. SKIFF. It seems to me that we are unnecessarily renewing the discussion upon a matter which we have already decided in Committee of the Whole, and also in Convention. In our discussion on the Bill of Rights, it will be remembered, there was a long discussion upon an amendment in relation to giving authority to the General Assembly to repeal acts which had conferred special privileges; but the Committee and the Convention refused to concur in the amendment. The amendment offered by the gentleman from Jefferson, [Mr. Wilson], it seems to me, is about the same thing. He offers an amendment, under which the Legislature might repeal a law which has been submitted to the people and approved by them. It seems to me, that after the formality and solemnity which have attended the passage of a law, if the Legislature may then repeal it, it would tend to place everything in doubt, and make everything unsettled. If the amendment now under consideration be adopted, the Legislature may undo what the people have done. If the people have acted upon this subject, I want to give them the privilege of undoing their own action, if they desire it. There is a principle of law involved in this question, which is not altogether settled. As I understand the matter, a party, who in any case acquires vested rights under a certain act of the Legislature, cannot be deprived of them by that body. If any individual, or set of individuals, obtain an act of incorporation for certain purposes, even though the law may be repealed, the rights which they have acquired under that law, will remain good. You cannot legislate them out of it. I think it would be an act of great injustice to incorporate a provision in the Constitution legislating corporations out of any rights which may be vested in them. It seems that gentlemen, however, are endeavoring to incorporate this idea into the Constitution, and I hope that those gentlemen who opposed it, when a proposition embodying the same thing was introduced as an amendment to the Bill of Rights, will now oppose its introduction here.

Mr. WILSON. The question which the gentleman from Jasper [Mr. Skiff] has argued, is not properly presented by the amendment. It will come up more properly when the seventeenth sestion, or the substitute which I intend to offer for that section, comes up for consideration. If I mistake not, the gentleman from Jasper supported the report of the Committee on "State Debts," which passed through the Committee of the Whole, and through the Convention, and was then ordered by the Convention to its engrossment and third reading. I find that we retained the power there in the hands of the Legislature to repeal laws creating State debts, if no debt shall have been contracted in pursuance thereof, notwithstanding the people may have approved them.

So far as this amendment is concerned, I have simply to say this, that I have no fears that any franchises will be taken away from any corporation, or its organization be destroyed, so long as it keeps within its legitimate sphere, and so long as it does not conflict with the interests of the community. I have no fears that the moneyed power, or the power consolidated and concentrated in these corporations, cannot take care of itself before the Legislature. I believe it has been able to do it so far in the history of the world, and it will have the ability to do it in all time to come. Corporations can guard their own rights, and they will do it. All we ask here is, that any law which the Legislature may pass, although it may be submitted to the people, may be repealable by the General Assembly. We must presume that the Legislature will act justly and honestly, and that they will not repeal an act of incorporation upon hasty and inconsiderate reflection; and we must not presume that that body is made up of scoundrels, who will rob corporations of their franchises. We are to presume that they will act faithfully to the interests of the corporations, the people and the State, and in the exercise of that faithfulness, and in the discharge of their duties, that they will not take away any of the franchises of a corporation, unless the interests of the State demand it.

But this question does not come up in its full bearings upon this amendment.

Mr. CLARKE, of Johnson. If it be the intention of the gentleman to strike out the words, "or repeal," in the next section, so as to take both from the Legislature and the people the power of repeal, I shall vote in favor of his present proposition. If the design, however, be to give to the Legislature the power to repeal all banking laws, which may be established by action of the Legislature, and by a vote of the people, I shall oppose it; as it seems to me, it brings up the question, which we discussed in the Bill of Rights, as to whether the power of repeal should be given to the General Assembly.

If the gentleman seeks to strike out these words so as to take the power of repeal from the Legislature or the people and leave the violation of charter to be decided by the courts, I shall support his proposition. I think in view of all the propositions, which are contained in this section to incorporate the power of repeal in connection with all the other provisions, would most certainly render this as anti-banking a constitution as the ingenuity of man could devise. We have provided in the first place that no man or set of men, shall issue bills for circulation, until they have deposited with the proper legal officers, state or government stocks to the amount of twenty per cent. over and above the amount of the circulation of the paper which they issue. In addition to that we have provided for individual liability, and that the branches of the state bank shall be liable for each other. Here are three or four financial checks. The people of the state have the means in their own hands, with which to redeem every dollar of circulation which any of these banks can issue. We have made the State Bank and its branches liable for the action of each other, and we have made the stockholders of these banks, whether under the State or general banking system, individually liable.

After you have provided all these checks, and provided for every possible contingency that can arise, so far as the interests of the people are affected, you propose now to say, that after this machinery is all put in operation, the legislature may, without any reason, and without any hearing, upon their own *ipse dixit*, turn round and repeal these charters, notwithstanding they have received the direct vote of the people. I am aware that in the course of this discussion gentlemen have assumed the position, that every man, who has a dollar to invest in banking institutions, and becomes a banker, is a scoundrel and thief, and we must legislate here upon that hypothesis. Now I believe that bankers, as a class, are just as honest as any other class of men; and I do not believe that they look to their interests any more than any other class of men. If we are going to legislate on that hypothesis in regard to everybody, then it seems to me that we have not only a poor opinion of the people of our state, but of human nature generally. It seems to me, that this is not the argument and position gentlemen should hold here. Banking is a legitimate class of business, and can be honestly pursued. And it is our duty and business to legislate upon it, as though we were legislating, not for rogues, but for honest men. Every man knows that frauds have been committed in horse trading, and it would be just as proper and reasonable to place the restrictions around horse-trading, which they propose here to place about banking.

By every act of mine here, and in every vote I shall give, I mean upon this subject, to look to the welfare of the bill-holders. But beyond that I am not willing to legislate here. I think that we have reserved to ourselves all the power that is necessary, over banking. If you add to the other restrictions which you have already placed in the constitution, this power of repealing charters whenever it suits the will of the legislature, you effectually prevent the establishment of solid and safe banks, as much so as if you were to say in plain English, that no banks should be established in this state. I think the experience of the country demonstrates this, that if you tinker with this subject, and introdnce the principles of individual liability, and the repeal of charters of banking institutions, whenever it shall suit the will of the legislature, you will drive out of this business men who would honestly engage in it as a legitimate business, and you will place the whole business iu the hands of sharpers, who will fleece and swindle the community. I undertake to say, if gentlemen go back to the origin of this war upon capital, and examine the history of the banking institutions of other states, they will find that the great bulk of stock, where these provisions were enforced, was in the hands of men who had no property or capital, mere men of straw; while the real stockholders were men who acted by proxy, and whose names were never known. I undertake to say that wherever these provisions existed the real owners of capital, the really moneyed men of these institutions did not allow their hands or faces to be seen. They operated through mere men of straw, so that when a crash should come, the responsibility should not fall upon them.

Although I do not profess to have any knowledge upon this subject of banking, yet in the course of twenty years, I have given this subject considerable attention; I have had something to do with this subject in another state. And I think that the effect of some of the provisions which gentlemen have introduced here, will be detrimental to the best interests of the people. I have come here to honestly and sincerely endeavor to make such a constitution as will permit the people to do what every man upon this floor concedes they should have the privilege of doing, upon this question of establishing banks. There is no question as to the object and purpose of bringing this convention together; it is conceded by all that that object was to make such a constitution as will enable the people, not the legislature, to create solvent legitimate banks. I must oppose this proposition, as I have opposed some other parts of this report, because I believe the effect of it is to disregard what I believe to be the wishes of the people in this respect.

The question was then taken upon the amendment offered by Mr. Wilson, and it was rejected.

Mr. DAY. I move to amend the section, so that it will read:

"But no general banking law, or law creating a State Bank, nor shall amendments thereto or acts in repeal thereof, take effect until the same shall have been submitted, separately, to the people at a general or special election to be held not less than three months after the passage of the law, and shall have been approved by a majority of all the voters voting for and against it."

The question was then taken upon the amendment and it was agreed to, upon a division: Ayes 14; noes 8.

Mr. JOHNSTON. I move to amend the section further, by striking out the words "for and against it," and inserting in lieu thereof "at said election," so that the section would read:

"But no general banking law or law creating a State bank, nor shall amendments thereto or acts in repeal thereof, take effect until the same shall have been submitted separately to the people, at a general or special election, to be held not less than three months after the passage of the law, and shall have been approved by a majority of all the voters voting at said election."

Mr. CLARKE, of Henry. I would suggest to the gentleman that his amendment proposes hardly a fair test. I do not know how you would find out the number of voters voting at an election, as some candidates might receive a greater number of votes than others. The question should be tested by the votes of those who vote for and against the proposition, and not by those who happen to vote upon other questions.

Mr. WILSON. If the doctrine contained in the amendment of the gentleman from Lee, [Mr. Johnston,] had been adopted, when the question of calling this Convention was voted upon, we would have never met here. Although there was a majority for the Convention of eighteen thousand of the votes cast for and against it, yet there was not a majority of all the votes cast at that election. I look upon the amendment as having the effect to cut off, to a great extent, if not entirely, the power of repeal by the people. You may get a full vote, if the legislature submit the question of general banking to the people, as that is a question in which every man voting would have an interest; but if you submit the question of repeal of some act of incorporation in which the people do not feel so much interest, you would not get a full vote. In such a case, the effect of the gentleman's amendment would be, that no act would ever be repealed under it. I hope that the amendment will not prevail, but that the section will be allowed to remain in its present shape.

Mr. JOHNSTON. My object in offering the amendment was simply this: that upon so important a question as that of voting for the incorporation of a general banking system, there should be a full expression of the voice of the people of the State. When it is known that it requires a majority of the voters of the State to create or repeal a State bank or a general banking system, we shall have a full expression of the voice of the people. I merely desire to obtain, upon so important a question as this, a full expression of the majority of the voters voting at an election, so that the election might not go by default.

The question was then taken upon the amendment offered by Mr. Johnston, and it was rejected.

There being no other amendments offered to section 16—

Repeal of Acts of Incorporation.

Section 17 was then read as follows:

"Subject to the provisions hereof, the General Assembly shall have power to amend or repeal all laws for the organization or creation of corporations, or granting of special privileges or immunities, by a vote of two-thirds of the House of Representatives, and also of the Senate; and no exclusive privilege, except as in this article provided, shall ever be granted."

Mr. ELLS. I move to strike out the words, "subject to the provisions hereof," at the beginning of the section. This amendment would remove the ambiguity which now exists in the section.

Mr. WILSON. I desire to offer the following substitute for the seventeenth section:

"The General Assembly shall have power to repeal all laws for the organization and creation of corporations; and no special or exclusive privileges shall ever be granted that may not be altered, revoked or repealed by a two-thirds vote of the House of Representatives, and also of the Senate."

I offer this substitute as an embodiment of my views upon the subject of repeal, and I do it for this reason. The committee have made a distinction, and very properly, too, between special and exclusive privileges or immunities. In this section they provide "that the General Assembly shall have power to amend or repeal all laws for the organization or creation of corporations, or granting of special privileges or immunities, by a vote of two-thirds of the House of Representatives and also of the Senate."

They further provide that no exclusive privileges shall ever be granted, except those provided for in this article; but they do not provide for the repeal of exclusive privileges. The committee, although they may have intended to cover the whole ground, have not done so; for exclusive privileges cannot be repealed under that section. I am in favor of letting this principle stand upon the broad ground of repealing every act passed by the General Assembly. There is a clause in the second section, under which exclusive privileges may spring up.

The second section as reported by the committee, is as follows:

"Corporations may sue and be sued, and their property shall be liable to taxation in the same manner as natural persons; and the liabilities, powers, privileges, and duties of stockholders in corporations may be fixed and defined by law, subject to the provisions hereof."

This section, in my opinion, leaves a door wide open, through which these exclusive privileges may spring up. I desire that the legislature shall have the power to repeal such privileges. And I may say further in support of this proposition, that I believe if this constitution goes to the people without the power of repeal embodied in it, it will drive thousands of votes from its support. There are men all over this State, who feel just as much, and perhaps more, interest in the doctrine of repeal, than do members upon this floor. This class, or at least a majority of the men comprising it, will give but a cold support to this constitution, and may vote against it, unless we retain the repealing power.

Mr. HARRIS. I do not rise to inflict a speech upon the committee. It will be recollected that I evinced some little interest in this same question when the Bill of Rights came up for consideration before the committee. I was then informed, by gentlemen all around me, that the principle contained in this section was right and proper, and that the Bill of Rights was not the proper place for it; but that it should be embodied in the article on Corporations. I hope gentlemen will come to the conclusion that this principle is just as correct, when embodied here, as it would be in the Bill of Rights.

Mr. SKIFF. I do not understand precisely what the gentleman from Jefferson, [Mr. Wilson,] means by the position he has taken upon this question. He says, if we incorporate anything in the constitution, prohibiting the legislature from repealing any act already passed, that the people will vote against it.

Mr. WILSON. The gentleman from Jasper, [Mr. Skiff,] misunderstood me. I did not refer to acts already passed. I refer to acts which may be passed under the new constitution.

Mr. SKIFF. I say that any act passed by one legislature may be repealed by a succeeding legislature.

Mr. WILSON. I wish to ask the gentleman a question. Suppose the legislature should under the new constitution charter a State bank, and it should go into operation, and there is no power retained in the constitution to repeal the charter, can a succeeding legislature repeal it?

Mr. SKIFF. I would answer the gentleman by referring him to the sixteenth section. It provides that "no general banking law, or law creating a State bank, nor shall amendments thereto, or acts in repeal thereof, take effect until the same shall have been submitted, separately, to the people, at a general or special election, to be held not less than three months after the passage of the law, and shall have been approved by a majority of all the voters for and against it."

Here is one exception where the General Assembly may repeal any law which it has passed.

This Convention will by this provision so tie up the hands of the legislature that comes immediately after us, and all succeeding legislatures, on this subject of banking, both for general banking or a State bank, that they can not pass any law whatever which can take effect, until it has been adopted by the people.

Mr. WILSON. The gentleman will find that the seventeenth section provides for laws creating every kind of corporation. It says, that subject to the provisions hereof, the General Assembly shall have power to amend or repeal all laws for the organization or creation of corporations, or granting of special privileges or immunities by a vote of two-thirds of the House of Representatives, and also of the Senate, &c.

Mr. SKIFF. I am answering the gentleman's question. He referred to a State Bank. I say that the Legislature ought not to be permitted to repeal a law creating a State Bank, after it has been submitted to the people and adopted by them, unless you require that the question of its repeal shall be submitted in the same way. That is the only way I want to have any law repealed which has been adopted by the people. If it comes in at a certain door, I want it to go out of the same door.

Mr. WILSON. I wish to refer the gentleman to one fact. Two years ago the Legislature passed a liquor law, and provided for submitting it to the people. The people passed upon the question. The last Legislature amended the law, and provided that it should go into effect if the people accepted it. There is no doubt that the Lsgislature had a right to repeal that law, nor can there be any doubt that a majority of the people desired its repeal. I would ask what necessity is there for submitting the question of the repeal to the people? When the people become tired of a law, they will make their opinions of it known through the legislature.

Mr. SKIFF. My views in relation to this matter of submitting laws to the people are these: Unless the constitution expressly grants this privilege, I do not think the legislature has any right to send a law to the people. This doctrine is held by men who possess higher legal attainments than I do.

Here we make an exception in relation to these corporations, that the legislature shall not charter any body whatever as a corporation. Why do we not go farther and say that they shall not pass a liquor law, without sending it down to the people, or that they shall not pass a law in relation to millers, and laws in relation to a thousand other acts of legislation, which they may pass? It is because we understand when a legislature has passed a bill by a majority in both houses, and it has received the signature of the Governor, it then becomes a law. If we are to submit any measures to the people for their approval before they become laws, I desire that they shall be repealed in the same way. I do not care what the law is—I am opposed to this idea of leaving everything to the people to be legislated upon.

Mr. CLARKE, of Johnson. I desire to amend the substitute by adding the following words at the end, "saving to the parties the rights acquired under such acts," so it will then read—

"The General Assembly shall hyve power to repeal all laws for the organization and creation of corporations, and no special or exclusive privileges shall ever be granted, that may not be altered, revoked or repealed by a two-thirds vote of the House of Representatives, and also of the Senate—saving to the parties the rights acquired under such acts."

Mr. WILSON, You might just as well strike out the whole of the substitute at once. If you save the rights which parties acquire under such acts, you can never repeal them in the world. The Legislature may go on and pass a general banking law, under which banks may organize, and yet if the legislature should repeal that law the rights which parties have acquired would still exist.

Mr. CLARKE, of Johnson. I offer this amendment in good faith, and for this reason: I think that we are about taking a step, which will have the effect of changing the whole character of our government. We are about to transform this government from a government of law and order to a government of mob democracy. If this power may be placed in the hands of the legislature, or the hands of the people, to destroy rights acquired under an act of the legislature, what else would we have but a government of mob democracy, and what rights have I, or any other man secured to us under the laws of this State?

If it be right to apply the doctrine here contended for in this instance, it is right to apply it in every other case. The provision in this section, gentlemen of the convention will see, applies to all special privileges. What do gentlemen mean by special privileges? They say here by this provision that where certain men form a partnership to do business under a common name, and perform ordinary acts of partnership, it is a special privilege. And yet the gentleman from Jefferson [Mr. Wilson] proposes by his substitute, after these partnerships have been formed, and after men have invested their money in them, under the sanction of law, that the rights they have acquired may be taken away from them, and that their property may be destroyed. What would follow the adoption of such a provision? Why, it would produce ruin and confusion, and it would strike at every branch of business and industry in the State. It would not affect banks alone, but every other branch of business, every corporation, every partnership, every association of men, formed for commercial, agricultural or business purposes.

I may be behind the age, and I seem to be, if the votes of this Convention upon this question are to be taken as evidence of my position. But, for one, I am too old-fogyish to sanction a doctrine like this. It seems to me that it changes the whole character of the government, makes it a government without law.

You are giving to the legislature or the people, as the case may be, the power to strike down my individual rights, and the individual rights of every man; and the legislature or the people, may, in a frenzy of passion, or under the influence of wrong impressions, and unfounded prejudices, and animated and urged on by the cries of demagogues, strike down the dearest and most cherished interests of the State. I am not willing to place in the fundamental law a power of this kind. The very object of government is to protect the people from these evils, it is not that every man shall have the right to exercise his sovereign will, independent of the rights, interest and happiness of his fellows.

The provision here proposed by the gentleman from Jefferson, would place every man upon his natural right to do just as he pleases. That is the legitimate effect of such a provision, because when by law you place the power in the hands of anybody, either in the legislature or any where else, to destroy private rights, you destroy the very end of government itself, which is to secure and protect those rights. I look upon this question as the most important one that can be presented in this convention. It comes home to every man, and it seems but a matter of justice, and propriety, and in accordance with the dictates of natural honesty, to say, if you place this power in the constitution, you will reserve to these men the power to enforce the rights which they have acquired under the sanction of law.

Mr. TRAER. I am inclined to differ with the gentleman from Johnson, [Mr. Clarke,] in his view of the operation of this clause. We know that Ohio and New York have this same principle incorporated into their constitutions, and we do not find that they have experienced there any of the evil consequences, which the gentleman has depicted, as likely to flow from its adoption here. I apprehend, that this idea of striking at the foundation of law, exists only in the imagination of the gentleman. I will say to my friend from Jefferson, if he will modify his motion, so as to leave out of his proposition the subject of banking, as that is already provided for in the sixteenth section, I will vote for it. I think it is unnecessary that we should cover that same ground again. I take the view of the gentleman from Jasper, [Mr. Skiff,] that where a law is approved by a vote of the people, it will be wrong and unnecessary to give the power to the legislature to repeal it, after having denied it to them in the sixteenth section. I hope the gentleman from Jefferson will so modify his motion as to leave out of his proposition the subject of banking; and I will then vote for it.

Mr. WILSON. My object is not to make this section harmonize with the sixteenth section, but to make the sixteenth section harmonize with this. I favor the doctrine of repeal, as provided for in the substitute I have offered. The gentleman from Johnson [Mr. Clarke,] has delivered us a good many homilies upon moral honesty. I undertake to say, that there are a good many members of this convention who will differ with the gentleman upon this question.

Mr. CLARKE, of Johnson. The gentleman has been arguing as though a person, who presented the proposition I did, was devoid of moral honesty. While I do not expressly claim that virtue for myself, I do claim it for my fellow members, who are supporting this doctrine.

Mr. WILSON. The gentleman from Johnson knows just as well as I do, that there is a distinction between the law concerning partnerships, and the law concerning corporations. He knows farther, that the law in relation to privileges has been well settled, and does not depend upon our constitution. Our statutes give the right to sue and be sued in the name of the firm, and you cannot prevent a man from entering into a partnership. We simply claim, when the legislature passes a law, which grants special privileges to a corporation, that they shall have the right to repeal it.

Mr. CLARKE, of Johnson. If an act authorizing partnerships should authorize them to use the common name, is not that a special privilege?

Mr. WILSON. Very well; suppose it is.

Mr. CLARKE, of Johnson. Is not an act authorizing a limited partnership, a special privilege?

Mr. WILSON. Very well; suppose it is.

Mr. CLARKE, of Johnson. Does not this clause reach these cases?

Mr. WILSON. Suppose there is an act authorizing a partnership to use a common name, and that act is repealed; does it destroy the partnership? No; it merely compels them to fall back upon their individual names. And an act repealing a special partnership, does not take away their privileges. You may pass a law of a different character, but they need not organize under it. And I say that if the United States, or this State, agrees to guarantee the rights of the citizens, the citizen of the State can sue the State, if that State does not secure those rights.

The gentleman undertook to contradict the position of the gentleman from Scott [Mr. Ells,] that a citizen could sue the State, under certain circumstances. He says he could not sue the State. I beg leave to refer the gentleman to the constitution of the United States, and the following provision:

"The judicial power shall extend to all cases in law and equity arising under this constitution, the laws of the United States, and treaties made, or which shall be made, under their authority," &c.

I would like to know if that does not give the citizen the right to sue the State, when the question involved affects constitutional rights?

Mr. CLARKE, of Johnson. When the gentleman gets through, I will try to teach him a little constitutional law.

Mr. WILSON. The gentleman can answer that question now.

Mr. CLARKE, of Johnson. I do not pretend, and have not assumed here, that I knew all the law known by this body, as a body, or by individual members. And when I replied to the gentleman from Scott, [Mr. Ells,] in relation to the citizens of a State suing a State, I said that the citizens of this State could not sue the State of Iowa. And I say so yet. And I say farthermore, to the gentleman from Jefferson, [Mr. Wilson,] that the highest judicial tribunal in the country, the Supreme Court of the United States, has decided under the section of the Constitution of the United States, which that gentleman has read, that even citizens of another State cannot sue this State, unless the law of this State gives them the right so to do; for the simple and plain reason that a State is sovereign, and cannot be sued without her own consent. This provision of the constitution has this application, and this force; that this State can sue the citizens of another State in the United States courts, but the citizens of another State cannot sue this State, unless there is some law authorizing it to be done. And it is a well settled principle, that a citizen of this State cannot sue the State, for the State is sovereign, and cannot be sued by its subject. I am willing to stake my reputation as a lawyer, to which the gentleman has appealed, that the construction I have put upon this section of the constitution is the well settled law of the land.

Now to come to the proposition before this body. This section provides that the general assembly may repeal all special privileges. What is my amendment? Merely to secure to parties the rights acquired under the act establishing these special privileges. That I say is but the dictate of common justice, yet gentleman complain of it. I have made no allegation here that the gentleman from Jefferson [Mr. Wilson,] was wanting in moral honesty in defending this section; nor have I intimated the same concerning other members of the convention. I want it understood that I am not in the habit of casting imputations of this kind. I suppose every member of this body acts upon his own honest convictions of duty. And while I yield to them the right to do so, I must claim a similar right for myself.

This provision reaches every special privilege that can be conferred by law; all acts of partnership; all limited partnerships, and every association of men that can be formed. Suppose that five men form a company, under the name of ——— Mill Company, for the purpose of erecting a mill. They provide, under the law, as they have a right to do, that their articles of partnership shall continue for five or ten years. When they do this they receive the sanction of law for the act. They go on in good faith, and invest their money; they buy a town lot, and commence building upon it, and they send off to obtain their machinery. But when it reaches here, and they are ready to place it in their mill, and put it into operation, the legislature passes a law repealing their partnership. What can they do? They cannot advance another step as a partnership, for the term upon which they agreed under the law has been abolished by the legislature. It is true, they may, as individuals, abandon the partnership, and in place of calling themselves the ——— Mill Company, place upon their sign John Smith, Richard Roe, Timothy Brown, and other names. But the convenience of the partnership name of the corporation is gone; and that I say is a right acquired by virtue of law, and which no legislature or vote of the people ought to take from them, unless they have violated the law under which they formed that partnership.

And so it is with a limited partnership. Suppose a man enters into a partnership in which he agrees to put into the business, say five thousand or ten thousand dollars. Under the law he can do so, and not be liable for the debts of the partnership beyond the amount of his contribution to the firm. Your Legislature repeals that law, saving to him none of his rights under it. If that partnership is in debt twenty thousand or fifty thousand dollars, he is liable to pay the whole amount, though when he was induced to invest his money in that partnership, it was upon the ground that he should be liable only to the amount of his investment. Now, has not this man acquired a special privilege under the law? And yet, under this section, it may be taken from him, and he will have no redress, though he may have done no wrong. And so you can apply this provision in detail to everything to which can be applied the term "special privilege." If this is not destroying private rights, then I do not know what provision you can devise that will do so.

I can sanction no such provision as this. Sitting here as a Constitution-maker, looking to the rights of the people, and endeavoring, through the Constitution, to protect the rights of the people, I cannot consent to place any provision in it which will, or may, strike down the rights of every man. It is not a question for us to consider whether this power will be exercised prudently and carefully. I believe, I presume, I am willing to admit, that no Legislature would do so great a wrong as this. But we are not sitting here to act upon the presumption that wrong will not be done. We are to place in this Constitution provisions that will prevent the destruction of acquired as well as natural rights. That is the object of a Constitution; and unless it becomes a fundamental law, as irrepealable as the laws of the Medes and the Persians, except in accordance with its own provisions, it will be nothing more than a statute, which may be set up and knocked down at pleasure.

I have not gone into the morality of this doctrine of repeal. I do not desire to open this subject of discussion, because I know if it is done, a great deal of time will be occupied; and hence I have endeavored, in what I have said upon this subject, both to-day, and when it was before the Convention the other day, to base my argument upon the plainest considerations that I could present—that it would endanger private rights, and operate detrimentally to the dearest interests of the people. If I chose to go into the moral bearing of this question, I could perhaps occupy an hour of the time of the Convention in giving reasons why this provision should not be adopted.

There is one consideration I will present, which strikes my mind pretty forcibly. There is a well-settled principle of law that these charters—these special acts of incorporation—these special privileges—are nothing more nor less than contracts. And yet it is proposed here that this Constitutional Convention of Iowa shall set before the people the temptation to violate contracts when they act in the aggregate. And if we allow them in the aggregate to violate contracts, what an example are we setting to them in their individual capacities! They will reason in this way: If the State can violate contracts, why may not we, individually, do so? What is the difference in the morality of the thing? I say, that if we adopt this provision, then we, as Constitution-makers, instead of elevating the standard of morality and correct business notions, would be lowering it. But I will not go into any farther discussion of this subject.

Mr. CLARK, of Alamakee. It seems to me that the argument of the gentleman from Johnson [Mr. Clarke] answers itself. He says, in the first place, that no corporate body, or even partnership, can be formed with a partnership name, without an act of the Legislature. Now, if it cannot be done without that act, then there is no natural right to do it. If his position is correct, that no body of men can form a corporation or partnership, with a partnership name, without a grant from the Legislature for that purpose. It must then be that mankind, individually, have no right to do this thing. If ten men want to form a partnership, and are obliged to go to the Legislature to obtain the privilege of doing so, then it is clearly a favor, and not a mere matter of right; and that fact is sufficient to establish the right of the Legislature to impose just such terms as it chooses upon its grant of this privilege and favor. Then, if the Legislature has the right to impose these conditions, when imposed they become a part of the grant. And I would ask what right is violated, or what contract is violated, if the Legislature repeals this grant according to the powers they have reserved to themselves?

Suppose that a number of men want to establish a banking corporation, or a turnpike company, or a railroad company. They go to the Legislature and ask the privilege to form a corporation for that purpose. The Legislature says to them, you can have that privilege, but in this grant we reserve to ourselves the right to annul your charter whenever we see fit. The men are at liberty to accede to or reject that charter, as they may deem best. If they accede to it, then do they not agree to take it upon those terms? And if they agree upon those terms, is not there an express contract that the Legislature that makes this grant shall have the power to annul it, and revoke it, whenever it sees fit to do so? Most clearly there is. We do not have this privilege as a matter of right; but we must go to the Legislature and ask of them the privilege of forming a corporation. There is no such right common to all mankind; but it must be asked as a favor of the Legislature; and in granting that favor, they have a right to impose their own terms. When these terms are imposed and accepted, then they become a part of the contract.

What, then, becomes of the sophistry of the gentleman from Johnson, [Mr. Clarke]—for it is nothing else? The gentleman gets up here and says that it is wrong, by legislative act, to take away the rights of any man. It is not proposed to take away any of his rights. He has no right to form a corporation without the consent of the Legislature. And the Legislature, in giving this consent, may reserve to itself the right to take it away whenever it sees fit to do so. The right goes no farther than the grant, with its conditions; and if it is revoked, there is no contract violated—no rights disregarded or trampled under foot.

Take the position contended for by the gentleman from Johnson, that the legislature making this law has no right to reserve to itself the privilege to amend the grant. Where will it lead us? It must inevitably lead to the conclusion that whenever a body of men obtain from a legislative body, no matter by what means, any exclusive privilege, that privilege is to last as long as time lasts, with no power in the body that granted that privilege to revoke it. I say that if the legislature should grant any privilege without conditions, good faith would require us to carry out the grant. All we seek to do is to prevent the legislature from granting any such unconditional privileges, and to lay upon them the obligation that when they grant these special privileges they shall grant them with the condition attached that the people, through their agents, reserve to themselves the right to recall that privilege or favor, whenever they see fit.

What then becomes of the sophistry of the gentleman when he appeals to this body not to adopt a principle which will lead to the violation of contracts? This is the very principle which will sustain contracts, and carry them out in good faith, for it will lead the people of this State to act in such a manner as will enable them always to carry out their contracts, and remove from them the temptation to break a contract or violate it, when they have made one which is virtually against their interests. It is for that reason that I am in favor of reserving in the constitution the right of the people, through their agents, the legislature, at all times to revoke all special grants and favors. I see no evils to flow from it, but rather good, inasmuch as the legislature will have the right to correct any evils which may have crept into these matters, in consequence of former unwise legislation.

Mr. PALMER. The subject of repealing acts granting special privileges and immunities appears to be the subject brought up by the amendment offered by the gentleman from Jefferson, [Mr. Wilson.] Now I believe the object of this article is to prevent the granting of exclusive privileges and immunities, except as may be herein provided. The last clause of the section under consideration says so in about so many words. We have passed upon a section in the bill of rights which provides about the same thing. The gentleman from Lucas, [Mr. Edwards,] offered an amendment which provided that no exclusive privileges or immunities shall ever be granted. This covers the whole ground. If we say that no exclusive privileges or immunities shall ever be granted, what necessity is there of providing how such privileges when granted shall be repealed? The section as reported by the committee, is not exactly right and will require some amendment. But the amendment of the gentleman from Jefferson, [Mr. Wilson,] and the additional amendment of the gentleman from Johnson, [Mr. Clarke,] are not only unnecessary, but inconsistent with provisions upon which we have already passed.

The substitute proposed by Mr. Wilson for section seventeen was read as follows:

"The General Assembly shall have power to repeal all laws for the organization or creation of corporations; and no special or exclusive privileges or immunities shall ever be granted, that may not be altered, revoked or amended by a two-thirds vote of the House of Representatives and also of the Senate."

The amendment proposed by Mr. Clarke of Johnson to the substitute, was to add the following clause:

"Saving to parties the rights acquired under such acts."

The question being then taken upon the amendment to the substitute, it was not agreed to, upon a division, ayes 8, noes 13.

The question then recurred upon agreeing to the substitute proposed for the section, and, being taken, upon a division, it was not agreed to, ayes 5, noes not counted.

Mr. SKIFF moved to strike out section 17.

Mr. PALMER. I move to amend the section, before the question is taken upon striking it out, in the second and third lines, by striking out the words "or granting of special privileges or immunities." The section will then read:

"Subject to the provisions hereof, the General Assembly shall have power to amend or repeal all laws for the organization or creation of corporations, by a vote of two-thirds of the House of Representatives, and also of the Senate; and no exclusive privileges exeept as in this article provided, shall ever be granted."

We have provided, in a preceding section, for the repeal of all bank charters. And as it is proposed to prohibit the granting of any other special privilenes or immunities, this part of this section is unnecessary, and I therefore move to strike it out.

Mr. CLARKE, of Henry. In regard to this amendment, I would say to the gentleman from Davis, [Mr. Palmer.] that if he will recollect the argument of the gentleman from Jefferson, [Mr. Wilson,] he will perceive that there may be exclusive privileges in religious societies, &c. And in order to prevent any difficulty in the matter, we desire to have such a provision here as will cause everybody to understand that any laws granting special privileges and immunities shall be repealable and subject to amendment.

Mr. PALMER. Does the gentleman contend that religious societies have special privileges, and are incorporated under special acts?

Mr. CLARKE, of Henry. They may be so incorporated most certainly. We have by the second section of this report exonerated all corporations, not for pecuniary profit, from paying taxes. In order to meet the objection raised by the gentleman from Jefferson, [Mr. Wilson.] I move to amend the portion of the section proposed to be stricken out by inserting after the word "special," the words "or exclusive," so that it will then read, "or granting of special or exclusive privileges or immunities." This will leave no room at all for a quibble. If the legislature charters a State bank, in doing so they are granting special and exclusive privileges, which this section will reach.

The question being then taken upon the amendment of Mr. Clarke of Henry, to insert the words "or exclusive," it was agreed to.

The question was then taken upon the motion of Mr. Palmer, to strike out the words "or granting of special or exclusive privileges or immunities," and it was not agreed to.

The question recurred upon the motion of Mr. Skiff, to strike out the seventeenth section.

Mr. WINCHESTER moved to amend the section by striking out the words, "the House of Representatives, and also of the Senate," and inserting the words "each branch of the General Assembly," so that the section would then read:

"Subject to the provisions hereof, the General Assembly shall have power to amend or repeal all laws for the organization or creation of corporations, or granting of special or exclusive privileges or immunities, by a vote of two-thirds of each branch of the General Assembly; and no exclusive privileges, except as in this article provided, shall ever be granted.

Mr. CLARKE, of Henry. That is a mere verbal amendment, I have no objection to it.

The question being then taken, the motion was agreed to.

The question was then taken upon the motion of Mr. Skiff, to strike out the section as amended, but it was not agreed to, upon a division; ayes 8; noes not counted.

There being no other amendment offered to that section—

Miscellaneous.

The next section was read as follows:

Sec. 18. No corporation shall hold any real estate hereafter acquired, for a period longer than twenty-five years, except such real estate as shall be actually occupied by such corporation in the actual exercise of its franchise, but the same shall escheat to the State for the benefit of the school fund.

No amendment being offered to this section—

The next section was read as follows:

Sec. 19. Private property shall not be taken by corporations, for their use or benefit, without compensating the owner for the actual damage resulting to him or her in the taking, and the manner thereof.

Mr. CLARK, of Alamakee. I move to strike out this nineteenth section. I have some reasons to offer why this section should be stricken out. As it is time that the committee should rise, I will move that the committee now rise, report progress and ask leave to sit again.

The question being taken upon the motion to rise, upon a division it was not agreed to, ayes 11, noes 13.

The question recurred upon the motion to strike out the nineteenth section.

Mr. CLARK, of Alamakee. I will endeavor to state to the committee some of my objections to this nineteenth section. In the first place, the eighteenth section of the bill of rights provides that private property shall not be taken for public use without just compensation. Now it has been always held that private property cannot be taken for private use even with just compensation. It can only be taken for public use, upon the principle that the public interest overrides the interest of the individual. But if this nineteenth section of the report of the committee on incorporations is adopted, private property may be taken for private uses by giving just compensation.

Mr. CLARKE, of Henry. It can be be taken only for public uses.

Mr. CLARK of Alamakee. If my friend from Henry [Mr. Clarke] is correct, that private property can only be taken for public uses, then there is no need for this nineteenth section, for all the necessary power is given under the eighteenth section of the bill of rights.

Mr. CLARKE of Henry. Does this section authorise corporations to take property at all? It merely says that the legislature shall not make a law allowing them to take private property without making just compensation to the owners of the property.

Mr. CLARK of Alamakee. I know it does not say that the corporations may take private property but it allows the legislature to pass a law giving them the right to take it. There can be no doubt that under the eighteenth section of the bill of rights private property can always be taken for public uses by compensating the owner thereof. That question has arisen over and over again, and it has been decided in several states that turnpike roads and railroads may come within the provisions of that section; that they are so far public in their nature that private property may be taken under the constitution for their construction. If that is all that gentlemen desire, then there is no need of this nineteenth section. But if it is intended to secure to banking corporations, or associations for another purpose of a private nature, the right to take private property for their use, even by compensating the owner for it, then I shall be opposed to it. I object to any constitutional provision that will compel me to sell my property, even at a fair compensation, without my consent. I may have secured a location for business, a homestead, a dwelling place, to which, for many reasons, I may feel peculiarly attached, and with which I could not be induced for any pecuniary consideration to part; I have a right to those attachments, and to refuse any man's money for that property. There is but one exception to that rule, and that is when the public good requires it, when the rights of the community, or the interests of the community demand that sacrifice at my hands. That is the only exception to the rule that I have the right to set my own price upon my property, and no man has the right to make me sell it without my consent. This nineteenth section reads:

"Private property shall not be taken by coporations for their use or benefit, without compensating the owner for the actual damage resulting to him or her in the taking and the manner thereof."

I do not understand what the last part of this section means: "And the manner thereof." It is evidently intended to mean, and it will be so construed, when you come to take it in connection with the eighteenth section of the bill of rights, to confer upon private corporations the right to take private property for private uses by compensating the owner. There is no necessity for this section without this construction, which will be sure to be put upon it if it is put into the constitution.

What are private corporations? What does Chancellor Kent say upon that subject? I will read from Kent's Commentaries, second Volume, 275, as follows:

"Public corporations are such as are created by the government for political purposes, as counties, cities, towns, and villages; they are invested with subordinate legislative powers, to be exercised for local purposes connected with the public good, and such powers are subject to the control of the legislature of the state. They may also be empowered to take or hold private property for municipal uses, and such property is invested with the security of other private rights. So, corporate franchises attached to public corporations are legal estates coupled with an interest, and are protected as private property. If the foundation be private, the corporation is private, however extensive the uses may be to which it is devoted by the founder, or by the nature of the institution. A bank, created by the government, for its own uses, and where the stock is exclusively owned by the government, is a public corporation. So, a hospital created and endowed by the government, for general purposes, is a public, and not a private charity. But a bank, whose stock is owned by private persons is a private corporation, though its objects and operations partake of a public nature, and though the government may have become a partner in the association by sharing with the corporations in the stock. (*a*)

(*a*) Marshall, Ch. J., U. S. Bank v. Planters' Bank, 9 Wheaton, 907. It has even been held, that a state bank may be considered a private corporation, though owned entirely by the state. Bank of South Carolina v. Gibbs, 3 McCord's Rep. 377.

The same thing may be said of insurance, canal, bridge, and turnpike companies. The uses may, in a certain sense, be called public, but the corporators are private, equally as if the franchises were vested in a single person. A hospital, founded by a private benefactor, is, in point of law, a private corporation, though dedicated by its charter to general charity. A college, founded and endowed in the same manner, is a private charity, though, from its general and beneficent objects, it may acquire the character of a public institution. If the uses of an eleemosynary corporation be for general charity, yet such purposes will not of themselves constitute it a public corporation. Every charity, which is extensive in its objects, may, in a certain sense, be called a public charity. Nor will a mere act of incorporation change a charity from a private to be a public one."

Now if this nineteenth section is adopted, if any private corporation desires my property for its exclusive benefit, it has the right to compel me to sell it for whatever disinterested men may say it is worth. I do not think this provision is right or should be retained in the constitution. If the construction I have placed upon it, be not the one that will be put upon it, then there is no necessity for it, for the eighteenth section of the Bill of Rights provides for all cases of public necessity. For these reasons, I move, therefore, that this section be stricken out.

The question being taken, the motion to strike out the nineteenth section was agreed to.

The next section, being the last, was then read, as follows:

Sec. 20. The word corporation, as used in this article, may be construed to mean any individual, association, or company, having or enjoying rights and privileges through provisions of law not possessed by every individual or partnership.

No amendment was offered to that section.

Mr. CLARKE, of Johnson. I have an additional section which I hope will meet with the approval of this committee. It is as follows:

"The State shall be responsible to the proper parties for the stocks deposited with the proper officer, as the basis of paper intended to circulate as money."

If the State receives this stock as trustee for the redemption of bills, there is no reason why the state should not be held responsible, if those stocks are lost through the misconduct of its officers, or otherwise.

Mr. PALMER. I move to amed by inserting after the word "stocks," the words "and other securities."

Mr. CLARKE, of Johnson. I will accept that amendment. What I desire is to have the State held responsible for those stocks which it may receive. If they decrease in value in the hands of the State, the State should not be held responsible for that.

Mr. HALL. I would suggest to the gentleman from Johnson to modify his proposition that the State shall be held responsible for the safe keeping and proper disposition of these stocks and other securities.

Mr. CLARKE, of Johnson. That is what I desire.

Mr. CLARKE, of Henry. I must say that I consider this proposed section as entirely unnecessary. I suppose that the State, having directed that the deposite should be made, and having indicated the officer in whose hands the deposite must be placed, becomes responsible and liable without any special constitutional provision to that effect. I do not think you will find such a provision as the gentleman from Johnson [Mr. Clarke] proposes, in the constitution of any State, even where they have provisions requiring the depositing of these stocks for security for banking.

This section can do no harm, but it will only be rendering doubly certain what I consider to be certain already.

Mr. CLALKE, of Johnson. I will withdraw my amendment now, and offer it when we are in Convention.

Mr. SKIFF moved that the committee rise, report back the report of the committee on incorporations as amended, and ask to be discharged from its further consideration.

The question being taken the motion was agreed to.

In Convention.

The PRESIDENT having resumed the chair—

The CHAIRMAN of the Committee of the Whole reported that the committee had had under consideration the report of the Committee on Incorporations, which was referred to them, had made sundry amendments thereto, and asked to be discharged from the further consideration of the same.

The report was received, and the Committee of the whole discharged accordingly.

On motion of Mr. HARRIS,

The CONVENTION then took a recess until 2 o'clock, P. M.

EVENING SESSION.

Two o'clock, P. M.

The CONVENTION met at two o'clock, and was called to order by the President.

Incorporations.

The PRESIDENT. The first busines in order will be the amendments reported by the Committee of the Whole to the report of the Committee on Incorporations.

The first amendment was to insert after the word "herein," the word "otherwise," so that the first section will read:

"No corporation shall be created by special law; but the general assembly shall provide by general laws, for the organization of all corporations hereafter to be created, except as herein otherwise provided."

The question was taken, and the amendment was concurred in.

The second amendment was to strike out in the first line of section two the word "their" and insert "the" in its place; aud to insert, also, between the words "property" and "shall" the words "of all corporations for pecuniary profit," so that it will read:

"Corporations may sue and be sued, and the property of all corporations for pecuniary profit shall be liable to taxation in the same manner as natural persons; and the liabilities, powers, privileges, and duties of stockholders in corporations may be fixed and defined by law, subject to the provisions hereof."

The question was taken, and the amendment was concurred in.

City and County Indebtedness.

The third amendment was to strike out of section four the following:

"Nor in any other corporation or corporations to an amount exceeding at one time, two hundred thousand dollars; nor shall the bonds or other evidences of indebtedness of any municipal or political corporation be issued or granted or its credit loaned, directly or indirectly, or pledged as security, to an amount in the aggregate exceeding two hundred thousand dollars at any one time;" so that the section would then read:

"No political or municipal corporation shall become a stockholder in any banking corporation, directly or indirectly."

Mr. SKIFF. I would propose, if it be in order, the following amendment to that part of the section which is proposed to be stricken out:

After the word "dollars," where it first occurs, to insert the words "provided that the same does not exceed five per cent. upon the taxable property of such corporation, as shown by the last preceding assessment," so that the section will then read:

"No political or municipal corporation shall become a stockholder in any banking corporation, directly or indirectly; nor in any other corporation or corporations, to an amount exceeding at one time two hundred thousand dollars; provided that the same does not exceed five per cent. upon the taxable property of such corporation, as shown by the last preceding assessment."

Mr. CLARKE, of Johnson. I would suggest to the gentleman from Jasper [Mr. Skiff] that it would be better for the Convention to take the vote first upon striking out, and if the amendment to strike out is agreed to, the gentleman can then offer his amendment by way of addition to the section as it will then stand.

Mr. HARRIS. It seems to me that it would be better to vote first upon the amendment offered by the gentleman from Jasper.

Mr. CLARKE, of Johnson. I am not particular in what manner we dispose of the question. I think we could vote more understandingly by taking up the amendments of the committee of the whole in their regular order, than by proposing to insert in connection with the question of striking out.

Mr. JOHNSTON. I presume the proper way will be to make the section perfect before taking the question upon striking out any part of it.

Mr. TRAER. I desire to ask the chair if the convention concur with the committee in striking out, whether an amendment will then be in order?

The PRESIDENT. An amendment that embraces different matter from that stricken out, would be in order.

Mr. EDWARDS. I would inquire if the question will not be first upon agreeing to the amendment made in committee of the whole, before any amendment can be made?

The PRESIDENT. The chair is of the opinion that an amendment made by the committee of the whole is susceptible to amendment by the convention, before the vote is taken upon agreeing to it.

Mr. CLARKE, of Henry. Do I understand that it is in order to offer amendments to this section now?

The PRESIDENT. The chair is of opinion that it is in order to offer amendments to this section, before the question is taken upon striking out.

Mr. SKIFF. I propose as an amendment to this section, the amendment which has already been read at the Secretary's desk.

I will detain the convention but a few minutes in explanation of the amendment I have offered. I wish to have this Convention recognise, in some way, the right of counties and cities in this State to take stock in railroad corporations. I think if the amendment made in committee of the whole should be concurred in, even that will recognise that right; but I want some restriction upon it, so that a new county may not subscribe as much stock as a large and wealthy county. The county of Lee, for instance, has about as heavy an assessment as any county in the State. I understand that some of the extreme northern counties have voted four hundred thousand dollars, when there are but two or three hundred voters in the county, and comparatively but a small amount of property there. I wish some restriction placed upon the counties in this respect. Some gentlemen have proposed, that we make the restriction ten per cent. upon the taxable property of the county; but I think five per cent. is sufficient. If the taxable property of Lee county amounts to three million of dollars, five per cent assessment would give one hundred and fifty thousand dollars—an amount large enough. If its taxable property amounts to four millions dollars, an assessment of five per cent. would realize two hundred thousand dollars. I would not have the assessment, no matter how large the amount of taxable property might be, exceed two hundred thousand dollars. I would prefer limiting it to one hundred thousand dollars.

I hope that some restriction of this kind will

prevail, and that the amendment of the Committee of the Whole, to strike out a part of this section, will not be concurred in.

Mr. GILLASPY. I am not willing to undertake to judge of the amount of stock that the several counties of this State should be allowed to hold; neither am I prepared to name the amount of stock my county would desire to take. We have already voted, as I have said before, one hundred thousand dollars to the Missouri and Burlington Railroad. The Keokuk and Fort Des Moines Railroad is to run through that county also, and in all probability the people may desire to vote one hundred thousand dollars to that road also. There is a strong desire to run the Northern Missouri Railroad to the town where I reside, and it may be that the people will desire to take stock in that road also. I am not prepared to say whether they will or not. I desire to give the people of my county the privilege of taking stock in these roads, if they desire so to do. I intend myself to vote against any proposition that comes up here restricting counties at all, in this matter, because I am not prepared to say what my county desires in this respect. This question was not mooted at all during the canvass there. The county I represent here occupies a very peculiar position, and the people there may or may not desire to vote stock in these various contemplated railroads. Not knowing what their desires may be, I am not disposed to close the doors against them. After we have talked so much about leaving all questions to the people—and it seems to be the prevailing opinion throughout the State, and in the Legislature, and everywhere else, that everything should be submitted to "the dear people,"—it does not seem in very good taste for gentlemen, at this hour, to undertake to say that they can judge what amount of taxation the people in the northern, southern, and western counties can bear. I, for one, am perfectly willing that Johnson county shall vote a million of dollars, if she desires; and I want Wapello and other counties to decide this question for themselves. I am satisfied, that my people at home feel themselves fully competent to decide for themselves; and as far as my vote shall aid them, they shall be allowed to exercise that privilege.

Mr. WILSON. I wish to make a correction here in relation to the question of constitutional law between myself and the gentleman from Johnson, [Mr. Clarke.] I see, by comparing the section of the Constitution, as printed in the code, and the section as printed in Story's Commentaries, that I was led into a misapprehension of the meaning of that section. I have since compared it with the decisions upon the section, and find that an action for the recovery of a claim cannot be brought directly against a State, without the interposition of a nominal party. The punctuation of the section, as printed in the code, is erroneous; hence the mistake made by me.

I wish to submit a few facts in relation to the proposition presented by the gentleman from Jasper, [Mr. Skiff.]

I have made an estimate of the amount of stock that can be raised in the tier of counties along the line of the Burlington and Missouri River Railroad, on the five per cent. basis, and find it to be as follows:

Counties.	*Am't of taxable property for 1856.*	*Am't of stock borrowed on five per cent.*
Des Moines........	$7,452,842 33	$372,642 11
Henry..............	3,912,217 00	195,610 85
Jefferson...........	2,008,767 00	100,438 45
Wapello............	2,682,813 00	134,140 65
Monroe............	1,742,671 00	87,133 55
Lucas..............	1,362,224 00	68,111 20
Clark...............	1,232,159 00	61,607 95
Union..............	494,657 00	24,732 85
Adams.............	569,222 25	28,461 11
Montgomery......	342,253 00	17,112 65
Mills................	631,165 00	31,558 25
Total.........	$22,430,990 58	$1,121,172 62

This table shows the amount of stock that the counties along the line of said road may take, under the operation of the proposition submitted by the gentleman from Jasper, [Mr. Skiff.] According to statements made by the chief engineer of the company, it will cost about ten thousand dollars per mile to prepare the road ready for the iron. This will give, in round numbers, two million seven hundred and fifty thousand dollars as the cost of preparing the road for the reception of the iron, from the Mississippi to the Missouri river. By this estimate, we discover that the stock which the counties may take, will fall short of the cost above given, one million six hundred and twenty-eight thousand eight hundred and twenty-seven dollars. But, notwithstanding this, the road can be built, although the counties may be restricted to five per cent. in making their subscriptions, as will appear by the following table:

Amount of county stock..............	$1,121,172 62
Probable value of land granted to the company..........................	1,250,000 00
Private stock now subscribed.......	150,000 00
Excess of stock taken by Mills county over the amount authorized by the five per cent. basis..................................	218,441 00
Total..........................	$2,739,614 62

In this table the land granted to the company is set down at two hundred and fifty thousand acres, and is valued at five dollars per acre. These figures lead me to the conclusion that, under the operation of the proposition of the gentleman from Jasper, [Mr. Skiff], the company referred to can command sufficient means to prepare the road for the iron. After the road is thus prepared, it is in a condition for first class mortgages, which are raised for the purpose of procuring the necessary iron. The iron being put down, the road is then in condition for second class mortgages, for the purpose of procuring rolling stock, the erection of the necessary buildings, &c.

If my estimates in relation to the land, or private stock, or any thing else, are above the real figures, the increased amount of the tax assessments in the various counties, before the vote could be taken on propositions to subscribe stock, will make up for the deficit. We find then that we have a sufficient amount at the rate of five per cent. to prepare the road for first class mortgages. That being the case, the amendment offered meets with my approval. I believe, if you take any tier of counties upon the line of any road now in prospect, that five per cent., together with their other resources, will be sufficient to prepare the road for first class mortgages.

This question of the right of counties to take stock in railroads, I know, is in a peculiar condition as it now stands. The gentleman from Johnson [Mr. Clarke,] thinks it a doubtful question, whether the Supreme Court will sustain the subscriptions. If they should decide against such right, it would compel the counties to repudiate. They will either have to do this, or we will have to recognize their right to vote such subscriptions. I do not like the idea of repudiation, neither do I like the idea of counties getting into debt. If it were a new question, and if there were no roads involved, I would not hesitate to say, that counties should be prohibited from taking stock. But it is no new question; and if we leave it in a doubtful shape, our counties may be compelled to go into repudiation. I do not believe that the people of the counties are in favor of repudiation, and for these reasons I am inclined to support the amendment offered by the gentleman from Jasper, [Mr. Skiff.]

Mr. CLARKE, of Johnson. I would not occupy the time of the convention in saying anything upon this subject, if I did not regard this question as involving the whole subject of the construction of internal improvements. I am opposed to the amendment of the gentleman from Jasper, for the reason that ten years hence, the restriction he has proposed may work great injury to the development of our resources, although it may be perfectly proper at this particular period in the history of the State. My own county is peculiarly situated in relation to this subject. It is true, we have one railroad in operation, to which the county has subscribed fifty thousand dollars, and the city fifty thousand dollars, in addition to the individual subscriptions. There are two other roads contemplated to be made through this place, in both of which the people of the city and of the county feel a deep interest. I do not know that they want to subscribe stock equal to this limit of five per cent. upon the value of the assessed property. But I am not willing here to determine this question, because there is another forum that can determine it, and if they determine it wrong, we can reverse its decision. Even admitting that this assessment of five per cent., upon the taxable property of a county, would be large enough to supply the wants of this county at present, ten years hence there may be a dozen railroads running through this place. This may be a railroad centre for the country around us, as Chicago is for the country around that city; and the people of our county may want to subscribe stock in all of these railroads. If so, she would be confined by the adoption of this amendment to a certain limited amount, which might fall far below the amount that she would have the power and ability to subscribe. I concede that there ought to be a limitation in this respect, but it ought to be placed in the hands of that power that can enlarge or diminish it, as the emergencies of the time may require.

If the proposition now before the Convention is not adopted, I shall offer a substitute which recognizes the right of a county to take stock, but leaves the amount which each county may take, and the mode and manner of taking it, to the legislature. I think that such an amendment as that will meet the views of the gentleman from Wapello, [Mr. Gillaspy.] The reason why we should recognize this right is just this, that the right of counties now to take stock is doubtful, to say the least of it. If the Supreme Court, in the cases which are now pending, should decide that this right does not exist, as the gentleman from Jefferson properly remarks, the counties are not in a position to save themselves from the reproach of repudiation; but if you recognize this right in the Constitution, it is then firmly established, and counties may go on and vote this stock to these companies. By this course, you save the stain of repudiation, and even the holders of the present bonds of the counties, if they should be declared illegal, could rely upon the intelligence and honesty of the people to make them valid and legal, and the result would be, that they would not depreciate in value.

I cannot support the restriction proposed, because I do not think it is proper to place it in the Constitution, and because, if it should be found too large or too small, it cannot be changed without an amendment of the Constitution. I think the safer plan would be to recognize here the right of placing such a restriction upon counties, but to leave the limit to the legislature. With this view of the subject, I shall vote against the amendment of the gentleman from Jasper, and shall, at the proper time, offer another amendment, which shall embody the views I have here presented.

Mr. PETERS. I was prepared, before the explanation of the gentleman from Jefferson, [Mr. Wilson,] to vote for the amendment of the gentleman from Jasper, [Mr. Skiff.] I was somewhat surprised at the magnanimity which the gentleman from Jefferson evinced, when he was explaining the effects of the limitation proposed. He takes into consideration only four roads in the State of Iowa, and he seems to think that these are the only ones that should be aided and assisted by means of county subscriptions. He goes on very carefully, to estimate the amount of land of which these roads have been the recipients, by grants from Congress, and then takes the comparative wealth of the counties through which they run, as a data from which to form a proper estimate of the amount of stock which other counties in the State should be allowed to subscribe. I apprehend, that there may be other roads in the State, in which the people may wish to take stock, and which are just as necessary as those roads which have already received assistance from the General Government.

It is urged, as a reason for placing the restrictions upon the counties, that the newer counties have but few inhabitants. Yet somebody is paying taxes upon the lands of these counties. The taxes are paid from some source. As far as I am individually concerned, I should favor the proposition of the gentleman from Johnson, [Mr. Clarke,] to allow the legislature to regulate this matter of limiting the amount of stock which counties shall take.

Mr. CLARKE, of Henry. We should have a clear and distinct understanding of the question now presented, before voting upon it. As far as I am concerned, I am in favor of either imposing some restriction, or placing in the Constitution a clause, that shall forever prohibit municipal corporations from becoming stockholders in other corporations. There are many others in this State who occupy this same position. We all of us see and feel that the power which corporations may exert for evil is very great, and we have expressed our fears lest it may prove an overwhelming one. While we have it in our power to check this evil, are we to leave the matter just as we find it? There have certainly been more speeches made on this floor upon this subject than upon any other which has come before us. There has been a more universal expression of opinion against the principle of counties and cities taking stock, than upon any other proposition that has been presented to this body. The question is, do members mean to place any constitutional restriction around these institutions? If they do not, then I make war against the whole thing from the beginning.

Now the proposition made by the gentleman from Jasper, [Mr. Skiff,] it seems to me, is one that should meet with the approval of a large majority of the Convention. If gentlemen are not prepared to go to the full extent, and preclude counties entirely from becoming stockholders in these corporations, they should, at least, meet those half way, who are in favor of allowing them to become stockholders, and say that they are willing to compromise this matter and establish some sum, one hundred thousand, two hundred thousand,or five hundred thousand dollars, and say, that beyond that point they shall not go. It is evident that there is not a majority upon this floor, who are in favor of restricting counties entirely, or of letting them incur an indebtedness to an unlimited extent. If the question should be made directly, upon the point of allowing counties to incur indebtedness to an unlimited extent, there would be a large majority who would go against it. The proposition presented by the gentleman from Jasper is correct; but I would submit to him, whether it could not be drawn up in a somewhat different form, which would better suit the views of the Convention.

Mr. CLARK, of Alamakee. I should not trouble the Convention with any remarks upon this question, which has been so fully and completely discussed in Committee of the Whole, had it not been for the remarks made by the gentleman from Johnson, [Mr. Clarke,] the other day, in which he attempted to place me in a false position upon this question. I wish to set myself right. I did say, and I now say, that, upon principle, I am opposed entirely to incorporating into the Constitution a provision allowing counties to become stockholders in any corporate capacity. But we have not the power to prevent the evil. Under the present construction of the Supreme Court, that right is now guaranteed to the people of the counties, and if, in the Constitution we may make here, we deny to them that right, the people will reject it; consequently, we have not the power, in this Convention, to carry out that principle. I shall vote for placing the amount of stock, which counties may take, as low as I conveniently can.

While I am upon the floor, I will notice the position in which the gentleman from Johnson has placed himself, in trying to make my position inconsistent. He concedes my proposition to the fullest extent, that the people in their primary capacity, when they come into a convention for the purpose of framing an organic law, have no rights, except the rights which each individual carries into the convention. If that be so, what is the next position which he takes? It is, that man has no natural rights to property, or control of property. Then put these two things together, and if man has no natural rights to property, and the convention, when it meets here to form a constitution, has no rights, except those which each individual brings with him, I ask the gentleman where he gets the right of allowing a majority of the people to control the property of the minority?

Mr. CLARKE, of Johnson. I suppose that men have *acquired* as well as *natural* rights, and when they go into a government they take with them those rights, both natural and acquired.

Mr. CLARK, of Alamakee. How can men acquire rights?

Mr. CLARKE, of Johnson. By their hands.

Mr. CLARK, of Alamakee. The gentleman virtually admits that I have a natural right to my hands, and that admission carries with it the right to the product of those hands.

Mr. CLARKE, of Johnson. I have not said any such thing

Mr. CLARK, of Alamakee. If nature gives me the right to my hands, as a necessary consequence, it gives me the right to the product of those hands.

The question was then taken by yeas and nays upon Mr. Skiff's amendment, which would make the section read as follows:

"No political or municipal corporation shal

become a stock-holder in any banking corporation, directly or indirectly, nor in any other corporation or corporations, to an amount exceeding, at one time, two hundred thousand dollars, provided that the same does not exceed five per cent. upon the taxable property of such corporation, as shown by the last preceding assessment."

The amendment was rejected; yeas 7, nays 25, as follows:

Yeas.—Messrs. Clark, of Alamakee, Harris, Skiff, Traer, Warren, Wilson and Young.

Nays.—The President, Messrs. Ayres, Bunker, Clarke, of Henry, Clarke, of Johnson, Day, Edwards, Ells, Gibson, Gillaspy, Gower, Gray, Hall, Johnston, Marvin, Palmer, Parvin, Patterson, Peters, Price, Robinson, Scott, Seely, Solomon and Winchester.

Mr. CLARKE, of Johnson. I move to amend by inserting after the word "indirectly," the following:

"But such corporations may become stockholders in corporations for works of internal improvement within the State, upon a vote of the citizens of such municipal corporations, under such restrictions, as to the mode and amount of subscription, as the General Assembly may prescribe."

The PRESIDENT. The chair would remark, that the amendment would not be in order, as it is an amendment to the amendment made in Committee of the Whole.

The question then recurred upon agreeing to the amendment made in Committee of the Whole to section four, which was to strike out all after the word "indirectly," so that the section would read—

"No political or municipal corporation shall become a stock-holder in any banking corporation, directly or indirectly."

The question was then taken by yeas and nays, and the amendment was concurred in; yeas 30, nays 2, as follows:

Yeas.—The President, Messrs. Ayres, Bunker, Clarke, of Johnson, Day, Edwards, Ells, Gibson, Gillaspy, Gower, Gray, Hall, Harris, Johnston, Marvin, Palmer, Parvin, Patterson, Peters, Price, Robinson, Scott, Seely, Skiff, Solomon, Traer, Warren, Wilson, Winchester and Young.

Nays.—Messrs. Clarke, of Henry and Clark, of Alamakee.

The next amendment reported by the Committee of the Whole, was to strike out in the fifth section the words "as far as possible," so that the section would then read—

"It shall be the duty of the General Assembly to provide by law for the restraint of municipal and political corporations in regard to assessments, taxations, borrowing money, contracting debts, issuing bonds, and loaning their credit, so as to prevent unnecessary burdens, and unjust taxation and frauds."

The question was then taken, and the amendment was concurred in.

Basis of General Banking.

The next amendment was in section seven, to insert the words "twenty per cent. below," so that the section will read—

"If a general banking law is passed, it shall provide, amongst other things, for the registry and countersigning, by an officer of the State, of all bills, or paper credit designed to circulate as money, and require security to the full amount thereof, to be deposited with the State Treasurer, in United States stocks, or in interest-paying stocks of States in good credit and standing, to be rated at twenty per cent. below their average value in the city of New York, for the thirty days next preceding their deposit; and also provide for the recording of the names of all stock-holders in such corporations, the amount of stock held by each, the time of any transfer, and to whom."

The question was taken, and the amendment was concurred in.

Liability of Stockholders.

The next amendment was in section eight, to insert after the word "liabilities" the words—

"Created during the time, that the person sought to be charged was a stock-holder in said banking corporation."

So that the section will read—

"Every stock-holder in a banking corporation, or institution, shall be individually responsible and liable to its creditors, over and above the amount of stock by him or her held, to an amount equal to his or her respective shares so held, for all of its liabilities created during the time that the person sought to be charged was a stockholder in such banking corporation."

The question was taken, and the amendment was concurred in.

State Bank.

The next amendment was to add the following to section nine—"or on stocks as authorized by the seventh section, or on both."

So that the section would read—

"The General Assembly may also charter a State bank, with branches to be founded upon an actual specie basis, or on stocks as authorized by the seventh section, or on both."

The question was taken, and the amendment was concurred in.

The next amendment was in section ten, to strike out all after the word "money," so that the section would read—

"If such a State bank be established, the branches shall be mutually responsible for each others liabilities upon all paper credit issued as money."

The question was taken, and the amendment was concurred in.

Frauds in Banking.

The next amendment was to add to section eleven the following:

"And all frauds, that may be committed by persons having the management and control of any bank or banks, established under this article, which shall materially affect the credit of said bank or banks, shall be punished as felony; and it shall be the duty of the General Assembly to provide by law for such punishment."

So that the section would read—

"It shall be the duty of the General Assembly, in case of its passing either or both of the banking laws herein provided, to provide also such other restrictions, and fix such other liabilities, and adopt such other guards and checks as shall be conducive to prevent frauds on the part of banking institutions, its officers and directors, and to secure to the people of this State a safe and reliable currency; and all frauds, that may be committed by persons having the management and control of any bank or banks, established under this article, which shall materially affect the credit of said bank or banks, shall be punished as felony; and it shall be the duty of the General Assembly to provide by law for such punishment."

Mr. CLARKE, of Henry. I would offer the following substitute for the amendment:

"And to this end the General Assemby shall provide laws, defining the offences, with suitable pains and penalties for the punishment of such frauds."

I do not think, that it is proper, in the constitution, to define offences, and so I offer this as a substitute for the amendment of the gentleman from Des Moines.

The question was then taken, by yeas and nays, and the amendment was not agreed to; yeas 9, nays 22.

Yeas.—The President, Messrs. Clark, of Alamakee, Clarke, of Henry, Gray, Marvin, Scott, Seely, Traer, and Warren.

Nays.—Messrs. Ayres, Bunker, Clarke, of Johnson, Day, Edwards, Gibson, Gillaspy, Gower, Hall, Harris, Johnston, Palmer, Parvin, Patterson, Peters, Price, Robinson, Skiff, Solomon, Wilson, Winchester and Young.

The question now recurred upon agreeing to the amendment made by the Committee of the Whole.

Mr. WINCHESTER. Permit me here to say, Mr. President, that I shall vote against this amendment, and all similar ones, because I do not believe in the incorporation of so much legislation into our constitution.

The question was then taken, by yeas and nays, upon concurring in the amendment of the Committee of the Whole, and it was not concurred in; yeas 16, nays 16, as follows:

Yeas.—Messrs. Ayres, Bunker, Clarke, of Johnson, Day, Gibson, Gillaspy, Hall, Harris, Johnston, Marvin, Palmer, Patterson, Peters, Price, Robinson and Solomon.

Nays.—The President, Messrs. Clark, of Alamakee, Clarke, of Henry, Edwards, Ells, Gower, Gray, Parvin, Scott, Seely, Skiff, Traer, Warren, Wilson, Winchester and Young.

Only Banks to Issue Paper Currency.

The next amendment reported by the Committee of the Whole was the following substitute for section fifteen:

"Any person, or body of persons, who shall issue for circulation as money, any bill, or other evidence of debt, without the authority of law, shall be deemed guilty of felony, and punished as may be provided by law."

The question was then taken, and the amendment was concurred in; yeas 18, nays 14, as follows:

Yeas.—Messrs. Bunker, Clarke, of Johnson, Day, Edwards, Ells, Gibson, Gillaspy, Gower, Hall, Harris, Johnston, Marvin, Patterson, Peters, Price, Robinson, Scott and Young.

Nays—The President, Messrs. Ayres, Clark of Alamakee, Clarke of Henry, Gray, Palmer, Parvin, Seely, Skiff, Solomon, Traer, Warren, Wilson and Winchester.

Submission of Banking Laws to the People.

The next amendment was in section sixteen, to insert after the word "law" in the third line, "to be held not less than three months after the passage of the law."

So that the section would read:

"But no general banking law, nor law creating a State bank, nor shall amendments thereto or acts in repeal thereof, take effect until the same shall have been submitted, separately to the people, at a general or special election, to be held not less than three months after the passage of the law, and shall have been approved by a majority of all the voters voting for and against it."

The question was taken, and the amendment concurred in.

Repeal of Acts of Incorporation.

The next amendment was in section seventeen, to insert between the words "special," and "privileges," the words "or exclusive" and to strike out the words: "the House of Representatives and also the Senate," so that the section would read:

"Subject to the provisions of this article, the General Assembly shall have power to amend or repeal all laws for the organization or creation of corporations, or granting of special or exclusive privileges or immunities by vote of two thirds of each branch of the General Assembly; and no exclusive privileges, except in this article provided, shall ever be granted."

The question was taken and the amendment was concurred in.

Miscellaneous.

The next amendment was to strike out the whole of section nineteen, which reads as follows:

"Private property shall not be taken by corporations for their use or benefit without compensating the owner for the actual damage resulting to him or her in the taking or manner thereof."

The question was taken and the amendment concurred in.

The PRESIDENT. The amendments made in Committee of the Whole have been all acted upon; and amendments to any part of the report are now in order.

City and County Indebtedness.

Mr. CLARKE of Johnson. I desire to offer the following as a substitute for section four:

"SEC. 4. No political or municipal corporation shall become a stockholder in any banking corporation, directly or indirectly; but such corporations may become stockholders in corporations for internal improvements within the State, upon a vote of the citizens of such municipal corporations, under such restrictions as to the mode and amount of subscriptions as the General Assembly may prescribe."

Mr. GILLASPY. I desire to say, in explanation of the vote I shall give, that I shall vote for the proposition of the gentleman from Johnson, believing that it comes nearer what I desire than any thing else I shall get upon this subject.

The question was then taken by yeas and nays, and the amendment was agreed to; yeas, 13, nays, 19, as follows:

Yeas: Messrs. Bunker, Clarke of Johnson, Edwards, Gibson, Gillaspy, Gower, Harris, Marvin, Peters, Scott, Seely, Winchester and Young.

Nays—The President, Messrs. Ayres, Clark of Alamakee, Clarke of Henry, Day, Ells, Gray, Hall, Johnston, Palmer, Parvin, Patterson, Price, Robinson, Skiff, Solomon, Traer, Warren and Wilson.

Mr. CLARKE of Henry. I move to amend section four by striking out all after the word "indirectly," where it first occurs and inserting as follows:

"Nor shall the bonds, or other evidences of debt, of any municipal or political corporation be given or granted, or its credit loaned, directly or indirectly, or pledged as security, for the benefit of any banking corporation; nor for any other corporation or purpose whatever, to an amount in the aggregate exceeding two hundred thousand dollars; but no municipal or political corporation shall give bonds or become indebted in any manner, to an amount exceeding in the aggregate five per cent. on the value of the taxable property within the limits of such corporation, which value shall be ascertained from the last state and county tax lists."

Mr. EDWARDS. I move as a substitute for the amendment of the gentleman from Henry, (Mr. Clarke) the following:

"But such incorporation shall be allowed to take stock in aid of works of internal improvement to an amount not exceeding ten per cent. upon the taxable property of such corporation by the last assessment lists."

Mr. CLARKE of Henry. I am sorry that the gentleman has moved this substitute, for while I would be very glad to take his proposition, if I could get nothing else, I would prefer to have my proposition have the first chance, and let his come in afterwards.

Mr. EDWARDS. We have had a vote already upon it.

Mr. CLARKE of Henry. I do not consider that a test vote for this reason: gentlemen told me afterwards, that the reason they voted against it, was, that they were in hopes to have aan entire restriction put upon this matter.

The question was upon the amendment to the amendment.

Upon this question Mr. EDWARDS called for the yeas and nays, and they were ordered accordingly.

The question being then taken, by yeas and nays, upon the amendment to the amendment, it was not adopted; yeas 10, nays 22, as follows:

Yeas: Bunker, Clarke of Johnson, Edwards, Gibson, Gower, Harris, Marvin, Peters, Seely and Traer.

Nays: The President, Messrs. Ayers, Clark of Alamakee, Clark of Henry, Day, Ells, Gillaspy, Gray, Hall, Johnston, Palmer, Parvin, Patterson, Price, Robinson, Scott, Skiff, Solomon, Warren, Wilson, Winchester and Young.

The question recurred upon the amendment of Mr. Clarke, of Henry.

Mr. YOUNG. We have had one vote upon a proposition similar to this, and it was voted down by a large vote. I am myself in favor of the principle of this proposition. I move to amend the latter part of the amendment by striking out the word "five," and inserting the word "eight," so that it will read: "to an amount in the aggregate, exceeding eight per cent. on the taxable property, &c."

Mr. TRAER called for a division of the question, which was ordered.

The question was then taken upon striking out the word "five" and upon a division it was agreed to, ayes 13, noes, 11.

Mr. CLARKE, of Johnson, moved to fill the blank with the word "eight."

Upon this question the yeas and nays were called, and ordered accordingly.

The question being then taken, by yeas and nays, upon filling the blank with the word "eight," it was not agreed to; yeas 13, nays 19, as follows:

Yeas—The President, Messrs. Bunker, Clarke, of Johnson, Edwards, Ells, Gibson, Gower, Marvin, Peters, Scott, Seely, Skiff and Traer.

Nays—Messrs. Ayres, Clarke, of Henry, Clark, of Alamakee, Day, Gillaspy, Gray, Hall, Harris, Johnston, Palmer, Parvin, Patterson, Price, Robinson, Solomon, Warren, Wilson, Winchester and Young.

Mr. YOUNG moved to fill the blank with the word "seven."

Upon this question the yeas and nays were ordered, and being taken, the motion was not agreed to; yeas 15, nays 17, as follows:

Yeas—The President, Messrs. Bunker, Clarke, of Johnson, Ells, Gibson, Gower, Harris, Marvin, Peters, Scott, Seely, Skiff, Traer, Warren and Young.

Nays—Messrs. Ayres, Clarke, of Henry, Clark, of Alamakee, Day, Edwards, Gillaspy, Gray, Hall, Johnston, Palmer, Parvin, Patterson, Price, Robinson, Solomon, Wilson and Winchester.

Mr. WILSON moved to fill the blank with the word "six."

Mr. HALL moved to lay the amendment upon the table. Not agreed to.

The question was then taken, by yeas and nays, upon the motion to fill the blank with the word "six," and it was not agreed to: yeas 16, nays 16, as follows:

Yeas—The President, Messrs. Bunker, Clarke, of Henry, Clarke, of Johnson, Clark, of Alamakee, Ells, Gibson, Gower, Harris, Marvin, Scott, Skiff, Traer, Warren, Wilson and Young.

Nays—Messrs. Ayres, Day, Edwards, Gillaspy, Gray, Hall, Johnston, Palmer, Parvin, Patterson, Peters, Price, Robinson, Seely, Solomon and Winchester.

Mr. CLARKE, of Johnson, moved a call of the Convention, which was ordered.

The following members answered to their names:

The President, Messrs. Ayres, Bunker, Clarke, of Henry, Clark, of Alamakee, Clarke, of Johnson, Day, Edwards. Ells, Gibson, Gillaspy, Gower, Gray, Hall, Harris, Johnston, Marvin, Palmer, Parvin, Patterson, Peters, Price, Robinson, Scott, Seely, Skiff, Solomon, Traer, Warren, Wilson, Winchester and Young.

The following were the absentees:

Messrs. Cotton, Emerson, Hollingsworth and Todhunter.

The PRESIDENT stated that Mr. Cotton was absent under leave.

On motion of Mr. PARVIN,

Mr. TODHUNTER was excused on account of sickness.

Mr. EDWARDS moved that Mr. Emerson be excused on account of sickness.

Mr. CLARKE, of Henry, moved that Mr. Hollingsworth be excused on account of sickness.

Mr. CLARK, of Alamakee. Mr. Emerson is able to attend the Convention if necessary.

Mr. PETERS. I know that Mr. Emerson does not consider himself able to be here, as he has been indisposed for two or three days.

Mr. HARRIS. I met Mr. Hollingsworth on the street as I was coming up here, and I asked him if he would be here to-day. He said he was not able to come, and was out only to try his strength,

Mr. TRAER. Mr. Hollingsworth told me he would try and come if it was necessary.

Mr. CLARKE, of Henry. I suppose Mr. Emerson and Mr. Hollingsworth would both come if it was necessary for them to be here.

Mr. CLARK, of Alamakee. Mr. Emerson told me he would come if it was important that he should be here.

The question being then taken upon excusing Messrs. Emerson and Hollingsworth, it was agreed to.

The question recurred upon filling the blank in the amendment of Mr. Clarke, of Henry, the blank being caused by striking out the word "five."

Mr. MARVIN moved to lay the amendment on the table, which was not agreed to.

Mr. CLARK, of Alamakee, moved to fill the blank with the word "four."

Mr. EDWARDS. I desire to give my reasons why I shall vote against this proposition. I regard it as unjust and not equitable. It is a proposition calculated to break down the new counties, for the benefit of the old, wealthy, and populous counties. I think a proposition to confine the wealthy and populous counties to the same amount as the new counties, is not just, and I will vote against it.

The question being taken upon filling the blank with the word "four," it was not agreed to.

Mr. CLARKE, of Henry. I voted in the majority to strike out the word "five." As there seems to be difficulty in filling the blank with any other number, I move to reconsider the vote by which that word was stricken out.

Upon this question the yeas and nays were ordered.

Mr. WILSON was excused from voting, having paired off with Mr. Solomon.

The question being then taken, by yeas and nays, upon the motion to reconsider, it was not agreed to; yeas 9, nays 21, as follows:

Yeas—The President, Messrs. Clark, of Alamakee, Clarke, of Henry, Ells, Gray, Marvin, Scott, Skiff and Warren.

Nays—Messrs. Ayres, Bunker, Clarke, of Johnson, Day, Edwards, Gibson, Gillaspy, Gower, Hall, Harris, Johnston, Palmer, Parvin, Patterson, Peters, Price, Robinson, Seely, Traer, Winchester and Young.

The question recurred upon filling the blank.

Mr. GIBSON. I move to fill the blank with the word "eleven." The reason why I make this motion, is this: I am opposed to any restriction in this matter. I believe it would be perfectly safe with the people of the counties. I voted against having any restriction, and I have uniformly voted for the highest number that has been proposed. I voted for striking out the word "five," as it was a restriction. I have voted for all the numbers from "ten" down to "six." It has been decided here that there shall be a restriction, and I want the highest number put in here that we can get. I believe there are some members upon this floor who have voted against each number proposed here, because they are opposed to any restriction at all. I do not propose this number "eleven" because I believe the citizens of all the counties would desire to take stock to the amount of eleven per cent. But I desire to give them an opportunity to take that amount, if they desire, or any proportion under, that they may think proper to take.

Mr. SCOTT. I am not in favor of throwing any such restriction about this matter in our Constitution. I do not believe any of us know the wants and wishes of any particular county in this State upon this subject. I myself do not know the wants and wishes of my own county. There may contingencies and emergencies arise that will change the features of this question. I am opposed to this Convention legislating. I see no propriety in it. It does seem to me as if members here thought this assemblage of thirty-six men were the wisest that had ever assembled in this State, and that so much wisdom could never be congregated in this State again. They forget that we are to have a Senate of thirty-six men, and a House of Representatives of more than twice that number; and that all matters must pass those two Houses before they receive the force and sanction of law. And without all the restrictions that can be thrown around this matter, may we not safely infer that the General Assembly will evince as much wisdom in regard to this matter, which is purely legislative, as will be shown about it in this body?

For that reason, I am opposed to putting any restrictions about this matter. I do not feel at liberty to say what sum my county should raise for this purpose. We have no railroads built there now, but there are as many as three different railroads projected, and I am confident that five, or even ten per cent., upon the taxable property of our county would not be as much as she would be willing to raise. I would leave each county at liberty to raise such sum as they may see fit and proper. I do not wish to have this Constitution legislative in its character, from beginning to end. I have been, from the start, opposed to putting, either directly or indirectly, guides and landmarks by way of restricting the action of the Legislature, or instructing them in regard to their duty. I think they will form a body of quite as much wisdom as we possess, and will have the common good of the State quite as much at heart as we have. Taking that view of the matter, I would say, let us confine ourselves to our own proper sphere, and let the Legislature do the same.

The question being then taken upon the motion to fill the blank with the word "eleven," upon a division, it was not agreed to, ayes 11, noes 18.

Mr. MARVIN moved to fill the blank with the word "nine."

Upon this question the yeas and nays were ordered, and being taken, the motion was not agreed to, yeas 13, nays 16, as follows:

Yeas—The President; Messrs. Bunker, Clarke of Johnson, Gibson, Gower, Harris, Marvin, Peters, Scott, Seely, Skiff, Traer and Warren.

Nays—Messrs. Ayres, Clark of Alamakee, Clarke of Henry, Day, Edwards, Gillaspy, Gray, Hall, Johnston, Palmer, Parvin, Patterson, Price, Robinson, Winchester and Young.

Mr. EDWARDS. I think the proposition of the gentleman from Henry, [Mr. Clarke,] with the blank filled with any amount, is the only difficulty in the way. There are members here who would have no objection to a proposition restricting to a certain amount, provided it would have an equally just bearing upon all the counties alike, according to their taxable property. But the proposition before us restricts old, wealthy, and populous counties to the same amount that the new counties of the State are allowed to subscribe, and we cannot consent to any such principle as that. I therefore move to lay the amendment of the gentleman from Henry upon the table.

Mr. CLARKE, of Johnson. If the gentleman from Lucas, [Mr. Edwards,] will withdraw his motion to lay upon the table, I will move to strike out the restriction of two hundred thousand dollars.

Mr. EDWARDS. I will withdraw my motion for that purpose.

Mr. CLARKE, of Johnson. I now move to strike out the portion of the amendment restricting the indebtedness to the sum of two hundred thousand dollars. The amendment will then read:

"Nor shall the bonds or other evidences of debt of any municipal or political corporation, be given or granted, or its credit loaned, directly or indirectly, or pledged as security for the benefit of any banking corporation; nor for any other corporation or purpose whatever, to an amount exceeding in the aggregate — per cent. on the value of the taxable property within the limits of such corporation, which value shall be ascertained from the last state and county tax lists."

Mr. CLARKE, of Henry. From the course of the debates the other day, I supposed, and had very good reason to suppose, that there was a large majority of the members here opposed to this town and county indebtedness from principle. A number of them so expressed themselves. A number said they were opposed to it in principle, but the evil had grown to such an extent that it could not now be eradicated. I was satisfied that every member here would go for some kind of restriction; at least I judged so from the course of the debate.

When the limitation of two hundred thousand dollars was proposed, some one got up and suggested that it should not be any given sum, but a per centage upon the taxable property. But others said to that, if you place this upon a per centage basis you will allow some counties to go into debt a half a million or more, and some cities in those counties will go into debt as much more. Another said, this State is growing in wealth from day to day, and what would be a good criterion now, will not be five or ten years from now. And it seemed to be the opinion that ten per cent. would, in a short time, be equivalent to no limit at all in this matter.

Now in order to compromise these conflicting views, and thinking gentlemen would be willing to compromise in this matter somewhat, I was willing, while I was totally opposed to municipal and political corporations taking stock at all, to meet gentlemen half way in this matter. As the gentleman from Des Moines, [Mr. Hall,] said, we have the wolf by the ears; what shall we do with him? We have him here, and cannot kill him, but we can confine him. I will join in with those who are willing to bind him and prevent him from doing the great mischief anticipated by the people at large.

I will say to gentlemen here, that perhaps no subject has been before this Convention, upon which I consulted with my constituents more than this subject. I have had those in my district, who heretofore have voted for issuing this stock, come to me and ask me to place some restriction in the constitution upon this matter. And other gentlemen here, of different parties, occupy the same position. Now because we cannot get just what we want, why not take the next best? Some here wish an entire prohibition; how many there are who wish that, I do not know. I would say to gentlemen of this Convention, do concede something to us. We are willing to concede something and meet you. Many of our constituents demand an entire prohibition of this question. Are you not willing to meet us on some common ground? Deal fairly with us; that is all we ask. Let us know what you will have.

The gentleman from Lucas, [Mr. Edwards,] I hope will understand my position. I want to place the restriction as low as I can, in regard to the per centage, in the first place; and then I want to have the sum of two hundred thousand dollars the limit at any rate. A per centage that would be equivalent to five hundred thousand dollars in Des Moines county, might not be above twenty-five or thirty thousand dollars in some other counties. But the smaller counties can issue their bonds for five per cent upon their taxable property, while Des Moines county would be allowed to raise two hundred thousand dollars, but not more than that. Some of those who were opposed to this restriction, went to figuring the other day, and told us how many millions of dollars all the counties would go into debt if we allowed them to take each two hundred thousand dollars. They showed us that we would practically be imposing scarcely any restriction. Yet such as it is we are willing to accept it. If we place this limit upon the counties taking stock, even if it practically does not amount to much, yet it will go abroad that a limit in relation to this matter has been imposed in this State, and the bonds of those counties which have already taken stock, will stand all the higher in the market.

And I will say to the gentleman from Lucas, [Mr. Edwards,] that I have no doubt that one hundred thousand dollars of bonds, with this restriction will be worth more in the market than one hundred and fifty thousand dollars without any restriction. I know that in some cases these questions have been put: To what extent is your county going? Is she limited in any way in this matter? Are there are other railroads through your county? Those questions are often, if not always, asked. The gentleman from Des Moines [Mr. Hall,] knows that when Henry county voted her third one hundred thousand dollars worth of stock, it sank in the market almost instantly. It is a good policy for the State to fix a restriction here somewhere. This is no legislation; it is only fixing a rule within which the legislature, if they see fit, may act, and within which the people of the county may vote these bonds if they see fit.

This is not a matter affecting the inhabitants of any one county. If that was the case, I would have nothing to say in favor of it. It is a question affecting the whole State, for what one county may do, all counties may do. And if all the counties go into this indebtedness, any general failure among them would embarrass the whole State, and in that light it is a matter of universal interest to us all. We in Henry county are interested in what is done in Potawattomie; and the people in Mills county are interested in what is done in Scott county. We want a rule of universal application all over the State restricting all the town and county corporations alike.

If the Convention say they are satisfied to take the per centage system, I will agree to it, though I do not think it is as good a restriction as to say that counties under a per centage system shall not go beyond the sum of two hundred thousand dollars. But still I am willing to concede that much to the gentleman from Lucas [Mr. Edwards] and others, and strike out the limitation of two hundred thousand dollars, and say that counties and cities shall not run into debt beyond five per cent. upon their taxable property. Let us meet each other somewhere, and not defeat each other. I have no doubt the friends of restriction are in the majority, if they do not defeat themselves by quibbling about the particular kind of restriction which shall be adopted here.

Mr CLARKE, of Johnson. As the Convention well knows, I am one of those who go for recognizing the right of the counties to go into debt. I am one of those who would prefer to leave this matter of limitation and restriction to the General Assembly.

If my motion to strike out the restriction of two hundred thousand dollars be agreed to, then we will be in a difficulty as to the amount of per centage we will put in here. As gentlemen, however, seem willing to compromise, I have a proposition which I will read as a kind of compromise in place of the proposition of the gentleman from Henry [Mr. Clarke]:

"But such corporations may become stockholders in incorporations for the construction of works of internal improvement within the State upon a vote of the citizens of such municipal or political corporation, not to exceed six per cent. upon the assessed value of the real and personal property of said corporations."

This proposition of mine leaves out the limitation of two hundred thousand dollars, but makes a limit upon the assessed value of the property of the county. I have placed it at six per cent. as the proper medium between the various numbers voted upon here. If we make a limit, and place it too low, it will be in the way of the future progress of this State. I have voted for the highest number heretofore, as I believed that the number "five" was too small. I believe some counties in this State will be centres for railroads, and the people of those counties will want to invest a larger amount of money and take a larger amount of stock than where only one road passes through the county.

Mr. CLARKE, of Henry. I will withdraw my amendment.

The question being taken upon granting leave to withdraw the amendment, it was granted, and the amendment was withdrawn accordingly.

Mr. CLARKE, of Johnson. I now move to amend section four of this report so that it will read as follows:

"No political or municipal corporation shall become a stockholder in any banking corporation, directly or indirectly; but such corporations may become stockholders in incorporations for the construction of works of internal improvement within this State, upon a vote of the citizens of such municipal or political corporation, not to exceed six per cent. upon the assessed value of the real and personal property of said corporation."

Mr. CLARK, of Alamakee. Does that give the county the right to give bonds to be used anywhere in the State?

Mr. CLARKE, of Johnson. I have no such intention in offering the amendment.

Mr. PARVIN. Every member of this body must be satisfied that the Convention have decided that they will not have anything of this kind in the Constitution; at all events I can interpret their votes in no other way. By a decided majority they struck out all of the fourth section after the word "indirectly," where it first occurs. A number of substitutes for the portion stricken out have been submitted and voted down, and the votes upon the filling of the blank in the substitute offered by the gentleman from Henry [Mr. Clarke] is an intimation of what the Convention intends to do in this matter.

Now, I am opposed to recognizing this practice by anything that we may put in the constitution. Those counties that have taken stock in these corporations have taken it under the constitution as it now stands, and under the laws as they have been interpreted by the Supreme Court. I am willing to leave that matter as it is at present. Those counties that wish to take stock hereafter, can do so as the others have done before them, with the constitution and the law as now existing. As this section has been in the main stricken out, the legislature will have this subject under their control, and if they see proper they can act upon the matter. I want nothing here to forbid counties taking stock; I would have nothing said about the matter at all. I represent a county that has taken stock in railroad companies, and, perhaps, may desire to take more. I am convinced they are satisfied with the constitution and laws as they now are upon this subject.

We have forbidden the State running into debt beyond a certain amount.

There are many members of this body who consider that counties running into debt, is pretty near the same in principle as the State running into debt. Yet all they ask is that the constitution shall say nothing about the matter, but leave it to the legislature and to the Supreme Court. This, I think must be the intention of the Convention, judging from the votes given here this afternoon. I cannot, therefore, see the use of offering substitute after substitute and amendment after amendment, when the Convention have decided, as I think they have, to put nothing of this kind into the constitution. I hope, therefore, this matter will be permitted to remain as it now is.

Mr. HARRIS. I have been voting for these restrictions upon the right of counties to take this kind of stock. I said, sometime since, that I would not vote for an entire prohibition, but I would vote for some restrictions. I have, however, become satisfied that the majority of this convention are not in favor of any restriction whatever. I shall, therefore, vote hereafter to leave the whole matter, as it now stands, and not spend any more time tinkering with it.

Mr. CLARK, of Alamakee. I am willing to vote for this amount of six per cent., but I am opposed to allowing the counties, as corporate bodies, to raise that amount of stock to be expended anywhere in the State.

Mr. CLARKE, of Johnson. I think the counties will themselves give all the necessary attention to that matter. I think that heretofore they have made it a condition, when they raised these stocks that the money should be expended in their respective counties. I imagine that we can very safely leave this matter to the counties themselves. We cannot enter into detail here, nor do I think there is any necessity for us to do so.

Mr. EDWARDS moved to strike out "six" and insert "eight," so that the counties could issue bonds to the amount of eight per cent upon the assessed value of the real and personal property in their limits.

The question being taken the amendment was not agreed to.

The question recurred upon the amendment proposed by Mr. Clarke of Johnson.

Mr. CLARKE, of Alamakee moved to amend so as to require the funds so raised to be expended within the counties respectively raising the same.

Mr. CLARKE, of Johnson. If that motion prevails, it will just end this whole matter, as none of the railroads will take the bonds of these counties upon such a condition.

The question being taken upon the amendment to the amendment, it was not agreed to.

The question recurred upon the amendment of Mr. Clarke, of Johnson.

Mr. SKIFF. I shall vote against this amendment, and when the proper time comes, I will move to reconsider the vote taken upon the proposition made by the gentleman from Johnson [Mr. Clarke] at the commencement of this afternoon's session, to leave this whole matter to the legislature to impose such restrictions as they may think necessary upon counties taking stock in these internal improvement incorporations.

Mr. HALL. I move to amend the amendment of the gentleman from Johnson [Mr. Clarke] by adding to it the following:

"Provided that property reserved as a homestead, and such as may be by law exempt from attachment by sale and execution, shall not be sold for taxes levied to pay interest upon loans voted under this section."

Mr. CLARKE, of Johnson. The gentleman from Des Moines, [Mr. Hall] would perhaps improve his amendment by adding to it these words: "And provided further, that said homestead and other property derives no benefit from these internal improvements."

Mr. HALL. I am fearful, if we are not careful, we will involve ourselves seriously in this matter. The legislature has provided that certain property shall be exempt from levy and sale against creditors; but for taxes it can be sold. The wife may be turned out of doors, and the family rendered homeless and houseless, to pay taxes. Where these taxes are necessary for the support of the government, it may, perhaps, be right and just that that should be done. But I think that no gentleman here will say that this property, so exempt, should be sold to pay taxes to meet the interest on debts created by the people in favor of these internal improvements. I would put this debt upon the same footing as are the debts of individuals. I am not in favor of this amendment or the original proposition. But I desire to learn the temper of the Convention in regard to protecting persons in the possession and enjoyment of a little property which the laws secure as against individual creditors.

The question being taken upon the amendment of Mr. Hall, it was not agreed to.

Mr. CLARKE, of Henry. I desire to offer, as a substitute for the amendment of the gentleman from Johnson, [Mr. Clarke,] something which will test the sincerity of the gentleman from Des Moines, [Mr. Hall,] in the position he has taken in regard to this matter. It is as follows:

"No political or municipal corporation shall become a stockholder in, or loan its credit to, or become security, directly or indirectly, for any other corporation."

Mr. JOHNSTON moved to lay the amendment to the amendment upon the table.

Mr. CLARKE, of Henry. I would ask, what would be the effect of that motion if adopted?

The PRESIDENT. The effect would be, to lay the substitute, proposed by the gentleman from Henry, [Mr. Clarke,] upon the table, and the question would then recur upon the amendment of the gentleman from Johnson, [Mr. Clarke.]

Mr. CLARKE, of Henry. With the permission of the Convention, I would like to say a very few words. I should be pleased to have a vote of the Convention directly upon the proposition I have submitted. It is one that I have had upon my table for some time. I would like to have a direct vote upon it. I want to ascertain—though not for any political purpose—what the sense of the Convention is, in regard to this question. I know that there are a number of gentlemen here who will vote for prohibition to its fullest extent. I do not know but what there is a majority here in favor of such a provision. I hope, therefore, my proposition will not be laid upon the table, but that we will be allowed to take a direct vote upon it.

Mr. JOHNSTON. I would like to say a single word on this subject, though I know the motion to lay upon the table is not debatable. I merely wish to say this, that after all the votes we have had this afternoon, after the expression of the opinion of the Convention, which has been given, I do not think it is necessary that we should take up the time of the Convention by matters which are introduced here, it seems to me, for the purpose of showing, perhaps, a little personal feeling upon the part of my friend from Des Moines, [Mr. Hall,] and my friend from Henry, [Mr. Clarke.]

Mr. CLARKE, of Henry. Not at all; nothing of the kind.

Mr. JOHNSTON. The truth is, I thought the amendment of the gentleman from Henry, [Mr. Clarke,] was produced by the feeling caused by the amendment of the gentleman from Des Moines, [Mr. Hall.] I voted against the amendment of the gentleman from Des Moines, and I shall vote against the amendment of the gentleman from Henry.

I was, as a member of the Committee on Incorporations, opposed to introducing into the Convention the principle of prohibition, in regard to these county and city loans. After a long consultation upon the subject when it came up, it was deemed best to report the old article of the Constitution, with some restrictions. As the chairman of the committee, [Mr. Clarke, of Henry,] has correctly stated, the members of that committee did not feel bound to support anything in the report, but considered themselves at liberty to move such amendments to it as they might consider best.

Now I still adhere to this doctrine of restriction. If this was entirely a new question I would have gone for entire prohibition, or at least great restrictions here. But it is not a new question. My constituents are deeply interested in this matter, and I would endeavor to care for their interests; but when I found that the friends of restriction—as the votes of this afternoon fully show—could not agree upon a single thing, I came forward on yesterday and moved to strike out the latter part of the section now under consideration, which was agreed to. Having taken my position, I have adhered to it all this afternoon; and if the question distinctly comes up whether or not the doctrine of prohibition shall be recognized in this Convention, I shall vote against it. As the matter stands now, I am desirous of leaving this matter where it is under the present Constitution; and, for this reason, the Supreme Court of this State, the highest tribunal known to our laws, has decided that it was constitutional for counties to vote these loans. It was under that decision that votes making those loans have taken place, for not a dollar was voted until it was decided to be constitutional. I would, therefore, have all future loans stand upon the same footing with those already made. For that reason I shall adhere to the old Constitution upon this subject.

The question was upon laying the amendment to the amendment upon the table.

Upon this question Mr. CLARKE, of Henry, called for the yeas and nays, and they were accordingly ordered.

The question being then taken, by yeas and nays, upon laying the amendment to the amendment upon the table, it was agreed to; yeas 22, nays 8, as follows:

Yeas.—The President, Messrs. Ayres, Bunker, Clarke, of Johnson, Gibson, Gillaspy, Gower, Hall, Harris, Johnston, Marvin, Palmer, Parvin, Patterson, Peters, Price, Robinson, Scott, Seely, Warren, Winchester and Young.

Nays.—Messrs. Clark, of Alamakee, Clarke, of Henry, Day, Edwards, Ells, Gray, Skiff and Traer.

The question then recurred upon the amendment of Mr. Clarke, of Johnson.

Mr. PALMER moved to lay that amendment upon the table.

Upon this question Mr. CLARKE, of Johnson, called for the yeas and nays, and they were ordered accordingly.

The question being then taken, by yeas and nays, upon laying the amendment upon the table, it was agreed to; yeas 16, nays 13, as ollows:

Yeas.—The President, Messrs. Ayres, Clark, of Alamakee, Day, Gibson, Gillaspy, Hall, Johnston, Palmer, Parvin, Patterson, Peters, Price, Robinson, Scott and Seely.

Nays.—Messrs. Bunker, Clarke, of Henry, Clarke, of Johnson, Edwards, Ells, Gower, Gray, Marvin, Skiff, Traer, Warren, Winchester and Young.

Mr. SKIFF. I move to reconsider the vote by which the proposition offered by the delegate from Johnson, [Mr. Clarke,] as a substitute for section four was rejected.

The substitute was then read as follows:

"No political or municipal corporation shall become a stock-holder in any banking corporation, directly or indirectly, but such corporations may become stock-holders in corporations for works of Internal Improvements within the State, upon a vote of the citizens of such municipal corporation, under such restrictions, as to the mode and amount of subscription, as the General Assembly may prescribe.

Mr. SKIFF. I voted in the majority, and against this proposition, as I should have preferred something else. But I have since ascertained, from the votes taken, that my wishes cannot be gratified. I am always willing, when I cannot succeed in carrying out my own particular views, to try and secure the next best thing. It is for this reason, that I make this motion to reconsider.

The question was taken, and the motion for a re-consideration was not agreed to.

Mr. CLARKE, of Henry. I now offer the following substitute for section four:

"No political or municipal corporation shall become a stock-holder in any banking corporation directly or indirectly, nor in any other corporation or corporations directly or indirectly, to an amount exceeding two hundred thousand dollars; nor shall the bonds or other evidences of debt of any municipal or political corporation be issued or granted, or its credit loaned directly or indirectly, or pledged as security for the benefit of any banking corporation; nor for any other corporation or purpose whatever, to an amount in the aggregate exceeding two hundred thousand dollars. But no municipal or political corporation shall give bonds, or become indebted in any manner, to an amount exceeding in the aggregate five per cent. on the value of the taxable property within such corporation, which value shall be ascertained by the last State and county tax list."

Mr. CLARKE, of Johnson. I move to strike out the words "two hundred thousand dollars" in the proposed substitute.

The question was taken, and the motion was not agreed to, upon a division; ayes 7, noes 7.

The question was then taken, by yeas and nays, upon the amendment offered by Mr. Clarke, of Henry, and it was not agreed to; yeas 5, nays 25, as follows:

Yeas.—Messrs. Clark, of Alamakee, Clarke, of Henry. Marvin, Skiff and Young.

Nays.—The President, Messrs. Ayres, Bunker, Clarke, of Johnson, Day, Edwards, Ells, Gibson, Gillaspy, Gower, Gray, Hall, Harris, Johnston, Palmer, Parvin, Patterson, Peters, Price, Robinson, Scott, Seely, Traer, Warren and Winchester.

Suspension of Specie Payments.

Mr. PALMER. I move to amend the thirteenth section by adding the following:

"But shall be forbidden under penalty of forfeiture of their corporate privileges."

So that it will read—

"Sec. 13. The suspension of specie payments by banking institutions shall never be permitted or sanctioned; but shall be forbidden under penalty of forfeiture of their corporate privileges."

The question was then taken, and the amendment was not agreed to, upon a division; ayes 8, noes not counted.

Restrictions in Banking Laws.

Mr. WILSON. I move to strike out the whole of section eleven, which reads as follows:

"It shall be the duty of the General Assembly, in case of its passing either or both of the banking laws herein provided, to provide also such other restrictions, and fix such other liabilities, and adopt such other guards and checks as shall be conducive to prevent frauds on the part of banking institutions, its officers and di-

rectors, and to secure to the people of this State a safe and reliable currency."

Mr. CLARKE, of Henry. If the gentleman will turn to the constitutions of other States, he will find that they have adopted a similar provision.

Mr. WILSON. I wish simply to say, in reply to the gentleman from Henry, I do not care how many constitutions you find, in which this provision is incorporated, it will have no effect. It is simply directory.

The question was then taken, by yeas and nays, and the motion to strike out the eleventh section was not agreed to; yeas 14, nays 17, as follows:

Yeas.—The President, Messrs. Bunker, Clarke, of Johnson, Edwards, Gower, Hall, Peters, Scott, Skiff, Traer, Warren, Wilson, Winchester and Young.

Nays.—Messrs. Ayres, Clark, of Alamakee, Clarke, of Henry, Day, Ells, Gibson, Gillaspy, Gray, Harris, Johnston, Marvin, Palmer, Parvin, Patterson, Price, Robinson and Seely.

Banking.

Mr. TRAER moved to strike out the following sections of the report:

Sec. 6. "Subject to the provisions hereof, the General Assembly may pass a general banking law, under which corporations may organize for banking purposes.

Sec. 7. If a general banking law is passed, it shall provide amongst other things, for the registry and countersigning, by an officer of the State, of all bills, or paper credit designed to circulate as money, and require security to the full amount thereof, to be deposited with the State Treasurer, in United States Stocks, or in interest paying stocks of states in good credit and standing, to be rated at twenty per cent. below their average value in the city of New York, for the thirty days next preceeding their deposit; and also provide for the recording of the names of all stockholders in such corporations, the amount f stock held by each, the time of any transfer, and to whom."

Sec. 8. Every stockholder in a banking corporation or institution shall be individually liable to its creditors over and above the amount of stock by him or her held, to an amount equal to his or her respective shares so held, for all of its liabilities created during the time that the person sought to be charged was a stockholder in such banking corporation; and in all cases where its stock shall be transferred, the liability of the transferer shall not cease, nor shall the liability of the transferee commence until the expiration of six months after such transfer shall have been duly recorded as provided by law.

Sec. 9. The General Assembly may also charter a State Bank with branches, to be founded upon an actual specie basis, or on stocks as authorised by the seventh section, or both.

Sec. 10. If such a State Bank be established, the branches shall be mutually responsible for each others' liabilities upon all paper credit issued as money.

"Sec. 11. It shall be the duty of the General Assembly, in case of its passing either or both of the banking laws herein provided, to provide also such other restrictions, and fix such other liabilities, and adopt such other guards and checks, as shall be condusive to prevent frauds on the part of banking institutions, its officers and directors, and to secure to the people of the state a safe and reliable currency.

Sec. 12. In case of the insolvency of any banking institution, the bill-holders shall have a preference over its other creditors.

Sec. 13. The suspension of specie payments by banking institutions shall never be permitted and sanctioned.

Sec. 14. Every banking corporation or institution shall cease banking and close its business within twenty-five years from the time of its organization or creation.

Sec. 15. Any person or body of persons who shall issue for circulation as money any bill or other evidence of debt, without the authority of law, shall be deemed guilty of felony and punished as may be provided by law."

Mr. TRAER. I wish to state that my object in making this motion is simply to put this question in a position, that the people can decide upon these restrictions for themselves. I believe that by striking out all after the sixth to the sixteenth section, so as to provide for chartering a State Bank and allow the question to go to the people and let them decide whether these restrictions are sufficient, we shall gain all we can possibly gain by passing these restrictions. It is with that view I move to strike out these sections.

Mr. BUNKER. I shall vote for striking out. It appears to me that this convention, to a great extent, are regarding banks as a positive evil. I do not so regard them, and I wish to place such restrictions around them as will benefit the public. I go therefore for striking out these sections.

The question was then taken by yeas and nays upon Mr. Traer's motion and it was not agreed to, yeas 9, nays 21, as follows:

Yeas—Messrs. Bunker, Clarke of Johnson, Gibson, Hall, Peters, Skiff, Traer and Warren.

Nays—The President, Messrs. Ayers, Clark of Alamakee, Clarke of Henry, Day, Edwards, Ells, Gillaspy, Gower, Gray, Harris, Johnston, Marvin, Palmer, Parvin, Patterson, Price, Robinson, Seely, Wilson and Winchester.

Mr. CLARKE of Johnson offered the following as a substitute for the sixth, seventh, and eighth sections of the report,

"Sec.—Banking institutions may be provided for by general law, under the following restrictions:

First—All bills, notes, or other papers, or evidence of debt, that may be issued for circulation as money, shall be based upon the stock of the United States, or the stocks of interest paying states, deposited with the proper officer of state, at the rate of not less than one hundred and twenty dollars, (estimating state stocks at their market value in New York, but in no instance above their par value) for every one hundred dollars of paper issued, which may be increased or diminished in value.

Second—All paper, of any such institution, intended to circulate as money, shall be registered in the office of the proper state officers and countersigned by such officer.

Third—In case of the insolvency of any banking institution, the bill-holders shall have a preference over other creditors; and the General Assembly may provide for the conversion of the stocks deposited by such institutions, into money, and the redemption of its bills.

Fourth—The suspension of specie payments of banking institutions shall never be sanctioned by law.

Fifth—Upon the failure of any banking institution to redeem its bills, or other paper issued to circulate as money, such institution shall forfeit all its rights, and it shall be the duty of the proper legal officers to commence proceedings in the manner prescribed by law, to close up its business, and liquidate its indebtedness; and such institutions shall have no powor after such failure, to redeem or transfer any of its property.

Sixth—The issue of any bills, or other evidences of debt, intended to circulate as money, by any banking institution, without being secured and countersigned as herein-before required, shall be deemed a forfeiture of all its rights by such institution, and the same shall be closed."

Mr. CLARK of Alamakee. I cannot see the advantage the convention and the people will gain by the adoption of the substitute offered by the gentleman from Johnson, (Mr. Clarke). I am opposed, myself, to incorporating a provision of that kind into the constitution upon the spur of the moment. The provision that was reported by the committee has been printed. We have all considered it attentively and understand it, I hope, thoroughly. I certainly shall feel very unwilling, under the circumstances, to vote for this substitute, even if it were as good as the provisions reported by the committee.

Mr. CLARKE of Johnson. This substitute was laid upon the clerk's desk two or three days ago. I offered it as an individual member and it is through no fault of mine, that it has not been printed. I do not suppose it will pass from the votes that have been given here, today; but I felt it my duty to present my views upon this question in the shape of the substitute which I have now offered.

The question was then taken by yeas and nays, upon the substitute offered by Mr. Clarke and it was rejected; yeas 7, nays 24, as follows:

Yeas—Messrs. Bunker, Clarke of Johnson, Gower, Peters, Traer, Warren and Young.

Nays—The President, Messrs. Ayers, Clark of Alamakee, Clarke of Henry, Day, Edwards, Ells, Gibson, Gillaspy, Gray, Hall, Harris, Johnston, Marvin, Palmer, Parvin, Patterson, Price, Robinson, Scott, Seely, Skiff, Wilson and Winchester.

On motion of Mr. PETERS,

The convention then adjourned till to-morrow morning at 9 o'clock.

THURSDAY, February 12th, 1857.

The Convention met at 9 o'clock, A. M., and was called to order by the President.

Prayer by the Chaplain.

The Journal of yesterday was read and approved.

Incorporations.

The PRESIDENT. The first business in order is the report of the Committee on Corporations upon its second reading.

Mr. WILSON. I move that the report, with the amendments thereto, be referred to a select committee of five.

Mr. CLARKE, of Henry. We should consider carefully, I think, the condition in which we will be placed, if this proposition should be adopted. We have gone through this report in Committee of the Whole, and discussed it section by section. Various amendments have been offered to it, and voted upon. If we send this report as amended to a select committee, the result will be that they will make another report. If they embrace in that report all these amendments, why then they will present nothing more than we already have; while if they make a different report, and leave out some of the amendments that have been agreed to, I ask gentlemen if we will not have these same amendments offered again, and have the same discussion renewed, that we have already had in committee of the whole?

We have no certainty that this special committee will agree upon a report. One member of the committee may come in and propose a more stringent article upon banking corporations than we already have; another member may propose to remove all restrictions in the constitution, upon this subject of banking, and allow the legislature to impose all restrictions and liabilities; and here then will come up another contest in the Convention. If this committee was to be raised for the purpose of taking what we have already done, and put it into proper form and shape, I would have no objection. But I understand that the object of the gentleman, in moving for the appointment of this committee, is to get rid of some of the amendments that have been made. If that be the object, I am opposed to it, for we have arrived at the result now before us, after the most full and complete discussion of the various amendments, and after we have taken a great many votes by yeas and nays; and I do not wish to travel over this same ground again. There are many things in the report as it now stands, that I would like to see altered; and especially I would like to amend the fourth section; but having gone through with this report, and fairly decided it, I am unwilling to consume another week in the consideration of another report from a select committee upon this same subject.

Mr. JOHNSTON called for the yeas and nays, and they were ordered accordingly.

The question was then taken by yeas and nays, and the motion to refer was agreed to, yeas 17, nays 15, as follows:

Yeas—The President, Messrs. Bunker, Clark of Alamakee, Clarke of Johnson, Ells, Gower, Hollingsworth, Marvin, Parvin, Peters, Scott, Seely, Solomon, Tracr, Warren, Wilson, and Young.

Nays—Messrs. Ayres, Clarke of Henry, Day, Edwards, Gibson, Gillaspy, Gray, Hall, Harris, Johnston, Palmer, Patterson, Price, Robinson, and Winchester.

The PRESIDENT announced the following named gentlemen as members of said special Committee: Messrs. Wilson, Hall, Young, Price and Bunker.

Order of Business.

The PRESIDENT. The next business in order is the consideration of the report of the Committee on Education and School Lands.

Mr. CLARKE, of Johnson. There have been two or three reports, which were made special orders, passed by for the purpose of acting upon the report on incorporations. I would suggest that one of these be taken up; either the report on the Executive, or that on the Legislative Department. There is a standing committee upon the Schedule, which cannot make any report until the character of these articles is determined. I move, therefore, that we take up the report of the Committee on the Executive Department.

Mr. PRICE. I would remark that the same objection still exists, that I urged the other day to taking up the report of the Committee on Executive Department. Mr. Todhunter, who is chairman of that committee, is confined to his room by illness.

Mr. PARVIN. The report of the Committee on the Judiciary was before the Committee of the whole some time since, and I would suggest to the gentleman from Johnson the propriety of taking up that report now.

Mr. CLARKE, of Johnson. I have no choice in regard to which of the reports we shall take up.

Mr. PARVIN. I move then, that we take up the report of the Committee on the Judiciary.

The PRESIDENT. If there be no objection, the report of the Committee on the Judiciary will be taken up.

There being no objection, the report was then taken up.

Judiciary Department.

The PRESIDENT. Some days since the majority and minority reports of the Committee on the Judiciary Department were referred to the Committee of the Whole, and partially considered therein. Owing to some misunderstanding with regard to the majority report, the two reports of the Judicial Committee were reported to the Convention by the Committee of the Whole, and re-committed to the Committee on the Judicial Department. Subsequently the gentleman from Henry, [Mr. Clarke,] submitted a report upon the part of the majority of that committee, and the gentleman from Johnson, [Mr. Clarke,] also submitted a minority report. The majority report is now before the Convention. What is the pleasure of the Convention with regard to this subject?

Mr. WILSON. I move that we go into Committee of the Whole upon the majority report.

The question was taken, and the motion was agreed to.

Committee of the Whole.

The Convention accordingly resolved itself into Committee of the Whole upon the majority report of the Committee on the Judicial Department, (Mr. Harris in the Chair.)

The committee then proceeded to consider the report by sections.

Number of Courts.

Section one was then read as follows:

"The judicial power shall be vested in a Supreme Court, District Courts, Circuit Courts, and such other inferior courts as the General Assembly may establish."

Mr. PALMER. I move to strike out in the first line the words "District Courts," and insert in lieu thereof the word "and," so that it shall read, "the judicial power shall be vested in a Supreme Court and Circuit Courts," &c.

Mr. WILSON. I would suggest to the gentleman, if it be his intention to have but two courts, he better retain the name as it stands in the constitution. I understand the proposition of the committee is to call our present district courts, circuit courts.

Mr. PALMER. I will move then to strike out the words "circuit courts," and insert "and" before "district courts."

My views have been already expressed on a former occasion upon this subject of the number of courts. I do not believe that the people of the State call for any material change in regard to the organization of our courts. The increase of business, however, may have rendered it necessary that the Supreme Court may be relieved somewhat; but this relief may be afforded by increasing the number of judges of this court. I have other grounds of objection to other sections of this report, which it may not be improper to notice here, as they are all involved in this one question of the number of courts.

I am opposed to the establishment of these District Courts, as they are called, or a Court which is constituted of Circuit Judges. I do not think that the Court of Appeals should be constituted of judges from whose decision appeals are taken. It is true that this report provides, that where any District Judge has made a decision below, he shall stand aside and take no part in the decisions of the Court of Appeals, when his judgments and decisions come up for revision. But still, I think the objection to such a system is not entirely removed. I would remove these judges of different Courts from association with each other. I would have them entirely separate and uninfluenced, even by association with each other, and by being members of the same Court.

I know of instances in this State, where the judges of Courts below have taken nearly as much interest in sustaining their decisions as the parties interested in the suits. I have known a judge below, when it was not asked to have his opinions placed upon the record, take the case, write out an elaborate argument, calling it an opinion, and file it among the papers of the case, that it might go up to the Supreme Court, to be there read, and exert an influence in the event of an appeal.

Judges have a pride of opinion about this matter, and are anxious that their decisions, in case of appeal, shall be sustained in the Court above. I would prevent judges of the District Court, or the Circuit Court—the lowest courts provided for in this section—from having any association with any of the judges, who are to try their cases upon appeal. To allow the judges, who are to try causes upon appeal, to associate with judges of the Courts below—to associate with them daily, and perhaps to sleep with them—would be to give them almost as much influence as if they were permitted to go into the Courts above and sit themselves upon the bench. I believe, if there is to be such a Court as an intermediate appeal Court, it should be composed of judges entirely distinct and separate from either the Supreme Court Judges or the judges of the other grades of courts.

Another objection which I have to this District Court system, is in regard to the election of the judges. This report provides that the State shall be divided into three districts; that four judges shall be elected in each of these districts, who shall be elected indiscriminately by the people of the districts at large; and that they shall officiate in districts of which they were not residents, previous to their election. This is a provision which, I think, does not prevail in any other State.

How would it have been relished by the people of this State, if, upon the organization of a State government, Congress should have refused to permit the State to organize under a Constitution which provided, that all the officers of the State government should be residents of the State at the time of their election; and should urge as a reason for so doing, that we might select men in some of the older States of better talent than we had, to fill the offices of importance in this State? How would the people of any new State relish the idea of having such a provision incorporated into their Constitution? It is true, that a new State may not have as much talent as an older one; but still, she has within her limits men who consider themselves capable of discharging the functions of the highest offices in her gift, and they would not consent, under any circumstances, that these offices should be filled by men outside of her limits. It may be that the older counties of this State, along the river, are as much superior to the new counties, in talents and learning, as they imagine themselves to be. Still, that affords no argument in favor of selecting from these counties judicial officers for the newer counties.

The fourth section of this majority report provides that,

"There shall be twelve District Judges, who shall also be Circuit Judges, one of whom shall reside, after his election, in each of the said circuits; shall be elected by the people of the districts at large, and to hold office for four years, (except as herein provided), and until their successors are elected and qualified; and shall have each a salary of not less than one thousand dollars, nor over three thousand dollars, and not changeable during their term of office."

So that, by this provision, if the counties, which are the most populous, choose to impose upon a district which is without their borders a judge who is not a resident of their own county, they can do so, notwithstanding the remonstrances and objections of the very district that is to be supplied with the judge. I think that this would be a wrong principle to adopt. If there is not talent enough in the new districts, let us provide that these districts shall furnish judicial officers to officiate within their own borders, and we will then soon invite talent enough there to discharge all the duties required of such officers. It will be an encouragement to talented men from every part of the country to emigrate to the new counties, when they know that their talents will be properly appreciated, and that they will not be neglected for persons residing in the older parts of the State.

Mr. WILSON. I have a substitute, which I wish to offer, which is much shorter than the report of the committee, and which comes nearer my views of what we require upon this subject.

Mr. CLARKE, of Henry. I would inquire if there is not an amendment already pending—the amendment of the gentleman from Davis? [Mr. Palmer.]

Mr. WILSON. I will offer it, then, after the amendment of the gentlemen from Davis is disposed of.

Mr. CLARKE, of Henry. I desire but a few minutes' time of the Committee to express my views in regard to this subject. If the Convention shall prefer the two Court system, I shall yield my wishes without any struggle. I concurred in this report, because I believed that the time had come when we needed the system here recommended. I concurred with the gentleman from Johnson, [Mr. Clarke], in believing that this system is adapted to the wants of a large State; and I believe, further, that the business of the State demands greater facilities than we now enjoy. I do not think, with the gentleman, that this system is alone adapted for a large State, and a greater amount of business than we now have. Those who have not practiced in our District Courts, of course cannot be supposed to have heard many of the complaints that have arisen there in regard to the system that now exists. But almost every lawyer, who has practiced in any part of the State, distant from the capitol, has heard more or less complaint in regard to the facilities that the present system affords for deciding questions of law that arise in the District Courts. There is not a District Court, held in any portion of the State, but what there are more or less exceptions taken of decisions of judges in the trial of causes. I venture to say, however, that if you go fifty miles from Iowa City, more than half of these cases are never taken up on appeal to the Supreme Court, for the reason, that the expenses attending such a course are so great as to debar parties from taking appeals. In my own limited practice, I have had numbers of cases where my clients wished to take up their cases on appeal, but I have always advised them not to do so, on account of the expense to which they would be necessarily subjected. I have sent cases to this place to lawyers to take charge of, and argue them; but not being familiar with the circumstances attending them, they would not give them that attention to which they were entitled.

What class of cases could be disposed of in this intermediate court? They are not cases that involve great questions—effecting title to real estate, or involving great fundamental principles of law. But they are questions, perhaps, in regard to overruling testimony, and those minor questions that spring up, purely legal, and of which parties wish to get a speedy and expeditious decision, in order to entitle them to a new trial again. If you will examine the decisions in our Supreme Court, you will find that one third of the cases now reported, require only the granting of a new trial, and the cases then are no nearer a final decision than when they started from the district. Look at the expense to which parties have been subjected, in order to reach this result. They subject themselves to the expense of sending lawyers here, paying their expenses while here—and what do they get? Merely a decision that they shall have a new trial, and that questions of law shall be ruled differently, which may, perhaps, enable them to introduce testimony which they offered in the court below, but which was rejected.

The people in distant parts of the State are beginning to demand a different system. It is generally expected that we will do something to relieve the Supreme Court of the burden that now rests upon it, and provide another tribunal for the settlement of these minor questions of law, which do not involve any great principles. Important questions relating to real estate, and other questions of law involving important interests, will, of course, be still taken up, as before, to the Supreme Court. What we desire now, by the establishment of this new system, is to have a court that will decide all these minor questions of practice, motions for new trial, &c., and relieve the Supreme Court from that class of work with which it is now so greatly encumbered, and save suitors and their attorneys the expense of coming up to the capitol to dispose of their cases.

Gentlemen will at once see, that we propose, by the plan here presented, to call upon the Circuit Judges to perform an extra amount of labor for the same salaries that they now receive. How is it to be done? We merely say, that the Legislature shall provide that these judges shall meet so many times in a year—say twice a year, at some point in the district; and that they shall then hear such cases as may come up to them on writ of error from the Circuit Courts. Several objections have been advanced by gentlemen to this plan. The gentleman from Davis [Mr. Palmer], has urged as an objection, that if you allow the Circuit Judge, who has made a decision in a court below, to meet the other judges when they come to try it upon appeal, having once committed himself, and having some pride of opinion in the matter, he will unduly influence the other judges in their decision. That may be an evil, but we have attempted to provide against it, as well as we could, by providing that a judge shall not be allowed to sit upon the bench during the trial of a case with which he had anything to do in the court below. In the Supreme Court they adopt a similar plan; and as I understand it, they find that it does not have the effect which the gentleman from Davis so much deprecates; it tends rather to excite a rivalry among the judges, to see who will be the most correct in his decisions; and the judge who criticizes the decision of another, gets his decision, in turn, severely criticized.

Is not this supposition just as natural as that made by the gentleman from Davis, [Mr. Palmer]? He supposes, in the objection he has made here, that every decision which is made in the Circuit Court, will be sustained in the District Court by the influence of the judge. In nine cases out of ten, these judges, if they were permitted to sit upon the bench of this Appellate Court, would decide cases just as they did before; and it is for this reason we provide that they shall not be permitted to vote upon questions which they have tried in the Circuit Courts. If a judge be an honest judge, he can give information in regard to the facts of a case, when it shall come up for trial, that will be of great benefit to the other judges upon the bench, if they see proper to receive information about the case, and not his prejudices. And if they would be governed by his facts instead of his prejudices, they would derive benefit rather than evil from an association with him. But the objection of the gentleman from Davis, if it be really a serious one, to the system itself, can be easily obviated. He can move to amend the report, by providing that a judge shall not be allowed to associate with the other judges, while a case from the Circuit Court, which he has decided, is undergoing investigation.

Another objection urged by the gentleman to the system we have reported, is in regard to the mode of the election of the judges. If there be a defect in the system in this respect, it can be easily removed. The Committee thought it would be better, inasmuch as we provide for District Judges, and inasmuch as the district at large is interested in these judges, that they should be elected at large, and taken from any part of the district from which the people should see fit to select them. I would ask if, in nine cases out of ten, they would not select in the Convention to nominate judges, one from each circuit? I would not deprive the people of a circuit, if they deemed it necessary, of the privilege of selecting a judge in another circuit. The gentleman knows very well that a judge could not be selected out of the circuit, unless the people consented to it. When the districts assemble in Convention, the delegates of one circuit will consult with those of another, in regard to the merits and fitness of the various candidates. And I do not think that in such a state of the case, it will be possible to palm off upon the people of a circuit, a judge whom they do not want. I think, on the other hand, that under this arrangement, the people of the different circuits will secure just such judicial officers as they desire to act for them.

I would direct the attention of gentlemen to the fact that, by this report, we have not increased the number of Supreme Court Judges. Owing to the rapid increase of the business of the State, the time will soon come, when it will be absolutely necessary to either increase the number of judges, or we must so manage that they will have less to do. By the system we propose, the Supreme Judges will have less to do, and we shall not need an augmentation of the bench in that respect. If we should still continue the present system, it is held by many gentlemen of the legal profession, and by some who have presided on the Supreme Court bench, that it will be necessary to increase the number of the Supreme Court Judges. The system we propose will be the most economical, because we lessen the besiness of the Supreme Court, thereby avoiding the necessity of creating an additional number of judges of that court.

The gentleman from Jefferson [Mr. Wilson,] remarked the other day, that the District Court had not enough business to employ all of their time. By the system we propose, we would give them enough to do. We would place them in a position, where they would hear in the first instance, except in certain cases provided for by law, all those questions that come up from justices' court, and finally settle them by the decisions they should render; and also decide all questions of practice, and all cases involving the question, whether a new trial shall be granted.

I wish gentlemen to consider another feature in connection with this matter. The gentleman from Jefferson has urged, as an objection against the plan we propose, that parties who desire it, will be precluded from taking their cases directly up to the Supreme Court. But it will be perceived that there is a provision in this report, by which the legislature may provide in all cases, where it is important they should do so, that suitors may take their cases by appeal, or writ of error, to the Supreme Court. So in this respect, the objection of the gentleman is entirely obviated, and the system will not necessarily put an obstruction in the way of those who wish to take their cases directly to the Supreme Court. If it can be demonstrated to the legislature that it is important to take a certain class of cases directly up to the Supreme Court, they can pass a law under which this arrangement will be made. We merely provide that there shall be a District Court system, so that those who wish may take their cases there, without being subjected to the unnecessary delay and expense of taking them up to the Supreme Court. I do not wish gentlemen to look upon this plan as any innovation upon the present system, for it does not materially change it. The present system remains precisely as it is now, except that cases which originate in Justices' Courts, are to be decided by this District Court, and there terminate. Other cases may go up to the Supreme Court just as they do now.

Again, gentlemen will see, that we propose by this system, that the legislature shall provide a practice act, that shall be uniform throughout the whole State. The objection has been raised to the establishment of this intermediate court, that a practice would spring up in one part of the State, entirely different from that prevailing in another part. But we obviate that objection by making it incumbent upon the legislature to provide an uniform practice all over the State.

Another feature of this system is, that we have omitted to make any provision for reports of cases decided in the District Court. The greatest evil that has attended the district system, wherever it has prevailed, in my apprehension, has been the publication of the reports of the cases that they have decided. Owing to the desire of the District Judges to see their decisions published, they have made provision for reporting their cases. We ought to make provisions for publishing only the decisions of the Supreme Court, for they make the law of the State. The decisions of the District Courts ought never to be reported, because they will be merely rules of law to regulate the practice of their circuits, until they are overruled by the decisions of the Supreme Court. The decisions of the Supreme Court will be the supreme law in every circuit and district; but the decisions of the District Court, until they are overruled or affirmed, will be merely rules to regulate the circuits in their respective districts. This District Court is, if I may so express it, a court of conciliation in one sense; a court to which the people may resort for cheap justice. If an important question arises in a circuit, involving a large amount of money, they can take it through the District Court, and from the District to the Supreme Court, or directly to the Supreme Court.

without the intervention of a trial in the District Court. The change in the present system, which we propose, is nothing of which gentlemen need be afraid. It is no innovation, and will not be attended with the inconveniences attending the establishment of an entirely new system. It is merely engrafting a new feature upon our present system, by requiring our District Judges to perform an extra amount of labor for the good of the people. If gentlemen will examine the plan closely, they will see, that it provides for the election of no additional officers. The clerks of the Circuit Courts will be the clerks of the District Courts.

There is another provision of the report, by which we provide that the present office of Prosecuting Attorney shall be dispensed with, and that there shall be merely a Prosecuting Attorney in each district, which will make only twelve Prosecuting Attorneys in the State.

Mr. WILSON. I would ask the gentleman from Davis [Mr. Palmer,] if he will not withdraw his amendment, and permit me to offer a substitute, that will reach the same object which he desires to accomplish; that is, of determining between the system proposed by the committee, and that existing at the present time?

Mr. PALMER. I will withdraw it.

Mr. HALL. I will renew the amendment.

Mr. WILSON. Can the gentleman from Des Moines [Mr. Hall,] move an amendment while I have the floor?

Mr. HALL. I can, and do object to the withdrawal of the amendment of the gentleman from Davis, [Mr. Palmer.]

Mr. WILSON. Then I move that the gentleman from Davis have leave to withdraw his amendment.

The question being taken upon granting leave to withdraw the amendment it was not agreed to.

The question then recurred upon the amendment of Mr. Palmer to strike out the words "Circuit Courts," and insert the word "and" before the words "District Courts," so that the section would read—

"The judicial power shall be vested in a Supreme Court and District Courts, and in such other inferior courts as the General Assembly may establish."

Mr. HALL. This question has been discussed a great deal already, and it does appear to me that gentlemen ought to be prepared now to vote, and decide this question. The amendment proposed by the gentleman from Davis [Mr. Palmer,] will settle one important point, and that is whether we are to have three courts or not—whether the intermediate court, provided in this report, shall be put into operation or not. When that point is established, and the committee have decided against it, then will be the proper time for offering a substitute for this report. And when I am satisfied that the majority of the convention are disposed to retain the present system, I will vote for a substitute that will approximate as nearly as practicable to the present system. I have said all I desire about this intermediate court. I have expressed my views upon that subject heretofore, and do not want to say anything farther, or very little more upon that subject.

I wish to say, however, that I believe that the necessities of the State require this increase of force in our Judiciary system. Those who reside in sparsely settled counties and districts do not see the necessity of this increase, as do those who reside in the more populous portions of the State. But the time will shortly come when they also will feel the want of this intermediate court. On an average, probably, the amount of business that goes to the Supreme Court is about three to five cases out of every hundred that is put upon the docket. In my judgment, the Supreme Court ought to be kept entirely at the seat of Government. I think the court of last resort ought to be located at the capitol, and not hold its sessions in any other place. That would give stability to it, and at least tend to give harmony and uniformity to its decisions, all of which is very desirable.

This intermediate court would be a court which would cost nothing, and still be a court more convenient to the litigant, and in that way give him confidence in the courts of justice, and securing correct principles of law and right. So far as electing these judges in large districts is concerned, that is a matter that we ought not to have a great deal of difficulty about. I would be willing to compromise upon that point, and then I should not think I had made any very great sacrifice. I would be willing to leave the districts perfectly independent in regard to that matter, inasmuch as with this intermediate court you give additional labor and no more expense. I do not think gentlemen can object to it upon that score unless they are opposed to it upon principle.

I would be unwilling to allow the assertions of the gentleman from Davis [Mr. Palmer] to pass by with even a tacit sanction upon my part; charging corruption and want of integrity in advance upon those who may sit upon the bench. He says that the judge who sits upon a case in the circuit court would become the lawyer and advocate in favor of his own decision, when it came into the district or intermediate court. Now, in the first place, as a genaral rule, and I may say as an almost universal rule, the great anxiety of a judge is to be right, and that is the main thing which influences him. He may sometimes be swayed by prejudice, feeling and passion, but those are exceptions, attributable to the laws of human nature, rather than defects in the system itself. It is an attribute of man to have these passions and prejudices, and you cannot legislate them out of existence. But there is a principle of integrity in the courts which I am willing to trust, and which will, as an almost universal rule, rise above all such considerations.

When we undertake to form a constitution, when we consider that we are here acting for the people of the whole State, we should endeavuor to add to their character, and not act here s if we supposed they were all knaves and scoundr ls. Let us act upon the presumption to which every man is entitled, that the people will be honest and faithful in the performance of their duty, and that however limited their districts may be, they will act honestly and judiciously in selecting persons to sit in their courts. We should endeavor to give the people confidence in the judiciary, so that the suitor, when he enters the temple of justice for the purpose of having his rights decided and adjudicated upon, and having the judiciary declare between man and man, and citizen and citizen, will feel satisfied that right will be done him and his opponent, and the principles of law and justice be made so clear and apparent that the ordinary mind may comprehend them.

As I said the other day, and it will bear repeating, it would be but justice to the circuit judge, as he is termed in this report, where he has been obliged to make a decision upon the spur of the moment on new questions which he has not thought of, or had an opportunity to investigate—it would be nothing more than justice to give him an opportunity of reviewing that decision as soon as practicable, and be present when the other judges review it, so that he may be convinced of his error, if he is wrong, and thus leave the ccurt a wiser and better man. The very association of these judges together will have a tendency to give uniformity to the decisions of the court. They will have a high and noble pride in having their decisions conform to what would be the decisions of the Supreme Court. It will be their earnest desire to have none of their decisions reversed by the Supreme Court sitting at the seat of government. This will be their ambition, prompted by the professional pride that they will carry with them upon the bench, and by the hope that their names may go down to posterity connected with as little error as possible. This will be found the ruling passion of these judges. In this country, where everything depends upon popular favor, and the good will of citizens, none are ambitious of becoming the instrument of error, oppression or wrong.

This objection grows out of a suspicion which is not warranted, and which we should not for one moment tolerate in this convention. Let us look upon the people as possessing the good and virtuous qualities which constitute the foundation of every good and efficient tribunal of justice. Let us here, as the representatives of the people, set the example of showing confidence in these judges. Let us give these men, whom we have endorsed as worthy, an opportunity to display the qualities and virtues we ascribe to them. Let us endeavor to incite a feeling which will prompt judges to inform themselves, and make themselves learned and eminent in the position in which the partiality of their fellow citizens have placed them.

It is the duty of this convention to give, if possible, to these circuit judges more opportunity for deliberation, and for displaying those good qualities, than they now possess. And if it was at all practicable, I would be willing to say —not here, but in the legislature—that the district judges should write out all of their decisions. Such a course would insure deliberation, and give confidence in their decisions. And confidence between the people and this branch of our government is worth everything, and without it the government itself becomes almost a reproach.

We want to secure a system that will accomplish this desirable object. And I do believe that the principle involved in this report will have that tendency, by making litigation cheap and convenient, and advancing the administration of justice to a very considerable extent. If gentlemen here are disposed to allow this additional facility to the people, if they are willing to place this additioaal labor upon the judges of district courts, they can say so at once, and we will then know what system we are going to adopt. If this convention should decide in favor of having this third court, as it is called, then we shall know how to proceed. I hope gentlemen will vote in committee of the whole as they intend to vote when this subject comes up in the convention; because if we once settle that we will not adopt this three court system, I will fall back upon the old system.

Mr. SCOTT. I do not rise, Mr. Chairman, to give my own personal views in regard to striking out this third court, for my views would be worth little in comparison with the views of legal gentlemen in this Convention. But I rise to give the views of my constituents. The bar of the district I represent here, have held meetings and unanimously instructed me to advocate and favor a three court system, or nearly the system of the State of New York. And when this question is pending here, I cannot do justice to my constituents without stating their views to the Convention.

The courts in every part of the State are probably administered as well as they can be under our present judicial system. But there is a clamorous complaint of the inefficacy of our judicial system in our district, and the bar there, as one man, unite in saying that the system is wrong, and that unless it is remedied, we, as members of this convention, will not have done our duty. That, I think, is the feeling in the whole of the northern part of the State, not only in my district, but in other districts there. They are in favor of the three court system, nearly upon the plan of the system in the State of New York. I, myself, am not personally conversant with these different judicial systems, not being of the legal fraternity. But I am instructed to go for the three court system. I hope that others here who agree with the views my constituency entertain upon this subject will unite together and remove the influences which are working against the interests of a portion of the State at least. I do hope that we will have a better judiciary system than the present one—that we will have a system that will not be frowned upon as the present one is in the portion of the State where I reside. There is a lack of confidence in the present system, and it certainly does not meet the demands of the people.

Mr. CLARK, of Alamakee. I have already expressed my views upon this subject, and they have not been changed. I am satisfied that all that portion of the State with which I am acquainted, is decidedly in favor of a change in our present judicial system, and they will feel very much disappointed if there is not a change. The interests and necessities of the people require this change. They have looked forward to this Convention as the means of procuring this change for them. If we adopt a constitution here without materially changing the judiciary of this State, I am satisfied there will be great dissatisfaction felt among that portion of the people of this State, who have expected, anticipated. and felt the necessity for this change.

One of the most serious objections urged in discussion here against this change is, that it held out inducements for litigation; in other words, that it cheapened litigation, and brought the courts almost to every man's door where he could litigate without any great expense, while the present judicial system removed that temptation. Now I suppose that one object of all governments should be to cheapen litigation, and bring it as near home, and make it as nearly practicable as possible for every person, no matter how humble and poor, to defend his rights by placing the means of defence within his reach. This, I suppose should be the object of our government, at least it should be the motive governing this Convention. And if that is the principle which is to govern us here, then we should certainly be in favor of the three court system.

I have heard no valid objection urged against that system. It brings the tribunal of justice within the reach of every man, who is interested in defending and maintaining his rights without subjecting the people to any of tha difficulties which were charged upon the former report of the committee. I appeal to gentlemen who are opposed to this three court system to agree to a compromise on this matter. If this system is adopted, those who desire to take appeals from the circuit to the district courts can do so and those who desire to go to the supreme court can do that also. We who are in favor of this system think its adoption would be beneficial to the State, that it would cheapen litigation and bring within the reach of every man the means of defending his rights, and, at the same time prevent, to a great extent, the ruinous expenses attending an appeal to the supreme court of this State. If any one desires to take an appeal directly to the supreme court, he can do so; and as he has the privilege of going into whichever court he pleases, we ask that we may have the same right and privilege. It seems to me there can be no objection to that.

One gentleman here is afraid that if we have a Supreme Court of four judges, they will sleep together. Now if he is fearful of any evil resulting from such a practice as that, he can move to have a provision inserted here that they shall not sleep together. (Laughter.) I would have no objection to that, though I do not think any evil will flow from such a practice.

It is said that the judge in the circuit court will be ambitious to sustain his decision when it comes up in the superior court, or court in bank. Now if gentlemen will look over the reports of the State of New York for fifty years past, they will find that that objection is not well founded. Under the old system there the circuit courts were often held by judges of the supreme court, not required to sit upon the supreme bench at the time. In the celebrated McLeod case, which grew out of the burning of the steamer Caroline, Judge Cowen came to Utica and presided upon that trial, and it will be found in looking over these reports, that it was the general practice, in the early history of New York, for the judges of the supreme court to do the greater part of the *nisi prius* business. And yet when cases came up to the supreme court on appeal, it was generally found that these judges were the first to advocate reversal of their own decisions. They did not consider themselves infallible. They thought it was impossible for any man, no matter how exalted his natural abilities were, no matter how extensive was his acquired knowledge, to render decisions upon the spur of the moment that would be so correct as when he had an opportunity to investigate the laws upon the subject; and they considered it a privilege to go into a court and correct the errors of their own decisions. I do not think, therefore, any inconvenience of this kind will be felt here. But if other gentlemen think there will be this trouble with this three court system, they can provide by law that these judges shall sit in appellate court upon no cases tried in their respective circuits.

It is said that the majority of cases will not stop in the district court. I am of a different opinion. The experience of New York shows that not more than one case out of twenty passes from the intermediate court to the court of last resort. That fact should of itself satisfy every man that this system will cheapen litigation, and will be beneficial to litigants generally. It is true that once in a while a case would go from the circuit court to the district court, and pass that court up to the supreme court. That will undoubtedly enhance the expenses in that particular case. But bear in mind that that one case where the expenses would be enhanced, is but one case out of ten or twenty that would go to the supreme court under the present system. So that, view this matter in any light you please, I cannot see any objection to be raised against this system. But I see a great many reasons which induce me, and the people in the part of the State which I represent, to demand this change.

Another reason for this change, and one which has been urged here, is, that the time is near at hand when the present Supreme Court can never dispose of the business before them, for it will be utterly impossible for them to do so. That difficulty, it is said, can be obviated, under the present system, by increasing the number of judges. But I do not think that will help them out of the difficulty. If the opinions of the court are to be worth anything, a majority of the judges must examine and deliberate upon the cases before them. And it will be necessary, in order to give that weight to the opinions which we all consider necessary, for each judge to consider and examine the case for himself. Now, I am opposed to a system of practice which will compel each judge of the Supreme Court, even though there might be ten or fifteen of them, to take up each case and look it over carefully before it could be decided. I am opposed to a system of practice, which, from the very necessities of the case, must cause business to increase upon the hands of the Supreme Judges to such an extent as to deprive them of the means of giving that deliberation to their action which is so essential, and which will cause cases to lie over from term to term, until the interest of the parties have almost passed away.

There are many cases where it is necessary to obtain a decision almost immediately. Take, for instance, the case of a creditor trying to enforce his demands against a debtor. He goes before the Circuit Court with an attachment; for some informality, that attachment is dismissed, and the case must go to some other court to be decided. If that case is to run along for years, the debtor may change his circumstances, so that the creditor will be in danger of losing his debt. This difficulty would not arise under the system I advocate. A warrant would be granted immediately, and the case be settled at once, and in a cheap manner, which would never be the case under the present system.

Mr. PALMER. I have greater objection to the details than to the main principles of the system here proposed. The gentleman from Henry [Mr. Clarke] seems disposed to adhere to this system in detail. He says that, in the election of these judges by the different districts, it is not probable any district would force upon any particular circuit a judge not acceptable to that circuit. I think they may do it; at all events, they can do it. Suppose there are three circuits in one district, two of those circuits being much the most numerous in population. Those two circuits may force upon the other circuit a judge totally unacceptable to them. That is my principal objection to the system here proposed.

The gentleman from Des Moines [Mr. Hall], says he does not adhere to the detail, but wants to see the main principles of the plan adopted. Now, as the changes proposed in this system have appeared in detail, to my mind, to be worse than the present system can be, I have preferred the present system to any that has yet been suggested. I do not know but a system might be devised something like this one, or this system might be amended, so as to be preferable to the present system.

The gentleman from Henry [Mr. Clarke], has also said that the District Courts, though courts of appeals, should not have their decisions reported. And yet he says they should be the final tribunal for the decision of causes from justices' courts. I think as important questions arise in cases originally brought before a justice of the peace as in cases originating elsewhere. There are questions of law arising in a justice's court involving as great principles as in more important cases originally commenced in higher courts. The decisions in those cases should be reported, and become established law throughout the State; or at least the principles they contain should become so settled that they may be regarded throughout the State as law. The system here proposed does not, I believe, embrace the provisions that this intermediate court shall be the highest court in certain cases, but it is left to the Legislature to say whether certain cases shall stop there, or be allowed to go on to a higher court; or under a certain restriction, certain portions of a case allowed to go to the highest court.

The gentleman from Des Moines [Mr. Hall], has said that I charged the judges of the lower courts with being liable to corruption, &c., in their association in the District Court with other judges. I meant to intimate nothing of the kind. I would not charge the judges with any disposition to do otherwise than to administer justice, and to decide equitably all the cases that may come before them, according to the exact justice and merits of each case. But I do say that it is one of the evils of the system here proposed, that the judges may be influenced by their daily association with those upon whose decisions they are to sit and decide. They may be led, unknowingly, to swerve from what justice and law would require. It is one of the evils I charged against the system, and I would remove it by constituting that court—if there is to be an intermediate court—upon a different plan from that proposed here.

It was the prayer of him who furnished to the world the brightest example mankind have ever known, "to be delivered from evil, and not led into temptation;" and I would deliver these judges from the temptation to which they will be exposed by association with those whose decisions they will be called upon to revise. It has been urged that the judges below should have an opportunity of having their decisions revised, and that they should be present when they are thus revised and reviewed. Now, it is because they are to be present that I object to the system proposed here. I think that is the worst feature of the system. I admit that it is to the interest and benefit of the judges themselves that their decisions should be reviewed; but it should be at such a distanee from them that they can have no influence whatever upon the judges who are to pass upon their decisions, and that can be accomplished in the Supreme Court.

Some gentlemen here may have formed their opinion of the qualifications of the District Judges, by comparing the number of their errors with the number of the errors of the Supreme Court. If they have done so, then I think they may judge somewhat erroneously. We all know that District Judges sit upon cases that they have not examined at all, perhaps, before they are called upon to try them. They know nothing about the questions arising in those cases. In the investigation of the case, and the hearing of the evidence, &c., questions of law may be sprung upon them of the utmost importance, and yet they will be compelled to decide almost instantaneously. They decide upon their recollection of the law, and sometimes err. When that case comes up before the Supreme Court, it is there argued elaborately; all the authorities which can be brought in support of or against the decision of the court below, are produced before the court; and the judges of the Supreme Court, before they utter a word upon the subject, have access to all the books that can be procured for their examination before they give their decision. It is not strange, then, that the decisions of the Supreme Court should be more according to law and equity, and that they should be less liable to err, than is the case in the decisions of the judges of the District Court. As I have before said, I think that, taking all things into consideration, we have had, on an average, considering the number of the judges of the different courts, about as good talent upon the district bench as upon the Supreme bench.

Mr. HALL. In the decision of the question now before us, let it be understood that the Convention, if it agrees to this motion, is opposed to the three court system. Let that be the only question settled. Let this question be considered as a test question, whether they are in favor of the two court or the three court system, so that we may get at something practical.

The question recurred upon the motion of Mr. Palmer to strike out of the first section the words, "Circuit Courts," and to insert before the words, "District Courts," the word "and," so that the section would then read,

"The judicial power shall be vested in a Supreme Court and District Courts, and in such other inferior courts as the General Assembly may establish."

The question being taken, upon a division, the motion to amend was agreed to; yeas 15, nays 10.

Mr. CLARKE, of Johnson, moved to further amend the section by striking out the word "inferior," so that the section would then read,

"The judicial power shall be vested in a Supreme Court and District Courts, and in such other courts as the General Assembly may establish."

Mr. HALL. I would suggest that we might just as well lay this report aside now.

Mr. CLARKE, of Johnson. If that can be done, I am willing to have it done. But perhaps such a motion might not succeed. I will therefore briefly give my reasons for the amendment I have offered.

As I remarked some days since, while I am opposed to this three court system, as unnecessary, and not called for by the wants of the people or the business of the courts, yet I am willing that the power to establish this third court should be placed in the hands of the Legislature to be exercised whenever the interests of the people may require. And for the purpose of so having it, I have moved to strike out this word "inferior." Then the Legislature would have power to establish just such other courts as may be deemed necessary. I offer this amendment as a compromise between the friends of the two systems. I think there ought to be power in the Legislature to increase the courts as the necessities of the people may require.

The question being taken upon striking out the word "inferior," upon a division, it was agreed to; ayes 16, noes not counted.

Mr. CLARKE, of Henry. I have a substitute to offer for this report. I offer the majority report of the Committee on the Judicial Department, with those portions stricken out that provide for this third court, I offer the following as a substitute for this report:

Section 1. The judicial power shall be vested in a Supreme Court, District Courts, and such other courts as the General Assembly may establish.

Sec. 2. The Supreme Court shall consist of a Chief Justice and two Associate Justices, two of whom shall be a quorum to hold court. They shall be elected by the people of the State at large, and shall hold their office for six years, (except as herein provided,) and until their successors shall be elected and qualified. The salary of each shall not be less than two thousand dollars, nor more than five thousand dollars per annum, to be fixed by law, and not changeable during their term of office, by the General Assembly.

Sec. 3. The State shall be divided into three judicial districts, to be bounded by county lines, and as nearly equal in population and territory as may be.

Sec. 4. There shall be twelve District Judges, one of whom shall reside in each of the said circuits; shall be elected by the people of the districts at large, and to hold office for four years, (except as herein provided,) and until their successors are elected and qualified; and shall have each a salary of not less than one thousand dollars, nor over three thousand dollars, and not changeable during their term of office.

Sec. 5. At the first election of judicial officers under this constitution—which shall be at the first general election after its adoption—they shall be so classified, under provisions of law, that one of the Supreme Court Judges shall go out of office every two years, and one of the District Judges in each district shall go out of office every year, and their successors shall be elected for the full terms. The Justice of the Supreme Court having the longest term at the first election, shall be Chief Justice; and after the expiration of his term, the Justice longest presiding shall be Chief Justice.

Sec. 6. The resident judge in each district shall hold the courts therein, except when otherwise provided by law, and District Courts shall be courts of law and equity, having jurisdiction in each, over all matters, civil or criminal, arising in their respective districts, under such regulations as the law may provide.

Sec. 7. The Supreme Court shall have appellate jurisdiction in chancery, and constitute a court for the correction of errors at law, in all cases coming from the District Courts; and shall have the right to appoint its own clerk and reporter.

Sec. 8. There shall be a clerk of the District Court elected in each county where a term of such court shall be appointed by law to be held.

Sec. 9. Each of said courts shall exercise a supervisory control over all inferior courts within the limits of their respective jurisdictions, and be conservators of the peace therein, they shall have power to issue all usual writs and process, and to enforce the same.

Sec. 10. No judicial officer, provided for herein, shall be eligible to any other office during the term for which he shall be elected; except that district judges shall be eligible to the office of justice of the Supreme Court; and their terms of office shall commence the first of January next after their election, but in cases of a vacancy the same may be filled by appointment by the Governor, until it shall be supplied at the next general election, when it shall be filled by election for the residue of the unexpired term.

Sec. 11. It shall be the duty of the General Assembly to make such provisions by law as shall be necessary for the carrying into effect of this article, and to provide for a regular system of practice in all the courts of the State. To provide for the election of an Attorney General to reside at the capitol, and for the election of Prosecuting Attorneys in each district, in lieu of the Prosecuting Attorneys in the several counties, and to prescribe their powers, duties, terms of office and salary.

Sec. 12. The style of all process shall be, "The State of Iowa;'" and all prosecutions shall be conducted in the name and by authority of the same.

Sec. 13. After the year 1860, the General Assembly may re-organize the judicial districts, and increase or diminish the number of districts, or the number of Judges of the Supreme or District Courts; but such increase or diminution shall not be more than one district, or one judge of either court at a time; and no re-organization of the districts, or diminution of the judges shall have the effect of removing a judge from office. Such re-organization of the districts, or increase or diminution of the judges shall take place every five years thereafter, if necessary, and at no other time.

Sec. 14. The Supreme Court, with one District Judge from each district, to be selected as shall be provided by law, shall form a court for the trial of all impeachments, except in cases where a Justice of the Supreme Court is upon taial, when the court shall be composed of the District Judges, a majority of whom shall constitute a quorum. Incompetency shall be a ground for impeachment, in a judicial officer; and all impeachments must be found by the General Assembly.

Mr. JOHNSTON. The Committee of the Whole have had under consideration the work of the majority of this committee, and they have before them now a substitute offered by the chairman of that committee. I am anxious to test the opinion of the Committee of the Whole in regard to the minority report. I therefore move to lay this majority report with the substitute offered by the gentleman from Henry, [Mr. Clarke,] upon the table, with a view of taking up the minority report.

The question being taken upon the motion to lay upon the table, it was agreed to, upon a division; ayes 16, noes not counted.

The Committee of the Whole then proceeded to consider the report of the minority of the Judiciary Committee, which was read as follows:

Section 1. The judicial power of this State shall be vested in a Supreme Court, District Courts, and such other courts as the General Assembly may from time to time establish.

Sec. 2. The State shall be divided into four judicial districts, to be bounded by county lines, and as compact and equal in population and territory as nearly as may be, in each of which districts, at the first general election under the Constitution, one Supreme Judge, and three District Judges, who shall be residents of their respective districts, shall be elected by the people. The Supreme and District Judges so elected, shall be so classified that one Judge of the Supreme Court, and one of the District Judges in each district, shall go out of office every two years. The Judge of the Supreme Court holding the shortest term of office under such classification, shall be Chief Justice of the Court during his term, and so on in rotation. After the expiration of their terms of office under such classification, the term of each Judge of the Supreme Court thall be eight years, and the term of office of each Judge of the District Court, six years, and until their successors are elected and qualified.

Sec. 3. The Supreme Court shall consist of the four Judges elected as required by the foregoing section, three of whom shall constitute a quorum, and they shall hold their Court at such time and place as the General Assembly may, by law, provide. The Judges of the Supreme Court shall be ineligible to any other office in the State, during the term for which they were elected; and the Judges of the District Court shall be ineligible to any other office in the State, except that of Supreme Judge, during the term for which they were elected.

Sec. 4. The Supreme Court shall have appellate jurisdiction only in all cases in Chancery, and shall constitute a Court for the correction of errors at law, under such restrictions as the

General Assembly may, by law, prescribe, and shall have power to issue all writs and process necessary to secure justice to parties, and exercise a supervisory control over all inferior judicial tribunals throughout the State.

Sec. 5. The District Court shall consist of a single Judge, and the District Judges of each District shall hold Court in each county of such District, alternately, at such time and place as the General Assembly may, by law, provide.

Sec. 6. The District Court shall be a Court of law and equity, which shall be distinct and separate jurisdictions, and have jurisdiction in all civil and criminal cases, arising in their respective Districts, under such restrictions as may be prescribed by law.

Sec. 7. The Supreme Court shall have the power to appoint a Clerk and Reporter of its decisions. The other officers of the Court shall be provided for.

Sec. 8. The Judges of the Supreme and District Courts shall be conservators of the peace throughout the State.

Sec. 9. The salary of each Judge of the Supreme Court shall not be less than three thousand dollars per annum, nor shall the salary of each Judge of the District Court be less than two thousand five hundred dollars per annum. After the year 1860, the General Assembly shall have the power to increase the salaries of the Judges of the Supreme and District Courts; but the salary of no Judge of either Court shall be increased or diminished during his term of office.

Sec. 10. In case the office of any Judge of the Supreme or District Courts shall become vacant before the expiration of the regular term for which he was elected, the vacancy may be filled by appointment, by the Governor, until it shall be supplied at the next general election, when it shall be filled by election, for the residue of the unexpired term.

Sec. 11. The Judges of the Supreme and District Courts shall be chosen at the general State election, and the term of office of each judge shall commence on the first day of January next after their election.

Sec. 12. After the year 1860, the General Assembly may re-organize the judicial districts, and increase or diminish the number of districts, or the number of Judges of the Supreme or District Courts, but such increase or diminution shall not be more than one district, or one judge of either court at a time, and no re-organization of the districts, or diminution of the judges, shall have the effect of removing a judge from office. Such re-organization of the districts, or increase or diminution of the judges of either court shall take place every five years thereafter, if necessary, and at no other time.

Sec. 13. The General Assembly may provide by law for the creation of a temporary court, for the trial of any judge of either the Supreme or District Courts, or any officer of State, who may be charged with incompetency or misconduct. If a judge of the Supreme Court is the subject of the charge, four judges of the District Court, selected from the respective districts, shall constitute a court to investigate the charge. If the complaint is against a judge of the District Court, or an officer of State, the Supreme Court shall have original jurisdiction of, and constitute a court to investigate the same. The complaint shall be made by petition, under oath, and the cause tried by the court. In either case, the judgment of the court shall not extend beyond deprivation of office, and ineligibility to hold any other office in the State, or either of them.

Sec. 14. The style of all process shall be, "The State of Iowa," and all prosecutions shall be conducted in the name and by the authority of the same.

Sec. 15. The General Assembly shall provide by law for the election of an Attorney General by the people.

Mr. WILSON. I offer the following as a substitute for the minority report.

"Sec. 1. The judicial power shall be vested in a Supreme Court, District courts, and such other inferior courts as the General Assembly may from time to time establish.

2. The Supreme Court shall consist of a chief justice, and two associates, two of whom shall be a quorum to hold court.

3. The judges of the Supreme Court shall be elected by electors qualified to vote for members of the General Assembly, and shall hold their courts at such time and place as the General Assembly may direct, and hold their offices for six years, and until their successors are elected and qualified, and shall be inelegible to any other office in the State during the term for which they may be elected. The Supreme Court shall have appellate jurisdiction only in all cases of chancery, and shall constitute a court for the correction of errors at law, under such restrictions as the General Assembly may by law prescribe. The Supreme Court may have power to issue all writs and process necessary to do justice to parties, and exercise a supervisory control over all inferior judicial tribunals, and the judges of the Supreme Court shall be conservators of the peace throughout the State.

4. The District court shall consist of a judge, who shall be elected by the qualified voters of the district in which he resides, at the general election, and hold his office for the term of five years and until his successor is elected and qualified, and shall be ineligible to any office during the term for which he may be elected in the State, except that of Supreme Judge. The District court shall be a court of law and equity which shall be distinct and separate jurisdictions, and have jurisdiction in all civil and criminal matters arising in their respective districts, in such manner as shall be prescribed by law. The judges of the district courts shall be conservators of the peace in their respective districts. The boundaries of the several judicial districts shall remain as they now are until changed by law.

5. The qualified voters of each judicial district shall at the general election elect one district attorney, and the qualified voters of each county one clerk of the district court, who shall

be residents therein, and who shall hold their several offices for the term of two years and until their successors are elected and qualified.

6. The judges of the supreme and district courts and the district attorneys shall each receive, after the first term for said officers under this constitution, as their only compensation a salary to be determined by law, which shall not be increased or diminished during the term for which they shall severally be elected.

7. The salary of the Supreme Judges for the first term shall be two thousand dollars; that of the district judges one thousand dollars; and that of district attorneys, one thousand dollars.

8. The style of all process shall be: "The State of Iowa," and all prosecutions shall be conducted in the name and by the authority of the same."

Mr. WILSON. I wish to state that although this substitute is moved by myself, yet there are some portions of it to which I do not agree. I am in favor of cutting down the districts at present to ten, and leave the legislature to increase them hereafter as the necessities of the time may require, provided the increase is not more than one district at a time.

Mr. CLARKE of Henry. The chief objection to these substitutes that have been offered here, is the fact that the only knowledge we can have of them is from hearing them read at the secretary's desk. We should have the substitute offered by the gentleman from Jefferson, [Mr. Wilson] printed and laid upon our tables before we proceed any further with it. I would prefer for the present, to go on with this consideration of the minority report and see if there is any thing in it to which we can agree. The substitute that I offered was merely the report of the majority, with those portions struck out in relation to the third or intermediate court. Every member here had that report before him, and could tell at once what was to be acted upon. But it is not so with the substitute proposed by the gentleman from Jefferson.

Mr. WILSON. Every member of this body has before him the constitution of the state as it now exists, and my substitute is a transcript from that constitution, with very few changes. I think we can act upon the substitute I have offered with very little difficulty, as it will not require a great deal of examination. The changes I propose in the article in the old constitution are merely such as will secure the election of the Supreme Court Judges by the people, and some other minor changes that can be seen at once.

Mr. CLARKE of Henry. If it is in order, I will move as a substitute for the plan submitted by the gentleman from Jefferson, the article in the old constitution.

The CHAIRMAN. According to the ruling that has prevailed in the Committee of the Whole heretofore, it is not in order to move a substitute for a substitute.

Mr. HALL. I move to lay the substitute of the gentleman from Jefferson, (Mr. Wilson) upon the table, so that we can get at something we know something about.

The question being taken upon the motion to lay the substitute upon the table, it was agreed to, upon a division; ayes 13, noes 10.

The question then recurred upon the minority report.

The CHAIRMAN stated the report was open to amendment.

Mr. CLARKE of Henry. I desire to offer a substitute for this report.

Mr. EDWARDS, I move that the committee rise and report progress and ask leave to sit again.

Mr. SOLOMON. We have laid upon the table the report that was referred to us for consideration. I should like to know what we have to report progress upon.

Mr. HALL. The tower of Babel, [laughter].

The CHAIRMAN. It is not for the chair to instruct the committee; he can only put the question to vote.

The question being taken upon the motion for the committee to rise, it was not agreed to.

The question recurred upon the minority report.

Mr. CLARKE, of Henry. I will offer as a substitute for this minority report, the article in the old constitution, which reads as follows:

1. The judicial power shall be vested in a Supreme Court, District Courts, and such inferior courts as the general assembly may from time to time establish.

2. The Supreme Court shall consist of a chief justice and two associates, two of whom shall be a quorum to hold court.

3. The judges of the Supreme Court shall be elected by joint vote of both branches of the general assembly, and shall hold their courts at such time and place as the general assembly may direct, and hold their offices for six years, and until their successors are elected and qualified, and shall be ineligible to any other office during the term for which they may be elected. The Supreme Court shall have appellate jurisdiction only in all cases in chancery, and shall constitute a court for the correction of errors at law under such restrictions as the general assembly may by law prescribe. The Supreme Court may have power to issue all writs and process necessary to do justice to parties, and exercise a supervisory control over all inferior judicial tribunals, and the judges of the Supreme Court shall be conservators of the peace throughout the State.

4. The District Court shall consist of a judge, who shall be elected by the qualified voters of the district in which he resides, at the township election, and hold his office for the term of five years, and until his successor is elected and qualified, and shall be ineligible to any other office during the term for which he may be elected. The district court shall be a court of law and equity, and have jurisdiction in all civil and criminal matters arising in their respective districts, in such manner as shall be prescribed by law. The judges of the district courts shall be

conservators of the peace in their respective districts. The first session of the general assembly shall divide the State into four districts, which may be increased as the exigencies require.

5. The qualified voters of each county shall at the general election elect one prosecuting attorney and one clerk of the district court, who shall be residents therein, and who shall hold their several offices for the term of two years, and until their successors are elected and qualified.

6. The style of all process shall be "The State of Iowa," and all prosecutions shall be conducted in the name and by the authority of the same.

Mr. CLARKE, of Johnson. The only material difference between the provisions in the present constitution in relation to the judiciary, and the provisions of the minority report is one which can be decided as well at this time as any other.

The difference is this: Under the present constitution the district judges are elected by single districts, the State being divided into fourteen or fifteen districts; while the minority report limits the number of districts to four, and provides that each district shall elect three judges, who shall perform their duties alternately. The object of that provision is simply this: In the first place, by enlarging the area of the districts, you thereby enlarge the extent of country from which to select these judges. The want of that, I apprehend, is one of the difficulties experienced in the present judicial system. I believe it is conceded upon all sides, without any disparagement to the attorneys living there, that some districts have not just the right kind of men to make judges who will give satisfaction to the bar and the people. The object of the minority report was to so increase the districts that there may be thrown together a larger body of lawyers from which to select judges.

The second reason for this proposed change is this: It is thought, by at least some members of the bar, and men in whose judgment I have a great deal of confidence, that by having three or four judges, if the legislature, had the power to increase the number of judges, it would be almost equal to a third court of the judges already in that district, or, at the farthest, with an increase of but one in the number of judges. And it is well known that one or two good judges connected with an indifferent judge, would be able to do much in controling his decisions, and settling his practice. Hence, the result would be, if there were three judges upon the bench, and the people should select one, or even two, indifferent judges, and one good judge, the good judge, as he went around the circuit, would have an opportunity of correcting their errors and settling their practice, and thereby would be saved the expense of taking many cases to the Supreme Court that would go there, if the districts were smaller and there were no interchange of judges in the circuits.

To me, the system looks feasable and practicable, and for one, I am willing to try it, for I think it is a system worth the trial. The result of it is, that instead of increasing the number of judges, the present number is diminished. We have, also, what is almost equal to another court, without any increase of expense, or of the actual number of courts. Therefore no objection can be raised against it on the score of economy.

I throw out these views for the consideration of the committee, without having any particular feeling about the matter myself. I think, from the examination I have given the subject, it would work well. Under the legislation of this winter we have some very large and some very small districts. Two of our judges, at least, if not more, have been cut off with merely nominal districts, for the reason that they failed to give satisfaction to the people and the bar in their districts. The object of this report is to re-district the State throughout, so as to give a larger number of persons from whom a selection of judges may be made, and enable the people to get rid of those judges who are incompetent and unfit for the places they now occupy. I throw out these considerations for what they are worth; and it seems to me that they are such as to be entitled to the examination of this Committee in determining this question.

Mr. PALMER. I hope that some gentlemen, who have so low a regard for the legal ability in some of the districts of this State, will remove to those districts, and see if the people there will have so high an estimation of their abilities as to elect them for judges.

Mr. CLARKE, of Johnson. I intended no reference to the rural districts at all, in what I said upon this subject. I alluded to a case in a district adjoining this one. More complaint has been made against that judge upon the ground of incompetency than perhaps any other judge in the State. And to satisfy the gentleman from Davis [Mr. Palmer], that I have no political allusions at all, I will say that that judge happens to be of my politics. In respect to this matter of the judiciary, I have no politics whatever. I am for a good judicial system, and good judges upon the bench; and hereafter, as heretofore, I shall never ask concerning a man's politics when I am called upon to vote for a judge. I have alluded to a district east of this place, which, perhaps, may be called one of the important districts of the State, and not to any of the districts west.

Mr. CLARK of Alamakee. I will merely remark here, that if I cannot have the three court system, I am in favor of having districts large enough for several judges.

Mr. JOHNSTON. I would inquire of the chair if this substitute is adopted, will it then be open to amendment?

The CHAIRMAN. Such is the opinion of the chair.

The question being then taken upon the motion to substitute the article in the old constitution for the minority report, it was agreed to.

Mr. PETERS. I now move to strike out all

that portion of this article which provides for a Supreme Court. My object in making this motion is to ascertain whether gentlemen upon this floor are consistent; and also to give the people of one section of the state the same rights and privileges that any other section enjoy. I want to put the distant portions of the state upon the same footing, as near as may be, with those portions near the capitol. I want to see if gentlemen believe in the arguments they have advanced here, to the effect that if we create a judicial tribunal it will have business, and the fact that it has business is an argument against creating it. I want to know if those objections are valid which were urged against the majority report of the committee on the judiciary.

Mr. JOHNSTON. I am opposed to the motion of the gentleman from Deleware, [Mr. Peters] but I will second it for the purpose of testing the sense of the committee upon it.

The question being taken upon so amending the article as to abolish the Supreme Court, it was not agreed to.

Mr. CLARKE of Johnson. I move to amend the first section by striking out the word "inferior" and inserting the word "other," so that the section will read:

"The judicial power shall be vested in a Supreme Court, District Courts and such other courts as the General Assembly shall from time to time establish."

Mr. PARVIN. I hope before the committee agree to this amendment they will consider the effect of it. The committee have already declared by a very decisive vote that they will not have a three court system. If this word "inferior" is stricken out of this section, the very next legislature will be besieged by every man in the state who wants a three court system.

Mr. CLARK of Alamakee. I will say to the gentleman from Muscatine [Mr. Parvin] that instead of this committee rejecting the three court system by a very decisive vote, there was but a majority of two against it.

Mr. MARVIN. I have not the least doubt myself that if this matter is left to the Legislature they will be beseiged for this three court system. Cries and demands for it have come up to us and if we do not heed them I trust the legislature may.

Mr. GILLASPY. I hope the committee will not strike out the word "inferior," I do not want to leave to the next General Assembly to create this new court. We have had one lesson from the General Assembly who have just gone home, and I do not want another. They have created more new judicial districts than we have had before for five years. If we leave this matter to the General Assembly they will have in ten years a supreme court as large as this convention.

Mr. CLARKE of Johnston. It is true the General Assembly has largely increased the number of districts; but that was done from necessity. There were in two of the districts two judges who caused so much disatisfaction that the people were not willing to have their cases tried before them, and in the district court,—of this I am advised by attorneys of all parties—they were so dissatisfied with the judge that they continued their cases from term to term until their dockets are filled with cases, to the great delay and injury of their business. The legislature, in order to give them courts in which to try these cases, have changed these districts leaving to these judges merely nominal districts, with the expectation that this convention would re-establish this whole matter. That accounts for the action of the late General Assembly. It was done under the pressure of the occasion, for there was a necessity for it, and it was done with the expectation that this convention would devise some system that would do away with these evils, and equalize the working of this department.

It seems to me that it is reasonable that we should leave to the legislature to increase the courts as the business and necessities of the state may require. A system that may answer our wants at this time, would not probably meet the necessities of the state in ten years from now; the commercial, manufacturing and other business facilities of the state will be increased by the construction of railroads, and litigation will increase proportionably, so that the present system will be totally inadequate to the wants of the people. Is it not wise and prudent to so place power in the hands of the law-making branch of the government, in the hands of the agents of the people, that they may be able to increase these courts as the interests of the state may requiae? I think such power is conferred upou the legislature of almost every state.

I am opposed to this three court system now, because I do not think it is demanded by the necessities and wants of the people. But it may be demanded five years hence, and I want the legislature to have the power to create these courts without imposing the necessity upon the people to call another convention to revise the constitution in that respect. I trust and believe that the legislature, as the representatives and agents of the people, will exercise this power carefully and properly.

Mr. GILLASPY. I will not undertake to say that the argument of the gentleman may not be correct to some extent, in reference to the district east of this. What he says may be very true with regard to that district. But I cannot see what the condition of things in that district has to do with the creation of a number of new districts in the interior of the State. What I know myself, I profess to know as well as anybody can know anything. I know the creation of the new districts has been brought about by gentlemen who desire to be elected judges of those districts. And I know that in instances when the people did not desire it, persons came up here and got the legislature to create these new districts, and before the election comes off they intend to move into the new districts in the hope of being elected judges. I know such interests have influenced the action of the legislature heretofore, and it may be the case hereafter.

And one of these persons unfortunately did not get the nomination. I am opposed to giving the legislature power to change the districts from time to time, and create new ones to any extent that their particular friends may desire. I think that ten judicial districts are sufficient for the State. And I know that so far as the people of my district are concerned, they are perfectly well satisfied with the present system. I shall therefore vote against anything of the kind here, until I am satisfied that the Convention is disposed to adopt some other system than the present one.

Mr. JOHNSTON. I have been opposed to this three court system from the first. But the truth is, that after hearing the very able arguments upon this subject—and if I may point to one in particular I would refer to the very able remarks of the gentleman from Alamakee, [Mr. Clark]—I feel we should give this matter a very favorable consideration. I have been opposed to inaugurating this three court system in the constitution, because I did not know exactly how my constituents stand upon that question, though so far as I am advised they are opposed to it. The time may come, however, when this third court may be necessary; and I, therefore, do not see any objection to the proposition of the gentleman from Johnson, [Mr. Clarke,] to leave this matter to the legislature.

When this system was first proposed I was struck with the same objection that the gentleman from Wapello, [Mr. Gillaspy,] has expressed. But that can be obviated by providing that the increase in the districts of the State shall not exceed a certain number until a given year, and then they shall increase as the population increases. If that is done, I will vote for striking out the word "inferior." But if no restriction is put upon the matter, I will vote against it.

Mr. GIBSON. I am opposed to this three court system. I think that, with a few amendments, the system we have at present, will be sufficient. And I would be in favor of restricting the legislature in relation to increasing the number of the districts, for I think it would be wrong to leave this matter entirely to the legislature. The county which I have the honor to represent here, is one of those which have been taken from one of the old districts, and put into a new district by the action of the last general assembly. I know that that change was made against the will of a large majority of the people of that county. And as my friend from Wapello [Mr. Gillaspy,] remarked, there could not have been any other object in this change than to create a district for certain politicians; at least that was the general understanding there, and it was not denied by the friends of one who was recognized as an aspirant for office in the new district. Our district was not too large before; our judge had not more to do than he could attend to conveniently. The change was uncalled for; the judge did not desire it. But it was evidently gotten up for the purpose of making a district to accommodate certain individuals.

I differ with my friend from Johnson, [Mr. Clarke,] as to this being a case of absolute necessity. There was no necessity whatever for the change. So far as Marion county was concerned, she was particularly opposed to being put into the new district, and she asked, through her representatives upon this floor, to be attached to another district, if she could not remain where she was, and her request was denied her. The wish of Marion county was denied here in order to accomplish the ends of certain political wire-workers who aspired to the judgeship. This being a fact fresh in my memory, I am in favor of placing some restrictions upon the legislature, so that they cannot force a county or district into a district where they do not desire to be.

Mr. TRAER. I must say that I cannot see that the question before us has anything to do with districting the State into judicial districts. As I understand it, the question is simply this: whether this Convention will leave the power in the hands of the legislature to create an additional court if they deem it necessary to do so. That I understand to be the only question involved in this matter. And I can see no necessity or reason for calling up any party issues here, or talking about districting the State, or the action of the late general assembly. This matter of districting the State will come up hereafter in another portion of the constitution. So far as I am concerned, I am in favor of curtailing the number of districts. But I think the discussion of that question is entirely out of place here, as it has nothing to do with this article.

Mr. PETERS. If the arguments of those gentlemen who have opposed the three court system are entitled to any weight, I should be bound to oppose the proposition to strike out the word "inferior," in this section. They tell us that if we establish another court it will probably have business to do; it will probably become corrupted; it will probably delay the rights of parties, and prevent litigants from arriving at a speedy determination of their causes. Now if these arguments are entitled to any weight, if the wants and necessities of the people of this State are amply provided for under the present system, I see no reason for asking the general assembly to come in and establish a new system. I apprehend that the same arguments that would apply in this chamber against these courts would apply with equal force to the general assembly.

Mr. CLARK, of Alamakee. I was in favor of the three court system, and I shall go in favor of striking out this word "inferior." If I cannot get what I want I will go for the next best thing I can get. I will not refuse half a loaf because I cannot get a whole one. I certainly think we should leave the constitution in such a shape that the legislature can create a third court if the people require it, and it will be beneficial to the State. What may be the best interests of the people of the State to-day, may not be in two years from now. And for the pur.

pose of meeting the changes which must inevitably take place in the wants and conditions of the people of this State, I am in favor of leaving this constitution in such a shape that the legislature may be able to provide all that may be necessary.

Mr. WINCHESTER. I do not rise for the purpose of giving my individual views in regard to a judicial system for this State. But when the legal members of this Convention differ so much among themselves concerning this matter, then, as a matter of course, the other members of the Convention, comprising the honest farmers and traders, must take the matter in hand and decide it. I regard this controversy here as caused almost wholly by the prejudices and predilections of members of the bar in this State, who have emigrated here from various States of this Union. I observe that the principal portion of those who are in favor of the three court system, are from the northern portion of this State, and have emigrated thither from New York and the New England States. On the contrary, those opposed to that system, and in favor of the present system, have emigrated from the Middle and Southern States of this Union, where the system at present existing in this State, has been, and is still, in operation. I was in favor of the three court system upon this ground, that a large majority of the members of the legal profession in my district were formerly from New York and the New England States. I therefore presumed that they would be in favor of the New York system of practice, although I have never received any instruction or expression of opinion from them in relation to this matter. I shall vote for striking out this word, "inferior," so as to give the legislature an opportunity to form new courts if they choose to do so. I shall vote also to restrict the number of the judicial districts of the State.

It has been said that the judicial department of the government is the most important of all. That may be so. I doubt not but it is so, in the opinion of some gentlemen; but I consider our whole fundamental law of such vast importance that I cannot distinguish between the importance of one department and that of another. I do not consider that the judicial department of the government is any more free from corruption, any more perfect or any more immaculate than the other departments. I am as much in favor of throwing restrictions and guards around that department as around any other. I shall consequently vote for such restrictions here as I may deem necessary, and among other things, for restricting the number of judicial districts.

Mr. GOWER. This question has been discussed here at some length, and the members of the bar seem to differ very much as to the policy of the different judicial systems proposed here. I have understood the business of the State could be performed by the present judges, and therefore I have voted against this three court system. But I can very well see how, as the business and prosperity of the State increase, the wants and necessities of the people may require a more extended judiciary. I shall, therefore, vote to strike out the word "inferior," and leave the legislature free to create such courts hereafter as may be deemed necessary.

Mr. CLARKE, of Henry. I am in favor of striking out and inserting what is here proposed. I would ask those gentlemen, who are in favor of the two court system, and who have voted against the report of the committee upon the supposition that perhaps their constituents might be opposed to it as an innovation, to give us this chance of leaving it to the legislature to constitute these courts, if your constituents should want them. I believe, as the gentleman from Johnson [Mr. Clarke,] has declared, that in five years hence, the system we propose will be demanded by the people, for I do not believe that the business of the State can then be carried on under the present system at all.

The question was taken, and the amendment of Mr. Clarke, of Johnson, was agreed to.

Mr. PETERS. I move that the committee rise.

The question was taken, and the motion was agreed to.

The PRESIDENT having resumed the chair—

The CHAIRMAN reported that the Committee of the Whole had had under consideration the subject referred to them, had made some progress therein, and asked leave to sit again.

Leave was granted.

On motion, the Convention then took a recess until 2 o'clock, P. M.

EVENING SESSION.

The Convention met at two o'clock P. M., and was called to order by the President.

The Convention then resumed, in Committee of the Whole, (Mr. Harris in the Chair,) the consideration of the Judicial Department.

Mr. PETERS. I move to take from the table the report of the majority committee on the Judicial Department.

The CHAIRMAN. The impression of the chair is, that it could not be taken up without a re-consideration of the vote, by which it was laid on the table.

Mr. PETERS. I move to re-consider the vote.

Mr. PALMER. I would ask whether the gentleman voted with the majority.

Mr. HALL. I move to re-consider the vote, by which this majority report was laid on the table.

Mr. JOHNSTON. The majority report of the committee was under consideration, for which the gentleman from Henry [Mr. Clarke,] moved a substitute. I made a motion to lay them both upon the table. The minority report then came up for the consideration of the committee, and the gentleman from Henry [Mr. Clarke,] moved to substitute the article in the present constitution for the report of the minority. That article is the subject now under consideration, and it has been amended in the first section.

Mr. SOLOMON. I have an entirely different recollection of this matter. As I understand it, the gentleman from Lee [Mr. Johnston,] moved to lay the majority report upon the table, but before making the motion he stated, that he did it for the purpose of getting up the minority report. After that statement, the majority report was laid upon the table, and the minority report then came up. The gentleman from Henry [Mr. Clarke,] then offered a substitute, and by some hook or crook the article on the Judicial Department in the present constitution has got in here, I hardly know how.

Mr. JOHNSTON. The gentleman from Henry [Mr. Clarke,] moved to introduce the article in the old constitution as a substitute for the minority report, which motion prevailed, and the first section was amended by striking out the word "inferior."

Mr. WILSON. I would suggest to the gentleman from Lee, that the gentleman from Henry presented two substitutes, one for the minority report, and one for the majority report, which is now laid upon the table.

Mr. HALL. This matter is not beyond the power of resurrection,and I will move, therefore, to take from the table the majority report of the committee. If the chair decides, that I cannot make the motion, I will take an appeal, and we will then get to the end of this matter, somewhere, and we can then turn back.

Mr. JOHNSTON. I have no doubt, that the report of the majority committee can be taken up on a simple notice. It has been merely laid upon the table, subject to the order of the committee. I presume it can be taken up at any time for the consideration of the committee.

Mr. SOLOMON. I am not at all surprised at the difficulty which seems to be felt here, for the fact is, that we laid the majority report upon the table, contrary to all rules of parliamentary practice. A motion to lay a report of a committee upon the table is out of order in Committee of the Whole. It is no more out of order to take a report from the table, than it was to lay it there.

Mr. HALL. It is not too late for repentance.

Mr. SOLOMON.—

"While the lamp holds out to burn
The vilest sinner may return."

Mr. PETERS. I find that the gentleman who made the motion to lay this report on the table, proposed to substitute in place of it the old constitution of this State with the provision, that the legislature might establish as many courts as they might deem necessary. He based his argument upon the proposition, that the report of the committee raising three courts was wrong and objectionable, and yet he would open a door by which the legislature might establish twenty courts, if they chose. I take the ground that a system of three courts is better than to leave the door open by which the legislature might establish as many as they please.

The question was then taken upon taking the majority report from the table, and it was not agreed to, upon a division ; ayes 11, noes 14.

Mr. EDWARDS. It appears to me, that we are making very slow progress in this matter. We have now been in Committee of the Whole twice upon this subject, which has been discussed so fully. I think that we had better take some course by which we will accomplish something definite. I would move therefore that the committee rise, and ask leave to be discharged from the farther consideration of this subject.

The question being taken, the motion was not agreed to.

Supreme Court.

The second section of the article in the present constitution was then read as follows :

"The Supreme Court shall consist of a Chief Justice and two Associates, two of whom shall be a quorum to hold court.

Mr. CLARKE, of Henry. I offer the following as a substitute for the second section :

"The Supreme Court shall consist of a Chief Justice and two Associate Justices, two of whom shall be a quorum to hold court. They shall be elected by the people of the State at large, and shall hold their office for six years, (except as herein provided,) and until their successors shall be elected and qualified. The salary of each shall not be less than two thousand dollars, nor more than five thousand dollars per annum, to be fixed by law."

Mr. PARVIN. I move to strike out all after the word "qualified." I will just state, that the Committee on the Legislative Department have reported a provision fixing the salaries of the judges. I believe this matter is generally provided for in the article on the Legislative Department in the constitutions of other States.

Mr. HALL. I hope the substitute will not be adopted. By a simple alteration in the first line of the section of the present Constitution, you can change the mode of electing these judges. There is no need of fixing the manner of election. The section is perfect, and the salaries are provided for in another place.

Mr. PARVIN. I will not press my amendment.

The question was then taken upon the substitute offered by Mr. Clarke, of Henry, and it was not agreed to.

Mr. TRAER. I propose to strike out "two," where it occurs in the second section, and insert "three" in its place, so that it will read—

"The Supreme Court shall consist of a Chief Justice and three associates, three of whom shall be a quorum to hold court."

The CHAIRMAN. The question will be taken first upon striking out, and then gentlemen can move to fill up the blank.

Mr. HALL. I shall vote for the motion of the gentleman from Benton, [Mr. Traer.] I believe the number four is the best possible number for a court of the last resort. I believe that we should have a court of more than three, because, with only three, if one judge is absent, we should have no bench at all. The addition of another judge to the bench will materially lessen the labors of the court. Gentlemen may perhaps wonder, why I consider a Supreme Court of four to be better than a court of three or five. It is because of the certainty and confidence in the decisions of a court, that it commands respect for its decrees and becomes worth something. In a division of the court, where the number of judges is three, and they stand two against one, or four judges, and two to two, you would have no decision at all, and there would be no governing principle, either for that court or any other court. But when you go a step farther and say, there shall be four judges, then you have three against one, and you add considerable strength and authority to their decisions. There is no number, in my opinion, equal to "four," and this should be the number of judges of a court of the last resort, whose decisions become law for other courts to follow. It should be one of the cardinal objects of this Convention to establish such a system as shall secure the respect and confidence of the people for the decisions of the Supreme Court.

Mr. PALMER. I understood the gentleman to say where the court was equally divided, that then there would be no decision. I think that we could prevent such a state of things by increasing the number of judges to five. I should like to have the decisions of the Supreme Court, in every case where we can, upon the law, but still the judges of the District Courts have shown themselves as competent as any judges upon the Supreme Bench.

Mr. CLARKE, of Johnson. I concur with the gentleman from Des Moines, [Mr. Hall,] in the view he has taken of this question. There is another consideration, in addition to those he has presented, bearing upon this question, to which I wish to call the attention of the Committee. With your court, as now constituted, all the decisions are reported, and where a case is decided by two judges, with a dissenting opinion by the other, it is reported, and stands in the books nominally as an authority, yet is really a case where two judges stand against two, because the judge who holds the dissenting opinion, takes sides with the District Judge, or judge below. Such authority as that is unreliable, and yet persons finding it in the reports, regard it as law, when, in fact, it is not, and never commands the respect and confidence of the bar, Under the other system, if the Supreme Court divide equally and stand two and two upon a question, the case is never reported and never finds its way into the books, and the decision of the court below stands as the law of that particular case.

As a question affecting the rights of the people, this is one that ought to be looked to carefully and seriously. I think it is better to have no decision from the Supreme Court than have a decision which is merely nominal, and which does not really settle any question.

The objection will be made, perhaps, that this system of having four judges is something novel and untried. I say very frankly, that I do not know any other State in the Union that has adopted this system. It was a subject that was very fully discussed in the Ohio Constitutional Convention, and from the conversation I have had with lawyers from that State, I learn that it is a matter of universal regret that the proposition was lost. The Supreme Court makes the law, and it is very important to the people that there should be no decision unless that decision becomes the law of the State.

Another objection is made to increasing the number of judges, upon the score of economy. It is true we increase the expense; but I think that the additional salary of another judge is nothing, in comparison with the amount, in the costs of litigation, which will be saved to the people by establishing a court which will settle questions at once and decisively.

There are many cases brought before the Supreme Court in which one of the judges may be interested: where, for instance, a new judge goes upon the bench. If he has been a lawyer in practice, he cannot sit in cases where he has been interested in the court below; and the result is, that many cases in the Supreme Court are tried by two judges; and if it should happen that those two judges should differ in opinion, then there is no decision at all. I remember a case of this kind which was tried last term from the county of Linn, in which I was one of the counsel. One of the judges had been counsel in the case before he went upon the bench. As it happened, the other two judges differed upon the most important points in the case, and they compromised in order to put the case in a condition to send it back for trial upon a minor question, leaving the real matter of litigation undisposed of. The result was, that the case went back to the District Court for trial, and the parties were thus under the necessity of bringing it up a second time to the Supreme Court. In the interval, however, the judge who was interested originally in the suit below, had gone off the bench, and a new judge had taken his place, so that this time we were enabled to obtain a decision. In this case the parties were put to the expense of bringing this case twice to the Supreme Court, before they could get a decision. In the system proposed by the gentleman from Des Moines, [Mr. Hall], no such difficulty would arise. When compared with the advantages which are likely to accrue from the adoption of the system proposed, it seems to me, that the mere expense of having an additional judge would be a matter of no great consideration.

Mr. HALL. My desire is, to give character to the decisions of the Supreme Court, so that when made, they shall command the respect and confidence of the community at large, and I think that a court of four judges is the most judicious number that we can possibly devise, to secure this result. No other number, in my opinion, will be so well calculated to inspire the people with confidence in the decisions of this court. You cannot select any number to which some objection may not be urged. I seek to establish a court whose decisions, when authoritatively made, shall be respected and obeyed as law all over the State. I ask gentlemen to consider this matter carefully, and I doubt not they will come to the conclusion that the Supreme Court should be composed of four judges.

Mr. CLARKE, of Henry. When this matter was first discussed in the Committee, the argument of the gentleman from Des Moines struck my mind with much force. If he can demonstrate, in the cases frequently happening in the Supreme Court, that three judges are divided in the way he says they are, why then his argument may be correct. I am satisfied, after reflection, that such is not the case. In looking over the reports of the Supreme Court, where there were three judges sitting upon the bench, you will scarcely find a dissenting opinion.

Mr. WILSON. In the first volume of Clarke's Reports, I find, in ninety-nine cases, only six dissenting opinions.

Mr. CLARKE, of Henry. Why should the people then have to pay the salary of this extra officer to assist in deciding these six cases, when, perhaps, if he had been there, the judges might have been divided two and two, and there would have been no decision. It may be a question, whether a court of four would not, in fact, multiply the cases in which no decision would be made. It very frequently happens now, that when one finds a majority against him, he gives up his opinion; but if he could persuade another judge to stand with him, he would not yield in the least.

If we go back to the old system of two courts I cannot see the necessity of augmenting the number of judges. I do not know that they can dispatch more business. If they can, then it seems to me that is a reason for increasing the number still more. Certainly the argument of the gentleman is just as strong for increasing the number to a dozen as to four. We require twelve men to sit upon a jury, and we must suppose that the opinion of twelve men would have more weight and force than that of four men. But I apprehend that is not the question. Three judges upon the bench are the best calculated to dispatch business, and in ninety-three cases out of ninety-nine, three judges concur in their decisions. I ask if the opinion of three judges, is not just as good sitting as three, as though there were a fourth to give a dissenting opinion? With this view of the case, I shall support the article as it is in the old Constitution, except that I favor the election of judges by the people, and the plan of districting the State.

Mr. WILSON. Gentlemen, in the course of the debate, have cited an instance of this character, where three judges sit upon the bench. One judge is interested, and he cannot, therefore, sit upon the trial of the case, and two judges are compelled to hear the case. There is danger, gentlemen say, of their being equally divided, because there is an even number of judges. This may happen, but it is an exceptional case, and rarely likely to happen. If you put three judges upon the bench, you must have a decision of some kind, because they cannot divide without having a decision; whereas, if you put four judges upon the bench, this rule becomes reversed, and in case of division, there may be two on one side and two upon the other. It seems to me that you would have fewer cases disposed of in that way than in any other.

Mr. PALMER, If this Supreme Court consists of four judges, it is presumed that they will do their duty, and sit upon the Bench at the same time. What is the object of an appeal, I would ask? It is to get the decision of the highest Court in the State upon the questions involved in the cases that come before them. If you adopt the plan of the gentleman from Johnson and the gentleman from Des Moines, a case may easily happen in which that object may be defeated, by an equal division of these four judges, and the party will be sent back without a decision in his case. But if you have five judges, they might divide the common ordinary cases between them, two of them taking a certain portion of the cases, while the other three should take the balance. In difficult cases the whole five might counsel together and decide upon them.

Mr. CLARKE, of Johnson. I remarked, when I occupied the floor a while since, that this proposition of a court of four judges was thoroughly discussed in the Ohio Constitutional Convention; but it was not adopted. I am advised since I made this remark, that the rejection of the proposition was not made upon its merits, but was made for another and a different reason; it was that under their peculiar system by sending out one Supreme Court Judge to hold courts in the Districts four would not constitute the number sufficient to discharge the duties devolving upon them. There was no doubt among the leading minds of the Convention, that this number of judges would make the best bench, and would secure the rights of the people more certainly than any other system; but in consequence of the proposition not meeting the other requisitions of their peculiar system of the judiciary, the plan of having four judges was discarded. I speak of this, in order that the statement made here, that this proposition had been discarded by the Constitutional Convention of that State might not prejudice the minds of members here against it. We are not placed in the position in which Ohio was placed at that time and we, therefore, can try this system to great advantage here. If it should fail and be found not to work well in practice, we can adopt a provision in either the minority or majority reports, which will give to the Legislature the right to increase the number of the Supreme Court Judges after a certain year. It will be a very easy matter in the course of a year or two to restore the bench to its present character. I trust gentlemen will not be startled at this proposition, because it is new. I confide very much in this matter in the experience of the gentleman from Des Moines [Mr. Hall.] He has occupied a seat upon the bench for a number of years, and can therefore speak advisedly upon this subject.

I desire to make a remark here in reply to the gentleman from Jefferson (Mr. Wilson,) that although there may be only six dissenting opinions in ninety-nine cases reported in the first volume of my reports, yet it is true that there are a great many other cases, where one judge does dissent, but writes no opinions, and there are many other cases where a judge doubts, and is standing alone, but yields his opinion under a kind of a protest. Such cases as these are common upon the bench in this State and I may say, upon the bench of every State, where there are three judges. This ought not to be the case. Put another judge upon the bench, and they will at least either make a decision, or disagree, and make no decision which will affect the interests and property of the people of the State. The decisions made by the Supreme Court affect the rights as well as the property of the State, and they should not be involved in any doubt and confusion. Men act upon these decisions, it is true. Here perhaps is a decision which is involved in considerable doubt, and it is discarded. Nobody has any faith in it and the next time it comes up, if there happens to be a new judge upon the bench, it may be reversed. Notwithstanding all this doubt, it stands as a rule of property and a rule of action in this State, and men are obliged to conform to it, although they have no faith in it. If we can devise a system, which will make the decisions of the Supreme Court more effectually binding upon parties and relieve them of all doubt, we shall have accomplished a most desirable result.

There is another thing which we should be careful to provide against in our fundamental law. How common it is, in looking over the reports of the different State, to find decisions made where the Courts doubt the propriety of the rule, and think it unjust and that it has grown up under an erroneous decision made years ago; yet although it is wrong in principle and in practice, the Court considers itself bound by it. If you put four Judges upon the bench, we would avoid such a state of things, because if there is any doubt about the practice and about the justice of a rule, one or two of the Judges will be likely to dissent, and the matter will be thoroughly investigated.

The expense of providing for the additional judge would be comparatively small when compared with the benefits likely to result from the adoption of the system, in removing the dangers and uncertainties of the law, to which I have alluded. I think the Convention ought, at least, to be willing to give us the privilege of trying this system.

The question was then taken on Mr. Traer's motion to strike out, and it was agreed to, upon a division; ayes 17, noes not counted.

Mr. HALL, I move to insert "three" in the blanks, so that the section would read,—

"The Supreme Court shall consist of a Chief Justice and three associates, three of whom shall be a quorum to hold Court."

I know it is difficult for gentlemen, who have not made it their business to some extent, to appreciate fully the views which I entertain upon this subject, which are the result of most mature deliberation and careful inquiry. We all know, and especially those gentlemen who have had any experience in the Supreme Court, that there are but few cases reported where the judges all concur in the decisions given. There is always more or less contariety and diversity of opinion. The great purpose I have in view is to secure the respect and confidence of the people for the decisions of the Courts when made. Gentlemen must recollect, that there is something more than the particular case in controversy, affected by the decisions of the Supreme Court. Their decisions do not stop with the particular cases in which they are made, but they become the rules of property, for the whole State. I recollect a case in point where a decision was made by two judges, one desenting upon an attachment lien giving it a preference over an unrecorded deed, which became the rule of property all over the State. Unless we provide a stable Judiciary, we may be slumbering securely upon our supposed rights, when in reality, a decision may be made by the Supreme Court, which will effectually destroy them.

Mr. PALMER proposed to fill the blanks with "four."

The question was first taken upon Mr. Palmer's motion, and it was not agreed to.

The question then recurring upon Mr. Hall's motion to fill the blanks with "three," it was taken, and the motion was agreed to.

There being no other amendment to the second section,

Section three was then read as follows:

"The judges of the Supreme Court shall be elected by joint vote of both branches of the general assembly, and shall hold their courts at such time and place as the general assembly may direct, and hold their offices for six years, and until their successors are elected and qualified, and shall be ineligible to any other office during the term for which they may be elected. The Supreme Court shall have appellate jurisdiction only in all cases in chancery, and shall constitute a court for the correction of errors at law under such restrictions as the general assembly may by law prescribe. The Supreme Court may have power to issue all writs and process necessary to do justice to parties, and exercise a supervisory control over all inferior judicial tribunals, and the judges of the Supreme Court shall be conservators of the peace throughout the State."

Mr. WILSON. I offer the following amendment. To strike out the words "joint vote of both branches of the General Assembly," and insert in lieu thereof, "qualified voters of the State," so that it would read:

"The judges of the Supreme Court shall be elected by qualified voters of the State, and shall hold their courts at such time and place as the General Assembly may direct, and hold their offices for six years, and until their successors are elected and qualified, and shall be inelegible to any other office in the State during the term for which they may be elected. The Supreme Court shall have appellate jurisdiction only in all cases of chancery, and shall constitute a court for the correction of errors at law, under such restrictions as the General Assembly may by law prescribe. The Supreme Court may have power to issue all writs and process necessary to do justice to parties, and exercise a supervisory control over all inferior judicial tribunals, and the judges of the Supreme Court shall be conservators of the peace throughout the State."

Mr. CLARKE, of Johnson. I shall vote for the amendment if I cannot get something else which I would like better. For the purpose of testing the question, I offer the following amendment as a substitute:

"The State shall be divided into four judicial districts, to be bounded by county lines, and compact and equal in population and territory as nearly as may be, in each of which districts, at the first general election under the Constitution, one Supreme Judge, who shall be residents of their respective districts, shall be elected by the people. The Supreme Judges so elected, shall be so classified that one Judge of the Supreme Court shall go out of office every two years. The Judge of the Supreme Court holding the shortest term of office under such classification, shall be Chief Justice of the Court during his term, and so on in rotation. After the expiration of their terms of office under such classification, the term of each Judge of the Supreme Court thall be eight years, and until their successors are elected and qualified."

I desire in offering this amendment to state my reasons for doing so, and I will do so as briefly as I can. It is conceded on all hands, that these judges ought to be elected by the people. But while I concur in this view, I have great apprehension lest the election of these judges might be thrown into the political arena, and that a seat upon the supreme bench might be made a reward for political services. I am well aware from my own experience in political life, that when a State Convention of any party assemble together for the purpose of making nominations for State offices, the question of the competency of the person to be nominated, is very often lost sight of entirely. I fear that this will be the case with judges, as it is with very many other officers. The question is not generally, whether a man is competent or honest, but whether he is a good partisan. I think the Convention will at once see that this kind of partisan feeling and interest ought not to put judges upon the bench.

There is another objection to the election of these judges by the State at large. I may say, without disparagement to any gentleman of the bar in the State, that there are very few members of the legal profession, whose reputation as practicing lawyers extends throughout the whole State. The result is, when people come to vote for judges, they will vote for them from partisan endorsement, and because they are the choice of the party to which they belong; not from any knowledge they may have of their abilities as lawyers. It seems to me, that the plan I have here proposed would obviate all these objections. At the district conventions for the nomination of judges, the leaders of the parties in the State at large cannot all be present, and these nominations will not be made the rallying point for the managers of the parties, but they will be left in a great measure in the hands of the people of the Districts.

Again, if this plan be adopted, every man competent to go upon the bench will be known throughout his district, and the result will be, that you will bring this question of the election of judges, directly home to the people themselves. If it should happen that either party should make a bad nomination, and the opposite party should make a good one, if the people of the district know the men, they will be most likely to lay aside all partisan considerations, as they would not do if the selections were made of candidates from any part of the State, whom they did not personally know. I think while we extend this right of electing judges to the people, we should be very careful that we do not make it so broad that it will be attended with bad results.

The proposition I have now presented makes the election of supreme court judges analagous to the election of district judges, bringing their election home to the people, and giving them an opportunity of selecting men whom they know, and who have acquired a reputation for integrity and legal capacity.

There is still another reason that has induced me to offer the proposition now under consideration. I am free to say that I never want to see a partisan bench in this State. Where there is more than one judge upon the bench, I should be glad to see it composed of men of opposite political parties, so that, being composed of men of various political opinions, it might command the confidence of all men. If we adopt the plan of electing these judges by districts, the probabilities are that the different districts will elect men of opposite parties, and while one district elects a republican, another will elect a democrat. Such a bench would not labor under the imputation, in any case, of having made a decision from partisan motives. I do earnestly wish to keep the election of our judges clear of all partisan considerations. I do not want either party to be responsible for the conduct and character of its judges, but I desire that the people universally shall feel that this is their court, in which they can repose the utmost confidence. These are briefly the considerations which have induced me to present the proposition now before the committee.

Mr. HALL. I do not feel willing that this question should pass to a vote without briefly expressing my own views upon the subject. And even if I should be as unfortunate as I was the other day, when I attempted to demonstrate that in raising funds for purposes of building railroads, and other internal improvements, the elective franchise was not politically applicable, still I feel it equally my duty to express my opinions upon the subject under consideration.

It is difficult, where we vote for any person, to separate from that act the idea of representation. It must be considered to some extent, that the person elected is the representative and organ of the party which elected him. In other words that the people and the person elected retain the relation of constituents and representative. It is difficult to separate these two ideas. To my mind, the only objection that can be raised or urged against electing judges by the people is, that prevailing idea that they represent the persons who elect them; and thus the court will become a representative court. If we could do anything to avoid that which would be serviceable, then this election by the people would become merely a mode of selecting men who are to meet together for the express purpose of declaring and expounding the law. If we elect the judges upon the State ticket system, we cannot shut our eyes to the fact that parties and partizans will, to a great extent, if not entirely, control the whole matter; and we will have a Democratic or Republican bench. The political parties are pretty equally divided in this State, and we will be sure to have one or the other kind of a bench; and there cannot be that confidence in the court that there would be if it could be got up on some different principle. It is useless to deny the fact that Democrats will not have the same confidence in an entirely Republican court that they would have in a Democratic court; or that the Republicans would have the same confidence in a Democratic court as in one of their own party, or even in a divided court. And if it was not acknowledging our weaknesses too much, or yielding to a truth that it is humiliating to admit, I should be willing to have a provision in the constitution saying, that when the State is any where nearly divided by two political parties, both parties should be represented upon the Supreme Bench.

By electing judges by districts it can scarcely fail to happen that there will be a mixed court; both parties will be represented upon the bench. And there will, in my opinion, be more confidence attached to that court, than if it was all taken from the one side or the other. This, certainly, would be something gained.

The next question, and the only question to be considered is, if there is any advantage in arranging this matter so that such a state of things would probably or certainly exist; would we lose anything by dividing the State into four equal parts, and allowing each fourth of the State to elect one judge, rather than have the whole State elect all four of the judges? Would one-fourth of the State, when they were electing their judge, be quite as apt to elect a competent man, a man of wisdom, knowledge and integrity, as the whole State would be? If they could, then there is no reason why these judges should not be elected by districts; nothing would be lost by that plan, and you would gain an additional advantage. But some gentlemen may say that some quarter of the State—take the south-western quarter of it—would not be quite as capable of selecting a proper person as the whole State would be. It appears to me they would be just as capable. If you select any person, he must be put upon the bench upon the recommendation of those who reside in his portion of the State, and the remote portions of the State must confide in those recommendations. There is no man in this State, I will venture to say, who has a State reputation as a lawyer, not one; if there is, I do not know him. Place any gentleman, I do not care who he may be, upon the ticket for the Supreme Court, and there will be thousands and tens of thousands of voters in this State who will have to take him upon trust, upon the representations made to them by others; in other words, upon party endorsement alone. They will vote for him because their party have nominated him, but not because they have any knowledge of him themselves. This will be the case with three out of four of the candidates. They will be distributed throughout the State, for there is no danger of their being all taken from any one portion of the State.

It appears to me that we can lose nothing by electing these judges by districts; while we will gain, from the fact that we at least take away three-fourths of the character of constituent and representative from the selection thus made. You will have judges upon the bench, each of whom will have no immediate constituents in three of the districts of the State. To that extent, at least, these judges will have no person to please or cater for, and nothing to fetter their minds or bias their judgment in favor of their constituencies. In my opinion, much would be gained by this plan; much confidence would be added to the character of the court by distributing the selection of judges throughout the State.

Mr. WILSON. I would call the attention of the committee to the argument just submitted to them. Gentlemen seem to be frightened at the idea of the relation of representative and constituency springing up between the judges and the people; but they are very much in favor of the same relation springing up between the bench and the political parties of the State. We frequently hear eulogies passed upon the intelligence and virtues of the people, while we as often hear of the corruption and venality of parties. Now it seems to me that if the relation of constituency and representative is to be sustained at all, it better be between the people and the judges, than between the political parties and the judges. I am opposed to any such thing; and the very argument that gentlemen presents in favor of their system, is a complete answer to it.

I do not want the feeling to grow up among our people in this State, or among the people of any other State, that the supreme bench of Iowa is simply the representative of the political parties of the State. I do not want such a sentiment to be entertained concerning the courts of any part of the country. I believe that that would be far worse than the idea of the relation of representative and constituent, existing between the judges and the people.

Here is another argument in favor of the theory of electing our judges by the people of the whole State. Under that system every voter in the State has a voice in selecting all of the judges; while under the district system he will have a voice in the selection of but one judge. The people of the State have demanded that they shall be allowed to select all the judges of the Supreme Court, not one judge only. Yet by this district system you propose to give each voter but a part of the right which the people demand.

And there is another thing. New York has been frequently referred to here, in connection with this district system. Yet at this very time New York is endeavoring to get rid of that district system. There is at this time a proposition pending before her legislature to abolish this system.

I think the people should be left to make their selection of judges from any portion of the State where men most capable for that office can be found. I can see no more reason for electing our supreme judges from different portions of the State, than for so selecting our other State officers. If we were to divide up all our State officers in the same way, we would select our Secretary of State from one district, the Auditor of State from another, the Treasurer from another, and so on, and let them rotate around as our district judges do. I am opposed to any such thing. Let us have a general ticket for the supreme judges, and let the people throughout the State have a voice in their election.

Mr. CLARKE, of Johnson. The strongest argument of the gentleman from Jefferson [Mr. Wilson,] is his last one, that of giving the whole of the people a voice in the selection of each and all of the judges, which they could not have under this district system. That is true. But the question for us to consider, is not whether it is important that the whole of the people shall elect these judges, but which system of election is best calculated to produce an effective bench, a bench of character and integrity, one in which the people will have confidence. That is the question, and to my mind it is the only important question for us to consider.

The gentlemen has argued that this mode of selection will restrict the people in their choice of judges. I do not think so. I go upon this presumption, that whether these judges are elected by districts, or by the people at large, it will be equally the interest, as I hope it will be the endeavor of the people, to select the best men that can be found.

Suppose they are elected by districts; if we go upon that presumption, and it is the only rational one we can assume, the presumption that the people of each district will select their best men, that the parties in each district will nominate their best men, the result will be the same; for you will get the best men in each district, and if you elect your judges by the state at large, we can only get the best men any way. I thing there is no force in that argument. You do not limit the right of selection; you do not restrict the power of the people to take their best men; but bring home to the people a practical knowledge of the men they are going to elect, and give them the means and opportunity to choose those who are really best fitted for the office.

I conceive the suggestion of the gentleman from Des Moines [Mr. Hall] to be true, that at every state election of the judges, at least one half of the people will know nothing personally concerning the candidate presented to them. If they vote for them, they will do so because their respective parties have nominated them; knowing neither of the candidates, they will of course prefer to vote for the men upon their own party ticket.

I contend that if you want to give the people an opportunity of voting intelligently upon this subject, of exercising the right of choosing between candidates for these offices, of saying emphatically by their votes whom they consider to be the best and most competent, the man of the highest integrity, you will do it by adopting this district system, because you put this selection within the reach of the general knowledge of every voter. I will cite by way of illustration, the gentleman from Des Moines [Mr. Hall] himself who has already occupied the Supreme Bench, and who is known throughout the State. I venture to say that you can hardly go into this State anywhere but what they know something about Jonathan C. Hall. But ask the people what they know about him? Ask any Democrat what he knows about him. He will tell you that he knows Mr. Hall is a Democrat and a prominent man in his party, and if he is upon his party's ticket he will vote for him. But ask him what he knows about Mr. Hall as a lawyer, and it is more than likely that he will say that he knows nothing about that, never saw him upon the bench, and never heard him speak as a lawyer. But take a district of twenty or twenty-five counties, including the one in which he lives, and I tell you that you cannot go into a house in that district, and ask a man what his notions of Mr. Hall as a lawyer are, but what he will say that he stands at the head of the bar in his District.

Now which is the best mode of selection, by a State ticket where a majority of the people of the State know nothing personally of the candidates presented to them, or by a district ticket where all the people know all the candidates personally? It is no disparagement to the bar of the State, to say that there is no lawyer in the State of such commanding talents, ability and reputation as to be known throughout the State. If gentlemen are in earnest about placing the people in a position where they can act intelligently when they come to choose these judges, then I say they must adopt this district system, as the most effective. But if they want to make a mere party matter of it, if they want to establish the certain rule that whoever is nominated must stand or fall upon his party creed then adopt the other system, and we shall be sure to have Democratic judges, Republican judges, American judges, or party judges of some kind.

Now as an humble individual who has something to do with these courts, I never want to be called upon to vote for politital judges, or to do business before that class of judges. I have been consisteut upon this point. Ever since we have had a state government, we have had no party contests upon this question in our district. The first judge we ever had was the late Judge Carlton, who, though a Democrat, was elected without opposition. The people were satisfied from their knowledge of the man, of his integrity and his ability as a lawyer, and so when he departed this life, Judge Smyth, who has since resigned, went over the track without opposition though then a Democrat, because the Whig lawyers were satisfied with the man, and would not come out to run any one against him.

I would be glad if the time would come when this feeling would prevail throughout the State, and if you adopt the district system I doubt not the time will very soon come, when the most able men will be nominated and placed upon our bench. If you want to elect your judges by politics, you can do so, and will be obliged to do so, by the State ticket system. I want to have one department of our State government in regard to which we can say, there is no political taint or bias, there is no partizan complexion to it; it is of such a character that when we go before it to have our dearest rights decided, we may rest assured that they will be decided upon principles of law and equity, and not upon political or party principles.

The illustration of the gentleman from Jefferson, [Mr. Wilson] in relation to the distribution of State offices according to this district system, has no analogy to the subject under consideration. Every man knows that our state officers are elected as politicians and are expected to represent and carry out the principles of the party to which they belong. But I hope the day will never come when persons will be put upon the bench to carry out political or party principles.

If we desire to elevate the character and standing of the bench, to secure the election of honest and capable men ; if we wish to keep the selection of our judges out of party politics—and I trust that such is the wish and desire of every member of this Convention—then this district system is far preferable to the other.

Mr. CLARKE, of Henry. It is well known to this Convention that I am opposed to this whole thing. I believe the system as reported by the majority of the committee on the judiciary, is the system best adapted to this State, and will finally be adopted by this Convention.

But let us look at this matter, and see to what gentlemen are endeavoring to lead us. I have no doubt but what those gentlemen who have taken the first steps in this matter of adding another judicial officer to the supreme bench, and are now defending the system of electing judges by districts, know very well where they intend to lead us. But I doubt if all here know where they are really leading us. What will be the effect of the motion of the gentleman from Johnson, [Mr. Clarke]? It is proposed that we shall have a fifth wheel to our judicial coach, something entirely unnecessary, not demanded by the people, and that every judge upon the supreme bench protests against.

Now what do these gentlemen want us to do? They want us to agree to elect these judges of the supreme court by districts. What then? How are we going to get at the thing? Are we going to get at it in any other way than to call for an election of judges immediately? It can be done in no other way. And from what district is this fourth judge coming? I ask gentlemen to explain this to me. That judge must be taken from some one district in the State. What district is going to have that judge? The district containing Iowa City, or the one in which Burlington is situated? We will see a battle here bye and bye. We will see, or we must expect to see, these gentlemen who are now standing cheek-by-jowl here, struggling and striving to determine from which district this pure, immaculate, holy judge will be elected, without a party vote.

I honor these gentlemen for their pure and holy aspirations. I hope they may live—and it will be wishing them a long life—until the time shall come in this State, when either of them will present himself as a candidate before the people, without any distinction of party. But I would ask the gentlemen, when or how they expect that time will come? Suppose that we give you this district system; what next? There must be nominations made for this office of supreme judge. And I think I have seen both of these gentlemen figuring pretty extensively in these awful political conventions. What! is that true? Is it possible that these gentlemen would ever permit themselves to be seen in these horribly corrupt political caucuses? It is indeed the fact. One would think from their speeches here that they had never been within a dozen miles of such a meeting. And yet both of them have figured, and lately, too, in State political conventions. And is a State caucus or convention less corrupt and more holy than a district caucus?

Here is the gentleman from Johnson, [Mr. Clarke,] wants to have a man upon our supreme bench well versed in all questions of law; and so it is with the gentleman from Des Moines, [Mr. Hall.] Does any man doubt that these gentlemen would be at the Convention or caucus as candidates, and perhaps also as delegates? I should smile to see the gentleman living in my district, come before the people and ask them to vote for him as judge, without any distinction of party. Whenever the Conventions assemble in their respective districts to nominate these judges the one would go to the democratic convention, and the other to the republican convention, as candidates from their respective districts, or as delegates, or as both. How are we going to keep party out of this question? We cannot do it; it is utter nonsense, it is perfectly absurd to attempt it.

If we adopt this system we must go farther, and say from what district this judge shall come. Or we may be called upon to say that our present judiciary shall receive their quietus upon the adoption of this constitution, and the whole bench shall be elected at that time. The gentleman from Des Moines, [Mr. Hall,] nods assent. Now, republicans, you understand what is before you. I am not in favor of cutting off the head of any man elected by the people until his full term of office has expired. That is my position, and I am not going to be led from it by any such maneuvering as this.

Mr. HALL. The gentleman from Henry, [Mr. Clarke,] is the most impracticable man I ever knew. He cannot find out from what district this fourth judge is to be elected. I thought this constitution we are making was to be good enough to be submitted to the people and go into operation right away, and not be postponed for four or five years. It was my impression that we were remodeling the institutions of the State to some extent; that we were now about to remodel our judiciary system; and no gentleman has gone farther, in endeavoring to bring about a change in that system, than the gentleman from Henry. When he proposed his system, did he expect to wait for five years for some of our district judges to go out of office? Does he expect, if we change our district system, to wait till every district judge throughout the State has served out his term of office? If so, what will we do in the meantime? Some judges' commissions have longer to run than others. What are we to do about that?

Mr. CLARKE, of Henry. I referred to the State officers now elected by the people.

Mr. HALL. The gentleman takes back more than half of what he said before. If the people have the right to elect these supreme judges, and have been kept out of that right for the last ten years, I think the sooner they have it given to them now the better. If the present supreme judges, in consequence of their republican propensities, are too immaculate to be reached by the people under this constitution, the gentleman and myself will be found upon opposite sides here. If the people want these men in office they can re-elect them. If they do not want them there, then they ought not to be upon the bench.

The question is whether these judges should be elected by the people in the several districts and come from different sections of the State, or whether they should be elected upon a general State ticket. I will not say that the gentleman from Henry has any selfish purpose in this matter. I will not insinuate quite as strongly in regard to the motives of that gentleman as he has upon mine. But if it should so happen that he should aspire to the office of supreme judge, I have no doubt it would be better for him to have a party nomination, and run in the entire State, in three-fourths of which he is not known, than to receive a district nomination, and run in a district where he is known. The truth is, it enables party conventions to pay off party services. They will nominate for party services, a man residing in some obscure corner of the State, while the editors of the party, all over the State, will be bound to say that he is the greatest man who ever trod the soil of Iowa; and thus he will step into office without difficulty. Now if you confine your election to the region of country where the individual resides, the people there will know all about him. They will not be overborne in their choice or selection, by a vote in a quarter of the State where the people know nothing about the candidate.

In this way the people will be more sure to elect competent men. That is the advantage of this system, and there is no disadvantage, unless gentlemen can show and prove that we cannot secure competent judges by the district system. I believe all the experience of this State justifies the conclusion that when the people of the State understand, they will vote for the most competent person, or he whom they believe to be the most competent, for judge. This has been demonstrated in repeated instances in this State. There may be times of high party excitement, when the lines will be more closely drawn. But as a general thing you cannot get the people to vote for an incompetent man, where they know him to be such. But where they do not know him, but are obliged to rely upon party endorsement, you may then saddle men upon the State, who have no qualifications for the position to which they may be elected. And it is qualification, and not length of time in office, that we should look to in these elections.

Mr. CLARKE, of Henry. I desire to relieve the gentleman from Des Moines [Mr. Hall,] from any anxiety he may feel in regard to my aspirations for office. I assure him he will not have me as a competitor in our judicial district, in any event. As to the question, whether I would run better in a district, or in the State at large, all I have to say is, that I am one of those individuals, who, however well I may run, am very unfortunate at the end of the race. And if I should hereafter aspire to run for any office, whether in my district, or in the State, at large, I hope there will be some one to take care of the poll books.

Mr. ELLS. I think it would be impossible—I put it upon the most extreme ground—to nominate four judges for the Supreme Bench, without giving those nominations a party complexion. I do not believe the democracy can do it; I know the republicans cannot do it; I, therefore, leave that consideration entirely out of the question involved in this amendment.

I think that both parties will need to look up the best men they have, in order to furnish competent men for the office of Judge of the Supreme Court. I think that to adopt this district system would be to deprive ourselves of the power to select our best men for these offices. I do not care whether they are whigs, or democrats, free soilers or what; if they are only good lawyers, pure, incorrupt, and incorruptible, that is all I wish to know about them. I do not care if they are all from one town, all live in one house, all belong to one family, and that the Smith family; if they are good men, and competent men, that is all I ask.

It seems to me, that the argument about party complexion, and party bias, would chime in completely with this district system. Those men who desire to control the party, can control a district when they could not control the State, and I think I can see as much of that feeling exhibited by men who disclaim anything of the kind, as by those who present this question broadly and freely to the whole people. I think such insinuations are out of character entirely, and ought not to be indulged in here.

You cannot separate this thing entirely from party influence. Each party will bring out their best men; that is right, and the people will select from them. We talk about there being no party feeling in this matter. Yet we must stand or fall by the party to which we belong. And feeling that I can make a better selection from the whole State, than from a single district, I shall favor the old system.

Mr. PALMER. The gentleman from Henry [Mr. Clarke,] compares this system to a five-wheeled coach. I do not so look upon it. I consider it a mere proposition to put the four wheels where they belong. And if the gentleman will "wait for the wagon" a little while, we will take him along, and show him where the fourth judge will be found.

Gentlemen have suggested here that there is evil to be apprehended from party feeling connected with the election of judges. I think this plan will go as far as any can, to remedy that evil, unless perhaps a provision is added to the section, that no voter shall vote for a candidate for the office of judge from party considerations; and particularly, that he shall not vote for a know-nothing, because he must really know nothing.

The question recurred upon the substitute proposed by Mr. Clarke, of Johnson, for the amendment of Mr. Wilson.

The amendment of Mr. Wilson was to make the section read as follows:

"The judges of the Supreme Court shall be elected by qualified voters of the State, and shall hold their courts at such time and place as the General Assembly may direct, and hold their offices for six years, and until their successors are elected and qualified, and shall be inelegible to any other office in the State during the term for which they may be elected. The Supreme Court shall have appellate jurisdiction only in all cases of chancery, and shall constitute a court for the correction of errors at law, under such restrictions as the General Assembly may by law prescribe. The Supreme Court may have power to issue all writs and process necessary to do justice to parties, and exercise a supervisory control over all inferior judicial tribunals, and the judges of the Supreme Court shall be conservators of the peace throughout the State."

The substitute proposed by Mr. Clarke, of Johnson, was as follows:

"The State shall be divided into four judicial districts, to be bounded by county lines, and compact and equal in population and territory as nearly as may be, in each of which districts, at the first general election under the Constitution, one Supreme Judge, who shall be residents of their respective districts, shall be elected by the people. The Supreme Judges so elected, shall be so classified that one Judge of the Supreme Court shall go out of office every two years. The Judge of the Supreme Court holding the shortest term of office under such classification, shall be Chief Justice of the Court during his term, and so on in rotation. After the expiration of their terms of office under such classification, the term of each Judge of the Supreme Court thall be eight years, and until their successors are elected and qualified."

The question being taken upon the substitute, upon a division, it was not agreed to; ayes 11, noes 15.

The question being then taken upon the amendment proposed by Mr. Wilson, it was agreed to.

No farther amendment being offered to this section—

District Courts.

Section four was then read as follows:

"The District Court shall consist of a judge, who shall be elected by the qualified voters of the district in which he resides, at the township election, and hold his office for the term of five years, and until his successor is elected and qualified, and shall be ineligible to any other office during the term for which he may be elected. The district court shall be a court of law and equity, and have jurisdiction in all civil and criminal matters arising in their respective districts, in such manner as shall be prescribed by law. The judges of the district courts shall be conservators of the peace in their respective districts. The first session of the general assembly shall divide the State into four districts, which may be increased as the exigencies require."

Mr. WINCHESTER moved that the word "five" in the first part of the section, be stricken out, leaving a blank, so that the section would then read—

"The District Court shall consist of a judge, who shall be elected by the qualified voters of the district in which he resides, at the township election, and hold his office for the term of—— years," &c.

The question being taken upon the amendment, it was not agreed to.

Mr. WILSON moved to amend the last clause of the first sentence of the section, by inserting etween the word "office," and the word "during," the words "except that of Supreme Judge;" so that it would then read—

"And shall be ineligible to any other office, except that of Supreme Judge, during the term for which he may be elected."

The question being taken, the amendment was agreed to.

Mr. CLARKE, of Johnson, moved to amend the last sentence in the section by striking out the word "four," leaving a blank, so that it would then read—

"The first session of the General Assembly shall divide the State into —— districts, which may be increased as the exigencies require."

The question being taken, the amendment was agreed to.

The question was upon filling the blank.

Mr. CLARKE, of Johnson, moved to fill it with the word "ten."

Mr. PALMER moved to fill the blank with the word "twelve."

The CHAIRMAN stated the question to be first upon filling the blank with the word "twelve."

The question being taken upon filling the blank with the word "twelve," upon a division, it was not agreed to; ayes 6, noes not counted.

The question then recurred upon filling the blank with the word "ten," and being taken, it was agreed to.

Mr. TRAER. I move to strike out the words "which may be increased as the exigencies require," so as to give the legislature no power to increase the number of districts.

Mr. PALMER. I hope that amendment will prevail. I would rather put a maximum in here, than to give the legislature any power to increase the number of districts.

The question being taken the amendment was not agreed to.

Mr. WILSON moved to strike out the word "township," in the first part of the section, and insert the word "general," so that it would then read—

"The District Court shall consist of a judge, who shall be elected by the qualified voters of the district in which he resides, at the general election," &c.

The question being taken, the amendment was agreed to.

No farther amendment being offered to this section—

Prosecuting Attorneys, &c.

Section five was then read as follows:

"The qualified voters of each county shall at the general election elect one prosecuting attorney and one clerk of the district court, who shall be residents therein, and who shall hold their several offices for the term of two years, and until their successors are elected and qualified."

Mr. PALMER offered the following as a substitute for section five;

"It shall be the duty of the General Assembly to make such provision by law as shall be necessary for the carrying this article into effect, to provide for a regular system of practice in all the courts of the State, to provide for the election of an Attorney General to reside at the Capitol of the State, to provide for the election of a Prosecuting Attorney in each district, and to prescribe their powers, duties, terms of office, and salaries."

The question being taken upon the substitute, it was not agreed to.

Mr. EDWARDS moved to amend the section by striking out the word "county," in the first line, and inserting the words "judicial district;" also striking out the word "prosecuting," and inserting the word "district," so that the section would then read:

"The qualified electors of each judicial district shall, at the general election, elect one district attorney," &c.

Mr. SOLOMON. I have prepared a substitute for this fifth section, embracing nearly the same idea the gentleman has expressed in his amendment. If he will withdraw his amendment, I will offer my substitute.

Mr. EDWARDS. I will withdraw my amendment.

The amendment was accordingly withdrawn.

Mr. SOLOMON. I offer the following as a substitute for section five:

"The qualified voters of each judicial district shall, at the time of electing their district judges, elect a prosecuting attorney, who shall be a resident of the district for which he is to be elected, and shall hold his office for the term of five years, and until his successor is elected and qualified."

I feel more strongly instructed by my district upon this point, than any other change which we will probably make in this Constitution. There are a number of new counties in my district which have felt the inconvenience of depending upon the prosecuting attorneys elected by the several counties, from their inefficiency and want of legal knowledge. And my constituents are almost unanimous in their desire for a change in this respect, so that we shall have an efficient prosecuting attorney, whose duty it shall be to proceed along with the court, and have his term of office and salary such as shall command the best talent and ability in the district. I offer this amendment as the embodiment of their wishes upon this subject. I have fixed the term of office at five years to prevent frequent changes in the office, a matter which I consider desirable. The duty of a prosecuting attorney, so far as I have learned anything about it, is a very important matter; and it requires considerable preparation and long practice to make an efficient prosecutor. I think that a tolerably long term will have a tendency to increase the efficiency of our prosecutions.

Mr. EDWARDS. I would suggest to the gentleman from Mills, [Mr. Solomon,] that his substitute does not provide for clerks of the District Courts, as the original section does.

Mr. SOLOMON. I know the two propositions differ in that respect, but I do not see how to remedy it. There is no complaint against the present plan of electing county clerks. I suppose it would be better to provide for district or county clerks in a separate section. They are provided for in this section of the old Constitution, because their terms of office are the same as those of the prosecuting attorneys. I would not like to have a clerk appointed or elected for the whole judicial district. My expectation was that some gentleman would move another section for that purpose.

Mr. PALMER. I do not think it is absolutely necessary that the clerk should be provided for here, any more than we should provide for the election or appointment of a sheriff. A sheriff is as much an officer of the court as is the clerk. We can, if we deem it best, leave this matter without any provision upon that point.

Mr. CLARKE, of Henry. I would ask the gentleman from Mills, [Mr. Solomon,] if he intends these district prosecuting attorneys to be in lieu of our present county prosecuting attorneys?

Mr. SOLOMON. That is my intention, as this will take the place of the present section upon this subject.

The question being then taken upon the substitute, it was adopted, upon a division; ayes 14; noes 8.

No further amendment being offered—

Style of Process.

Section six was then read as follows:

"The style of all process shall be 'The State of Iowa,' and all prosecutions shall be conducted in the name and by the authority of the same."

No amendment was offered to this section.

The CHAIRMAN announced that the article had been considered by sections, and was open to further amendment.

Temporary Court for trial of State Officers, &c.

Mr. CLARKE, of Johnson. I desire to offer an additional section, to come in after section five, to read as follows:

"The General Assembly may provide by law for the creation of a temporary court, for the trial of any judge of either the Supreme or District Courts, or any officer of State who may be charged with incompetency or misconduct. If a judge of the Supreme Court is the subject of the charge, four judges of the District Court, selected from the respective districts, shall constitute a court to investigate the charge. If the complaint is against a judge of the District Court, or an officer of State, the Supreme Court shall have original jurisdiction of, and constitute a court to investigate the same. The complaint shall be made by petition, under oath, of five citizens, and the cause tried by the court. In either case, the judgment of the court shall not extend beyond deprivation of office, and ineligibility to hold any other office in the State, or either of them."

I will state briefly the reasons which induce me to offer that proposition. Under the system which at present prevails in this State, and in most of the States, of impeaching and trying State officers by the legislature, the experience of every man, I think, has demonstrated that it is little less than a farce, and never has amounted to anything but political, partizan squabbling. The result of the trial has generally been according to the political complexion of the majority in the legislature. I think that provision ought to be made for the trial of officers who hold high stations, and I think that all will concede that they ought to be tried by a judicial tribunal like other offenders. I think the majority, if not all, of the judiciary concur in the propriety of the creation of some such court as this.

Mr. CLARK, of Alamakee. I think we have adopted a provision to make District Judges eligible to the office of Judge of the Supreme Court. If that is so, then the question suggests itself to my mind whether it would be proper to allow District Judges to constitute a court to try a member of the Supreme Court upon a charge which, if he is convicted, would oust him from his office and create a vacancy.

Mr. CLARKE, of Johnson. When a District Judge ceases to belong to that court, and goes upon the Supreme Court bench, he will be a Judge of the Supreme Court, and there can be no conflict or interference of one with the other. My proposition amounts to this: whenever five citizens file a petition, under oath, charging any of these officers with misconduct, this court is to convene, and try the parties according to law. I suppose some legislation will be necessary, besides this provision. But I think it would be better for the State, and the interests of the State, that there should be some court where these matters can be decided free of party feeling.

Mr. CLARKE, of Henry. I will suggest what, it appears to me, will be the effect of this provision, and then gentlemen can vote as they think proper. The effect will be just this: whenever a suitor shall become offended with any judge upon the bench, all he will have to do will be to make complaint that the judge is incompetent, and put him upon his trial. We throw a shield of protection around other citizens, and we ought to require here that at least some formula of complaint shall be gone through with before we put our judicial officers upon trial. In other cases there must be an impeachment, which must be found by the General Assembly, before a public officer is placed upon trial. I am afraid of coustitutiug a court for trial and impeachment.

Mr. GOWER. I am very much of the impression that there are judges in the State, at this time, who require some more prompt attention than they are likely to receive from our Legislature. It strikes me that this provision would not endanger the safety of the judges at all, and may work beneficially for the people, and the State generally. I never expect to be any but an humble citizen of this State, but I have an interest in this matter. And if there is any judge in this State guilty of malpractice or incompetency, I would have him dealt with, as any other officer. I do not perceive that there is any danger to be apprehended from the effect of this provision. The gentleman from Henry [Mr. Clarke], seems to think that prosecutors or suitors would, from some pique or anger, in consequence of a loss of a suit before a judge, arraign him under this provision. But what is the tribunal before which he mnst be arraigned? It is a court composed of other judges, where he will be equitably dealt with, and if he is not guilty, will suffer no evil consequences.

Mr. PARVIN. I move to amend the amendment by striking out the words "incompetency or." If the people of any district choose to elect an ignorant judge—one totally incompetent, a fool, even—let them keep him to preside over them. I would have no judge tried for anything but malfeasance.

The question being taken upon the amendment to the amendment, it was not agreed to.

Mr. WILSON. I do not like the phraseology of this amendment; nor do I like that of the substitute I have in my hand. But there seems to be a disposition to have somethiug of the kind. I therefore offer this as a substitute:

"The Supreme Court, with one District Judge from each district, to be selected as shall be provided by law, shall form a court for the trial of all impeachments, except in cases where a Justice of the Supreme Court is upon trial, when the court shall be composed of the District Judges, a majority of whom shall constitute a quorum. All impeachments must be found by the General Assembly."

Mr. CLARKE, of Johnson. I am not very particular about this matter. But it seems to me that the substitute of the gentleman from Jefferson, [Mr. Wilson], if adopted, would leave this thing just where it is now. The experience in this matter, is, that the difficulty always exists in getting the impeachment. If you adopt this substitute, you make a much more bulky court than is necessary, increase to a great extent the expenses, and by no means render the decisions more satisfactory. If the District Judge is tried by the Supreme Court, constituted of four judges, and they are equally divided, then you have no decision for or against the party accused, while the accused will have all the advantages of an acquittal, as if there was no doubt about the case. If you increase the number of judges, you will constitute a court in the form of a jury, and gain nothing by it.

I think the best and safest court you can establish is the one I have proposed. There must be five persons to concur, under oath, in presenting a petition against the judge. And I think, wheu five responsible men make these charges, on specifying what those charges are, he should be arraigned for trial before some court. You may go before your Legislature, with the affidavits of these five men, and ten chances to one the whole affair will be smothered. The people have as much regard for our judicial officers as for any officer in the State, and there will be no wanton attack upon our judges, where you require the concurrence, in the charges, of five men, under oath.

Mr. WILSON. It will be very difficult for the gentleman from Johnson, [Mr. Clarke,] to guarantee that none but responsible men will present this petition, the more especially where incompetency is one of the grounds of the petition. A man may be defeated in a law suit before a judge: he has his friends and they will deem the judge's ruling in that very case as a sufficient ground to declare him incompetent. You thereby place our judges at the mercy of any five men in the State, who may have ,or fancy they have, cause for being dissatisfied with him.

Mr. CLARKE, of Johnson. Does the gentleman from Jefferson [M. Wilson,] suppose that a court constituted as I propose, would find a judge guilty of incompetency, because of any charge he may have given in any single case? I do not suppose such a court would do that. You will create a court which will be responsible for what it does, and therein consists the advantage of this practice over that of impeachment and trial by the General Assembly. If the members of the General Assembly do wrong or refuse to hear and redress the people in this respect, when they dissolve, the responsibility is gone, they miingle again with the people, and there is no power to reach them. But if you establish a court that is fixed, and it does wrong, the people can hold them responsible.

I think the charge of incompetency to be sustained would have to extend over more than one case, and reach to decisions upon more than one subject. It is true it is a general charge, and one, perhaps, that would be difficult to prove; but one which I think will not be often made. But in preparing constitutional provisions and law for the future, you must make your work broad enough to cover all cases that may arise. I think it is probable that there may, in future, be some one on the bench, so far incompetent that he ought to be removed. And in the trial, the same rules of law will govern, and the accusers are open to the same questions as to whether they are influenced by malice or any thing else, against the party accused, as in other cases.

Mr. WILSON. In reply to the question, the gentleman has asked me, I will say that I have no doubt that the Supreme Court would act justly and properly in the premises. But because they will do so, does that do away with the liability of those charges being presented against persons? You may have a charge presented against a judge every day, and the Supreme Court may decide it groundless, and correctly so. Yet there is the fact that these charges have been made, and the judge may be injured in reputation from that very fact alone. That is what I object to; it is this placing in the power of any person who may feel himself aggrieved, this easy method of preferring charges against the judge who decided the case against the preson, and put him to the detriment of a hearing before the Supreme Court. It is that to which I am opposed, and I think the Convention, to act properly, must vote down the proposition.

Mr. PARVIN. I hope the Convention will let the manner of impeaching officers remain as it now is. This matter of impeachment is too serious an affair to warrant the providing a shorter way of getting it done, than we now have. If a judge is deserving of impeachment, there is no reason to doubt that the legislature will impeach him. I would prefer it as it now is under our present Constitution.

The question being then taken upon the substitution proposed by Mr. Wilson, it was not agreed to.

The question was then taken upon the section proposed by Mr. Clarke, of Johnson, and it was not agreed to.

Filling Temporary Vacancies.

Mr. EDWARDS, proposed the following section.

The General Assembly may provide by law that the judge of one district may hold the courts of another district, in case of necessity or inconvenience, and in case of temporary inability of any judge from sickness, or other cause, to hold the courts in his District, provision shall be made by law for holding such courts.

Mr. PALMER. I believe some such provision as this is necessary. Our Supreme Court, I believe, has decided that under the Constitution, as it now stands, the legislature cannot provide for the calling of any member of the bar to the bench, to fill a temporary vacancy.

Mr. EDWARDS. There is no provision made by the committee to reach this matter, and for that reason I have offered this section.

Mr. CLARKE, of Alamakee. I do not think there has been any such decision by the Supoeme Court as that to which the gentleman from Davis, (Mr. Palmer,) has alluded. I know it is the practice in my part of the State for District judges to exchange with each other. I do not think there is any necessity for such a provision as this in the Constitution.

Mr. EDWARDS. I will say that, perhaps, so far as the first portion of my proposition is concerned, it may be provided for in some other way; but so far as the inability of the judge, from sickness, or other cause, to hold his term of the court, the law makes no provision for the calling of a member of the bar to the bench temporarily. The result is, that the people and the litigants of the district are subjected to great expense and delay. I know there is such a provision in the constitution of every State but of Iowa.

Mr. PALMER. The fourth section now provides that "the District Court shall be a court of law and equity, and have jurisdiction in all civil and criminal matters arising in their respective districts, in such manner as shall be prescribed by law." I think this exchange of judges could not take place without some constitutional provision, if we leave the fourth section as it is.

Mr. HALL. I think that is the law now, and the proposed section would be but re-enacting what has been the law ever since I have been in Iowa.

Mr. CLARK, of Alamakee. If this proposed section is intended to authorize the legislature to provide for calling a member of the bar to preside temporarily as judge, I must oppose it. If we adopt the practice of having our judges elected by the people, I am opposed to creating a member of the bar a temporary judge, and for a number of reasons. In the first place, a member of the bar who is capable of presiding as judge, always has more or less business in the district. And it seems to me that it would be seriously objectionable to take him from that business and put him upon the bench temporarily. If there is a vacancy of that nature to be filled, I apprehend, the Governor, or some other person, would be better qualified to fill it than the legislature.

Mr. EDWARDS. I will state that, in my practice, in other States, I have known several instances where the law has made provision, in cases where the regular judge could not attend for the members of the bar to select one of their number to act as judge temporarily. It is well known to the profession that there can hardly be any term of court in any county, but what some member of the bar would be without any particular business before that court. Heretofore no complaint has been made against these temporary judges.

Mr. CLARK, of Alamakee. I am not in favor of putting anything in this constitution, that will allow a District Judge to evade the duty imposed upon him by law. If you adopt this practice, you will find that our District Judges will be very often absent from their posts. There has never been any difficulty experienced, where my acquaintance in this State extends, in relation to this matter. If it becomes impossible for our District Judge to hold his term of court, we get some other District Judge to hold it. I can see no necessity, but rather much evil to result from the practice proposed here.

The question being taken upon the section proposed by Mr. Edwards, it was not adopted.

Jurisdiction of the District Courts.

Mr. HALL. The present Supreme Court of this State have decided that it is not in the power of the legislature, under the fourth section of the present constitution, to limit the jurisdiction of the District Courts, and prevent an indictment being found for the most diminutive offense. That portion of the fourth section now reads—

"The District Court shall be a court of law and equity, and have jurisdiction in all civil and criminal matters arising in their respective districts, in such manner as shall be prescribed by law."

I move to strike out the word "all," before the word "civil," so that it shall read, "and have jurisdiction in civil and criminal matters," &c.

It was upon that word "all," that the decision of the Supreme Court was based. Strike it out, and the legislature can pass an act giving to justices of the peace original jurisdiction, and the District Court only appellate jurisdiction in some cases.

The question being taken, the motion to amend was agreed to.

Mr. CLARKE, of Johnson. I move to amend the same clause of the fourth section by inserting after the word "equity," the words "which shall be distinct and separate jurisdictions," so that it will then read:

"The District Court shall be a court of law and equity, which shall be distinct and separate jurisdictions, and have jurisdiction in civil and criminal matters arising in their respective districts, in such manner as shall be prescribed by law."

I offer this amendment for this reason: The Supreme Court decided, I think, prior to the adoption of the Code, and they have incidentally decided since, that law and equity could not be mixed up together. The Code does, however, so mingle them; it was the intention of those who framed the Code, to combine law and equity, and have both involved in the same suits. The effect of the decisions of the Supreme Court, it seems to me, are such as to affect the manner of pleading and treating these classes of cases. For the purpose of settling this matter, and making it plain, I move to insert the words I have indicated. I think the practice under the Code, and the experience of the bar, are such as to recommend the proposition I have submitted.

The question being taken the amendment was adopted.

Organization of Judicial Districts.

Mr. CLARKE of Johnson. I offer the following as an additional section, to come in between the fifth and sixth section of this article:

"After the year 1860, the General Assembly may reorganize the Judicial Districts, and increase or diminish the number of Districts, or the number of Judges of the Supreme or District Courts, but such increase or diminution shall not be more than one District or one Judge of either court at a time, and no reorganization of the Districts, or diminution of the Judges, shall have the effect of removing a Judge from office. Such reorganization of the Districts, or increase or diminution of the Judges, of either court shall take place every five years thereafter, if necessary, and at no other time.

Mr. PALMER. This proposed section may need a little change, as I see it is taken from the minority report of the committee on the judicial department, and was drawn up in view of another system than the one we are now engaged in perfecting. We want to limit the number of Judges, so that they shall not be increased five or six at a time, as was done this winter. However, we can pass upon it informally here in Committee of the Whole, and then put it in proper shape when we come to act upon this article in convention.

Mr. CLARKE of Henry. I would suggest that it would be more appropriate to have this provision come in at the end of the fourth section. The latter portion of the fourth section now reads:

"The first session of the General Assembly shall divide the State into ten districts, which may be increased as the exigencies require."

I would suggest to the gentleman from Johnson [Mr. Clarke] to move to strike out the words: "which may be increased as the exigencies require," and then add the provision he proposes to the clause thus amended.

Mr. CLARKE of Johnson. I will modify the amendment in the manner proposed.

The question was stated to be upon the amendment to the fourth section, so that the latter portion of it will read ar follows:

"The first session of the General Assembly shall divide the State into ten districts; and after the year 1860, the General Assembly may reorganize the Judiciel Districts, and increase or diminish the number of districts, or the number of Judges of the Supreme or District Courts, but such increase or diminution shall not be more than one district or one judge of either court at a time, and no reorganization of the districts or diminution of the judges, shall have the effect of removing a judge from office. Such reorganization of the districts, or increase or diminution of the judges of either court shall take place every five years thereafter, if necessary, and at no other time."

Mr. SCOTT. I would suggest that the words "at a time," in the clause, or "one judge of either court at a time," are rather ambiguous. I think that the words: "at any one session" would be better.

Mr. CLARK of Alamakee. I am in favor of something of this kind proposed. But this thing suggests itself to my mind, whether or not, in the rapid increase of this State, the necessities of the people may require an addition of more than one district in every five years. The last part of the proposed amendment provide that

"Such reorganization of the districts, or increase or diminution of the judges of either court shall take place every five years thereafter, if necessary, and at no other time."

Mr. CLARKE, of Johnson. That may be modified when we get into Convention, if the principle is incorporated here. We may, in Convention, change the length of the term of the judges, and shall want to have this provision correspond with the length of that term.

The question being taken upon the amendment, it was adopted.

System of Practice.

Mr. CLARKE, of Henry. I offer the following additional section to come in as section seven of this article:

"It shall be the duty of the General Assembly to make such provision as shall be necessary for the carrying into effect of this article, and to provide for a general system of practice in all the courts of this State."

The question being taken, the section was adopted.

Intermediate Courts.

Mr. PALMER. The first section of this article, as it now stands, reads as follows:

"The judicial power shall be vested in a Supreme Court, District Courts, and such other courts as the General Assembly may from time to time establish."

I wish to amend it so that there can be no court created except one inferior to the Supreme Court. I therefore move to insert, after the words, "and such other courts," the words, "inferior to the Supreme Court." The section will then read:

"The judicial power shall be vested in a Supreme Court, District Courts, and such other courts, inferior to the Supreme Court, as the General Assembly may, from time to time, establish."

Mr. TRAER. I would ask what court can be made higher than the Supreme Court?

Mr. PALMER. The word "supreme" is used merely as a name, and not to fix the position of the court. In the State of New York, there is a Supreme Court, and then a higher court—the Court of Appeals. My object is to have this Supreme Court remain the highest court in the State.

Mr. CLARKE, of Johnson. As I understand the object of this amendment, it is to prevent the Legislature from making a court higher than the Supreme Court, but leave them the power to establish an intermediate court, between the District and Supreme Courts.

The question being taken, the amendment was adopted.

Mr. TRAER moved that the Committee now rise, report this article as amended, to the Convention, and ask to be discharged from the further consideration of the subject.

The question being taken, the motion was agreed to.

In Convention.

The PRESIDENT having resumed the chair,

The CHAIRMAN of the Committee of the Whole reported that he had been instructed by that Committee to report to the Convention, for their adoption, the fifth article of the present Constitution, being the article upon the judicial department, with sundry amendments thereto, and ask to be discharged from the further consideration of the subject.

The PRESIDENT. The Chair would inquire what has become of the majority report of the Standing Committee on the Judicial Department, which was referred to the Committee of the Whole?

The CHAIRMAN. That report was laid upon the table on motion of the gentleman from Lee, [Mr. Johnston], and the Committee then proceeded to consider the article I have been instructed to report to the Convention.

The PRESIDENT. According to parliamentary practice, the Committee of the Whole has no table, and therefore had no right to entertain such a motion. The only way for them to get rid of any subject referred to them, is to rise, report the same to the Convention and ask to be discharged from its further consideration.

The CHAIRMAN. I have made such a report as the Committee directed me to make.

The PRESIDENT. If it be the pleasure of the Convention, the Chair will receive the article of the present Constitution as amended in Committee of the Whole, as a substitute for the report referred to them; and it will be taken as the basis of the future action of the Convention in relation to this subject.

No objection being made, the report of the Committee of the Whole was received, and the Committee discharged.

On motion of Mr. PETERS,

The Convention then adjourned.

FRIDAY, February 13th, 1857.

The Convention met at 9 o'clock, A. M., and was called to order by the President.

Prayer by the Chaplain.

The journal of yesterday was read and approved.

Miscellaneous.

Mr. CLARKE, of Henry. I am requested to ask leave of absence for the gentleman from Muscatine, [Mr. Parvin.]

Leave was granted.

The PRESIDENT laid before the Convention a communication from the Citizen's Library Association of Iowa City, extending to the members of the Convention the privileges of their Reading Room.

On motion of Mr. CLARKE, of Henry, it was

Ordered that the thanks of the Convention be tendered to the Citizens' Library Association for the generous proffer of the privileges of their room.

Order of Business.

The PRESIDENT. The report of the Committee of the Whole, being the substitute which they have reported, for the majority report of the Committee on the Judiciary, is now before the Convention upon its second reading, and is open to amendment.

Mr. WINCHESTER. I move that the consideration of that report be postponed for the present, and that it be laid upon the table. If this motion prevails, I will then move that we go into Committee of the whole upon the report of the Committee on the Legislative Department.

Mr. WILSON. I hope that motion will not prevail, but that we will dispose of the report on the Judicial Department to-day.

Mr. YOUNG. If the report on the Legislative Department should not be taken up, I hope the report of the Committee on the Executive Department will not be taken up, as the chairman of that committee, [Mr. Todhunter,] is confined to his room by sickness.

The question was then taken upon Mr. Winchester's motion, and it was not agreed to.

The Judicial Department.

The PRESIDENT. The article on the Judicial Department adopted by the Committee of the Whole will now be read through by sections, and amendments will be in order.

The first section was then read:

"The judicial power shall be vested in a Supreme Court, District Courts, and such other courts, inferior to the Supreme Court, as the General Assembly may from time to time establish."

Mr. CLARKE, of Johnson. I would ask if the question is upon agreeing to the amendments made to the article as it now stands in the present constitution?

The PRESIDENT. The majority report of the Committee on the Judicial Department was referred to the Committee of the Whole, to which they made one amendment, and they then laid it aside. They then proceeded to consider the article in the old constitution, and they have reported it back, amended in one or two particulars, to the Convention, as a substitute for the report of the majority committee. The substitute now comes before us as a whole, and the question is upon agreeing to the report made by the committee of the whole. It is now open for amendment.

The second section as amended was then read as follows:

"The Supreme Court shall consist of a Chief Justice and three associates, three of whom shall be a quorum to hold court."

Mr. WILSON. This section is now open for amendment, I believe. I move to strike out the word "three." wherever it occurs in that section, and insert "two" in its place.

Mr. TRAER. Does parliamentary law require that we should concur in substituting this article of the old constitution for the majority report?

The PRESIDENT. The committee of the whole reported the article upon this subject in the present constitution as the basis for the action of the Convention.

Mr. TRAER. I was about to observe, if the question is, whether the Convention will concur in the amendments made to the second section, the motion of the gentleman from Jefferson, [Mr. Wilson,] would be unnecessary. If they do not concur in those amendments to the substitute, then the section will stand as it is in the present constitution.

The PRESIDENT. The Convention will bear in mind that the report of the majority committee was referred to the committee for their action, to which they made one amendment and then laid it aside, taking up and acting upon the article on this subject in the present constitution, as a substitute for this report. The substitute is now before the Convention, open for amendment.

Mr. CLARKE, of Johnson. I am well satisfied that the whole proceeding yesterday upon this matter was unparliamentary, and out of order. The committee could not lay the report of the majority upon the table, and take up something else, and act upon it. It seems to me that in order to make our journal intelligible, this whole report as amended by the committee should go upon the journal.

The PRESIDENT. The Secretary has entered it at large upon the journal.

Mr. CLARKE, of Johnson. I hope the amendment offered by the gentleman from Jefferson, [Mr. Wilson,] to the second section, will not prevail. I know that the system we propose has an element of novelty in it, and I am aware that the argument used against many propositions, that they are not to be found in any of the constitutions of the other States, will apply to this; but that to my mind is no argument. I should be glad to have it said of Iowa, that we have learned something since other States have adopted their constitutions.

I have another remark to make upon this subject, and it is this: If we adopt the provision which has been reported by the committee of the whole, that after 1860 the General Assembly may increase or diminish the number of judges of the Supreme Court, if it is found upon a year's trial, that the system which we recommend does not work well, and is attended with the dangers which its opponents predict will ensue from its adoption, it can be very easily changed and the court can either be reduced to three judges, or increased in number. For one, I concur with the view which the gentleman from Des Moines, [Mr. Hall,] has taken of this subject. I am satisfied after reflection that a court composed of four judges is the best system. I confess, when the plan was first suggested to me, it had too much novelty in it to recommend itself to my favor, and I was at first opposed to it; but after a little more reflection and examination of the effect it will have, I have become satisfied that it would strengthen, in a great measure, the character of the court, and secure the confidence of the people in its decisions. I hope gentlemen will at least be willing to give it a trial for a year, and if it does not work well, we can then very easily remedy the difficulty that may result from its working, if there should be any.

Mr. GILLASPY. I am opposed to the system of a Supreme Court of four judges, although it might be expected, by honorable gentlemen of the legal profession upon this floor, that I would not oppose it. In the first place, I am unable to see, from the arguments of the gentleman from Des Moines, [Mr. Hall,] and the gentleman from Johnson, [Mr. Clarke,] that the addition of another judge would aid materially in the decisions of the court. On the contrary, I think that so far as those decisions are concerned, we would be in a worse situation than that in which we are now placed. I learned for the first time, since I came to this convention, that the Supreme Court of this State is in bad repute. I had supposed, that it had always stood very high in the public estimation, and I had abunaant reasons for this belief, from the fact that so many members of the convention were anxious to vote themselves the reports of the decisions of the Supreme Court.

I would be disposed to vote for an increase of judges, if it were necessary; but I do not believe that it is. I understand that in Ohio, under the old constitution, they had four Supreme Court Judges—and that State is one which has been pointed out by various gentlemen upon this floor as a model State for us to follow—but in their last constitutional convention they changed the number to five, as they found that odd numbers worked better than even ones. I am opposed to adopting four as the number of judges, and shall vote for the same number that we now have.

Mr. HARRIS. Not having an opportunity heretofore to express an opinion in regard to this matter, I would like to make a single remark before the vote is taken. I have no desire whatever to conceal my opinions about this matter, but I am disposed to express them freely and frankly. I was disposed to favor the idea of having three judges upon the Supreme Court bench, until the intimation was thrown out by the gentleman from Henry [Mr. Clarke,]—I could not tell whether by authority or not—that there was an understanding here among the majority that the old bench were to remain until the expiration of the time, for which they were elected by the legislature.

Mr. CLARKE, of Henry. I should suppose, that the gentleman might have known, from my course upon this floor, that I am not the oracle of the republican party, or of the majority here. I speak for myself alone, and stand here as independent as the gentleman from Appanoose, in that respect. I express my own sentiments, without intending to express the views of others.

Mr. HARRIS. I am very free to say, that I should be opposed to the principle of keeping these judges upon the bench while a portion of the District Judges were to go out. In saying this, I do not wish to say a word against the present bench, because I believe they have discharged their duties faithfully, and honorably to themselves, and will, under existing circumstances, no doubt, have strength enough to be re-elected. I am opposed to the recognition of the principle, that they should be continued in office under this new constitution. If they are to be continued in office, then I would favor the system of four judges, or any other system, that would enable us to put this constitution in operation. If this is not the case, then I am in favor of three judges.

Mr. CLARK, of Alamakee. I do not know how it may be with a majority of either party of this convention, but as for myself, individually, I am not pledged to legislate in this constitution to keep any man in office.

Mr. CLARKE, of Henry. I desire to be understood as speaking for no party here, but only so far as I am individually concerned. I shall favor no course that will legislate out of office those that are in office now. I do not believe that it is necessary, in framing the constitution upon which we are engaged, that we should do any such thing. In my action here, I shall avoid any course which will have a tendency to throw out of office the men whom the people have placed in office, until their terms of office expire; unless it is absolutely necessary to do so in order to carry out the provisions of the constitution. I believe the effect of having four Supreme Judges would be to legislate out of office the present judges, who have just taken their seats upon the Supreme Court Bench. I shall, therefore, vote against providing for that number of judges for this court.

I do not believe that the people expect or need this number of judges for that court. I do not think that this number is desired by the bench, because it would be no advantage to them to have a fifth wheel to their coach. A good argument for retaining the present system of three judges is to be found in the fact, that in ninety-three cases out of ninety-nine reported in the first volume of Clarke's Reports, the three judges all concurred in the opinions they pronounced, and they are entitled to all the force and validity that any human tribunal can give. I say that it is not necessary to have four judges upon the bench, as some gentlemen would have us believe, in order that we may have decisions which shall command the respect and confidence of the people. As I have already said, I am opposed to the system of four judges, for the reason that it will legislate out of office the present judges upon the bench. If we adopt the old system, then we shall leave the judges just where they are now, so far as they are not affected by the district system.

Mr. HARRIS. I have no disposition to prolong the discussion of this question, but I wish to say, that party considerations should not prevail in this matter. I am confident that I would not discriminate in favor of one more than another. I am in favor of the election of judges by the people, and I would not have any man in office, who did not hold his right to that office by the free gift of the people.

Mr. HALL. Gentlemen appear to be controlled a great deal, in this matter, by the fact that they are fearful, if a change from three to four judges be made, the present Supreme Judges will not have the privilege of holding on to their offices for the balance of the term for which they were elected. It may be a consideration that will satisfy the minds of some gentlemen in forming this constitution, that the present bench should hold their offices for three years and a half longer, rather than that it should be so constituted as to give more strength and validity to their decisions than they now have. It may be a consideration with them to look after the interests of two or three men, rather than the interests of the whole people. I am not influenced by any consideration of that kind. I have no complaints to make against the present Supreme Court. I have the highest esteem for the members upon our present Supreme Bench; I have great confidence in them as lawyers and as judges. And if the people have that confidence in them, which I have no doubt they will have, it will be the easiest thing in the world for them to inaugurate this system we now propose, and retain our present judges upon the bench. The gentlemen who have declaimed so loud and vehemently, in regard to the sagacity and capacity of the people to select these officers, certainly should not now begin to shrink from returning this power of electing judges to the people, where I conceive it properly belongs. No such considerations as seem to influence some gentlemen here in determining this system shall influence me. I will vote for this measure upon principle; I will vote for giving this power of appointing Supreme Court Judges into the hands of the people.

Gentlemen may say—judges of your party are not upon the bench, and, therefore, you have nothing to lose by the adoption of this principle. I repel the idea, that I am actuated by any such feelings; I would take the same course that I now do, under any circumstances that might possibly exist. It does appear to me, standing here in the relation we do to the people, that other and higher considerations should influence the members of this convention, than mere party considerations. We all know, that the decisions of the Supreme Court of the State become authority for all the inferior courts, and become equally binding upon the courts, upon the legislature, and upon every branch of government. The Supreme Court, in fact, settles and establishes more law for the people than the legislature itself does, for it is the department of government that construes the meaning of every instrument we make, and defines and establishes the law, regulating all business transactions between man and man. It is strength and confidence in the decisions of the Supreme Court when made that we want. When this court makes a decision, it becomes a rule of property for every man in the State. *Their construction of the* constitution, and their construction of legislative enactments, become the *law for the entire State.*

These are the considerations that have induced me to take the course I am now pursuing; and it is not because of some little inconvenience which I may have witnessed in the working of the present system. I desire to see a court established whose decisions will be regarded with confidence by the people, and considered as of binding effect. Under the system of a Supreme Court, consisting of four judges, you can never have a rule established, which will become a rule of property, real or personal, in the State, unless you have the concurrence of three judges out of four. There must be three out of four to establish such a rule, and not two out of three. As I have stated heretofore, there is no other number that can be found, where the ratio of concurrence is so great, compared with the dissenting opinion, as the number four. This is a truth that no gentleman can deny. Do we not gain more by that number, when we look at the great purposes for which a court is instituted, than we lose from the fact that they may be sometimes divided two and two? There have been rules made by two judges, since Iowa became a State, some ten years ago, that struck at the very foundation of titles, and to my certain knowledge they have been taken up to a higher court and overruled. Let me say to gentlemen, they will find in those cases, where there are dissenting opinions since this State has had an organized court, that these opinions were given in the most important cases, and upon principles in which the people were more deeply interested than upon any other questions, striking, as they did, at the foundation of property and individual rights. I am confident in the opinion that more security and character will be given to the decisions of the Supreme Court by having four judges upon the bench, than we can possibly gain by any other number. It is from these considerations that I ask the Convention to fix the number of judges at four.

Gentlemen have alluded, in this connection, to the experience of Ohio upon this question of the best number of judges to constitute a Supreme Court bench. It is true that, for nearly fifty years, Ohio had four judges, and they then altered the number to five. I think I can speak authoritatively, when I say that the change has not proved entirely satisfactory, and many of her most intelligent citizens, who have thought and reflected upon the subject, are satisfied that the number four would be the most practicable number.

I do not believe that gentlemen should be actuated by partizan considerations in this matter, because there may be danger of losing some of their friends upon the bench. I think that gentlemen ought to hesitate long before acting upon this principle, for it seems to me it would be but an act of justice to return a right to the people, which has been wrongfully withheld from them for ten years. If it were just and right at the start to give this power to the people, it is just and right now, and you should not act as though *you were afraid you cannot withhold it from them a little longer.*

Mr. BUNKER. I regret that any side issues, which have no earthly connection with it, should have been lugged into the consideration of this question. I hope this Convention will perceive that it makes no difference in relation to the holding of office of our present Supreme Court Judges, whether the fourth judge is provided in this constitution or not. If a majority of the Convention wish to continue the present judges in office, until their term of office expires, they can easily do it by a provision in the constitution. If they do not wish to do it, I cannot see what connection this fourth judge has with the subject under consideration. We can provide for the election of the fourth judge without interfering at all with the three already upon the bench. I wish, therefore, to say to my friend from Appanoose [Mr. Harris] that if he is in favor of the system of three judges, instead of four, I hope he will act accordingly.

I wish this question to be voted upon on its simple merits. I go for a court of three judges, because I believe it to be the best system we can adopt. My belief is, if we elect four Supreme Court Judges, and put them upon the bench, that instead of having a majority decision in most cases, we will have the four judges equally divided. When it was shown yesterday that we had very few dissenting opinions in our Supreme Court, of three judges—only six cases in ninety-nine—the gentleman from Johnson, [Mr. Clarke] claimed that there were many cases where one judge found himself alone against the other two, and therefore, yielded up his opinions. This may be all true; but I believe if we had four judges, that we would have these dissenting opinions still more frequently.

Mr. GILLASPY. I desire my position to be distinctly understood upon all questions that come up here for decision. Yesterday, when a vote was taken upon this subject, I paid particular attention to it, and there were some seven or eight majority in favor of a court of four judges. If there is anything that has "come over the spirit of the dreams" of gentlemen since yesterday, when it was their intention, by some hook and crook, to legislate the Supreme Court out of office, and they are now to take the back track, I want them to show their hands. I undertake to say, it is the universal feeling throughout the State, that the Supreme Court ought to be elected by the people. There is now a Supreme Court just elected by the legislature, to serve for a term of six years. I ask gentlemen if they are disposed to withhold that right which the people claim, for a period of six years? If so, I want it distinctly understood; and I am willing to take the responsibility at the proper time, to give that right to the people, so far as my vote shall go, notwithstanding I voted in favor of having a court of three judges. I watched this thing closely yesterday, and as I said before, there were seven or eight majority in favor of a court of four judges. I desire now to see how these matters will result to-day. When the proper time comes, I shall vote to give the people the right they claim, and I am not going to deprive them of that right for six years, because there are some men upon the bench who have their party friends in the Convention. I did entertain the hope that no partizan feeling would govern the action of any member upon this floor. Upon that same principle, if the judges should hold for a still longer term, you might deprive half of the citizens of this State of the right of ever selecting their Supreme Court Judges at the ballot box. I know the people demand the right, as soon as the constitution goes into operation, of selecting their Supreme Court Judges, as well as every other officer in the State. It was said the other day, if we re-district the State, that we shall have to legislate the District Judges out of office. I am perfectly willing, so far as I am concerned, that it shall be done, if it must be done. In the district in which I live, the District Judge is my fellow-townsman, and is a Democrat; yet I am willing that he should go by the board for the good of the State. I would be the last man to cast a vote upon this question upon mere party considerations.

I hope gentlemen will reflect, and not do any thing which will look so much like backing out of the votes they gave yesterday.

Mr. CLARKE, of Johnson. I regret very much the turn which this discussion has assumed, for the reason, that I think it has nothing to do with the question now before the Convention. Allow me here to state that I do not sit here to legislate in office or out of office, any man or set of men. The first consideration with me in my vote upon this question is, which is the better system; and as I have already indicated to the Convention the convictions of my judgment, that this is an improvement upon the present system, I am going to vote for it. If there is any gentleman upon this floor, who has a direct personal and pecuniary interest in this question, it is self; and if the question of legislating the present bench in or out of office comes up, I am directly interested in it, holding as I do an appointment from that bench. If I looked at my personal interest upon this question, the apprehension that this was a move to throw out of office the present bench, might lead me personally to vote against it, because a new bench might oust me from my position. But I allow no such considerations as these to influence my action upon this matter. I trust, that my friend from Wapello, (Mr. Gillaspy,) who is opposed to the proposition for which the gentleman from Des Moines, (Mr. Hall,) and myself are contending, will not succeed in driving gentlemen who take sides with us, from their position by the threats which he has thrown out here. When the proper time comes to decide the question, whether we shall oust the Supreme Court Bench and have an election of judges under this constitution, I shall vote upon that question, as my judgment dictates. There will be no backing out then with me, nor shall I be influenced by mere political considerations. I do not take the position, which the gentleman from Henry, (Mr. Clarke,) has taken in announcing here how he shall vote upon that question. I have not determined how I shall vote. If this proposition is adopted—and I trust it will be—I am strong in the conviction that the change it will work in the judicial system, will be a decided improvement upon the present system.

I have made these remarks for the purpose of setting myself right upon this question, and I repeat again that if the proposition carries it can do no harm, it it does no good; because we have in our power the means of eradicating the defects of the system when they appear.

In Ohio, it is true, the number of Supreme Court Judges has been changed from four to five. I stated distinctly yesterday the reason of that change, upon authority derived from a gentleman, who was a member of the Ohio Constitutional Convention. The only reason for the change was, not because they were dissatisfied with the working of four judges upon the bench, but because under their system of dividing the State into five judicial districts, with a Supreme Court in every district, it was found that four judges could not perform the work required at their hands. I do trust that upon this question we will not have a party vote here. So far, I believe, upon every question upon which a vote has been taken in this Convention, there has been no such thing as a party vote. If by making four judges it necessarily resulted that we were going to oust the present bench, there might be some force in the argument of the gentleman from Henry, (Mr. Clarke, and some effect in the threats of the gentleman from Wapello, (Mr. Gillaspy.) But as this question does not come up here, and as it is more properly a question for future consideration, I trust that it will have no influence upon the minds of the Convention.

Mr. CLARKE of Henry. I desire to be perfectly understood upon this point. I say that the question does come up here, and no person has any right to act without reference to the subsequent acts he may be called upon to perform. When I am called upon to take one step, I always wish to look ahead and see what the second and third steps are going to be. I think I demonstrated yesterday that if we provided for the election of these judges by districts, and if we concluded to have this fourth judge we would have next to decide from what district he should come, and then there would be discussion in which gentlemen who have declared themselves in favor of ousting the bench would say, let us elect all the judges, one from each district. I fancied it was coming to that, but that proposition was voted down and we now come back to the question of the fourth judge. I foresaw that the same question will come up here, and we may as well meet it now as at any time. I am not afraid to meet it at any time.

The next question we have to meet is in regard to the election of this judge. Gentlemen say that he is to be elected by the people, and that, having remodeled the system under the old constitution, it is right and proper that the question of the election of all the judges should go to the people. I ask gentlemen if this is not the argument they intend to use? I ask them with what consistency they can get up and say, let the people elect this fourth judge, while the other judges retain their positions? It is in vain for the gentleman from Johnson, (Mr. Clarke) to say that he regrets the introduction of this question, as being premature. If we have to meet this question at all, we may as well meet it now as at any other time. My argument is, that gentlemen here having concluded not to remodel the old system but adopt it just as it stands in the constitution, with the exception of providing that the judges shall be elected by the people, there is no necessity, of course, for our removing these judges, any more than there would be of removing from office our United States Senators. We do not touch them or alter any feature of the judiciary system, so far as they are concerned.

The gentleman from Des Moines [Mr. Hall], claims the election of the Supreme Court Judges as a right of the "dear people." Where was the voice of this gentleman upon this question in the first Convention that assembled in this State for the purpose of framing a Constitution? Why was he not then as eloquent as he is now in favor of the rights of the "dear people?" And why did he not then secure to the people the election of their judiciary? What was the argument used then against giving this right of electing judges to the people? It was, that the people would select, from party motives, men to fill these offices; but if you left the matter to the Legislature, they would select the best men in the State. We have judges upon the bench who were elected under the present Constitution, have acted under it, and the results of their labors are before us in the shape of their decisions.

Now, the position I occupy upon this question—and in this I am actuated by no party motives, for I leave them out of the question entirely—is just this: If one, or all of these judges, who occupy this position, were Democrats, and competent men, I would not depart one hair's breadth from the ordinary course to get them out of office. I say that we shall be departing from what is necessary, or what would be expected by the people, if we incorporate into the Constitution anything that will require a re-election of these judges, before their term of office expires.

But to come back to the question of the four judges upon the bench. I wish to present a proposition to these gentlemen who pretend that their whole object in this matter is to get such a number of judges as will add weight and character to their decisions. They deny here that they have any political or personal considerations connected with this question. And one gentleman, in order that we may have the full weight and authority that will be given to the decisions of the Supreme Court by having four judges upon the bench, is willing to go so far as to sacrifice his own position. Let me ask these gentlemen if there is not a better and cheaper way for giving this additional weight and authority to the decisions of the Supreme Court, which gentlemen talk so much about. That is, instead of saying that two shall constitute a quorum of the Supreme Court Bench, we shall require that all three shall concur in every decision before it shall become the law of the State. If you put four judges upon the bench, and they divide equally, there is no decision. If you put three judges there, and one of them does not concur with the other two, there is no decision; so that one balances the other two. But where you require all three judges to concur, there is a decision. If gentlemen really wish to have a court whose decisions shall have weight and stability, why not adopt the plan I have suggested, instead of creating a fourth judge, at an expense of from three to five thousand dollars.

Mr. HALL. I will detain the Convention but a very few minutes. I will state, that I was a member of the Constitutional Convention of 1844, and I did oppose then the election of judges by the people; and I was just as honest then in opposing it, as I am now in favoring the proposition of electing these judges in this way. I consider the course I took then as reflecting no reproach upon my history. The experience I have had since that time, and the new ideas that have developed themselves in the progress of the country, have worked a change in the opinions I entertained upon this subject. At that time there was but one State that elected her judges by the people, and that was Mississippi. I opposed, as I said before, the election of the judges by the people at that time, although the great mass of the Democracy favored it, and they succeeded in the first, as in the second Constitution, in securing the election of District Judges by the people. So much for that history. Experience has since taught me that it is better to entrust the election of all our judicial officers to the people. This conclusion results, then, from this experience: that since the organization of the government, this privilege of electing Supreme Court Judges has been wrongfully or unnecessarily withheld from the people. If we have done wrong in this respect, let us now correct it. If this right has been unjustly withheld from the people let us now render justice to them. Gentlemen say it will be right to retain the present judges in office from four to six years. If gentlemen can justify keeping them in upon any principle, I have no objection. So far as my vote is concerned, I will make reparation for the wrong which I did in 1844, by restoring the right of electing the judges to the people in less than six years, if I can do so. As to having increased strength given to the decision of the court, by requiring the concurrence of three judges, I would be very glad if we could have the concurrence of three out of four judges, before their decision is regarded as the rule of law. Gentlemen speak of the additional expense. I can satisfy any gentleman that two clients of mine have lost more by this vacillation of the decisions of the courts—yes, one of them has lost more—than would pay the additional salary of a judge for five years. This may have no weight in the minds of gentlemen. But it is nevertheless the fact that the decision, to which I have before referred, has changed the rule of property in such a way as to injure individuals to an amount five times that of the salary of a judge. I do not say that this has been the result in the great aggregate of cases; but it has been the result in a number of cases.

The question was then taken, by yeas and nays, upon the motion to strike out "three" and insert "two," as the number of associate judges, and the number required to form a quorum, and it was agreed to, yeas 20. nays 12, as follows:

Yeas—The President, Messrs. Ayres, Bunker, Clark of Alamakee, Clarke of Henry, Edwards, Ells, Gillaspy, Gower, Gray, Harris, Hollingsworth, Johnston, Scott, Seely, Traer, Warren, Wilson, Winchester and Young.

Nays—Messrs. Clarke of Johnson, Day, Emerson, Gibson, Hall, Marvin, Palmer, Patterson, Peters, Price, Robinson and Solomon.

Number of Courts.

Mr. PETERS. I move to amend the first section of this substitute, by striking out the words "other courts inferior to the supreme court," and inserting the words, "inferior courts," so that it will read as in the present constitution, as follows:

"The judicial power shall be vested in a Supreme court, district courts, and such inferior courts as the General Assembly may from time to time establish."

Mr. SOLOMON. I will state that I allowed this section to be passed over this morning, from not fully understanding the explanation of the chair, in reference to the position this subject occupied; and consequently I failed to move an amendment to this section before the gentleman from Jefferson, [Mr. Wilson,] had moved his amendment to the second section.

I have very serious objections to this first section as it now stand, and would like to have the Convention decide upon it at this time. The section of the old constitution was amended in committee of the whole, by striking out the word "inferior," so as to allow the legislature power to establish courts of any grade. The reason assigned by the gentleman, [Mr. Clarke of Johnson,] who moved that amendment, was that it would enable the General Assembly of the State, whenever the necesities of the State demanded it, to create this intermediate court, which seems to be desired by some gentleman upon this floor. That is a worthy object, and if the section as it now is amended, would secure that object and nothing more, I would have no objection to it. But that is not the case. A succeeding section provides that the State shall be divided into ten districts, and for the election of district judges in those respective districts; and they never can be superseded by the General Assembly; those district courts must exist until this constitution is superseded by another. This article also provides for a supreme court.

Now if the legislature has the power to create an intermediate court, they may make it of an entirely new class of judges, and provide for their election, and for all that is necessary to constitute a separate and distinct court. My objection is, that it gives the legislature the power to establish a mammoth judiciary, which will eat up the substance of the people.

I am in favor of the object that gentlemen express a desire to attain; but I would prefer to have the legislature compelled to create this new intermediate court of judges whose election is already provided for. I object to having another and a distinct arm of the judiciary fastened upon the people of this State, independent of the constitution, and in spite of the object that gentlemen here say they have in view.

Mr. CLARKE, of Johnson. I think I can perceive the difficulty under which the gentleman, [Mr. Solomon,] labors in regard to this matter. But the truth is, that you cannot go into all matters of detail in the constitution. It will not do for us here to provide that if any additional courts besides those already provided for in the constitution, are created by the General Assembly, the duties of those courts shall be performed by the judges of the district court. And for this simple reason; that in the course of time the business and litigation of the State will have so increased, that the judges of the supreme and district courts will have as much as they can do to discharge the duties of their respective courts.

Let me illustrate: in all, or nearly all, the river counties of this State, there are now three terms of the district court. So it is in this county; so in the county of Washington, and so, I believe, in the county of Linn, under a law passed this winter, and so in other counties. And the time will come when you must have four terms of the district court every year, in the larger counties of this State. I believe they have now four terms of the district court in the county of Dubuque. It must be plain to the mind of every member of this Convention, that when that time comes, these district judges will not be able to hold this superior or intermediate court, if it be created.

Again, the time may come, when it will be necessary to establish a separate chancery court in this State. If the anticipations expressed here be realized, in regard to the increase in the population and business of the State, you will need various kinds of courts that I will not enumerate. You must leave this matter to be determined by the wisdom of the people through their agents, the legislature. It may be well to provide that until a given time, the duties of a new court may be discharged by the judges of the district courts. But it will not do to enter into the details, the minutiæ, of this matter here.

If the gentleman will look at this subject in this light, he will see that it will not do to provide for all these details in the constitution, for by doing so we might so tie up the hands of the legislature, that in five years the necessities and wants of the people would demand an amendment of this portion of the constitution. We may perhaps obviate the difficulty, by providing that if the legislature should create a new court within a given time, the duties of that court shall be performed by the judges of the district courts. But the time will come before many years, when those courts will have all the business they can possibly perform.

Gentlemen will bear in mind that we have limited the districts of the State to ten in number, and a single judge in each district. If they estimate the number of counties in this State, and provide for holding a term of the court four times a year in each county, they will see at once that these judges cannot have much time to meet as a superior court and decide the cases that would come up to them there on appeal. If the gentlemen will submit an amendment providing that for a given number of years, the judges of the District Court shall perform the duties of this new court, such an amendment might be advisable and a proper one.

Mr PETERS. My object in moving to restore this section to the form in which it stands in the present constitution, was that we might have some assurance that we would have a stable judiciary system. Gentlemen who have upon this floor opposed this three court system, have referred to the action of the late General Assembly as evidence to show that if we leave this constitution in such a condition as will allow the legislature to create such a third court as they may see fit to create, every man in the State, who is anxious to be a judge, will go before the legislature and endeavor, by log-rolling and scheming, to get them to establish such a court as will be likely to ensure their election, thus opening the doors for the creation of a system of judiciary, as large and extended, as the legislature at any time may see proper to establish. Now if that is the object gentlemen have in view in supporting this section as now modified, then I would suggest to them that they better strike out all in relation to any court, other than the Supreme Court, and say that the legislature shall have power to establish such other courts as they may from time to time see fit to create.

We have come in here, Mr. President, and asked the convention to give us a third court, one that will be nearer home, and more entitled to the respect and confidence of the people, who live remotely from the capitol. And in answer to this request, we have held out to us a promise which in itself, amounts to nothing. It gives the legislature the right to establish courts wherever they please. They may establish one in the county of Dubuque, perhaps one where Sioux City is situated, and yet such a court as would not meet the requirements of the people. It may be such a court as our district courts are at present, composed of one judge, and receive no more of the confidence of the people, than do our district courts.

It must be evident to all here, that the people of the State, living remotely from the capitol, will not be satisfied with a system of judiciary like our present one. Member after member has got up here and stated that their constituents had instructed them to ask for a change in the system as it at present exists. And still gentlemen get up here and say that the people have demanded no change. I am aware of the fact that the gentlemen who oppose this three court system are in the majority in this body. I am aware of the fact that they can vote us down in this matter. But I simply wish to remind them that this is not the last chance we have to cast a vote upon this question. I wish to give them notice that when this constitution goes before the people, the second judicial district will vote against it by a large majority, if nothing is done here to give them what they so urgently ask. They have felt the inconvenience of the present system, and have called for a change in it. If gentlemen will insist upon forcing upon them the present system as it now exists, I can only say that the people of that district, as well as the people further north, will vote against this constitution.

I know that if this constitution should be adopted and the legislature have the right to establish inferior tribunals to the Supreme Court, peradventure, if the capitol should be removed to Fort Des Moines, Johnson county might then come in and ask for a judicial tribunal, upon the plan that the report of the judiciary committee recommended. So far as any argument is concerned against the system we advocate, I have yet to hear of any except in this, that gentlemen say that all we have to do, who live remotely from the capitol, is to file our bill of exceptions, and enclose a fifty dollar fee to some attorney residing at the capitol, who will attend to our business for us. This may seem a plausible argument to those who live near the capitol and who attend the Supreme Court. But it will not appear as plausible to those who live remotely from the capitol.

I hope if we are to have a system of the judiciary, we may have such a system that, when it is submitted to the people, they will know what it is. I would prefer the present system, to leaving this matter open, so that the legislature may create just such courts as they may see fit to create.

Mr. CLARKE of Johnson. The imputation that the delegate from Deleware, [Mr. Peters], has cast upon me is very unjust. He seems to intimate that I am opposed to this three court system because I live near the capitol. I thought I answered that when I replied to the gentleman from Mills [Mr. Solomon] the other day. In order to meet the wishes of gentlemen, I have moved, and the Committee of the Whole have sanctioned, a proposition which will enable the gentleman to get this third court, when the people desire to have it. It seems to me, therefore, that I ought not to be assailed with these imputations.

Mr. PETERS. I had no intention to cast imputations upon any gentlemen.

The PRESIDENT. The chair will remark that he did not consider the gentleman from Deleware [Mr. Peters] as saying any thing to cast imputation upon the gentleman from Johnson, [Mr. Clarke].

Mr. CLAKE, of Johnson. He made the remark that if the capital was removed to Fort Des Moines, the gentleman from Johnson would then ask for another court.

Mr. PETERS. Not the *gentleman* from Johnson but the *people* of Johnson.

Mr. CLARKE, of Johnson. Now if it be true that the people would vote down this constitution, if they did not get this third court, then they should be satisfied now, for the amendment which I offered and which was adopted will give them what they desire. All they will have to do will be to demand of their agents, the legislature, the creation of this court, and they will get it. It seems to me that the position of the gentleman is a contradictory one, for while he says he favors the three court system, he will vote against a constitution which gives him the opportunity to have what he asks.

Mr. HARRIS. I wish to protest against this lash that some gentlemen are disposed to hold over our heads, by telling us that if we do not do thus and so, some particular section of the State are going to do wonderful things when this constitution comes before the people. I know that it is the right and privilige of the portion of the State that my friend from Deleware, [Mr. Peters] represents, to vote as they please. And he must concede to us the right to do the same.

I think the remark made by the gentleman from Hardin [Mr. Winchester], the other day, is true—to use an old phrase, "as true as preaching,"—that this whole thing in regard to the judiciary is decided according to the local prejudices of the attorneys upon this floor. While I will not undertake to say what are the sentiments of the constituents of members from any other portion of the State but my own, I beg leave to be considered the best judge of what my constituents desire. I believe if this thing was fully discussed, and fairly presented to the people of this State, the universal verdict would be, the fewer the courts and the more simple the judiciary, the better; because the people would then know what kind of mill they must be ground through when they go into court.

I believe our present system is more simple than any other that prevails in any State of this Union, and that it is as effective as any other, in securing full and ample justice to our citizens. And I believe another thing in regard to this matter: notwithstanding I stand here opposed to gentlemen of long and tried experience —to gentlemen to whose wisdom and knowledge in judicial matters I ought perhaps to bow—yet I believe that the creating of a multiplicity of courts, in which the suitor may be ground, and ground, and ground, for a number of years, does not have the tendency to secure rights and protect property; but, on the contrary, it has the tendency rather to fritter away the means of our people.

As I have before remarked, I believe there is a great deal of truth in the saying of a celebrated jurist, that a court was of more importance to prevent disputes by settling the law, than for any other purpose. It is necessary that parties should know what their rights are, and upon what they have to depend; and that I regard as the great desideratum in this matter. And hence, so far as this thing is concerned of giving the power to the Legislature to create more courts than we now have, unless they be of a minor character—such as county courts, and courts of probate—I am disposed to support the present system of judiciary in our State.

It has been said here that there was some feeling in one of the districts of this State with regard to the present system. But when we come to canvass the matter a little, we find that the people had put upon the bench a judge with whom some of the lawyers were disposed to quarrel, and they desired to get rid of him. Now, if you expect ever to get a judge upon the bench that some lawyers will not quarrel with, you will be most egregriously mistaken. It is as natural for some lawyers to quarrel with a judge, when he does not decide to suit them, as it is for them to breathe. And the fact that one or two lawyers in a district may be opposed to the judge, is no evidence at all that he is incapable of filling the position to which he is called. I am opposed to whatever may have the tendency to make our judiciary more complex, and make the mill longer in grinding out the grist that is put in it.

I believe, that in a case brought up before the court, when the facts have been fairly tried before a jury of competent men, then so far as the facts are concerned, the matter should stop. I believe we ought to have a court for the correction of errors, when the court has not decided according to the facts presented. And when that is done, I believe the matter ought to be ended. So far as the rights of citizens are concerned, in nine cases out of ten, the great bulk of the litigation, the winner in the end is really the loser. That is the result of my experience, though my experience may not be entitled to much weight. I have been at least an attentive observer in the courts, and have not been without some practice in matters of this kind. And I say, that so far as the actual dollars and cents are concerned, in the great bulk of the cases brought into our courts, the winner of the case is really the loser.

Cases may arise where a man is brought up to answer to charges of which he is not guilty, and it is right and proper that he should have the opportunity to receive benefits from an investigation that will secure him his rights. But in criminal cases it more frequently happens that parties are more afraid of receiving justice than of not getting their due. But there are cases that arise, in which property is involved, and it is but just that a man should have his rights, be they what they may. But I believe that in nineteen-twentieths of the cases litigated in our courts, when you get through, the winner of the case will find that he has lost money by the operation.

Mr. PETERS. The gentleman from Appanoose, (Mr. Harris), seems to be very much opposed to the idea that I should represent the will of my constituents upon this question.

M. HARRIS. Not so; I said that I did not like to have gentlemen hold the lash over us, and say, if we did not do thus and so, the Constitution would be voted down. We have the same right to represent our constituents upon this question, that other gentlemen have.

Mr. PETERS. I think I understand the gentleman; I stated here the other day that the main reason with us for calling this Convention, was to procure a change in our judiciary. Others claimed that the reason with their constituents was the subject of banks. So far as the subject of banks is concerned, I have this to say, that if a vote was taken in my district to-day, there would be at least one thousand majority against banks. I say, again, that the call of this Convention was in consequence of the desire of the people, of my district at least, for a change in our judiciary system, rather than any thing else, and unless we do adopt some change that will work for their benefit, they will, as a matter of course, vote against the adoption of this Constitution. I urge this as a reason for members to examine the proposition before the Convention, for the purpose of seeing whether we are actually in the wrong in this matter, or there is some merit in our position.

I understand that the proposition for a three court system is intended to give those who live remotely from the capitol the right to appeal to a court within their reach, to a judiciary which will be entitled to some respect and confidence; while those who live nearer the capitol will have the privilege, if they consider it such, to appeal directly from the district to the Supreme Court. It is not intended to force the people to go through a mill they do not like, to use the comparison of the gentleman from Appanoose, [Mr. Hrrris,] but it gives them the opportunity to have a court which would be entitled to more respect than the present District Court. Under our present system, if a judge commits an error, however plain the error may be, however distant we may live from the capital, we must go there to seek our remedy; thus involving so much expense, delay and trouble that the party aggrieved is often forced by necessity to bear the consequences of this error and let the case stop. For my part I can see nothing in the proposition we submit that will endanger the rights of any one, as we simply extend to those more remote portions of the State an extra judiciary which does not cost them a dollar; and yet gentlemen oppose it, though I must say, I have heard no reason, that to my mind, appears to be a valid one, against it.

Mr. SOLOMON. As I believe the object of the gentleman fromDelaware, (Mr. Peters,) and, mine, are the same, I will read an amendment I had proposed to submit to this section, and ask him to accept it in lieu of the one he has offered. I propose to add to the section the following:

"Provided the creation of such court or courts does not involve the election of judges other than those provided for in this article." The section if thus amended, will read:

"The judicial power shall be vested in a Supreme Court, District Courts, and such other courts, inferior to the Supreme Court, as the General Assembly may from time to time establish: provided the creation of such court or courts does not involve the election of judges other than those provided for in this article."

Mr. PETERS. I will accept the amendment.

Mr. SOLOMON. This amendment expresses my object in raising the point I did here this morning. I desire to see this amendment prevail, and it is for the purpose of securing safety and economy to the people. Although I have had, perhaps, as much provocation this morning, as any gentleman upon this floor, to enter upon side issues, instead of the question before us, I shall not do so, as I consider it undignified and inconsistent with our duties upon this floor.

I believe the provision I have offered will prove economical to the people, from the fact that it will prevent the legislature from establishing a new court, electing new judges and giving them new salaries to perform duties which can be performed, and which it is the intention of this Convention, shall be performed, by the judges already provided for. It may also prevent that other matter which seems to be dreaded by members here, and perhaps very properly—the outside pressure upon the General Assembly, from time to time, to get an intermediate court created for the purpose of forming some new offices to be filled. My amendment, therefore, secures the object avowed by the gentleman who moved the amendment to this section, in the Committee of the Whole (Mr. Clarke, of Johnson,) merely by its different reading, preventing any abuse by the legislature.

Mr. CKARK, of Alamakee. I am in favor of some system which will give us another court. But I would iuquire of the gentleman from Mills, (Mr. Solomon,) if his amendment will not have the effect of defeating that object?

Mr. SOLOMON. I hope not; it is not so intended.

Mr. CLARK, of Alamakee. I do not know how another court can be established, without providing some means of procuring some judges or justices to preside over it, and having the judges of the District Court to form a *nisi prius* court, distinct and separate from the appellate court. I think there will be no third court unless the legislature, in framing this superior or appeal court, has the power of establishing and creating the judges of that court. And if they create judges for that court, they must be created as judges of that court, and not as judges of the District Court. If the amendment read so as to allow the legislature, in establishing that court, to prescribe certain rules and practice by which the District Judges, as such, might preside in that court, then I would have no objection to it. It seems to me that it is necessary to have some provision of that kind in the Constitution. It should be borne in mind that the present Constitution—the one we are framing—so far as we have prepared it, does not divide the districts up at all: it merely provides that there shall be ten districts, and the judge of each district is elected as a *nisi prius* judge in that district, and for no other purpose. The question arises in my mind, whether, under the Constitution with this amendment incorporated into it, the legislature will have power to create a third court, and provide judges to hold that court. It seems to me that there is a difficulty there. If that difficulty is obviated I would then be in favor of this amendment.

Mr. BUNKER. I would enquire of the gentleman from Mills, [Mr. Solomon,] whether this amendment would not prevent the legislature from establishing county courts, organizing our probate courts, or courts of record? It appears to me that the amendment might deprive us of our ordinary probate courts.

Mr. SOLOMON. I do not apprehend any difficulty of that kind.

The question being then taken upon the amendment, it was not agreed to.

No further amendment being offered,

Term of Office, Jurisdiction, &c., of Supreme Court.

"Section third was then read as follows:

The Judges of the Supreme Court shall be elected by the qualified voters of the State, and shall hold their courts at such time and place as the General Assembly may direct, and hold their offices for six years, and until their successors are elected and qualified, and shall be ineligible to any other office during the term for which they may be elected. The supreme court shall have appellate jurisdiction only in all cases in chancery, and shall constitute a court for the correction of errors at law, under such restrictions as the General Assembly may by law prescribe. The Supreme Court may have power to issue all writs and process necessary to do justice to parties, and exercise a supervisory control over all inferior judicial tribunals, and the judges of the Supreme Court shall be conservators of the peace throughout the State."

Mr. PALMER. I move to amend by striking out the word "six," and inserting the word "four," so that the term of office shall be four years. I think that six years is too long a time for any office in this State.

Mr. CLARKE, of Johnson. I am opposed to striking out the word "six." I would be in favor of a provision by which one of these judges would be elected every two years. If the amendment of the gentleman from Davis, [Mr. Palmer,] does not prevail, I will offer an amendment to that effect. I desire it for this reason: if the judges are all elected at one time, as the section now contemplates, and as the practice is under the present Constitution, the result will be that we will have an entirely new set of judges upon the bench at one time. If you provide that after the first election, the judges shall be classified, so that one of them would go out in two years, one in four years, and one in six years, and after that each judge be elected for six years, you would have your Supreme Bench changed gradually, and always have two old judges, familiar with the business of the court, upon the bench. That, I think, would be better than the present practice, to elect an entirely new bench at the same time.

The question being then taken upon the amendment proposed by Mr. Palmer, it was not agreed to.

Mr. CLARKE, of Johnson. I move to amend this section by adding the following:

"After the first election of Supreme Judges under this Constitution, they shall be so classified, under provisions of law, that one of the Supreme Judges shall go out of office every two years. The justice of the Supreme Court having the shortest term at the first election, shall be chief justice; and at the expiration of his term, the justice holding the shortest term shall be chief justice."

I suppose, when we get through this article, it will be necessary to refer it to a Committee on Revision, to put it into shape. The ideas I have presented in this amendment are taken from one of the reports of the Committee on the Judicial Department.

Mr. TRAER. I would suggest that this subject better be referred to the Committee on Schedule.

The question being taken upon the amendment, it was agreed to.

No farther amendment being offered to the third section—

District Courts.

Section four was then read as follows:

"The District Court shall consist of a judge, who shall be elected by the qualified voters of the district in which he resides, at the general election, and hold his office for the term of five years, and until his successor is elected and qualified, and shall be ineligible to any other office except that of Supreme Judge, during the term for which he may be elected. The District Court shall be a court of law and equity, which shall be distinct and separate jurisdictions, and have jurisdiction in civil and criminal matters arising in their respective districts, in such manner as shall be prescribed by law. The judges of the district courts shall be conservators of the peace in their respective districts. The first session of the General Assembly shall divide the State into ten districts, and after the year 1860, the General Assembly may reorganize the Judicial Districts, and increase or diminish the number of Districts, or the number of Judges of the Supreme or District Courts; but such increase or diminution shall not be more than one District or one Judge of either court at a time, and no reorganization of the Districts, or diminution of the Judges, shall have the effect of removing a judge from office. Such reorganization of the Districts, or increase or diminution of the Judges, of either court shall take place every five years thereafter, if necessary, and at no other time."

Term of Office.

Mr. GILLASPY. I move to amend this section by striking out the word "five," wherever it occurs. I am in favor of electing our District Judges for four years. I am in favor of having our general elections take place every two years, the election of our District Judges every four years, and have our Supreme Judges elected for six years. I am in favor of that for this reason: Under the present constitution we have a general election every year, and some years we have three elections. Now that is totally unnecessary, and the people in my section are dissatisfied with it. We had three elections last year; nothing but excitement from the eighth of January, 1856, until the November election of the same year. We had a district election, the general election in August, and the presidential election in November. I am in favor of electing all the state officers for two years, the district judges for four years, and the supreme judges for six years. If we adopt that plan, then we will have a general election once in two years. I hope, therefore, the Convention will agree to my amendment.

The question being taken upon striking out the word "five," wherever it occurs in the fourth section, it was agreed to.

Mr. GILLASPY moved to fill the blanks with the word "four," so that the District Judges would hold office for four years, and the districts of the State would, after the year 1860, be re-organized every four years, and at no other time.

Mr. CLARKE, of Johnson. It seems to me, Mr. President, that this is a question that requires some consideration. I had not supposed that the vote would have been taken upon the motion to strike out this word "five," without some discussion upon it. I do not want to talk upon this subject all the time, but I am very much interested in this question of the judiciary. We aim, or should do so, by the provisions of this constitution, to obtain men of the best talent for judges. It is conceded that we have not obtained them under the present constitution, for the reason that the salaries, and other objections to the system, have kept the best men, men of the most extensive practice and acquirements as lawyers, from leaving the field of their practice. It seems to me that a long term would be one of the strongest inducements to a lawyer of good practice and extensive business, to give up his practice and accept the office of judge. I think I may lay it down as a proposition, which will meet the assent of every lawyer upon this floor, that a man with an extensive practice, is not willing to give up that practice to permit it to be scattered, for the purpose of going upon the bench for a year, or two years, or even four years.

The length of the term is one of the things to be looked at. It does seem to me that five years is short enough, as an inducement of this kind. I think the effect of shortening the term will be to prevent the best lawyers of the State from taking seats upon the bench, unless they are lawyers of a somewhat superannuated character, old men, who seek the bench as a place of rest. We do not want that class of men for judges. We want men in the prime of life, in the full vigor of manhood. The duties of a judge are onerous and laborious; and if you shorten the term of office, you will keep from the bench such men as should be upon it, to discharge properly the duties incumbent upon that station. I would ask lawyers upon this floor if they would give up a practice of five or ten thousand dollars a year, for a seat upon the bench for four years?

The PRESIDENT. It would be in order to move to fill the blank with the word "six."

Mr. CLARKE, of Johnson. I prefer five years, myself. I had not supposed the question would have been taken upon the motion to strike out, without there being some discussion. I did not vote myself, as I was busy all the time the vote was being taken. I hope some gentleman who voted in the majority will move to reconsider, that we may look at all the bearings of this question.

Mr. GILLASPY. The argument of the gentleman from Johnson [Mr. Clarke] is a very singular one. He would have the members of this convention understand that nobody has any interest in this matter at all, except the members of the bar. Now, I consider that every man in the State of Iowa has an interest in this matter; and those men upon this floor who do not belong to the legal profession, have feelings and interests in this matter. The gentleman has lost sight of the great principle of the cause of the "dear people."

Mr. CLARKE, of Johnson. Not at all.

Mr. GILLASPY. I undertake to say the people are as capable of determining upon the qualification of their judges, as they are of the qualifications of their other officers; and if the people shall elect to the bench of any district, a man who performs the duties of his office ably and efficiently, they will be inclined to elect him for another four years, thus making the term of office, practically, eight years in length. I know they will do it; such has been the practice everywhere. On the other hand, if the people should be so unfortunate as to put upon the bench a member of the legal profession, not qualified to act as a judge, I think it would be a godsend to allow them to get rid of him at the end of four years.

I believe it is the intention of this Convention to raise the salaries of these district judges. But I should be opposed to doing so, to the extent talked of here, if we are to elect a man to that office for nearly a life-time. The report of the committee, which came in the other day, proposed to elect our supreme judges for eight years. I am willing to vote that the length of the term of a supreme judge shall be six years. As to the district judges, it does seem to me we ought to leave the control of this matter to the people. If they get a good man upon the bench, whose decisions give character and credit to the judiciary, and satisfaction to the people, they will re-elect him, if he deserves it, at the end of the four years.

Let us pay them such a salary as will be an inducement to the best men in the State to accept the office. I think that under the old constitution even, we obtained the best talent in the State for any office, although they were not well paid for it. Gentlemen have said here that the district judges throughout our State were not excelled by any in the Union, even at a salary of only a thousand dollars. But I am in favor of raising their salaries, because I think they are too low. And I am in favor of having them elected for only four years, in order not to have their times of election conflict with our general elections. If a judge is a good man, the people will re-elect him; if he is a bad one, they ought to have a chance to elect another.

Mr. CLARKE, of Johnson. I have no desire to prolong this discussion. But I would ask the Convention to look at this matter a little closely. As I understand it, we have thrown this whole thing into the political arena. From the discussion of yesterday it seems to be conceded that the judges, both of the supreme and the district courts, are to be put up and bandied about between the political parties. What more is now proposed? To cut down the term to a merely nominal term. What will be the result of that? I say unqualifiedly that a man who is fit to be a judge, who possesses the mind and talent and experience that will fit him to be a judge of character and integrity, is not going to enter this political arena for the purpose of obtaining this office. We have an illustration of my position in my own county at the present time. We are now without a judge. The gentleman to whom the appointment has been tendered by the governor, declines taking it, unless he can be assured he will be elected when the election to fill the vacancy comes off. There are various candidates, upon both sides, who desire the office. And it is a question in my mind whether a man who seeks for the office of judge, ought to have it. And this will be the feeling among the fit men of the bar in this district. They will not go out and log-roll and caucus to secure delegates from their respective counties in order to secure the nomination for themselves. The moment they do that, they become tarnished, and sink below the level of what I think a judge should be.

By shortening the term of the office of district judge, you increase the necessity of this thing, in order that a man may receive an equivalent in the length of the time he is in office, for the practice he surrenders in accepting it.

There is another thing. A man who fills the office of judge creditably and profitably, must sometimes come in conflict with the prejudices and passions of the people. It is a notorious fact that those judges who have been the most upright in the discharge of their duties, have been unpopular. Reduce the length of their term of office, and you will have demagogues seeking the place of judge, who will gradually undermine his place in the confidence of the people, and they will log-roll to get his place. I say your courts will lose character if you adopt this system.

I have heard no complaint so far, from any quarter, in relation to the length of the term as it now stands. I think the people are satisfied. And I hope that gentlemen here who have been referring us so much to the experience of the past, and who, as they say, are so unwilling to make any changes, except those that the people have demanded, will leave this matter as it is. There may be some inconvenience, on account of the times of their election; that is possible. But the inconvenience of the thing is nothing when compared with the integrity and purity of the bench.

I look at this shortening the term of office of our judges as lessening the probability of our getting the right kind of men for that office. And the danger of changing the judges upon the bench is one that should be carefully guarded against. Every lawyer knows that just as often as you change your judges—unless the people are very fortunate—just that often you change the practice in our courts. That ought to be avoided as much as possible.

Suppose a man goes upon the bench for four years. If he is the right kind of a man for the office, he will cease his connection with any political party; he attends no political conventions; he makes no political speeches; he stands before the altar of justice as free from political and partizan feeling, as a minister of the gospel before the altar of his Maker. He will know no party; he will know no man. Now if he is standing there, discharging his duty honestly in the sight of God and man, there will be various demagogues gradually undermining him. He is not log-rolling, not canvassing to secure a nomination, and he will be put aside, and another put in his place. The injury resulting to the system, by thus reducing the length of the term, will not be compensated by any benefits to the people. I must look upon this proposition as one that will result detrimentally to the character and standing of our judiciary.

Mr. CLARK, of Alamakee. I am in favor of limiting the term of our district judges to four years, and for this reason: I believe that in the first place the shorter the terms in which we limit all our officers, the more amenable and responsible they are to the people who give them their offices. And the farther we depart from that principle the more independent our officers become of the people who elect them. I believe it is the true principle of all republican governments, as far as possible, to make the officers directly accountable and amenable to the people who put them in office. They are the mere servants of the people, and the shorter their terms are, the more dependent they are upon those who put them in office. Yet I am not in favor of having the term of office so short, that there will be a change in the office to such an extent, as to deprive the officer of the benefit of the experience, which, to a certain extent, he may acquire in that office.

I believe four years is long enough for any district judge. It is true there is only one year's difference between that and the present term of office, which is five years; yet if we give such a salary to these officers as they ought to receive, such as their talents and ability ought to command, and such as it will command in other capacities, we will be able to secure such talent as we desire. And if we want first class talent we must do this, no matter what may be the length of the term. If we do not give men sufficient salary to induce them to abandon their present business, and accept the office of district judge, we shall not get the talent that should be obtained.

The objection is equally strong to giving up a good practice for a term of eight years as for a term of four years. If a lawyer is induced to give up his practice to accept the office of district judge, upon a salary that will not compensate him for the change, a term of eight years will be more injurious to him than a term of four years. If he is induced to give up his practice for the consideration, in part, of the honor that would be conferred on him, he would be more ready to do it for a term of four years, than for a term of eight years. I believe that, for the same amount of salary, we will get as good talent for a term of four years, as we would for a term of five or eight years. And I believe that, at the same time, we will obviate one difficulty, which we must experience if the term of office is longer; and that is, that we are not always sure we will get a good judge. It is not always the case that a good lawyer makes a good judge. I think our past experience demonstrates that fact. It is impossible for the people always to tell, before they try a man, whether he will be a good judge or not. If we place the term of office at five, eight or ten years, and we happen to make a mistake in regard to the fitness of the person we may elect to be judge, we will have an officer fastened upon us for a term of years, which the necessities of the people do not require. With such a judge, four years is a term plenty long. If, on the other hand, we get a good judge—one with whom the people are satisfied—there will be no difficulty about re-electing him. I apprehend that any man who commands a position to become a candidate for that office, will be influenced as much by that consideration, as with a positive term of eight years before him. No man who is competent to fill the office should remain there if he does not give satisfaction. If, upon trial, he does not find himself qualified for the office, he should not desire to be kept in it. And I believe that men of the right abilities for the office will have that feeling in regard to it.

It seems to me that four years will be long enough, and will be more conducive to the benefit and interests of the people than a longer term.

The question recurred upon filling the blank with the word "four," so as to fix the term of office for district judge at four years, and provide for a reorganization of the districts every four years.

Upon this question, Mr. CLARKE, of Johnson, called for the yeas and nays, and they were ordered accordingly.

The question being then taken, by yeas and

nays upon the motion to fill the blank with the word "four," it was agreed to; yeas 24, nays 7, as follows:

Yeas—Messrs. Ayres, Clark, of Alamakee, Day, Edwards, Emerson, Gibson, Gillaspy, Gray, Harris, Hollingsworth, Johnston, Marvin, Palmer, Patterson, Peters, Robinson, Scott, Seely, Solomon, Traer, Warren, Wilson, Winchester and Young.

Nays—The President, Messrs. Bunker, Clarke, of Henry, Clarke, of Johnson, Ells, Gower and Hall.

Number of Districts.

Mr. GOWER. I move to strike out the word "ten," as the number of districts into which this State is to be divided, and insert the word "thirteen."

Mr. HARRIS. If the gentleman will make his motion to fill with the word "twelve," I should be inclined to vote for it.

Mr. GOWER. I wish, b fore the vote is taken, to give my reasons for the motion I have submitted to this Convention. When this question was voted on yesterday, it had not attracted my attention, and I was not fully prepared to act understandingly upon it. Since that time, however, I have investigated the subject more fully. I have been to the office of Secretary of State, and from him I learned that there are now thirteen judicial districts in this State. He told me. that under the action of the last General Assembly, there were fourteen districts organized, but the bill organizing the twelfth district failed to become a law.

I find, upon examination of the "Abstract of the Census Returns," for 1856, which have been furnished us, that last year we had a population of 509,414, so far as returns were made—Warren and Woodbury counties not having made their returns; they may be put down as having at least 10,000 inhabitants. The natural increase in the population of the State by June, 1857, will make the population of Iowa at least 600,000. There are one hundred and three counties, organized and unorganized, in this State. If we divide the State into thirteen judicial districts, each District Judge will have, on an average, the guardianship of eight counties, and 46,154 of population, which, it seems to me, will be enough for any one man to attend to. This plan will, besides, preclude the necessity of breaking up our present arrangement.

Mr. CLARKE, of Johnson, called for the yeas and nays upon the question, and they were ordered accordingly.

The question being then taken, by yeas and nays, upon the motion to strike out "ten" and and insert "thirteen," it was not agreed to; yeas 6, nays 25, as follows:

Yeas—Messrs. Bunker, Clarke, of Johnson, Ells, Gower, Palmer and Peters.

Nays—The President, Messrs. Ayres, Clark, of Alamakee, Clarke, of Henry, Day, Edwards, Emerson, Gibson, Gillaspy, Gray, Hall, Harris, Hollingsworth, Johnston, Marvin, Patterson, Price, Robinson, Scott, Seely, Solomon, Traer, Warren, Wilson and Winchester.

No further amendment being offered to this section—

District Prosecuting Attorneys.

Section five was then read as follows:

"The qualified voters of each judicial district shall, at the time of their electing District Judges, elect a Prosecuting Attorney, who shall be a resident of the district for which he is elected, and shall hold his office for the term of five years, and until his successor shall have been elected and qualified."

Mr. WILSON. I move to amend the section by striking out the word "five," and inserting the word "four," so as to make the term of the Prosecuting Attorney correspond to that of the District Judge.

The question being taken, the amendment was agreed to.

Mr. CLARKE, of Johnson. As there seems to be some controversy about creating the office of District Attorney, I think the whole matter should be left to the Legislature. I therefore move to strike out this fifth section.

Mr. PRICE. I hope the motion of the member from Johnson [Mr. Clarke], will not prevail. I feel deeply interested in the change in our judicial department in this respect—more deeply interested than in any other. I am very well satisfied with the different sections as they now stand. But in the district which I have the honor to represent, we certainly feel a very deep interest in this change from county prosecutors to district prosecutors. We have ascertained that a proper administration of the criminal law cannot be had under the present system. The county prosecutor with us is merely a nominal officer. No gentleman, who has ever read a page of law, would feel himself justified in accepting the office. And in many counties in my district, we have found that many men have been elected to the office of county prosecutor who had no qualifications, legal or otherwise, for the office. There is no inducement to any lawyer to take the office. And the result of having a merely nominal office, is, that the criminal law cannot be enforced. We have, in fact, no Prosecuting Attorney, and the whole system of criminal jurisprudence is liable to be treated without respect, and to be utterly disregarded; at least, that is my experience.

With those gentlemen who live in large counties, where a salary can be given large enough to secure the services of good lawyers, the present system may work well enough. But we of the western portion of the State feel the necessity for this change. We would thereby have an efficient prosecuting attorney for the district, for we could secure some gentlemen of sufficient legal attainments to fill the office with credit to himself, and with benefit and advantage to the people at large, of the different counties. For that reason I trust the motion of the gentleman from Johnson will not prevail.

Mr. HARRIS. I certainly feel as much interest in this question, as in any other connected with the subject of the judiciary. There certainly has been experienced a lamentable evil, in the section from which I came, in regard to the present system. For the most of the time, in my practice as a defending lawyer, I cannot say that I have had reason to complain of it, and I do not think my clients have had any reason to complain. But all over the State, and especially in the western portion of it, there is a great outcry against the failure to procure a proper enforcement of the criminal law of the State. And I apprehend that the remark made by my friend from Potawatamie, [Mr. Price,] in regard to some of the older counties does not hold good; that is, that they are able there to secure the best talent for the office of prosecuting attorney. There have been instances in this State where the office of prosecuting attorney has been filled with the best class of our lawyers; my friend from Des Moines, [Mr. Hall,] I believe once filled the office for two years. But I think the experience of all the State will go to show that the office has generally gone begging among the poor lawyers; and the class of lawyers from which it has usually been filled, has not been the best in the State.

There is another fact to which I wish to allude. The salaries now given are not sufficient. Now if the salaries given by each county for its county prosecuting attorney, could be put together for the whole district, and given to one officer for the district, you would then be able to secure the services of an able man, one fitted to discharge faithfully the duties of the office. In going around through the district he could always get some other business, and have the means derived from that to assist him.

I do think something of this kind is necessary. I know that so far as the people I represent are concerned, they have as much interest in this matter, and I was as frequently spoken to about it, as in relation to any other subject. I did not prompt attention to this matter; it came up from the people of my district, from men in the different counties, who had no expectation of holding the office, and desired only to see the law faithfully executed.

There is another reason assigned here on the part of some gentlemen that we ought not to make this change, because we need a prosecuting attorney in each county, in cases that come before justices of the peace, and in other cases. Now so far as my knowledge goes in regard to this matter, there is not one case in ten in these primary examinations where the prosecuting attorney is called upon. For in every instance where any individual feels any interest, where his rights or the rights of his friends have been outraged, he employs some attorney in whom he has confidence, to present the case to the magistrate. They merely endeavor to have the offender recognized and committed for trial, and then stop with the case, and let the matter go into court, when the State will take charge of it. They look to the prosecuting attorney to take charge of it in the courts. And it often fails there because the prosecuting attorney is not able to cope with the defense, who are generally the best lawyers about the court. And a young man, without experience, cannot be expected to meet successfully that class of lawyers. It is very natural that the cases should result as they generally do.

Another reason assigned for retaining the county prosecutor, is that he may give advice to the county officers. Now gentlemen here know that that is all a farce. If a county officer needs any advice, he goes to a lawyer in whom he has confidence, and upon whose opinion he can rely. This office of prosecuting attorney merely seems to give some young lawyer, or lawyer of no ability an opportunity to get his name upon the records of the court.

Mr. SOLOMON. In addition to what I said yesterday upon this subject, I would say that I hope the motion of the gentleman from Johnson [Mr. Clarke,] will not prevail. I feel a greater interest in this than in any other provision of this report. I can say that prior to the passage of the law providing for the calling of this convention, I heard this subject extensively discussed among the people of my district. It was a general subject of complaint among people, who generally approved of the constitution in every other respect.

Now in regard to whether a district attorney would be better than a county attorney, I can say this; from my short experience in the profession, I am satisfied the change would be a beneficial one. I think so, in the first place, from this fact, that where there is a bad criminal case which should be ably prosecuted, the first thing done by the defence is to change the venue from one county to another, the object oftentimes being to take the case to an adjoining county, where less efficiency, perhaps, exists in the prosecution, or where for various reasons the prosecution will not be so strong. I think if a district prosecutor was elected, whose duty it would be to be present at every court in the whole district, it would do away with this almost universal practice of changing the venue in criminal cases.

Another reason I have for this provision is this; the grand jury system is at the very foundation, at the very threshold of all criminal prosecutions. Our grand juries are composed of men taken from the people of the counties at large, who are not lawyers, and who generally are men who have remained at home, who have not attended courts, and who are therefore very little acquainted with the application of law to its violations. It is therefore necessary that there should be able counsel furnished our grand jurors by the State, who could, when a case comes before them, and the testimony is presented, tell the jury whether it was likely the State would be able to sustain the prosecution. This I think is one of the strongest arguments in favor of an able prosecutor. And I take it for granted that such a prosecutor could not be obtained as readily by the county system, as by the district system.

I think it is for the benefit of the community that the State should have able prosecutors. It will have a tendency to deter the commission of crime. The facility with which criminals are able now to scrape under our present system, has a great tendency, I have no doubt, to induce crime rather thon prevent it. I hope that this sectien will be retained, because I believe the people throughout my section of the State desire this change in our judiciary system.

Mr. PETERS. I will merely remark that I shall oppose the striking out of this section.

Mr. GILLASPY. I hope the motion to strike out this section will not prevail. I am glad to see members of the profession occupying the same position I do upon this question. It seems to me that if the members upon this floor had before them a statement of the amount of costs paid by the people of this State in the shape of taxes in consequence of incompetent prosecutors, there would not be a dissenting voice in regard to this section. I have no complaint to make about my county, we have a very able prosecutor there now. But I know that the people generally are in favor of this change. In the district of the gentleman from Appanoose, [Mr. Harris] in Monroe county, at one of their elections they could not obtain a candidate from either party who belonged to the profession, for the office of prosecutor, and they were obliged to elect a farmer, a man who had never seen an indictment in his life.

Mr. HARRIS. I will say that that has been quite frequent in my district.

Mr. GILLASPY. We have paid taxes enough since the time this State was a territory, in consequence of incompetent prosecutors, to build a railroad from one end of the State to the other, and if gentlemen will examine the records of the several counties they will find ample evidence to satisfy them that such is the fact. In my county the little king of a county judge does not consult any body. If there is a case in which he has any interest, he goes to work without consulting our prosecuting attorney, employs some other attorney at the expense of the county to take charge of the matter. Now I want to do away with all this thing, and have a man elected who is competent to fill the office. That can only be done by giving him such a salary as will justify a member of the profession to take hold of the matter, and prosecute all cases as they should be prosecuted. If you do that you will have prosecutions and convictions, whereas you now have prosecutions and acquittals. There has not been a criminal conviction in my county for the last five years. That does not relate to the prosecuting attorney we have now. I do not know what he will be. I have no fault to find with him. I hope for the best. I hope the convention will not strike out this section.

Upon the motion to strike out the fifth section, providing for district prosecuting attorneys, instead of county attorneys, Mr. Gillaspy called for the yeas and nays, and they were ordered accordingly.

The question being then taken by yeas and nays, the motion to strike out was not agreed to; yeas 6, nays 26, as follows:

Yeas—Messrs. Bunker, Clarke of Johnson, Ells, Gibson, Gower and Gray.

Nays—The President, Messrs. Ayers, Clark of Alamakee, Clarke of Henry, Day, Edwards, Emerson, Gillaspy, Hall, Harris, Hollingsworth, Johnston, Marvin, Palmer, Patterson, Peters, Price, Robison, Scott, Seely, Solomon, Traer, Warren, Wilson, Winchester and Young.

No further amendment being offered to the fifth section—

Style of Process.

Section sixth was read as follows:

"The style of all process shall be: "The State of Iowa," and all prosecutions shall be conducted in the name and by the authority of the same."

No amendment being offered to this section—

General System of Practice.

Section seven was then read as follows:

"It shall be the duty of the General Assembly to provide for the carrying into effect of this article, and to provide for a general system of practice in all the Courts of this State."

No amendment was offered to this section.

Sheriffs, District Clerks, &c.

Mr. PALMER offered the following additional sections:

Section 8. The qualified voters of each county shall elect at such times as may be prescribed by law, one sheriff and one clerk of the district court, who shall be residents therein, and hold their several offices for the term of two years, and until their successors shall have been elected and qualified.

Sec. 9. When any vacancy shall occur in the office of any judge of the Supreme or District Courts, before the expiration of the regular term for which he was elected, the same shall be filled by appointment by the Governor, until it shall be supplied at the next general election, when it shall be filled by election for the residue of the unexpired term.

Mr. GILLASPY. I would suggest that this subject should be referred to the committee on the schedule, and not be brought in here. It seems to me it would be better to have the committee on the schedule report upon the election of all officers, county recorders, and all others.

Mr. PALMER. I will state my object in offering these sections here. These officers of the courts, I think, should be provided for here in this article, rather than in the articles upon the schedule. It might perhaps be brought in the article upon miscellaneous subjects, under the head of county organizations.

Mr. CLARKE, of Johnson. I think it is necessary to provide here for filling vacancies for merely the residue of the term, instead of the full term, as is now the case. I therefore offer a substitute for the sections offered by the gentlemen from Davis, [Mr. Palmer] :

"In case the office of any judge of the Supreme or Districts Courts shall become vacant before the expiration of the regular term, for which he was elected, the vacancy may be filled by appointment by the Governor, until it shall be supplied at the next general election, when it shall be filled by election for the residue of the unexpired term."

Mr. HALL. It appears to me, that it is unnecessary to provide in the constitution for the election of all these ministerial officers. This matter can be provided for by the legislature.

The question was then taken on the substitute offered by Mr. Clarke, of Johnson, and it was not agreed to.

The question then recurring on the amendment offered by Mr. Palmer, it was taken, and the amendment was not agreed to.

Attorney General.

Mr. CLARKE, of Johnson. We have provided for the election of district attorneys, and I think it is better now to provide for the election of an attorney general. I, therefore, offer the following as an additional section:

"Sec. 8. The general assembly shall provide by law for the election of an attorney general by the people."

Mr. PALMER. Is not that officer provided for by the report of the committee on the executive department?

Mr. CLARKE, of Johnson. The attorney general is not an executive officer, but an officer of the judicial department. This is the proper place to provide for this officer, quite as much so as to provide for the election of district attorneys.

Mr. HARRIS. I have but very little feeling in regard to this matter, but I was always of the opinion, that the attorney general was a sort of fifth wheel to the wagon, and of no account. The legislature created this officer, and if it be deemed necessary, they can provide for him. This officer may be really indispensable, but I am disposed to think otherwise.

The question was then taken by yeas and nays, and the section was agreed to; yeas 18, nays 13, as follows:

Yeas.—The President, Messrs. Bunker, Clark, of Alamakee, Clarke, of Henry, Clarke, of Johnson, Edwards, Ells, Gower, Gray, Hollingsworth, Marvin, Scott, Seely, Traer, Warren, Wilson, Winchester and Young.

Nays.—Messrs. Day, Emerson, Gibson, Gillaspy, Hall, Harris, Johnston, Palmer, Patterson, Peters, Price, Robinson and Solomon.

Salaries of the Judges.

Mr. CLARKE, of Johnson. I offer the following as an additional section:

"The salary of each judge of the Supreme Court shall not be less than three thousand dollars per anuum, nor shall the salary of each judge of the District Court be less than two thousand five hundred dollars per annum. After the year 1860, the general assembly shall have the power to increase the salaries of the judges of the Supreme and District Courts; but the salary of no judge of either court shall be increased or diminished during his term of office."

On motion of Mr. PALMER,

The convention then took a recess until two o'clock, P. M.

EVENING SESSION.

The convention met at two o'clock, A. M., and was called to order by the President.

Adjournment Sine Die.

Mr. WINCHESTER. I offer the following resolution:

Resolved, That the convention will adjourn *sine die* on the twenty-second instant.

Mr. BUNKER. I move to lay the resolution on the table, and upon that question I demand the yeas and nays.

On motion of Mr. HALL, a call of the conventian was ordered.

The secretary then proceeded to call the roll, and the following gentlemen answered to their names:

The President, Messrs. Ayres, Bunker, Clark, of Alamakee, Clarke, of Henry, Clarke, of Johnson, Day, Edwards, Emerson, Gibson, Gray, Hall, Harris, Hollingsworth, Marvin, Palmer, Patterson, Peters, Price, Robinson, Scott, Seely, Traer, Warren, Wilson, Winchester and Young.

The following were the absentees:

Messrs. Cotton, Ells, Gillaspy, Gower, Johnston, Skiff, Solomon and Todhunter.

Mr. WILSON. I move that all farther proceedings under the call be dispensed with.

Mr. HALL. I hope that the sergeant-at-arms will be sent for the absentees, and that they will be brought in.

Mr. HARRIS. I hope that the motion of the gentleman from Jefferson [Mr. Wilson,] will not prevail. I know, that one of the absentees, Mr. Gillaspy, is very anxious to vote upon a resolution of this kind.

The PRESIDENT stated that Mr. Cotton was absent on leave.

A motion was made, that Mr. Todhunter be excused on account of illness, which was agreed to.

Mr. YOUNG asked leave of absence for Mr. Skiff, which was granted.

Mr. WILSON. I will withdraw the motion I made for dispensing with farther proceedings under the call.

The sergeant-at-arms was then dispatched for the absentees, Messrs, Johnston, Solomon and Gillaspy.

Mr. TRAER. I understand that the resolution, if it passes, will have no more effect than any other resolution we may pass here, as we can rescind it at any time. This question may be sprung upon us now, but I do not think that it will amount to any thing.

Mr. GIBSON. The resolution, I believe, provides for adjouring on the twenty-second instant, but the twenty-second comes on Sunday.

Mr. WINCHESTER. I will amend my resolution then by saying Monday the twenty-third instant.

On motion of Mr. CLARKE, of Johnson,

All farther proceedings under the call were dispensed with.

The PRESIDENT. The question will be first taken on laying the resolution upon the table.

The question was then taken by yeas and nays, and the resolution was laid on the table; yeas 20, nays 9, as follows:

Yeas—The President, Messrs. Ayres, Bunker, Clark, of Alamakee, Clarke, of Henry, Clarke, of Johnson, Day, Edwards, Ells, Emerson, Gibson, Gray, Hollingsworth, Palmer, Scott, Seely, Traer, Warren, Wilson and Young.

Nays—Messrs. Gillaspy, Hall, Harris, Johnston, Patterson, Peters, Price, Robinson and Winchester.

Mr. TRAER. I wish to call up the resolution of the gentleman from Jasper, [Mr. Skiff], in regard to limiting the time of speaking in the Convention.

The PRESIDENT. The Chair is of the opinion that it would not be in order now, as there is a motion pending in regard to the order of business.

Mr. TRAER. I am not very particular about the matter. I would like to confine some of these gentlemen to some reasonable time, who are voting for adjourning all the time, and yet taking up the time in making speeches.

Salaries of Judges.

The PRESIDENT. The business now before the Convention is the consideration of the article on the Judicial Department, and the business first in order is the amendment offered by the gentleman from Johnson, [Mr. Clarke], which reads as follows:

"The salary of each Judge of the Supreme Court shall not be less than three thousand dollars per annum, nor shall the salary of each Judge of the District Court be less than two thousand five hundred dollars per annum. After the year 1860, the General Assembly shall have the power to increase the salaries of the Judges of the Supreme and District Courts; but the salary of no judge of either court shall be increased or diminished during his term of office."

Mr. WILSON. I move to strike out the words "three thousand," and insert in lieu thereof, "twenty-five hundred."

Mr. TRAER. I would suggest that this whole subject is covered by the report of the Committee on the Legislative Department. Perhaps it would be just as well to leave this matter to them. I am opposed to fixing the salaries at any particular rate.

Mr. HARRIS. I think the gentleman could accomplish his purpose better by letting the matter come directly up now, and refer it to the Committee on the Schedule. If we wish to fix the salaries at any particular sum, we can let the Committee on Schedule regulate them.

Mr. CLARKE, of Johnson. We are not sitting here to make political capital for any party, nor any body of men; but we are sitting here to discharge our duties with reference to the public good. I am anxious to establish a judiciary system that shall be worth something, and which will hold out encouragement to the best men in the State to accept places under it.

The action of the Legislature, this last winter, it seems to me, ought to satisfy every member of the Convention that they evaded their responsibilities, and shifted them upon us. It is worse than futile to re-district the State, and turn out the present judges in the hope of getting better men, unless we give them the assurance that they will be paid salaries that will enable them to accept places upon the bench. I am not particular about having the exact sum named in the proposition, but I desire to pay these judges such salaries as will enable the people of the State to secure the services of men of talent and integrity. I am not mistaken in saying that any man, who is fit to fill either the place of a District or a Supreme Court Judge, is able to make, at his practice, double, if not treble, the amount of the salary he would receive as judge. If that be true, it seems to me that the Convention, if they seek to have new judges who will be men of character, ought to be willing to say to them—if you take this position, you shall at least be paid for your services such salaries as will enable you to support your families. It is a notorious fact that nearly every judge in the State, now upon the bench, has been compelled to engage in some other business in order to support his family. It was but a few days ago that one of our Supreme Court Judges was compelled to resign his place upon the bench, because the salary was too inadequate to enable him to support himself and family. A District Judge was compelled to resign because in consequence of the insufficiency of his salary; he was compelled to go into other business, that would produce litigation, and which, consequently, unfitted him for a seat upon the bench. It seems to me that we gain nothing unless we fix these salaries here, and at such a standard as will command the services of the best men we have.

There is another thing to be taken into consideration here. It is true that these amounts look large, when compared with the amounts named in the present Constitution. It is equally true, that since this Constitution was made, the business of the courts has increased to double and treble what it was before. And it is equally true, that the expense of living in this State has doubled within the last ten years. I do not know how long present prices of living will keep up; but it seems to me that any reduction in the cost of living you can anticipate with the prospective increase of business, and that these salaries are none too large to induce the best men to take these positions. I do not believe, with some gentlemen here, that men are so anxious to hold these offices. I do not believe they will be in demand by the best talent in the State, because I believe that men who are fit for judges, and who possess ability and integrity, are not the men who will be clamorous for them, but will rather prefer a private station.

I trust that the Convention, if they do strike out this proposition, will name some reasonable amount for these salaries. I think we ought to provide that the legislature shall not go beyond a certain amount, but that the legislature, within that limit, shall increase these salaries as the public necessities may require. I make these remarks from no personal feeling. I am not looking to the interests of the present judges, but I am looking to the interests of the judicial system of the State.

Mr. CLARK, of Alamakee. I am in favor of allowing the judges liberal salaries, and I do not know that the sums named by the gentleman from Johnson, [Mr. Clarke,] are too large for the present time. But it seems to me it would be better to leave some discretionary power over this matter with the legislature. Five years ago, three thousand dollars for the supreme court judges, would have been deemed an exorbitant salary; but times have changed since then, and the expenses of living have greatly increased. It is uncertain how long this state of things will last. If there should be a tendency to go back to the old prices of five and ten years ago, as there may be, then the salaries named here would be deemed exorbitant. In that case, the legislature should have power vested in them to reduce the amount of the salaries of the judges, so as to make them conform somewhat to the prices of other labor. Holding that view, I shall be in favor of so modifying the proposition before the Convention, as to give the legislature some discretionary power in the matter.

Mr. CLARKE, of Henry. I desire to make a single remark with regard to the salaries of the district judges. Some of these judges are now occupied the whole of their time, in the discharge of their duties; and I think they should be paid the salaries that are set down here. But there are other districts where the judges are not so hard worked, and, of course, they ought not to receive the same salary. I think that the better way would be to entrust the legislature with the power of regulating this matter of salaries. If the best talent of the State cannot be secured at these small salaries, they should be proportionately increased, according to the amount of labor which each individual is required to perform. I certainly should not favor the idea that a judge, who is occupied for only one month in a year, should receive the same salary as the judge who is engaged the whole year round.

The question was then taken, by yeas and nays, on the amendment offered by Mr. Wilson, to strike out "three thousand dollars," and insert two thousand five hundred dollars, in the amendment offered by Mr. Clarke of Johnson, and it was agreed to; yeas 23, nays 5, as follows:

Yeas—The President, Messrs. Bunker, Clark of Alamakee, Clarke of Henry, Day, Edwards, Gibson, Gillaspy, Gray, Hollingsworth, Johnston, Marvin, Palmer, Parvin, Patterson, Price, Robinson, Scott, Seely, Traer, Warren, Wilson, Winchester and Young.

Nays—Messrs Clarke of Johnson, Ells, Emerson, Hall and Peters.

Mr. WINCHESTER. I offer the following as a substitute:

"The salary of each judge of the supreme court shall not be less than two thousand dollars not more than three thousand dollars; the salary of each district judge shall not be less than one thousand five hundred dollars nor more than two thousand five hundred dollars; nor shall their salaries be increased or diminished during their terms of office."

Mr. GILLASPY. I wish to give the reason why I shall vote against this substitute, and it is this. To my mind, we might just as well say that the chief justice shall have three thousand dollars a year, because we give the power to the legislature to fix it at that amount. I am opposed to this substitute, therefore. I believe gentlemen ought to take the responsibility of fixing the salaries here, and so far as I am concerned, I am prepared to do so.

The question was then taken, by yeas and nays, upon the substitute offered by Mr. Winchester, and it was rejected; yeas 5, nays 25, as follows:

Yeas—Messrs. Clark of Alamakee, Clarke of Johnson, Emerson, Patterson and Winchester.

Nays—The President, Messrs. Ayres, Bunker, Clarke of Henry, Day, Edwards, Ells, Gibson, Gillaspy, Gray, Hall, Harris, Hollingsworth, Johnston, Marvin, Palmer, Peters, Price, Robinson Scott, Seely, Traer, Warren, Wilson and Young.

Mr. BUNKER. I move to fill the blank for the salary of the district judge with "two thousand dollars," and to make the salary of the supreme court judges "two thousand five hundred dollars."

Mr. GILLASPY. I move to fill the blank for the salaries of the supreme court judges with "two thousand dollars."

Mr. HALL. I think that we ought to fix the salaries here. It will prevent these judges from being dependent upon the legislature from year to year for their salaries.

The PRESIDENT. The question will first be upon filling the blank with "two thousand five hundred dollars."

Mr. CLARKE, of Henry. I should be in favor of a lower sum than two thousand five hundred dollars, as the sum below which the legislature should not go. The amendment is properly guarded in this respect, that these salaries shall not be diminished or increased during their term of office. There will be no danger of leaving this question of salaries to the legislature.

Mr. CLARKE, of Johnson. If we leave it to the legislature the question is not settled until the legislature fixes the salaries, and you hold out no inducements to your best men to fill these vacant places you propose to make. What I desire to accomplish here is, to say to these new judges, if you take these places, you shall get a reasonable salary.

The question was then taken, by yeas and nays, upon filling the blank with "two thousand five hundred dollars," and it was not agreed to; yeas 14, nays 16, as follows:

Yeas—The President, Messrs. Bunker, Clarke of Johnson, Edwards, Ells, Emerson, Hall, Hollingsworth, Marvin, Patterson, Price, Traer, Warren and Young

Nays—Messrs. Ayres, Clark of Alamakee, Clarke of Henry, Day, Gibson, Gillaspy, Gray, Harris, Johnston, Palmer, Peters, Robinson, Scott, Seely, Wilson and Winchester.

Mr. GRAY. I move to fill the blank with "two thousand dollars."

The question was then taken, by yeas and nays, and the motion of Mr. Gray was agreed to; yeas 18, nays 12, as follows:

Yeas—Messrs. Ayres, Clark of Alamakee, Clarke of Henry, Day, Gibson, Gillaspy, Gray, Harris, Hollingsworth, Johnston, Palmer, Patterson, Robinson, Scott, Seely, Traer, Wilson, and Young.

Nays—The President, Messrs. Bunker, Clarke of Johnson, Edwards, Ells, Emerson, Hall, Marvin, Peters, Price, Warren and Winchester.

Mr. GRAY moved to strike out "two thousand five hundred dollars," and insert "one thousand five hundred dollars."

The question was then taken, by yeas and nays, upon the motion to strike out two thousand five hundred dollars, as the salary of the district judges, and insert one thousand five hundred, and it was agreed to; yeas 20, nays 9; as follows:

Yeas—Messrs. Ayres, Clark of Alamakee, Clarke of Henry, Day, Edwards, Gibson, Gillaspy, Gray, Harris, Hollingsworth, Johnston, Palmer, Patterson, Robinson, Scott, Seely, Traer, Warren, Wilson and Young.

Nays—The President, Messrs. Bunker, Clarke of Johnson, Emerson, Hall, Marvin, Peters, Price and Winchester.

Mr. GIBSON. I move that the word "less" be stricken out wherever it occurs, and that the word "more" be inserted in its place; and I desire briefly to give my reasons for such a proposition.

The General Assembly, in consequence of their late action, have offered, in the shape of a law, a direct insult to every district judge in the State of Iowa. They raised the salaries of the supreme court judges from the sum of one thousand to the sum of two thousand dollars; and that of the district judges from one thousand to only twelve hundred dollars, which I say was an insult to the district judges. I am willing to take the responsibility of fixing this matter, so far as I am concerned, and I hope the Convention will do the same thing, and not leave it to the action of the legislature.

Mr. HALL. I think the members of the convention must feel exceedingly poor, this afternoon, and they must look forward with some degree of alarm, lest the State may become insolvent; for they have fixed the salaries of the supreme court and district judges so low that they will not be able to command the services of the best men of the legal profession for these places, for their private business will pay them far better. You cannot secure the services of a respectable pilot or engineer on a steamboat at the prices you propose to pay these judges. Gentlemen have become wonderfully economical all at once. If they can only get judges to take a place upon the bench, it is no matter who they are, or from what quarter they come. Now you cannot get the gentleman from Wapello [Mr. Gillaspy] to leave his private business for a seat upon the bench at the prices that you now propose to pay these judges.

But gentlemen say, in answer to the argument that the salaries of judges should be increased on account of the increased expenses of living, that this state of things is not going to last always. But we are not going backwards in this State; on the contrary, from a thinly settled State, we are becoming a densely populated one, increasing in wealth and population faster than any new State ever did. If you establish the salaries of these district judges at fifteen hundred dollars, they will remain so for a long time. Notwithstanding you are devolving upon them a large increase in the amount of business and enlarging their responsibilities, you are scarcely increasing their salaries at all. I do not believe that the people of this State will be at all grateful to us for cheapening the salaries of those officers who manage the machinery of government, and control the affairs of government to a very large extent, below the compensation which an ordinary steamboat captain, or pilot, or an engineer on our railroads gets. I recollect very well an incident that occurred while I had the honor of occupying a seat upon the Supreme Court Bench. While on my way home from this city, I met at Rock Island a man who formerly resided at Burlington, and who was considered a great loafer there, and who, I believe, is now residing at Fort Madison, in one of the charitable institutions there. When I met him, he said he was doing very well, and was employed as a runner for railroads at ninety dollars a month. Now that was a larger salary than the State paid me. I ask gentlemen if they desire to put their judicial officers in such a position that they shall receive no more compensation for the services they render than is given by railroad companies to persons in the lower grades of employment?

It does appear to me that the Convention ought to be governed in this matter by a liberal and rational policy. One of the Supreme Court Judges left the bench, last year, because he could not afford to retain the office any longer;

and the District Judge of this district has resigned for the same reason. Those gentlemen, and all other judges who have capacity, can do infinitely better to resign and go into other business. It is a false and mistaken idea of economy, in my opinion, to pay your judges upon the bench these meager and insufficient salaries.

I shall vote against the amendment because I believe the salaries it provides for these judges are too low. The disparity between the salaries of the district and supreme court judges is too great when you take into consideration the fact, that there are to be but ten districts in the whole State, and you put these judges to the expense of being away from home the most of their time. They should have, in my opinion, as much as the supreme court judges, for their expenses will be as great as those of the judges of the supreme court, and they will be away from their families fully as much. The inconveniences of sending these judges of the district court over a large district of country will be fully as great as in the case of the supreme court judges. Why then make this difference of five hundred dollars in the salaries of these two classes of judges? It does appear to me, that we should pay the judges of the district court as high salaries as the supreme court judges. If we pay the supreme court judges two thousand dollars a year, I should be willing to pay the district court judges the same amount.

Mr. GILLASPY. I have great confidence in the judgment of the gentleman from Des Moines, [Mr. Hall] but for my part I have not come here to ascertain what the salaries of steam boat captains and pilots are, nor what they can get. I have no doubt that the gentleman is conversant with them, living upon the river as he does. The gentleman is getting along very fast it seems to me, for it is only a year or two since that he was upon the supreme court bench at one thousand dollars a year salary and he was willing to remain there; and so far as I know, might have been there yet, had he had his own way. No difficulty has been heretofore found in getting supreme court judges at one thousand dollars salary and it seems to me if we double the pay, that we will have no difficulty in getting competent men to sit upon the bench. I am satisfied that the labors of the supreme court from this time will be greater than those perhaps of a majority of the judges of the district court. I can only speak from a knowledge of my own district. I am satisfied that one thousand five hundred dollars is sufficient to induce as good a lawyer as we have in my district to accept a place upon the bench, and I presume that we have as good lawyers there as any where else. I am satisfied that fifteen hundred dollars will pay any lawyer for accepting this position. It may be that in one or two districts upon the Mississippi river—unless we take into consideration this fact when we re-district the State—the judges there may have to perform a sufficient amount of labor to entitle them to a higher rate of compensation. I am satisfied that in every solitary district there will be scores of applicants ready to take these offices; and that gentlemen of the finest attainments will be willing to accept these places at a salary of one thousand five hundred dollars.

Mr. PETERS. I move that this whole subject be referred to a select committee of five.

Mr. TRAER. I wish to explain the votes I have given upon this question, and satisfy my friend from Des Moines (Mr. Hall) that I have not voted in favor of his proposition, from the fact, that I was in favor of paying low salaries. I stated at the outset that I was opposed to fixing the salaries of the judges in the constitution with the exeption merely of fixing them for the present time. I am satisfied that the gentleman from Des Moines is right in his estimates upon this matter, and I believe if we wish to have good judges we must pay them a fair price for their services. I would apply this rule to every kind of business. No matter what business transactions you may be engaged in, if you expect good workmen, you must pay them fair prices; and this rule will apply just as well to the judiciary as to any other department of government or any of the ordinary transactions of life. I am in favor of paying these judges fair salaries, and I think two thousand five hundred dollars a year is not too high a salary for them. I am opposed however to establishing salaries for these officers in the constitution for any term of years. I believe the better way would be to regulate this matter in the schedule, for the present, and let the legislature take care of this question hereafter. I think with my friend from Alamakee [Mr. Clark] that times may change, and the expenses of living may not be as high in a few years as now. The salary of one thousand dollars a year was sufficient at the time it was fixed, and it would go as far then as two thousand dollars will now.

I am opposed, therefore, to incorporating any provision in the Constitution that shall permanently fix these salaries. I do not know what gentlemen can do in Wapello county, or what kind of talent they have there; neither do I care; but it is a fact that, in the region of country I represent, almost every lawyer can make from one to three thousand dollars a year in the practice of the law, and some make a great deal more. If we desire to have the best talent of the bar upon the bench, it is necessary, I think, that we should pay them salaries sufficient to make it an inducement for them to accept such places. I hope gentlemen will take the right view of this question, and vote against this proposition of fixing these salaries in the Constitution, and leave this question in such a way that the legislature may change the salaries as the necessities of the times may demand.

Mr. MARVIN. Perhaps I may be permitted to speak upon this question without being suspected of supposing that I shall ever be benefitted, individually, by any particular course I may pursue here. I am certainly surprised at the votes given here. I know that there are thousands of farmers to-day in this State who would not leave their homes and families, pay the expenses necessary to be incurred in attendance upon court, and hire out their services, at the salaries that we offer to pay our best judges. There are farmers in this Convention who would not do it. If there are thousands of farmers throughout the State who would not leave their business and families, and the enjoyments of the home circle for a salary of two shousand dollars, can we expect that men of fine attainments, who have spent their lives in acquiring sufficient knowledge to fill these stations of importance, with honor to themselves and benefit to the people, will be induced to accept these places unless we pay them as much or more than they can make by their profession at home? The rates of living for a judge will amount to something over seven hundred dollars a year; and when you add to this sum his traveling, and other incidental expenses, you will swell the amount to at least one thousand dollars. When I employ a man to do certain work for me, I desire to secure the services of some one upon whom I can place the utmost reliance and confidence; and for the services of such a man I am willing to pay a high price. And this rule I should apply in every kind of business. When I vote for a judge of the supreme court, I desire to vote for a man who will do honor and credit to the station he fills. I am, therefore, in favor of paying our judges such salaries as will be an inducement to the best men we have to accept a place upon the bench.

Mr. HARRIS. I think that the remarks made by my friend from Jones, [Mr. Marvin,] are worthy of some consideration at the hands of the Convention. I hope that in what I may say, or in the manner in which I shall vote here, gentlemen will not consider me as acting from interested motives. I certainly am not actuated by any motives of that kind. I do know, that just at this time, there is a lamentable want of the right kind of talent upon the bench in some parts of this State. I should not suppose that gentlemen would be deterred from doing what they believed to be just and proper, in placing the salaries these officers are to receive at such sums as will secure the best talent we have in the State.

The gentleman from Wapello, [Mr. Gillaspy,] says it does not matter to him whether the compensation is sufficient, if they can only get the services of men who will perform this duty.

Mr. GILLASPY. I stated distinctly that, in my judgment, the salary was sufficient, and that if we obtained the services of men who would perform this duty at the salary now fixed, that was all I asked.

Mr. HARRIS. It does not matter to the gentleman from Wapello, [Mr. Gillaspy], who are to perform this duty. I wish to establish the principle here, that "the laborer is worthy of his hire." The argument is made here that the Legislature, this winter, have made a disparity between the salaries of judges, that they ought not to have made. Now, if this be the case, I apprehend they will have an account to settle with their constituents. As one of these constituents, I have no objection to calling them to an account. But it does look to me, as the matter is now presented, that the salaries of one class of these judges should not be less than fifteen hundred dollars. I am not afraid to trust this matter of fixing the salaries of the judges to the Legislature. They may have acted unwisely hitherto, so far as the fixing of these salaries is concerned. But gentlemen must recollect that this is a matter that has not been much agitated before the people; and with light which the discussion of this subject will throw before the people, the matter of salaries would be soon regulated in accordance with the demands and necessities of the time. The population and business of the State will probably increase with unprecedented rapidity, and, of course, the business of the courts will increase in a proportionate ratio. We should leave it to the Legislature, then, to regulate the salaries of our judicial officers, as the increase of their business and responsibilities shall make it necessary.

Mr. GILLASPY. The gentleman from Jones, [Mr. Marvin], in his appeal to the farmers upon the floor of this Convention, has asserted a doctrine that I never understood before; that is, in order to get talent, you must go where there is wealth; that in order to get a talented man, you must find a wealthy man. I was never aware before that that was a fixed fact: nor do I believe now that it is.

In regard to what I said about catching the legal profession with a thousand dollar bait, I did not mean to cast any reflection upon the gentleman from Appanoose, [Mr. Harris.] But if I mistake not, I have seen the gentleman, in times past, nibbling about a hook with a thousand-dollar bait on it, and he never did get it.

Mr. HARRIS. The gentleman from Wapello, [Mr. Gillaspy], has been more successful than I have, for he has never failed, I believe, to get the bait every time.

Mr. MARVIN. I said that if we adopt this rate of salary, we would have to go for our judges to the wealthy classes, who had retired from business, because the poorer lawyers would want more salary to support themselves and family.

Mr. HALL. The gentleman from Wapello, [Mr. Gillaspy], seems to understand this matter almost to perfection. I want to refer the gentleman to the history of his own district. They have starved out every judge they have ever elected there; not one has served out his time.

Mr. GILLASPY. We have one there now.

Mr. HALL. And he is getting, in about a year, ragged at the elbows and knees.

Mr. GILLASPY. He is one of the best judges in the State.

Mr. HALL. I have nothing to say against his attainments. The gentleman has taken the liberty to allude to myself. It was well understood among my friends, that I was tendered the position I held for a short time upon the Supreme Bench, without any solicitation upon my part.

And it was just as well understood that I declined receiving the appointment for a longer period. I never solicited the appointment from any quarter, nor wrote a line, nor asked any one to solicit it for me. I kept an accurate account of my expenses, during the time I held that position, and I found that it cost me thirty-three per cent. more, to live and support my family, than I received from the State.

I think if we fix the salary of the Supreme Judges at $2,000 a year, the disparity proposed between their salaries and the salaries of the District Judges are too great. And I think the gentleman will find lawyers in his district, fit for the office, very scarce who will take the place with the salary proposed. They will not be fit for the office in my opinion, though they may be in his opinion.

Mr. GILLASPY. In their own opinion; not in mine.

Mr. HALL. I understood the gentleman as endorsing that assertion. The disparity, as fixed by this amendment is too great. I do not believe that we ought to fix the salary so that gentlemen who accept the position must do so for the sake of the honor attached to it. The policy of the State should be to get men who would honor the position, rather than be honored by it. That is what we should desire and seek. Men have arisen in other States, who have shed lustre around the bench upon which they sat. And men should be sought in this State who would shed this lustre upon the bench here, and be an honor to the position; and thus alone is the position made honorable; the only honor that belongs to the position is derived from the talent and ability with which it has been filled.

It is essentially necessary that this position should be put at least upon an equality, if not a little above other employments that men can engage in. Because we have had judges heretofore, it is no sign we have treated that branch of our government, as it should have been treated; nothing of the sort should be inferred. I know, if I am to believe the assertions of our present judges, that they have been unwilling to have accepted the position, except because of the hope that, when the time came for the legislature to fix the salaries, they would be raised to the proper standard. The legislature this winter did raise their salaries to two thousand dollars, and dated them back six months, to last August, making them about two thousand two hundred and fifty dollars a year for the present year.

And I think I may be safe in saying that the question of salaries, so far as our District Judges are concerned, was left open with the expectation that this Convention would do something in the matter, and that we should probably put them upon a footing with our Supreme Judges. I say, therefore, if we desire to provide properly for this branch of our government, let us put it upon the footing of other classes of men, who engage in these high employments. This is all I ask; and I think it is necessary. By so doing we shall, at least, have the same competition, that exists in other grades of employment equally valuable. This is certainly desirable. You cannot get men competent for District Judges, for the prices you propose to establish in this article.

I believe in the doctrine laid down by the distinguished Daniel Webster, that for the purpose of obtaining a good judiciary, it was necessary to work them hard, give them plenty to do, and pay them well; give them full employment, keep them engaged, and be sure and pay them well. For, as he said, lawyers, as a general thing, always live well, but they always die poor.

Mr. HARRIS. I would not trouble the convention again, but for the position that my friend from Wapello [Mr. Gillaspy,] has sought to place me in upon this question. I would not have made the remarks I did in regard to that gentleman, if I had not considered his attack upon me as entirely unprovoked. So far as to my having been a candidate for office, that is true; my name was presented to the nominating convention, not this year, nor last year, but four years ago, in connection with the matter the gentleman has reference to. And the gentleman knows it was not presented there with my consent. I strove to place upon the bench one of those hopeful scions of the law that he speaks of, from his own town, until I fell under the displeasure of my own district in trying to do so. I withdrew my name from before the convention against their will, and incurred the displeasure of some of them by doing it, and that, too, when there was a probability of my getting the nomination. Those are the facts of the case, well known all over that portion of the State. If the gentleman has made anything by his attack upon me, he is welcome to all the advantage he can derive from it.

Mr. GILLASPY. I was merely in sport in what I said, and took the remarks of others in the same spirit.

Mr. WILSON. I wish to enter a protest against being placed in the class favoring these niggardly salaries, as they have been termed by some gentlemen here. I am not in favor of starving either our district judges, or our supreme judges. I am in favor of giving to any and all of our officers for their services, a good living compensation. And I look upon this provision as a protection for our judges; it is fixing a limit, and declaring that below a certain sum the legislature shall not go, but above that they can go as far as they please, even to ten thousand dollars a year. If the judges demand more than they receive, if the amount of services performed, the cost of living, and the price to be paid for getting suitable talent, require higher salaries, then let them be fixed by the legislature, who are the direct representatives of the people, and should have the control of this matter. The great complaint of the old constitution was that it tied the hands of the legislature too closely. I am willing to say here, below a certain amount they shall not go; but they may take the responsibility of going as much above that amount as they please.

Mr. CLARKE, of Johnson. If I understand the pending amendment, it will not permit any increase at all hereafter. As I understand the position of this thing now, the salaries of the judges of the Supreme Court are fixed at two thousand dollars, and of the District Court at one thousand five hundred dollars.

Mr. PALMER. Until 1860.

Mr. PETERS. I hope gentlemen here who have been promising us for several days, that they will give us better District Courts than we now have, from the fact that their salaries will be increased, will take this matter into consideration. The remarks upon this subject have been full and complete. For my part I would be willing to vote for two thousand five hundred dollars as the lowest salary for district judges, and put the supreme judges upon the same footing.

The question then recurred upon striking out the word "less," and inserting the word "more," as moved by Mr. Gibson, so that the legislature shall not have power to increase the salaries of the judges.

Upon this question Mr. HALL called for the yeas and nays, and they were ordered accordingly.

The question being then taken, by yeas and nays, the motion was not agreed to; yeas 6; nays 24, as follows:

Yeas—Messrs. Ayres, Day, Gibson, Gillaspy, Palmer and Robinson.

Nays—The President, Messrs. Bunker, Clark, of Alamakee, Clarke, of Henry, Clarke, of Johnson, Edwards, Ells, Emerson, Gray, Hall, Harris, Hollingsworth, Johnston, Marvin, Patterson, Peters, Price, Scott, Seely, Traer, Warren, Wilson, Winchester and Young.

Mr. WARREN. I move to reconsider the vote by which the blank, in the clause relating to the salaries of the judges of the District Courts, was filled with the sum of one thousand five hundred dollars. I voted in the majority for the express purpose of moving a reconsideration, when the time should come for me to do so. I think the discussion that has taken place here is sufficient to indicate the propriety of the motion I now submit.

Mr. CLARKE, of Henry. I would suggest to the gentleman from Jackson [Mr. Warren,] that it would be better to amend the section by inserting the proposition to leave this matter to be fixed by the general assembly, and after they have done so, then have it that the salaries shall not be increased or diminished during the term of office to which the salary is attached. Let these sums stand as the minimum, below which the legislature shall not go.

Mr. WARREN. I cannot accept that proposition. I am unwilling to trust the legislature. I am fearful they would be too much like this body. My object in submitting the motion to reconsider is to move an increase of the amount fixed for the salary.

The question was upon the motion to reconsider the vote fixing the salary of district judges at one thousand five hundred dollars.

Upon this motion Mr. GILLASPY called for the yeas and nays, and they were ordered accordingly.

The question being then taken, by yeas and nays, the motion to reconsider was agreed to; yeas 21; nays 9, as follows:

Yeas—The President, Messrs. Ayres, Bunker, Clarke, of Johnson, Day, Edwards, Ells, Emerson, Hall, Marvin, Patterson, Peters, Price, Robinson, Scott, Seely, Traer, Warren, Wilson, Winchester and Young.

Nays—Messrs. Clarke, of Henry, Clark, of Alamakee, Gibson, Gillaspy, Gray, Harris, Hollingsworth, Johnston and Palmer.

The question recurred upon the proposition to fill the blank with the sum of one thousand five hundred dollars.

Mr. WARREN moved to fill the blank with the sum of two thousand dollars.

Mr. HARRIS moved to fill it with one thousand eight hundred dollars.

The question was stated to be upon the resolution to fill with two thousand dollars.

Mr. CLARKE, of Henry. I do not know but what I have voted heretofore under a misapprehension of the question. But if I have understood members aright, when we have been discussing this question, it has been reiterated here again and again, that the district judges had not enough to do for one third of their time; with that understanding and with the further knowledge that the district judge in my district was fully occupied, I thought it was well to discriminate between the different judges. If one of them had but little to do, and would devote two thirds of his time to other pursuits, I could not perceive the same reason for giving him a salary of two thousand dollars a year, as the judge who is so situated as to have all his time taken up with the duties of his office. With this view I desired to leave this matter to the legislature, that they might have the opportunity to discriminate, in fixing the salaries for the different judges if they should consider it necessary.

The State may be so districted that the amount of labor, falling upon the several judges, shall be equalized. But that may not be done, and the legislature should discriminate in the matter. I believe many of the judges would be receiving high salaries for their present services, at one thousand five hundred dollars a year. But I was willing to give all of them that sum, and restrict the legislature from going below that amount. But I did not want the time of this convention taken up in fixing the salaries with the discrimination that ought to be made; that discrimination I would leave to the legislature.

I believe in high salaries, to a certain point, as much as any man does. But I do not believe at all in having any sinecures, in creating offices and having them filled by certain individuals at high salaries, with nothing to do. I believe that when there is business to be done that there should be an office and an officer; and if there is a great deal of business to be done in that office, I would pay the officer a high salary for doing it. But I would leave the legislature to say what those salaries should be. At the same time to guard against partial legislation, I am willing to say to the legislature, you shall not go below a certain sum, in establishing salaries for our judges, but above that sum we will leave it to them to establish whatever salary they may think proper. It was with that view that I voted for inserting the sum of one thousand five hundred dollars instead of two thousand dollars, as the point below which the legislature should not go, in establishing the salaries of our district judges.

In regard to the judges of the supreme court, the case is different. Their duties are alike; they occupy the same bench, and each has to devote the same number of hours to business that the others do. And there is no reason for this Convention or the legislature to discriminate between them in regard to the matter of salaries. I am willing to establish their salaries at two thousand dollars a year. I do not think it ought to be below that sum; and, understand me, I do not think the salaries of some of our district judges should be below two thousand dollars. But if my information is correct, there are some district judges in this State whose salary would be a high one even at fifteen hundred dollars a year.

Mr. HALL. I suppose the principles established by the Convention, of limiting the number of districts to ten at the start, and not permitting the number to be increased before 1860, and then only one at a time, was to secure plenty of work for our district judges. That was, at least, my purpose in supporting that proposition. And but for the extent of territory in this State, I would be willing to vote for even a smaller number of districts, and a smaller number of judges to do the work. As it is, however, I do not think the number of districts should be any smaller.

And there is another thing to be considered. The judge who is deciding cases, arising in every department of business and life, should be in a position which would not require him to engage in any kind of business in relation to which he would be called upon to give a decision. And whether he may have more or less to do, he should be paid for the whole of his time. The man who employs another should find work for him to do. And if you employ a man as a judge, satisfy yourself that you have given him work enough to do, as much as he ought to do, and then make him do it. But do not say he shall be half a judge and half a speculator, or half a judge and half a horse jockey. We should place our judges in such a position that they will not become interested in any business, questions relating to which come before them for decision. I will go as far as any man here to give our judges plenty to do. That is my principle: pay them well and work them well. Give them but little time for study and examination—as little as possible—and have them efficient; treat them as you do your other servants; give them all they can do, and then pay them well for doing it.

Mr. EMERSON. It will be seen, by the votes I have given since this matter of salaries has been before this Convention, that I have been in favor of the highest amount. I do not think the proposition of the gentleman from Johnson, [Mr. Clarke,] was any too high. Gentlemen say here, refer the matter of fixing these salaries to the legislature; put the district judges at fifteen hundred dollars, and then the legislature may put them, if they please, at two thousand dollars. Now, I think, if gentlemen here look at the matter in this light, look at the sum of fifteen hundred dollars as being sufficient, and as much as a district judge should have, they would vote the same way if they were in the legislature. It seems to me it would behoove every judge to be a bachelor; for, certainly, if he had a family, he could not feed and clothe them; or even if he could, I do not suppose any gentleman upon this floor will say that he could more than feed and clothe his family.

Then is it proper and right to place your judges in a situation where it will be physically impossible for them ever to lay up a dollar "for a rainy day?" Is it right, in fixing their salaries, to fix them at just what they can barely live upon? Is there any gentleman upon this floor who would like to be put upon bread and meat in such a way that there was no probability of his ever laying up a dollar by his vocation, and at the end of the year he was to be just where he started, and if he continues to be judge through life, be just merely able to clothe himself and famfly? Let us estimate this matter. Take the town of Dubuque, for instance; in the first place, anything like a good dwelling house will cost him, for rent, from seven hundred to one thousand dollars a year, merely covering him from the weather. Then, if he is to receive a salary of fifteen hundred dollars, he will have from five hundred to eight hundred dollars to feed and clothe his family.

I object to this course being pursued with regard to our judges. Indeed, I have been considerably disappointed at the position and standing that lawyers occupy in this State. If, as the gentleman from Wapello, [Mr. Gillaspy,] said, the lawyers are to be baited and caught, each of them with a thousand dollars—

Mr. HARRIS. The gentleman said "all of them."

Mr. EMERSON. All of them; then I shall never educate any of my children to be lawyers, that is certain. I do not believe there is a lawyer in the State who is fitted to do justice to the people upon the bench, who is not worth at least two thousand dollars to himself, with his practice. And my impression is that a lawyer who has not a practice worth two thousand dollars, cannot get a living at his profession, and should leave it as soon as possible for something else; and he is not fit for the position of a judge to administer justice. I think there are few lawyers, in the town from which I come, who would be willing to take three thousand dollars a year for their practice. I am well satisfied there are a number of firms there who would not do justice to themselves, were either of them to accept three thousand dollars a year. And again, there are some men there who, I think, would be doing well if they got one-third that amount. Yet I would rather pay a competent lawyer five times as much as I would other men, who do not get business to do because the community do not look upon them as competent to give advice and attend to their cases. And how are you to get men to accept the office of judge, when the business of the firm to which they belong is worth from five thousand dollars to eight thousand dollars a year, and some of them have ten thousand dollars worth a year—how are you going to get such men to sit on the bench for one thousand five hundred dollars a year? You cannot do it, for they could not accept the office and do themselves and their families justice.

And yet are not these the very men we want upon the bench? And if they are the very class of men you want upon your bench, in order to dispense justice, are you not compelled to pay them such a price as will call them to that position? This is a mere matter of dollars and cents. At what price can you obtain this legal talent in this State? I suppose we will agree, all of us, that we stand in need of, that we must and ought to have, the best legal talent in the State upon the bench. Now at what price can you obtain that talent? And by what rule are you to ascertain that price? Is it not by ascertaining what the business of such men as we want is worth to themselves? If that is the proper rule, then when we know what is the income of that class of legal talent that we desire, we can begin to make out our calculations as to the price we shall find it necessary to pay to get their services.

As I have before remarked, I do not think the income of the class of talent we should have upon our bench, can be less than two thousand dollars a year, and most probably it will be higher than that sum. Now if that be true, should not every gentleman here be ready to say that we ought to pay at least that amount, if we desire to secure competent men for judges? And if the income of that class is greater, then we must pay the higher price before we can obtain their services. It seems to me, therefore, that the the amendment of the gentleman from Johnson [Mr. Clarke,] should meet with no opposition here. We should adopt the minimum of two thousand dollars, for that is the least that that kind of ability can be obtained for, and no man can live for less, if he has a family to support, while he is upon the bench.

Mr. PETERS. I would move to insert "two thousand five hundred dollars," as the salary of our district judges. And I would merely call the attention of the convention to one fact, that if we are to judge the liberality of the next legislature, by the liberality of the last one, we must come to the conclusion that they would place these salaries down to the lowest sum that the constitution should provide.

The PRESIDENT. The chair would say to the gentleman from Delaware, [Mr. Peters,] that as the amount he has named has been stricken out by the convention, it would not be in order to fill the blank with the same sum.

Mr. CLARKE, of Johnson. I hope the convention will agree to put the salary of the district judges at two thousand dollars. Though that is the amount which has been inserted here for the salary of our supreme judges, we can reconsider that matter.

Mr. ELLS. This question, in my estimation, rises entirely above dollars and cents. So far as I am concerned, I wish to so act here as to secure to the State of Iowa the best legal talent for our supreme and district judges. The only question is, what amount will secure this talent? Whatever the sum may be, I am willing to pay it, let it be two thousand dollars, three thousand dollars, or five thousand dollars. I think there is more depending upon our having our best lawyers upon the bench, than there is depending upon our other State officers. If our supreme bench is incompetent, the State itself will sink in the estimation of every other State in the Union. If the decisions of our courts do not take rank with the first class decisions of the country, then your State must sink to the level of those decisions. Not only is the title of property, and the validity of all contracts, dependant upon the reputation of your courts, but the reputation of your State is dependant upon it.

I do not care about the amount of the sum to be paid for our judges. If two thousand dollars will secure the services of the best legal talent of the State, then that is sufficient. If it will not, then place the sum at the figure that will secure that talent. I do not know what lawyers make in this State; but I feel satisfied that you could not induce any lawyer of talent to go upon the Supreme Bench for two thousand dollars. A third rate county court lawyer will make more money in a year than that. I am satisfied, that in Iowa, where lawyer's fees are higher than they are in Ohio, his income should be from three thousand to five thousand dollars a year; and the income of many lawyers is from eight thousand to ten thousand dollars a year.

It is true, as gentlemen say, that the Legislature can go above the amount we place here. But the Legislature will say, and with great reason, too, that the Constitutional Convention refused to go above that amount; they fixed that as the ultimatum, and thereby left it to be inferred that that was all they thought necessary and requisite to be paid. I would say to members of this Convention, to fix the amount here at what they would be willing to vote if they were in the Legislature, and that, I have no doubt, would be from eighteen hundred to two thousand dollars for our district judges, and from twenty-five hundred to three thousand dollars for our supreme judges. I, myself, intend to vote here as I would if I were in the Legislature; and for that reason I voted, in the first place, for three thousand dollars for our supreme judges, and have steadily voted against any less sum, and shall continue to do so from this time forth, believing that, in doing so, I am representing, not only the good sense and wishes of my own district, but of the people of the whole State.

I wish to say, in reply to one remark of the gentleman from Henry, [Mr. Clarke], that there are many districts where the services of the judges are not onerous, and where less compensation would be sufficient, that I had supposed that the object of re-organizing the districts was to make the duties of the several judges more nearly equal. The man who has the less to do, will have to travel over a large amount of territory, and his expenses of travel will equalize the difference between the amount of services performed by him and that performed by other judges in smaller districts.

Mr. CLARK, of Alamakee. I believe there are two extremes to this question, as well as to all others, and that it is about as easy to reach the one extreme as the other. And I think there is equally as much danger of injury resulting from our going to the one extreme as to the other. Now, I am willing and anxious, if we are to fix the amount of salaries here definitely, to so fix them that they will have the tendency to command the best talent in the State. Yet, while I am willing to do that, I am not willing to fix those salaries at prices which will be beyond what is necessary to obtain that talent and ability. For, if we do that, we will, instead of securing the best talent, work contrary to what we intend.

Ever since we have had a government of the United States, we have always had two parties in the field, and most all our officers have been elected by party influence and strength. It is true, we could elect judges without drawing party lines and distinctions, if we would; but it has never yet been done. And if we place the salaries of our judges beyond what would be a fair compensation in the largest district, the result would be as in other cases, instead of its being the means of drawing out the best talent of the country, it will throw into the hands of parties, the means which parties always resort to, whether they are compelled to do so or not, of making these paying offices the right arm of the party, and throwing into the party that amount of capital, which will be used for the purpose of promoting, or paying off, those men who, from party considerations and party services, are entitled to these nominations, instead of securing the best talent for our judiciary. This has been the result in other cases, and I have no doubt it will be the result in this case to a certain extent, if we go beyond what is actually required to remunerate fairly and honorably the talent we need upon the bench.

I do not believe we can fix this matter in a better shape than it was before we reconsidered the vote we took awhile since. That vote fixed the amount below which the legislature should not go, and left to the legislature the right to put it as much higher as they should see proper. The legislature is to be elected at least once in every two years. They come fresh from the people, bringing with them a knowledge of the wishes of the people, and the wants and interests of the people, and are conversant with the changes that must inevitably occur in the condition of affairs in this State. It does seem to me that we cannot fix upon a better rate of salaries than the one we fixed here, leaving the legislature to arrange it hereafter.

I have examined the Constitutions of the States, some recently made; and they did not attempt to establish the salaries of judges at all. They leave that matter entirely to the legislature. That is the case in New York, and they have no difficulty there, and no complaint is made. They certainly command as good talent as they have in this State.

It has been justly remarked, that the history of this State has provied that it is bad policy to place this matter at a certain number of dollars and cents, and make the wants and necessities of the people conform to that number. There has been a very great inconvenience felt from this very practice in the old States. There was not range and latitude enough given to the legislature; it did not allow them to make those changes, which the condition and necessities of the people required.

I have no doubt, myself, that had we permitted the amounts to remain here as they were fixed, there would have been no serious difficulty or inconvenience felt by the people of this State. I have that confidence in the wisdom of our legislature, though they may err sometimes, as to believe that they will fix these salaries at an amount that will command the best talent of this State, as they will certainly be more competent and qualified to judge of what is needed in the future than we can now be.

Mr. EDWARDS. I believe, from what has been said by gentlemen on both sides of this question, that in order to do justice to the views of gentlemen, and to that branch of government which we are disposed to encourage and uphold, the proposition to fix the salaries of District Judges at one thousand and eight hundred dollas and of Supreme Judges at twenty-four hundred dollars would be favorably received. I think the gentleman from Van Buren, (Mr. Day,) made a motion to that effect. And so far as I have been able to understand the sentiments of members sitting near me here, I think they would be willing to compromise upon those amounts.

Mr. BUNKER. As I understand that proposition, it is to fix the salaries at those amounts until the year 1860.

Mr. DAY. At the time I gave my last vote, I was not satisfied with salaries proposed for District Judges; I thought they were too low. I do not know why they should not have as much as the Supreme Judges. They are traveling about a great deal more, which costs them considerable. The Supreme Judges all sit at the capital and have nothing to do. I would prefer to have the salaries of both Supreme and District Judges fixed at the same rate, at two thousand dollars.

Mr. CLARKE, of Henry. While I individually concur in the views expressed by the gentleman from Johnson [Mr. Clarke] and the gentleman from Des Moines [Mr. Hall] I know this fact: that the people of this State are not prepared for those views. You cannot force the people; there is no use in trying to do so. We cannot cram the constitution down their throats; they must and will vote upon it. If you fix these salaries at a high rate, and leave nothing to the people through their legislature, you will create difficulty. I find that the people of this State are peculiarly wedded to the idea of low salaries. While I am myself opposed to low salaries, yet I have some regard for the wishes and temper of the people.

Gentlemen will recollect that while they propose to jump from a salary of twelve hundred dollars to two thousand dollars for our district judges, they will be doing so for ten judges; and the same argument will be brought forward to induce us to increase the salaries of senators, members of the house of representatives, governor, lieutenant-governor, auditor, treasurer, secretaries, and other officers. If the salaries of these judges were the only salaries to be increased, I would not mind it so much. But this is merely the first step. As I said this morning, let us look at the second, and third, and fourth steps, and see to what this first step will lead us.

I believe our best policy is to leave this matter to the legislature, merely establishing here a minimum. I go with the gentleman from Wapello [Mr. Gillaspy], to establish this minimum, and take it out of the power of any party in the legislature to cut down the salary of a judge after he has been elected. And I would also leave it so that the salary of a judge should not be increased, in consequence of the popularity he may have with the dominant party in the legislature. We should seek here to throw a safeguard about the officer, to protect him from legislative action; and then we should seek to throw a protection about the rights of the people, to prevent that officer from log-rolling before the legislature to have his salary increased.

Am I not right in that, gentlemen; you who have thrown in my face again and again, that the legislature are the people, am I not right in this? You have said to me, leave something to the legislature. When I desired to incorporate into the Bill of Rights provisions that I thought necessary for the protection of my fellow-beings, you have said to me, trust the legislature. And when I said that the legislature had once passed a law to prevent me and you from having the benefit of the testimony of an entire class of our population, you have told me that another legislature repealed that law, and you have appealed to me to have some confidence in the legislature, as the direct representatives of the people.

Now, I ask you to have confidence in the legislature. We have established a minimum here; We have said that the supreme judges shall not have less than two thousand dollars, and the district judges less than fifteen hundred dollars a year. Are you not willing to trust the legislature with something? If the people of this State really desire to have these salaries increased; if they cannot get men of talent and ability for these offices, then rest assured that they will find it out, and will say to the legislature, increase these salaries until they will secure the talent we wish.

I am not arguing against all high salaries. I coincide with those who argue here, that to secure good talent and ability salaries should be high. But I am willing to leave to the legislature to judge in this matter, when, and how, and where it is necessary to increase these salaries. Gentlemen complain of the action of the last legislature; they say that they did not place the salaries of district judges above the sum of twelve hundred dollars. I am not here to arraign their action. They either acted honestly and understandingly, or they did not. They had the whole case before them—it has not been before us—and they acted in the capacity of the representatives of the people, and saw fit to establish the salaries of our district judges at twelve hundred dollars. And when we increase those salaries to fifteen hundred dollars, are we not going far enough ahead of the people, acting through their agents, the legislature? And yet gentlemen get up here and claim that their peculiar ideas—not the ideas of the people—must be incorporated in the constitution, whether or no, and these officers must have these high salaries whether the people want them to do so or not.

I tell you that it is the last feather that breaks the camel's back. And if you crowd your high salaries on here, and leave nothing for the legislature to do, the people will let you know that you have gone farther than they intended you should go. They will say to you—you have put on so many thousand dollars more a year taxation; we have enough of that now; all that we wanted you to do, was to remove the restrictions upon the power of the legislature to incorporate banks, and you have gone and placed a burden of thirty thousand dollars or forty thousand dollars more a year of salaries than we had before. That is the kind of talk that tells among the people.

I beg gentlemen here to consider this matter, and leave something to the people and their legislature to do. They will do all that is necessary. If they can get men to fill offices for one thousand five hundred dollars which are now filled for one thousand two hundred dollars, and have been heretofore filled for one thousand dollars, that will be enough; if not, then this matter will rectify itself.

Mr. CLARKE, of Johnson. In view of the appeal of the gentleman from Henry, [Mr. Clarke,] let us look at the increase in the amount of these salaries. We have now fourteen judges at a salary of one thousand two hundred dollars a year each, making a sum total of sixteen thousand eight hundred dollars. The action of this convention has cut down the number of districts from fourteen to ten, making ten judges in place of fourteen, which, at a salary of two thousand dollars a year each, would make an increase of only three thousand two hundred dollars a year for the salaries of our district judges. Now even in view of this awful bugaboo of three thousand two hundred dollars, I do not think there is any danger that the people of this State will vote down this constitution. It seems to me that these figures are a sufficient answer to the argument—if it is an argument—of the gentleman from Henry.

What have we done in this matter? We have divided the State into ten districts. There are one hundred and three counties in this State, which will make an average of ten counties to a district. In all these counties, at no very remote period, if it is not the case now, there must be held at least two terms of the court every year. And I ask gentlemen to consider where they will get a competent man to fill the office of judge, who will travel over ten counties, twice a year, for one thousand five hundred dollars, when, by going to three or four of the courts in his district, he can make double that sum as a practicing lawyer.

We propose to increase the labors of the judges, so as to keep them busy eight months in the year, allowing them two months in the summer and two months in the winter for rest. And I say there is no man, with sufficient legal talent for the bench, who will accept the office of judge for one thousand five hundred dollars a year.

But all the districts will not average ten counties each, for you can get no man who can attend to all the business in that number of heavy counties upon the Mississippi river. The western districts will, therefore, be larger, and the eastern districts smaller, as regards extent of territory. The judges of some of the western districts will be obliged to travel over fifteen or twenty counties. And where is the man who will take this labor and discharge the duty of district judge for the pittance of one thousand five hundred dollars? It does seem to me that this will be an effective method to keep competent men off the bench.

It is said that in New York, and some of the other States, they do not pay higher salaries than we propose to pay in this State. Admit it. There is no analogy between our position and that of New York. In that State they have elderly men upon the bench; men who have acquired fortunes in the practice of their profession, and take seats upon the bench as positions of honorable retirement. They do not accept these positions for the salaries attached to them; they do not expect to live upon these salaries. They accept them as positions of honor, in which the labor is light compared to what the duties of the same offices are here.

In this state our lawyers are all poor men. If they go upon the bench they will expect to make a living there, as they will have no other business with which to support their families. The men upon our bench in this State are men in the prime of life, with families to provide for, and you must make your salaries conform to the circumstances in which you are placed; if you do not, the result will be that the bench will be thrown in the hands of men who cannot make the same amount by their practice. That has bean our experience for the last ten years. I appeal to every man upon this floor if, with few exceptions, our district bench especially has not been occupied by men who cannot command the same amount in their practice, as the salary amounts to. Every man of ability and integrity is compelled to stand back and say: I am excluded from the bench; it matters not what my talents, reputation and position as a lawyer before the community may be, the amount of salary offered here, is a bar to exclude me from the post of honor in my profession.

I undertake to say that lawyers are like other men. There is in every profession a foremost place, and lawyers have their right to look at a position upon the bench as a reward for efficient labors and services, and exalted acquirements in their profession. But under this rate of low salaries, you will throw the bench in the hands of inferior men, when we might secure able men and men of talent, by an increased expenditure each year of only three thousand two hundred dollars.

I would ask gentlemen if they will risk this matter with the legislature after the experience of last year? I think not. It is a notorious fact that the legislature did not put up the salaries of district judges, because they knew this body was to come after them, and they sought to avoid the responsibility and shift it upon us. For one I am willing to take that responsibility, and not shift it back upon the legislature that is to come after us. I do not wish to play ball with this subject and have it bandied back from the legislature to the convention, and then from the convention to the legislature again. Let us do our duty as men, and I believe the people will sustain us.

As the proposition before us now stands, we have fixed the salaries of supreme judges at two thousand dollars, where the last legislature put it, and we put the salaries of district judges at one thousand five hundred dollars, three hundred more than it now is. Where is the man competent to fill that place, who would be influenced by this increase of three hundred dollars? I apprehend not one can be found. But if you will fix the salary in your constitution at some reasonable amount, and say that the legislature shall not cut it down and thereby compel the judges upon the bench to return to their profession and endeavor to gather up their scattered practice, you will then be able to get men who will fill the place with honor, and credit and benefit to the State.

Mr. WILSON. Suppose the salary should be two thousand dollars and the judge should go upon the bench with that salary. Could the legislature cut it down?

Mr. CLARKE of Johnson. No sir: but you have cut down the term of office to four years, and there is no man, who is competent to go upon the bench, who will accept the office with the expectation of being kicked out at the end of four years. He must go on with the expectation, that if he performs his duties, he will be retained in his position. I do not want to have it understood that when he has the business of his court all arranged, when he is familiar with the practice, and the bar are familiar with him, he is to be exchanged at the end of four years, for some one who will have to begin anew in all these things, and then be himself superseded at the end of his term by some one else

Mr. HALL. I rise merely to reply to the interrogations of the gentleman from Henry, [Mr. Clarke.] The remarks which I made the other day, to which he alludes, were made upon the article of incorporations. In the discussion in regard to the provisions of a bill concerning banking, that was to be framed by the legislature, and then be submitted to the people, I expressed a confidence in what the legislature should prepare for submission to the people, and said that there were sufficient guards, without so many constitutional provisions as we were making.

But we are now considering a subject of a very different character. We are establishing a separate and distinct branch of the government, co-ordinate with the legislature. It should be the policy and feeling of this convention to make this branch of the government as independent of the other branches as is practicable, and not have it dependant upon them at all. The judicial branch of this government should be as independent as the legislative branch, not dependant upon it at all. And you will not have a good and well balanced form of government without doing that. And for that reason, I would be willing, and it would be proper to do so, to so prepare this branch of our government that it should not be affected by the other branches of the government, that it should be entirely independent of them. It is the great conservative branch of the government, that branch upon which more interests depend than upon any other. Why then make it the servant of any other branch of the government? Why starve it down to the lowest possible amount you can? Why thin the porridge of the children of your judges, more than that of any other officers? Men seem to think that judges and their families can get along upon a bare subsistence, and they seem willing to vote as little of comfort and luxury to the families of their judges, and think they are doing God's service to take away all they can from them. And yet what we propose to add to the means of the judges would not amount to one-ninth part of a cent to each person in the State. If gentlemen will change their votes for that amount, then the quicker we know it the better; it will be a new page in the history of this State, whatever there may be of credit in it.

The question then recurred upon the motion of Mr. Warren to fill the blank with the sum of two thousand dollars, as the salary of the district judge.

Upon this question Mr. GILLASPY called for the yeas and nays, and they were ordered accordingly.

The question being then taken, by yeas and nays, the motion was agreed to; yeas 16; nays 14; as follows:.

Yeas.—The President, Messrs. Bunker, Clarke of Johnson, Day, Ells, Emerson, Hall, Marvin, Patterson, Peters, Price, Robinson, Solomon, Traer, Warren and Winchester.

Nays.—Messrs. Ayres, Clark of Alamakee, Clarke of Henry, Edwards, Gibson, Gillaspy, Gray, Harris, Hollingsworth, Johnston, Palmer, Seely, Wilson and Young.

Mr. EDWARDS moved to reconsider the vote by which the salaries of the supreme judges were fixed at two thousand dollars a year.

Upon this question Mr. GILLASPY called for the yeas and nays, and they were ordered accordingly.

The question being then taken, by yeas and nays, upon the motion to reconsider, it was not agreed to; yeas 15; nays 16, as follows:

Yeas—The President, Messrs. Bunker, Clarke of Johnson, Edwards, Ells, Emerson, Hall, Hollingsworth, Marvin, Peters, Price, Solomon, Traer, Warren and Winchester.

Nays—Messrs. Ayres, Clark of Alamakee, Clarke of Henry, Day, Gibson, Gillaspy, Gray, Harris, Johnston, Palmer, Patterson, Robinson, Scott, Seely, Wilson and Young.

The question then recurred upon the amendment proposed by Mr. Clarke of Johnson, as amended.

Mr. WILSON offered the following as a substitute for that amendment:

"The salaries of the supreme and district judges shall be determined by the general assembly."

Mr. CLARKE, of Henry. I shall go for the substitute, then for the amendment of the gentleman from Johnson, [Mr. Clarke.] as it now stands. I have been looking over and making some calculations as to what will be the probable increase of the total amount of salaries under this constitution, and, as I make it out, it will amount to something over fifty thousand dollars a year. Now I suppose one great object for which we were sent here was to lessen the burdens of the people—not to take them off in one direction and put on heavier burdens in another.

Yet where we have cut down the number of districts in order to lessen the burdens upon the people, the gentleman from Johnson, [Mr. Clarke,] wants to put a heavier burden upon the people in another direction, and then says, we have only increased your burdens by some three thousand dollars. Now, if we carry out the ideas of gentlemen here, especially of gentlemen of that school, we will have to create additional salaries of forty thousand dollars or more, in addition to what the gentleman proposes here, and which will amount to some forty-five thousand or fifty thousand dollars. I prefer leaving the matter entirely to the legislature. If we cannot agree upon a minimum different from the one now proposed here, let us leave the whole matter of the salaries of the judges to the legislature, to arrange as they may see fit and proper. The judges are but the creatures and servants of the people. Let the people, through their agents, the legislature, fix their salaries. They can do it in a more satisfactory manner, I am sure, than we are doing here.

Mr. CLARKE, of Johnson. The argument of the gentleman from Henry, [Mr. Clarke,] is an enigma to me. He says if the amendment I have proposed, and which has been fully discussed, is adopted here, it will entail an annual increase of burden of forty thousand or fifty thousand dollars upon the people. I do not understand what he means by that. I have made a calculation as to the salaries of our district and supreme judges: the ten district judges, at a salary of two thousand dollars each—an increase on what they now receive—will make twenty thousand dollars; and three judges of the supreme court at two thousand dollars—the same as they now receive—will make six thousand dollars; making a total for both district and supreme judges, of twenty-six thousand dollars per annum. I do not know what the gentleman means by telling us of this large increase of forty thousand or fifty thousand dollars a year. I hope the Convention will not be frightened out of their propriety by any enigmas of this kind, that the gentleman may bring forward here, and of which he has not told us the meaning.

Now, as I have said before, if you cut down the number of judges from fourteen to ten, and increase their salaries from twelve hundred to two thousand dollars per annum, the whole increase of expenditures will be but thirty-two hundred dollars. If I have not figured correctly, the gentleman can set me right. We have increased neither the number nor the salaries of the supreme judges; and, so far as I am advised, we have not increased the salaries of any other officers, except district attorneys, for which the gentleman himself voted, and for which he argued.

It seems to me the gentleman ought to be a little consistent. And if this policy of economy is to control this Convention, for fear the people will vote against the Constitution on account of the increased expenses of government, it seems to me it would have more force, and apply with more weight to the appointment of district prosecutors, than to anything we have done here this afternoon. So far as the question of economy is concerned, I do not think the people sent us here to reduce the expenses of government. I do not believe that on the day of election, when the members of this Convention were chosen, a single man thought of reducing the expenses of government. I think we would be doing a service to the people by making a Constitution upon which a stable government can be established, to meet their necessities and protect their interests. I think the cost of that government is but a small matter.

Mr. GILLASPY. I do not desire to take up the time of this Convention. But this is a question upon which I stand pledged to my constituents It was well understood by them that this question would be brought up before us; and so I believe it was throughout the State of Iowa. I admit, if present prices were to last for all time to come, there might be some propriety in these enormous salaries. But let things go back to where they were five years ago, with everything in proportion, and I would ask gentlemen where they would stand in regard to this mattor of salaries. I stand pledged to the people of my district to vote for two thousand dollars for the supreme judges, and fifteen hundred dollars for the district judges. And if I were not to make that fact known to the Convention, I should feel that I was not doing my duty to my constituents. If others choose to take the responsibility to increase those salaries, they can do so. I do not believe things will remain as they are now in this State. And I am opposed to taking into consideration here this speculative spirit, which is now stalking rampant through the land, and I shall vote against any proposition of the kind. I believe—indeed, I know—that it is the expectation of the people of my district that we will undertake this matter of fixing salaries, and not seek to shirk the responsibility and put it off upon the legislature that may come after us. I am ready to take the responsibility of doing so, and I hope other members of this Convention will do the same.

Mr. CLARKE, of Henry. The gentleman from Johnson [Mr. Clarke] certainly either misunderstands me, or he misrepresents me. I did not say that these judges would cost the people fifty thousand dollars more a year than they now do. I said that we would be called upon here to increase the salaries of other officers; and in looking over the list of officers: the governor, lieutenant-governor, secretary, auditor, treasurer, attorney general, members of the house of representatives, senators, &c., together with these judges, the amount of increase of salaries would be some forty-five thousand dollars a year.

Now, my plan is to increase these salaries somewhat, and fix a minimum where we can, say that the salary shall not be less than a given sum, and then leave to the legislature, as the exigencies of the times may demand, if present prices continue, and men cannot be got to fill these offices for these salaries, to raise them to the proper amount.

My idea is that we are taking a step too much in advance of the people. We must look to the legislature for an expression of the feelings of the people. And the legislature that has just left these halls, expressed the feelings of the people upon this question. And now it is proposed that we shall go far in advance of that expression, so far that I am afraid that, when we take this matter in connection with other matters that will be urged against this constitution, it will have the effect to swamp the whole thing.

Let gentlemen establish some other standard than their own estimate of the value of these services. Let them adapt themselves somewhat to the public sentiment. I have been called upon to do it over and over again, and I have attempted to do it where principle was not at stake. If we go beyond public sentiment, there is nothing that will so certainly endanger this constitution as an argument of dollars and cents brought against it. That is my idea. It is not because I shall urge this argument against the constitution. I should be glad enough to have high salaries. But I know that a great number of my constituents would be opposed to it. And if any demagogue, or person opposed to the constitution, should get up and say to them—the expenses of our State government will be increased by the operation of this constitution over fifty thousand dollars a year, it would be a strong argument against it in the minds of the people. That is what I mean by what I have said upon this question. I would let the salaries of these judges be left to the legislature, with the salaries of our attorneys and other officers.

Now in reply to what the gentleman said concerning my vote in regard to these district attorneys.

I asked the gentleman from Mills, [Mr. Solomon], if his proposition to create ten district attorneys was to do away with our present system of county attorneys, and I understood him to say that such was his intention. And it was with that understanding that I voted for it. I go for a greater economy in the administration of the affairs of our government; in that I am consistent. And where we cut off in one direction I would not put it on in another. Having cut down these districts to ten, I would leave these salaries to be arranged by the legislature. Of course in our schedule we would provide for the salaries of our present incumbents, to continue until the legislature shall fix it.

The question recurred upon the substitute offered by Mr. Wilson.

Upon this question, Mr. GILLASPY called for the yeas and nays, and they were ordered accordingly.

The question being then taken, by yeas and nays, upon the substitute, it was not agreed to; yeas 10, nays 20, as follows:

Yeas—The President, Messrs. Clark, of Alamakee, Clarke, of Henry, Gray, Palmer, Scott, Seely, Traer, Wilson and Young.

Nays—Messrs. Ayres, Bunker, Clarke, of Johnson, Day, Edwards, Ells, Emerson, Gibson, Gillaspy, Hall, Harris, Hollingsworth, Johnston, Marvin, Patterson, Peters, Price, Robinson, Solomon and Winchester.

Mr. BUNKER offered the following as a substitute for the amendment as amended:

"The salaries of the Supreme Judges shall be twenty-five hundred dollars each, and the salaries of the District Judges shall be two thousand dollars each, until the year 1860, after which their salaries may be fixed by the Legislature, but shall never exceed four thousand dollars each."

Upon this question, Mr. GILLASPY called for the yeas and nays, and they were ordered accordingly.

The question being then taken upon the substitute proposed by Mr. Bunker, by yeas and nays, it was not agreed to; yeas 5, nays 23, as follows:

Yeas—The President, Messrs. Bunker, Clarke of Johnson, Ells and Emerson.

Nays — Messrs. Ayres, Clark, of Alamakee, Clarke, of Henry, Day, Edwards, Gibson, Gillaspy, Gray, Hall, Harris, Hollingsworth, Johnston, Palmer, Patterson, Peters, Price, Scott, Seely, Solomon, Traer, Wilson, Winchester and Young.

The question recurred upon the amendment proposed by Mr. Clarke, of Johnson, amended to read as follows:

"The salary of each Judge of the Supreme Court shall not be less than two thousand dollars per annum, nor shall the salary of each Judge of the District Court be less than two thousand dollars per annum. After the year 1860, the General Assembly shall have power to increase the salaries of the Judges of the Supreme and District Courts; but the salary of no judge of either court shall be increased or diminished during his term of office."

Mr. WILSON. I move to amend by striking out all the first part, relating to the amounts fixed for salaries, so that the provision will read—

"After the year 1860, the General Assembly shall have power to increase the salaries of the Judges of the Supreme and District Courts; but the salary of no judge of either court shall be increased or diminished during his term of office."

Upon this question, Mr. HALL called for the yeas and nays, and they were ordered accordingly.

The question being then taken, by yeas and nays, upon the amendment to the amendment, it was agreed to; yeas 16, nays 13, as follows:

Yeas—The President, Messrs. Clark, of Alamakee, Clarke, of Henry, Day, Edwards, Gibson, Gillaspy, Gray, Harris, Hollingsworth, Johnston, Scott, Seely, Traer, Wilson, and Young.

Nays — Messrs. Ayres, Bunker, Clarke, of Johnson, Ells, Emerson, Hall, Marvin, Palmer, Peters, Price, Robinson, Solomon and Winchester.

The question then recurred upon the amendment of Mr. Clark, of Johnson, which had been amended to read as follows:

"After the year 1860, the General Assembly shall have power to increase the salaries of the Judges of the Supreme and District Courts; but the salary of no judge of either court shall be increased or diminished during his term of office."

Mr. HALL. I think we have come out of the very hole we went in, and I therefore move that the Convention adjourn.

The question being taken, the motion was agreed to, and—

The CONVENTION accordingly adjourned until to-morrow morning at nine o'clock.

SATURDAY, February 14th, 1857.

The Convention met at 9 o'clock, A. M., and was called to order by the President.

Prayer by the Chaplain.

The journal of yesterday was read and approved.

Miscellaneous.

Mr. SCOTT presented the petition of E. G. Hutchinson and eighty-five others, in regard to the constitutional limits of counties, which was referred to the Committee on Miscellaneous Subjects.

Mr. CLARKE, of Henry, offered the following resolution:

Resolved, That a standing committee of three be appointed for the revision, correction, engrossing and enrolling of reports, which have passed their second reading.

Mr. JOHNSTON. The only difficulty about this matter is, that there may be more work of this kind than one committee can do. I would suggest to the gentleman that he amend his resolution so as to provide for the appointment of two committees, one upon revision, and one upon enrollment. The labors of the committee on revision will be very great.

Mr. CLARKE, of Henry. This kind of work can be easily divided. It is all clerical, and the reports can be disposed of as they come in. I see no necessity for the appointment of more than one committee.

The question was taken, and the resolution was agreed to.

Printing of the Debates.

Mr. CLARKE, of Henry. There is one matter which I would like to bring before the Convention. I was appointed to act upon a committee which had the reporting and printing of our debates under consideration. Arrangements were made to have the printing of our debates done at Davenport. I apprehended at the time that the difficulty, under which we are now laboring, would occur. We were assured, by the gentleman who undertook this job, that the reports of our debates and proceedings should appear on the third day after they took place. Now some three weeks have elaped since the last sheet of our proceedings has been laid upon our tables. I would suggest that a committee be appointed, whose duty it shall be to make inquiries in regard to this matter, and report to us as soon as practicable, the cause of this delay. We are losing by it the advantage we expected to derive from the appointment of our reporter, and the reporting and printing of our proceedings.

Mr. CLARK, of Alamakee. I move that a committee be appointed to inquire into this matter. It may perhaps be proper to move that the committee on printing be appointed to take this matter into consideration. I am not very particular in regard to the mode in which this matter may be disposed of. It is evident that we need a committee of some kind to take this matter into consideration.

The PRESIDENT. The chair will observe to the gentleman from Alamakee, that we have a committee already appointed to superintend the printing of these reports.

Mr. CLARK, of Alamakee. I will then offer the following resolution:

Resolved, That a special committee of three be appointed to inquire into and report the cause of the delay in the printing of the reports of this Convention.

My reason for offering this resolution is, that at the time this question was before the Convention, when we voted for giving this job of printing to the person who is now engaged upon it, we were assured that we should have spread upon our tables the proceedings of this convention, within at least forty-eight hours after they took place, extraordinary, or rather unavoidable accidents excepted. I believe that so far we have had our debates and proceeding published up to the sixth day, the printer being at least three weeks behind. If there is any good cause for this delay in the printing of our debates, then of course the publishers are excusable. If these slips of our debates are intended to circulate information of our proceedings among the people, certainly they should be kept advised of what we are doing here from time to time, as our proceedings transpire here, and as we progress in our business. The object of having these slips placed upon our tables was, in the first place, that the convention might see the report of our proceedings as they transpire; and in the next place, that they might distribute over the State the information contained in these slips, so as to enable the people to ascertain what their representatives were doing here. That was the object which we had in view, in incurring the expense of having our proceedings reported and printed.

Mr. GILLASPY. I am truly glad to see gentlemen, at this late day, take some interest in this matter. It has been a subject upon which I have reflected much. I would ask gentlemen upon this floor, in what way they intend to correct the debates, when they shall close their labors here, and when they will be some two or three hundred miles away from this city. Not one-third of our proceedings are as yet published and when we all leave here, I wish to ask whether we will not be left to the tender mercies of the reporters and printers, without an opportunity of correcting the proof sheets? We are certainly now deprived of one great advantage that we expected to derive from the printing of these debates; for as I understood the matter, we were to have our proceedings printed in time to circulate at home among our constituents. It was a novel idea in the first instance, that we had to get our debates printed at Davenport, when there were State and other printers in this city, who could have done this printing, and laid proof slips of the debates every morning upon our tables. I hope gentlemen, who have had this matter in charge, will see that there is some remedy provided, by which the delay that has hitherto attended this printing will be avoided.

Mr. CLARKE, of Johnson. As chairman of the committee that had this matter in charge, I can, perhaps, give the gentleman some information touching the delay complained of. In this contract, which the convention made for the printing, they provided that unavoidable delays should not affect the rights of these parties. I can say to the Convention that an unavoidble delay, created by the act of God, has prevented the printers from getting paper from any point, short of Ohio, in order to do this work, and they have furnished us the slips we have already had by getting paper from various places, as they could pick it up. They dispatched a messenger to Ohio, to get the paper, and I suppose that paper is somewhere between Chicago and Davenport; but in consequence of the freshet that washed away the bridges upon the Chicago and Rock Island Road, it is impossible to get any thing over it. I presume, that is the cause, and the only cause of delay.

Mr. SCOTT. I will ask the gentleman, if the State does not furnish the paper?

Mr. CLARKE, of Johnson. It is true that it is the duty of the State to furnish the paper; but as they had not on hand the quality and size necessary for this work the printers were authorized to send to Ohio after it; and I suppose it is now somewhere between Chicago and Davenport. A gentleman of our town, who arrived here yesterday, said that he was on the road several days, and that it is now impossible to get any thing over it until the damage on the road is repaired. Large bridges have been washed away, and there is an interval of about fifty miles where the track was destroyed, and over which it is impossible to get any thing. As I said before, the State has no paper of the right size, suitable for this work, and the paper that could be had any where in this vicinity could not be used except at great loss, by cutting it down at least one half. Our printers could not get suitable paper at Chicago, but were obliged to send to Ohio for it.

Mr. CLARK, of Alamakee. The explanation of the gentleman from Johnson does not satisfy me. If there is no paper to be had suitable for printing our reports, as they were intended to be printed at first, I think that we had better make our reports conform to the paper. If we are going to have our debates printed, they should be printed during the session of this convention. It is of considerable importance to the members of the convention that they should have the reported proceedings laid before them, that they may see, from time to time, what has been done. We had the promise that they should appear before us in our city papers every morning; but we get only a mere synopsis—a skeleton of our action here. We had the promise, also, that printed slips of our proceedings should be laid before us, unavoidable delay alone excepted, in at least forty-eight hours after they took place. How does the matter stand? Four weeks of the convention have passed away; these contractors must have known within a very few days after they undertook this work, whether there was paper here suitable for the printing of these reports. Within the time that has now elapsed, it seems to me that they could have procured the paper from Ohio, or even from the city of Washington, before this late day. The delay, therefore, in my opinion, is an unnecessary one.

There is another difficulty in regard to this matter. The gentleman from Johnson, [Mr. Clarke] himself, admits that this paper cannot be obtained within ten or twelve days. I certainly think that some action should be taken upon this matter by the convention, for I am satisfied that there is no need of this delay. The necessity for sending out of the State for paper might have caused a delay of a few days, but these printers have had time enough after the action of the convention upon this subject, to have sent to Ohio and obtained the paper when the roads were in good condition. It seems to me there must have been some other cause for this delay. If this delay is to continue for two weeks longer, I apprehend there should be some action taken by the convention, and some other means should be devised to complete this work. If it is for the interest of the State to print these reports, it is necessary that we should have them printed as I said before, as we progress in our business, even if we are compelled to cut down the paper we have one half. If there was a necessity which warranted the expense of publishing these reports in the first place, that necessity should lead us to adopt the next best measure, or abandon the printing entirely, as has been suggested by my friend on my left [Mr. Gillaspy]. Suppose this convention adjourn, and these reports are not printed; it will be utterly impossible to have them corrected after the members of this body go home.

Mr. ELLS. I am not informed in regard to the cause of delay in the printing, but I apprehend, that it is owing to causes which will be entirely satisfactory to gentlemen, when they shall be made apparent. The gentlemen who have charge of this work are energetic men, and never, without just reason, delay their work. They have had great difficulty in procuring their paper, as the gentleman from Johnson, [Mr. Clarke,] has already informed you. I myself have had, since the 20th of December, on the way from Dayton, Ohio, to Davenport, a quantity of almanacs, which have not yet arrived. If it takes forty days to get a lot of almanacs, which ought to be on hand the first of the year, it would take much longer to get forty, fifty or sixty reams of paper.

Mr. CLARK, of Alamakee. The explanation of the gentleman from Scott does not satisfy me. If his agent trusted to chance to have his almanacs forwarded, it affords no excuse to the contractors of this work for the delay of which we complain. They were to progress with this work—unavoidable accidents alone excepted and that means, such as the common prudence and foresight of men cannot guard against—and lay proof sheets before us within a reasonable time after the proceedings took place.

Mr. HALL. I move to lay the resolution upon the table.

The question was taken, by yeas and nays, and the motion was not agreed to. yeas 11; nays 20; as follows:

Yeas—Messrs. Bunker, Clarke, of Johnson, Edwards, Ells, Hall, Hollingsworth, Palmer, Price. Seely, Warren and Young.

Nays—The President, Messrs. Ayers, Clark of Alamakee, Clarke of Henry, Day, Emerson, Gibson, Gillaspy, Gray, Harris, Johnston, Marvin, Patterson, Peters, Robinson, Scott, Solomon, Traer, Wilson and Winchester.

Mr. HALL. It appears to me, that there is no necessity for the appointment of this committee. I cannot see, that any possible good can result from this course of action. I have no doubt, that these gentlemen have a good and satisfactory excuse for not sending these slips here. By the appointment of this committee the subject will occupy the attention of two or three members of the convention for several days, and the result will be, that we will learn just what we have now learned, that it was impossible to furnish these slips on account of the interruption of the railroad communication by the recent freshets. These printers have been about as expeditious in the transaction of their business and have not been much more behind, than we have, but I apprehend they have a great deal better excuse than we have.

Mr. CLARKE, of Henry. So far as these contractors are concerned, they may have an excuse which will be a good one under their contract. But I would ask if they cannot go on with their work, by taking the paper of the State and cutting it down to a size which will answer their purpose, until they get the paper, which they have ordered? I would ask how much waste there will be in cutting down this paper? I apprehend not a great deal; and this committee will have it in their power to inquire what the expense will be in cutting it down, and if it be not too great, they can report the fact to us, and we can get the paper, and order it to be reduced and let the printing go on, until they procure the paper they want.

Mr. WILSON. I would say to the gentleman from Henry [Mr. Clarke] that he cannot have a very good idea of printing books and furnishing proof. They may use paper cut down for our proof slips, but they cannot afford to keep the matter standing until they get the paper they want. There is not an establishment in this State that can keep the amount of matter standing that will be required to bring out a work of this kind. They go on and set up some four or five signatures, or sheets, furnish us with proof slips, and then they must distribute the type before they can set up new matter.

Mr. CLARKE, of Henry. Why not let them cut the paper down for the whole of the two thousand copies they strike off? They will not have to go over more than one-third of the book before they would get paper of the proper size, and then they would not have to cut down paper for the rest of the book.

Mr. HALL. I have no doubt that these gentlemen are acting in good faith towards us, and are doing the best they can to expedite matters. When they commenced this work, as I understand it, they first furnished proof slips for the convention, and then they struck off the number of copies, as revised, which had been ordered by us. They commenced the work with a certain kind of paper, and they expected, no doubt, long before this, to have procured a corresponding quality of paper for the balance of the work; but they have been disappointed in getting it, in consequence of the obstructions upon the road between Davenport and Chicago. It would be a matter of regret to them, and to us all, if one part of the volume should be printed upon one kind of paper, and another part upon another.

The question was then taken, by yeas and nays, upon the resolution of Mr. Clark, of Alamakee, for the appointment of a committee of three to whom this matter should be referred, and the motion was agreed to; yeas 20, nays 11; as follows:

Yeas—The President, Messrs. Ayres, Clark of Alamakee, Clarke of Henry, Day, Emerson, Gibson, Gillaspy, Gray, Harris, Johnston, Marvin, Patterson, Peters, Robinson, Scott, Solomon, Traer, Wilson and Winchester.

Nays—Messrs. Bunker, Clarke of Johnson, Edwards, Ells, Hall, Hollingsworth, Palmer, Price Seely, Warren and Young.

The PRESIDENT therefore appointed the following gentlemen: Messrs. Clark, of Alamakee, Gillaspy and Young.

Adjournment Over.

Mr. SCOTT. I notice that quite a number of members are absent this last day of the week, and I therefore move that the Convention adjourn till Monday at two o'clock, P. M.

Mr. PETERS. I move to amend, that we adjourn over till the second Monday in May.

Mr. SCOTT. I will withdraw the motion I made, so that the gentleman from Delaware [Mr. Peters,] may have the privilege of offering his resolution, if he desires it, independent, and by itself.

Mr. PETERS. I offer the following resolution then:

Resolved, That this convention do now adjourn till the second Monday of May next.

Mr. HARRIS. I move to amend the resolution by saying *sine die* on the second day of March next.

Mr. HALL demanded the yeas and nays.

Mr. MARVIN. I would suggest to the gentleman from Appanoose, [Mr. Harris,] that he say the third day of March.

Mr. HARRIS accepted the amendment.

The question was then taken, by yeas and nays, upon Mr. Harris' amendment to adjourn *sine die* on the third day of March, and it was not agreed to; yeas 9; nays 22, as follows:

Yeas—Messrs. Edwards, Gibson, Hall, Harris, Johnston, Marvin, Palmer, Patterson and Price.

Nays—The President, Messrs. Ayers, Bunker, Clark of Alamakee, Clarke of Henry, Clarke of Johnson, Day, Ells, Emerson, Gillaspy, Gray, Hollingsworth, Peters, Robison, Scott, Seely, Solomon, Traer, Warren, Wilson, Winchester and Young.

Mr. CLARK, of Alamakee. I move to amend the resolution so as to provide, that when we do adjourn, we adjourn to meet at Dubuque.

Mr. HARRIS. I would move to amend by fixing the time of meeting on the first Monday in June. Some of us could not go home and return to the convention in May, without great sacrifice to our business. I would ask for a division of the question. I do not wish to vote for any other place but this for our meeting.

The PRESIDENT. The question will be first taken upon the motion of the gentleman from Alamakee, [Mr. Clark,] in relation to the place of meeting, which he has designated as Dubuque. Then the amendments as to time will properly come in.

The question was then taken upon the motion of Mr. Clark, of Alamakee, and it was not agreed to.

The PRESIDENT. The question now recurs upon the amendment offered by the gentleman from Appanoose, [Mr. Harris,] to change the time designated in the resolution offered by the gentleman from Delaware [Mr. Peters,] from the second day of May to the second day of June.

The question was then taken, by yeas and nays, upon Mr. Harris' proposition, and it was not agreed to; yeas 6; nays 25, as follows:

Yeas.—Messrs. Edwards, Gray, Harris, Palmer, Patterson and Robinson.

Nays.—The President, Messrs. Ayres, Bunker, Clark of Alamakee, Clarke of Henry, Clarke of Johnson, Day, Ells. Emerson, Gibson, Gillaspy, Hall, Hollingsworth, Johnston, Marvin, Peters, Price, Scott, Seely, Solomon, Traer, Warren, Wilson, Winchester and Young.

Mr. HALL. I offer the following substitute for the resolution of the gentlemen from Delaware, [Mr. Peters.]

Resolved, That when this convention adjourn, on Monday next, it will adjourn to meet at Davenport in the first Monday of June next."

Mr. PETERS. I move to strke out "Davenport," and insert "Dubuque."

The question was taken upon Mr. Peters amendment, and it was not agreed to, upon division; ayes 12; noes 13.

Mr. WINCHESTER. I move to strike out of the substitute the words "first Monday of June," and insert in lieu thereof, the words "first Monday of May."

The question was taken upon Mr. Winchester's motion, and, upon division, it was agreed to; ayes 14; noes 12.

Mr. CLARK, of Alamakee. I move to strike out of the substitute the words "Davenport city," and insert in their place "Iowa City."

Mr. HALL. As we have had some difficulty about our printing coming to us, we might go to the printing.

Mr. SCOTT. I would ask if our going to Davenport would furnish us with more paper?

Mr. PETERS. I wish to say that, if we adjourn to Dubuque, there are presses in that city that will publish our proceedings at length every day.

The question was then taken, by yeas and nays, upon the amendment offered by Mr. Clark, of Alamakee, and it was agreed to; yeas 16, nays 15, as follows:

Yeas—The President, Messrs. Ayres, Bunker, Clark, of Alamakee, Clarke, of Johnson, Gillaspy, Gray, Harris, Hollingsworth, Johnston, Palmer, Price, Traer, Wilson, Winchester and Young.

Nays—Messrs. Clarke, of Henry, Day, Edwards, Ells, Emerson, Gibson, Hall, Marvin, Patterson, Peters, Robinson, Scott, Seely, Solomon and Warren.

The substitute, as amended, was then read as follows:

"*Resolved*, That when this Convention adjourn, on Monday next, it will adjourn to meet at Iowa City on the first Monday of May next."

Mr. EDWARDS. I hope that this resolution will not prevail. Yesterday, with a different state of the weather, I should have voted for the proposition, but to-day I shall vote against it, for the reason, that if we were to consent to an adjournment, to meet again the first of May, most of the delegates here could not reach their homes in the next ten or twelve days. From the intelligence I have received, I am satisfied that I could not reach my place of residence in that time, for the streams are very high, and, from present appearances, the probabilities are that we will have another general freshet, which will be likely to carry away bridges, and render traveling almost impossible for a while. If we were to adjourn now, most of us would be kept on the road for several days, at considerable expense. I am satisfied that if gentlemen will only go to work, and talk less, we can accomplish all our work by the last of this month. We have now finished half of the articles in the Constitution, and they are now ready, with the exception of some one or two points in each article, to go to the Committee on Revision. I am inclined to think, from what I have learned from members, that there are very few important changes to be proposed in the reports of the various committees, in regard to the remaining articles of the Constitution; and I am satisfied, if the Convention would so shape its action as to bring the question directly upon the adoption of the reports of the committees, or upon the question of abiding by the articles upon these subjects in the present Constitution, with the slight amendments which may be necessary, and if they would work more and talk less, that they will accomplish all that they were sent here to accomplish in ten days more, and then be able to go home. If this Committee on Revision, and the Committee on the Schedule, would go to work this day and put in proper shape the work already done, then take up the balance of the reports of the committees, and take a direct vote upon articles as they stand in the present cConstitution, and which were reported by the ommittees in order to obtain the sense of the Convention, there would be no difficulty in our adjourning by the last Monday of the month.

Mr. WILSON. I am willing to vote directly upon the resolution now before the Convention, and I hope that all such resolutions will be voted down. I came here to perform the work assigned me, and to perform it, too, before I go home. I do not want any adjournment such as some gentlemen have proposed here. The people sent us here to accomplish our work, and it is our duty to perform it, as soon as we can, and then go home. If, instead of wasting the time of the Convention with the discussion of such a resolution as this, we had proceeded with the regular order of business, I have no doubt that the report on the judicial department would have been finished to-day. Members are very anxious to adjourn. If they want to do so in good time, let us immediately proceed with the business before us, and get through with it as soon as may be. I believe, with the gentleman from Lucas, [Mr. Edwards], that if we go to work as we ought to do, and let these resolutions alone, we will be able to complete our labors by the first of March. If we, however, occupy half a day every two or three days, with resolutions of this kind, we may expect to remain here until the first Monday in June or July. I am for going to work immediately. Let us vote all these resolutions down, perform the labor we were sent here to do, and then go home. I am well satisfied that any member who should vote in favor of an adjournment, would be, and ought to be, repudiated by his constituents.

Mr. GILLASPY. The remarks of the gentleman from Jefferson, [Mr. Wilson], will look very well upon paper. I am glad to see that gentlemen are getting in earnest, and ready to work. It will be recollected by members upon this floor, that we had under consideration, in Committee of the Whole, for three or four days, the article on incorporations, and the Convention were better prepared, in my opinion, to act then than they will be at any time hereafter; but to my astonishment, the gentleman from Jefferson [Mr. Wilson], moved to refer this article to a select committee. Such a course could tend only to delay, for when, some day in the future, we have a report upon this subject from that committee, this Convention will be called upon to consume several days more in discussing the very same principles that we have already discussed, and we will have the very same speeches reiterated again and again. I say that it does not look very well for the gentleman, who made such a proposition as this, to get up now and make buncombe speeches about adjourning, to go upon paper for the eyes of his constituents. If the gentleman had desired to carry out what he says he desires, and what the people expect, he should have voted for my resolution, and put himself upon the record in favor of adjourning on the eleventh instant, and then have gone to work in right earnest. I am as much opposed as the gentleman to the waste of time in these discussions upon adjournment; but I am also opposed, when this Convention has had under consideration, for a week or ten days, a single proposition in Committee of the Whole, and then in Convention, to refer it to a select committee, which, after a delay of several days, will send it back to us remodeled and reformed, to consume four or five days more of the time of the Convention. I do not believe this is the proper course to expedite business. I believe, as the gentleman says, that the people of the State will hold the members of this Convention responsible for all needless and unnecessary delay. They ought to do it, and I believe they will.

Mr. WILSON. I wish to say a word in reply to the gentleman from Wapello, [Mr. Gillaspy.] He may be a very acute gentleman, but he has certainly widely missed the mark in what he has just said.

Mr. WINCHESTER. I rise to a point of order, unless the gentleman intends to make a personal explanation. Cries of "Go on;" "Go on."

The PRESIDENT. The gentleman has leave to proceed.

Mr. WILSON. The motion which was made—not on yesterday morning, but on the morning of the day before yesterday—to refer the report of the Commitiee on Incorporations to a select Committee was not made for the purpose of delaying the convention. I think the gentleman will find, when the report of that select committee is brought in here, that, instead of making delay, it will expedite the business of the convention. I believe he will find that that report will be in a shape that will be more satisfactory to this convention, and to the people of this State, generally, than the shape in which the article on incorporations was likely to pass the convention at that time.

And further than that, I believe it is well known, to all the members of this conventron, that I have not occupied the attention of this body to the extent that some other members have by moving to adjourn *sine die*, or until May or June. Those are the members who have taken up more time of the convention than have any others.

Mr. TRAER. And do not do any work.

Mr. WILSON. That comes in very well; "and do not do any work" of the convention, either.

Mr. GILLASPY. Does the gentleman apply that remak to me?

Mr. WILSON. As well to the gentleman from Wapello, [Mr. Gillaspy,] as to others. The gentleman introduced a resolution to adjourn on the

19th of this month. I do not believe we could possibly have got through our work by that time. I do not believe the gentleman offered the resolution with any such expectation. And he gets up here and speaks of bumcombe speeches. I charge upon him the offering of bumcombe resolutions, so that he can go to his constituents, and say—see here: I was in a hurry; I wanted to get through; I wanted to be economical. That will be the result; that was the only object ntended, I am satisfied of that. As I have before remarked, we need fix no day for our final adjournment. If we go on with our work as we ought. I believe we can get through by the first of March. I am not in favor of setting any particular time for adjournment. But I am in favor of our going on with the business before us just as rapidly as we can. When this resolution has been disposed of, I hope we will take up the resolution to confine members to one or two speeches, and these short ones, upon any proposition.

Mr. HALL. I am too good-natured to take offense at curtain lectures; I am willing to "grin and bear" them. I have been a school-boy and a school teacher, and have heard such lectures before, as the gentleman from Jefferson, [Mr. Wilson,] has just given us.

We have now been in session for four weeks, and have done but little. There are many questions before us, yet unacted upon, that the people consider of great importance. And I do not believe that the Convention would lose anything, or that the people would lose anything, if we were to adjourn over for a few weeks. If we were likely to get through within a reasonable time, I would be willing to remain here. But the Convention votes down every proposition which seems to squint at a termination of the session. I would be willing to offer a resolution, that when we adjourn on the twenty-fifth of this month, it be to meet again on the first Monday in May next. I would be willing to amend the resolution now pending in that way, so that at least we may have some definite understanding about getting away from here. I am willing to work as much and as long as any body else, and to go as far as the farthest in advancing the proceedings of this convention. As to these school-boy lectures, I take them in the most perfect good nature.

Mr. GILLASPY. I acknowledge the profound judgment and sagacity of the gentleman from Jefferson, [Mr. Wilson.]

Mr. WINCHESTER. I rise to a point of order. The gentleman from Wapello, [Mr. Gillaspy,] has already spoken two or three times upon this question.

The PRESIDENT. The chair considers the remarks of the gentleman from Wapello in the nature of a personal explanation.

Mr. GILLASPY. That is what I desire to make. I understand the gentleman from Jefferson exactly. And I hope he may be successful in the attainment of the object, which I believe he has in view. I doubt very much, however, that he will be able, when he gets home before his constituents, to excuse himself for the vote which he cast against my resolution, which he calls a buncombe resolution. And yet there lacked but two votes to show that it was the sense of this convention that we could get through by the day named in my resolution. I think I understand the gentleman exactly, and that the only excuse he intends to give for his vote against it is, first that it was offered by a democrat, and next that it was offered for buncombe. Now I am willing to leave to this convention, and to the people of this State, to say whether it was a buncombe resolution or not. I believe that my judgment is that of the people of this State, and that a decision of a full convention would have been that it was a proper and legitimate resolution, and not a resolution for buncombe, as the gentleman from Jefferson styles it.

I am willing the gentleman should so regard it. But I declare, before the people of this State and before high Heaven, that I had no such thought in offering that resolution. I offered it, because I believed it to be my duty to do so, as an honest representative of the people of my county, upon the floor of this convention. I would appeal to members of this convention, to say if we have not long since transcended the expectation of the people of this State, in regard to the length of the session of this convention. I undertake to say that the constituents of the gentleman from Jefferson expected to see him home long before this time, with a constitution to be submitted to them. I know that my constituents believed that we would have been through our labors here at least ten days ago.

Now I am perfectly willing that the gentleman from Jefferson shall go home, and endeavor to excuse himself for procrastinating the session of this convention, because "the gentleman from Wapello offered a buncombe resolution." He is welcome to make all he can out of that.

Mr. MARVIN. It cannot be supposed for a moment that any motion or speech, made on such an occasion as this, is calculated to enhance one's personal popularity at home. I might disclaim any such expectation, as others have done, if I deemed it at all necessary.

But I wish to say this in regard to the proposition to adjourn over. I have found many gentlemen here who desire to be at home. I have said privately to them—hold on patiently; perhaps by the first of March we can get through; if we are not through at that time, then I will vote for adjourning over for a time. But I would ask members if we are in a condition at this time to adjourn over? We have, it is true, no reports of committees under consideration. But if we go home, and carry the reports that have been made to us, to our constituents, they will ask, what action have you taken upon this report, and upon that report? Why, we have not acted upon them at all. What have you been doing? We will find that we cannot tell exactly where we stand upon any of the subjects before us.

Now it seems to me that if we will go on in good earnest, cut down all speeches to fifteen minutes in length, and allow no member to speak more than once upon any one subject, we will be able to get along by the first of March, that we can see our way through, if not adjourn *sine die.* If we adjourn over at this time, we must remain for a week or fortnight in this city on accouut of the freshets, and if we decide to come back on the first of May, we may have another freshet then, and be another fortnight on our way here. I think if we will only shorten our speeches, we will get through our work in much less time than now seems probable. I do not like to see our time wasted and thrown away as it is here. If by the first of March we see a prospect of getting through in a little while, we will not want to go home, for if we do go, we will have to stop there at least thirty days, and when we come back, each one will want to say what his constituents told him about each subject upon which we will be called to act. My constituents told me to take all the time that was necessary, and not hurry my work too much.

Mr. HARRIS. If gentlemen are disposed to characterise an effort to fix the time for final adjournment on the first of March, as intended for buncombe, I have no objections at all. My manufacturing buncombe is a matter I must settle with my constituents at home, and not with members here. I came here with no limitation as to the time I should take to do our work here; but it was expected that we would get through as soon as possible, and I intended to at least try and do so. But it does seem to me that it will accomplish no good result, to send those of us who live three hundred or four hundred miles from here in the south western part of the State, over the roads in the condition they are at present. I am free to say that I should feel disposed to stay here two or three weeks before I would start home just at this time. I think the time passed this morning has been worse than uselessly spent. I think if we would go on with our work as we ought, we can get through in two or three weeks, and then go home.

Mr. WILSON. I move that the resolution be indefinitely postponed; and upon that motion I call for the previous question.

The call for the previous question having been seconded, the main question was then ordered to be put.

The question was upon the motion to postpone indefinitely.

Upon this question—

Mr. HALL called for the yeas and nays, and they were ordered accordingly.

The question being then taken, by yeas and nays, the motion to postpone indefinitely was agreed to; yeas 19, nays 12, as follows:

Yeas—The President, Messrs. Bunker, Clark of Alamakee, Clarke of Henry, Clarke of Johnson, Edwards, Ells, Gillaspy, Gray, Harris, Hollingsworth, Johnston, Marvin, Palmer, Price, Seely, Traer, Wilson and Young.

Nays—Messrs. Ayres, Day, Emerson, Gibson, Hall, Patterson, Peters, Robinson, Scott, Solomon, Warren and Winchester.

Mr. SCOTT.—I now renew my motion, that the convention do now adjourn till next Monday afternoon at two o'clock.

Upon this question—

Mr. GILLASPY called for the yeas and nays, and they were ordered accordingly.

The question being then taken, by yeas and nays, upon the motion to adjourn till Monday, it was not agreed to; yeas 9, nays 22, as follows:

Yeas—Messrs. Bunker, Clarke of Henry, Clarke of Johnson, Ells, Peters, Price, Scott, Seely and Solomon.

Nays—The President, Messrs. Ayers, Clark of Alamakee, Day, Edwards, Emerson, Gibson, Gillaspy, Gray, Hall, Harris, Hollingsworth, Johnston, Marvin, Palmer, Patterson, Robinson, Traer, Warren, Wilson, Winchester and Young.

Limitation of Debate.

Mr. EDWARDS offered the following resolution:

"*Resolved,* That no member shall be permitted to speak more than once on any question, and then not to exceed twenty minutes."

The PRESIDENT. As this resolution is in the nature of a rule, it must lie over one day before it can be acted upon.

Mr. WILSON. The gentleman from Scott [Mr. Ells,] offered a resolution, with regard to this same subject, on Monday last, I believe. It has never been taken up and acted upon. I move that the convention now proceed to consider that resolution.

The motion was agreed to, upon a division; ayes 17; noes not counted.

The resolution, as amended upon a former occasion, was then read as follows:

"*Resolved,* That no member shall be allowed to speak more than twice on any one subject, and not more than twenty-five minutes at one time, after said subject has been once considered in Committee of the Whole."

Mr. EDWARDS. I offer, as a substitute for this resolution, the one I submitted a few minutes since, as follows:

"*Resolved,* That no member shall be permitted to speak more than once on any question, and then not to exceed twenty minutes."

Mr. CLAKE, of Henry. I would enquire of the chair how far a substitute, to be in order, can differ from the original resolution? This substitute is an entirely different thing, in my opinion. If there is any object in having a rule requiring such matters as these to lie over one day before consideration, I think it ought to be applied to this substitute, for it is entirely different from the original resolution.

The PRESIDENT. The chair is of opinion that as both the substitute and the original resolution relate to the same subject-matter, that is, the limitation of debate, it is in order to offer it at this time. The only object, in having a rule requiring these matters to lie over one day before final action, is to give notice to members that such subjects will be brought forward for consideration. That notice has already been given by the original resolution, which was introduced several days since.

Mr. WILSON. I move the previous question.

Mr. JOHNSTON. I hope the gentleman will withdraw his call for the previous question. I should like to amend this substitute a little, so as to allow less time for speaking. As it stands now I shall be compelled to vote against it, as the limit proposed is no limit at all.

Mr. WILSON. I will withdraw my motion for the previous question.

Mr. WINCHESTER. I move to amend the substitute by striking out the word "twenty," and inserting the word "ten."

Mr. PALMER called for a division of the question, which was ordered.

The question was first upon the motion to strike out the word "twenty," and being taken was agreed to, upon a division; ayes 16; noes not counted.

The question then recurred upon the motion to fill the blank with the word "ten."

Mr. PALMER moved to fill it with the word "fifteen."

Mr. CLARKE, of Henry. I move to fill the blank with the word "thirty." I do not think that we can find upon record any where that gag-laws have been the order of the day, in bodies like this, as it is proposed to apply here. I do not know that any gentlemen, who have spoken in this convention, have consumed more time than was necessary, in the discussion of the questions that come before us for consideration. We come here to discuss and compare opinions upon those matters upon which we are called to act. Some people are so conceited that they think they know all that is necessary about every subject, and need no further information upon them. And such persons wish to apply the gag-rule to every one who desires to express his opinion, or to get information from others, in relation to the questions upon which he is called to act. I claim that I have the right to hear the opinions of members here, that I have the right to sit here and listen to them, and thus get information upon all questions upon which I am called to act. I did not come here to sit and vote merely as an automaton. I came here to express my ideas before others, if I had any, and to hear theirs in return, and then I should be prepared to act judiciously and understandingly.

Mr. WINCHESTER. I shall vote in favor of the least time. I know that there are some persons so conceited that they think they know everything; there are others that are so conceited that they think that others know nothing, and never will know anything unless they tell them. I claim that there are some as well able to act without making any speeches at all, as those who speak an hour at a time, four times a day, and spend four hundred dollars of the people's money in doing so every day.

Mr. CLARKE, of Henry. It is just that class of gentlemen, like the gentleman who has just taken his seat, that I like to hear speak. I do not think they do their duty here, if they know all about the matter before us, if they sit silently by and let us vote without the benefit of their great stock of information, which we need so much.

Mr. SCOTT. I am in favor of limiting the time of speaking. I always dislike to hear a long prosy address, and such never has any good effect. I am, therefore, in favor of reducing the time of speaking; but I would not reduce it so that gentlemen here, who have been in the habit of speaking two or three hours upon a subject, shall be entirely debarred from any opportunity for speaking. We have honorable gentlemen here, some of the ablest men in the Convention, who cannot give us their ideas in fifteen minutes. And those I have the most confidence in, are men who have been in the habit of speaking in public, and cannot give their ideas in fifteen minutes. And there are others who have been in the habit of speaking, to whom I would be willing to apply a five-minute rule.

I do not need more than fifteen minutes for anything I may have to say. But I have friends here, upon whom I rely, who need more than fifteen minutes. But there is my friend from Hardin, [Mr. Winchester,] and myself, can undoubtedly tell all that we have to say upon any topic in fifteen minutes, perhaps in less time.

Mr. TRAER. I would suggest that if any gentleman is making a speech upon any subject, and, in doing so, throws more light upon the action we should take upon it, if he cannot get through in fifteen minutes, the Convention will allow him additional time. For my own part, I think fifteen minutes is long enough. Gentlemen who are in such a hurry to get home that they are continually moving resolutions of adjournment, will find that we can get along much faster in this way than in the other.

Mr. HALL. I think fifteen minutes will be long enough for any gentleman to speak. I have, upon several occasions, noticed the clock when gentlemen have been speaking, and I think none of them except myself—for I do not know how long I do speak—and the gentleman from Dubuque, [Mr. Emerson,] the other day, have ever spoken more than half an hour. I think the gentleman from Johnson, [Mr. Clarke,] spoke about twenty minutes at one time. As we sit here but about two hours in the forenoon, and a little longer in the afternoon, I do not think fifteen minutes will be too short a limit to our speaking.

Mr. CLARK, of Alamakee. There will be one good result from such a resolution as this: it will enable every member to know when he has got to the end of his speech.

Mr. SCOTT. I do not think that will be the result, for the gentleman from Alamakee, [Mr. Clark], and others, will call upon the Convention for permission to go on, and the exceptions will constitute the rule.

Mr. CLARKE, of Henry. I withdraw my motion to fill the blank with the word "thirty," and will let gentlemen here arrange this matter as they please.

The question was stated to be upon filling the blank with the word "fifteen."

Mr. GILLASPY. I would be willing, myself, to vote in favor of fifteen, or even ten minutes. But I have no desire, by any vote of mine here, to gag any gentleman. I do not desire to deprive any gentleman of the opportunity of speaking, and I do not think that fifteen minutes would be too much for some of them. I will say, in advance, that if the limit of fifteen minutes should be adopted, if any gentleman desires to occupy more time than that, I would be in favor of giving it to him, as a courtesy which is due him.

The question was then taken upon filling the blank with the word "fifteen," and it was agreed to.

The question then recurred upon the substitute as amended, which was read as follows:

"*Resolved*, That no member shall be permitted to speak more than once on any question, and then not to exceed fifteen minutes."

The question being taken upon the substitute, it was agreed to.

Adjournment sine die.

Mr. HALL offered the following resolution:

"*Resolved*, That this Convention will adjourn, *sine die*, on or before the fourth day of March, 1857."

Mr. TRAER. Is this resolution in order? I thought this whole subject had been indefinitely postponed.

The PRESIDENT. The Chair is of the opinion that the resolution is perfectly in order.

Mr. GILLASPY. I move to amend this resolution by striking out the words "fourth of March, 1857," and inserting "twenty-fifth of this month."

Mr. CLARKE, of Henry. I am sorry to see my friend from Wapello, [Mr. Gillaspy], supporting such a proposition as this. I thought he was in favor of the greatest liberty. I was in hopes that, as he was the only liberal man (besides myself) in this Convention, he would stand by me.

Mr. BUNKER. I am opposed to this whole course of speechifying and offering resolutions to adjourn by a certain day. I prefer to teach by example, rather than by precept. In my opinion, every resolution of this kind that is offered here only procrastinates the time when we shall be ready to adjourn. I trust, therefore, that this resolution, with the amendment, will be voted down.

Mr. TRAER. I would like to inquire if the Chair decides that after a subject is indefinitely postponed, it can be immediately brought forward again?

The PRESIDENT. The Chair is of the opinion that the resolution of the gentleman from Des Moines, [Mr. Hall] is in order. The twelfth standing rule of this Convention provides that "a motion to adjourn and a motion to fix a day on which the Convention shall adjourn, shall always be in order."

Mr. TRAER. The indefinite postponement of a subject must have some effect. The rule laid down in Cushing's Manual is this:

"In order to suppress a question altogether, without coming to a direct vote upon it, in such a manner that it cannot be renewed, the proper motion is for indefinite postponement; that is, a postponement or adjournment of the question, without fixing any day for resuming it. The effect of this motion, if decided in the affirmative, is to quash the proposition entirely; as an indefinite adjournment is equivalent to a dissolution, or the continuance of a suit, without day, is a discontinuance of it. A negative decision has no effect whatever."

This question of fixing a day for adjournment, and the question of adjourning over to a certain day, have both been up here, and have both been indefinitely postponed. The point of order I raise, is, that the question cannot be brought up again during this session.

The PRESIDENT. The Chair regrets very much to be compelled to differ with the gentleman from Benton, [Mr. Traer], but is still of the opinion that this resolution is in order.

Mr. TRAER. I regret very much to differ with the Chair upon this matter; but I am compelled so to differ, and must, therefore, take an appeal from the decision of the Chair.

Mr. SOLOMON. The motion to indefinitely postpone was upon a question entirely dissimilar from the one now before the Convention. That question was to adjourn until the first Monday in May next, to create a vacation in our sessions; while the question now before us is to continue our sessions until a certain day, and then adjourn *sine die*.

Mr. SCOTT. I hope the appeal will be persisted in, and that the Convention will sustain the decision of the Chair.

Mr. TRAER. It is not from any desire to differ with our presiding officer, or any other gentleman here, that I make this appeal. But this Convention will bear me witness that these questions of adjourning to a certain day, and adjourning *sine die* on a certain day, have been brought forward here, not only this morning, but heretofore, and have taken up more time than, if rightly used, would have been required to complete the consideration of one or more articles of the Constitution. I want to test this matter, and see if we are to have these questions brought in here, morning after morning, with amendments, and substitutes, and motions to lay on the table, &c., and thus have our time taken up to no purpose at all. Gentlemen talk here about others taking up too much time in discussion, and they are themselves pursuing a course which takes up more time uselessly than anything else that we have had before us.

I want to know if this convention are in favor of going to work, or whether they are willng to take up the time of this body in this way. I want to see if they will sustain the rule they have themselves adopted, that when a subject is indefinitely postponed, it cannot be brought forward again in the same session. This question of adjournment has been brought forward here in all the different shapes in which it can be presented, and I am convinced that it is with the direct intention of delaying the proceedings of this Convention.

I do not want to be discourteous to the President, or to any member of this convention; but I want to see a right course pursued here, and I think it is right to put this matter down effectively, so that we may go on with our work.

Mr. CLARK, of Alamakee. Does the gentleman from Benton [Mr. Traer] think that we have got ourselves into such a condition that we cannot adjourn at all?

Mr. TRAER. I think we can adjourn whenever we see fit.

The question was stated to be upon this question: "Shall the decision of the chair stand as the judgment of this convention?" and being taken, it was agreed to.

The decision of the chair was therefore sustained.

The question then recurred upon the amendment of Mr. Gillaspy, to strike out the words "fourth of March, 1857," and insert the words "twenty-fifth of this month."

Mr. YOUNG moved to lay the whole subject upon the table.

Upon this motion Mr. HALL called for the yeas and nays, which were ordered accordingly.

The question being then taken, by yeas and nays, the motion to lay on the table was not agreed to; yeas 14, nays 16; as follows:

Yeas—The President, Messrs. Bunker, Clark of Alamakee, Clarke of Johnson, Edwards, Ells, Gray, Hollingsworth, Marvin, Scott, Seely, Traer, Wilson and Young.

Nays—Messrs. Ayres, Clarke of Henry, Day, Emerson, Gibson, Gillaspy, Hall, Harris, Johnston, Palmer, Patterson, Peters, Price, Robinson, Solomon and Winchester.

The question then recurred upon the amendment proposed by Mr. Gillaspy.

Mr. YOUNG. I move to postpone this whole subject until the fourth of March next.

Mr. HARRIS. I hope the gentleman will withdraw his motion, and allow members an opportunity to test the sense of this convention in regard to his matter. I voted against laying this subject upon the table because I wanted to take a test vote upon this question. I am opposed to the amendment of the gentleman from Wapello [Mr. Gillaspy], but I shall vote for the original resolution.

Mr. PALMER. I believe we have the power to rescind this resolution at any time, if it is adopted. But to show that I am in favor of adjourning by that time, I shall vote for the resolution to adjourn *sine die* on the fourth of March.

Mr. BUNKER. I shall vote against this resolution, and against all other resolutions of this kind, for the very reason that the gentleman from Davis (Mr. Palmer) gives for voting for it. As he has said, we can rescind this resolution, if adopted, at any time, and that fact alone must satisfy every member of this convention that the only effect of resolutions of this kind is to procrastinate the sessions of this convention. His statement is an acknowledgment that all the time spent in discussing these questions is worse than thrown away.

Mr. YOUNG. I am sorry I cannot accommodate the gentleman from Appanoose, [Mr. Harris,] by withdrawing the motion to postpone until the fourth of March. We have been fighting all the morning, until now, nearly twelve o'clock, upon these resolutions. Every member here must admit that we have not got any of our work into shape so that we can say on what day we should adjourn. There is no man more anxious to go home than I am. But I came here with the expectation of doing up all the work before us, and then going home. Gentlemen have spent more time here in discussing resolutions to adjourn, than would have been necessary to pass upon the subject we had under consideration yesterday.

I hope gentlemen will keep resolutions of this kind away from here, until we can say when we ought to adjourn. I do not think there is any member here who desires to stay longer than is necessary. The people sent us here to do our work in as short a time as we could, but not to gag ourselves down to a certain day for adjournment, when not one-half of the reports of the committees have been acted upon, and some of our committees have not reported at all; and not a single subject has yet been acted upon finally, to give the committee on schedule, one of our most important committees, the least foundation upon which to base their report.

I hope this will be the last resolution thrown in here with no other purpose than to consume time. Let us go on with our work, and when we get so we see to the end of it, we can adopt a resolution to adjourn *sine die*. I hope gentlemen will not continue to bring in these resolutions just for the purpose of manufacturing buncombe at home, and then get up here and make speech after speech to consume the time of this convention.

Mr. PETERS. Being the mover of a resolution to adjourn to the second Monday in May, I think it proper that I should say a few words here. If any gentleman intends to charge me with offering that resolution for the purpose of manufacturing buncombe, or for any other purpose of the kind, I can only say that he is mistaken. As to long windy speeches, and occupying the time of this convention, the members here will bear me witness that I have kept my seat as much as any member in this body. I have done it with the feeling that by keeping my seat I have gained one point towards the completion of the work we come here to perform.

But in conversing with several members of the convention I learned that they considered it absolutely necessary for them to leave this convention and return home, at least for a time. I have also noticed that some of the questions brought before this convention, discussed and voted upon here, have been questions that were not before the people, and that they did not expect would be brought in here. And I thought that by adjourning, and going home for a few days or a few weeks, we might return here better prepared to take up the subjects that would come before this convention and act judiciously upon them, and thus conduce to the shortening the actual sessions of this convention. I believed the time we would be obliged now to spend here in discussing and settling these questions would be longer than it would be if we were to go home and consult our constituents, and then come back prepared to act understandingly upon these subjects.

So far as the charge of offering resolutions and making long speeches for buncombe, applies to me, I wish to enter my protest against the whole matter.

Mr. HALL called for the yeas and nays, upon the motion of Mr. Young, to postpone the whole subject of final adjournment until the fourth of March, and they were ordered accordingly.

The question being then taken, by yeas and nays, upon the motion to postpone, it was not agreed to; yeas 13, nays 18, as follows:

Yeas—The President, Messrs. Bunker, Clark of Alamakee, Clarke of Johnson, Edwards, Gray, Hollingsworth, Marvin, Scott, Seely, Traer, Wilson and Young.

Nays—Messrs. Ayres, Clarke of Henry, Day, Ells, Emerson, Gibson, Gillaspy, Hall, Harris, Johnston, Palmer, Patterson, Peters, Price, Robinson, Solomon, Warren and Winchester.

Mr. YOUNG moved that the convention do now adjourn.

Upon this question Mr. HALL called for the yeas and nays, and they were ordered accordingly.

The question being then taken, by yeas and nays, upon the motion to adjourn, it was not agreed to; yeas 11, nays 20, as follows:

Yeas—The President, Messrs. Bunker, Clarke of Johnson, Ells, Hollingsworth, Marvin, Scott, Seely, Traer, Wilson and Young.

Nays—Messrs. Ayres, Clark of Alamakee, Clarke of Henry, Day, Edwards, Emerson, Gibson, Gillaspy, Gray, Hall, Harris, Johnston, Palmer, Patterson, Peters, Price, Robinson, Solomon, Warren and Winchester.

The question then recurred upon the motion of Mr. Gillaspy, to amend the resolution by striking out the words "fourth of March, 1857," and inserting the words "twenty-fifth of this month."

Upon this motion Mr. GILLASPY called for the yeas and nays, and they were ordered accordingly.

The question being then taken, by yeas and nays, upon the motion to amend, it was not agreed to; yeas 13, nays 18; as follows:

Yeas—Messrs. Ayres, Clarke of Henry, Day, Emerson, Gillaspy, Hall, Johnston, Patterson, Peters, Price, Robinson, Solomon and Winchester.

Nays—The President, Messrs. Bunker, Clark of Alamakee, Clarke of Johnson, Edwards, Ells, Gibson, Gray, Harris, Hollingsworth, Marvin, Palmer, Scott, Seely, Traer, Warren, Wilson and Young.

The question then recurred upon the resolution of Mr. Hall to adjourn *sine die* on or before the fourth of March, 1857.

Upon this question Mr. HALL called for the yeas and nays, and they were ordered accordingly.

The question being then taken, by yeas and nays, upon the resolution, it was agreed to; yeas 22, nays 9; as follows:

Yeas—The President, Messrs. Ayres, Clarke of Henry, Day, Edwards, Emerson, Gibson, Gillaspy, Hall, Harris, Johnston, Marvin, Palmer, Patterson, Peters, Price, Robinson, Scott, Solomon, Warren, Winchester and Young.

Nays—Messrs. Bunker, Clark of Alamakee, Clarke of Johnson, Ells, Gray, Hollingsworth, Seely, Traer and Wilson.

Mr. CLARKE, of Henry. I wish to make a personal explanation in regard to my vote upon the resolution just adopted. I consider that the convention has passed a rule this morning contrary to the seventh section of the bill of rights, which secures to all perfect freedom of speech, and for that reason I was willing to vote for an adjournment at as early—

Mr. CLARKE, of Johnson. I rise to a point of order. There is nothing now before the convention for consideration.

Mr. CLARKE, of Henry. I am only making a personal explanation,

Mr. CLARKE, of Johnson. I do not wish to press the rules against others more strictly than they are applied to me.

The PRESIDENT. The gentleman can proceed by leave of the convention.

The question being taken, leave was not granted to Mr. Clarke, of Henry to proceed.

Judicial Department.

The convention then resumed the consideration of the subject of the judicial department.

Salaries of Judges.

The question was upon agreeing to the amendment of Mr. Clarke, of Johnson, which had been amended to read as follows:

"After the year 1860, the General Assembly shall have the power to increase the salaries of the judges of the Supreme Court and of the District Courts; but no salary of a judge of either court shall be increased or diminished during the term of his office."

Mr. DAY. I would inquire if the last vote taken upon this subject on yesterday unsettled the salaries of these judges?

The PRESIDENT. It left the salaries as the legislature of this winter fixed them; Supreme Judges at two thousand dollars, and District Judges at one thousand two hundred dollars each a year.

Mr. DAY. I will move to reconsider the vote by which the portion of this section which designated the amounts of the salaries was stricken out.

Mr, GRAY. I desire to offer the following as

a substitute for the entire amendment proposed by the gentleman from Johnson, [Mr. Clarke.]

"The salaries of the Supreme Judges shall be two thousand dollars each, and those of the District Judges one thousand six hundred each per annum, until the year 1860; after which time they shall receive such compensation as the General Assembly may by law establish, which shall not be increased or diminished during the term for which they shall be severally elected."

The PRESIDENT. The motion to reconsider comes first in order, and unless it is withdran must be first taken.

Mr. HALL. I hope the gentleman frem Van Buren, (Mr. Day,) will not withdraw his motion to reconsider. I think the Judiciary Department of the government ought to be placed in an independent position, at least so far that the legislature shall not have power to reduce their salaries below a certain amount. We know that these judges provided for here will not have been in office much more than a year by 1860; and if the legislature should happen to be adverse to them, they can cut down their salaries, and thus drive them from the bench.

Mr. DAY. I cannot withdraw my motion to reconsider.

Mr. WILSON. I would inquire of the chair what will be the question, if the motion to reconsider should prevail?

The PRESIDENT, The question will then be on the motion of the gentleman from Jefferson, [Mr. Wilson,] to strike out all this part relating to the amounts of salaries to be here established.

Mr. CLARKE, of Henry. Mr. President;

The PRESIDENT. The gentleman from Henry.

Mr. CLARKE, of Henry. I am happy, very happy, that I am permitted to speak once more in this august assembly. I have been listening here this morning to the various motions that have been made, and resolutions that have been offered. I have seen, with surprise, a resolution passed here, right in the face of that portion of the report of the committee on the bill of rights, respecting the liberty of speech, here in our midst, where it should be enjoyed fully and freely, and to the fullest extent, if anywhere. It is because I desire to get out as speedily as possible, of such fetters, meshes and restraints, that I shall vote for the shortest time for the session of this body. And I shall, for the same reason, go against every thing like reconsideration, taking the back track upon anything after we have acted upon it, if it will possibly answer to go into our constitution. If the convention can swallow a whole resolution like the one they adopted this morning, then I am ready to get through and leave as soon as possible. If we are to be bound down, restrained and tyrannized over by a majority that may be in these seats, while so many members are absent, then I shall endeavor to get as soon as possible out of a place where gentlemen refuse me the opportunity to explain my apparently inconsistent votes. I shall, therefore, go against this reconsideration, as it may lead to a longer consideration of this question, and thereby keep us longer subjected to such a resolution as the one passed this morning.

I am willing to leave this matter of fixing these salaries to the legislature. We do not propose to change the amount they have fixed for the salary of a judge of the Supreme Court. And if this constitution is adopted by the people, which I begin very much to doubt, then the legislature will have to fix the salaries for some ten district judges. And they can do that as well as they could fix the salaries for the supreme judges. Gentlemen complain that the present judges of the district court do not receive enough, only one thousand two hundred dollars, and they propose to raise it to one thousand six hundred dollars, or one thousand eight hundred dollars. If we reduce the number of districts from fourteen to ten, and throw the duties of the other four judges upon these ten, then the legislature will clearly perceive that as their duties are increased, their salaries should be increased also. I have nothing to fear from leaving this matter to the legislature; but I have something to fear from the reconsideration of subjects that have been once acted upon.

Mr. HALL. All I have to say is that there was once a law in force which provided that common scolds should be ducked in the nearest horse-pond. I am glad that that law is not in force now, or some of the members of this convention might suffer somewhat from its operation. [Laughter].

The question was upon the motion to reconsider.

Upon this motion,

Mr. HALL called for the yeas and nays and they were ordered accordingly.

The question being then taken, by yeas and nays, upon the motion to reconsider it was not agreed to; yeas 14, nays 16; as follows:

Yeas—Messrs. Ayers, Clarke of Johnson, Day, Ells, Emerson, Gray, Hall, Harris, Palmer, Patterson, Peters, Robinson, Solomon and Winchester.

Nays—The President, Messrs. Bunker, Clark of Alamakee, Clarke of Henry, Edwards, Gibson, Gillaspy, Hollingsworth, Johnston, Marvin, Scott, Seely, Tracer, Warren, Wilson, and Young.

The question was upon agreeing to the amendment of Mr. Clarke, of Johnson, as amended.

Mr. GRAY. I offer the following as a substitute for that amendment.

"The salaries of the supreme judges shall be two thousand dollars each, and those of the district judges one thousand six hundred dollars each, per annum, until the year 1860; after which time they shall receive such compensation as the General Assembly may by law establish, which shall not be increased or diminished during the term for which they shall be severally elected."

Mr. PATTERSON. I would inquire if that substitute is open to amendment?

The PRESIDENT. Amendments to it will be in order.

Mr. PATTERSON. Then I move to amend

it by striking out the words "one thousand six hundred dollars," and inserting the words "one thousand eight hundred dollars," as the salary of the judges of the district court.

Mr. CLARKE, of Johnson. If the gentleman from Linn [Mr. Gray] will modify his substitute in the manner proposed by the gentleman from Lee (Mr Patterson) I will accept it in lieu of my amendment, as a compromise of this question.

Mr. GRAY. Individually I would have no objection to doing so. But I offer my substitute as a kind of middle ground, upon which the extremists upon this subject might harmonize their differences, if possible. The majority of my friends with whom I have consulted incline to the respective sums I have named in my substitute. I must therefore, decline at present to accept the amendment proposed by the gentleman from Lee [Mr. Patterson].

The question was upon the motion of Mr. Patterson to amend the substitute by increasing the salary proposed for each judge of the district court from one thousand six hundred dollars to one thousand eight hundred dollars.

Upon this question, Mr. HALL called the yeas and nays, and they were ordered accordingly.

The question being then taken by yeas and nays, upon the motion to strike out the words "one thousand six hundred dollars" and insert the words "one thousand eight hundred dollars," it was not agreed to; yeas 12, nays 18, as follows:

Yeas—Messrs. Ayres, Bunker, Clarke of Johnson, Day, Ells, Hall, Patterson, Robinson, Solomon, Traer, Warren and Winchester.

Nays—The President, Messrs. Clark of Alamakee, Clarke of Henry, Edwards, Emerson, Gibson, Gillaspy, Gray, Harris, Hollingsworth, Johnston, Marvin, Palmer, Peters, Scott, Seely, Wilson and Young.

The question then recurred upon the substitute.

Mr. SOLOMON. I move to amend the proposed substitute by inserting after the words "supreme judges," the words: "who shall have been elected by the people," so as to confine these salaries to those judges elected by the people under this constitution. I will state briefly my reason for this motion. It seems to be universally recognized as a principle that the salary of no officer shall be changed during the term for which he may be elected. I desire to put this principle into practical effect here. If it is a true principle, and it seems to be universally admitted to be such, then let us enforce it in this case, and make these proposed salaries applicable only to those who hold office under this constitution. It is for that object that I make this motion to amend.

Mr. WILSON. I hope the amendment will not prevail. I am willing, by way of compromise, to vote for the substitute proposed by the gentleman from Linn, [Mr. Gray,] for I believe it is the best and fairest compromise we can make. If gentlemen fear that our district judges will be starved out with their present salaries, they may as well let them draw this increase of compensation from the time this Constitution goes into effect. We are not yet certain that this Convention will proceed to re-district the State. As this article now stands, that work must be performed by the next General Assembly. I am willing to vote for this substitute, as it now stands, by way of compromise.

Mr. HALL. I did not see the necessity of amending this provision as it was amended on yesterday. This substitute is a sort of compromise to the ear, but it breaks the promise to the heart. We cannot get these new districts well organized, and these courts fairly established, much before the year 1860. The first legislature that convenes under this Constitution, if it is adopted, will have this whole matter at their mercy, notwithstanding we may put this provision in here. Why not, then, leave the whole matter directly under their control at once, and put the supreme judges in the hands of the legislature, and let them fix their salaries as they please? This substitute is a mere mockery. I would prefer to vote for the amendment of the gentleman from Johnson, [Mr. Clarke,] as it now stands amended, and leave this matter openly and plainly to the legislature. I shall vote against this substitute.

Mr. SOLOMON. I would ask, if the opposition expressed by the gentleman from Des Moines, [Mr. Hall,] is to my proposed amendment, or to the whole of the substitute?

Mr. HALL. To the entire substitute. If the majority of the Convention prefer to place this branch of the government under the control of the legislature, let them do so directly.

Mr. SOLOMON. I desire to have this whole matter left to the legislature; that is my position exactly. The salaries of these judges have already been fixed by the legislature, and I would let them remain, to be changed hereafter or not, as the legislature may see fit.

Mr. WILSON. Have not the salaries of the present judges been increased during their term of office?

Mr. SOLOMON. I neither know nor care how that is.

Mr. WILSON. What did the last legislature do in relation to this matter?

Mr. SOLOMON. I do not know, and do not want to know, what they did.

Mr. GILLASPY. I started out in favor of two thousand dollars for the supreme judges, and fifteen hundred dollars for the district judges. But I am inclined, judging from the desires of this Convention, from the votes they have given upon this subject, to vote for the substitute proposed by the gentleman from Linn, [Mr. Gray,] as a compromise.

The question was upon the amendment proposed by Mr. Solomon.

Upon this question Mr. HALL called for the yeas and nays, and they were ordered accordingly.

The question being then taken, by yeas and nays, upon the amendment proposed to the substitute, it was not agreed to; yeas 12, nays 18, as follows:

Yeas—Messrs. Ayres, Clarke of Henry, Day,

Emerson, Gibson, Gillaspy, Harris, Johnston, Palmer, Patterson, Peters and Solomon.

Nays—The President, Messrs. Bunker, Clark, of Alamakee, Clarke, of Johnson, Edwards, Ells, Gray, Hall, Hollingsworth, Marvin, Robinson, Scott, Seely, Traer, Warren, Wilson, Winchester and Young.

The question recurred upon the proposed substitute.

Mr. CLARKE, of Henry. I think that some change or amendment should be made in this substitute. I suppose it is intended to apply to district judges elected under this Constitution. We have some fourteen judges now, and I suppose we do not want to have anything to do with them.

Mr. EDWARDS called for the previous question, which being seconded, the main question was then ordered to be put.

The question was upon the substitute proposed by Mr. Gray, to the amendment of Mr. Clarke, of Johnson, as amended.

Upon this question Mr. HALL called for the yeas and nays, and they were ordered accordingly.

The question being then taken, by yeas and nays, upon the proposed substitute, it was agreed to; yeas 20; nays 10, as follows:

Yeas—The President, Messrs. Ayres, Bunker, Clark, of Alamakee, Clarke, of Henry, Day, Edwards, Gillaspy, Gray, Harris, Hollingsworth, Johnston, Marvin, Palmer. Patterson, Scott, Seely, Traer, Wilson and Young.

Nays—Messrs. Clarke, of Johnson, Ells, Emerson, Gibson, Hall, Peters, Robinson, Solomon, Warren and Winchester.

The question then recurred upon the amendment as amended.

Mr. TRAER called for the previous question, which being seconded, the main question was then ordered to be put.

Mr. CLARKE, of Henry. I think this amendment should be amended so that it shall not apply to our present district judges.

Mr. HALL. Let it apply to them.

Mr. CLARK, of Alamakee. If this amendment is not made, I shall be compelled to vote against this substitute.

Upon the question of agreeing to the amendment as amended, the yeas and nays were called by Mr. Hall, and they were ordered accordingly.

The question being then taken, by yeas and nays, the amendment as amended was agreed to; yeas 21; nays 9, as follows:

Yeas.—The President, Messrs. Ayres, Bunker, Clarke, of Henry, Day, Edwards, Gillaspy, Gray, Harris, Hollingworth, Johnston, Marvin, Palmer, Patterson, Scott, Seely, Traer, Warren, Wilson, Winchester and Young.

Nays.—Messrs. Clark, of Alamakee, Clarke of Johnson, Ells, Emerson, Gibson, Hall, Peters, Robinson and Solomon.

Districting the State.

Mr. WILSON. I move to farther amend this article by striking out of the fourth section the words, "the first session of the general assembly shall divide the State," and insert the words "the State shall be divided," so that it will read "the State shall be divided into ten judicial districts," &c. This will leave to the convention to decide hereafter whether they will proceed to divide the State into districts, or leave it to the legislature to do so.

Mr. CLARKE, of Johnson. I would suggest the following as a substitute for the whole provision:

"The State shall consist of ten Judicial Districts; and after the year 1860, the General Assembly may re-organize the judicial districts, and increase or diminish the number of districts, or the number of Judges of the said Court, and may increase the number of Judges of the Supreme Court; but such increase or diminution shall not be more than one district, or one Judge of either Court, at any one session; and no re-organization of the districts, or diminution of the Judges, shall have the effect of removing a Judge from office. Such re-organization of the districts, or any change in the boundaries thereof, or increase or diminution of the number of the Judges, shall take place every four years thereafter, if necessary, and at no other time."

Mr. WILSON. I will accept the amendment.

The question being then taken upon the amendment as modified, it was agreed to.

Mr. CLARKE, of Johnson. I am laboring under considerable bodily indisposition, and I think it very doubtful whether I shall be able to attend this convention this afternoon. I would be glad to have this subject laid over until Monday. I believe the same courtesy has been extended to other members, who are chairmen of committees, that I now ask to be extended to me.

Mr. GILLASPY. I shall be disposed, and I have no doubt the convention will be disposed, to accede to the request of the gentleman from Johnson, [Mr. Clarke,] and let this subject lie over. I think we can take up something else, and go on with it.

Mr. TRAER moved that the convention adjourn until Monday next at 2 o'clock P. M.

Upon this question Mr. WINCHESTER called for the yeas and nays, and they were ordered accordingly.

The question being then taken, by yeas and nays, upon the motion to adjourn till Monday afternoon, it was not agreed to; yeas 15; nays 15, as follows:

Yeas.—Messrs. Bunker, Clarke of Johnson, Ells, Hall, Hollingsworth, Marvin, Palmer, Peters Robinson, Scott, Solomon, Traer, Warren, Wilson and Young.

Nays.—The President, Messrs. Ayres, Clark of Alamakee, Clarke of Henry, Day, Edwards,

Emerson, Gibson, Gillaspy, Gray, Harris, Johnston, Patterson, Seely and Winchester.

On motion of Mr. HARRIS,

The convention then took a recess until this afternoon, at two o'clock.

EVENING SESSION.

The convention met at two o'clock, P. M., and was called to order by the President.

Mr. GRAY. For the purpose of giving the members and officers of the Convention an opportunity for a little rest, and for recruiting the tired energies of nature, I move that we adjourn until two o'clock on Monday next.

On motion of Mr. WINCHESTER,

A call of the Convention was ordered.

The Secretary then proceeded to call the roll, when the following gentlemen answered to their names:

The President, Messrs. Ayres, Bunker, Clarke, of Henry, Day, Ells, Emerson, Gibson, Gillaspy, Gray, Harris, Hollingsworth, Johnston, Palmer, Patterson, Peters, Price, Scott, Seely, Solomon, Traer, Warren, Wilson, Winchester and Young.

The following gentlemen were the absentees:

Messrs. Clark, of Alamakee, Clarke, of Johnson, Cotton, Edwards, Gower, Hall, Marvin, Palmer, Parvin, Robinson and Todhunter.

Mr. AYRES asked leave of abrence for Mr. Marvin, which was granted.

Mr. HARRIS moved that Messrs. Clarke, of Johnson, and Todhunter, be excused, which motion was agreed to.

On motion of Mr. TRAER,

All further proceedings under the call were dispensed with.

Mr. WINCHESTER called for the yeas and nays upon the motion to adjourn, and they were accordingly ordered.

The question was then taken, by yeas and nays, upon the motion to adjourn until Monday afternoon at two o'clock, and it was agreed to; yeas 17, nays 9, as follows:

Yeas—Messrs. Bunker, Clarke, of Henry, Ells, Emerson, Gray, Harris, Hollingsworth, Palmer, Peters, Price, Scott, Seely, Solomon, Traer, Warren, Wilson and Young.

Nays—The President, Messrs. Ayres, Day, Gibson, Gillaspy, Johnston, Patterson, Robinson and Winchester.

The Convention accordingly adjourned until two o'clock, P. M., on Monday next.

MONDAY, February 16th, 1857.

The Convention met at 2 o'clock, P. M., and was called to order by the President.

The journal of Saturday was read and approved.

Personal Explanation.

Mr. EDWARDS. I rise for the purpose of making a personal explanation. I hold in my hands a copy of the "Iowa Capital City Reporter," of the fourth inst., which contains a communication based upon some remark that I am reputed to have made upon the banking question. I am represented as advocating the doctrine of a "paper basis," for banking. This is entirely incorrect. I made use of no such remark. I stated that I was in favor of a specie basis. It is true that the reporter for the two daily papers here made the mistake, but I regarded the error as unintentional and so glaring upon its face, that I did not think it worth while to call the attention of the reporter to the fact.

Judicial Department.

The PRESIDENT. The business first in order is the consideration of the report of the Committee on the Judicial Department. The amendments that were offered to the report in Committee of the Whole have all been acted upon, but the report is still open for amendment. What is the pleasure of the Convention in regard to it?

Number of Judicial Districts.

Mr. HARRIS. I would like to have the fourth section read, which fixes the number of the judicial districts.

The fourth section as amended was then read as follows:

"The District Court shall consist of a judge, who shall be elected by the qualified voters of the district in which he resides, at the general election, and hold his office for the term of four years, and until his successor is elected and qualified, and shall be ineligible to any other office except that of Supreme Judge, during the term for which he may be elected. The District Court shall be a court of law and equity, which shall be distinct and separate jurisdictions, and have jurisdiction in civil and criminal matters arising in their respective districts, in such manner as shall be prescribed by law. The judges of the District Courts shall be conservators of the peace in their respective districts. The first session of the General Assembly shall divide the State into ten districts, and after the year 1860, the General Assembly may reorganize the Judicial Districts, and increase or diminish the number of Districts, or the number of Judges of the Supreme or District Courts; but such increase or diminution shall not be more than one district or one judge of either court at a time, and no reorganization of the districts, or diminution of the judges, shall have the effect of removing a judge from office. Such reorganization of the districts, or increase or diminution of the judges of either court shall take place every four years thereafter, if necessary, and at no other time."

Mr. HARRIS. I move to strike out "ten" and insert "thirteen" in its place.

The PRESIDENT. The chair is of the opinion that that motion would not be in order. The gentleman from Appanoose can attain his object by moving to refer the matter to the Committee on the Judicial Department, with instructions to make that change.

Mr. HARRIS. I will make that motion then. This is a matter in which I feel some interest, and to which I paid some attention even before the motion was made to insert the number "ten" in this section. Since that time I have taken pains, upon the basis of that number of districts, to try and arrange the districts of the State in a manner which would be satisfactory to myself, but after some six or seven trials in endeavoring to make an equal proportion between the large counties and keeping the western districts within a reasonable size, I was forced to give up the attempt entirely. Since that time I have tried the number thirteen, and I have succeeded in arranging that number of districts in a manner which, I think, will prove satisfactory to the members of the convention. Even with that number, if you undertake to have a basis of population, unless you make six, seven, or eight districts upon the Mississippi, and not go back more than one county from the river, you will then be under the necessity of putting fifty, seventy, eighty, and perhaps a hundred thousand inhabitants in some districts there. Hence I think that gentlemen will conclude that population cannot be taken as the basis for dividing the judicial districts. Taking thirteen as the number of districts, I make no district of less than four counties.

It is said by gentlemen here that you can put together fifteen or twenty of these counties, that are remote from the river, and where there is not a large amount of business or population. But when gentlemen will take the map and notice the distance that the judges will have to travel, and the inconveniences to which they will be subjected, I apprehend they will come to a different conclusion. I will give gentlemen an illustration of the privations to which judges are subjected in the new counties. It is an incident which happened in the section of the State where I live. At that time there were twenty or thirty counties in one judicial district, and the legislature refused to make it smaller. The judge for that district was going to the Missouri river; and he found himself at one time entirely away from any neighborhood or settlement, between two creeks which he found he could not cross; and he was compelled to lie in the woods over night. I came very near being placed in the same position myself, while traveling from one county to another.

I make this statement, for the purpose of showing the inconveniences to which judges and lawyers are compelled to submit, when traveling over a large section of country. I know that some half dozen gentlemen, who voted for ten districts this morning, when I called their attention to the matter, and showed them the map, and explained how things would stand, admitted that a larger number of districts would be necessary. I have spent some twelve or fifteen hours over this matter since the last sitting of the Convention, and I am satisfied that justice cannot be done to all parts of the State without having a larger number of districts than ten. I will simply state, that in the calculations I have made, I have not taken into account the political character of any county, and I have not had the vote of a single county before me, but I made my estimates from the map and population of the counties, without regard to any political questions whatever.

Mr. CLARKE, of Johnson. I shall vote for the motion for another reason than that assigned by the gentleman from Appanoose, [Mr. Harris], and I think it will be perhaps necessary to add another instruction to the Committee. The amendment which was adopted upon my motion on Saturday provides for the organization of the districts in 1860 and every five years hearafter, but the increase shall be only one judge at a time. It may be a question, whether that will allow a re-organization to take place often enough for the business of this State; and I would therefore suggest, that the Committee take that matter into consideration also. I would suggest, too, after this matter is finally settled, that it be referred to a special committee to re-cast the whole article.

Mr. HARRIS. I do not wish to make this a test question in any way. I simply wish to refer it to a committee, who will investigate it thoroughly, and if, after a careful investigation, they should report that the proposition I submit ought not to be adopted, I will cheerfully submit.

The PRESIDENT. The Chair would suggest to the gentleman from Appanoose, [Mr. Harris] that he modify his motion so that the committee shall be instructed to inquire into the expediency of making the change, &c.

Mr. WILSON. If the gentleman will change his motion in that respect, then I will interpose no objection to it.

Mr. HARRIS. I accept the suggestion, and will modify my motion accordingly.

The question was then taken, and the motion of Mr. Harris was agreed to.

Order of Business.

The PRESIDENT. The next business in order will be the report of the Standing Committee on Education and School Lands.

Mr. WINCHESTER. I move that that report be laid upon the table, and that the report of the Committee on the Legislative Department be taken up. The chairman of that committee is now present.

The question was taken, and the motion of Mr. Winchester was agreed to.

Legislative Department.

The report of the Committee on the Legislative

Department was then taken up and read the second time.

In Committee of the Whole.

On motion of Mr. CLARKE, of Johnson.

The Convention then resolved itself into Committee of the Whole upon the report of the Committee on the Legislative Department, (Mr. Patterson in the chair.)

The CHAIRMAN. The report will now be read through by the Clerk, by sections, for amendments.

Section first was then read as follows:

"The legislative authority of this State shall be vested in a Senate and House of Representatives, which shall be designated the General Assembly of the State of Iowa; and the style of their laws shall commence in the following manner: 'Be it enacted by the General Assembly of the State of Iowa.'"

No amendments being offered to this section,

Biennial Sessions.

Section second was then read as follows:

"The sessions of the General Assembly shall be biennial, and shall commence on the second Monday of January next ensuing the election of its members; unless the Governor of the State shall, in the interim, convene the General Assembly by proclamation."

Mr. GOWER. I move to amend the section by providing that the sessions of the General Assembly shall be annual for three years after the adoption of this Constitution.

The question was taken, and the motion was not agreed to.

Mr. PALMER. I move to strike out the word "biennial" and insert "annual," so that the section would then read—

"The sessions of the General Assembly shall be annual, and shall commence on the second Monday of January next ensuing the election of its members; unless the Governor of the State shall, in the interim, convene the General Assembly by proclamation."

Mr. HALL. I do not think that this matter should be permitted to pass without something being said upon it. The question whether we shall have annual or biennial sessions is one of considerable importance. We all know, during the ten years in which this State has had an existence, that we have had, from necessity, a great deal of legislation, and we know, too, that at the present time there is a greater necessity for legislation than we have ever had during the history of the past. We are now inaugurating a system of railroads, to some of which immense grants of lands have been made by the General Government; and we are also inaugurating a system of banking, and a great many other institutions new in the history of the State. We have just entered upon a system for building up in this State benevolent and charitable institutions, upon which we are expending large sums of money. It strikes me, therefore, that for a period of years it would be wise in us to adopt a system of annual sessions of the Legislature. If all these institutions progress, as we have every reason to believe they will, there will be a necessity for annual sessions for several years to come. I hope gentlemen will reflect upon this matter, and adopt such a plan as will fully answer the wants and necessities of the State.

Mr. PARVIN. A majority of the committee on the Legislative Department at their first meeting were in favor of annual sessions, but at a subsequent meeting and after pursuing their investigations a little further, they came to a different conclusion. The convention, as every member will observe, have cut off much of the legislation that has heretofore prevailed, by making it the duty of the General Assembly to pass general laws in regard to those subjects which have heretofore been provided for by special enactments.

In considering this question whether we should have, under our new constitution, annual or biennial sessions, there are two things necessary to be considered. The first is in regard to the expenses attendig annual sessions of the legislature; the next is whether there is really any necessity for them. Annual sessions are attended with considerable expense, but then that consideration should not stand in the way, if there is an actual necessity for the meeting of the legislature every year. It was the opinion of a majority of the Committee, that there would be no necessity for the meeting of the legislature more than once in two years, from the fact that we have cut off all local legislation, and general laws do not need revising oftener than once in two years. If you will look at the acts passed at the last session of the General Assembly—and this rule will hold good should you go back to the formation of our present constitution—you will find that more than half of them were such as this report specifies shall be provided for by general laws. I think every person will agree with me, in the opinion, that once in two years is often enough to revise general laws. It is a fact, as gentlemen all know, that when a law is passed, differing very much from what has been heretofore passed, there is always more or less complaint; just so certain as the legislature pass an act which makes a every great change from former laws upon the same subject, the very next winter a repeal will be demanded; when if two years had elapsed, the people would have become accustomed to it, and become convinced of its necessity and utility.

Gentlemen have urged as a reason against biennial sessions, that there have been several special sessions of the legislature, and that this necessity for them will continue to exist in the future. But still this does not weigh, in my estimation, in favor of having annual sessions. Even with the called sessions, we would have eight sessions in ten years, and this would be a gain upon the present system. But with the provision we have made here for cutting off all local legislation, I do not think there will be any necessity for sessions of the legislature oftener than once in two years.

Mr. PALMER. I believe that in most of the States, where the plan of biennial sessions has been tried, they have abandoned it, and again instituted annual sessions. I think that there are many subjects of legislation that will require the meeting of the legislature annually. If there is but little business to be done, the legislature may dispatch it in a few days, adjourn, and go home. I have seen, in other States, the necessity that many times existed, of having annual sessions of the legislature. As has been mentioned, we have had a session of the legislature almost every year since the organization of the government, notwithstanding our Constitution provides for biennial sessions.

I have discovered an error in the hasty legislation of the last session, and I do not know in what manner it can be remedied. A bill was passed, fixing the times for holding the district courts in our county, but by some error—I do not know how it originated—the courts are to be held in three different counties in one district upon the same day. Such errors as these may require annual sessions of the legislature. Hardly a session goes by without some material error being committed by the legislature. Besides, new and different circumstances may arise during the year which will require a change in the legislation of the next year. The population of the State is increasing with wonderful rapidity, and our interests are constantly varying with the changes going on around us, and require a corresponding variation in our legislation. A new State like our own, growing so rapidly in population and wealth, needs annual sessions more than an old State, whose laws have become fixed and permanent, and where they can get along with biennial sessions much better than we can.

Mr. EDWARDS. I coincide with the views entertained by the gentleman from Muscatine, [Mr. Parvin,] that biennial are preferable to annual sessions of the legislature for the obvious reason, that in this country the people are governed too much. Now there is always great difficulty growing out of annual sessions of the legislature. They meet here, and for want of business, they pass a great many laws, which are repealed before the people have an opportunity to become acquainted with them. I hold that it is better to have bad laws and become well acquainted with them, than to be perpetually changing our laws.

The necessity of having annual sessions is obviated by the very plan which has been submitted here in this article, of doing away with a great amount of special legislation, that always takes up one half of the sessions of the General Assembly. They do not cut off so much of this special legislation as I would like, for there are many other subjects of special legislation, that might have been included in this article besides those they have enumerated. When the article shall be fully perfected, I think the argument will be decidedly in favor of adopting the plan of holding biennial sessions.

If we adopt this plan, the power is still given to the Governor of convening the legislature, if any necessity should arise rendering it necessary for him to do so. If we cut off the vast amout of special legislation as now proposed, biennial sessions of the legislature will, in my opinion, fully meet the wants and requirements of the people of the State, besides saving them a large amount of expense.

Mr. GIBSON. I am opposed to the plan of having annual sessions of the Legislature. I think the less special legislation we have, the better for the people. They will understand the laws better, and be better governed by them. If the provision be adopted requiring the Legislature to pass general laws upon certain subjects, it will supersede the necessity, to a very great extent, of having so much local and special legislation as we have had in years past. Under a system of having sessions every year, one half of the people do not become acquainted with the laws that are passed; and they very often remain in force only a few months when the next Legislature that meets repeals them. We thus have a continual change in our laws, and one half of the people in the State do not really know what the laws upon the statute books are.

The system of biennial sessions will save a great deal of expense to the State. There will be perhaps one hundred and fifty members in both Houses, and if they sit sixty days, at three dollars a day, the per diem for a session will amount to twenty-seven thousand dollars, to say nothing of the mileage, which will be, at least, half that amount. There are, too, the expenses of printing, and other incidental expenses to be taken into the account. I should judge that a session could not be held short of fifty to sixty thousand dollars. Here is a considerable item of expense to be saved, unless there is some advantage to be gained by it, which will counterbalance this great expense.

By adopting biennial sessions we will get rid of this large expense, and give to the people a better opportunity to become acquainted with the laws which are passed. If we provide, by general law, for internal improvements, charitable institutions, and a great many other matters that are now provided for by special acts, and have as little legislation upon the statute-book as possible, I think the people will understand the laws much better.

Mr. HARRIS. I certainly agree with the position taken by the gentleman who has just taken his seat, [Mr. Gibson.] If any gentleman will take the trouble to look over the acts of any General Assembly of this State, he will find that three fourths of the laws that have been passed are local, and such as will be cut off by the provision contained in this report in regard to general laws.

The thirty-first section of this report reads as follows:

"The General Assembly shall not pass local or special laws in the following cases:

For the assessment and collection of taxes for State, county, or road purposes;

For laying out, opening, and working on roads or highways;

For changing the names of persons;

For the incorporation of cities or towns;

For vacating roads, town plats, streets, alleys, or public squares;

In all the cases above enumerated, and in all other cases where a general law can be made applicable, all laws shall be general, and of uniform operation throughout the State."

Gentlemen will see that by this provision, we will cut off a large amount of legislation, which has consumed, heretofore, so much of the time of our General Assembly. Gentlemen say that we are building railroads, and there may be a necessity for having annual sesssions of the legislature upon that account. But we do not know when we may need a General Assembly for the purpose of legislating in regard to railroads. I apprehend that we shall not be troubled with matters of that kind, for we shall not be likely to receive another grant of lands from the general government in aid of railroads in this State. If there should be a necessity at any time for any legislation upon matters of this kind, the Governor can call an extra session by proclamation, and the legislature can convene here with just as little expense as they can at any annual session.

As to the case spoken of by my friend from Davis [Mr. Palmer] I can only say it was the misfortune of the people of his district, and it was a penalty upon them for their carelessness in sending men here who did not attend to their business properly. I do not think that such cases as the gentleman has cited afford any good reason why we should have annual sessions of the legislature.

Mr. HALL. I am as unwilling as any gentleman to adopt anything as a part of our system, which would unnecessarily tax the people. When gentlemen get up and cypher out the additional expense to which the State will be subjected, in having annual instead of biennial sessions, it is somewhat alarming, it is true. And it strikes one at first sight, that this expense may be unnecessary. But when you look at the fact, and find that although constitutionally we have but biennial sessions, yet in reality we have annual sessions, and are subjected to this very identical expense of which the gentleman complains, that alters the case very materially.

I know that in the older States, where they have adopted the system of biennial sessions, they have uniformly had annual sessions, and have not saved to the State a single dollar by having this biennial system. I am told that the necessity for annual sessions is obviated by the fact that the committee have reported in favor of cutting off speciale legislation.

I undertake to say, that they have not obviated the necessity of legislation upon general acts, for the legislature are to judge, if general laws can be made applicable. It is for the purpose of passing general laws, that we want this legislature to convene, because all these acts come under the head of general laws.

Again, we are stepping upon ground which is new, and we are placing the government in a position which has not been fully tried. We do not know how well this provision may answer the purpose,and we are not entirely certain that the legislature that may first draft the laws upon general principles and set the machinery in motion throughout the State will guage it so accurately that it will need no repairing. We are now stepping as it were from infancy into manhood; and we are going to adopt a sysfem of internal improvements throughout this State, which will involve very large interests, larger than many of us have computed. We are going into a system that will involve the destiny of the whole State, either for good or evil, and upon which legislation will be necessary. We are about commencing a system of building charitable institutions, and raising money by taxation for the prosecution of our public works.

It will be almost impossible, while appropriations are being made for these improvements, to have them carried on in a manner that shall ensure safety to the State and security to the people, unless we have annual sessions of the legislature for a few years, to provide for the thousand emergencies that may arise, calling for legislation. While these improvements are progressing at the rate they are now, they will involve the necessity of annual sessions after the adoption of this constitution, for a few years at least. I am willing to limit these annual sessions to a few years, but I do feel that there will be an absolute necessity for having them for a while yet; while we impose such onerous duties upon the legislature, we ought to give them an opportunity of discharging them within a reasonable time before the public interests shall suffer. I do not wish to advocate the system of annual sessions, upon any other grounds than those of public interest and necessity. With the experience of those who have gone before us, it does appear to me that it would be absolute weakness upon our part if we did not provide for the wants and necessities of the times by adopting the system of annual sessions for a few years to come at least.

Mr. MARVIN. I do not rise for the purpose of prolonging, to any great length, the discussion which we already have had upon this question. It has been my conviction for years, that annual sessions were preferable to biennial sessions in any State. One view I would suggest, in addition to those that have already been presented, is this: We know that when our legislative assemblies sit any great length of time, they dispatch their business at the close of the session in a hurry, and pass laws hastily, often-times without giving them that reflection and mature thought which they deserve. A great many members of the legislature have more or less business to attend to at home. Some have their law business, some their mechanical business, and some their farming business to attend to. If the legislature meets in the beginning of January, they will, before the opening of spring, get in a hurry to go home. If the sessions should be biennial, there would be an accumulation of business within two years; there would be a disposition to crowd matters into a short space, and get through with the business in a hurry. My plan would be to have annual sessions, and let them be short. I really believe that most of the legislatures, that assemble here to make laws, could do all their business in thirty or forty days, and then return to their homes, and accomplish their business with better satisfaction to the people, than if they sat here sixty or eighty days.

Mr. HARRIS. It has been said by gentlemen here, that two or three States that made these changes from annual to biennial sessions have changed back again, and that biennial sessions, where they had them, worked a great hardship. I have no doubt that gentlemen are sincere in this belief; but my information does not lead me to that conclusion. I find the same provision in the constitution of Ohio—a State which has been so often referred to in the course of this debate—that we propose to insert here; and I find another provision in their constitution which I would like to see introduced here, that the legislature shall not adjourn even for the holidays. My friend from Jones [Mr. Marvin,] says that one reason why we should have annual sessions is, that the legislature is not going to meet until the first Monday of January, and that the members would be so anxious to adjourn before the spring came on, that they cannot give the business that attention which will be necessary. If the gentleman has ever been a member of the legislature, he must know that meeting here upon the first of January, will give just about as much time for the transaction of business, as to meet here the first day of December. I recollect when I was here a few years ago, that we spent a week in debating the question, whether to adjourn two weeks over the holidays. A large minority of the members were determined to leave, and they considered themselves as so many free apprentices, entitled to the holidays. Gentlemen will recollect that the legislature last winter adjourned over two weeks for the holidays. It was true they had hard work to get through with their business in their allotted time, but that was their own look-out. In regard to this matter, I would say that the people should be more careful in sending business men to the legislature, and not send men who wish to spend time in holidays.

I do not believe that there is any necessity for these annual meetings of the legislature. I do not believe that the interests of this State, if they are carefully consulted, will show that there is any necessity for them.

In regard to this matter of passing general laws, I would say, that there is a provision in the old Constitution that the General Alsembly might provide for general legislation; but here is a direct provision that they shall not legislate upon any of these subjects. I undertake to say, that it will shorten the sessions at least one-half, and I believe three-fourths, of the time of the General Assembly, when it is understood that they cannot legislate upon town charters, &c., because there is more time consumed in debating the provisions of town charters, in which three-fourths of the members are not concerned, than there is in discussing general laws.

I think, therefore, under these circumstances, there is no necessity for having annual sessions. As I said before, in the case of any absolute or imperative necessity, demanding legislative action, the Governor may call the legislature together.

Mr. CLARKE, of Henry. I reiterate what I said the other day, that we should be very careful, in preparing this Constitut on, to be sent down to the people, how we load it down with taxation. I believe it is conceded that the legislative department is the most expensive department of the State government. It is increasing in numbers, and the proposition is made here that their compensation shall be increased. Heretofore, the legislature of this State have held biennial sessions, but in some instances the Governor has called special sessions. The section we are now considering is in the article of the present Constitution, upon this subject, in which there is a provision that, in an emergency, the Governor can call the General Assembly together. That, I think, is sufficient, and I think there is no necessity for our making a change in this particular. I have not, myself, heard a demand made for that change. I do not know what other gentleman may have heard, through their constituents; but for myself, I have never heard any demand for a change in that particular. If we make that change, it is going to involve the people of this State in great additional expense. The gentleman who last occupied the attention of the Convention, [Mr. Harris,] spoke in regard to this matter from the experience which he has himself had as a member of the legislature of this State. I believe, when we take away from the legislature, under the operation of this Constitution, the mass of local and special legislation which is now devolved upon that body, the legislative business of this State will be carried on to the full satisfaction of the people, by having biennial sessions. If gentlemen could show me that there was an absolute necessity for annual sessions, and that it was good policy to adopt this system, my vote might be cast differently; but as the case now presents itself to my mind, I shall certainly vote for biennial sessions. I shall continue to vote for the provisions of the old Constitution, wherever I can, and where I think a change is not demanded.

The question was then taken upon the motion made by Mr. Palmer, to strike out "biennial," and insert "annual," and it was not agreed to upon division; ayes 8, noes not counted.

There being no other amendments made to the second section—

Time of Electing Members.

The third section was then read as follows:

"The members of the House of Representatives shall be chosen every second year, by the qualified electors of their respective districts, on the second Tuesday in October, except the years of the Presidential election, when the election shall be on the Tuesday next after the first Monday in November; whose term of office shall continue two years from the Tuesday next after the first Monday in November."

Mr. WINCHESTER. I move to strike out all after the word "October," to the word "November," where it first occurs; so that the section would then read:

"The members of the House of Representatives shall be chosen every second year, by the qualified electors of their respective districts, on the second Tuesday in October; whose term of office shall continue two years from the Tuesday next after the first Monday in November."

Mr. GILLASPY. I move to amend the amendment by providing that the elections shall be held on the Tuesday next after the first Monday in November, so that the section would then read:

"The members of the House of Representatives shall be chosen every second year, by the qualified electors of their respective districts, on the Tuesday next after the first Monday in November, whose term of office shall continue two years from the Tuesday next after the first Monday in November."

Mr. GILLASPY. In explanation of the amendment I offer, I desire to make but a single remark. If we fix the time of the general election, in order to have the terms of office uniform, we must fix the elections in October or in November. In the region of the State which I represent here, the people are dissatisfied with the numerous elections we have, and there seems to be a general feeling manifested there in favor of fixing the general election upon the day of the presidential election, so as to obviate the necessity and expense of having two elections. I know it may be said by some members that the weather is too cold and unpleasant in November. My experience is, that everybody turns out at the presidential elections, and there is no necessity for having two elections so close together every four years, as we will have, if we fix upon October as the month for general elections. I think, if we adopt the amendment I have proposed, that we will save time.

Mr. PARVIN. I am not particular myself, whether these elections are fixed in October or November, but so far as I have conversed with other persons on the subject, they seem to think that the weather in November is too cold and blustering for elections to be held during that month, and that October would be a more suitable month. It was thought by the committee that it was not necessary to have two elections so near every four years. To remedy that, they made provision that on the year of the presidential election the general election should be holden on that day, and they made provision in the last line of the section, that the term of office of the members should commence and end on the day of the Presidential election.

Mr. WINCHESTER. I agree with the gentleman from Wapello, [Mr. Gillaspy,] that all elections should be uniform, and at the same time every year. I think that November is altogether too late a month in the year in which to hold these elections. I reside in a new portion of the State, where it is sparsely settled, and where the election precincts are a great distance apart; and I know, that at the last presidential election there were at least one-fifth of the voters there who did not get to the polls on account of the cold and blustering weather. Some of them lived fifteen and twenty miles from the polls, and rather than encounter the unpleasant weather they remained at home.

Mr. YOUNG. I hope the amendment of the gentleman from Wapello (Mr. Gillaspy) will not prevail. He speaks of his section of country as being in favor of holding the elections in October, the time designated by the constitution for holding all general elections, with the exception of the year of the presidential election. I think it would be bad policy for us to throw the State and presidential election together for the sake of saving the time and expense of holding them. When we have a presidential election I think we ought not to couple any other elections with it. We had experience of the bad policy of such a course in the election of the members of this body. I suppose every member here run right upon the heels of the presidential ticket. As far as I have had any observation, I know that has been universally the case in regard to holding elections in November. I agree with the gentleman from Hardin, [Mr. Winchester], that it is entirely too late to hold our elections in November, for the weather is then cold and unpleasant, and people will not turn out to attend. There is certainly no pleasanter month in the year than October for the purpose of holding elections.

I hope the amendment offered by the gentleman from Hardin [Mr. Winchester] will prevail, and that the amendment offered by the gentleman from Wapello, [Mr. Gillaspy], will be rejected.

Mr. GILLASPY. It may have been the case in the Mahaska district that the geutleman ran upon the heels of his ticket, but that was not the case of myself, in my district; for I ran ahead of the presidential ticket. But I do not know as this has any thing to do with this question. I would be glad if the presidential election were in October. What I desire now is to have the elections uniform once in every two years. When we undertake to be economical, we ought to carry out the principle in every particular. Every election costs the people a large amount and I see no necessity of having a State election in October and a presidential election in November. If we can avoid, by having less frequent elections, the turmoil and excitement always consequent upon them, the better will it be for the people. If we adopt the second Tuesday in November as the time for holding these elections, it will obviate this difficulty to a great extent.

Mr. PALMER. I think this section is well enough as it is. It provides for elections being held on the second Tuesday in October of each year, except the years of the Presidential election, when it is to be held on the day of that election. So far as the term of office is concerned, it is made to commence, in both cases, on the Tuesday after the second Monday in November. There is, therefore, no difficulty upon that point. As to the time, I think it is well enough to have the election in October, where we can do so, and not have two elections come so close together. The objection is a very obvious one to having two elections coming close together every four years, requiring the voters to go, as the gentleman from Hardin [Mr. Winchester] has said, from twenty to twenty-five miles to the place of election, or else lose their votes. It is not likely they would go that distance, if they were called upon to vote twice in a month's time. It would most probably be the case, that on every fourth year, instead of going to our State elections in October—if it is held at that time—they would neglect that and go to the Presidential election as the more important one. They vote for members of the General Assembly oftener, and do not care so much about it as they do about the Presidential election.

I am in favor of having our elections on the second Tuesday in October in those years other than the years of the Presidential election, on account of the weather, and the convenience of our farmers. I believe our farmers then have got through their harvesting, and have no business so urgent as to render it necessary, to any great extent, that they should stay at home and not go to the polls. The weather is so moderate in this State at that time of the year, as not to keep them from the elections on account of the inclemency of the weather. I am opposed to having all the elections on the Tuesday after the first Monday in November, because it will then frequently be, as it was last fall, cold and stormy. It was quite a cold day last fall, and many voters were kept from the polls, so far as my knowledge extends, on account of the severity of the weather.

I am in the situation of the gentleman from Wapello [Mr. Gillaspy], in respect to following upon the heels of the Presidential electors. I ran ahead of the electors in my district, and so I depended not at all upon the influence of the Presidential election for my votes. I was glad to see a pretty full vote upon that occasion, because I wanted a full expression of the opinion of the people. But I believe if the election of delegates to this Convention had come off four weeks before it did, there would have been two thirds, or three fourths more votes cast than there were at the time the election was actually held.

The question recurred upon the motion of Mr. Gillaspy to amend the amendment, and being taken, it was not agreed to.

The question was then taken upon the amendment proposed by Mr. Winchester, and it was not agreed to, upon a division; ayes 3; noes not counted.

Mr. CLARKE, of Henry. I move to amend this section by striking out the words "continue two years from the Tuesday next after the first Monday in November," and insert "commence on the first day of January next succeeding such election, and continue two years;" so that the section will then read—

"The members of the House of Representatives shall be chosen every second year, by the qualified electors of their respective districts, on the second Tuesday in October, except the years of the Presidential election, when the election shall be on the Tuesday next after the first Monday in November; and their term of office shall commence on the first day of January next after their election, and continue two years."

It seems to be a pretty general idea here to have the terms of office of the various officers of this State commence with the year, on the first of January. In some instances it is necessary that officers should have some time after their election in which they can qualify themselves. And when the election is in November, there is not too much time for that purpose before the first of January. I have, therefore, offered this amendment that we may have uniformity in this matter.

Mr. PARVIN. I can see but one objection to the amendment of the gentleman from Henry, [Mr. Clarke,] and that is, that the legislature is to meet on the first Monday in January. The case might arise when the Governor might wish to convene the legislature a month or six weeks sooner than the time fixed in the constitution for their meeting. In that case, if we adopt this constitution, the Governor would have to summon the old members together, they would come to the capitol, be in session a few weeks, and then they would have to give place to the new legislature. This difficulty may never arise, but there is a possibility of it. That is the only objection I can have to the amendment.

Mr. MARVIN. If we adopt the report as it now stands, and have the term of office commence, as it will every fourth year, on the day of election, no one can tell who is elected, because the judges have two days in which to make returns of the election. I am in favor of having the term of office commence some time after the day of election, with the first of December, or the first of January following.

The question being then taken upon the amendment of Mr. Clarke, of Henry, it was agreed to.

No further amendment being offered to this section—

Qualification of Representatives and Senators.

Section four was then read as follows:

"No person shall be a member of the House of Representatives who shall not have attained the age of twenty-one years, be a free white male citizen of the United States, and shall have been an inhabitant of this State one year next preceding his election, and at the time of his election shall have had an actual residence of thirty days in the county or district he may have been chosen to represent."

No amendment being offered to this section—

Section five was read as follows:

"Senators shall be chosen for the term of four years, at the same time and place as Representatives; they shall be twenty-five years of age, and possess the qualifications of Representatives as to residence and citizenship."

Mr. GILLASPY. I move to strike out of the section the word "five," and insert the word "one," so as to make the age for senators twenty-one years instead of twenty-five years. I think the people in the several districts of this State will be perfectly competent to judge of the qualifications of the various candidates for representatives and senators.

The question being then taken upon the amendment, it was not agreed to, upon a division, yeas 10, noes not counted.

No further amendment being offered to this section—

Number of Senators.

Section six was then read as follows:

"The number of Senators shall not be less than one-third, nor more than one-half the Representative body. The present Senators shall remainin office during the term for which they were elected, and shall be divided into two classes. Those Senators whose term of office expires on the first Monday in August, 1858, shall be one class, and those Senators whose term of office expires on the first Monday in August, 1860, shall be the other class; so that one-half shall be chosen every two years."

Mr. YOUNG moved to strike out all but the first sentence, which reads as follows:

"The number of Senators shall not be less than one-third, nor more than one-half the Representative body."

Mr. PARVIN. I would like to hear some reason given for this motion. The section merely provides that the senators shall remain in office during the term of office for which they were elected. The people have elected them to that office, and I think they should be allowed to hold it.

Mr. YOUNG. I suppose that if we frame a constitution here that shall be adopted by the people, we will call a legislature together to act upon it and put it into working operation. One half, at least, of our present senators have served the time for which they were elected. When members of the legislature are elected, they do not expect to serve more than two sessions. One half of our senators, and all the members of the lower house, have served two regular sessions and one extra session.

We have met here for the purpose of amending our Constitution, and bringing new subjects and questions before the people. It appears to me that it would be inconsistent to ask the legislature last elected to come here and act upon what we are now preparing for the people. I think our next legislature should be elected with the express purpose of acting upon the Constitution we may get up here, if it should be adopted. We do not know what may be the position of any individual member of the present legislature upon the matters that are to be presented to them in this Constitution. They were not discussed at the time we elected the last legislature. I know that in my section of the State, when the question of electing the members of the present legislature was before the people, there was a universal opinion that the senator then elected in our county, would hold office only until the adoption of the Constitution as amended by this Constiuttion. It is for that reason that I have made this motion to strike out.

I want this Constitution to go into operation with a new legislature. I want to give the people an opportunity to elect a new legislature to carry out the principles and views contained in their new Constitution.

Mr. TRAER. I am rather in favor of this amendment, for this reason: so far as I am individually concerned, I am opposed to interfering with the legislature; but my motives for voting for this amendment arise from the fact that I consider this portion of the section unnecessary. Under the present arrangement our senators are already qualified, and will continue so, provided we elect them at the end of two years. Section seven provides, in case of an increase in the number of senators, how they shall be classified and arranged. I think, therefore, it is unnecessary to have this matter in the Convention at all. Farther than that, if we should pursue any course here interfering with the present legislature, or with the senate only, and it becomes necessary to classify them, we can provide for that in the schedule. I am opposed to putting anything in the Constitution unless it is necessary to have it there. However, I am not very particular about this matter. But I shall vote for this amendment for the reason I have given. I have given these reasons because, as a member of the committee who made this report, if I vote against any portion of it, I desire to state my reasons for doing so.

The question being taken upon the amendment of Mr. Young, it was agreed to, upon a division, as follows: ayes 15, noes 13.

No farther amendment being offered to this section—

Classification of Senators.

Section seven was then read as follows:

"When the number of senators is increased, they shall be annexed by lot to one of the two classes, so as to keep them as nearly equal in number as practicable."

Mr. CLARKE, of Henry. I would suggest to gentlemen who have commenced the work of amendment, that they better go on and complete it with this section.

Mr. HALL. I would move that the sixth section be amended so as to correspond with the sixth section of the old Constitution, which reads as follows:

"The number of senators shall not be less than one-third, nor more than one-half the representative body; and at the first session of the General Assembly, after this Constitution takes effect, the senators shall be divided by lot, as equally as may be, into two classes; the seats of the senators of the first class shall be vacated at the expiration of the second year, so that one-half shall be chosen every two years."

Mr. PARVIN. I do not wish to be troublesome, but I think the gentleman from Benton, [Mr. Traer,] will see the necessity for something like what the committee reported. He said he voted to strike out the latter part of the sixth section of the committee's report, because he could not see the necessity of it. If it was the intention of the Convention that all of the senate shall be elected to the next legislature, then the amendment for which the gentleman voted was necessary. They are classified under the old Constitution; but that will be done away if this is adopted. There is certainly a necessity for their classification being provided for here.

I was a little surprised to hear the remarks of the gentleman from Benton, because I think there was a necessity for the classification that was provided for in the section that has been amended, because there must be a classification of some kind. If the convention intended that these senators should be legislated out of office, then the provision for classification was necessary; if they did not intend that, then it was equally necessary to provide for some kind of classification. I have yet to learn that the convention is decided in regard to turning out of office our present senators.

Mr. PALMER. I think the committee of the whole have decided that question by striking out the latter part of the sixth section of the committee's report. There have been several modes suggested to meet the difficulty presented to us. I think the best way would be to insert the following before the seventh section:

"The senators shall be so classified by lot that one-half shall be chosen every two years."

The section will then read:

"The senators shall be so classified by lot that one-half shall be chosen every two years. When the number of senators is increased, they shall be annexed by lot to one of the two classes, so as to keep them as nearly equal as practicable."

If the gentleman from Des Moines, [Mr. Hall] will withdraw his proposed amendment, I will offer the one I have indicated.

Mr. HALL. I will withdraw my amendment and accept the one suggested by the gentleman from Davis, [Mr. Palmer.]

The question was upon the amendment of Mr. Palmer, as above stated.

Mr. TRAER. I desire to say that I was under the impression when I voted to strike out the latter part of section six—and I see no difficulty in the way yet—that it was unnecessary to have anything in the constitution, in this part of it at least, in regard to the classification of senators. In the first place, if we see proper to continue the present senators, they are already classified, they need no classification hereafter, no division by lot.

The gentleman from Davis, [Mr. Palmer,] seems to think that that vote was equivalent to a vote deciding that the whole senate shall be legislated out of office. I beg to differ with the gentleman upon that point. I state distinctly that, though voting for that amendment, I am in favor of retaining the present senators in office, and they shall remain there, so far as my vote is concerned. I voted with the majority upon that amendment, and the conclusion of the gentleman from Davis is not therefore correctly drawn from the premises. If we do vote hereafter to legislate the present senators out of office, then we can re-district the State and regulate this matter in the schedule, where it properly belongs. I saw no particular necessity for having it in here, and for that reason I voted for striking it out.

The gentleman from Appanoose, [Mr. Harris,] wishes to hear some reason why the present senate should not be legislated out of office. I do not consider that that question comes up properly in this place, and therefore I do not see fit to offer any argument at this time upon that subject. I think, however, there can be arguments offered, at least to satisfy my mind. I think there is no good reason for legislating any body out of office. I do not think the people expected it, and so far as I am concerned, I shall vote against it.

Mr. HALL. It would be a strange state of public sentiment for the people to call a convention to alter and amend their constitution, and send their delegates here to produce radical and material changes in their present constitution, and then have a legislature, elected long before the constitutional delegates were, to become the organ to carry out the new constitution. That is what no man would do in his private business. He would not employ a person to perform duties before he knew what the duties were that the person would have to perform. And I must have very conclusive evidence presented to me, before I shall believe that the people of this State expected or desired that the legislature, which was chosen long before the delegates to this convention, should be the instrument by which the new legislation should be brought forward, which the changes in our constitution would require. Such a state of things would be something irregular and unnatural.

I believe the people desire and wish to have an opportunity of selecting their public servants, those individuals who are to come up here and carry out the new principles and the new policy contained in this new constitution. They should have an opportunity to send a legislature up here fresh from their midst. If they were capable of selecting the legislature they had before, they are capable of selecting the legislature that is to come after us. It is not going to put the public to any additional expense or cost. It is merely giving the people the privilege of sending such persons to represent them, in carrying out these changes and amendments in their constitution, as they may desire to have charge of that business.

I am willing to allow the people to do that. I I do not wish to place any restriction upon the people in this respect.

The gentleman from Muscatine [Mr. Parvin] said that it would be unconstitutional to legislate them out of office.

Mr. PARVIN. The gentleman is mistaken: I said no such thing.

Mr. HALL. I may have misunderstood the gentleman; but I am not mistaken in supposing that there have been some views to that effect thrown out here. Now, the instrument we are framing is itself to be the constitution, and nothing done under it, and in pursuance of its provisions, if it is adopted, will be unconstitutional. If it is not adopted, then it will only be so much waste paper.

Why should we keep the present legislature in office? Can gentlemen answer that question, and give one sound reason why it should be done? Why should we not have a new legislature under this constitution? Will the people send persons here to represent them any less ably than those they last elected to the legislature? Will not persons be selected with reference to the new duties this constitution will impose upon them? If not, why? There must be some reason why we would not have this privilege, if it is not to be had.

I insist that this right belongs to the people, and they should have it.

Mr. SCOTT. I would inquire of the gentleman from Des Moines (Mr. Hall) if he is in favor of having the supreme judges also ousted out of office, and have others elected at a new election?

Mr. HALL. I stated plainly when the subject was up before this convention, that if we should decide here that that right had been improperly kept from the people for ten years past, I was in favor of giving it to them as soon as possible. And when the people are to select their agents, the sooner they do so the better. The people choose their representatives under this new constitution, at every new election. One half of the senate is thrown back to the people at every election. Why should we retain one-half of the present senate over one election? This power has never been abused or injured under the old constitution. It is better, the more frequently we can get the voice of the people in regard to any subject in which they can feel an interest. Gentlemen get up here, and seek instructions from their constituents, for the purpose of learning the will of the people and obeying it, and no voice is considered so potent and powerful as the voice of the people, the voice which comes through the ballot box. I would refer all the power we can to the people, and let them have a voice in choosing all their public servants, as soon as possible.

Mr. TRAER. I certainly can see no particular force in the argument, and the only one offered here in regard to ousting the present Legislature, and that is, that we should refer the Legislature back to the people, that they may elect men with reference to the principles to be contained in this Constitution, and the measures to be carried out under it. It appears to me that the men who compose our present Legislature will be just as likely to understand the wishes of their constituents, and of the people generally, as any other body of men that could be elected. What men will compose the new Legislature, if we pursue the course contended for here? Will they not be men of the same stamp with those who compose the present Legislature? Will they have any better opportunity to understand the feelings and wishes of their constituents than those who have been already elected? The Legislature that met here this winter can read this Constitution, consult their constituencies, and learn their wishes just as well as those who may be elected by the people after going through the ordeal of a new election. That argument has, therefore, no weight with me.

I understand very well all this argument of "the dear people;" all this talk about placing power in the hands of the people. I understand all this thing very well. I have heard it ever since I was a boy, and I have always found that in nine cases out of ten it was all sheer buncombe. I am as much in favor of giving, under this Constitution, all necessary power to the people as the gentleman from Des Moines [Mr. Hall] can be. I believe my love for "the dear people" extends quite as far as his does. But I can see no good logic in this argument of legislating men out of office, because if we do not, the gentleman from Des Moines, myself, and others, will not get a seat in the Legislature. I say that I will go as far to give power to the people as my judgment dictates, and the wishes of my constituents, heretofore expressed, may justify. But I shall vote against doing anything of the kind urged here, and I believe that in doing so I shall carry out the wishes and desires of the majority of those I represent here. I am willing to meet the responsibility in that particular. If I go wrong, I shall have to answer for it.

For these reasons I shall vote just as I have already indicated. If there are other arguments against my position—arguments of sufficient weight to change my mind—I shall probably have honesty enough to acknowledge that fact here, and vote in some other way. But with my present light, I shall vote as I have said.

Mr. HARRIS. I do not intend to raise an issue with any gentleman with regard to the patriotism, the wisdom, or the integrity of the Legislature which has just adjourned from this city. But as it appears to be a matter of some consequence to know whether that Legislature would be just as capable as any other, I can refer the gentleman to the opinion of Governor Grimes in regard to that Legislature. I believe he was under the necessity of interposing, in many instances, in reference to their doings here. I would, therefore, refer the gentleman to his Excellency in regard to that Legislature.

The gentleman says—not in precisely so many words, but it amounted to the same thing—that this making an appeal to the people, this referring this matter to the people, is all buncombe; and that it is got up here for nothing but buncombe. If he thinks so, then he can take the position of not only continuing in office the Legislature, but all the rest of the officers of this State, for life. We hold that all officers should be frequently elected by the people, and that there should be no interposition between the people and their servants to prevent them from reviewing their conduct when they see proper. I say that that is the principle of our government. And the only question to be decided here is, whether we are willing to let this matter go back to the people, or interpose between them and those they may desire to select to sustain and put in operation what we may do here.

The gentleman says he is willing to take the responsibility. He can do so, if he desires, and continue the present Legislature in office. But I wish to tell that gentleman, and other gentlemen here, that I should not wish to bear that responsibility before my constituents. And I apprehend that when this matter comes to be discussed before the people of this State, there will be a more weighty responsibility attached to it than gentlemen here seem to be aware of.

Gentlemen ask us with an air of triumph,—Would you put the supreme judges out of office? I say, yes, I would; and that, too, just as quickly as I would any other officers. I do not hold the supreme judges to be any more sacred, or farther above the people and the ballot box, than any other officers. If they have discharged their duties and met their responsibilities properly, and in a manner that the people expected of them, then they have nothing to fear. If they have not, I ask what responsibility they expect to get clear of by holding on to their power a while longer? They must some time pass in review before the people, and will not be adjudged more favorably on account of time.

Mr. SCOTT. The gentleman from Appanoose [Mr. Harris] has seen fit to represent that I have *interrogated the gentleman from Des Moines* [Mr. Hall] with an air of arrogance.

Mr. HARRIS. I did not say arrogance.

Mr. SCOTT. Well: with an air of triumph. Perhaps it might have been with an air of triumph that I interrogated the gentleman from Des Moines (Mr. Hall), and if I mistake not, the gentleman from Des Moines offered good and cogent reasons why the supreme judges should be kept in office. I suppose they were good and well taken, and well grounded. I have no issue with the gentleman from Appanoose [Mr. Harris], but I wished to know if the gentleman from Des Moines (Mr. Hall) had changed his opinions in regard to this matter. I do not know that the gentleman from Appanoose did say that the supreme judges should be kept in office. But I am confident, though I may be mistaken, that the gentleman from Des Moines offered good and cogent reasons why they should be permitted to remain in office; and the same reasons will apply to members of the legislature. They have been elected for a specific term, and they should not be thrown out until that specific term has been fulfilled. I mean that they cannot honestly and morally be turned out.

Perhaps it was with an air of triumph that I asked the gentleman from Des Moines if he had changed his opinions upon that point in five or six days. He urged good reasons the other day on the one side, and he can offer no better on the other side to-day. I only asked for information. I wished to know if he had changed his views.

Mr. HARRIS. Is the gentleman in favor of districting the State into judicial districts?

Mr. SCOTT. I have told the gentleman already, that I have not investigated that matter.

Mr. HARRIS. I understood the gentleman from Des Moines (Mr. Hall) to say positively, the other day, that he was in favor of turning out the supreme judges.

Mr. PARVIN. I have listened all this time to hear some good reason for turning these officers out of office. As I wish to keep them in office, I desire to give my reasons very briefly. I think the gentleman from Des Moines (Mr. Hall) must either consider that the present legislature are incompetent to act under this new constitution, or that they are dishonest and will not do as well as others would. No other reason, I think, could be drawn from his argument. If this convention fixes the constitution as the gentleman from Des Moines argues, they must provide for new men to act under it, and put it into operation. And yet those men who elected the delegates to this convention, elected but a short time before, members of the legislature; and those men, I think, are as well qualified to act justly and understandingly as would be others more recently elected.

The people elected them for a definite period of time, under a constitution then and now in force. That constitution may be done away with by the institution of the one we are now framing; but they elected those members under that *constitution, as they had been doing for the last* ten years. These men, having been elected for a definite period of time, have the right to remain in office during the term for which they were elected. We are not providing a constitution for a new tribe, or a new race of men, but for the same class of people that the present legislature were elected to represent. When we are asked to turn out all the officers that the people have elected, and send them back to the people, I am afraid of the responsibility. But I am not afraid to carry out the wishes of those who sent me here. The present legislature is the very body that ought to carry out this new constitution. It was elected just before the present convention was elected. Let us not take the responsibility of saying here that the people last August did not know whom they wanted for their representatives, and that they know better to-day. We might just as well put in the constitution that representatives shall be elected every six months.

It is said that we are taking power from the people. I say we would be taking power from the people, if we were to say here that what they did last August shall be undone. I am opposed to doing that, because I think the men elected last August are just as competent as any we can get now. I feel that they are just as honest and faithful as new men would be. I believe the people want them to remain in office, and I do not want them to have the trouble of electing them over again. I do not think we have any right to devolve that trouble back upon the people, and make them do the work over that they did last August. The responsibility is in putting them in, and not in keeping them in.

Mr. GILLASPY. I concur with the gentleman from Mahaska, [Mr. Young,] when he said that the universal opinion was, that when they elected the senators, they would go out of office when this new constitution was adopted. That was the opinion in my county, that in the event a new constitution should be made and adopted, the representatives then elected should only serve until that constitution was adopted.

I believe the gentleman from Benton [Mr. Traer,] will not certainly charge me with desiring to come here to the legislature. But I know that the people of my region of the State expect that the present members of the legislature will go out of office, and that we will begin anew with the new constitution. And I know farther, that some of the supreme judges expect the same thing with regard to themselves. And I know the Governor expects it himself. I believe the people are just as competent to elect representatives now as they were last August. And I would be perfectly willing that our members of the senate and of the house of representatives shall be again sent back to the people. And I shall endeavor by every action of mine here to discharge honestly my duty to my constituents. Hence I support the amendment of the gentleman from Mahaska, [Mr. Young.]

Mr. TRAER. I wish to say in answer to my friend from Wapello, [Mr. Gillaspy,] that I suppose if I had charged him with the desire to get into the legislature, he might have had some ground of complaint. I certainly did not charge that upon him, or any gentleman here, but only said that it was one reason that would be assigned for making this change in regard to our present legislature. The gentleman says he has never been a candidate for the legislature. And for a very good reason; he has been in more profitable business, ever since I have been in the State.

Now I wish to say in regard to this question, which has been discussed here, that I understood, when I was elected as a delegate to this convention, that I was to come here, not for the purpose of framing a new constitution for the State of Iowa, or to legislate the present general assembly out of office, or legislate any of the State officers out of office; but we were to meet here to make a few important changes in the constitution, then adjourn, and go home. So far as my constituents are concerned, I do not believe that one of them, whether democrat or republican, expected that any such change as this would be made. And I hold that the proper course for this convention to have persued was to have made these changes, and have gone home before this time.

Gentlemen have been talking to us for three or four days back about the probabilities of a tremendous public sentiment being manufactured out of the length of the time this convention has been in session. And I do not know but what there has been some buncombe manufactured out of that. But at the very time they are talking about getting through in a few days more, they are hatching up measures that will keep us here six weeks, if they are persisted in, bringing up questions that will cause as much excitement and discussion as any that can come before us.

I am in favor of making a few necessary and prominent changes in the constitution. For instance, I am in favor of one concerning incorporations, and pernaps one in the article upon the judiciary, making the judges elective by the people. These, and perhaps a few other amendments, I undertake to say, were all that was expected of us, and looked for by the people.

And as to my taking the responsibility upon me to vote a certain way, I believe that if I vote as I have indicated, I shall go home with less responsibility than will the gentleman from Appanoose, [Mr. Harris,] if he votes for turning every man out of office, getting ready himself, perhaps, to accept office.

Mr. HARRIS. Is the gentleman in favor of keeping in office the members of the House as well as of the Senate?

Mr. TRAER. I think I expressed myself plainly and distinctly upon that question.

Mr. HARRIS, I think I understood the gentleman to say, in regard to this matter of apportionment in this constitution, that he was in favor of a new apportionment.

Mr. GOWER. I agree with the gentleman from Benton, [Mr. Traer,] that we were sent here to make but few changes in the constitution, and not to meddle with those officers the people have elected. I see by the old constitution, that it is provided that—

"The members of the House of Representatives shall be chosen every second year, by the qualified electors of their respective districts, on the first Monday in August, whose term of office shall continue two years from the day of the general election."

It does not go on and say, "or until this Constitution is changed," but that their "term of office *shall continue* two years from the day of the general election." There was nothing in the act calling us together here, that I know of, that authorizes us to meddle with that matter at all. Nor do I know that there is anything in our office that would justify us in doing so. And when I was at home, no longer ago than last Saturday, the matter was spoken of there, and there was an expression of a wish that this thing should not be done; and I myself hope it will not be done.

Mr. YOUNG. It does seem to me, from the position taken by some gentlemen here, that we are not to have a legislature to act expressly with reference to this Constitution, if we get up one that the people will adopt. Gentlemen argue here that we have no right to interfere with the present legislature at all, because they were elected by the people. That may be very good doctrine. But carry it out, and see where it will lead us. We will have no right to change the time of the meeting of the legislature. If we are to retain the present members of the legislature in office, we must let them go on in their regular course in office.

My opinion, when I came here, was, that we would make a constitution, submit it to the people, and after its adoption we must, as a matter of course, have some legislation before any important changes in the Constitution could be carried into effect. According to the argument of some gentlemen here, we cannot carry this Constitution into effect before two years from this winter, unless the Governor shall call an extra session of the legislature. I do not think that is what the people expect, but that we will have a session of the legislature provided for here sooner than that. If we do not have a session until two years from this winter, we must then have a legislature. I do think it would be folly to retain the present legislature.

I do not believe the legislature are as corrupt and dishonest as some gentlemen have endeavored to represent them here. If I believed so, I would go for having no legislature at all. But I believe that the legislature, as a general thing, are composed of honest men, and that our last legislature was as honest as any. Still, I do not think they are as prepared to act upon the amendments which this Convention may make to our Constitution, as men elected directly with reference to the questions brought before the people upon the adoption of this Constitution.

I have no doubt in my own mind that two kinds of banking will be permitted by the constitution. That appears to be the general impression here. And the members of the legislature should come up here with an expression from the people as to what kind of banking system they desire. I think the nearer we get to the people the better. I do not think there is any inconsistency in throwing out the present legislature. There is no similarity between the State officers and the supreme judges and the members of the legislature. The members of the legislature are intended to make laws, and the State officers to carry them out.

Mr. EDWARDS. I am opposed to ousting the present members of the General Assembly for this reason: If we adopt a provision in the constitution to oust the present legislature, then we must provide here to district the State for senatorial and representative purposes. I am opposed to incorporating any such matters into the constitution, for the reason, that if we send a constitution to the people, and they ratify it, it is to be presumed that it will remain for many years the fundamental law of the State.

Now our State is continually changing in respect to population, wealth, and the developement of its resources. If we were to district the State for senatorial and representative purposes, in this constitution, it would have to stand as long as the constitution stands. Now, districts that are at present sparsely settled will probably, in the course of a few years, become filled with a dense population, and there should be a new districting of the State.

The gentleman from Des Moines (Mr. Hall) has said a great deal in regard to the "dear people," in regard to giving the power to the people to elect a new set of men to the legislature. Now, the "dear people" elected, only last summer, these men to the legislature; and if we legislate them out of office, the same people will elect the same men, or the same number of men, and send them back again. It was but the last August that the people exercised this power, and the gentleman would have them do it again next year.

I must say that I was amused at the position taken by the gentleman, when I thought of the lecture that he read to us at the commencement of our sessions here, when he said that the people expected us to make but one or two changes in the constitution. Now we find him pressing as many innovations upon the constitution as any other member upon this floor. And when we come to compare notes, we will find that he has said a great deal about our having to stay here so long. Now, what is "sauce for the goose is sauce for the gander," and if the gentleman is right in his cry about sending the legislature back to the people, the gentleman has certainly occupied a different position heretofore in opposing innovations upon the constitution.

Mr. HALL. I do not know whether I am to impute the remarks of members in this committee to defective memories, or to indifference to what they may say. No man was ever so completely mistaken as the gentleman from Clayton, [Mr. Scott.] He could not have listened at all to what I said the other day, or his recollection must go my contraries. The gentleman from Benton, [Mr. Traer,] seems to think that my action here is governed by some expected laurels that I may win by being a member of the next legislature. He is as much mistaken as the gentleman from Clayton.

I do not like this kind of flings at the motives of gentlemen. Their positions should be met with at least something like argument. I looked at this matter, as I thought, in a philosophic point of view, in that point of view in which it would be looked upon, had not gentlemen some secret, hidden, concealed motives in this matter. If they acted as they talked, then they would act as I propose to do.

We are forming a constitution; a fundamental law of the land; what I would term the higher law of government for the people. We find that the people have become dissatisfied with their present constitution, and have sent us here for the purpose of revising and amending it. There is no rule in that constitution to control our action here. We expect to frame an instrument that will be equal, that when adopted by the people, will be the creation and establishment of a new code, if I may so term it, which will institute a new form of government, in many particulars. Gentlemen concede that radical changes must be made by us here, and thost changes must affect the people. And because I have said so, and because it is true, gentlemen taunt me with having been a mere buncombe talker in reference to "the dear people." Now if there is weight in my opinion, if there is reality and substance that we cannot fail to act upon, then I claim that it is not a mere *ad captandum* argument, thrown out for the purpose of catching the public mind.

Those officers whom gentlemen want to execute the new powers and duties created under this constitution, will owe their authority to the instrument under which we are acting; they do not get their authority from the power under which they will be acting; they were not elected under the instrument which we propose to submit to the people. In reference to that the gentleman from Benton says that it was the general understanding in his district that the members elected in August last were to act under the constitution we might frame here. Now his constituency may have the sagacity and foresight to understand beforehand what this convention would do, and act with reference to what might be done here. My constituents were not so wise as that, and could not tell what the result of our deliberations here would be. They did not know what new duties would be imposed upon the legislature, and they did not take for granted that their representatives were so wise, that they could be trusted to do what they pleased.

The proposition I submit is this: that as we are forming, as it were, a new government, a new organic law, changing our old form of government in vital points in which the people are interested, we should open the door to the people to send persons to the legislature that would represent their views and opinions upon these points. Gentlemen say that the present legislature are good enough, and wise enough, and will do what is right. I have no desire to take issue with gentlemen upon that point; it is not for me to decide that; I wish to be excused from deciding that question. If the people are satisfied that such is the case, then they can return them. If not, then I do not wish to prevent them from electing others.

Is it mere demagoguism, mere buncombe, for me to stand up here and say that the people of Des Moines county, or any other county in this State, when this constitution shall have been submitted to them, and they shall have adopted it, should have the privilege of selecting their agents to meet at their capitol to carry out the new principles we may have introduced into their organic law? Is that demagoguism, *ad captandum* argument, buncombe? If so, then I have lived a long time to very little purpose, so far as knowing what an appeal to the people means. This is one of the vital principles belonging to our government.

Gentlemen say to the people that they—the people—are satisfied with their representatives; they assume that they are wholly and entirely satisfied with the representatives they have already chosen. Perhaps gentlemen can say that they will be satisfied with them for four, six, or even eight years to come, for they will probably get no worse during that time, and will be as good as they are now. You propose to make this Legislature the representative of the people by virtue of this Constitution; you keep them in power by virtue of our action here, not as the true representatives of the people, but as the appointees of this Convention. That is the position gentlemen take here. They will keep alive those officials who would otherwise cease to exist, because they assume that the people want them to do so. They ask us to legislate authority into this Constitution that shall put vitality into these officers who would otherwise cease to exist; and when, if we did not do so, the people would have an opportunity of sending up here other representatives under this very Constitution we are now framing.

Gentlemen may think this is carrying their argument too far, but to my mind it is not. I think there must be something not yet spoken of, which leads gentlemen to be so strongly positive with regard to the great satisfaction it would give the people to have their present Legislature continued in office under the new Constitution.

Mr. TRAER. I do not wish to make another speech upon this question. But I wish to relieve, if I can, the mind of the gentleman from Des Moines, [Mr. Hall] in reference to this matter. I think the gentleman has drawn inferences that are not warranted at all. He says, that by not legislating the present General Assembly out of office, we will make them nothing more nor less than our appointees. Now, I have a great deal of confidence in the experience, ability, integrity, and all that, of the gentleman from Des Moines; but I cannot come to any such conclusion as he has drawn.

I ask the gentleman from Des Moines if the people did not elect these men to serve for such a length of time? Did not the Constitution under which we are acting, provide that these men should hold their office for a certain term? Now the position I have taken is to leave them to fill out that term. We do not propose to say that they should hold office for four or six years. The people did not send us here to legislate out of office the men they have put in office. We were sent here to make certain amendments, and after we have made those amendments to the Constitution we were sent here to make, I am in favor of going home.

Mr. HALL. Will these men hold their places under the old Constitution, or the new one?

Mr. TRAER. Under the new one, if it is adopted; under the old one, if the new one is rejected.

Mr. HALL. Will they have been elected under the old or the new Constitution?

Mr. TRAER. Suppose we do not change the old Constitution at all in this respect, but leave it as it is now, will there be any change?

Mr. HALL. Certainly not.

Mr. TRAER. Then they will hold their power under the same principle under which they were elected, whether you call it the new or the old Constitution.

The next position the gentleman takes, is, that my constituency must be very sagacious, and all that. I say to the gentleman, that last year, when the question was presented whether we should have a Constitutional Convention or not, this question was canvassed. The question was put to the candidate for Senator—"In case you are elected to the Senate, and the new Constitution permits a general banking system, are you in favor of that system?" That question was asked all the candidates; and I suppose they were elected to carry out those principles. Therefore, I am not in favor of turning them out of office. The people do not expect us to so, but to carry out other purposes, which they did have in view when they sent us here, and then go home.

So far as the gentleman's classical quotations are concerned, I do not know as I should be able to answer them, if I should try. I do not know as they have any place in this constitution, or anything to do with it, or that they will have anything to do with it, even if we amend it.

Mr. HARRIS. I would ask the gentleman this question; if the present legislature is continued in office, will not questions come up before them for them to legislate upon, that were not expected to come up before them when they were elected?

Mr. TRAER. I am willing to grant that. But those representatives are going home right among the people; and I would ask, will not they be as well informed of the wishes of the people, as any men that could be elected.?

Mr. HARRIS. They may be informed; but there may be a possibility that the opinions of the representatives, and the opinions of the majority of the people, may not be the same with regard to what they may have to do under this constitution.

Mr. TRAER. So far as I am concerned, and so I believe it is with the republican party, we are in favor of following instructions. And when they are instructed to go for a certain measure, they will obey those instructions, be it for a certain kind of banking law, or anything else.

Mr. JOHNSTON. I wish to make a few remarks upon this question. The question before the committee is not really the one that has been discussed. All the discussion is upon the amendment of the gentleman from Mahaska, [Mr. Young,] which was adopted some time since. I will, however, in this place, say one word in regard to my position as a member of the committee that made the report now under consideration.

At the time this subject was being considered by the committee, I felt perfectly indifferent about it; and I do yet. I have very little feeling upon the subject, either one way or the other. I acceded to the wishes of the majority to have this section put in here. But seeing a desire upon the part of some gentlemen here to have it stricken out, I had no objection to that being done. There are some reasons to be given for both sides of the question. That which influenced the committee, to a great extent, was the fact that it was important, after the adoption of this constitution, to have some persons of experience, and who knew something, not only about the rules of legislation, but of the affairs of the State. It was considered that they were the proper persons to come in and assist in carrying out the provisions of this constitution. That argument had great weight with members of the committee, and with myself.

On the other hand there was another argument equally strong, probably a little stronger, in favor of having new persons elected. The argument was simply this; that questions would be presented by this very committee to the people of the State, which did not arise at the time these last senators were chosen. Take, for instance, this question of a banking law. We do not propose to go into the details of a banking law in this constitution. We propose to merely incorporate here the general outlines of a system, perhaps not even that; perhaps only authorize the legislature to pass a banking law creating banks in this State. It may be very important to the people of this State to know for whom to vote to represent them in ihe next legislature.

There is another important question, in addition to this question of banking; and that is the question of county indebtedness. If the article on incorporations goes into the constitution, and is submitted to the people of this State, as it passed the committee of the whole, leaving that subject entirely open to the people, it may be very important for the people to know the views of senators in regard to that question, whether they are in favor of prohibiting or recognizing their right to vote loans to these corporations for purposes of internal improvement.

I merely refer to these matters to show that it is important, after all that has been said, to have a new set of men brought forward to assist in carrying out this new constitution. So far as I am personally concerned, it is a matter of no consequence to me, or to the people of my district. Those men who would be legislated out of office by this measure are my personal friends; but that matters not. I think the people should have the right, and the opportunity of voting for new men, when these new questions are to be presented to the legislature for consideration.

Mr. CLARKE, of Johnson, moved that the committee rise, report progress, and ask leave to sit again, which was agreed to.

In Convention.

The PRESIDENT having resumed the chair,

The CHAIRMAN reported that the Committee of the Whole had had under consideration the subject referred to them, had made some progress therein, and had instructed him to ask leave of the convention to sit again.

The report of the committee of the whole was received, and leave granted accordingly.

On motion of Mr. HARRIS,

The convention then adjourned until to-morrow morning at nine o'clock.

TUESDAY, February 17th, 1857.

The Convention met at 9 o'clock, A. M., and was called to order by the President.

Prayer by the Chaplain.

The journal of yesterday was read and approved.

The PRESIDENT announced the names of the following gentlemen as members of the Committee on Revision, Engrossment and Enrollment: Messrs. Clarke of Henry, Johnston and Wilson.

Legislative Department.

The PRESIDENT. The regular order of business is the further consideration, in Committee of the Whole, of the report of the Committee on the Legislative Department.

Committee of the Whole.

The CONVENTION then resolved itself into Committee of the Whole, (Mr. Patterson in the chair) upon the report of the Committee on the Legislative Department.

Classification of Senators.

The CHAIRMAN. The question pending when the Committee last rose was upon the amendment proposed by the gentleman from Davis [Mr. Palmer], to come in before the seventh section, so that the section as amended will read—

"The senators shall be so classified by lot, that one-half shall be chosen every two years; and when the number of senators is increased, they shall be annexed, by lot, to one of the two classes, so as to keep them as nearly equal as practicable."

The question was taken, and it was agreed to upon division; ayes 16, noes not counted.

There being no further amendments offered to that section,

Powers and Duties of the House.

Section eight was then read, as follows:

"Each house shall choose its own officers, and judge of the qualification, election, and return of its own members. A contested election shall be determined in such manner as shall be directed by law."

There being no amendments offered to this section,

Section nine was then read, as follows:

"A majority of each house shall constitute a quorum to do business; but a smaller number may adjourn from day to day, and may compel the attendance of absent members in such manner and under such penalties as each house may provide."

There being no amendments offered to this section,

Section ten was then read, as follows:

"Each house shall sit upon its own adjournments, keep a journal of its proceedings, and publish the same; determine the rules of its proceedings, punish members for disorderly behavior, and, with the consent of two-thirds, expel a member, but not a second time for the same offense; and shall have all other powers necessary for a branch of the General Assembly of a free and independent State."

There being no amendment offered to this section,

Section eleven was then read, as follows:

"Every member of the General Assembly shall have the liberty to dissent from or protest against any act or resolution which he may think injurious to the public or an individual, and have the reasons for his dissent entered on the journals; and the yeas and nays of the members of either house, on any question, shall, at the desire of any two members present, be entered on the journals."

There being no amendments offered to the eleventh section,

Privilege from Arrest.

Section twelve was then read, as follows:

"Senators and representatives, in all cases, except treason, felony, or breach of the peace, shall be privileged from arrest during the session of the General Assembly, and in going to and returning from the same."

There being no amendments offered to this section.

Vacancies.

Section thirteen was then read, as follows:

"When vacancies occur in either house, the Governor, or the person exercising the functions of Governor, shall issue writs of election to fill such vacancies."

There being no amendments offered to this section,

Public and Secret Sessions.

Section fourteen was then read, as follows:

"The doors of each House shall be open, except on such occasions as, in the opinion of the House, may require secresy."

There being no amendments offered to this section,

Adjournment Over.

Section fifteen was then read, as follows:

"Neither House shall, without the consent of the other, adjourn for more than three days, nor to any other place than that in which they may be sitting."

No amendments being offered to that section,

Introduction and passage of Bills.

Section sixteen was then read, as follows:

"Bills may originate in either House, and may be altered, amended, or rejected by the other; and every bill, having passed both houses, shall be signed by the Speaker and President of their respective houses."

There being no amendments offered to the sixteenth section—

Veto.

Section seventeen was then read as follows:

"Every bill which shall have passed the General Assembly, shall, before it becomes a law, be presented to the Governor. If he approve, he shall sign it; but if not, he shall return it with his objections, to the House in which it originated, which shall enter the same upon the journal and proceed to reconsider it; if, after such reconsideration, it again pass both Houses, by yeas and nays, by a majority of two-thirds of the members of each House present, it shall become a law, notwithstanding the Governor's objections. If any bill shall not be returned within three days after it shall have been presented to him, Sunday excepted, the same shall be a law in like manner as if he had signed it, unless the General Assembly, by adjournment, prevent such return."

Mr. GOWER. I have for some time thought that the requisition of a vote of two-thirds of the General Assembly to pass a law over a veto was of questionable propriety. I have heard the subject spoken of very frequently, and I have heard much complaint of the power which the President has in the general government, of exercising the veto power. I wish to offer an amendment, that it shall require seven-twelfths instead of two-thirds, to pass a law over the Governor's veto.

Mr. MARVIN. I would make the motion that a majority of all the members shall be required to pass a law over the Governor's veto.

Mr. CLARKE, of Johnson. I would second the motion in a little different shape. I would prefer a motion in this form. I wish to strike out the words "two-thirds," and insert "present," so that it would read, "if after such consideration it again pass both Houses, by yeas and nays, by a majority of the members of each House present," &c.

I desire to say upon this subject that I have never been favorable to the exercise of this veto power. I regard it as anti-republican in its character, and yet I admit that there is some force in the argument, that this veto power has done some good, though it has done much harm.

The only advantage, it seems to me, that there is in the exercise of this power, is to again call the attention of the legislature to the bill upon which this power has been exercised, thereby giving them an opportunity for reflection and reconsideration, if they have been hasty in their action. It appears to me, if after such reflection and reconsideration, they shall still be of the opinion that it is for the interests of the people that the bill should pass, then the legislature, as the agents of the people, ought to have the power to pass it. If there is anything flagrant in an act which is thus vetoed, after the reasons of the Governor are given for his veto, if the legislature possess the ordinary judgment and prudence of men, they will consider those objections, and will come to a conclusion as to whether they are well founded or not. I move to strike out the words "two-thirds" and insert "present," so that it will require a majority of the "members of each house present," to pass a law over the Governor's veto.

Mr. PARVIN. I have no wish to enter upon a discussion of the propriety of the proposed amendment. I only rose to say that after the committee had fully considered this matter, they came to the conclusion that they could not do better than adopt the section, upon this subject, as it stands in the present constitution. I consider that there is no danger in the exercise of this veto power, and that it is a safe and salutary restriction upon the hasty action of the legislature. I think the gentleman who offered this amendment will concede that the exercise of this power was a benefit to his constituents the last winter. It was exercised several times, and I have not yet heard much complaint of its exercise. It is a subject which has attracted public attention in every State in the Union, and for which provision has been made in the constitutions of all the States. After looking at the subject in all its phases, the committee came to the conclusion that they could adopt no better plan than that of adhering to the provision upon this subject in the present constitution, which they considered to be a safe and salutary restriction upon hasty and inconsiderate legislation.

Mr. HARRIS. I would ask what motion is really before the committee? There have been three different motions made.

The CHAIRMAN. Two of them were not seconded, and the motion now before the committee is that made by the gentleman from Johnson, [Mr. Clarke.]

Mr. HARRIS. I hope that will not prevail, and I hope the provision upon this subject will remain just as it stands in the present constitution. I know that a great deal has been said about its being anti-democratic and anti-republican. I believe if gentlemen will sit down and examine the history of the vetoes that have taken place, either in the national or the state governments, they will find that they have been almost universally sustained by the people. I look upon the executive in these cases as more directly the representative of the will of the people, than are the general assembly. He generally acts for the whole people, and the expression of all the people is taken in his election.

There is another thing to be considered in connection with this matter. Many of the acts which are vetoed are passed by a system of log-rolling. One member, who has a favorite project which he desires to carry, combines his influence with another member, who has also some project to get through the legislature, and by this system of log-rolling they get their measures passed. The Governor has only the interests of the people in view, and has no interest in aiding special matters of legislation, which may be passed by any log-rolling system. I could refer our friends upon the other side to the history of the last General Assembly, as a sufficient reason for supporting the veto power at this time. I believe the exercise of this power has been sustained, in nine cases out of ten, whenever it has been used by the Governor.

Mr. PALMER. I am in favor of the amendment offered by the gentleman from Johnson, [Mr. Clarke.] I believe that this veto power contains a bad principle. A provision has been adopted in many of the old constitutions, giving the Governor a veto power over legislation, which cannot be overcome by a majority of the legislature. I would go so far as to give him a qualified veto, as is proposed by the gentleman from Johnson, and no farther. When a bill has passed both houses of the legislature, let the Governor examine it carefully, and if he finds anything there which is unconstitutional or absurd, let him point out those particulars, and return it, with his objections, to the house in which it originated; and if, upon due consideration and sober second thought, they should consider that it was right and proper, let them pass it. It is well enough, I think, that the Governor should have a revising power over the errors which may be committed by hasty and inconsiderate legislation. For instance, about two years ago a bill was passed through both branches of the legislature of our State, with scarcely any objection, chartering some bridge company in the northern part of the State. It came before the Governor, who, after examining it, pronounced it unconstitutional, and returned it with his objections to the General Assembly, and it was voted down with scarcely a corporal's guard to sustain it. The veto power, when it is qualified, may operate well; but it is giving too much power into the hands of the executive officer of the State, to entrust him with the unqualified exercise of this power.

Gentlemen have said that it has operated well so far in the history of the country. Grant that it has operated, as a general thing, pretty well; it is wrong in principle, and may work badly. We all know that a Governor of a State is elected by the people, without their having any great knowledge of his legislative powers; but when they vote for members of the General Assembly, they know they are voting for men who are to make their laws, and they vote for them with an express understanding of the opinions they entertain in regard to certain leading measures of legislation. When the people elect a majority in both branches of the Assembly in favor of a law of any kind, the Governor should not be allowed to interpose a veto, which would require a two-thirds vote to overcome it. I think that in most of the States where they have had this provision of a two-thirds vote to overcome the Governor's veto, and where they have recently formed new Constitutions, they have discarded this principle. Some of them have left this principle out altogether, while others have adopted it, but qualified, as it is proposed to do here. Upon an examination of the constitutions of the different States, I find that in thirteen States the veto power exists as it is in our old Constitution; and in eighteen others, either no veto is allowed at all, or else they have the qualified veto, which is now proposed by the gentleman from Johnson, [Mr. Clarke.] In ten of these States, the qualified veto exists; while in the other eight, no veto at all is allowed. In the State of Ohio, the Governor is not allowed the exercise of the veto power. In the State of Maryland, it is made the duty of the Governor to sign every bill that passes the Legislature; and in several of the States besides Ohio, the Governor is not allowed the exercise of this power, and is not even allowed to sign the bills.

It is singular that while so much is said in the free States about the aristocracy of the Southern slave-holding States, out of fifteen slave-holding States there are but four that have this veto power, where it requires a vote of two thirds of the Legislature to pass a bill, after it has been vetoed. All the others provide either that there shall be no veto power given to the Governor, or else they provide for a qualified veto. I hope that this Convention will, after mature deliberation, come to the conclusion that the best plan is that which is proposed by the amendment of the gentleman from Johnson.

The question was then taken upon the amendment offered by Mr. Clarke, of Johnson, and it was rejected; ayes 9, noes not counted.

Mr. GOWER. I move to strike out "two thirds," and insert "seven twelfths," so that it will require seven twelfths of the members to pass a law over the Governor's veto. I have examined this subject with some degree of attention, and I have come to the conclusion that the veto power oftentimes is a salutary check upon hasty and inconsiderate legislation. But I think that seven twelfths of the members are sufficient to pass a law over the Governor's veto.

The question was then taken upon the amendment offered by Mr. Gower, and it was not agreed to.

No other amendments being offered to this section—

Final passage of bills.

Section eighteen was then read as follows:

"No bill shall be passed unless by the assent of a majority of all the members elected to each branch of the General Assembly, and the question upon the final passage shall be taken immediately upon its last reading, and the yeas and nays entered on the journal."

No amendment being offered to this section—

Publication of Receipts and Expenditures.

Section nineteen was then read as follows:

"An accurate statement of the receipts and expenditures of the public money shall be attached to and published with the laws at every regular session of the General Assembly."

No amendments being offered to this section—

Impeachment.

Section twenty was then read, as follows:

"The House of Representatives shall have the sole power of impeachment, and all impeachments shall be tried by the Senate. When sitting for that purpose, the senators shall be upon oath or affirmation; and no person shall be convicted without the concurrence of two-thirds of the members present."

No amendment being offered to this section, twenty-one was then read, as follows:

"The Governor, Secretary of State, Auditor, Treasurer, Judges of the Supreme and District Courts, Superintendent of Public Instruction and Attorney General, shall be liable to impeachment for any misdemeanor in office; but judgment in such cases shall extend only to removal from office, and disqualification to hold any office of honor, trust and profit, under this State; but the party convicted or acquitted shall nevertheless be liable to indictment, trial and punishment, according to law. All other civil officers shall be tried for misdemeanors in office, in such manner as the General Assembly may provide."

Mr. YOUNG. I move to strike out the words "Superintendent of Public Instruction." I believe it is generally conceded that we shall not hereafter have the office of "Superintendent of Public Instruction." I make this motion in order to test, in some degree, the sense of the Convention upon this subject. If the Convention retain these words here, I suppose it will be some indication that they design retaining the office of Superintendent of Public Instruction.

Mr. HALL. I would suggest to the gentleman that he modify his amendment so as to provide for all other State officers not enumerated in this section.

Mr. YOUNG. I will change my motion so as to strike out all after the word "Courts," in the second line, to the word "shall," and insert, "and other officers of the State," so that the section would read—

"The Governor, Secretary of State, Auditor, Treasurer, Judges of the Supreme and District Courts and other officers of the State, shall be liable to impeachment for any misdemeanor or malfeasance in office; but judgment in such cases shall extend only to removal from office, and disqualification to hold any office of honor, trust or profit, under this State; but the party convicted or acquitted shall nevertheless be liable to indictment, trial and punishment, according to law. All other civil officers shall be tried for misdemeanors and malfeasance in office, in such manner as the General Assembly may provide."

The question was then taken upon the amendment offered by Mr. Young, and it was agreed to.

There being no other amendments offered to this section—

Appointments to Offices of Profit.

Section twenty-two was then read, as follows:

"No senator or representative shall, during the time for which he shall have been elected, be appointed to any civil office of profit under this State, which shall have been created, or the emoluments of which shall have been increased during such term, except such offices as may be filled by elections by the people."

No amendments being offered to this section—

Eligibility to General Assembly.

Section twenty-three was then read, as follows:

"No person holding any lucrative office under the United States, or this State, or any other power, shall be eligible to the General Assembly; Provided, that officers in the militia, to which there is attached no annual salary, or the office of justice of the peace, or postmasters, whose compensation does not exceed one hundred dollars per annum, or notary public, shall not be deemed lucrative."

Mr. CLARKE, of Henry. In regard to this section, it has been suggested that it should define whether a person holding any lucrative office under the United States, or any other power, shall be eligible to a seat in the General Assembly.

Mr. PARVIN. I cannot see what would be gained by an amendment, such as the gentleman suggests. There is no law to prevent a man, if he be white, from becoming a candidate for any office. If the gentleman will go back farther, and say that a man holding any lucrative office under the United States, or any other government, shall not be voted for, I have no objection.

Mr. CLARKE, of Henry. I move to amend the section, by adding after the words "eligible," the words "hold a seat in;" so that it will read—

"No person holding any lucrative office under the United States, or this State, or any other power, shall be eligible to hold a seat in the General Assembly," &c.

In answer to the gentleman, I would say, that other States have declared that all votes cast for persons under similar restrictions as those contained in this section were void. My object is to prevent persons who hold lucrative offices from holding a seat in the general assembly.

Mr. MARVIN. I would like to understand, whether, as the section now reads, it does not amount to the same thing. It says: "That no person holding any lucrative office under the United States, or this State, or any other power, shall be eligible to the general assembly." I wish to ask if we are not to understand by this that no person as here described can take a seat in the general assembly.

Mr. CLARKE, of Henry. I would suggest to the gentleman that the clause as it now stands is ambiguous. The same question would be raised here, as was raised in Wisconsin in the case of the election of James R. Doolittle to the United States Senate. He was elected a judge under such a provision as this. He resigned his office, and now he is elected United States Senator. The question was raised in the Assembly that he could not be elected United States Senator during the term for which he was elected judge. A similar question arose in the United States Senate in the case of Senator Trumbull from Illinois. The only object I have in proposing this amendment is to remove any ambiguity of construction that may be given to this clause.

The question was then taken upon the amendment offered by Mr. Clarke, of Henry, and it was not agreed to.

No other amendments being offered to section twenty-three—

Section twenty-four was then read as follows:

"No person who may hereafter be a collector or holder of public moneys, shall have a seat in either House of the General Assembly, or be eligible to any office of trust or profit under this State, until he shall have accounted for and paid into the treasury all sums for which he may be liable."

No amendments being offered to section twenty-four—

Appropriations.

Section twenty-five was then read as follows:

"No money shall be drawn from the treasury but in consequence of appropriations made by law."

No amendments being offered to section twenty-five—

Per Diem and Mileage.

Section twenty-six was then read as follows:

"Each member of the General Assembly shall receive a compensation to be fixed by law, for his services, to be paid out of the treasury of the State. Such compensation shall not exceed three dollars per day for the period of sixty days from the commencement of the session, and shall not exceed the sum of two dollars per day for the remainder of the session; when convened in extra session by the Governor, they shall receive such sums per diem as shall be fixed for the first sixty days of the ordinary session. They shall also receive three dollars for every twenty miles they travel, in going to and returning from their place of meeting, on the nearest traveled route."

Mr. WILSON. I offer the following substitute for section twenty-six:

"Each member of the General Assembly shall receive a compensation to be fixed by law for his services, to be paid out of the treasury of the State. Such compensation shall be three dollars per day for each member, for the first session of the General Assembly under this Constitution; and three dollars for every twenty miles they travel, in going to and returning from their place of meeting, on the nearest traveled route."

Mr. CLARKE, of Johnson. I have prepared a substitute for this section, which I would like to offer, and which I would ask the gentleman from Jefferson [Mr. Wilson,] to accept as a substitute for his. It covers the same ground that the one he has offered does, but goes a little farther.

The substitute was then read, as follows:

"Each member of the first General Assembly under this constitution shall receive the sum of three dollars per diem, after which the compensation of the members of the General Assembly shall be fixed by law,—and the sum of three dollars for every twenty miles they travel in going to and returning from their place of meeting, on the nearest mail route,—after which they shall receive such compensation as may be fixed by law. But no General Assembly shall have the power to increase the compensation of its own members. The General Assembly shall have no power to sit more than one hundred days, in any one session; and when convened in extra session, they shall receive no greater compensation than is fixed by law for the regular sessions."

Mr. WILSON. I am not satisfied with the proposition which the gentleman from Johnson, [Mr. Clarke] has presented. In relation to mileage, it provides that the members of the General Assembly shall receive mileage by the nearest mail route. When we get our railroads in operation, we may have some very long mail routes.

Mr. CLARKE, of Johnson. I inserted this provision with the view of preventing members from going by the way of Illinois.

Mr. WILSON. I prefer the proposition I have submitted to that which the gentleman has presented, if it remains in its present shape. If he will change it to meet my views more fully, I will accept it in lieu of that which I have offered.

We have now provided that the sessions of the Legislature shall commence on the first Monday in January. The members who generally compose the Assembly are persons engaged in the various departments of life, lawyers, merchants and farmers. The lawyers generally want to go home about the time of the spring term of court; the farmers want to get home in time for their spring work, and the merchants want to get away early in order to make their spring purchases in the East; so that they are all compelled, through pressure of business, to adjourn early in the spring.

It seems to me that there is no necessity for the incorporation of any provision in the constitution limiting the sessions of the Legislature; the very fact that I have mentioned, that all classes are desirous of bringing about an early adjournment in the spring, is a sufficient guarantee against a long and protracted session. I do not believe that we would have a session running over a peried of a hundred days, even if we do not limit the session in the constitution. If we insert a provision in the constitution, that the session shall not exceed a hundred days, it affords color for an excuse for staying here that length of time. I believe we should have shorter sessions of the Legislature than we otherwise would, if we say nothing about this matter in the constitution.

Mr. CLARKE, of Johnson. The only objection I have to the proposition of the gentleman from Jefferson [Mr. Wilson] is, that it does not go far enough. The only reason why I made provision in the proposition I offered for limiting the sessions to a hundred days, was, that I supposed it was necessary to fix some limit. I did not want too short sessions, because I believed they would produce hasty legislation, which would result in injury to the people. I was inclined to the opinion that perhaps for the first and second sessions of the legislature, after the adoption of this constitution, there would be a great deal of work to do. The business of creating banking corporations and providing for internal improvements, might take up a good deal of time; and hence I fixed this limitation of a hundred days, as a safe-guard in that respect. If this provision does not meet the minds of the committee, I am willing to strike it out.

The next provision I have made is, that when the legislature is convened in extra session, they shall receive no greater compensation by the day than is fixed by law for the regular session.

I understand that the Legislature, at the expiration of their extra session, held last summer, voted themselves pay for a full session. I wish to obviate that difficulty.

Mr. WILSON. I do not think that there can be any difficulty in regard to this, for if the compensation is fixed for a general session, that same compensation will be attached to the extra session.

Mr. PARVIN. I cannot see in what respect the substitutes offered by gentlemen here are better than the section reported by the committee. We all agree that some provision should be made for cutting off such a charge as was made at the extra session. The committee thought, and I believe gentlemen here will agree with us, that they had sufficiently guarded against any such thing, when they say that the Legislature, "when convened in extra session by the Governor, shall receive such sums per diem as shall be fixed for the first sixty days of the ordinary session." The committee were in favor of limiting the sessions of the legislature, and they thought that sixty days would be ample time within which the legislature could do their business.

Mr CLARKE, of Johnson. I ask the Clerk to read the following substitute for the proposition offered by the gentleman from Jefferson [Mr. Wilson]. I have modified the one which I sent up to the clerk's desk in such a manner that I think it will fully meet the views of the gentleman.

The substitute was then read, as follows:

"Each member of the first General Assembly under this constitution, shall receive the sum of three dollars per diem, and the sum of three dollars for every twenty miles they travel in going to and returning from their place of meeting, on the nearest traveled route; after which they shall receive such compensation as shall be fixed by law; but no General Assembly shall have the power to increase the compensation of its own members, and when convened in extra session, they shall receive no greater compensation per diem than is fixed by law for the regular session."

Mr. WILSON. With the alterations the gentleman has made in his substitute, I will accept it in lieu of my own.

The question was then taken, and the substitute was agreed to.

There being no further amendments to section twenty-six,

Publication of Laws.

Section twenty-seven was read, as follows:

"No law of the General Assembly of a public nature, shall take effect until the fourth day of July next after the passage thereof. If the General Assembly shall deem any law of immediate importance, they may provide that the same shall take effect by publication in the newspapers of the State."

Mr. WILSON. I desire to amend the section by adding the following words:

"And no local laws shall be so published at the expense of the State."

I think that the adoption of such an amendment will cut off considerable expense that has been brought upon the State by the publication of local laws. Persons who wish local laws passed, and wish them to take immediate effect, should provide for their publication themselves.

Mr. PALMER. I would favor the amendment if the distinction could be easily drawn between local and general laws. It would be a question to my mind, whether a law fixing the times for holding a court in certain districts, was local or general. The publishing of such laws as that ought to be paid out of the State treasury.

Mr. WILSON. I would suggest to the gentleman that a law of such a character would come under the head of laws of public nature. It would not be treated as a local law in any sense.

Mr. HALL. I hope that, in a body like this, we will not legislate in these trifling matters. I think the general assembly can take care of these little matters. It is a mere matter of convenience, and it is too picayunish for us to trouble ourselves with such a matter as this.

The question was then taken upon the amendment offered by Mr. Wilson, and it was not agreed to.

Mr. PALMER. I move to insert in the second line, before the word "if," the word "but," so that the latter clause of this section may come in as an exception to the first clause. The section, as amended, would then read:

"No law of the General Assembly of a public nature, shall take effect until the fourth day of July next after the passage thereof. But if the General Assembly shall deem any law of immediate importance, they may provide that the same shall take effect by publication in newspapers in the State."

The motion was not seconded.

Mr. HALL. I move to amend the section by providing that no laws shall take effect until sixty days after their passage.

Mr. WILSON. I would suggest to the gentleman that sixty days time is hardly sufficient for the distribution of these laws, and their circulation among the people.

Mr. HALL. I will say ninety days then.

Mr. WILSON. I think, judging from the past history of the State, that that time would not be sufficient. The general assembly usually adjourns about the first of February; and yet we scarcely ever receive the laws in our county before May or June. It seems to me that ninety days would not be sufficient time, and that we ought at least to say four months after the adjournment of the legislature.

Mr. PALMER. I would suggest to the gentleman from Des Moines, [Mr. Hall,] that he amend by saying "ninety days after the adjournment of the legislature."

Mr. HALL. I move to strike out the words "fourth day of July next after the passage thereof," and insert at the end of the first sentence, "ninety days after the adjournment of the general assembly," so that the section will read:

"No law of the General Assembly, of a public nature, shall take effect until ninety days after the adjournment of the General Assembly. But if the General Assembly shall deem any law of immediate importance, they may provide that the same shall take effect by publication in newspapers in the State."

The question being taken, the amendment was not agreed to.

No further amendment being offered to that section—

Laws Granting Divorce.

Section twenty-eight was then read as follows:

"No divorce shall be granted by the General Assembly."

No amendment being offered to this section—

Lotteries Prohibited.

Section twenty-nine was then read as follows:

"No lottery shall be authorized by this State; nor shall the sale of lottery tickets be allowed."

No amendment being offered to this section—

Acts to Embrace but one Subject.

Section thirty was then read as follows:

"Every act shall embrace but one subject, and matters properly connected therewith; which subject shall be expressed in the title. But if any subject shall be embraced in an act which shall not be expressed in the title, such act shall be void only as to so much thereof as shall not be expressed in the title."

Mr. PALMER. I move to strike out the word "subject" wherever it occurs in this section, and insert the word "object." I believe it was the intention of the framers of this constitution that the word should be "object." A virtual violation of the section by the legislature led to a great deal of difficulty. For instance, there would be acts passed in relation to certain state roads, therein named. There was one omnibus act of this kind, embracing provisions for the establishment of many state roads, and also to vacate others already established. It related to but one subject, it is true, that of state roads, but it related to more than one object. There was some question before the supreme court as to the meaning of the word "subject," and it was the opinion of many that that act was in compliance with the original provision of the constitution. It appears to me that if we can embrace so many different provisions under the word "subject," it ought to be stricken out, and some other word substituted for it, which would confine the action of the legislature within some more limited range.

Mr. CLARKE, of Johnson. This subject has been before the supreme court, in the case referred to by the gentleman from Davis, [Mr. Palmer.] The session before the last of the General Assembly passed what is known as the "omnibus road bill," providing for the laying out, establishing and vacating some thirty, forty or fifty roads. Under that act roads were established, and damages were allowed to a certain individual, which the county judge refused to pay. And a proceeding, by writ of mandamus, was commenced in the name of a third person to test that matter. In that proceeding, this whole matter was discussed in the supreme court. The proceedings were dismissed in the district court, and in the supreme court a decision was rendered by two judges, sustaining the law as constitutional; that though it embraced a variety of objects, it embraced but one subject. From that decision the chief justice dissented. That decision now stands, though there are two judges in favor of it, and two against it. I think the construction put upon the act by the majority of the court was a correct one. But as they leave the subject open to discussion here, it might be well for this Convention to consider this section, in connection with the section that succeeds it. That section reads—

"The General Assembly shall not pass local or special laws in the following cases:

For the assessment and collection of taxes for State, county, or road purposes;

For laying out, opening, and working on roads or highways;

For changing the names of persons;

For the incorporation of cities or towns;

For vacating roads, town plats, streets, alleys, or public squares;

In all the cases above enumerated, and in all other cases where a general law can be made applicable, all laws shall be general, and of uniform operation throughout the State."

If the supreme bench should eventually reverse that decision, and decide that each act providing for laying out and vacating State roads, must provide for only one road, we gain very little by the section I have just read.

I do not say that the amendment of the gentleman from Davis [Mr. Palmer] will affect this matter beneficially. But the word "subject" is a broader word, and more extensive in its application, than the word "object." It is found in the constitution of New York, and in some other constitutions, I think. The supreme court drew a distinction between the two words, and the question is now a debateable question in the courts, and among the bar. I think we should do something to remove these doubts and difficulties, if we can. I am not very particular about the matter myself, but I throw out these suggestions for the consideration of the Convention.

The question being taken to strike out the word "subject," and inserting the word "object," it was not agreed to.

No further amendment being offered to this section—

Special acts of Legislation.

Section thirty-one was then read as follows:

"The General Assembly shall not pass local or special laws in the following cases:

For the assessment and collection of taxes for State, county, or road purposes;

For laying out, opening, and working on roads or highways;

For changing the names of persons;

For the incorporation of cities or towns;

For vacating roads, town plats, streets, alleys, or public squares;

In all the cases above enumerated, and in all other cases where a general law can be made applicable, all laws shall be general and of uniform operation throughout the State."

Mr. EDWARDS. I move to amend this section by striking out the last sentence, which reads—

"In all the cases above enumerated, and in all other cases where a general law can be made applicable, all laws shall be general and of uniform operation throughout the State."

I make this motion because the section as it now stands is ambiguous, and will bring on a direct conflict between the legislative, executive and judicial departments of the State. The Legislature may pass a law, and the Governor may veto it upon the ground that it is unconstitutional, one of those cases for which the Legislature are required to provide by a general law. I know a case directly in point that occurred in the State of Indiana. These cases here enumerated are taken principally from the constitution of Indiana. The Legislature there passed a law removing a county seat. The Governor vetoed it upon the ground that the Legislature should have provided for the removal of county seats by a general law. The Legislature passed the bill over the Governor's veto. The parties in favor of the old county seat afterward filed their application for an injunction against the law, and the case was finally taken into the supreme court.

I think all cases of special or local legislation should be enumerated and set forth in the Constitution. And in doing that, we should not leave such an ambiguous provision as the sentence I have proposed to strike out, that will bring on a conflict between the legislative, executive and judicial branches of the government. It opens the doors to controversies, and will prove a fruitful source of litigation.

I would like to reply to one remark made by the gentleman from Des Moines, [Mr. Hall,] on yesterday. He stated that, by the Code of Iowa, there had been general laws passed, covering all the cases enumerated in this section. While that may be true, at the same time the Legislature, especially at the last session, has passed a great many special or local acts, for which provision had been made by general law, such as the incorporation of towns, the vacation of alleys and streets, and the laying out of public roads. It is, therefore, necessary that we should provide against special and local legislation, and the strongest necessity for doing so, is the fact that we propose to provide for biennial instead of annual sessions of the legislature. I think, therefore, it would be wise and proper to strike out the sentence I have indicated.

Mr. PALMER. I trust the motion of the gentleman from Lucas, [Mr. Edwards,] will not prevail. I believe the object of the first part of the section is to make it the duty of the legislature to pass laws of a general nature, so as to dispense with local laws upon the subjects named in the first part of the section. We know that a great portion of many sessions of our Legislature is spent in local legislation. We want to make it the duty of the Legislature to pass general laws, so far as they can, to apply to all these local questions, and to provide for them, so that when any local object is sought to be accomplished by law, those desiring that object, may, under some general law, obtain what they seek.

I consider that, under the foregoing clauses of this section, it would probably be the duty of the Legislature to do this very thing—to pass general laws to provide for these local objects. Then why not say so?

I think that there can be no danger of the Legislature and the executive coming into conflict upon this subject. If the Legislature passes a law for any object, which the Governor thinks might be provided for under a general law, he can say so; and if the General Assembly find any difficulty in providing any general law to accomplish that object, they can apply to the Governor for his views upon the subject, or for the draft of a bill, such as he might specify, to remedy the difficulty, or accomplish the object desired. If there should be any difference of opinion between the Governor and the General Assembly, in reference to the constitutionality of any act on account of its local character, he might accompany his opinions with the draft of a bill, of a general character, to accomplish the object desired.

The question was then taken upon the amendment proposed by Mr. Edwards, and it was not agreed to, upon a division; ayes 5; noes not counted.

Mr. CLARKE, of Johnson. I move to amend the first clause of this section, by inserting after the word "cases," the words "but shall provide by general laws;" so that the section will then read—

"The General Assembly shall not pass local or special laws in the following cases, but shall provide by general laws for the assessment and collection of taxes," &c.

I offer this amendment in order to remove all doubt which has been thrown about this matter by the decisions of the Supreme Court.

Mr. PARVIN. If the gentleman from Johnson [Mr. Clarke,] will refer to the last clause of the section, he will find that the object he aims to attain by his amendment, is there fully provided for. It reads—

"In all the cases above enumerated, and in all other cases where a general law can be made applicable, all laws shall be general, and of uniform operation throughout the State."

That is precisely what he professes to be seeking.

Mr. CLARKE, of Johnson. The difficulty is this; it is left discretionary with the general assembly, under the clause to which the gentleman refers, to pass these general laws. I prepared this amendment at the time the motion of the gentleman from Lucas [Mr. Edwards,] was pending, to strike out the clause the gentleman from Muscatine [Mr. Parvin,] has read, supposing that motion would prevail. That portion of the section reads as follows:

"In all the cases above enumerated, and in all other cases where a general law can be made applicable, all laws shall be general, and of uniform application throughout the State"

You leave to the general assembly to decide whether or not a general law can be made applicable. If they want to pass a special law upon any of these, or of other subjects, they may conclude that a general law would not be applicable. With the amendment I propose, it is made imperative upon them to provide by general laws for these subjects. If my amendment prevails, it seems to me it would be better to strike out that clause, as otherwise there would be some tautology.

Mr. PARVIN. There is no ambiguity in regard to the cases specified. The ambiguity is only in reference to cases not specified. There is a little ambiguity in the phrase "in all other cases," and there may be some question whether or not the general assembly would not be at liberty to exercise their discretion. But that is all.

Mr. CLARKE, of Johnson. If the gentleman will move to strike out the words "and in all other cases where a general law can be made applicable," and leave the section so that it will read, "in all the cases above enumerated, all laws shall be general, and of uniform operation throughout the State"—it would then bear the construction he puts upon it. But as it now stands I think it is left to the general assembly to decide whether or not a general law will accomplish the purpose desired. If these words I have indicated are stricken out, then my amendment would not be necessary.

The question was then taken upon the amendment of Mr. Clarke, of Johnson, and it was not agreed to, upon a division; ayes 9; noes 10.

County Seats and Boundaries.

Mr. MARVIN. There is one other subject which I think should be provided for by general law, and placed beyond the discretion of the general assembly. That is, the location of county seats. I move to amend the section, by adding to the cases enumerated the following:

"For the location of county seats."

Mr. TRAER. I had prepared an amendment differing somewhat from that of the gentleman from Jones, [Mr. Marvin.] It was to insert the following:

"For changing the boundaries of counties, or locating county seats."

I am well aware, and I suppose every gentleman here is aware, that great injustice has been done to the people of counties, in the western part of the State, by the changing of their county seats by the legislature.

There have been cases where a few individuals who desired to make a certain point the county seat, have got the boundaries of certain counties changed, in order to make the point they favor occupy a central location, and, perhaps, thereby placing some others in a very undesirable location, where they would be obliged to travel a very great distance to get to the county seat. A few years ago the legislature passed a law establishing the boundaries of some two or three counties, and adding one county to another. This winter that arrangement was changed, and the two counties were separated again.

I would fix it here so that the legislature could not change the lines of any county by the passage of any local or special act, but have it all provided for under general law, and left to the vote of the people of the respective counties. This will do away with a great deal of local legislation, and a great deal of log-rolling which took place at the last session. I trust, therefore, the gentleman from Jones will accept the amendment I have indicated.

Mr. MARVIN. I cannot accept the amendment the gentleman from Benton, [Mr. Traer,] has proposed; but I will change my amendment so that it will read, "For locating or altering county seats."

Mr. SCOTT. I am in favor of the amendment of the gentleman from Jones, [Mr. Marvin.] I would have the location of county seats left especially to the people of the vicinity where the county seat is located. I do not want the legislature to control this matter. We have labored under a great deal of difficulty in the county where I reside, in regard to the location of our county seat. The county seat was first located at Prairie Laporte; then at Garnavillo; now at Elkador; next spring a vote is to be taken between the respective merits of Gutenburg and Elkador; and there are other places that are putting forward their claims, for instance, Monona, McGregor, Clayton Centre, Volga City, and perhaps Strawberry Point. Whichever place will send the strongest delegation to press its claims before the legislature would be likely to succeed. In this way our court-house is no more fixed than if it were upon wheels. I think the people can judge better as to where the county seat should be located, than the General Assembly can.

Mr. TRAER. I will move to amend the amendment of the gentleman from Jones, [Mr. Marvin] by adding to it the words "and fixing the boundaries of counties." The object of the amendment the gentleman has offered, seems to be to prevent the legislature from changing the location of county seats by local legislation. Any person familiar with the manner the legislature has gone on for the last two or three years, must know this: if certain individuals desire to make a certain point the county seat, they go to work and ascertain the views of the people of the county. If they find out that a majority of the people of the county are against the location they propose, what do they do in that case? They go before the legislature, and by a system of log-rolling, they get the legislature to cut off a certain portion of that county, so as to leave a majority in the county in favor of the point they are in favor of. That has been done in several instances. That was tried in reference to my county, but the effort was not successful.

And that will be done just so long as you leave the legislature at liberty to change the boundaries of counties. You leave them the power to change the location of county seats, by allowing them to change the boundaries of the counties, so as to change the vote of the county, and enable certain interested parties to carry the county seat to a point, where, without this change, it could not be carried. I think, if any change is to be made in the boundaries of any county, those people it is proposed to cut off, should be allowed to have some voice in the matter. I have seen too much expense and litigation attending legislation in this respect. And I think if we can reach it here, we ought to do so. I am decidedly in favor of fixing this matter here, because I think it will correct all the mischief in this respect, we have heretofore felt.

Mr. CLARK, of Alamakee. I am in favor of providing in this constitution, so as to prevent the legislature from passing any special laws to change the boundaries of counties, or to locate or change county seats. I presume much inconvenience is not felt in the older counties of this State, from the action of the legislature upon this subject. But it is different in the new counties. Their county lines, boundaries and seats, undergo perpetual change. And these changes are not made in accordance with the wishes of the people except in few instances.

A few men will buy a piece of land, and lay out a town. They then send their agents to the legislature, and get the boundaries of one or more counties changed, so as to make their town the central point of the county. And before the great mass of the people in these counties know anything about it, the law is passed.

This creates excitement, and at the next session of the legislature, the people send on other persons to get that law changed. It enables a few dishonest men to get the advantage and control of this matter, against the wishes of a majority of the people of these counties. Some two or three weeks must intervene before information can be sent to the people of what is going on, and an expression of their wishes be sent back again; and especially nearly the close of a session, ample time is secured to accomplish the purpose of these few men.

I think this thing should be settled by a general law, under which the people can determine it as the interests of the county may require, much better than it can be done by this special, log-rolling kind of legislation. It will also have this farther beneficial effect: it will take from the legislature that kind of legislation which is always found to occupy a large share of their sessions. For that reason I am for taking this subject from the legislature and leaving it with the people.

Mr. SOLOMON. I am in favor of the object sought, but I have some fears, in my own mind, in regard to the manner proposed here, in which to secure that object. There is a principle of popular sovereignty involved in this question, which I think we ought to secure to the people. This question of the location of county seats, is a matter which interests the people of the respective counties alone, and it should be left to them in their sovereign capacity to decide. No one questions that. All those who favor the amendment of the gentleman from Jones [Mr. Marvin] favor it for the reason that they suppose it will secure this object; and the change of boundaries of counties should be brought about in the same manner. All here will agree upon that point.

Now let us see what is proposed by this amendment.

At the first sight, I was decidedly in favor of it. And if it would secure the object sought, I would be in favor of it yet. It proposes a provision that the General Assembly shall make no special law, but only a general law in regard to this matter. I cannot cite exactly what would be the general law; but let me say that, in pursuance of a general law in reference to this subject, great injury has been done, and the very thing which the gentleman desires to prevent, has been done in this State to a very great extent under a general law. If I mistake not, the legislature has made the district judges, or some other authority, the power to decide, of themselves, or to appoint commissioners to go into counties and locate county seats. I think I am correct in that; that was the general law. And thus the legislature, instead of using their power to do that which the gentleman deprecates, did worse: they delegated it to others—to a judge, who, by means of his own commissioners, could locate a county seat wherever he pleased. This, I think, is wrong.

I would therefore suggest to the gentleman to withdraw his amendment in this place, and submit in some other place, the proposition that no county seat or boundary shall be changed, except by a direct vote of the people. That will secure his object, but his amendment here will not, because the legislature will still have the power to grant this authority to county commissioners under a general law.

Mr. TRAER. I desire to change the phraseology of my amendment to the amendment, by substituting the word "changing" for "fixing," so that it will apply only to the changing of county boundaries.

I notice, upon looking at the map, that some counties there laid down, which are not yet organized, are not large enough to meet the constitutional requirements of a certain number of square miles, and it will be necessary that their boundaries should be changed.

What I desire, is this: that after a county is organized for judicial purposes, the boundaries shall not be changed, unless a majority of the people interested desire the change. I desire to take that matter out of the hands of the Legislature, and leave it with the people, where it belongs. And in answer to the gentleman from Mills, [Mr. Solomon], I will say, that I think this question of the people voting upon these matters will be secured by a general law. I do not think that is a point we need express in the Constitution, at all. The probability is, that the Legislature, in preparing the general law, will leave it to the people.

Mr. SOLOMON. Does not the gentleman know that some previous Legislatures have not done so, but have clothed judges with the power to appoint commissioners?

Mr. TRAER. I think the gentleman is not right in his application of that fact to the amendment I have proposed. The amendment of the gentleman from Jones [Mr. Marvin], is in relation to the changing of county seats, and he can attend to his amendment for himself. My amendment to the amendment proposes to settle this matter of county boundaries. There is a general law now, I think, in regard to fixing the county seats, which provides that the people shall have a vote upon that question. I recollect of such a vote being taken in my county. But there is no general law in regard to changing the boundaries of counties after they have been organized. That is the point I wish to reach by my amendment; to prevent the Legislature enttrely from forming any special laws upon that subject. I would have the Legislature pass a general law, under which the people are to vote in favor of such a change before it takes place.

Mr. GILLASPY. There is a provision in the old Constitution, in article eleven, which, it seems to me, has worked very well in this State. I refer to section two, of article eleven, which reads as follows:

"No new county shall be laid off hereafter, nor old county reduced to less contents than four hundred and thirty-two square miles."

If the amendment of the gentleman from Benton, [Mr. Traer], should prevail, I would like to ask what effect it will have upon former legislation upon this subject?

Mr. TRAER. It is beyond our power to reach that.

Mr. GILLASPY. I am myself in favor of taking this matter out of the hands of the Legislature. To my certain knowledge there have been more wrongs and outrages perpetrated upon the people of this State by this kind of legislation, than in any other way. I know very well that this winter, at the instance of four or five individuals, without any consultation with the people of the county in which they were disposed to operate, in the absence of the members representing that county, other parties took the matter in hand, and restored what was formerly Humboldt county. Several old counties had been thrown together to make what was called Webster county, and Fort Dodge was made the county seat. Half a dozen men, who desired to make another county seat, came before the Legislature and got them to restore Humboldt county, without letting the people know anything about it. And the next Legislature may go to work and make another change.

I am in favor of any provision that will take this matter out of the hands of the Legislature. It does seem to me that if it should be left with them, we will have innumerable difficulties all over the State. And there could be nothing worse than to leave the changing of boundaries and locating county seats to the Legislature. It should be left to the people, and not to the Legislature. They could change half the counties in this State, and build up new county seats in them all, in less than ten years. I think this matter of county boundaries and county seats should be left entirely to the people of the respective counties.

Mr. MARVIN. My object in offering the amendment I submitted, was not to indicate what general law the Legislature should pass upon this subject, but to provide that there should be a general law, so that the Legislature might not be continually harassed by this kind of business. I suppose, if they pass a general law, which is not acceptable to the people, it will be soon changed and corrected. I do not desire here to state what kind of general law should be passed by the Legislature.

Mr CLARKE, of Henry. I am rather surprised that certain gentlemen here have so suddenly lost all their confidence in legislative bodies. After having held them up here before us as the very embodiment of public opinion, as the very best guardians of the rights of the people, you find those gentlemen now exhibiting their distrust of the Legislature in everything. And as soon as it comes to some little matter of local legislation, they want to bind them down to legislate in a certain direction.

Now I have no objection at all to compel the Legislature to provide general laws, under which this question of county seats shall be settled. But when you come to the other question, started by the gentleman from Benton, [Mr. Traer,] in regard to county boundaries, I think the matter assumes an entirely different aspect. The people of the State at large are not particularly interested in the location of any county seat in any particular county. But the people of the State are interested in regard to the number and the size of the counties in the State. This question of county boundaries is one, therefore, which may very properly be left to the Legislature, to be dealt with by them as the exigencies of the future may require.

It is enough, in my opinion, if you put in your Constitution a provision requiring the Legislature to make a general law, leaving this matter of county seats to the people of the different counties that may be interested in the subject. Here, for instance, is the county of Keokuk, where, as I have been informed, there is a kind of continual warfare in regard to the county seat, it being one year in one place, and another year in another place. And there may be instances where the people desire to get the county cut in two. There is the large county of Lee, for instance, large enough for two or three counties. There may be cases where the people may desire to join two or three counties into one, or may want to have them divided by rivers and other streams, instead of having them square and compact as they are now. I would not interfere with this matter at all. The restriction in the old Constitution is that—

"No new county shall be laid off hereafter, nor old county reduced to less contents than four hundred and thirty-two square miles."

Now if this amendment is put in here, we should have this old restriction in also, to guard against these local divisions among the people. I would therefore make a distinction between county seats and the boundaries of counties. I would leave this matter to the legislature to settle as they may see fit. If they see proper to leave it to the people, they can do so; if to commissioners, I would let them do that. The legislature may use as much wisdom as we here can; and perhaps they may find that this course will not work well. If you put this restriction in the constitution, the legislature must abide by it. If you leave it to be settled by the legislature, and they can make a general law, leaving the people to settle the matter, if it does not work well then the law can be changed.

Mr. HALL. I think there can be no doubt as to the wisdom and propriety of a general law to locate and establish county seats. But when you come to the establishment, altering and changing of county boundaries, I would like to have gentlemen tell me what kind of a general law could be made that would be applicable to such purposes. I have been unable to think of any possible form in which you could frame a general law, to give to the people of the counties, or those who may be interested in the matter, the right to decide this question. For instance, here is a county that desires to be divided. You might say that the people of the whole county should decide the question. But then here is a tier of townships in one county which desire to be added to another county for the sake of convenience. How is that matter to be decided? By the vote of the towns, or by the vote of the county? Are the people who desire the change, and are to be affected by it, to decide the matter themselves, or are they to be controlled by the rest of the county? It would be a very difficult matter to establish any general rule in this matter, that would not produce much more agitation, contention and injustice than is to be apprehended from the action of the legislature.

According to my judgment, you cannot prepare any general rule that will be applicable to this subject. Counties are communities established for the public convenience. The State is divided up into a hundred or more political subdivisions, for the convenience of the respective sections for the transaction of their business. This is a matter of governmental policy, designed to afford as much convenience to one portion of the State as to another. To enable them to transact their governmental business, the county seat is a necessary consequence. Every county must have a point, a public place in which to transact county business, hold their courts, have their public offices, keep their records, receive their taxes, &c. It is true, it is well enough to limit the counties, and say they shall not be less than a certain number of square miles, in order to preserve a certain uniformity in these political organizations. But I do not believe that you could frame a general law upon the subject of county boundaries, that would be at all satisfactory.

These counties are to be divided, changed and modified. Whom are you going to allow to decide the matter? One end of a county may be thickly, and the other end sparsely, settled, and the latter portion of the county may be entirely overcome by the former, though it is superior in area and wealth. I do not think this matter has been very greatly abused by the legislature; I do not think there has been any good cause of complaint, or if there has been, it might turn out that those who complained, did so from some interested motives.

Mr. CLARK, of Alamakee. I can see nothing in the arguments of those who oppose this amendment, to convince me that the course here proposed is impracticable, or that any other course would be a better one. The gentleman from Henry, [Mr. Clarke,] thinks there ought to be some limitation in the constitution in regard to the size of counties, that they should not be less than a given size. I am as much in favor of that as he is. But the plea that legislative bodies should be trusted, and that we must not show a want of confidence in them in regard to this matter, is entitled to no weight at all. We know that legislative bodies do act improperly upon this subject. They may be willing to do justice, but they know nothing about the matter before them, except from the title of the bill referring to it. The whole thing is moved by wire-workers, interested speculators, who manage the affair secretly, without the knowledge of the great mass of the people to be affected by it. That is what we seek to obviate.

It is true that you cannot make any general or special laws that some persons will not take the advantage of, or which will not work hardships in certain cases. The gentleman from Des Moines [Mr. Hall,] asks, if you desire to take a tier of townships from one county, to be joined to another, will you have it decided by a majority vote of the people of the two counties? He speaks of that as if it would be a great injustice. Now it may be inconvenient and injurious to some to allow the question to be decided in that way. But I ask the gentleman if it is not far preferable, and carrying out democratic principles as far as practicable, to leave the question to be decided by the vote of the majority of voters in the two counties, as the only persons interested in the matter, than to have the matter decided as it now is?

Mr. HALL. Suppose the county of Dubuque wanted to incorporate the county of Delaware within her limits, could not she do it by her own vote alone, against the vote of every man in Delaware county, if the question was decided in that way?

Mr. CLARK, of Alamakee. I admit that she might do it. But in doing it, would she injure Delaware county very much? But I do not think there is any great danger that such a thing would take place. It is in itself an improbable suggestion. I do not believe it would be for the interest of Dubuque to attach Delaware to her. I do not believe that this provision will engender a spirit of conquest, or desire to acquire territory, in the several counties. I believe they would be governed by principles of interest. You cannot convince me, any more than you could the members of the legislature from Dubuque, that it would be for their interest to attach Delaware to their county. Or if you could, I apprehend that the same logic, and the same train of reasoning could convince the members from Delaware also.

Now I admit that there is a chance that this power may be abused. But you cannot frame any law that cannot be abused, whether special or general. Now let us see where is the most likelihood of abuse; whether from leaving the subject in such a shape that the legislature, without having any direct interest in the matter, and one-half, or perhaps three-fourths, knowing nothing at all about the bill they pass —whether in that way, or in the way we propose. Suppose that the legislature should be clothed with the power to change the location of county seats. Would it not be the more likely that Dubuque county, if she wanted to annex Delaware county, would come down here and get a law for that purpose passed through the legislature before the people of Delaware county would know anything about it? Which of the two systems opens the widest door to fraud and unfair dealing? Which of the two systems would be most likely to give the people, interested in this matter, a voice in its decision? Which of the two systems would be most likely to deprive them of that voice? I think that every reflecting mind must see in a moment that, although if the system we advocate is adopted, there may be cases in which injustice may be done, yet in nine cases out of ten it would prevent that injustice.

Every person who is at all acquainted with the history of this State, and the history of other States, knows that county boundaries are changed, county seats are located and relocated against the wishes of the people who are interested in that matter. It is felt to be an evil to a very serious extent, in our new counties. If a few speculators have an interest in building up a particular place, all they have to do is to get some one in the legislature to watch every opportunity to introduce and have passed a bill to divide up one or more counties and change the county seats. Their object is to do the thing secretly, have everything arranged, and press the matter through before the people interested in it are aware that such a movement has been put on foot.

Now these things are not right; and when I make this assertion, I do not lay myself open to the charge of distrusting the legislature more than I have reason to do. For I hold that whatever has been done under the old constitution, will be done under the new constitution, if the provisions of both in regard to this subject are the same. What has been under certain circumstances, will be again under the same or similar circumstances. The same causes will produce the same effects, all other things being equal. That is a universal law.

We have felt great inconvenience and injustice under the provision of the constitution as it now stands, and we want it changed. Another objection is, that the legislature may pass a general law authorizing district judges to appoint commissioners to perform these duties. That may be obviated by amending the amendment so as to require the legislature to submit any general law they may pass upon this subject to a vote of the people interested in the matter. It seems to me that that would reduce the matter as near as possible to the requirements of the doctrine of the greatest good to the greatest number.

There is another argument, which gentlemen who oppose this amendment have not attempted to answer, and that is, that it will close the doors of our legislative halls to the entrance of that class who come here to obtain the means for private, pecuniary, and selfish gratification. It will throw out of our legislative halls a large class of that kind of legislation, which is never intended, and which is not calculated to benefit the great mass of the people, but merely to put something into the pockets of the few at the expense of the many.

For these reasons, I am in favor of this proposed amendment.

Mr. TRAER. I feel very much interested in this matter from the fact that I have been requested by a number of my friends, who reside in the newer portions of the State, and who have been very much troubled in regard to this very matter—and who, by the way, had to come here over a distance of two hundred or three hundred miles to seek to prevent these frauds—to endeavor to have some provision inserted in the constitution to remedy this evil. And I hope that this amendment, or some other, the effect of which will be the same, will be adopted.

I look upon the argument of the gentleman from Des Moines [Mr. Hall] as about the only argument of any great force against this proposition. His argument is, that it would be impossible to make a general law that would reach this case without doing some injustice. Now, it appears to me that there is a law upon the statute book, that provides for something of a very similar nature, which I wish to read. I think there is at least a comparison to be drawn, and we may possibly adopt a principle of the same kind in this case. It is in regard to towns and villages, and contains a principle which, I think, can be applied to counties.

"Ground subsequently laid out, platted, and recorded as above described, may be added to any town plat adjacent thereto, with the consent of all the proprietors of the part to be so attached, and of the people of the town to which it is to be attached.

"Whenever the county court of the county in which the town lies is satisfied that all the proprietors of the part sought to be attached have given their consent thereto, and that a sum of money sufficient in the estimation of the court to defray the expenses of an election, has been deposited with the clerk, it shall cause an order to be entered, that the question be submitted to a vote of the people of the town at a time therein fixed, which may be on the day of any other election, if thought expedient.

"Notice that such question will be submitted to the voters at such election, must be published in the same manner, and at the same time, as is prescribed for the general notice of such elections.

"Returns of the election shall be made to the county court, and if the result has been in favor of incorporating the addition into the town, an order to that effect, describing such addition, shall be entered upon the records of the court, a transcript of which order shall also be recorded in the town records, and thenceforth such addition shall be deemed a part of said town, and the judge of the county court shall issue his proclamation accordingly."

The question is to be submitted to a vote of the people of the particular locality interested, and the majority of the voters are to decide the question. Notice of the elections are to be given, and the elections carried on as in the case of all other elections. It seems to me there is a principle there which might be applied to counties, to remove the objection of the gentleman from Des Moines.

Take the case the gentleman has supposed, that the county of Dubuque desires to attach to herself a portion of the county of Delaware. If you leave this matter to the whole vote of the two counties, Dubuque would carry her point. If the matter is left to the people who are to be taken from Delaware, then I should think there would be no difficulty in the way. If a majority of them should vote in favor of it, I should be in favor of their being attached to the county of Dubuque. That is the principle I should like to see embodied in a law regulating this matter, but I do not think it is necessary to put it into the Constitution.

I wish to provide that the Legislature shall not pass special laws changing the boundaries of counties, but leave the Legislature to pass a general law for that purpose. I have no doubt that if we trust this matter to the Legislature, they will get up a law that will be satisfactory.

My friend from Alamakee [Mr. Clark], has told you how a great deal of fraud has been committed by parties interested in getting these special laws passed by the Legislature; and he has shown how, if this matter is left as it now stands, frauds will undoubtedly be committed hereafter. As I said before, the provision of the Constitution, as it now stands, furnishes a place for speculators to creep in, and use their influence in order to effect certain objects they have in view, against the wishes of the people. I might refer to the organization of the county of Worth, by the Legislature. There were half a dozen influences brought to bear upon the Legislature. One party, who owned a large quantity of land in Worth county, wanted a piece stricken off Mitchell county and added to Worth, so as to have his land in a central position in the county. One man who wanted to change the county seat of Cerro Gordo county, managed to get a piece taken off the northern part of the county, so as to make his land in Cerro Gordo county occupy a central position. And so it was with other parties. And the man who gets up the best oyster supper, &c., is the most likely to get his project through. The will of the people was not consulted at all. I do not think a single petition was sent up here by the people of the counties interested.

What I desire to accomplish here is, to get such a provision in the Constitution as will leave to the people interested in the change, to say whether or not the change shall take place. And I think the gentleman from Des Moines, [Mr. Hall,] who has advocated leaving other matters to the people, ought to vote for this proposition, for that principle is certainly as much involved in this as it can be in any other place. I hope this amendment will be adopted, if not here, in some other part of the Constitution, where it will have the same effect.

Mr. HALL. I distinguish between a representative vote and votes which are pecuniary in their nature. No gentleman has satisfied me that a general law can be made to meet this question. I undertake to say that gentlemen may have all the time until this Constitution is adopted and the next Legislature adjourns, and they cannot frame a satisfactory law upon this subject. There are ten thousand interests springing up which must be affected by such a law. Suppose a county has been organized; in a short time it becomes indebted to a large amount, and the old citizens desire to become attached to a county not so much indebted; the people will vote for that as a matter of course; but would it be right to leave it with them to decide?

It strikes me that if you should prepare a general law, under which the boundaries of counties can be arranged, you but throw a firebrand among them for them to fight over. You introduce a system of internal agitation among our political and municipal corporations. You establish that which may crush the very dearest interests of these communities, and destroy their progress and advancement. There should be some power to regulate these political boundaries. There may be a general law regulating it to some extent, and so far I am willing to leave to the legislature to prepare such a general law. But that a general law can be made that will be altogether applicable, I say is out of the question. No gentleman here can draw up a plan of a general law, in which I cannot show a dozen instances of its impracticability. Why, then, bring this matter in here? Evils may be great as they are, but they may be greater yet. It strikes me that it would be unwise in us to undertake to say that the political—the county boundaries in this State shall be fixed only under a general law.

Mr. CLARK, of Alamakee. The gentleman from Des Moines [Mr. Hall] says that no scheme can be devised in which he cannot find a half a dozen flaws. If he concedes that a law can be made in which he can find only half a dozen flaws, then I think it would be a very good law, taking into consideration his ingenuity and skill in such things. A man of his ingenuity is capable of finding half a dozen flaws, at least, in any plan that the wit of man could devise. Now, while he may find that many in the system we advocate, I apprehend that any man of only one-tenth part of his ingenuity can find a hundred objections to the present system. It is all intrigue, log-rolling, the few taking advantage of the many; that is the history of the matter. and the cases that have been decided upon equitable principles, are the exceptions to the rule.

I wish it to be borne in mind, that in adopting the proposed amendment to the constitution, we do not take this matter entirely out of the hands of the legislature. We only say they shall not make special laws upon the subject. Laws that are good for one part of the state we desire to be good for other portions of the State. It is only the general principle we undertake to settle; the details we leave in the hands of the legislature, where they now are.

Every objection that can be raised by the gentleman from Des Moines to the proposed amendment, can be raised with equal force against the present system. He says that one county will absorb another. It cannot do it without the legislature passes a law giving it the power. Now we must trust to the legislature to some extent. We can do that, even if we do not have as much confidence in that body as the gentleman from Des Moines has expressed upon many occasions.

He says that if we adopt this amendment and provide that there shall be none but general laws upon this subject, the large counties will eat up the smaller ones. The legislature will not be beset by these different interests, this lobbying and caucussing; that will be all cut off; and when this general law is made, the legislature will so frame it that Dubuque cannot eat up Delaware. They will place safeguards around it to protect the rights of every individual.

The object to be attained is the one we point

out: to cut off this special legislation, this lobbying, these facilities now held out to a few speculators to steal a march upon the few *bona fide* settlers in the county.

We want to do this for the benefit of the legislature, and through the legislature for the benefit of the great mass of the people of this state. I do hope that a provision of this kind will prevail. I believe it is one of the very best that we can incorporate into our constitution. Go into our new counties, and you will find the people there complaining of the practice under the present constitution. You will find them afraid to invest their money there to build up a town, for instance, on account of this system of changing county boundaries and county seats, without their knowledge and against their wishes. That practice has become so common that the people consider it unsafe to invest their money for the purpose of improving a town in the county. What to-day is the county line may not be to-morrow. The change may take place without their knowledge; while they are sleeping their rights may be stolen from them.

If you require a general law to be passed to regulate this matter, you shut the door against all this kind of practice, which arrests the wealth, growth and prosperity of our state. It leaves in the hands of the legislature the power, and we impose upon them the duty, so to frame that general law, as to obviate the difficulties and objections raised by the gentleman from Des Moines.

I am willing to so far trust the legislature as to say that they shall have this power. I can see no difficulty that can flow from the adoption of this proposed amendment.

Mr. PETERS moved that the committee rise, report progress, and ask leave to sit again.

The question being taken, the motion was not agreed to.

The question recurred upon the motion of Mr. Traer to so amend the amendment offered by Mr. Marvin, as to require the legislature to pass general laws for changing the boundaries of counties.

Mr. CLARKE, of Henry. If the gentleman from Alamakee [Mr. Clark] was the true exponent of the object to be gained by the adoption of this amendment, and it was to go no further than he has set forth, I think I could go with him to that extent. I do not agree with the gentleman from Des Moines in believing that a general law could not be framed under which these county lines can be regulated and changed. I can perceive very clearly how that can be provided for by general law, by providing that in all these cases commissioners should be appointed to decide the matter; or that the question should be submitted to the inhabitants of each county to be affected by the proposed alteration, and that a majority of the votes cast in each county should be required in order to complete the alteration.

As I said before, I consider that this is a question in which the people of the State at large are interested, and the agents of the people at large should have it in their hands. And if we merely say, and go no farther, that the General Assembly shall make a general law for the establishment and changing of county lines, they will have it in their power to amend that general law at any time, and the power over this matter will be as fully in the hands of the General Assembly under this system as under the system of special legislation.

But if we go farther, as some gentlemen here have intimated, and say that the General Assembly shall, by a general law, leave this matter in the hands of the people of the county affected, then I shall be opposed to it. I will go with gentlemen to this extent: that every law made by the General Assembly for changing these county boundaries, shall be submitted to the people of the counties affected by the change, and it shall not become a law until it shall have received a majority of votes cast for or against it. I will go as far as the farthest here, to prevent these frauds that have been complained of, but while I do that, I do not wish to take this matter of changing county boundaries from the people of the State at large, and leave it entirely to the people of the counties affected. I say, with the gentleman from Des Moines (Mr. Hall), that if you do that, there is no large county in the State but what, under that system, could absorb every adjoining county; as long as they had the controlling majority they could add to their territory.

Mr. CLARK, of Alamakee. That could be obviated by limiting the size of the counties.

Mr. CLARKE, of Henry. If gentlemen are willing to stop with a provision in the Constitution that the Legislature shall not pass any special laws for the changing of the boundaries of counties, I do not know but what I would be willing to go as far as that. But I am unwilling to go as far as the gentleman from Mills, [Mr. Solomon], and the gentleman from Benton, [Mr. Traer] desire me to go. I think the Legislature should have some power in this matter, and that it should not be left exclusively to the people of the county effected by the change.

The question being then taken upon the amendment to the amendment, upon a division, it was agreed to; ayes 12, nays 7.

The question was then taken upon the amendment as amended, and, upon a division, it was agreed to; ayes 14, nays 5.

Mr. PALMER moved to amend the fourth clause by adding the words, "counties, towns, or cities," so that it should read—

"For changing the names of persons, counties, towns, or cities."

The question being taken upon the amendment, it was not agreed to.

No further amendment being offered to that section—

Extra Compensation.

Section thirty-two was then read as follows:

"No extra compensation shall be made to any officer, public agent, or contractor, after the service shall have been rendered, or the contract entered into; nor shall any money be paid on any claim, the subject matter of which shall not have been provided for by pre-existing laws; and no public money or property shall be appropriated for local, or private purposes, unless such appropriation, compensation, or claim, be allowed by two thirds of the members elected to each branch of the General Assembly."

No amendment being offered to this section—

Oath of Members.

Section thirty-three was then read as follows: "Members of the General Assembly shall, before they enter upon the duties of their respective offices, take and subscribe the following oath or affirmation: 'I do solemnly swear, (or affirm, as the case may be,) that I will support the Constitution of the United States, and the Constitution of the State of Iowa, and that I will faithfully discharge the duties of Senator, (or Representative, as the case may be), according to the best of my ability.' And members of the General Assembly are hereby empowered to administer to each other the said oath or affirmation."

No amendment being offered to this section—

State Census.

Section thirty-four was then read as follows: "The General Assembly shall, in the years 1858, 1862, 1864, 1866, 1868, and 1875, and every ten years thereafter, cause an enumeration to be made of all the white inhabitants of the State."

No amendment being offered to this section—

Apportionment of Members.

Section thirty-five was then read, as follows: "The number of Senators and Representatives shall, at the next session following each period of making such enumeration, and the next session following each United States census, be fixed by law, and apportioned among the several counties, according to the number of white inhabitants in each."

Mr. TRAER. I move to strike out the words "and Representatives," so that the section will read—

"The number of Senators shall, at the next session following each period of making such enumeration," &c.

The special committee on the basis of representation propose an amendment to this article to come in after the next section. Their amendment refers especially to the House of Representatives, and relates to this same matter. I, propose, therefore, to strike out the words "and Representatives," and leave this section to apply to Senators alone. If the committee should decide, when the subject comes before them, against the amendment of the special committee, then these words can be inserted in this section again, when we get into convention upon this report.

Mr. PARVIN. I do not see the necessity of striking these words out of this section. The object of the gentleman can be accomplished by a section in the report of the committee on the schedule. As I understand it, his object is to have one or two additional members in the general assembly for the present general assembly, and the next one. I think, therefore, his object can be better accomplished in the schedule than here.

Mr. TRAER. The gentleman from Muscatine [Mr. Parvin,] entirely misapprehends the application of the amendment of the special committee. That amendment was intended as a general principle, to be placed in the constitution, to operate for all the time the constitution should be in force; it is not a temporary matter at all. I do not know as it is necessary to discuss what are the principal features of that amendment at this time, as it is not now before the committee.

Mr. YOUNG. I move that the committee rise, report progress, and ask leave to sit again. My object in making that motion is this: there is something of considerable importance in the motion to amend now pending before the committee, and I think it would be well to bestow some deliberation upon it, before we act upon it.

The question being taken, the motion that the committee rise was agreed to.

In Convention.

The PRESIDENT having resumed the chair,

The CHAIRMAN of the Committee of the Whole reported that the Committee had had under consideration the subject which had been referred to them, had made some progress therein, and had instructed him to ask leave of the convention to sit again.

The report of the committee of the whole was received, and leave granted accordingly.

On motion of Mr. TRAER,

The convention then took a recess until two o'clock this afternoon.

EVENING SESSION.

The convention met at two o'clock, P. M., and was called to order by the President.

The Convention then resumed in Committee of the Whole, (Mr. Patterson in the chair) the report of the Committee on the Legislative Department.

The CHAIRMAN. The question pending when the committee rose was upon striking out the words "and representatives," in the twenty-fifth section.

The question was then taken, and the amendment was agreed to.

Mr. CLARKE, of Henry. I move to strike

out the word "white" in this section, so that it will read—

"The number of Senators shall, at the next session following each period of making such enumeration, and the next session following each United States census, be fixed by law, and apportioned among the several counties, according to the number of inhabitants in each."

I would move to strike out the word "white" also in the thirty-fourth section, but we have passed by that.

The question was taken, and the amendment was not agreed to.

No further amendments being offered to this section—

Number of Members and Senators.

The thirty-sixth section was then read as follows:

"The senate shall not consist of more than fifty members, nor the House of Representatives of more than one hundred."

Mr. WILSON. I move to amend the section by striking out the word "fifty," and inserting in its place the words "thirty-six," and striking out the words "one hundred," and inserting the words "seventy-two," so that the section will read:

"The Senate shall not consist of more than thirty-six members, nor the House of Representatives of more than seventy-two."

Mr. SOLOMON. By a vote just taken, the committee have decided not to fix the basis of representation in the House at this time. They have done so avowedly for the purpose of investigating and considering the report of the special committee, which was formed to examine into and report upon a basis of representation for the House of Representatives. Now in opposition to the gentleman's amendment, I will simply say that if it should prevail, it would render the report of that committee entirely useless, and it could not by any means be adopted. I would like to see this question deferred in some way, until that report can be considered, although I myself dissent from the report. If this motion of the gentleman from Jefferson, [Mr. Wilson,] shall prevail, it will fix the number of members of the House at seventy-two. It is very likely that the report of this committee will fix the number of representatives at a greater number than that named by the gentleman. I think the better way would be to defer the consideration of this question for a while.

Mr. WILSON. I see no difficulty in the way, even if the amendment be adopted, of applying the principle which this special committee on the basis of representation may recommend. All that the friends of that proposition will have to do, is to increase the ratio of representation now contemplated by them. I am opposed to increasing the number of representatives in either branch of the general assembly. I believe the number is large enough now, and I am, therefore, opposed to increasing it.

Mr. PALMER. I am of the opinion that every organized county, as soon as it contains a certain number of inhabitants, say four or five thousand, should have a representative of its own, in the lower house of the general assembly. I know that questions of legislation frequently come up, which may affect the interests of one county one way, and the county immediately adjoining directly the other way. If we give to several new and sparsely settled counties only one representative, it may operate greatly to the disadvantage of some of these counties. For instance, two or more counties form a representative district, and the person they send to the legislature will be the representative of only one of these counties, because he cannot be the representative of both. He may be called to legislate upon questions which affect the county of which he is a resident. The interests of that county may require him to act in one way, directly adverse to the interests of the other county in his district. He cannot serve the interests of both these counties when they thus come in conflict. If he subserves the interests of his own county, in that case he does not represent the interests of the other county. I think, therefore, it will be a hardship to establish such a representation as would deny to certain counties, which are not thickly populated, a representative. Each county should have a representative to represent its particular interests in the lower house of the general assembly. The number of counties in the State is about a hundred, which will be rather increased than diminished. If the number of seventy-two is fixed here, it cannot be increased, however numerous the population might be in the different counties.

Mr. TRAER. I entertain the hope that this amendment will not prevail. I was a member of the committee that drafted this report and presented it to the convention. I believe the committee were unanimous in the opinion that a State as large as Iowa, required at least a hundred members in the lower house of the general assembly. I think that nothing is to be gained by striking out the numbers reported by the committee and inserting others.

It may be argued here, and I suppose it will be the strongest argument that will be adduced in favor of a reduction in the number of members proposed by the committee, that the greater the number of representatives, the greater will be the expense. This argument may have some weight; and yet I think that when we take into consideration the wants of the people of the State of Iowa, the argument of a few dollars more expense should have very little weight in a matter of this kind. I, for one, am in favor of a full and general representation. I want every voter of this State to have a fair representation in the House of Representatives. For that reason, believing as I do, that without a house of that size it would be impossible to give to all parts of the State an equal and fair representation, and believing farther, that a house of large size is less apt to become corrupt and led astray in matters of legislation than a smaller house, I am in favor of the number specified in the report. I hope this committee will not strike out that number. There are no good reasons why it should be done.

Again: every State in the Union of the size of Iowa, has a larger number of representatives than we propose in this report. I see no reason why a State occupying the position Iowa does, when she bids fair soon to become one of the very foremost States in the Union, should not have a representation which will fairly and fully represent all parts of the State. I think that when members come to look at the question in this light, they will certainly come to the conclusion that a House composed of a hundred members is small enough. For these reasons, I shall vote against the amendment of the gentleman from Jefferson, [Mr. Wilson.]

Mr. CLARKE, of Henry. In regard to this amendment, I wish to suggest to the gentleman from Jefferson, [Mr. Wilson], that he had perhaps better let the number remain as it has been reported by the committee. The time will very soon come—sooner than any of us may conceive—when there will be more than seventy-two organized counties that will demand and be entitled to a representative. I would prefer that every county in the State should have a representative. If there are one hundred and four counties in the State, I would make the number of members of the lower House one hundred and four, so that every county might have a representative in the most numerous branch of the Legislature. So far as the Senate is concerned, it is not a matter of so much importance what the number is. I should not care if it were limited to twenty-five. I think the proportion of twenty-five senators to a hundred representatives would be just as good as that of any other proportion. But so far as the House of Representatives is concerned, I agree with the gentleman from Davis, [Mr. Palmer], that we shall require that number of representatives in the lower House, if we have anything like a full representation of the people of different portions of the State. Every county will certainly demand a representative.

Mr. SOLOMON. This is a subject in which I feel a deep interest. We have involved ourselves in a difficulty here from which, in my opinion, it will be hard to extricate ourselves. I am opposed to this motion to strike out, because, if it prevails, it will be an expression of this body against a principle which I desire, at least, to have discussed, and, if possible, adopted. I would like very much to avoid, if I can, the settling of this question just at this point, and for that purpose I would submit a substitute for this section.

The CHAIRMAN. The Chair is of the opinion that the question must be first taken upon the amendment offered by Mr. Wilson.

The question was then taken upon the amendment offered by Mr. Wilson, and it was not agreed to.

Mr. SOLOMON. I now offer the following substitute for the section:

"Until the year 1866, every organized county in this State shall have at least one member in the House of Representatives, and the other members shall be apportioned throughout the State according to the population. After the year 1866, the apportionment shall be according to the population."

Mr. PALMER. I move to amend the substitute by inserting after the words, "counties in this State," the words, "containing five thousand inhabitants," so that it will read as follows:

"Until the year 1866, every organized county in this State containing five thousand inhabitants shall have at least one member in the House of Representatives, and the other members shall be apportioned throughout the State according to the population. After the year 1866, the apportionment shall be according to the population."

Mr. TRAER. I hope the gentleman will withdraw his substitute for the present.

Mr. SOLOMON. I have no objections to withdrawing it, if I am not cut off from the privilege of offering it at some other time. I do not deem it the right of any member of this Convention to offer any proposition, directly in collision with a propositien which the Convention, by their vote, have declared to be an expression of their sentiments. If the Convention go on and fix the number of representatives which the State may have, it may effect this proposition in such a manner that I cannot, under that rule, offer it.

Mr. TRAER. I think the gentleman could offer it even then.

Mr. SOLOMON. I will withdraw my proposition for the present.

Mr. CLARKE, of Henry. I offer the following amendment:

"Nor shall the House of Representatives consist at any time of a greater number of representatives than there shall be counties in the State."

Mr. SOLOMON. I am opposed to this proposition because, if adopted, it will cut off my proposition. If it prevail, I think it will deprive each organized county in the State of the opportunity of having a representative. The inequality between the smaller and the larger organized counties is so great, that we should never adopt the principle. The friends of the proposition that each organized county should have at least one member, cannot expect that that principle will form the sole basis of representation. I do not expect it, neither do I desire it, for it would be too much in conflict with that grand principle which establishes the propriety of giving representation according to population. I desire to see, besides the principle of allowing each organized county in the State a representative, another principle prevail, which will allow the balance of the House of Representatives to be apportioned according to population among the heavier counties. This will secure an absolute right to the new counties, and also do justice to the older counties. I hope, for that reason, that the amendment will not prevail.

Mr. CLARKE, of Henry. I will withdraw the amendment I offered.

Mr. SOLOMON. I move to strike out section thirty-six.

The question was taken, and the motion was not agreed to.

Mr. SOLOMON. I move to strike out the words "one hundred," so as to leave a blank for the number of representatives of the lower house. I hope the Committee will then pass on and leave it as it stands.

The question was taken, and the motion was agreed to, upon division; ayes 15, noes 13.

Basis of Representation.

Mr. HARRIS. I offer, to come in here, as sections thirty-seven and thirty-eight, the report of the special Committee on the Basis of Representation.

Sec. 37. The House of Representatives shall be based upon the several counties of the State in the following manner: *Provided,* That no representative district shall contain more than four organized counties, and shall be entitled to one representative. Any district containing one or more counties, and having a number of inhabitants equal to one-half of the ratio fixed by law, shall be entitled to one representative, and any one county containing in addition to the ratio fixed by law, a fraction of one-half of that number shall be entitled to one additional represesentative. Provided, further, That no floating district shall hereafter be formed.

Sec. 38. At its first session under this Constitution, and at every subsequent session, the General Assembly shall proceed to fix the ratio of representation and also to form into districts, as above provided, those counties which will not be entitled to a representative singly under the provision of the preceding section.

Mr. TRAER. Mr. Chairman: As chairman of the committee that made this report, I shall embrace this opportunity to lay before the committee some of the reasons which governed the special committee in their action upon this matter. I will state that this question came up in the deliberations of the committee upon the legislative department, when it was discussed at some length. The committee were divided in opinion; the majority were opposed to the principle. By agreement, however, it was arranged that this matter should be referred to a special committee. The result of their action, you have in the report which has just been read.

The basis of representation, as it existed under the old constitution, was the same in both branches of the general assembly, that of population. The people in the newer portions of the State have been dissatisfied with the basis as it existed under the present constitution, from the fact that it operated unequally, and they were unable to get a representation equal to that which the older counties enjoyed. The question came up and was discussed in my district, when I was a candidate for election. I claim that there is a necessity for a change in the representative system of this State, for several reasons; among which, the most prominent, is the fact that in the newer portions of the State the population is increasing so rapidly, that an apportionment, based upon an equal division, according to the number of inhabitants, will so change in two years, owing to the increased rapidity which characterize the settlements of the newer counties, that at the expiration of that period the representation will be rendered very unequal, the population doubling in the new counties in less than one half of the time that it does in the old counties. This fact shows that a system of representation, based solely upon population, without regard to this increase, must of necessity operate very unequally in the different portions of the State.

You will perceive, Mr. Chairman, that this inequality in representation exists, to a greater extent, in the senate than in the house of representatives. The apportionment being made for the senate only once in four years, makes the disparity in the number of population in those districts still greater. Thus, in some of the older portions of the State, the population in the senatorial districts, which entitled them to a senator at the time the apportionment was made, has increased but a very small fraction of the whole ratio; while in the newer counties that ratio has been doubled, and in some cases has increased to three times the original number.

I now propose to show, from some calculations which I have made, and which are based upon the present apportionment for the senate, that such is the case. The facts to which I allude are as follows; (and we are to suppose that this apportionment was made upon a correct estimate, and divided equally among the inhabitants of the State, as near as possible): The county of Des Moines, constituting the fourth senatorial district, with twenty thousand one hundred and ninety-eight Inhabitants, has two senators; while the twenty-fifth district, which I have the honor to represent, has thirty-one thousand six hundred and twelve inhabitants, and only two senators. Here we see that the population has increased one third in two years.

Again, the seventh district, composed of Henry county, with fifteen thousand three hundred and ninety-five inhabitants, has one senator, while the thirty-third district, with twenty-seven thousand seven hundred and forty-one inhabitants, has but one senator; showing a difference of almost one-half. The sixth district, with a population of thirteen thousand three hundred and five, has one senator, while the thirty-fourth district, with a population of twenty-four thousand and eighty-seven, has but one senator, showing a difference in the representation in those districts of one-half. Thus gentlemen will see that the difference is very considerable in the amount of representation between the older and newer portions of the State.

And when we take into consideration that this apportionment is made only once in four years, and that the difference, which I have shown to exist, will not only be doubled but trebled in that time, it will be apparent to every person that great injustice is done to the newer portions of the State by the present system of apportionment. With this state of facts before them, the Committee came to the conclusions which are embodied in the report before referred to.

Now, sir, having shown the reasons which induced the Committee to report this proposition, I propose to consider, to some extent, the proposition itself, arguing from the facts and premises laid down in the foregoing remarks. I come to the following conclusions: first, that any apportionment made under the present system of representation must necessarily work injustice to the new counties; that it will be impossible to so district the State that injustice will not be done to certain portions thereof. I therefore propose that we should adopt a principle of representation for the House, which, while it will give the new counties a little more representation than they would be entitled to otherwise, will only serve to balance what they lose under the present unequal apportionment in the Senate. In short, I propose that those counties, to which this principle will apply, shall make up in the House what they will lose in the Senate, thereby equalizing the differences which have heretofore existed.

What are the provisions of this report? When strictly considered, the only difference between this report and the system now in force is simply this: this gives the new counties the advantage of the fraction on the first representative, while the old system requires the whole amount of the ratio, before the county would be entitled to a member. In the second place, it provides that there shall not be more than four counties in any one district. This will effectually prevent the system of placing ten or fifteen counties in one district, to be represented by one individual, who could not, be his talents ever so great, become acquainted with the wants of his constituents. I am in favor of this provision in the report. I claim that there is connected with every organized county, certain interests which cluster around it as a distinct organization, which require a representative in the General Assembly. And the only reason that prevented the Committee from reporting in favor of a system which would give each county at least one representative, was the fact that such a system would make the House too large. Therefore the Committee fixed upon this plan of allowing the Legislature to settle the ratio and graduate the number of members to suit their convenience, provided that they did not exceed the limit fixed in the Constitution. The advantage of this system is, that it will operate equally well with any ratio which the Legislature may see fit to adopt. It will do away with the old system of districting the State by the General Assembly, prevent a lerge amount of corruption and gerrymandering for party purposes, and render the representation just and equitable throughout the State. And last, though not least, it will do away with the system of floats with which the newer portions of the State have been cursed for years past.

Now, sir, all we ask is, that justice may be done in this matter, which we are satisfied the sense of justice and magnaminity of the members of the convention will prompt them to grant. Our motto is, "let justice be done though the heavens fall." I will not detain the committee longer, but will return my thanks for the courtesy which has been extended to me. Feeling perfect confidence in the wisdom and impartiality of gentlemen, I will submit this proposition to their decision, with every assurance that that decision will be all that I, myself, or the friends of this measure, could ask.

Mr. PARVIN. My fellow-members of the Committee on the Legislative Department, feel under great obligations to the gentleman from Benton, [Mr. Traer,] for the ability and energy which he has manifested upon this subject ever since their first meeting, when he introduced this subject; and, although the committee were opposed to him, yet he urged his scheme with so much ability and energy, that the committee agreed unanimously to recommend the appointment of a special committee, to whom this subject might be referred. That there is something wrong in regard to the representation of the new counties, which are settling so rapidly, is manifest to every one. In endeavoring to remove that error, we must be careful that we do not fall into a greater one. The difficulty in having one man representing a dozen counties is, that their local interests are changing so continually that it is almost impossible for any one man to represent them all to their entire satisfaction. I do not think that we are going to avoid this difficulty, unless we adopt the system of borough representation, which I think is exceedingly objectionable. One great reason that gentlemen urge for the adoption of this system is, that the apportionment is not fixed now so often as it should be. But if gentlemen will just look at the thirty-fourth section, which we passed upon this morning in committee of the whole, they will find that the general assembly hereafter is to apportion the State every two years from 1858 until 1870, after which time there will be an apportionment every five years. We have decided that we will have only biennial sessions, consequently, under the thirty-fourth section, at every session there will be an apportionment of representation. Therefore the second section reported by this special committee is unnecessary, if the thirty-fourth section adopted by the committee of the whole, is agreed to by the convention.

The first section relates to the basis of representation. Shall we fix representation upon the population, or shall we fix it upon the borough system? The first section of this report provides that no representative district shall contain more than four counties. There are counties in this State four of which would not possess half of the ratio of population. I suppose that you can find four counties organized that have not two thousand inhabitants, perhaps not one thousand, perhaps less than that number. The ratio of population fixed by the last House of Representatives was seven or eight thousand. I ask if it is just that these counties with so small a population shall come in here with a representation equal to that of counties with seven or eight thousand, when if they waited for two years and should increase in population, the general assembly would fix a ratio so that they would secure the representation to which they were justly entitled?

There would be some propriety in the argument of the gentleman from Benton, [Mr. Traer,] that we should make provision for the future increase of population—such as we know will be the case, from the fact that these new counties are settling faster than the old ones—had we not provided by the thirty-fourth section, that an apportionment of representation should be made every two years. Will the convention sanction the principle of borough representation, or will they sanction the principle of representation based upon population? I can see no other question at issue here. I do not wish to do any injustice to these new counties. They are settling very rapidly; but I believe the provision we have adopted here, providing for an apportionment every two years, will be amply sufficient to provide for any increase of their population.

Mr. HARRIS. Knowing that my friend from Muscatine (Mr. Parvin) was opposed to the scheme originated by the gentleman from Benton (Mr. Traer) I expected to hear from him a very strong argument against the proposition; and therefore I have listened to his remarks with some interest.

The gentleman did not make use of the words "organized counties" when he was discussing the question as to whether more counties should be put together to have but one representative. The report of the special committee speaks of "organized counties," and does not have reference to counties which are merely laid out, and have a place upon the map, but which, as yet, have no place in municipal or civil government, and which are attached to other counties for judicial and representative purposes. We claim that counties which are organized, and which have a government of their own, should have a representation to attend to their local home interests in the legislature. We claim that counties of this description should at least have the privilege of having a voice in the legislature to present their claims and interests. Is this a matter of such injustice that any gentleman living in one of the large and populous cities of this state, should cry out against the principle of allowing the newly organized counties the representation which we ask for them? If this be injustice, then I have only to say here, that I am one of those that are ever ready to stand up and defend that injustice.

I ask gentlemen seriously, what harm or injustice can there be in saying, that no representative district shall be composed of more than four organized counties? I appeal to the gentleman from Muscatine, or any other gentleman here, representing those strong counties, which, in the plenitude of their power, send up four or five representatives to the legislature, what great harm can result from the adoption of the provision recommended in this first section of the report made by the special committee? On the other hand, we who represent the sparsely settled portion of the State, know that great good may be frequently done our people and our interests in consequence of having somebody to represent us in the Legislature, who can sympathise with our wants, and speak for us when the proper time comes for demanding any act of justice at the hands of the General Assembly.

The gentleman from Muscatine [Mr. Parvin] says that there may be four counties with not more than two thousand inhabitants. I apprehend that you will find very few instances of this kind, where four organized counties have not a population of two thousand inhabitants. I ask gentlemen, even if that be the case, if they are prepared to say that that extent of territory, when it is composed of counties, that have an organized government, and have their own interests to look after, should not have the privilege of having at least one representative to look after their interests in the legislature? Take my own county of Appanoose, and the county of Wayne. Appanoose has a population of ten thousand, and Wayne has a population of four thousand. If you make the basis of representation seven thousand, which will likely be the number fixed upon, then by putting the two together they would be entitled to two representatives. What would be the result? Why Appanoose, having a greater population, can control and swallow up Wayne county. The principle of representation which we propose here, simply steps in and says, that Appanoose shall have but one representative.

This report also provides, that when any county contains, in addition to the ratio fixed by law, a fraction of one-half of that number, it shall be entitled to an additional representative. Consequently, the gentleman's own county, when it shall have this fraction, would have the very same advantage that any of the new counties would have. What would the gentleman have? Would he have the fraction frittered away with the other counties, and have these floating districts, that cause so much log-rolling and corruption in the legislature? I say there is no injustice done to the old counties by the provision we have here made in this report, because they have the same advantage from this fraction that the new counties have, and of course this arrangement will result as much in their favor, as it will in our own. But the advantage we derive from this proposition is, that it simply gives each county its own representative, in the place of having the representation bartered off among half a dozen politicians. Another advantage we derive from this proposition is, that it will have a tendency to give these counties that are weak a stronger representation than they otherwise would have, without doing any injustice to the stronger ones.

Again, the proposition would have the tendency to compel these stronger counties, that have not the full fraction, to give away their fractions to the smaller counties that do not come up to the ratio, so as to place them upon some show of equality in the legislature; or in other words, to prevent the stronger counties, that would otherwise have the weaker ones attached to them, from swallowing up the weaker counties entirely. The disparity that exists, between the representation of the smaller and larger counties, in the senate will continue. We do not propose to meddle with that, but we will give the stronger counties the advantage which they will derive from it All we ask is, that any four organized counties shall have the privilege of sending one representative to the general assembly, and shall not be dependent upon the older counties. The idea that the new counties are to gain any particular advantage from the fraction is sheer nonsense, because the old counties will have just as much advantage from it as the new counties.

I hope gentlemen representing the older counties will examine this matter carefully, before they decide upon it, and give us the rights which we, of the new counties, claim are justly due us.

Mr. PARVIN. I wish to say but one word in reply. I know that under the apportionment of the last general assembly, Muscatine has but one floating representative. By this report the gentleman from Benton [Mr. Traer;] would give us two floating representatives.

Mr. HARRIS. Is there any injustice done to Muscatine in that?

Mr. PARVIN. I will tell gentlemen of this convention that Muscatine does not ask any favors of this kind. This report gives Muscatine a favor, which she has not asked. We ask for no more representation, than our population would give us.

Mr. SOLOMON. I do think that this subject is worthy of the careful consideration of this body. I presume it is the unquestionable prerogative of the framers of the organic law of this State to fix the basis of representation for the general assembly. We have the precedent set us in previous constitutions, and I believe this course is adopted in all the States. The duty then devolves upon us, who are to be the authors of the organic law for years to come, to inquire carefully into what we shall lay down as the basis of representation for the general assembly. It is necessary for us to consider this matter carefully. While I do not profess to be able to shed any light before this convention upon this or any other subject that may come before them, still, as an humble representative of a very respectable portion of this State, and one which is immediately interested in this question, I beg the indulgence of this body, while I present my views upon the subject now under consideration.

Before I go on with my argument I will submit a substitute for the report which has been offered by this Committee.

"Until the year 1866, every organized county in this State shall have at least one member in the House of Representatives, and the other members shall be apportioned throughout the State according to the population; after the year 1866 the apportionment shall be according to the population."

This proposition varies somewhat from the last basis of representation in one branch of the General Assembly in this State. If gentlemen will look into this matter, they will see that I do not propose to destroy the popular voice in the General Assembly at all. The General Assembly is made up of two separate and distinct bodies, whose action is entirely independent of each other. The report of the special committee fixes the basis of representation for the Senate the same that it is now, according to population, throughout the State. But in regard to the other branch it proposes what may perhaps be considered an innovation. It is only in one branch of the General Assembly that we desire to bring in a new principle. The popular voice is preserved in the Senate. If any danger should arise to the people at large, as a whole, from this principle of giving to organized counties their rights, by giving to them some slight preference, it can be checked in the Senate. There we have a check upon this principle, if there be anything wrong in it. Then, by admitting this basis of representation for each organized county, you only furnish to such county a voice through which that county may be heard and felt in one branch of the General Assembly. If it is heard to the disadvantage of the balance of the State, it may then be checked in the Senate. One door through which every bill, before it becomes a law, must pass, is the Senate, and the whole people of the State have an equal voice there. If any injury shall have been done in the other House by this principle, it may be checked in the Senate; consequently the people are not robbed of their rights by its adoption.

I know it will be urged, as an argument in opposition to this principle, that it seeks to give to men rights which they have not as members of the body politic. Here is the starting point. Let us examine it a little. What does it mean? I admit, with every man, that it is a safe principle that the representation in every State, should be according to the population; that a man, wherever he may be, should be clothed at all times with power equal to his neighbor citizens. But this is only in a general sense. It is a broad principle, and it should never be violated, but ever be protected.

There is, however, another principle. We are established as a State, and when men come to speak upon questions which affect the whole State, and affect every part of it alike, then each man should be heard alike. But besides having a corporate existence as a State, we have established and permitted corporations of a different character—political communities—as cities and counties. These bodies are established for certain purposes. They are distinct, and have interests of their own, which not only differ materially, but they are antagonistic to the interests of surrounding communities. Now the only question in this whole case is this: Does this political institution, the county, which is a corporate body, does this municipality, does this organization, entitle the citizens thereof to a separate and distinct voice, independent of that to which they would be entitled as mere citizens of the State! I think it does, and here is where I get my reasons for urging this change.

Now I am free to admit, that if the population of this State, or of any other State, was equally distributed throughout its whole territory, no fairer basis of representation could be invented than that of population. How is it in our own State? I want to ask you if four fifths of the population of the State do not now reside in the valley of the Mississippi? According to the basis in our present Constitution, four-fifths of the legislators of this State come from the Mississippi valley. The Mississippi valley controls, then, the legislation in both branches of the General Assembly. I would ask, then, if the Legislature is the voice of the State?

Do the new counties in the west have an opportunity to say "aye" or "no," effectively, upon any measure before the Legislature? Here is Lee county, on the Mississippi—a large county—a very respectable county—and one that is entitled, from her population, to a heavy voice in the Legislature. That county has had, I think, as many as six members in the House of Representatives at one time, and it has five now. And while Lee county had, in the last Legislature, five members of the House of Representatives, seven of our western counties—in one of which I reside—had but one member. Lee county had five representatives, while Mills, Montgomery, Adams, Union, Page, Taylor, and Ringgold counties had but one, and that one representative lived in Mills county—the other counties, of course, having no direct voice in the lower branch of the General Assembly.

Now, although there is great disparity between these counties as regards population, still, they have important interests in other respects. Take, for instance, this subject of railroads in our State. I undertake to say that my county—Mills county—feels as deep an interest in regard to railroads as Lee county, or Des Moines county. And as proof of this, while my county is put with six others to have but one representative, and Lee county alone has five representatives, yet my county has taken as much stock in the Burlington and Missouri railroad as the counties of Wapello and Des Moines.

Mr. MARVIN. Does Mills county take this stock as a county, or is it taken by individuals?

Mr. SOLOMON. She takes it as a county—as a municipality; and this shows the interest she feels in that branch of internal improvements.

Now, from the debates we have had here, I think I have good reason to believe that something may be inaugurated in this Constitution which will place these railroad interests in the General Assembly. If that is so, then that is one reason why each county that is organized should have a voice in that General Assembly. And suppose you give them that voice? Do you destroy the power of Lee county, of Dubuque county, or of any other county in this State, according to the rights to which its population entitles it? No, sir; because, if the lower House, which is made up of a large body of representatives from new counties, should undertake to impose anything upon the State to which the majority of the people are opposed, it can and will be checked in the Senate, unquestionably.

Now, mind you, we do not ask that the whole House of Representatives shall be apportioned according to counties. But we ask that each new organized county shall have at least one member, and the remainder of the House shall be apportioned according to population.

This seems to strike the minds of some gentlemen as impracticable, from the fact that it will make the House of Representatives a great deal larger body than at present. I want to investigate this point a little. I am free to say that I believe there should be a great difference in point of numbers between the Senate and the House of Representatives. What advantage is there in having two bodies of men assembled under the same roof, and possessing equal powers, and very nearly equal in numbers, and which shall deliberate in the same way, and formed upon the same basis of representation? I think the very fact of there being two Houses would indicate that they should be organized upon different and distinct principles. The one is intended as the deliberative branch of the General Assembly—the check upon the other. The other, then, should be furnished with the means of bringing up everything fresh from the people, from every locality and portion of the State. If the House of Representatives is to be composed of but seventy-two members, who are to sit down side by side with the Senate, in the same building, to deliberate upon the same subjects, to be governed by the same rules, and to come from the people in the same way, I would ask, where is the benefit to be derived from having two such deliberative bodies? One benefit, perhaps, is to give a little more time for the same kind of deliberation; that is all.

But in the other case, if you form the House of Representatives upon a different plan, and bring its members from every county in the State, you will have men there representing the various views of the different sections of the State, which they will force upon the consideration and deliberation of that body. All the bills they pass, however, must be sent to the Senate for their sanction. I do not think, therefore, that the fact that the House of Representatives will be increased in numbers is any argument against my proposition.

I should think that a House of Representatives numbering one hundred and fifty members and a Senate numbering fifty, or even only thirty-six members, would not be an unjust proportion And that proportion and that disparity would admit of my principles and my views upon this subject.

I do not think that justice can be done in any other way, to the various sections of the State. The new counties that do not send a representative here, independent of the surrounding counties, have no voice here at all. We are ushering into this State a new era with regard to at least two subjects. We are breaking down the barrier against paper currency in this State—this convention are assuming the responsibility to do that thing. They are placing it in the power of the commercial cities and towns upon the Mississippi river, without the new counties having an opportunity to say "aye" or "no" in the matter, to take hold of and control entirely this subject of currency. You must recollect that the legislature is to frame a law permitting or inaugurating a definite system of banking, and that law is to be submitted to the people, four-fifths of whom are in the Mississippi valley.

I know that the proposition in regard to representation which we advocate, will be attacked if it is deemed worthy of opposition at all, under the stigma of the old "rotten borough system." The gentleman from Muscatine [Mr. Parvin] left off the word "rotten," but I will put it on, because I have heard it so often used. Now let us see whether there is any parallel between the two systems. Take that system as it prevailed for some time in Massachusetts. That State gave to each town—not to each county, but to each town—certain privileges in regard to representation. We propose to give representation to counties which have a separate and distinct municipal existence, and should be entitled to more respect than towns are. That is the difference between the system we advocate and the one stigmatized as the "rotten borough system," which this system is said to resemble. It has been attempted in this convention to clothe the new counties with the power of assuming corporate debts; in other words, to clothe them almost entirely with powers which States alone have heretofore exercised. I ask gentlemen who have sought to do this thing, and who have looked to the individuality of these municipalities, to go with me one step farther, and give them their representation in the General Assembly. What will be the use of giving them certain powers over and above what they now have, or even their present powers, without a voice in the legislature to make known their wants? But I will not say anything further on this subject at the present.

I do not know that I can hope that this proposition will prevail. I am very well aware of the fact that from the manner in which this body was chosen, that considerations will creep into the deliberations here, opposed to giving those privileges to the more thinly populated portions of the State, which we who come from the new counties claim should be extended to us. Therefore, I scarcely expect, unless this body proceeds with a spirit of greater magnanimity than usually actuates men, to succeed in carrying this proposition. But I will at least urge it in justice to my constituents.

Mr. MARVIN. I desire to explain my position upon this subject. I am in favor of the proposition, with some amendments which may be offered at the proper time, which is now before the convention. I do not live in what may be strictly called one of the new counties of the State. But I believe it is but justice to them to grant this thing. I have an interest, however, in making single districts. I know that more or less corruption will creep into every legislative body, when they attempt to make floating districts. I do not care which political party may be in power; when they attempt to make a floating district they will go to work and carve out—the republicans putting a strong republican district with one that is doubtful, and the democrats a strong democratic district with one that is doubtfully democratic—so that their influence may be felt in the elections. Now I do not like this way of doing things. I would take this matter from the general assembly so that they could not have anything of this kind. For that reason I would be in favor of the propositions before the convention, to strike out these floating districts, and give every county having one-half of the ratio, a representative. But still I shall ask to amend this proposition so that a county, before it shall have two representatives, must have one and three-fourths ratios, instead of one and a half, as the proposition now stands. I will say further, in reply to those who seem to consider this a new thing, that I find the same principle in the constitution of the State of Ohio.

Mr. HALL. I hear a great deal of complaint among gentlemen here, in regard to the older portions of the State. I come from what has been termed one of the "mother counties" of this State, old Des Moines county. I believe the very soil upon which the building in which we are assembled now stands, was once a portion of Des Moines county. I do not think these complaints are just. I do not think there is any disposition on the part of the older portions of the State, to do any act oppressive or unjust towards the newly settled portions of the State. I should feel chagrined, coming from the county that I have the honor in part to represent, if I thought such was the case.

I believe the true policy is to to adopt some system of representation, for both branches of the general assembly, which will approximate as nearly as practicable to the actual population of the districts that elect the members of the general assembly. The plan proposed by the select committee upon the basis of representation, and now proposed as an amendment to the report of the committee on the legislative department, proposes to fix a certain number of population as the ratio for a representative, say six, seven, or eight thousand. When we come to a county that has not the ratio, the next enquiry is, has it more than one-half of the ratio? It begins in the new counties with the fraction and ends in the old counties with the fraction. It is just as fair one way as the other. It may for a short time give the new counties a small preponderance, as there may be more new counties with only half the ratio, than old counties with a half a ratio over. But the new counties are growing more rapidly; there is more room for settlement there; they are filling up more rapidly in proportion to their numbers, than the older counties, and will soon reach a certain point in population where they will have a full ratio, and no more representation than they now have with only half a ratio.

Now I can see no earthly injustice in the proposition. You get rid of this floating system. The people can tell what they are doing, and have not to depend upon the will of the legislature for the districting of the State. I do think the present system is an outrageous one. For instance, under the late apportionment, here is a floating member given to the counties of Lee, Van Buren and Henry, containing a population of over sixty thousand, because Henry had a little fraction of a thousand, Lee had a fraction of a thousand, and Van Buren another thousand over the ratio, and there is a float thrown in to keep them up. I believe that each representative should come from some specified district. I think we cannot adopt a fairer and more just principle than the one proposed by this select committee, by which you get rid of all this chicanery and gerrymandering. It is a system that will work fairly, and can be subject to no just ground of complaint whatever.

This rule cannot perhaps be made to operate with the same certainty in the Senate as in the House of Representatives; hence you fix the number in that body more definitely, and at a smaller amount. But it can approximate in that branch of the legislature, so that these gerrymandering schemes, now prevalent to some extent in this State, and more especially in other States, will, as far as possible, be avoided. I hope the principle in this report of the special committee will prevail.

I do not know as there would be any great objection to increasing the fraction, though I am willing to give to each county that has over the ratio, population equal to one-half a ratio, an additional number. However, if the fraction is increased, to suit the views of the gentleman from Jones, [Mr. Marvin,] from one-half to three-fourths, I will still vote for it.

Mr. SOLOMON. It will be noticed that in my amendment I limit the operation of this principle to the year 1866. My object is this: I think that it is only our present condition that demands the inauguration of this principle, and that from the rapidity with which our State is filling up, the various portions will become nearly equal in population by 1866, and the necessity for this rule will have passed away. It is for that reason that I have limited the operation of the principle to that time.

The question was upon the amendment to the amendment.

The amendment offered by Mr. Harris was as follows:

"The House of Representatives shall be based upon the several counties of the State in the following manner: Provided, That no Representative district shall contain more than four organized counties, and shall be entitled to one Representative. Any district containing one or more counties, and having a number of inhabitants equal to one-half of the ratio fixed by law, shall be entitled to one Representative, and any one county containing in addition to the ratio fixed by law, a fraction of one-half of that number shall be entitled to one additional Representative. Provided farther, That no floating district shall hereafter be formed.

At its first session under this Constitution, and at every subsequent session, the General Assembly shall proceed to fix the ratio of representation, and also to form into districts, as above provided, those counties which will not be entitled to a Representative singly under the provision of the preceding section."

The amendment to the amendment, offered by Mr. Solomon, was as follows:

"Until the year 1866, every organized county in this State shall have at least one member in the House of Representatives, and the other members shall be apportioned throughout the State according to the population; after the year 1866 the apportionment shall be according to the population."

The question being taken upon the amendment to the amendment, upon a division, it was not agreed to; ayes 10; noes 15.

The question being then taken upon the amendment, it was agreed to.

Formation of Districts.

Section thirty-seven was then read as follows:

"When a Congressional, Senatorial, or Representative District shall be composed of two or more counties, it shall not be entirely seperated by any county belonging to another district; and no county shall be divided in forming a Congressional, Senatorial, or Representative District."

No amendment being offered to this section—

Elections by the General Assembly to be viva voce.

Section thirty-eight was then read as follows:

"In all elections by the General Assembly, the members thereof shall vote *viva voce;* and the votes shall be entered on the journal."

No amendment being offered to this section—

Salaries of State Officers.

Section thirty-nine was then read as follows:

"The annual salary of the Governor shall not exceed twenty-five hundred dollors; Secretary,

Treasurer, and Auditor of State, fifteen hundred dollars each; Judges of the Supreme Court, twenty-five hundred dollars each; Judges of the District Courts, two thousand dollars each."

Mr. WILSON. I offer the following as a substitute for this section:

"The Governor, Secretary, Treasurer, Auditor of State, and Attorney General, shall, at stated times, receive for their services a compensation, to be established by law, which shall neither be increased nor diminished during the period for which they shall have been elected."

The section, as reported by the committee, provides also for the salaries of the supreme judges, and the district judges. That portion of the section has been disposed of in the article upon the judicial department. I am opposed to fixing any of the other salaries in the constitution. I do not think it is the proper place for such things. I believe it is a subject of legislation, and ought to be exclusively such. I believe that these salaries ought to be varied according to circumstances, and we can make no constitutional rule that can apply to them. The constitution should contain only the frame work of the government, the principles upon which the government is to be based. The salaries have nothing to do with these at all, and I hope the subject will be left out of the constitution entirely, and left to the legislature to determine.

Mr. HARRIS. If the gentleman will allow the salaries to be fixed for the first term, and then let the legislature fix them, I will go for his proposition.

Mr. WILSON. Unless there is a constitutional provision fixing the salaries of State officers, they would receive the same that State officers now receive.

Mr. HARRIS. Would they receive that salary as a matter of right by law, or as a matter of courtesy?

Mr. WILSON. As a matter of right. The law will remain unrepealed unless it comes in conflict with the constitution. This section I have proposed will not come in conflict with the law. Unless the law is changed here, the State officers will receive the salaries given them now by law.

The question being taken upon the substitute offered by Mr. Wilson it was adopted.

Mr. HARRIS moved that the committee rise, report back to the convention the report of the committee on the distribution of powers and the legislative department, as amended, and ask to be discharged from its further consideration.

The question being taken, the motion was agreed to.

In Convention.

The PRESIDENT having resumed the chair,

The CHAIRMAN reported that the Committee of the Whole had had under consideration the report of the standing committee upon the distribution of powers and the legislative department, had made sundry amendments thereto, and had instructed him to report the same as amended to the convention, and ask to be discharged from its further consideration.

The report of the Committee of the Whole was received and the committee discharged accordingly.

The Convention then proceeded to the consideration of the amendments made in committee of the whole.

Members of the House of Representatives.

The first amendment of the Committee of the Whole was to strike out of section three the words "continue two years from the Tuesday next after the first Monday in November," and insert the words, "commence from the first day of January next succeeding the election, and continue two years;" so that the section would then read,

"The members of the House of Representatives shall be chosen every second year, by the qualified electors of their respective districts, on the second Tuesday in October, except the year of the Presidential election, when the election shall be on the Tuesday next after the first Monday in November; whose term of office shall commence from the first day of January next succeeding the election, and continue two years."

The question being then taken, the amendment of the committee of the whole was concurred in.

Members of the Senate.

The next amendment of the committee of the whole was to strike out of section six the words,

"The present senators shall remain in office during the term for which they were elected, and shall be divided into two classes. Those Senators whose term of office expires on the first Monday in August, 1858, shall be one class, and those Senators whose term of office expires on the first Monday in August, 1860, shall be the other class; so that one-half shall be chosen every two years."

The section would then read as follows:

"The number of Senators shall not be less than one-third, nor more than one-half of the representative body."

Upon concurring in this amendment, Mr. PARVIN called for the yeas and nays, and they were ordered accordingly.

The question being then taken by yeas and nays, the amendment of the committee of the whole was concurred in; yeas 19; nays 11; as follows:

Yeas.—The President, Messrs. Ayres, Clark, of Alamakee, Clarke of Johnson, Emerson, Gibson, Gillaspy, Hall, Harris, Johnston, Marvin, Palmer, Patterson, Peters, Price, Robinson, Solomon, Traer and Young.

Nays.—Messrs. Clarke, of Henry, Edwards, Gower, Gray, Hollingworth, Parvin, Scott, Seely, Warren, Wilson and Winchester.

Classification of Senators.

The next amendment of the committee of the whole was to prefix to section seven the words, "The Senators shall be so classed by lot that one-half shall be chosen every two years."

The section would then read as follows:

"The Senators shall be so classed by lot that one-half shall be chosen every two years. When the number of Senators is increased, they shall be annexed by lot to one of the two classes, so as to keep them as nearly equal in number as practicable."

The question being taken, the amendment was concurred in.

Impeachment.

The next amendment of the Committee of the Whole was to strike out of section twenty-one the words, "Superintendent of Public Instruction and Attorney General," and insert the words "and all other officers of the State."

The section would then read as follows:

"The Governor, Secretary of State, Auditor, Treasurer, Judges of the Supreme and District Courts, and all other officers of State, shall be liable to impeachment for any misdemeanor in office; but judgment in such cases shall extend only to removal from office, and disqualification to hold any office of honor, trust or profit under this State; but the party convicted or acquitted shall nevertheless be liable to indictment, trial, and punishment according to law. All other civil officers shall be tried for misdemeanors and malfeasance in office in such manner as the General Assembly may provide."

The question was upon concurring in the amendment.

Mr. WINCHESTER. I do not exactly like the language of that amendment. I would therefore move a substitute for the amendment, to strike out the words "Secretary of State, Auditor, Treasurer, Superintendent of Public Instruction and Attorney General," and insert the words "and all other State officers," so that the section would then read:

"The Governor, Judges of the Supreme and District Courts, and other State officers shall be liable to impeachment for any misdemeanor or malfeasance in office," &c.

The question being taken upon the substitute for the amendment of the Committee of the Whole, it was adopted.

The amendment as amended was then concurred in.

Per Diem and Mileage of Members.

The next amendment of the Committee of the Whole was to substitute the following for section twenty-six of the committee's report:

"Each member of the first General Assembly under this constitution, shall receive the sum of three dollars per diem while in session; and the further sum of three dollars for every twenty miles travel in going to and returning from the place where such session is held, by the nearest traveled route; after which they shall receive such compensation as shall be fixed by law; but no General Assembly shall have the power to increase the compensation of its own members. And when convened in extra session they shall receive the same mileage and and per diem compensation as fixed by law for the regular session and none other."

The question being taken, the amendment was concurred in.

Laws taking Effect.

The next amendment of the Committee of the whole was to strike out of section twenty-seven the words "the fourth day of July next after the passage thereof," and insert the words "ninety days after the adjournment of the General Assembly by which it was passed," so that the section would then read,

"No law of the General Assembly of a public nature, shall take effect until ninety days after the adjournment of the General Assembly by which it was passed. If the General Assembly shall deem any law of immediate importance, they may provide that the same shall take effect by publication in newspapers in this State."

The question was upon concurring in the amendment.

Mr. HARRIS. I move to amend the amendment of the Committee of the Whole, by inserting in the original section, after the words "General Assembly," where they first occur, the words "passed at a regular session," and then leave that portion of the section as it now stands. Also, to insert after the words "passage thereof," this sentence: "laws passed at a special session shall take effect ninety days after the adjournment of the General Assembly by which they were passed." The whole section will then read as follows:

"No law of the General Assembly, passed at a regular session, of a public nature, shall take effect until the fourth day of July next after the passage thereof. Laws passed at a special session shall take effect ninety days after the adjournment of the General Assembly by which they were passed. If the General Assembly shall deem any law of immediate importance, they may provide that the same shall take effect by publication in newspapers in the State."

The question being taken upon the amendment to the amendment, it was agreed to.

The amendment of the Committee of the Whole, as amended, was then concurred in.

County Seats and Boundaries.

The next amendment of the Committee of the Whole was to insert in section thirty-one, after the words "alleys, or public squares," the sentence, "for changing county boundaries, or locating and changing county seats," so that the section would then read as follows:

"The General Assembly shall not pass local or special laws in the following cases:

For the assessment and collection of taxes for state, county, or road purposes;

For laying out, opening and working roads or highways;

For changing the names of persons;

For the incorporation of cities and towns;

For vacating roads, town plats, streets, alleys, or public squares;

For changing county boundaries, or locating or changing county seats.

In all the cases above enumerated, and in all other cases where a general law can be made applicable, all laws shall be general, and of uniform operation throughout the State."

Mr. MARVIN. I would call for a division of the question, so that we may have the vote upon that portion that relates to county boundaries, and that portion relating to county seats taken separately.

The PRESIDENT. A motion to amend the amendment of the Committee of the Whole would be in order.

Mr. CLARKE, of Henry. I move to amend the amendment by striking out the words "changing county boundaries, or," so that that portion will then read "for locating or changing county seats."

Mr. CLARK, of Alamakee. I hope this motion to amend will not prevail, for if it does, the whole object, or nearly the whole object, of the amendment of the Committee of the Whole will be destroyed. If this amendment is agreed to, then all that a man has to do in order to get a county seat changed, is to slip down here and get the Legislature to change the present boundaries of the county, so as to throw the present county seat out of the centre of the county, and thus render it inconvenient for the county after its boundaries are changed. The evils experienced from the change of county seats by this log-rolling in the Legislature, are, in fact, not so serious as those resulting from a change of county boundaries, splitting counties up, taking off in one place, and putting on in another. I would not give three cents for the amendment we quarreled about so much in Committee of the Whole this forenoon, if this amendment prevails.

Mr. CLARKE, of Johnson. I desire to say that I am opposed to this portion of the amendment of the Committee of the Whole, for the reason that it can be made of no utility. I do not see how a law can be devised under which this system can be carried out. There can be no general law, because where county boundaries are changed, it is probably because, as the gentleman from Des Moines [Mr. Hall,] said this morning, some portion of one county wants to be attached to another county, as a matter of convenience. And if you pass a general law submitting the question to the vote of both counties, the desire of those who seek the change may be defeated.

Mr. CLARK, of Alamakee. There is no proposition to submit anything to the people; it is all left to the Legislature.

Mr. CLARKE, of Johnson. I was supposing that that was the only way in which this could be done, and I can see no way of making the proposition practical. There is no danger, I think, of misconduct upon the part of the Legislature. It seems to me that no portion of a county can have its boundaries changed without the people of the county opposed to it having a knowledge of the fact. The member or members of the district or counties affected will certainly have time—and it will be their duty—to give notice to all the parties interested, so that they can be heard by petition or remonstrance. I think there is no change made except upon petition of those interested; and if there are those who are opposed to it, they can let it be known. I am in favor of the county seat question being provided for by general law; but I do not see how you can provide by general law for regulating the matter of county boundaries.

The question was upon striking out the words "changing county boundaries, or."

Upon this question, Mr. HALL called for the yeas and nays, and they were ordered accordingly.

The question being then taken, by yeas and nays, upon the motion to strike out, it was agreed to; yeas 18, nays 12, as follows:

Yeas—The President, Messrs. Ayres, Clarke, of Henry, Clarke, of Johnson, Edwards, Ells, Gower, Hall, Harris, Hollingsworth, Johnston, Marvin, Parvin, Patterson, Price, Robinson, Warren and Young.

Nays—Messrs. Clark, of Alamakee, Emerson, Gibson, Gillaspy, Gray, Palmer, Peters, Scott, Seely, Solomon, Traer and Wilson.

The question recurred upon concurring in the amendment of the Committee of the Whole, as amended.

Mr. CLARK, of Alamakee, demanded a call of the Convention, which was ordered.

The roll having been called, the Secretary announced the following as the result:

Present—The President, Messrs. Ayres, Clark, of Alamakee, Clarke, of Henry, Clarke, of Johnson, Edwards, Ells, Emerson, Gibson, Gillaspy, Gower, Gray, Hall, Harris, Hollingsworth, Johnston, Marvin, Palmer, Parvin, Patterson, Peters, Price, Robinson, Scott, Seely, Solomon, Traer, Warren, Wilson, Winchester and Young.

Absent—Messrs. Bunker, Cotton, Day, Skiff and Todhunter.

On motion of Mr. PARVIN,

Further proceedings under the call were dispensed with.

The question recurred upon concurring in the amendment of the Committee of the Whole as amended, and being taken, the amendment was concurred in.

Apportionment of Senators.

The next amendment of the Committee of the Whole was to strike out of section thirty-five, after the word "Senators," the words, "and Representatives," so that it would then read—

"The number of Senators shall, at the next session following each period of making such enumeration, and the next session following each United States census, be fixed by law, and apportioned among the several counties according to the number of white inhabitants in each."

The question being taken, the amendment was concurred in.

Number of Representatives and Senators.

The next amendment of the Committee of the Whole was to strike out of section thirty-six the words "one hundred," leaving a blank, so that the section would read as follows:

"The Senate shall not consist of more than fifty members, nor the House of Representatives of more than ——."

Mr. PALMER moved to fill the blank with the words, "number of counties in the State."

Mr. TRAER. I rise to a point of order, and that is, that as the Convention have not yet concurred in the amendment of the Committee of the Whole creating a blank, there is no blank to be filled.

The PRESIDENT. The Chair is of opinion that the motion of the gentleman from Davis, [Mr. Palmer], can be entertained as an amendment to the amendment of the Committee of the Whole.

Mr. CLARKE, of Johnson. It seems to me that there is going to be difficulty in this matter, if we are not careful what we do. The sections we have adopted in the Committee of the Whole, reported from the Select Committee on the Basis of Representation, it seems to be contemplated that a county may have more than one representative. The first of these sections reads as follows:

"Every county and district which shall have a number of inhabitants equal to one half of the ratio fixed by law, shall be entitled to one representative; *and any one county containing in addition to the ratio fixed by law, one half of that number, or more, shall be entitled to one additional representative.*"

Now, if the motion of the gentleman from Davis, [Mr. Palmer] prevails, it would follow that there never could be more members in the House of Representatives than there are counties in the State; and, consequently, it would destroy the principle contained in the sections reported by our Special Committee upon the Basis of Representation.

Mr. PALMER. I thought the blank should be filled. I will, however, move that there be a division of the question; that it be taken first upon striking out, and if that be agreed to, then upon inserting.

Mr. HARRIS. All we have to do is to refuse to concur in the amendment of the Committee of the Whole, and the whole difficulty is obviated. The motion to strike out, as I understand it, was carried merely as a matter of courtesy to the gentleman from Mills, [Mr. Solomon], who desired to test a proposition he wished to submit, to give to each county a representative. His proposition having failed, there was no necessity for this amendment to strike out the words "one hundred."

Mr. PALMER withdrew his amendment to fill the blank with the words "number of counties in the State."

The question recurred upon concurring in the amendment of the Committee of the Whole to strike out the words "one hundred."

Mr. CLARKE, of Johnson. I move to amend the amendment so as to strike out the words "nor the House of Representatives of more than one hundred," so that the section will then read—

"The Senate shall not consist of more than fifty members."

Mr. TRAER. I do not understand that the principle involved in the report of the Special Committee on the Basis of Representation will be in conflict with this section as reported by the Committee on the Legislative Department. The report of the Special Committee proposes to leave to the Legislature the fixing of the ratio. But we can, by this section, so restrict the Legislature that they shall not provide for more than a certain number of members of either House of the General Assembly. Suppose we adopt this section, which provides that there shall not be more than fifty Senators and one hundred members of the House of Representatives. All the Legislature will have to do will be to raise the ratio from time to time, as our population increases, so that there will not be more than that number in either House. I do not, therefore, see any necessity for the amendment proposed by the gentleman from Johnson, [Mr. Clarke.]

Mr. CLARKE, of Henry. I think that in process of time the idea of the gentleman from Mills, [Mr. Solomon,] will demand and receive some consideration. We must take into consideration in this matter, not only the principle of population, but the principle of territory; both ideas must be represented here. It was with that view that I suggested that the number of counties should be the limit of the House of Representatives, as in the progress of time, having so many counties in the State, the people of the State would consider that the most numerous branch of the General Assembly should be sufficiently large to admit of one representative from each organized county.

There are only about thirty-six counties in the State at this time that have five thousand inhabitants each. Suppose that number is taken as the ratio; in a very few years double that number of counties, seventy-two, will have that number each, and in a few years after one hundred counties will have that amount of population each. And I believe we must come to some such proposition as that submitted by the gentleman from Mills, in regard to the basis of representation.

I do not think that in a State like this we can keep up the idea of having our representation based alone upon population. I think the amendment which was proposed by the gentleman from Davis, [Mr. Palmer,] to fill the blank with the words "number of counties in the State," is right. I can see no difficulty to result from adopting that principle. You compel the legislature to keep within the number of counties. Suppose there are one hundred counties in the State; the legislature will then have to establish some ratio that will keep the number of members of the House of Representatives within the number of counties. All we desire is to impose some limit upon the size of the House of Representatives. I know that the people are becoming uneasy in regard to the number of members we will have in our General Assembly, and they desire to have some restriction imposed. They know that from the emigration and rapid growth of our State, without some restriction, we will in a few years have as large a body for the House of Representatives as they have in Massachusetts. And I do not think the people of this State desire we should have that.

I would be in favor of the amendment of the gentleman from Davis, [Mr. Palmer.] Or if we have but one hundred counties now, then restore the number stricken out.

Mr. HARRIS. The difficulty with the gentleman from Henry, [Mr. Clarke,] is that he has not been discussing the question before us. It has certainly been decided by a very emphatic vote that, in regard to this matter of basis of representation, we will not take into consideration the population with the number of counties. The only question is upon concurring in the amendment of the committee of the whole to strike out the words "one hundred," and have the blank filled with some other number. If we do not desire to strike out those words, then refuse to concur in the amendment, and there will be no conflict with the principle adopted in committee of the whole, in relation to the basis of representation.

The question was then taken upon the amendment offered by Mr. Clarke of Johnson, to the amendment, and it was not agreed to.

The question was then upon the amendment of the committee of the whole, and being taken, the amendment was not concurred in.

Basis of Representation.

The next amendment in committee of the whole was to insert the following sections:

"Sec. 37. The House of Representatives shall be based upon the several counties of the State in the following manner: Provided, That no Representative district shall contain more than four organized counties, and shall be entitled to one Representative. Any district containing one or more counties and having a number of inhabitants equal to one half of the ratio fixed by law, shall be entitled to one Representative, and any one county containing in addition to the ratio fixed by law, a fraction of one-half of that number shall be entitled to one additional Representative. Provided farther, That no floating district shall hereafter be formed.

"Sec. 38. At its first session under this constitution, and at every subsequent session, the General Assembly shall proceed to fix the ratio of representation and also to form into districts as above provided, those counties which will not be entitled to a Representative singly under the provision of the preceding section."

Mr. PARVIN. I move to amend the thirty-eighth section by striking out the words "under this constitution, and at every subsequent session," and inserting the words "after the taking of each census," so the section will read:

"At its first session, after the taking of each census, the General Assembly shall fix the ratio of representation, and also to form into representative districts those counties which will not be entitled singly to a representative."

I offer this amendment to make this section accord with the thirty-fifth section, which relates to senators. I want the apportionment for both houses made at the same time.

Mr. HALL called for the yeas and nays upon the amendment to the amendment, and they were ordered accordingly.

The question being then taken, by yeas and nays, upon the amendment to the amendment, it was not agreed to; yeas 11, nays 20, as follows:

Yeas—The President, Messrs. Ayres, Clarke of Henry, Clarke of Johnson, Ells, Gower, Gray, Parvin, Scott, Winchester and Young.

Nays—Messrs. Clark of Alamakee, Edwards, Emerson, Gibson, Gillaspy, Hall, Harris, Hollingsworth, Johnston, Marvin, Palmer, Patterson, Peters, Price, Robinson, Seely, Solomon, Traer, Warren and Wilson.

Mr. TRAER. I move to amend section thirty-eight by inserting before the word "session" the word "regular," so that the section will then read:

"At its first session under this constitution, and at every subsequent regular session, the General Assembly shall fix the ratio of representation, and also form into representative districts those counties which will not be entitled singly to a representative."

The question being taken upon the amendment to the amendment, it was agreed to.

Mr. CLARKE, of Henry. I move to amend section thirty-seven, by striking out the words "one-half," and inserting the words "two-thirds," as the fractional ratio to entitle a county to a representative.

Mr. HARRIS. I hope that amendment will not prevail, for it will defeat the object which was had in view by the gentleman from Benton, [Mr. Traer] and others, who supported these sections in committee of the whole. It was suggested there by the gentleman from Jones, [Mr. Marvin,] that he should move an amendment of this kind. But I trust it will not prevail.

Mr. TRAER. Before a district could have an amount over and above the ratio, equal to two-thirds of that ratio, the probability is that each county in the district would have enough of population to entitle it to a representative. So that the difficulty the gentleman apprehends cannot occur in regard to districts. I would ask him if he would apply the principle of his amendment to counties?

Mr. CLARKE, of Henry. I would be willing to apply it to the old counties.

The question being then taken upon the amendment to the amendment, it was rejected.

The question recurred upon the amendment of the committee of the whole, to insert the two sections before stated.

Upon this question Mr. TRAER called for the yeas and nays, and they were ordered accordingly.

The question being then taken, by yeas and nays, the amendment of the committee of the whole was concurred in; yeas 29, nays 2, as follows:

Yeas—The President, Messrs. Ayres, Clark of Alamakee, Clarke of Henry, Clarke of Johnson, Edwards, Ells, Emerson, Gibson, Gillaspy, Gower, Gray, Hall, Harris, Hollingsworth, Johnston, Marvin, Palmer, Patterson, Peters, Price, Robinson, Scott, Seely, Solomon, Traer, Wilson, Winchester and Young.

Nays—Messrs. Parvin and Warren.

Salaries of State Officers.

The last amendment of the committee of the whole was to substitute the following for section thirty-nine.

"The Governor, Secretary of State, Auditor, Treasurer, and Attorney General shall, at stated times, receive for their services a compensation to be established by law, which shall neither be increased nor diminished during the period for which they shall have been elected."

Mr. CLARKE, of Henry. I would suggest that we try to make this section conform to the section we adopted in the article upon the judicial department, so that our action may be uniform. We provided in that article that the salaries of the supreme judges should be two thousand dollars, and the salaries of the district judges one thousand six hundred dollars, until the year 1860, after which they should receive such compensation as may be provided by law.

I therefore move to substitute for the amendment of the committee of the whole, the following:

"The annual salary of the Governor shall be two thousand dollars: of the Secretary of State, Auditor, Treasurer and Attorney General one thousand five hundred dollars each; of the Judges of the Supreme Court two thousand dollars, and of the Judges of the District Court one thousand six hundred dollars each respectively, until the year 1860, after which they shall receive such compensation as may be provided by law; but the compensation of none of them shall be increased or diminished during the term for which they shall have been elected."

This will establish the salaries of all our officers for the present, so that each candidate may know what salary he will have if elected.

Mr. WILSON. I hope the amendment of the gentleman from Henry, [Mr. Clarke,] will not prevail. The salary of the governor, I believe, is now established at two thousand dollars, under the action of the late general assembly. The salary of the treasurer, auditor and secretary is established at one thousand five hundred dollars each, just the same as proposed by the gentleman in his amendment, so that there is but very little difference between his amendment and the law as it now stands. And any man elected under that law will receive that compensation. The section in relation to the salaries of our judges was adopted more as a compromise than anything else, and the salaries of the district judges were raised from what they are now, one thousand two hundred dollars, to one thousand six hundred dollars. I hope this convention will not undertake to fix the salaries of all our State officers in the constitution.

Mr. CLARKE, of Henry. It was for that very reason tnat I supposed no gentleman here would have any objection to fixing these salaries in the Constitution, so that our action may be uniform. If there is any opposition to my amendment, I will withdraw it.

Mr. CLARKE, of Johnson. What is the salary of the Governor as now established?

The PRESIDENT. I understand it to be eighteen hundred dollars, though I cannot speak from the record.

Mr. CLARKE, of Johnson. I understood, from the gentleman from Jefferson, [Mr. Wilson,] that it was two thousand dollars.

Mr. WILSON. I was so informed; I do not know.

Mr. CLARKE, of Johnson. If it is two thousand dollars, then I will vote for the amendment of the gentleman from Henry, [Mr. Clarke.]

Mr. CLARKE, of Henry, withdrew his amendment.

The question recurred upon the substitute of the Committee of the Whole for the thirty-ninth section.

Mr. HALL. I do not believe in making every branch of the government entirely dependent upon the Legislature. That seems, however, to be the view of the Convention, and I have no complaint to make. But I do believe in having the co-ordinate branches of the government as independent as possible. I believe we ought to fix the salary of the Executive, and not let him be dependent at all upon the Legislature. And that is my opinion also in regard to the judicial department. But it seems we are to throw the whole matter into the power of the Legislature, and let each department electioneer out the best way it can. Now I think that, inasmuch as they are independent and co-ordinate branches of government, the Constitution ought to make them independent of each other in this respect.

Mr. WILSON. The old Constitution left the salaries of the state officers dependent upon the Legislature, except that the salaries could not go above a certain sum for ten years after the adoption of the Constitution. At the end of that time the Legislature raised their salaries, and I believe will always be disposed to give them fair and reasonable compensation.

Mr. HALL. There certainly can be no objection to placing the two departments of the government, co-ordinate with the Legislature, upon an equality with the Legislature. I do not care what the old Constitution did in this respect; it did wrong. And I think it would be wisdom upon the part of this Convention to keep in view the independence of the co-ordinate branches of the government, and at least fix the salaries of the Governor.

The question was upon the amendment of the Committee of the Whole.

The thirty-ninth section read as follows:

"The annual salary of the Governor shall not exceed twenty-five hundred dollars; Secretary, Treasurer and Auditor of State, fifteen hundred dollars each; Judges of the Supreme Court, twenty-five hundred dollars each; Judges of the District Courts, two thousand dollars each."

The substitute proposed by the Committee of the Whole read as follows:

"The Governor, Secretary of State, Auditor, Treasurer and Attorney General, shall, at stated times, receive for their services a compensation, to be established by law, which shall neither be increased nor diminished during the period for which they shall have been elected."

Mr. HALL called for the yeas and nays upon the substitute, and they were ordered accordingly.

The question being then taken by yeas and nays, the substitute proposed by the Committee of the Whole was not concurred in; yeas 13, nays 18, as follows:

Yeas—The President, Messrs. Ayres, Clark, of Alamakee, Clarke, of Henry, Gibson, Gower, Marvin, Scott, Seely, Traer, Wilson, Winchester and Young.

Nays—Messrs. Clarke, of Johnson, Edwards, Ells, Emerson, Gillaspy, Gray, Hall, Harris, Hollingsworth, Johnston, Palmer, Parvin, Patterson, Peters, Price, Robinson, Solomon and Warren.

The PRESIDENT stated that the amendments of the Committee of the Whole had been gone through with, and the report as amended was still open to amendment.

County Boundaries.

Mr. CLARK, of Alamakee. I move to add to section thirty-one the following:

"And no special law, changing the boundary lines of any county, shall have effect until, upon being submitted to the people of the counties affected by the change, at a general election, it shall be approved by a majority of the votes in each county, cast for and against it."

The whole section will then read—

"The General Assembly shall not pass local or special laws in the following cases:

For the assessment and collection of taxes for state, county or road purposes;

For laying out, opening and working roads or highways;

For changing the names of persons;

For the incorporation of cities and towns;

For vacating roads, town plats, streets, alleys or public squares;

For locating or changing county seats;

In all the cases above enumerated, and in all other cases where a general law can be made applicable, all laws shall be general, and of uniform operation throughout the State; and no special law, changing the boundary lines of any county, shall have effect until, upon being submitted to the people of the counties affected by the change, at a general election, it shall be approved by a majority of the votes in each county, cast for and against it."

This will obviate all the objections raised against the provision in the amendment of the Committee of the Whole, which was stricken out. The object is to cut off this log-rolling to secure special legislation to change the boundaries of the counties.

Mr. PETERS. I move to amend the amendment by adding to it the following:

"Nor shall any county seat be removed, unless the proposition shall receive a majority of two-thirds of all the votes cast for or against it."

The section if so amended will read—

"The General Assembly shall not pass local or special laws in the following cases:

For the assessment and collection of taxes for State, county, or road purposes;

For laying out, opening, and working roads or highways;

For changing the names of persons;

For the incorporation of cities and towns;

For vacating roads, town plats, streets, alleys, or public squares;

For locating or changing county seats.

In all the cases above enumerated, and in all other cases where a general law can be made applicable, all laws shall be general, and of uniform operation throughout the State; and no special law changing the boundary lines of any county shall have effect until upon being submitted to the people of the counties affected by the change, at a general election, it shall be approved by a majority of the votes in each county, cast for and against it; nor shall any county seat be removed, unless the proposition shall receive a majority of two-thirds of all the votes cast for and against it."

The question being taken upon the amendment to the amendment, it was not agreed to.

The question recurred upon the amendment.

Upon this question Mr. CLARK, of Alamakee called for the yeas and nays, and they were ordered accordingly.

The question being then taken, by yeas and nays, the amendment was agreed to; yeas 20; nays 11, as follows:

Yeas.—Messrs. Ayres, Clark of Alamakee, Clarke of Henry, Ells, Emerson, Gibson, Gillaspy, Gower, Gray, Hollingsworth, Marvin, Palmer, Parvin, Robinson, Scott, Seely, Solomon, Traer, Wilson and Young.

Nays.—The President, Messrs. Clarke of Johnson, Edwards, Hall, Harris, Johnston, Patterson, Peters, Price, Warren and Winchester.

Eligibility to House of Representatives.

Mr. TRAER. I move to amend section four by inserting after the word "State," the words "and of the county and district he may have been chosen to represent," and strike out after the word "election" the words "and at the time of his election shall have had an actual residence of sixty days in the county or district he may have been chosen to represent;" so that the section will then read—

"Sec. 4. No person shall be a member of the House of Representatives who shall not have attained the age of twenty-one years, be a free white male citizen of the United States, and shall have been an inhabitant of this State, and of the county or district he may have been chosen to represent, one year next preceding his election."

Mr. WARREN. I offer, as a substitute for the amendment of the gentleman from Benton, [Mr. Traer,] the following: To strike out the words "one year next preceding his election; also to strike out the words "thirty days," and insert "one year;" so that the section will then read—

"No person shall be a member of the House of Representatives who shall not have attained the age of twenty-one years, be a free white male citizen of the United States, and shall have been an inhabitant of this State, and at the time of his election shall have had an actual residence of one year in the county or district he may have been chosen to represent."

Mr. TRAER. I think a person should be in a district at least one year before he can be elected to the legislature. I am opposed to this idea of a person coming into this State, and being taken up, and sent to the legislature, before he has had any opportunity to find out the wishes and wants of the county or district he may undertake to represent.

Mr. GILLASPY. I do not know what the practice is in the district of the gentleman from Benton, [Mr. Traer.] Now I am opposed to all this thing. I am astonished, at this late hour of the convention, to see gentlemen here, who have talked so much about trusting the people, try to take every thing from them. I am willing to leave the people of my district to judge who shall represent them in the legislature. If they are disposed to send a man to the general assembly, who has not been in the district more than sixty days, let them do so. If that rule had been in force in the first part of our history as a State, we should hardly have been able to get a general assembly at all. I think such a provision as this would work a hardship to the new counties, as it might debar them from choosing their best men to represent them.

Mr. TRAER. I have no desire to discuss this matter. My object is not the same as some gentlemen seem to suppose it to be. My sole object is to protect the people against wire-working politicians.

I do not intend to impugn the motives of the gentleman from Wapello, [Mr. Gillaspy,] in opposing this amendment. But he told me yesterday evening that he intended to move to my county. [Laughter.]

Mr. GILLASPY. If the gentleman from the rural district has any fears, I will take back all I said about going to his county.

The question was upon the amendment to the amendment.

Mr. TRAER. I accept the amendment of the gentleman from Jackson, [Mr. Warren.]

The question then recurred upon the amendment as modified, which was to so amend the section that it would read as follows:

"Sec. 4. No person shall be a member of the House of Representatives who shall not have attained the age of twenty-one years, be a free white male citizen of the United States, and shall have been an inhabitant of this State, and at the time of his election shall have had an actual residence of one year in the county or district he may have been chosen to represent."

Mr. GILLASPY called for the yeas and nays, and they were ordered accordingly.

The question being then taken, by yeas and nays, the amendment was agreed to; yeas 16; nays 15, as follows:

Yeas.—The President, Messrs. Clarke of Johnson, Edwards, Gower, Gray, Hall, Hollingsworth, Marvin, Palmer, Parvin, Scott, Solomon, Traer, Warren, Winchester and Young.

Nays.—Messrs. Ayres, Clark of Alamakee, Clark of Henry, Ells, Emerson, Gibson, Gillaspy, Harris, Johnston, Patterson, Peters, Price, Robinson, Seely and Wilson.

On motion of Mr. PALMER,

The convention then adjourned until to-morrow morning at nine o'clock.

WEDNESDAY, February 18th, 1857.

The Convention met at 9 o'clock, A. M., and was called to order by the President.

Prayer by the Chaplain.

The journal of yesterday was read and approved.

Personal Explanation.

Mr. CLARK, of Alamakee. I hold in my hands a copy of the "Keokuk Evening Times," in which I see a letter dated "Iowa City, February 3, 1857," and signed "White Man." The writer of that letter uses the following language:

"One of their leading men—Clark of Alamakee—went so far to-day, as to say, that although he did not approve, yet he would not condemn amalgamation."

In calling the attention of the Convention to this matter, I wish merely to place myself right upon the record.

I never made use of such an expression as here attributed to me, and I said nothing from which it could legitimately be drawn. I have always been opposed to amalgamation, and I trust I always shall be. As for being a leading man here, I certainly never had any ambition that way, nor have I made any effort to reach that distinction.

Legislative Department.

The PRESIDENT. The report of the Committee on the Legislative department, with the amendments reported to the Convention by the Committee of the Whole, is now upon its second reading and open to amendment. The clerk will proceed to read it by sections.

Section one was then read, as follows:

"The legislative authority of this State shall be vested in a Senate and House of Representatives, which shall be designated the General Assembly of the State of Iowa; and the style of their laws shall commence in the following manner, "Be it enacted by the General Assembly of the State of Iowa."

No amendments being offered to this section,

Biennial Sessions.

Section two was then read, as follows:

"The sessions of the General Assembly shall be biennial, and shall commence on the second Monday in January next ensuing the election of its members; unless the Governor of the State shall, in the interim, convene the General Assembly by proclamation."

Mr. CLARKE, of Johnson. I move to amend the second section by striking out the word "biennial," and inserting the following:

"Be annual for the first five years after the adoption of this constitution and biennial thereafter," so that it will read:

"The sessions of the General Assembly shall be annual for the first five years after the adoption of this constitution, and biennial thereafter, and shall commence on the second Monday in January next ensuing the election of its members; unless the Governor of the State shall, in the interim, convene the General Assembly by proclamation."

I offer this amendment, first because I was pledged to support it in the canvass which resulted in giving me a seat upon this floor. I openly avowed myself before the people as in favor of annual sessions of the legislature. My opponent took the opposite ground, and having, therefore, been elected upon this, with other questions, I feel myself pledged to go for annual sessions. That is one reason that induced me to offer this amendment. The second is this: I think it will be clear to the minds of the Convention, that for the first few years after the adoption of this constitution, we will need annual sessions. The very object and purpose of calling this convention was to give to the legislature power over various important subjects which was not given to them by the present constitution.

I apprehend, if this constitution is adopted, that one of the first things that will demand the attention of the legislature, will be the creation of banking institutions. To judge from the difference of sentiment in this convention upon that subject, I do not apprehend that the first legislature will adopt a system that will be perfect; and I think that twelve months experience will require the calling of the legislature together for the purpose of perfecting that system, whatever it may be. We can judge of the action of the legislature upon that subject by our own experience here, by our own diversity of sentiment, from the fact that there is scarcely a third of the convention who agree upon any definite system in relation to banking. We all have our peculiar views upon that subject, and the probability is that the same diversity of feeling will exist when the legislature assembles. If this should be the state of feeling in the legislature, the result will be that if any banking system is adopted at all, it will be the effect of compromise, and as a consequence, the system will be an imperfect one. I think every gentleman will concur with me in saying that we shall need a session upon that subject within a year after the adoption of the constitution.

We shall need annual sessions, too, for a while, upon the subject of internal improvements, if this subject is left open for the action of the General Assembly, as it is by the amendments to the Constitution, which we have been considering, and which will come up for the consideration of the General Assembly. Some action must be taken upon this subject, and something must be done to push through to completion all these works of internal improvements. Upon that subject we shall need frequent legislation. The interests of railroad companies will require additional facilities, perhaps, or it may be that the interests of the people will require that additional checks be placed upon these companies. These two subjects, of themselves, are sufficient, in my judgment, to lead us to provide for annual sessions, at least for the length of time named in the proposition I have submitted.

There are many other subjects that will demand the attention of the Legislature every year, for the first few years after the adoption of the Constitution. It is no answer to all this to say, that there is a provision in the Constitution authorizing the Governor to call special sessions, when the public necessities require. That is no answer, and for this reason: In the first place, you may not have a Governor who is willing to take the responsibility of calling such a session. Another reason is this: he is governed by the same prejudices, habits and interests which govern other men. Suppose that his prejudices are against all improvements called for by the people, and which the public necessities require, I ask gentlemen, would he take upon himself the responsibility of calling special sessions?

Another objection I have to this system i

this: that you are making this legislative department, which is the peculiar representative of the people in the government, and which is supposed to echo their voice, entirely dependent upon the Governor—a co-ordinate branch of the government, and but a single man. I am unwilling to place the power of the people—this department of the people—in the hands of one man. The experience of the past has shown that, although we have had a Constitution providing for biennial sessions, yet we have had annual sessions nearly all the time. I think we have had eight sessions in ten years.

There is still another objection to this section. We have adopted a provision in this article—or else it is in the article upon the executive department, which will probably be adopted—giving the Governor power to specify the acts upon which the General Assembly may act. In another way, then, you tie the power of the people, by tieing up the hands of the General Assembly which represents the people, and making it dependent upon the will of one man. All this, I believe, tends to centralization of power, and despotism. It is a new thing in the history of republican governments, that they should be tied up and placed in the power of one man; and that the will of one man may prevent the action of the people. It does not seem to me to be republican or democratic, using neither of these words in a party sense.

Having committed myself to the support of annual sessions, I have offered this proposition as a kind of compromise, believing that the convention will see the necessity of at least providing annual sessions for five years, after the adoption of this constitution. This certainly can do very little harm in five years, and if at the end of that time it is deemed unnecessary, the constitution then removes the difficulty.

Mr. PARVIN. The gentleman from Johnson, [Mr. Clarke,] having now discharged his duty and fulfilled his promise made before the election, I hope will feel himself at liberty not to start this question again. I thought the vote yesterday was decisive in regard to this matter, for the convention expressed themselves distinctly as being in favor of biennial sessions, by a pretty fair majority. I am not aware that any change has taken place in the minds of the convention since that time. The gentleman alludes to the fact that there have been called sessions; and he says that he is unwilling to place the power of calling extra sessions in the hands of any one man. Yet he represented that we have had eight sessions in ten years. I believe he is mistaken in that matter, for I think we have had but seven sessions in ten years, two of which were called sessions. Whether it be seven or eight sessions in that time, still we have had two sessions less than we would have had, if there had been a provision in the constitution, such as the gentleman wants.

The reason, as I stated yesterday, why we needed only biennial sessions, is the fact that we have cut off a large amount of the business of the General Assembly, by the action of the convention in regard to local legislation. I think the State will be decidedly the gainer by the adoption of the system of biennial sessions. But the gentleman from Johnson says that we need annual sessions for a few years for the purpose of legislative action in regard to banks; that banking laws which may be passed at one session may need amendment the next. I think that a good reason why we should not have annual sessions is, that when the legislature have passed a general banking law, the people should have time to see whether it works well, before it should be changed or repealed. I consider that every two years is often enough to revise all general laws. Let the people understand them before they ask for amendment or repeal. I do not wish to detain the convention upon this subject with any extended remarks. I see no reason, from any thing that has been said by the gentleman from Johnson, [Mr. Clarke,] for changing my vote of yesterday.

Mr. CLARKE, of Johnson. I move a call of the house.

The call was ordered, and the clerk then proceeded to call the roll, when the following gentlemen answered to their names:

The President, Messrs. Ayres, Clark of Alamakee, Clarke of Henry, Clarke of Johnson, Ells, Emerson, Gibson, Gower, Gray, Hall, Harris, Hollingsworth, Marvin, Palmer, Parvin, Patterson, Peters, Price, Robinson, Scott, Seely, Solomon, Traer, Warren, Wilson, Winchester and Young.

The following were the absentees:

Messrs. Bunker, Cotton, Day, Edwards, Gillaspy, Johnston, Skiff and Todhunter.

On motion of Mr. CLARKE, of Johnson,

Messrs. Todhunter, Skiff, Bunker and Day were excused.

On motion of Mr. SCOTT, all farther proceedings under the call were dispensed with.

Mr. HALL. I think if gentlemen will consider that the proposition of having annual sessions for at least five years, really gives but two more sessions than we would have under the system of biennial sessions, they would not object to it. It merely makes an addition of two sessions in that period of time. I desire gentlemen to consider the great amount of legislation that will be necessary for a few years to come. As was remarked by the gentleman from Johnson, [Mr. Clarke,] we are opening new fields of legislation; we are about establishing systems of banking and internal improvements, &c., with which our citizens are not very familiar; and it cannot be expected that, at the very first start, legislation will be as perfect as it will be after we have had more experience in the working of these systems. They must be perfected within at least five years, or the expectations of the convention will not be carried out.

Again: gentlemen should recollect that five or six years have elapsed since the Code, as we now term it, has been put in force. The edition of that work is nearly exhausted, and there will have to be, within the next three years, a complete revision of the laws of this State, or there will not be provision made for the wants of the people. If gentlemen will look at the amount of legislation which the new Constitution will impose upon the State, and consider the fact that several years have elapsed since the revision of our laws, which are now scattered through the journals of different Legislatures; and also consider the fact that we must make provision for an entire code, they will see the necessity of more than ordinary legislation for the first three or four years after the adoption of this Constitution. The public interests, in my opinion, will suffer unless we make provision for meeting all these demands.

I would be unwilling to leave this matter open, or leave it for biennial sessions and special sessions, to be convened by the Governor. We have already agreed upon a provision of limiting the action of the Legislature, at special sessions, to the matters particularly indicated by the Governor's message at the opening of the session. They are confined exclusively to action upon the subjects for which they are convened. With the total refusal, on the part of the Convention, to authorize sessions sufficient for the purpose of carrying out the great objects of legislation, the Governor would not be authorized to call the Legislature together for the purpose of perfecting the system of banking, and aiding internal improvements, and of revising and perfecting the laws which previous Legislatures had passed.

The matter of additional expense created by annual sessions, to which gentlemen have alluded in the course of this discussion, I consider as of little consequence, in view of the interests at stake. It is better for the State to expend fifty thousand dollars than to do wrong to a single man. It appears to me, in view of all the considerations I have presented, that it would be better for us to provide for annual sessions of the Legislature for a few years, at least, after the adoption of this Constitution. At this crisis in our State affairs, I hope that gentlemen will consider this matter, and that they will vote for two or three annual sessions, if they are not prepared to vote for more.

Mr. CLARKE, of Henry. I did suppose, when the vote was taken in committee of the whole, upon this question, that it was decisively settled. I do not know of anything since that vote was taken, that has occurred to change my views in regard to this matter. I entertain the opinion which I have already expressed, that we should make just as few changes as possible, so far as matters of governmental policy are concerned. I do not believe that it is expected by the people throughout the State, that we are going to change the present plan of biennial sessions. They believe that under this system of biennial sessions, when the legislature meet, knowing that they are not to have a session the next year, they will make up their minds to dispatch the business before them in a careful and thorough manner.

If you provide for annual sessions, an immense amount of business will go over from one session to another. I believe the most effective way of carrying on legislative business expeditiously, is through biennial sessions.

Again: if you establish annual sessions, you oblige the legislature to meet every year, and you have all this additional expense of mileage and extra sessions; whereas, by leaving this question as it stands in the present constitution, if at any time it should be discovered that there was anything in our banking laws, for instance, that was working badly for the interests of the people, it would be in the power of the governor to call an extra session. So the gentleman from Des Moines [Mr. Hall] need not borrow any trouble in regard to the interests of the State suffering very materially, if we do not provide for these annual sessions.

Then there is that other argument which was advanced here, and to which the gentleman made no reply; that by the operation of this constitution there will be less legislation than there has been heretofore. The first legislature that meets after the adoption of this constitution, will go on and provide by general laws, for nearly two-thirds of the legislation that has usually been transacted by the legislature. But this will not occupy a great deal of their time. When they have once passed their general laws, then all these local questions that the legislature have had to act upon heretofore, and which have consumed so much of their time, will be disposed of.

I do not believe that the first Legislature that meets under this Constitution will have to sit the length of time we have provided here, to complete all the business they will have to do under the Constitution. If their sessions will be shorter than heretofore, where, then, is the necessity of inaugurating a different system in the State? Why call upon the people of the State to bear the additional expense of these annual sessions? I can see no good reason for it. In fact, we have, all of us, been at work upon the supposition that we were going to lessen the amount of our legislation. If this idea has been erroneous, let us know it. Let us look over the provisions we have adopted, and see if we have been acting upon an erroneous idea. If we have not been so acting, then certainly there can be no necessity for adopting the system of annual sessions.

Mr. TRAER. I feel inclined to oppose this amendment. I would say here, that if the only question involved in this amendment was the mere expense of holding these sessions of the Legislature, it would be a matter of very little consequence to me. I subscribe to the doctrine advanced here by some gentleman the other day, that there was great danger in having too much legislation. I believe, that whenever, in changing their constitutions, other States have changed from annual to biennial sessions, they have done so for the purpose of getting rid of too much legislation. That is the ground upon which I base my opposition to this amendment. Suppose that we have annual sessions, we inaugurate some new law, and, before it can be fairly tried, the next Legislature comes on, and if there is any objection made to it, they will repeal it; whereas, if it were left to operate for two years, the people would become satisfied with it, and regard it as a just and beneficent measure.

It appears to me that, under the provisions we adopt with regard to special legislation, a session once in two years is sufficient to transact all the general legislation of this State And, it appears to me that by requiring, in a special session, that the Legislature shall be confined to those subjects contained in the Governor's message, they will be more likely not to act upon matters which will not result in benefit to the State. I think, therefore, that on this account, it would be better to have special sessions, than to provide here for regular annual sessions. By adopting the plan of biennial sessions, we shall save the State considerable expense, If you adopt the system of annual sessions, the Legislature will be required to meet every year, whether there is any business before them or not.

For these reasons, I shall vote against the amendment offered by the gentleman from Johnson, [Mr. Clarke.]

Mr. GIBSON. I voted against an amendment similar to this in committee of the whole, and I see no good reason for changing that vote. I believe that annual sessions are entirely unnecessary. If it becomes necessary to have them, we can have them by a special call from the Governor, as provided for by the article we are now considering. I feel that there is a great deal more danger to be apprehended from too much than from too little legislation; and I think that experience has taught us within the last few years that this is the case. If annual sessions were absolutely necessary, I would not object to the expense; but unless they are absolutely necessary, then I think that we are doing wrong to incur the expense of having annual sessions. We are adding expense upon expense: we are providing for an increased number of officers, with an increase of compensation. This increased expense will amount to a good deal more than most gentlemen are aware of, so much, in fact, that the mass of the tax-payers of the State will complain bitterly when they come to pay it.

We have made provision here for doing away with a great deal of special legislation. We have provided, that every subject of legislation which can come under a general law, shall not be legislated upon by special act. What idea does such a provision carry with it? Does it not convey the idea, that we wanted to dispense with as much legislation as possible? And yet gentlemen now turn around, and say they will double the sessions of the legislature. Is there any good reason for this course? The expenses of the legislature for a session, as near as I can compute them, including the per diem of members, the mileage, and the other expenses necessarily incurred by the meeting of such a body, cannot fall very far short of fifty thousand dollars. Is this State to be taxed fifty thousand dollars for a session every year? If it is absolutely necessary to incur the expense, in order to legislate upon matters of pressing importance, there is a provision in this article reported by the committee, authorizing the Governor to call the legislature together for that purpose. It is a general remark in the section of country that I have the honor to represent, that there is far more danger to be expected from too much than too little legislation.

Gentlemen have advanced, as an argument in favor of annual sessions, that the laws passed at one session may need amending and perfecting at another. We had better live under laws that are not perfect, than be continually changing them. If the laws are constantly changed by having annual sessions, we will scarcely know what laws are passed at one session, before they will be changed at the next. In view of these considerations, I am decidedly opposed to the amendment of the gentleman from Johnson, [Mr. Clarke.]

Mr. CLARKE, of Johnson. Some gentlemen here, it seems to me, are determined to fancy that we are sent here to make a strait jacket for the people, in which they shall not be able to move, or in any way help themselves. They seem to think, that we are sitting here to legislate for half a million of people, when the fact is that we ought to look into the far future, and make a system of government, that will accommodate itself to a million, or a million and a half of people. Iowa is one of the largest States of the Union, a new State, whose interests are diversified, and which, in the course of the next twenty years, will require an amount of legislation, about which this convention can have no conception. Within the next five years, too, questions will arise vitally affecting the interests and well being of the people. And in making a fundamental law, therefore, we should anticipate just such a state of things. It is no argument against this proposition, to say that other and older States have biennial sessions. That may be true, and biennial sessions may be very proper in those States, where their system of government is perfect, and where their laws form a perfect code, and where their resources are, in a great measure, developed. But our State is placed in a far different position, with none of her resources developed, and none of her interests fully known. We do not know in what position we will be placed within the next five years.

As I said before, the law making power is a power in which the people are more directly interested than any other, and which more directly affects their interests, and, therefore, it ought to be under their control. It is no answer to this argument to say, when you have biennial session that you give power to the governor to call special sessions. Let me take a case that may happen. Suppose that some great banking or internal improvement corporation is established under a general law, which is found to be defective, and which gives them rights and powers which are dangerous to the interests of the people. Immediate legislation may be required, in order to prevent the injury which may result to the people by the action of this corporation. Suppose that your governor, whoever he may be, should happen to be friendly to that corporation. I ask the members of the convention, if he is going to call an extra session in order to obviate the defects in the law creating such corporation, and to prevent the people from being wronged? I think that he will not take that responsibility, especially when it is against his own interests to do so. Such a thing as this may happen; and I am not willing to place such a power as might be exerted in such a case as this, in the hands of one man.

Let me make a single remark upon this question of economy, upon which the gentleman who last addressed the Convention, [Mr. Gibson,] laid so much stress, as a reason against adopting the system of annual sessions. Gentlemen seem to imagine that we are sitting here to form a government, which can be carried on without expense. I do not understand that this was our purpose and object. I suppose that we were sent here to make a government that should protect the rights and welfare of the people, and that the expenses of such a government were entirely a matter of secondary consideration. If the argument of the gentleman from Marion, [Mr. Gibson,] be true, it destroys itself, because the very same argument would prevent us from having any legislature whatever, for, by having none, we would save all the expense incident thereto. Or to go a step farther, in answer to the argument upon the other side, that the governor can call the legislature together at a special session—why not place the power entirely in the hands of the governor for calling the legislature together? If he is to judge when it is for the interests of the people to have new legislation, why is it not proper to leave it altogether to him, to say in what instances the legislature shall be called together, and constitute him a monarch over the people?

Gentlemen talk a great deal about their love for "the dear people," when discussing this and other subjects. I do not talk much about the people, but I presume I have their interests in view as much as do these gentlemen who are continually using the term, "the dear people." It does appear to me that these gentlemen show a dread of the people, when they urge here, as an argument against annual sessions, that if a law is passed at one legislature by one political party, it may be repealed, at a succeeding one, by another party. These things ought not to influence our action here. It is for the people to choose their representatives, and send men here who will truly represent their interests. I submit, it is a matter of convenience and necessity in order to put this new government which we are instituting here into working order, and obviate the defects that will necessarily arise in the legislation of the first few years, that we should have annual sessions.

Mr. WINCHESTER. I am somewhat surprised, and no less pleased, that "a change should have come over the spirit of the dream" of the gentleman from Henry, [Mr. Clarke,] even at this late day of the session. He says now, sir, that he is opposed to making any changes in the constitution, excepting those which are absolutely necessary, those which cannot be dispensed with. Now I submit it to this convention, whether the gentleman has not proposed as many changes to this constitution as any other member of this convention. No one will deny that this convention has marked out a vast amount of labor for succeeding legislatures for a year or two to come. If the legislature is confined to biennial sessions, they must necessarily hold very lengthy ones. As we are all aware, in the course of fifty or sixty days, members of the legislature become very tired, and business hangs heavily upon their hands. They will then either rush through it without due consideration, or they will leave it over to another session. This is a question which was canvassed somewhat in my section of the State before this convention assembled, and was considered as more important than many changes which we have already made. I shall support the measure of holding annual sessions. Some of us came here with the expectation that there would be a change in this respect from biennial to annual sessions. Others came here opposed to any change, in favor of adhering to biennial sessions. I think that as a matter of compromise those gentlemen should concede something to us, and that it would be nothing but justice to us and to our constituents, to permit us to have annual sessions for the first three or five years.

Mr. CLARKE, of Henry. I wish to make a few remarks, Mr. President. It really amuses me to see how some members upon this floor will insist upon assigning to "the gentleman from Henry" his position. It really amuses me, too, that some gentlemen, who shall apparently be listening to the discussions going on in this body, will entirely misconstrue the position of the "gentleman from Henry." I hold that there is no man upon this floor who has been more unfairly dealt with than I have in the positions which I have taken. Whenever I have risen here and made a stand for a principle, gentlemen have insisted upon it that because I have taken that stand, I have had some particular class of persons in view, notwithstanding the fact that I have reiterated, over and over and over again, that I was standing upon a principle, irrespective of its effect upon any particular class of persons.

Now, the gentleman rises here and says that he rejoices that a change has come over the spirit of my dreams, although I have announced at all times that, so far as mere matters of governmental policy were concerned, I was in favor of adhering to the old constitution as closely as I could; and when I reiterated here, having repeated the same thing just now, that I expressly excepted all matters of principle. Upon them the humblest member has a right to stand and to insist upon being heard, and if he does not do it he does not do his duty to himself, to his constituents or to his country. Now, I say again that so for as my labors here are concerned, I shall endeavor to abide by the old constitution, and the systems there laid down, because the people have become accustomed to them. Where they have not demanded a change, I am not in favor of making a change. And now I say to the gentleman that he cannot put his finger upon a single matter of any importance where I have advocated a change, excepting in the judiciary system; and I expressly stated to the convention that I did not propose in that system to make any innovation, but merely require of the present judges, under the present system, additional work; that they should meet and decide some questions—

The PRESIDENT. The chair will remind the gentleman that this is foreign to the matter before the convention.

Mr. CLARKE, of Henry. These remarks have been explanatory of my position, and I suppose that any gentleman has a right to make an explanation. I want gentlemen to understand me. So far as this question is concerned, I say that I have heretofore distinctly stated that I occupied the same position that I now occupy. I do not believe this change to be demanded by the people of the State, and I shall therefore vote against it.

Mr. HALL. I understand the proposition to be to hold annual sessions for five years; or perhaps three years will be long enough to hold annual sessions. Now, gentlemen will recollect, that at the time of the adoption of the present constitution, the sessions of the legislature were limited to fifty days, that is, after the expiration of that time members received only meager *per diem*, which was an implied reproach contained in the constitution itself, against holding longer sessions than fifty days. Every person who lived here and observed the condition of things after the adoption of that constitution, knows perfectly well that public convenience actually suffered in consequence of the meager legislation doled out by that constitution immediately following its adoption. Any person acquainted with the history of this state, or who will take the trouble to look back into the old files of newspapers, must be aware of the difficulties we had to encounter, although we had an extra session the second year. Go back and look at the interests of the State then to be provided for, and then look at the amount of legislation now demanded; look back upon what was then the condition of the state, and you will appreciate the absolute necessity of this amendment, if we intend to have public interests and public rights attended to.

Gentlemen say there will be general laws. Well, sir, these general laws must be perfected and enacted. If not enacted right at the first session, shall we be compelled to wait two years before the error can be remedied? The very fact that we are to have this general legislation, that we are to enter upon general systems, new and untried, and that much experience will be necessary before those systems can be perfected, ought to be enough to satisfy any man, that we shall need annual sessions for the first three years, at least, and that even that may be inadequate, and that unless we provide for it, we shall be doing injustice to ourselves and injustice to the people. All these plans are to be perfected by the legislature. They are new and untried; and in addition to these general laws upon other subjects, we shall have a banking system to provide, which is a matter of immense importance. Iowa is a new State. We are continually laying out roads in every direction. The legislature is to provide by general legislation to meet the public convenience, upon a plan superior, if possible, to any we have had. Then there are other subjects—the incorporation of cities, for instance. We have had an incorporation law, but it has been inadequate. These must all be framed, submitted to the people, tested, and if inadequate, amended.

Then, in addition to these matters, which must be legislated upon immediately after the adoption of the new constitution, we must have a revision of the laws of the State. A new code must be prepared and presented. A new volume must be prepared to go to the people of the State and the world. And if in the multiplicity of subjects upon which the legislature must act, there should be any error, must we wait two years before it will be possible to remedy the evil? It strikes me not. It strikes me that it is the part of wisdom, of economy, and of duty, that we should provide for a sufficient number of sessions in the few years following the adoption of the constitution to meet the extraordinary legislation which this constitution will demand. It strikes me that we should provide for annual sessions.for five years, or, at any rate for three, which may, perhaps, be adequate. I am as much opposed to innovation as any gentleman; but when I see a necessity, I will not shrink from that necessity, and omit to do my duty under the plea of precedent.

I stand here for this proposition as a matter of right, believing it to be a matter of necessity, and that alone influences me in advocating it.

Mr. WILSON. I should judge from the speeches that gentlemen make in favor of the doctrine of annual sessions, that they had come to the conclusion that this convention was about to introduce a complete revolution in this State, and that everything was to be changed, from the most unimportant to the most important statute.

Mr. HALL. I said no such thing. Why do gentlemen continually misrepresent me? I gave a catalogue of what I expected would be changed.

Mr. WILSON. I will say to the gentleman from Des Moines, [Mr. Hall,] that I used the term in the plural, and did not refer to him any more than to other gentlemen who favor the doctrine of annual sessions. Neither did I say that they had expressed the opinion that there was to be such a revolution in our affairs, but I said that if we were to be guided by their speeches, we should come to that conclusion. Now, sir, I do not think that will be necessary. The changes we have made here are important, it is true, but one session of the Legislature can provide for these changes. They can provide all the statutes rendered necessary by these changes. We want a banking law—perhaps two of them. We shall want general laws to provide for the locating or changing of roads, for the incorporation of towns and cities, to change the location of county seats, &c. Taking all these together, it will not take more than eight or ten statutes to provide for the whole of them,—probably not so many. It seems to me that one session of the Legislature can attend to that thoroughly and completely.

Now, sir, the very argument which the gentleman has introduced to show the necessity of annual sessions, it seems to me, rebuts itself. He says the people will discover defects in the different statutes which may be presented. I say that the people cannot tell whether these defects are real or imaginary, if the laws are not tried for a sufficient length of time. If a session is called to meet in January, and if they pass a set of statutes to take effect in July, and then if you bring the Legislature together again the next January, it will not leave time enough for the people of the State to test these laws, and to decide whether they will answer the purpose or not. But if you leave it for two years, that will allow of the experience of eighteen months to discover whether the supposed defects are real or not. I believe that is the better policy. The great difficulty attending annual sessions is, that the Legislature will change laws or repeal them before the people have had an opportunity to test them. We ought to provide against that as much as possible; and in relation to these general laws, as in relation to anything else. This is a wrong—an error—which has sprung up in legislation; and out of that has sprung the doctrine of the gentleman from Benton, [Mr. Traer,] that we have too much legislation. We are "governed too much," in other words. If we have an opportunity to test our laws, we shall find that we need fewer laws than would be enacted under the system of annual sessions.

I believe that the only statutes required for the purpose of carrying into effect the changes which have been made in the present Constitution, will be a banking law or laws, general laws of incorporation, for the laying out of roads, for the changing of names, for the locating of county seats, and the practice act. This would require but few statutes, and it seems to me that one session can enact these and put them into force, so as to give the people an opportunity of trying them, without calling for an annual session.

Another thing in relation to the practice act. Six months will not be sufficient to test the qualities of any practice act, if the Legislature adopts a practice act for the law side of the court and for the chancery side. It will be tested in some portions of the State, but in other parts it cannot be tested. It cannot be fairly tested in less time than eighteen months; and biennial sessions would give the requisite time. I hope the Convention will adhere to the biennial sessions. If it is necessary to have one extra session, it can be called by the Governor, to cure the defects in the laws passed by the first session.

Mr. HARRIS. Having taken the position upon this matter before the Committee, that there is no necessity for departure from the old Constitution in this particular, I had supposed that the matter might rest as entirely settled there. I had supposed that gentlemen had said what they desired to say with regard to this matter, and that they would be content to vote when the subject came before the Convention. I had not expected that we were to be under the necessity of contending this whole matter over again. If gentlemen had been content to assign the reasons for their votes, in order that they might stand right upon the record, I should have been silent. But not only has the question then presented been called up, but we have been called upon to reflect and consider, and entreated to change our reasons for other reasons pertinaciously presented here to induce a change in the decision of the Convention. Now, sir, I am disposed to be as accommodating as any man can be or ought to be, and if I could really feel that there was any necessity for the changes that gentlemen have spoken of, I should certainly acquiesce. One gentleman has asked us to come up here as a compromise, considering it a question where a compromise is demanded and necessary, for the reason that we ought not to do anything placing our constituents and their constituents in a different position. We believe that the interests of the whole State require that the Constitution, in this respect, should be left where it was; and we do not understand that we are imposing any disability upon the constituents of any member here more than upon our own in leaving it there.

One gentleman says that we act and talk here as if we were trying to get up a strait-jacket for the purpose of controlling the Legislature, and controlling the officers of the State. Now, sir, I am free to say that that is just what I wish to do. I believe that if there is any class of men in the community who are really under the necessity of being laced in the strait-jacket, it is the Legislature. I believe that latitudinarianism, when extended to legislation, under the Constitution, is as dangerous as when extended anywhere else. If there is any class of officers of the State—if there is any part of the governmental machinery of the State that I would place a strait-jacket upon, to use the language of the gentleman, it would be the Legislature. Hence, sir, that language does not deter me from still defending biennial sessions, because I am in favor of a strait-jacket upon the Legislature; and I am not sure that the history of the past legislation of this State will not show that some of them require another kind of a strait-jacket.

Mr. CLARKE, of Johnson, (in his seat.) The gentleman has been a member of the Legislature, and ought to know.

Mr. HARRIS. Yes, sir. I have been a member of the Legislature, and I have had some reason to know with regard to this matter. And as an evidence of what I say, I will state to gentlemen that if they will consult the records of the sessions when I was a member, they will find myself and some others taking the position in the outset, that we would put down, so far as our influence might go, all that class of legislation provided for by general laws—the incorporation of villages, the change of the names of county seats, the change of the names of individuals, and other matters of that character. We adhered to it for some time, until we ascertained that the applications were so numerous, and especially those coming from the other branch of the Legislature, that we were under the necessity of yielding that point, and refraining from further opposition, or else losing our influence upon much more important questions in the form of general laws. We found that we should lose our influence upon matters of general policy, affecting the entire interests of the State, under the personal feeling engendered by these local questions, if we persisted in requiring parties to obtain their ends through the general laws already in force. We found that persons would come to the Legislature, at an expense to the State of two or three dollars per day, costing them nothing, to obtain that which they could obtain through the courts, because, if they went into the courts they would be under the necessity of paying fees for it. That is my history of the action of the Legislature, and of the reasons which compelled me to change my position upon this question.

Gentlemen have said that there have been public laws upon these subjects, but that they were inadequate. I would not be disposed for a moment to dispute their impressions with regard to that matter. I believe that they have a right to think as they do—the same right that I have to think the contrary. My opinion is that those laws were not inadequate; but it was easier, and much less expensive to these parties to have an attorney in a member of the Legislature, whose services could be paid for by electioneering, to attend to these things before the Legislature, at the expense of the treasury of the State, than to have an attorney in the courts of the county, whose fees could not be so easily paid. There is where the inadequacy was. There is where the whole difficulty was. I think we have provided for cutting off most of these things.

Here is another history of the session I was a member of the Legislature: A gentleman from the northern part of the State sent in a petition to have his name changed. That petition was presented in the Senate. I, with others, took the position that there was no necessity for acting upon that; and after spending as much time in talking about it as it would have taken to pass the bill, we laid it upon the table. We wished to make an example of it, in order to get clear of that class of legislation. But afterward there came up a bill from the other House for changing certain names, and it so happened that it concerned the family of a member of the House, so that it was passed as a matter of courtesy there, and as a matter of courtesy we were under the necessity of permitting it to go through. We were then appealed to, not to make a discrimination between different individuals, but to take up from the table the similar bill, which we had spent some time in placing there. Thus were we brought to the necessity of opening the door for that class of legislation. It was not that the laws were inadequate, but simply because it was not peremptory, so that the Legislature could get around it. It provided a remedy by general laws, but did not prevent the Legislature from passing special laws.

It is said that the laying out of roads, and legislation of that character, is immense. I do not think any very great hardship has resulted from waiting for two years heretofore; and it must be recollected that the adoption of the new Constitution is not to interfere with those already laid out. It is only in the new counties that there will be any inconvenience from so short a delay, and I apprehend that they can wait, without any very great injury, from one session to the next.

As to the number of sessions we have had, I have been a citizen of the State for something over eight years, and although I have not taken much pains to consult the history of the State previous to that time, I have been since that period a tolerably attentive observer of our public affairs. I believe that we have had but one extra session in eight years, that of the last summer. That is my recollection; and gentlemen will certainly not undertake to contend that we shall now require an amount of legislation under the slight transition which we are about to make in reorganizing the government, any thing like that required in taking our position as an independent State, and all that class of legislation connected with the transition from a territorial to a State government. Yet I think we have got along tolerably well with the extra sessions we have had.

I will notice one other objection urged with some force by gentlemen here. It is this: We are just inaugurating a system of internal improvements; and when the railroad interest of this State has become immense, as it soon will be, a great deal of legislation will be required upon that. My own impression is that the prosperity of the railroads, and other internal improvements of this State, will depend far more upon the enterprise, energy, and determination of the private citizens who may embark in them, than it will upon the legislation of the State. The remark which has been made here that we are governed too much, does not apply, in my mind, with such force, and so emphatically to any thing else as to this question of public improvements. The less the State attempts to dabble in and control these things, the better it is for the interests of the State. Comparing the history of the public improvements of any State where they are controlled by the State, with that of any State where they are left to individual enterprise, will satisfy any gentleman that it will not take much legislation to provide for those interests. I believe that the less legislation we have upon the subject, after providing a general plan, the better it will be for the State, the better for the individual, and the better for the success of the improvements themselves.

Mr. GOWER. I feel some interest in this matter of annual sessions. I have lived thirty years in the course of my life under annual sessions, and I believe it was the general impression that we had too much legislation. For some twenty years, in the latter part of my life, I have lived under biennial sessions, and under that system we have had legislation enough, so far as I have been able to discover. When this subject was first moved upon this floor, it was moved that annual sessions should be held for five years. I felt that it was unnecessary to have annual sessions so long, and moved to amend by restricting them to three years. I thought that possibly three annual sessions might be desirable, and I now think that would be sufficient to arrange matters, if it is necessary to have annual sessions at all. It appears to me that a biennial session is frequent enough.

Mr. MARVIN. I do not know how my constituents would wish me to vote here. Gentlemen talk of their constituents in relation to this matter. I do not suppose I have talked with one out of fifty upon it. Those with whom I did talk upon it, generally came to the conclusion that annual sessions are preferable; but that does not represent my constituents. My feelings are decidedly in favor of the motion now before the convention. If I supposed that annual sessions would tend to increase legislation, I would not advocate even two extra sessions. But I believe it will not have that tendency. The great objection to too much legislation is that we have too much hasty legislation. Our legislators come together, and after a certain length of time they become uneasy, and cease to give the subjects which come before them the consideration which they should. I believe that short annual sessions would not increase the amount of legislation, but would increase the care which members would bestow upon that legislation.

Gentlemen seem to suppose that we are to have many general laws that will save the legislature so much time and expense, that for a few years to come we shall not have much legislation. It strikes me that to perfect a system of general legislation will require for a few years as much time as the legislature has heretofore been called upon to spend in special legislation. And compared with the expense of a regular session of the legislature, the disadvantage to the State at large in not having certain laws passed, may be much more than the expense of a regular or an extra session. For instance, take the school law, which every member of the convention, and every man in the State considers entirely insufficient for the wants of the State. Suppose that a school law should be under consideration in the legislature, as it was last winter, and for want of time to mature it sufficiently, it shall be passed over for two years. I verily believe that the loss to the people of the State in not having an efficient school law would be more than the sessions of four legislatures. We cannot compute the disadvantages that may arise to the people, and especially to the children of this State, when we deprive them of that intellectual improvement which they ought to have an opportunity to make. Their loss cannot be computed in dollars and cents.

If we are allowed to hold but one session of the legislature in two years, matters of great and general interest and importance, upon which the legislature will be compelled to act, will so occupy their time, especially if the members are no more united in their opinions upon such measures than we are in this body, that it might easily happen that no school law would be passed until the time when members became uneasy and anxious to get home to their business, when it might be passed by altogether. I believe that if we had annual sessions for a few years, we shall have less legislation, and that that would be the subject of greater reflection, and would give greater satisfaction to the people.

Members have referred to States that have abolished the annual session principle, as in Ohio; and how stands it there? The new plan has been in operation for five or six years, and every year but one they have had a session of the legislature. The legislature of Ohio is now in session, having adjourned over from last winter, finding that they could not complete their work. And I believe I state truly the general sentiment of the people of Ohio, when I say that if they were called upon to day to decide whether they would return to annual sessions, they would do so; and our wants for a few years will be much more pressing than theirs. It is not the wish of those who advocate this measure to keep the strait jacket off from the legislature, but off from the people. Ought the people to be compelled to move in a certain track, to be put in this strait jacket? I am willing to put any restrictions upon the legislature, that may seem necessary, but I am unwilling to impose restrictions upon the people.

Mr. GILLASPY. I, sir, do not know what the views of my constituents are upon this subject. So far as I have conversed with them, there seemed to be a general feeling in favor of annual sessions for a certain period, and in view of that fact I am inclined to support what I understand to be the amendment last offered by the gentleman, to have annual sessions for three years.

The PRESIDENT. No amendment was moved by the gentleman.

Mr. GILLASPY. I should be inclined to favor three years. I find upon an examination of the various constitutions of the United States that the States are equally divided, leaving out Iowa, one-half having adopted biennial, and the other half annual sessions. I find that eleven of the free states have annual sessions; and that a great number of those having the system of biennial sessions, have an extra session every intermediate year. I believe that there will be questions presented in the constitution which the present convention are about to make, which will require annual sessions; and I believe that we might as well provide for it as to leave it an open question whether the governor shall call an extra session of the general assembly. I will move, if it be in order, to strike out "five" years, and insert "three."

Mr. CLARKE, of Johnson, called for the yeas and nays, which were ordered accordingly.

The question being taken, by yeas and nays, the amendment to the amendment was rejected; yeas 15, nays 17, as follows:

Yeas—Messrs. Ayres, Edwards, Ells, Emerson, Gillaspy, Hall, Harris, Johnston, Marvin, Palmer, Patterson, Peters, Robinson, Traer and Winchester.

Nays—The President, Messrs. Clark of Alamakee, Clarke of Henry, Clarke of Johnson, Gibson, Gower, Gray, Hollingsworth, Parvin, Price, Scott, Seely, Skiff, Solomon, Warren, Wilson and Young.

The question recurred upon the amendment to hold annual sessions for five years.

Mr. CLARKE, of Johnson, called for the yeas and nays, which were ordered accordingly.

The question being taken, by yeas and nays, the amendment was not agreed to; yeas 9, nays 23, as follows:

Yeas—Messrs. Clarke of Johnson, Ells, Hall, Marvin, Peters, Price, Skiff, Winchester and Young.

Nays—The President, Messrs. Ayres, Clark of Alamakee, Clarke of Henry, Edwards, Emerson, Gibson, Gillaspy, Gower, Gray, Harris, Hollingsworth, Johnston, Palmer, Parvin, Patterson, Robinson, Scott, Seely, Solomon, Traer, Warren and Wilson.

Veto.

Mr. CLARKE, of Johnson, moved to amend the seventeenth section so that to pass a bill over the governor's veto, a vote of a majority of the members in each house shall be required, instead of a majority of two-thirds of the members present, and called for the yeas and nays, which were ordered accordingly.

The question being taken, by yeas and nays, the amendment was rejected; yeas 8, nays 24, as follows:

Yeas—Messrs. Clarke of Johnson, Edwards, Gibson, Marvin, Palmer, Price, Wilson and Young.

Nays—The President, Messrs. Ayres, Clark of Alamakee, Clarke of Henry, Ells, Emerson, Gillaspy, Gower, Gray, Hall, Harris, Hollingsworth, Johnston, Parvin, Patterson, Peters, Robinson, Scott, Seely, Skiff, Solomon, Traer, Warren and Winchester.

Age of Senators.

Mr. GILLASPY. I move to amend section fifth, by striking out "five," and inserting "one," so that it shall read that senators shall be twenty-one years of age, instead of twenty-five; and I do it because I regard this as a relic of fogyism, and I want to get rid of everything of that kind. I call for the yeas and nays.

The yeas and nays were ordered accordingly.

The question being then taken, by yeas and nays, the amendment was rejected; yeas 16, nays 16, as follows:

Yeas—The President, Messrs. Clark of Alamakee, Clarke of Henry, Ells, Gibson, Gillaspy, Gray, Harris, Johnston, Patterson, Peters, Scott, Seely, Solomon, Traer and Wilson.

Nays—Messrs. Ayres, Clarke of Johnson, Edwards, Emerson, Gower, Hall, Hollingsworth, Marvin, Palmer, Parvin, Price, Robinson, Skiff, Warren, Winchester and Young.

Veto.

Mr. GOWER. I move to insert in section seventeen, the fraction "seven-twelfths," for "two-thirds." As it now stands, a vote of two thirds is required to pass a bill over the constitutional objections of the Executive. Now we may have one hundred and fifty senators and representatives, and two-thirds would give twenty-five more than one half. Thus it would require twenty-five members to pass a bill over the veto. It strikes me that that is more than is necessary. If there is a question of importance before the Legislature, due weight should be given to the opinion of every member. I think that two-thirds is more than is necessary, and for that reason would reduce it one-half, making it seven-twelfths, requiring only twelve more than one-half the members.

The question being taken, the amendment was rejected.

Meeting of the General Assembly.

Mr. GIBSON moved to amend the second section by striking out "second," and inserting "first," so as to provide for the meeting of the Legislature upon the first Monday in January.

The question being taken, upon a division the amendment was rejected; ayes 8, noes 15.

Term of Residence.

Mr. GRAY. At the solicitation of some friends, I move to reconsider the vote by which the amendment offered by the gentleman from Benton, [Mr. Traer,] was adopted yesterday, in the sixth section, I believe, requiring twelve months' residence in the county to qualify a member for a seat in the Legislature. It is thought to be an unnecessary restriction.

Mr. SOLOMON. In seconding the motion to reconsider, I desire to say that I voted yesterday under a misapprehension, supposing that it was to fix the residence in the State. I think that thirty days is long enough for the county.

Mr. CLARKE, of Johnson, called for the yeas and nays, which were ordered.

The question being taken, by yeas and nays,

the motion to reconsider was agreed to, yeas 18, nays 16, as follows:

Yeas—Messrs. Ayres, Clark, of Alamakee, Clarke, of Henry, Ells, Emerson, Gibson, Gillaspy, Gray, Harris, Johnston, Palmer, Patterson, Peters, Price, Scott, Seely, Solomon and Wilson.

Nays—The President, Messrs. Clarke of Johnson, Edwards, Gower, Hall, Hollingsworth, Marvin, Parvin, Robinson, Skiff, Traer, Warren, Winchester and Young.

The question recurred upon the adoption of the amendment of Mr. Traer.

Mr. WINCHESTER moved to amend the amendment by striking out "one year," and inserting "ninety days."

Mr. CLARKE, of Henry. I consider that just as objectionable as the other. For my part, I cannot see why there should be any necessity for requiring different qualifications for the candidate than for the elector. We have a provision that a man may become an elector by residing in the precinct or county twenty days. A residence of twenty days entitles a man to elect; and I cannot see why we should establish any other term for a man to become a candidate. Certainly the people in every county are well qualified to judge with regard to the person whom they wish to represent them. I am willing to give them the largest latitude within the boundaries from which they take their candidate. I am willing to trust this matter entirely with the people. As I voted to allow them to select a man twenty-one years of age to represent them in the Senate, so I will vote to allow them to vote for any one who is an elector within the precincts which he may be called upon to represent.

Mr. TRAER. I am not very particular about the exact length of time. I think it would be better that it should correspond with the term of residence in the State. I am under the impression that the operation of this amendment would be different from what the gentleman from Henry represents it. I made the motion with a view to protect the interests of the people, not to curtail their authority in nominating. It is a well known fact that politicians get nominated sometimes without the consent of a large majority of the people whom they are to represent. We know that there are certain systems of wire working by which gentlemen get nominated, and having once obtained the nomination of the party which is in the ascendancy, they are likely to be elected, although, at the same time, a large majority of the district would choose some other man if they had an opportunity. I have no doubt that gentlemen know of instances where persons have moved into a district, and in the short space of thirty or sixty days have become candidates to represent that district in the Legislature, and when the result proved that they knew nothing of the wants or the wishes of the people whom he was elected to represent. I say that this is intended as a protection to the people, to prevent designing politicians from getting the nomination, and thus working themselves into the Legislature without knowing either the wishes or the wants of the people whom they should represent. I am in favor of allowing the people to nominate and elect men who know what their wants are. And I take the position that no man, within thirty days after coming into a district, can know what are the real wants of that district. It was for that reason that I offered the amendment; but, as I said before, I am not particular about the term of one year. I would be satisfied with six months. Anything short of that I shall vote against. I want it distinctly understood that the position assumed by the gentleman from Henry for this question, is entirely a different one from what the mover of the amendment intended. He places it upon the ground that we are attempting to restrict the choice of the people. I place it upon the ground that we are attempting to protect them from designing men. That is my reason for offering the amendment, and I think that will be the effect of it.

Mr. GOWER. I have in my mind an occurrence in my own county which took place two years ago last July, when a convention met to nominate a member to the legislature. Our friends brought up a man who had just come into our county and nominated him. I did not concur with the nomination, because I was not sufficiently acquainted with the merits of the man; but after his nomination, I advocated his election, and voted for him although I was not acquainted with him. Sir, his election was most disastrous to the wishes of his friends. I shall vote against reducing the time from one year, for I think we ought to require our candidates to reside in the county that length of time before they can be elected.

Mr. CLARKE, of Johnson. I rise to ask the the gentleman to withdraw, for the present, the motion to change the time to ninety days, and let us take a vote upon the question of twenty days.

I am in favor of the proposition as it now stands, to require one year; but if I cannot get that, I shall vote, of course, for the next longest time. I am in favor of the term of one year for this reason: I regard it as a protection to the people. I desire to protect them from a danger which may in a few years over-burden them, and that is the creation of these great corporations, which may find it for their interest to have certain men in the legislature, and may send their men for that purpose into the different counties. It is notorious that in the legislature of last winter, men came here to get judicial districts formed, and in one instance, a man went home, moved into one of these new districts, and got the nomination for the judgeship of that district. This is a common thing. The instance which the gentleman from Cedar [Mr. Gower] cites, is a common thing. I do think this is as much a matter of protection to the people as anything else.

I think the whole convention will concede that the man who comes to the legislature ought to have resided sufficiently long in the county or district, to know the people, to know their wants and their wishes. I know it is a very common thing to take up a new man, not because he happens to be a man of superior intelligence or integrity, but because he happens to be in favor with the politicians of the one side or the other. I repeat the request, that the gentleman withdraw his motion, to allow us to vote first upon the term of one year, and if that fails, I shall then vote with him.

The PRESIDENT. The question is susceptible of division. The question can first be taken upon striking out "thirty days."

Mr. CLARKE, of Johnson. I call for a division of the question.

Mr. CLARK, of Alamakee. I am in favor of letting the people protect themselves upon this question. I do not believe there is any necessity for this motherly fostering care of the people which gentlemen profess to have so much at heart, when they favor the plan of requiring a residence in the county of a year, before the people can have the privilege of putting him in nomination for certain offices. I believe that the people are capable of taking care of themselves—wholly so—and I can see but one effect to follow this restriction. If there are certain men in a county, who wish to become candidates for that office, this will enable them, to a certain extent to keep the market and keep out competition. If I was a candidate for election to the senate, and was afraid of competition, it would be very natural that I should be in favor of having the constitution say, in so many words, that no man should be a candidate against me for that office unless he had resided in the county for one year. Now, I have that confidence in the people at large that I believe they are capable of deciding these questions, of knowing who are best qualified and calculated to protect their interests, and to represent their interests in the legislature of the State. As a general thing it may be wise not to take up persons who have been in the county but a little while, but that is a matter of which the people of the county are as capable of judging as we are, and the people will not vote for a man who has just come into the county as readily as for one whom they know. But it may easily happen in the new counties that the only man who has happened to be in the county for a year, and who is therefore exclusively privileged to represent the county, may not be so well fitted for that office as some other man who has been there less than twelve months.

I believe, that as a matter of principle, the question should be left to the people, that they should have the privilege of saying who is best qualified to represent them in the legislative halls of their State.

As to the suggestion of the gentleman from Benton, [Mr. Traer,] that sometimes a man succeeds in getting the nomination of a convention against the wishes of the great majority of the party in the county, I see no great force in it. I do not believe that is the case as a general thing. When we hear that cry, it generally comes from some other aspirant for the same office, because it has been decided against him by the convention. The man who has been in the county but sixty days would not stand half the chance of satisfying the convention, compared with one who had been known to them for twelve months or more. He would not have the influence in the community; he would not have the acquaintance of the community. He would not have the means for wire-pulling possessed by the man who has been there at least a year.

Nor do I see much force in the reasons urged by my friend from Johnson [Mr. Clarke,] further than this. There seems to be some change in the spirit of the dreams here, since this convention commenced its session. It is beginning to see more clearly some of the danger of these corporations for the purpose of carrying on works of internal improvement, and some of the abuses which may grow out of them. I am glad it is coming to its senses upon this point. I do not believe that the amendment that is proposed will cure the evil. I believe, if it has any effect, it will be merely to lop off some of the outer branches. I believe it to be the wishes of the people to cure the evil, to lay the axe at the root of the tree, instead of simply attempting to lop off some of the outer branches. I do not believe this restriction will have the effect of protecting the interests of the people in any county of this State. On the contrary, I think it will curtail their free choice in making a selection from the county of the man whom they believe it will be for their best interest to elect. It is really rather a modest request of this convention to ask of the sovereign people to yield to us the privilege of determining for them whom they shall have to represent them, for fear they might abuse the privilege, as much as to say to them—you are not capable of self government; you are not capable of selecting your own delegates or representatives; and so we will put you in leading strings; we will impose a supervisorship over you; we will constitute ourselves your guardians, since you are not to be trusted. I do not believe in this principle. I believe it is wrong. I believe it to be an unwarranted depreciation of the people of this State, that such a provision should be inserted.

Mr. GILLASPY. I voted yesterday against requiring a man to live in a county twelve months, before he should be eligible to a seat in the house of representatives. I perceive, however, that there is a feeling upon the part of members of this convention to prescribe rules to the people in their selection of candidates for the various offices in this State. Now I am opposed to that. I believe the people are competent, and I see no good reason why they should not be allowed to select any elector in their county to represent them in the capacity of legislator. But the convention has said this morning to the people—it matters not what your opinions or interests may be, you shall not select any man in your county to represent you in the senate of Iowa unless he is twenty-five years of age. And the convention said by their action yesterday—

no matter what your interests and wishes may be, you shall not select a man to represent you in the house of representatives, except he shall have been a resident of the county he is to represent twelve months.

Mr. SOLOMON. We voted under a mistake.

Mr. GILLASPY. Some members may have done so, but I do not think all did. I believe the people are competent to decide, and will decide correctly in the choice of their representatives. The gentleman from Benton [Mr. Traer.] tells us that his whole course of manœuvering here is——for what? To prevent new comers in the county, wire-working politicians from taking advantage of the people, and getting into the legislature against their wills. That may be the way things are done in Benton county, but such is not the case in the part of the State I have the honor to represent. But if the doctrine is true that wire-workers and politicians can thwart the will of the people, I would ask the gentleman if men, who have been in the State for ten or twenty years, are not better able to pull the wires, and get up conventions to carry out their political designs, than any who may have just come here? Some of our best citizens, who have lived in our Mississippi counties for years, are of late emigrating to the western counties of this State. Yet, according to the course proposed here for the convention to pursue, a man who has just moved into one of our frontier counties, though an old resident of the State, and better versed in the wants and necessities of the people than any other man in that county may be, could not represent that county in the legislature until he had been there for twelve months.

Now, I think this is not right. I think the people should have the power to select those they choose to represent them. In my county they have that right now, and I do not think I should be justified in standing up here and dictating to my county what they shall do hereafter in this respect—that they shall not exercise that power I believe they should be allowed to exercise. I believe this Convention should allow the people to select whom they may see fit to send to the Legislature, and they and their representatives should be responsible for the result of their action.

Mr. SOLOMON. I am getting to entertain more and more confidence in the gentleman upon my left, who has just taken his seat, [Mr. Gillaspy.] His principles of action are founded upon deep philosophy, and I see that fact exhibited more and more in every speech he makes here. He goes for allowing every man, who is entitled to vote in this State, to become a candidate for the Legislature. That is one of the soundest principles I have heard advocated upon this floor. Why should we allow men to vote for and select men for representatives, who are not well qualified to judge of the qualifications a representative should possess, and, consequently, to make representatives themselves? We allow men to go into our western counties, remain there twenty or thirty days, and then vote for members of the Legislature. If there were fifty such voters in a county, they might exercise a predominating influence upon the voice of the people of that county. If you give certain men the power to exercise a predominating influence upon this subject of choosing a representative, and then impose upon them a disability in regard to filling that office with one of their own number, your principle is inconsistent in my opinion.

Let me say once for all, that I am opposed to any disparity being put upon any man in this State for anything. I think the principle is a wrong one. I think the people should be allowed free choice in their selection of representatives. I am opposed to the principle which prescribes men from holding office on account of their age. I voted with the gentleman from Wapello, [Mr. Gillaspy], for admitting a man to a seat in the Senate who is twenty-one years of age. I think this body have mistaken the true principle, after having voted that down. Some of the ablest men in my section of the country—men the best qualified to represent it in the Legislature, or in any other capacity—have scarcely attained the age of twenty-one years. That is my experience, at least. Ability shows itself at an early day, and will not be kept down.

Gentlemen urge as a reason why we should establish this principle, that unless we do, these mammoth corporations will send their hired emissaries into these new counties, and the people will take them up and send them here, when they will establish such rules and regulations as these corporations may dictate. In answer to that, I will say, that I have no fears that the people of any county or district in this State will, in the course of any very short period after the establishment of any mammoth corporation, send to the Legislature, or elect to any other position in this State, a man who belongs to or favors such a corporation.

Gentlemen also argue that, unless we establish this principle, men will go from one section of the State to another, and before the people get well acquainted with them they will be sent to the legislature. Now I believe if any man in any portion of this State, occupies such a position at home that it is impossible for him to get into the legislature, he may go west and try it there, and he will find that almost before he reaches there, although we have no railroads or telegraphs, we will know almost everything he has done in the eastern portion of this State. That is the kind of people we are in the west; we make it our business to know all these things. The constitution clothes us with privileges and franchises that we are proud of, and we endeavor to obtain all the information we need, in order to exercise our powers and privileges understandingly. If a man in the eastern portion of the State does anything wrong, he will not better himself by going to the western counties of the State. If he is a good man, and the wrong act is one of minor importance, he should remain at home. If he is not a good man, he will make nothing by leaving home, for his bad deeds will follow him wherever he goes.

I once heard of a man who stole a sheep. It was discovered, and he concluded to move to some other place. He sought a new location, but had been there but a short time before it began to be buzzed around that he had stolen two sheep. That soon became common talk, a fixed fact in the minds of the neighborhood. He made up his mind to pull up stakes and go to some other place. He did so, but the sheep followed him. But a short time elapsed before it began to be noised abroad that he was a sheep-stealer, and it soon became a fixed opinion in the minds of all the neighborhood that he had been a sheep-stealer all his life. He finally made up his mind to return to his old home, for everybody there knew that he had stolen sheep but once. I give this in illustration of the principle, that if a man has committed an error, he should remain in the place where he has committed it, because, if it was an oversight or an accident, he may outlive it.

Mr. EDWARDS I am somewhat puzzled to know which is the people's side of this question. Gentlemen upon both sides claim that they are laboring for the good of "the dear people." I understand the question involved here, is a mere question of policy and expediency. If it is proscription to require a man to reside one year in a district before he shall be allowed to represent it, it would be proscription to require him to live there thirty days. The only question is, which term is best, thirty days, sixty days, ninety days, six months, or a year? The one time is in principle just as much proscription as the other.

Now I hold that if there is anything in this question connected with "the dear people," the longest term of proscription is the best one as regards public policy and expediency. I am opposed to this thing of opening the doors for the purpose of inviting demagogues and time-serving politicians to float upon the surface from one county to another in order to obtain office and emoluments. I am in favor of that principle which requires of a man a residence long enough to become identified with the interests of a neighborhood, and to learn its wants, before he thrusts himself forward to occupy the place of law-maker and especial guardian of their interests. That rule is a bad one that does not require that.

But the gentleman from Mills, [Mr. Solomon,] carries the matter a little further. He is willing to open wide the door, and give the elective franchise to all persons. I would ask the gentleman if he intended to extend the elective franchise to negroes?

Mr. SOLOMON. I said that if you give to any man the privilege of being an elector, he should have the privilege of filling any office to which he might be elected. I leave it to the gentleman and his friends to say whether people of color shall have the elective franchise bestowed upon them.

Mr. EDWARDS. We will leave that to "the dear people," and let the majority of them decide. The principle of the gentleman, even as he has explained it, is still wrong. Suppose that eligibility to a seat in the House of Representatives is extended to all the voters of the State. Have we not witnessed in other States a system of villainy and fraud carried on, importing voters from one State, district, county or town, into another, because no time for residence had been prescribed? Now the people demand that certain checks and barriers shall be thrown around the elective franchise, to protect the purity of the ballot box. And we will fail in our duty, if we do not require a residence of a man long enough to enable him to become identified with the interests of the people.

The gentleman from Mills, [Mr. Solomon,] has also made some remarks in regard to the motion to make twenty-one years the age required of Senators. I believe that such a rule as that would be wrong. I believe that there is such a thing as men becoming wiser and more experienced, as they grow old, than when they were young. I believe in the idea that Shakespeare conveys in the expression he uses in reference to the Roman Senate, when he says, "most potent, grave and reverend seigniors." I believe the Senate should be a check on the lower House, the popular branch of the Legislature. Young men are sent there without that discretion that members of the Senate are supposed to possess; and the Senate, as the more deliberative body, has more experience, and will act as a check upon the loose legislation of the lower House. I believe that there is something in experience, and that we should have men of more experience to occupy seats in the Senate, than in the lower House. I think that the position of gentlemen here amounts to nothing when they come to apply the test. We should adopt a principle which will protect the elective franchise, protect the people in their dearest rights. And as to the time to which this residence shall be limited, it is a mere question of policy whether it shall be a long or a short time.

Mr. PARVIN. The question now under discussion is, whether we shall limit the term of residence to six months, or twenty days, as it now is. I think that is not a matter of much importance. Many of the gentlemen who have argued this subject, have appeared willing to impose no restriction at all, but let the electors choose whom they please to represent them in the General Assembly of the State. We may well exclaim—oh, that our fathers had been more wise! for this principle of restriction goes as far back as the formation of the government of the United States. In framing the Constitution of the United States, how came it that our forefathers provided in it that no man should be eligible to the office of President of the United States unless he was a native born citizen of the United States, and of the age of thirty-five years? Why place these restrictions in the Constitution? Is it likely that the citizens of the United States would elect a man to that responsible office who did not possess these qualifications? It seems that our forefathers thought it was possible, and hence they placed that restriction in the Constitution. Why not send for Kossuth, and make him President of the United States? Why require that a man shall be of a certain age before he shall be a Senator of the United States? Why place any restriction in the Constitution at all in regard to the age of members of our House of Representatives? Why say, even, he shall be twenty-one years of age? If we leave it to the people, is it likely that they will elect a minor to represent them? If they do, let them do it; it is their own business. Now this is the language of some gentlemen here.

I did misunderstand the gentleman from Mills, [Mr. Solomon,] before he made his explanation, in reply to what the gentleman from Lucas [Mr. Edwards,] said. I thought he took the position of throwing the doors wide open, and letting all the sons of Africa come in, and become electors and representatives of the people of Iowa. I thought he was for allowing all, white and black, red and yellow, all the great families of mankind, to come in and exercise these privileges without restriction. That is what I understood him to advance as his position. But his explanation is altogether different.

Now I am in favor of some restriction. The committee proposed thirty days as the limit in the section under consideration. I was willing to vote for as long a time as should be considered necessary. I am willing now to vote for a longer time than that. I do not care whether it be six months or a year; I am willing to vote for a longer time than has been reported. I think there should be some restriction.

Mr. TRAER. Before the question is taken upon the motion to strike out, I would like to reply to one or two arguments advanced by gentlemen upon the other side. The first is the argument of the gentleman from Alamakee, [Mr. Clark,] which may be entitled to some weight. He said that the effect of this proposition would be to prevent the people from securing the best talent in a county or district to represent them. Now I want to say to the gentleman from Alamakee, [Mr. Clark,] that it may be necessary for the people of Alamakee to import talent to represent them in the legislature. But, so far as my district is concerned, I believe that we can furnish a sufficient amount of talent, without any importation, to represent us in the legislature.

There is another view to be taken of this subject of the people selecting representatives to represent them in the legislature. If the action of their representatives extended merely to the particular district, and the people of that district, from which they were selected, then this matter would be presented to us in a different light; then we might leave entirely, without any restriction whatever, to the people to select whom they might see fit to represent them in the legislature.

But when we take into consideration that every representative. who comes here, represents not only the district in which he resides, but to a certain extent he represents all the State, and that he is to vote upon questions that will affect all portions of the State, then this question of restriction presents itself with some force. Now the people in Johnson county may have some choice in regard to the representatives to be chosen from Muscatine or Des Moines, although they cannot have any direct voice in that selection. Now, I say it is perfectly right and legitimate for this convention to put some restriction in this constitution. I do not think it is taking away the rights of the people at all. The provision is intended to protect the rights of other parts of the State, by restricting certain parts of the State in their selection of persons for high offices. That is my view of this matter.

I wish to say a word in reply to the gentleman from Mills [Mr. Solomon]. I was perfectly astonished to see the gentleman get up here, and make an argument as long as he did, directly in the face of what he said and did on yesterday. If he examines the yeas and nays, he will find that he voted with me.

Mr. SOLOMON. I know that I did.

Mr. TRAER. And the only reason he has given to-day for changing that vote, is, that the gentleman from Wapello [Mr. Gillaspy] has made an argument here, and he submits to him.

Mr. SOLOMON. I will state that when my friend from Linn [Mr. Gray] moved to reconsider that vote of yesterday, rose and said that I desired to second the motion, as I voted under a misapprehension of the question on yesterday.

Mr. TRAER. The gentleman stated that the gentleman from Wapello [Mr. Gillaspy] made a speech that expressed his ideas exactly, and therefore he would vote with that gentleman. I certainly think there is some lofty tumbling to get round to exactly the opposite position to the one taken on yesterday. When I take a position, I generally stick to it, unless there is seme pretty good reason for changing it: and if there is, I would make that reason known. As I understand the gentleman, he gave no reason at all for his change.

Mr. SOLOMON. I still insist that I voted under a misapprehension on yesterday. If I had understood the question properly, I should not have voted on yesterday as I did. I say this now, as I did before the gentleman from Wapello [Mr. Gillaspy] made his speech.

Mr. TRAER. I merely called the attention of the Convention to the matter; I do not think it amounts to much. As I said this morning, I am not wedded to my proposition, and am willing to change or modify it.

As I now understand it, the question is now upon striking out the words "thirty days," and inserting the words "one year."

The PRESIDENT. A division of the question has been ordered. The first question is upon the motion to strike out the words "thirty days."

Mr. CLARK, of Alamakee. I am happy to find one subject upon which the gentleman from Benton, [Mr. Traer,] and myself can agree. I am sensible myself, and I suppose the people of my county are also sensible, that we need better legislative capacity than we have heretofore had. And when the gentleman says that we need that in our county, I will agree with him at once. We do want to throw the doors open and let all the talent come into our county that can be induced to come there; and the people have discernment to discover and appropriate that talent to their use. I presume that that state of things does not exist in Benton county; that there is no need of more legislative talent there; that they have already all they desire, and that they will continue to have all they need, as long as the gentleman from Benton honors them with his presence there. I presume that is the reason his county is so differently situated from mine. I have no doubt that may be so.

I can see no reason at all in the argument that gentlemen use here in favor of the restriction proposed here, that there are other restrictions proposed in this article. They say there is a restriction placed upon voters, that they shall not vote until they have resided in the county for a certain length of time. That is all very true; there is a good reason for it, and as long as there is a reasonable rule, I am willing to stand by it. But when there is no reason for a restriction of that kind, I will not vote for it. Without a restriction of that kind upon the right of voting, men might go into two or more counties or districts and vote at the same election. That rule does not apply then to selection of officers. The people have the means of knowing all about the man whom they have presented to them for their election. And the reasons for requiring a man to reside in a county for a certain length of time before he shall be allowed to vote, does not exist in regard to candidates for office. There is a good reason for the rule in the one case, and no good reason for it in the other.

Mr. CLARKE, of Johnson, called for the yeas and nays upon the motion to strike out "thirty days," and they were ordered accordingly.

The question being then taken, by yeas and nays, upon the motion to strike out, it was not agreed to; yeas 13, nays 19, as follows:

Yeas—The President, Messrs. Clarke of Johnson, Edwards, Gower, Hall, Marvin, Palmer, Parvin, Robinson, Traer, Warren, Winchester and Young.

Nays—Messrs. Ayres, Clark of Alamakee, Clarke of Henry, Ells, Emerson, Gibson, Gillaspy, Gray, Harris, Hollingsworth, Johnston, Patterson, Peters, Price, Scott, Seely, Skiff, Solomon and Wilson.

Mr. SCOTT moved that the convention take a recess until two o'clock this afternoon, but withdrew the motion at the request of—

Night Sessions.

Mr. GILLASPY, who offered the following resolution:

"*Resolved*, That this Convention, in addition to its regular sessions, will meet each evening at 7 o'clock, until adjournment *sine die.*"

Mr. CLARKE, of Henry. I have but one remark to make in regard to this resolution. While I am just as anxious as any gentleman can be to do all our business and go home, I do not think we will gain anything by these night sessions. Our members now, one after another, are being struck down by sickness, and if we go into these night sessions it is possible we may soon find ourselves without a quorum, though in that way gentlemen may gain their object, and get an adjournment.

Mr. WILSON. There was a committee of revision and correction appointed on yesterday, and that committee will certainly have enough to keep it employed all the time its members are not required to be in attendance here. One or two reports have already passed their second reading, and are ready to be referred to that committee. The only time that committee will have, will be after we have adjourned in the afternoon. It is necessary that all the reports of our standing committees, as they shall have been amended by the convention, shall go through the hands of the committee on revision, and then be reported back to this convention for the third reading. And unless time is allowed after adjournment in the afternoon for this revision, the convention will have to wait, after all their reports have had their second reading, until the committee has time to revise these reports.

Mr. CLARKE, of Johnson. I have in my pocket the plan of a judiciary system, upon which the convention has acted, and which was re-committed for revision. If we are to meet here at night as well as in the daytime, I cannot possibly take time to re-write it, and put it into shape.

Mr. PALMER. I am in the condition of the gentleman from Jefferson, [Mr. Wilson.] I am on a committee that cannot act until we see what is the action of other committees, and find out what their reports are. We are just beginning to prepare for holding our meetings, and we may require several meetings before we can perfect our report. It will certainly be very inconvenient for the committee on miscellaneous subjects to meet here, if we have night sessions.

Mr. SOLOMON. I hope this resolution will not prevail. I think it is necessary for members here to have some time for recreation and rest.

Mr. CLARKE, of Johnson. I rise to a point of order; and that is that the subject we have had under consideration this morning, the report of the committee on the legislative department, has not been disposed of in any way.

The PRESIDENT. The chair did not understand that there was any objection to the resolution; if it is objected to, it cannot be entertained.

Mr. CLARKE, of Johnson. I will move then that the sergeant-at-arms be instructed to furnish each member and officer of this convention with a lantern. [Laughter.] I do not claim the credit of that suggestion; it belongs to the gentleman from Des Moines, [Mr. Hall.]

Mr. HALL. Will the gentleman from Wapello [Mr. Gillaspy,] accept the suggestion?

Mr. GILLASPY. No, sir; I have no desire to rob the State any more than we have already done.

Mr. TRAER. I would also suggest that the sergeant-at-arms be required to contract with the agents of the omnibus line, to take the members and officers of the convention to and from the State house. [Renewed laughter.]

Mr. HALL moved to lay the resolution upon the table.

The question being then taken, the motion to lay upon the table was agreed to.

Daguerreotypes of the Convention.

Mr. CLARKE, of Johnson, presented the following communications, which were read:

IOWA CITY, February 18, 1857.
To the Constitutional Convention:—

GENTLEMEN: Permit me, in behalf of the State Historical Society, to request you to furnish your daguerreotypes, to be preserved in its picture gallery.

Yours respectfully,
C. B. SMITH,
Corresponding Secretary.

IOWA CITY, February 18, 1857.
To the Honorable Members of the Convention:—

The undersigned would respectfully request the members of the convention to call at his office, as soon as circumstances will permit, and have their miniatures taken for the purpose of lithographing; also duplicate copies to be placed in the State Library, and for the Historical Association. Specimens may be found at the desk of Mr. Clarke of Johnson.

Respectfully,
J. R. HARTSOCK,
Artist.

Mr. CLARKE, of Johnson. The design is to have the likenesses of the members and officers of this convention placed in one frame, for preservation in the library of the State Historical Society, which is designed, under the law passed this winter, to be a permanent institution, and to be connected with the State University. The artist, Mr. Hartsock, has left with me three sizes of specimens of his work, with his prices for each. If the convention are disposed to go into this plan, and adopt this mode of preserving their likenesses, the members ought to seek opportunity without delay to have their miniatures taken. I understand, also, that Mr. Hartsock intends, if this succeeds, to get up a lithograph, showing the convention in actual session, the appearance of the hall, and likenesses of the officers and members.

Mr. HARRIS. I was talking with the artist this morning, and he was careful to say that it would be attended with no expense to any member.

Mr. CLARKE, of Johnson. The expense of lithographing will be borne by the artist. But the pictures to be hung up in the frame, will cost from one to three dollars, according to size.

The communications were received, and laid upon the table.

On motion of Mr. HARRIS,

The convention then took a recess until two o'clock this afternoon.

EVENING SESSION.

The convention met at two o'clock P. M., and was called to order by the President.

The consideration of the report of the committee on the legislative department, as amended in committee of the whole, was resumed by the convention.

Impeachment of State Officers.

Section twenty-one was read as follows:

"The Governor, Judges of the Supreme and District Courts, and all other State officers, shall be liable to impeachment for any misdemeanor in office; but judgment in such cases shall extend only to removal from office, and disqualification to hold any office of honor, trust or profit under this State; but the party convicted or acquitted shall nevertheless be liable to indictment, trial, and punishment according to law. All other civil officers shall be tried for misdemeanors and malfeasance in office in such manner as the General Assembly may provide."

Mr. EDWARDS. I move to strike out the word "misdemeanor," and insert in its place the word "malfeasance."

Mr. WILSON. I hope that motion will not prevail. Certainly the word "misdemeanor" is a more comprehensive term than the word "malfeasance," which is now sought to be inserted in its place.

The question was then taken, and the amendment was rejected.

Mr. CLARKE, of Henry. I move to amend by adding after "misdemeanor" the words "or malfeasance." As it now stands, the word "misdemeanor" is ambiguous, to say the least of it. In law the definition of "misdemeanor" is—

"An offence of a less atrocious nature than a crime. It applies to all offences inferior to felony, and also to all offences for which the law has not provided a particular remedy." (Bouvier's Institute.)

Blackstone says: "*Crimes* and *misdemeanors* are mere synonymous terms; but, in *common usage*, the word *crime* is made to deonte offences of a deeper and more atrocious dye, while small faults and omissions of less consequence are comprised under the gentler name of *misdemeanors*."

"The definition of *malfeasance* is, in *law*, the performance of some injurious act which the party had contracted not to do, or had no right to do." (Bouvier's Institutes.)

The question was then taken upon the amendment offered by Mr. Clarke, of Henry, and it was agreed to.

Special Legislation.

Mr. CLARKE, of Johnson. I desire to amend the thirty-first section, and I would ask the clerk to read it.

The section was then read as follows:

"The General Assembly shall not pass local or special laws in the following cases:

For the assessment and collection of taxes for state, county or road purposes;

For laying out, opening and working roads or highways;

For changing the names of persons;

For the incorporation of cities and towns;

For vacating roads, town plats, streets, alleys or public squares;

For locating or changing county seats;

In all the cases above enumerated, and in all other cases where a general law can be made applicable, all laws shall be general, and of uniform operation throughout the State."

Mr. CLARKE, of Johnson. I move to amend by striking out, in the seventh line, the following words:

"And in all other cases where a general law can be made applicable."

So that the section would then read:

"The General Assembly shall not pass local or special laws in the following cases:

For the assessment and collection of taxes for state, county, or road purposes;

For laying out, opening and working roads or highways;

For changing the names of persons;

For the incorporation of cities and towns;

For vacating roads, town plats, streets, alleys, or public squares;

For locating or changing county seats.

In all the cases above enumerated, all laws shall be general, and of uniform operation throughout the State."

This same question was presented the other day in the Committee of the Whole, but in a little different shape. I desire to make this provision effective, and at the same time I desire to cut off as much local legislation as possible. I have no doubt, if the words which I propose to strike out remain here, that they will leave a discretionary power with the Legislature upon this subject. I trust that those gentlemen, who were in favor of cutting off this local legislation, will say so here, and make it imperative upon the General Assembly to provide general laws for the cases here enumerated. As the section now stands, a discretionary power may be exercised by the Legislature upon this subject; and that will be the construction put upon it, in my opinion, by the Court. If gentlemen want to make it imperative upon the General Assembly to carry out the provisions of this section, they ought to strike out these words.

The question was then taken by yeas and nays, upon the amendment offered by Mr. Clarke, and it was rejected; yeas 13, nays 18, as follows:

Yeas.—Messrs. Clarke of Johnson, Edwards, Gower,, Hall, Hollingworth, Johnston, Marvin, Palmer, Patterson, Solomon, Warren, Winchester and Young.

Nays.—The President, Messrs. Ayres, Clark, of Alamakee, Clarke, of Henry, Ells, Emerson, Gibson, Gillaspy, Gray, Parvin, Peters, Price, Robinson, Scott, Seely, Skiff, Traer and Wilson.

Time of Elections.

Mr. YOUNG. I desire to offer an amendment to the third section, by striking out from the first clause, which reads—

"The members of the House of Representatives shall be chosen every second year, by the qualified electors of their respective districts, on the second Tuesday in October, except the year of the Presidential election, when the election shall be on the Tuesday next after the first Monday in November."

The following words:

"Except the years of the Presidential election, when the election shall be on the Tuesday next after the first Monday in November."

My object in offering this amendment is to make all our state elections uniform. I think it is a matter of the highest importance that our state elections should be kept separate and distinct from the presidential elections, and that they should be held on the same day in every year, whatever month we may happen to agree upon. As the section now stands, we would have elections for three years in October, and for one year in November. The state and presidential elections, in my opinion, should, in all cases, be kept separate and distinct. We may have state interests that would conflict with those of the presidential election, and for that reason I make the motion to strike out the words I have indicated.

Another reason I have for making this motion is, that it is essential that our tax-collectors should be elected and prepared to take charge of his duties before the time of the collection of taxes comes around.

Mr. GILLASPY. I regret very much that this amendment has been offered. It is well understood that I was in favor of fixing these elections in November, but I yielded that point and acquiesced in the report of the committee which, in the committee of the whole, was carried by an overwhelming vote. I wish to know now, whether this convention is going to take the back track and say that what they did yesterday was wrong. The gentleman speaks of the election of tax-collectors of counties. I undertake to say that one month cannot make a great deal of difference in their qualifications. I do hope that the people of this State will not be burdened with two elections, one in October and one in November, every four years, and that this convention will adopt the report of the committee If the report be adopted, I am perfectly satisfied, and I believe my people will be satisfied with it, because it accomplishes the great object they have in view, and that is, to do away with the frequent elections that cause so much trouble and excitement. The people of the State are just as much interested in the election of a President of the United States, as they are in the election of a Governor or a representative. I hold that they are capable of judging rightly in this matter, and that they will do so, place as many officers upon the ticket to be elected, as you see fit and proper. It is the unnecessary expense of having two elections every four years within a month of each other, that I object to, and that my people object to.

I hope that the convention will not now retrace their steps, when they decided by a large majority, in committee of the whole, to adopt the report of the Committee on the Legislative Department. I hope, therefore, that the motion of the gentleman from Mahaska, [Mr. Young,] will not prevail.

The question was then taken, by yeas and nays, upon the amendment of Mr. Young, and it was rejected, yeas 13, nays 19, as follows:

Yeas—The President, Messrs. Ayres, Clarke of Johnson, Edwards, Ells, Gower, Gray, Hollingsworth, Marvin, Scott, Wilson, Winchester and Young.

Nays—Messrs. Clark of Alamakee, Clarke of Henry, Emerson, Gibson, Gillaspy, Hall, Harris, Johnston, Palmer, Parvin, Patterson, Peters, Price, Robinson, Seely, Skiff, Solomon, Traer and Warren.

Number of Senators and Representatives.

Mr. WILSON. I move to strike out of section thirty-six the words "fifty" and "one hundred," and insert "thirty-six" and "seventy-five" in lieu thereof, so that the section will read:

"The Senate shall not consist of more than thirty-six members, nor the House of Representatives of more than seventy-five."

I make this motion for the reason I stated yesterday, that I am opposed to any increase in the present number of members of the legislature; and I am informed that if we take the ratio of representation established by the last legislature, under the plan adopted by the convention in relation to the apportionment of representatives, it will just increase the number to seventy-five. I am willing to make an increase of three representatives, but I am unwilling to increase the number any more than that, so far as I am concerned. I therefore make the motion to amend as I have stated.

Mr. CLARKE, of Henry. I regret that I cannot go with my friend from Jefferson, [Mr. Wilson,] in support of his proposition. I am in favor of giving the people the greatest latitude, whether the ratio which is established should give them one hundred members or less.

The question was then taken, by yeas and nays, upon the amendment offered by Mr. Wilson, and it was rejected; yeas 6, nays 25, as follows:

Yeas—The President, Messrs. Gibson, Gower, Skiff, Warren and Wilson.

Nays—Messrs. Ayres, Clark of Alamakee, Clarke of Henry, Clarke of Johnson, Edwards, Emerson, Gillaspy, Gray, Hall, Harris, Hollingsworth, Johnston, Marvin, Palmer, Parvin, Patterson, Peters, Price, Robinson, Scott, Seely, Solomon, Traer, Winchester and Young.

Eligibility to General Assembly.

Mr. CLARKE, of Henry. I desire to offer an amendment to section twenty-three, which reads as follows:

"No person holding any lucrative office under the United States, or this State, or any other power, shall be eligible to the General Assembly: Provided, that offices in the militia, to which there is no annual salary, or office of justice of the peace, or postmasters, whose compensation does not exceed one hundred dollars per annum, or notary public, shall not be deemed lucrative."

I think that some gentlemen voted under a misapprehension in committee of the whole, when they voted against the amendment I am about to propose. The construction I would put upon this section is, that persons who have been elected to the legislature, and who hold some office of trust or profit, could have their seats contested upon the ground that they were not eligible to an election. Others put a different construction upon it, and the chairman of that committee, [Mr. Parvin,] as I understand, supposes that the section means eligibility to hold office. He supposes that any postmaster could be elected to the legislature, and if he resigned that office, could hold his seat in the Assembly. Webster gives the following definitions of eligibility:

"1. Worthiness or fitness to be chosen; the state or equality of a thing which renders it preferable to another, or desirable.

2. The state of being capable of being chosen to an office."

It is the decision in Congress, that the word "eligibility" refers to the capability of being chosen to an office. Then, again, Webster gives the following definitions of the word eligible:

"1. Fit to be chosen, worthy of choice, preferable.

2. Legally qualified to be chosen; as a man is or is not *eligible* to office."

If the convention wish the ambiguity to remain in these sections, very well; but if they wish to say that persons shall not be eligible to an election, it should be so expressed; or if, on the other hand, they wish to say, that persons shall not be eligible to hold office, they should so express it. Gentlemen will see, by referring to the old constitution, that this section is a transcript of the section upon the same subject there, and yet difficulties have arisen under it, which we ought to guard against here. By making the twenty-third section correspond with the twenty-fourth, using the language contained in it, we will avoid the ambiguity now contained in the twenty-third section, and accomplish the object we desire. If gentlemen will take the pains to read the twenty-fourth section, they will see that it provides that—

"No person who may hereafter be a collector or holder of public moneys, shall have a seat in either house of the General Assembly, or be eligible to hold any office of trust or profit under this State, until he shall have accounted for and paid the treasurer all sums for which he may be liable."

I would move, therefore, that the language used in this section be applied to section twenty-three, and that the word "eligible" shall be stricken out, so that the section shall read—

"No person holding any lucrative office under the United States, or this State, or any other power, shall have a seat in either house of the General Assembly," &c.

The section thus modified will allow the people, if they see fit, to select a candidate for the General Assembly, who may hold some other office, and elect him. The difficulty which I wish to guard against is the holding of two offices, which are inconsistent with each other. If a person holding an office under the government is elected to the General Assembly, if he is so disposed, he can give up the former office, and he will then be properly qualified to occupy a seat in the legislature. The amendment I propose allows the people a greater latitude in the selection of their officers, and allows persons holding offices to vacate their old ones, and accept new ones.

The question was then taken upon Mr. Clarke's amendment, and it was rejected, upon a division; ayes 7, noes 12.

Committee on Revision.

Mr. TRAER. I move that the article as now amended be referred to the committee on revision.

Mr. CLARKE, of Johnson. I suppose we have made quite a number of amendments to this article, which ought to take the usual course. If they need re-writing, they should first go to the committee on the legislative department, in order that it may see that they all come in at their proper places. After the article and amendments are re-written, and put into shape, they can then be engrossed, and ordered to a third reading.

Mr. TRAER. I do not understand that this committee have to re-write any thing. I do not see any necessity for referring this article to the committee on the legislative department.

Mr. CLARKE, of Johnson. If there is any defect in this article which needs rectifying, it is out of the power of the committee on revision to correct it, after the article has been ordered to be engrossed, and read the third time.

Mr. EDWARDS. I understand the proper course would be to refer it to the committee on revision, and if there is any thing wrong, and which needs amending, they can send it back here.

Mr. SOLOMON. I desire to see a slight alteration made in one section before this article is ordered to be engrossed. I would ask the gentleman from Benton [Mr. Traer,] to withdraw his motion for a moment.

Mr. TRAER. I will withdraw my motion.

Basis of Representation.

Mr. SOLOMON. A special committee was appointed the other day to prepare a basis of representation for the House of Representatives, and they made a report which met with the almost universal approbation of the convention. Understanding that report in a certain way, I favored it myself, and I understand that those who favored it, or spoke upon it, entertained the same view of it that I did. I think some change in the phraseology is necessary to give it the effect and bearing which we all desire, and I will point it out, if the convention will hear me.

I will state in the first place, that I understand the basis to be this, and that the convention desired to establish this privilege; that in assigning representatives through the State, any organized county which has a number of inhabitants equal to one-half the ratio fixed by law, shall be entitled to a member in the House of Representatives; and where a fraction over was also found in any county equal to one-half the ratio, she also shall be entitled to the same privilege. I do not think, that the phraseology of the section in question, secures this It reads—

"Any district containing one or more counties, and having a number of inhabitants equal to one-half of the ratio fixed by law, shall be entitled to one Representative, and any one county containing in addition to the ratio fixed by law, a fraction of one-half of that number shall be entitled to one additional Representative."

The convention will please observe that the arrangement of the districts is given to the legislature. Suppose then that two counties, which have each the number of inhabitants equal to one-half the ratio fixed by law, and which, according to the obvious intention of the section, would be entitled to two representatives, should be put together by the legislature, and thrown into one district, as may be done. I apprehend if we would change the phraseology of the section, so as to say that any organized county having a number of inhabitants equal to one-half the ratio fixed by law shall be entitled to one representative, it would secure the end desired. I desire to offer the amendment I have indicated.

The PRESIDENT. The chair will observe, that no amendment would now be in order. The gentleman can accomplish his purpose, if some member who voted in the majority will move to

proposition he desired to introduce, and therefore he could not offer it.

The PRESIDENT. The Chair understood the gentleman from Appanoose, [Mr. Harris,] as objecting to the reception of the amendment which the gentleman proposed to offer; and as the amendment could not be entertained unless by the unanimous consent of the Convention, the Chair assigned the floor to another gentleman.

Mr. SOLOMON. I desire to present an amendment to which the gentleman from Appanoose will not object.

The PRESIDENT. The amendment can be entertained by the unanimous consent of the Convention.

Mr. SOLOMON. I now offer the following amendment to the section on the basis of representation, so that it will read—

"Every county having a number of inhabitants equal to one-half of the ratio fixed by law shall be entitled to one representative."

That will secure the object I have in view, and do away with the objections which I now have to the section.

Mr. GOWER objected to the introduction of the amendment.

Mr. SOLOMON. If objection is made, I shall move to reconsider.

Mr. GOWER. I will withdraw the objection.

Mr. SOLOMON. Then I will offer the amendment.

Mr. HARRIS. I think the matter, as it stands, is broad enough to cover the whole ground; but the amendment does not alter the principle at all. I suppose there is no particular objection to it.

The PRESIDENT. The amendment will be made by the Secretary.

Mr. TRAER moved that the report, as amended, be referred to the Committee upon Revision.

Mr. PALMER. I would inquire whether the Committee have authority to transpose sections, to put two or more sections into one, &c.? I see that there is considerable disorder in this article as it stands printed.

The PRESIDENT. It is the opinion of the Chair that that is a part of the duty of the Committee.

Mr. PALMER. Then I will call the attention of the Committee to the disorder in these different sections. The third and fourth sections relate to the eligibility of members; and, again, in sections twenty-three and twenty-four, we come to the same subject. I think these should be placed together. The sixth and seventh sections are also closely connected in subject, and I think they would properly constitute one section.

Mr. CLARKE, of Johnson. What became of the proposition of the gentleman from Mills, [Mr. Solomon]?

The PRESIDENT. It was incorporated into the report of the Committee.

Mr. CLARKE, of Johnson. Was it adopted by a vote of the Convention?

The PRESIDENT. It was, by unanimous consent.

Mr. CLARKE, of Johnson. I was not aware of it. I intended to vote against it. I think it injures the whole feature of the proposed improvements. I understood the consent to be only to admit the proposition that it might be discussed and voted upon.

The PRESIDENT. The chair had decided that the amendment was not in order, and that it could only be made by the unanimous consent of the convention; no objection being made at the time, the chair instructed the Secretary to incorporate the amendment in the report.

The motion to refer to the committee on revision was agreed to.

Executive Department.

Mr. TRAER moved that the convention proceed to the consideration of the report of the committee on the executive department.

Mr. HARRIS. Before that question is put, I wish to inquire whether there is any reasonable probability that the chairman of the committee [Mr. Todhunter,] will be able to resume his seat within a short time. If not, we may properly go on with the report; but if there is, I should prefer to wait until he can be here.

SEVERAL MEMBERS. No; there is not.

The motion to take up the report upon the executive department was agreed to.

On motion of Mr. TRAER—

Committee of the Whole.

The convention proceeded to consider the report in committee of the whole. [Mr. Gibson in the chair.]

The Secretary proceeded to read the report by sections.

Governor.

Sections one and two were read as follows:

"The supreme executive power of this State shall be vested in a Chief Magistrate, who shall be styled the Governor of the State of Iowa.

The Governor shall be elected by the qualified electors at the time and place of voting for members of the General Assembly, and shall hold his office   years from the time of his installation, and until his successor shall be qualified."

Mr. SKIFF moved to fill the blank with the word "two."

Mr. PARVIN moved to fill the blank with "four."

The question being taken upon the motion of Mr. Parvin, it was agreed to, upon a division; ayes 18, noes 13.

No farther amendment being offered to this section—

Lieutenant Governor.

Section three was read as follows:

"There shall be a Lieutenant Governor, who shall hold his office years, and be elected at the same time of the Governor. In voting for Governor and Lieutenant Governor, the electors shall designate for whom they vote as Governor, and for whom as Lieutenant Governor. The returns of every election for Governor and Lieutenant Governor shall be sealed up and transmitted to the seat of government, directed to the Speaker of the House of Representatives, who shall open and publish them in the presence of both Houses of the General Assembly."

Mr. GILLASPY moved to strike out the words "Lieutenant Governor."

The motion was agreed to, upon a division; ayes 15, noes 8,

Mr. GRAY. The words "Lieutant Governor" occurs several times.

Mr. GILLASPY. My motion was to strike it out wherever it occurs.

Mr. WARREN. I move to strike out the whole section. We can afterwards add whatever is necessary about the returns of election to the second section.

Mr. PARVIN. Having stricken out the words "Lieutenant Governor," the first three lines become unnecessary; but then follows a provision as to the mode in which returns shall be made, which it is necessary to retain with regard to the election of Governor.

Mr. WARREN. The amendment could better be made to the second section.

Mr. GILLASPY. I think with the gentleman from Muscatine, [Mr. Parvin,] that if we strike out the first three lines, and the words "Lieutenant Governor" wherever they occur, the remainder of the section is proper, and should stand with the section providing for the election of Governor.

Mr. WILSON. I will offer a substitute, which probably the gentleman from Jackson [Mr. Warren,] will accept in lieu of his motion:

"The returns of every election for Governor shall be sealed up and transmitted to the seat of government, directed to the Speaker of the House of Representatives, who shall, during the first week of the session, open and publish them in presence of both Houses of the General Assembly. The person having the highest number of votes shall be Governor; but in case any two or more have an equal, and the highest number of votes, the General Assembly shall, by joint vote, choose one of said persons so having an equal, and the highest number of votes, for Governor."

Mr.. JOHNSTON. (In his seat.) That is right; that is from the old constitution.

Mr. WILSON. I would move this as a substitute for the third and fourth sections.

Mr. WARREN accepted the substitute, and the question being taken thereupon, it was agreed to.

Contested Elections.

Section five was then read as follows:

"Contested elections for Governor, or Lieutenant Governor, shall be determined by the General Assembly in such manner as may be prescribed by law."

Mr. WILSON moved to strike out the words "or Lieutenant Governor" from section five, which motion was agreed to

No further amendment being offered to section five—

Eligibility to Office, Age, &c.

Section six was read as follows:

"No person shall be eligible to the office of Governor, or Lieutenant Governor, who shall not have been a citizen of the United States, and a resident of the State two years next preceding the election, and attained the age of thirty years at the time of said election."

On motion of Mr. WILSON, the words "or Lieutenant Governor" were stricken out.

Mr. SOLOMON moved to strike out "thirty," and to insert twenty-one; so as to require the governor to be twenty-one years of age when elected.

Mr. SCOTT. I hope this motion will prevail. I heard with a great deal of pleasure the able arguments from almost all parts of this Convention in favor of the proposition to extend the elective franchise. I wish also to extend the right of holding office, so as to give, as far as possible, the largest liberty. No one can say that I am personally interested in this, because I am certainly past thirty years of age; but still I say that the people should be allowed to select among any of the electors resident within the State for a proper length of time, any one whom they see fit to represent them, to fill any of these offices, no matter what his age may be, whether twenty-five, thirty or fifty. I have yet to learn that age gives a man thought or ability, after he arrives at majority. I think history will bear me out in saying that many of the world's ablest men have been ripe at the age of twenty-five and before reaching the age of thirty years, they have seen their best days. History will show that some of our greatest and best men passed the culminating point at thirty years, and were on the wane from that time. And for this reason I hope the convention will support the motion of the gentleman from Mills [Mr. Solomon] and take off this restriction.

Mr. SKIFF. I will move to amend the amendment by striking out all of that clause about the age of the governor; being the words, "and attained the age of thirty years at the time of said election."

Mr. SOLOMON accepted the amendment.

Mr. PALMER. We have adopted as a qualification of senators the provision that they shall be twenty-five years of age. If this motion prevails, we shall require of a man to fill the office of governor less experience than to fill the office of senator. It seems to me there is some inconsistency in that. I believe I woud vote that the governor should be twenty-five years of age.

Mr. WILSON. I hope the gentleman will not make Young America bear the weight of the whole senate upon this motion. If the convention agree to this, it will be easy to recur to the provision with regard to senators, and make it consistent. I hope we shall not be required to err again, merely because we may have erred once.

Mr. MARVIN. If it is a fact that we have men in Iowa who are in their zenith at twenty-five, and then begin to decline, I think it is a very good reason for inserting a provision in the report upon the subject. If we have such fast young men, that they destroy their intellect and physical strength at twenty five, let us wait until they are thirty and see what they are; and if then they retain the strength of manhood, we may reasonably hope that they will last four years longer.

Mr. SCOTT. The decline of which I spoke, I wish it to be understood, does not arise from any malfeasance or mispractice; it may be over exertion in behalf of the commonwealth. There are individuals who, in consequence of over exertion, have reached their culminating point at thirty years, and even at twenty-five; men whose energies have all been expended in behalf of the welfare of the community, valuable men in the community, men of the finest talents, the greatest ability, the soundest judgment at twenty-five years of age, but who at thirty are almost in their dotage, and who at forty-five are past being of use to the community, compared with what they were at twenty-five. I hope gentlemen will not misunderstand me. I do not refer to those fast young men of whom he speaks, whom we should not take into consideration in connection with this office for a moment. I trust we shall never have one of that class to fill the gubernatorial chair in this State. If such men should ever come to a State like this, it is not probable that they would ever be called upon to fill any office of trust, honor, or emolument, in the State. But when I spoke of fast young men, I meant highly cultivated and intelligent young men, such as we have in this convention under thirty years of age, men well qualified to fill important offices of honor and trust. It is to give such men an opportunity of aspiring to the same places with myself and others, that there may be no unjust discrimination on account of their age, against those who may be equal or superior to ourselves, that I desire the amendment to prevail, that the people may, if they choose, elect one of that class to fill this important office.

Mr. PARVIN. This is a contest entirely between Young America and Old Fogyism, and as I am getting old I believe I will adhere to the landmarks of our fathers, and the qualifications they have prescribed. I shall vote against striking out.

Mr. CLARKE, of Henry. This has been an old warfare for many generations, the contest between old men and young men. There is an old proverb that "young men think old men are fools, and that old men know that young men are." That is the supposition upon which we have been acting, which has crept into the constitution, and has been the cause of these precedents to which the gentleman refers us. I recollect, sir, these precedents; and I recollect, too, that when the question was asked of one of the most eccentric of American statesmen, and one of the shrewdest and wisest, whether he did not come within the restriction, he replied, "Go and ask my constituents." That reply always struck me with a great deal of force. I say that the constituents can tell whether these restrictions ought to apply to a man or not. The constituents can tell, if he be twenty-one years of age, or seventy-five years of age, whether he is a suitable man to reflect their opinions, and to represent them. I say again that I am in favor of giving the greatest latitude to the people, not to the office-seekers. I say let the people select their representatives wheresoever they will, if they only seek them from their own number, the qualified electors of the State. I go no further than the gentleman from Mills, [Mr. Solomon,] in that respect, and perhaps I ought to congratulate myself that the gentleman from Mills stands up shoulder to shoulder with me for this proposition.

This is the principle that men will come to yet, when this Old Fogyism, this relic of old Federalism, this hedging and guarding the people at every point, this fear to trust the people, will all be swept away like a cobweb, and the people will be allowed to select their representatives wherever they can find them from their midst, without being trammelled by all these qualifications. I am not afraid to trust the people to the fullest extent. I have confidence that they will understand their own interests, if you will only act broadly upon that principle, and not be forever jealous of them. People are just beginning to see where this is leading them. They are beginning to creep along now towards their full liberty, are beginning to embrace republicanism in all its purity, in its full length and breadth and height, and this it is which leads them to the opinion that when we throw the doors open and leave these things free and unrestrained to the people, they will right themselves, that they do not require this eternal guarding and hedging. I am, therefore, in favor of striking out, and in inserting, if it is desired, twenty-one years of age.

Mr. EDWARDS. I move to amend by adding, "provided that bachelors shall not be eligible to the office of Governor."

Mr. SOLOMON. I have no objection to that. It will not be very likely to affect me personally.

Mr. GILLASPY. I am upon the side of Young America; and I am certainly astonished to find the *young* gentleman from Muscatine [Mr. Parvin] [laughter] occupying the position he does. I had supposed from the rapid advance the gentleman had been making during the last few years, he would certainly be with us. From an old line democrat he has advanced to the republican party, with all its new ideas; but now we see him lingering behind and clinging to the old relic of fogyism, that the people are not capable of deciding as to qualifications of candidates for office, or as to the age of persons to be elected to the various offices of this State. The gentleman from Davis [Mr. Palmer] intimated that we were to be governed by the vote of this convention with regard to the qualifications of Senators. Now I have no doubt that before this convention adjourns, it will wipe out that twenty-five years in the senatorial qualifications. I believe that a man competent to come here as a member of the General Assembly—and we have all known men twenty-one years of age who would be competent to come here—would be competent to act as Governor of the State. Why, sir, the people of the Union have elected a man but one year over thirty-five to the second office in the gift of the people of the United States. They have had so much confidence in Young America. And when the government of the United States can do that, I believe that the State of Iowa ought to be willing that any candidate, who is an elector, whom the people may desire to nominate, may be eligible to the office of Governor, or any other office within the gift of the people of the State. It may be that old men know more than young men, but it does not always follow that old men are any better qualified to discharge the duties of an office than some young men may be. I want to leave it open for the people of the State to decide for themselves. I know many young men, and am glad to see young men upon the floor of this convention—and I do not mean to include myself in that class, being passed the middle age of life—but I am proud to say that we have young men upon this floor who I think would do honor to the State as Governor of the State; and I know many young men throughout the State, and I believe we have them in every county of the State, who, although under twenty-five years of age, would make respectable Senators. I hope the doctrine of Young America may prevail. It is the doctrine of the age; and the man who is not up to it is behind the age.

Mr. PARVIN. My good and old established friend from Wapello [Mr. Gillaspy] has stated the truth in saying that a few years ago I was a democrat. Now I ask that gentleman and this committee, if the constitution which now governs us was not a democratic constitution, made by the sterling, simon-pure democracy of Iowa; and I ask if this qualification act was not a part of that constitution. Upon that little affair, I stand upon the democratic ground; and without pressing the inquiry any further, I will merely say that it is he and his friends who have gone astray in this matter, which is only characteristic of their course in other respects. They have wandered after strange gods; and I may say of them in the language of the Scripture, "Ephraim is joined to his idols; let him alone."

Mr. GILLASPY. I recollect very well that when the gentleman belonged to the democratic party, that party held to the doctrine of progression. I do not believe that a party should stand still for all time to come, and any man who may practice upon that principle as a partisan, or in any other capacity in life, is behind the age, and must expect to be lost sight of by the whole community around him; and I believe that is the fix the gentleman from Muscatine is getting into.

Mr. CLARK, of Alamakee. I am opposed to the amendment of the gentleman from Lucas, [Mr. Edwards,] preventing bachelors from holding the office of Governor. In the first place it is perfectly useless; for a person who has been a candidate for a certain office, without an election, long enough to be called an old bachelor, certainly need not be feared as a competitor by any candidate for the office of Governor of the State. Consequently, it would be wholly unnecessary to incorporate into the Constitution a provision of this kind. In the next place, I am inclined to look upon that class of persons with a great deal of indulgence, and I certainly would be the last one to place anything in the Constitution of the State proscribing them, or in any way making them in any more unfortunate position than nature seems to have assigned them. I shall therefore vote against the amendment.

Then as to the old fogy doctrine which has been brought forward, as it is proposed that none under the age of thirty shall be eligible to the office of Governor, I am in favor of turning the tables, and extending the restriction so that no person *over* the age of thirty shall be eligible.

Mr. EDWARDS. I merely offered this amendment in order that my Young America friends may be consistent. I think that a gentleman who is in the class of old bachelorism has as much old fogyism as any one can have. My object is to bring these gentlemen down a little and compel them to get married.

Mr. CLARKE, of Johnson. I think that the amendment of the gentleman from Lucas, [Mr. [Edwards,] is a personal reflection upon the gentleman from Davis, [Mr. Palmer.]

Mr. PALMER. I will waive all objections to it upon the ground of personality. [Laughter.] While I am not in favor of the proposition, I think that all who are opposed to old bachelors holding office ought to vote for it. The gentleman from Alamakee, [Mr. Clark,] has said that there is no danger of their getting into office, if they cannot get married. I think we have the strongest evidence that they are pretty hard to beat, because we have just elected a man notoriously a bachelor, to the highest office in the gift of this Republic, notwithstanding the most strenuous opposition. So I think if any gentleman has any apprehensions that the public interests will suffer by permitting the office of Governor to be filled by an old bachelor, he better vote for this amendment.

Mr. MARVIN moved that the Committee rise, report progress, and ask leave to sit again.

The motion was not seconded.

Mr. EDWARDS, by unanimous consent, withdrew his amendment.

The question then recurred upon the amendment to strike out the clause, "and attained the age of thirty years at the time of said election;" it was rejected, upon a division; ayes 13, noes 16.

Mr. TRAER moved to strike out "thirty," and insert "twenty-five."

The motion was not agreed to, upon a division; ayes 10, noes 15.

No further amendment being offered to section seven—

Powers and duties of the Governor.

The following sections were read:

"Sec. 7. The Governor shall be commander-in-chief of the militia, the army and navy of this State.

Sec. 8. He shall transact all executive business with the officers of government, civil and military, and may require information in writing from the officers of the Executive Department upon any subject relating to the duties of their respective offices.

Sec. 9. He shall take care that the laws are faithfully executed.

Sec. 10. When any office shall, from any cause, become vacant, and no mode is provided by the Constitution and laws for filling such vacancy, by granting a commission, which shall expire at the end of the next session of the General Assembly, or at the next election by the people."

No amendment being offered to these sections,

Extra Sessions of the General Assembly.

Section eleven was read as follows:

"He may, on extraordinary occasions, convene the General Assembly by proclamation, and shall state to both Houses, when assembled, the purpose for which they shall have been convened; and when so convened, they shall have no power to legislate upon any subject save that suggested in the message of the Governor."

Mr. SKIFF moved to strike out the words, "and when so convened they shall have no power to legislate upon any subject save that suggested in the message of the Governor." The section would then read—

"He may, on extraordinary occasions, convene the General Assembly by proclamation, and shall state to both Houses, when assembled, the purpose for which they shall have been convened."

Mr. SKIFF. It may be that matters may come up which it will be necessary to attend to. I do not think that the Legislature, when in session, ought to be restricted in relation to the subjects of its action by the will of the Governor. We might just as well say to the Governor that he may legislate in the vacation of the General Assembly, as give him the power to tell the Legislature upon what they shall legislate.

Mr. SOLOMON. I shall be compelled to differ from my friend. I am opposed to striking that out. I think this is a question germain to one we had up this morning, in reference to annual or biennial sessions of the Legislature. We clothe the Governor with power to convene the General Assembly by proclamation, and we require him to state in his proclamation the objects and purposes for which they are so convened. At the time the Legislature are elected, they are elected upon certain issues. They take their seats and go through with one session, and perform their duties to their constituents upon those issues. This section is intended to provide that whenever any new cases may arise, necessary for immediate action, and requiring, in the opinion of the Governor, an extra session, he may call them together. I think the people would be relieved from a great deal of unnecessary and improper legislation if, the matters upon which the Legislature are called together, having been attended to, that object having been secured, and the Legislature having done all that they were elected to do, there should be no power to act upon other subjects. They were elected to serve only one term, and those special objects, and those only, have brought them together again. The amendment would enable the Governor of the State to be loose and reckless in regard to the objects and purposes set forth for their convening; because, as a matter of course, it would be totally immaterial what subjects he set forth in his proclamation, if they can afterwards legislate upon any subject they think proper. My object is to hold the Governor responsible for the extra session,—to place his reasons upon the record. If he assumes the high prerogative of calling together the Legislature of the State, he ought to be compelled to set forth in a clear light his reasons for so doing. If not so compelled, he may set forth anything he pleases as the ostensible reason, and then the Legislature can act upon the real objects of the Governor, which he did not dare to set forth in his proclamation. I think it is eminently proper that, if the former part of the section shall be adopted, the latter part should be also, so that the Legislature may be confined in their action to the objects of the meeting as set forth in the proclamation of the Governor.

Mr. SKIFF. The twelfth section reads—

"He shall communicate, by message, to the General Assembly, at every regular session, the condition of the State, and recommend such matters as he shall deem expedient."

While we do not restrict the General Assembly in that case, while we do not say that at the regular sessions of the legislature, they shall adopt or reject the recommendations of the Governor and pass upon no others, it seems to me that it is very proper to omit to impose the restriction upon the same legislature at an extra session. Here is a deliberative body of men called together to discharge certain duties. The Governor may think they should be convened for a particular purpose, which, as a general rule, he will engraft into his message. But he may be negligent, or from interested motives he may omit what really ought to have been put in, and then there would be no remedy. Let him call them together, and as in other cases let him send in his message to the General Assembly and recommend what he thinks ought to be done, and then leave it to them to act without confining them to those recommendations. To say that they shall pass upon nothing else seems to me a little too much like the one man power. The body of the people are represented by the legislature. A great deal has been said about trusting the representatives of the people. I think that now is a good time to put the good doctrine into practical operation. I do not like to see so much power vested in the Governor, as to tell the General Assembly exactly what they may vote upon. He might just as well go a little farther and tell the legislature how they shall vote, that they shall pass this law or not pass that one. I want the legislature left as free as practicable.

Mr. HALL. I look upon this matter in a different light from some other gentlemen. In my view that message will become a constitution or law to that legislature. And when they pass a law, instead of going to the constitution to see whether it is valid or not, it will be necessary to go to the message, and it will be necessary to consider the question whether the Governor in his message went far enough to authorize the legislature to pass the law; for if he did not, the law would be void. This seems to me calculated to introduce a miserable system of legislation, and I am in favor of having it stricken out.

Mr. CLARKE, of Henry. I am in favor of striking out for this reason. Whenever a Governor shall call the General Assembly together, they must assemble at a great expense to the State. After they are once here, there may be subjects of legislation presented to them not mentioned or thought of by the Governor, and the people may require legislation upon those subjects.

Another reason is, as has been suggested, that we are putting too much power into the hands of the Governor, in leaving him to decide in advance of the meeting of the legislature upon what subjects they shall legislate. It is giving him a power no potentate in the world now exercises It is going beyond the power of proroguing. It is holding the legislature as the creatures of the Governor, to allow him to tell them that they shall meet and legislate upon any particular subject, and then go home. I want no such power over the legislature of Iowa to be given to any man. I want no such restrictions. I say that if the representatives of the people come up here, they should come here with all the majesty of the people. As their representatives they are prepared to act for them. I am willing to leave to the Governor the power to call them together upon an emergency; but when it is called I would not hamper or trammel the legislature at all in acting upon what is wanted by the people.

Mr. SOLOMON. I move the following substitute for the whole section:—

"He may on extraordinary occasions convene the General Assembly by proclamation in which he shall state fully and distinctly the purpose for which they are convened; and when so convened they shall have no power to legislate upon any subject save that suggested in the proclamation of the Governor."

The difference between the original and the substitute is this. The original requires that when the legislature are assembled, he shall state the reasons for which he calls them together. The substitute requires him to state those reasons in the proclamation by which he calls them together. Now I wish to explain why I think this is proper and necessary. I stood this morning with those who are in favor of annual sessions of the legislature; and I did so because I thought it was proper and necessary that the legislature should convene every year and come fresh from the people, so that they might pass such laws as the people desire. Gentlemen who oppose this amendment will place themselves upon the record in this light. They desire to have a legislature elected to hold office for two years from the election, and then to come together and legislate for two different sessions for the people. If they desire general legislation every year, then let us have annual sessions; and let not this great expense be entailed upon the State for legislation by men elected two years before. If a legislature called by the Governor is to have plenary powers to go on and do anything which any legislature *de novo* may do, let us have them come directly from the people. This provision is designed to vest a power in the Governor to call them together in certain emergencies or exigencies in the State. I trust that those gentlemen who consider legislation once in two years sufficient for this State, will vote with me upon this proposition.

Mr. CLARKE, of Johnson. I am in favor of this motion to strike out, because I believe it to be right. It seems to me there is a wonderful inconsistency between the arguments of gentlemen upon this matter, and their arguments heretofore in regard to annual sessions. We were told then that we need not make provision for annual sessions, for the Governor would have the power to call extra sessions, whenever they were necessary. The convention voted down the proposition for annual sessions. It is now proposed to give to the Governor the super-added power of specifying what the legislature shall do, when thus convened in extra session, making them the mere creatures, the tools of the executive.

Suppose that, under this provision, when the legislature meets here, they take a more extended view of the Governor's message calling them together, than he does, and they proceed to pass acts of legislation accordingly. The Governor says: I meant no such thing when I called you together, and therefore I will veto these acts. Does he not thus become a one-man power in this State? Will he not have the control, not only of the executive department, but also of the legislative department?

If we desire to destroy this third branch of our government, let us say so, and understand it, and I will vote to abolish it. But do not let us provide for a Governor who shall have power not only to execute the law, but also to make it. I undertake to say this: that with the wide and diversified interests of a State as large as Iowa, the Governor is not to be presumed to know all the immediate and pressing wants of every locality, and of every district, as the members in the legislature representing those localities and districts may know them. When some great emergency calls the General Assembly together, there may be some pressing necessity for them to attend to, which may not be provided for by law, and may not be embraced in the message convening them together.

We seem to be making all the different branches of the government dependent on one another, instead of having them independent in their respective spheres. Instead of guarding the right of the people in each particular point, we seem to be endeavoring to make the executive the controlling power in the government. As I have shown heretofore, the judiciary are dependent upon the legislative department, as it can fix their salaries or starve them out, if it shall so desire. And when we come to the legislative department we propose to place it under the control of the executive. The Governor thus becomes the great power of the State for four years.

It does seem to me that there can be nothing contrived better calculated to take away and destroy the efficiency of the law-making branch of the government, which I consider the most important one, as the one coming most directly from the people, and entirely acquainted with their wants. I will not say that we will always have governors who will act improperly; but that may happen, and it has happened in a neighboring State in a recent instance. We should provide for contingencies of this kind. It does seem to me that, without annual sessions, and with the veto power, the governor will exercise the whole power of the State, for at least one-half of the four years of his term of office.

Mr. SOLOMON. I am well aware that the power to convene and to prorogue the law-making branch of the State is an extraordinary power. And when I see a proposition presented by a committee, conferring upon the governor of the State the power to convene the legislature at his discretion, I want to compel him to spread before the public the reasons operating upon his mind for so doing. Gentlemen who opposed the proposition for annual sessions, did so upon the ground that such a proposition would entail needless expense upon the community, and we would have our laws so frequently changed that they would be worse than no laws at all. I offered this substitute here to meet their objections. If they desire to confer this extraordinary power upon the Governor of the State, I think he should be compelled to give his reasons for convening the legislature. And I would also, when the legislature had acted upon what the Governor considered the extraordinary necessity for their assembling together, have them stop and not go on recklessly and spend the people's money for months, when it was designed that they should not be in session but once in two years. I know that this is an important power, but if it is to be conferred, I would restrict and circumscribe it.

The question was upon the following substitute for the eleventh section, offered by Mr. Solomon:

"He may, on extraordinary occasions, convene the General Assembly by proclamation, in which he shall state fully and distinctly the purposes for which they are convened, and when so convened, they shall have no power to legislate upon any subject, save that suggested in the proclamation of the Governor."

The question being taken upon the substitute, it was not agreed to.

The question recurred upon the amendment of Mr. Skiff, to strike out from the eleventh section the following words:

"And when so convened, they shall have no power to legislate upon any subject save that suggested in the message of the Governor."

So that the section would read—

"He may, on extraordinary occasions, convene the General Assembly by proclamation, and shall state to both Houses, when assembled, the purpose for which they shall have been convened."

The question being taken the amendment was adopted.

No farther amendment being offered to the eleventh section—

Messages to the General Assembly.

Section twelve was then read as follows:

"He shall communicate, by message, to the General Assembly, at every regular session, the condition of the State, and recommend such matters as he shall deem expedient."

Mr. GILLASPY. I move to amend by inserting after the word "State," the words "and river," so that the section will read—

"He shall communicate, by message, to the General Assembly, at any regular session, the condition of the State and river," &c. [Laughter.]

Mr. SKIFF. I move to amend by inserting "Des Moines" before river."

Mr. JOHNSTON moved to amend by adding also, "and Salt river." [Renewed laughter.]

Mr. TRAER moved to add to the words "Des Moines River," the word "improvement," so that the section would read—

"He shall communicate, by message, to the General Assembly, at every regular session, the condition of the State, and the Des Moines River Improvement, and recommend such matters as he shall deem expedient."

Mr. GILLASPY withdrew his amendment.

No further amendment being offered to this section—

When the Governor may Adjourn the Legislature.

Section thirteen was read as follows:

"In case of disagreement between the two

Houses with respect to the time of adjournment, the Governor shall have power to adjourn the General Assembly to such time as he may think proper; Provided, it be not beyond the time fixed for the regular meeting of the next General Assembly.

No amendment being offered to this section—

Eligibility to Office.

Section fourteen was read as follows:

"No person shall, while holding any office under the authority of the United States, or this State, execute the office of Governor or Lieutenant Governor, except as hereinafter expressly provided."

Mr. WINCHESTER moved to strike out the words "or Lieutenant Governor," which was agreed to.

No farther amendment being offered—

Term of Office.

Section fifteen was read as follows:

"The official term of the Governor and Lieutenant Governor shall commence on the of and on the same day every year thereafter."

Mr. WILSON. I move to fill the first blank by the words "second Monday of January next succeeding the election of Governor under this constitution;" so that the section will then read—

"The official term of the Governor shall commence on the second Monday of January next succeeding the election of Governor under this constitution, and on the same day every year thereafter."

Mr. CLARKE, of Henry, moved to amend the amendment by striking out the words "second Monday," and insert the words "first day;" so that the section would then read "commence on the first day of January," &c.

Mr. WILSON. The votes for Governor will not have then been canvassed by the legislature.

Mr. HARRIS. I would also suggest that the retiring Governor should have an opportunity of sending a message to the legislature.

Mr. HALL. I do not think this section is at all necessary. The second section reads as follows:

"The Governor shall be elected by the qualified electors at the time and place of voting for members of the General Assembly and shall hold his office four years from the time of his installation, and until his successor shall be qualfied."

That fixes the time for his term of office to commence, and you cannot fix it more definitely. I, therefore, move to strike out the whole section.

Mr. SKIFF. It seems to me that if we strike out this section, it will be left a little indefinite as to when the Governor shall assume the duties of his office. It is nowhere else provided in this article at what time the Governor elect shall assume the chair of State. The second section merely says:

"The Governor shall be elected by the qualified electors at the time and place of voting for members of the General Assembly, and shall hold his office four years from the time of his installation, and until his successor shall be qualified."

It does not tell us when his installation shall take place, or fix any time for that. It does not tell when the first Governor to be elected under this new constitution is to be installed, and we cannot, therefore, tell when to begin to reckon the four years of his term.

Mr. WILSON. If the term commences on the second Monday in January, as I propose, then the matter is easy enough.

Mr. SKIFF. I am in favor of the proposition of the gentleman from Jefferson, [Mr. Wilson,] but the gentleman from Des Moines [Mr. Hall,] has moved to strike out the whole section.

Mr. CLARKE, of Henry. There seems to be some question in regard to this matter. I would, therefore, suggest that the official term of the Governor shall commence on the first day of the January after his election, and continue for four years from that time.

Mr. WILSON. The difficulty is that we have determined that the legislature shall convene on the second Monday in January, and they must canvass the votes of the Governor. He may, therefore, be in office one week before his vote is canvassed.

Mr. CLARKE, of Henry. I think there will not be any difficulty about that. The old governor is still governor until his successor is qualified.

Mr. WILSON. But this section will say that the term of office of the governor shall commence on the first day of January, if the proposition of the gentleman from Henry, [Mr. Clarke,] is adopted. Does he propose then to pay two salaries for that week? You will have two governors; there will be no interregnum, for there will be two governors.

Mr. CLARKE, of Henry. I apprehend that there will be no such difficulty. As to the double filling of the office, that occurs all through the constitution. I would ask gentlemen who are the officers in those cases where the constitution provides that they shall hold until their successors are elected and qualified? Some days must elapse before they are qualified. Who then are the incumbents? No one thinks of raising that question. The one who holds the office is the officer, and he continues as such until his successor is elected and qualified.

The question was then taken upon the motion to strike out section fifteen, and, upon a division, it was agreed to; yeas 15, noes 7.

Reprieves, Pardons, &c.

Section sixteen was then read as follows:

"He shall have power to grant reprieves, commutations and pardons, after conviction, for all offences except treason and cases of impeachment, subject to such regulations as may be provided by law. Upon conviction for treason, he shall have power to suspend the execution of the sentence until the case shall be reported to the General Assembly at its next meeting, when the General Assembly shall either grant a pardon, commute the sentence, direct the execution of the sentence, or grant a further reprieve. He shall have power to remit fines and forfeitures, under such regulations as may be prescribed by law; and shall report to the General Assembly at its next meeting each case of reprieve, commutation, or pardon granted; and also all persons in whose favor remission of fines and forfeitures shall have been made, and the several amounts remitted."

Mr. CLARKE, of Johnson. I move to amend this section by inserting after the words, "or pardon granted," the words, "and the reasons therefor;" so that portion of the section will read:

"He shall have power to remit fines and forfeitures, under such regulations as may be prescribed by law; and shall report to the General Assembly at its next meeting each case of reprieve, commutation or pardon granted, and the reasons therefor."

Mr. MARVIN. I will say that that subject was under consideration in the committee, and it was supposed that that matter should be left to the legislature, and they would do all that was sufficient. That, I think, was the only reason why that clause was not inserted here, if I recollect aright.

Mr. CLARKE, of Johnson. I can only say that my object is to prevent the improper exercise of this pardoning power, as it prevails in many States. I may say further, perhaps, without any breach of confidence, that in a conversation with our present executive, he suggested that such a provision as I have moved here should be inserted in this article, as its tendency would be to prevent improper pardons. The legislature heretofore has never made any such provision, and we may as well make the matter safe by inserting the provision here.

The question being taken upon the amendment, it was adopted.

Vacancy in the Office of Governor.

Section seventeen was then read as follows:

"In case of the death, impeachment, resignation, removal from office, or other disability of the Governor, the powers and duties of the office for the residue of the term, or until he shall be acquitted, or the disability removed, shall devolve upon the Lieutenant Governor."

Mr. WARREN. I move to amend the section by striking out the words, "Lieutenant Governor," and inserting in their stead the words, "Secretary of State, until said disability shall cease, or the vacancy shall be filled." The section will then read:

"In case of the death, impeachment, resignation, removal from office, or other disability of the Governor, the powers and duties of the office for the residue of the term, or until he shall be acquitted, or the disability removed, shall devolve upon the Secretary of State, until said disability shall cease, or the vacancy shall be filled."

Mr. MARVIN. I trust the amendment of the gentleman from Jackson, [Mr. Warren,] will not be adopted. It would be far better to provide that the duties of the office of Governor, in case of a vacancy, shall devolve upon the president of the Senate.

Mr. CLARKE, of Johnson. I will move to amend the amendment by substituting for "Secretary of State," the words "president of the Senate." I think that would be far preferable for this reason: if the duties of the office of Governor should be devolved upon the Secretary of State, it would give him two offices, and then everything like a check upon these two offices is removed. The president of the Senate may be absent from the seat of government at the time this vacancy arises in the office of Governor; but that objection will apply to the Governor himself as well as to the president of the Senate, because he is not required to live at the seat of government. This is not an important matter; but I think the president of the Senate, or some other officer besides the Secretary of State, should be called upon to discharge the duties of this office in case of a vacancy.

Mr. HALL. There is no such office as president of the Senate, except during the session of the General Assembly.

Mr. TRAER. As I understand it, the president of the Senate holds his office for two years.

The question being then taken upon the amendment to the amendment, upon a division, it was agreed to; ayes 13, noes 9.

The question was upon the amendment as amended.

Mr. SKIFF. I think some provision should be made in case both the governor and the president of the Senate should happen to be disqualified. A provision of that kind was made in case of the Lieutenant Governor, and it may as well be put in here in regard to the president of the Senate. I call the attention of members to the subject.

Mr. CLARKE, of Henry. I think it would be better to take the vote upon the amendment as amended, which is now pending, and then we can farther amend the section afterwards, to meet the difficulty the gentleman from Jasper, [Mr. Skiff,] has suggested.

The question being then taken upon the amendment as amended, it was agreed to.

Mr. MARVIN. I move farther to amend this section by adding to it the following:

"And if the President of the Senate, for any of the above causes, shall be rendered incapable of performing the duties pertaining to the office of Governor, the same shall then devolve upon the Speaker of the House of Representatives."

The section will then read:

"In case of the death, impeachment, resignation, removal from office, or other disability of the Governor, the powers and duties of the office for the residue of the term, or until he shall be acquitted, or the disability removed, shall devolve upon the President of the Senate; and if the President of the Senate, for any of the above causes, shall be rendered incapable of performing the duties pertaining to the office of Governor, the same shall devolve upon the Speaker of the House of Representatives."

I would state that it is merely adding the latter part of section nineteen to this section.

The question being taken the amendment was agreed to.

No farther amendment being offered to this section—

Duties of Lieutenant Governor.

Section eighteen was then read as follows:

"The Lieutenant Governor shall be President of the Senate, but shall only vote when the Senate is equally divided; and in case of his absence, or impeachment, or when he shall exercise the office of Governor, the Senate shall choose a President pro tempore."

Mr. CLARKE, of Henry, moved to strike out this section.

The question being taken, the motion to strike out was agreed to.

President pro tempore of the Senate.

Section nineteen was then read as follows:

"If the Lieutenant Governor, while acting as Governor, shall be impeached, displaced, resign or die, or otherwise become incapable of performing the duties of the office, the President pro tempore of the Senate shall act as Governor until the vacancy is filled, or the disability removed; and if the President of the Senate, for any of the above causes, shall be rendered incapable of performing the duties pertaining to the office of Governor, the same shall devolve upon the Speaker of the House of Representatives."

On motion of Mr. CLARKE, of Henry,

The section was stricken out.

Great Seal of the State.

Section twenty was then read as follows:

"There shall be a seal of this State, which shall be kept by the Governor, and used by him officially, and shall be called the Great Seal of the State of Iowa."

No amendment being offered to this section—

Grants and Commissions.

Section twenty-one was read as follows:

"All grants and commissions shall be in the name and by the authority of the people of the State of Iowa, sealed with the great seal of this State, signed by the Governor and countersigned by the Secretary of State."

Mr. SKIFF. I would like to have some gentleman explain this section. As I understand it, when a patent to any of the school lands, swamp lands, or any other lands of the State, is made to any person, the Governor shall sign it, and it shall be countersigned by the Secretary of State. I believe this clause is in our present constitution, but I think it is not understood by our present officers as I understand it, but land patents are signed by the register of the State. Now I should like to understand whether the Secretary of State is to sign these land patents. I believe he has not done so for some two or three years past.

No amendment being offered to this section—

State Secretary, Auditor, Treasurer, &c.

Section twenty-two was read as follows:

"A secretary of State, Auditor of Public Accounts, Treasurer of State, Superintendent of Public Instruction, and Attorney General shall be elected by the qualified electors, who shall continue in office two years. The Secretary of State shall keep a fair register of all the official acts of the Governor, and shall, when required, lay the same, together with all papers, minutes, and vouchers relative thereto, before either branch of the General Assembly, and shall perform such other duties as shall be assigned him by law."

Mr. GILLASPY moved to strike out the words "Superintendent of Public Instruction, and Attorney General."

Mr. CLARKE, of Henry. I would like to have the gentleman from Wapello [Mr. Gillaspy] state his reasons for this motion.

Mr. GILLASPY. I have always, so far as I was able, been disposed to accommodate others. Now I suppose there is no gentleman upon this floor, besides the gentleman from Henry [Mr. Clarke] who has any desire to hear my reasons for moving to strike out the words I have indicated. But as he has expressed a desire to hear my reasons, I am disposed to accommodate him.

In the first place I have always believed, and believe yet, that the office of Superintendent of Public Instruction was an office for which we had no need whatever. I have always believed that the proper policy of this State was to create as few officers, to eat up the school fund of this State, as possible. I believe that the school fund commissioners and the superintendent of public instruction are all unnecessary. The duties assigned to the superintendent of public instruction have been of that character that no man living could perform them. So much for that office.

As to the office of Attorney General, I consider it a perfect sinecure, and an office of no benefit to the State.

Mr. CLARKE, of Johnson. It is provided for in another article.

Mr. GILLASPY. I have nothing to do with that now. I am giving the gentleman from Henry, [Mr. Clarke,] my reasons for moving to strike out these words here. I will say that I

Mr. WILSON. The report of the committee on education provides for a board of education, instead of this officer.

Mr. SKIFF. Am I to understand that the committee on education recommend the abolition of the office of superintendent of public instruction?

Mr. WILSON. I make this motion for the purpose of having this matter left over until we come to act on the report of the committee on education, in order that the convention may not forestall action on this matter.

The question being then taken upon the motion to strike out the words "superintendent of public instruction," it was agreed to.

Mr. CLARKE, of Johnson. I now move to strike out the words "attorney general," because we have made provision for that officer in the report of the committee on the judicial department, and we certainly do not want it in the constitution in two places. It is well known that I am in favor both of the office of superintendent of public instruction and of attorney general.

The question being taken upon the motion to strike out the words "attorney general," it was agreed to.

Mr. CLARKE, of Johnson. I move to strike out the words "the Secretary of State shall keep a fair register of all the official acts of the Governor, and shall, when required, lay the same, together with all papers, minutes, and vouchers relative thereto, before either branch of the General Assembly, and shall perform such other duties as shall be assigned him by law," and insert in lieu thereof the words "and perform such duties as may be required by law," so that the section will then read—

"A Secretary of State, Auditor of Public Accounts, and Treasurer of State shall be elected by the qualified electors, who shall continue in office two years, and perform such duties as may be required by law."

I make this motion for this reason: The portion I have moved to strike out provides only for the duties of Secretary of State. Now, it seems to me that we should not prescribe the duties of that officer any more than the duties of the other officers. I would leave the prescription of the duties of the officers to the law-making power.

Mr. CLARKE, of Henry. I would suggest that some doubt might arise hereafter, if we strike out all relating to the duties of Secretary of State. I think gentlemen sometimes vote here without fully understanding what they are voting upon.

The question being taken upon the amendment offered by Mr. Clarke, of Johnson, it was adopted.

No farther amendments being offered to this section—

Signing Bills of the General Assembly.

Section twenty-three was then read, as follows:

"Every bill which shall have passed the General Assembly shall be presented to the Governor; if he approve, he shall sign it; but if not, he shall return it, with his objections, to the house in which it shall have originated, which house shall enter the objections at large upon its journals, and proceed to reconsider the bill. If, after such consideration, a majority of all the members elected to that house shall agree to pass the bill, it shall be sent, with the Governor's objections, to the other house, by which it shall likewise be reconsidered; and if it shall be approved by a majority of all the members elected to that house, it shall be a law. If any bill shall not be returned by the Governor within ten days (Sundays excepted), after it shall have been presented to him, it shall be a law without his signature, unless the general adjournment shall prevent its return, in which case it shall be a law unless the Governor, within ten days next after such adjournment, shall file such bill with his objections thereto, in the office of the Secretary of State, who shall lay the same before the General Assembly at its next session, in like manner as if it had been returned by the Governor. But no bill shall be presented to the Governor within two days next previous to the final adjournment of the General Assembly."

Mr. JOHNSTON. I move to strike out this section, because the subject to which it relates is fully provided for in the article upon the legislative department.

The question being taken, the motion to strike out was agreed to.

Mr. CLARKE, of Johnson, moved that the committee rise, report the article as amended to the convention, and ask to be discharged from its farther consideration.

The motion was agreed to.

In Convention.

The PRESIDENT having resumed the chair,

The CHAIRMAN reported that the Committee of the Whole had had under consideration the report of the Committee on the Executive Department, had made sundry amendments thereto, and had instructed him to report the same back to the convention, and ask to be discharged from its further consideration.

The report was received and the committee discharged accordingly.

On motion of Mr. WINCHESTER,

The Convention then adjourned until to-morrow morning at 9 o'clock.

THURSDAY, February 19th, 1857.

The convention met at 9 A. M., and was called to order by the President.

Prayer by the Chaplain.

The journal of yesterday was read and approved.

Executive Department.

The convention proceeded to consider the report of the standing committee on the executive department, as amended in committee of the whole.

Term of the Governor.

The first amendment of the committee was to fill the blank in section two, with "four," fixing the term of office of the Governor at four years.

Mr. HARRIS. I hope we shall not agree to that amendment.

Mr. GILLASPY. Before that question is put, sir, I wish to say that I hope the convention will not agree to the amendment. I believe that it is just as important to the people of this State to elect a Governor once in every two years, as to elect any other State officer in that time. I think every gentleman upon this floor must be well aware that the case may arise,—and I believe the time has been under this rule of four years—when Governors may hold office at least two years against the wish and will of a majority of the people of the State. I can see no reason for electing your Secretary of State, your Auditor of State, and your Treasurer of the State, for two years and your governor for four. In a great many States, and it may ultimately be so in this State, the office of Auditor of the State is of more importance to the people than the office of governor. I am satisfied that the people of the State are almost universally opposed to the election of governor for four years. There has been great complaint about it, since the organization of this convention. So far as I know, they are unitedly, without distinction of party, in favor of the plan of electing the governor for two years. If we have a good governor who keeps up with the age, there is no trouble about re-electing him, and he will serve four years; but if he is not up to the age, as a matter of course, the quicker we get rid of him the better. I hope that the convention will not deprive the people of the State of the privilege at the regular State election, of voting for all the officers of the State. We elect members of Congress every two years; we elect our auditor, our Secretary of State, and our Treasurer, every two years; and I can see no good reason why we should not elect our governor at the same time. I ask the convention to reflect upon the matter, and hope the election of the governor will take place every two years.

Mr. PALMER. I think that a long term of service is peculiarly inappropriate to this office. It is not an office requiring experience in that particular capacity. It is presumed that a man somewhat acquainted with the affairs of State will generally be chosen to fill the office. As I am in favor of rotation in office, I would vote for the shortest time, in order to encourage that laudable ambition which may exist with many to subserve the public interests. I do not think that the action of public men should be such as to discourage those who aspire to places of honor and profit, but rather to encourage them. As I have said, this is not an office which requires so much experience in that particular capacity to fill, as many other offices. There is some reason for making the term of office of the judge of the supreme court six years; because it is supposed that the longer a person fills that office the better qualified he will be to discharge its duties. But as the gentleman from Wapello [Mr. Gillaspy] has said, there is no reason why we should make the term of this office longer than that of secretary of State, or auditor. Indeed I think there is not so much reason for a long term, because a man who has filled the office of auditor or secretary of State one or two years would be presumed to be better qualified to fill it, since the longer he fills the office, the better acquainted he becomes with its details. I am in favor of making all of these offices two years in length. We must have a general election every two years, of members of the lower house, and I think that would be the proper time to fill most of the State offices. They may as well be filled for two years as for a longer time, and perhaps the shorter the time the better it would be for the public good.

Mr. SOLOMON. I have no desire to detain the convention from a vote; but I have some serious apprehensions about this question, as the long term seemed to prevail so extensively in the committee of the whole. I am utterly opposed to the term of four years; and I found my objections upon this: We have determined that the lower House of the General Assembly shall be elected every two years, and that the Senate shall be renewed every four years. In committee of the whole we have clothed the Governor with the veto power. This gives him the power of checking legislation, and preventing all legislation in which two-thirds of the legislature do not concur. Now shall we establish that interval of four years, or reduce it to two years? It seems to be conceded that we should not allow the legislative power in the country to extend beyond two years in the one branch, and four years in the other. Now when the people have expressed their will by the election of a legislature, I believe they ought, also, at the same time, to express the same will in the election of Governor. But if you elect the Governor for four years, take away from him this veto power. We are a vast State. We are increasing rapidly. We are changing hourly. There is an influx of population into this State which will, perhaps, for the next ten years, be unsurpassed in the whole country, excepting California. We have not before been surpassed in our increasing improvements; and I think we should not be so fettered down that we can change our executive officers only once in four years. Can there be any valid objection urged against giving the people the right even to re-elect.

The argument in favor of electing the Governor for four years, I apprehend to be this, that we should give the Governor long enough time to carry out a certain settled policy; but if we turn him out at the end of two years he will not have had time to inaugurate and establish any settled policy, and consequently, as a State, we shall be without it. I apprehend that this is a fallacy. If the Governor undertakes to carry out certain views and principles in the execution of his powers, and if these views and principles are acceptable to the people, and he is the proper man to fill the office, I undertake to say that the people will re-elect him. On the contrary, if his views and principles are not with them, they should have the opportunity of turning him out, which I think they ought to do.

The question was upon concurring with the committee of the whole in filling the blank with "four."

Mr. CLARKE, of Johnson, called for the yeas and nays, which were ordered.

The question being then taken by yeas and nays, the amendment was not concurred in; yeas 11, nays 19, as follows:

Yeas—Messrs. Bunker, Clarke of Henry, Clarke of Johnson, Edwards, Gower, Gray, Hollingsworth, Parvin, Scott, Skiff and Winchester.

Nays—The President, Messrs. Ayres, Clark of Alamakee, Ells, Emerson, Gibson, Gillaspy, Hall, Harris, Johnston, Marvin, Palmer, Patterson, Peters, Robinson, Seely, Solomon, Traer and Wilson.

Lieutenant Governor.

The next amendment of the committee was to strike out sections three and four, and to insert the provision in the old constitution, so as not to incorporate a provision for a Lieutenant Governor.

Mr. GRAY. Before the vote shall be taken upon that amendment, I propose to say a word upon this question. The proposed amendment dispenses with the Lieutenant Governor as recommended by the standing committee. The gentleman who is most responsible for this report, whose work it is, indeed, is the gentleman from Warren, [Mr. Todhunter,] now detained from his seat by indisposition. To him belongs the entire credit of this report. As one of the committee, I was disposed to consider this matter immaterial. I consented to the whole report, as did every other member of the committee, except in the matter of the veto power. In that single case, the gentleman from Van Buren [Mr. Ayres,] and myself dissented from this report, although we did not conceive it of sufficient importance to put in a minority report. On yesterday, by what seemed to be a very decided vote, the convention struck out this provision for a Lieutenant Governor. My intention in rising this morning is to ask gentlemen to consider well the importance of the matter before striking this out. As the chairman of the committee is not now present, I feel it my duty to state briefly some reasons for disagreeing to the report of the committee.

I find, by reference to the state constitutions, that this office is provided for in many States of the Union—in Vermont, Massachusetts, Rhode Island, Connecticut, New York, Ohio, Indiana, Illinois, Michigan and Wisconsin—ten of the free States, and Kentucky, Louisiana, Texas and Missouri, of the Southern States. It seems to me that, so far as the expense of that office is concerned, it is merely nominal. If I understand the matter correctly, it amounts to no more than the pay of a Senator in the General Assembly. The amount, therefore, is insignificant. If, then, there be any convenience in having that office, if there is any public utility in it, I appeal to gentlemen to let the report stand. It seems to me that there are some advantages connected with the office.

It provides for a certain organization of at least one branch of the General Assembly, and thus may prevent the dead lock of the legislative power which we have sometimes seen. We have seen a delay of weeks in the business of Congress, arising from an inability to elect a presiding officer.

Again, it enables every Senator to represent, upon the floor of the House, his own separate district. That would not be the case if one of their own number should be called upon to preside.

Again, this officer will be elected directly by the people, instead of by the Legislature. We all seem to agree in placing elections, as far as possible, directly in the power of the people.

I do not know that I need to say anything further. I did not rise to make a speech; but merely, in justice to the Chairman of the Committee, of which I am an humble member, to ask gentlemen to consider the matter in its various aspects before voting to strike it out. I know it is a matter in which he took considerable interest.

Mr. CLARKE, of Henry. I concur with the remarks of the gentleman who has just taken his seat. As to the matter of expense, it will not add a single cent to the expenditure of the State. The President of the Senate, as I understand it, now draws double pay. All that is proposed for the Lieutenant Governor is the pay of a Senator while he is presiding. It does not, therefore, add a single cent to the expenses of the State.

Gentlemen do not reflect that they may be taking from the people the power of selecting their own chief magistrate. When a man is a candidate for the office of Lieutenant Governor, the people always vote for him with the understanding that circumstances may arise which will make him their Governor. But if you give to the Senate the power of selecting the man who may be the Governor of the people, you take from the people this power and put it into the hands of the Senate.

We may certainly look to the experience of other States. This matter has been somewhat scoffed at here. Gentlemen pretend to have within them a light superior to any they can borrow. I am willing to look to the experience and wisdom of other States; and, as the gentleman has observed, I find that, in a majority of the free States, this system prevails; and if this office is found beneficial elsewhere, and if we are not to be subjected to any expense at all, why should we not introduce this provision into our Constitution? We certainly see where we can derive benefit from it, and no man can point out to me where it can possibly work any harm.

Mr. CLARKE, of Johnson. The question, as I understand it, is, upon concurring with the amendment made in Committee of the Whole, striking out this provision for a Lieutenant Governor. I am in favor of the amendment, and shall vote for concurring. There are a great many objections which present themselves to this feature. In the first place, it is making a place for a partisan. I think no gentleman upon this floor will contradict me when I say that no man but a mere partisan is ever elected to this place; and it matters not to which party he may belong. If we create the office of Lieutenant Governor, he is nominated by one of these party conventions, where the question never is asked: Is he a fit man to preside over the deliberations of a legislative body? but, is he a partisan, and will he do the work of the party, although it may be against the popular will, if he is elected to that place. We have had some striking instances of the character of this office within the last year. I need but point to the recent election of Senator in the State of Wisconsin, where the Lieutenant Governor, a mere partisan, refused to ratify the action of the joint convention for the election of a United States Senator, because he had a notion of constitutional law upon a question which has been decided by the Senate of the United States against him. If you want to create an officer to act in that way, to carry out the behests of a party, no matter to which party he belongs, then create this office. Let me refer to another very recent case, in the State of Indiana last winter, when the wishes of the Senate, the wishes of the Legislature, and the wishes of the people of that State, were all set at defiance and disregarded by their Lieutenant Governor. If you want to make a place for a partisan who will do the work of the party, whatever the will of the people and of the Legislature may be, create this office.

My second objection is: that the Senate is the most competent body of persons to select their presiding officer. It is reasonable to presume that when they come to select a president of the Senate, they will look to a man's qualifications for the place, to his ability as a parliamentarian, to his intelligence, to his integrity. None of these qualifications are looked to or sought after in making a political nomination for a Lieutenant Governor. A man in that position is called upon to act upon every question which comes before the Senate, and it may be to give a casting vote in relation to it, and thus to decide questions in relation to which the people had not thought when he was elected. I regard it as a very responsible position; and in nine cases out of ten, so far from that officer reflecting the opinions and wishes of the people, he is elected without any regard to these considerations.

In the third place, if you elect this officer for a term of years—if you establish the term of two years for this office this argument will not so well apply—you may have an occasion where the Senate, the highest deliberative body of the government, may be presided over by an officer whose partisan interests and opinions may be in direct conflict with the wishes of the majority. While the people change the character of the legislature, they will not be able to reach the Lieutenant Governor, the presiding officer of the Senate, and in a close contest, upon a tie vote, affecting great political, commercial, or pecuniary interests, he may be against the majority of the legislature, and thus act as a check upon the popular will.

I do not think there is much force in the argument of the gentleman from Linn, [Mr. Gray] that establishing this office will prevent delay in the organization of this body. Suppose that you have a presiding officer elected by the people, who takes his seat, not by virtue of the votes and voice of the members of that body, but who is placed over them as a kind of tyrant, whose will is superior to theirs upon very many questions. And suppose that you do prevent delay in the organization of that branch; that does not affect the other branch, and if that is not organized, if partisan differences, or any other kind of differences there prevent their organization, the Senate cannot proceed to business until the other branch is organized. And we find that the trouble in the organization of legislatures and of Congress, has generally resulted and been created in the lower House. Very few of the higher branches of any State government have ever had any trouble in the election of a presiding officer. Generally there are influences existing and influences operating which do not affect the higher branch.

Now, Mr. President, we have the light of the past thrown into our faces here. We are told that a certain number of the State Constitutions those of a majority of the free States provides for this office. That may be true. I only wonder that gentlemen who derive so much light from these constitutions upon this branch of the subject, have not been willing to obtain the same light in other instances. A day or two ago we were trying to increase the length of time within which a man should be eligible as a candidate for the legislature, and we referred to the fact that in many of the State constitutions this time was much more extended than in our present constitution. Gentlemen then did not look to the light of other days; but now that light is thrown into our faces because it suits their own peculiar views. As I have said before, I say now, that while we may borrow from the time past, we do not follow their light implicitly. There may be and ought to be some new things in this constitution, in advance of the experience and history of the past. Since these party excitements have existed in the country, the office of Lieutenant Governor has been found to be a check upon legislation, a check upon the will and wishes of the people. I am, therefore, opposed to the creation of this office.

There is another argument. The gentleman from Des Moines, [Mr. Hall,] and myself, a few days ago, tried to increase the Supreme Court in order to give it efficiency, stability and character. We were told that if we increased the number of these officers we should burden the people with it, and they would vote down the constitution. Yet the very same gentlemen are in favor of this proposition and have spoken in its favor; and they have already made ten new additions, ten district attorneys, and are now preparing to make the eleventh. I hope that gentlemen will be a little consistent upon this subject, and when they brand us with being willing to swamp the people in debt, by creating an expensive government, they will look to it that they are not doing the same thing. Gentlemen say, it is true, that the cost of adding this office will only be the cost of another Senator. Does that follow? This proposition does not provide any such thing as that, and the salary of this officer may be made equal to that of the Governor. I think that the question of expense is as forcible here as anywhere. But that with me is a small consideration. If I believed that this officer was necessary, that he was useful, that instead of being a check to the legislature and the will of the people, he would promote legislation, or would advance the interests of the whole people, the question of economy would have little weight with me. But I believe if we look at the history of any State where they have had this officer, we shall find that in any emergency he has acted in the face and eyes of the will of the people, and done things improper, illegal, and dishonorable, to subserve the purposes of the party to which he belongs. I do not wish to subject the legislation of this State to the liability of such obstacles.

Mr. WILSON. I voted yesterday to strike out "lieutenant governor," from the report of the Committee on the Executive Department. Upon reflection, I have come to the conclusion to vote against the amendment of the committee. I believe there are more advantages connected with the office of Lieutenant Governor than disadvantages. The argument presented by the gentleman from Johnson [Mr. Clarke] in the cases of Wisconsin and Indiana, which he has cited, if it is good for anything, seems to me to be good for too much. If it is an argument against the establishment of a lieutenant-governorship, it is also an argument against the establishment of a senator; because I am satisfied you can find as many cases of corruption and wrongful action upon the part of the senatorial body, as upon the part of the lieutenant-governor. You can find just as much corruption and wrongful action upon the part of any other officer of the State as upon the part of the lieutenant-governor. If, then, the argument is good for anything, it goes to the abolition of all offices. That is an evil inherent in all political power, and which we cannot guard against.

As to the argument of the partizan character of the incumbent of this office, I need simply say that partisans fill all of our offices.

Yesterday I voted in favor of making the President of the Senate the acting governor in case of the death or disability of the Governor elected. It seems to me that that leads us too far. We give to one county in the State, in that case, the right to elect a governor for the whole State. We give, for instance, to Dubuque county, a county always Democratic, the power to elect a governor of the State of Iowa, when the State may have become Republican. The governor and lieutenant-governor will always, I presume, be the same in politics, and why not have the successor of the governor of the same politics, instead of bringing in one of the antagonistic party?

If you change it from the President of the Senate to the Secretary of State, you derange the executive department, because the Secretary of State cannot well fill both offices. Their duties are separate and distinct,. Where, then, can we lodge the power to succeed the governor? I see no better plan than in the office of lieutenant-governor. The cost of that office will not be much, as has already been intimated by the gentleman from Henry. I am in favor of determining what his pay shall be, fixing it at either the same as the senators', or perhaps increasing it by one half, which would make the cost to the State over and above that which it now pays one half of the amount paid to the President of the Senate. If the President of the Senate now gets four dollars per day, and the lieutenant-governor takes his place at six dollars per day, then the increased cost will be two dollars per day during the sessions of the legislature. It seems to me that the advantages connected with that office will be such that the people can well afford to bear that slight additional burden. I shall therefore vote to disagree with the amendment of the committee of the whole. I believe, upon reflection, that the advantages in favor of this are far superior to the disadvantages.

Mr. CLARKE, of Henry, rose to address the Convention a second time, but objection was made.

Mr. CLARK, of Alamakee. I voted yesterday to strike out the office of Lieutenant-Governor. I had not reflected upon it well, and I am inclined to the opinion that I did not vote right. Upon hearing the argument thus far upon the question, and upon reflection, I am disposed to favor the office of Lieut.-Governor, for one reason, if there were no other: I believe that an executive officer, whoever he may be that shall perform the duties of that office, whether Governor or Lieutenant-Governor, ought to be elected directly by the people, in all cases, at least so far as it is possible to provide for it. We elect the Governor by the direct votes of the people—by the popular will—by the popular voice. In case of his removal or disability, I see no reason why the person filling his place should not be elected directly by the whole people as much as the Governor himself. As has been remarked, if the Governor's office should become vacant some other person must fill that place, and if it is to be the Secretary of State, there is an inconsistency in his holding the two offices. If it is to be the President of the Senate, then he will not have been elected by the direct vote of the people; and if the President of the Senate acts as Governor, he holds two offices, which must be incompatible with each other. I believe that any one man, holding and occupying the office of President of the Senate, if he performs his duties thoroughly and faithfully, does all that one man should be required to perform, and does as much as any one man is capable of doing. I believe that the person who acts as Governor, whether the person elected to that office, or some person provided for the contingency in the manner we now contemplate, should give his whole time to its duties. The person who fills the office of the Governor elect, necessarily requires for the discharge of the duties of that office, as much time as the Governor elect would have himself required; and if it be necessary, in having a Governor to discharge certain duties, to require him to give his whole time to that business, I see no reason why the person who takes the place of the Governor should not also be required to devote his time to the same business whenever it may devolve upon him to perform it. For these reasons I shall change my vote.

Mr. HARRIS. As gentlemen are giving their experience this morning, I will take a little time in giving mine. I did not vote in favor of striking out on yesterday. I voted for the report presented here with regard to this addition of Lieutenant Governor. It is true that I had thought very little about the matter; but I had come to the conclusion, that under certain circumstances, it might be a benefit to have that officer. Some two years ago, in the organization of the Senate of this State, I made up my mind that probably the office of Lieutenant Governor, in its effects upon the organization of the Senate, would be a benefit rather than an injury. There is one argument which seems to have a good deal of force with the gentleman from Johnson, [Mr. Clarke.] He says that it is frequently found that a Lieutenant Governor, who is the presiding officer of the Senate, differs in opinion—differs in politics—with the Senate over which he presides, and is a tyrant placed over them. Now, if that be true, to what conclusion must gentlemen inevitably come? He is elected by the whole people of the State, and it is reasonable to assume that he represents the sentiments of the whole people of the State, taken in the aggregate, at the time of his election. Then if his sentiments differ from those of the majority of the body over which he presides, we are bound to conclude that that body does not represent the sentiments of the people of the State, and that majority must have been placed there by the low trick of demagoguism, generally called gerrymandering, by which people are swindled out of their right to be represented, and to have their sentiments reflected by the majority of the Legislature. If, then, the contingency of which the gentleman speaks, should occur, it would be a reason, to my mind, why we should be in favor of the office instead of being opposed to it.

The argument that no man but a partisan ever gets that office has certainly been sufficiently answered by the gentleman from Jefferson [Mr. Wilson]. But I must say here that I have been somewhat astonished since I have held a seat upon this floor, at the oft-repeated claims to no-partyism put in by the gentleman, or his desire to keep everything clear from party, when I must say that the general impression is that the gentleman is as strong a partisan as any man upon this floor. And, sir, I apprehend that he deceives no man more than he does himself, when he rises here and lectures the rest of us for trying to fill the office with partisans, and all such things. I do not wish to misrepresent that gentleman; I do not wish to say that he is any more of a partisan than the rest of us; but I must say that if it is not so I have often been at fault in the information I have obtained, and I believe that fault prevails generally throughout the State. This cry that the people will fill the offices with partisans has no influence with me. I believe that when any great question is presented which is to act for weal or woe upon the destinies of this State, any man who is not a partisan is a cypher. Men always take sides, provided they are awake to the interests of their country, provided those feelings of patriotism that should swell the bosom of every American citizen, find an abiding place in his heart. And whenever men separate, one man taking one side, and another the opposite side, then I understand that they become partisans; so that every man who is not an absolute cypher in the government is a partisan. It is right that it should be so. I do not believe that any man who takes sides is a demagogue, that he is a dishonest partisan, and I do not apply that term to the gentleman from Johnson [Mr. Clarke] whom I suppose to be as honest in these matters as the rest of us.

I say then that this cry of partisanship which has been raised here has no influence with me, and I do not believe that it will have much weight with any reflecting man, for the simple reason that all men must be convinced that while the spirit and letter of our government remain substantially as they are, we must necessarily have our offices filled with partisans; and the only question is, which party reflects the sentiments of the people most nearly. I believe they are capable of judging in regard to these things; and hence the reason assigned by the gentleman from Johnson [Mr. Clarke] is to my mind a reason why we should have this office.

A great deal has been said about the expense. I do not recollect the expense of the delays in organizing the Senate in the last few years; but they alone might cost the State as much as the salary or *per diem* of a Lieutenant Governor.

There is some force in the argument that when we elect a Governor we should obviate the contingency of his office becoming vacant, or that there is at least no harm in making provision for a contingency of that kind. I shall certainly vote against the amendment of the committee of the whole.

Mr. GIBSON. It strikes me, sir, that the office of Lieutenant Governor is entirely unnecessary. Now what are the arguments of gentlemen in favor of the proposition? The gentleman from Jefferson [Mr. Wilson] presents us one of his arguments, and perhaps one of the strongest ones, that without this system there is a possibility and probability that the Governor of the State may be of one political party, while the President of the Senate, who may become Governor, may be of the other. Let us examine that matter a moment. He referred to Dubuque for instance, as it is always democratic, and of course he must have assumed that the Governor was republican. Now what possibility is there that the Senate would elect a democrat from Dubuque to preside over them, unless there is a majority in the Senate belonging to that political party. If there is a democratic majority in the Senate, then they can take the presiding officer from Dubuque, or any where else in the State; for it is not confined to Dubuque.

Mr. WILSON. I would like to ask the gentleman this question: whether he thinks that if there had been a disability which would prevent the Governor from acting two years ago, the will of the people of this State would not have been defeated by the election of Mr. Fisher, the President of the Senate at that time?

Mr. GIBSON. I do not know that the will of the people would have been defeated in that case at all. I am not at all certain of that.

Mr. CLARKE, of Henry. I would like to ask a question. Suppose that the Senate should remain as now organized, and that at the next election a democratic Governor should be elected, who should die a week after the election; would the will of the people be represented by having Mr. Hamilton placed in that office?

Mr. GIBSON. That might be so, and it might not. I would not undertake to decide it either way. Now my impression is that the presiding officer of a body is not intended to be the sovereign of that body. Perhaps I take a different view of it from some gentlemen, but I regard the presiding officer of a deliberative body as the servant of that body. Does not that body place him as their presiding officer to carry out their will and their wishes? Does he not serve that body in that capacity according to their will? Is he not governed by the will of the majority of the body? Then what becomes of the argument that we must elect a man from the whole State to preside over the Senate, and deny to that body the right to select their officer to carry out their will? The same argument would apply as aptly to the Secretary and Assistant Secretary, to the Doorkeeper, Sergeant-at-arms, Fireman, and Messengers. They are nothing other than officers of the deliberative body, and if it is necessary for this officer to hold his place independent of the body, it becomes equally necessary to have all the offices filled in the same manner. It seems to me that the last would be so apparently and entirely wrong, that no one would advocate it. This officer, as I understand it, has no duty to perform, except to preside over the Senate, except in the event of death, removal, or disability of the Governor, an event which may happen, but which it is not very probable will happen. We have had an occurrence of that character but once since the organization of the State government. And had we had a Lieutenant Governor during the entire existence of the State, with that single exception, his sole duty would have been to act as presiding officer of the Senate. So that I think this is creating an office which is entirely unnecessary. As I am trying to be consistent, I claim to be opposed to the creation of any and all offices that are not absolutely necessary. I am opposed to increasing the number of officers unnecessarily. I am opposed to increasing the expenses of the State to an unnecessary amount. Now if we decide to have a Lieutenant Governor, I suppose there is not a gentleman upon this floor who would say that he ought to be confined to the mere nominal price paid the President of the Senate. I believe it is usual in those States which have Lieutenant Governors to give them an annual salary of a certain amount, always perhaps a little less than that of the Governor, but not very much less. I shall, therefore, vote against striking out the amendment of the committee of the whole, believing that the office of Lieutenant Governor is entirely unnecessary.

The question being taken by yeas and nays, upon concurring in the amendment of the committee of the whole, striking out the provision for Lieutenant Governor, it was not agreed to; yeas 14, nays 19, as follows:

Yeas—The President, Messrs. Ayres, Bunker, Clarke of Johnson, Edwards, Gibson, Gillaspy, Hollingsworth, Johnston, Parvin, Patterson, Warren, Winchester and Young.

Nays—Messrs. Clark of Alamakee, Clarke of Henry, Ells, Emerson, Gower, Gray, Hall, Harris, Marvin, Palmer, Peters, Price, Robinson, Scott, Seely, Skiff, Solomon, Traer and Wilson.

The remaining provisions in relation to that office were restored.

The amendment to section eleven, striking out the last two lines restricting the power of the legislaturo at the extra session, was concurred in.

The amendment to strike out section fifteen, fixing the commencement of the term of office, was not agreed to, upon a division; ayes 10, noes 10.

The amendment to section sixteen, requiring the Governor to report the reason for all reprieves, commutations, or pardons granted by him, was agreed to.

The amendment to section seventeen, devolving the duty of acting as Governor, first upon the President of the Senate, and then upon the Speaker of the House of Representatives, was not agreed to, upon a division; ayes 7, noes 17.

The next amendment of the committee, to strike out section eighteen and nineteen, in relation to the Lieutenant Governor, was not agreed to.

Duties of Secretary of State.

The next amendment was to amend section twenty-two, by striking out the following:

"The Secretary of State shall keep a fair register of all the official votes of the Governor, and shall, when required, lay the same, together with all papers, minutes and vouchers relative thereto, before either branch of the General Assembly, and shall perform such other duties as shall be assigned him by law."

And insert in lieu thereof the words—

"And perform such duties as may be required by law."

The question being taken upon the amendment, it was concurred in.

Superintendent of Public Instruction.

The next amendment of the Committee of the Whole was to strike out the words "superintendent of public instruction and attorney general," so that the section would then read as follows:

"A Secretary of State, Auditor of State, and Treasurer of State, shall be elected by the qualified electors, who shall continue in office two years, and perform such duties as may be required by law."

Mr. YOUNG. Will a division of the question be in order? We have provided for the Attorney General in another place, but there is no other provision made for a superintendent of public instruction.

The PRESIDENT. The question is susceptible of a division, because there was a vote taken upon each branch of it in Committee of the Whole. If desired, the question will first be taken upon striking out the words "superintendent of public instruction."

Mr. YOUNG. I call for a division, and for the yeas and nays upon striking out the words "superintendent of public instruction."

The yeas and nays were ordered accordingly.

The question being then taken, by yeas and nays, upon the amendment of the committee of the whole, to strike out the words "superintendent of public instruction," it was concurred in; yeas 25, nays 7; as follows:

Yeas—The President, Messrs. Ayres, Clark of Alamakee, Clarke of Henry, Clarke of Johnson, Edwards, Ells, Emerson, Gibson, Gillaspy, Gower, Hall, Harris, Johnston, Marvin, Palmer, Patterson, Price, Robinson, Scott, Solomon, Traer, Warren, Wilson and Young.

Nays—Messrs. Bunker, Gray, Hollingsworth, Parvin, Seely, Skiff and Winchester.

The question then recurred upon the amendment of the Committee of the Whole to strike out the words "Attorney General."

The question being taken, the amendment was concurred in.

Signing Bills of the General Assembly.

The next amendment of the Committee of the Whole was to strike out the following section:

"Sec. 23. Every bill which shall have passed the General Assembly shall be presented to the Governor; if he approve, he shall sign it; but if not, he shall return it with his objections to the house in which it shall have originated, which house shall enter the objections at large upon its journals and proceed to reconsider the bill. If, after such consideration, a majority of all the members elected to that house shall agree to pass the bill, it shall be sent, with the Governor's objections, to the other house, by which it shall likewise be reconsidered; and if it shall be approved by a majority of all the members elected to that house, it shall be a law. If any bill shall not be returned by the Governor, within ten days (Sundays excepted), after it shall have been presented to him, it shall be a law without his signature, unless the general adjournment shall prevent its return, in which case it shall be a law, unless the Governor, within ten days next after such adjournment, shall file such bill, with his objections thereto, in the office of the Secretary of State, who shall lay the same before the General Assembly at its next session, in like manner as if it had been returned by the Governor. But no bill shall be presented to the Governor within two days next previous to the final adjournment of the General Assembly."

The question being then taken, the amendment striking out this section, was concurred in.

The PRESIDENT announced that all the amendments made in the committee of the whole had been considered.

Term of the Governor.

Mr. HARRIS moved to fill the blank in the

second section with the word "two," so that the section would read as follows:

"The Governor shall be elected by the qualified electors at the time and place of voting for members of the General Assembly, and shall hold his office two years from the time of his installation, and until his successor is elected and qualified"

Upon this question,

Mr. CLARKE, of Johnson, called for the yeas and nays, and they were ordered accordingly.

The question being then taken, by yeas and nays, the motion was agreed to; yeas 23, nays 9, as follows:

Yeas—The President, Messrs. Ayres, Clark of Alamakee, Ells, Emerson, Gibson, Gillaspy, Gray, Hall, Harris, Johnston, Marvin, Palmer, Parvin, Patterson, Price, Robinson, Scott, Seely, Skiff, Solomon, Traer and Wilson.

Nays—Messrs. Bunker, Clarke of Henry, Clarke of Johnson, Edwards, Gower, Hollingsworth, Warren, Winchester and Young.

Term of Lieutenant Governor.

Mr. TRAER moved to fill the blank in the first part of section three with the word "two," so that it would then read as follows:

"There shall be a Lieutenant Governor, who shall hold his office two years, and be elected at the same time with the Governor."

The question being taken, the motion was agreed to.

Age of Governor and Lieutenant Governor.

Mr. GILLASPY moved to strike out the word "thirty," in section six, and insert the words "twenty-one," so that the section would then read:

"No person shall be eligible to the office of Governor or Lieutenant Governor, who shall not have been a citizen of the United States, and a resident of the State for two years next preceding the election, and attained the age of twenty-one years at the time of said election."

Mr. CLARKE, of Johnson, called for a division of the question, which was ordered.

The question was stated to be upon the motion to strike out the word "thirty."

Upon this question,

Mr. CLARKE, of Johnson, called for the yeas and nays, and they were ordered accordingly.

The question being then taken by yeas and nays upon the motion to strike out the word "thirty," it was not agreed to; yeas 15, nays 18, as follows:

Yeas—Messrs. Clark, of Alamakee, Clarke, of Henry, Ells, Gibson, Gillaspy, Harris, Johnston, Palmer, Peters, Price, Scott, Seely, Solomon, Traer and Wilson.

Nays—The President, Messrs. Ayres, Bunker, Clarke, of Johnson, Edwards, Emerson, Gower, Gray, Hall, Hollingsworth, Marvin, Parvin, Patterson, Robinson, Skiff, Warren, Winchester and Young.

Commencement of Term of Governor, &c.

Mr. CLARKE, of Henry. I move to amend section fifteen so that it will read as follows:

"The official term of the Governor and Lieutenant Governor shall commence on the second Monday of January next after their election, and continue for two years, and until their successors are elected and qualified."

Mr. MARVIN. I would suggest to the gentleman to make it the first Monday after the organization of the Legislature; they may not organize the first week after they meet.

Mr. CLARKE, of Henry. The difficulty apprehended by the gentleman does not really exist, for this section only provides that these two officers shall hold until their successors are qualified. The former Governor will be Governor until his successor is qualified.

The question being taken upon the amendment of Mr. Clarke, of Henry, upon a division, it resulted, ayes 14, noes 14.

The PRESIDENT announced the vote, and stated that the Chair, having the casting vote, it would be given in the affirmative, making ayes 15, noes 14.

The amendment was therefore agreed to.

Duties and pay of Lieutenant Governor.

Mr. CLARKE, of Henry, moved to further amend section fifteen by adding to it the following:

"The Lieutenant Governor, while acting as Governor, shall receive the same pay as provided for Governor; and while presiding in the Senate, shall receive as compensation therefor, the same mileage and per diem pay provided for a Senator, and none other."

Mr. TRAER. I move to strike out the latter clause of the amendment, that portion relating to the compensation of the Lieutenant Governor while presiding in the Senate. I think it would be nothing more than right that, while presiding in the Senate, he should receive more than the pay of a Senator.

Mr. PALMER. I have drawn up a provision upon this subject, which I had intended to offer as a separate section, to come in at the close of this article. It is nearly the same as this amendment, except that it provides that, while presiding over the Senate, the Lieutenant Governor shall receive a compensation not to exceed double the pay of a Senator; and, while acting as Governor, he shall receive the same salary as Governor. I will read the section I had prepared:

"The Lieutenant Governor shall receive, during the time he presides in the Senate, a per diem allowance and mileage, not exceeding double the amount which is at the time allowed to a member of the Senate; and he shall receive no other salary, except when he discharges the official duties of the Governor, when he shall receive the same salary which is allowed by law to the Governor."

Mr. CLARKE, of Henry. I would prefer my amendment to the one read by the gentleman from Davis, [Mr. Palmer.] My amendment is more concise. I will, however, modify my amendment so that the Lieutenant Governor shall receive, while presiding in the Senate, "the same mileage and double the per diem pay provided for a Senator."

Mr. SCOTT. If the Lieutenant Governor is to receive the same pay as is provided for the Governor, it might be construed that he was to receive two thousand dollars a year, whether he performed the functions of Governor for a month, or even a week.

Mr. TRAER. I think it would be well to specify somewhat in regard to the time he is to receive the salary of Governor.

Mr. CLARKE, of Henry. The amendment says expressly that, "while acting as Governor," he shall receive the same pay as provided for Governor.

Mr. TRAER. I think it does not specify particularly enough the time for which he is to receive the salary provided for the Governor.

Mr. CLARK, of Alamakee. There can be no misconstructiou in regard to this matter. He is to receive, "while acting as Governor," the "same pay as provided for Governor," during that time.

Mr. TRAER. I have no objection to offer. I merely made the suggestion in order that the amendment might be worded so that there could be no misconstruction.

The question being taken upon the amendment, by yeas and nays, it was agreed to; yeas 21, nays 12, as follows:

Yeas—The President, Messrs. Ayres, Clark, of Alamakee, Clarke, of Henry, Ells, Emerson, Gower, Gray, Hall, Harris, Marvin, Palmer, Parvin, Patterson, Peters, Price, Robinson, Seely, Skiff, Traer and Wilson.

Nays—Messrs. Bunker, Clarke, of Johnson, Edwards, Gibson, Gillaspy, Hollingsworth, Johnston, Scott, Solomon, Warren, Winchester and Young.

No farther amendment was offered to the report.

On motion of Mr. PALMER, the report as amended was then referred to the Committee on Revision, Engrossment and Enrollment.

Education and School Lands.

On motion of Mr. SKIFF,

The Convention then resolved itself into Committee of the Whole, [Mr. Parvin in the chair,] and proceeded to consider the majority report of the Committee on Education and School Lands.

The majority report was read as follows:

Your Committee to whom was referred the subject of Education and School Lands, have had the same under consideration, and after careful investigation and mature deliberation, the majority beg leave to report the following:

Section 1. The Educational interests of the State to include Common Schools and other Educational Institutions, shall be under the management and control of a Board of Education, which shall consist of sixteen members.

Sec. 2. No person shall be eligible as a member of said Board who shall not have attained the age of twenty-five years, and been two years a citizen of the State.

Sec. 3. The General Assembly shall district the State into sixteen Educational Districts, and one member of said Educational Board shall be chosen by the qualified electors of each district, and shall hold their offices for the term of four years, and after the first election under this constitution, the Board shall be divided by lot into two equal classes, and the seats of the first class shall be vacated after the expiration of two years, and one-half of the Board shall be chosen every two years thereafter.

Sec. 4. The first session of the Board of Education shall be held at the seat of government, after which said Board may fix the time and place of meeting.

Sec. 5. The sessions of said Board shall be limited to twenty days, and but one session shall be held in one year, except upon extraordinary occasions, when, upon the recommendation of two-thirds of the Board, the Governor may order a special session.

Sec. 6. The Board of Education shall organize by appointing from their body a presiding officer, and the appointment of a Secretary and other inferior officers usual in Legislative Assemblies. They shall keep and publish a journal of their proceedings, which shall be distributed in the same manner as the journals of the General Assembly.

Sec. 7. All rules and regulations made by said Board, shall be published and distributed to the several Counties, Townships, and such School Districts as may be provided for by said Board, and when so passed, published and distributed, they shall have the force and effect of law.

Sec. 8. Said Board shall have full power and authority to legislate and make all needful rules and regulations in relation to Common Schools and other institutions of learning that are instituted to receive aid from the School or University funds of the State.

Sec. 9. Said Board may appoint a Chancellor, who shall have jurisdiction over all questions that may arise under the laws, rules and regulations of the Board, and from all decisions and judgments of said Chancellor, an appeal may be taken to the Supreme Court.

Sec. 10. The Board of Education shall provide a system of Common Schools, by which a School shall be organized and kept in each district at least three months in each year. Districts failing to organize and keep up a School, may be deprived of their portion of the School Fund.

Sec. 11. The Board of Education shall establish one University, which shall be located at some central point in the State, *Provided*, that until such time as such location may be made, and suitable buildings erected, said University shall continue as at present located.

Sec. 12. The University lands, and the proceeds thereof, and all moneys belonging to said fund shall be a permanent fund for the sole use of said University. The interest arising from the same shall be annually appropriated for the support and benefit of said University.

Sec. 13. The General Assembly shall encourage, by all suitable means, the promotion of intellectual, scientific, moral and agricultural improvement. The proceeds of all lands that have been, or hereafter may be, granted by the United States to this State, for the support of Schools, which shall hereafter be sold or disposed of, and the five hundred thousand acres of land granted to the new States, under an act of Congress, distributing the proceeds of the public lands among the several states of the Union, approved A. D., 1841, and all estates of deceased persons who may have died without leaving a will or heir, and also such per cent. as may be granted by Congress, on the sale of lands in this State, shall be, and remain a perpetual fund, the interest of which, together with all rents of the unsold lands, and such other means as the General Assembly may provide, shall be inviolably appropriated to the support of Common Schools throughout the State.

Sec. 14. The money which shall be paid by persons as an equivalent for exemption from Military duty, and the clear proceeds of all fines collected in the several counties for any breach of the penal laws, shall be exclusively applied, in the several counties in which such money is paid or fine collected, among the several School Districts of said counties, in proportion to the number of youths subject to enumeration in such districts, to the support of Common Schools, or the establishment of Libraries, as the Board of Education shall from time to time provide.

Sec. 15. The General Assembly shall take measures for the protection, improvement, or other disposition of such lands as have been, or may hereafter be reserved, or granted by the United States, or any person or persons, to this State, for the use of a University, and the funds accruing from the rents or sale of such lands, or from any other source for the purpose aforesaid, shall be, and remain, a permanent fund, the interest of which shall be applied to the support of said University, for the promotion of literature, the arts and sciences, as may be authorized by the terms of such grant. And it shall be the duty of the General Assembly as soon as may be, to provide effectual means for the improvement and permanent security of the funds of said University.

Sec. 16. The financial agents of the School funds shall be the same, that by law receive and control the State and County revenue for other civil purposes.

Sec. 17. The money subject to the support and maintenance of Common Schools shall be distributed to the districts in proportion to the number of unmarried youths, between the ages of five and twenty-one years.

Sec. 18. The Board of Education shall each receive the same per diem and mileage as their compensation as members of the General Assembly.

Sec. 19. A majority of the Board of Education shall constitute a quorum for the transaction of business, *Provided*, no rule, or regulation, or law, for the regulation and government of the School System, shall pass without the sanction of the majority of all the members of the Board, which shall be expressed by the yeas and nays, on the final passage.

A. H. MARVIN, Chairman.

The minority report from the same committee was also read as follows:

"The majority of the committee to whom was referred the subject of education and school lands, having agreed to a report in favor of a Board of Education, elected by districts, and clothed with exclusive legislative powers in all cases involving common schools, colleges and universities; also, in favor of a Chancellor's Court empowered to determine all questions arising out of the action of said Board, or in any way connected therewith—the undersigned, being unable to agree with said majority in their reasonings and conclusions, asks leave to make a counter report. Without attempting to discuss the *details* of said system of educational government embraced in said report, the undersigned would briefly state that he objects to the proposed amendments to the constitution—1st. Because they assume to do that which properly belongs to the legislative department of the State; 2d. Because said Board of Education are clothed with powers dangerous, as *precedents*, to the liberties of a free and enlightened people; 3d. Because the system therein proposed could not be altered or amended without an amendment to the constitution of the State. For these and other obvious reasons, the undersigned disagrees with the majority of said committee, and respectfully submits for the consideration of the convention, the following, as Article 10, of the constitution:

Article 10.—*Education and School Lands.*

Section 1. The General Assembly shall provide for the election or appointment of a Board of Education, to be composed of twelve persons, who shall be the Trustees of the University, and shall have the general charge and control of education in the State. They shall have power to appoint a Secretary of the Board, who shall be their executive agent, and perform such duties as may be imposed upon him by the Board of Education or the laws of the State.

Sec. 2. Knowledge and learning, generally diffused throughout a community, being essential to the preservation of a free government, it shall be the duty of the General Assembly to encourage, by all suitable means, moral, intellectual, scientific, and agricultural improvements, and to provide by law for a general and uniform system of common schools, wherein tuition shall be without charge, and equally open to all. The proceeds of all lands that have been or hereafter may be granted by the United States to this State, for the support of schools, which shall hereafter be sold or disposed of, and the five hundred thousand acres of land granted to the new States, under an act of Congress distributing the proceeds of the public lands among the several States of the Union, approved A. D., 1841, and all estates of deceased persons, who may have died without leaving a will or heir, and also such per cent. as may be granted by Congress on the sale of lands in this State, shall be and remain a perpetual fund, the interest of which, together with all the rents of the unsold lands, and such other means as the General Assembly may provide, shall be inviolably appropriated to the support of common schools throughout the State.

Sec. 3. The money which shall be paid by persons as an equivalent for exemption from military duty, and the clear proceeds of all fines collected in the several counties for any breach of the penal laws, shall be exclusively applied, in the several counties in which such money is paid or fine collected, among the several school districts of said counties, in the proportion to the number of inhabitants in such districts, to the support of common schools, or the establishment of libraries, as the General Assembly shall, from time to time, provide by law.

Sec. 4. The General Assembly shall take measures for the protection, improvement, or other disposition of such lands as have been or may hereafter be reserved or granted by the United States, or any person or persons, to this State, for the use of a university; and the funds accruing from the rents or sale of such lands, or from any other source, for the purpose aforesaid, shall be and remain a permanent fund, the interest of which shall be applied to the support of said university, with such branches as the public convenience may hereafter demand, for the promotion of literature, the arts and sciences, as may be authorized by the terms of such grant. And it shall be the duty of the General Assembly, as soon as may be, to provide effectual means for the improvement and permanent security of the funds of said university.

All of which is respectfully submitted,

GEORGE W. ELLS."

The CHAIRMAN stated that the majority report was open to amendment.

Mr. WILSON moved to substitute the minority for the majority report.

Mr. MARVIN. I hope this will not be done without some discussion. I will say that the committee are indebted for the principal features of the majority report, to the member from Des Moines [Mr. Hall]. I would be very much pleased if he could have an opportunity, before this question is decided, to give his views in full upon this subject. I am not myself prepared at this time to make any remarks.

Mr. HALL. The report of the majority of the committee on education and school lands contains every principle, I believe, that is in the minority report, with the exception of one provision in the first section of the minority report. That first section provides for a board of education, the same as does the majority report, but it prescribes a different mode of electing the members of that board. If I understand the two reports, the majority report provides that this board of education shall be elected by the people, one member being elected by the people of each district. The minority report allows the board to be appointed by the legislature, or selected in any other manner in which the legislature may prescribe.

Both reports agree that the educational interests of the State shall be placed in the charge of a board of education. So far as the main principles of the two reports are concerned, they are about the same; there is no great difference between them.

I have given some attention and reflection to this subject. I have carefully examined the rise and progress of our common schools in this State, ever since they came into existence; I have made myself somewhat familiar with the subject. I have improved what opportunities I had afforded me, to ascertain if there was any cause why our common school system was not more successful; why those difficulties existed which have been complained of; and if possible, after having ascertained those troubles and difficulties, and constant changes, as far as practicable, to provide some adequate remedy for them. And I think, if gentlemen will look upon this as a practical question, as a question that they desire to have treated as its importance deserves, as a question that presents a subject which they desire to be acted upon, they will find that the majority report contains the true principle for the accomplishment of that purpose.

I shall not stop to call the attention of this convention to the importance of the subject of education: that is conceded by every one. No gentleman upon this floor will yield, perhaps, his zeal upon this question to that upon any other question. It belongs to, and is the most important benefit we can confer upon, the rising generation. One-half of the souls now living in this State are interested in this matter; and as the rising generation comes forward all will be interested in it. It is a matter which pertains to the character of the country. And now when we can do something to facilitate this great object, which we all have in view, and we can do some good to the country, we should so act that we can say hereafter that we have been of some service to our State.

The principle we have endeavored to get at in this majority report is to extend the benefits of this system of education to those to whom it belongs. It is believed that in this State, as in all other States, there is a feeling which will sustain this interest of education; that scattered over every part of our State are men who are deeply interested in this great cause, that look upon it as the great principle of reform and improvement in all things; and no matter in what cause or in what scheme of reform they are engaged, they look to the subject of education as, after all, the great reforming principle. We have in this State, in every county, and scattered through every part of it, persons who, if they were not tied down by others who have not that interest in the subject with themselves, would unite in creating and perfecting a harmonious system, and elevate it beyond what it will ever be if it is left to the masses to control and govern.

The object of this majority report is, as far as practicable, to place this cause of education in the hands of these persons who feel such a deep interest in it; and in order that they may have the means to bestow that attention and care to the subject which its importance demands, the report seeks to remove from them the fetters which now bind them down so that they cannot devote their time and attention to this subject. If a man has any kind of private business that he wishes to have done, what means would he select to accomplish it? He would not throw it promiscuously among those persons who would be, perhaps, one half opposed to him. He would select those who had an interest in the work, and would do all they could to carry it out.

In endeavoring to do what we deem necessary in this matter, I am well aware that we will have to combat old and deep-seated prejudices; we have to give up some of our old ideas that we have entertained for a long time. The fact that we propose to take what is considered a prerogative from the legislature stares us at once in the face. We propose to create an independent power here, to create a legislature upon the subject of education, that will be independent of, and above the political legislature, so far as that subject is concerned.

We have had experience of the action of our political legislature in this respect; and we have had enough of that experience in Iowa. We know that this subject will receive but a small moiety of the attention of the legislature. We know that the matter has been neglected; we know that a system has been put upon the people, and laws been enacted without due deliberation; and the consequence has been that the whole subject has been constantly subjected to change. We have tried experiment, and we know the reasons why it has resulted as it has. We know that from the vast variety of business before the legislature, they have not been able to give that attention and deliberation to the subject which the important cause of education demanded at their hands. And there is no gentleman upon this floor but what would admit that if you would select twelve or fifteen members of the legislature, and devolve upon them the duty of perfecting a system of schools, they would do it better than the whole body would do it. Any of us here would rather trust to the deliberations of those twelve or fifteen members for ten days, for good to the cause of education, than to the legislature for the sixty or seventy-five days they are in session.

This report seeks to obviate this difficulty by taking from the mass of the community a board of education, to be chosen with reference to their peculiar qualifications, and the relations which they occupy towards this great cause. It undertakes to divorce the cause of education from the politics of the State; it seeks to take it away from those agitating questions which are continually arising before the people and the legislature, and turn it over to a tribunal which can have no object in view but that for which they were elected.

Gentlemen may say that there will be party nominations for these offices in the different districts. That may be so; but when they come to perform their duties under this report, have they anything to do connected with politics? Have they a solitary question of which they can make a political question? They have nothing to do with the funds; they have nothing to do with the treasure which belongs to the schools, and the university of this State. They cannot appropriate one dollar of it. Their only subject to act upon is the arranging of a system of education for the State. They have no other purpose or duty; nor have they any other power. They are to arrange a system of education for the State; decide upon the extent of education that shall be afforded by the common schools, and academies and colleges, perhaps; they are to perform all these duties, but they have not the control, nor can they appropriate one dollar of the school fund. The General Assembly of the State will control that fund, will appropriate the proceeds for purposes of education. This board will render back to the State a consideration in the schools which they will prepare and establish, and in the children which they will educate for that purpose.

You here see the workings of this system; you turn the common schools and the academies to this board; you turn over the children to this board, while you allow the General Assembly to furnish the means. There can be no conflict or difficulty between them; the line of demarcation is complete and clear.

Now if you look at the history of this question, as it has arisen in the different states of this Union, you will find that the common schools have progressed, and the system of education advanced, as the subject has been separated from and kept out of the way of all matters connected with politics. And whenever the system is in its greatest perfection, it is comparatively free from these political, fluctuating and changing influences. This is the experience of men everywhere; and I have not suggested this change in the system of education in this State to any man who did not approve of it, until I came upon this committee. I speak of the principle of separating the educational interests of the State from the political differences of the various branches of the state government.

I do not wish to occupy the time of the Convention to any considerable extent; indeed, I cannot do so, for I feel too unwell this morning. I am not able to present this matter as I ought; and, with these few remarks, I will leave it to the Committee.

Mr. ELLS. I am myself unwell this morning, and I have been indisposed for several days. I attended here this morning merely for the purpose of voting, and am not prepared to discuss any question at all. I will, however, say a few words, hoping that those gentlemen who are prepared to discuss this question will take it up and discuss it as it should be discussed.

The cause of education is one in which the true philanthropist takes a deep interest. Indeed, sir, he holds it second only to that of religion itself; for without education it is almost impossible for the moral reformer to reach the hearts and consciences of the masses. Ignorance, superstition, degradation and despotism, have been the prolific source from which have sprung the moral, political and physical diseases that now curse nineteen-twentieths of the human race. No man can read the history of the world, imperfect as that history unquestionably is, without being forced to this conclusion. He will also find, in those countries of Europe where education has taken the deepest root, and been the most generally diffused among the masses, that the people are correspondingly steady, firm and abiding in their attachment to free and liberal institutions of all kinds. The Germans are a striking illustration of the truth of this assertion. With them, education is the rule, and ignorance the exception; while with the volatile Frenchman, the reverse is the rule.

In the United States the same characteristics are manifested. Any gentleman who has traveled north and south of Mason and Dixon's Line, will bear me witness of the truth of this assertion. In view of these facts, Mr. Chairman, I feel free to say that the cause of education is fraught with mightier consequences to the people of this State than any other upon which we are called to act in this connection.

Now, sir, in laying the foundation for an educational system, we must discard all narrow views and prejudices, and not only provide for the wants of the present generation, but for all future generations. I desire to see the common schools of this State so constituted that a thorough knowledge of all the natural sciences will be taught in the most practical manner. Should this point be attained they will contrast most favorably with the superficial education that characterizes a vast number of the graduates of the chartered colleges of these United States. Gentlemen must pardon me for the low estimate I put upon those institutions where the *fees* are the primary object of the tutors and professors. A four years' course, together with the matriculation fees, will insure a diploma to any *numbskull* whose father pays promptly at the end of the terms.

I am not speaking at random, or from any dislike to chartered institutions. My remarks are intended for practical effect, being the result of many years' observation in the State of Ohio. The city of Dayton, where I resided about eight years, has a regular system of *graded* common schools—commencing with the primary and ending with the high school. In these schools tuition is free—consequently there is no *pecuniary* inducement for the teachers to advance the pupils from the lower to the higher grade for the sake of the fees.

At the end of each quarter the scholars in the district school are examined by a competent and thorough board of examiners, and only those who are thoroughly acquainted with the branches taught in the primary or district school are permitted to enter the next grade. Here the children of the rich and poor are all placed on a common level—no preference is shown. Nor are these examinations the result of previous training in questions and answers for examination day. So far from this being the case, questions are often asked that are not in the text books, but involving the same principles. The good results of a system of this kind, no man can calculate. Nothing short of this ought to satisfy the mind of any member of this convention or any friend of education in the State.

Now, sir, let us examine these two reports and see if either of them are as organically calculated to—

Here the gentleman gave way to—

Mr. CLARKE, of Johnson. I regret exceedingly that the authors of these counter reports, upon the subject of education and school lands, should be both so indisposed as to be unable to give that consideration to the subject which its importance demands. And for the purpose of giving them an opportunity to recover so as to be better able to advocate the merits of their several reports, I will move that the committee rise, report progress, and ask leave to sit again.

The question being taken, the motion was agreed to.

In Convention.

The PRESIDENT having resumed the chair—

The CHAIRMAN reported that the committee of the whole, to which had been referred the report of the committee on education and school lands, had instructed him to report that they had had the subject under consideration, had made some progress therein, and asked leave to sit again.

The report was received, and leave granted accordingly.

Amendments to the Constitution.

On motion of Mr. CLARKE, of Johnson,

The convention then proceeded to consider the report of the committee on amendments to the constitution.

The majority report was read as follows:

"The committee to whom was referred so much of the constitution as relates to future amendments of the constitution, have had the same under consideration, and a majority of the committee ask leave to recommend the following:

Sec. 1. Any amendment or amendments to this constitution may be proposed in both houses of the General Assembly, and if the same shall be agreed to by a majority of the members elected to each of the two houses, such proposed amendment shall be entered upon their journals, with the yeas and nays taken thereon, and referred to the legislature to be chosen at the next general election, and shall be published as provided by law for three months previous to the time of making such choice; and if in the General Assembly so next chosen, as aforesaid, such proposed amendment or amendments shall be agreed to by a majority of all the members elected to each house, then it shall be the duty of the General Assembly to submit such proposed amendment or amendments to the people in such manner and at such time as the General Assembly shall provide; and if the people shall approve of and ratify such amendment or amendments, by a majority of the electors qualified to vote for members of the General Assembly voting thereon, such amendment or amendments shall become a part of the constitution of this State.

Sec. 2. At the general election to be held in the year one thousand eight hundred and sixty-seven, and in each tenth year thereafter, and also at such times as the General Assembly may by law provide, the question "Shall there be a convention to revise the constitution and amend the same?" shall be decided by the electors qualified to vote for the members of the General Assembly; and in case a majority of the electors so qualified voting at such election, shall decide in favor of a convention for such purpose, the General Assembly at its next session shall provide by law for the election of delegates to such convention.

(Signed) W. A. WARREN, Chairman,
JOHN T. CLARK,
DAVID BUNKER."

The minority report was read as follows:

"The committee on amendments to the constitution have had the same under consideration, and the undersigned beg leave to make the following minority report:

That in our opinion, it is inexpedient to submit the matter of amendment of the constitution to the people once in ten years, unless the people so require, through their legislature; and we therefore submit the following to be substituted in place of Section two in the majority report:

If, at any time, the General Assembly shall think it necessary, to revise or amend this constitution, they shall provide by law for a vote at the next ensuing election for members of the General Assembly; in case a majority of the people vote in favor of a convention, said General Assembly shall provide for an election of delegates to a convention to be held within twelve months after the vote of the people in favor thereof.

H. D. GIBSON,
TIMOTHY DAY."

Mr. WINCHESTER. I do not think it is necessary to go into committee of the whole upon these reports. I move that the tenth article of the present constitution be substituted for these reports.

The PRESIDENT. The report under consideration is the report of the majority committee.

Mt. WINCHESTER. I move then that the article in the present constitution be substituted for the majority report.

Mr. HARRIS. I have a substitute which I desire to offer for the second section.

Mr. CLARKE, of Johnson. I do not know the reasons which the gentleman from Hardin [Mr. Winchester,] has for making this motion. I hope, however, it will not prevail. The article in the present constitution, which I will refer to in a moment, makes no farther provision for amending the constitution than by calling a convention together for that purpose. I think that some other provision ought to be made, by which defects in the constitution may be supplied, without putting the people to the expense of calling another convention.

The first section of the majority report meets my views much nearer than the article in the present constitution, while at the same time it is sufficiently guarded so as to provide against any hasty changes in the fundamental law. I trust the convention will consider this subject, and take the reports of the majority and minority, and determine which of them is the most practicable. The minority report is substantially the same as that in the article upon this subject in the present constitution. I do think that we ought to make some provision by which the new constitution may be amended, without putting the people to the expense of calling a new convention. I hope, therefore, that the motion of the gentleman from Hardin will not prevail.

Mr. GIBSON. The proposition in the minority report is, with one exception, the same as that contained in the article upon this subject in the present constitution, which provides for the holding of a convention, within six months after the vote of the people calling such a convention. The report of the minority provides for holding the convention within twelve months after such a vote of the people. The object of this provision was to give sufficient time, after the vote of the people was taken for or against the calling of a convention, for a session of the legislature to convene and make such arrangements as would be necessary for the meeting of the convention.

The majority report provides for an expression of opinion in regard to the propriety of calling a convention once in ten years. This may be all very well. But it may be that the people may desire such expression oftener than once in ten years. For instance, there will be a vote taken in 1867, and at that time there may be no apparent necessity for calling a convention to amend the constitution. But some circumstances may arise within a year or two, or within the next five years, which will render it absolutely necessary to call a convention to amend the constitution. In that event, as I understand it, the majority report prohibits the possibility of calling a convention for the next ten years, or taking a vote thereon. What we seek to embody here is, not to have this matter referred to the people, unless it becomes necessary, and this can be made clearly apparent through the legislature. If the people want to amend their constitution sufficiently to justify the calling of a convention, they will be certain to let their representatives know it, and they reflect their will in this matter. If there be no necessity for calling a convention, then it will be unnecessary to refer this matter to the people. But, as I have already said, cases may arise in less than ten years, when it may become absolutely necessary to call a convention to amend the constitution. For these reasons, I prefer the minority report to the second section of the majority.

Mr. HARRIS. I would like, as far as I can, to adhere to the article upon this subject in the present constitution, without incurring some of the inconveniences that will arise under it. The subject of amending the constitution, without the expense and trouble of calling a convention for that purpose, and which is substantially provided for in the first article of the majority report, was agitated somewhat in my part of the State during the canvass, and in fact before this convention was called together. I am in favor of this section of the majority report, and I would like to see it adopted. I think we should have the privilege of making such alterations in the constitution as the people might indicate, without being subjected to the expense of calling a convention for that purpose. I think it can be done as provided for in this first section of the majority report, without any danger of hasty changes, and in such a way that the sentiments of the people would not be misrepresented.

Gentlemen will see that two general elections are necessary to be held, before these changes, if made in the constitution, can become a law. The people surely in that time can become satisfied in regard to the necessity of these changes, and there can be no danger of a surprise. For that reason, I am in favor of the first section o the majority report, but the second I cannot support.

I have proposed a substitute for the second section, which I shall offer, if the amendment now under consideration does not prevail. In the first place, I have provided that the question of a Constitutional Convention shall be submitted once in twenty years, and at any other time when two-thirds of the general assembly shall pass a law therefor. Gentlemen may take exceptions to the two-thirds rule in this matter, but I do not think it will work any hardship, especially when we have a provision to amend the constitution as often as once in twenty years. I should not suppose that gentlemen would want to change the constitution oftener than that. But if any case should arise rendering the calling of a convention absolutely necessary, there will be no difficulty about securing a two-third vote for that purpose.

Mr. WINCHESTER. My objection to the majority report is confined simply to the first section. If this section is adopted every legislature that comes here may agitate the question of amendments to the constitution, and take up, by so doing, a great deal of the time of the legislature. The question would run along for two or three years, consuming a great deal of time, and the expenses of publication, &c., as provided for by this section, would be enormous.

Mr. GILLASPY. I favor the motion of the gentleman from Hardin, [Mr. Winchester,] for adopting the article upon this subject in the present constitution. I cannot support the first section of the majority report, and I would not have an election upon the subject of calling a convention for the next twenty years to come. If this section be adopted I hope it will be amended, so as to require a two-thirds vote of each house upon any proposition submitted to the people, before it becomes a part of the constitution, because a bare majority may at any time submit innumerable amendments to be voted upon by the people, which may affect, to a great degree, the prosperity of the State. I would not be at all astonished if you were to submit to-morrow an amendment to the constitution upon the subject of county indebtedness, that there would be a vote against it, in which case it would sincerely affect the interests of the whole State. And so it might be with any other subject that would come up. I shall vote for the proposition of the gentleman from Hardin, [Mr. Winchester.]

Mr. TRAER. I look upon this question as one of the most important that can come before this Convention, involving, as it does, the rights of the people to a greater extent than any question that has been or can be presented here. I am a little surprised that my friend from Wapello [Mr. Gillaspy] should take the position he now does, as I believe he has invariably been upon the side of the people heretofore. Now he comes in and tells us it is dangerous to submit this question to the people, as they might possibly vote in favor of something that would prove ruinous to the interests of the State. This is a different kind of logic from that which the gentleman has generally used when speaking of the rights of the people; and I must say that it is a new kind of democracy to me.

I have paid some little attention to this subject of amendments to the constitution, and I have invariably found that where this question has arisen, with regard to amendments of the constitution by the legislature, or amendments by the people, what we call the simon pure, the old fogy democracy, were in favor of something of the kind here proposed. I refer particularly to the action of the last Massachusetts constitutional convention upon that subject. You will find there that the men who represented the extreme wing of the democratic party, not the free soil, but the real old-fashioned democracy, passed such a proposition as this with an amendment that would take entirely out of the hands of the legislature, in case the people called a convention, the power of saying in what manner their delegates should be elected. That is the position I take, and that is the position we should take here.

I hold that the people have an inherent right to change their fundamental law at any time without their representatives or any other body interfering with that right. I believe that the general principle laid down and generally acted upon in these cases, is that, if there is an article upon amendments placed in the Constitution, or, in other words, if there is any provision here that does not expressly give the people the right to amend their Constitution without the action of the Legislature, it leaves the people subject to the action of the Legislature; or, in other words, they have not the right to amend their Constitution independent of the Legislature.

I favor the proposition that the people should have the right to amend their Constitution at any time, independent of the Legislature. I am in favor of incorporating into the Constitution an article, submitting the question of amendments to the Constitution to the people at least once in ten years, and giving them the right to elect their delegates, and to hold a convention independent of the Legislature. I take that position, and I would refer gentlemen to the history of this State for the last six years to show that this position is correct.

It is a well known fact to every individual, who has been a resident of the State for that length of time, that the people of this State have endeavored, during that time, to get a constitutional convention called; and it is also a well known fact that, in two instances, at least, the will of the people, as expressed repeatedly upon this subject, has been thwarted through their representatives in the Legislature, who have been compelled to submit to the dictates of certain gentlemen, directed against the will of the majority. This question came up, as near as I can recollect, about six years ago, in the election of representatives to the General Assembly. I will not say how it was in Wapello county, or any other county in that section, but I know it was the case in the section of the State I represent, that the question arose in regard to the amendment of the Constitution, so as to admit of banking in this State. The election of certain gentlemen, in my section, to the House, depended upon the fact whether they were in favor of a constitutional convention. Unfortunately for the people the democracy gained the ascendancy, and they were unable, at that time, to accomplish their object. Two years rolled around, when the question came up again, and through the action of the people, a large majority of the members elected to the Legislature were in favor of a constitutional convention. They passed a bill through that body carrying out the wishes of their constituents, but it was vetoed by the Governor upon constitutional grounds. They passed it again, obviating the constitutional objections, but the Governor put it in his pocket and did not return it, and in this manner the express will of the people was thwarted.

I am perfectly willing that the Legislature, as is provided in the first section, shall have the right to change the Constitution; but, at the same time, I desire to have the question so shaped that the people can have a Convention, without the Legislature having anything to do about it. I wish to refer gentlemen for a moment to the Rhode Island case, which was carried up to the Supreme Court of the United States, and there decided. The question involved there was, whether the people, by any means, could amend their constitutional law without the consent of the Legislature, unless they incorporated into the Constitution in the first place a provision giving them that right. It was decided by Judge Taney, that there was no other way for the people to amend their Constitution but by revolution, unless the right to amend it was reserved to them by the Constitution itself. That principle carried out here will produce the same result, unless we reserve that right to the people.

I am opposed to the article in the present Constitution, for I believe it has not operated well heretofore, and I believe it will not hereafter. I am in favor of the majority report, with some additional amendment, which will reserve to the people the right to amend their Constitution. I believe that to be true democratic doctrine, whether it be the doctrine of the Democratic party or not.

I hope that the motion to substitute the article upon this subject in the present Constitution for this majority report, will not prevail.

Mr. BUNKER. As one of the majority of the Committee, I desire to make a few remarks, showing what the views of the Committee were in reporting the provisions they have. In the first section we provide that—

"Any amendment or amendments to this Constitution may be proposed in either House of the General Assembly, and if the same shall be agreed to, by a majority of the members elected to each of the two Houses, such proposed amendment shall be entered on their journals, with the yeas and nays taken thereon, and referred to the Legislature to be chosen at the next general election, and shall be published, as provided by law, for three months previous to the time of making such choice."

The object of this clause of the section, is to obviate the expense of calling a Convention together for the purpose of making minor amendments to the Constitution. And gentlemen will see that, by the following clause, we guard against hasty legislation, by requiring the action of two legislative bodies previous to the amendments being submitted to the people and their taking effect. We provide thus:

"And if, in the General Assembly, so next chosen, as aforesaid, such proposed amendment or amendments shall be agreed to, by a majority of all the members elected to each House, then it shall be the duty of the General Assembly to submit such proposed amendment or amendments to the people, in such manner, and at such time as the General Assembly shall provide; and if the people shall approve of and ratify such amendment or amendments, by a majority of the electors qualified to vote for members of the General Assembly, voting thereon, such amendment or amendments shall become a part of the Constitution of this State."

The formalities we have here provided for amendments to the Constitution are about as great as the formalities of amending it by the present mode.

In regard to the second section of this report, which provides for submitting the question of a constitutional convention to the people, I believe the committee were of the opinion that, under our form of government, all rights should be retained inherent in the people, and they should have the power to act upon their fundamental law, without the intervention of anybody whatever. And we thought ten years would be a proper period of time for a submission of this question directly to the people.

In relation to another portion of the second section, the gentleman from Marion [Mr. Gibson] alleges that it might be desirable to submit the question of a constitutional convention to the people oftener than once in ten years. I think the gentleman has not carefully examined this question, and although he was a member of the committee, I think he has not properly examined the majority report upon this subject. This second section provides, that

"At the general election to be held in the year one thousand eight hundred and sixty-seven, and in each tenth year thereafter, and also at such times as the General Assembly may, by law, provide, the question—'shall there be a convention to revise the constitution and amend the same?'— shall be decided by the electors qualified to vote for members of the General Assembly; and in case a majority of the electors so qualified, voting at such election, shall decide in favor of a convention for such purpose, the General Assembly at its next session shall provide by law for the election of delegates to such convention."

The gentleman cannot fail to see, from this section, that the question of a constitutional convention shall be submitted to the people once in every ten years, and at any other time that the general assembly may provide by law. But I do not think it worth while to discuss this question at length. The object of the first section is to secure amendments to the constitution, without the expense of calling a convention; and the object of the second section is to reserve to the people the right to alter the fundamental law, without the intervention of any other power.

On motion of Mr. Young,

The convention then took a recess till two o'clock, P. M.

EVENING SESSION.

The convention met at 9 P. M., and was called to order by the President.

Amendments to the Constitution.

On motion of Mr. YOUNG,

The Convention proceeded, in committee of the whole, to the consideration of the report of the Committee upon amendments to the Constitution (Mr. Young in the chair).

Mr. WINCHESTER moved to substitute the article upon amendments in the old constitution for the report of the committee.

Mr. SOLOMON. I desire to offer an amendment to the substitute, which I will read to the chair.

Mr. HARRIS. I wish to say, that after considerable consultation with those who I supposed would support the majority report, they have decided to make some amendments to that report, which may make it much more acceptable than it now is. For this reason I hope the motion to substitute the section from the constitution will not prevail; for if we fail to render the report of the committee satisfactory, it will then be time enough to return to the former provision.

Mr. SCOTT. I hope this motion will not prevail. It is certainly using a committee, which has labored long and arduously, very shabbily. As there is very little difference, as I understand, betwen the old constitution and this report, by a very slight change, we can make the report of the committee accord with the wishes of a majority of the convention. I shall be very sorry to see this motion prevail, because I think it is not doing justice to the committee.

Mr. GILLASPY. I occupy the same position

I did this forenoon. I shall vote for the substitute offered by the gentleman from Hardin [Mr. Winchester]. The same objections that I have to that apply to the first section in the report of the committee.

While I am up, I desire to return my thanks to the distinguished gentleman from Benton [Mr. Traer] for the knowledge which he has imparted to myself and to this convention on the subject of democracy, and of democratic principles generally. I have no doubt that the gentleman is better prepared to enlighten this body upon the subject of democracy and the democratic party than he is with regard to the new party towhich he has lately attached himself. He knows more about the democratic party from the fact that it is an old party, better known before the country. But for one I would much rather have heard him give us his views upon the subject of the principles of his own party, the party of latter-day republicanism, than in regard to the democratic party, about which I had some slight knowledge before.

Mr. TRAER. Will the gentleman allow me—

Mr. GILLASPY. No, sir. I desire to say that I have no fears of the action of the people in regard to any amendments that may be submitted to them by the legislature. But I take the ground that it is wholly unnecessary, and that the people do not desire to have these things brought before them. I intended, if article ten should be adopted from the old constitution, to move to amend by throwing off the clog the gentleman has alluded to, the legislature. I believe that the people of the State have the right to decide for themselves when they will have a change in the constitution; and I believe the proper way to accomplish that object is to permit them to elect their delegates, and send them up here to revise the constitution. If the principles laid down in the report of this committee were to prevail, I am satisfied that the people will be harassed from year to year, at every election, by various propositions, and it is very probable that they would sometimes be called upon to vote upon half a dozen different propositions to amend the constitution. There would be no end to it. I am satisfied that the people would be opposed to it. I believe that if we agree to the proposition contained in this report, it would be dangerous to the institutions of this country, for you allow a bare majority to pass these amendments. This constitution is to go to the country as a republican constitution, there being a majority of republicans in this convention. Now if what we are told is to take place shall be fulfilled, if the new party is to destroy and disannul all the work of the party which preceded them, I undertake to say that it would be the policy of the democratic party to eradicate or annul all the changes made in the present constitution. Now a bare majority are to have the power to submit amendments to the people. I am opposed to allowing amendments to the constitution to be made in that way, to be voted upon by the people at the suggestion of the General Assembly. I say it is no more than right and fair to provide that a two-third vote of each House shall be required before any proposition can be submitted to the people for the amendment of the present constitution. I am in favor of that for this reason. If there should be anything in the present constitution about to be adopted here, so obnoxious to the people that they desire a change, which they desire the legislature to submit to them to vote upon, there can be and will be a two-third vote at both sessions of the General Assembly submitting that proposition. If there cannot be a two-third vote, it would be, in my judgment, improper and impolitic to allow a bare majority of the legislature to submit at all times, and upon all occasions, any propositions to amend which they might see fit, and thus harrass the people of the country by requiring them to vote at every election upon some proposition or other for the amendment of the constitution. I am opposed to it, and shall be perfectly satisfied with article ten of the old constitution, with that clog, the legislature, stricken out, so as to allow the people to decide for themselves when they will have an amendment of the constitution, and how they will have it.

Mr. TRAER. I think the gentleman misrepresents me with regard to the subject of democracy.

Mr. GILLASPY. [In his seat.] Not intentionally.

Mr. TRAER. I did not intend in my remarks this morning to speak of the democracy of this time, but only of democracy as I think it ought to be. I made a distinction between the self-named democracy and the simon-pure democracy; and I wanted to show what that difference was. I said I was surprised to see the gentleman, after haranguing the convention as much as he, and some others, have done upon the rights of 'the dear people,' take the position that he feared the people would be imposed upon if these questions were submitted to them. That was the ground I understood him to take, although he now seems to be getting off upon another subject. Now I am perfectly willing to strike that out entirely. I do not care to give the legislature any power at all to touch this matter. What I am in favor of, is an arrangement by which the people can amend the constitution at any time, without applying to the legislature in any shape or form. That is my position. I wish to leave it entirely to the people. And I wish to put some provision into the constitution to prevent the legislature from assuming the right to deprive the people of the right to say when and where and how they will amend their constitution.

Mr. CLARK, of Alamakee. I have no personal feelings upon the question now before the committee, although I was a member of the committee which made this report. I, for one, do not assume that even this body is perfect, or that the constitution which may come from our hands will be perfect. And in the next place, if it were perfect when it comes from our hands, it may not be adapted to the wants of the people a few years hence. We are increasing in population. We are changing our position as to wealth and improvements. Everything is changing; nothing is standing still. We are progressing; and the constitution which may be perfectly adapted to our wants to-day may not be adapted to our wants five or ten years hence. These considerations led the committee to adopt as one part of their report, a provision by which the legislature might submit a proposition for any amendments which they might consider it necessary to make in the constitution, that they might just draw up the form of the amendment, and have it entered upon their journal, with the yeas and nays thereupon. Then there would be a distinct question or proposition laid before the voters of the State, upon which at their next election of representatives they would be called to vote upon, not directly, but by their selection of representatives. They would know that the amendment would again come before the legislature, and if they were in favor of the amendment they would endeavor to elect a legislature in favor of it, or if opposed to it, to elect a legislature which should be opposed to it. Now is there anything wrong in this? Is there anything wrong in principle in it? We do not take the people by surprise. They are not required to vote in a hurry. The amendment is proposed at one session of the legislature, and published in the papers. Then it goes over until another legislature is elected, partly perhaps on that very issue, and if that legislature again approve it, after all this has been done, the question is finally submitted to the people for a direct vote. Now with all these provisions and safeguards, I see no danger in adopting such a provision in our constitution.

There has been a provision adopted in another part of the constitution to-day, providing for the election of a Lieutenant Governor, a question upon which this body is divided, and it may well be considered a doubtful question whether the interests of the people really require a Lieutenant Governor. Perhaps after a few years experience the people may wish to change that. It could be very readily and easily accomplished in the manner proposed, without subjecting the people of the State to the great expense which is now being incurred in consequence of the session of this convention. The mode is simple, direct and easy, and it seems to me desirable that such a provision should be contained in the constitution. With all due deference to the objections made by my friend from Wapello, [Mr. Gillaspy,] I shall beg leave to disagree with him upon some of the conclusions he comes to, and some of the principal arguments which he uses here.

I must confess that I have been somewhat amused at the different positions which certain gentlemen seem to take as different questions arise before this body. And when the gentleman from Wapello, [Mr. Gillaspy,] urged as an objection to the amendment that the country would be flooded with proposed amendments to the constitution, so that after a while the people would be going crazy upon the subject, it seemed as if the gentleman might be afraid that the people would so alter the constitution that the present provision for internal improvements might be altered, changed, or overturned. Now I ask the gentleman seriously if he proposes to fix the constitution so that the people cannot alter it. I ask him seriously if he wishes to incorporate a provision for internal improvements, and then, if the people should vote for it without sufficient reflection, have it so fixed that they cannot change it if they should wish to alter it.

Mr. GILLASPY. I am opposed to making the constitution subject to amendment and repeal like a common statute.

Mr. CLARK. I ask the gentleman whether he does not propose to submit this constitution, when it is framed, to the people for their adoption; and whether there is any difference in principle between submitting this constitution, and amendments to the constitution? Is he in reality afraid of the votes of the people of the State? Is he now about to repudiate and kick over the great dish of milk he has given in his frequent declarations that the people are safe upon all questions, that our rights are all safe in the hands of the 'dear people?'

Mr. GILLASPY. I wish to correct the gentleman. I have said distinctly that I have no fears of the result of the vote of the people; but that I believe it to be unnecessary to harrass the people by these several votes. I have the utmost confidence in them. If the gentleman wants to misrepresent me upon the record, I say it is unfair. Give my language and I have no objection.

Mr. CLARK. I certainly have no wish to misrepresent the gentleman or to place him in a false position. If he did not mean what his language naturally implied, I am very happy to hear it.

Mr. GILLASPY. I meant what I said.

Mr. CLARK. If the inferences which I drew did not legitimately follow from his language, then I have learned the English language to very little purpose. Now let us follow this out a moment, and where shall we be? What evil is there to flow from a provision of this kind in the constitution? Is there any valid objection that can be urged against it? If my friend from Wapello has any better objection than that the people are not safe to be trusted, I hope he will let us have the benefit of it. Now if the people are safe to be trusted; if we act upon the principle that our government is predicated upon the will of the people, and that our sovereign power traced back to its source, rests upon the individual, capable of self-government, if that is the ground upon which my friend from Wapello plants himself, I ask the gentleman where there can be a valid objection to this provision in the constitution, to allow the people at any time, upon the shortest notice, the privilege of altering the constitution when they have found it to fail to meet their wants, or to cease to provide for their interests? Can there be any objection to placing the question directly before the people, and giving them the opportunity to make a change? Can there be any valid objection raised? It seems to me not; and if not, then I am in favor of the provision in the first section of that article. I am in favor of it because the experience of the past, the experience of other States, has proved the necessity of such a provision in the constitution. And the history of the past, the history of other States, which have had that provision in their constitutions, proves that there is no danger of its abuse.

This is not a new feature in a State constitution. Neither the committee, nor myself as a member of the committee, claim the merit of inventing anything of the kind. It is taken from other constitutions where it has been in practical operation for five, ten, and twelve years. No complaint, no inconvenience, no injury ever resulted from a provision of that kind; and no serious injury ever can result, for the simple reason that it places the whole power of the amendment in the hands of the people. Then I am in favor of that section.

As to the next section I am certainly in favor of it, for the simple reason that I am willing to place to the greatest extent the control of the fundamental law, the foundation of all the law of our State, in the hands of the people, and independent of any power of the legislature to control their will. I am unwilling to place the constitution of the State out of the direct control of the people, out of their reach, in the hands of a representative body. I believe it should be retained in their possession, within their control; that they should have the privilege themselves to reach that question, without the necessity of legislative enactment. The experience of the past proves the necessity of it. I think that there might be a case in this State in which it would be necessary perhaps to use that power, and when the legislative body might refuse to call a convention in accordance with the wish of the people. That such a case has occurred within the short history of our government as a government, is a sufficient reason to me for introducing a provision which shall render impossible a repetition of an occurrence of that kind. The revolution in the State of Rhode Island, which ended in treason by the decision of the Supreme Court of the United States, and which resulted in incarcerating one of her first free born sons in the walls of a dungeon, grew out of this defect in their constitution. The people had their constitution formed in the early days of our history, before we had had much experience in a republican form of government, and they had failed to reserve to the people themselves the right of calling a convention, excepting through the legislative bodies. The people did not succeed in getting the enactment, but they met in convention, formed a constitution, and elected their officers under it. Mr. Dorr, who happened to be elected Governor, was incarcerated in the walls of a dungeon as a traitor against his State, convicted of treason. Now I am in favor of a provision in the constitution, which shall obviate the necessity of again subjecting any class of the people of the United States to a contingency of that kind. I think all power should be inherent in the people, and that they should have the right to reach the fundamental laws of their land without being compelled to ask it as a privilege from the hands of any legislative body. I am in favor of what the gentleman has been talking about heretofore; I am in favor of making the people directly the controllers of the government; of allowing them, themselves, without asking it as a favor of their legislative bodies, the right to say when they will change, alter, or modify their constitution. I believe that such a provision, if not absolutely necessary, at all events will never do any harm, unless we adopt the principle that the people do not know what they want; the principle that the people are not capable of self government, that to submit the control of the fundamental laws of the land to the great body of the people will be dangerous. For these reasons I am in favor of the report of the committee.

Mr. GILLASPY. The gentleman has stated, sir, that he did not intend to misrepresent me. I thought it was distinctly understood by this convention that I said I was in favor of the tenth article of the old constitution, but that while I favored that article I opposed the manner in which the amendments of the constitution were brought before the people. I favored it for this reason; not for any fear I had of the action of the people; but that I was desirous of amending article tenth of the old constitution so that the amendment of the constitution should be brought about directly by the people, without any interposition of the legislature, that the people should have the sole power; and I suppose the convention, with the exception of the gentleman from Alamakee [Mr. Clark] understood me. I do not wonder that that gentleman did not understand my language, because he does not always understand his own. I understand that he had so far forgotten his own language that on yesterday morning he rose in his place and disclaimed having said something, which he actually did say ten days ago, about the amalgamation of the whites and blacks, when he virtually endorsed that doctrine. Now I understand that he said yesterday morning that he did not intend by his speech to say any such thing. I am not astonished therefore that the gentleman should not understand my language when he does not always understand his own.

Mr. CLARK, of Alamakee. I ask the gentleman if he did not use substantially this language this forenoon:—"I am opposed to submitting amendments to the people, for the reason that if they are submitted to the people they may change the provision in relation to internal improvements."

Mr. GILLASPY. That is the fact.

Mr. CLARK. Then I ask the gentleman if I misstated him? I stated that he said so, and it seems that he did say so. Now I leave it to the convention to decide whether I misunderstood him or not.

As to the question of amalgamation, I noticed with regret that the gentleman was not in his seat when I made the explanation yesterday morning, for I suppose that he was the gentleman who wrote that article.

Mr. GILLASPY. I was not the gentleman.

Mr. CLARK. I say again that I never made use of the language ascribed to me; and I never made use of any language from which such a deduction could legitimately be drawn.

Mr. GILLASPY. Does the gentleman assert that I was the author of that article?

Mr. CLARK. I did not say whether he was or was not. I said that I supposed yesterday morning that he was, and noticed that he was not in his seat. I did not say in the remarks referred to, that I was in favor of amalgamation, nor did I use any language which would authorize any gentleman to say that I was in favor of amalgamation.

Mr. SKIFF. I move that this discussion be referred to the Committee on Military Affairs. [Laughter.]

Mr. WILSON. It seems to me that if the gentleman from Wapello, [Mr. Gillaspy,] would make some of his old speeches over again he would convince himself that this first section of the majority report ought to be adopted. He has been telling us, during the whole session, that he came from a district which required but one amendment to the Constitution—that in relation to banking. He did not wish to go to work and revise the Constitution throughout.

Mr. GILLASPY. I will just ask the gentleman if I ever said that I only wanted one amendment?

Mr. WILSON. I am satisfied that that has been the burden of the song sung by the gentleman ever since he took his seat in this body. Now if the first section of this report had been embodied in the old Constitution, probably the gentleman would not have been grieved in being compelled to sit here so long as he has. That amendment might have been submitted to the people separately, and his constituents might have had an opportunity to pass upon that without sending the gentleman up here to revise the Constitution. If the people of the State do not desire a general revision of the Constitution, but simply wish amendments to be made in one or two particulars, how easy it would be, by a provision of this kind, to submit them separately to the people, through the medium provided in this section, and have them passed upon. It does away with the excuse of calling a convention whenever the people wish to change the Constitution in only one or two particulars.

The gentleman meets with another difficulty. He is willing to support the old constitutional provision in relation to amendments. It seems to me that that is even worse than the section he objects to. The old Constitution provides—

"If at any time the General Assembly shall think it necessary to revise or amend this Constitution, they shall provide by law for a vote of the people for or against a convention, at the next ensuing election for members of the General Assembly."

That is, if the General Assembly deem it proper, they shall submit the question to the people. The wishes of the people are not consulted in that section at all. Yet the gentleman is willing to abide by that, while he is not willing to let the people pass upon one distinct proposition submitted to them by the majority of the Legislature.

Mr. GILLASPY. Was the gentleman in his seat when I said that I was in favor of amending that, leaving it to the people and not to the Legislature?

Mr. WILSON. I cannot exactly comprehend how the gentleman will amend that section so as to leave it entirely to the people, unless by letting the people hold a mass convention at any time to determine whether there shall be amendments made or not. There must be some agency in this matter. The first section proposes to divide this agency between the people and the Legislature, that the Legislature may submit the proposition to the people, which shall be published three months in the newspapers thoughout the State, before the next election of members to the General Assembly. The question is thus presented to the people. The candidates will take their positions upon it; and the people, in voting for the candidates, will, in effect, vote for or against the amendment itself. When the new Legislature meets, they pass upon the amendment again, and if they again approve of it, they send it directly to the people for their ratification. It seems to me that that contains all the safeguards that are necessary, and at the same time gives to the people an opportunity to amend their Constitution whenever they may deem it proper, without calling a convention and going to the expense of revising the whole Constitution. For, although a convention may be called together by the people with the intention upon their part that the Constitution shall be amended only in one or two particulars, you will find that when the Convention assembles it will be judged necessary to make a general revision of the whole. You will find that that has been the custom in all the states where conventions have been called for the purpose of revising the Constitution. They have not stopped with one or two amendments. They have pursued the same course which we have adopted here. They have parceled out the Constitution among a series of committees, and those committees have reported in favor of a general revision, as we have done here. We wish to avoid the necessity of that by this section. It seems to me that this article provides a complete remedy against that wrong; for I believe it to be a wrong to place the Constitution in such a shape that a general revision must be taken in hand by the Convention, when the people only desire one or two changes in relation to some particular matters. I hope that the section will be adopted by the Committee.

Mr. PALMER. I believe that the committee all concur in the provisions of section one of the majority report. I am disposed to be in favor of the provisions of that section, although I do not approve of the provisions of the second section. I do not believe we should require the people, every ten years and as much oftener as the legislature may choose, to say whether they will amend their constitution or not. I think it should be the object and pride of every delegate to a constitutional convention, to form such a constitution as would stand the test of time and secure the approval of the wisdom of ages. We do not meet here to make a temporary law. Our object is to establish permanent and fundamental laws. Now I think if we should adopt the first section of the majority report, together with the section recommended by the minority of the committee, it would make a very good article upon this subject. I think there is no danger that we shall be very much troubled under this first section, from being compelled to vote upon amendments to the constitution. All proposed amendments have to pass both Houses of the General Assembly at two successive sessions, before they can even be submitted to the people. I have more confidence in our General Assembly than to think that two General Assemblies in succession will thus pass a provision which it is not expedient or necessary to vote upon.

It has justly been observed that this convention need not have been called, if a provision like this in the first section of the report of the majority of the committee had formed a part of our present constitution. What was it that caused a calling of the convention? It was simply an objection to one single article of the constitution; for we heard hardly an objection to any other part of the constitution. Then if the legislature, in accordance with a provision like this, could have submitted to the people a suitable article providing for banking, that article would doubtless have been adopted by a large majority of the people, and the State might have been saved the expense of calling this convention.

Now it is proposed in the second section of the majority report, to put in a provision which would be as inconsistent as if the legislature, when they have passed any important law, should insert in it a section, providing that every future legislature should take into consideration the propriety of repealing or amending that act. Is there a necessity for that? It should be the object of legislators to pass laws which would not require re-examination by every subsequent legislature every few years. And I think it would be still more improper to incorporate upon the constitution a similar provision, by inserting the second section of the majority report, which provides that we shall not only have a vote every ten years, but as much oftener as the legislature shall think proper.

Mr. GIBSON. What is the question before the Committee?

Mr. SOLOMON. I submitted an amendment, but it has not yet been read. The substitute as I propose to amend it will read:

"If at any time the General Assembly shall think it necessary to revise or amend this constitution, they shall provide by law for a vote of the people for or against a convention, at the next ensuing election for members of the General Assembly. In case a majority of the people shall have voted at such election in favor of a convention, the said General Assembly shall provide for an election of delegates to a convention to be held within twelve months of the vote of the people in favor thereof."

This is the old constitution with some slight changes. I offer the amendment solely for the purpose of making certain that which has been deemed uncertain by our legislatures and persons who have looked at the language of our present constitution. The amendment simply makes this tenth article practical. As it stood in the old constitution it provided, that "in case a majority of the people vote in favor of a convention, the said General Assembly shall provide for an election of delegates to a convention to be held within six months after the vote of the people in favor thereof." The intention evidently was that at one session of the General Assembly, a law should be passed providing that the people should take a vote for or against a convention to form a new constitution, and that is all that it was intended that the legislature should do. It is then intended that under that law the people shall vote; and in case a majority shall vote in favor of a convention, the legislature succeeding that vote should provide for the election of delegates, the manner in which they should be elected, their number, &c.

It is a provision also that the convention shall be held within six months after the vote. Now the election for or against the constitution is to be held in August, under our laws as they stand. And it was found to be impracticable for the succeeding legislature to pass a law and have it in force in time for an election to be held under it. Hence I deem it necessary to change the time from six to twelve months, in order to give the necessary time. I suppose that, of course, this amendment will prevail, as it merely makes the provision unambiguous and practical; but whether the substitute itself will prevail, I cannot say. I am willing to say, however, that I am in favor of it, and I desire, briefly, to give my reasons.

I think gentlemen misunderstand this matter of the amendment of the constitution; for certainly either they misunderstand it or I do. I have always looked upon the constitution of a State, or of the United States, as something more than a mere statute. I look upon the organic law of the State as something that should be permanent, which should be durable, and different in its character from mere statute laws. The intention of the constitution is to set metes and bounds to the legislature. This is the intention of the constitutions throughout the entire confederacy. Now it seems to me eminently improper that the instrument which is to define the powers of the legislature should be formed by that legislature; that the instrument which is to define the powers of any body should be formed by that body. I think the present system is the best.

I am opposed for another reason to the report of the committee as it now stands. As the report now stands there is nothing to preclude or to prevent subsequent legislatures from becoming constitution-makers. In fact it becomes a part and parcel of their legitimate duty to inquire into it, and see if any amendment is needed, and if so to go to work to correct it. The report of the committee seems to me, therefore, to place the constitution, and the statutes made under it, and subservient to it, upon rather too great an equality. It has been charged to-day against the democratic party, although I have never learned it in any of the lessons I have learned upon that subject, that the democratic party, as a party, throughout the country, and in each individual State, had not been the supporter of the constitutions. Why, sir, if I know anything of the democratic party at the present day, it is that party which says to its opponents —hands off from the constitution. And if I know anything of the other party, it is that party which seeks to carry out what it considers expedient, without a just and proper warranty from the constitution. That is what I deem to be the national distinction between the democratic party and their opponents. Now, sir, the democratic party desire a constitution carefully made in the first place, and then to stand as the land-mark, as the law-forbidding to the legislature, until it is repealed by the same power which formed it. I look upon the constitution as too sacred to come fully made from the hands of the legislature.

This amendment provides that the legislature may submit to the people any amendment or amendments; and it has been urged that if we had had such a provision, this convention need not have been assembled, since the main object of the convention was to secure a change in the banking system. That may possibly be true. But do you not suppose that the legislature at the same time that they took up the banking question would have done like ourselves, and taken up other things? I am not surprised at the desire of some members to place this constitution on a level with statute law, for they seem to indicate by their course that they have no other conception of a constitution than that it should be a statute. Many of the amendments offered here have too much of that tendency. I am not in favor of blending these two things together. There are always influences surrounding a legislature which make it unfit for preparing and framing the organic law of the land. That should be left to a body of men convened at sometime when there is little or no political excitement, and no such influences as surround the legislature, and will continue to hover around them under whatever constitution we may submit. The gentleman from Benton [Mr. Traer,] has stated here that he sees a distinction between the so-called democracy of the country, and what he thinks is the simon-pure democracy. Now let me say to the gentleman that he has not seen anything new. That distinction has been discovered for some time. It is a *color*-able distinction, and I thank God for the distinction.

Mr. GIBSON. I would prefer the amendment to the amendment; but I am inclined to vote against both as a substitute for the report. As one of the committee upon amendments to the constitution, I was in favor of the first section of this report. I so expressed myself in committee, and so expressed myself in the minority report. Myself, and one other member of the committee, [Mr. Day,] dissented from the last section. Upon examination of the first section, however, it strikes me that it would be proper to amend it a little; and if it were in order for me to offer an amendment, I should like to do so. For the information of the Convention I will read what I propose to offer as an amendment when the opportunity is afforded. I propose to add after the word "provide" in the ninth line, the following:

"*Provided*, that there shall not be more than one proposition submitted at any one session of the legislature."

It strikes me that that would obviate a great deal of the objection which is made to this section, that the legislature will go into a constitution-making operation. If it is so restricted that the legislature can only pass on one amendment, an amendment of one article of the constitution, so that each amendment shall come up singly upon its own merits, I think there would be no danger whatever. Besides, there are sufficient guards thrown around this, to give it, in my opinion, all the sanctity which ought to belong to the constitution, as much as if it were proposed by a convention assembled like ourselves, and perhaps even more. This article provides that at a general session of the legislature, a proposition for an amendment may pass both houses to accomplish the specified object. This is placed upon the journal, and it then goes no further. The people see it, and they understand it. There it stands at the next election of members of the legislature. If then this is a proposition which is not required by the people, they will show their disapprobation of it, as has been already remarked, in that election, for the candidates of that succeeding legislature will take issue upon that ground. If then a majority of the next legislature is in favor of the amendment, they pass upon it and refer it to the people to be voted upon at the next general election. It must then be published for three months preceding the general election. In how much plainer or how much firmer manner could you bring this matter before the people? They are the sovereign authority as claimed by the gentleman, and I believe no one has undertaken to dispute it. I profess, for one, to believe as much in the sovereignty of the people as any other gentleman upon this floor. If then the people are sovereign, is there any other plan by which we can get the express will of the people, better, upon a single subject, than in the manner proposed?

It is apparent to every one that when we submit this constitution, it will contain defects. I do not think that we can claim to be perfect, or to be capable of framing a perfect instrument. We may find upon future examination, a defect in some article or section, which, if we had it in our power we would remedy; but having adjourned we have nothing more to do with it. What shall then be done? Must the State incur the expense of calling another convention in a few years to remedy the defect in certain articles of the constitution, or else endure them as they are, when known to be defective? In two or three days the legislature might fully discuss the matter, and might prepare such an amendment as the wants of the people might require. They would then place it upon their journal. The next succeeding legislature would adopt it, and submit it to the people, and the people would vote upon it. I cannot conceive of any way in which the proposed amendment could come more fully before the sovereign people than in the manner now proposed.

Of the second section there was a difference of opinion in the committee. That difference does not amount to a great deal. It was simply the question whether the matter should be submitted to the people to vote upon every ten years. The minority of the committee thought that unnecessary. They thought the matter would be sufficiently safe in the hands of the legislature; that when the people made it known to the legislature that there was a necessity for calling a convention to amend the constitution, the legislature would submit the question to the people. It was argued that it would be unnecessary to make any provision whatever for calling a convention, for the reason that all the amendments it would ever be found necessary to make, could be provided by the legislature in the plan proposed in the first section. I am of opinion that it would be unnecessary to submit the matter to the people every ten years, to decide whether to hold a convention or not; but that whenever the people really desire it, the legislature will submit the question to the people.

Gentlemen have arrayed themselves against this proposition, the gentleman from Benton [Mr. Traer] particularly, that the people have suffered a great deal in Iowa for the want of this very provision. This strikes me as rather singular, because if they had had the means in the constitution, how could they have remedied the evil sooner than this? If the vote were to be taken every ten years, a convention could not have been called sooner than this; for the question could not have been submitted until 1856, and the convention could not have been called before this. It is said that the rights of the people have been trampled upon for the last six years; that they have been demanding a convention under the provision of the old constitution, and were not allowed it. How that may be, I will not undertake to assert; but one thing is evident; whenever it is apparent that the people really make a demand the legislature must obey.

I am not trying to make political capital here. True, I claim to be a partisan, but I do not want to be ranked as a partisan here, trying to make capital either for myself or anybody else. I want to act to the best of my ability, and as far as I know how, as a pure, true, honest and faithful representative, and leave the result to those more versed in wire working and political maneuvering than I am. The statement of the gentleman was no doubt meant to reflect upon the democratic party because they refused to pass an act submitting the matter of the amendment of the Constitution to the people. What is he going to make by it? Has he any means of establishing the fact that there was a majority of the people in the State in favor of calling a convention sooner than it was called? If he has, I am not aware of it. I do not know how he arrives at that conclusion. It is well known that the people were divided. Some of them wished for a convention and others were opposed to it; and when the convention was called, the matter was decided by a majority not very large. A warfare had been waged against the old Constitution from the very first year of its existence, and at last the gentlemen have accomplished their object and called a convention to revise and amend the Constitution.

It strikes me, under these circumstances, that if the substitute does not prevail, we can amend this first section so as not to have a multitude of amendments offered at the same time, by which a system of log-rolling might be gotten up, and certain abuses passed under the influence of combinations. I think this amendment will sufficiently guard and protect this matter in every respect.

Mr. HARRIS. I have no disposition to read curtain lectures here; but it does seem to me that we are taking up a little too much time about this matter. As I understand it, there is but one simple proposition before the committee, and that is, whether they are in favor of allowing the people to vote upon amendments to the Constitution proposed by the Legislature, without calling a convention. If the committee are opposed to that, then they can go for something else. I do dot think there is any necessity of talking about this matter at all.

I will merely say that I am disposed to favor the report of the majority of the Committee on Amendments to the Constitution, with some alterations, which I think can be made in it without difficulty, if the proposed substitute is not adopted. I am not in favor of free and unbridled license in this matter, and I believe amendments can be proposed which will meet with the approbation of the committee generally.

Mr. CLARKE, of Henry. I do not agree with the gentleman from Appanoose, [Mr. Harris,] that we have been and are consuming time needlessly and uselessly upon this matter. I think the main point to be discussed is, whether we shall take the provision in the old Constitution, or whether we shall take the report of the committee. And it is a question of much more importance than any question of verbal amendments, &c., which seem to engross so much of the time of this Convention. This is the question we have to discuss now.

And I must say that I regretted very much the rather ungenerous attack upon my friend from Wapello, [Mr. Gillaspy.] I do insist upon it that that gentleman is perfectly consistent. I must say that I admire the course of that gentleman in this body. You always know where to find him. He always speaks straight forward and right out just what he intends and means in every respect. I admire that gentleman much more than I do those gentlemen—not here, of course, but in other deliberative bodies—whose whereabouts you never can ascertain until about the time the vote is taken, when they can see which way the majority is going. The gentleman from Wapello is just as bold and decided when in the minority as when with the majority. And there is another good thing about him. He is willing to get up and give his own opinions, and to listen to the opinions of others, and not occupy a silent seat and sneer at what others may say, like some who come up with an air of wisdom, as if they thought themselves superior to the gods.

Mr. WILSON. I would suggest to the gentleman from Henry, [Mr. Clarke,] that he is putting it on a little too thick. [Laughter.]

Mr. CLARKE, of Henry. I hope the gentleman from Jefferson, [Mr. Wilson,] will apply none of my remarks to himself.

Mr. WARREN. I would call the gentleman from Henry, [Mr. Clarke,] to order. The gentleman from Wapello, [Mr. Gillaspy,] can defend himself.

[Cries of "go on; go on."]

Mr. CLARKE, of Henry. Now, when the gentleman from Wapello gets up here and says that he wants to save the people from the trouble of being called out at unreasonable times to vote upon propositions which may be sent down to them from the Legislature, I believe he is honest and sincere; and when the gentleman gets up here and says he does not like to live under such an uncertain constitution, which may be changed as easily as a statutory act, I believe he is honest and means just what he says; and if that was the effect of this proposition, or if I could think that such would be the effect of it, I would go with the gentleman to the fullest extent; "the dear people," to the contrary, notwithstanding.

Now, that is not what the people want; a constitution that may be amended and torn to pieces by every legislature that may meet under it. If the committee that prepared and offered this report had not thrown sufficient guards about this matter, I would go with the gentleman from Wapello. But the gentleman from Wapello errs in supposing that this will be a sort of plaything for the General Assembly, and that they can at their will make these changes and alterations, and call upon the people continually to vote upon them. If the gentleman will carefully examine the provisions of this report, he will discover that it is so much guarded that it will take almost as much time to affect an amendment in this constitution as it would under the old one.

What must be done to obtain an amendment to the constitution under this article? In the first place, the matter must come up before a General Assembly and be discussed there; a majority of the members elected to each house must agree to the amendment; the publication of the proposed amendment must be made for three months before the election of the next general assembly. We have provided that the general assembly shall meet only every two years; and this second general assembly must pass the proposed amendment by a majority of all the members elected to either house. The people, when voting for the members of this general assembly, vote with direct reference to the pending amendment. The question is asked the candidate, Are you in favor of this amendment or not? And the people will vote according to their answers.

Thus is one safeguard provided here for the people. If they are opposed to the amendment, when they come to elect this second general assembly, they can send to the legislature a majority who would vote down the amendment.

So the gentleman from Wapello will perceive that our "dear people" are safe, and he and I have gained all we want in that particular. We have protected the people by requiring that they shall vote directly in reference to this matter, before it shall be brought up in the general assembly to torment them before their time. If the majority of the last general assembly concur with the former one in the amendment, then it goes down to the people again.

And I will say to gentlemen, that if they will examine the constitutions of all of the states, they will find that all but six of them have provisions similar to this one. They adopted this provision after going through much experience and tribulation, having had conventions assembled to hold long sessions at great expense. Massachusetts, which has suffered as much from this matter as other states, has this provision in her constitution; New York has it in her constitution: while New Hampshire, Vermont, Kentucky, Virginia, Florida, and one other state, are the only states that have not this provision. Even Missouri has it in her constitution. I am in favor of this first section, as amended.

The question recurred upon the amendment

proposed by Mr. Solomon to the substitute proposed by Mr. Winchester to the majority report of the committee.

The substitute was as follows:

"If at any time the General Assembly shall think it necessary to revise or amend this constitution, they shall provide by law for a vote of the people for or against a convention, at the next ensuing election for members of the General Assembly. In case a majority of the people vote in favor of a convention, said General Assembly shall provide for an election of delegates to a convention, to be held within six months after the vote of the people in favor thereof."

The amendment was to the last sentence. Strike out the word "vote," and insert the words "shall have voted at such election;" also, strike out the word "six," and insert the word "twelve," so that the substitute, if so amended, would read as follows:

"If at any time the General Assembly shall think it necessary to revise or amend this constitution, they shall provide by law for a vote of the people for or against a convention, at the next ensuing election for members of the General Assembly. In case a majority of the people shall have voted at such election in favor of a convention, said General Assembly shall provide for an election of delegates to a convention, to be held within twelve months after the vote of the people in favor thereof."

The question being taken upon the amendment to the substitute, it was not agreed to.

The question being then taken upon the substitute, it was not agreed to.

Mr. GIBSON moved to amend the first section of the majority report by inserting after the words "General Assembly shall provide," the words "provided there shall not be more than one proposition submitted at one session of the legislature;" so that the section would then read as follows:

"Any amendment or amendments to this constitution may be proposed in either house of the General Assembly, and if the same shall be agreed to by a majority of the members elected to each of the two houses, such proposed amendment shall be entered on their journals, with the yeas and nays taken thereon, and referred to the legislature to be chosen at the next general election, and shall be published as provided by law for three months previous to the time of making such choice; and if in the General Assembly so next chosen, as aforesaid, such proposed amendment or amendments shall be agreed to by a majority of all the members elected to each house, then it shall be the duty of the General Assembly to submit such proposed amendment or amendments to the people in such manner and at such time as the General Assembly shall provide; provided there shall not be more than one proposition submitted at one session of the legislature; and if the people shall approve and ratify such amendment or amendments, by a majority of the electors qualified to vote for members of the General Assembly voting thereon, such amendment or amendments shall become a part of the constitution of this State."

Mr. GOWER. I would like to have these amendments to the Constitution submitted to the people whenever they are acted upon favorably by two-thirds of each House of any General Assembly; and if the people approve them I would have them become a part of the Constitution. I therefore offer the following as a substitute for the first section:

"Upon the petition of a respectable number of citizens of this State, the General Assembly may, by a vote of two-thirds therein concurring, propose amendments to this Constitution, which may be submitted to the people at their general election; and if a majority of those voting at said election shall vote in favor of said amendments the same shall become a part of the Constitution of this State."

Mr. GIBSON. The phraseology of this substitute is rather indefinite. It says, "Upon the petition of a respectable number of citizens of this State," &c. A number may be very few and yet be respectable. A half dozen may be a very respectable number, and yet it is not very numerous.

Mr. GOWER. I think if a petition of any number of our citizens is presented to our Legislature, that is a respectable number; and it is for the Legislature to consider if the prayers of the petitioners is worthy of their action; and if two-thirds of the Legislature act in favor of the amendment prayed for, I think it should be submitted to the people for their action.

The objection I have to this first section is the one that has been noticed by the gentleman from Henry, [Mr. Clarke.] It is too tedious, unnecessarily so, in its operation. Under the substitute I propose, we can get an expression of the wishes of the people much more speedily, and I think quite as effectively.

The question was then taken upon the substitute proposed by Mr. Gower, for the first seccion, and it was not agreed to.

The question recurred upon the amendment proposed by Mr. Gibson.

Mr. HALL. I would propose the following as a substitute for this first section:

"In case the General Assembly shall deem the amendment of any article of this Constitution important, they may provide by law for the submission of the amendment proposed to the vote of the people at the next succeeding general election; and if the proposed amendment shall receive a majority of all the votes given at said election, the amendment so proposed shall be declared adopted, and shall become a part of the Constitution of this State. No more than one article of this Constitution shall be amended under this section in any one year. All amendments proposed under this section shall be definitely and specifically defined, using the very words proposed for the amendment, which, with the law submitting it, shall be published at least three months prior to the election."

This report, I think, was mostly drawn from the provisions in the constitution of the State of New York. It would meet my views entirely if we had annual sessions of the Legislature, as they have in New York. But we have provided for biennial sessions only, and hence it would take a long time to make even the most trivial amendment to our Constitution; and I, therefore, think it is essential to make the change in this section that I have proposed. The amendment I propose will just exactly meet the case provided for by the New York Constitution. The very next election after an amendment has been passed upon by the Legislature it can be submitted to the people, and if a majority of the people, voting at that election, vote for the amendment, it will then become a part of the Constitution.

This is a very simple and ready plan of correcting any defects that may be found in the Constitution. There can be a general revision in that way, and only one article is to be amended at a time. It seems to me that the proposition I have submitted must meet the views of those gentlemen who have spoken upon this subject.

Mr. HARRIS. The proposition of the gentleman from Des Moines, [Mr. Hall,] seems to contemplate that no amendments proposed to the Constitution shall relate to subjects outside of the Constitution. If that is the understanding, then I shall be in favor of his amendment.

Mr. HALL. If there are any little errors or defects in this Constitution, the amendment I propose will enable the people to correct them speedily; or it will enable them to substitute a new section, or to amend and change one in any one of the articles. That is the proposition; it is for temporary amendments.

Mr. HARRIS. I would prefer simply to see the section we have had reported to us by the committee so amended as to require two-thirds of all the members elected to each House of the General Assembly to vote in favor of any proposed amendment, instead of a majority, as the section now stands.

Mr. WILSON. Does the gentleman from Appanoose, [Mr. Harris,] propose two-thirds as the vote of the second General Assembly elected by the people for the express purpose of preparing this amendment to the Constitution? I think if the people have elected a Legislature directly upon that issue, that a majority vote is sufficient.

Mr. HARRIS. I am willing that the principle of the two-third vote shall apply only to the first legislature, and have a majority vote sufficient in the legislature chosen by the people after the subject has been presented to them.

Mr. CLARKE, of Johnson. Then you will never amend your constitution.

Mr. CLARKE, of Henry. I would suggest to the gentleman from Des Moines [Mr. Hall] that it is a great deal easier for members to consider amendments to a section than substitutes for the whole of the section. The substitute he has proposed embraces many points, some of which I concur with him in considering worthy of adoption, while there are others to which I disagree. Now if these different subjects were proposed, each separate and distinct, by way of amendment to the section, we could then sooner and more easily arrive at a conclusion in the matter.

It is an objection the gentleman raises, that of biennial sessions. But I do not agree with him in saying that but one article of the constitution shall be amended at any one session of the legislature. I would suggest that if we have the questions proposed directly to the people—and in other constitutions they never go back to the people—and there is a check of a two-thirds vote put upon the legislature, so that two-thirds of each house concurring they may propose an amendment and send it immediately to the people to be voted upon, if it receives a majority of the votes cast, it is to become a part of the constitution. This is all that we can ask here. And we can get at that much more easily if we can have the different points presented to us here as separate amendments, than the whole in a substitute. I shall therefore vote against the substitute.

Mr. CLARKE, of Johnson. I shall vote against the substitute though in one respect I prefer it to the section as reported by the committee. The main objection I have to the substitute is this; from the explanation given by the gentleman who proposed it, [Mr. Hall], it is contemplated to give the legislature power to cure mere defects in the constitution as we leave it. Now I want something in the constitution which will enable the people to reach not merely defects, not the mere phraseology of the constitution, but to enable them to enlarge it and make it more suitable to the increased population and business wants of the State.

Hence I prefer the report of the majority as it is, and do not see that there can be any improvement upon it. It is true that this majority report will perhaps cause five years to pass before an amendment can be perfected to become a part of the constitution, for it must pass two legislatures and be submitted to a vote of the people. I would prefer, if the matter could be so arranged, to have these amendments submitted to the people after one legislature has passed upon them, and let the people then decide upon them. But I am willing to take this report, for fear I cannot get what I desire.

It seems to me that under the provisions reported by this committee, there is no danger of hasty and ill-advised changes in the fundamental law, by which the rights or interests of the people can be injuriously affected. It seems to me that if we provide that all amendments or changes in the constitution when they shall have passed a General Assembly shall be thrown before the people and become questions for their consideration when they come to select candidates for the next General Assembly, if the questions proposed by way of amendments are at all material and important, the members of the legislature will be chosen with reference to them.

I think this is fair. It is placing this matter where it properly belongs, in the hands of the people, and no gentleman need be alarmed for fear of hasty legislation in retaining this power where it legitimately belongs.

As to the second section of this report, I am somewhat doubtful about the necessity of having a convention every ten years to revise the constitution. I think it very likely, however, from the present aspect of our work here, that we shall need another convention in much less time than ten years. But it seems to me, that if we place in the constitution a general clause authorizing the legislature to provide for taking a vote of the people upon the subject of calling a convention, there need not, and ought not to be, any fixed time within which this power shall be exercised.

But, as I said before, I am willing to take this for fear I shall not be able to get anything better. We are spending some time upon this subject, and, perhaps, it is well enough to do so. But I dissent wholly from the views of the gentlemen upon the other side, that there should be no provision made in the constitution for its amendment, unless by calling a convention for that purpose. I think the experience of the past ten years in Iowa, that if there had been a provision similar to the one before us, in the old constitution, the necessity for calling this convention would have been obviated, and all this eloquence would have been lost to the world.

I hope this convention will look at this matter in a practical point of view. We are entering upon untried fields; we are about to try new systems of economy; we are opening the door to legislation that will be new to the people of this State. We do not know how it may affect their interests. We do not know but what, when these internal improvements are in the course of construction, when these banks of issue are at work, throwing their paper before the country, some emergency may arise which will call for speedy action in the amendment of this constitution. I want to provide a way to do it, and it does seem to me that the provision made by this majority report is fair and safe.

Mr. HALL. The gentleman from Johnson [Mr. Clarke] clearly does not understand the substitute I have offered. It follows out the principle of this report, except that it avoids the necessity of the action of two legislatures upon the amendment. I cannot myself see the necessity of one legislature proposing an amendment to the constitution, publishing it with the view that it shall enter into the next canvass for the election of members of the legislature, and this very amendment is to be the subject of the action of the second legislature, and if they approve of it, they shall then provide for submitting to the people this amendment, which was proposed more than two years before, which has been acted on by the electors in the mean time, then acted upon by a subsequent legislature, and is then to be published and voted on by the people. All this looks to me as rather unnecessary.

Now, I would not object to this at all, if we had annual sessions of the legislature. But with only biennial sessions of the legislature, it seems to me that it is putting off too long what may be essential amendments to the constitution. We obtain, under this report with biennial sessions in about four years and a half what we would obtain in about two years, if we had annual sessions.

The substitute I propose simply says, that if the legislature deem it important and necessary, to amend any one article of the constitution, they shall propose the amendment in so many words, and at the next general election the people of the State shall vote upon that amendment and if a majority of all the votes cast at that election shall be in favor of the amendment, it shall then become a part of the constitution. The process is a simple, plain and practical one, and the object sought is brought about in just one-half the time that it can be done in the other way.

There is no argument in the idea that propositions for amendment will be made by the legislature merely out of a feeling of levity, and without thought. We should treat this matter as if men of integrity and honesty, men who would understand and abide by the oaths they will take, will be in the general assembly.

I believe a provision for amending the constitution should be introduced here, and I do not believe it should be fettered as the majority report does fetter it. I believe the legislature should be allowed larger liberty to propose these incidental amendments, which may be found necessary after this constitution goes into operation. This is all I propose to accomplish by my substitute, and all I desire to accomplish.

My proposition preserves the main principles of the report of the committee. If the gentleman from Johnson, [Mr. Clarke,] had thoroughly understood my proposition, he could not have better expressed its working than he did in stating what he desired to accomplish. I understood him to be in favor of getting rid of this two years' delay, and that is what I propose here. Otherwise, my proposition is substantially the report of the committee.

Mr. CLARKE, of Johnson. I agree with the gentleman in what he has said as being important for us to provide here. Still, I do not think I have misapprehended his substitute. As I understand it, it only provides for one amendment to be submitted to the people for their action at any one time. If the gentleman will modify his proposition in that respect, then I shall be more inclined to favor it.

Mr. HALL. I will do that very cheerfully, and modify my proposition so that every amendment to an article shall be submitted as a separate and distinct proposition.

Mr. CLARKE, of Johnson. The only trouble then will be this: Suppose that there are two articles which require immediate amendment; they cannot both be amended in the same year.

Mr. HALL. I will modify my substitute to that effect, and provide only that the vote shall be taken by the people upon each amendment separately, and let them be made to one or more articles of the Constitution.

Mr. CLARKE, of Johnson. If the gentleman will do that, then I will be satisfied with his substitute..

Mr. CLARKE, of Henry. I suppose amendments would be in order to this section before we take the question upon the substitute.

The CHAIRMAN. The ruling in Committee of the Whole has been to defer amendments until after the vote has been taken upon substitutes. But the Chair is of opinion that amendments to the section, for which this substitute is proposed, would now be in order.

Mr. CLARK, of Alamakee. It seems to me that we should decide whether we will take this substitute, or the majority report as the basis of our action. After we have done that we can go on and make such amendments as we deem proper.

Mr. SPRINGER. (The President.) The offering of a substitute for a section is equivalent to a motion to strike out and insert. When this motion is made, and before putting it to the question, it is in order to amend both the section proposed to be stricken out and that which is proposed to be inserted.

The CHAIRMAN. Is it in order to move amendments to both the report and the substitute?

Mr. SPRINGER. Either or both of them can be amended now. That rule is not only laid down in Cushing's Manual, which is our authority here, but it is also laid down in Jefferson's Manual; and I notice that it is distinctly laid down in the reports of the Massachusetts Convention.

Mr. PALMER· I suppose it would be first in order to amend the section as it now stands.

Mr. SPRINGER. So I understand it.

The CHAIRMAN. The question will then be first taken upon the amendment of the gentleman from Marion, [Mr. Gibson,] to the first section.

The amendment was stated to be as follows:

Insert after the words "General Assembly shall provide," the words "provided there shall not be more than one proposition submitted at any one session of the Legislature."

So that the section will then read—

"Any amendment or amendments to this Constitution may be proposed in either House of the General Assembly; and if the same shall be agreed to by a majority of the members elected to each of the two Houses, such proposed amendment shall be entered on their journals, with the yeas and nays taken thereon, and referred to the Legislature to be chosen at the next general election, and shall be published, as provided by law, for three months previous to the time of making such choice; and if, in the General Assembly so next chosen as aforesaid, such proposed amendment or amendments shall be agreed to, by a majority of all the members elected to each House, then it shall be the duty of the General Assembly to submit such proposed amendment or amendments to the people in such manner, and at such times as the General Assembly shall provide; provided that there shall not be more than one proposition submitted at any one session of the Legislature; and if the people shall approve and ratify such amendment or amendments by a majority of the electors qualified to vote for members of the General Assembly, voting thereon, such amendment or amendments shall become a part of the Constitution of this State."

Mr. GIBSON. My object in offering this amendment was to so provide that the General Assembly should not propose more than one amendment to the Constitution at any one session, and thereby prevent the throwing of a multitude of propositions before the people at the same time, by which the minds of the people would become, to some extent, confused; and also to prevent, as much as possible, a system of log rolling, by which some amendments to the Constitution, favoring one section of the State, would be made to assist in getting through other amendments favoring other portions of the State, and the interests of the people and the desires of the State at large would be overcome by the practice of swapping votes. I want to remedy this thing, and have but one article of the Constitution amended at any one session of the Legislature.

The question being taken upon Mr. Gibson's amendment, it was rejected.

Mr. CLARKE, of Henry. I move to amend this first section by inserting after the word "majority," where it first occurs, the words "of two-thirds;" also strike out the words "and referred to the legislature to be chosen at the next general election;" and the words "previous to the time of making such choice; and if, in the General Assembly so next chosen as aforesaid, such proposed amendment or amendments shall be agreed to, by a majority of all the members elected to each house, then it shall be the duty of the General Assembly to submit such proposed amendment or amendments to the people in such manner, and at such time as the General Assembly shall provide;" and insert in lieu of these last words proposed to be stricken out, the words, "after which it shall be submitted to a vote of the people." The section would then read as follows:

"Any amendment or amendments to this constitution may be proposed in either house of the General Assembly; and if the same shall be agreed to by a majority of two-thirds of the members elected to each of the two houses, such proposed amendment shall be entered on their journals, with the yeas and nays taken thereon, and shall be published, as provided by law, for three months; after which it shall be submitted to a vote of the people, and if the people shall approve and ratify such amendment or amendments by a majority of the electors qualified to vote for members of the General Assembly, voting thereon, such amendment or amendments shall become a part of the constitution of this State."

I propose this amendment of the section to obviate the objection made by the gentleman from Des Moines [Mr. Hall] that by our plan of biennial sessions of the legislature it would require four years or more to obtain an amendment to the constitution. I think the people will be prepared to vote upon these amendments after they shall have been published three months in the papers of the State; and if a majority of the people of the State, voting directly upon the proposed amendments to the constitution, shall be in favor of them, they should be allowed to make those amendments.

Some other amendments will be necessary in this section. For instance, if the gentleman from Des Moines [Mr. Hall] wishes to propose an amendment, requiring that each proposed modification or change of the constitution shall be separately submitted to the people, I shall have no objection.

Mr. WILSON. I certainly prefer this section as it was reported by the committee, to anything that has been proposed in lieu of it. And I greatly prefer it to the amendment of the gentleman from Henry [Mr. Clarke]. If we adopt the provision requiring a two-thirds vote in the legislature, before that body shall submit any amendment to the people, we shall never get an amendment to the constitution submitted to them. I see no reason why a two-thirds vote should be required to submit an amendment to the people, when the people have to pass upon it, after it has been so submitted. A majority vote, certainly, ought to be sufficient to submit any amendment to the people and they can then approve or reject it, as they think proper.

I believe that, with all the amendments we may make to this section, we shall not make it any better than it now is. I think we should stand by the report of the committee. It throws all the safeguards necessary around this subject of amending the constitution, and at the same time does away with the objections which have been raised by gentlemen upon this floor, that this amending the constitution through the legislature looks too much like statutory enactments. It provides a sufficiently careful method of amending the constitution. First, the legislature are to act upon any proposed amendment; if they act favorably upon it, then it is to be published for thee months before the next general election; then the people are to act in selecting the members of the next General Assembly; that General Assembly are to act upon the proposed amendment, and if they act favorably, it is to be again submitted to the people. Now it seems to me that a majority vote, all the way through, is sufficient.

I do not believe that we can better this section any, let us try as much as we may. I am satisfied that its provisions have operated well in those States where they have been adopted, among which is New York, from whose constitution, I believe, this section was taken.

Mr. CLARKE, of Henry. They have annual sessions in New York.

Mr. MARVIN. The difficulty appears to grow out of the length of time required, before we can secure an amendment to the constitution, though its necessity may be ever so obvious. It cannot be done in this State, under this provision, in much less than five years. It can be done in less time in New York, under the same provision, because they have annual sessions of the legislature. I would propose an amendment to this section, which, I think, will obviate the difficulty to which I have referred. The amendment I propose is to strike out the words "and referred to the legislature to be chosen at the next general election;" and also the words "previous to the time of making such choice; and if, in the General Assembly so next chosen as aforesaid, such proposed amendment or amendments shall be agreed to, by a majority of all the members elected to each house."

The section would then read as follows:

"Any amendment or amendments to this constitution may be proposed in either house of the General Assembly; and if the same shall be agreed to by a majority of the members elected to each of the two houses, such proposed amendment shall be entered on their journals, with the yeas and nays taken thereon, and shall be published, as provided by law, for three months; then it shall be the duty of the General Assembly to submit such proposed amendment or amendments to the people in such manner and at such time as the General Assembly shall provide; and if the people shall approve and ratify such amendment or amendments by a majority of the electors qualified to vote for members of the General Assembly, voting thereon, such amendment or amendments shall become a part of the constitution of this State."

Mr. WILSON. I desire to say a word in reply to the gentleman from Jones [Mr. Marvin]. He seems to think that it would take five years under this section to obtain an amendment to the constitution. I do not so understand it. This section provides that "any amendment or amendments to this constitution may be proposed in either house of the General Assembly," and that may be done at any time. For instance, at the session of the General Assembly held this winter, there might have been an amendment proposed to the constitution. if there had been such a section as this in it, that amendment would be submitted to the people at their next general election, when they would pass upon it in their selection of the next General Assembly, and if that General Assembly should pass favorably upon the proposed amendment, they could submit it to the people whenever they think proper to do so, at a special election, or at the April election; that is left for the general assembly to determine. So that in that way it would not take more than two years for the people to secure any amendment to the constitution they might desire.

The question was stated to be upon the amendment proposed by Mr. Clarke, of Henry.

Mr. CLARKE, of Henry. All I desire to accomplish is to get this report so as to meet the views of a majority of the convention. Perhaps I do not understand the amendment of the gentleman from Jones [Mr. Marvin.]

Mr. MARVIN. The only real difference between my proposition and the proposition of the gentleman from Henry, is that he requires a two-thirds vote in the General Assembly, and I require but a majority vote.

Mr. CLARKE, of Henry. In regard to that, the gentleman from Jefferson [Mr. Wilson] is mistaken, in supposing that a two-thirds vote cannot be obtained.

Mr. WILSON. I do not say that it never can be obtained, but I made use of the general expression that it could not be obtained.

Mr. CLARKE, of Henry. It has been generally held by every one who has discussed the matter of amendments to the constitution, that they should not be made except in imperative cases, and in such cases two-thirds of the members of both houses would most generally concur. If it was a mere party movement, it would be impossible to get a two-thirds vote. But if it was a matter of general intererest, not a party matter at all, but a matter in which the interests of the State were involved, there certainly would be no difficulty in obtaining a two-thirds vote. But party, or trivial questions could not obtain this two-thirds vote, and for that reason, I incorporated that provision in my amendment.

In regard to the other points raised by the gentleman from Des Moines [Mr. Hall], I concur with him that an objectionable feature in this report, is the time required in which to procure an amendment to the constitution. It may take four or five years before we could obtain an amendment, though ever so important, and for the want of which the interests of the State may suffer most seriously. I think there are sufficient guards about this subject of amending the constitution; this two-thirds vote will guard it sufficiently.

Mr. WILSON. I will simply say, that in case the amendment of the gentleman from Henry [Mr. Clarke] should not be adopted, I propose to offer an additional section, which I have copied from the constitution of Indiana, and which is the section which was referred to by the gentleman from Des Moines [Mr. Hall]. It is as follows:

"If two or more amendments shall be submitted at the same time, they shall be submitted in such manner that the electors shall vote for or against each of such amendments separately, and while any amendment or amendments which shall have been agreed upon by one General Assembly shall be awaiting the action of a succeeding General Assembly, or of the electors, no additional amendment or amendments shall be proposed."

Mr. CLARKE, of Henry. I will withdraw my amendment for the amendment of the gentleman from Jones [Mr. Marvin.]

Mr. CLARKE, of Johnson. I desired to propose a slight change in the amendment of the gentleman from Jones, which I trust will be accepted. I propose to strike out the following:

"—and referred to the legislature to be chosen at the next general election, and shall be published as provided by law, three months previous to the time of making such choice; and if, in the General Assembly so next chosen, as aforesaid, such proposed amendment or amendments shall be agreed to, by a majority of all the members elected to each house, then it shall be the duty of the General Assembly to submit such proposed amendment or amendments to the people in such manner and at such time as the General Assembly shall provide."

And insert the following:

"—and shall be published as provided by by law, for three months, after which it shall be submitted to the people."

Also to insert after the word "thereon," where it last occurs, the word "separately." The section will then read:

"Any amendment or amendments to this constitution may be proposed in either house of the General Assembly; and if the same shall be agreed to by a majority of the members elected to each of the two houses, such proposed amendment shall be entered on their journals with the yeas and nays taken thereon, and shall be published as provided by law, for three months, after which it shall be submitted to the people; and if the people shall approve and ratify such amendment or amendments, by a majority of the electors qualified to vote for members of the General Assembly, voting thereon, separately, such amendment or amendments shall become a part of the constitution of this State."

Mr. MARVIN. I will withdraw my amendment for the amendment of the gentleman from Johnson (Mr. Clarke).

The question was stated to be upon the amendment proposed by Mr. Clarke, of Johnson.

Mr. WILSON. Does the gentleman provide in his proposition that these amendments to be submitted by the General Assembly to the people, shall be published as provided by law?

Suppose that the General Assembly make provision for publication only in one newspaper?

Mr. CLARKE, of Johnson. That can be amended.

Mr. WILSON. I would suggest that they be published in one newspaper in each county.

Mr. CLARKE, of Johnson. There is one objection to the proposition of the gentleman from Jefferson (Mr. Wilson). We will be making a very large bill of expenses if we require this publication in every county in the state. I think the manner of publication may be properly left to the General Assembly.

Mr. WILSON. Is there any better way of publishing these amendments to the people, than to have them published in one newspaper in each county?

Mr. CLARKE, of Johnson. There may not be a better way, but I think there may be a cheaper one. I would prefer to leave to the General Assembly to provide the mode of publication. I think it would be going a little too much into detail for us to do that here.

Mr. CLARKE, of Henry. I would propose to amend the amendment by striking out the word "separately," and adding the following to the section:

"Provided that if more than one amendment be submitted, they shall be submitted in such manner and form that the people may vote for or against each amendment."

The section would then read as follows:

"Any amendment or amendments to this Constitution may be proposed in either House of the General Assembly; and if the same shall be agreed to by a majority of the members elected to each of the two Houses, such proposed amendment shall be entered on their journals, with the yeas and nays taken thereon, and shall be published as provided by law for three months, after which it shall be submitted to the people; and if the people shall approve and ratify such amendment or amendments by a majority of the electors qualified to vote for members of the General Assembly, voting thereon, such amendment or amendments shall become a part of the Constitution of this State; provided that if more than one amendment be submitted, they shall be submitted in such manner and form that the people may vote for or against each amendment."

The question was taken upon the amendment to the amendment, and it was not agreed to.

The question was then taken upon the amendment proposed by Mr. Clarke, of Johnson, and it was rejected.

No other amendments being offered to the section—

The CHAIRMAN stated the question to recur upon the substitute proposed by Mr. Hall for the first section of the report of the majority of the committee.

Mr. HALL. I have modified my amendment so that it will read as follows:

"In case the General Assembly shall deem the amendment of any article of the constitution important, they may provide by law for the submission of the amendment proposed to the people at the next succeeding general election; and if the proposed amendment shall receive a majority of all the votes given at said election, the amendment so proposed shall be declared adopted, and become a part of the constitution of this State. All amendments proposed under this section shall be definitely and specifically defined, using the very words proposed for the amendment, which, with the law submitting it, shall be published at least three months prior to the election. If two or more amendments shall be submitted at the same time, they shall be submitted in such manner that the electors shall vote for or against each of said amendments separately; and while any amendment, or amendments, which shall have been agreed upon by one General Assembly, shall be awaiting the action of the electors, no additional amendment or amendments shall be proposed."

Mr. WILSON. I do not see much difference between this proposition and the one which has just been voted down. I wish to call the attention of members to one thing. Under the operation of this proposed substitute, it will take some two years to procure an amendment to the constitution. Under the operation of the section as reported by the committee, with all the safeguards thrown around it, it will take but a little more than two years, probably some three or four months more. Now if there is only that difference of time, I think the committee better stand by the report; it is decidedly the safest.

Mr. HALL. The gentleman is certainly mistaken. The proposition I have submitted is substantially that of the committee, except as regards the time, and the separate votes upon the amendments. A legislature now in session may pass a law, and if it is published the people can vote upon it, and the constitution will be amended as soon as their vote will be proclaimed. But under the report of the committee, a legislature now in session may propose an amendment, and it would be published, and the legislature that meets in 1858 would pass upon it, and if they approved it, it might be submitted to the people at their October election in 1858.

Mr. WILSON. The gentleman is certainly mistaken as to the report of the committee. It provides that—

"Any amendment or amendments to this Constitution may be proposed in either House of the General Assembly, and if the same shall be agreed to, by a majority of the members elected to each of the two Houses, such proposed amendment shall be entered on their journals, with the yeas and nays taken thereon, and referred to the Legislature to be chosen at the next general election, and shall be published, as provided by law, for three months previous to the time of making such choice, and if, in the General Assembly so next chosen as aforesaid, such proposed amendment or amendments shall be agreed to, by a majority of all the members elected to each House, then it shall be the duty of the General Assembly to submit such proposed amendment or amendments to the people in such manner, and at such time as the General Assembly shall provide."

They may provide for the submission of these amendments to the people at a special election. There are two legislatures to act upon each amendment.

Mr. HALL. Under my proposition there is but one.

Mr. WILSON. I will take the gentleman's own proposition. Suppose the legislature is in session next winter, and it starts a proposed amendment to the constitution. At the October election in 1858 the people would vote directly in reference to it, and the legislature of 1859 could submit it to the people at a special election. And there would not be a difference of more than three or four months between the time under the operation of the section of the committee's report, and the time under the operation of the substitute of the gentleman from Des Moines, [Mr. Hall.]

Mr. HALL. It makes a difference of one year.

Mr. PARVIN. While I am in favor of having a clause in the constitution, by which it can be amended without the necessity of calling a convention for that purpose, I would not throw the doors wide open, so that upon any little excitement the constitution might be changed without due reflection and deliberation.

The objection I have to the substitute of the gentleman from Des Moines, [Mr. Hall,] is that it does so open the doors to this change, in my opinion; it does it by providing that amendments may be proposed by one legislature, which may submit them to the people, and they may be passed under some local or temporary excitement. Now while I desire a provision which will permit of the constitution being changed, without calling a convention, I do not wish to have those changes made upon the spur of the moment.

I hope, therefore, that the committee of the whole will adhere to the report of the committee, and require the amendments to be made to the constitution to pass through two legislatures before they become a part of the constitution. I would have any amendment, passed by one general assembly, discussed by the people until another general assembly meets. Anything of a transitory nature would wear out by that time, and the second general assembly would not pass it, or if they did, the people would not ratify it. I have voted against all the amendments that have been proposed here, because I have not heard any yet that I thought were better than the report of the committee.

The question being then taken upon the substitute proposed by Mr. Hall, for the first section of the report of the majority of the committee, upon a division, it was not agreed to, ayes 14, noes 15.

No other amendments being offered to the first section—

Section two was then read as follows:

"At the general election to be held in the year one thousand eight hundred and sixty-seven, and in each tenth year thereafter, and also at such time as the General Assembly may, by law, provide, the question, 'Shall there be a convention to revise the constitution, and amend the same?' shall be decided by the electors qualified to vote for members of the General Assembly; and in case a majority of the electors so qualified, voting at such election, shall decide in favor of a convention for such purpose, the General Assembly, at its next session, shall provide by law for the election of delegates to such Convention."

Mr. TRAER. I move to amend this section by adding after the word "purpose," the following:

"The qualified electors of the State shall proceed at the next general election to choose delegates to said Convention upon the basis provided for the State Senate; and said Convention when assembled shall have full powers to revise and amend the constitution; and to do all things necessary to carry out the objects for which they were convened. Said delegates shall receive compensation *per diem* the same as that allowed to members of the General Assembly."

I offer this amendment in order to carry out the views I expressed this morning in regard to giving the people the right to amend the constitution without referring the matter to the General Assembly at all. I desire to secure to the people of this State the right to make and revise their organic law without the interference of the legislature. I look upon the representatives, when assembled here in legislature, as agents acting for the people; and in order that they may have some power to act, it is necessary to guarantee to them certain rights, which we do in the constitution. In other words, the constitution gives them authority to act as agents for the people.

I believe we all agree upon one question, that the people are the source of power; or in other words, that all political power was originally vested in the people of this government. If that be the case, and we are all agreed upon that point, then the question arises—how, or in what way, are we going to delegate this power to our representatives in the legislature? I hold that we should do the same, as any individual would do, when he makes another individual his agent to carry out certain prescribed objects; reserve the right of countermanding the authority we give our agents at any time we may see fit. That is just what I desire to do in the constitution. We delegate to our Representatives the right through the constitution to represent us; and according to the amendment just adopted, we are going to guarantee to them the right to amend the fundamental law to a certain extent.

What I desire to get at, is to incorporate in the Constitution a clause which will enable the people, whenever they see fit, to resume that right and act without the authority of the legislature. When we have agents to act for us, I hold it is a contradiction in terms that we should give them the right to say when we may or may not act.

As I said before, the only question that arises is this: Can the people of the State of Iowa—after we have made this Constitution and placed the article in it which gentlemen here propose—amend it without the authority or consent of those whom they have delegated to represent them in the Legislature? I hold that they can. As I referred, in the morning, to the decision in the Rhode Island case, I would refer gentlemen again to it, from the fact that it substantiates the doctrine that I laid down, that the only way, unless such a provision I have proposed be adopted, that the people would have to change this Constitution after it was adopted, if the Legislature should refuse to act in this case, would be to change their fundamental law by other means—that of revolution.

Such is the decision of Chief Justice Taney of the Supreme Court of the United States.

I think gentlemen will see the object I have in view without any further remarks from me at this time. I desire to have other gentlemen express their opinions upon this subject. If the amendment I have offered now be voted down, I shall bring it up again in Convention, where I will have an opportunity of placing gentlemen upon the record.

I desire to know who are and who are not in favor of maintaining the rights of the people. This talking about, and acting upon, the rights of the people, is quite a different thing.

Mr. GIBSON. The gentleman from Benton, [Mr. Traer], rather amuses me in the position he has taken in this matter. He has taken occasion to represent the Democratic party as refusing to provide for calling a Convention to amend the Constitution. What is the condition of matters now? Does not his own party have a very large majority in the State? And this Constitution that they are now framing, I suppose, as a matter of course, they will claim to be a Republican Constitution. Now, then, while they have the possession of both branches of the Legislature, and full possession of the State, what is the trouble? Why, the gentleman from Benton [Mr. Traer] acts as though he was afraid that in a year or two the State would change hands, and would get into the hands of the Democratic party, and that they would not be allowed to change the fundamental law which they are fixing up here. If they make a good constitution here, why this cry against the legislature—against the usurpation of the sovereignty of the people by the legislature, and a desire to have this question go directly before the people? Is the gentleman afraid to trust the people? Is he afraid to trust his Republican legislature?

It seems to me that there is a gross inconsistency here. I have yet to learn that whenever there is a majority of the sovereign people of the State in favor of a measure, the legislature will not grant it. The legislature, as I understand it, are nothing but the servants of the people to carry out their wishes, and the people have a right to demand of them what they want, and that body dare not refuse them. This is the doctrine of the Democratic party; but whether it is the doctrine of the Republican party, I am not able to say, as I am not very well versed in the politics of that party. Perhaps I may be after a while, and I hope I may. I can certainly see no good reason or propriety in retaining the provision that the people shall vote upon this subject every ten years.

Mr. WILSON. I would inquire of the gentleman whether his opposition to the Republican party is the result of ignorance?

Mr. GIBSON. It may possibly be so. What I was about to say was this: that I can see no good reason for retaining that clause in this section, requiring the people to vote for or against an amendment of the Constitution, unless there is some expression in favor of it. It is saying to the people that they must decide this question once in ten years, or, in other words, it is saying in substance to the people, you are changeable, and what you do now you will want to undo in ten years. I take it for granted that it is sufficient to leave this matter in the hands of the Legislature; and I suppose it will be in the future as it is now, whenever the people really demand a convention, and demand amendments to the Constitution, the Legislature will grant that privilege.

Mr. HALL. The gentleman from Benton, [Mr. Traer,] has seen proper to allude to the celebrated case of Luther vs. Borden, in the 7th of Howard's Reports. I wish to read a little of the doctrine contained in that case, as I think it may enlighten the gentleman. I will read a few extracts:

"But in 1776 the American people adopted principles more especially adapted to their condition. They can be traced through the confederation and the present Constitution, and our principles of liberty have now become exclusively American. They are distinctly marked. We changed the government where it required change; where we found a good one we left it. Conservatism is visible throughout. Let me state what I understand these principles to be.

The first is, that the people are the source of all political power. Every one believes th s. Where else is there any power? There is no hereditary legislature, no large property, no throne, no primogeniture. Every body may buy and sell. There is an equality of rights. Any one who should look to any other source of power than the people would be as much out of his mind as Don Quixote, who imagined that he saw things which did not exist.

"Our American mode of government does not draw any power from tumultuous assemblies. If anything is established in that way, it is deceptive. It is true that at the Revolution governments were forcibly destroyed. But what did the people then do? They got together and took the necessary steps to frame new governments, as they did in England when James the Second abdicated. William asked Parliament to assemble and provide for the case. It was a revolution, not because there was a change in the person of the sovereign, but because there was a hiatus which must be filled. It has been said by the opposing counsel, that the people can get together, call themselves so many thousands, and establish whatever government they please. But others must have the same right, We have then a stormy South American liberty. supported by arms to-day and crushed by arms to-morrow. Our theory places a beautiful face on liberty, and making it powerful for good, producing no tumults. When it is necessary to ascertain the will of the people, the Legislature must provide the means of ascertaining it.

"Always these conventions were called together by the Legislature, and no single constitution has ever been altered by means of a convention gotten up by means of mass meetings. There must be an authentic mode of ascertaining the public will, somehow and somewhere. If not, it is a government of the strongest and most numerous. It is said that, if the Legislature refuses to call a convention, the case then resembles the Holy Alliance of Europe, whose doctrine it was, that all changes must originate with the sovereign. But there is no resemblance whatever. I say that the will of the people must prevail, but that there must be some mode of finding out that will."

Mr. TRAER. I would ask the gentleman whether he reads from the opinion of Judge Taney, or from Mr. Webster's argument.

Mr. HALL. I read from the argument made by Mr. Webster in that case.

Mr. TRAER. The gentleman from Des Moines [Mr. Hall], when he rose, said he was going to give me some good democratic authority upon this question. But what authority has he presented here? Why, the gentleman who was always arrayed in opposition to the political views of Mr. Webster, now comes forward and offers his opinions as evidence of what democracy is. I do not understand by what process of reasoning the gentleman finds out that Webster was a democrat. I base the opinion I have expressed upon this question upon Chief Justice Taney's opinion, and not upon Mr. Webster's argument. It is an opinion which I suppose will have some weight in reference to this question, and I will now read it. Judge Taney says:

"No one, we believe, has ever doubted the proposition, that, according to the institutions of this country, the sovereignty of every State resides in the people of the State, and that they may alter and change their form of government at pleasure. But whether they have changed it or not, by abolishing an old government and established a new one in its place, is a question to be settled by political power. And when that power has decided, the courts are bound to take notice of that decision and follow it."

Again he suggests—

"If it be asked. what redress have the people if wronged in these matters, unless by resorting to the judiciary? the answer is the same as in all other political matters. In these, they go to the ballot boxes, or legislature, or executive, for redress of such as are within the jurisdiction of each, and to such as are not, to conventions and amendments of constitutions.

And when the former fail, and these last are forbidden by statute, all that is left in extreme cases where the suffering is intolerable, and the prospect of relief is good, by action of the people without the forms of law, is to do as did Hampden and Washington, venture action without the forms and abide the consequences."

Unless we provide in the constitution some such method as I have suggested, by which the people will retain the right to amend the constitution without the consent of the legislature, there will be no way to amend it unless they go through the legislative form for that purpose, except by revolution, and they would then become amenable in every effort to amend it, as they did in Rhode Island, to the charge of treason. If we delegate this power to our agents without retaining any authority to take that power back again, we cannot get it back, Judge Taney says, without revolution. I claim that we should insert a provision in the constitution that should retain the power to amend it in the hands of the people, and enable them, in case they get a democratic Governor, who will veto all their bills in regard to the amendments to the constitution, to amend it without his consent.

Gentlemen say, that by the amendment I have offered here, I am afraid to trust the people. My object is to incorporate a provision in the constitution, that shall protect the people. The gentleman from Marion [Mr. Gibson] tells me that I am afraid to trust the present republican party. My desire in this matter is not to protect the republican party, or any party, but to protect the people.

I leave it to every intelligent democrat upon this floor, if the wishes of the people were not thwarted in their efforts for a constitutional convention four years ago, by the action of the democratic Governor of this State. I defy any gentleman to prove the contrary. I say that the legislature expressed the will of the people, when they passed a bill providing for submitting the question of a constitutional convention to the people of this State. The will of the people in this respect was not only expressed through the ballot box, but through the action of their representatives; and yet the Governor vetoed the bill. The Governor placed himself in direct opposition to the will of the people, basing his action, as he alleged, on constitutional grounds. The legislature immediately remedied the objections which the Governor found in the law and the Governor then defeated the wishes of the people by pocketing the bill.

Mr. HALL. I do not rise here to defend Mr. Webster as a constitutional lawyer, for his opinions upon questions of constitutional law need no defence. All I contend for here, is to have this constitution left in a manner that, when it is amended, it shall be amended according to law. If I understand what democracy is —I mean American democracy—it is based upon the constitution and the laws, and it does not wish to leave anything for the people to do, when they are acting under the laws, that shall affect the interests of the country. That is what I understand by American democracy. This mass meeting legislation, which the gentleman approves, is not the kind of democracy I have been accustomed to revere; it is that democracy around which guards and checks are thrown for a great purpose. Even if these guards and checks are sometimes used improperly it is no argument against the propriety of having them. The best principle that can possibly be suggested may be abused when in bad hands; but this affords no argument against the exercise of the principle. I would be unwilling, in making this constitution, to adopt any principle, to call for any action, to impose any duty upon the people, unless in accordance with law, so that every person will know, what it should be. That is what I call democracy.

I assert again, the doctrine laid down in Mr. Webster's argument is the great American doctrine, the doctrine of our forefathers. It is the principle upon which our institutions rest, and which gives security to all; and it is that alone which can give permanency to our institutions. I do hope that the convention will take no step that will authorize mass meetings or conventions throughout the State to usurp, as it were, the authority of amending or adopting a new constitution. You never know when public sentiment is with you, as one mass meeting may declare one way, and another meeting another way. You have no rule to decide the matter, and you enter at once upon a wide field of conjecture, in which the stronger will overpower the weaker. I do not think it is necessary to go into an argument to show that this convention should not adopt any such wild scheme as that presented by the gentleman from Benton [Mr. Traer].

Mr. TRAER. What is the difference whether the will of the people is collected by constitutional or statute law?

Mr. HALL. I did not say that it would make any difference. I said distinctly that it should be according to law.

Mr. TRAER. My amendment provides for placing in the constitution a provision, by which the will of the people shall be collected. The gentleman from Des Moines wants to leave it to the legislature to say how the will of the people shall be collected. Mr. Webster says, that the will of the people, when regularly collected, is just as supreme as the will of the Emperor of Russia. The gentleman from Des Moines and myself agree upon that point. The only question then is, in what way shall we collect that will? I propose to provide in the constitution a way in which the people may go to work, and vote upon this question. Of course, a vote cast by the people will amount to just the same, whether it is ascertained under constitutional or statute law. I propose to incorporate a provision in the constitution whereby the people may have an opportunity to express their will through the ballot box, and when they have declared it, if a majority are in favor of calling a convention I propose that they shall then hold an election for delegates, without asking the permission of the legislature. The gentleman from Des Moines proposes that the calling of such a convention shall be done by the authority of the legislature.

The gentleman and myself do not disagree in the doctrine laid down by Mr. Webster. The decisions of the court upon the Rhode Island case was that all amendments to the constitution, which were not made in the manner pointed out by that instrument, would be illegal; and I hold that if we do not incorporate into our constitution such an amendment as I have presented, that we cannot amend the constitution without the consent of the legislature. The question then presented is, whether we shall provide for getting this expression without the consent of the legislature.

Mr. WILSON. There is one thing in the proposition submitted by the gentleman from Benton [Mr. Traer] which it seems to me ought to meet with the approbation of the gentleman from Des Moines [Mr. Hall]. The proposition submitted by the gentleman from Benton, as I understand it, is to strike out all after the words "General Assembly," and then insert his proposition.

The only effect the amendment of the gentleman will have is this: that after the legislature shall have submitted the question to the people, and after the people have determined to call a convention,, they can then come together and elect their delegates, without waiting the further action of the legislature, and proceed to amend the constitution, and exercise all the powers that is necessary for a body of that kind to exercise.

Mr. TRAER. The gentleman will notice that I have provided, that in case the legislature refuse to take any action, that then the people, once in ten years, shall take the matter in their own hands.

Mr. WILSON. I was referring to the submitting tho question of a convention to the people; and I was saying, if in any intermediate year, the legislature should submit the question of calling a convention to the people, and they should vote in favor of it, that they need not wait for the legislature to make provision in regard to it, but they could hold their convention without any further action by the General Assembly.

The question was then taken upon Mr. Traer's amendment, and it was rejected.

Mr. GIBSON. I offer the second section of the minority report as a substitute for the second section of the majority report.

The substitute was then read as follows:

"If, at any time, the General Assembly shall think it necessary to revise or amend this Constitution, they shall provide by law for a vote at the next ensuing election for members of the General Assembly; in case a majority of the people vote in favor of a Convention, said General Assembly shall provide for an election of Delegates to a Convention to be held within twelve months after the vote of the people in favor thereof."

Mr. PALMER. I think there is a little inconsistency in this section, especially in view of the provision we have just adopted, which provides that the legislature may make amendments to the constitution. The substitute now offered provides that the General Assembly, if they deem it necessary that amendments be made to the constitution, may call a convention. I think the difficulty I have suggested may be remedied by inserting after the word "necessary," the words "to call a convention;" so that the section would read—

"If, at any time, the General Assembly shall think it necessary to call a convention to revise or amend this Constitution, they shall provide by law for a vote at the next ensuing election for members of the General Assembly; in case a majority of the people vote in favor of a Convention, said General Assembly shall provide for an election of Delegates to a Convention to be held within twelve months after the vote of the people in favor thereof."

The question was taken upon the amendment offered by Mr. Palmer, and it was rejected.

Mr. CLARKE, of Henry. I understand that the objection raised by the gentleman from Benton [Mr. Traer,] is entirely obviated by the second section of the majority report, which provides that, at certain times, there shall be a convention without the interposition of the legislature. But, nevertheless, as we have provided in the second section for amendments to the constitution at intermediate times, I propose to strike out the words in the second line—

"And also at such times as the General Assembly may by law provide."

I think, also, that instead of calling a convention in 1867, we had better provide for calling it in 1870.

The question was then taken upon the amendment offered by Mr. Clarke of Henry, and it was rejected.

The question was then taken upon the substitute offered by Mr. Gibson, and it was rejected.

Mr. WILSON. I offer the following to come in as an independent section:

"If two or more amendments shall be submitted at the same time, they shall be submitted in such manner that the electors shall vote for or against each of such amendments separately."

The question was taken, and the amendment was agreed to.

Mr. PALMER. I move to strike out the words "1867" in the first line of the second section, and insert "1870;" so that it will read—

"At the general election to be held in the year one thousand eight hundred and seventy, and in each tenth year thereafter, and also at such time as the General Assembly may, by law, provide, the question—"shall there be a Convention to revise the Constitution, and amend the same?"—shall be decided by the electors qualified to vote for members of the General Assembly; and in case a majority of the electors so qualified, voting at such election, shall decide in favor of a Convention for such purpose, the General Assembly, at its next session, shall provide by law for the election of delegates to such Convention."

The question was taken, and the amendment was agreed to.

Mr. PALMER. I move to strike out the word "tenth" in the third line, and insert "twentieth" in lieu thereof.

The question was taken, and the amendment was rejected.

Mr. SKIFF. I move that the committee rise.

The question was taken, and the motion was agreed to.

In Convention.

The PRESIDENT having resumed the Chair,

The CHAIRMAN reported that the committee of the whole, to whom had been referred the report of the committee on amendments to the constitution, had had the same under consideration, had made some amendments thereto, and instructed him to report the same back to the convention, with said amendments, and ask to be discharged from its further consideration.

The report of the committee of the whole was received. and leave granted accordingly.

Instructing Committees to Report.

Mr. WINCHESTER. I offer the following resolution:

"*Resolved*, That all standing and special committees, except the committee on revision, that have not reported, be requested to do so on or before Monday next."

Mr. CLARK, of Alamakee. I move to lay the resolution on the table.

Upon this motion Mr. WINCHESTER called the yeas and nays, and they were ordered accordingly.

The question was then taken, by yeas and nays, upon the motion to lay the resolution upon the table, and it was not agreed to; yeas 14, nays 20, as follows:

Yeas—The President, Messrs. Bunker, Clark of Alamakee, Clarke of Henry, Edwards, Ells, Gray, Hollingsworth, Palmer, Patterson, Robinson, Seely, Wilson and Young.

Nays—Messrs. Ayres, Clarke of Johnson, Day, Emerson, Gibson, Gillaspy, Gower, Hall, Harris, Johnston, Marvin, Parvin, Peters, Price, Scott, Skiff, Solomon, Traer, Warren and Winchester.

Mr. EDWARDS. I move to amend the resolution by excepting the committee on schedule and the committee on revision from its operation.

Mr. CLARK, of Alamakee. I see no necessity for amending the resolution. It amounts to nothing, and it is only a resolution of request. I am opposed to taking up the time of the convention with these foolish resolutions.

Mr. WINCHESTER. I thank the gentleman for the compliment.

The question was taken upon Mr. Edwards motion, and it was agreed to.

Mr. PALMER. I move further to amend the resolution by excepting from its operation the committee on miscellaneous subjects.

Mr CLARK, of Alamakee. I move to amend by excepting them all.

Mr. HARRIS. I would like to except the judiciary committee.

Mr. CLARKE, of Henry. I hope that the special committee on the bill of rights will be excepted.

Mr. CLARK, of Alamakee. Better except all the committees.

Mr. PALMER. I withdraw my motion.

Mr. SCOTT. I move that we adjourn.

The question was taken, and the motion to adjourn was not agreed to.

Mr. JOHNSTON. As I understand it, the resolution is now amended so that the Committee on the Schedule and the Committee on Revision are excepted. I think it is high time that we had before us the reports of all the committees; and for the purpose of making it effective, I move to amend it by striking out the word "requested" and insert "instructed."

Mr. PARVIN. The amendment makes a very material change in the resolution, and I shall vote against it.

The question was then taken, by yeas and nays, upon Mr. Johnston's amendment, and it was agreed to; yeas 23, nays 11, as follows:

Yeas—The President, Messrs. Ayres, Clarke of Johnson, Day, Edwards, Emerson, Gibson, Gillaspy, Gower, Hall, Harris, Johnston, Patterson, Peters, Price, Robinson, Seely, Skiff, Solomon, Traer, Warren, Winchester and Young.

Nays—Messrs. Bunker, Clark of Alamakee, Clarke of Henry, Ells, Gray, Hollingsworth, Marvin, Palmer, Parvin, Scott and Wilson.

Mr. WILSON. I move to amend the resolution by striking out "Monday."

The question was taken, by yeas and nays, upon Mr. Wilson's motion, and it was not agreed to; yeas 11, nays 23, as follows:

Yeas—The President, Messrs. Clark of Alamakee, Clarke of Henry, Ells, Gray, Hollingsworth, Marvin, Palmer, Scott, Seely and Wilson.

Nays— Messrs. Ayres, Bunker, Clarke of Johnson, Day, Edwards, Emerson, Gibson, Gillaspy, Gower, Hall, Harris, Johnston, Parvin, Patterson, Peters, Price, Robinson, Skiff, Solomon, Traer, Warren, Winchester and Young.

The PRESIDENT. The question now recurs upon the adoption of the resolution.

Mr. SKIFF. I move that the convention adjourn.

Mr. JOHNSTON. And upon that question I call for the yeas and nays.

Mr. SKIFF. I will withdraw the motion to adjourn.

Mr. SCOTT. I will renew the motion.

Mr. GILLASPY. I ask for the yeas and nays upon that motion.

The yeas and nays were ordered.

The question was then taken, by yeas and nays, upon the motion to adjourn, and it was not agreed to; yeas 11, nays 23, as follows:

Yeas—The President, Messrs. Clark of Alamakee, Clarke of Henry, Edwards, Gower, Gray, Hollingsworth, Scott, Seely, Skiff and Traer.

Nays—Messrs. Ayres, Bunker, Clarke of Johnson, Day, Ells, Emerson, Gibson, Gillaspy, Hall, Harris, Johnston, Marvin, Palmer, Parvin, Patterson, Peters, Price, Robinson, Solomon, Warren, Wilson, Winchester and Young.

Mr. CLARKE, of Henry. I move to amend the resolution by excepting from its operation the special committees on the Right of Suffrage and the Bill of Rights.

Mr. TRAER demanded the previous question which was seconded, and the main question ordered.

The PRESIDENT. The question is first upon the amendment proposed by the gentleman from Henry, [Mr. Clarke,] to except the Committees on the Right of Suffrage and the Bill of Rights from the operation of the resolution.

The question was then taken, by yeas and nays, and the amendment was not agreed to; yeas 11, nays 23, as follows:

Yeas—Messrs. Bunker, Clark of Alamakee, Clarke of Henry, Ells, Gower, Gray, Hollingsworth, Marvin, Parvin, Seely and Traer.

Nays—The President, Messrs. Ayres, Clarke of Johnson, Day, Edwards, Emerson, Gibson,

Gillaspy, Hall, Harris, Johnston, Palmer, Patterson, Peters, Price, Robinson, Scott, Skiff, Solomon, Warren, Wilson, Winchester and Young.

The PRESIDENT. The question now recurs upon the adoption of the resolution.

Mr. CLARKE, of Henry. Does it not require a day to lie over, before it can be acted upon?

The PRESIDENT. The Chair is of the opinion that the resolution is in order.

Mr. SOLOMON. I would ask if it is not in accordance with the rules that reports of Standing Committees shall be made during the morning hour?

The PRESIDENT. There is a rule tacitly adopted in the Convention, that reports of Standing Committees should be considered in order in the morning hour, but independent of that, the Chair is of the opinion that reports of Standing Committees are always in order.

The question was then taken, by yeas and nays, upon the adoption of the resolution as amended, and it was agreed to; yeas 22, nays 12, as follows:

Yeas—The President, Messrs. Ayres, Clarke of Johnson, Day, Edwards, Emerson, Gibson, Gillaspy, Gower, Hall, Harris, Johnston, Palmer, Patterson, Peters, Price, Robinson, Skiff, Solomon, Warren, Winchester and Young.

Nays—Messrs. Bunker, Clark of Alamakee, Clarke of Henry, Ells, Gray, Hollingsworth, Marvin, Parvin, Scott, Seely, Traer and Wilson.

On motion of Mr. CLARK, of Alamakee,

The convention then adjourned till to-morrow morning at 9 o'clock.

FRIDAY, February 20th, 1857.

The Convention met at 9 o'clock, A. M., and was called to order by the President.

Prayer by the Chaplain.

The journal of yesterday was read and approved.

No petitions or memorials were presented.

Committee on the Schedule.

Mr. YOUNG. As the committee on the schedule will probably have a meeting this evening, and as one of its members—Mr. Toddhunter—is now unwell, and will in all probability remain so until after the convention adjourns, I would ask that some one be appointed upon that committee, that we may have a complete number of working members. I therefore move that an additional member of the committee on the schedule be appointed by the chair.

The question being taken, the motion was agreed to.

The PRESIDENT appointed Mr. Wilson as the additional member of that committee.

Militia.

Mr. SKIFF, from the committee on the militia, made the following report:

"The committee to whom was referred that portion of the constitution relating to the militia, have had the same under consideration, and have unanimously instructed me to report the same back without amendment, and recommend its adoption by this convention.

Respectfully submitted,

H. J. SKIFF.

The article on militia in the present constitution is as follows:

Section 1. The militia of this State shall be composed of all able-bodied white male citizens between the ages of eighteen and forty-five years, except such as are, or may hereafter be exempt by the laws of the United States, or of this State, and shall be armed, equipped and trained as the General Assembly may provide by law.

Sec. 2. No person or persons conscientiously scrupulous of bearing arms, shall be compelled to do militia duty in time of peace: *Provided*, that such person or persons shall pay an equivalent for such exemption in the same manner as other citizens.

Sec. 3. All commissioned officers of the militia, (staff officers excepted,) shall be elected by the persons liable to perform militia duty, and shall be commissioned by the governor."

The report was received and laid upon the table.

Number of Judicial Districts, &c.

Mr. CLARKE, of Johnson, from the Committee on the Judicial Department, made the following report:

"The Committee on the Judicial Department, to whom was referred the article on the Judicial Department, adopted by the convention, with instructions to inquire into the expediency of increasing the number of judicial districts from ten to thirteen, &c., beg leave to report—

"That, after due consideration of the subjects referred to them, the committee recommend that the number of judicial districts be increased from ten to eleven;

"And that the General Assembly have power to re-organize the judicial districts, and increase or diminish the number of judges of the district court, and increase the number of judges of the supreme court, every four years, instead of five years, as provided in section ten of this article, so that the power to make the contemplated changes in the districts or judges may be exercised at the end of the terms of the judges.

"All of which is respectfully submitted,

W. PENN CLARKE, Chairman."

Mr. CLARKE, of Johnson. I move that the convention now proceed to consider this report, together with the article on the judicial department. There are two blanks in section ten which should be filled, and then the article can be referred to the committee on revision.

The question was taken and the motion was agreed to.

The convention then proceed to consider the report of the committee on the judicial department, together with the article on the judiciary as previously amended by the convention.

Section ten was then read, as follows:

"Sec. 10. The State shall be divided into —— judicial districts; and after the year 1860, the General Assembly may reorganize the judicial districts, and increase or diminish the number of districts or the number of judges of the said court, and may increase the number of judges of the supreme court; but such increase or diminution shall not be more than one district or one judge of either court at any one session; and no reorganization of the districts or diminution of the judges, shall have the effect of removing a judge from office. Such reorganization of the districts, or any change in the boundaries thereof, or increase or diminution of the judges, shall take place every —— years thereafter, and at no other time."

Mr. CLARKE, of Henry. I move to fill the first blank with the word "eleven," that being the recommendation of the committee, as the number of districts into which the State is to be divided.

Mr. CLARK, of Alamakee. I move to insert the word "thirteen."

The question was stated to be upon the motion to fill the blank with the word "thirteen."

Mr. SKIFF. I would like to hear from the judiciary committee upon this subject. From all the information that I have with regard to this subject, I had supposed that there will be more judges needed in this State than eleven or even twelve. Taking into account the time required by the judges for holding their courts, I think more than eleven will be needed. As I understand it, the judges of the circuit court ought not to be employed in holding their courts more than half the year; the other half they ought to have for other matters. I would like to hear from the committee on the judiciary why they recommend eleven rather than a higher number.

Mr. CLARKE, of Johnson. I would say, for the information of the gentleman from Jasper, [Mr. Skiff,] that the committee on the judiciary have examined this subject to some extent, and we find that ten districts would afford sufficient time to enable the judges to discharge their duties. But that would require that some of the districts, in the western part of the State, should be very large, and require a great amount of travel on the part of the judges. The committee thought, therefore, that it would facilitate business to increase the number of districts to eleven, so as to diminish, to some extent, the size of the large western districts. The committee are satisfied, upon investigation, that with eleven districts, the western districts will not be too large to afford the judges time for other business for at least one-half the year.

By this arrangement the times for holding the courts can be so fixed that the judges, the members of the bar, and the people attending those courts, will not be compelled to travel either early in the spring or late in the fall, when the traveling is bad and dangerous.

With these views the committee recommend the number eleven, as they think that will afford districts enough until 1860, when the Legislature will have power to increase the number of districts one at any one session.

Mr. PRICE. I was in hopes, when this report was recommitted to the judiciary committee, that, so far as the increase in the number of districts was concerned, the committee would report some provision which would be of benefit to the people; at all events, somewhat better than the old report.

Now the idea of having but eleven districts in this State may suit the notions of gentlemen who live in the eastern portions of the State, or it may suit the wants of the eastern portions of the State, so far as the judiciary is concerned; but I am very well satisfied that it will not meet the wants or expectations of the people of the western portions of the State. If the State is divided into but eleven districts they must necessarily be so large in the western part of the State, that the objects to be obtained by having a judiciary at all will be almost defeated. It might do very well if judges had nothing to do but to travel; if, as has been suggested by a friend near me, the only qualification required in a judge was bottom but no brains, then this might do very well. This might do if, in the western part of the State, a judge was called upon to devote his whole time to travel, and not to study, or the dispensing of justice.

If we have but eleven districts, our judges in the western part of the State will necessarily have districts so large as to embrace at least fifteen counties. And I undertake to say that no man, however good a lawyer he may be—however rapid and ready in his deliberations and decisions he may be—can discharge the duties of a judicial office with fifteen or eighteen counties in his district; he cannot do it; it is a physical impossibility. As has been already well suggested, the western portion of this State is thinly populated—sparsely settled—and there is proportionably a large extent of territory to be traveled over, and thus the labor of traveling will be even more than when the districts are so densely populated as to take up all the time of the judge. Now, if there is to be a choice between the time to be employed in administering justice and that to be devoted to travel, I say let the time of the judge be devoted to the administration of justice.

I am in favor of inserting the word "thirteen" in this blank as the number of districts into which the State shall be divided. With less than that number of districts, it seems to me, we cannot do. I hope this convention, and especially those members coming from the western portion of the State, will look a little to the wants and interests of the people of the western sections of the State, and not confine their attention to the eastern horizon, but be a little merciful to us who live upon the western borders.

Mr. PARVIN. I feel the full force of the remarks of the gentleman from Pottawattamie, [Mr. Price;] and I think no gentleman will disagree with him, in the remarks he has made, that we ought not to look at the eastern portion of this State alone. I was in favor of ten districts, but the committee decided upon recommending the number "eleven," and I gave up to them. I do not think that keeping the number of districts down to eleven will do the western portion of the State any injustice. I think we can add to the districts in the eastern portion of the State, where they are now small in size, and let the western districts remain as they are. The judicial district in which I live consists of three counties, under the action of the late General Assembly. Now, perhaps five counties would leave the district small enough; and even six counties might not be too many. The district above us is composed of but three counties; it may just as well have five counties in it.

I think our district is composed of Muscatine, Cedar and Jones counties. I venture to say that the business of these three counties would not keep a judge employed more than three months in the year; at all events it might all be dispatched in four months. Now, is it necessary to have a district as small as that? Most assuredly it is not. Let two or three other counties be added to this district, and let the same be done in other cases where it can be done. And in this way we can get along without increasing the size of the districts in the western portion of the State, and have but eleven districts in all. I do not wish to increase the size of districts where the population is sparse, and where a large amount of travel is required. But here in the east, where we have less travel, we can increase the size of the districts. I would have been pleased had the committee reported the number "ten," because I think we could dispense with three of our judges very well. However, I shall support the recommendation of the committee.

Mr. CLARK, of Alamakee. While I have the utmost respect for the opinion of the gentleman from Muscatine, [Mr. Parvin,] I beg leave to disagree with him in the conclusions to which he arrives in this matter. In the first place, I think we have thirteen organized judicial districts in this State at this time, and, if I am not mistaken, there is a fourteenth district, but not fully organized. This shows that, in the judgment of the people, as expressed through their representatives—the legislature—it is necessary to have fourteen districts at this time.

And, in addition to that, the tenth judicial district is fully large enough for two districts. Both the eastern and western portions of the district are anxious to have it made into two districts. There was a move of that kind on foot last fall, and, had it not been for the meeting of this convention, by which it was supposed this matter would be arranged, there would have been petitions sent to the legislature asking for a division of that district. One judge cannot do all the business in that district. The necessity we felt there last fall still exists, and is not obviated by any proposed arrangement contained in the report of this committee.

There is another reason why we should have more districts than ten, or even eleven. If I understand the provisions of the constitution, as we have already passed upon them, we can have no additional districts provided by the legislature until after the year 1860; and then only one at a time. Now, granting for the sake of argument, that eleven districts are all that we actually need now, let us look at what our necessities and wants are likely to be in the future. Four years must pass before we can have an additional district. Look at the increase in the population of this State. The vast regions of country in the western portions of the State, which are now uninhabited, will then be settled, and will call for additional labor from our district judges. In order to divide the State into but eleven districts, our western districts must be very large, and embrace a very large space of territory. It is true that the population there is sparse at the present time; but within two or three years, those counties now unorganized will be completely organized, and the judges of each district will be compelled to hold court in ten, twelve, and perhaps fifteen counties. Now, this is an emergency which should be provided for in some way.

Again, as our western counties fill up with population, and as the business increases, the labors of the judge will increase in proportion. And what would be now very easy for a judge to attend to, would not be three or five years hence.

Looking at this matter in this light, it seems to me we must all be satisfied that eleven districts are not enough. I do not think that thirteen are really enough; but, as a compromise, I would be willing to agree that the State should be divided into but twelve districts.

Another reason why I am opposed to this proposition for eleven districts is this: it is well known that I am in favor of an intermediate court, and nearly one-half of the members upon this floor are in favor of that also. But we have made a compromise upon this question, and instead of adopting the three court system in the constitution, we have left that matter to the legislature of the State, and they can create this third court if they see fit. If they create that third court, it would be advisable to have the State so divided into districts that the judges of the district courts could perform the duties of that intermediate court. Suppose we have but eleven districts, and the State is divided into four districts for this intermediate court. One of the new districts would have but three judges. And, therefore, unless we have some other number, the plan I am in favor of would be defeated and delayed until after the year 1860. If we made that compromise in good faith on both sides, let us complete the arrangements and meet the expectations of all who entered into it. I will admit that if we have thirteen districts, one of these larger districts would have five judges; but that would be no serious trouble.

I do not believe we can do justice to the wants of the people of this State by adopting a less number for our districts than twelve or thirteen. I do not intend to charge any man with intentional bad faith, for I believe all intend to be honest. But we will not carry out the intentions and objects of that compromise, so far as to allow the legislature to create a third court, unless we so frame the rest of the constitution that they may carry out that compromise, and reduce it to practical effect.

For these reasons I am in favor of at least twelve districts; first, because I think the necessities and wants of the people require that many districts; and, in the next place, I do not believe we can carry out the other provision of this article, which allows the legislature to create this third court, unless we do adopt that number.

Mr. EDWARDS. I shall sustain the report of the judiciary committee, in relation to the number of judicial districts. I think that eleven districts are amply sufficient to meet the wants of the people of this State. I believe that the territory of Iowa, embraced within the limits of its organized counties, is not larger than the State of Indiana, and that State has never had over ten judicial districts. That State is densely populated, and the courts in the various counties generally sit for a period of two weeks.

There are eighty-three counties in this State, and the districts will not average eight counties to the district. And in one-half of the counties the term would not extend to over three days. Now putting each district down at eight counties, and the time occupied by the court in each county, and the whole time occupied by the court in each year will not be over four months; or one-third of the year is all that is devoted by the judge to the discharge of his duties upon the bench.

Now if you wish to prepare the judge for the proper discharge of the duties devolving upon him, the better plan is to keep him employed in the discharge of the duties of his station. The oftener he holds his court, the better will he be prepared to perform the duties of his office. And half of the year devoted to the constant employment of the judge in the duties of his office is not too much. And the argument upon the other side in regard to the new sections of the State, I think can be met by this consideration.

I have seen a disposition upon the part of the members here from the old counties, and I think it is very honorable and creditable to them, to do ample justice in every respect to the new counties. And I believe if it was asked for, upon the part of the members generally from the more newly settled counties of the State, they would grant what would be asked for in this case.

But I think this would be highly unnecessary. We have raised the salaries of the district judges from one thousand two hundred dollars to one thousand six hundred dollars a year, without any material increase of the labor to be performed by them. And I can see no good reason why we should increase the number of districts above the number recommended by the committee.

The committee have made provision in their report that if it is found necessary, after the year 1860, that the number of districts should be increased, the legislature can make that increase. So far as the State is concerned at the present time, I think that eleven districts are amply sufficient. That will make the districts comprise, on the average, from seven to eight counties each, and in most of the new counties the term of the court will not exceed three days.

Mr. SKIFF. It seems to me as though we were taking matters out of the hands of the Legislature, by thus reducing the number of districts in the State. The Legislature that has just closed its session increased the number of districts some three, I believe.

The PRESIDENT. They made four new districts.

Mr. SKIFF. They increased them four. Now if the representatives of the people, meeting here at the capitol during the present winter, did not know as much about what their constituents wanted as we do, then I think it was a very strange thing.

Mr. EDWARDS. One of these new districts contains but three counties; and one near here contains but two counties.

Mr. CLARKE, of Johnson. There are three such districts.

Mr. SKIFF. I think the representatives of the people are better qualified to judge of these matters than this Convention is. This Convention did not meet together, as I understand it, for any such purpose as districting the State, unless we changed our judiciary system. If we had changed that system then we would necessarily have had to re-district the State. But we have left the system the same, and I think it would be getting along a little too fast to go to cutting down the number of districts.

The judicial district in which I live comprises eight counties. I have heard a great many of the lawyers there say that the district was too large, that the amount of business there was too great for the judge to dispose of. It would take a judge a great deal more than half the year to go round and attend to the business. Many counties there now have business that has been waiting a year or more. In Polk county, for instance, one of the principal attorneys told me that there were one hundred and sixty cases on the docket, and it has not been cleared off for a long time. And so it is in other counties in the district; the dockets have not been clear for some time past, and the business is accumulating. If there was a re-districting of the State, I think we could not have more counties in our district than we now have and do anything like justice to the suitors at large.

If other gentlemen here are from districts that are too small, and can take more counties in their districts, well and good; let them do so. I can only speak in regard to my own district; and what I have said has been after consultation with those persons who understand the matter pretty well. If the number of judges and districts are to be decreased, I shall most seriously object to having any more counties put in our district, for I think it is large enough now.

Mr. YOUNG. I live in the same judicial district as the gentleman from Jasper, [Mr. Skiff,] and I do not think the difficulty that he speaks of exists there. The best evidence I have that the people are satisfied with the district, is that there is a new judge to be elected there, and I see, from our paper, that there are about twenty candidates for the office. Now I think if the district was so large, and the labor so great as the gentleman seems to think, we would not have so many men aspiring to the office of judge in that district.

There is one reason why the business of the district may have accumulated. They had, in Polk county, a judge whom clients, lawyers and everybody else wanted to get rid of. That was the whole object in view in re-arranging that district; not because the district was too large, but because they wanted to get rid of Judge McFarland. I have been informed by the lawyers of my own town, and of other places, that the district was not too large. I have, in fact, been told, that we could take into the district two small counties lying west of us, and then not have too large a district. The counties comprising the district at the present time are of about medium size, and there are eight of them. I think we can add to it the two counties west of us, and then not have a district too large for the judge to attend to its business.

I am in favor of the recommendation of the committee, not to increase the number of districts beyond eleven. I am satisfied, in regard to the legislation of this winter increasing the number of districts, that it was not done because of the necessities of the case, but to enable certain localities to make such changes as they desired.

Mr. HARRIS. Whenever I have had a fair hearing and a proper expression of the sense of the Convention upon any question, I am always disposed to let the matter rest there. But notwithstanding that, while I do not impugn the motives of the committee at all, which has made this recommendation, I do not think that justice can be done to the western portions of the State with only eleven judicial districts. However, I was disposed to let the matter abide the recommendation of the committee. But gentlemen who have thought and felt a great deal in regard to this matter, insisted that it would not do at all, and they would, therefore, attempt to increase the number of districts. I did suggest to them that we should not make a stand for more than twelve districts. I do not believe that, if any gentleman will take the map and examine it carefully, he can come to the conclusion that the State could be apportioned fairly into less than twelve districts. Yet some of my friends are not satisfied with that, and insist that even thirteen is as small a number of districts as we can well get along with; and, for that reason, I shall vote with them. And I shall not think that justice will be done to the State with less than twelve districts at any rate. However, as I said before, this matter having been carefully canvassed, if the Convention shall decide that eleven districts are sufficient, I shall not complain.

I wish to offer a few remarks here in reply to some that have been made here this morning. And first and foremost, in regard to the size of the districts. I said to this convention the other day, that I had devoted some eight or ten hours to an attempt to prepare a plan for districting the State. I first tried the plan of ten districts, but did not succeed at all. I did get up a plan for twelve districts, which I submitted, as I stated at that time, to a majority of the convention, and I found, with but one or two exceptions, each one thought his own district was too large. Some of them thought the State might be so districted, and perhaps into even a less number of districts, so as to do ample justice to other portions of the State; but yet their immediate districts were too large. That satisfied me at once that the districts were too large for even as many as twelve, because I went individually around to one member and an other in that way, and that was the result of our consultation.

I then tried the plan of thirteen districts; and I will say here that I put none at less than four counties. Gentlemen say there are thirteen districts now; why re-district the State? I will tell them the reason. It is true that we have now thirteen districts; but there are a number of districts here upon the Mississippi river, that comprise only three counties each. Gentlemen will at once see the necessity of re-districting the State, in order to have some fair division of the territory.

The gentleman from Lucas [Mr. Edwards,] says there are only eighty organized counties in the State, and with ten judicial districts there will be an average of but eight counties to the district. But we do not place this matter upon the average of counties to the district. Will gentlemen say that the territory embracing Linn, Johnson, Des Moines, Muscatine, Lee, and Van Buren counties, should be embraced in one district? No gentleman will insist upon that. In drafting a plan for thirteen districts, I put from four to seven counties in the Mississippi districts, while in the western part of the State I embraced from fifteen to sixteen counties in a district. And I believe that in that part of the State, I had no district of less than eight counties.

And I will say so far as the number of organized counties is concerned, my impression is, though I may be mistaken, that the Secretary of State told me that there were at this time about ninety organized counties in this State. I had a conversation with him upon the subject, but I did not charge my memory particularly with it at the time, because I did not suppose that any particular consequence would be attached to that matter.

Mr. EDWARDS. There are but eighty-three organized counties.

Mr. HARRIS. The Secretary of State certainly named a higher number than that. He might have said that there were about ninety counties; I will not be positive that he said there were fully ninety organized counties. However, supposing that there are only eighty-three counties. Are you going to divide them up equally in proportion to the amount of business? Certainly not. As was well asked by the gentleman from Potawattamie, [Mr. Price,] are you going to make a man rely upon his bottom more than upon his brains? I have seen something of that. I have traveled with a judge when he had to fly from county to county, doing the business in some counties in half a day each, and taking the rest of the day to go to some other county.

Now I do insist that counties that are organized, that have an amount of business necessarily resulting from a population of from four, eight, ten, twelve, or fifteen thousand inhabitants, over eight counties is more than one judge can take charge of, and deal justly, either as regards himself, or those to whom he is called upon to administer justice.

I do not believe that less than thirteen districts will do justice to the State. But still, as I said before, I will not be tenacious upon that point. I am not disposed, when the convention, after due deliberation, have come to a decision upon this question, to run counter to their decision. But I did think that this dividing the State into but ten districts was decided upon without much consideration. In fact I knew, from conversation that I had with various members, that it had been done without proper consideration, and they had relied upon assertions that the legislature of this winter, in making new districts, had acted without due consideration. That I believe was the reason that this provision for ten districts was ordered to be inserted here. For that reason I made the motion I did the other day, to have this subject re-committed to the judiciary committee.

Mr. CLARKE, of Henry. I believe that I originally made the motion to fix the number of districts in this State at ten. But afterwards, upon consulting with gentlemen, the gentleman from Appanoose (Mr. Harris) and others from newer counties, I found that the almost universal opinion was, that the number of districts ought to be increased. Standing here, as I do, the representative of a county where the population is dense, and from a district where we have heretofore had but four counties, I do not wish to urge my own peculiar ideas and views. I came here to meet gentlemen from different portions of the State, and compare views, and learn from them what the wants of the State are. And I hold that it is my duty to yield somewhat of my own ideas in regard to the demands of the State, to those of gentlemen who from their position and situation can better judge than I can of what their portions of the State desire.

And when gentlemen come here, like the gentleman from Potawattamie, [Mr. Price], and the gentleman from Appanoose, [Mr. Harris], and the gentleman from Alamakee, [Mr. Clark], and tell us that they desire to have the number of districts increased, I am willing to increase it, and when the subject was before the judiciary committee, I was in favor of the number twelve. And on looking over and considering this matter and weighing the arguments that have been adduced here, I think that if the necessities of the State do not now demand that number of districts, they will in two years or even less time than that, before the legislature can act upon that subject.

I certainly believe that those gentleman who have tried and labored under the inconveniences of these large districts, must be better informed in regard to this matter than I can be, as I have not had to suffer many of these inconvences of which they speak. I am in favor, therefore, of thirteen districts, as the gentleman from the northern part of the State seems to desire it.

Mr. WINCHESTER. I have some confidence in the opinions of the members who compose the committee on the judicial department. They have had this matter under consideration for a long time; it has been fully discussed in the convention; it was again referred to the committee for consideration, and they have again reported upon it. I think the number eleven to be fully sufficient. I live in a sparsely settled portion of the State, in a district containing, as at present organized, eight counties. The courts have been heretofore held in each of these counties from once to twice a year, not over twice a year in any one of them, and the length of the term has never exceeded three days, thus taking some forty-eight to fifty days to hold the court twice a year in each county.

This report provides that the number of districts may be increased after the year 1860. I do not apprehend that the business of these counties will be so greatly increased as to become burdensome to the judges in that length of time, but that they will have, as they now have, from three-fourths to five-sixths of the year to travel or remain at home. It was the policy advocated by the eminent statesman John Randolph, that the least number of judges, that could possibly be got along with, was the best. That was the position taken by him in the last political position he ever occupied, that of a member of the constitutional convention of Virginia. I have uniformly voted for the least number of judges that I thought competent to transact the business of the State. It is well known to those who are conversant with the Bible that the book of Kings is larger than the book of Judges.

Mr. HARRIS. I move to fill the blank in section ten with the word "twelve."

The PRESIDENT. The question must be first taken upon the highest number, that proposed by the gentleman from Alamakee [Mr. Clark], being the number "thirteen."

Mr. HARRIS. I would ask the gentleman from Alamakee to withdraw the motion he has proposed, and let the number "twelve" be offered as a compromise.

Mr. CLARK, of Alamakee. I will do so for the sake of a compromise.

Mr. HARRIS. I now move to fill the blank with the number "twelve."

Mr. GIBSON. I thought this question was nearly disposed of the other day, when, as I thought, it had already been sufficiently discussed. And I was in hopes, from the votes given by this convention, that the plan of ten judicial districts would have been sustained. But it seems that there are some gentlemen who differ upon this subject, and thinkt that the number of districts ought to be increased. Consequently the matter was referred back to the committee on the judicial department, to undergo a renewed and more thorough examination, and that committee have reported for one additional district.

Now I was one of those here who believed that ten judicial districts in the State were enough. But perhaps eleven may be needed. I suppose the committee have given the matter due consideration; and with that deliberation and consideration upon their part, and their report that eleven districts are absolutely necessary, I will not be tenacious in my course upon this subject, about one district. I would prefer, however, to reduce the present number of districts to ten, as I think that that uumber is sufficient, and that the wants of the State will not require more than that number. I am of the opinion that ten efficient judges would be abundantly able to perform all the labors and duties pertaining to their stations in this State.

The gentleman from Mahaska, [Mr. Young,] has alluded to the district in which he now resides, and he stated that that district was formed, not because it was too large, not because the judge was not able to perform all the duties of his office in the old district, but because in the minds of some of the people at least, the judge was not just the man they wanted there. Now I do not propose to defend any man or any set of men in this matter. If this was the fact, and the judge had proved recreant to the trust imposed upon him, was the proper mode to get rid of him to divide up his district so as to leave him three sparsely settled counties, and without business to keep the court three months in the year? If he had done wrong, why was he not impeached and turned out of office? This seems to me to be a very poor argument in favor of a new district.

I am of the opinion that it will be necessary to have the State re-districted and apportioned according to population and territory, making a fair compromise between the two interests. But I am of a different opinion from the gentleman from Mahaska, [Mr. Young,] as to the object of forming the new district to which he has referred, leaving but three sparsely settled counties in one of the districts. I do not think that it was so much on account of objection to the judge of that district, as to make room for some party favorite.

Mr. YOUNG. I will except Marion county of that district; but I will say that every other county in the district desired to get rid of Judge McFarland.

Mr. SKIFF. Was the gentleman from Mahaska, [Mr. Young,] in that district?

Mr. YOUNG. I was not.

Mr. GIBSON. I will say that while there were persons in Marion county who did not like Judge McFarland in some respects, yet the prevailing opinion among the people, both republicans and democrats, is that he has dispatched the business in a shorter time, and has done more business than any other judge we ever had. This may not be the fact in Mahaska county.

Mr. WILSON. The gentleman from Appanoose, [Mr. Harris,] seems to be frightened at the size of the contemplated districts in this State, and is afraid his district will be increased. Now let the gentleman take his own figures, and examine the matter. Suppose that two counties are added to his district. The time of the judge of that district will not be occupied more than seven months in the year, thus leaving five months to the judge after he has performed all the business of his district.

I know that in the district in which I reside twenty-five weeks in the year are sufficient in which to perform all the business of the district. And so I presume it is in a majority of the districts throughout the State; the same rule will prevail, that the judges have upon their hands from four to six months in the year, when they are not occupied in the discharge of the duties of their office.

Now I believed, in the first place, that ten

judicial districts were sufficient. I believed that ten judges could do all the business in those districts. But, as a member of the committee on the judicial department, I was willing to compromise, and report back to the convention the number "eleven." I believe that that is a sufficient number, and I see no necessity for going beyond that number. I saw no absolute necessity for going that far, except as a compromise. I shall, therefore, vote for the number reported by the committee.

Mr. PATTERSON. I understand that the judiciary committee have recommended "eleven" as the number of districts for this State and the question is now upon the motion of the gentleman from Appanoose [Mr. Harris] to fill the blank with the word "twelve," so as to provide for twelve districts. When the question of fixing the salaries of the judges was up, I voted to make the salary of the district judge $2,000 a year. And it was then urged, I think, that we ought to give our judges more labor to perform if they were to have a high salary. Now I thought that was the true policy; I believe it so still. I am, therefore, opposed to increasing the number of districts, beyond what the committee have reported. I think that number is sufficient, and I hope the convention will concur in the recommendation of the committee, and vote down the number now proposed. I am willing to give my friends in the west nearly all they may desire; but I am not willing to give them another district.

The question recurred upon the motion of Mr. Harris to fill the blank with the word "twelve," as the number of judicial districts in this State.

Upon this motion—

Mr. CLARKE, of Johnson, called for the yeas and nays, and they were ordered accordingly.

The question being then taken, by yeas and nays, the motion was not agreed to, yeas 14, nays 20, as follows:

Yeas—Messrs. Clark of Alamakee, Clarke of Henry, Gillaspy, Gray, Harris, Johnston, Palmer, Peters, Price, Scott, Seely, Skiff, Solomon, and Traer.

Nays—The President, Messrs. Ayres, Bunker, Clarke of Johnson, Day, Edwards, Ells, Emerson, Gibson, Gower, Hall, Hollingsworth, Marvin, Parvin, Patterson, Robinson, Warren, Wilson, Winchester, and Young.

The question then recurred upon filling the blank with the number "eleven."

The question was then taken by yeas and nays, and the motion to fill the blank with that number was adopted; yeas 31, nays 3, as follows:

Yeas—The President, Messrs. Ayres, Bunker, Clarke of Henry, Clarke of Johnson, Day, Edwards, Ells, Emerson, Gillaspy, Gower, Gray, Hall, Harris, Hollingsworth, Johnston, Marvin, Palmer, Parvin, Patterson, Peters, Robinson, Scott, Seely, Skiff, Solomon, Traer, Warren, Wilson, Winchester, and Young.

Nays—Messrs. Clark of Alamakee, Gibson, and Price.

Re-organization of the Districts.

Mr. CLARKE, of Johnson. I move to fill the second blank with the word "four," which is the recommendation of the committee. I desire to say in explanation of their action, that this provision of the constitution when it was referred back to them made the time, when the districts were to be organized, every five years after the year 1860. We have found it necessary to make this change of the term from five to four to correspond with the termination of the terms of office of the judges, as the article provides, that no re-organization of the districts, diminution or increase of the judges shall have the effect of removing a judge from office. Hence we thought it necessary to have that power exercised at the end of the terms, so as to make the system work evenly.

Mr. CLARK of Alamakee. I can see no good reason in the change asked for by the gentleman from Johnson [Mr. Clarke]. If the Legislature see fit at any time to pass a law diminishing the number of the districts, they can say that it shall take effect at the expiration of the term of office of the judge. I see no reason in the argument for saying that the Legislature shall not carry out the wishes of the people, and make the laws conform to the interests and necessities of the people, only once in four years. In the first place, I think it is doubtful policy in the convention to say how many districts there shall be. I think this matter very properly belongs to the legislative department.

But gentlemen urge as a reason for adopting this measure, that we can look over this State as well as the Legislature. To look into the future and say how many districts the State will require four or five years hence, is claiming a great deal more ability and judgment than, as modest men, we should claim. It is assuming that this convention has the ability to look ahead, and tell the people what they want, better than the Legislature years hence can tell. If we are to have but this number of districts, as proposed by the gentleman, and the Legislature is to have the power of adding only one district at a time, it strikes me, that power over this subject should be conferred upon them oftener than once in four years.

Mr. CLARKE, of Johnson. The object of the provision, as it now stands, is to prevent such legislation as we had this last winter, of remodeling districts for the purpose of getting rid of indifferent judges. The object of the provision must be obvious to every member of the convention, and it is this, to give some stability to this system, so that when any districts are settled, they at least should remain so for a given length of time.

Mr. CLARK, of Alamakee. I hold it to be

pretty good reasoning, that if the legislature could be trusted by the gentleman from Johnson a few days ago, they should be trusted by him to-day. A short time ago, when we were talking about giving the legislature the power to legislate upon certain provisions, that might gratify the wishes of the gentleman, his position was that, coming fresh from the people, they were not to be feared. Now, forsooth, when he wants to get up a scheme which suits his own peculiar views, he turns round and says that the people are not to be trusted. He alludes to the proceedings of the last legislature, where there was a re-modeling of the districts in order to get rid of bad judges. If we are going to make a constitution which will entirely suppress bad legislation, let us go still farther, and make a constitution doing away with the necessity of a legislative body at all. To say that, because a legislative body may sometimes err, they shall not have the power to create these districts, when the necessities of the people require them, is, to my mind, a very poor argument. I can see no force in the position of the gentleman, that the legislature shall not have power over this subject, only once in four years. If the legislature this last winter did a wrong act, and if for that reason the gentleman would take from them power to do so for four years together, why not say eight, sixteen or a hundred years? If we are going upon the principle that we will not trust the legislature for four years together, why not extend the time still further? I believe the gentleman's position is predicated upon sophistry instead of logic. I believe, if we intend to have a legislature that shall have the confidence of the people, we ought to entrust them with power which will enable them always to meet the wants and wishes of the people. That is my opinion upon that subject. If we desire that the legislature shall make laws for the people, which will prove beneficial, we must give them a latitude in their legislation, which will enable them to do so.

I go upon the principle, that confidence begets integrity. What else is there that holds together a community? You show to an individual that you consider him worthy of confidence, and you will create a desire in him to be worthy of that confidence. The same rule will hold good with reference to legislative bodies. When we make a constitution, in which we say to the legislature we distrust you, we are afraid that you will make laws that will compromise the rights and interests of the people, and, therefore, we will with-hold from you the power to make laws, so that you cannot exercise power only once in four years—so far as the principle goes, it will have directly the opposite tendency of that claimed by the gentleman from Johnson, [Mr. Clarke,] because if the legislature are disposed to make wrong laws, I apprehend that when they have the privilege, they will then exercise it to an unlimited extent.

Mr. CLARKE, of Johnson. My consistency is very dear to me, and if, when the record of my life is opened in the great book above, it does not show that I have always steadily pursued one object, and that, the greatest good of the greatest number of my fellow citizens, so far as my sphere of action can reach them, I shall be greatly disappointed. I beg leave to ask the gentleman from Alamakee]Mr. Clark,] whether he is so obtuse that he cannot see the difference between my speaking my individual sentiments, and speaking as the organ of the committee? I ask him further, if he is so obtuse, as not to see that the report which was passed upon by the convention, and was referred to the committee of which I am chairman, with instructions upon certain subjects, and which now comes back to the convention, is the action of the committee, and not the expression of my individual feelings, or opinions upon this subject?

The gentleman has charged me with inconsistency upon this subject. What I have said in support of this report I have stated as the organ of the committee, and not with a view to the previous action of the Convention in reference to it. I have all along, in the deliberations of this body, advocated giving to the people, and especially to the law-making power, the largest liberty upon this subject as well as upon all other subjects. I am willing to trust all these things to the people. But the Convention has decided upon a different course. They have adopted a certain system, and it was only referred back to the committee of which I am chairman, to inquire into certain matters and report upon them. That committee has acted, and four of the five have concurred in that report; and, as their chairman, I am representing the feelings of the committee, and not my own individual opinions. In this view of the subject, I think that my course will be found not to be so very inconsistent as the gentleman imagines it to be.

Whether I have explained this matter satisfactorily I do not know, for the gentleman does not seem to have a very high opinion of my abilities.

Mr. CLARK, of Alamakee. The gentleman certainly misunderstood me in this matter, for I have the highest respect for his abilities. I desire to ask the gentleman a single question. If he advocates the adoption of the four-year system, not from his own convictions of right, but because he is the organ of the committee, I ask him how he is going to represent and carry out the views of the majority and follow his own convictions of right?

Mr. CLARKE, of Johnson. I am going to vote for carrying out the wishes of the majority of the committee as a compromise measure.

Mr. WILSON. It seems to me that the speech made by the gentleman from Alamakee, [Mr. Clark,] day before yesterday, in favor of restraining the power of the Legislature to change county boundaries, is a complete answer to the speech which he has made to-day, against restraining the power of the Legislature in connection with judicial districts. He was not willing the other day to trust the legislature with power over the subject of county boundaries, for fear they might abuse it. And he feared if he went to bed at night in one county he might wake up the next morning and find himself in a new county; and he gave as a reason, that a few men in particular localities controlled the action of the legislature in this respect. The same argument that the gentleman used then, would apply with equal force to a re-organization of judicial districts. A few men in a district, perhaps, want a change, and they want a new district which will be more convenient for their business. They go to work, get a bill for that purpose before the legislature, get their members interested in the project, and the result is, that the matter is referred to the members of the counties composing that district, who report in favor of a change, and the bill is passed through both houses of the general assembly, when, in fact, only a few persons interested in its passage are aware that such a measure is before the legislature. It is for the purpose of guarding against such results as these that the committee have reported this provision. They wished to restrain, as far as possible, the legislature from coming up every two years and creating new districts. While I am willing to concede to the legislature all the qualities that are necessary to an honest and upright body, I say that after all they are liable to be deceived, and they may think they are carrying out the will of the people, when, in fact, they are only carrying out the will of a few individuals, who are directly interested.

Mr. CLARK, of Alamakee. I contend that the position I take now is consistent with my argument the other day. I contended then for giving the greatest latitude to the legislature, subject to the checks which I wished to throw around them to prevent log-rolling. I am willing to place the same checks upon legislation as connected with these judicial districts. With such a check, I would go for giving the legislature the largest liberty, in order that they might fully and fairly represent the wishes of the people.

Mr. HALL. My object has been, during the discussions we have had upon this subject, to make the judiciary independent, if possible, of legislative authority, as far as practicable, and give it that significance and importance in government, to which it is entitled. I hope that we will make, in regard to the judiciary, that great distinction which wisdom has found to be beneficial; that is, to have that department of the government as independent as possible.

The proposition now under consideration is to divide the State into eleven judicial districts and elect judges who shall hold their offices for four years, who shall discharge their duties in the districts in which they were elected, and for the time they were elected. The object of this provision is to give permanency and some little stability to this branch of the government. At the end of four years, when these judges have served out their time, then the legislature may add another district, and new judges may be elected in these districts, who will continue to hold their positions and administer justice, independent of the legislature, during the time for which they were elected. There can be no possible complaint of this system, unless it so happens, as it has happened, that the legislature should feel disposed to punish some judge and put him upon the retired list, set him aside with nothing to do, make new districts and give the people another opportunity of selecting some judge who will suit them better. I am not disposed to place in our constitution this power of punishing a judge, because there may be judges in this State who become unpopular in their district, and do not satisfy the leading men of the dominant party; or because some aspirant would prefer to legislate them out of office. Such a procedure as this would destroy the respect of the people for that branch of the government, and diminish the confidence which they have in it. Nothing of this kind can maintain that respect and dignity of character which this branch of the government ought to have. It does appear to me that the system recommended here will operate well.

But gentlemen take ground against it, because they want an increase in the department, and they say that we will need more judges, that eleven judges cannot transact the business they will be called upon to perform. I do not believe a word of it. There is not, nor has there been, a judge in this State, who is occupied half of the time in discharging the duties of his office. The judgeship is a mere incident in a man's life, and he looks to some other business for his main employment. He looks to the office of judge in the light of a little patrimony, to which he devotes a portion of his time, leaving the balance of it for some other business. This ought not to be the case in this State. A judge should make the duties of his office his only business. We should require our judges to work well, pay them well, and make them judges from necessity, if not from inclination. If you give them plenty to do, they will give up all other business and devote their time to their office, in order to qualify themselves for discharging the duties which they will be called upon to perform. The more you give a judge to do, the better he will be able to discharge his duties to the satisfaction of himself and the community, because he will study diligently and labor hard to accomplish what is before him. You elect a judge, and the first year he will be a little slow in discharging his duties; but as he progresses in the discharge of his duties he will be enabled to dispatch his business with rapidity, so that at the end of the second or third year, he will have made great improvement in the rapidity with which he discharges his duties, and he will be enabled to meet the duties devolving upon him, as the business increases in his district. I believe that eleven judges are sufficient to discharge all the duties that can possibly devolve upon them.

This idea of making new districts often, is to my mind fallacious, for if a judge had ten counties in his district, it would take him but forty weeks in the year, if he devoted four weeks to each county exclusively. We know that the new counties do not require that the judge should spend within their limits any such length of time.

I am satisfied that the salaries we have fixed for these judges are too low; but if they are willing to take these offices, let us put upon them the labor which they ought to perform, to enable them to accomplish their labors satisfactorily to the community.

Mr. CLARKE, of Henry. I desire to make a few remarks upon this question. I do not know whether there is anything on this side of the house to affect members. But so it is, for some reason or other, when gentlemen upon this side ask the privilege of making explanations here, objections come from the other side of the house. In a number of instances it has happened, that the gentleman who made objections, would get up and speak three or four times upon the same question without being called to order. I suppose that there are peculiar privileges pertaining to that side of the house. I am very happy that I am permitted to speak without being called to order, not having spoken upon this question before.

In regard to this matter of preventing the legislature from changing the districts, the same reasons do not apply that apply for preventing the legislature from changing the boundaries of counties. Every county is an organization within itself, for certain purposes; and among others, for governmental purposes. The judicial districts are simply thrown together for the facility of transacting judicial business, and it makes no difference to any one county whether another county is attached to the district, if they only have their regular term of the court. The only difference, then, is in the duties of the judge. If anybody can demonstrate that any other interests than simply the interests of the judge are affected in this matter, I would like him to do it.

The only question, then, is, what can these judges accomplish, and how much ought they to accomplish for the salaries which are paid them? In regard to that matter, I apprehend that the people of the State, or of any particular district, are not going to ask or consent that the judge in their district shall be loaded down with more work than he can perform, or that the district shall be so changed that he will have nothing to do. It has been said that, in one instance, a judge became so obnoxious to a portion of his district, that they did have their district changed. If that was the case, it was a very good reason for getting rid of an obnoxious judge, and I would not deprive the people of that privilege. But that is no objection to the proposition we make here.

The only question that can be raised here in regard to this matter, is, whether every legislature shall have the power of making the alterations and changes which the people demand. I was a little surprised at the remarks of the gentleman from Jefferson, [Mr. Wilson,] in endeavoring to arraign the gentleman from Alamakee, [Mr. Clark,] for inconsistency. The argument which that gentleman made in regard to changing county boundaries had very great force and effect, as every member here must acknowledge. We could all see a reason why men would tamper with the legislature, and, by a system of log-rolling, get the boundaries of counties changed, for the purpose of making new county sites for speculative purposes. But can any gentleman tell me that the same reason will apply to judicial districts? No gentleman here could make the same argument, and give the same reasons, for throwing checks around the legislature, in regard to judicial districts.

The only argument upon this point was that of the gentleman from Des Moines, [Mr. Hall,] and the danger of frequent changes to which he referred in connection with this matter, is, I apprehend, purely an imaginary one. If it really exists, let us throw some restraint around this second legislature. If his argument is good for anything, it certainly is as good in its application to the legislature which meets every fourth year as to the legislature that meets every second year. I do not think there is any necessity for limiting the legislature in this way. I believe they ought to be left free in this respect, so that if the people need any changes at any time, whether it be every second or every fourth year, they can have them.

The question was then taken, by yeas and nays, upon concurring with the recommendation of the judicial committee, that the blank should be filled with "four," and it was agreed to; yeas 25, nays 8, as follows:

Yeas—The President, Messrs. Ayres, Bunker, Clarke of Johnson, Day, Edwards, Ells, Gibson, Gillaspy, Gower, Gray, Hall, Hollingsworth, Johnston, Parvin, Patterson, Robinson, Seely, Skiff, Solomon, Warren, Wilson, Winchester and Young.

Nays—Messrs. Clark of Alamakee, Clarke of Henry, Harris, Marvin, Palmer, Peters, Price and Scott.

On motion of Mr. WINCHESTER,

The article on the Judicial Department as amended, was then referred to the Committee on Revision.

Amendments to the Constitution.

The PRESIDENT. The next business in order is the consideration of the amendments made in committee of the whole, to the report of the committee on amendments to the constitution.

The first amendment made by the committee of the whole was the following to come in as section second:

"If two or more amendments shall be submitted at the same time, they shall be submitted in such manner that the electors shall vote for or against each of such amendments separately."

The question was then taken, and the amendment was concurred in.

The next amendment was to strike out of section two the words "one thousand eight hundred and sixty-seven," and insert in lieu thereof the words "one thousand eight hundred and seventy," so that the section would read:

"At the general election to be held in the year one thousand eight hundred and seventy, and in each tenth year thereafter, and also at such times as the General Assembly may, by law, provide, the question, 'Shall there be a convention to revise the constitution and amend the same?' shall be decided by the electors qualified to vote for members of the General Assembly; and in case a majority of the electors so qualified, voting at such election, for and against such proposition, shall decide in favor of a convention for such purpose, the General Assembly, at its next session, shall provide by law for the election of delegates to such convention."

The question was taken, and the amendment was concurred in, upon a division; ayes 14, noes 6.

Mr. CLARKE, of Johnson. I offer the following as a substitute for the first section:

"Section 1. Any amendment or amendments to this constitution may be proposed in either house of the General Assembly, and if the same shall be agreed to by a majority of the members elected to each of the two houses, such proposed amendment or amendments shall be entered on their journals, with the yeas and nays taken thereon, and shall be published, as provided by law, for three months, after which such proposed amendment or amendments shall be submitted to a vote of the people at a general election; and if the people shall approve of and ratify such amendment or amendments, by a majority of the electors qualified to vote for members of the General Assembly, voting thereon separately, such amendment or amendments shall become a part of the constitution of this state."

The question was then taken, by yeas and nays, upon the substitute, and it was rejected; yeas 12, nays 22 ,as follows:

Yeas—The President, Messrs. Clarke of Henry, Clarke of Johnson, Edwards, Gower, Gray, Hall, Hollingsworth, Johnston, Marvin, Scott and Winchester.

Nays—Messrs. Ayres, Bunker, Clark of Alamakee, Day, Ells, Emerson, Gibson, Gillaspy, Harris, Palmer, Parvin, Patterson, Peters, Price, Robinson, Seely, Skiff, Solomon, Traer, Warren, Wilson and Young.

Mr. TRAER. I renew my amendment made in committee of the whole, to amend the second section, by striking out all after the word "purpose" in the fifth line, and inserting the following:

"The qualified electors of the state shall proceed at the next general election to choose delegates to said convention, upon the basis provided for the State Senate, and said convention when assembled shall have full power to revise and amend the constitution, and to do all things necessary and proper to carry out the objects for which they were convened. Such delegates shall receive as compensation per diem the same as that allowed to members of the General Assembly."

So that the section as amended would then read:

"At the general election to be held in the year 1870, and in each tenth year thereafter, and also at such times as the General Assembly may by law provide, the question, "Shall there be a convention to revise the constitution, and amend the same?' shall be decided by the electors qualified to vote for members of the General Assembly; and in case a majority of the electors so qualified, voting at such election, shall decide in favor of a convention for such purpose, the qualified electors of the state shall proceed at the next general election to choose delegates to said convention, upon the basis provided for the State Senate; and said convention when assembled shall have full power to revise and amend the constitution, and to do all things necessary and proper to carry out the objects for which they are convened. Such delegates shall receive as compensation per diem the same as that allowed to members of the General Assembly."

The question was then taken by yeas and nays, upon the amendment offered by Mr. Traer, and it was rejected; yeas 9, nays 25, as follows:

Yeas—The President, Messrs. Clark of Alamakee, Clarke of Johnson, Day, Harris, Johnston, Seely, Solomon, Traer and Warren.

Nays—Messrs. Ayres, Bunker, Clarke of Henry, Day, Edwards, Ells, Emerson, Gibson, Gillaspy, Gower, Gray, Hall, Hollingsworth, Marvin, Palmer, Parvin, Patterson, Peters, Price, Robinson, Scott, Skiff, Wilson, Winchester and Young.

Mr. PALMER. I move to substitute the following for section three:

"If at any time the General Assembly shall think it necessary to call a convention to revise or amend this constitution, they shall provide by law for a vote of the people upon that question at the next ensuing general election; and in case a majority vote in favor of a convention, said General Assembly shall provide for an election of delegates, the convention of the said delegates to be held within twelve months after the vote of the people in favor thereof."

I think that preferable to the present provision. The present section leaves it discretionary, whether the vote shall be taken oftener than every tenth year, and this section leaves it entirely discretionary with the General Assembly when the question shall be submitted to the people, and does not make it the duty of the people to vote every tenth year upon the subject. I think the legislature can express the opinions of the people upon this subject, and that coming from the people they will know when the people desire to vote upon the question. Whenever it is desired by the people, they can provide for their taking a vote.

Mr. CLARKE, of Henry. If I understand the object of the second section at all, it is not really to provide for an amendment of the constitution, because I think that wherever they have had this first section, amendments have always been made under that provision. But it probably grew out of the Rhode Island trouble, and I think it is to guard against that state of things, lest the legislature should refuse to order a convention, and to make an amendment which the people desire. The people may desire a convention, and the legislature may be in the way. This is to retain the power in the hands of the people. There is one portion of the section which, in my opinion, should be stricken out, that allowing the question to be submitted at any intermediate time. We have a provision for amendments by the legislature, and if we retain the provision for a vote of the people once in ten years, that will give them the power to hold a convention independent of the legislature; they can vote upon the question every tenth year, whether the legislature will it or not, whether they shall hold a convention to revise the constitution.

Mr. PALMER. The instance of Rhode Island cited here, is not a fair one upon this subject. It is well known that the people of Rhode Island never had a constitution of their own; that their government was under a charter granted from the King of England, up to the time of the formation of their late constitution. The legislature never did represent the mass of the people of that state. They represented only the holders of certain amounts of property; and the people who held no property, never had any voice in electing the legislature. In the other states, where the people have voted universally for the legislature, without distinction on account of property, I believe that a provision, similar to the one I have offered, has worked well in their constitution.

Mr. CLARK, of Alamakee. I am in favor of retaining the provision in the constitution which places the people above their representatives, which places them above and independent of their legislature, upon the question of the revision or amendment of the constitution; that they may at all times retain in their own hands that power, and not be dependent upon any other power for it. There may not be a case in this state for fifty years, when the people will wish to exercise the right; but that does not disprove the wisdom of incorporating such a provision in the constitution. That the case may occur, no person can deny; and if the case may occur, I apprehend that it is the dictate of wisdom and of duty to provide for that contingency. The people should have the right of amending or altering the constitution; and as there may be a case in which they cannot obtain the desired legislative enactments, I think there should be left in the constitution a provision giving them that right. The legislature may have some outside pressure, and may not represent the wishes of the people; or we may have a governor who will veto a provision of that kind, and defeat the wishes of the people. It certainly can do no harm to incorporate a provision of this kind in the constitution, and for these reasons I am in favor of it.

The question being taken, by yeas and nays, the substitute was rejected; yeas 16, nays 18, as follows:

Yeas—Messrs. Clarke of Johnson, Day, Edwards, Gibson, Gillaspy, Gower, Hall, Harris, Johnston, Palmer, Patterson, Peters, Price, Robinson, Scott and Winchester.

Nays—The President, Messrs. Ayres, Bunker, Clark of Alamakee, Clarke of Henry, Ells, Emerson, Gray, Hollingsworth, Marvin, Parvin, Seely, Skiff, Solomon, Traer, Warren, Wilson and Young.

Mr. CLARKE, of Johnson. I desire to say, in explanation of my vote, that I voted for the substitute, not because I preferred it to the original section as it stands, but because I think that section, as it now stands, puts off the vote too late, from 1867 to 1870. If some gentleman would move a re-consideration, and bring the section back to where it stood, that the first vote may be taken in 1867, I shall be in favor of the section rather than the substitute.

On motion of Mr. TRAER,

The report was ordered to be engrossed for a third reading, and referred to the committee on revision.

Militia.

The convention proceeded to the consideration of the report of the standing committee upon the subject of the militia.

The report was read as follows:

"The committee to which was referred that portion of the constitution relating to the militia, have had the same under consideration, and have unanimously instructed me to report the same back without amendment, and recommend its adoption by this convention.

"Respectfully submitted:

"H. J. SKIFF."

The article in the present constitution is as follows:

"Section 1. The militia of this state shall be composed of all able-bodied white male citizens between the ages of eighteen and forty-five years, except such as are, or may hereafter be, exempt by the laws of the United States, or of this state, and shall be armed, equipped and trained, as the General Assembly may provide by law.

Sec. 2. No person or persons conscientiously scrupulous of bearing arms, shall be compelled to do militia duty in time of peace: *Provided*, that such person or persons shall pay an equivalent for such exemption in the same manner as other citizens.

Sec. 3. All commissioned officers of the militia, (staff officers excepted,) shall be elected by the persons liable to perform militia duty, and shall be commissioned by the governor."

Mr. TRAER. I move to strike out "eighteen," and to insert "twenty-one." I am opposed to compelling a man to serve in a military capacity until he is allowed the right to vote.

Mr. CLARK, of Alamakee. I move to strike out "eighteen," and insert "fifteen," so as to make it conform to the principles of Young America.

A division was called for, the question being first upon striking out "eighteen."

Mr. JOHNSTON. Upon consultation with the majority of the committee on the militia, it was deemed proper that this article should be reported back without any amendment; but I believe the majority are in favor of striking out "eighteen," and inserting "twenty-one." There is a disposition to prevent us young men from holding offices in the State, and we are determinee that the old fogies shall do the fighting. [Laughter.]

Mr. CLARK, of Alamakee. I withdraw my amendment.

Mr. TRAER. I will observe in favor of my motion, that striking out "eighteen," and inserting a higher number does not necessarily involve a prohibition against young men of eighteen years of age serving in a military capacity. I made the motion simply because we are compelling a person to perform military duty as a man, when we do not recognize him as a man under our constitution. I am in favor of giving them the privilege of serving in the militia, but not in favor of compelling them to do it. I am in favor of equal justice; and if we compel them to serve in a military capacity, we ought to allow them to vote.

Mr. SKIFF. As I am the chairman of the committee on militia, I suppose I shall be expected to make a speech. I am almost disposed to call the gentleman from Lee [Mr. Johnston] to account for attempting to call in question that report. He was consulted at various times on this subject, and we were very arduous in our labors in getting up that report, and I supposed that he wished it to be carried as we reported it. But for him now to take a stand in favor of mutilating that report touches my pride somewhat. I really hope it will not be altered. I consider our report as perfect as it can be made. I hope that the word "eighteen" will not be stricken out for any other number, for we have the wisdom of ages upon our side; we have the example of all the states of the Union. I have no desire to adopt any new course in military matters; for every one knows that innovations in military tactics are always looked upon with distrust. That is the way I look upon this amendment—with very great distrust indeed. I want those young men of eighteen to be compelled to come into the service of the country. I think the country needs their services.

The question was then taken upon the motion to strike out "eighteen," and it was not agreed to.

Mr. SCOTT. I rise to move that the word "white," be stricken out from this section; and for that I think I have very good reasons. As a convention, we have granted, or probably will grant, certain powers corroborating the action of the last legislature, in regard to the colored population of this state; according to them privileges which they have never received before. I wish also to grant and delegate to them the power of defending their own common country with us. One reason for making this motion is, that they have been heretofore, especially in the last war, so efficient in vindicating the cause of our country. Another reason which does not directly apply to my district, but which is applicable, I believe, to the district of the gentleman from Wapello, [Mr. Gillaspy,] and some other districts, is, that there are some colored people who might be spared even to put into the front ranks in case of an invasion, and might prove a very effective part and portion of the military of this state. I hope gentlemen will take the view of it that I do, and grant them, in the constitution, the right to form part of our militia. It is their fit and proper place, and I am sorry to see them restrained from occupying it.

Mr. CLARKE, of Henry. I think that is the only place in the constitution where that word ought to be. It is a sort of justice meted out to them in this respect; while in every other place where it exists it seems to be restrictive. They are like the young men whom it was wished to exonerate, inasmuch as they are not allowed to vote, and not allowed to be represented. I would like to have them all put in the same category. I voted to strike out "eighteen" and should have voted in favor of inserting "twenty-one." Wherever a citizen is allowed all the privileges of the community in which he lives, has the shield of the constitution thrown around him, and the laws to protect him, he ought certainly to submit not only to contribute from his purse to the support of the constitution and the laws, but also, at all times, to be ready to answer the call of his county, and go into the ranks to oppose the enemy. But when you take from him all these privileges, when you give him no constitutional rights, no guards, when, by your laws, you ostracize him and throw him without the pale of society, when you deprive him of all its protection, I ask, is it right, is it just, that you should call upon him to serve in the militia, to defend that country in which you have made him an alien? You take from him all that makes the country dear to us; you deprive him of all those motives which induce others to defend their country, those influences which make them patriots; and I say it is unjust to him to call upon him to defend those institutions which have this effect upon him. I shall oppose the motion of the gentleman to strike out the word "white," from this section.

Mr. GILLASPY. I believe I should fail in my duty to my constituents if I were to sit still during the discussion of a question of this importance to them, and fail to rise in my place to give to my friend the credit of being one of the most honorable and honest men in this convention. My friend from Clayton, [Mr. Scott,] proposes to have the colored population of this country placed in the front ranks of the army that they may be killed off. My friend from Henry, [Mr. Clarke,] true to his colors, is in favor of retaining the word "white." He believes that this colored population ought to have rights and privileges that the white people of this country do not enjoy. He is willing to put them upon an equality so far as voting for office and social position are concerned; but when you talk of war, and there is a probability that they may be maimed, he is opposed to having them act in that category, showing all the time that he is an honest and fast friend to that portion of our population. I hope that gentlemen disposed to favor the proposition will vote for the motion of my friend from Clayton, [Mr. Scott.] As for myself, I am opposed to seeing the only colored person in my town, being a female, put into the front ranks of the army of this state. [Laughter.]

Mr. CLARKE, of Henry. I certainly, sir, feel very much flattered by the endorsement of the gentleman from Wapello, [Mr. Gillaspy.] And I must say to my friend from Wapello that, in considering the reasons for opposing this motion, I also had in view, as I have had heretofore, the interests of the gentleman from Wapello. I knew his particular feelings of opposition to this measure, especially with regard to that one individual in whose welfare he takes so deep an interest; and knowing that his feelings were tender upon that point, and that he was extremely unwilling to jeopardize her, and thereby lose the privilege of having even one colored constituent in his town—while I stood up here to defend the rights of the class, I also had in view the interests of my friend from Wapello. But I hope he will not be alarmed if the motion should prevail; because if he should look a little further, he will see that the word "male," comes in, which will save him from needless alarm upon this subject.

Mr. WINCHESTER. I shall vote uniformly upon this question to support the report of the committee. I believe this is the most important article which we have been called upon to consider. I have great respect for the members of that committee and their opinions; for I believe that committee is composed of some of the most weighty members of this body, weighty not only in stature but in wisdom. Having, therefore, great respect for their opinions, I shall vote uniformly in support of their report.

The motion to amend was not agreed to.

On motion of Mr. TRAER,

The article was ordered to be engrossed for a third reading, and referred to the committee on revision.

On motion of Mr. SKIFF,

The committee took a recess until 2 o'clock P. M.

EVENING SESSION.

The convention met at 2 P. M., and was called to order by the President.

Court of Common Pleas.

Mr. EDWARDS. I offer the following resolution:

"*Resolved*, That the committee on the judicial department be instructed to provide in that article of the constitution for the creation of a court of common pleas, and report by Monday next."

It will be recollected that there were many gentlemen upon this floor who were very anxious to have a change in the judicial department of our state government. They were unable to accomplish their object. But upon consultation with, and at the request of, many friends of the three-court system, this course has been decided upon, and they have consented to agree to a system of courts of this kind, provided it can be adopted. I have, therefore, prepared a resolution of instruction for the purpose of bringing the subject before the convention, at an early day, that it may be discussed, if necessary, in order to obtain the sense of the convention upon the resolution of instruction. Gentlemen can vote for or against the resolution of instruction, and we will thereby save time, and get an expression of the sense of the convention.

I will, in as brief a manner as I am capable of doing, give what I consider to be the advantages of this system.

It is well known to gentlemen here, that such a system has been adopted in the states of Ohio and Indiana. I have practiced under both systems, that of Indiana, and the one here in this state. When the system was first established in Indiana, I was opposed to it, and as a member of the legislature I did all I could to defeat it. But experience afterwards proved that it was the favorite court of the state; and whatever experience proves to my mind to be beneficial to the people in its results, I am ready to acquiesce in.

One of the advantages that this system possesses is, that it meets the wants of the great mass of the people, and more especially those classes that are poor. It is a system of courts that goes home directly to the people, and especially to the poor people. Now, we have to premise here something what the law will be, if this system is adopted. We can only provide in the constitution that the legislature shall create a court of that kind, and then we can presume, from the experience of the past, and a knowledge of the law in other States, what the law will be here.

The law in Ohio and Indiana is this: The court of common pleas has concurrent and original jurisdiction with the district courts, in all cases of one thousand dollars and under; it has original jurisdiction in all probate business; it sits once in every three months, and may be a court for one county alone, or for a district of several counties. I believe the districts in those States, so far as I know anything about the matter, have not extended over more than six counties. The average salaries of judges in courts of this kind are about one thousand dollars a year.

Now, in nine-tenths of all the cases that are litigated in our courts, I venture to say, the sum in controversy does not exceed one thousand dollars. But under the present system of compelling parties to go to the district court in all cases of one hundred dollars and upwards, the process of obtaining justice, which should be so provided by the fundamental law that it could be obtained as speedily and cheaply as possible, is greatly delayed, and rendered oppressively expensive.

There are mistaken ideas in the minds of many gentlemen who pre-suppose that we are to guard against the purse-strings of the State in one particular, while in another we are to disregard the wants of the people and of litigants. I think if we are true friends of the people we will provide, especially in all cases of judicature, that justice shall be speedily obtained. Now these courts of common pleas meet once in every three months, and sit as long as there is any business to be done. Then the citizens of each county has the right, in all cases of one thousand dollars and under, to have his case tried at that court at least in three months. The court is also to attend to probate business.

Another consideration, is, that this court has such a character as to invite competent men to come upon the bench to discharge the duties of that position. It is provided by law that this court is to have jurisdiction in all minor cases of felony and misdemeanor. Now that is one branch of the subject.

As the practice is now in the district court, cases cannot come up oftener than once in six months. They are generally continued and extended from year to year. The demands of justice are not met either upon the part of the State or the unfortunate defenders. They are kept in prison, or have to give bail. Now in a court of this nature, the accused can have an opportunity, every three months, to be tried.

The creation of this court contemplates the abolition of the office of county judge—an office that I regard as possessing more power than a Spanish prefect, more power than the court of King's Bench. He has discretionary power over the funds of the people of the country, and can make such appropriations as he may see proper to make.

And we suppose that by law the office of school fund commissioner will be abolished, and the business of that office can be entrusted to the treasurer of the county. Then by this abolition of the offices of school fund commissioner and of county judge, we provide for the expense necessary to carry on the system of common pleas courts.

There are several gentlemen who desire to express their views upon this subject, and I will omit any further remarks until other gentlemen have spoken.

Mr. HARRIS. I thought I would not say anything until my friend from Lucas [Mr. Edwards,] had got through with his remarks. It strikes me that this resolution is not in order, because the article upon the judicial department is not now before the committee on the judiciary. I do not know whether or not that committee has been discharged from the further consideration of the subject. But they have no control now whatever over the article on the department of the judiciary. I understand that the article upon the judicial department has been ordered to a third reading, and I do not think a resolution of this kind would be now in order.

The PRESIDENT. The Chair is of opinion that the resolution is in order.

Mr. HARRIS. Then I will make one or two remarks upon this subject, but I do not propose to take up much time in discussing it. I was in hopes this matter would not be disturbed again. I shall certainly feel disposed to vote against this resolution, for the reason that, if we launch out again upon the sea of discussion, we will be likely to consume some three or four days upon it. If my recollection is correct, the question of a court of common pleas was before the committee, and voted down. And if there has been any question decided by this convention beyond all cavil or doubt, it is that the majority of this convention are opposed to any material change in our present system of the judiciary.

I shall, therefore, with all due deference to the gentleman from Lucas, [Mr. Edwards,] vote against this resolution.

The PRESIDENT. The resolution proposes to instruct the committee on the judicial department to report a provision to establish this court of common pleas.

Mr. HARRIS. That is the way I understand it; and, therefore, I shall vote against it.

Mr. GILLASPY. I move to amend the resolution by adding to it the following:

"And to provide that no person shall be eligible to the office of district judge who shall not have attained the age of fifty years, or the office of supreme judge until he shall have attained the age of seventy-five years."

The question being taken upon the amendment, it was not agreed to.

The question recurred upon the resolution.

Mr. PETERS. I suppose the object of this resolution is to bring before the convention the question of abolishing our present system of county courts, and to provide for some manner of changing them, so as to give us a court within the reach of litigants, without the expense and delay that now attends our district courts. I suppose this resolution was brought forward for the purpose of testing the sense of this convention upon this question, before it becomes too late under our rules to reconsider the vote which was taken this morning, ordering the report of the committee on the judicial department to its third reading. I hope the convention will see the necessity of some such change as this resolution proposes.

Mr. PALMER. The resolution is rather indefinite, I think. It speaks of a court of common pleas. I think it should instruct the committee as to what kind of a court of common pleas it should be. When I lived in Ohio, our circuit court there was frequently called a court of common pleas. Now it may be a court very differently organized from our ordinary courts of common pleas. I suppose from the remarks of the gentleman [Mr. Edwards,] who offered the resolution, that he wants the courts of common pleas in the counties to supercede the county courts. Now I believe that as the article upon the judiciary now stands, the legislature has power to constitute such a court as this if they think proper to do so.

I think we have spent time enough upon this article of the constitution; I do not think that this convention is going over the whole ground again, without some very pressing necessity for it.

The question was upon the resolution.

Upon this question—

Mr. EDWARDS called for the yeas and nays, and they were ordered accordingly.

The question being then taken, by yeas and nays, the resolution was rejected; yeas 8, nays 26, as follows:

Yeas—Messrs. Edwards, Emerson, Hall, Marvin, Patterson, Peters, Robinson and Scott.

Nays—The President, Messrs. Ayres, Bunker, Clark of Alamakee, Clarke of Henry, Clarke of Johnson, Day, Ells, Gibson, Gillaspy, Gower, Gray, Harris, Hollingsworth, Johnston, Palmer, Parvin, Price, Seely, Skiff, Solomon, Traer, Warren, Wilson, Winchester and Young.

Miscellaneous.

The PRESIDENT stated the unfinished business before the convention to be the further consideration, in committee of the whole, of the report of the committee on education and school lands.

Mr. PATTERSON moved that the convention resolve itself into committee of the whole upon that report.

Mr. JOHNSTON. I hope my colleague will withdraw that motion, and permit me to make statement to the convention.

Mr. PATTERSON. I will withdraw the motion.

Mr. JOHNSTON. I understand that the gentlemen who feel particularly interested in the majority and minority reports of the committee on education and school lands—[Messrs. Hall and Ells]—are indisposed to proceed to a discussion of them this afternoon, and would prefer that they should lie over until Monday. I have no disposition myself to press this matter, and would be willing to accommodate them. This subject of education is one of some importance, and is the only one of importance now before the convention. And though I have been heretofore in favor of expediting matters as much as possible, I am still in favor of accommodating these gentlemen. This convention can find something else to engage their attention.

We passed a resolution on yesterday, requiring the several committees which have not yet reported to do so on Monday next. And it might be well to give those committees some time, this afternoon or to-morrow, to make out their reports. There are three select committees, one on incorporations, one on the bill of rights, and one upon the right of suffrage. And I understand that the committee on miscellaneous subjects, and the committee on the schedule, desire to meet and prepare their reports. It might be well, perhaps, to give these committees this afternoon or to-morrow to examine the subjects before them, so as to be able to report on Monday.

Mr. PALMER. In order that these committees can have time to work this afternoon, move that this convention do now adjourn.

The question being then taken upon the motion to adjourn, upon a division, it was agreed to; yeas 19, noes not counted.

The convention accordingly adjourned until to-morrow morning at 9 o'clock.

www.ingramcontent.com/pod-product-compliance
Lightning Source LLC
LaVergne TN
LVHW021057110826
845150LV00001B/96

* 9 7 8 1 4 2 5 5 6 6 7 1 5 *